OXFORD MEDIEVAL TEXTS
General Editors
D. E. GREENWAY   B. F. HARVEY
M. LAPIDGE

WILLIAM OF MALMESBURY

GESTA REGVM ANGLORVM
THE HISTORY OF
THE ENGLISH KINGS

William of Malmesbury
GESTA REGVM
ANGLORVM
The History of the English Kings
VOLUME I

EDITED AND TRANSLATED BY
R. A. B. MYNORS†

COMPLETED BY
R. M. THOMSON
and
M. WINTERBOTTOM

CLARENDON PRESS · OXFORD

This book has been printed digitally and produced in a standard specification in order to ensure its continuing availability

OXFORD
UNIVERSITY PRESS

Great Clarendon Street, Oxford OX2 6DP

Oxford University Press is a department of the University of Oxford.
It furthers the University's objective of excellence in research, scholarship,
and education by publishing worldwide in

Oxford New York

Auckland Cape Town Dar es Salaam Hong Kong Karachi
Kuala Lumpur Madrid Melbourne Mexico City Nairobi
New Delhi Shanghai Taipei Toronto
With offices in
Argentina Austria Brazil Chile Czech Republic France Greece
Guatemala Hungary Italy Japan South Korea Poland Portugal
Singapore Switzerland Thailand Turkey Ukraine Vietnam

Oxford is a registered trade mark of Oxford University Press
in the UK and in certain other countries

Published in the United States
by Oxford University Press Inc., New York

© Estate of R.A.B. Mynors, R.M. Thomson and M. Winterbottom, 1998

Not to be reprinted without permission
The moral rights of the author have been asserted
Database right Oxford University Press (maker)

Reprinted 2006

All rights reserved. No part of this publication may be reproduced,
stored in a retrieval system, or transmitted, in any form or by any means,
without the prior permission in writing of Oxford University Press,
or as expressly permitted by law, or under terms agreed with the appropriate
reprographics rights organization. Enquiries concerning reproduction
outside the scope of the above should be sent to the Rights Department,
Oxford University Press, at the address above

You must not circulate this book in any other binding or cover
And you must impose this same condition on any acquirer

ISBN 978-0-19-820678-1

PREFACE

IN January 1953 Roger Mynors wrote to R. W. (now Sir Richard) Southern: 'I enclose, in hopes that it may be some use to you, a typescript of the introductory letters in the Troyes (Clairvaux) MS of the *Gesta regum*, the second of which in particular contains some account of the genesis of the work. That the text of the MS represents an earlier draft of it than any of Stubbs's three "editions", is beyond question.' In the event, the exact status of what Mynors labelled the T branch of manuscripts of the *Gesta regum* is still in dispute. What is not doubtful is the significance of the branch, and the justification of the present edition is largely that it exploits T's evidence in full for the first time.

Mynors himself, during the fifties, produced a draft text of the whole work, with a brief apparatus criticus; and it was apparently at this time too that he translated almost all of it. The aim was to produce a volume in the series of Nelson Medieval Texts, with historical notes added by Southern. That project came to nothing, and the Mynors typescript was laid aside for three decades. In the mid-eighties, however, after discussion with R.M.T., Mynors passed the text and translation to M.W. Subsequently he discussed some of the problems with him. Mynors also at this time completed the translation, and wrote a summary of his notes on the manuscripts, taken from the margin of his Rolls Series edition of the *GR*. The two volumes he eventually gave, newly bound, to M.W.; they contain, in Mynors' tiniest hand, the collations on which his text rested.

M.W. re-collated the most important of the manuscripts after making a sample collation of all the witnesses. He is primarily responsible for the text, which is constructed on slightly different principles from those followed by Mynors. As for the translation and the index, both of us worked on them intensively, especially towards the end when R.M.T.'s tenure of a Visiting Fellowship at Corpus Christi College, Oxford, from July 1995 to February 1996 enabled us to go over them from start to finish. We are very grateful to the College for providing this opportunity to work together so closely. The resulting translation must lack the stylistic unity of Mynors' original. Mynors believed strongly that a translation should be elegant even at the cost of literalness. We have preferred to stay closer to the Latin. But we are very conscious, as Mynors was, of the difficulties presented by the *GR*, and of the pitfalls its smooth surface conceals.

The complex problems presented by the *GR* go beyond what could conveniently be relegated to footnotes. There will therefore be a companion volume, written by R.M.T., providing a general introduction (including a detailed statement of our view of the relationship of the four versions of the text) and a chapter by chapter commentary.

We owe much to the help of Dr Martin Brett, in particular for his great service to scholarship in this area in organizing the production of a computer-generated concordance to almost all the works of William. We are very grateful to the libraries which opened their doors to us or supplied microfilms, and to the staff of the Classics Office at Oxford, not least Rachel Woodrow, who typed the first draft of the index. We are very conscious of the support and encouragement of the General Editors during a long period of gestation, of the friendly co-operation of Anne Gelling, and of the high skills of Joshua Associates. Finally, we were most fortunate in our copy editor, John Cordy, to whose meticulous skill and impeccable taste we are greatly indebted.

No one could work on William of Malmesbury without feeling the highest admiration and affection for a great scholar; and we feel the same about Roger Mynors. It has been our aim to produce a book worthy of them both.

R.M.T.
M.W.

CONTENTS

ABBREVIATED REFERENCES ... ix

INTRODUCTION

  1. The Manuscript Tradition ... xiii
  2. Editions and Translations ... xxii
  3. Principles of the Present Edition ... xxii
  4. Orthography ... xxvi

SIGLA ... xxix

PLAN OF THE *GR* ... xxxi

TEXT AND TRANSLATION
  Letters ... 2
  Book 1 ... 14
  Book 2 ... 150
  Book 3 ... 424
  Book 4 ... 540
  Book 5 ... 708

APPENDICES

  I. Additions of B and C ... 802
  II. Additions of the Aa Group ... 834

INDEX ... 841

ABBREVIATED REFERENCES

AA SS	*Acta Sanctorum*
AG	William of Malmesbury, *De Antiquitate Glastonie Ecclesie*, cited by page from the edition of J. Scott, *The Early History of Glastonbury* (Woodbridge, 1981)
ASC	*The Anglo-Saxon Chronicle* (cited by year)
CCSL	*Corpus Christianorum Series Latina*
Clover–Gibson	*The Letters of Lanfranc, Archbishop of Canterbury*, ed. Helen Clover and Margaret Gibson (OMT, 1979)
Colgrave–Mynors	Bede's *Ecclesiastical History of the English People*, ed. Bertram Colgrave and R. A. B. Mynors (OMT, 1969)
Counc.	*Councils and Synods*, I (AD 871–1204), ed. D. Whitelock, M. Brett, and C. N. L. Brooke, 2 parts (Oxford, 1981)
Eadmer, *Hist. Nov.*	Eadmer, *Historia Novorum*, cited by page from the edition of M. Rule (RS, 1884)
Fulcher	Fulcher of Chartres, *Gesta Francorum Iherusalem Peregrinantium*, ed. H. Hagenmayer (Heidelberg, 1913)
GND	The *Gesta Normannorum Ducum* of William of Jumièges, Orderic Vitalis, and Robert of Torigni, ed. and trans. E. M. C. van Houts, 2 vols. (OMT, 1992, 1995)
GP	William of Malmesbury, *Gesta Pontificum Anglorum*, cited by page from the edition of N. E. S. A. Hamilton (RS, 1870)
GR	William of Malmesbury, *Gesta Regum Anglorum* (cited by chapter and section)
H & S	*Councils and Ecclesiastical Documents relating to Great Britain and Ireland*, ed. A. W. Haddan and W. Stubbs, 3 vols. (Oxford, 1869–78)
HE	Bede, *Historia Ecclesiastica*
HN	William of Malmesbury, *Historia Novella*, cited

ABBREVIATED REFERENCES

	by chapter from the edition of K. R. Potter (NMT, 1955)
JW	Cited by year from *The Chronicle of John of Worcester*, ed. R. R. Darlington and P. McGurk, ii (OMT, 1995), and, for the period after 1066, from *Florentii Wigorniensis monachi Chronicon ex Chronicis*, ed. B. Thorpe, 2 vols. (London, 1849), ii
Leland, *Coll.*	*Joannis Lelandi antiquarii De Rebus Britannicis Collectanea*, 2nd edn., 6 vols. (London, 1774)
Liebermann, *Gesetze*	F. Liebermann, *Die Gesetze der Angelsachsen*, i (Halle, 1903)
MGH	*Monumenta Germaniae Historica*
Constit.	*Constitutiones*
Ep.	*Epistolae*
Lib. de Lite	*Libelli de Lite Imperatorum*
Poetae	*Poetae Latini aevi Carolini*
SS	*Scriptores (in folio)*
Mir.	William of Malmesbury, *De Laudibus et Miraculis Sanctae Mariae*, cited by page from the edition of J. M. Canal (Rome, 1968)
NMT	Nelson's Medieval Texts
ODML	*Dictionary of Medieval Latin from British Sources* (Oxford, 1975–)
OMT	Oxford Medieval Texts
Otto, *Sprichwörter*	A. Otto, *Die Sprichwörter und sprichwörtlichen Redensarten der Römer* (Leipzig, 1890)
PL	*Patrologia Latina*
RS	Rolls Series
Sawyer	P. H. Sawyer, *Anglo-Saxon Charters* (Royal Historical Society, London, 1968), cited by document number
SK	D. Schaller and E. Könsgen, *Initia Carminum Latinorum Saeculo Vndecimo Antiquiorum* (Göttingen, 1977)
Thomson, *William of Malmesbury*	R. M. Thomson, *William of Malmesbury* (Woodbridge, 1987)
VD	William of Malmesbury, *Vita Dunstani*, cited by page from *Memorials of Saint Dunstan*, ed. W. Stubbs (RS, 1874), pp. 250–324

VW	William of Malmesbury, *Vita Wulfstani*, cited by book and chapter from the edition of R. R. Darlington (Camden Society, 3rd series xl, 1928)
Walther, *Initia*	H. Walther, *Initia Carminum ac Versuum Medii Aevi Posterioris Latinorum* (Göttingen, 2nd edn., 1969)
Walther, *Proverbia*	H. Walther, *Proverbia Sententiaeque Latinitatis Medii Aevi: Lateinische Sprichwörter und Sentenzen des Mittelalters*, 5 vols. (Göttingen, 1963–7)
William of Poitiers, ed. Foreville	Guillaume de Poitiers, *Histoire de Guillaume le Conquérant*, ed. Raymonde Foreville (Paris, 1952)

INTRODUCTION

1. THE MANUSCRIPT TRADITION[1]

The *Gesta regum* is transmitted in four versions, all of them in some sense authorial. The character of the versions will be discussed in the introduction to the Commentary (but see below, pp. xxii–xxiv). We first give a brief description of the manuscripts witnessing to each of the versions in turn, and say something about their interrelationship.

The T version

There are two main witnesses, each breaking off in mid-folio at the end of 401. 2:

Tt   Troyes, Bibliothèque Municipale 294 bis, s. XII[2], Clairvaux. Stubbs, p. xc.

Tp   Paris, Bibliothèque Nationale lat. 6046, s. XIV, N.E. France or Flanders(?). Stubbs, pp. lxxxvi–lxxxviii; *GND* i, p. cii. Six quires are lost, five of them in *GR*, resulting in the omission of 70. 2 *Offam* to 87. 3 *stetit*, 165. 6 *propter barbariem* to 170. 4 *mirum*, 258. 1 *hominem* to 267. 4 *oblitus uena-*, 283. 2 *contra patriam* to 298. 1 *pontificatus autem*, and 381. 2 *itaque nota* to 388. 2 *profecto*. Stubbs saw that the MS is hybrid.[2] It is a T text from 59. 2 to 121. 4,[3] and from the start of Book iii to the

---

[1] This section gives the sort of concise picture of the tradition of which we think Roger Mynors would have approved, and does not go into detail where the essentials are not concerned. The conclusions reached rest on a sample collation of the MSS made and assessed by M.W. The dates and provenances, except for the MSS of the 'Libellus', are R.M.T.'s. Occasionally notes left at his death by Roger Mynors have been quoted. References to Stubbs in this section are to the first volume of his edition of the *GR* (RS, 1887, 1889).

[2] Mynors noted that 'it would appear that the scribe was copying a composite exemplar, not (it seems) because one type of text had been "corrected" from another but because quires of two texts had been juxtaposed'. Though the MS is so late, the existence of a composite of this kind much earlier has been demonstrated by Dr M. M. Woesthuis's work on the *Chronicon* of Helinand of Froidmont, who lived from *c.*1160 to after 1229, and one of whose main sources was a *GR* MS of this type. We are very grateful to Dr Woesthuis for this information.

[3] The MS follows B (and AC) in the order *quod . . . profecto non dicit* at 59. 2, but a line later agrees with TtTc's *et nullas usque* (*nullasque* ACB). At 121. 4 the last T reading is the omission of *etiam*; the MS then fails to follow TtTc in the order *confortauit laetitia*.

end of the manuscript. Otherwise it is a B text (Bp: see below, p. xx).

An abbreviated[4] T text is given by an anonymous series of extracts (called by Tc 'Libellus de gestis Anglorum'), published by Hieronymus Commelin[5] in Heidelberg in 1587 from a MS (said by Mynors to be very like the Tournai MS mentioned below) lent him by the Fleming Paul Knibbe. The MSS known to us are:[6]

<dl>
Tc
</dl>

    Brussels, Bibliothèque Royale II. 2541 (formerly Phillipps 11604), c. 1200, St Martin's, Tournai. Stubbs, pp. c–cii.
    London, British Library Add. 39646, s. XII ex., Braine-sur Vesle. Stubbs, p. civ; *GND* i, pp. cvii–cviii.
    New York, H. P. Kraus (formerly Phillipps 237), s. XII ex., Bonne Espérance. Stubbs, p. ciii.
    Paris, Bibliothèque Nationale lat. 6187, s. XIII in. (early s. XIV: R.A.B.M.).
    Paris, Bibliothèque Nationale lat. 17656, after 1179, N. France. Stubbs, pp. ciii–civ; *GND* i, p. civ.
    Paris, Bibliothèque Nationale nouv. acq. lat. 2864, c. 1195, Hautmont.
    San Marino, Calif., Huntington Library H.M. 627 (formerly Phillipps 4621), s. XII 3/4, Aulne. Stubbs, pp. cii–ciii.
    Valenciennes, Bibliothèque Municipale 792, s. XIV in., Vicoigne.[7]

Collation shows that Tt and Tp, so far as they overlap, are twins.[8] Their immediate common ancestor we call T^1.[9] Though Tt is much

---

[4] Stubbs (pp. cv–cvii) gives details of the extracts, which end abruptly at the end of 286 (though individual MSS append differing and miscellaneous material). Rather than reproduce Stubbs's information, we merely give two minor corrections after checking his table against Tc: 'Libellus' 2. 15: 171; 3. 6: 234.

[5] *Rerum Britannicarum . . . scriptores vetustiores ac praecipui* (Heidelberg, 1587).

[6] We are much indebted to Dr E. M. C. van Houts for information on these MSS, especially that in the Huntington Library, which goes beyond what is contained in her *GND*. Her dates do not always agree with those of Mynors.

[7] It was presumably when Mynors was examining this text of the 'Libellus' that he found the lost ending of the *Gesta Stephani* in the same book (see K. R. Potter's edition in NMT [1955] = OMT [1976], p. xii).

[8] Tt cannot of course descend from Tp. It has many errors not shared by Tp (or Tc), e.g. 61. 1 *preponderabat; equanimiter* before *occultum*; 61. 4 *paradisiacum*; 65. 1 *legendi*; 65. 3 *eruditionis exquisitiores* (and so on).

[9] We cannot tell if the truncation found in TtTp goes back only to T^1 or further. It must in any case be the result of the loss of folios at the end of a MS. Damage to a folio in an ancestor of Tt has resulted in the omissions seen at 386. 2 and 387. 7, where TpTc are not available. In

older than Tp, it is by no means to be assumed that it is more sincere.[10]

The only MS of the 'Libellus' we have employed is Tc. It is of course an intermittent witness, but it is independent of T¹.[11] Their common ancestor we call T where only Tt and Tc witness to it, and T⁺ where all three agree. All the MSS whose provenance is traceable originate from France or Flanders, and the natural assumption is that T was (or was a transcript of) the presentation copy sent to Normandy for the Empress Matilda, a letter to whom prefaces Tt (see Letter ii and Commentary).

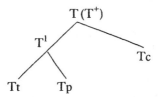

The A version

The major witness to this version in its purest state is

A1   London, British Library Arundel 35, s. XII 2/4, Winchester.[12] Stubbs, p. lxvii. It has lost its last quires, and breaks off at 411. 2 *curialibus suis*.

This is almost certainly the source[13] of four further texts:

another passage where Tt is our only witness it shows signs of variants in an ancestor: Letter ii. 3 *uel ubi unde* for *ubi*. At 249. 3 Tt (but not TpTc) gives *uel omnino* for *omnium*.

[10] At 93. 1 Tp preserves the incorrect addition (from below) *et salute animarum*; Tt (like Tc) tries to repair the error. (At 96. 1 it seems to be Tt's corrector who tries to remedy an omission.) At 333. 2 T¹ omits *gestu*; Tt, but not Tp, supplies *oculo* (after *insolenti*).

[11] T¹ errors avoided by Tc are normally excluded from our apparatus. They include 65. 1 *cuius* (for *cuiuis*); 68. 2 *uocatur* (for *uocentur*); 95. 3 *anno regni*; 280. 2 *et ut* (for *ut et*). Some, but certainly not all, of Tc's improvements over T¹ will be the result of intelligent conjecture.

[12] 'As is shown by the use of majuscules for the name of Swithun at 108(. 2). It was at Winchester apparently in the 13th century, when notes were added on ff. 76 and 103, and is probably the "Gesta regum Angliae secundum Gulielmum quendam" recorded there by a foreign visitor at present unidentified in Vatican MS Reginensis lat. 2099 f. 306' (Mynors). It is also indicative that at 122. 3 'ubi Grimbaldum (capitalized in A1) abbatem constituit (sc. Alfred)' an early corrector has replaced *abbatem* with *patronum ecclesie*.

[13] So Mynors asserted in a letter to N. R. Ker dated 9 May 1953, though he left no proof. Our sample collations are consistent with the conclusion without enforcing it. But the following readings (for which we partly rely on Stubbs and on Mynors's collations) are compelling:

29. 2 *nichil*] *nic* A1 (at the end of a folio) Ag; *nil* Ap; *nichil* At, partly *in rasura*; *h̄l* Ao

390. 1 *supellex*] *sup* A1ApAg (all leaving a gap); *sūp ta* At; *sūpta* Ao

At   Cambridge, Trinity College R. 7. 10 (748), s. XII med., English. Stubbs, p. lxviii.
Ap   London, British Library Add. 23147, s. XII ex., English. Stubbs, pp. lxvii–lxviii. Ends 445. 3 *composuit*.
Ao   Oxford, All Souls College 35, s. XIII¹, English. Stubbs, pp. lxix–lxxii.
Ag   Oxford, Bodleian Library Laud. misc. 548, *c.* 1200, Newark, Surrey. Stubbs, pp. lxviii–lxix.[14]

Ao and At share a common parent lower than Al.

We now come to a separate and somewhat mysterious branch of the A tradition, Aa. The witnesses are:

Aap   Paris, Bibliothèque Nationale lat. 6047, *c.* 1200, English and French hands. Stubbs, p. lxxvi.
Aac   London, British Library Cotton Claud. C. IX, s. XIII¹, Battle, Sussex.[15] Stubbs, pp. lxxiii–lxxiv (he called it Aa¹).
Aa²   London, British Library Harley 261, s. XIII 1/4, Rochester. Stubbs, p. lxxiv (Hardy regarded it as the parent of a sixteenth-century book that is now Harley 528).
Aa³   Princeton, University Library Scheide 159 (formerly Phillipps 26641), s. XIII ex., Robertsbridge, Sussex. Stubbs, pp. lxxiv–lxxv. It ends at 446. 2 *Flandren-*, but is completed by a Parker scribe.[16]
Aah   Oxford, Bodleian Library Hatton 54, s. XIV in., Rochester. Stubbs, pp. lxxv–lxxvi.

This whole Aa group is marked not only by many shared errors against Al and the other versions, but by a series of additions (sometimes adaptations). These will be discussed further in the Commentary.

401. 2 *inuestigari*] *inuestiga* Al (at the end of a column) AtAp (Ap adds *-re* above the line, apparently in a later hand); *inuestigare* Ag; *inuestigata* Ao (changed to *-ari* in a different ink)
403. 4 *militum*] *mi* Al (at the end of a line) Ag; Ap has an erasure of (?) one letter; *(manu)m ini(quam)* Ao (and At?)
405. 4 *quaslibet*] *quas et* Al (separated by a gap and a line end) Ag; *quas* (end of line) *et* (preceded by a space) Ap; *quaslibet etiam* Ao
Further, the early correction mentioned in n. 12 above is in the text of AgAoAt (so Stubbs), and in Ap.

[14] For the owner, John Twyne, see A. G. Watson, *The Library*, 6th ser., viii (1986), 150.
[15] 'The royal letter to the abbot of Battle at the end is possibly in the same hand and rubrication as the text' (Mynors).
[16] See Carl T. Berkhout, *Princeton University Library Chronicle*, lv (1994), 277–86. We are grateful to Dr Tim Graham for the help he has given us in this matter.

Here it suffices to say that there are two layers of additions. Some (Appendix II*a* below) are found in all five witnesses. These are all quite short; they include that at 112. 1, which can hardly be other than the work of William, and many references back that are characteristic of the author himself. Others (Appendix II*b*) are found only in AacAa²Aa³Aah; they include striking long additions like the *Commendatio Alfredi* (124. 1) and the material following 297. Their authenticity is much less certain.

It is natural to deduce that Aap is nearer than the other four to the original state of A, and collation confirms. At the same time Aap avoids many errors made by Al. At least some of these improvements could in principle be the result of contamination from other versions (or of conjecture); but contamination seems to be restricted, for there is little sign of the sharing of errors with Tt and B that marks the other Aa MSS. We have therefore regarded Aap as a trustworthy and independent witness to the A version. Aac and its fellows[17] are independent both of Al and of Aap, but so contaminated as to be worthless. Their interrelationships are not therefore of practical importance. But it is probable that Aah is, as Stubbs thought, a copy of Aa².

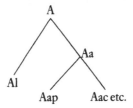

The C version

The witnesses are:

Ck   Cambridge, Trinity College, Collection Dr S. D. Keynes, written at Glastonbury in 1411 by John Merylynch, monk of the house. Contains Merylynch's *Tabula* for the *GR*, then 4.2 *[placu]it omnibus* to 42.3 *pretendere; ubi* (the rest has been lost).

Cs   Cambridge, University Library Ii. 2. 3, s. XII², Buildwas.

---

[17] To these should be added Cambridge, Trinity College R. 5. 34 (725), a Parker transcript of the sixteenth century. This is stated by Stubbs, p. lxxii (calling it Ar), to be a copy of At (if not of Al). It is in fact basically an Aa text. At 297 it actually contains more added material than its fellows.

	Stubbs, pp. lxxxvi–lxxxvii. Ends 419. 7 *calamitatem*, but is completed by a Parker hand from an Aa (non-Aap type) MS.
Cr	London, British Library Add. 38129 (formerly Phillipps 8239), s. XV, St John's Hospital, Exeter. Stubbs, pp. lxxxii–lxxxiii (his Ce²).
Cm	London, British Library Arundel 161, s. XIV¹, English. Stubbs, pp. lxxxv–lxxxvi.
Ce	London, British Library Royal 13 D. II, s. XII², Margam, Glamorgan. Stubbs, pp. lxxx–lxxxii (his base text; called by him Ce¹). Omits 449.
Cd	London, British Library Royal 13 D. V, s. XIII 2/4, St Albans (where it was used by Matthew Paris). Stubbs, pp. lxxxiii–lxxxiv.
Ca	Oxford, Bodleian Library MS D.D. All Souls College b. 32, no. 22, s. XII ex., English. Two bifolia are preserved, containing parts of the end of Book iv and of the beginning of Book v.
Cf	Oxford, All Souls College 33, s. XII², English? Stubbs, pp. lxxxiv–lxxxv. Ends 445. 3 *composuit*.
Cp	Paris, Bibliothèque Nationale lat. 6048, s. XII², French. Stubbs, p. lxxxvii (his Ce³). Contains only 72.2 *restituerit* to 376. 2 *ammiratus na-*.

Cs is almost certainly the parent of Cf.[18] They both contain, by happy chance, an interpolation mentioning one Gilbert of Minières, an ancestor of Roger Mynors (we print it in Appendix I, against our normal practice, *pietatis causa*). Equally, the presence of (part of) this interpolation in the tiny fragment Ca ensures that this too belongs to the same sub-group.[19] Further, Cd is parent of Cm.[20] It remains to relate Cs and Cd with the substantial remaining C MSS, CrCeCp (consideration of the fragment Ck must be delayed).

A conventional stemma cannot be drawn. The manuscripts would seem to descend from a developing exemplar (C), and they lie on a spectrum. At one end, Ce comes closest to TA, from which C and B ultimately descend (see p. xxiii below); at the other, Cs comes closest

---

[18] Sample collation suggests but does not quite prove this point. It seems to be a coincidence that Cf stops with the same word as Ap.

[19] So too did the MS from which Cambridge, Corpus Christi College 139 (s. XII ex., Sawley) drew its extracts. We have not seen this book, and rely for information on *MGH SS* x. 461–4, 471–2.

[20] So Stubbs. Sample collation confirms. Another copy of Cd (according to Stubbs, p. lxxxiv) is what he calls Cd², British Library Royal 13 B. XVII, s. XVI.

to B. This shows up clearly in our apparatus, where CsB not infrequently agree in error against TACe. It is our view that this is not the result of any inherited virtue in Ce, but, on the contrary, a sign of its high level of contamination from T and/or A. The source cannot usually be determined in a particular case. But it is remarkable that, in two of the places where Ce presents a variant written in by the original scribe, the only known source is T.[21] This contamination has not resulted in many cases of agreement *in error* between T and/or A and Ce; the deduction would seem to be that the contamination has been done with discrimination.[22]

To judge the quality of CpCrCd, we examined their behaviour in 32 cases where Cs and B agree in error against TACe. Ce is followed in 18 of these places by Cp, in 10 by Cd and in 9 by Cr. This suggests that Cp is much less pure,[23] Cd and Cr rather less pure than Cs.

We come now to the fragment Ck.[24] Its provenance encourages the a priori speculation that its exemplar was a manuscript presented by William to Glastonbury: perhaps, then, C itself. Collation shows that it is not copied from any extant C manuscript. Its most striking readings are a handful shared with Ce against the others: 9.2 *leniores* (correct); 31.1 *tum* (after *simplex*) (also correct); 39.1 *Westseaxana* (perhaps correct); 37.1 the number omitted, with a blank space, in the C addition. But it normally avoids Ce's private errors. It seems in fact to be a very correct gemellus of Ce. It would seem likely then that their common exemplar was C itself, in a state resulting from discriminating correction, conceivably made by William himself during his researches at

---

[21] See the apparatus at 61.3 *extremum* (where the variant agrees with T¹) and 74.3 (*cupiditas*) (Tt). For the other cases see on 15.4 *excussimus* (TtB), 72.1 *Ethelbertus* (Ce's variant is *Eadelredus*; cf. Tt's *Adelredus*), 256.4 *ampliora* (B) and 348.1 *affusi* (T¹A). For other signs of contamination in Ce, note 135.9 (where Ce has in the wrong place a line omitted by CsB; CdCr have it in the right place) and 188.7 (where CsB wrongly omit *filiam*, Cr adds it after *Emma*; Ce adds *filia* after *Emma*); also 355.2 (where Ce, but also CpCr, add in the wrong place *fecundas*, which CsB omit).

[22] The alternative hypothesis to the one we put forward is that Ce is at the 'sincere' end of the spectrum, and that Cs has been much contaminated from B, CpCrCd less so. That would involve the (not quite impossible) supposition that a corrector was prepared to delete words he did not find in B (e.g. 178.4 *primo facinora multa*, 184.2 *ex monachis*, 199.3 *eius*, 208.1 *pestem*, 356.2 *antiqui*, 357.6 *tempore*, 376.4 *subinde*, 376.6 *innixi*), however much the sense demanded their presence.

[23] It should be made clear that we are speaking here of the purity of Cs so far as contamination from TA is concerned; in other ways (as the Mynors fragment demonstrates) it is far from pure.

[24] We are extremely grateful to Dr Keynes for providing us with a photocopy and for granting us permission to discuss the manuscript here.

Glastonbury. The other primary C manuscripts will descend ultimately from earlier stages of C.

The occasional agreements in error of Cs and Cp may go back to C, though some stemmatic relationship against the others is not ruled out. But the agreements in error of Cd and Cr are so striking that we have no doubt of their stemmatic relationship. It is complicated, however, by widespread contamination of Cd (not of Cr) from Aa (non-Aap type) and B that has, most unusually, affected even the major class indicators.[25]

In these circumstances, we have followed Mynors' draft text in constructing C from Cs and Ce, the two MSS at opposed ends of the spectrum of contamination. If we are right, readings peculiar to CsB are in effect original CB readings; but, again if we are right, they will normally be errors, removed in the exemplar of Ce by a shrewd corrector. Equally, some CsCp agreements (whether or not supported in CdCr) may be genuine C readings, though we ignore them in our apparatus. For our intermittent use of the C MSS apart from CsCe see below, p. xxv.

The B version

The witnesses to this last version are:

Bq   Cambridge, Trinity College R. 7. 1 (739), s. XIII 2/4, English. Stubbs, p. lxxix.

Bc¹   London, British Library Harley 447, s. XIII 2/4, Bury. Stubbs, p. lxxvii.

Bc²   London, British Library Royal 13 B. XIX, s. XII ex., French and English hands. Stubbs, pp. lxxvii–lxxviii.

Bk   Oxford, Bodleian Library Bodley 712, s. XIV, English. Written for Robert Wyvil, bishop of Salisbury 1330–75. Stubbs, pp. lxxviii–lxxix.

By   Oxford, Bodleian Library Laud. misc. 729, s. XIII¹, English. Stubbs, pp. lxxix–lxxx (with an account of its very fragmentary state).

Bp   Paris, Bibliothèque Nationale lat. 6046, in part (see on Tp above, pp. xiii–xiv).

---

[25] Thus Cd has the Aa version at 167.1, the Aa (non-Aap type) addition at 15.1 (omitting *apud Doferam*), and the B insertion at 140. It is virtually an 'edition' of the *GR*, produced by someone of intelligence (there are a number of conjectures that we have not found elsewhere in the MSS).

Bph   Philadelphia, Free Library Lewis E. 247, s. XII 4/4, English.[26] Ends at the end of 276.
Bs   Stafford, County Record Office D1229/D3/4, s. XIV, English. A single leaf, giving 245. 2 *-rumque continet* to 249. 3 *remeandum uel*.

The witnesses split into two distinct families. On one side we have Bc¹Bc²By. Mynors could find no evidence that the first two of these are not independent of each other,[27] and we concur. Their agreement we call Bc. By is so fragmentary that sample collation gave little evidence for its attachments. What there is suggests that this too may be an independent descendant of Bc. Mynors saw too that Bs[28] is close to Bc¹ (arguably to Bc).

The second, perhaps purer[29] branch consists of Bk[30]BpBphBq. Again the gaps in two of these witnesses made our sample collation less helpful than it should have been. Individually or together Bp and Bph sometimes give the truth against the rest of the B MSS, apparently by sporadic contamination or conjecture.

Mynors seems to have reconstructed B from BqBc¹. We have, for the sake of convenience, used BkBc¹. By and Bs are too fragmentary to use, and we have ignored Bq, perhaps unwisely. For our intermittent use of Bc², Bp, and Bph see below, p. xxv.

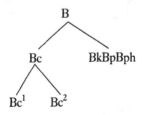

[26] Formerly Acton Griscom E. 17. See Griscom's *The Historia Regum Britanniae of Geoffrey of Monmouth* (London, New York, Toronto, 1929), pp. 39–40, for a description of its mutilated state.

[27] Very remarkable divergences between them occur in Book ii, where Bc¹ follows TtA in omitting 142–3, but CBkBc² contain them, while in 150–1, which TtABc¹ again omit altogether (Bc¹ omitting 152–3 also), C and BkBc² have different versions (see below, Appendix I).

[28] We are grateful to Dr Ian Rowney for first drawing R.M.T.'s attention to it.

[29] Bk seems at times to be less sincere than Bc: observe e.g. 74. 1 *quatere*] *quarere* Bk, *querere* Bc; 223. 1 *orbes*] *urbes* Bk, *oculos* Bc (both places in which Bc seems to offer ham-fisted assistance). But appearances may be deceptive, as Bp gets both passages right. For the same sort of thing in Bk, note 111. 3 *aduncinare*] *aduncare* Bc, *capere* Bk (but Bp and Bph are lacking here).

[30] We have a complete collation only of Bk. It is a MS marked by incorporated variants like 95. 3 ⟨*ecclesia uel*⟩ *basilica*; one such variant, at 340. 2 (*potuit* ⟨*uel uoluit*⟩), reflects contamination between versions. It also contains a long addition after 287 (see Commentary there; also on 270).

2. EDITIONS AND TRANSLATIONS

The *Gesta regum* has been little edited. The *editio princeps* (if we leave out of account the extracts published by Commelin: above, p. xiv) was the work of Sir Henry Savile[31] (1596); it was reprinted at Frankfurt five years later. Hardy[32] was right to diagnose this as largely based on Bc², and Stubbs (pp. xciv–xcvii) to show that he must have had other sources as well. Hardy himself made a remarkable advance in his edition of 1840,[33] and the admiration of Stubbs (pp. xcvii–xcviii) and Mynors was well merited. Hardy knew of many of the manuscripts, and saw the broad lines of their relationships. Stubbs, in an edition[34] that was one of the few scholarly fruits of his long episcopal period, gave full details of almost all the manuscripts, and his prefaces provide magisterial accounts of the versions and of the sources. But his text is not in itself an advance on Hardy's, and the apparatus criticus is unsystematic.

In 1815 the Revd John Sharpe, rector of Castle Eaton, Wiltshire, published a remarkable translation of the book. After Hardy's edition appeared, another cleric, the Revd Joseph Stevenson, vicar of Leighton Buzzard, revised Sharpe's translation in order to adapt it to the newly established text.[35] The resulting book, published in London in 1854, has been invaluable to us in revising Mynors's draft. Both for elegance of style and for attention to the minutest touch in William's Latin, this is a work of the highest distinction.

3. PRINCIPLES OF THE PRESENT EDITION

Our view, to be argued fully in the Commentary, is that two drafts of the *GR* were written over a number of years up to about 1126. From

---

[31] In *Rerum Anglicarum Scriptores post Bedam praecipui, ex vetustissimis codicibus manuscriptis nunc primum in lucem editi* (London, 1596).
[32] *Willelmi Malmesbiriensis monachi Gesta Regum Anglorum atque Historia Novella ad fidem codicum manuscriptorum recensuit Thomas Duffus Hardy* (London, 1840), p. xxi.
[33] There are valuable historical notes. Reprinted in *PL* clxxix. 946–1440.
[34] RS xc (two vols.), 1887, 1889.
[35] *The History of the Kings of England and the Modern History of William of Malmesbury*, transl. J. Sharpe (London, 1815); *The Church Historians of England*, Vol. iii Part I, containing The History of the Kings of England and of his own times, by William of Malmesbury . . . revised by J. Stevenson (London, 1854). Sharpe's translation had already been updated in a similar way by J. A. Giles in the Bohn Library (London, 1847).

the first (W^1) was generated what we know as the T version; the second (W^2), copied from the first, gave rise to our A witnesses. The copying that separated the drafts meant that T retained 'correct' readings (most easily recognized in documents and other cited material independently available to us) which were corrupted or deliberately changed in A (and in the later versions). William then embarked on a major revision of W^2, which was completed around 1135. From this revised draft was made a fair copy (W^3), which gave rise to our C witnesses, and, after a renewed process of correction and revision, to the archetype of our B version. The copying that led to W^3 resulted in new errors against TA, some of which were removed in the revision that led to B.

The aim of the present edition is to print, so far as is practicable, what is common to C and B.[36] Each version contains private additions and adaptations that must go back to William himself. But each is marred by private transcriptional errors, particularly prevalent in B. Though B may well witness to the final stage of William's work on the book, that witness has been corrupted in the process of transmission, and a text based on B would need much correction from the other versions before it became tolerable to read. C would make a more reliable base text, and that is how Hardy and then Stubbs used Ce. But when it differs from all the other three versions in details of wording it would seem perverse to follow it. In these circumstances it has seemed best to print an eclectic text, as close as possible to the text agreed between C and B, but purged of mistakes which crept in between W^1 and W^2 (i.e. between T and A) and between W^2 and W^3 (i.e. between A and C) and which William himself never corrected. The diagnosis of such mistakes is a delicate matter. Where we feel that a T or a TA reading has a good but not quite compelling claim to be considered superior, we distinguish it with an asterisk in the apparatus. We do not try to conceal that we are presuming to print a text that never existed in its entirety at any stage of William's work, though it is one that we hope he would have regarded as by and large close to his wishes. We are particularly conscious that we have usually relegated to the apparatus readings found only in B even where there

[36] Thus we print the agreed reading of CB against TA if it is tolerable. If either B or C, but not both, agrees with TA, we normally follow TAB against C and TAC against B. Cases where B and C differ from each other and also from TA have been dealt with on their individual merits. They include i pr. 5 *insulae pene totius*, 48. 4 *repugnantibus*, 49. 4 *uulgatissimum quoque est*, 49. 6 *posteris*, and 121. 11 *sed et ad* (see the apparatus at each point).

xxiv   PRINCIPLES OF THE PRESENT EDITION

is good reason to suppose them to be William's considered work. It is for this reason that we have marked such readings with a dagger. It is essential therefore that the reader keep a constant eye on the apparatus, paying particular attention to T variants, which may represent William's first thoughts, and to B variants, which may represent his last thoughts.

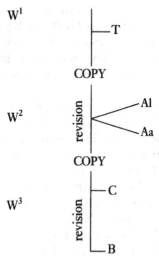

Where TA differ over a stretch of text from CB, and in some other similar cases, we have employed parallel columns in the main text to display the variants. The apparatus gives details of less extended differences between TA and CB, as well as of readings private to individual versions. There are two Appendices. In the first we give passages private to C or B that extend further than a few words. In the second, we give the more important of the changes found in Aap and, separately, those found in the Aa MSS generally (see above, pp. xvi–xvii).

We now summarize the way in which we reconstruct the four versions.

For the **T version** we cite, according to the vagaries of the gap-ridden witnesses, Tt, T¹, T, and T⁺. Where Tt is the only witness, we give almost all its variants. Where Tt and Tp are available, we give variants on which the two agree (= T¹), but normally ignore their private variants unless they are both, but divergently, different from the other versions. Where Tt and Tc are available (their agreement we call T), we do the same. Where all three witnesses are available (their agreement we call T⁺), we do not normally give variants private to Tt, Tp, and Tc (or even T¹) unless they are all, but divergently, different from the other versions.

For the **A version** we construct A from AlAap, but normally ignore their private variants. If Aap is for any reason cited separately, we upgrade it to Aa when the reading is shared by Aac. After the defection of Al at 411. 2, we substitute for it the witness of its copies Ag and At (their agreement we call a).

For the **C version** we construct C from CsCe, but normally ignore their private variants. We usually only give the readings of Cp, Cd, and Cr in passages where C alone is available or where Cs and Ce vary from each other and from the other versions. After the end of the old part of Cs in 419. 7, we construct [C] from Ce and Cr. For the last chapter of all only Cr is used.

For the **B version** we construct B from BkBc¹, but normally ignore their private variants. If Bc¹ is for any reason cited separately, we upgrade it to Bc when the reading is shared by Bc². We normally only give readings of Bp and Bph where B alone is available or where Bk and Bc¹ vary from each other and from the other versions.

It should be noticed that we do not normally record corrections made to an individual witness where they diverge from the reading of the version to which it belongs: thus e.g. 'A' may mean 'AlAap[a.c.]'.

We are well aware that the procedure we have followed runs the risk of masking genuine T, A, C, and B readings where contamination or conjecture has resulted in one of the two witnesses from which a version is constructed aligning itself with other versions. We console ourselves with the thought that such masked readings will normally be errors, and that a practice in which we have markedly differed from the draft left behind by Mynors gives some opportunity for them to show themselves. Mynors's sparse apparatus dealt merely in versions: that is, it attributed a reading to T, A, C, or B (or some combination of them) with no indication as to whether the reading was also available in individual witnesses to another version. We have followed this practice so far as not normally to give a variant unless it has the unqualified support of a version. But we do add the evidence of any individual witness to another version that agrees with the variant. Hence many readings attributed (especially) to TAl (these will often be TA readings that have been 'corrected' in Aa) and to CsB (for these see above, p. xix).

It is to be observed that no deductions should be drawn from silence as to the reading of any *individual* witness. It does *not*, for example, follow from the attribution of a variant to TAl that all the individual witnesses to the other versions agree with the printed text.

Certain parts of the *GR* are transcriptions from books and documents for which we have independent witness; others are found in a very similar form in other works of William. In these cases, our apparatus does *not* aim to provide complete information about the variants in these independent sources; it usually does no more than draw attention to readings found elsewhere that have a good claim to be thought 'correct', or to coincidences between readings found elsewhere with which part of the *GR* tradition agrees.

Readers should notice the conventions we have adopted concerning the letters in the text which give cues to the entries in the apparatus criticus. Where the passage referred to exceeds a few words, the letter is given twice, once at the start of the passage, and again at the end of it. Where only one letter is given, its reference is *solely* to the word to which it is appended, unless the form of the entry makes it clear that the reference extends further. We register variants in the order of words by giving the variant order without further explanation. Thus if *et omnia* is printed, the apparatus would give the variant as *omnia et*; this entry does *not* mean that the word *et* is added after *omnia*.

The footnotes to the text and translation in the main identify only those of the many allusions made by William to classical and other texts that he signals himself and/or that we print between inverted commas. For many other identifications, see the volume of Commentary.

We hope that readers will be helped by our innovation in dividing the chapters, sometimes very long, into numbered sub-sections.

4. ORTHOGRAPHY

We are not sure what principles, if any, governed the orthography of Mynors' draft text of the *GR*. It has seemed to us desirable to impose, so far as possible, a consistent practice. The natural place to look for William's own principles is his autograph of the *Gesta pontificum*, providentially available as Oxford, Magdalen College lat. 172. Analysis shows that William preserved in his narrative passages a fairly consistent orthography, though he was ready to abandon his normal practice, especially for proper names, when citing from other sources, and particularly from documents. He is on the whole consistent in his spelling of individual words; and some general principles can be discerned.[37]

t normally replaces *c* before *i* where another vowel follows *i*, however odd the result may seem (*fatio, sotius*): hence e.g. *fautium* (but *faucibus*), *felitior* (but *feliciter*).

William conforms to classical standards in the use of final *e* and *ae* (normally represented by a hooked *e*); so adverbs are consistently distinguished from feminines. The use of *e* and *ae* initially varies from word to word: thus *ae* (hooked *e*) is regularly used for *aetas, aequus* and *aecclesia*, but usually not for *edes, emulus, estimo*. Internally *e* is much preferred to *ae* or *oe*, though e.g. *caelum, laetus* are normal. The prefix *prae*- is normally abbreviated, but when it is not it is spelt *pre-*.

Internal *m* and *n* are normally used as in Classical Latin, but note e.g. *aliquandiu* and *quanuis*. Abbreviation often masks the distinction. *-mpn-* for *-mn-* is common, but e.g. *erumna* and *sollemnis* predominate.

y seems never to be employed.

There are some intrusive aspirates (e.g. *nichil*), and William is indecisive over e.g. *pulc(h)rum* and *sepulc(h)rum*.

his (also *eis*, rarely *iis*) is used, not *hiis*. Also *eisdem*, not *(h)isdem*.

Some words seem always to be abbreviated, e.g. *gratia* (hence difficulty for the editor: we have chosen to write e.g. *epistola, michi, presbiter*).

Prefixes are normally assimilated, but note exceptions like *admitto, admodum, exsanguis, exsequi, exsors* (and even *obprobrium, subrigo*).

Some Greek words have been 'medievalized', e.g. *laberinthus, panagericus, rethorica*. In others, though by no means all, *f* replaces the original phi (thus *sarcofagus*).

To come to proper names: a similar pattern emerges. William is fairly consistent in spelling the name of a particular individual, though his spellings may vary for the same names applied to different people (thus most Æthelreds become *Ethelredus*, but the Unready is regularly *Egelredus*). There is in general a good deal of vacillation over *-th-* and *-d-*.

In the Latinization of Anglo-Saxon proper names, much of William's practice is accounted for by the principle that initially and internally *æ, ea*, and *eo* become *e* (though note e.g. *Ethelardus* for

---

[37] It may be noted that N. E. S. A. Hamilton's splendid edition in RS lii is remarkably accurate in details of spelling, as in other ways.

Æthelheard). There is great variety in the treatment of Æthel- (*Ethel-*, *Adel-*, *Egel-*, *Edel-*). Cen- becomes *Ken-*, Cw- *Qu-*, Cyne- *Kine-*, Ecg- *Eg-*, Pleg- *Plei-*, and Wig- *Wi-*. At the end of a name, *-us* or *-a* is often added without further modification. But -burh becomes *-burga*, -erht *-ertus*, -gifu *-gifa* or *-giua*, -heah *-egus*, -here *-erius*, -ig(e) *-ius*, -ine *-inus*, -iu *-ius*, -walh *-walkius*, and -yth *-ida* (*-itha*).

Internal *w* is frequently, and not always consistently, replaced by *u* (e.g. *Eduardus*).

The Anglo-Saxon form is often preserved when William is transcribing documents, or giving lists that go back to documents.

Among French names, *Rotbertus* and *Willelmus* are the regular forms.

In printing our text of the *GR*, we have tried so far as possible to be consistent: that is, a word that is not a proper name is spelt the same way each time it appears, and although a proper name may be spelt differently for different bearers of the name, we have aimed to be consistent for each individual person. Where we can, we have followed the norms of the *GP*.[38] Where a word or name did not appear in the *GP*, we have tried to act in accordance with William's general principles, while naturally giving weight to any strong indication given by the *GR* MSS. We shall no doubt not please everyone in acting thus; but there was nothing to be said for following the orthography of any individual manuscript of the *GR*. Even A1, produced soon after William wrote, does not represent his practice at all consistently.

---

[38] We have sometimes diverged from this rule when William is citing documents and other sources (see above p. xxvi). Similarly, we have not corrected the anomalous genitive forms of OE proper names found in the manuscripts at 143.2, 150B.3 and 185.2 (contrast 39).

SIGLA

T version

    Tt   Troyes 294 bis, s. XII^2
    Tp   Paris lat. 6046, s. XIV
    Tc   London, British Library Add. 39646, s. XII ex.
    T^1 = agreement of TtTp
    T   = agreement of TtTc
    T$^+$ = agreement of TtTpTc

A version

    Al   London, British Library Arundel 35, s. XII 2/4
    Aap   Paris lat. 6047, *c*.1200
    Aac   London, British Library Cotton Claud. C. IX, s. XIII^1
    A   = agreement of AlAap
    Aa   = agreement of AapAac

After the defection of Al:

    Ag   Oxford, Bodleian Library Laud misc. 548, *c*.1200
    At   Cambridge, Trinity College R. 7. 10 (748), s. XII med.
    a = agreement of AgAt
    [A]   = agreement of aAap

C version

    Ce   London, British Library Royal 13 D. II, s. XII^2
    Cs   Cambridge, University Library Ii. 2. 3, s. XII^2
    C   = agreement of CeCs

After the defection of Cs:

    Cr   London, British Library Add. 38129, s. XV
    [C]   = agreement of CeCr

Also employed:

    Ca   Oxford, Bodleian Library MS D.D. All Souls College b. 32, no. 22, s. XII ex.
    Cd   London, British Library Royal 13 D. V, s. XIII 2/4
    Cp   Paris lat. 6048, s. XII^2

SIGLA

B version

Bk	Oxford, Bodleian Library Bodley 712, s. XIV (1330–75)
Bc¹	London, British Library Harley 447, s. XIII 2/4
Bc²	London, British Library Royal 13 B. XIX, s. XII ex.
B	= agreement of BkBc¹
Bc	= agreement of Bc¹Bc²

Also employed:

Bp	Paris lat. 6046, s. XIV
Bph	Philadelphia, Free Library Lewis E. 247, s. XII 4/4

Other witnesses*

β	Oxford, Bodleian Library Lat. class. d. 39, s. XII²
γ	London, British Library Harley 258, s. XVII
δ	Oxford, Bodleian Library Dugdale 21, s. XVII
ϵ	Oxford, Bodleian Library Wood empt. 5, s. XIII
ζ	London, British Library Cotton Tib. A. XV, s. XI¹
η	London, British Library Royal 11 D. VIII, fo. 249ʳ, s. XII in.
θ	London, British Library Harley 633, s. XII²
κ	Cambridge, University Library Kk. 4. 6, s. XII 1/4
λ	London, British Library Lansdowne 417, s. XIV–XV
μ	London, British Library Arundel 178, s. XVI
ξ	Oxford, Queen's College 368, s. XVII
π	London, Public Record Office E 164/24, s. XIII
ρ	Oxford, Bodleian Library Rawlinson B. 252, s. XVII
σ	Oxford, Bodleian Library Wood empt. 1, s. XIV
τ	London, British Library Cotton Tib. A. V, s. XV
ϕ	Oxford, Bodleian Library James 23, s. XVII
ψ	London, British Library Cotton Claud. E. V, s. XII 1/4
Γ	South-western version of c. 129 (see apparatus ad loc.)

*Folio numbers for β can be traced in Thomson, *William of Malmesbury*; for η and θ (William's *Liber pontificalis*) in W. Levison, *Neues Archiv für ältere deutsche Geschichtskunde*, xxxv (1910), 333–431; and for the charter collections in Sawyer (references in the apparatus).

a.c.	before correction
p.c.	after correction
s.l.	above the line
mg.	in the margin
v	variant
*	See above, p. xxiii
†	See above, p. xxiv

PLAN OF THE *GR*

BOOK I

General theme: 'the history of the English from their conquest of Britain to the reign of Ecgberht'.

In particular: Roman England and the English conquest 1–8; the histories of the four most powerful English kingdoms: Kent 9–15, Wessex 16–43, Northumbria 44–73, and Mercia 74–96; of the two least powerful: East Anglia 97, East Saxons 98; survey of kingdoms and bishoprics 99–105.

Digressions: (1) *Linked to the main theme*: origins of Malmesbury abbey 19. 3, 30; (early history of Glastonbury 19–29, 35–6, 38–9); character and death of Bede 54–63; the achievement of Alcuin 66, 69–70. (2) *Independent*: none. (3) *Linked to other digressions*: praise of St Aldhelm 31; the Frankish kings and their descendants 67–8.

BOOK II

In general: 'the history of the kingdom to the Norman Conquest'.

In particular: Reign and achievement of Alfred 120–4; of Æthelstan 131–40; privileges of Glastonbury 142–3, 150–1, 184–5; Edgar 148–60; Æthelred II 164–77; Cnut 181–7; Edward the Confessor 196–200, 220–8.

Digressions: (1) History of the later Carolingians 110, 112, 128; the origins and early history of Normandy 127, 178; English royal saints, male and female 207–19. (2) Norman stories 145; Gerbertian legends 167–9, 172; French history 187; legends of Emperor Henry II 189–94; Gregory VI 201–3. (3) *Visio Karoli* 111; miraculous stories from Italy 170–1; miraculous stories from Germany 173–5; other miraculous stories, two of Rome 204–7.

BOOKS III–V 'will tell of the three Norman kings, together with such events as befell in their time in other countries'.

BOOK III

In general: The reign of William I.

In particular: Norman background 229–38; conquest of England 238–58; foreign affairs 261; private life and character 267, 273, 277–9; problems of the Anglo-Norman Church 270–2; William's children 274–6; his death 283.

Digressions: (1) History of the county of Anjou 235; Danish royal house 259; Norwegian 260; Robert Guiscard and the Normans in the South 262; the dispute between Canterbury and York 295–303. (2) Miracle in Brittany 237; legends and stories of Gregory VII 263–6; legend of Maurilius of Rouen 268; Berengar of Tours 284–5; the Investiture Dispute 288–9. (3) Miracles concerning the Eucharist 286; Arthur's grave 287; miracles of mice 290–1; Marianus Scotus 292; a German miracle 293.

BOOK IV

In general: The reign of William II and 'certain events of his time, whether disasters in this country or great doings overseas . . .; in particular the Christians' pilgrimage to Jerusalem'.

In particular: William II 305–21; natural and other disasters and portents 322-33; his death 333; Robert Curthose back home 389.

Digressions: (1) transfer of episcopal sees in England 338–41. (2) Cistercian Order 334–7; Goscelin 342; Crusade, concluding with accounts of Bohemond, Raymond, and Robert Curthose 343–89. (3) Descriptions of Rome, Constantinople, Antioch, and Jerusalem: 351–3, 354–6, 359, 367–8.

BOOK V

In general: The reign of Henry I selectively to *c.* 1125.
Digressions: (1) King Sigurd's crusade 410; Henry V and Investitures 420–38. (2) William IX of Aquitaine and Bishop Peter of Poitiers 439. (3) Norman monastic reformers 440; English monastic reformers 441–4; incorruption of English saints 445.

TEXT AND TRANSLATION

EPISTOLA I

*Incipit Epistola Conuentus Malmesberiensis ad regem
Dauid de Gestis Anglorum*

DOMINO suo regi magnificentissimo et piissimo Dauid conuentus Malmesberiae salutes et fideles orationes. Generis uestri amplitudo et mentis in bonis magnitudo ad nos usque suaui manauit fama. Quapropter amorem uestrum in animos nostros rapuimus, et prosperitati uitae uestrae certantibus uotis fauemus. Habet enim hoc uirtus proprium, ut quamlibet graues difficultates, quamlibet remotas terrarum longinquitates perrumpat, et bonos quosque in sui animi rationem et fauorem allitiat. Amamus ergo in uobis quod dicitur, quia sitis alloquio dulcis, accessu non difficilis, cui sit naturale uultus benignitate trepidos inuitare, fastum 2 regii supercilii morum comitate premere. Itaque qui solus est Rex, omnium regum corda regens, constituens omnia transitoria preter bonitatis meritum, illam*ᵇ* olim sanctitate famosam, regali uirtute laudatam, omni honestate ornatam, antecessorum uestrorum prosapiam uestro non immerito iure sullimauit regio. Quanuis enim genus mortalium pronius insideat prauitati, et iuniores multo ardentius et incautius*ᶜ* senioribus semper in ea studeant, recessit a genere uestro huiusmodi omen infelicitatis. Cum uero solus habeamini tantorum regum et principum heres, non minus ipsis fundati estis fidei religione, potentiae uirtute, munificentiae misericordia, morum stabilitate.

3 Hinc est quod Anglorum Regum*ᵈ* Gesta uestra regia auctoritate dominae nostrae imperatrici nepti uestrae destinare non timuimus, quae hortatu dominae nostrae sororis uestrae Mathildis reginae scribere fecimus, rex illustris et prestantissime merito*ᵉ* meritoque uenerande domine. Suscipiat ergo excellentia uestra, regum optime, a pauperculo et desolato cetu uestro hereditarium munus, et dominae imperatrici una cum nostro legato uestra etiam auctoritate deferri curate. Quod si non uobis reddidissemus, iure argui

---

ᵃ *This and the following letter are preserved only in Tt, from which they were printed by E. Könsgen, Deutsches Archiv für Erforschung des Mittelalters, xxxi (1975), 204–14*   *ᵇ* *Mynors; illa Tt*   *ᶜ* *Könsgen, Mynors; cautius Tt*   *ᵈ* *Könsgen, Mynors; rerum Tt (before correction?)*   *ᵉ* *Perhaps to be deleted (so translated)*

LETTER I

A Letter from the Convent of Malmesbury to King David about the History of the English

TO THEIR lord the most glorious and religious King David the convent of Malmesbury offer greetings and faithful prayers.

Your Majesty's illustrious lineage and your great and generous spirit in good works have reached us by report which it was sweet to hear. This quickly filled our hearts with affection for you, and we rival one another in prayers for your long life and prosperity; for it is a property of excellence to be able to transcend obstacles however serious and distances however great, and attract all men of good will to its own way of thinking and feeling. So what we love in you is that you are, they say, so mild in address, so easy of access, with a natural kindliness of mien which encourages the diffident and a characteristic courtesy which does away with the haughty air of royalty. Thus it was well deserved when the only true King, who rules the hearts of all kings, and has appointed that all things should pass away except the merit won by goodness, exalted to royal rank in you that line of your ancestors which had of old been renowned for sanctity, famed for royal valour, and adorned with honour in all its forms. For let mortal men tend as they will towards wrongdoing, and let young men always show themselves more hot-blooded and headstrong in that direction than their elders: your own family has been spared this forerunner of misfortune. Rated as you are the sole heir to such a line of kings and princes, your foundation in religious faith, in virtue backed by power and compassion expressed by generosity, and in firm consistency of character is no less than theirs.

This explains the confidence with which we seek your Majesty's authorization in offering to your niece our lady the Empress Matilda this *History of the English Kings*, the writing of which we arranged with the encouragement of our lady your sister Queen Matilda, O illustrious and most glorious king and justly our honoured lord. We therefore beg your Majesty, best of kings, to accept from your poor desolate convent this offering which is yours by inheritance, to add your own authorization, and to arrange for the gift, together with our messenger, to be sent forward to our lady the empress. Had we not given it to you

deberemus iniuriae, et uos ingratitudinis possetis reos expostulare. Hic enim cognoscetis quam splendidis progenitoribus uos non indignus nepos et ipsa proneptis accesseritis, et quam emulo gestu diuinae mentes uestrae illorum sectatae sint uestigia, prius-
4 quam cognoscerent nomina. Sane quaedam quae diebus regum in aliis acciderunt terris preter materiam apposuimus, quae uiderentur[a] et ignari nescisse et ignaui preterisse. Pro quibus omnibus si quantulumcumque amicitiam et aduocationem uestram meruerimus, habunde mercedem tulerimus. Quanuis enim amplissimus fructus bonorum operum sit pura conscientia, nonnichil tamen aduocatio et fauor principum nutrit et fouet ingenia: uester precipue, cuius mens benigna, manus munifica, regalis uita sine querela predicatur.
5 Est certe familiae uestrae gentilitium ut ametis litterarum studium. Nam ut sileamus de ceteris, quorum litteraturam liber iste non taceat, domina nostra germana uestra hoc inter alias uirtutes suas habebat continuum, ut litteris assisteret, cultores earum proueheret. Cuius imitari beniuolentiam regalis erit animi ingenuique propositi, tum[b] in reliquis[c] tum in dilectione monasterii sancti
6 Aldelmi cognati uestri. Quod ita demum fiet, si et sequamini quae bene fecit et expleueritis quae minus fecit. Profecto enim credimus quod non se putauit totam morituram nec omnino in cineres abituram, dum illum relinqueret superstitem qui sua errata pro uirili portione corrigere sciret, pro regali potentia posset, pro fraterno affectu uellet. Dum uero ipsa uiueret, uiguit in aecclesia nostra totius honoris perfectio, totius sanctitatis religio, totius caritatis lar-
7 gitio. Hoc solum in habundantia totius bonitatis superfuit, quod absque pastore gregem aecclesiae nostrae liquerit. Qua de causa oues ipsas,[d] quas domina nostra congregauit, iniuste dispersas noueritis. Quapropter supliciter uestram regiam potestatem imploramus, ut preter ea quae per epistolam uobis mandamus, non indignanter obaudiatis et muneris nostri latorem apud imperatricem regali cura commendetis,[e] quatinus de uobis nobis sit gloria, in quibus tantae spei nostrae constat fidutia.

Valeat in Christo regalis dignitas uestra.

[a] *Probably read* uideremur *(so translated) pr. 4 n. k); so too at Letter ii. 6 (after* silentium*)* [b] *William no doubt wrote* cum *(see below, i* [c] *Könsgen;* reliquiis *Tt* [d] *Könsgen;* ipsae *Tt* [e] *The text appears to be corrupt. As in Letter ii. 7 there should be a distinction between the words written in the epistle and those to be conveyed orally by its bearer (on the problems of the monastery). Read e.g.* obaudiatis muneris nostri latorem, et *(or* eumque*) apud*

as your due, we should rightly be accused of wrongdoing, and you could fairly denounce us as guilty of ingratitude. For here you will learn how illustrious are the forebears whom you follow as their not unworthy grandson and she as their grand-niece, and how well judged was the rivalry, how percipient the intentions of you both, as you pursued their footsteps before you even knew their names. Some things we 4 have indeed added which happened in the time of those kings in other countries, although outside our subject-matter, of which we might seem ignorant if we had been unaware of them or idle had we passed them by. If in return for all this we secure in the smallest degree your friendship and support, we shall be abundantly rewarded. For though the most abundant reward of good works is a clear conscience, the support and favour of princes does much to feed and foster gifted men: and your favour in particular, whose beneficent purpose, generous hand, and kingly way of life are extolled with no dissentient voice.

It is without doubt a characteristic of your family to love the 5 study of letters, for, to say nothing of other members whose culture does not pass unnoticed in this book, our lady your sister among her other virtues never ceased to support good literature and advance those who were devoted to it. To imitate her goodwill will befit your kingly spirit and your noble purpose, not in other points alone but more particularly in your love for the monastery of St Aldhelm your kinsman. And the best way to accomplish this 6 will be to follow what she so admirably did, and equally to fill in what she left undone. For we are convinced that she thought she would not wholly die nor pass entirely into dust, provided she might leave behind her a man who would know how to correct her mistakes to the best of his capacity with the power of a king to do so and the readiness of a loving brother. While she lived, our church enjoyed in full measure complete honour, unsullied holiness, loving and unstinting generosity. One thing alone was wanting 7 in this abundant goodness: she left our church a flock without a shepherd. As a result, the sheep whom our lady gathered into the fold are, we must tell you, unjustly scattered. And this is why we humbly beseech your royal Majesty further to be so good as to comply especially with what we ask in our letter, and also with kingly forethought to recommend to the empress the bearer of our gift, that we may enjoy some reflected glory from you, to whom we entrust the fulfilment of all our hopes.

We wish your royal Majesty farewell in Christ.

EPISTOLA II

Alia epistola ad Imperatricem

Gloriosissimae imperatrici et dominae suae Mathildi cetus fratrum Malmesberiae Deo et sanctae Mariae sanctoque Aldelmo seruientium salutes et fideles orationes. Regalis pietas et uerae pietatis sancta religio reuerentissimae matris uestrae Mathildis reginae iam dudum post eius discessum nos premonuere nil minus de uestra quam de ipsius bonitate sperare. Et quia spei nunc pene satisfecit rei ueritas in hoc, quod sitis apud regem nostrum totius rectitudinis stipes, totius clementiae origo, totius misericordiae status, gratias Deo uotis omnibus exhibemus.
2 Et iuste quidem. Cum enim ipsa uiuens toti*ᵃ* pene nostro*ᵇ* seculo subueniret et in eius pietate fere omnium penderet solatium nostramque regali dote possideret aecclesiam, uberius nos eius misericordia fouebamur. Quippe ipsius regimine ibi habundanter fulgebat religio ubi totius caritatis preminebat plenitudo. Infamis igitur Fortuna, talibus nostrae aecclesiae successibus inuidens, tanto nos acrius affecit eius fine dolore et merore, quanto familiarius eius regimine pollebat ipse locus gloria et honore. Et uix *ᶜ*tantae desolationi
3 nostrae respirauit spei*ᶜ* consolatio felicis aduentus uestri in Angliam, prestantissima domina, quia satis deceret uos imperatricem dominari ubi*ᵈ* mater uestra merito ueneranda insignis regina dominabatur. Maxime uero, cum de uita eius nil aliud reprehendi possit nisi quod ipsam aecclesiam sine rectore dimiserit, iustissimum est*ᵉ* tam potentis filiae sapientia corrigi quo beatissimae matris ignorantia hactenus potuit reprehendi. Quapropter dominationem uestram in quanto possumus animo rapimus, et hoc libro, quem iussu dominae nostrae de Anglorum regum gestis scribere fecimus, nos et nostra regiae aduocationi uestrae summittimus.
4   Solebant sane huiusmodi libri regibus siue reginis antiquitus scribi, ut quasi ad uitae suae exemplum eis instruerentur aliorum

---

ᵃ Könsgen, Mynors; tot *Tt*   *ᵇ Written above the line in Tt, and perhaps to be deleted*   *ᶜ⁻ᶜ The wording of this phrase is hardly secure*   *ᵈ Mynors;* uel ubi unde *Tt*   *ᵉ* est id *would be clearer*

LETTER II

Another letter, to the Empress

To the most glorious empress, their lady Matilda, the community of brethren who at Malmesbury serve God and St Mary and St Aldhelm offer greetings and faithful prayers.

The queenly piety, and the religious life born of true piety, that marked your most revered mother Queen Matilda had long ago led us to expect after her passing no less from your goodness than from hers. And now that our hopes have almost been fulfilled by the reality, inasmuch as you are in our king's counsels a root of all rectitude, a fount of all mercy, and a prop and stay of all compassion, we give God thanks in all our prayers. And rightly so; for while she herself 2 during her lifetime was the support of almost our whole world (since the relief of almost all men depended on her piety), because by royal gift she possessed our church, we enjoyed her compassion more fully than other men. Under her rule the light of religion shone abundantly in the place where her charity in its fullness was pre-eminent. And so cursed Fortune, jealous of the great prosperity of our church, struck us all the more violently with grief and mourning at her death, in proportion to the glory and honour which were so familiar a source of strength to this same place under her rule. So great 3 was our desolation that we scarcely took heart again with the hope, most excellent lady, of your prosperous arrival in England; for it seemed to us right and proper that you as empress should rule where your mother, to whom we were rightly devoted, ruled as a famous queen. Above all, since no exception can be taken to anything else in her life except that she left our church without a head, it is the height of justice that the wisdom of so powerful a daughter should set right the one point in which a truly blessed mother has so far by her ignorance laid herself open to criticism. We therefore express the greatest possible affection for your imperial Majesty, and with the offer of this book on the history of the English kings, the writing of which we arranged on our lady's instructions, we entrust ourselves and all that is ours to your royal patronage.

It is true that in the old days books of this kind were written for 4 kings or queens in order to provide them with a sort of pattern for their own lives, from which they could learn to follow some men's

prosequi triumphos, aliorum uitare miserias, aliorum imitari sapientiam, aliorum contempnere stultitiam. Quod beatissimam matrem uestram non latebat, cum eius sanctissimus animus adeo litterarum negotiis operam dedisset. Semel igitur nobiscum inito sermone de beatissimo Aldelmo, cuius se consanguineam non immerito gloriabatur, seriem eius prosapiae sciscitata est. Acceptoque responso quod eadem esset quae regum Westsaxonum fuisset, rogauit ut totam eius progeniem breui sibi libello disponeremus, se indignam[a] asserens more antiquo uolumine gestorum regum 5 Anglorum honorari. Nec potuit nostra negare humilitas quod tam imperiosa uolebat auctoritas. Exigua igitur scedula seriem et nomina simul et annos regum Anglorum complecti fecimus. Tum uero grandiusculae narrationis illecta desiderio, facile dulcedine qua pollebat effecit ut plenam de antecessoribus eius meditari fecissemus historiam. Maius itaque moueri fecimus de regibus opus,[1] profuturum, ut dicebat, illorum notitiae, suae gloriae, nostrae aecclesiae utilitati et famae.

6 Sed uix imperatis institeramus cum illam repente Fortuna, profectibus Angliae inuidens, immortalitatis, ut speramus, sedibus dedicauit. Quo merore consternati, decreuimus stili abiurare studium, cum uideremus exisse de medio hortatricem studiorum. Enimuero procedente tempore rupere silentium tum amicorum petitio, tum rei utilitas, quia uidebatur et erat indignum ut tantorum uirorum 7 sepeliretur memoria, immorerentur[b] gesta. Nunc autem liber iste, cum totus de uestris tractetur[c] progenitoribus, et quam potenter rerum Opifex imperiale genus uestrum ad uos usque produxerit,[d] nulli mortalium iustius quam uobis mitti potest. In eo etiam experiri potestis quod nullus eorum quorum liber presens continet memoriam, nec rex aliquis nec regina aliqua, regalius uel splendidius uobis Anglorum regni hereditarii iura expectauerit. Suscipiat igitur imperialis clementia uestra exiguum munus, et munere nostro dominationem nostri. Preterea quae uobis per libri latorem mandamus, pro anima matris uestrae et antecessorum uestrorum omnium, imperialiter audite, et nobis misericordiam impendere curate.

Valeat imperialis uestra dignatio.

---

[a] *Winterbottom;* non indignam *Tt;* non dignam *Brett*   [b] *Perhaps* commorerentur *(cf. VD p. 272)*   [c] *One expects* tractet   [d] *Mynors (cf. i pr. 6);* perduxerit *Tt*

[1] Cf. Virgil, *Aen.* vii. 45.

successes, while avoiding the misfortunes of others, to imitate the wisdom of some and to look down on the foolishness of others. Of this your most blessed mother was well aware, since her sainted mind had devoted so much attention to the business of literary studies. Thus on one occasion we were engaged in conversation with her on the subject of St Aldhelm, whose kinswoman she claimed with proper pride to be, and she asked for information about his family. When told in reply that his lineage was the same as that of the kings of the West Saxons, she asked us to set out his whole family history in a short essay for her benefit, claiming that she was unworthy to receive the tribute of a volume on traditional lines on the history of the English kings. In our humble position we could not refuse a 5 request backed by such imperious authority. We therefore arranged for the drawing up of a brief list of the English kings, both names and dates. She was then attracted by the project of a somewhat fuller narrative, and with that charm which was one of her strong points she easily induced us to contemplate a full history of her predecessors. So we came 'to set on foot a greater enterprise'[1] about our kings, one that would (as she put it) make them better known, bring her credit and be both useful and honourable to our foundation.

Scarcely however had we started on our task when on a sudden Fortune, grudging the success achieved by England, removed her, as we trust, to the realm of immortality. Prostrated by grief, we decided to abandon the attempt to write, seeing that the lady who had encouraged our endeavours had been taken from our midst. Then, as time went on, our silence was broken, partly by requests from our friends, partly by the value of the project, for it both seemed and was quite wrong that the memory of those great men should remain buried and their deeds die with them. So now this book, which deals entirely 7 with your forebears, and with what power the Creator has advanced your imperial house down to yourself, cannot be offered to any living person with more justice than to you. In it you can also discover that none of those chronicled in this present book, whether king or queen, has more royal or more glorious claim to the hereditary crown of England than yourself. May your imperial Majesty therefore deign to accept our humble gift, and by our gift the right to rule over us. Lend your imperial ear, furthermore, for the sake of the souls of your mother and all your predecessors, to the requests which we make by the bearer of the book, and do not forget to show us compassion.

We wish your imperial Majesty farewell.

EPISTOLA III

^aEpistola ad Rotbertum comitem^b

Domino uenerabili et famoso comiti Rotberto, filio regis,^c Willelmus Malmesberiae monachus salutes^d et, si quas ualet, orationes. Virtus clarorum uirorum illud uel maxime laudandum in se^e commendat, quod etiam longe positorum animos ad se diligendum inuitat; unde inferiores superiorum uirtutes fatiunt suas, dum earum adorant uestigia ad quarum aspirare non ualent exempla. Porro totum ad maiorum redundat gloriam, quod ipsi et bonum fatiunt et minores ad se amandum accendunt. Vestrum est igitur, o duces, si quid boni facimus,^f uestrum profecto si quid dignum memoria scribimus; uestra industria nobis est incitamento ut, quia pericula uestra paci nostrae impenditis, uos uicissim per labores nostros omni aeuo inclarescatis.

2 Hinc est quod Gesta Regum Anglorum, quae nuper edidi, uobis potissimum consecranda credidi, domine comes uenerabilis et merito amabilis. Nullum enim magis decet bonarum artium fautorem esse quam te, cui adhesit magnanimitas aui, munificentia patrui, prudentia patris; quos^g cum emulis industriae liniamentis representes,[1] illud peculiare gloriae tuae facis, quod litteris insistis. Quid quod etiam notitia tua dignaris litteratos quos uel inuidia famae uel tenuitas fortunae fecit obscuros? Quia enim natura indulget sibi, quod quis probat in se ipso non improbat in altero. Consentaneos igitur sibi mores experiuntur in te litterati, quos citra intellectum ullius acrimoniae benignus aspicis, iocundus admittis, inuitus^h dimittis. Nichil plane in te mutauit fortunae amplitudo, nisi ut pene tantum benefacere posses quantum uelles.

3 Suscipe ergo, uirorum clarissime, opus in quo te quasi eⁱ speculo uideas, dum intelliget tuae serenitatis assensus ante te summorum procerum imitatum facta quam audires nomina. Continentiam

---

^a *This letter is found only in C (where it appears at the end of Book iii), and B (where it precedes Book i)* ^b *Cs;* Epistola Willelmi monachi Malmesberiensis ad Robertum comitem *Bc¹; no headings in CeBkBc²* ^c filio regis Ro(d)berto *B* ^d salutem *Bk,* sal *Bc* ^e in se laudandum *B* ^f facimus boni *B* ^g quod *B* ^h munus *B* ⁱ ex *B*

---

[1] For this difficult phrase cf. 11. 2.

LETTER III

A letter to Earl Robert

To his honourable lord the famous Earl Robert, son of the king, William monk of Malmesbury sends greetings and, for what they are worth, his prayers.

The excellence of great men has one laudable feature which perhaps more than any other recommends it; it inspires the affection even of those who are far off, so that men of lower degree adopt as their own the virtues of those above them, reverencing the footprints of qualities they cannot hope to follow. Great men in fact deserve all the credit, both for the good they do and for the affection they inspire in lesser men. Yours is the credit therefore, O leaders of men, if we do anything good, and yours if we write anything that deserves to live; it is your energy, since it is by the perils you undergo that you buy our peace, which spurs us on to secure you in return by our own labours a lasting renown.

Hence it is, my honourable and deservedly lovable lord, that I have thought it right to dedicate especially to you the *History of the English Kings* which I have lately put out. There is no one for whom patronage of the liberal arts is more appropriate than yourself, in whom combine the noble spirit of your grandfather, your uncle's generosity, your father's wisdom, whose pattern you reproduce as their rival in activity,[1] while adding a special element to your own reputation, your devotion to letters. What is more, you think worthy of your notice men of letters who have been thrust into obscurity by jealous competitors or limited resources. Human nature is self-indulgent, and a man does not reject in others what he approves in himself. Thus men of literary tastes find in you a congenial character: with no suggestion of any harsh feeling you look kindly upon them, you give them a warm welcome, and part from them with regret. In fact, your grand position has made no change in you, except that you are now able to do almost as much in the way of kindness to others as you could wish.

Receive therefore, most distinguished of men, a work in which you can see yourself as in a mirror; for you will understand and will agree that you were imitating the actions of the greatest princes before you

autem operis prologus primi libri exponit; quem[a] si placuerit legere, materiam totam poteris de compendio colligere. Illud a uestra dignitate impetratum uelim, ut non michi uertatur uitio quod sepe per excessum alias quam in Anglia[b] peregrinatur narratio; uolo enim hoc opus esse multarum historiarum breuiarium, quanuis a maiori parte uocauerim Gesta Regum Anglorum.

[a] quod *B*   [b] Grecia *B*

even heard their names. The contents of the work are set out in the prologue to the first book; and if you will be so good as to read that, you will be able to get a summary view of the subject-matter as a whole. One request I would make of your highness: not to blame me if my narrative has often exceeded its limits and goes roaming outside England; for I would like this work to serve as a summary of many fields of history, although to suit the greater part of it I have called it *A History of the English Kings*.

LIBER PRIMVS

Prologus in libro primo

RES Anglorum gestas Beda, uir maxime doctus et minime superbus, ab aduentu eorum in Britanniam usque ad suos dies plano et suaui sermone absoluit;[a] post eum non facile, ut arbitror, reperies qui historiis illius gentis Latina oratione texendis animum dederit.[b] Viderint alii si quid earum rerum[c] uel iam inuenerint[d] uel post haec inuenturi sint;[e] noster labor, licet in querendo sollicitas 2 duxerit excubias, frustra ad hoc tempus consumpsit operam. Sunt sane[f] quaedam uetustatis inditia cronico more et patrio sermone per annos Domini ordinata. Per haec senium obliuionis eluctari meruerunt quaecumque tempora post illum uirum fluxerunt. Nam de Elwardo, illustri et magnifico uiro, qui Cronica illa Latine aggressus est digerere, prestat silere, cuius michi esset intentio animo si non 3 essent uerba fastidio. Nec uero nostram[g] effugit conscientiam domni Edmeri sobria sermonis festiuitate elucubratum opus, in quo a rege Edgaro orsus usque ad Willelmum primum raptim tempora perstrinxit, et inde licentius euagatus usque ad obitum Anselmi[h] archiepiscopi diffusam et necessariam historiam studiosis exhibuit. Ita pretermissis a tempore Bedae ducentis et uiginti tribus[i] annis, quos iste nulla memoria dignatus est, absque litterarum patrocinio claudi- 4 cat cursus temporum[j] in medio. Vnde michi cum[k] propter patriae caritatem, tum propter[l] adhortantium auctoritatem uoluntati[m] fuit interruptam temporum seriem sarcire et exarata barbarice Romano sale[n] condire; et, ut res ordinatius procedat, aliqua ex his quae sepe dicendus Beda dixit deflorabo, pauca perstringens, pluribus ualefatiens.

5 Procedat itaque primus libellus de Anglorum gestis succinctus, ex quo Britanniam occupauere usque ad regem Egbirhtum,[o] qui uaria sorte profligatis regulis insulae pene totius[p] nactus est monarchiam. Sed cum quattuor ex Anglis potentissima pullulauerint[q] regna,

---

[a] describit *A*   [b] dederint *A*   [c] rerum earum *B*. *This version's frequent reordering of words will henceforth be ignored except in special circumstances*   [d] inuenerunt *A*   [e] sunt *A*   [f] sane sunt *Tt*   [g] uestram *Tt*   [h] Radulfi *B†*   [i] quattuor *Tt*; et tribus *C*   [j] annorum *Tt*   [k] tum *TtAaC; the autograph of GP shows that William used* cum . . . tum, *not* tum . . . tum *in this sense, and it will be printed without comment where there is appreciable manuscript evidence for it*   [l] *Tt adds*

BOOK ONE

Prologue

THE history of the English, from their arrival in Britain to his own time, has been told with straightforward charm by Bede, most learned and least proud of men. After Bede you will not easily, I think, find anyone who has devoted himself to writing English history in Latin. If others have discovered anything of the kind before now, or make the discovery hereafter, I wish them joy of it; for my own part I have kept continual watch, but hitherto my labours in the quest have been a waste of time. There are, it is true, some records in the form of annals in the mother tongue, arranged in order of date; and thanks to these the period since Bede has contrived to escape the dotage of oblivion. As for Æthelweard, a distinguished figure, who essayed an edition of these Chronicles in Latin, the less said of him the better; I would approve his intention, did I not find his language distasteful. Nor have I overlooked the careful work of Eadmer, sober and elegant in style, in which, after a rapid survey of the period from King Edgar to William I, he enlarges his scale, and provides students with a full and invaluable narrative of events down to the death of Archbishop Anselm. But he thus omits two hundred and twenty-three years after Bede which he thought unworthy of remark, and in that interval history limps along with no support from literature. It was therefore my design, in part moved by love of my country and in part encouraged by influential friends [Tt *specifies them as* 'Queen Matilda and the brothers of our church'], to mend the broken chain of our history, and give a Roman polish to the rough annals of our native speech. To make clear the sequence of events, I will give a selection from the work of Bede, to whom I shall often have to refer, touching on a few points and letting most go by.

2

3

4

Let me begin then with a concise first book on the history of the English from their conquest of Britain to the reign of Ecgberht, who, after various strokes of fortune had dismissed the lesser kings, made himself sole ruler of almost the whole island. Now, among the English,

5

Matildis reginae et fratrum ecclesie nostre *(cf. Letter i. 3)*   *ᵐ* curae *Tt*   *ⁿ* salo (solo *Aap*^{a.c.}*) A*   *ᵒ* Egbirhtum regem *Tt*   *ᵖ* totius pene insule *TtA (which William may have changed to avoid the sense 'the whole peninsula'); totius insul(a)e pene C (cf. 54. 3 n.s)*   *ᵍ* om. *Tt*

Cantuaritarum,*a* Westsaxonum, Northanimbrorum, Mertiorum, quae omnia singillatim, si erit otium,*b* persequi meditamur, prius de illo dicendum quod et adoleuit maturius et exaruit*c* celerius. Quod profecto fiet expeditius si regna Orientalium Anglorum et Orientalium Saxonum post aliorum tergum posuero, quae et nostra cura et posterorum memoria putamus indigna.*d*

6 Secundus liber ad aduentum Normannorum producet lineam regalium temporum. Tres reliqui in gestis trium regum uersabuntur, his adiectis*e* quae diebus illorum*f* alibi acciderunt et celebrem sui notitiam celebritate gestorum exigunt.

7 Haec ita polliceor, si conatui nostro diuinus fauor arriserit, et me preter scopulos confragosi sermonis euexerit, ad quos Elwardus, dum tinnula et emendicata uerba uenatur, miserabiliter impegit. Si quis uero, ut ille ait, 'si quis*g* haec quoque captus amore leget',[1] sciat me nichil de retro actis preter coherentiam annorum pro uero pacisci; 8 fides dictorum penes auctores erit. Quicquid uero de recentioribus aetatibus apposui, uel ipse uidi uel a uiris fide dignis audiui. Ceterum in utranuis partem presentium non magnipendo iuditium, habiturus, ut spero,*h* apud posteros post decessum amoris et liuoris, si non eloquentiae titulum, saltem industriae testimonium.

1. Anno ab incarnatione Domini quadringentesimo quadragesimo*i* nono uenere Angli et Saxones Britanniam. Aduentus causam, licet usquequaque decantatam, *j*non ab re fuerit hic intexere; et,*j* ut quod intendo clarius*k* elucescat, altius ordiendum.

Romani Britanniam, per Iulium Cesarem in Latias leges iurare compulsam, magna dignatione coluere,*l* ut et in annalibus legere et in ueterum edifitiorum uestigiis est uidere. Ipsi etiam principes, qui toti pene orbi imperitarent, huc aucupatis occasionibus libenter annauigare, hic aeuum solebant transigere. Denique Seuerus et Constantius, imperatores amplissimi, ambo apud insulam diem functi et supremo*m* sunt honore*n* funerati. Quorum Seuerus, ob prouintiam ab incursatione barbarorum muniendam, celebrem illam et uulgatissimam fossam de 2 mari ad mare duxit. Constantius, ut aiunt, uir*o* magnae ciuilitatis Constantinum ex*p* Helena stabularia susceptum, egregiae spei iuuenem,

a Cantuariarum *Tt*   *b* uita *Tt*   *c* aruit *B*   *d* parum putamus digna *B†*   *e* additis *Tt*   *f* aliorum *Tt*   *g* si quis *om. Tt*   *h* ut spero *om. Tt*   *i* sexagesimo *Al (Aap is damaged here)*   *j–j* non erit ab re hic retexere sed *T (more pointedly)*   *k* certius *T*   *l* coluerunt *T (this type of variant will henceforward be ignored)*   *m* summo *B*   *n* honore sunt *T*   *o* uir ut aiunt *T**   *p* ab *Al*, ad *Aap*

four kingdoms grew to greatest power, Kent, Wessex, Northumbria, and Mercia, and I have in mind to deal with each of these in turn, if time permits; but first I must tell of that which grew earliest to maturity and first decayed. This will be easier if I leave to the end the kingdoms of the East Angles and East Saxons, which I consider unworthy of my own labours, and of the attention of posterity.

My second book will bring down the history of the kingdom to the Norman Conquest. The three remaining books will tell of the three Norman kings, together with such events as befell in their time in other countries, and as by their celebrity demand a mention here.

This is my undertaking, if only the favour of Heaven smile on my adventure, and steer me past the rocks of rough and rugged style, on which Æthelweard, in his search for jingling phrase and borrowed finery, so piteously was wrecked. But if anyone, as the poet says, 'if any moved by love read these poor words',[1] let him be warned that I guarantee the truth of nothing in past time except the sequence of events; the credit of my narrative must rest with my authorities. But whatsoever I have added out of recent history, I have either seen myself or heard from men who can be trusted. In any case, I do not greatly value the judgement of my contemporaries either way; posterity, I trust, when love and envy are no more, if it cannot praise my style, at least will pay a tribute to my industry.

1. In the year of our Lord 449 the Angles and Saxons arrived in Britain. The reason for their coming is universally familiar, but it may be appropriate to insert it here; only, to make my story clear, I must begin somewhat further back.

The Romans, having under Julius Caesar compelled Britain to accept the rule of Rome, held it in high regard, as we can read in the annals and see for ourselves in the remains of ancient buildings. Even their emperors, though they ruled nearly the whole world, gladly sought any opportunity to make the voyage hither and here spend their time. Severus and Constantius, for instance, princes of great distinction, both died in the island and were solemnly buried here. It was Severus who, to protect the province from barbarian incursions, built the famous rampart, of which everyone has heard, from sea to sea. Constantius, who was reputed a most cultivated prince, left as his heir a young man of great promise, Constantine, his son by Helena, a

---

[1] Virgil, *Ecl.* vi. 9–10.

reliquit heredem; qui ab exercitu imperator consalutatus, expeditione in superiores terras indicta, magnam manum Britannorum militum abduxit. Per quorum industriam triumphis ad uota fluentibus breui rerum potitus, emeritos et laboribus functos in quadam parte Galliae ad occidentem super littus oceani collocauit;*a* ubi hodieque posteri eorum manentes immane quantum coaluere, moribus linguaque nonnichil a nostris Britonibus degeneres.

2. Succedentibus annis in eadem insula*b* Maximus, homo imperio aptus si non contra fidem ad tirannidem anhelasset, quasi ab exercitu impulsus purpuram induit, statimque in Galliam transitum parans ex prouintia omnem pene militem abrasit. Constantinus etiam*c* quidam, non multo post ibidem spe nominis imperator allectus, quicquid residuum erat militaris roboris exhausit. Sed alter a Theodosio, alter ab Honorio interfecti rebus humanis ludibrio fuere; copiarum quae illos ad bella secutae fuerant pars occisa, pars post fugam ad superiores Britannos*d* concessit. Ita cum tiranni nullum in agris preter semibarbaros, nullum in urbibus preter uentri deditos reliquissent, Britannia omni patrocinio iuuenilis*e* uigoris uiduata, omni exercitio artium exinanita, conterminarum gentium inhiationi diu obnoxia fuit.

3. Siquidem e uestigio Scottorum et Pictorum incursione multi mortales cesi, uillae incensae, urbes*f* subrutae, prorsus omnia ferro incendioque uastata.*g* Turbati insulani, qui omnia tutiora putarent quam prelio decernere, partim pedibus salutem querentes fuga in montana contendunt,*h* partim sepultis thesauris, quorum plerique in hac aetate defodiuntur,*i* Romam ad petendas suppetias ire intendunt.*j* Romani, miseratione infracti nichilque antiquius estimantes quam fessis sotiorum rebus*k* opem porrigere,*l* semel et iterum proturbato*m* hoste operam suam exhibuere. Postremo, longinquae peregrinationis pertesi, aduentum in posterum excusant:*n* discerent ipsi potius a martio patrum calore non degenerare, animis et armis patriam defensare. Aditiunt uerbis formam*o* muri pro sui tuitione construendi, ad

---

a locauit *T*   *b* in eadem insula *om. T*   *c om. T*   *d* Brit(t)ones *A*
e militaris *B*   *f* urbesque *(om. incensae) T*   *g* fedata *T*   *h* fugam . . . intendunt *T*   *i* Perhaps read effod- *(cf. 209. 1; contrast 168. 3)* thesauros . . . defossos) *B*   *j* contendunt *(om. ire) T*   *k* rebus sociorum *TB*   *l* impendere *B*   *m* perturbato *TcB; T adds* longius   *n* incusant *B*   *o* normam *T**

stable-girl. Constantine, having been acclaimed emperor by the army, planned an expedition against the Continent, and took a large body of British troops away with him. By their valour he soon mastered the Empire, as one triumph after another answered his prayers, and when their task was done and they had earned retirement, he established them in a part of Gaul towards the west on the ocean coast, where to this day their descendants still live and have grown into a great people, though in manners and language they have sunk somewhat below the Britons of our own island.

2. In the years that followed in Britain, Maximus, a worthy candidate for empire had he not treacherously aspired to absolute power, assumed the purple as though under compulsion from the army and, making immediate preparations to cross into Gaul, stripped the province of nearly all its troops. Soon after, a second Constantine, chosen emperor there for the promise of his name, drained away what little military strength was left. These men showed how Fortune makes a mockery of human affairs, for they were put to death, one by Theodosius, the other by Honorius; and of the forces which had followed them into battle, half were killed and the remainder after the disaster joined the Bretons on the Continent. Thus these petty dictators had left no men in the countryside save half-barbarians, and none in the towns save those whose god was their belly; and Britain, robbed of the youthful strength of her defenders and despoiled of all skill in the arts, long lay exposed to the greed of neighbouring peoples.

3. Almost immediately, for instance, an invasion of the Picts and Scots caused widespread loss of life; villages were burnt and towns destroyed, and the whole countryside was laid waste with fire and sword. The islanders in confusion, thinking discretion the better part of valour, sought safety in flight and made their way to the hill country, or buried their valuables, of which many are being dug up in our day, and hastened to Rome to ask for help. The Romans, overcome with compassion and thinking it most important to assist allies in their exhaustion, gave effectual help by throwing back the enemy time and again. Ultimately they grew tired of these distant expeditions, and begging to be excused for the future advised the Britons themselves to maintain the martial valour of their forebears and defend their own country with fortitude and force of arms. They also taught them how to build a wall for their defence, to keep watch and ward on the

propugnacula excubandi, in hostem si necesse sit procursandi, et cetera quae disciplina militaris exigit exsequendi. Post monita, lacrimis miserorum comitati, discedunt; abeuntes felix Fortuna prosequens uotis suorum restituit. Tum uero Scotti, desperati reditus audito nuntio,[a] incunctanter et plus solito in Britones irruere, murum complanare, paucos resistentes opprimere, predas non ignobiles domum agere; at uero[b] uulgus terrae reliquum ad palatium aduolat, regis sui fidem implorans.

4. Erat eo tempore rex Britanniae Wrtigernus nomine, nec manu promptus nec consilio bonus, immo ad illecebras carnis pronus omniumque fere uitiorum mancipium, quippe quem subiugaret auaritia, inequitaret[c] superbia, inquietaret[d] luxuria. Denique, ut in Gestis Britonum legitur,[1] filiam suam spe regni sollicitatam stupro fregerat, et ex ea[e] filium tulerat. Hic in tantis tumultibus rem paruiponderans, opesque regni comesationibus abliguriens, scortorum[f] lenociniis deperibat. Excitatus tamen aliquando perstrepentium uocibus, super statu publico in medium consulit, sententias magnatum[g] suorum explorans. Itaque, ut ad summam redigam, placuit omnibus Anglos et Saxones e[h] Germania euocandos, armis ualidos, sedibus uagos: geminum futurum commodum, ut armis[i] inuicti facile hostes propulsarent, et hactenus locorum incerti pro ingenti annumerarent benefitio[j] si uel squalidum solum ieiunumque cespitem ad habitandum suscepissent;[k] ceterum numquam eos aliquid contra patriam[l] molituros, quia[m] genuinam feritatem morum emolliret memoria benefitiorum. Probato consilio mittuntur in Germaniam legati, spectabiles sane uiri et qui digne personam patriae induerent.

5. Germani, audientes rem uotis mille petitam[2] a se ultro expostulari, uicino pede paruere, celeritatem negotii laetitiae stimulis maturantes. Valedicentes igitur aruis genitalibus, renuntiantes parentum affectibus, fortunae uela committunt, placidoque uentorum fauore[n] tribus longis nauibus, quas illi ceolas dicunt,[o] Britanniam allabuntur.

[a] C adds et [b] om. T [c] inquietaret Al[p.c.]Aap [d] inquinaret Tt*; inequitaret AlAap[p.c.]Bk [e] ex eaque Tt [f] Scottorum AaB [g] optimatum (om. suorum) Tt [h] a B [i] animis Tt (cf. 239. 2 armis ualidi, animis inuicti) [j] munere annumerarent Tt; beneficio ann. B [k] susciperent Tt [l] aliquid BkBc² (and BpBph), aliquos Bc¹ [m] quoniam B [n] fauore uentorum Tt [o] uocant B

[1] Hist. Brittonum 20.   [2] Cf. Lucan vii. 238–9.

battlements, to make forays if need be against the enemy, and to perform the other requirements of the art of war. This said, with the tears of the poor Britons for a send-off, they took their leave; fortune smiled on their departure and restored them to their anxious families. Whereupon the Scots, hearing that they were not expected to return, without delay and in greater force than before descended on the Britons, laid low the wall, overwhelmed the few who resisted, and carried off considerable booty. What remained of the common people flocked to the palace, begging help from their king.

4. The king of Britain at the time was Vortigern, unready and unwise, devoted to carnal pleasures and the servant of almost every vice, enslaved by avarice, dominated by pride and distracted by lechery; we read, for example, in the *History of the Britons*,[1] that he had tempted his own daughter with the hope of sharing his kingdom, and had actually deflowered her himself and got a son by her. Amid all these disasters he paid no attention to business, and wasted the substance of his realm on riotous living, abandoned to the blandishments of his wantons. However, he was roused at length by the clamour of the petitioners, and took advice in council on the state of affairs, asking his magnates for their opinions. To cut a long story short, it was unanimously decided to summon from Germany the Angles and Saxons, who were warlike nomads and thus offered a twofold advantage: being invincible in battle they would easily drive out the enemy, and having hitherto no local attachment, they would reckon it a rich reward if they were given as their dwelling-place even rough ground or barren moorland; in any case, the memory of such kindness would soften their native ferocity of manners, and they would never raise a finger against the fatherland. This plan being approved, a mission was sent to Germany, consisting of course of eminent men and worthy representatives of their country.

5. When the Germans heard themselves actually invited to do something for which 'they had prayed a thousand times',[2] they hastened to comply; joy spurred them to speed on the business. So, bidding farewell to their native land and renouncing the ties of kindred, they entrusted their sails to fortune, and in three of the long ships which they call *ceolae* with favouring winds they reached the coast of

Venerunt autem et tunc et sequenti[a] tempore de tribus Germaniae populis, Anglis Saxonibus Iutis. Omnis enim fere terra quae trans oceanum Britannicum sub septemtrionali axe iacet, quia tantum hominum germinat, non iniuria Germania uocatur,[b] licet multis[c] prouintiarum limitibus distincta. Quapropter, sicut hi quibus id muneris est lasciuientes arboris ramos solent succidere, ut reliquorum uitae suco suo possit sufficere, sic incolae aliquorum expulsione matrem[d] alleuiant,[e] ne tam numerosae prolis[f] pastu exhausta succumbat; sed, ut facti minuant inuidiam, sorte ducunt eliminandos. Inde est quod illius terrae homines inuenerunt[g] sibi ex necessitate uirtutem, ut natali solo eiecti peregrinas sedes armis[h] uendicent, sicut Wandali, qui olim protriuerunt Affricam; sicut Gothi, qui possederunt Hispaniam; sicut Longobardi, qui adhuc obsident Italiam; ut[i] Normanni, qui partem Galliae armis domitam incolentes uocauerunt Normanniam. Ex hac ergo[j] Germania primo uenit Britanniam[k] manus parua quidem, sed quae paucitatem suam uirtute fulciret, ducibus Hengesto et Hors, commodae indolis fratribus haud obscura stirpe apud suos oriundis; erant enim abnepotes illius antiquissimi Woden, de quo omnium pene barbararum gentium regium genus lineam trahit, quemque gentes Anglorum deum esse delirantes, ei quartum diem septimanae, et sextum uxori suae Freae, perpetuo ad hoc tempus consecrarunt sacrilegio. In quibus uero locis Britanniae Angli uel Saxones uel Iutae habitationem locauerunt, Beda[1] non tacet. Nostrum propositum est, quanuis affluat materia, stilo non indulgere, sed tantum necessaria quaeque libare.

6. Venientibus igitur Anglis undique occursum: a rege impertitae gratiae, a populo effusus fauor, data fide acceptaque, et tradita Tanatos insula incolatui[l] eorum subuentum. Accessit et pactum, ut illi iunctis umbonibus sudores suos patriae impenderent, recepturi emolumenta militiae ab his quorum saluti uigilias pretenderent. Paululum morae in medio, et ecce Scottos aduentantes, facilique negotio cessuram sibi ut supra predam estimantes, Angli inuadunt; illi uix dum collato pede fugam componunt, fugitantes eques insecutus[m] a tergo cecidit.

[a] consequenti (om. et, as Bk) Tt   [b] uocatur Germania Tt   [c] om. A
[d] frequenter matrem Tt*   [e] alleuant TtACeBk (but cf. GP pp. 376, 432)
[f] sobolis Tt   [g] inuenerint C   [h] Tt adds sibi   [i] One expects sicut
[j] igitur Tt   [k] B adds Germania   [l] accolatui Tt* (cf. 398. 6)
[m] consecutus C

[1] HE i. 15.

Britain. There came, both then and later, men of three German peoples: Angles, Saxons, Jutes. Almost all the country lying across the British ocean to the northward, although divided by many provincial boundaries, is aptly known as Germany because it is the germinating place of such a horde. For this reason, just as experts cut back a tree's 2 rampant branches that it may have sap enough to support the vigour of what remains, so do the natives drive out some of their number to relieve the motherland, lest she succumb exhausted beneath the effort of feeding such a numerous progeny; only, to make the action less invidious, they choose by lot those who must go. This is the reason why the men of that country have made a virtue out of necessity: when expelled from their native soil they win a foreign home by force of arms—the Vandals, for instance, who long ago overwhelmed Africa, the Goths who conquered Spain, the Lombards who still hold Italy, and the Normans who inhabit the part of Gaul which they have conquered and called Normandy. It was from this Germany, then, that 3 there first came to Britain a band of men whose prowess made up for their scanty numbers. Their leaders were Hencgest and Horsa, two brothers of spirit equal to the task, sprung of distinguished lineage amongst their own folk; for they were great-great-grandsons of the patriarch Woden, from whom the royal family in almost all barbarian nations traces its descent, and whom the English peoples vainly supposed to be a god, consecrating to him the fourth day of the week and the sixth to his consort Frig, an idolatrous practice which persists to the present time. The parts of Britain in which Angles, Saxons or Jutes took up their abode are recorded by Bede;[1] my own intention, however plentiful my matter, is to keep my pen in check, to touch on what is necessary and nothing more.

6. On their arrival, the English were welcomed on every hand: the king lavished favours on them, the people received them with open arms, pledges of loyalty were given and received, and quarters were provided for them by the offer of the Isle of Thanet. It was further agreed that in battle array they would devote all their efforts to the country's cause, looking to receive the reward of their prowess from those whose security was to be shielded by their vigilance. No long time elapsed before the Scots reappeared, expecting booty to drop into their lap with ease as it had before; whereupon the English fell upon them. Battle was hardly joined when they took to flight, and as they fled the cavalry pursued them and cut them in pieces from the rear.

Sic non semel certatum, cumque semper uictoria consentiret Anglis, ut fere fit in rebus mortalium, et istis successus accendit audatiam et illis timor aluit ignauiam, eoque res processit ut nichil magis Scotti quam cum Anglis manus conserere cauerent.

7. Interea Hengestus, non minus acer ingenio quam alacer in prelio, aliquos ex[a] suis non abnuente rege patriam remittit, qui regis et populi inertiam, insulae opulentiam exponant,[b] ampla uenire uolentibus premia proponant. Illi mandata gnauiter exsequuntur, breuique[c] cum sedecim nauibus reuertuntur, adducentes filiam Hengesti, uirginem ut accepimus quae esset [d]et naturae miraculum et[d] uirorum spectaculum. Regressis adornatur conuiuium; iubet Hengestus filiam fungi pincernae[e] munere, ut regis accumbentis oculos pasceret. Nec id frustra fuit: nam ille, ut[f] semper in feminarum decorem adhinniebat, statim et formae gratia et gestuum elegantia sautiatus animum, potiendi puella[g] spem imbibit, nec distulit quin nuptias peteret, patrem uolentem cogens. Ipse enim astu primo[h] negare, tam humiles nuptias rege indignas allegans; postremo, quasi grauatus, in sententiam transiit, [i]totam Cantiam pro munere accipiens,[i] ubi iam dudum omnis iustitia[j] sub cuiusdam Guorongi laborabat regimine, qui tamen sicut omnes reguli insulae Wrtigerni substernebatur[k] monarchiae. Nec contentus hac liberalitate barbarus,[l] sed abutens regis imprudentia, persuadet uti a Germania fratrem et filium uirtutis uiros euocet, scena composita ut, quia ipse ab oriente prouintiam[m] defensitaret, illi quoque ab aquilone Scottos frenarent. Ita rege coniuente ipsi, circumnauigata Britannia, Orcades insulas adiere, easque gentes cum Pictis et Scottis pari erumna inuoluentes, in aquilonali parte insulae, quae nunc Northanimbra[n] uocatur, tunc[o] et deinceps assedere; nullus tamen ibi regio insigni uel nomine usus usque ad Idam, de quo regalis Northanimbrorum adoleuit linea.[p] Sed haec inferius;[1] nunc quod ceperam attexam.

---

[a] in *BkBc²(and Bp)*, de *Bc¹ (om. Bph)*   [b] exponunt *Tt*   [c] generaliter executi breui *B*   [d-d] miraculum *Tt*   [e] pincerne fungi *Tt*   [f] ut ille *TtA*   [g] potiende puell(a)e *TtA (cf. GP p. 412* feminae . . . potiendae*)*   [h] primo astu *(om.* enim*) Tt*   [i-i] et totam . . . accepit *Tt*   [j] omn. iust. *after* Guorongi *Tt*   [k] *TtAap^p.c. Bc^1p.c.;* -bantur *ACB*   [l] contemptus hac libertate (libertate *also Cs), omitting* barbarus *Tt*   [m] prou. ab oriente *Tt*   [n] Northanimbria *B*   [o] et tunc *B (cf. 397. 2; but contrast 161. 3)*   [p] prosapia *B*

They fought on these terms more than once and, since victory always smiled upon the English, one side—as often happens in human affairs—grew bolder through success, and the other more frightened and so more cowardly, until at length there was nothing the Scots were more anxious to avoid than a hand-to-hand engagement with the English.

7. Hencgest meanwhile, who was no less astute than he was ardent in battle, sent some of his men home to their own country without protest from the king, to expose the unwarlike nature of the prince and people and the riches of the island, and offer handsome rewards to any who might wish to join him. They carried out their orders with alacrity, and soon returned with sixteen ships, bringing with them Hencgest's daughter, a maiden, we are told, who was a masterpiece of nature and the cynosure of all men's eyes. A banquet was arranged on their return, and Hencgest ordered his daughter to act as cup-bearer, that the king might feast his eyes on her as he sat at meat. The ruse succeeded. The king, who always lusted after fair women, was at once deeply smitten with the girl's beauty and graceful movements, and conceived the hope of securing her for his own. Without delay he asked her father for her hand. Hencgest was only too willing to yield to this pressure. First he cunningly said no, urging that such a lowly match was unworthy of a king; finally he agreed as though under pressure, and was given as a present the whole of Kent. All justice there had long been at a low ebb under the rule of a certain Guorongus, who however like all the petty kings in the island was subject to the monarchy of Vortigern. Not satisfied with this generous treatment, and making full use of the king's unwisdom, the barbarian secured an invitation for his brother and son, both men of might, to come from Germany, pretending that, while he defended the province on the east, they would restrain the Scots towards the north. So, with the king's agreement, they sailed round Britain, making for the Orkney Islands, and having brought tribulation alike on the inhabitants of those parts and on the Picts and Scots, they settled henceforward in the northern part of the island, now called *Northanhimbra*. The name and emblems of a king, however, were unknown there before the time of Ida, from whom the Northumbrian royal line is descended. But of this later;[1] I must now go on with my story.

---

[1] 44. 2.

8. Guortemer filius Wrtigerni, haudquaquam ultra dissimulandum ratus quod se Britonesque suos Anglorum dolo preuerti cerneret, ad expulsionem eorum mentem intendit, simulque patrem ad idem audendum incendit.[a] Hoc igitur auctore post annos septem aduentus eorum fedus fedatum, et per uiginti annos frequenter leuibus preliis, sed quater ut Cronica[1] tradit[b] omnibus copiis depugnatum. Prima congressione aequa utrimque fortuna discessum, dum hi Hors fratrem Hengesti, illi Catigis alterum regis filium magno iustitio[c] desiderarent. In ceteris cum Angli superiorem semper manum referrent, pax conuenit, incentore belli Guortemer fatali sorte sullato, qui, multum a facilitate patris abhorrens, egregie regnum moderaretur si Deus siuisset.[d]

2 Sed eo extincto Britonum robur emarcuit, spes imminutae retro fluxere; et iam tunc profecto pessumissent, nisi Ambrosius, solus Romanorum superstes, qui post Wrtigernum monarcha regni fuit, intumescentes barbaros eximia bellicosi Arturis opera pressisset.[e] Hic est Artur de quo Britonum nugae hodieque delirant, dignus plane quem non fallaces somniarent fabulae sed ueraces predicarent historiae, quippe qui labantem patriam diu sustinuerit infractasque ciuium mentes ad bellum acuerit, postremo in obsessione Badonici montis, fretus imagine Dominicae matris quam armis suis insuerat, nongentos

3 hostium solus adorsus incredibili cede profligarit. Contra Angli, quanuis uario fortunae lusu rotarentur, uacillantes suorum aties aduentu compatriotarum supplere, audentioribus animis in ferrum ruere, paulatim cedentibus accolis per totam se insulam[f] extendere, simul Dei non aduersante consilio in cuius manu est omnium imperiorum mutatio; sed haec processu annorum, nam[g] uiuente Wrtigerno nichil contra eos nouatum. Interea Hengestus, uitio quodam humani ingenii ut quo plus habeas plus ambias, fraude subornata generum ad conuiuium cum trecentis suorum inuitat; cumque frequentioribus poculis inuitatos ad tumultum animasset, et ex industria unumquemque salsa[h] dicacitate perstringeret, primo ad iurgia, mox ad arma uentum. Ita Britones ad unum omnes iugulati animas inter uina uomuere; rex ipse captus

4 datis tribus prouintiis libertatem redemit, seruitutem exuit. Post haec,

---

[a] accendit B [b] tradunt Tt [c] iudicio TtBk [d] om. Tt, leaving a space [e] precessisset Tt [f] insulam se Tt [g] iam Tt [h] falsa B

[1] ASC s.aa. 455, 456, 465, 473.

8. Vortimer, son of Vortigern, seeing himself and his fellow Britons outreached by the crafty English, decided that this could no longer be overlooked, and set himself to drive them out, kindling his father at the same time to a like endeavour. So it was his doing that seven years after their arrival the pact was unpicked, and for twenty years there were frequent skirmishes and, according to the Chronicle,[1] four pitched battles. From the first conflict they emerged with equal honours, one side deeply mourning the loss of Hencgest's brother Horsa; the other, of Catigis, Vortigern's second son. In the other three the English always got the upper hand, and so peace was made, after the death of Vortimer, the moving spirit of the war, who was far from his father's easy-going temper, and would have made a good ruler had God permitted.

With his decease the Britons' strength withered away, and their hopes dwindled and ebbed; at this point, in fact, they would have collapsed completely, had not Vortigern's successor Ambrosius, the sole surviving Roman, kept down the barbarian menace with the outstanding aid of warlike Arthur. This Arthur is the hero of many wild tales among the Britons even in our own day, but assuredly deserves to be the subject of reliable history rather than of false and dreaming fable; for he was long the mainstay of his falling country, rousing to battle the broken spirit of his countrymen, and at length at the siege of Mount Badon, relying on the image of our Lord's Mother which he had fastened upon his arms, he attacked nine hundred of the enemy single-handed, and routed them with incredible slaughter. On the other side, the English, although the sport of Fortune's wheel, made good their wavering ranks by reinforcements of their fellow-countrymen, and more boldly rushed into the fray; so, little by little, as the natives retreated, they spread over the whole island, not without the favouring providence of God, in whose hand is every change of lordship. But this happened in the course of time; while Vortigern lived, no new attack was made upon them. Hencgest meanwhile—for it is a common human failing that the more you have, the more you want—laid a plot against his son-in-law, and invited him and three hundred of his men to a feast. Plying them heavily with wine, he roused them to uproar, then of set purpose whipped up each individual with some cutting jest; and so from high words they came to blows. Thus the Britons had their throats cut one and all, belching out life and liquor as they lay; the king himself was taken prisoner, and had to buy himself out of slavery by the surrender of three provinces. Later,

anno tricesimo nono aduentus sui, Hengestus diem clausit, uir qui successus suos non minus fraudibus quam uiribus urgens multumque genuinae seuitiae indulgens, omnia cruentius quam ciuilius agere mallet. Reliquit filium Eisc*ᵃ* qui, magis tuendo quam ampliando regno intentus, paternos limites numquam excessit, consumptisque annis uiginti quattuor filium Oht eiusdemque filium Irmenricum habuit successores, sibi quam auo aut proauo*ᵇ* similiores. Amborum temporibus quinquaginta tres anni deputantur in Cronicis;[1] ceterum si singillatim uel communiter regnauerint non discernitur.

9. Post illos Ethelbirhtus, Irmenrici filius, rerum potitus quinquaginta annos et tres iuxta Cronicam, iuxta Bedam quinquaginta sex exegit.*ᶜ*[2] Viderit lector quomodo hanc*ᵈ* dissonantiam componat; nos*ᵉ* eam, quia ammonuisse suffecerit, in medio relinquimus. Hic primis pubescentis regni temporibus adeo uicinis regibus fuit ridiculo ut uno et altero pulsus prelio uix suos terminos tutaretur. Postmodum, cum adultiori aetati consultior etiam militiae accessisset peritia, breui*ᶠ* omnes nationes Anglorum preter Northanimbros continuis uictoriis domitas*ᵍ* sub iugum traxit, et, ut exterorum*ʰ* quoque familiaritatem asciceret, regis Francorum affinitatem filiae eius nuptiis sibi conciliauit. Tum uero Francorum contubernio gens*ⁱ* eatenus*ʲ* barbara ad unas consuetudines confederata siluestres animos in dies exuere[3] et ad leniores*ᵏ* mores declinare. His addebatur Letardi episcopi, qui cum regina uenerat, celebs admodum uita, qua regem ad Christi Domini cognitionem etiam tacens inuitabat; quo factum est ut postea beato Augustino predicanti regius animus iam emollitus facile cederet, et primus de numero patrum suorum sacris sacrilegis renuntiaret, ut quos regni premebat potentia fidei quoque obumbraret gloria. Haec est profecto*ˡ* clara nobilitas, haec superba uirtus, honestate uincere quos honore uincas. Quin etiam, curam*ᵐ* extendens in posteros, leges patrio sermone tulit, quibus bonis premia decerneret, improbis per remedia seueriora occurreret, nichil super aliquo negotio in futurum relinquens ambiguum.

ᵃ eius *Al, om. Aa*   *ᵇ* atauo *TtA*   *ᶜ* transegit *B*   *ᵈ om. B*   *ᵉ* nam nos *C*   *ᶠ om. C*   *ᵍ* domitos *TtA*   *ʰ* exteriorum *TtA;* externorum *B*   *ⁱ om. Tt*   *ʲ om. A*   *ᵏ* Ce *(cf. HN 462* morum lenitate*);* leuiores *TtACsB*   *ˡ* profecto est *Tt*   *ᵐ* uita *Bk,* iura *Bc(and BpBph)*

[1] A deduction from the *ASC* dates of the reign of Æsc (488 + 24 = 514) and the start of Æthelberht's (565).

in the thirty-ninth year after his arrival, Hencgest died; pursuing his successful career as much by fraud as force, and giving free rein to his natural cruelty, he was a man who in all his actions preferred bloodshed to diplomacy. He left a son Eisc, more intent on maintaining his kingdom than extending it, who never transgressed the boundaries left him by his father, and after twenty-four years was succeeded by his son Ohta, and Ohta's son Eormenric, both of whom resembled him rather than their grandfather or great-grandfather; the Chronicles[1] allot fifty-three years to the two of them, but whether they reigned separately or together is not clear.

9. After them Æthelberht, the son of Eormenric, succeeded to the throne, which he held for fifty-three years according to the Chronicle—Bede says for fifty-six.[2] This discrepancy the reader must settle for himself; I am content to call attention to it, and let it be. In the early years of his infant reign he was such a joke to the neighbouring kings that after defeat in one or two battles he could scarcely defend his frontiers. Later, when he grew older and had acquired more military skill, he soon tamed by a series of victories all the English peoples except the Northumbrians, and brought them under his rule; and by way of winning the friendship of some external power as well, he secured an alliance with the king of the Franks by marrying his daughter. Then it was that, by intercourse with the Franks, a nation hitherto barbarous and now united in one way of life daily 'unlearnt its woodland wildness'[3] and turned to more civilised ways. To these influences must be added the rigid purity of life of Bishop Liudhard, who had come over with the queen, which even without words encouraged the king to learn about Christ the Lord. As a result, the king's heart was already softened when later he yielded easily to the preaching of St Augustine, so that he became the first of all his dynasty to renounce the cult of idols. Thus those who bowed beneath his power as a king were overshadowed equally by his renown as a believer; and this is true aristocracy, and virtue in all its splendour, to excel in goodness those whom you excel in rank. Besides this, taking thought for posterity, he passed laws in the mother tongue designed to reward the good and keep the wicked in check by sterner measures, leaving nothing in any transaction doubtful for the future.

---

[2] *ASC* s.a. 565; Bede, *HE* ii. 5.   [3] Cf. Virgil, *Georg.* ii. 51.

10. Excessit anno post acceptam fidem primo et uicesimo, Edbaldo filio regni tradens insignia. Ille mox ubi paterni metus abrupit frena,[a] exsufflata Christianitate, nouercae quoque pudorem expugnauit; sed, ne omnino in preceps ferretur, diuinae miserationis austeritas[b] obicem opposuit. Confestim enim regulis quos pater sub iugum miserat rebellantibus,[c] regni mutilatus dispendio, et per horas crebro afflatus demonio, contumacis[d] perfidiae tormenta[e] pendebat. Quibus offensus successor Augustini[f] Laurentius, dum post premissos comites prouintia cedere meditaretur, Dei animatus uerbere sententiam reuo-
2 cauit. Qua de re conuentus rex, dum fidem dictorum pontificis plagae facerent, non aspernanter, ut aiunt, inflexus, et Christianismi[g] gratiam hausit et incestis nuptiis ualedixit. Verum ut in punienda perfidia terribilis exempli nota posteris inureretur, auitis finibus egre licet retentis numquam ad paternum fastigium potuit aspirare. Ceterum tota uita integer in fide nichil quod famam lederet commisit; monasterium quoque extra muros Cantuariae, quod pater fundauerat, ingentibus prediis et amplissimis donariis illustrauit.
3 [h]Quorum laudes et merita omnes Angli suspicere et predicare debebunt, quod Christianam fidem leni credulitate et credula lenitate Angliae inualescere permiserint. Quis enim non iocunde speculetur quantum aequitati conueniat, quantum dulcedini concinat responsum illud regis Ethelbirhti, quod eum primae predicationi Augustini Beda[1] retulisse narrat?—non posse se nouae sectae tam cito animum adhibere, relictis cultibus quos semper exercuerit cum tota Anglorum gente; ueruntamen nulla illos molestia exacerbandos, quin potius predicationis permissu et amplo uictu iuuandos, quod tam longam a natali solo peregrinationem susceperint ut Anglis quae optima putabant indulgenti benignitate communicarent. Nec infra promissionem factum fuit remissius, donec sensim explorata fidei ueritate et ipse
4 cum subiectis numero fidelium sotiatus est. Quid iste? Nonne primo tempore magis carnis illecebra quam animi obstinatione deuians, magnam tamen uitae pontificum exhibebat uenerationem quorum

---

[a] frena abrupit *Tt* [b] austeritatis miseratio *Tt* [c] rebellantibus regulis *(om. quos . . . miserat)* *Tt* [d] om. *Tt* [e] penas *B* [f] beati Augustini *Tt* [g] Christianissimi *AaB (and Tt*[a.c.]*?)* [h–h] *(p. 32) om. Tt*

---

[1] *HE* i. 25.

10. In the twenty-first year after his conversion, Æthelberht died, leaving the crown to his son Eadbald. No sooner had Eadbald cast off the restraints of filial respect than he threw Christianity to the winds, and even violated the honour of his stepmother. Only the merciful severity of Providence debarred him from rushing headlong into the abyss; for immediately the princes whom his father had subdued rebelled, and he paid the price of obstinate infidelity by the loss of part of his kingdom and the hourly visitation of an evil spirit. Disgusted by these excesses Laurence, Augustine's successor, sent his companions home and was planning to follow them and leave the province, when he was encouraged by God's scourge to change his mind. He told the story to the king, who, as the story goes, was humbly 2 moved (for the bishop's stripes added weight to his words), received the grace of Christianity, and bade farewell to his incestuous union. But in the punishment of his infidelity it was right that his terrible example should be branded on the memories of posterity; and so, although he did just succeed in retaining his ancestral territory, he never could aspire to his father's eminence. For the rest of his life, however, he remained upright in the faith, and did nothing that could damage his reputation. He also enriched with great estates and generous gifts the monastery outside the walls of Canterbury, which his father had founded.

The worthy deeds of these two men should be admired and praised 3 by every Englishman, for it was their union of mild government with openness of mind that allowed the Christian faith to take firm root in England. Who would not contemplate with pleasure the fairmindedness, the sweet friendliness of the answer which King Æthelberht gave, as Bede tells us,[1] to the first preaching of Augustine?—that he could not so quickly abandon the worship which he and the whole English nation had always practised, and give his allegiance to the new cult; but that no difficulty should be put in the way of these people, indeed they should rather be encouraged, with leave to preach and plentiful provision, seeing that they had made so long a pilgrimage from their native soil, in order, out of their generous kindness, to share with the English what they thought the best thing in the world. And he was as good as his promise, until, having gradually come to learn the truth of the Christian faith, he and his subjects were added to the number of believers. What of Eadbald? At first he went astray 4 more, surely, from the weakness of the flesh than from perversity of heart, and even so paid great respect to the life of those bishops whose

negligebat fidem? Denique, ut dixi, ob unius facile conuersus iniuriam magno momento Christianitatis augmentis fuit. Ambo igitur laudabiles, ambo profusiora preconia emeriti, siquidem bonum quod ille magnanimiter inchoauerit,[a] iste benigne confouerit.[h]

11. Cui post uiginti quattuor[b] regni annos[c] defuncto successit filius[d] Ercomberhtus [e]ex Emma filia regis Francorum susceptus, et[e] eodem [f]quidem annorum numero[f] sed meliori auspitio principatu functus, religione in Deum, pietate in patriam iuxta insignis. Cum enim[g] auus et pater citra destructionem idolorum fidem nostram coluissent, hic, parum et inferius deuotione regia[h] arbitratus, si non destrueret propensiore[i] consilio quod illi tacito[j] dampnarant iuditio, omnia deorum sacella complanauit ad solum, ut nullum sacrilegii ad posteros manaret uestigium, preclare: poterat enim uulgus fanaticae superstitionis ammoneri quam diu loca puluinarium suorum non desineret intueri. Atque ut gentem suam, uentri[k] tantum indulgentem, parcitati gulae doceret insuescere, precepit per omne regnum obseruari quadraginta dierum sollemne[l] ieiunium. Magnam prorsus tunc temporis rex rem[m] aggressus, quem nec delitiarum luxus[n] eneruare nec regni sollicitudo a Dei cultu potuit auocare. Per haec Dei fauore tutus,[o] rebusque domi et foris[p] ex sententia cedentibus, tranquillissime consenuit. Cuius filia Ercongota, tanto soboles non indigna parente[1] emulisque uirtutum liniamentis patri respondens, Kala monasterium apud Gallias sanctitudinis suae luce[q] uestiuit.

12. At uero filius Egberhtus, per nouem annos patrio throno retento, nichil memorabile fecit tam breuis imperii compendio, nisi quis aduentum Theodori archiepiscopi et Adriani abbatis temporum illius imputet gloriae, doctorum uirorum et qui omnem litteraturam imis medullis combiberant. Quod nisi esset usquequaque detritum, libenter pergerem referre quantum lucis tunc per eos orbi Britannico infulserit, quomodo hinc Greci hinc Latini palestras litterarum certantibus studiis in unum contulerint, et insulam tirannorum quondam nutriculam familiare philosophiae domicilium effecerint.[r]

---

[a] *One expects* inchoauerat   [h] *See above, p. 30*   [b] XXV B†   [c] annos regni T*t*B*c (and* B*k*[p.c.]*)*   [d] *om.* T*t*   [e-e] *om.* T*t*   [f-f] num. ann. uno minus B†   [g] namque cum T*t*   [h] infra deuotionem regiam T*t*   [i] propensiori B† *(cf.* 77*)*   [j] que *(perhaps rightly)* illi tacente T*t*   [k] eatenus uentri T*t** *(cf. 9. 2)*   [l] sollemne quad. dierum T*t**   [m] rem *before* prorsus T*t*   [n] luxus deliciarum T*t*   [o] securus T*t*   [p] et domi forisque rebus B   [q] claritate T*t*   [r] *For B's addition here, see Appendix, p. 802*

faith he neglected. In the end he was, as I have said, easily converted by the punishment undergone by one of them, and played an important part in the growth of Christianity. Both therefore are to be praised and deserve high honour, for the good which one of them generously started was nurtured by the kindly favour of the other.

11. After ruling for twenty-four years, Eadbald died, and was succeeded by Earconberht, his son by Emma, daughter of the king of the Franks, who reigned for the same number of years but with better success, being distinguished equally by devotion to God and love of his country. For while his father and grandfather in their practice of our faith had stopped short of destroying idols, Earconberht thought it unworthy of the piety befitting a king not to destroy deliberately what they had tacitly condemned; and he levelled all the temples with the ground, so that no trace of idolatry should survive in the days yet to come. Quite rightly; for the common people could always be reminded of their fanatical superstition, as long as they could contemplate without interruption the places sacred to their rites. Further, in order to accustom his people to moderation in eating—for they were simply [Tt they had hitherto simply been] the slaves of their own stomachs—he ordained that the solemn Lenten fast should be observed throughout his kingdom. It was indeed a great campaign that the king then undertook, but luxury and comfort could not soften him, nor could the cares of state distract him from the worship of God. Thus it was that, protected by God's favour, and successful both at home and abroad, he grew old in perfect peace. His daughter Earcongota, 'worthy offspring of so great a sire',[1] who resembled her father in the pattern of her virtues, became a nun at Chelles, a monastery in Gaul, and bathed that house in the radiance of her sanctity.

12. His son Ecgberht occupied his father's throne for nine years, but accomplished nothing notable in this short reign, unless one sets to the credit of his times the arrival of Archbishop Theodore and Abbot Hadrian. They were learned men, steeped to the very marrow in all literary culture; and if the story were not universally known, I would gladly go on to tell of the light that then shone through them upon the world of Britain, how Greeks and Latins competed to provide joint training-schools in literature, and turned the island which had once been a nursery of tyrants into the familiar habitation of philosophy.

[1] Cf. Lucan vi. 420.

13. Successit Egberhto frater Lotharius, alite mala regnum ingressus, quippe per undecim annos infestante Edrico filio Egberhti, frequenter*a* et uaria sorte ciuilibus bellis conflictatus nouissimeque*b* iaculo corpus*c* traiectus, ipso uulnere inter medendum*d* uitam effudit. *e*Sunt qui non taceant fratres ambos cita morte merito crudelitatis absumptos, quod Egberhtus filios patrui innocentes*f* occiderit, Lotharius martires propalatos irriserit; quanuis prior et factum ingemuerit et matri fratruelium partem insulae Tanatos ad edificandum monasterium concesserit.*e*

14. Nec Edricus successu tirannidis longum gloriatus est, sed citra biennium regno et uita spoliatus patriam lacerandam hostibus exposuit. Continuo enim quidam Cedwalla cum fratre Mollone, alias sane bonus et efficax, digladiabile odium in Cantuaritas spirans, quantis potuit conatibus prouintiam inuasit, olim diuturna pace feriatam, sed tunc intestino bello dissidentem, impune sibi cessuram*g* arbitratus.
2 Sed non ita ut sperabat imparatos aut animi uacuos prouintiales offendit: siquidem post multa incommoda uicatim et oppidatim accepta tandem animati ad manus ueniunt, congressuque superiores Cedwallam in terga uertunt, fratreque in tugurium quoddam compulso domunculam ipsam succendunt. Ita Mollo, dum erumpendi in hostem deesset audatia, et totis circa tectum habenis regnarent incendia, inter flammas halitum*h* ructauit. Non tamen Cedwalla destitit aut a prouintia pedem retulit, quin dolorem suum crebris accolarum dispendiis sarciret, rei quoque ultionem in successorem Inam transfunderet, sicut suo loco dicetur.[1]

15. *i*In tam*i* desperatis rebus Cantiae sexennio circiter a regia successione claudicatum; septimo demum anno Wihtredus filius Egberhti, cum apud suos inuidiam pressisset industria et apud hostes pacem locasset pecunia, magna spe ciuium allectus in regem uoti compotes fecit. Domi enim*j* ciuilis et bello inuictus Christianam religionem sanctissime coluit, potestatem amplissime porrexit, et, ut nichil felicitati deesset, post triginta tres*k* annos longeuus, quod beatissimum

---

a frequenti *Tt*   *b* -que *om. B*   *c* femur *Tt*   *d* inter medendum *om. Tt*   *e–e* *om. Tt*   *f* ut dixi *add. B†* (see passage referred to in c. 12 n. r above)   *g* censuram *Tt*   *h* animam *B*   *i–i* interea *B*   *j* nam domi *Tt*   *k* *om. B†*

---

[1] 35. 2.

13. Ecgberht was succeeded by his brother Hlothhere, who came to power under an evil star, for the hostility of Ecgberht's son Eadric exposed him for eleven years to the varying fortunes of repeated civil wars, and at length he was pierced by a javelin and died of the wound while in the doctors' hands. Some openly say that both brothers deserved by their cruelty to be so soon cut off, inasmuch as Ecgberht killed his uncle's innocent children, while Hlothhere mocked at the martyrs when they were on public view: though Ecgberht did regret what he had done, and gave his cousins' mother part of the Isle of Thanet to build a minster there.

14. Nor did Eadric live long to boast the success of his tyrannical rule, but within two years was despoiled of crown and life, and left his country to be torn in pieces by its enemies. For immediately a certain Cædwalla, in other ways a worthy and active man, breathing relentless hatred against the men of Kent, invaded the province together with his brother Mul on the largest scale he could, expecting to make an easy prey of a country that had long enjoyed peace and idleness, though at that time torn by civil strife. He did not, however, find the men of the province so unprepared or spiritless as he expected; for after suffering many losses village by village and town by town, at length they recovered their spirit and came to grips with the enemy, defeated him in open conflict, and put Cædwalla to flight. His brother they drove into a cottage, and set fire to the building. Thus Mul, lacking the courage to break out and face the enemy, and surrounded by flames raging in full career, was burnt to death. Cædwalla, however, did not abandon his campaign or retire from the province, until he had assuaged his grief by inflicting frequent losses on the inhabitants, and handed on the duty of vengeance to his successor Ine, as shall be told in its place.[1]

15. In this desperate state of affairs, there was a break for about six years in the royal succession of Kent, till at length in the seventh year Ecgberht's son Wihtred, silencing envy at home by his prowess and securing peace abroad by bribery, was chosen king amid the high hopes of his people. He proved the answer to their prayers. Civilized at home and invincible in war, he was a devoted adherent of the Christian religion, extended his power far and wide, and, to fill the cup of his felicity, after thirty-three years died at a great age, leaving three children who outlived him and were his heirs, something

mortales putant, superstitibus eisdemque[a] heredibus liberis tribus fato
2 functus est. Quorum Edbertus uiginti tribus, Edelbertus undecim,
Alricus triginta quattuor annis paterna terentes instituta, haud deco-
loro[b] exitu regnum continuauere,[c] nisi quod Edelbertus fortuito urbis
incendio, et Alricus infausto aduersus Mertios prelio, [d]gloriam temporum suorum[d] non parum obnubilauere.[e] Ita si quid accidit probri[f]
non tacetur, si quid prosperi parum[g] in cronicis notatur, [h]siue quod
consulto factum est,[h] siue quod naturae uitio comparatum est,[i] quod,
3 cum sit bonorum breuis gratia, 'aeternum quae nocuere dolent'.[1] Post
illos [j]nobile germen regum exaruit, generosus sanguis effriguit,[j] tunc
impudentissimus quisque, cui uel lingua diuitias uel factio terrorem
comparauerat, ad tirannidem anhelare, tunc regio insigni indigni
abuti. Quorum Edelbertus[k2] idemque Pren, cum biennio Cantuaritis
imperitaret, in Mertios maiora uiribus conatus[l] et ab eisdem captus,
uinculis manus corpus captiuitati prebuit; nec multo post ab hostibus
laxatus sed a suis non receptus, dubium quo fine defecit. Deinde eiusdem calamitatis et factionis heres Cuthredus octo annis solo scilicet
nomine regnauit. Hinc regiae dignitatis abortiuum Baldredus, postquam Cantiam octodecim annis obsedit,[m] ab Egbirhto rege Westsaxonum prelio pulsus in exilium concessit.
4   Ita regnum Cantiae, quod ab anno incarnationis Domini quadringentesimo[n] quadragesimo quarto steterat, annis trecentis septuaginta
quinque alterius potestati accessit. Sed quia primi regni, quod de
Anglis excreuit, prosapiam paucis persecuti quasi scintillam de antiquitatis fauilla[o] excussimus,[p] nunc regnum Westsaxonum stilus uentilabit,
quod a primo proximum, longo tamen interuallo, inchoauit. Ipsum
est quod, multo situ marcescentibus ceteris,[q] inuicto usque ad aduentum Normannorum uigore floruit, et alia (ut ita dicam) strangulata faucibus auidis absorbuit.[r] Hoc ergo si lineatim ad Egbirhtum prouexero,
de reliquis duobus, nausiam longitudinis euitans, aliqua subtexam,
quae cum in primo libro debitum finem[s] inuenerint, secundus solos
Westsaxones intuebitur.

[a] eiusdemque *Al*, eisdem *Aap (and Bk)* [b] decolore *Al*; decolorato *Bk (both 'correcting' the unusual word* decolorus*)* [c] continuare *Tt* [d-d] claritatem fortune *B* [e] obnubilauelerunt *(sic) Tt* [f] probri accidit *Tt* [g] non multum *Tt* [h-h] om. *Tt* [i] uidetur *Tt* [j-j] nobilis regum sanguis effriguit, generosum germen exaruit *Tt* [k] *Rightly* Edbrihtus *(cf. 95. 2)* [l] ausus *B* [m] *Bf adds* potius quam rexit *(cf. 164. 1)* [n] CCC *B* [o] quasi antiqui-tatis scintillam *B* [p] elicuimus *TtCe^vB* [q] ceteris marcescentibus *Tt* [r] obsorbuit *Tt(A)Cs (cf. variant at GP p. 20)* [s] om. *Tt*

which mortal men regard as the highest good fortune. Of these Eadberht ruled continuously for twenty-three years, Æthelberht for eleven, Alric for thirty-four, following their father's footsteps and not without success, except that Æthelberht's time was somewhat darkened by an accidental conflagration of his capital, and Alric's by an unsuccessful battle against the Mercians. It is always so: disgraces are never forgotten, good fortune barely finds a mention in the chronicles, whether this be intentional or due to a flaw in human nature, for the memory of benefits is short, while 'damage rankles aye'.[1] After them, the generous stock of kingship withered and its noble blood grew cold; then every ruffian who had become rich by lies or formidable by faction aspired to rule, and worthless men misused the emblems of royalty. One of them, Æthelberht,[2] surnamed Præn, after lording it for two years among the men of Kent, attempted more than he could perform against the Mercians; captured and bound, he was cast into prison, and not long after, being released by his enemies but rejected by his own men, met his end no one knows how. His heritage of discord and disaster passed to Cuthred, who reigned for eight years, king merely in name. After him, the royal dignity miscarried, and Baldred, having beset Kent [B *adds* rather than ruled it] for eighteen years, was defeated in battle by Ecgberht king of the West Saxons, and went into exile.

Thus the kingdom of Kent, which had stood since the year 444, after three hundred and seventy-five years was absorbed into the power of another. We have succinctly surveyed the descent of the first monarchy sprung from the Angles, coaxing a spark from the ashes of the past; my pen shall now discuss the kingdom of the West Saxons, which began next after the first, though some time after. This is the kingdom which, while all the others languished deep in decay, flourished unconquered down to the coming of the Normans, throttled the rest and engulfed them in its greedy maw. I will therefore bring its story in the direct line down to Ecgberht, and, not to be tedious and long-winded, will add a brief account of the other two; these will find their appropriate end with my first book, and the second shall be solely devoted to the West Saxons.

---

[1] Ausonius, *Caesares* 92–3 (p. 166 Green, p. 190 Peiper).
[2] i.e. Eadberht.

16. Regnum Westsaxonum, quo neque*a* magnificentius neque diuturnius ullum Britannia uidit, a quodam Cerditio primum ebulliens, mox in magnum fastigium euasit; qui gente Germanus, amplis maioribus (quippe a Wodenio decimus), cum domesticis conflictationibus ingentes spiritus aluisset, statuit patria decedere et armis famam dilatare. Id, animo communicato cum filio Cenrico, meditari ausus, consentiente adolescente, qui proximis gloriae passibus patrem urgeret, in Britanniam cum quinque ceolis copias traiecit.

2 Actum anno Dominicae incarnationis quadringentesimo nonagesimo quinto, post mortem Hengesti octauo; ipsoque die a Britonibus bello exceptus, uir ueteris militiae non difficulter arietantem multitudinem contudit et fugere compulit. Quo successu et sibi profundam in reliquum securitatem et prouintialibus quietem peperit; nam numquam post illum diem lacessendum arbitrati, in eius iura uolentes concessere. Non tamen ille ignauo indulgens otio feriabatur, quin potius crebras circumquaque uictorias extendens anno post aduentum suum uicesimo quarto in occidentali parte insulae, quam illi Westsexam uocant, monarchiam adeptus est; qua quindecim*b* annis functus fatum compleuit, regno toto preter insulam Wehtam ad filium deuo-

3 luto. Ea enim indultu regiae munificentiae potestati Wihtgari nepotis sui accessit. Is cum sanguinis propinquitate tum bellandi artibus auunculo iuxta carus,*c* celebrem in eadem insula primo principatum, post etiam sepulturam accepit. Porro Cenricus, patre non inferior uirtute, regnum nonnichil ampliatum post annos uiginti sex*d* filio Ceaulino contulit.

17. Huius spectatissimum in preliis robur annales ad inuidiam efferunt, quippe qui fuerit Anglis stupori, Britonibus odio, utrisque exitio. Horum exempla pro compendio subitiam. Ethelbirhtum Cantuaritarum regem, alias laudabilem sed tunc *'*pro antiquitate familiae primas sibi partes uendicantem ac per*f* hoc auidius alienos fines incursantem,*'* probe aggressus fusis auxiliis ad sua fugauit. Britannos,*g* qui temporibus patris et aui uel pretento deditionis umbone uel claustrorum muralium obiectu Gloecestrae et Cirecestrae et Bathoniae exitium effugerant,*h* infesta*i* persecutus animositate*j* urbibus exuit et in

---

a nec B   *b* XVI B†   *c* B† adds eius enim ex sorore nepos erat (note that Bc, like BpBph, omits nepotis sui above)   *d* uiginti quattuor annos Tt; annos quattuor et uiginti ACs; annos XXV Bk   *e–e* primas partes dominationis pro antiquitate familiae presumentem et per hoc alienos fines auidius incursitantem Tt   *f* pro A   *g* Britannes Bk (and BpBph), Britones Bc   *h* effugarant Tt   *i* auide B   *j* animositate persecutus Tt

16. The kingdom of Wessex, the greatest and most lasting Britain ever saw, received its first impulse from a certain Cerdic, and swiftly won its way to great eminence. A German of noble birth, being tenth in descent from Woden, Cerdic first developed great ambitions in domestic conflict, and then decided to leave his native country and spread his fame by force of arms. As he dwelt on this bold plan, he shared his enterprise with his son Cynric, and when the young man agreed—for he followed closely in his father's footsteps on the path to glory—he brought his force over with five *ceolae* into Britain. This was in the year of our Lord 495, being the eighth year after Hencgest's death. On the very day of his arrival, the Britons met him in battle, but as a veteran fighter he had no difficulty in overthrowing the clumsy charges of the multitude, and putting them to flight. This success produced for the future unbroken security for himself and peace for the inhabitants; for from that day forward they never dared attack him, and readily submitted to his rule. But he did not waste his time in sloth and idleness; on the contrary, after extending his victories unbroken in all directions, in the twenty-fourth year after his arrival he secured the throne in the western part of the island, which they call Wessex, and after holding it for fifteen years, died, leaving his son the whole kingdom except the Isle of Wight. The island, by the king's generous gift, passed to his nephew Wihtgar, who, having endeared himself to his uncle no less by skill in war than by ties of blood, [B *adds* for he was his nephew by his sister,] found in the island of his inheritance first a distinguished seat of power and then a distinguished place of burial. Meanwhile Cynric, his father's equal in valour, made some additions to the kingdom, before handing it on, after twenty-six years, to his son Ceawlin.

17. Ceawlin's famous might in battle is lauded by the annals to excess; an object of wonder to the English and of hatred to the Britons, he was the ruin of them both. I will add a few brief examples. When Æthelberht king of Kent, praiseworthy as he was in other respects, presumed upon the antiquity of his family to claim the lordship and made forays too readily into the territory of other princes, Ceawlin boldly attacked him, routed his auxiliaries, and drove him back into his own country. The British, who in the days of his father and grandfather, protected either by a show of surrender or by the defence of walls, had escaped the fate of Gloucester, Cirencester, and Bath, he savagely pursued, expelled them from their cities, and drove them

2 confragosa saltuosaque loca hodieque detrusit. Inter haec tamen, quia fatalis alea incertis iactibus in huius uitae tabula mortales eludit, tantos bellorum euentus*a* obfuscauit luctus domesticus. Denique Cuda fratre immatura morte intercepto, eiusdemque nominis filio ante se in pugna extincto, ambobus predicabilis spei iuuenibus, multum felicitati suae decessisse non*b* semel suspirauit. Postremo ipse,*c* diebus ultimis regno extorris, miserandum sui spectaculum hostibus exhibuit. Quia enim in odium sui quasi classicum utrobique cecinerat, conspirantibus tam Anglis quam Britonibus apud Wodnesdic ceso exercitu anno tricesimo primo regno nudatus in exilium concessit et continuo decessit.

3 Tunc fluitantes regni habenas direxerunt nepotes eius, filii Cudae, Celricus annis quinque,*d* Celwlfus quattuordecim. Quorum tempore inferior sed uirtute prestantior omnem aetatem in bellis detriuit, quippe qui nulli umquam ignauiae locum dederit, quin sua et tutaretur*e* et protenderet.

18. Post illum filii*f* Celrici, Kinegislus et Quicelmus, regni infulas aequa lance induerunt, ambo strenui, ambo mutuis pietatis inter se certantes offitiis, ut merito propter insolitam regibus concordiam fuerint presentibus miraculo, futuris exemplo. Denique bella quam plurima, nescias maiore uirtute an moderatione, gesserunt uel contra Britannos uel contra Pendam regem Mertiorum, hominem, ut suo loco dicetur,[1] ad furta belli peridoneum. Qui proprios egressus terminos, dum Cirecestram suis partibus applicare conatur, impetum concordium
2 regum non ferens cum paucis profugit. Quicelmum sane non mediocris culpa respergit, quod Eduinum Northanimbrorum regem, probatae prudentiae uirum, subornato sicario insidiis appetiuerit. Sed si consideretur illa gentilis sententia 'dolus an uirtus quis in hoste requirat?',[2] facile excusabitur nichil preter solitum fecisse, quod uellicatorem potentiae quoquomodo uoluerit de medio subtrahere. Nam et antea de regno Westsaxonum plurima*g* decerpserat et tunc, accepta irritatus iniuria, quoniam recruduerant odia, multa prouintialibus inflixit dis-
3 pendia. Euaserunt tamen reges, quibus non multo post per*h* Birinum episcopum caelestis influxit doctrina, regni anno uicesimo quinto, post aduentum beati Augustini quadragesimo. Inflexus ilico Kinegislus et*i*

---

a successus *B*   *b* plusquam *Bt*   *c* ipse *after* ultimis *Tt*   *d* VI *Bt*   *e* tutaret *B*   *f* filius *TtA*   *g* plura *B*   *h* beatum *B*   *i* om. *B*

---

[1] c. 74.   [2] Virgil, *Aen.* ii. 390.

into the land of rocks and forests, where they yet remain today. But our 2
life is a dice-board, on which Fortune with her unexpected throws
makes game of mortal men, and all these victories in the field were
overcast by tragedy at home. His brother Cutha was taken off by an
untimely death, and his son, also Cutha, died in battle before his eyes;
both were young men of remarkable promise, and often did he lament
these grievous blows to his good fortune. At length he himself at the
end of his days was driven from his throne, and became a piteous spectacle to his enemies. Both nations had heard the trumpet call to vent
their hate against him; English and Britons conspired together and cut
his army to pieces at *Wodnesdic*; and in the thirty-first year he was
deprived of his kingdom, went into exile, and forthwith died. The trail- 3
ing reins of power were taken by his nephews, Cutha's sons, Ceolric
for five years, Ceolwulf for fourteen; the younger but more valiant of
them spent all his life in war, never allowing any weakness to stop
him from maintaining and extending his own territory.

18. After him Ceolric's sons, Cynegils and Cwichelm, assumed the
crown in equal shares; valiant both of them, each striving to outdo
the other in affectionate services, so that by this unwonted concord
among kings they properly became a wonder to contemporaries and
an example to posterity. Many were the battles they fought, with no
less restraint than valour, against the British and against Penda king
of the Mercians, a man well suited to the stratagems of war, as shall
be told in its place.[1] He had crossed his own frontiers in an attempt
to win Cirencester for his side, but unable to bear the onslaught of
these united princes he fled with few companions. Cwichelm, it is 2
true, is stained with no little guilt, for he made a treacherous attempt
by means of a hired assassin on the life of that wise and respected
prince, Edwin king of the Northumbrians. But if we bear in mind
the pagan sentiment 'Valour or guile? All's one 'twixt foe and foe',[2] he
will easily be excused for having done nothing unusual in trying to
remove a dangerous rival by any means in his power. Some time before,
Edwin had seized considerable parts of the West Saxon kingdom, and at
that moment, hostilities having broken out again, he showed his
resentment at the losses he sustained by doing great damage to the
inhabitants of the province. The kings, however, escaped, and not 3
long after, the springs of heavenly doctrine were opened to them by
Bishop Birinus, in the twenty-fifth year of their reign and the fortieth
since the arrival of Augustine. Cynegils was converted at once, and

mollito regali supercilio, sacerdoti se in baptismo libens substrauit. Recalcitrauit aliquantisper Quicelmus, donec ualitudine corporis ammonitus*ᵃ* ne salutem animae negligeret, deuotionem consortis et ipse emulatus eodem anno carne solutus est. At uero Kinegislus sexennio post, longae quietis gratia functus, anno regni tricesimo primo uitam clausit.

19. Successit hereditati filius eius Kenwalkius, primo regni auspitio pessimis,*ᵇ* medio et ultimo tempore optimis principibus comparandus. Potestate siquidem initiatus adolescens, qui regio luxu insolescens facta paterna in secundis poneret, sine retractatione Christianismum*ᶜ* et legitimum matrimonium abiurauit. Sed a Penda rege Mertiorum, cuius sorori repudium dederat, bello impetitus et uictus, ad regem Orientalium Anglorum confugit; ubi et propria calamitate et hospitis sedulitate fidem persuasus, triennio post resumptis uiribus regnoque recepto iocundum miraculum suae mutationis ciuibus exhibuit, in tantum fortis ut, qui antea*ᵈ* nec suos fines impune defensitarat, nunc 2 usquequaque*ᵉ* imperium prorogaret. Britannos antiquae libertatis conscientiam frementes, et ob hoc crebram rebellionem meditantes, bis omnino protriuit, *ᶠ*primum in loco qui dicitur Wirtgeornesburg, secundo iuxta montem qui dicitur Penne,*ᶠ* et in Wlferium Pendae filium paternam ultus iniuriam, plurima illum parte regni truncauit;*ᵍ* religiosus adeo ut primus antecessorum suorum in Wintonia templum Deo per id seculi*ʰ* pulcherrimum construeret, quo loci posteritas in sede episcopali fundanda, etsi augustiori*ⁱ* peritia, per eadem tamen cucurrit uestigia,*ʲ* [29. 2] ita munificus*ᵏ* ut nichil patrimoniorum cognatis negaret, quippe qui filio fratris pene tertiam regni partem magnanima liberalitate communicaret. Has animi regalis*ˡ* dotes stimulis monitionum animabant sanctissimi suae prouintiae episcopi Angilbertus, de quo multa in Gestis Anglorum¹ *ᵐ*quae probes*ᵐ* inuenies, et nepos eius Leutherius, post ipsum in Westsaxonia septenni*ⁿ* pontifitio 3 functus. Quod eo non pretermisi, quia de annis presulatus eius*ᵒ* Beda nichil expressum reliquit, michi ex Cronicis² cognitum dissimulare

---

ᵃ monitus *Tt*   *ᵇ* pessimus *TtB*   *ᶜ* Christianissimum *Tt*ᵃ·ᶜ *AaB*   *ᵈ* ante *B*   *ᵉ* longiuscule *B†*   *ᶠ⁻ᶠ* om. *TtA*   *ᵍ* multauit *B†*   *ʰ* temporis *B* (cf. 122. 2 n.)   *ⁱ* angustiori *TtAa (and Bk?)*   *ʲ Here C inserts a long passage on Glastonbury (see Appendix, p. 802) conventionally numbered 19 (in part)–29 (in part)*   *ᵏ* ita munificus *TtA*; ita fuit munificus *C*; nec solum in ecclesiasticis uerum etiam in secularibus ita munificus extitit *B*   *ˡ* regales *B*   *ᵐ⁻ᵐ* Bede *B*   *ⁿ* septenni annis *A*; septem annis *C*   *ᵒ* om. *Tt*

bending his kingly pride gladly humbled himself before the priest in baptism. Cwichelm resisted for a time, until, warned by bodily weakness not to neglect the health of his soul, he imitated his brother in devotion, and the same year was delivered from the flesh. It was six years later, after enjoying a long period of peace, that Cynegils died, in the thirty-first year of his reign.

19. He was succeeded by his son Cenwealh, who at the outset of his reign challenged comparison with the worst of princes, in the middle and later periods with the best. Introduced to power as a young man, so that the royal splendour went to his head, and he paid little heed to what his father had done, he abandoned without remorse both Christianity and lawful wedlock; but being attacked and defeated by Penda king of the Mercians, whose sister he had divorced, he took refuge with the king of the East Angles. There, by his own misfortunes and his host's exertions, he was converted, and three years later repaired his forces and recovered his kingdom, rejoicing his subjects with welcome evidence of his change of heart. So strong did he become, that he who before had not succeeded in defending even his own frontiers, now extended his sway in all directions. The British, brooding over the memories of their former independence and therefore constantly plotting rebellion, he twice completely crushed, first at a place called *Wirtgeornesburh*, secondly near the hill called *Penne*, and avenged on Penda's son Wulfhere the injuries done by his father, depriving him of a large part of his kingdom. So devoted was he to religion, that he was the first of his line to build a church in Winchester, very handsome for its date; and posterity, in founding a cathedral in that same place, has shown perhaps more ample craftsmanship, but has only followed the lead of Cenwealh; [29. 2] so generous too [B He was so generous not only in church but also in lay matters] as to deny nothing of his inherited possessions to his kinsmen, for with true liberality he bestowed almost a third of his kingdom on his brother's son. These gifts of kingly character were encouraged with their lively admonitions by the two holiest bishops of his province: Agilbert, about whom you will find much to admire in the *History of the English*,[1] and his nephew Leuthere, who followed him for seven years in the see of Wessex. I mention the fact for this reason, that Bede has left nothing explicit about the length of his term of office; and having learnt it myself from the Chronicles,[2] it seemed against my principle to conceal

---

[1] Bede, *HE* iii. 7 etc. [2] *ASC* s.a. 670.

preter religionem uidebatur; simul, quia se ingerebat occasio, amplectenda erat predicabilis uiri mentio, qui Malmesberiense monasterium, in quo terreni incolatus pretendimus militiam, acri et pene[a] diuino mentis intuitu ex humili ad amplissimum statum euexit,[b] *'quod a[c] Meildulfo, natione ut aiunt Scotto, eruditione[d] philosopho, professione monacho, adeo angustis sumptibus elaboratum ut inhabitantes egre cotidianum uictum expedirent, ipse diu multumque librato consilio Aldelmo, eiusdem loci monacho, pro iure tunc episcoporum regendum contradidit. De qua re, ut omnem sermo noster dubietatis deprecetur offensam, uerba eius hic aliqua intexam.'[e]

30. [f]'Ego Leutherius gratia Dei episcopus, pontificatus Saxoniae gubernacula regens, rogatus sum ab abbatibus qui sub iure parrochiae nostrae cenobiali monachorum agmini pastorali sollicitudine preesse noscuntur, uti terram illam cui inditum est uocabulum Meildulfesburh Aldelmo presbitero ad degendam regulariter uitam conferre largirique dignarer. In quo uidelicet loco a[g] primo aeuo infantiae atque ab ipso tirocinio rudimentorum liberalibus litterarum studiis eruditus[h] et in gremio sanctae matris aecclesiae nutritus uitam duxit; et ob hoc potissimum hanc petitionem fraterna caritas suggerere uidetur. Quapropter, predictorum abbatum precibus annuens, ipsum locum tam sibi quam successoribus suis normam sanctae regulae sollerti deuotione sequentibus, fraterna petitione coactus, ultroneus concedo.[i]

'Actum publice iuxta flumen Bladon septimo[j] kalendas Septembris anno incarnationis Dominicae sexcentesimo septuagesimo quinto.'[k]

31. Cum igitur industria abbatis accederet fauori pontificis, tunc res monasterii in immensum efferri, tunc monachi undique congregari; currebatur ad Aldelmum totis compitis, his uitae sanctimoniam, his litterarum scientiam desiderantibus. Erat enim uir ille cum religione simplex, tum[l] eruditione multiplex, et qui famam uirtute preiret, liberalium artium epotator, ut esset mirabilis in singulis et in omnibus singularis. Mentior, si non hoc testantur de Virginitate codices immortalis[m] eius ingenii indices, quibus meo iuditio nichil dultius, nichil splendidius;[n] quanuis, ut est nostri seculi desidia,

---

[a] pene et *AC (but cf. 385. 3)*   [b] prouexit *B*   [c-c] quodam *Al*, quod a quodam *Aa*   [d] *B adds* ut aiunt   [e] obtexam *B*   [f] *Versions of this document (Sawyer 1245) are to be found in GP pp. 347–9 and* ελπφ   [g] *om. B*   [h] *om. B*

the facts; also because, given the opportunity, I could not fail to mention that famous man, who by his keen and almost supernatural insight raised from lowliness to great estate the monastery of Malmesbury, in which I profess to serve during my time on earth. It was founded by Meildulf, by birth (it is said) an Irishman, in training a philosopher, by profession a monk; but with such slender endowments that the inmates could hardly find their daily bread. Leuthere, after long and careful thought, made it over, as bishops in those days were entitled to do, to the administration of Aldhelm, a monk of the house. And, to relieve my remarks of any imputation of unreliability, I will incorporate here some words of his on this subject:

30. 'I, Leuthere, by God's grace a bishop, and helmsman of the see of Saxony, have been asked by the abbots who with pastoral forethought rule the monastic congregations within my diocese, to give and grant unto the priest Aldhelm the land known as *Meildulfesburh*, that he may live there under the Rule. For in that place he has dwelt from early childhood and the very beginnings of his education, being learned in liberal studies and fostered in the bosom of holy mother Church, and this reason in particular moves his loving brethren to make their request. Now therefore, yielding to the prayers of the aforesaid abbots and moved by the petition of my brethren, I grant this place of my own free will to him and to his successors such as shall devoutly follow the holy Rule.

'Delivered in public by the river Bladon on 26 August in the year of our Lord 675.'

31. The bishop's favour being thus seconded by an energetic abbot, the monastery grew exceedingly, and monks came together from all quarters; men hastened by every road to Aldhelm, some in quest of his holiness of life, others of his literary skill. Single-hearted in religion, in learning many-sided, he was a man whose reputation could not keep pace with his virtues; such was his thirst for the liberal arts that he was a master in each and unique in all. For the truth of my words, see those books *On Virginity*, the evidence of his undying genius, than which in my judgement there is nothing more delightful nor more brilliant, although—such are the sluggish wits of our

---

[i] *Tt adds* et cetera *ACsBc¹; tunc BkBc²ᵃ·ᶜ·*   [j] oct(au)o *B*   [k] secundo *C*   [l] *CeBc²ᵖ·ᶜ·;* cum
[m] immortales *ABk*   [n] piperatius *Tt*

quibusdam pariant nausiam non attendentibus quia iuxta mores gentium*ᵃ* uarientur modi dictaminum. Denique Greci inuolute, Romani circumspecte, Galli splendide, Angli pompatice dictare solent. Sane, quoniam dulce est*ᵇ* maiorum inherere gratiae, eorumque exemplis*ᶜ* ignire memoriam, non inuitus euoluerem quantos hic sanctus pro aecclesiae nostrae priuilegio sudores insumpserit, quot*ᵈ* miraculis uitam insignierit, nisi quia*ᵉ* alias auocamur;*ᶠ* et facta eius etiam lippienti meratius*ᵍ* apparent oculo quam nostro possint adumbrari pincillo. Innumera signa, quae modo apud eius fiunt memoriam, ostendunt presentibus preteritae *ʰ*illius uitae*ʰ* sanctimoniam. Habet ergo*ⁱ* ille laudes suas, habet meritis partam gloriam; nostra oratio prosequatur historiam.

32. Kenwalkius, post triginta unum annos*ʲ* moriens, regni arbitrium uxori Sexburgae delegandum putauit; nec deerat mulieri spiritus ad obeunda regni munia. Ipsa nouos exercitus moliri, ueteres tenere in offitio, ipsa subiectos clementer moderari, hostibus minaciter infremere, prorsus omnia facere ut nichil preter sexum discerneres. Veruntamen plus quam femineos animos anhelantem uita destituit, uix annua*ᵏ* potestate perfunctam.

33. Sequens biennium*ˡ* in regno transegit Escuinus, regali prosapiae proximus, quippe qui fuerit Kinegisli ex fratre Cuthgislo abnepos; quo decedente uel morte sua uel ui aliena (neutrum enim expedite inuenio), uacantem aulam successione legitima impleuit Kentwinus Kinegisli filius, ambo notae in bello*ᵐ* experientiae, siquidem ille Mertios, iste Britannos anxia clade perculerit,*ⁿ* sed temporis breuitate miserandi; nam imperium secundi non ultra nouennium prorogatum, primi biennium*ᵒ* superior sermo absoluit. Et hoc secundum Cronicorum fidem; ceterum non eos regno integro*ᵖ* imperitasse sed inter se diuisisse Beda confirmat.¹

34. Tunc regiae indolis nobile germen Cedwalla emicuit, Ceaulini ex fratre Cuda pronepos, immodicae spei iuuenis et qui nullam

ᵃ Tt adds naturaliter   *ᵇ* uidetur *B*   *ᶜ* exemplisque illorum *Tt*   *ᵈ* quantis *Tt*   *ᵉ* quod *B*   *ᶠ* ad aliud euocamur *Tt*   *ᵍ* mer. lippienti *(*limp-*Cs) C*   *ʰ⁻ʰ* couersationis *(sic)* eius *Tt*   *ⁱ* om. *B*   *ʲ B adds* regni   *ᵏ* annua uix *C*   *ˡ* triennium *B†* (*cf. n. o below*)   *ᵐ* bellis *Tt*   *ⁿ* perculerint *C*   *ᵒ* triennium *CB* (*cf. n. l above*)   *ᵖ* integro regno *Tt*

generation—some find they cloy, not observing how literary style is bound [Tt *adds* by nature] to vary with varying national characters. The Greeks, for instance, like an involved style, the Romans are 2 lucid, the Gauls brilliant, the English rhetorical. Indeed so delightful is it to dwell upon our devout forebears, and to rekindle their memory by giving examples of what they did, that I would gladly tell at length of all the labours undertaken by this holy man for the privileges of our house, all the miracles that adorned his life, were I not summoned to other topics; and his acts appear clearer to the eye, even of the purblind, than from anything my pencil could sketch. The countless wonders which now take place at his tomb demonstrate in the present the holiness of his life in the past. He has his meed of praise, the glory won by his deserts; we must pursue our narrative.

32. After thirty-one years Cenwealh, on his death bed, thought fit to leave royal power to his wife Seaxburh, nor did she, though a woman, lack the energy to face the duties of the throne. She personally raised fresh troops, and kept the old in their allegiance; she ruled her subjects mercifully, and showed a threatening front to her enemies; did everything, in short, in such a way that there was no difference to be seen, except her sex. She died, however, this woman of mettle more than womanly, after scarce a year in power.

33. For the next two years the throne was occupied by Æscwine, the nearest to the royal house, being Cynegils's great-great-nephew through his brother Cuthgils; when it fell vacant on his death, either from natural causes or by violence (I find neither expressly stated), by right of succession it was filled by Centwine, Cynegils's son. Both had distinguished military records, for one had soundly defeated the Mercians, the other the British, but both had their days cut pitifully short: the reign of the second was not continued beyond nine years, the first had but two years, as we have already said. In this I follow the Chronicles; Bede,[1] however, asserts that they did not rule over the unbroken kingdom, but divided it between them.

34. Then arose that noble offshoot of the royal stock, Cædwalla, great-nephew of Ceawlin through his brother Cutha, a young man of

---

[1] *ASC* s.aa. 674–6, 682, 685; *HE* iv. 12.

occasionem exercendae uirtutis preterire nosset. Qui cum iam dudum efficatioribus*a* studiis bilem principum suae patriae irritasset, factione conspiratorum in exilium actus est. Hanc ille amplexatus iniuriam, ut omni milite spoliaret prouintiam, quicquid bello idoneum erat abduxit;*b* namque seu miseratione fortunarum eius infracta seu uirtute delectata, tota pubes exulem secuta. Excepit primum impetum furentis rex Australium Saxonum Edelwalkius, manum conserere ausus; sed cum omni populo quem ductauerat fusus, sero prerupti consilii penitentiam fecit. Animis suorum erectis, Cedwalla*c* maturato insperatoque*d* reditu emulos potentiae adorsus regno abegit. Ita per biennium regno*e* potitus, preclara rei bellicae facinora consummauit. Australibus Saxonibus*f* digladiabili*g* odio infestus, successorem Edelwalkii Edricum repetita *h*occurrentem audatia*h* exitio dedit. Wehtam insulam fidutia Mertiorum rebellantem parum abfuit quin deleret. Preterea Cantuaritas*i* aggressus crebras de illis uictorias reportauit; postremo, ut supra diximus,[1] fratre amisso regione decessit, plurimo accolarum sanguine*j* dampnum consolatus suum. Inter haec arduum memoratu est quantum etiam ante baptismum inseruierit pietati, ut omnes manubias, quas iure predatorio in suos usus transcripserat, Deo decimaret. In quo etsi approbamus affectum, improbamus exemplum, iuxta illud: 'Qui offert sacrifitium de substantia pauperis, quasi qui immolat filium in conspectu patris.'[2] Iam uero quod Romam baptizandus contenderit, ibique a Sergio papa*k* Petrus uocatus adhuc*l* in albis positus supremum arbitrium feliciter incurrerit, notius est quam ut nostro indigeat illustrari relatu.

35. Eo Romam eunte regnum per Inam nouatum, qui Kinegisli ex fratre Cuthbaldo pronepos magis pro insitiuae uirtutis industria quam successiuae sobolis prosapia in principatum ascitur, fortitudinis unicum*m* specimen, prudentiae simulacrum, religione parem nescias; quibus artibus uitam componens, domi gratiam foris reuerentiam mercabatur. Adeo annis duobus de quadraginta potestate functus, sine ullo insidiarum metu*n* securus incanuit, sanctissimus publici amoris lenocinator. Prima illi in Cantuaritas expeditio, in quos nondum de incendio Mollonis ira defremuerat. Prouintiales paulisper*o* resistere

---

a efficacibus *B*   *b* corrasit *B†*   *c* Cedualla *before* animis *Tt; om. B*
d impatoque *Tt*   *e* eo *B†*   *f* Sax. Austr. *Tt*   *g* ueteri *B*   *h–h* aud. occ. ultimo *Tt*   *i* Cant. pr. *Tt; B† adds* ut supra in rebus eorum digessi, *omitting* ut supra diximus *below*   *j* sanguine accolarum *Tt*   *k* *B† adds* baptizatus et *(cf. GP p. 354)*   *l* adhucque *B†*   *m* *om. C*   *n* motu *Tt*   *o* parumper *Bk (and BpBph),* parum *Bc*

---

[1] 14. 2.   [2] Ecclus. 34: 24.

the highest promise, and not one to let slip any opportunity to put his valour into practice. His more effective energy had long made the magnates of his country hostile, and at length a faction of conspirators drove him into exile. Accepting this outrage as a chance to denude the province of its troops, he carried off with him whoever was fit for service; whether through pity for his misfortunes or admiration for his valour, all the young and able-bodied followed the fugitive. His first furious onslaught fell on Æthelwalh, king of the South Saxons, who dared to engage him, but too late did penance for his rash decision, being routed with all his people. This encouraged Cædwalla's supporters; he returned early and unexpected, fell upon his rivals, and drove them from the kingdom. Holding the throne in this way for two years, he achieved distinguished successes in the field. The South Saxons he pursued with relentless hatred, and Æthelwalh's successor Eadric, who withstood him with renewed boldness, he destroyed. The Isle of Wight rebelled, relying on Mercian support, and was nearly wiped out. The men of Kent he attacked and frequently defeated; but at length, as we have said above,[1] after his brother's death he left the province, having made up for his loss by heavy slaughter of its inhabitants. With such a record, it is hard to do justice to his devotion to religion even before he was baptised, which led him to give God the tithes of all the spoils he had converted to his own use by right of seizure. In this, while we approve the intention, we must disapprove the action, as it is written: 'Whoso bringeth an offering of the goods of the poor, doeth as one that killeth the son before his father's eyes.'[2] As for his journey to Rome to be baptised, how he was christened Peter by Pope Sergius, and while still a catechumen was called in a happy hour before the supreme tribunal—all this is too well known to need light shed on it by any words of mine.

35. On his departure for Rome, the kingdom received a fresh start from Ine, the great-nephew of Cynegils through his brother Cuthbald, who was called to the throne more for his acquired prowess and energy than for any blood link with the royal line. A paragon of valour, the image of wisdom, and in religion without peer—these were the arts by which he ruled his life, and won favour at home and respect abroad. For thirty-eight years he ruled, growing old in peace without fear of privy enemies, and attracting the affection of his subjects in uprightness of life. His first expedition was against the men of Kent, for resentment at Mul's death by burning had not yet cooled.

ausi, mox omnibus temptatis et uiribus in uentum effusis, cum nichil in pectore Inae quod ignauiae conduceret*a* repperissent, dispendiorum suorum intuitu deditioni consuluere:*b* temptant regium animum muneribus, sollicitant promissis, nundinantur pacem triginta milibus auri mancis, ut pretio mollitus bellum solueret, metallo prestrictus*c* receptui caneret. Qua ille pecunia suscepta delicti gratiam fecit in regnum reuersus. Nec solum Cantuaritae*d* sed et Orientales Angli hereditarium exceperunt odium, omni nobilitate primo pulsa, post etiam bello fusa.

3 Haec de preliorum eius successu dicta modum agnoscant*e* suum; ceterum quantus*f* in Dei rebus fuerit inditio sunt leges ad corrigendos mores in populum latae, in quibus uiuum ad hoc tempus puritatis suae resultat speculum; inditio sunt monasteria regiis sumptibus nobiliter excitata, precipue *g*Glastoniense,

*h*nostris quoque diebus insigne,*i* quod in quodam palustri recessu construxit, ut scilicet eo tenatius supernis monachi*j* inhiarent quo castigatius terrena oculis haurirent.*h*

*h*cui quantum splendoris adiecerit libellus ille docebit quem de antiquitate monasterii eiusdem elaboraui.*h*

4 Affuit*k* consilio pater Aldelmus, cuius ille precepta audiebat humiliter, suspitiebat*l* granditer, adimplebat hilariter. Denique et priuilegium quod pro libertate monasteriorum suorum ab Apostolico Sergio impetrauerat libens confirmauit, et multa Dei famulis eius hortatu contulit,*m* et ad extremum episcopatu renitentem honorauit, licet uitam tanti uiri mundo cita mors inuiderit; uix enim annis quattuor episcopatu functus animam celo thurificauit, anno Dominicae incarnationis 5 septingentesimo nono. Fuere qui dicerent eum fuisse regis nepotem ex Kentenio fratre, sed non placuit nobis pro uero arrogare quod magis uidetur opinioni blandiri uolaticae quam stabilitati conuenire historicae, presertim cum nusquam ab antiquo scriptum reperiatur, et Cronica[1] palam pronuntiet Inam nullum fratrem habuisse preter Inigildum, qui paucis annis ante ipsum decessit. Non eget Aldelmus ut mendatiis asseratur:*n* tanta sunt de illo quae indubiam depromant fidem, tot sunt quae non ueniant in litem.

a induceret *B*   *b* consulere *B*   *c* restrictus *B*   *d* Cantiani *Tt*
e cognoscant *B*   *f* quantum *B*   *g* The *C* version of the passage from here to the end of 36 is printed in the Appendix, pp. 814–18. Stubbs's chapter numbering has been modified
h–h nostris . . . haurirent *TtA;* cui . . . elaboraui *B*   *i* *Tt;* insignis *Al,* insignissimum *Aa*   *j* monachi supernis *Tt*   *k* aderat *B*   *l* suscipiebat *Al (but cf. GP p. 354, VWii. 7)*   *m* indulsit *B*   *n* inseratur *Tt*

The men of that province resisted for a time, but soon had tried every shift and spent their efforts on the empty air; finding in Ine's disposition no sign of relenting, they counted up their losses, and decided to give in. They tempted the king with gifts and wooed him with promises, bargaining for their peace with thirty thousand mancuses of gold, in hopes that, yielding to payment, he would break off his campaign, and dazzled by the precious metal would give the signal for retreat. On receipt of the proffered sum he forgave them the outrage, and returned to his kingdom. Nor was it only the men of Kent: the East Angles too had to bear the brunt of a hereditary feud, their whole nobility being first driven back and then routed in battle.

But let this account of his military successes here find its end; for the rest, his stature in things of God is clear from the laws he published to improve the standard of behaviour, in which a living image of his own high character can to this day be seen reflected; clear too from the noble monasteries built by him at kingly cost, above all Glastonbury,

TtA a house outstanding in our times too. He built it in a sequestered marsh, intending that the more confined the monks' view on earth, the more eagerly they would hold to heavenly things.

B Ine's additions to whose splendour will be found described in the little book I have composed on the ancient history of the house.

A close adviser of Ine's was father Aldhelm, whose words he listened to in humility, reverenced greatly, and cheerfully obeyed. Thus he was glad to confirm the privilege which Aldhelm had obtained from Pope Sergius to preserve the liberties of his monasteries, and on Aldhelm's advice he contributed much to the servants of God. In the end, he made him a bishop, for all his reluctance. But Aldhelm's early death deprived the world of his living qualities: he held office for scarcely four years before offering up his soul to heaven, in the year 709. Some said that he was Ine's nephew by his brother Kenten, but I am not happy to assert as truth a story that seems rather to flatter a fleeting rumour than to have a firm foundation in history, especially as there is no ancient written authority for it and as the Chronicle[1] is quite clear that Ine had no brother apart from Ingild, who predeceased him by a few years. Aldhelm has no need of lies to buttress his reputation: there are too many other things concerning him that brook no dispute and carry the hallmark of truth.

---

[1] s.a. 718.

36. Habuit sane Ina sorores Cuthburgam et Quenburgam. Cuthburga Alfrido regi Northanimbrorum nuptum tradita, sed non post multum*ᵃ* coniugio diducto, *ᵇ*monasterioque apud Winburnam constructo sub magistra regulae Hildelida*ᵇ* *ᵇ*primo apud Berkingum sub abbatissa Hildelida, mox ipsa magistra regulae Winburnae Deo placitam*ᵇ* uitam transegit. Vicus est modo ignobilis, tunc temporis insignis, in quo frequens uirginum chorus terrenis desideriis castratis superos suspirabat amores. Accessit sacri celibatus studio librorum Aldelmi de Virginitate lectio, Berkingensium*ᶜ* quidem nomini dedicata sed omnibus eandem professionem anhelantibus ualitura.

2 Habuit et uxorem Ethelburgam, feminam sane regii generis et animi, quae dum crebro uiri instillaret auribus ut mundanis rebus uel extremis annis ualefacerent, et ille hortantem de die in diem differret, astu tandem uincere parat. Cum enim quadam uice apud uillam ingenti tumultu regales luxus explicuissent, post tridie cum discessissent, uillicus ex reginae conscientia palatium quanta potest deformitate, tam fimo pecudum quam aggere ruderum, infamat; postremo in lecto ubi 3 cubuerant porcam nouiter enixam collocat. Interea, cum iam plus*ᵈ* miliario processum esset, illa maritum uxoriis delinimentis aggreditur, rogans ut illuc unde abierant necessario pedem referant; magni discriminis rem fore si non exaudiat. Re non difficulter impetrata, rex uidens locum pridie*ᵉ* Sardanapallicis delitiis parem nunc feda solitudine deformem miratur, tacitoque iuditio oculi rem examinantes ad mulierem rediere.*ᶠ* Tunc illa occasionem*ᵍ* aucupata laetumque subridens, 'Et ubi sunt,' ait,*ʰ* 'domine coniunx, hesterni strepitus? ubi aulea Sidoniis sucis ebria? ubi parasitorum discurrens petulantia? ubi dedala uasa pondere metallorum mensas ipsas onerantia? ubi terra marique 4 exquisita ad*ⁱ* gulae lenocinium obsonia? Nonne omnia fumus et uentus? *ʲ*nonne omnia transierunt?*ʲ* et ue his qui heserint,*ᵏ* quia simul transibunt. Nonne omnia sicut fluuius preceps et currens in mare? et ue his qui heserint,*ᵏ* quia simul trahentur. Cogita, queso, quam miserabiliter defluent carnes, quae modo in delitiis nutriuntur. Nonne nos qui ingurgitamur uberius, putrescemus miserius? Potentes potenter tormenta patientur, et fortioribus fortior instat cruciatio.'[1]

ᵃ non multo post *B* *ᵇ⁻ᵇ* monasterioque ... Hildelida *Tt;* primo ... placitam *ACB* *ᶜ* ipsarum *Tt* *ᵈ* om. *B* *ᵉ* pridem *B* *ᶠ* redire *B* *ᵍ* occasione *TAl* *ʰ* inquit *B* *ⁱ* quesita *(om. Bk—and BpBph)* ob *B* *ʲ⁻ʲ* om. *A* *ᵏ* (h)eserunt *B*

[1] Wisd. 6: 7 and 9.

36. Ine did leave two sisters, Cuthburh and Cwenburh. Cuthburh married Aldfrith, king of the Northumbrians, but was soon divorced and then

Tt lived in a monastery built at Wimborne, where Hildelith enforced obedience to the Rule,	ACB lived a godly life first at Barking under Abbess Hildelith, later herself enforcing the Rule at Wimborne,

a place then famous, now insignificant, where a large group of virgins, divorced from earthly desires, yearned for the love of God. Their enthusiasm for the holy life of celibacy was furthered by their reading of Aldhelm's books *On Virginity*, dedicated specifically to the women of Barking [Tt to them] but of service to all of the same profession.

Ine also had a wife, Æthelburh, a woman of royal lineage and character, who frequently dropped in her husband's ear the plea that they should bid farewell to the world, even late in life. He put her off from one day to another, and she eventually made a plan to overcome him by guile. They had a noisy bout of royal extravagance at some vill. Next day, after their departure, the bailiff, with the queen's cognisance, used animal dung, piles of rubble, all the mess he could find to defile the palace. His master-stroke was to place a newly delivered sow in the royal bed. When they were a mile or more on their way, Æthelburh used her wifely wiles to beg him to allow them to go back. It was imperative, she said, and if he ignored her request it would be of much consequence. The king gave way easily enough, and found himself before the extraordinary sight of a place, only yesterday fit for the excesses of Sardanapalus, now deserted and turned upside down. He gazed for a while in silent thought, then looked back at his wife. She took her chance. With a pleasant smile she said: 'And where now, my lord and husband, are the revels of yesterday? Where the tapestries drunk with Phoenician juices? Where the pert parasites running hither and thither? Where the elaborate vessels weighing down the very tables with their ponderous metal? Where the delicacies hunted down on land and sea to pander to greed? Are not all these things smoke and wind? Have they not all passed away? And woe to those who cleave to them, for they will pass away also. Are they not all like a rushing river, running to the sea? And woe to those who cleave to them, for they will be swept away also. Consider, I beg you, how miserably the flesh will decay, that now is fed on luxuries. Will not we who guzzle too freely rot the more wretchedly? Mighty men shall be mightily tormented, and a sore trial shall come upon the mighty.'[1]

Nec plura locuta maritum compulit in sententiam exemplo, quam multis annis frustra insusurrauerat uerbo.

37. *a*Nam post triumphales*a* bellorum manubias, post multarum uirtutum gradus, summum culmen perfectionis meditatus, Romam abiit.*b* Ibi ne pompam suae conuersionis faceret, non publicis uultibus expositus*c* crinem*d* deposuit, sed ut solius Dei oculis placeret, amictu plebeio tectus clam consenuit. Nec deerat tanti 'dux femina facti';[1] quae cum antea uirum ad hoc audendum incitasset, tunc merentem uerbis lenire, labantem exemplis erigere, prorsus quod ad*e* salutem eius spectaret nichil dimittere. Ita mutua caritate conexi, temporibus suis uiam hominum ingressi sunt, non sine magnis, ut accepimus, miraculis, quibus diuina dignatio felitium coniugum sepe respondit meritis.

38. Successit principatui Ethelardus, Inae consanguineus, licet surgentes eius primitias frequenter interpolaret Oswaldus regii sanguinis adolescens. Prouintialibus enim in rebellionem excitatis bello regem persequi conatus;*f* sed*g* non multo post illo fatali sorte sullato, Ethelardus per quattuordecim annos quietissime retentum regnum Cuthredo cognato reliquit.*h*

40. *i*In quo ille pari annorum numero et uirtute non dispari aduersus Ethelbaldum regem Mertiorum et Britones iugi exercitio uictorias adipiscens non minimum sudoris consumpsit.*i*

40. *i*Hic aduersus Ethelbaldum regem Mertiorum et Britones*j* iugi exercitio uictorias adipiscens non minimum*k* sudoris consumpsit, ac post annos quattuordecim*l* regni gubernacula reliquit.*i*

41. Arripuit illud*m* Sigebrihtus, uir apud suos seuitia immanis idemque foris ignauia perinfamis; quocirca communi omnium odio conspirante, post annum solio deturbatus meliori locum fecit. Sed ut fere in talibus fit, cum magnitudine calamitatis aliquos ad gratiam sui reuocasset, eorum uirtute prouintia quae Hamtunscire dicitur in obsequio detenta. Verum cum nec sic cessaret, et nece cuiusdam Cumbrani, qui fidelissime sibi adheserat, ceteros in exitium suum*n*

---

a-a post triumphales autem *C*, *which now rejoins TtAB*   *b* adiuit *C, which adds* anno Dominice incarnationis DCC*mo* tricesimo *(tricesimo Cs,* XX *Cd,* XXV *Cr; Ce omits the whole number, leaving a blank space)*   *c* om. B   *d* comam *B*   *e* om. *B*   *f* Tt adds* est   *g* *B adds* eo (om. illo)   *h* *There follows in C a passage conventionally numbered 38 (in part)–39; see Appendix, p. 818*   *i–i* in . . . consumpsit *TtA*; hic (om. C) . . . reliquit *CB*   *j* *C adds* idem Cuthredus   *k* parum *C*   *l* XVI *Bt*   *m* regnum *TtA*   *n* sui *B*

She needed to say no more: a tableau forced agreement from a husband who for many years had refused to listen to her whispered words.

37. For after his spoils of victory in battle, and after the ascent of many steps in virtue, Ine planned to achieve the summit of perfection, and set out for Rome [C *adds* in AD 720/725/730]. There, in order not to make a display of his conversion, he did not cut his hair before the public gaze, but grew old in secret, dressed like a man of the people, that he might please no eye but God's alone. Nor was a woman lacking 'to lead the high emprise';[1] his queen had earlier urged her husband to take this bold step, and now she consoled him in grief with her encouragement, roused his despondency by her example, in a word left nothing undone that could contribute to his salvation. United thus by love for one another, at their appointed times they went the way of all mankind; not without many miracles, as we have heard, by which the divine Mercy has often answered the merits of fortunate couples.

38. Ine was succeeded by his kinsman Æthelheard, though in his early days he suffered much interference from Oswald, a young man of the royal blood. Oswald moved the men of his province to rebellion, and tried to make war on the king; but not long after, he met his death, and Æthelheard held the throne in perfect peace for fourteen years, leaving it to his relative Cuthred.

40. TtA In which [reign] he, over the same number of years and with comparable fortitude, devoted great efforts to a prolonged and victorious campaign against the Mercian king Æthelbald and the Britons.

40. CB He [C The same Cuthred] devoted great efforts to a prolonged and victorious campaign against the Mercian king Æthelbald and the Britons, and after fourteen years let fall the reins of government.

41. Rule was now seized by Sigeberht, a monster of cruelty at home and a byword for cowardice abroad; universally unpopular, he was turned off the throne after one year, and made way for a better man. But, as often happens in such cases, the greatness of his fall regained him some supporters, and thanks to their valour the region known as Hampshire was not lost to his service. Even so, he could not rest, and when by the murder of a certain Cumbra, one of his most faithful adherents, he had driven the remainder to take up arms for his destruction,

---

[1] Virgil, *Aen.* i. 364.

armasset, ad abdita ferarum spelea secessit;[a] ibi[b] quoque infortunio eum prosequente, a subulco confossus interiit. Ita crudelitas regis, omnem pene nobilitatem peruagata, in homine ultimae[c] sortis stetit.

42. Suscepit regni gubernacula Kinewlfus, clarus et[d] ille quidem[1] morum compositione militiaeque gestis, sed 'uno solo aduersus Offam regem Mertiorum propter Benesingtune prelio quarto et uicesimo regni anno uictus, multisque perinde dampnis afflictus,[e] fedo etiam[f] exitu finem uitae sortitus. Nam cum uno et triginta annis nec[g] ignaue nec[g] immodeste regnasset, seu rerum gloria elatus, quod nichil sibi obuiaturum crederet, seu posteritati[h] suae metuens, contra quam Kineardum Sigebrihti fratrem increscere cerneret, illum prouintiae terminos coegit[i] excedere. Qui cedendum tempori ratus, dissimulato 2 animo quasi uolens profugit. Mox, cum furtiuis conuenticulis perditam improborum manum contraxisset, solitudinem regis auspicatus[j] (nam animi causa rus concesserat), cum expeditis eo superuenit;[k] ubi, dum illum alienis[l] amoribus inseruientem audisset, ex insidiis domum foris[m] obsedit. Rex ancipiti discrimine permotus,[n] cum presentibus ponderato consilio, fores occlusit, sperans latrones uel mulcere alloquio uel terrere imperio. Cum neutrum procederet, ira percitus in Kineardum insiluit, minimumque abfuit[o] quin uita priuaret; sed a multitudine circumuentus, dum cedere dampnum gloriae arbitratur, mortem probe ultus occubuit. Pauci ex clientela eius qui aderant, dum 3 non manus dare sed herum uindicare intendunt, obtruncati. Extemplo fama mali tanti principum perlabitur aures, qui non longe agebant excubias. Quorum qui maximus aeuo et prudentia Osricus, ceteros cohortatus ne necem domini sui in insignem et perpetuam suam[p] ignominiam inultam dimitterent, districtis gladiis in coniuratos irruit. Kineardus primo causam suam agere, magna polliceri, cognationem pretendere; ubi nichil proficit, ad resistendum commanipulares accendit. Dubium certamen fuit, his pro uita illis pro gloria summa ope[q] conantibus; tandem diu cunctata uictoria in iustiorem partem declinauit. Ita miser ille, nequiquam[r] fortiter fatiens, animam amisit, non longum insidiarum successu[s] gloriatus. Corpus regis Wintoniae

---

[a] concessit B   [b] illuc B   [c] extremae Tt   [d] et before morum Tt (then et militie)   [c-e] om. Tt   [f] om. Tt   [g] neque Tt   [h] potestati Bk (and Bp), potentatui Bc[1], potentia tui Bc[2] (Bph avoids error)   [i] terminos prou. cogit Tt   [j] aucupatus Savile, probably rightly (cf. VD p. 262 occasionem aucupatus)   [k] superuenerat B   [l] meretriciis Tt   [m] Cf. HN 480 a foris obsessi   [n] om. Tt   [o] defuit Tt; obfuit B   [p] sui Tt   [q] om. Tt   [r] nequaquam B   [s] successu insidiarum Tt

he sought refuge in the secret lairs of the wild beasts; there too misfortune pursued him, and he was stabbed to death by a swineherd. Thus was his cruelty, which had ranged at will among the nobles, brought to a stand by the lowest of the low.

42. The reins of kingship were taken in hand by Cynewulf, 'he too of good report'[1] for character and exploits in war; but by defeat in a single battle against Offa king of the Mercians near Benson in the twenty-fourth year of his reign, he suffered heavy losses, and finally came to a disgraceful end. When he had reigned thirty-one years with spirit yet restraint, either success went to his head and he thought nothing could withstand him, or he had fears for his succession, menaced as he was by the growing power of Sigeberht's brother Cyneheard; and so he compelled him to leave the province. Cyneheard thought it best to bow before the storm, and disguising his feelings left as though of his own accord. Then, having gathered in secret rendezvous a band of ruffians, he waited till the king was alone, on holiday in the country; appeared on the scene with a swift force; and then, when he had heard that the king was devoted to his amours, laid siege to his house. The king was much concerned to find himself in these straits, and after taking counsel with his men, barred the doors, hoping either to pacify the rebels by smooth words or to coerce them by his authority. When neither course made any progress, he fell into a rage, rushed upon Cyneheard, and almost killed him; but he was surrounded by superior numbers and, thinking it disgraceful to yield, gave a good account of himself and then met his death. The few of his supporters who were present, more intent on vengeance than surrender, were cut to pieces. Soon the report of this disaster reached the ears of the princes, encamped not far away; and Osric, their leader in counsel as in years, called on his followers not to leave their lord's death unavenged to their own great and lasting shame, and with drawn sword fell upon the rebels. Cyneheard at first argued his case, made them handsome offers, pleaded his kinship; but when he made no progress, roused his fellow-soldiers to resist. The struggle hung in doubt, one side fighting for life with all their might, the other for glory; but after long suspense victory came down on the side of justice. So that poor wretch, after a vain display of valour, lost his life and the chance to boast for long of the success of his treachery. The king's body was

---

[1] Perhaps not a quotation.

sepultum, illius Reopendune, *quod erat tunc cenobium nobile, nunc (ut audiui) pauco uel nullo incolitur habitatore.*

43. Post illum*b* regnauit Brihtricus annis sedecim, pacis quam belli studiosior, artifex amicitias componere, externos blande appellare, domesticis coniuere, in his dumtaxat quae*c* uigorem regni*d* non eneruarent; atque ut ampliorem gratiam apud propinquos locaret, filiam Offae regis Mertiorum eo tempore potentissimi in coniugium*e* accepit, de qua (quod sciam) nichil liberorum tulit. Cuius affinitate fultus Egbirhtum, solum regalis prosapiae superstitem, quem ualidissimum suis utilitatibus metuebat obicem, Frantiam fugandum curauit. Nam et ipse Brihtricus et ceteri*f* infra Inam reges, licet natalium splendore*g* gloriantes, quippe qui de Cerditio traherent originem, non parum 2 tamen a linea*h* regiae stirpis exorbitauerant. Illo igitur expulso, securo resolui ceperat*i* otio cum gens Danorum piratica, rapto uiuere assueta, occulte tribus nauibus aduecta, pacem prouintiae confudit.*j* Quae scilicet manus soli ubertatem, inhabitantium uirtutem speculatum uenerat, ut postea eius multitudinis quae totam pene inundauit Britanniam aduentu compertum est. Tunc enim furtiue*k* *l*in alta pace regni*l* appulsi, regium uicum qui proximus inuolauere, uillicum suppetias ferentem leto dedentes; sed mox timore concurrentium amissa preda,*m* ad naues refugerunt. Post Brihtricum, *n*qui apud Werham iacet,*n* Egbirhtus conscendit thronum auitum,*o* omnibus ante se*p* regibus merito preferendus. Et nos ergo, quia usque ad eius*q* tempus*r* narrationem extendimus, iam nunc ad Northanimbros, sicut polliciti sumus,[1] animum flectamus.

44. Et supra paucis libauimus,[2] et nunc necessario repetimus, quod Hengestus confirmato in Cantia regno*s* fratrem Ohtam et filium Ebusam, acris et probatae experientiae uiros,*t* ad occupandas aquilonales Britanniae partes*u* miserit. Illi imperatis*v* insistentes conuenientem studiis suis exitum habuere; namque sepenumero cum prouintialibus congressi, profligatisque qui resistendum putauerant, reliquos in fidem acceptos placidae quietis*w* gratia mulcebant. Ita cum

a–a om. *Tt*   *b* Kineuulfum *Bf*   *c* qui *AapB*   *d* regum *Bk*, regium *Bc(and BpBph)*   *e* coniugem *(om.* in*) B*   *f* om. *B (then* reliqui reges*)*   *g* splendore natalium *Tt*   *h* linea *after* stirpis *Tt*   *i* occeperat *Tt (cf. GP p. 284 n. 3)*   *j* confundit *B*   *k* fortune *B*   *l–l* om. *Tt*   *m* preda amissa *Tt*   *n–n* om. *Tt*   *o* thronum auitum conscendit Egb. *Tt*   *p* *Bf* adds in Westsaxonia   *q* hoc *Tt*   *r* tempora *B*   *s* regno in Cancia *Tt*   *t* iuuenes *Tt*   *u* aquilonares partes Brit. *Tt*   *v* preceptis *B*   *w* lenitatis *Tt*

buried at Winchester, Cyneheard's at Repton, in those days a famous monastery, but now, as I have heard, with few or no inhabitants.

43. After Cynewulf for sixteen years Brihtric was king, a man more devoted to peace than war, an adept at making friends, smooth with foreigners and willing to wink at the conduct of his household, at any rate when the force of his rule was not affected. To acquire greater influence among his neighbours, he married a daughter of Offa, king of the Mercians, the most powerful king of the period, by whom he had, as far as I know, no children. Relying on this connection, he managed to drive across to France Ecgberht, the sole survivor of the royal house, whom he feared as the most effective obstacle to his own advancement. For Brihtric himself and the other kings since Ine, although boasting proud lineage as descendants of Cerdic, had diverged considerably from the direct line of the blood royal. Having thus driven out Ecgberht, 2 he was beginning to relax in peace and quiet, when a pirate tribe of Danes, accustomed to live by rapine, arrived secretly in three ships and threw the province into confusion. This party had come to spy out the fertility of the soil and the courage of the inhabitants, as later became clear on the arrival of the host that spread over almost the whole of Britain. This time, however, they made a furtive landing, the kingdom being completely at peace, and descended on the nearest royal estate, killing the bailiff when he came to its protection; but soon, as the defence rallied, they took fright, abandoned their loot, and escaped to the ships. After Brihtric, who lies buried at Wareham, Ecgberht ascended the throne of his ancestors, and showed himself a better man than all who had ruled before him [B *adds* in Wessex]. I for my part, having brought the story down to his time, must now turn my attention, as I promised,[1] to the Northumbrians.

44. We have already briefly told,[2] and must now repeat, how Hencgest, having established his rule in Kent, sent his brother Ohta and his son Ebusa, two active men of long experience, to seize the northern parts of Britain. Pressing on with their task, they met with the success which their efforts deserved; for after frequently engaging the natives of the region and routing those who had thought fit to resist them, they came to terms with the remainder, and won their affections with the blessing of peace. When therefore by their own

---

[1] i pr. 5 (cf. 7.3).   [2] 7.3.

et suis artibus et subiectorum fauore nonnichil potestatis corrasissent, numquam tamen regium nomen temerare meditati, eiusdem medio-
2 critatis formam in proximos posteros deliniauerunt.*a* Annis enim uno minus centum Northanimbri duces communi habitu contenti sub imperio Cantuaritarum priuatos agebant;*b* sed non postea stetit haec ambitionis continentia,*c* seu quia semper in deteriora decliuis est*d* humanus animus, seu quia gens illa naturaliter inflatiores anhelat*e* spiritus. Anno itaque*f* Dominicae incarnationis quingentesimo quadragesimo septimo, post mortem Hengesti sexagesimo, ducatus in regnum mutatus, regnauitque ibi primus Ida,*g* haud dubie nobilissimus, aetate et uiribus*h* integer; uerum utrum ipse per se principatum inuaserit an aliorum consensu*i* delatum susceperit, parum diffinio, *j*quia ueritas est in abdito;*j* ceterum satis constat magna et uetere prosapia oriundum, puris et defecatis moribus multum splendoris generosis contulisse natalibus: adeo bello inuictus domi seueritatem
3 regiam genuina mansuetudine animi*k* temperabat. Possem hoc loco istius, et aliorum alibi, lineam seriatim intexere,*l* nisi quod ipsa uocabula barbarum quiddam stridentia minus quam uellem delectationis lecturis infunderent. Illud tantum non immerito notandum, quod cum Wodenio fuerint tres filii, Weldegius Wihtlegius Beldegius, de primo reges Cantuaritarum, de secundo Mertiorum, de tertio Westsaxonum et Northanimbrorum, preter duos quos procedens sermo nominare perget,[1] originem traxerint. Hic ergo Ida, sicut absolute inuenio, a Beldegio nonus, a Wodenio decimus, quattuordecim*m* annis in regno permansit.

45. Successor eius Alla, ex eodem quidem genere sed diuerso a Wodenio tractu*n* sanguinem ducens, regnum efficaciter prouectum sudorum*o* suorum titulis per triginta annos nobiliter ampliauit. Huius tempore uenales ex Northanimbria pueri—familiari scilicet et pene ingenita illi nationi consuetudine, adeo ut, sicut nostra quoque secula uiderunt, non dubitarent arctissimas necessitudines sub pretextu minimorum*p* commodorum distrahere—uenales ergo ex Anglia pueri, Romam deducti, saluti omnium compatriotarum occasionem dedere;

---

a declinauerunt *B*; *for* deliniare *thus cf. 444. 1 = GP p. 173* *b* se agebant *Tt*^{p.c.}   *c* abstinentia *Tt*   *d* decliuis est in deteriora *Tt*   *e* anhelabat *TtBc*^{1a.c.}   *f* ergo *B*   *g* Ida primus *Tt*   *h* uiribusque *(om. et) B*   *i* consensu aliorum *Tt*   *j-j* om. *Tt*   *k* animi mansuetudine *Tt*   *l* seriatim lineam contexere *Tt*   *m* XII *B†*   *n* diuerso tractu a Weidegio *Tt*   *o* studiorum *B*   *p* inimicorum *B*

skilful policy and the support of the conquered they had got together a considerable power, they never thought, in spite of that, to trespass on the name of king, but handed down as a tradition to their immediate successors the same modesty of status. For one year less than a century, the Northumbrian rulers were satisfied to be like other men, and accepted private status under the suzerainty of Kent. But these strictly limited ambitions lasted no longer, either because the spirit of man tends always to the worse part, or because the people of Northumbria are naturally proud and spirited. So, in the year of our Lord 547, being the sixtieth after the death of Hencgest, the principality was changed into a kingdom, and the first king was Ida, a man undoubtedly of high birth, and of youth and strength unimpaired; but whether he laid hands on the kingly power of his own accord, or accepted it when offered by others, I do not definitely affirm, for the truth is obscure. In any case, it is well known that he sprang of old and distinguished family, and by his pure and untarnished character added great lustre to his eminent birth; such was the native kindliness with which, while unconquered in the field, he tempered at home the severity of the royal power. I might include the detailed lineage of Ida here and of other kings elsewhere, were not the names themselves with their barbarous and discordant sound likely to give my readers less pleasure than I could wish. One point at any rate deserves to be noticed: that, Woden having had three sons, Wældæg, Wihtlæg and Bældæg, the kings of Kent are descended from the first of these, the kings of the Mercians from the second, and from the third those of the West Saxons and Northumbrians, with two exceptions to be named as I proceed.[1] Ida, then, as I find definitely stated, was ninth in descent from Bældæg and tenth from Woden, and reigned for fourteen years.

45. His successor Ælle, who was of the same family, but derived his descent from Woden by a different line, vigorously extended the kingdom, and for thirty years increased its reputation by the fame of his achievements. It was in his time that the slave-children from Northumbria, by a custom so familiar and almost ingrained among the Northumbrians that, as has been witnessed even in our own day, they did not hesitate to put their nearest and dearest on the market in hopes of some trifling profit—the children from England, as I was saying, taken to Rome for sale, provided the means for the salvation of all

---

[1] Ælle (45. 1) and presumably his son Edwin (47. 4 etc.); Edwin's descendants Osric and Oswine were kings of Deira only.

nam, cum miraculo uultus et liniamentorum gratia oculos ciuitatis[a] inuitassent, affuit forte cum aliis beatissimus Gregorius, tunc apostolicae sedis archidiaconus, qui miratus tantam in mortalibus decoris compositionem, miseratus tam abiectam in captiuis conditionem, consulit[b] astantes: 'Qui genus, unde domo?'[1] Responsum est esse genere[c] Anglos, prouintia Deiros [d](est enim Deira prouintia Northanimbriae),[d] Allae regi subditos, paganismo[e] deditos; quorum extremum dolentibus[f] suspiriis prosecutus, reliquis eleganter applausit, ut Angli angelis similes de ira eruerentur et alleluia cantitare docerentur. Nec mora, impetrata a Benedicto papa licentia ad predicandum, iter[g] adoriri magnanima eximii uiri spirauit industria; et profecto conceptum opus pietas explesset, nisi iam profectum factiosus ciuium[h] amor reuocasset. Erat enim uir ille cum uirtutibus clarus, [i]tum ciuibus carus,[i] quippe qui spem illorum, quam de eo a puero combiberant, incredibili uirtute superarit. Ita boni intentio tunc quidem frustrata, postmodum sub pontificatu eius laudabilem finem accepit, sicut suis lector locis inueniet.[2] Me interim ista inseruisse non piguit, ne[j] lecturorum[k] conscientiam defraudarem de Alla, cuius mentionem perstrinxit patris Gregorii uita; qui, quamquam maxima occasio Christianitatis genti Anglorum fuerit, nichil umquam siue[l] Dei consilio siue[l] quodam infortunio de ea[m] audire meruit. Sane ad filium eius manauit electio.

46. Alla mortuo, adeptus est regnum Ethelricus Idae filius, post detritam in penuria aetatem extrema canitie prouectus, sed ueloci morte de medio post quinque annos sullatus: miserabilis princeps, et quem fama obscura prorsus occuleret,[n] nisi filii conspicuus uigor patrem in speculam extulisset.

47. Itaque cum longo senio satietati uitae satisfecisset, Ethelfridus regnum ascendit maior filiorum, qui teneritudinem annorum maturitate morum consolaretur; cuius gesta per scriptorum facetiam prolata in publicum non nisi ordinis loco stili nostri expectant offitium: adeo

---

[a] ciuitatis oculos *Tt* [b] consuluit *Aac, perhaps rightly* [c] gente *Tt*
[d–d] que pars Northanimbrie est *Tt* [e] paganis(s)imo *TtBkBc*[ta.c.] [f] ingentibus *Tt* [g] *Tt adds* Anglis [h] Romanorum *Tt* [i–i] om. *Tt* [j] nec *AaB* [k] lectorum *Tt* [l] seu (sine *Tt*) . . . seu *B* [m] ipsa *B*
[n] reconderet *B (cf. Virg. Aen. v. 302)*

[1] Virgil, *Aen.* viii. 114.

their fellow-countrymen. Their surprising beauty and graceful forms had attracted the attention of the citizens, when among others appeared by chance the most blessed Gregory, at that time archdeacon of the Apostolic See. Marvelling at such perfection in a mortal frame, and sad to see them as captives so forlorn, he asked the bystanders 'what their race and whence they came.'[1] He was told that they were Angles by race, of Deiran origin (Deira is a province of Northumbria), subjects of King Ælle, and pagans. This last remark he received with a sigh of regret; to the rest he riposted wittily that Angles who look like angels ought to be rescued from the wrath to come (*de ira*) and taught to sing *Alle*luia. Without delay he obtained from Pope Benedict permission to preach, and with generous energy—great man that he was—aspired to set forth on the journey. Surely his piety would have carried through the task once begun, had not his fellow-citizens, devoted but passionate, recalled him when he had already started. For his eminent goodness was equalled by his popularity among his fellows, so far had his amazing merit outstripped the high hopes they had formed of him as a boy. Thus were his good intentions frustrated for the moment, only to be gloriously fulfilled later when he became pope, as the reader will find told in its proper place.[2] Meanwhile I have brought in this story without misgivings, for fear that I might leave my future readers unaware of Ælle, who is mentioned in passing in the Life of St Gregory; for although the prime cause of the Christian mission to the English people, he was not thought worthy, whether by divine wisdom or through some misfortune, to hear of Christianity himself. The choice passed to his son.

46. On Ælle's death, Ida's son Æthelric succeeded. He had spent his life in grinding poverty and was now a very old man; but he was quickly carried off by death after a five-year reign—a pitiful ruler, who would undoubtedly be buried in oblivion, had not his son's conspicuous energy brought the father into prominence.

47. When therefore the poor ancient had had enough, and more than enough, of life, Æthelfrith his elder son ascended the throne, young in years but in character mature, whose exploits have been described by ingenious authors, and receive here the attention of my

---

[2] Reference apparently to *GP* p. 5; in what follows William probably alludes to one of the Lives of Gregory: cf. *The Earliest Life of Gregory the Great*, ed. Bertram Colgrave (Lawrence, 1968), p. 90.

in eius et sequentium laudibus Bedae uigilauit ingenium, et illius quidem in confines sibi Northanimbros eo familiarius quo propinquius prospitiebat intentio; nostra uero lacinias illius carpet et componet oratio.[a] Ne quis sane michi uitio uertat quod tam diffusa in arctum contrahitur historia, nouerit factum consilio, ut qui nausiauerint in illis obsoniis, in his mendicantes respirent reliquiis. Est enim uerbum usu tritum, antiquitate uenerandum: 'Cibi qui minus suffitiunt auidius sumuntur.'

2 Ethelfridus igitur, ut dicere ceperam, regnum nactus primo acriter sua defendere, post etiam improbe aliena[b] inuadere, gloriae occasiones undecumque conflare. Multa per eum prelia[c] inchoata prouide et consummata egregie, dum nec illum a necessitate frenaret inertia nec ad temeritatem precipitaret audatia. Testis est horum Degsa lapis, in illis regionibus percelebris locus, in quo rex Scottorum Edan, qui successibus Ethelfridi inuidens detractantem etiam in bellum impulerat, non sine magno uictoris discrimine uictus fugam iniit; siquidem germanus Ethelfridi Tetbaldus,[d] caput periculis obiectans eo studiosius quo fratri operam ostentare affectabat impensius, luctuosam uictoriam reliquit, cum omnibus commanipularibus suis desideratus. Testis et

3 Legionum Ciuitas, quae[e] nunc simpliciter Cestra uocatur, quaeque[f] ad id temporis a Britannis possessa contumacis in regem populi alebat superbiam. Ad cuius oppugnationem cum intendisset animum, oppidani, qui omnia perpeti quam obsidionem mallent, simul et numero confisi, effuse in bellum ruunt; quos ille insidiis exceptos fudit fugauitque, prius in monachos debachatus qui pro salute exercitus[g] suplicaturi frequentes conuenerant. Quorum incredibilem nostra aetate numerum fuisse inditio sunt in uicino cenobio tot semiruti[h] parietes aecclesiarum, tot anfractus porticuum, tanta turba ruderum quantam uix alibi cernas; [i]uocatur locus ille Bancor, tunc monachorum famosum receptaculum, nunc mutatus in episcopium.[i]

4 Ita Ethelfridus[j] rebus ad uoluntatem foris scaturientibus, domesticum metum et intestinum periculum[k] propulsare desiderans, Eduinum Allae filium, non aspernandae probitatis iuuenem, regno et prouintia eliminat. At ille multo tempore incertis iactatus sedibus multosque[l]

---

[a] carperet et componeret narratio *Tt* [b] sua acriter . . . aliena improbae *Tt*
[c] pr(a)elia per eum *A* [d] Thetaldus *(or sim.) B* [e] *om. Tt* [f] uocata que *Tt*
[g] exercitus salute *TtB* [h] semirupti *Tt* [i-i] *om. Tt* [j] *om. Tt*
[k] *om. TtB (et int. metum B)* [l] pluresque *Tt*

pen only because the course of my narrative demands it. His praise indeed and that of his successors earned the attention of Bede, and Bede was particularly concerned with the Northumbrians, his own neighbours, who were familiar because they were so near; whereas my own account will but choose and put together snippets of his. Nor let anyone hold it against me that such a long story is here abridged; this is done, let me assure him, on purpose, that stomachs too weak for the feast spread by Bede may find relief here, like beggars picking up the fragments. It is a familiar saying, and hallowed by its antiquity, that food which does not satisfy is eaten with more appetite.

Æthelfrith then, as I began to say, on inheriting the kingdom, started by zealously defending his own possessions, and then unjustly invaded those of others, inventing on all sides opportunities to shine. Many were the campaigns he undertook from policy and completed with success, being neither restrained by idleness from doing what had to be done, nor plunged into perils by rashness. Witness the stone of Degsa, a landmark in those parts, where Aedan king of the Scots was vanquished and put to flight, when his jealousy of Æthelfrith's success had forced his rival, even against his will, into the field. The victor came into great peril; for Æthelfrith's brother Theodbald, exposing himself readily to danger as a means of displaying all the greater zeal in his brother's cause, was lost with all his companions in arms, and left a cloud over the day of victory. Witness too the City of Legions, now called simply Chester, which down to that date had been a possession of the British and had fostered their obstinate resistance to the king. When the king planned to reduce the city, the townsmen, being of the sort that prefer to endure anything rather than a siege, and at the same time trusting in their numbers, rushed out to battle in disorder. The king ambushed them and put them to flight, venting his fury first of all on the monks, who had gathered in crowds to pray for the success of the army. Their numbers would seem incredible in our own day, as is evident from the ruined walls of churches in the monastery near by, the complex arcading, and all that great pile of ruins, such as you would hardly find elsewhere. The place is called Bangor, in those days a famous refuge for monks, but now changed into a bishop's see.

While news of successes streamed in from abroad, Æthelfrith was anxious to be quit of domestic anxiety and dangers at home, and banished from the realm and region Ælle's son Edwin, a young man whose prowess could not be overlooked. Edwin was long tossed about

olim amicos procliuiores in hostem quam* in fidem expertus *(quia, ut
ille dixit,

cum fueris felix, multos numerabis amicos;
tempora si fuerint nubila, solus eris),*b1*

tandem ad Redwaldum regem Orientalium Anglorum uenit; apud
quem deploratis casibus suis, cum resedisset regia dignatione tutus,
aduenere legati Ethelfridi, uel traditionem* transfugae uel bellum
denuntiantes. Ille uxorii pectoris consilio* roboratus, ne fidem amico
datam ullius minis* corrumperet, super Ethelfridum paratis copiis
insperatus aduolat, nichilque minus quam insidias opinantem premeditatus aggreditur. Quod tunc solum uirtus deprehensa potuit, intercluso
fugae spatio remedium in manus uertit. Quanuis igitur pene inermis,
quanuis ancipiti periculo circumuentus, non prius tamen occubuit
quam interitu Reinerii filii Redwaldi mortem suam compensasset.
Hunc exitum*f* post regni*g* uiginti quattuor annos habuit Ethelfridus,*h*
usu quidem bellorum*i* nulli secundus sed diuinae religionis penitus
ignarus. *j*Habuerat ex Acca filia Allae, sorore Eduini, filios duos, Oswaldum duodennem Oswium*k* quadriennem,*l* qui tunc occiso genitore*j*
nutritiorum*m* diligentia fuga lapsi Scottiam euadunt.*n*

48. Sic Eduinus, emulis omnibus fusis*o* fugatisue,*p* pluribus laboribus emeritus regni fastigium iam non rudis ascendit. Cuius dominio
cum*q* mox Northanimbrorum ceruicositas dignanter*r* assurrexisset,
accessit ad cumulum felicitatis mors matura Redwaldi; namque*s*
prouintiales, qui olim apud se exulantem promptae audatiae et impigri
animi*t* explorassent Eduinum,*u* ultro coniurata fide in eius ditionem conspirant. Ille, Redwaldi filio inani*v* regis nomine concesso,*w* cetera moderabatur pro arbitrio. Ea tempestate spes atque opes Anglorum in illo sitae;
nec erat quaelibet Britanniae prouintia quae non illius spectaret nutum,
parata ad obsequium, preter solos Cantuaritas. Hos enim immunes excursionis reliquerat, quippe qui iam dudum ad nuptias Ethelburgae,
sororis Edbaldi regis eorum, mentem appulerat; quam cum longo

a quem *Tt*   *b–b* om. *Tt*   *c* redditionem *Tt*   *d* consiliis *C*   *e* ullo
modo *Tt*; illius minis *A*   *f* *Tt* adds belli   *g* om. *Tt*; regnum *B*   *h* Eth.
habuit *Tt*   *i* belli *Tt*   *j–j* filii eius Oswaldus et Oswius alter quadriennis alter
duodennis *Tt*   *k* Oswinum *AB*   *l* quadrimum *Bc*, quadrinum *Bk (and
BpBph)*   *m* nutritorum *B*   *n* inuadunt *Tt*   *o* cesis *TtB**   *p* uel
expulsis *B*   *q* cum dominio *C*   *r* om. *B*   *s* nam *B*   *t* animi esse
*Tt**   *u* om. *Tt*   *v* Inam *Al(Y*nam *Cs)*, inani nam *Aa*   *w* commisso *Tt*

from place to place, finding that many of his erstwhile friends favoured his adversary above the claims of loyalty, for, as the poet says:

> Let Fortune smile, you'll count your friends in scores;
> If clouds o'ercast the sky, you'll be forlorn.[1]

At length he came to the court of Rædwald, king of the East Angles. There he told the sad story of his misfortunes, and had begun to feel secure in the king's sympathy, when messengers arrived from Æthelfrith demanding the surrender of the fugitive with war as the alternative. Rædwald, emboldened by the counsel of his stout-hearted wife, refused to break faith with a friend no matter what the threat, raised forces and descended unexpectedly on Æthelfrith, making a planned attack on an enemy who was expecting nothing so little as an ambush. To a brave man caught in such a trap, only one course remained: his escape cut off, he had to seek safety in action. Although almost unarmed, although menaced with danger on every side, he did not fall till he had made up for his own death by the death of Rædwald's son Rægenhere. Such was the end, after reigning twenty-four years, of Æthelfrith, a man second to none in experience of battle, but quite ignorant of true religion. He had had by Acha, Ælle's daughter and sister of Edwin, two sons, Oswald then twelve years old and Oswiu four, who at that time after their father's death made their escape thanks to their foster-parents, and fled to Scotland.

48. So Edwin, having routed all his rivals, was a veteran of many campaigns and no longer inexperienced when he succeeded to the throne. The stubborn Northumbrians soon welcomed his overlordship, and the cup of his good fortune was filled by the timely death of Rædwald. The East Anglians, who had come to know Edwin as a man of ready vigour and enterprise when he was in exile among them long before, made a sworn league among themselves, and agreed to accept Edwin as their overlord. Edwin allowed Rædwald's son the empty name of king, and had everything else his own way. At that time all the prosperity and hopes of the English centred on him, and there was not a province in Britain but hung upon his nod ready to obey, except only the men of Kent. He had left them immune from his raiding activities, because he had long ago turned his mind towards a marriage with Æthelburh, sister of their king Eadbald; and when after

---

[1] Ovid, *Trist.* i. 9. 5–6.

tempore petitam tandem aliquando impetrasset, eo consilio ut non contempneret habitam quam diu suspirauerat dilatam, tanto duo illa[a] regna confederata sunt offitio ut nichil esset uel in potestatibus diuer-
3 sum uel in moribus barbarum.[b] Eadem preterea[c] occasione Paulino predicante Domini Christi fides illis partibus infusa primo regem ipsum penetrauit; quam[d] cum regina marito inter coniugales affectus[e] crebro inculcaret, et antistitis ammonitio suo loco non deesset, diu ille cunctabundus et anceps[f] semel tamen susceptam imis inseruit precordiis:[g] tunc uicinos reges[h] ad fidem inuitare, tunc aecclesiarum edifitia excitare, nichil quod ampliandae fidei congrueret negligere. Interea et deuotioni regiae serenus Deitatis fauor[i] arridebat, adeo ut non solum Britanniae gentes Angli Scotti Picti, sed et incolae[j] Orcadum et Meuaniarum, quas nunc Anglesei, id est Anglorum insulas, dicunt, et arma eius metuerent et potestatem adorarent. Nullus tunc predo publicus, nullus latro domesticus, insidiator coniugalis[k] pudoris procul, expilator alienae hereditatis exul: magnum id in eius laudibus
4 et nostra aetate splendidum. Itaque imperii sui[l] ad eos limites incrementa perducta sunt ut iustitia et pax libenter in mutuos amplexus concurrerent, osculorum gratiam grata uicissitudine libantes, et feliciter tunc Anglorum respublica[m] procedere potuisset, nisi[n] mors immatura temporalis beatitudinis nouerca turpi Fortunae ludo [o]uirum abstulisset patriae.[o] Aetatis enim anno octauo et quadragesimo, regni septimo decimo, repugnantibus[p] regulis quos sub iugum miserat, Cedwalla Britonum et Penda Mertiorum, cum filio interemptus miserabile uarietatis humanae fecit exemplum, [q]nullo prudentia inferior quod nec[r] Christianam fidem nisi diligentissime inspecta ratione uoluit suscipere, susceptaeque nichil comparabile existimare.[q]

49. Occiso Eduino, filii Ethelfridi idemque nepotes Eduini[s] Oswaldus et Oswius, iam adulti, iam iuuentae uernantis[t] florem[u] induti, repatriauerunt, simulque qui aetate prestabat Eanfridus, cuius mentio superius excidit. Regnum itaque in duo discretum; siquidem Northanimbria, iam dudum[v] in geminas secta prouincias, ex Deiris

[a] illa duo *TtBc* [b] uel in moribus barbarum *before* uel in pot. diu. *Tt. Whatever the order,* barbarum *is used oddly.* [c] preterea eadem *Tt* [d] quod *B* [e] affectus coniugales *Tt* [f] et anceps *om. Tt* [g] totis precordiis indidit *Tt (cf. 123. 1)* [h] regem *C* [i] fauor Dei. serenius *Tt* [j] incole *Tt;* insul(a)e *ACB* [k] maritalis *Tt* [l] eius imperii *Tt* [m] respublica Anglorum *Tt* [n] si non *Tt* [o-o] patrie illum abstulisset *Tt* [p] expugnantibus *C;* rebellantibus *B†* [q-q] *om. Tt* [r] ne *B* [s] *Tt* adds* de sorore Acca [t] uernantis iuuent(a)e *TtB* [u] *om. B* [v] iam pridem *Tt*

long suit he had at last won her hand, with the intention of treasuring her now as his own, for whom he had sighed so long while she was withheld, those two kingdoms were so closely united in spirit that there was no divergence in their government, no barbarian discord in their way of life. Given the same opportunity, the faith of Christ the Lord, preached by Paulinus, was introduced into that region, and first gained a footing in the king himself. Long was he in doubt, and hesitated; but the queen often pressed it upon her husband in the intimacy of marriage, and the admonitions of the bishop were not wanting in their turn; and so he accepted the faith, and once accepted absorbed it in his inmost heart. Then he began to summon neighbouring kings to share the faith, himself putting in hand the building of churches, and neglecting nothing that might contribute to the propagation of the Gospel. All this time, too, God's kindly favour smiled upon the religious king, so that not only the nations of Britain, English, Scots, and Picts, but the inhabitants of the Orkneys and Mevanians (now called Anglesey, 'Isles of the Angles') feared his arms and reverenced his power. In those days there was no highway robber nor domestic thief; gone was the crafty assailant of the sanctity of marriage, banished the despoiler of other men's inheritance—a thing greatly to his praise, and remarkable today. And so the increase of his government was carried to such heights that Justice and Peace gladly met in mutual embrace and happily kissed one another. With good hap indeed could the English commonwealth then have gone forward, had not untimely death, that stepmother of temporal felicity, by a mean stroke of fortune robbed the country of its hero Edwin. In the forty-eighth year of his age and seventeenth of his reign the princes whom he had subdued, Cadwallon king of the Britons and Penda king of the Mercians, rebelled; he and his son were killed, and provided a pitiful example of human vicissitude. He yielded to none in wisdom, for he would not even adopt the Christian faith till he had carefully examined the principle of it, though once adopted, he reckoned it above all comparison.

49. On Edwin's death, Æthelfrith's sons and Edwin's nephews [Tt *adds* by his sister Acha], Oswald and Oswiu, who were already of age and flourishing in the springtime of young manhood, returned to their country, and with them their elder brother Eanfrith, whom I omitted to mention earlier. The kingdom was therefore divided in two; and indeed Northumbria had long been cut up into two provinces, Ælle having arisen from among the

Allam, ex Bernitiis Idam creauerat. Quapropter tunc filius patrui Eduini Osricus Deiram, Eanfridus filius Ethelfridi Bernitiam sortiti, hereditarium ius se obtinuisse*^a* gloriabantur; ambo in Scottia sacris*^b* Christianis*^c* initiati, ambo uix dum potestatis compotes*^d* fidei transfugae, non multo post infestante Cedwalla 'fidei' relictae penas dedere.*^e*

2 Annuum tempus inter has moras*^g* exactum Oswaldum, magnae spei iuuenem, ad imperandi scientiam exercuit. Is fide quam ferro instructior (nam apud Scottos, ubi cum multa nobilium indole exulauerat, baptismi gratiam meruerat), Cedwallam rerum gestarum memoria elatum, uirum (ut ipse dictitabat)*^h* in exterminium Anglorum natum, primo impetu castris exuit, mox cum omnibus copiis deleuit. Cum enim quantulumcumque exercitum undecumque conflasset,*ⁱ* his sermonibus in bellum excitauit, ut*^j* aut uincendum sibi commilitones*^k* aut moriendum nossent,*^l* nichil de fuga meditantes, exprobrandi pudoris rem uentilari allegans, Anglos cum Britannis tam iniquo marte confligere *^m*ut contra illos pro salute decertarent*^m* quos ultro pro gloria lacessere consuessent; *ⁿ*itaque libertatem audentibus animis et effusis uiribus asserant; ceterum de fugae impetu memoriam nullam.*ⁿ*

3 Quare tam acriter et tanto conflictu*^o* utrobique concursum ut recte dictum sit illum diem fuisse quo numquam Britannos*^p* tristior, numquam Anglos afflasset hilarior: adeo alteri omnibus uiribus consumptis*^q* ulterius respirare non ausi, alteri sacra religione cum regis magnanimitate consentiente in immensum prouecti. Denique ex eo tempore cultus*^r* idolorum ad cineres torpuit,*^s* et ipse regnum latioribus quam Eduinus terminis citra ullam necem hominum octo annis*^t* quiete*^u* cohercuit. Huius regis laudes historia¹ panagerico prosequitur stilo,*^v* quarum nos competentes particulas uelut quodam complectemur epilogo.

4 Quantus enim in eius pectore fidei feruor coaluerit facile ex hoc animaduertes,*^w* quod si quando antistes Aidanus Scottice auditoribus facienda proponeret et interpres deesset, confestim rex ipse, quanuis indutus clamidem uel auro rigentem uel Tirios murices estuantem, id munus dignanter*^x* corripiens barbari sermonis inuolucrum patria

---

^a obtinuisse se *Tt*   *^b* sacri *A*   *^c* om. *Tt*   *^d* potestate percepta *Tt*   *^{e–e}* perfidiae merita recepere *Tt*   *^f* credulitatis *B†*   *^g* *Tt adds* ut ferunt   *^h* iactabat *Tt;* dictabat *B*   *ⁱ* agregasset *Tt*   *^j* om. *Tt*   *^k* om. *Tt*   *^l* nossent *after* meditantes *Tt*   *^{m–m}* et... decertare *Tt*   *^{n–n}* om. *Tt*   *^o* tantis animis *Tt*   *^p* Britones *C*   *^q* effusis *Tt*   *^r* et cultus *Tt**   *^s* usque friguit *Tt*   *^t* octo annis *after* regnum *Tt*   *^u* quiete *C;* cum quiete *TtAB; perhaps* sub quiete (*cf. 108. 1*)   *^v* modo *T*   *^w* animaduerteres *C*   *^x* non aspernanter *B†*

Deirans, and Ida from the Bernicians. And so at this moment Osric, son of their uncle Edwin, was given Deira, and Æthelfrith's son Eanfrith, Bernicia, and each could boast that he had obtained his due by inheritance. Both had become Christians in Scotland, both were hardly on the throne before they broke their faith, and not long after, when attacked by Cadwallon, paid the penalty of that breach. These 2 developments lasted for a year, [Tt *adds* as they say] and gave Oswald, a young man of great promise, some practice in the art of command. Better furnished with faith than with steel (for he had received the sacrament of baptism among the Scots when he with many sons of the nobility was an exile amongst them), he attacked Cadwallon, who was exulting in the record of his own exploits and seemed a man born, as he himself used to say, to annihilate the English; the first attack drove Cadwallon from his camp, and soon he was destroyed with all his forces. Oswald had collected from every possible source such an army as he could, and encouraged his comrades in arms to do battle with the assurance that they must conquer or die without a thought of flight. It was a most disgraceful circumstance, he said, that the English should be struggling against the British on such unequal terms as to be forced to fight for their lives against men whom they had been used to challenge freely for the sake of glory. They must therefore assert their independence with bold hearts and all their strength, and not devote a thought to the means of escape. Such was the keenness, such the force of the attack on both sides that 3 it may be said with truth that no day ever dawned more lamentable for the British or happier for the English. One side lost all their strength, and never dared to breathe again; the other, with its union of true religion and a generous-hearted king, was prodigiously increased. So it was that henceforward the worship of idols sank into ashes, and Oswald himself for eight years, without any bloodshed, maintained his realm in peace within wider frontiers than Edwin's. This famous king receives a panegyric from the historian[1] of which I will include certain parts by way of epilogue.

How great the flame of religious faith burning in his bosom, may 4 easily be seen from this, that if ever Bishop Aidan put before his audience what they ought to do in the Scottish tongue, and an interpreter was needed, at once the king himself, though he might be wearing a cloak stiff with gold thread or glowing with Tyrian purple, graciously took upon himself that duty, and made plain in his native tongue

---

[1] Bede, *HE* iii. 1 seq.

lingua expediret. Vulgatissimum quoque est*a* quod crebro appositis obsoniis,*b* cum conuiuae in cibos dentes acuerent, mentes intenderent, ipse uoluptatem*c* frenarit, penuria sua pauperum mercatus gaudia; unde arbitror etiam temporaliter absolutam esse celestis sententiae fidem, quam diuinum quondam resultauit oraculum: 'Dispersit,
5 dedit pauperibus; iustitia eius manet in seculum seculi.'[1] Nam quod auditor mirari debeat et infitiari non ualeat,*d* dextra illa regalis, tantarum elemosinarum largitrix, hodieque cum brachio cute et neruis incorrupta uiget; totum uero corpus reliquum preter ossa in cineres dissolutum*e* communionem mortalitatis non euasit. Et sunt quidem nonnullorum sanctorum corporales exuuiae nullius omnino labis consciae. Quapropter estiment*f* alii quo examine iuditium suum ponderent; ego istud gratius et euidentiori miraculo diuinius esse pronuntio; nam usu etiam pretiosa degenerant, et quicquid uidetur rarius predi-
6 catur uberius. Iam uero superfluus essem si dicere affectarem quam sedulus fuerit preces in altum porrigere, uotis caelos onerare: adeo est amplior laus ista in Oswaldo quam ut nostra oratione indigeat cumulari. Quando enim togatus negligeret qui, rebellione per Pendam regem Mertiorum excitata, cum stipatoribus fusis ipse quoque ferratam siluam in pectore gereret, nec atrocitate uulnerum nec mortis confinio potuit argui quin pro animabus fidelium suorum Domino Deo suplicaret? Ita uir in seculo ingentis gloriae, magnae apud Deum gratiae, animam exuens gratiosam sui posteris*g* profudit
7 memoriam per miraculorum*h* frequentiam. Merito: res est*i* enim non pertrita sed 'coruo rarior albo',[2] hominem habundare diuitiis et nolle lasciuire uitiis. *j*Itaque defuncti brachia cum manibus et capite insatiabili uictoris ira desecta et stipiti appensa. Et corpus quidem, ut dixi, totum placido naturae sinu confotum in terreum elementum abiit; brachia uero cum manibus auctore Deo,*k* teste ueraci historico,[3] inuiolata durant. Ea a fratre Oswio apud Bebbanburg (urbem ita uocant Angli) composita scrinio, monstrata miraculo idem asserit. Quo loci quia opinione fluctuo utrum ad hunc diem seruentur, precipitem

---

a uulgatissimum est quoque *T*; uulgatum quoque est *C*; est etiam uulgatissimum *B†*   *b* dapibus *B*   *c* uoluntatem *Al*, uoluntate *Aap*   *d* audeat *B*   *e* resolutum *T*   *f* uiderint *T*   *g* pastoris *C*; apud posteros *B†*   *h* meritorum *B*   *i* om. *T*   *j-j* (p. 76) om. *Tt*   *k* *B adds* et

[1] Ps. 111 (112): 9.
[2] Juvenal vii. 202.
[3] Bede, *HE* iii. 6.

what had been wrapped up in a barbarian language. Often too—this is a well-known story—when the feast was on the board and the guests were plying their sharp teeth and concentrating their busy minds entirely upon the food, the king restrained his appetite, and by impoverishing himself purchased the happiness of the poor; for which reason I think that even in this world he proved the truth of that heavenly oracle, which the divine spokesman once re-echoed: 'He hath dispersed, he hath given to the poor; his righteousness endureth for ever.'[1] Here then is something to make the hearer marvel, but deny it he cannot. That kingly right hand, by which such generous alms were lavished, survives in our own day, with arm, skin, and sinews incorrupt; all the rest of the body, except the bones, has fallen into dust, not having escaped the common lot of mortality. There are indeed several saints whose bodily remains are quite free from all taint of corruption. Let others therefore consider in what scales their judgement should be weighed; for my part, I declare this to be more clearly a sign of God's grace and His power than a more obvious miracle; for even precious things suffer by familiarity, and what is seldom seen receives more lavish praise. I should now be tedious, did I aspire to tell how constant he was in the offering of prayer and in loading Heaven with his vows. Such merit in Oswald is far too great to need increase from any words of mine. When was he likely to neglect his prayers in ordinary life, who, when Penda king of the Mercians had stirred up a rebellion, after his bodyguard had been scattered and he himself carried a forest of spears in his breast, could not be deterred by his cruel wounds or by the near approach of death from interceding with our Lord God for the souls of his faithful followers? So died a man who stood high in the glory of this world and in favour with God, and left posterity good reason to remember him with gratitude for his frequent miracles. And rightly: it is no trivial thing, but 'than white raven rarer',[2] for a man to abound in riches and yet refuse to wanton in wickedness. So it came about that, after his death, his arms, with his hands and head, were cut off by the victor with insatiate fury and fastened on a pole. Thus his whole body, as I have said, was laid to rest in the peaceful lap of Nature, and passed into the element of earth; but his arms and hands, by God's power, remain inviolate, as the truthful historian affirms.[3] He also tells us that they were placed in a shrine by his brother Oswiu at a place called by the English Bamburgh, and shown there as a miracle. Whether they are kept in that place to this day, I am far from certain, and therefore do not venture a

affirmationem non emitto. Si quid alii historiographi temere sunt professi, ipsi uiderint; michi fama uilius*a* constet, ne quicquam nisi absoluta fide dignum pronuntiem.

8 Caput, tunc ab eodem germano Lindisfarni humatum, nunc Dunelmi inter brachia beatissimi Cuthberti teneri aiunt. Ossa reliqui corporis cum regina Ostrida, uxor Ethelredi regis Mertiorum, filia regis Oswii, caritate patrui ducta Bardenio monasterio suo, quod est in regione Mertiorum non longe a Lindocolina ciuitate, inferre uellet, iuerunt in repulsam monachi parumper,*b* inuidentes mortuo quietem ossuum quem oderant uiuum, quod super eos bellico iure acceperat regnum. Sed intempesta nocte per lucernam de caelo super reliquias emissam edocti fatuum lenire tumorem,[1] in aequitatem transiere, ultro expostulantes*c* quod ante reiecerant; frequentabanturque ibi uirtutes diuinitus, sentiebatque precellentissimi martiris opem quicumque
9 implorasset languidus. Reuiruit ex cadentis sanguine campi cespes plus solito floreus, quo sanatus sonipes, quem posti affixum sinuosis anfractibus ignis uitabundus effugit. Nec uacauit a uirtute lauaturae reliquiarum eius puluisculus, quo mentis impos integritati rationis est redditus. Occurrit medelae qui recentem cruorem capitis imbiberat stipes, quo loto*d* hausit sanitatem desperatus. Diu illud monasterium tanti thesauri conscium claruit habitantium sanctimonia et necessariorum copia, presertim postquam Ethelredus rex ibidem coronam tonsurae monachicae accepit, ubi et mausoleum eius usque *e*diem hodiernum*e* uisitur. Porro post multos annos ossa beatissimi Oswaldi, cum ea loca infestarent barbari, Gloecestram translata; locus iste, *f*tunc monachos nunc*f* canonicos habens, non multo incolitur habitatore.

10 Fuit igitur Oswaldus qui genti suae primitias sanctitatis dederit, quippe nullus ante illum Anglus miraculis, quod sciam, uiguerit.*g* Qui post actam sancte uitam large dando elemosinas, crebras in Dei obsequela*h* protelando excubias, postremo zelo Dei aecclesiae cum gentili committens ante (quod optabat) effudit spiritum quam (quod timebat) Christianitatis uideret detrimentum. Nec fraudabitur profecto martirum gloria qui, primo bonae uitae intendens, postmodum

---

a illius *Bk*, ullius *Bc(and BpBph)*   *b* om. *B*   *c* postulantes *B*
d loco *C(corr. in Ce)Bc*   *e–e* hodie *B*   *f–f* om. *C*   *g* claruerit *B. One expects* uiguerat   *h* obsequia *B*

---

[1] Unidentified.

definite opinion; if other historians have committed themselves, I leave that to them, hoping that I shall always put a lower value on mere rumour, and set down nothing except what deserves complete acceptance.

His head was at that time buried by the same brother at Lindisfarne, but is said to be now at Durham, held in the arms of St Cuthbert. As for the remaining bones of his body, Queen Osthryth, wife of Æthelred king of the Mercians and daughter of King Oswiu, was moved by affection for her uncle to wish to transfer them to her monastery of Bardney, which is in the province of the Mercians not far from Lincoln. The monks opposed this for a time, grudging peace in death to the bones of a man they hated when alive, because he had assumed rule over them by right of conquest. A light from Heaven, however, that shone upon the relics at dead of night taught them 'to bate their foolish pride';[1] they abandoned their prejudices, and demanded of their own volition what they had previously rejected. Many were the miracles performed there by divine authority, and every sick man who invoked the aid of that most famous martyr felt his power. From his blood, where he fell, the turf grew green again and fuller than its wont of flowers; a horse was cured by it, and as the turf hung tied to a pillar, fire curled round to avoid it and dared not touch. A little dust steeped in the water used to wash the relics made a precious lotion, with which a lunatic was restored to his sound senses. The stake which had drunk up the fresh blood from his head acquired healing power, and a man whose life was despaired of regained his health from the washings of it. The monastery that enshrined such a treasure long flourished in the sanctity of its inmates and the ample provision made for them, especially after King Æthelred was crowned there with the monastic tonsure; the king's grave is shown there at the present day. At length, after many years, those parts being harassed by the barbarians, St Oswald's bones were translated to Gloucester, a house in those days of monks, but now of canons and with few inmates.

So it was Oswald who bestowed upon his countrymen the first-fruits of sanctity, for no Englishman before him, so far as I know, worked miracles. He spent his life in holiness, in generous almsgiving, in long and frequent vigils in God's service, and at the end joined battle with the pagan king in his zeal for the church of God, thus, as he hoped, he laid down his life in good time, and did not, as he feared, live to see the cause of Christ suffer defeat. Nor will he be disappointed of the martyrs' glory who followed their footsteps, being from the first

gloriosae morti*a* corpus impendens, eorum triuit uestigia; et cumulatiori pene laude, quod illi singuli se singulos, ille secum Deo consecrauerit*b* totos Northanimbros.*j*

50. Eo igitur humanis rebus exempto, Oswius frater eius apud Bernitios, Oswinus filius Osrici, de quo superius dixi,[1] apud Deiros regnum occuparunt;*c* quibus cum primo de prouintiarum diuisione modeste conuenisset, suspenso federe in sua pacifice discessum. Verum non multo post, per homines quibus nichil magis cordi erat quam discordias serere, pax incertis pactionibus sepe ludificata, ultimo penitus abrupta, in uentos abiit: facinus miserabile, fuisse qui regibus concordiam*d* sodalitatis inuiderent, nec abstinerent quin eos prelio, 2 quantum in ipsis erat, committerent. Ibi tunc*e* Fortuna, multis antea illecebris Oswinum adulata, scorpiacea cauda persequebatur;*f* namque, pro penuria exercitus*g* bello abstinendum ratus, suburbanum rus clanculo concesserat,*h* statimque a suis proditus ab Oswio interemptus est, uir egregie factus ad emerendam gratiam ciuium largitione pecuniae, animae quoque suae (ut ferunt) non negligens mentis deuotione. Ita Oswius, integri regni compos, nichil non postea molitus est quo existimationem suam purgaret, quo maiestatem augeret, atrocis facti offensam probitate posteriorum uirtutum*i* imminuens.

3 Et primus quidem idemque amplissimus laudum eius cumulus extat, quod fratrem et auunculum nobiliter ultus Pendam regem Mertiorum—illud uicinorum excidium, illud perduellionum seminarium—exitio dedit; ex quo tempore tam Mertiis quam omnibus pene Anglis uel ipse presedit uel presidentibus imperauit. Hinc totus ad offitia pietatis conuersus, ut Dei benefitiis in se confluentibus digna sedulitate responderet, *j*Christiani cultus*j* infantiam pro nece germani in regno suo palpitantem uiuacitate regia*k* erigere et pleno spiritu*l* animare contendit, eandemque mox doctrina*m* Scottorum adultam sed in multis aecclesiasticis obseruationibus fluctuantem *n*primo per Angilbertum et Wilfridum, postremo*n* per Theodorum archiepiscopum 4 canonico statu informauit. De cuius in Angliam*o* aduentu princeps

---

a mortis *Al*^{a.c.}*Aap*   *b* consecrauit *B*   *j* See above, p. 72   *c* occupauit *Tt*   *d* gratiam *B*   *e* om. *Tt (the collocation is odd)*   *f* prosequebatur *Aac, perhaps rightly (cf. GP p. 218, VW ii. 22)*   *g* om. *Tt*   *h* concessit *B*   *i* morum *B*   *j-j* Christianismi *C*   *k* sua *Tt*   *l* spiritu pleno *Tt*   *m* doctrinam *B*   *n-n* om. *Tt*   *o* in Angliam *om. Tt*

[1] 49. 1.

devoted to a virtuous life, and in the end making with his body the offering of a glorious death; indeed his praise is fuller, almost, than theirs, for they devoted themselves to God singly, each for himself, but Oswald devoted with himself the whole people of Northumbria.

50. So, when Oswald was taken from the world of men, his brother Oswiu assumed the crown in Bernicia and Oswine son of Osric, of whom I have spoken above,[1] in Deira. At first, having come to a reasonable understanding as to the boundary of their territories, they left their agreement in the balance and retired peacefully to their own land. It was not long, however, before men who enjoyed nothing so much as to sow the seeds of discord brought the peace frequently into jeopardy because the agreement was so vague, until at length it collapsed entirely and was scattered to the winds. It was a sorry sight to see men display such ill-will towards the friendly agreement of princes, and unable to abstain from doing what they could to embroil them in war. At that stage, Fortune, who had previously lavished her treacherous smiles on Oswine, turned against him with her scorpion tail. Having decided not to offer battle because his army was so small, he had retired secretly to a property of his not far from the city, and was at once betrayed to Oswiu by his own servants and put to death. He was a man exceptionally well adapted to win popularity by his open-handedness, whose devotion showed, it is said, that he did not neglect his immortal soul. So Oswiu became sole king, and thereafter did all he could to clear his reputation and increase his royal authority, lightening the guilt of this outrage by a subsequent display of virtue. 2

His first and greatest claim to fame is the notable vengeance he exacted for his brother and uncle by destroying that menace to his neighbours, that hotbed of hostilities, Penda king of the Mercians. From that time forth, the Mercians like almost all the English were either ruled by him directly, or subjected to rulers over whom he was suzerain. He then turned wholly to religious duties, by way of a proper response to the benefits that God showered upon him: on account of his brother's murder, Christianity in his kingdom was like an infant gasping for breath, and he did his best with royal zeal to revive it, and fill it again with the breath of life. Later when, thanks to the teaching of the Scots, it was fully grown, but was wavering on many points of ecclesiastical observance, he had it taught the true law, first by Agilbert and Wilfrid, and then by Archbishop Theodore. For Theodore's arrival in England our thanks are principally due to 3 4

Oswio debetur gratia, licet Egberhtus rex Cantuariae pro iure prouintiae multum illius delibet*ᵃ* gloriae. Quin et Deo famulantibus frequentia constituens habitacula*ᵇ* huius quoque boni patriam non reliquit exsanguem. Quorum precipuum monasterium,*ᶜ* tunc feminarum nunc uirorum,*ᵈ* ab Eboraco triginta milibus in boreali parte situm, antiquo uocabulo Streneshalh, modo*ᵉ* Witebi nuncupatur;*ᶠ* quod ab insignis religionis femina Hilda ceptum Ethelfleda,*ᵍ* eiusdem regis filia, in regimine succedens magnis*ʰ* fiscalium opum molibus auxit, ubi et patri post uiginti octo annos regni defuncto funerea*ⁱ* iusta persoluit. *ʲ*Illud cenobium, sicut et omnia eiusdem regionis, tempore Danicae uastationis*ᵏ* (quam dicemus inferius)*ˡ* deletum, multa sanctorum corpora perdidit: *ˡ*nam et sanctissimae uiraginis Hildae ossa*ˡ* tunc Glastoniam translata, et aliorum sanctorum alias nonnulla. Nunc mutato nomine paululum pro tempore restauratum antiquae opulentiae uix tenue presentat uestigium.*ʲ*

51. Oswio, cui duo erant filii, minor*ᵐ* legitime susceptus reprobato notho successit, Etheldridae uxoris sanctissimae meritis quam suis commendatior; denique duabus omnino rebus, quas *ⁿ*quidem in Gestis Anglorum² legerim,*ⁿ* predicandus, uel quod dominae*ᵒ* ⟨Deo⟩*ᵖ* uacare uolenti serenus indulserit, uel quod beatum Cuthbertum lacrimis religiosa assentatione profusis in episcopatum promouerit.*ᵠ* Ceterum horret animus meminisse impietatis quam in beatissimum Wilfridum*ʳ* grassatus euomuit, quando bonitatis illius nausiam concipiens patriam clarissimo lumine uiduauit. Idem in suplices*ˢ* proteruus, quo morbo nullum tirannorum*ᵗ* carere uideas, Hibernenses, genus sane hominum innocens et genuina simplicitate nichil umquam mali moliens, uasta clade protriuit. At contra in rebelles ignauus triumphosque patris eludens*ᵘ* imperium Mertiorum amisit; quin et ab eorum rege Ethelredo filio Pendae in pugna*ᵛ* fugatus fratrem quoque amisit. *ʷ*Veruntamen haec postrema iuuentutis lubrico, in Wilfridum uero commissa episcoporum et uxoris consilio ueritas rerum assignari

---

ᵃ deliberet *Tt*   *ᵇ* freq. Deo fam. hab. const. *Tt*   *ᶜ* cenobium *Tt (cf. GP p. 198)*   *ᵈ* monachorum *B, GP p. 198*   *ᵉ* nunc *Tt (so GP p. 198, AG p. 68)*   *ᶠ* nuncupatum *Tt*   *ᵍ* om. *Tt*   *ʰ* magis *Tt*   *ⁱ* funera *TtCsBk*   *ʲ⁻ʲ* om. *Tt*   *ᵏ* infestationis *B*   *ˡ⁻ˡ* *AB; the passage is expanded in C (see Appendix, p. 820)*   *ᵐ* *B†* adds Egfridus *(otherwise unnamed until after his death)*   *ⁿ⁻ⁿ* ego audierim *Tt*   *ᵒ* *One expects* uxori *(Southern) or* reginae; Domino *Savile*   *ᵖ* *Supplied by Winterbottom (cf. e.g. GP p. 369),* Domino *Mynors*   *ᵠ* promouit *Tt*   *ʳ* Wilf. beat. *Tt*   *ˢ* simplices *Tt*   *ᵗ* fere tyrannum *Tt*   *ᵘ* illudens *Tt*   *ᵛ* fuga *Al;* bello *AaB*   *ʷ⁻ʷ* *(p. 80) om. Tt*

Oswiu, though Ecgberht king of Kent as ruler of the province claims much of the credit. He also founded numerous dwelling-places for the servants of God, and this was another good thing with which he left his native country well endowed. Of these the chief was the monastery originally of women but now of men, situated thirty miles north of York, and called of old *Streneshalh* but now Whitby. This had been started by that great religious leader Hild, and subsequently increased with large financial resources by her successor as head of it, the king's daughter Ælfflæd, who there celebrated her father's funeral, when he died after twenty-eight years on the throne. This house, in common with all other houses in the same region, was destroyed in the Danish invasions, to be described later,[1] and forfeited the bodies of many saints; for the bones of the most holy virgin Hild were at that time translated to Glastonbury, and the bodies of other saints to other places. At present, with its name altered, and restored on a modest scale as circumstances permit, it displays little more than faint traces of its former opulence.

51. Oswiu had two sons, of whom the elder was rejected as a bastard, and the younger [B *adds* Ecgfrith], being legitimate, succeeded. He is recommended more by the merits of his saintly queen Æthelthryth than for any of his own; I find, for instance, only two things to his credit in the *History of the English*,[2] one that he kindly gave his lady her freedom when she wished to devote herself to God, and the other that he advanced St Cuthbert, after he had shed tears of pious assent, to be a bishop. All the same, my mind is revolted to think of the torrents of impiety he vented in his attacks on St Wilfrid, when, sickened by his virtue, he robbed his country of its brightest ornament. Highhanded as he was towards suppliants, a disease from which you will find no tyrant free, he devastated the Irish, an innocent race of men who in their native simplicity have no evil designs against any man. Against insurgents, on the other hand, he showed no spirit, and making his father's triumphs vain, he lost his rule over the Mercians; indeed, being routed in battle by the Mercian king, Penda's son Æthelred, he lost his brother too. But the truth of history bids me assign these last disasters to the heedlessness of youth, and his treatment of Wilfrid to the counsel of the bishops and his queen, especially

---

[1] Especially from c. 118.
[2] Bede, *HE* iv. 19 and 27–8.

iubet, presertim cum Beda, adulari nescius, eum in libro de uita abbatum suorum[1] piissimum et Deo dilectissimum uocet.[m] Postremo, quinto decimo regni anno,[a] expeditionem in Pictos agens, cum illis in montes abditos consulto cedentibus peruicaciter instaret,[b] cum omnibus fere copiis interiit; pauci fuga lapsi rem domi nuntiarunt, quanuis diuinus Cuthbertus pro futurorum conscientia et iturum retinere temptauerit et[c] ipsa hora occisionis spiritum [d]e celo sibi[d] influentem[e] hauriens interfectum absens non tacuerit.

52. Egfridi necem cum insignior ubique fama loqueretur, etiam ad fratris Alfridi[f] aures 'anxia precipiti peruenit epistola penna'.[2] Is, quia nothus (ut diximus[g])[3] erat, factione optimatum, quanuis senior, regno indignus estimatus[h] in Hiberniam, seu ui seu indignatione, secesserat. Ibi, et[i] odio germani tutus et magno[j] otio litteris imbutus, omni philosophia composuerat animum.[k] Quocirca, imperii habenis habiliorem[l] estimantes, qui quondam expulerant ultro expetiuerunt; necessitas
2 medelam ad preces refudit. Nec eos ille[m] sua spe frustratus est; nam per decem et nouem annos summa pace et gaudio prouintiae prefuit, nichil umquam, preter in persecutione magni Wilfridi, quod liuor edax digne[n] carpere posset admittens.[o] Non tamen isdem terminis quibus pater et frater[p] regnum tenuit, quod Picti, recenti uictoria insolenter abusi, Anglosque longa[q] pace ignauiores aggressi, fines eorum ab aquilone decurtauerant.

53. Habuit successorem filium Osredum, octo annorum puerum, qui annis undecim[r] regnum inumbrans turpemque uitam sanctimonialium stupris exagitans, tandem[s] cognatorum insidiis cesus eandem fortunam in ipsos refudit.[t] Siquidem Kenred duobus et Osricus undecim annis regnantes hoc tantum memorabile habuere, quod domini sui licet[u] merito, ut putabant, occisi sanguinem luentes fedo exitu auras polluere. Meruit sane quo laetior abiret Osricus,[v] 'multumque' ut gentilis ait[w] [4] 'aliis iactantior umbris', quod[x] Celwlfum

---

[m] See above, p. 78   [a] anno regni Tt   [b] insisteret B   [c] temptauit et in B   [d-d] celo Tt   [e] effluentem B   [f] Alfridi fratris ad (ad s.l.) Tt   [g] dixi A   [h] putatus Tt; existimatus A   [i] B adds ab   [j] grandi B   [k] animum composuerat Tt   [l] aptiorem Tt   [m] ille eos Tt   [n] digne after carpere Tt; om. B   [o] admittens before quod Tt   [p] et frater om. Tt   [q] om. B   [r] undecim annis Tt   [s] tandemque Al[a.c.]B   [t] effudit Tt   [u] quamuis Tt   [v] Osricus before quo Tt   [w] ut poeta dixit Tt   [x] supremae scilicet uoluntatis arbitrium quo Tt (ob seems to be required before supremae)

[1] Hist. Abbatum 1.   [2] Juvenal iv. 149.

since Bede, who is incapable of flattery, calls him in his book on the lives of his abbots[1] a man of great piety and very dear to God. At length, in the fifteenth year of his reign, while he was conducting an expedition against the Picts, and had obstinately pursued them when they deliberately retreated into their mountain recesses, he was destroyed with almost all his forces, and few escaped to tell the tale; although St Cuthbert, with his habitual foresight, had tried to restrain him at the outset, and at the hour of his death, inspired by a heaven-sent spirit, had announced even at that distance that he was dead.

52. When more public rumour began to spread everywhere the news of Ecgfrith's death, 'on headlong wing the anxious missive came'[2] to the ears of his brother Aldfrith also. Being illegitimate, as we have said,[3] he had been regarded by the nobles although the elder as unworthy of the throne, and either under compulsion or in indignation had retired to Ireland. Protected there by the hatred felt for his brother and enjoying ample leisure for the study of literature, he had formed his mind by wide acquaintance with philosophy. Being in consequence considered more suitable for the reins of power, he received an invitation from those who had previously cast him out; their only hope of safety lay in pleading with him. Nor did he disappoint their hopes: for nineteen years he ruled the province in unbroken peace and happiness, and never did anything, save for his persecution of St Wilfrid, which carping jealousy could properly attack. Yet he did not maintain his kingdom within the same bounds as his father and brother, for the Picts, presuming insolently on their recent victory, had attacked the English, who were unduly softened by a lengthy peace, and had curtailed their boundaries on the north.

53. He had as his successor a son Osred, a child eight years old, who after darkening the throne for eleven years and spending his shameful existence in the ravishing of nuns, was at length treacherously put to death by his kinsmen, and handed on the same fate to them also. Cenred reigned for two years, Osric for eleven, with one memorable feature only, that although they had killed their lord, so they thought, with good reason, each paid the penalty by poisoning the air with a horrible death. Osric, it is true, deserved 'to make the happier end,' 'among the other shades far prouder he' as the heathen poet puts it,[4] in that, while still

---

[3] 51. 1 (though he is not named there).   [4] Statius, *Theb.*ix. 559.

2 Kenredi fratrem uiuens sibi successorem[a] adoptauerat. Conscendit igitur tremulum regni culmen[b] Celwlfus ab Ida septimus,[c] et idoneus ad cetera et cui non deerat[d] litterarum peritia acri animo et alacri studio comparata. Vadatur sermonis mei ueritatem[e] Beda, qui, eo tempore quo maxime scaturiebat litteratis[f] Britannia, huic potissimum Anglorum Historiam[g] elimandam obtulit, eligens nimirum in illo auctoritatem [h]bene dicta roborandi propter imperium et scientiam perperam dicta emendandi[h] propter ingenium.

54. Cuius[i] anno quarto idem historicus,[j] post multos in sancta aecclesia libros elaboratos, caelestem patriam quam diu suspirauerat ingressus est, anno Dominicae incarnationis septingentesimo tricesimo quarto, aetatis suae quinquagesimo[k] nono: uir quem mirari facilius quam digne predicare possis, quod in extremo natus orbis angulo[l] doctrinae corusco terras omnes perstrinxerit. Nam et Britannia, quae a quibusdam alter orbis appellatur, quod oceano interfusa[m] non multis cosmographis[n] comperta est, habet in remotissima sui plaga locum
2 natiuitatis et educationis eius,[o] Scottiae propinquum. Plaga, olim et suaue halantibus monasteriorum floribus dulcis et urbium a Romanis edificatarum frequentia renidens, nunc uel antiquo Danorum uel recenti Normannorum[p] populatu lugubris, nichil quod animos multum allitiat pretendit.[q] Ibi est Wira, nec egenae latitudinis nec segnis gurgitis amnis, qui pelago influus naues serena inuectas aura placido hostii excipit gremio.[r] Cuius utrasque ripas Benedictus quidam aecclesiis insigniuit et monasteria ibidem construxit, alterum Petri alterum Pauli nomine, caritatis et regulae unione non discrepantia.
3 Huius industriam et patientiam mirabitur qui leget librum quem Beda composuit de uita eius et reliquorum abbatum suorum. Industriam, quod copiam librorum aduexerit, quod artifices lapidearum edium et uitrearum fenestrarum primus omnium Angliam asciuerit, totum pene aeuum[s] talia transigendo peregrinatus; quippe studio aduehendi cognatis aliquod insolitum amor patriae et uoluptas elegantiae asperos fallebant labores; neque enim ante Benedictum lapidei tabulatus domus in Britannia nisi perraro uidebantur, neque perspicuitate uitri

---

[a] successorem sibi (om. uiuens) T*t* [b] culmen regni T [c] octauus B†
[d] deesset Bk(and BpBph), deceret Bc [e] ueritatem sermonis mei TB [f] litteratis (litteras Tc) scaturiebat T [g] historiam Anglorum T [h-h] propter imperium, scientiam corrigendi T [i] huius T [j] historiographus T
[k] sexagesimo (om. nono) T [l] mundi angulo natus T [m] interfuso T* (cf. Hegesippus ii. 9. 1) [n] historicis T*t*, historiis Tc [o] eius et educationis T

alive [Tt in that by his will], he had adopted Ceolwulf, Cenred's brother, as his successor. So Ceolwulf ascended the tottering throne, seventh in 2 descent from Ida; he was a suitable candidate in other respects, and in particular had acquired some knowledge of letters by keen intelligence and industry. The truth of my assertion is vouched for by Bede who, at a time when Britain was exceptionally rich in men of literary culture, selected Ceolwulf to whom to offer his *History of the English* for polishing, choosing him, I take it, as possessing the power to confirm what was well put through his authority, and the ability to correct what was ill put through his intelligence.

54. It was in the fourth year of his reign that the historian of whom I speak, after compiling many books in the service of the Church, passed to that heavenly country he had desired so long, in the year of our Lord 734 and the fifty-ninth of his age. He was a man more easily admired than praised as he deserves, for he who dazzled all countries by the brilliance of his learning was born in the furthest corner of the world. For even Britain, called another world by some because, cut off as it is by the Ocean, to many geographers it has remained unknown, can show the place of his birth and upbringing in its most distant region, not far from Scotland. It is a district once fragrant with religious 2 houses as a garden is with flowers, and brilliant with many cities of the Romans' building; but now, made wretched by ravages of the Danes of old or Normans in our own day, it offers nothing that can much attract us. There flows the river Wear, not mean in width nor slow of stream, whose tidal waters receive in the peaceful harbourage of its mouth the boats that gentle breezes carry thither. Both its banks were enriched with churches by a certain Benedict, who also built two monasteries there, one called St Peter's, the other St Paul's, but both united in the bond of love and discipline. Benedict's energy and long- 3 suffering will be much admired by readers of Bede's life of him and of his other abbots. His energy, as the importer of a quantity of books, and as the first man to invite to England craftsmen skilled in building in stone and in glazing windows (for he spent almost his whole life in travel with such aims as these); and in his eagerness to bring his kinsmen something new, love of his country and delight in craftsmanship made his onerous labours light; before the days of Benedict, houses of coursed stone were a very rare sight in Britain, nor could the sun's

p Northan(h)imbrorum *B* GP *p. 328*   *q* pretendens *T*   *r* sinu *T*   *s* euum pene *B*,

4 penetrata lucem edibus solaris iatiebat radius. Patientiam, quod in possessione cenobii sancti Augustini apud Cantuariam libenter uenienti Adriano cesserit, non reueritus beati Theodori archiepiscopi supercilium sed ueneratus magisterium; quod, dum per alienas terras cursitat diu absens, subintroductum a monachis Wirensibus se inconsulto abbatem aequanimiter, immo magnanimiter tulerit, domumque reuersus parilem illi honorem in consessu,[a] in omni porro potestate communicauerit; quin et ictus paralisi tam ualide ut nichil artuum[b] ei esset flexibile, tertium constituerit, quod alter, de quo diximus, eadem non mitius[c] decoqueretur ualitudine. Cumque morbus increscens iam quateret uitalia, sotio ad se delato solo nutu ualedixit. Sed nec ille prestantius ualuit rependere offitium, utpote qui propinquiorem tendebat ad exitum; nam[d] ante Benedictum defunctus est.

5 Successit Celfrithus, sub quo 'res monasterii in immensum auctae.'[e] Is, cum diuturno senio uiuendi renuntiasset[f] desiderio, Romam ire perrexit, senilem animam, ut sperabat, dominis effusurus apostolis; sed enim, uoti effectu carens, naturae debitum apud Lingonis ciuitatem iniit. Reliquiae ossuum posterioribus annis ad monasterium suum, deinde Danicae tempore[g] uastationis cum ossibus beatae

6 Hildae Glastoniam portatae. Horum abbatum gratiam, quae per se satis eminet, conspicuus alumnus eorum Beda in splendidiorem excellentiam urget, siquidem scriptum sit: 'Gloria patris[h] filius sapiens',[1] quod alter eum monachauerit, alter educauerit. Quod quia ipse Beda pro compendio notitiae subiecit, omnem uitam suam quodam epilogo comprehendens, ipsius uerba lector recognoscat[i] licebit, [j]ne meis[j] sermonibus uel plus uel minus ipsa nouae formae procudat[k] necessitas. Ait ergo in fine Aecclesiasticae Anglorum Historiae[2] uir cum in ceteris tum in hoc laudabilis, quod uel quantulamcumque sui cognitionem posteritati[l] non inuiderit:

55. 'Haec de historia Britanniarum, Domino adiuuante, digessi Beda, famulus Christi et presbiter monasterii beatorum apostolorum[m] Petri et Pauli quod est ad Wiremudan. Qui natus in territorio eiusdem monasterii, cum essem annorum septem, cura propinquorum datus

---

[a] consessum *Tt*, concessum *Tc*   [b] om. *T*   [c] minus *B*   [d] siquidem *B*   [e‑e] cenobiales possessiones in summum prouect(a)e *B*   [f] satisfecisset *T*   [g] tempore Danic(a)e *TB** (cf. 50. 5)   [h] patris est *Jerome, VD p. 273*   [i] recognoscit *Ce* (recognoscere *Cd*), (lectorem) cognoscere *Cs*   [j‑j] nec in eis *B*   [k] procudet *Bc (and Bp)*, prouidet *Bk (and Bph)*   [l] posteris *B*   [m] beatorum apostolorum *ABc, Bede;* apostolorum beatorum *Tt;* apostolorum *TcC;* beatorum *Bk*

rays cast their light into buildings through translucent glass. His long- 4 suffering, in that on the arrival of Hadrian he gladly made way for him in the possession of St Augustine's at Canterbury, not so much fearing the resentment of Archbishop Theodore as venerating his authority; again, when during a long absence on foreign travel he found another abbot foisted in by the monks of Monkwearmouth without consulting him, he took it calmly, even generously, and on his return shared all the powers of the office equally with him, seating him beside himself; further, when smitten with an arthritis so severe that none of his joints would bend, he appointed a third, because the second, of whom I have been speaking, was no less severely brought low by the same complaint. When the disease increased and was already attacking his vital parts, he had his colleague brought to him, and bade him farewell with a nod of the head, which was all he could do; but the other was no better at returning this courtesy, for he was heading towards an earlier end, and died before Benedict. The next 5 abbot was Ceolfrith, under whom the monastery flourished exceedingly. Ceolfrith, losing his desire for life in a prolonged old age, determined to go to Rome, to breathe his last (so he hoped) at the feet of the Apostles; but his purpose failed of its effect, and in the city of Langres he paid the debt of Nature. His relics in later years were carried to his own monastery, and then, during the Danish devastations, went with the bones of St Hild to Glastonbury. The merit of these abbots, 6 sufficiently eminent in itself, is raised to a more excellent splendour by their great pupil, Bede; for it is written: 'A wise son is the glory of his father',[1] and one of them made him a monk, the other taught him. And because Bede himself has briefly put this on record, when summarizing his whole life in a sort of epilogue, the reader will be able to recognize the familiar words, and I shall not, in the need to rewrite what he says, run the risk of adding or omitting something. These then are his words[2] at the end of the *Ecclesiastical History of the English*, and it is not the least of his claims upon us that he did not grudge posterity at least some knowledge of himself.

55. 'So much then for the history of Britain, as set in order with God's help by me, Bede, a servant of Christ and priest of the monastery of the blessed Apostles Peter and Paul at Monkwearmouth. Born on the land of that house, at the age of seven by the care of my

---

[1] Jerome, *Ep.* lii. 7.   [2] Bede, *HE* v. 24 (p. 566 Colgrave–Mynors).

sum educandus reuerentissimo abbati Benedicto, ac deinde Celfrido; cunctumque*ᵃ* ex eo tempus uitae in eiusdem monasterii habitatione peragens, omnem meditandis scripturis operam dedi, atque inter obseruantiam*ᵇ* disciplinae regularis et cotidianam cantandi in aecclesia 2 curam, semper aut discere aut docere aut scribere dulce habui. Nono decimo autem uitae meae anno diaconatum, tricesimo gradum presbiteratus, utrumque per ministerium reuerentissimi episcopi Iohannis iubente Celfrido abbate, suscepi. Ex quo tempore accepti presbiteratus usque ad*ᶜ* annum aetatis meae quinquagesimum nonum meae meorumque necessitati ex opusculis uenerabilium patrum breuiter haec annotare, siue etiam ad formam sensus et interpretationis eorum adicere curaui.'

56. Deinde enumeratis triginta sex uoluminibus quae in septuaginta octo libris edidit, addidit:

'Teque deprecor, bone Iesu, ut cui propitius donasti uerba*ᵈ* tuae scientiae dulciter haurire, dones etiam*ᵉ* benignus aliquando ad fontem omnis scientiae peruenire et parere*ᶠ* semper ante fatiem tuam.'[1] 'Praeterea omnes ad quos haec historia peruenire potuerit nostrae nationis, legentes siue audientes, supliciter*ᵍ* precor*ʰ* ut pro meis infirmitatibus et mentis et corporis apud supernam clementiam sepius interuenire meminerint, et hanc michi in suis quique*ⁱ* prouintiis suae remunerationis uicem rependant, ut qui de singulis prouintiis siue locis sullimioribus quae memoratu digna atque incolis grata credideram diligenter annotare curaui, apud omnes fructum piae intercessionis inueniam.'[2]

57. Deficit hic ingenium, succumbit eloquium nescientis*ʲ* quid plus laudem, librorum numerositatem an sermonum sobrietatem: infuderat eum proculdubio non indigo haustu diuina sapientia, ut angusto uitae spatiolo tanta elaboraret uolumina. Quid quod ferunt eum Romam iuisse, ut libros suos uel aeclesiasticae doctrinae conuenire presens assereret uel, si resultarent, apostolico nutu corriperet? Veruntamen quod Romae fuerit solide non affirmo, sed eum illuc inuitatum haud dubie pronuntio; quod haec epistola clarum fatiet, simul et quanti penderit eum Romana sedes,*ᵏ* ut eum tantopere desideraret:

ᵃ cumque C	*ᵇ* obseruationem B	*ᶜ* om. AB	*ᵈ* dona B	*ᵉ* et B
ᶠ placere A	*ᵍ* simpliciter T	*ʰ* deprecor B	*ⁱ* quoque Tt, om. Tc
ʲ nesciens C	*ᵏ* curia B			

[1] Bede, *HE* v. 24 (p. 570 Colgrave–Mynors).   [2] Praef. (p. 6 Colgrave–Mynors).

kinsmen I was entrusted for my education to the most reverend Abbot Benedict, and after him to Ceolfrith; and all the rest of my life I have spent in the same monastery, devoting all my pains to the study of the Scriptures. In the intervals of regular monastic observance and the daily task of singing in choir, to learn, to teach, or to write have ever been my joy. In my nineteenth year I became a deacon, in my thirtieth a priest, both through the ordination of the right reverend Bishop John, at the bidding of Abbot Ceolfrith; and from the time of my priest's orders until my fifty-ninth year, it has been my care to make these brief selections from the works of the holy Fathers to meet my own needs and those of my friends, or even to add something to clarify their sense and interpretation.'

56. Then, after listing thirty-six works published by himself in seventy-eight volumes, he goes on: 'And I beseech Thee, O merciful Jesu, that he to whom in Thy mercy Thou has given sweet draughts of Thy wisdom, may some day receive of Thy loving-kindness the right to approach the fountain of all wisdom and to appear before Thy face for evermore.'[1] 'Moreover, I humbly beg all those of our nation to whom this history may come, whether they read it themselves or hear it read, that they forget not to make frequent intercession with the heavenly Mercy for my weaknesses of mind and body, and pay me each in his own province this guerdon in return, that I, who have striven diligently to set down about every region and every place of standing the things which I thought worthy of record and pleasing to the dwellers in it, may obtain from all men the benefit of their generous prayers.'[2]

57. At this point my invention fails, my powers of speech give way beneath me, as I wonder which to praise the more, the great number of his writings or the modesty of his style. Without a doubt, the divine wisdom had come upon him in good measure, to enable him in one short lifetime to complete so many great books. Men even say that he went to Rome, to maintain in person that his writings agreed with the doctrine of the Church, or correct them by papal authority if they diverged. That he actually was in Rome I do not affirm for certain; that he was invited thither I maintain beyond cavil, as the following letter will show, which indicates also how highly he was esteemed by the Holy See, that his presence should be so greatly desired.

58. *"Sergius episcopus, seruus seruorum Dei, Celfrido religioso abbati salutem.

'Quibus uerbis ac modis clementiam Dei nostri atque inenarrabilem*[b] prouidentiam possumus effari, et dignas gratiarum actiones pro immensis circa nos eius benefitiis persoluere, qui in tenebris et[c] umbra mortis positos ad lumen scientiae perducit?' Et infra: 'Benedictionis interea gratiam, quam nobis per presentem portitorem tua misit deuota religio, libenti et hilari animo, sicuti[d] ab ea[e] directa est, nos sus-
2 cepisse cognosce. Oportunis ergo ac dignis amplectendae sollicitudinis[f] tuae petitionibus arctissima deuotione fauentes, hortamur Deo dilectam religiositatis tuae bonitatem ut, quia exortis quibusdam aecclesiasticarum causarum capitulis, non sine[g] examinatione longius innotescendis, opus nobis sunt ad conferendum arte litteraturae imbuti, sicut decet[h] deuotum auxiliatorem sanctae matris uniuersalis aecclesiae, obedientem deuotionem huic nostrae hortationi[i] non desistas accommodare, sed absque aliqua immoratione[j] religiosum Dei famulum Bedam, uenerabilis monasterii tui presbiterum, ad limina apostolorum principum dominorum meorum Petri et Pauli, amatorum tuorum ac protectorum, ad nostrae mediocritatis conspectum non moreris dirigere, quem, fauente Domino sanctis tuis precibus, non diffidas prospere ad te redire, peracta premissorum capitulorum cum auxilio Dei desiderata sollemnitate. Erit enim, ut confidimus,[k] etiam[l] cunctis tibi[m] creditis profuturum quicquid aecclesiae generali claruerit per eius prestantiam impertitum.'

59. Ita iam[n] celebris erat fama ut in[o] questionibus enodandis indigeret eo sullimitas Romana, nec uero umquam Gallicanus tumor inuenit in Anglo quod argueret merito: adeo Latinitas omnis eius fidei et magisterio palmam dedit. Nam et fidei sanae et incuriosae sed dulcis fuit eloquentiae, in omnibus explanationibus diuinarum scripturarum magis illa rimatus quibus lector Dei dilectionem et proximi combiberet
2 quam illa quibus uel sales libaret uel linguae rubiginem limaret. Porro de uitae illius sanctitate dubitare quemquam arcet illius dicti irrefragabilis[p] ueritas, quod protulit mundo diuae sophiae maiestas: 'In maliuolam animam non introibit sapientia, nec inhabitabit in corpore subdito peccatis.'[1] Quod de mundana sapientia profecto non[q] dicit,

---

[a] *This letter is also found in* ζ *(today not wholly legible) and* κ; *see also Leland, Coll. ii. 396–7 and Thomson, William of Malmesbury, pp. 172–3.*   [b] memorabilem *B*   [c] *B adds* in *(so* κ*)*   [d] sicut *T,* κ   [e] eo *B*   [f] solitudinibus *B*   [g] *TtB,* ζ(?); sui *TcAlC,* κ, *Leland;* sua *Aa*   [h] *B adds* Deo   [i] adhortationi *B*   [j] remoratione *BkBc²ᵃ·ᶜ· (and BpBph),* ζ; rememoratione *Bc¹Bc²ᵖ·ᶜ·*   [k] credimus *B*   [l] *om. B; et* ζ

58. 'Sergius, bishop, servant of the servants of God, to the pious Abbot Ceolfrith, greeting.

'How can we express the mercy of our God and His unspeakable providence, how can we pay Him worthy thanks for His immense goodness towards us, in leading into the light of knowledge those sitting in darkness and the shadow of death?' And further on: 'In the mean time, the offering which in your Christian charity you have sent us by the bearer of this letter, we accept gladly in the spirit in which it was sent. We therefore grant with sincere devotion the well-judged requests which you, our dear brother, have thought fit to submit, and at the same time exhort you, worthy and dear to God as you are, that whereas certain questions have arisen in the Church which cannot without examination be published abroad, and we need the aid of scholars for their discussion, you therefore, as becomes a faithful supporter of holy Church, the mother of us all, should not hesitate devoutly to obey this our request, and without delay to send to the threshold of the chief of the Apostles, my lords Peter and Paul, your lovers and patrons, and into my unworthy presence that religious servant of God, Bede, a priest of your venerable house; and be sure that, God granting assent to your holy prayers, he will safely return to you, when once with God's help the needful proclamation of these canons has been made. For we are sure that whatever through his excellent wisdom is vouchsafed to the Church in general will redound no less to the benefit of all those who are committed to your charge.'

59. So great was his reputation at that time that in the solving of its problems mighty Rome itself had need of him, nor could the proud Gauls ever find in this English scholar aught deserving of criticism; the whole Latin-speaking world gave him the prize for learning and for faith. His faith was sound, his style unpretentious but agreeable; in all his biblical commentaries he sought out material from which his reader might absorb love of God and his neighbour, rather than the means of displaying a pretty wit or sharpening a rusty pen. The holiness of his life is put beyond doubt by the unquestioned truth of that saying which divine Wisdom in its majesty made known to the world: 'Into a malicious soul wisdom shall not enter, nor dwell in the body that is subject unto sin.'[1] Clearly this is not said of worldly wisdom,

(?), κ, *Leland*   *m* om. B   *n* tam *Tt(but not Tc)B*   *o* uel B   *p* irr. dicti *TB*   *q* profecto non *after* quod *T*

---

[1] Wisd. 1: 4.

quae indifferenter hominum cordibus illabitur, et qua creberrime pessimi, nullasque[a] ad extremum diem ponentes[b] metas sceleribus, pollere conspitiuntur, iuxta illud Dominicum: 'Filii huius seculi prudentiores filiis lucis in generatione sua sunt';[1] sed illam sapientiam nominat[c] quae 'disciplinae[d] effugit[e] fictum, et quae separat se a cogitationibus quae sunt sine intellectu',[2] intellectu[f] dico[g] bene uiuendi et bene dicendi, unde pulcherrime Seneca in libro[h] de causis commemorat Catonem, oratoris offitium diffinientem, dixisse: 'Orator est uir bonus dicendi peritus.'[3] Emundabat ergo aecclesiasticus orator prius conscientiam,[i] ut sic accederet ad recludendam[j] misticorum scriptorum[k] intelligentiam. Qui enim fieri potest ut seruiret uitiis qui medullas intimas hauriret, qui totas cogitationes consumeret, in Scripturarum expositionibus? Nam, ut ipse fatetur in libro tertio super Samuelem,[4] expositiones suae, si non aliud afferrent lectoribus emolumentum, hoc sibi non mediocriter ualerent, quod, dum haec omni studio agebat, lubricum[l] seculi et inanes cogitationes post tergum ponebat; defecatus itaque[m] uitiis subibat in interiora uelaminis, quae intus exceperat animo foras efferens sermone castigato.

60. Veruntamen animi eius pura sanctitas et sancta puritas magis proximo[n] tempore obitus excelluit: siquidem continuis septem ebdomadibus stomachi indignatione cibos nausians, egroque et angusto suspirio halitum producens, adeo ut eum incommoditas lecto prosterneret, non tamen litteralium studiorum reiecit operam. Totis enim diebus preter debitum psalmodiae pensum assiduis ad discipulos lectionibus ruminandisque et absoluendis questionum difficultatibus grauedinem ualitudinis decipere, suspensa interim cogitatione, nitebatur. Euangelium quoque Iohannis, quod difficultate sui mentes legentium exercet, his diebus lingua interpretatus Anglica, condescendit minus imbutis Latina; subindeque monebat discipulos, dicens: 'Discite, filioli, dum uobiscum sum; nescio enim quam diu subsistam, et si post modicum tollat me Factor meus, et reuertatur spiritus meus[o] ad eum qui misit illum[p] et in hanc uitam uenire concessit.[q] Diu uixi; bene consuluit michi Dominus meus[r] in hoc uitae spatio;[s] cupio iam[t] dissolui, et esse cum Christo.'

[a] et nullas usque T^+ [b] figentes T^+ [c] nominauit A [d] Apparently taken by William with fictum   [e] effugiet B, Vulg.   [f] om. TcB   [g] om. T', et Tc   [h] in libro om. T^+ [i] B adds suam   [j] recludendum C   [k] secretorum B [l] et lubricum T^+ [m] quoque A [n] om. C; after obitus B [o] om. T^+ [p] illum misit T^+ [q] concessit uenire A [r] om. T^+ [s] tempore T^+ [t] om. ABk

which finds its way without distinction into men's hearts, and is often seen to thrive in the wicked and in those who till their last day set no limits to their crimes, in accordance with our Lord's words: 'The children of this world are wiser in their generation than the children of light.'[1] No; He means that wisdom which 'flees deceit, and removes from thoughts that are without understanding'[2]—the understanding, I take it, of how to live rightly and speak rightly. How admirable is Cato's definition of the function of an orator, recorded by Seneca in his book on cases: 'An orator is a good man with skill in speech.'[3] Thus our orator of the Church used first to clear his conscience, that so he might draw near to unlock the mysteries of Scripture. How is it possible that he should be in bondage unto sin, who gave himself body and mind to the exposition of Holy Writ? For, as he himself admits in his third book on Samuel,[4] if his commentaries brought his readers no further profit, they would at least mean no small advantage for himself, in that, while wholly devoted to his task, he put behind him the deceits and empty cogitations of the world. So, purified from his sins, he entered within the veil, and what he received within it in his heart, he brought forth to the world with well-disciplined pen.

60. But the purity and holiness of that heart stood out more clearly as the hour of his death approached. For seven weeks on end of severe internal disorder he had refused food, and could draw breath only in difficult short gasps, so that the disease confined him to his bed; but he did not abandon his literary work. All day long, apart from his allotted task of psalmody, by constant lessons with his pupils and by pondering and solving difficult questions, he tried to mask the severity of his illness by refusing to think of it. During those weeks, he came to the help of those ill-equipped with Latin by rendering into English the Gospel of St John, which sets such a problem to readers by its difficulty; and from time to time he used to warn his pupils with the words: 'Learn your lesson, children, while I am with you, for I know not how long I may continue. I do not know if after a little space my Creator will take me, so that my spirit returns to Him who sent it, and who suffered it to come into this life. I have lived long. My Lord has been good to me in this my span of life; I long now to be released, and to be with Christ.'

---

[1] Luke 16: 8. [2] Wisd. 1: 5.
[3] Seneca the Elder, *Controversiae* i pr. 9.
[4] *In I Sam.* prol. (*CCSL* cxix. 10, lines 54–9).

61. Plerumque spe metuque libratis, cum neutrum preponderaret, inferebat: 'Horrendum est incidere in manus Dei uiuentis. Non ita inter uos uixi ut pudeat me^a uiuere, sed nec mori timeo, quia bonum Dominum habemus', sanctissimi Ambrosii morientis dictum mutuatus.[61] Felix qui tam secura loquebatur conscientia^c ut nec^d uiuere erubesceret^e nec mori metueret,^f hic^g non reueritus aspectus hominum, illic^h occultum Dei aequanimiter expectans arbitrium. Sepe, ui doloris pressus, his exemplis respirabat: ⁱ"Diligit Deus hominem quem corripit, flagellat autem omnem filium quem recipit."[2] 'Aurum probat fornax, et uirum iustum caminus temptationis.'[3] 'Non sunt condignae passiones huius temporis ad futuram gloriam, quae reuelabitur in 2 nobis.'[4] Prosequebantur dicta lacrimae suspiriorumque^j difficultas. Iam uero noctibus, quia deerant qui docerentur uel uerba exciperent, lucubrabat ipse sibi pernox in gratiarum actione et psalmorum cantu, implens sapientissimi uiri dictum, ut numquam minus solus esset quam cum solus esset.[5] Si quando uero sopor irreperet palpebris,^k qui erat^l modicus et grauis, confestim excussus turbatusque affectum Deo semper^m intentum hac uoce prodebat: 'Suscipe, Domine, seruum tuum in bonum;ⁿ non calumnientur me superbi; fac cum seruo tuo 3 secundum misericordiam tuam.'[6] Haec et alia ex reliquiis memoriae preteritae ultro ^oori occurrebant^o exempla, quae promebat per temporum interualla, prout leniebatur infesti morbi angustia. Feria uero tertia ante Ascensionem Domini,^p inualescente ad extremum^q incommodo, modicus tumor in pedibus^r apparuit, haud dubius^s uicinae mortis presagus et index. Tunc accita congregatione, inunctus et communicatus, osculo cunctis libato, futuram sui memoriam a singulis implorans, nonnullis etiam familiariorem^t amicitiam emeritis xeniola, 4 quae in secretis habebat, largitus est. Die uero Ascensionis, cum iam anima fragilem usum corporis exosa egredique gestiens palpitaret, contra oratorium in^u quo consueuerat orare^v cilicio subiecto decumbens, illibato sensu et hilari uultu Spiritus sancti gratiam inuitabat, dicens: 'O Rex gloriae, Domine uirtutum, qui triumphator hodie

---

^a me pudeat *T*⁺, *Ep. Cuthb. p. 582* Colgrave–Mynors (and *Polyhistor* p. 81.8)
^b imitatus *A*   ^c conscientia loquebatur *T*⁺   ^d *B adds* eum   ^e puderet *B*   ^f timeret *T*⁺*B*   ^g illinc *TtTc*, illic *Tp*   ^h istinc *TtTc*, istic *Tp*
^{i–i} *T*⁺; *om. ACB (but cf. Ep. Cuthb. p. 582)*   ^j et suspiriorum *T*⁺   ^k palp. irreperet (repleret *Tc*) *T*⁺   ^l *T*⁺* adds* et   ^m semper Deo *T*⁺   ⁿ in bono *B*; *om. A*   ^{o–o} accurrebant horum *B*   ^p *om. T*⁺   ^q supremum *T*^t (and *Ce*^v), summum *Tc*   ^r *T*⁺*B add* eius   ^s dubie *B*   ^t familiorem *TtTcAl*^{a.c.}; familiarem *B*   ^u *om. T*⁺   ^v orare consueuerat *T*⁺

61. Often, when hope and fear were balanced and neither prevailed, he would say: 'It is a fearful thing to fall into the hands of the living God. I have not so lived among you as to be ashamed of life, but I do not fear to die either, for the Lord we serve is good', borrowing a remark made by the most holy Ambrose on his deathbed.[1] Happy the man who spoke with such a clear conscience that he could live without embarrassment and die without fear, not abashed before men's faces in this world and peacefully awaiting God's secret judgement in the next. Often, when in the grip of pain, he could find relief in such texts as these: 'Whom the Lord loveth he chasteneth, and scourgeth every son whom He receiveth.'[2] 'Gold is tried in the furnace, and a just man in the fire of temptation.'[3] 'The sufferings of this present time are not worthy to be compared with the glory which shall be revealed in us.'[4] His words were followed by tears and heavy sighs. At 2 night-time again, when there was no one at hand to be taught or to take down from dictation, he would spend the whole night awake by himself, in thanksgiving and the singing of psalms, fulfilling the remark of a very wise man in that he was never less alone than when he was alone.[5] If sleep ever came upon his eyelids, which was short and laboured, he would suddenly wake up, and in some confusion display a heart ever set upon God by ejaculating: 'Be surety for Thy servant, Lord, for good: let not the proud oppress me. Deal with Thy servant according unto Thy mercy.'[6] These and similar apt quotations 3 from what remained in his memory rose unbidden to his lips, and he used to utter them from time to time when there was a remission in the cruel onset of his disease. However, on the Tuesday before Ascension Day, when his distress was reaching its extreme, a moderate swelling appeared on his feet, the unquestioned indication of approaching death. At that point he summoned the community, received the last sacraments, and giving each a kiss, begged them all to remember him in their prayers; to some also, who had won his closer intimacy, he gave small presents which he had privily kept by him. On Ascension 4 Day itself, as his soul was now trembling on the brink, weary of its frail body and longing to depart, he lay on a hair blanket over against the chapel in which it had been his custom to pray, and with senses unimpaired and cheerful countenance besought the grace of the Holy Spirit with these words: 'O King of Glory, Lord of Might, who on

---

[1] Paulinus, *Vita Ambrosii* 45 (*PL* xiv. 43).
[2] Heb. 12: 6.
[3] Cf. Prov. 27: 21, Ecclus. 2: 5.
[4] Rom. 8: 18.
[5] Cicero, *De Officiis* iii. 1 (of Scipio Africanus).
[6] Ps. 118 (119): 122, 124.

super omnes caelos ascendisti, ne derelinquas nos orphanos, sed mitte promissum Patris in nos, spiritum ueritatis.' Hac oratione finita supremum efflauit, subsequente et omnium naribus oppletis[a] odore, qualem nec cinnama[b] nec balsama spirant,[c] sed paradisiaco et quem[d] uernalis ubicumque locorum exhalat laetitia. Humatus est tunc in eodem monasterio, sed modo[e] cum beato Cuthberto Dunelmi[f] situm fama confirmat.

62. Sepulta est cum eo gestorum omnis pene[g] notitia usque[h] ad nostra tempora: adeo nullus Anglorum studiorum eius emulus, nullus gloriarum[i] eius[j] sequax fuit, qui omissae monetae lineam[k] persequeretur.[l] Pauci, quos aequus amauit Iesus,[1] quanuis litteris non ignobiliter informati, tota uita ingratum consumpserunt silentium; alii, uix primis labris illas gustantes, ignauum confouerunt otium. Ita, cum semper pigro[m] succederet pigrior, multo tempore in tota insula studiorum[n] detepuit feruor. Magnum ignauiae testimonium dabunt uersus epitaphii, pudendi prorsus et tanti uiri mausoleo indigni:[2]

> Presbiter hic Beda requiescit carne sepultus:
> dona, Christe, animam in caelis gaudere per aeuum,
> daque illum[o] sophiae debriari fonte, cui iam
> suspirauit ouans intento semper amore.

63. Poteritne ulla excusatione hic pudor extenuari,[p] ut nec in eo[q] monasterio ubi illo uiuente totius litteraturae exultabat gimnasium potuerit inueniri homo qui memoriam eius[r] formaret, nisi exili et miserabili stilo? Sed de hoc satis dictum; nunc quod in manibus erat repetam.

64. Celwlfus, citra grauitatem Christianam estimans[s] terrenis negotiis immori, post octo annos regni regem exuens in Lindisfarnensi aecclesia[t] monachum accepit; quo loci quanta meritorum[u] gratia conuersatus sit, testatur celebris iuxta beatum Cuthbertum sepultura et multa superne demissa miracula.

[a] expletis *TcC*   [b] timiama *T*⁺   [c] suspirant *B*   [d] qualem *TcB*   [e] om. *B*   [f] modo *B*   [g] pene omnis gestorum *T*⁺*B**   [h] om. *T*⁺   [i] gratiarum *B*   [j] om. *T*⁺   [k] lineas *B*   [l] prosequeretur *A*   [m] pigro semper *T*⁺   [n] studiorum *after* tempore *T*⁺   [o] illi *A (and Leland, Coll. iii. 118, where the epitaph is also preserved)*   [p] attenuari *B*   [q] in eo *om. Al,* eo *om. Aa*   [r] illius *B*   [s] existimans *T*⁺*B*   [t] cenobio *Aa, om. Al*   [u] religionis *T*⁺

this day didst ascend in triumph above all the heavens, leave us not comfortless, but send upon us the promise of the Father, even the Spirit of Truth.' When he had finished this prayer, he breathed his last; whereon a fragrance ensued that filled the nostrils of all present—no scent of cinnamon or balsam, but a fragrance of Paradise, and such as all Nature breathes in the gladness of spring. At that time he was buried in his own monastery, but now, it is asserted, he lies at Durham with St Cuthbert.

62. With Bede was buried almost all historical record down to our own day; so true is it that there was no English competitor in his field of study, no would-be rival of his fame to follow up the broken thread. A few, whom favouring Jesus loved,[1] achieved a not discreditable level of learning, but spent all their lives in ungrateful silence; while others, who had scarcely sipped the cup of letters, remained in idleness and sloth. So, as each proved more idle than the last, zeal for these studies languished long in the whole island. A good specimen of this decadence will be found in his verse epitaph, a shameful effusion, quite unworthy the monument of so great a man:[2]

> The reverend Bede here buried is.
> Christ grant him everlasting bliss,
> At wisdom's well to drink his fill,
> For which he longed with loving zeal.

63. Can anything excuse this shameful state of affairs? In that same convent where, while he lived, burgeoned a school of every branch of learning, could no one be found to enshrine his memory except in this piteous doggerel? Enough of this: I must return to my subject.

64. Ceolwulf, thinking it too much for a serious Christian to be still immersed in earthly business on his deathbed, resigned the crown after a reign of eight years, and took the monastic habit at Lindisfarne, where he lived a most saintly life, as is clear from his exalted resting-place beside St Cuthbert, and the many miracles vouchsafed by Heaven.

---

[1] Cf. Virgil, *Aen.* vi. 129–30.
[2] SK 12463.

65. Prouiderat ante ne uacillaret respublica, substituto in regnum Egberhto[a] patrui[b] filio; quod ille acceptum, bonorum terens orbitas,[c] uiginti annis egregio moderamine cohercuit. Habuit fratrem aequiuocum, Eboraci archiepiscopum, qui et sua prudentia et germani potentia[d] sedem illam in genuinum statum reformauit. Namque,[e] quod cuiuis Gesta Anglorum[1] legenti in promptu est, Paulinus, eiusdem urbis[f] primus antistes, ui hostilitatis loco pulsus et apud[g] Rofecestram diem obiens, ibidem illud insigne pallii, quod ab Honorio papa susceperat,[h] reliquit. Plures post eum tantae urbis presules, simplici episcopatus nomine contenti, nichil altius anhelauerant; at uero Egberhtus intronizatus, animosioris ingenii homo, cogitans[i] quod sicut superbum est si appetas indebita, ita ignauum si debita negligas,[j] pallium multa throni apostolici[k] appellatione reparauit. Hic omnium liberalium artium armarium,[l] ut ita dicam, et[m] sacrarium fuit, nobilissimamque bibliothecam Eboraci constituit;[n] cuius rei testem idoneum aduoco Alcwinum, qui a regibus Angliae pro pace missus ad [o]Karolum Magnum imperatorem,[o] et benigno[p] apud eum fotus hospitio, in epistola ad Eanbaldum, tertio loco Egberti successorem, ait:[q2] 'Laus et gloria Deo, qui dies meos in prosperitate bona conseruauit, ut in exaltatione filii mei carissimi gauderem, qui laboraret uice mea in aecclesia ubi ego nutritus et educatus[r] fueram et preesset[s] thesauris sapientiae in quibus me magister meus dilectus Egbertus archiepiscopus heredem[t] reliquit.' Item Karolo Augusto:[3] 'Date michi exquisitiores[u] eruditionis scolasticae libellos, quales in patria habui per bonam et deuotissimam magistri mei Egberti archiepiscopi industriam; et, si placet sapientiae uestrae, remittam aliquos ex pueris nostris, qui excipiant inde quaeque necessaria et reuehant in Frantiam flores Britanniae, et non sit tantummodo in Eboraca ortus conclusus, sed etiam in Turonica emissiones paradisi.'[4]

66. Hic est Alcwinus qui, ut dixi, pro pace [v]Frantiam missus ibi apud Karolum[v] seu terrae amenitate seu regis humanitate captus resedit, magnique apud eum habitus imperialem animum, quantum

---

[a] *Rightly* Edberhto *(but William makes this error consistently)* [b] patris sui T', patrui sui Tc [c] orbitam B [d] pec(c)unia B [e] nam B [f] *om. A*   [g] apudque *(om.* et*)* T^+ [h] acceperat T^+ [i] cogitans *before* animosioris T^+, GP *p. 246*   [j] negligas debita T^+, GP *p. 246*   [k] apost. thr. T^+ [l] armarium *after* dicam T^+B [m] immo T^+ [n] et nobilissimam *(so GP p. 246)* Ebor. bibl. instituit T^+ [o-o] regem magnum Carolum B [p] et benigno *om.* T^+ [q] dixit T^+ *(cf. GP p. 246)*   [r] eruditus T^+, *Alc.*, GP *p. 246*   [s] preesse Tt *(not* $TpTc$*)*CsB, GP *p. 246 (om.* et*), and so Alc. with a different constr.*   [t] *om. A*   [u] exquisitores A [v-v] ad Karolum directus et ibi T^+

65. He had already taken steps to maintain the government by making Ecgberht, his uncle's son, king in his own place, and Ecgberht, accepting the kingdom, followed good examples and ruled it very well for twenty years. He had a brother of the same name, the archbishop of York, who by his own wisdom and his brother's influence brought that see back into its proper state. For, as any reader of the *History of the English*[1] can see, Paulinus the first bishop of that city, being driven out by the violence of the enemy and dying at Rochester, left there the pallium which he had received as mark of distinction from Pope Honorius. After him, many prelates in that great city had been content with the plain title of bishop, and aspired no higher; but Ecgberht on his enthronement, being a man of more lively mettle, reflected that, while it is conceited to demand what you do not deserve, it is a poor spirit, equally, that lets slip what it has a right to, and made repeated appeals to the Holy See, until he got back the pallium. Ecgberht was, one might say, a storehouse and treasury of all the liberal arts, and founded at York a splendid library. Of this I can call a qualified witness in the person of Alcuin, who, when sent by the English kings on a mission of peace to the emperor Charlemagne, by whom he was kindly entertained, writes as follows to Eanbald, Ecgberht's next successor but one:[2] 'Glory and praise to God, who has granted me prosperity and length of days, and has given me joy in the promotion of my beloved son to labour in my place in the church where I was born and bred, and to be master of the treasures of wisdom wherein my beloved master, Archbishop Ecgberht left me his heir.' In the same way to Charles Augustus:[3] 'Allow me to have the rarer volumes of academic learning, such as I had in my own country thanks to the excellent and devoted energy of my master, Archbishop Ecgberht. And, if your wisdom so pleases, I will send some of my students to extract whatever is needed and bring the fine flower of Britain back to France, so that if there be in York a garden enclosed, there may be no less in Tours plants of the orchard.'[4]

66. This is that same Alcuin who, as I said, was sent into France to treat of peace; he there took up his abode at Charles's court, charmed either by that beautiful country or by the kindness of the king. Being held in high regard, he gave the emperor, in moments of leisure from

---

[1] Bede, *HE* ii. 20.
[2] Alcuin (*MGH Ep.* iv), *Ep.* cxiv (p. 167. 3–9).
[3] Alcuin, *Ep.* cxxi (p. 177. 4–10).
[4] Cf. S. of S. 4: 12–13.

ab aulicis curis uacabat, dialectica et rethorica et etiam astronomia probe composuit. Erat enim omnium Anglorum, quos quidem legerim, post beatum Aldelmum et Bedam doctissimus, multisque libris ingenii periculum fecit.*a*

67. Sane, quoniam ad id locorum uenimus ut Karoli Magni mentio ultro se*b* inferret,*c* uolo de linea regum Francorum, de qua multa fabulatur antiquitas, ueritatem subtexere; nec multum a proposito elongabor, quia progeniem eorum nescire dampnum duco scientiae, cum et confines nobis sint et ad eos maxime Christianum spectet imperium. Et forte quibusdam non iniocundum uidebitur, si hoc percurrant compendium, quibus magna uolumina euoluere non erit otium.

68. Franci a feritate morum Greco uocabulo*d* dicti, quod iussu primi Valentiniani*e* imperatoris Alanos in Meotidas paludes refugientes eiecerint. Parua gens prius et exilis, incredibile quantum breui adoleuit decenni uectigalium indulgentia: hoc enim pacto ante bellum salutis discrimen inierant. Ita accedente libertate *f*in immensum aucti,*f* primo maximam partem Germaniae, procedente tempore totas Gallias occupantes signa sua comitari coegere; unde Lotharingi et Alemanni et ceteri Transrenani populi qui imperatori Teutonicorum subiecti sunt magis proprie se Francos appellari iubent, et eos quos nos Francos putamus Galwalas antiquo uocabulo quasi Gallos nuncupant. Quibus et ego assensum commodo, sciens quod Karolus Magnus, quem regem Francorum fuisse *g*nemo qui in inficias eat,*g* ea gentilitia lingua usus sit quam Franci Transrenani terunt. Legenti uitam Karoli[1] in promptu occurrit quod sermo meus a uero non exulat. Anno igitur incarnati Verbi quadringentesimo uicesimo quinto Franci primum regem habuerunt Faramundum. Nepos Faramundi fuit Meroueus, a quo omnes*h* post eum reges*i* Merouingi uocati sunt. Eodem modo et filii regum Anglorum a patribus patronomica sumpserunt, ut filius Edgari Edgaring, filius Edmundi Edmunding uocentur, et ceteri in hunc modum; communiter uero athelingi dicuntur. Naturalis ergo lingua Francorum communicat cum Anglis, quod de Germania gentes ambae germinauerint. Feliciter et potenter regnauerunt Merouingi

---

a For B's addition here see Appendix, p. 820   *b* se ultro T⁺   *c* ingereret B   *d* Greco uocabulo om. B†   *e* Valentiani TcB   *f-f* multum euecti B   *g-g* The phrase, variously presented by the MSS, is paralleled at 239. 3; VW i. 16; Mir. p. 115 line 106 n. Aac corrects to the classical nemo est qui inficias eat.   *h* cuncti B   *i* B† adds Francorum usque ad Pipinum

the business of the court, a good grounding in dialectic, rhetoric, and even astronomy. For as a man of learning he outshone all Englishmen whom I ever read, save only St Aldhelm and Bede, and put his gifts to the test by writing numerous books.

67. Now, having reached the point at which mention of Charlemagne naturally came up, I should like to add a true account of the lineage of the Frankish kings, the subject of so many hoary myths; nor will it take me far from my intended course, for I regard ignorance of their descent as a serious gap in knowledge, seeing that they are not only our neighbours but the people mainly responsible for the Christian empire. Perhaps some who lack the time to read long books will find pleasure in running through this brief sketch.

68. The Franks were so called in Greek from their habitual ferocity, because under orders from the emperor Valentinian I they drove out the Alans who were taking refuge in the marshes of Lake Maeotis. Few and weak at first, it was incredible how soon they grew into a powerful nation through ten years' respite from taxation, that being their stipulation before the battle in return for risking their lives. Having thus gained their freedom, they grew enormously, and seized first most of Germany, then later all Gaul, compelling the vanquished to serve in their own forces. Hence the people of Lotharingia and Alemannia, and the other peoples across the Rhine who are subject to the Teutonic emperor, more correctly demand to be given the name of Franks, while to those whom we reckon as Franks they give the ancient name of *Galwalas*, that is, Gauls. I too agree with them, knowing that 2 Charlemagne, who was, as no one would deny, king of the Franks, spoke as his native tongue the language used by the Franks across the Rhine. Any reader of Charles's *Life*[1] will easily see the truth of my remarks. So in the year of the Incarnation 425 the Franks first had a king, Faramund. Faramund's grandson was Merovech, from whom all subsequent kings [B *adds* of the Franks down to Pippin] were called Merovings. In the same way the sons of English kings took patronymics from their fathers' names: Edgar's son is called Edgaring, Edmund's Edmunding, and so on, while in general they are named æthelings. Thus the native tongue of the Franks is related to English, because 3 both races germinated from Germany. The rule of the Merovings was

---

[1] Apparently an allusion to Einhard, *Vita Karoli* 29.

usque ad annum incarnationis Domini sexcentesimum octogesimum septimum. Tunc enim Pipinus filius Ansegisi*a* comes palatii apud Transrenanos Francos*b* factus est. Is, captatis occasionibus quibus ambitum palliaret, dominum suum Theodericum regem,*c* Merouingorum fecem, sub iugum misit; et, ut facti leniret infamiam, spetietenus illi*d* regis
4 nomine donato, cuncta intus et foris regebat pro libito. Huius Pipini genealogia supra infraque contexitur ita: Ansbertus senator ex filia Lotharii patris Dagoberti Blithilde genuit Arnoldum; Arnoldus genuit*e* sanctum*f* Arnulfum Metensem episcopum; Arnulfus genuit*g* Flodulfum,*h* Walthchisum, Anschisum;*i* Flodulfus genuit Martinum ducem,*j* quem interfecit Ebroinus; Walthchisus genuit sanctissimum*k* Wandregisilum abbatem; Anschisus dux genuit Ansegisum; Ansegisus genuit*l* Pipinum; filius Pipini fuit Karolus Tudites,*m* quem illi Martellum uocant, quod tirannos per totam Frantiam emergentes contuderit,
5 Saracenos Gallias infestantes egregie depulerit. Hic, paternae sequax sententiae, reges tenuit in clientela, comitis contentus nomine; reliquit filios duos, Pipinum et Karlomannum. Karlomannus, incertum qua de causa seculum relinquens, tonsoratus est in Monte Cassino. Pipinus a Stephano papa,*n* successore Zachariae, apud Sanctum Dionisium in regem Francorum et patritium Romanorum coronatus est; nam imperatoribus Constantinopolitanis iam dudum a solita uirtute degenerantibus, nec ullam Italiae et*o* aecclesiae Romanae opem ferentibus, quae multis annis tirannidem Longobardorum suspirauerant, idem papa iniurias
6 illorum potestati Francorum applorauit. Quapropter Pipinus Alpibus transcensis Desiderium regem Longobardorum*p* ita coartauit ut ablata Romanae aecclesiae restitueret et, ne repeteret, sacramento firmaret. Frantiam reuersus post aliquot annos obiit, superstitibus*q* Karolo et Karlomanno. Karlomannus post biennium finem*r* habuit. Karolus, nomen Magni ab effectu sortitus, duplo quam pater habuerat regnum ampliauit, triginta et eo amplius annis simplici nomine regis*s* fastigatus et ab imperatoria appellatione, quanuis sepe ab Adriano papa in-
7 uitaretur, temperans.*t* Verum, eodem Apostolico defuncto, cum consanguinei eius Leonem sanctissimum, qui successerat, plagis in aecclesia beati Petri affecissent, adeo ut*u* linguam mutilarent et lumina terebrarent, Romam ad reformandum statum aecclesiae ire maturauit. Ibi in

a Angisi *A;* Ansegis *Bk,* Angesis *Bc*   *b* om. *C*   *c* om. *B*   *d* a *B*
e om. *T⁺B*   *f* om. *T⁺*   *g* om. *T⁺*   *h* Anodulfum *T⁺*   *i* om.
T⁺   *j* om. *T⁺*   *k* om. *T⁺*   *l* Ansegisum Ansegisus genuit *om. T⁺, correctly*   *m* Tutides *TpC*   *n* om. *C*   *o* uel *B*   *p* eorum *B†*
q *T⁺A** add liberis *(cf.* 256. 3*)*   *r* *T⁺* adds uite   *s* regis nomine *T⁺B*
t abstinens *B*   *u* *T⁺* adds et

strong and successful up until the year 687. At that point Pippin, son of Ansegisel, became count of the palace among the Franks across the Rhine. Seizing any opportunity to put a fair front on his ambition, he suppressed his lord, King Theuderic, the offscouring of the Merovings; then, in order to reduce the infamy of his behaviour, he gave him the name of king in appearance only, and ruled everything at his own good pleasure both inside and outside the palace. The 4 genealogy of this Pippin both upwards and downwards runs as follows: Ansbert the senator by Blithhild, daughter of Dagobert's father Chlotar, begot Arnold. Arnold begot St Arnulf, bishop of Metz. Arnulf begot Chlodulf, Walthchis, and Anschis. Chlodulf begot Duke Martin, who was killed by Ebroin; Walthchis begot the most saintly abbot St Wandregesil; Duke Anschis begot Ansegisel. Ansegisel begot Pippin. Pippin's son was Charles Tudites, whom they call Charles Martel, 'the Hammer', because he crushed the tyrants who were arising all over France, and notably drove back the Saracens who were infesting Gaul. Following his father's policy he 5 maintained the kings under his control, but was content with the name of count; he left two sons, Pippin and Carloman. Carloman, leaving the world for a reason unknown, received the tonsure at Montecassino. Pippin was crowned at Saint-Denis by Pope Stephen, the successor of Zacharias, as king of the Franks and patrician of the Romans; for since the emperors of Constantinople had lapsed long before from their accustomed valour, and brought no aid to Italy and the Roman Church, which had for many years groaned under the tyranny of the Lombards, that same pope appealed to the power of the Franks to end this wrongdoing. Pippin accordingly crossed the 6 Alps, and so constrained Desiderius, king of the Lombards, that he had to restore what he had taken from the Roman Church and swear an oath never to reclaim it. Returning to France, Pippin died some years later, leaving behind Charles and Carloman. Two years later Carloman died. Charles, who earned by his achievements the name of Great, doubled the size of his father's kingdom, being for thirty years and upwards distinguished by the simple name of king, and not presuming to take the title of emperor, though often invited to assume it by Pope Hadrian. However, after Hadrian's death, when 7 his kinsmen had laid violent hands in St Peter's on his successor, the most holy Leo, even to the extent of cutting out his tongue and putting out his eyes, Charles hastened to visit Rome in order to reform the state of the Church. After wreaking vengeance on the

improbos ultionem exsecutus tota hieme resedit, Apostolicum per Dei miraculum plane loquentem et*a* uidentem proprio tribunali restituens. Inter has moras Quirites, collato cum presule consilio, die Natalis Domini Augustum inopinate acclamant; quod cognomen licet inuitus ut insuetum admisisset, postea tamen animositate qua*b* decebat contra imperatores Constantinopolitanos defendens, Ludouico filio*c* heredi-
8 tarium contradidit. Ex eius genere regnauere in illa regione quae nunc proprie Frantia dicitur, usque ad Hugonem cognomento Capet, a quo descendit modernus Ludouicus. Ex eadem progenie regnarunt*d* in Alemannia et Italia usque ad annum Domini nongentesimum duodecimum. Tunc enim quidam*e* Conradus rex Teutonicorum illud imperium arripuit. Huius nepos fuit Otto*f* maximus, nichil probitatis debens omnibus ante se imperatoribus; ita uirtute et gratia*g* mirabilis hereditatem imperii posteris reliquit suis; nam modernus Henricus*h* ex eius sanguine lineam trahit.*i*

69. Sed ut ad inchoatum reuertar,*j* Alcwinus, licet in Frantia a Karolo Magno monasterio beati Martini prelatus esset, non immemor compatriotarum, imperatorem in amicitia eorum continere, illos crebris epistolis ad bonum incitare. Dictorum eius hic pleraque intexam, *k*quibus palam fiat*k* quam cito post obitum Bedae in eius etiam aecclesia studium librorum emarcuerit, et post mortem Egberhti regnum Northanimbrorum propter peruicatiam malorum morum pessum ierit.

70. Ait ergo*l* ad Wirenses, *m*apud quos*m* Beda*n* uixerat et obierat, ex obliquo fecisse arguens quod ne fatiant rogat: 'Assuescant pueri astare laudibus superni Regis, non uulpium fodere cauernas, non leporum fugaces sequi cursus; discant nunc Scripturas sacras, ut aetate perfecta alios docere possint. Recogitate nobilissimum nostri temporis magistrum Bedam presbiterum, quale habuit in iuuentute discendi studium, qualem nunc habet*o* inter homines laudem, et multo maiorem apud Deum remunerationis gloriam.'*p* [1] Item ad Eboracenses: 'Non pro auri auaritia (testis est mei*q* Cognitor cordis) Frantiam ueni nec remansi in
2 ea, sed aecclesiasticae causa necessitatis.' [2] Item ad Offam regem

a et clare (dare *Bk*) *B†*   *b* quam *A*   *c* Ludouicum filium *B*   *d* *T*⁺ adds imperatores   *e* om. *B*   *f* oto ille *T¹*, ille otho *Tc*   *g* gratiaque (om. et) *B*   *h* *B†* adds gener (genitor *Bk*, but not *Bph*) Henrici regis Anglie   *i* traxit *B*   *j* regradiar *Tt*, regrediar *Tp*   *k–k* om. *B*   *l* ait ergo om. *T¹* (but adding ait after assuescant below)   *m–m* in quibus *T¹*   *n* *T¹* adds et   *o* habeat *T¹* (and *A* of *Alc.*)   *p* gratiam *B*   *q* mei after cordis *T¹*, *Alc.*

malefactors, he resided there for the whole winter, and restored to his throne the Holy Father, who could now by a miracle both speak and see plainly. While he was there, the Roman people, in concert with the pope, on Christmas Day unexpectedly hailed him as Augustus. Though at first reluctant to assume this title because of its unfamiliarity, he later came to defend it with proper spirit against the emperors of Constantinople, and handed it on as an heirloom to his son Louis. His descendants were kings in the region now properly called France, as far as Hugh surnamed Capet, the ancestor of the Louis of our own day. Other members of the family ruled in Alemannia and Italy until the year of our Lord 912. At that date the empire was seized by a certain Conrad, king of the Teutons, whose grandson was Otto the Great, the equal in prowess of all preceding emperors, whose remarkable valour and popularity enabled him to leave the empire as an inheritance to his own descendants. Our own contemporary, Henry, [B *adds* son-in-law of Henry king of England] traces his descent from Otto.

69. But to return to my theme. Although in France, and made by Charlemagne head of the monastery of St Martin, Alcuin did not forget his countrymen; he maintained the emperor in friendly relations with them, and often wrote to rouse them to good works. I will insert here several of his remarks, which show how soon after Bede's passing, even in his own church, the study of letters withered away, and how, Ecgberht once dead, the kingdom of Northumbria went to pieces through perseverance in doing evil.

70. He writes as follows to the monks of Monkwearmouth, among whom Bede had lived and died, showing indirectly that they were guilty of the practices from which he asks them to desist: 'Let your young men form the habit of attending to the praises of their heavenly King, instead of digging out the fox from his earth or coursing the flying hare; let them at this stage learn the Holy Scriptures, that when they are grown up, they may be able to teach others. Remember the priest Bede, the most distinguished scholar of our time, what zeal for learning he showed in his youth, what fame he now has among men, and how much greater glory and reward in the presence of God.'[1] Or again, to the monks of York: 'It was not for greed of gold—the Searcher of my heart is my witness—that I came to France or have remained here, but for the necessities of the Church.'[2] Again, to Offa

---

[1] Alcuin, *Ep.* xix (p. 55.19–25). [2] Alcuin, *Ep.* xliii (p. 89.4–5).

Mertiorum: 'Ego paratus eram cum muneribus Karoli regis ad uos uenire,[a] et patriam reuerti; sed melius michi uisum est propter pacem gentis meae in peregrinatione remanere, nesciens quid fecissem inter eos inter quos nullus securus esse uel in salubri consilio proficere potest. Ecce loca[b] sancta[c] a paganis uastata, altaria periuriis fedata, monasteria adulteriis uiolata, terra sanguine dominorum et principum fedata.'[d][1] Item ad Ethelredum regem, qui tertius post Egberhtum regnauit: 'Ecce aecclesia sancti Cuthberti sacerdotum Dei[e] sanguine aspersa, omnibus spoliata ornamentis; locus cunctis in Britannia uenerabilior paganis gentibus datur ad depredandum;[f] et ubi primum post discessum sancti Paulini ab Eboraco Christiana religio in nostra gente sumpsit exordium, ibi miseriae et calamitatis cepit initium. Quid significat pluuia sanguinis quam Quadragesimali tempore in Eboraca ciuitate, quae caput totius regni est,[g] in aecclesia beati principis apostolorum uidimus de borealibus domus sereno aere de summitate[h] tecti[i] minaciter cadere? Nonne potest putari a borealibus partibus uenire sanguinem super terram?'[j][2] Item Osberto patritio Mertiorum:[k] 'Nostrum[l] regnum[m] Northanimbrorum pene periit[n] propter intestinas dissensiones et fallaces iurationes.'[3] Item ad Ethelardum Cantuariensem archiepiscopum: 'Hoc dico propter flagellum quod nuper accidit partibus insulae nostrae, quae prope trecentis et quadraginta annis a parentibus inhabitata[o] est nostris. Legitur in libro Gildae, sapientissimi Britonum,[p] quod idem Britones propter auaritiam et rapinam principum, propter iniquitatem et iniustitiam iudicum, propter desidiam predicationis episcoporum, propter luxuriam et malos mores populi patriam perdidere. Caueamus haec eadem uitia nostris temporibus inolescere, quatinus benedictio diuina nobis patriam conseruet in prosperitate bona quam nobis[q] sua[r] misericordissima pietate perdonare[s] dignatus[t] est.'[4]

71. Planum, ut arbitror, factum est quantam labem, quantam pestem obliuio litterarum et lubrici mores perditorum hominum Angliae inuexerint; quae uerba ad cautelam legentium posita hunc in ista historiola[u] locum habeant.

[a] redire *Tt, Alc.* [b] *om. Tt* [c] sanctissima *Tt, Alc.* [d] maculata *Bt*; infecta *Alc.* [e] *om. B* [f] predandum *Tt* [g] caput est totius regni *Al, Alc.*; est caput totius regni *Aa* [h] summo *B* [i] tecti *after* cadere *Tt, Alc.* [j] populum *Tt, Alc., GP p. 209* [k] *om. Tt (cf. 94. 2)* [l] *Tt adds* uero [m] *Tt, Alc. add* id est [n] perit *TtBc*[1] [o] habitata *Bc(and Bph)*, habita *Bk* [p] Gildi Brit. sap. *Tt, Alc.* [q] in nobis *B; C adds* Deus [r] in sua *Tt, Alc.* [s] donare *B* [t] dignata *Alc.* [u] historia *C*

king of the Mercians: 'I was prepared to come to you with gifts from King Charles, and to return to my own country; but it seemed better for my people's peace that I should remain in foreign parts, not knowing what good I should have done among those who make all peace of mind, all progress in sound policy, impossible. The holy places are laid waste by the infidel, the altars defiled by perjury, the monasteries outraged by adultery, and the land made foul with the blood of lords and chieftains.'[1] He also writes to King Æthelred, who reigned third 3 after Ecgberht: 'Behold the church of St Cuthbert spattered with the blood of the priests of God, and robbed of all her ornaments; that shrine more venerable than any other in Britain is handed over for a prey to pagan nations; and where first, after St Paulinus' departure from York, the Christian religion in our land had its beginning, has come the onset of misery and disaster. What means that rain of blood, which in the season of Lent, in the city of York which is the capital of the whole kingdom, in the church of the blessed prince of the Apostles, we saw fall threateningly on the north side of the building beneath a clear sky from the pinnacle of the roof? Can we not suppose that bloodshed is coming from the northern regions upon the earth?'[2] And to Osberht, patrician of the Mercians: 'Our kingdom of 4 Northumbria has almost perished, by reason of internal discord and oath-breaking.'[3] To Æthelheard archbishop of Canterbury: 'This I say by reason of the scourge that has lately befallen parts of our island, wherein our forefathers have lived for close on three hundred and forty years. It is written in the book of Gildas, wisest of the Britons, that it was through the avarice and rapine of their princes, through the iniquity and injustice of their judges, because their bishops would not preach and their people were wanton and corrupted, that those same Britons lost their country. Let us beware that the self-same vices do not re-establish themselves in our own day, that so the divine blessing may preserve for us in full prosperity the country which God in His most merciful goodness has seen fit to give us.'[4]

71. I have made plain, I think, how great was the disgrace, how grievous the sickness brought upon England by the eclipse of education and the depravity of wicked men. Let this remark stand here in my history as a warning to my readers.

---

[1] Alcuin, *Ep.* ci (p. 147. 17–21). [2] Alcuin, *Ep.* xvi (pp. 42. 37–43. 3; 43. 17–20).
[3] Alcuin, *Ep.* cxxii (p. 180. 16–17). [4] Alcuin, *Ep.* xvii (p. 47. 14–22).

72. Egberhtus itaque, fratris in religione[a] emulus comamque tonsus, [b]Osulfo filio, illeque, post annum a ciuibus innocenter cesus,[b] Molloni locum fecit; is,[c] undecim annis satis impigre regno functus, insidiis Alhredi occubuit.[d] Alhredus decimo regni quod inuaserat anno cedere a prouintialibus compulsus est. Ethelbertus quoque,[e] filius Mollonis, eorum consensu rex leuatus, quinto anno ab eisdem expulsus est. Tunc rex Alfwoldus acclamatus post undecim annos perfidiam prouintialium[f] ingemuit, sine culpa trucidatus; quod et celebris apud Haugustaldum [g]sepultura et diuina pretenderunt miracula. Ei[h] nepos suus, filius Alhredi, Osredus succedens uixque anno emenso expulsus regnum Ethelberto, qui et Ethelredus dictus est, uacuauit.[i] Is filius Mollonis, qui etiam Athelwaldus uocabatur, fuit, regnumque post duodecim annos exilii recipiens quattuor annis tenuit; quibus exactis fatum superiorum effugere non ualuit misere occisus. Quare offensi plures episcopi et optimates a patria fugere.[j] Quidam merito plexum affirmant quod in occisione iniusta Osredi consensum suum obligauerit, cui sufficere potuerit quod principatu eiectus sedem illi restituerit.[g] De huius regni exordio Alcwinus ita[k] memorat: 'Benedictus Deus, qui facit mirabilia solus! Nuper Ethelredus filius Adelwaldi de carcere processit in solium, et de miseria in maiestatem; cuius regni nouitate detenti sumus ne ueniremus ad uos.'[1] De nece ita ad Offam regem Mertiorum: 'Sciat ueneranda dilectio uestra quod dominus rex[l] Karolus amabiliter et fideliter sepe mecum locutus est de uobis, et in eo habetis fidelissimum amicum: ideo et uestrae dilectioni digna dirigit munera, et per episcopales sedes regni uestri. Similiter[m] et Edelredo regi et ad suas episcoporum sedes dona direxit; sed heu proh dolor, donis datis et epistolis in manus missorum, superuenit tristis legatio per missos, qui de Scottia per uos reuersi sunt, de infidelitate gentis et nece regis. Ita Karolus, retracta donorum largitate, in tantum iratus est contra gentem illam, ut ait, perfidam et peruersam et homicidam dominorum suorum, peiorem eam paganis estimans, ut, nisi ego intercessor essem pro ea, quicquid eis boni abstrahere potuisset et mali machinari, iam fecisset.'[2]

---

[a] regione *Tt*   [b-b] om. *Tt*   [c] cessit. Ille *Tt*   [d] cesus est *Tt*
[e] Egbertus quoque qui et Adelredus *Tt (see below, 2); the correct name is* Ethelredus
[f] eorundem *Tt*   [g-g] om. *Tt*   [h] et *CsB*   [i] euacuauit *TtC, but cf. 121. 7, VD p. 300*   [j] refugere *B*   [k] ita Alcuinus *Tt*   [l] om. *A*   [m] sedliter *Al, sed Aa*

[1] Alcuin, *Ep.* viii (p. 33. 15–17).   [2] Alcuin, *Ep.* ci (p. 147. 3–16).

72. So Ecgberht, emulating his brother's religious life, received the tonsure and made way for his son Oswulf, and Oswulf, being killed for no just reason by the citizens after a year, was replaced by Moll; Moll reigned with some energy for eleven years, and was treacherously killed by Alhred. Alhred, in the tenth year of his usurping reign, was forced by his people to retire; and similarly Moll's son Æthelberht, who was raised to the throne by common consent, was driven out by them after four years. Ælfwald was then hailed as king, but eleven years later had cause to rue the treachery of his people, being put to death for no fault of his own. This is proved by the popularity of his resting-place at Hexham, and by miracles divinely wrought. His nephew, Alhred's son Osred, succeeded, but after 2 scarcely a year was driven out, and left the empty throne to Æthelberht, also called Æthelred. He was son of Moll, also called Æthelwald; ascending the throne after twelve years of exile, he held it for four, at the end of which, unable to escape the fate of his predecessors, he too was wretchedly put to death. Several bishops and nobles were indignant at this, and fled the country; some declare that he deserved his fate, because he had pledged his consent to the murder of Osred, when he could have been satisfied with Osred's expulsion, which restored him to the throne. Of the beginning of Æthelred's reign Alcuin writes as follows: 'Blessed be God, who only doeth marvellous things! Æthelred, the son of Æthelwald, has lately been promoted from prison to the throne, from misery to magnificence; and this change in the kingship has hindered me from coming to you.'[1] And of his death, to Offa king of the Mercians: 'I would have you 3 know, beloved lord, that my lord King Charles has often spoken with me of you in friendship and good faith, and in him you have a most faithful friend. So it is that he is sending suitable presents to you, his well-beloved, and to the episcopal sees within your kingdom. He has likewise despatched gifts to King Æthelred and his episcopal sees; but alas, when the gifts and letters were in the hands of his emissaries, the sad news was brought by messengers returning from Scotland through your country, that his people had proved treacherous and had killed their king. Charles therefore has withdrawn his generous gifts, and was so angry with that perverse and perfidious people, as he calls them, who assassinate their lords,—for he counts them worse than pagans—that unless I had pleaded for them, he would by now have taken from them all the good, and done them all the evil, that he could.'[2]

73. Post Ethelredum nullus ad regnum ascendere*a* ausus, dum quisque superiorum sibi casum timeret, et otio inglorio tutus uictitare quam ancipiti discrimine pendulus regnare mallet; plerosque enim regum Northanimbrorum familiari pene exitio uitam exisse. Ita cessante rectore per triginta tres annos, prouintia illa*b* risui et predae finitimis fuit. Siquidem ubi Dani, quos ex uerbis Alcwini loca sanctorum populatos fuisse supra[1] ostendimus, domum regressi ceteris insulae copiam habitatorumque ignauiam nuntiarunt, barbari, raptim copioseque insulam petentes, illas usque*c* in id tempus partes occupauere. Nam et regem multis annis habuere proprium, qui tamen ad regis Westsaxonum spectaret arbitrium; transactis enim illis*d* triginta tribus annis, hanc etiam regionem cum ceteris obtinuit rex Egbirhtus, anno Dominicae incarnationis octingentesimo uicesimo septimo, regni sui uicesimo octauo. Cuius quia tempus attigimus,*e* iam nunc promissionis nostrae[2] recordati, de regno Mertiorum pauca subitiemus, quia et placet nobis dicendi parsimonia et non arridet multa dicendorum materia.

74. Anno Dominicae incarnationis sexcentesimo uicesimo sexto, post mortem Hengesti anno centesimo tricesimo nono, Penda quidam, filius Pibbae, a Wodenio decimus, stirpe inclitus, bellis industrius, idemque fanaticus et impius, apud Mertios regis nomen presumpsit, cum iam quinquagenarius frequentibus contra finitimos excursionibus nutrisset audatiam. Itaque arrepto regno eger quiete animus, et qui nesciret quantum scelus esset sotiali uincere bello,[3] urbes proximas quatere,*f* compatriotarum fines regum inequitare,*g* prorsus magno tumultu et terrore agere. Quid enim non auderet qui lumina Britanniae Eduinum et Oswaldum, reges Northanimbrorum, Sigbertum, Egricum,*h* Annam, reges Orientalium Anglorum, in quibus generis claritas et uitae sanctitas conquadrabat, temeritate nefaria extinxit? Kenwalkium quoque, Westsaxonum regem, bello bis terque lacessitum in exilium compulit; quanuis ille merito perfidiae culpam luerit, qua in Deum fidem illius abnegando et in ipsum Pendam sororem eius*i* repudiando peccauerat. Iam uero onerosum dictu*j* est quod omnibus occasionibus cedium inhians, et uelut coruus ad nidorem cadaueris aduolans, ultro*k* Cedwallae in auxilium accurrerit,

a accedere *Tt* *b* om. *C* *c* om. *C* *d* om. *Tt* *e* attingimus *TtAlBc*[*t a.c.*] *f* quarere *Bk*, querere *Bc (Bph avoids error)* *g* inquietare *TtAaCs* *h* Egfridum *A* *i* illius *Tt* *j* dictum *Tt(after corr.?)Aap* *k* om. *A*

73. After Æthelred, no man dared ascend the throne; everyone feared to share the fate of his predecessors, and preferred a life of ease, inglorious but safe, to the suspense and dangers of the kingship; for most of the kings of the Northumbrians had, they knew, come to a bad end which seemed almost hereditary. In the absence of a ruler for three and thirty years, the province lay exposed to the mockery and pillage of its neighbours. On their return home, the Danes, whose devastation of the shrines of the saints I have made plain above[1] in the words of Alcuin, told their fellows of the island's riches and the poor spirit of its inhabitants; and the barbarians, hastening across in large numbers, seized the region and held it up to the time of which I am speaking. For many years they even had their own king, who was, however, under the overlordship of the king of the West Saxons. When the thirty-three years were over, this region too like the rest passed under the sway of King Ecgberht, in the year of our Lord 827 and the twenty-eighth of his reign. Having reached the time of Ecgberht, I must remember my promise,[2] and add a short statement about the kingdom of the Mercians; I like brevity in itself, and there is not much material to attract me.

74. In the year of our Lord 626, being the one hundred and thirty-ninth year after the death of Hencgest, a certain Penda, son of Pybba and tenth in descent from Woden, highborn and warlike but a bigoted pagan, assumed the royal style among the Mercians, being already in his fifties and well schooled in enterprise by frequent raids on his neighbours. With his restless spirit, not understanding 'how great his guilt who wins in civil war',[3] he proceeded, having seized the throne, to set the neighbouring cities shaking, to raid the territory of his fellow princes, and in general to spread disorder and dismay. Limitless indeed his boldness, who with criminal violence extinguished those luminaries of Britain, Edwin and Oswald, kings of the Northumbrians, Sigeberht, Ecgric, and Anna, kings of the East Angles, in whom nobility of blood was matched with holiness of life. Cenwealh too, the king of the West Saxons, after two or three attacks, was driven into exile, though he, it is true, met with his just reward for treachery towards God, whose faith he had rejected, and towards Penda himself, whose sister he had divorced. It is an unpleasant task to tell how, seizing as he did every opportunity for bloodshed, like a raven flying to the stink of carrion, he volunteered to help Cædwalla,

---

[1] 70. 3. [2] i pr. 5. [3] Cf. Lucan i. 366.

3 et ad recuperandum regnum magno emolumento fuerit. Ita per triginta annos in cognatos grassatus, nichil aduersus exteras gentes memorandum commisit. Sed inuenit tandem effrenis cupiditas*a* idoneum meritis*b* finem; siquidem ab Oswio, qui Oswaldo fratri*c* successerat, magis per Dei uirtutem quam per manum militarem cum auxiliis fusus, infernalium animarum numerum auxit. Habuit ex regina Kineswida filios quinque,*d* Wedam,*e* Wlferium, Ethelredum, Merewaldum, Mercelinum;*f* filias duas,*g* Kineburgam et Kineswidam, ambas sancta continentia precellentes. Ita parens perpetuo in Deum rebellis sanctissimos caelo fructus effudit.

75. Successit illi in parte regni Weda filius Oswii dono Australibus Mertiis prelatus, strenuus ephebus et eiusdem Oswii, etiam patre uiuente, gener. Nam filiam eius ea conditione acceperat ut Christianitatem amplectens idolis abrenuntiaret; cuius fidei participem prouintiam suam arridente regni serenitate, socero suffragante, facere procurasset, nisi tam laeta principia mors per insidias uxoris, ut dicitur,*h* festinata succideret. Tunc regnum Oswius suscepit quod sibi et uictoriae in patrem et affinitatis in filium iure*i* competere uidebatur. Sed animositas prouintialium non ultra triennium potuit ferre regnantem; expulsis enim eius ducibus, Wlferioque Pendae filio in omen regni acclamato, libertatem*j* recepit.

76. Wlferius ne spem ciuium falleret sedulo satagere, magnis et animi et corporis uiribus utilem se principem ostentare: denique Christianitatem uix in regno suo palpitantem et*k* per fratrem initiatam fauore suo enixissime iuuit. Primis fere annis a rege Westsaxonum grauiter afflictus, sequentibus consilii uiuacitate iniuriam propulsans, etiam ipsum Wehtae insulae dominio mutilauit; eandemque, ritus sacrilegos adhuc anhelantem,*l* ad rectum tramitem inflectens non multo post regi Australium Saxonum Edelwalkio, quem in baptismo susceperat, gratia fidei dedit. Verum enimuero haec, et quaecumque eius bona, inficit et deprimit grauis simoniae nota, quod primus regum Anglorum sacrum
2 episcopatum Lundoniae cuidam Wine ambitioso*m* uenditarit. Habuit in matrimonio filiam*n* Ercomberhti regis Cantuariorum Ermenhildam, et ex ea genuit Kenredum et Werburgam, uirginem sanctissimam, quae

---

a temeritas *TtCe*ᵛ *b* *Tt adds* suis *c* fratri Osualdo *Tt* *d* quinque *Tt*
(cf. *JW* i. 264 *Thorpe); om. ACB* *e* sc. Peadam (so also below) *f* Mercelmum
ACs, as JW i. 264–5 *Thorpe* *g* suas *C* *h* ut dicitur *om. Tt* *i* *Tt;* iure in
filium *ACB* *j* *Tt adds* suam *k* palpitantem et *om. Tt* *l* adhuc sacrilegos
efflantem *Tt* *m* ambitiose *A* *n* *ACs add* regis

and was of great assistance to him in the recovery of his kingdom. In thirty years of aggression against his kinsmen, he did nothing worthy of note against foreigners. At length however his unbounded greed met with the end it deserved: he and his allies were routed, more by God's help than through military might, by Oswiu the brother and successor of Oswald, and went to swell the number of souls in hell. He had by his queen Cyneswith five sons, Peada, Wulfhere, Æthelred, Merewald, and Merchelm, and two daughters, Cyneburh and Cyneswith, both saintly virgins of repute. Thus their father, though a lifelong rebel against God, produced most saintly fruit for Heaven.

75. In half his kingdom he was succeeded by his son Peada, whom Oswiu had made ruler over the southern Mercians. Young and vigorous, Peada had already in his father's lifetime become Oswiu's son-in-law, receiving his daughter in marriage on condition that he would abandon idols and embrace the Christian faith; and in the favourable conditions of peace he would with his father-in-law's assistance have contrived to convert his whole realm, had not such a promising start been cut short by death, accelerated, it is said, by his wife's machinations. Oswiu then took over the kingdom, which seemed to be his by the double right of victory over the father and family ties with the son. But the people's resentment after three years could endure his reign no longer; they drove out his generals, made Penda's son Wulfhere king by acclamation, and regained their liberty.

76. Wulfhere was very careful not to disappoint his subjects, showing himself a worthy king by great gifts both of mind and body, and to Christianity, which in his kingdom was gasping for breath, having just been started by his brother, he gave all the encouragement in his power. In his early years harassed by the king of the West Saxons, he later kept the aggressor at bay by his energy and skill, and even deprived him of the lordship of the Isle of Wight. The island was still devoted to pagan practices, but he turned it into the right path, and not long after gave it to his godson Æthelwalh, king of the South Saxons, as a reward for his faith. But these and his other good actions are overcast and weighed down by the guilt of simony; for he was the first English king who sold the holy see of London, to a claimant named Wini. He married Eormenhild, daughter of Earconberht king of Kent, and by her had Cenred, and Wærburh, the most holy virgin

Cestrae iacet. Frater eius Merewaldus Ermenburgam, filiam Ermenredi fratris eiusdem Ercomberhti, uxorem habuit, suscepitque ex ea filias Milburgam, quae Weneloch, et Mildritham, quae Cantiae in monasterio sancti Augustini requiescunt, et Mildritham,[a] et filium Merefinnum. Kineburgam, Pendae filiam, Alfridus rex Northanimbrorum duxit uxorem;[b] quae postmodum, carnali copula fastidita, sanctimonialem[c] habitum suscepit[d] in monasterio quod fratres sui Wlferius et Ethelredus construxerant.

77. Wlferio post decem et nouem annos defuncto, regnauit frater eius Ethelredus, animi religione quam pugnandi exercitatione celebrior: denique una et ipsa illustri expeditione in Cantiam contentus ostendisse uirtutem,[e] reliqua uita otio inseruiit, nisi quod regem Northanimbrorum Egfridum[f] metas regni transilientem pugna adorsus domum redire ammonuerit, Elwino fratre ceso.[g] Hanc sane cedem[h] propensiori consilio, beato Theodoro archiepiscopo satagente, congestis pecuniae talentis apud Egfridum redemit. Post haec regni anno tricesimo in Bardenia regulariter tonsus, primo in monachum, mox in abbatem alteratus est. Hic est qui, contemporaneus Inae regis Westsaxonum, priuilegium quod sanctus Aldelmus a Roma, ut prediximus,[1] attulit sua quoque auctoritate roborauit. Regis[i] Northanimbrorum Egfridi Ostgidam[j] sororem habuit uxorem, ex qua filium Celredum suscepit.

78. Statuit sibi successorem Kenredum, filium fratris Wlferii, qui pietate in Deum probitate in patriam perinsignis magna morum sinceritate uitam cucurrit, quintoque regni anno Romam ire pergens, reliquum temporis illic religiose compleuit, maxime miserando exitu militis compunctus, qui, ut Beda[2] refert, cum confiteri scelera sua sanus superbisset, in mortis ianua constitutus aperte uidit demones auctores ad suplitia quibus animum indulserat blandientibus ad scelera.

79. Post illum regnauit Celredus, patrui sui Ethelredi filius, sicut uirtute contra Inam mirabilis, ita immatura morte miserabilis: siquidem non ultra[k] octo annos regno satisfatiens, Licitfeldae conditus est, relicto Ethelbaldo herede, pronepote Pendae ex Alwio

---

[a] *Properly* Mildgitham   [b] *om. Tt*   [c] sancti *Bk Bc*[2] *(and Bph),* sanctimonialis *Bc*[1]   [d] suscepit habitum *Tt*   [e] uirt. ost. contemptus *Tt*   [f] Eg. reg. Nor. *Tt*   [g] monuerit ceso El. fr. *Tt*   [h] *om. Tt*   [i] *C adds* eiusdem   [j] *Properly* Ostridam *(cf. 49. 8)*   [k] *om. C*

[1] 35. 4.

[2] *HE* v. 13.

who reposes at Chester. His brother Merewald married Eormenburh, daughter of Eormenred brother of the Earconberht just mentioned, and by her had three daughters, Mildburh who lies buried at Wenlock, Mildred, who lies in Canterbury in the monastery of St Augustine, and Mildred, and a son Merefin. Cyneburh, Penda's daughter, became the wife of Aldfrith king of the Northumbrians; but later she wearied of this union in the flesh, and took the nun's habit in a monastery which her brothers Wulfhere and Æthelred had founded.

77. After a reign of nineteen years, Wulfhere died, and his brother Æthelred came to the throne, a man better known for his saintly disposition than for his skill in war; content to display his valour with a single, and a brilliant, expedition into Kent, he spent the rest of his life enslaved to comfort, except that when Ecgfrith king of the Northumbrians crossed his frontiers, he attacked him and warned him off, killing his brother Ælfwine. This killing, however, when wiser counsels prevailed, he redeemed under pressure from Archbishop Theodore by a heavy payment of money to Ecgfrith. Later, in the thirtieth year of his reign, he received the monastic tonsure at Bardney, and became first a monk and then abbot. It was this king who, being a contemporary of Ine king of the West Saxons, confirmed by his own authority the privilege brought, as we have already said,[1] by St Aldhelm from Rome. His wife was Osthryth, sister of Ecgfrith king of the Northumbrians, by whom he had a son Ceolred.

78. He appointed as his successor Cenred, son of his brother Wulfhere, a man distinguished by his piety towards God and uprightness towards his people, who, having maintained great integrity of character all his life long, proceeded in the fifth year of his reign to go to Rome, and there passed the rest of his time in religious exercises; he had been greatly struck by the pitiful end of a warrior who, as Bede recounts,[2] had been too proud when in health to confess his sins, and then, when at the gates of death, openly saw, hounding him on to punishment, those very demons to whom he had abandoned his heart when they were luring him into crime.

79. After him reigned Ceolred, his uncle Æthelred's son, who is to be admired for his valour against Ine, and no less pitied for his untimely death; after holding the throne no more than eight years, he was buried at Lichfield, leaving as his heir Æthelbald, Penda's great-nephew

fratre. Hic alta pace et multo tempore, id est quadraginta uno annis, rerum perfunctus et nouissime a subiectis occisus fortunae rotam uoluit. Auctor necis eius Bernredus nichil memorandum dedit, nisi quod, mox ab Offa necatus, dignum finem insidiarum tulit. Huic Ethelbaldo Bonefatius archiepiscopus Mogontiacensis, natione Anglus, qui postea martirio coronatus est, misit epistolam, cuius hic[a] partem subdam,[1] ut uideatur quam libere arguat uitia iam in gente Anglorum inoleuisse quae Alcwinus timebat uentura esse. Simul et erit documentum ingens, in ostensis mortibus quorundam regum, quam districte Deus reos[b] puniat quos diu librata ira expectat.

80. 'Domino carissimo et in Christi amore ceteris regibus Anglorum preferendo Ethelbaldo Bonefatius archiepiscopus, legatus Germanicus Romanae aecclesiae, perpetuam in Christo caritatis salutem.

'Confitemur coram Deo quia, quando prosperitatem uestram et fidem et bona opera audimus, letamur; quando autem[c] aliquid aduersum uel in euentu bellorum uel de periculo animarum de uobis cognoscimus, tristamur. Audiuimus[d] enim quod elemosinis intentus furta et rapinas prohibes et pacem diligis et defensor uiduarum et pauperum
2 es, et inde Deo gratias agimus. Quod uero legitimum matrimonium spernis, si pro castitate faceres, esset laudabile; sed quia in luxuria et adulterio etiam cum sanctimonialibus uolutaris, est uituperabile et dampnabile; nam et famam gloriae uestrae coram Deo et hominibus confundit, et inter idolatras constituit, quia templum Dei uiolasti. Quapropter, fili carissime, penite[e] et memorare quam turpe sit ut tu, qui multis gentibus dono Dei dominaris, ad iniuriam eius sis libidinis seruus. Audiuimus preterea quod optimates pene omnes gentis Mertiorum tuo exemplo legitimas uxores deserant et adulteras et sanctimoniales constuprent, quod quam sit peregrinum ab honestate doceat
3 uos alienae gentis institutio: nam in antiqua Saxonia, ubi nulla est Christi cognitio, si uirgo in paterna domo uel maritata sub[f] coniuge fuerit adulterata, manu propria strangulatam cremant et supra fossam sepultae corruptorem suspendunt, aut cingulotenus uestibus abscisis[g] flagellant eam castae matronae et cultellis pungunt, et de uilla in

[a] huic *Tt*   [b] reos Deus *Tt*   [c] om. *C*   [d] audimus *B*   [e] penitere *TcCsB*   [f] cum *B*   [g] abscissis *B*

[1] Boniface, *Ep.* lxxiii (pp. 146–55 Tangl, excerpted and adapted).

through his brother Alwih. Æthelbald governed in profound peace and for a long period—forty-one years; but at length he spun Fortune's wheel, and his subjects put him to death. The man responsible, Beornred, has left nothing worthy of remark, except that he was soon killed by Offa, and met an end worthy of his treachery. It was to this Æthelbald that Boniface, archbishop of Mainz, an Englishman by origin who later won the crown of martyrdom, sent a letter of which I will subjoin an extract,[1] to show how openly he demonstrates that the vices whose onset was feared by Alcuin had taken root already in the English nation. At the same time, in displaying the deaths of some of these kings, there will be a solemn demonstration how strictly God punishes the guilty, over whom His anger long hangs, waiting to strike.

80. 'To Æthelbald, his well-beloved lord, dear to him in the love of Christ above all other English kings, Boniface, archbishop, legate in Germany of the Roman Church, wishes perpetual well-being of love in Christ.

'We confess before God that, when we hear of your prosperity and faith and good works, we rejoice; when we learn any ill news concerning you, be it of battles lost or of souls in peril, we are sad at heart. Now we have heard that, being devoted to almsgiving, you repress theft and rapine, that you are a lover of peace and a champion of the widow and the poor; and for these things we give thanks to God. As for your rejection of lawful wedlock, if this were done for the sake of purity, it would be worthy of praise; but as you wallow in adultery and lust, even with nuns, it is greatly to be condemned and reprobated, for it confounds your fame and honour in the sight of God and man, and sets you among the idolaters as a defiler of God's temple. Wherefore, my beloved son, repent, and remember what a disgrace it is that you, who by God's gift are master over many peoples, should in defiance of God be the servant of your passions. We have heard, moreover, that almost all the nobles among the Mercians, taking you as their example, desert their lawful wives, and live in sin with adulteresses and nuns. How far removed this is from honourable conduct, you may learn from the traditions of an alien nation. In Old Saxony, where there is no knowledge of Christ, if a maiden in her father's house or a married woman in the hand of her husband commits adultery, they burn her, strangled by her own hand, and over the grave they hang the corruptor of her who is buried below, or else they cut away her garments down to the waist, and the virtuous married

uillam missae occurrunt nouae flagellatrices,*ᵃ* donec interimant. Insuper et Winedi, quod est fedissimum genus hominum, hunc habent morem, ut mulier uiro mortuo se in rogo cremati pariter arsura precipitet. Si ergo gentiles, Deum ignorantes, tantum zelum castimoniae habent,*ᵇ* quid tibi conuenit, fili carissime, qui Christianus et rex es? Parce ergo animae tuae, parce multitudini populi tuo pereuntis exemplo, de quorum animabus redditurus es rationem.

4 'Attende et illud, quod si gens Anglorum, sicut in Frantia et Italia et ab ipsis paganis nobis improperatur, spretis legitimis matrimoniis per adulteria defluit, nascitura ex tali commixtione sit*ᶜ* gens ignaua et Dei contemptrix, quae perditis moribus patriam pessumdet, sicut Burgundionibus et Prouintialibus et Hispanis contigit, quos Saraceni multis annis infestarunt propter peccata preterita. Preterea nuntiatum est nobis quod, multa priuilegia aecclesiarum et monasteriorum auferens,
5 ad hoc audendum duces tuo*ᵈ* exemplo prouoces. Sed recogita, queso, quam terribilem uindictam Deus in anteriores reges exercuit eius culpae conscios quam in te arguimus. Nam Celredum predecessorem tuum,*ᵉ* stupratorem sanctimonialium et aecclesiasticorum priuilegiorum fractorem, splendide cum suis comitibus epulantem spiritus malignus arripuit, et sine confessione et uiatico, cum diabolo sermocinanti et legem Dei detestanti, animam extorsit. Osredum quoque, regem Deirorum et Bernitiorum, earundem culparum reum ita effrenem egit ut regnum et iuuenilem aetatem contemptibili morte amitteret. Karolus quoque princeps Francorum, monasteriorum multorum euersor et aecclesiasticarum pecuniarum in usus proprios commutator, longa tortione et uerenda morte consumptus est.'

81. Et infra: 'Quapropter, fili carissime, paternis et subnixis precibus deprecamur ut non despitias consilium patrum tuorum, qui pro Dei amore celsitudinem tuam appellare satagunt.*ᶠ* Nichil enim bono regi salubrius quam si talia*ᵍ* commissa, cum arguuntur, libenter emendentur, quia per Salomonem dicitur: "Qui diligit disciplinam, diligit sapientiam".[1] Ideo, fili carissime, ostendentes consilium iustum, contestamur et obsecramus per uiuentem Deum et per filium eius Iesum Christum et per*ʰ* Spiritum sanctum ut recorderis quam fugitiua

---

ᵃ flagellantes *T* *ᵇ* habeant *TAlCs* *ᶜ* sic *B* *ᵈ* Tt*Ce;* tuos *TcACsB* *ᵉ* om. *CB* *ᶠ* satagant *B* *ᵍ* om. *T* *ʰ* om. *AapB*

[1] Prov. 12: 1.

women flog her and pierce her with knives, and she is sent from one village to the next, where fresh tormentresses meet her, until they do her to death. Besides which it is a custom among the Wends, a most horrible race of men, that when her husband dies, and his body is burnt, a woman should throw herself upon the pyre to be burnt with him. If therefore the pagans, who know not God, show such zeal for chastity, what is appropriate for you, my beloved son, who are a Christian and a king? Have pity then on your own soul, have pity on the multitude of people led to destruction by your example, of whose souls you will have to give an account.

'Observe this also, that if the English nation does as we are accused of doing in France and Italy and by the very heathen themselves, and spurning lawful wedlock becomes rotten with adultery, there will arise from such mingled unions a coward race, despising God, whose corrupt behaviour will be the ruin of their country; as has happened to the peoples of Burgundy, Provence, and Spain, whom the Saracens these many years have harassed for their former sins. We have been informed, moreover, that by abolishing many privileges of churches and monasteries, you encourage your nobles by your example to the same presumptuous acts. Consider, I beseech you, how terrible was the judgement which God visited on earlier kings who were guilty of the same fault which we rebuke in you. Ceolred, your predecessor, who violated nuns and trampled on the privileges of the Church, an evil spirit seized as he was feasting gloriously with his nobles, and tore his soul from him, without confession or sacrament, while he was conversing with the devil and blaspheming God's law. Osred too, king of the Deiri and Bernicians, who was guilty of the same offences, was so far driven wild that he lost his kingdom and his life, young as he was, and came to a shameful end. Charles too, prince of the Franks, who overthrew many monasteries and converted the revenues of churches to his own use, was consumed by prolonged torments and died a shameful death.'

81. And further on: 'For which cause, my beloved son, we beseech you with a father's earnest prayers, not to despise the counsel of your fathers, who for the love of God are urgently appealing to your majesty. For a good king, nothing is more conducive to his well-being than the ready correction of such errors when they are pointed out for, as Solomon says, "Whoso loveth instruction, loveth wisdom."[1] And so, dear son, as we give you true counsel, we do urge and implore you by the living God, and by His Son Jesus Christ, and by the Holy Spirit, that

sit uita presens, et quam breuis et*a* momentanea delectatio spurcae carnis, et quam ignominiosum sit ut breuis uitae homo mala exempla in perpetuum posteris relinquat. Incipe ergo melioribus moribus uitam componere et preteritos errores iuuentutis corrigere, ut hic coram hominibus laudem habeas, et in futuro aeterna gloria gaudeas. Valere celsitudinem tuam et in bonis moribus proficere optamus.'

82. Huius epistolae competentes particulas huic libello pro rerum notitia insui,*b* partim auctoris uerbis partim meis, longas sententias ut uidebatur abbreuians; cuius facti non iniuste ueniam*c* paciscar, quia ad historiae ordinem festinantibus uelocitate dictionis consulendum erat. Porro misit idem Bonefatius Cuthberto archiepiscopo eiusdem tenoris epistolam,[1] hoc aditiens, ut clericos et sanctimoniales de tenuitate et
2 pompa uestium argueret. Preterea, ne miraretur quod alienum negotium ageret, cum sua nichil interesset quomodo et quibus moribus Anglorum gens uiueret, sciret se a Gregorio papa tertio sacramento astrictum ne conterminarum gentium mores apostolicae notitiae subtraheret; quapropter, blandis*d* ammonitionibus non succedentibus, acturum se ne huiusmodi uitia papam laterent. Sane de tenuitate uestium clericalium Alcwinus[2] Ethelardum archiepiscopum successorem*e* Cuthberti oblique castigat, monens ut, cum Romam uadens Karolum Magnum imperatorem, nepotem Karoli de quo superius[3] Bonefatius locutus est, uisitaret, non adduceret clericos uel monachos uersicoloribus et pompaticis uestibus indutos, quod non solerent Francorum clerici nisi religiosis uestibus amiciri.

83. *f*Nec inanes esse potuere tanti uiri[4] epistolae, quas ille legationis suae et*g* compatriotarum amoris intuitu uigilatis sensibus emittebat. Namque et Cuthbertus archiepiscopus et rex Ethelbaldus concilium coegere, emendaturi superflua quae ille increpasset. Cuius sinodi actionem, multo giro uerborum uolutatam, nunc supersedeo intexere, quia (ut opinor) conuenientius alium laboris nostri locum occupabunt, cum ad recensitionem episcoporum*h* uentum fuerit;[5] sed quia regum res in manu habemus, scriptum Ethelbaldi, deuotionis eius*i* index, quod in eodem concilio factum est, subnectam:

a B adds quam   *b* inserui T*t*B*¹* (but cf. 449. 2)   *c* iniuriam B   *d* om. B   *e* antecessorem T*t*   *f–f* (p. 120) om. T*t*   *g* om. Al, memor Aa   *h* epistolorum A   *i* om. A

[1] Ep. lxxviii.   [2] Alcuin, Ep. ccxxx (p. 375. 10–15).
[3] 80. 5.   [4] i.e. Boniface.   [5] GP c. 5.

you forget not how fleeting is our present life, how brief and momentary the pleasures of our filthy flesh, and how shameful it is that man, with his brief life, should leave a bad example to posterity for ever. Begin therefore to mend your ways, to set your life in order and correct the former errors of your youth, that here among men you may win praise, and in the world to come may rejoice in glory everlasting. We bid your Majesty farewell, and wish you progress in well-doing.'

82. I have included in my book the appropriate portions of this letter as evidence of the facts, partly in the author's words and partly in my own, shortening the long sentences at my discretion; an action for which I justifiably expect to be excused, since readers eager to hurry on to historical narrative had to be given the advantage of speed. Furthermore, Boniface sent Archbishop Cuthbert a letter[1] in the same terms, adding that he should remonstrate with clerks and nuns for their delicate and elaborate garments. He adds, for fear the archbishop [2] should wonder at his minding other people's business, since the English way of life was nothing to do with him, that Pope Gregory III had bound him by oath not to conceal the behaviour of surrounding nations from the knowledge of the Holy See; and therefore, he says, if kindly warnings fail, he will see to it that vices of this kind are not hidden from the pope. And indeed, on this matter of the fine raiments of clerks, Alcuin[2] indirectly rebukes Archbishop Æthelheard, Cuthbert's successor, when he warns him, on his visit to Rome to see the emperor Charlemagne, grandson of the Charles mentioned above[3] by Boniface, not to bring with him clerks or monks arrayed in many-coloured and elaborate garments, for Frankish clerks, he says, habitually confined themselves to garments proper to persons in religion.

83. Nor could it be of no effect, a letter from that great man,[4] full of well-pondered comments, sent by him in virtue of his office as legate, and moved by love for his countrymen. In fact, Archbishop Cuthbert and King Æthelbald summoned a council, to correct the excesses against which he had protested. The proceedings of this synod are wrapped up in much circuitous language, and I forbear to include them here, because they will, I think, more suitably find a home elsewhere in my work, when I come to give an account of the bishops;[5] but since our present subject is the history of the kings, I will subjoin a document issued by Æthelbald in the same council, which shows his devotion to the Church.

84. *"*Plerumque contingere solet pro incerta temporum uicissitudine ut ea quae multarum fidelium personarum testimonio consilioque roborata fuerint, fraudulenter per contumatiam plurimorum et machinamenta simulationis sine ulla consideratione rationis periculose dissipentur, nisi auctoritate litterarum et testamento cirographorum aeternae memoriae inserta sint. Quapropter ego Ethelbaldus rex Mertiorum pro amore caelestis patriae et remedio animae meae studendum esse preuidi,*b* ut eam per*c* bona opera liberam efficerem ab omni uinculo 2 peccatorum.*d* Dum enim michi omnipotens Deus per misericordiam clementiae suae absque ullo antecedente merito sceptra regiminis largitus est, ideo libenter ei ex eo quod dedit retribuo. Huius rei gratia hanc*e* donationem me uiuente concedo, ut omnia monasteria et aecclesiae regni mei a publicis uectigalibus et operibus et oneribus absoluantur, nisi in structionibus arcium uel pontium, quae nulli umquam relaxari possunt. Preterea habeant famuli Dei*f* propriam libertatem in fructibus siluarum et agrorum et in captura piscium, nec munuscula prebeant uel regi uel principibus nisi uoluntaria, sed liberi Deo seruiant' et cetera.*ff*

85. Bonefatio successit Lullus, et ipse natione Anglus, de cuius sanctitate et*g* uita beati Goaris loquitur,[1] et hi uersus,[2] quos iam inde a pueritia memini me audisse, protestantur:

> Antistes Lullus, quo non est sanctior ullus,
> pollens diuina tribuente Deo medicina,
> occurrit morbis, ut totus predicat orbis.

86. Veruntamen, ut historiam repetam, successit Ethelbaldo Offa, quinto genu Pendae abnepos, uir ingentis animi et qui omnia quae mente concepisset efficere proponeret, regnauitque anno uno minus quadraginta. Huius gesta cum considero, animus heret in dubio utrum probem an improbem: ita in uno eodemque homine modo uirtutibus se uitia palliabant, modo uirtutes uitiis succedebant, ut ambigeres quo teneres nodo mutantem Prothea uultus.[3] Singulorum documenta sermo percurret.*h* Cum rege Westsaxonum Kinewlfo

---

a Two versions of this charter (dated by William to 747) are recorded as Sawyer 92: (1) H & S iii. 386–7 (749); (2) H & S iii. 247 (719). William's version is in fact nearer to the latter, which is preserved in μ.   *b* prouidi C, μ   *c* om. A   *d* delictorum A, μ   *e* om. A   *f* om. A   *ff* See above, p. 118   *g* in A   *h* percurrit C

[1] Wandalbert, Mir. S. Goaris 4–7 (AA SS, Iulii [2 Jul.], pp. 338–9).

84. 'Whereas it often happens, in the uncertainty and mutability of life, that what has been established in the presence and on the advice of many trustworthy persons is perilously undone by fraud, through the effrontery of many and their deceitful contrivance, no consideration being had of reason, unless it is consigned to eternal remembrance by written authority and the witness of chirographs: now therefore I, Æthelbald king of the Mercians, for love of the heavenly country and for my soul's health, have foreseen the need to ensure that my soul by good works might be freed from all the bondage of its sins. Seeing therefore that almighty God in His goodness and mercy, with no merit on my part preceding, has granted me the sceptre of a kingdom, I gladly pay Him back out of that which He has given. For which cause I offer this concession in my own lifetime, that all the monasteries and churches in my realm be freed from public taxes and from public works and burdens, excepting only for the building of fortresses and of bridges, from which no man can ever be released. Moreover, let the servants of God enjoy their own free use of the fruits of field and woodland, and of the taking of fish. Let them not furnish presents to the king or to nobles except of their own volition, but let them be free to serve God', and so forth.

85. Boniface was succeeded by Lull, another Englishman, whose saintliness is attested by the Life of St Goar,[1] and by these lines,[2] which I remember hearing since my boyhood:

> Bishop Lull, of goodness full,
> Great doctor he by God's decree
> And makes men well, as all can tell.

86. But to resume my narrative. Æthelbald was succeeded by Offa, who was in the fifth generation after Penda, a man of immense ambition, with whom to conceive an idea was to plan its accomplishment; and he reigned one year short of forty years. When I think of his achievements, I am in doubt whether to praise or to condemn; to such an extent did vices at one moment cloak themselves with virtues, and virtue at another take the place of vice, in one and the same man, that it is hard to know 'what noose will tether Proteus' changing shape'.[3] Examples of both will be given as we proceed. Having declared war

---

[2] Walther, *Initia* 1333.
[3] Cf. Horace, *Ep.* i. 1. 90.

aperto marte congressus palmam leuiter obtinuit, quanuis esset ille bellator non ignobilis. Idem, cum magis sibi dolo estimaret successurum, regem Ethelbrihtum, magnarum promissionum lenociniis ad se accitum et intra palatium suum fraudulentis assentationibus delinitum, inopinate capite spoliari[a] fecit, regnumque Orientalium Anglorum, quod ille tenuerat, indebite peruasit.

87. Reliquias beati Albani, ad illud tempus obscure reconditas, et reuerenter eleuari et in scrinio, quantum regia magnanimitas poterat, gemmis et auro decorato componi precepit, basilica pulcherrimi operis ibi edificata et monachorum congregatione adunata. Idemque in Deum peruicax sedem archiepiscopatus olim Cantuariae fundatam in Licitfeldam transferre conatus est, inuidens scilicet[b] Cantuaritis archiepiscopatus fastigium. Quapropter Ianbrihtum[c] archiepiscopum, multis sudoribus fatigatum crebraque sedis apostolicae et noua et uetera edicta[d] proferentem, tandem omnium prediorum,[e] quae intra 2 terminos suos erant, et episcopatuum ditione priuauit. Per Adrianum igitur apostolicum, quem ueri similibus assertionibus diu fatigauerat, sicut occupatis animis multa illicita subtrahi et surripi possunt, obtinuit ut archiepiscopatus Mertiorum apud Licitfeldam esset, omnesque pontifices Mertiorum prouintiae illi subicerentur (quorum haec fuere nomina: Denebertus Wigorniensis episcopus, Werenbertus Legecestrensis, Edulfus Sidnacestrensis, Wlfeard Herefordensis), et episcopi Orientalium Anglorum[f] Alheard Helmanensis, Titfrid Dammucensis; uocabatur autem episcopus Licitfeldensis Aldulfus. Remanserunt uero archiepiscopo Cantuariensi episcopi quattuor, Lundoniensis, 3 Wintoniensis, Rofensis, Selesiensis. Horum episcopatuum quidam adhuc manent, quidam [g]alias translati, quidam[g] uenali ambitu[h] alteris uniti; nam Legecestrensis et Sidnacestrensis et Dammucensis[i] incertum quo euentu hodie non extant. Nec porro in his rapacitas Offae stetit, sed multarum aecclesiarum, inter quae[j] Malmesberiensis, predia[k] publicus expilator[l] abrasit. Sed non diu canonicas regulas haec temerauit iniquitas: namque mox successor Offae Kenulfus, nulli ante se regi potentia uel religione impar, missa Leoni Adriani successori epistola Ethelardum successorem Ianbrihti in pristinam dignitatem 4 subleuauit. Vnde Albinus[m] in epistola ad eundem Ethelardum:

[a] spoliari capite *Tt*   [b] *om. Tt*   [c] Ianbritum *Tt;* Lamb- *ACB, with various spellings (similar difficulties at 87. 3, 88. 7)*   [d] dicta *CsB*   [e] presidiorum *B*   [f] et (*om. A*) . . . Anglorum *om. Tt*   [g-g] *om. C*   [h] habiti *B*   [i] et Dammucensis *om. Tt (cf. GP p. 16)*   [j] *AB add* et, *perhaps rightly*   [k] preda *B*   [l] epilator *T'*   [m] Alcuinus *B*

on Cynewulf king of the West Saxons, he easily won the day, although Cynewulf was no mean fighter. On the other hand, when he thought treachery more likely to be profitable, he invited King Æthelberht to visit him, attracting him with handsome promises; once within his palace walls, he lulled his suspicions with spurious affability, and suddenly had him beheaded, after which he overran without any right the kingdom of the East Angles, which Æthelberht had held.

87. The relics of St Alban, which had up to that time been hidden in obscurity, were reverently exalted by Offa's order, and laid in a shrine adorned with gold and jewels as richly as his royal generosity could compass, an abbey church of most beautiful workmanship being built there, and a community of monks brought together. At the same time, he showed his obstinacy towards Heaven, by trying to move to Lichfield the archiepiscopal see that had long ago been established at Canterbury, no doubt because he envied the men of Kent the distinction of an archbishopric. Archbishop Jænberht tired himself out in his efforts to resist, putting forward many decrees of the Apostolic See, both new and old, but at length Offa deprived him of supremacy over all the estates that were within his borders, and over the bishoprics. Thus he secured from Pope Hadrian, whom he had long wearied with claims that looked convincing—for it is always possible fraudulently to extract many an illicit concession from busy men—that the Mercians should have their own archbishopric at Lichfield, and that to that province should be subordinate all the Mercian bishops, whose names were as follows: Deneberht of Worcester, Wernberht of Leicester, Eadwulf of *Sidnacester*, Wulfheard of Hereford, and the bishops of the East Angles, Alhheard of Elmham and Tidferth of Dunwich; the bishop of Lichfield was Aldwulf. There remained to the archbishop of Canterbury four bishops: London, Winchester, Rochester, and Selsey. Of these sees, some still exist, some have been moved elsewhere, and some have been united with others from mercenary motives; for Leicester, *Sidnacester*, and Dunwich—it is not certain why—have disappeared. Nor did Offa's greed stop there; the estates of many churches, Malmesbury among them, fell victim to his widespread depredations. His wickedness, however, did not long infringe the rule of law. Soon after, Offa's successor Cenwulf, who was the equal of any of his predecessors in power and piety, sent a letter to Hadrian's successor Leo, and raised Jænberht's successor Æthelheard to his original eminence; on which subject Alcuin says in a letter to Æthelheard:

'Audita prosperitate itineris uestri et reuersionis in patriam, et quomodo ab Apostolico suscepti fuistis, toto cordis affectu gratias egi Domino Deo nostro, qui magno clementiae dono prospero itinere uestram uiam direxit, et dedit uobis gratiam in conspectu Apostolici, uotique compotem redire in*a* patriam concessit, et primi doctoris nostri sacratissimam sedem ad pristinam dignitatem per te iterum exaltare dignatus est.'[1] Regalis igitur epistolae partem, simul et pontificalis, apponere dignum reor, quanuis anticipare temporum seriem uidear; sed ideo hoc fatiam, quia difficilius contexo interrupta quam absoluo instituta.

88. 'Domino beatissimo et uere amantissimo Leoni, sanctae et apostolicae sedis Romanae pontifici, Kenulfus gratia Dei rex Mertiorum cum episcopis ducibus et omni sub nostra ditione dignitatis gradu sincerissimae dilectionis in Christo salutem.

'Gratias omnipotenti Deo semper agimus, qui aecclesiam suo pretioso sanguine adquisitam inter diuersas mundi huius procellas nouis semper, prioribus ad uitam sumptis, suescit ducibus ad portum salutis attrahere, eamque noua luce infundere, quatinus nullo sit tenebrarum
2 errore fuscata, sed uiam ueritatis inoffenso pede gradiatur; unde merito omnis per orbem exultat aecclesia, quia cum omnium uerus remunerator bonorum gloriosissimum gregis sui pastorem Adrianum perpetuo remunerandum super aethera duxisset, suis tamen ouibus pia erexit prouidentia preuium, qui scit ouile Dominicum ad caulas non inferius uitae*b* agitare. Nos quoque merito, quos extremitas orbis tenet, eodem modo pre ceteris gloriamur, quia illius sullimitas nostra salus est, illius prosperitas*c* nobis perhennis exultatio; quia unde tibi apostolica dignitas, inde nobis fidei ueritas innotuit. Quapropter oportunum arbitror tuis sanctis iussionibus aurem obedientiae nostrae humiliter inclinari,*d* et quae tuae pietati rite nobis sequenda uideantur toto nisu implenda, quae uero rationi contraria deprehensa fuerint
3 citius declinanda ac interim a nobis omnimodis resecanda. Sed modo ego Kenulfus gratia Dei rex excellentiam tuam humilis exoro ut te sine offensione animi uestri de profectu nostro, ut optamus, liceat alloqui, quatinus in gremium me pietatis tuae tranquilla pace percipias, et

---

a om. *T¹A, Alc.*   *b* uitae *after* caulas *Cs, much more naturally (and with rhythm)*   *c* proceritas *T⁺Al*   *d* inclinare *Tt^v (not TpTc)*

[1] Alcuin, *Ep.* cclv (p. 412. 16–22).

'When I heard of your prosperous journey and safe return home, and of your reception by the pope, I gave thanks with a full heart to the Lord our God, who by His generous mercy directed your going to a successful issue, and gave you grace in the sight of the pope, permitting you to return home with your prayers answered; who has also seen fit once again to exalt the most holy see of our first teacher, through you, to its original eminence.'[1] I therefore think it right to append part of the king's letter and part of the pope's, although I may seem to be taking things out of their chronological order; I will do it, however, for this reason, that it is more difficult to knit up a story once interrupted than to finish what one has begun.

88. 'To his most blessed and right well-beloved lord, Leo, pontiff of the holy and apostolic Roman see, Cenwulf, by the grace of God king of the Mercians, with the bishops and thegns and every rank and dignity under our sway, sends the greeting of most sincere affection in Christ.

'We give thanks continually to almighty God, whose way it is to steer the Church that He has purchased with His precious blood amid the various tempests of this world into the harbour of salvation by ever appointing new helmsmen when the old are taken up into life, and to pour new light upon her, that she may never be overcast by any darkness of error, but may walk without stumbling in the path of truth. Hence it is that the whole Church throughout the world rightly rejoices; for when He who truly rewardeth all good men had taken to his eternal reward in Heaven Hadrian, that most glorious shepherd of His flock, He yet in loving providence raised up one to go before His sheep, who knows no less well how to bring the Lord's flock into the fold of life. With good reason do we also, who dwell at the ends of the earth, boast in like manner above all others that the Church's exaltation is our salvation, and its prosperity gives us abiding joy; for your Apostolic dignity and our true faith take their origin from one and the same source. For this cause I think it meet that our obedient ears should be humbly turned towards your holy bidding; we should fulfil with all our strength whatever your Holiness considers we should properly follow, while what is found to be contrary to reason we should at once reject, and cut away from us altogether. But now I Cenwulf, king by the grace of God, humbly beseech your Excellency that I may have leave, without causing you any displeasure, to address you, as I hope, for my own good, that you may receive me with peace

quem meritorum nulla facultas erigit, larga benedictionis tuae ubertas ad plebem suam regendam locupletet, ut una mecum gentem, quam uestra apostolica auctoritas fidei rudimentis imbuit, per intercessionem tuam contra impetus exterorum Omnipotens erigat, et per se
4 regnum, quod ipse Deus dedit nobis, dilatare dignetur. Hanc benedictionem omnes qui ante me sceptro prefuere Mertiorum meruerunt ab antecessoribus tuis adipisci; hanc ipse humilis peto et a uobis, o sanctissimi,^{a} impetrare cupio, quatinus in primis adoptionis sorte me tibi filium suscipias, sicuti te in^b patris persona diligo et totis obedientiae uiribus semper amplector. Decet enim inter tantas^c personas fides sancta seruari et inuiolata caritas custodiri, quia paterna pietas filiorum felicitas in Deo esse credenda est, secundum illud Ezechiae: "Pater filiis notam faciet ueritatem tuam, Domine."[1] In quibus uerbis te, amande genitor, imploro ut filio tuo tametsi^d indigno ueritatem Domini tuis uerbis sacrosanctis notam facere non deneges, ut per tuam sanam eruditionem, Deo adiuuante, ad melioris uitae propositum merear peruenire.
5 'Quin etiam, dulcissime, cum omnibus episcopis nostris et^e cuiuscumque apud nos dignitatis persona deprecor, uti nobis de multimodis inquisitionibus, super quibus^f maximam subtilitatem uestram dignum duximus perquirere, benigne respondeas, ne sanctorum traditio patrum et ab illis tradita nobis regula quasi incognita per aliquid uitietur in nobis, sed sermo tuus directus nobis in caritate et mansuetudine ueniat, ut per Dei misericordiam profuturum in nobis percipiat
6 fructum. Primum namque est quod pontifices nostri ac peritissimi quique in nobis dicunt, quod contra canones et apostolica statuta, quae nobis a patre beatissimo Gregorio dirigente statuta sunt, sicut uos scitis, auctoritas Dorobernensis metropolitani in duas scindatur^g parrochias, cuius eodem patre mandante ditioni subiacere debent episcopi duodecim, sicut per aecclesias nostras legitur in epistola quam fratri et coepiscopo Augustino direxit de duobus Lundoniae et Eboracae metropolis episcopis, quam etiam apud uos haberi non dubitamus. Sed ipse primum pontificalis apex, qui tunc Lundoniae sub honore et ornamento pallii fuerat conscriptus, pro eo Dorobernensi^h
7 oblatus est atque concessus. Nam quia beatae recordationis Augustinus,

---

^{a} sanctissime *Tc (cf.* dulcissime *in 5 below)* ^{b} m(ich)i T^+ ^{c} tantos A
^{d} $Tt^{p.c.}TpTcBc;$ tam si $Tt^{a.c.}ACBk$ *(corr. from* tam) ^{e} *One expects* et omni ^{f} B
adds et ^{g} scinditur B ^{h} Dorouernensis T^+

---

[1] Isa. 38: 19.

and quietness into your affectionate embrace, and that the generous abundance of your blessing may endow for the governance of his people one who is exalted by no merits of his own; that so, through your intercession, the Almighty may exalt against the attacks of enemies from without myself and my people, who by your Apostolic authority are imbued with the elements of the faith, and may deign of Himself to enlarge the kingdom which God Himself has given us. This blessing all those who have gone before me on the throne of the Mercians were found worthy to obtain from your predecessors, and this it is that I humbly beg and seek to obtain from you, most holy father, that above all you may receive me as your son by right of adoption, even as I love you as my father and am ever devoted to you with the whole force of my duty. Between such persons as ourselves, it is right that faith should religiously be kept and love maintained inviolate, for we must believe that the love of a father is under God the happiness of his sons, according to the words of Hezekiah: "The father to the children shall make known Thy truth, O Lord."[1] Taking this for my text, dear father, I beseech you: do not refuse by your most holy words to make the Lord's truth known to your son, however unworthy, that by your wholesome teaching with God's help I may be found worthy to attain to a better way of life.

'Moreover, beloved sir, together with all my bishops and every person of any dignity about me, I beg you of your kindness to reply to us in respect of the divers enquiries we have thought proper to address to your subtle wisdom, that the tradition of the holy Fathers and the rule handed down to us by them be not infringed by us at any point through ignorance; but let your words come addressed to us in love and gentleness, that by God's mercy they may bear fruit within us for our good. The first is this, that our bishops and all our most learned men declare it to be against the law, and against the Apostolic rules laid down for us, as you know, under the supervision of our blessed father Gregory, for the authority of the metropolitan of Canterbury to be divided into two provinces, seeing that by that holy father's disposition there should be twelve bishops under his control, as is read in our churches in the letter sent by him to Augustine, his brother and fellow-bishop, about the bishops of the two mother-cities of London and York, of which we do not doubt you have a copy. But, at the first, the pontifical dignity which had been destined for London, with the honourable distinction of the pallium, was offered and granted instead to the see of Canterbury. For it was in that city that Augustine

qui uerbum Dei imperante Gregorio Anglorum genti ministrabat et gloriosissime aecclesiis prefuit Saxoniae, in eadem ciuitate diem obiit, et corpus illius in basilica beati Petri apostolorum principis, quam successor eius Laurentius sacrauit, conditum fuisset,[a] uisum est cunctis gentis nostrae sapientibus quatinus in illa ciuitate metropolitanus honor haberetur ubi corpore[b] pausat qui his partibus fidei ueritatem inseruit. Cuius itaque, sicut uos scitis, dignitatis honorem primum rex Offa, propter inimicitiam cum uenerabili Iaenberhto et gente Cantuariorum acceptam, auertere et in duas parrochias dissipare nisus; et piissimus coepiscopus et antecessor uester Adrianus rogatu predicti regis facere cepit quod prius nemo presumpsit, et Mertiorum presulem

8 pallio extulit. Neutrum tamen ex his culpamus, quos Christus (ut credimus) aeterna uictoria triumphat. Sed tamen excellentiam uestram humiles exoramus, quibus a Deo merito sapientiae clauis collata est, ut super hac causa cum sapientibus uestris queratis, et quicquid uobis uideatur nobis postea seruandum rescribere dignemini, ne tunica Christi inconsutilis alicuius inter nos dissensionis scisma patiatur, sed per uestram sanam doctrinam, ut desideramus, ad uerae pacis unitatem dirigatur. Magna enim humilitate simul et dilectione haec tibi scripsimus, papa beatissime, clementiam tuam profusius precantes quatinus ad ea quae a nobis necessario explicita sunt benigne et iuste respondeas.

9 'Sed et illam epistolam, quam Ethelardus archiepiscopus[c] coram cunctis prouintialibus episcopis nostris multiplicius de suis ac totius Britanniae causis et necessitatibus tibi scripsit, pio amore perscrutari digneris, et quicquid de rebus quae in ea scripta[d] sunt fidei normula poscat, pagina nobis ueritatis patefacere memineris. Ergo preterito anno legationem meam etiam et episcoporum per Wadan abbatem misimus; at ille, accipiens illam[e] legationem, segniter, immo insipienter, deduxit. Sed modo tibi modicum amoris gratia munus per Brine presbiterum et Fildas et Ceolberht ministros meos, pater amande, mitto, quod[f] est centum uiginti mancusas, cum litteris, precans te ut benigne suscipias et benedictionem tuam nobis donare digneris. Omnipotens Deus te longeuo tempore ad laudem suae sanctae aecclesiae custodiat incolumem'.

[a] *Why not* fuit?   [b] corpus *Al*, corpus eius *Aa*   [c] *T*[+]* adds* noster   [d] *So the MSS*   [e] ipsam *T*[+]   [f] id *Tt (not TpTc), cf. 89. 2*

died, of blessed memory, he who at Gregory's command brought the word of God to the English nation and ruled most gloriously over the churches of Saxony, and his body was buried in the basilica of St Peter, chief of the Apostles, which his successor Laurence consecrated; and therefore it seemed right to all the wise men of our nation that the metropolitan dignity should be established in that city, where rest the bodily remains of him who implanted the true faith in these regions. It was King Offa at first, as you know, who on account of his hostility towards the venerable Archbishop Jænberht and the Kentish nation, attempted to divert the seat of this honourable dignity and split it into two provinces, and your most holy fellow-bishop and predecessor Hadrian at the request of that king essayed to do what no man had presumed to do before, and honoured the bishop of the Mercians with the pallium. Not that we blame 8 either of them, and both, we are confident, are crowned by Christ with victory everlasting. None the less, we humbly beseech your Excellency, who have deservedly received from God the key of wisdom, to make enquiry into this matter with your wise counsellors, and be so good as to write back to us of the order which you think we should maintain in future, that Christ's seamless tunic may suffer no rent from any difference between us, but may be directed by your sound doctrine to the unity of true peace, as we desire it should. For it is with great humility and love, most blessed father, that we write thus to you, urgently beseeching you of your mercy to reply in kindness and justice to the considerations which of necessity we put before you.

'Deign moreover, we beseech you, in loving duty to peruse the letter 9 which Archbishop Æthelheard together with all the bishops of our province wrote to you in detail concerning the problems and needs of himself and of all Britain, and whatsoever is demanded by the rule of faith in relation to the things therein written, forget not to make known to us by the written word of truth. For this cause I despatched a mission last year from myself and the bishops under Abbot Wada; but after receiving his mission, he conducted it slothfully and even without understanding. But now, in love towards you, I send with this letter, beloved father, a modest present, by the hand of the priest Bryne and of Fildas and Ceolberht my servants, to wit one hundred and twenty mancuses, beseeching you to receive them kindly and to grant us your benediction. May almighty God long preserve you in health to the praise of His holy Church.'

89. 'Domino excellentissimo filio Kenulfo regi Mertiorum prouintiae Saxoniae Leo papa.

'Veniens ad sacratissima limina beatorum apostolorum Petri et Pauli, tam orationis uota fideliter soluens quamque[a] nostrae apostolicae sedi causam sui sacerdotii suggerens, reuerentissimus et sanctissimus frater noster Ethelardus archiepiscopus Dorobernensis aecclesiae obtulit nobis uestrae regalis excellentiae sillabas; quibus in duabus epistolis a uobis directis, plenis fidei rectae, magnam humilitatem uestram reperientes omnipotenti Deo referimus grates, qui uestram prudentissimam excellentiam in omnibus ornauit ac decorauit erga beatum Petrum apostolorum principem et nobiscum habere dilectionem et in omnibus apostolicis humiliter consentire censuris. Porro in una ex illis epistolis repperimus qualiter gratia nostrae apostolicae functionis, si iuxta fuissetis, animam uestram pro nobis posuissetis benigne; immo et nostrae prosperitati multum in Domino congaudeatis, et, quando nostrae dulcissimae ammonitionis litterae ad uestrae unanimitatis[b] perueniunt aures, cum omni suauitate cordis et[c] gaudio spirituali, quasi filii paternum munus, suscipere fatemini. Ferebatur[d] uero et hoc, quod aliquantulam[e] ex uestra facultate benedictionem nobis offerri demandastis, id est centum uiginti mancusas, quas cum magno amore pro animae uestrae salute suscepimus. Et predictus archiepiscopus cum sotiis suis honorifice ac benigne a nobis susceptus est, et adiuuari eum in suis necessitatibus libenter fecimus.[f] Interea credentes uestrae prudentissimae excellentiae, ubi ferebatur in ipsis tuis regalibus apicibus quod nostris apostolicis sanctionibus nullus Christianus contraire presumit, ideo totis nisibus nostris ea quae tuo regno expediunt emittere atque predicare conamur, ut ea quae uobis prelatus frater noster[g] Ethelardus archiepiscopus, seu tota sinodus euangelicae atque apostolicae doctrinae sanctorumque patrum necnon predecessorum sanctorum nostrorum pontificum, canonica censura predicante, uestrae regali excellentiae seu cunctis principibus gentis uestrae et uniuerso populo Dei edisserit, nequaquam in orthodoxa eorum doctrina quippiam resistere debeatis, Domino ac Redemptore nostro in euangelio dicente, ubi ait: "Qui uos recipit, me recipit; et qui recipit prophetam in nomine prophetae, mercedem prophetae accipiet."[1] Quanto magis pro

---

[a] quam B   [b] humanitatis TtTc, humilitatis Tp   [c] de T+   [d] ferebatur T+ (cf. below); fatebatur ACB   [e] aliquantulum CB   [f] fecimus libenter T+   [g] uester B

89. 'Pope Leo to the most excellent lord, his son Cenwulf, king of the Mercians in the province of Saxony.

'On his arrival at the most holy threshold of the blessed Apostles Peter and Paul, where he both duly paid the vows of his devotion and brought to our Apostolic See the matter of his priestly office, our most reverend and right holy brother Æthelheard, archbishop of Canterbury, delivered to us a missive from your excellent Majesty, wherein were two letters from you, full of true faith, in which we saw how great is your humility. For this cause we give thanks to almighty God, who has in all things adorned and perfected your excellent wisdom, to make you bear love just as we do towards St Peter, prince of the Apostles, and in all things humbly to accept the mandates of the Holy See. Moreover, in one of your letters we discovered, how for the sake of our Apostolic office you would, had you been at hand, have laid down your life in our behalf, of your charity; and further, how you rejoice greatly in the Lord to hear of our prosperity, and how, when our letter full of most kindly counsel is read before you in your sincere affection, you confess that you receive it with all gladness of heart and spiritual joy, as a son receives a present from his father. We read this also, that you have given orders for some small beneficence out of your own abundance to be offered to us, to wit one hundred and twenty mancuses, which we have accepted with deep affection for your soul's health. And the aforesaid archbishop, with his company, was honourably and kindly received by us, and we gladly caused him to be given aid in his necessity. For the time, putting our faith as we do in your excellent wisdom displayed in the statement in your Majesty's own letter that no Christian presumes to act contrary to our Apostolic decrees, we therefore essay with all our strength to publish and utter only such things as are expedient for your kingdom. Whatsoever therefore is laid down by our brother and your prelate, Archbishop Æthelheard, and the whole body of evangelical and apostolic doctrine, and that of the holy Fathers and our predecessors, by canonical authority, for your royal Excellency and all the magnates of your realm and the whole people of God, this ought you never to resist in anything, so long as their doctrine remains orthodox, remembering the words of our Lord and Redeemer in the Gospel, when He says: "He that receiveth you, receiveth me; and he that receiveth a prophet in the name of a prophet shall receive a prophet's reward."[1] How much

---

[1] Matt. 10: 40–1.

ipso sepe dicto archiepiscopo, quem nobis ualde nimisque collaudastis, sicuti et est uidelicet clarissimus, *ᵃdignissimus, carissimusᵃ* atque peritissimus, et quia illum scitis prudentem, bonis ornatum moribus, Deoque et hominibus dignum, ecce, fili dulcissime et amantissime atque prestantissime, rex bone, in his tuis assertionibus collaudamus Deum omnipotentem, qui talem uobis demonstrauit antistitem qui, sicut uerus pastor, indicere uerbis secundum doctrinam sanctarum Scripturarum dignam penitentiam ualet, et eruere, qui sub ditione sacerdotali eius existunt,ᵇ animas eorum ex inferno inferiore et ab igne inextinguibili, deducens eos et infra ducens in portum salutis, et offerre pro illis hostiam dignam et immaculatam in conspectu diuinae maiestatis omnipotenti Deo.

5 'Et quia multum nobis prenominatus archiepiscopus in omni sanctitate sua et uitae conuersatione ultro citroque placuit, ualde nimis ei credentes, ex auctoritate ei beati Petri apostolorum principis, cuius uel immeriti uices gerimus, talem prebuimus presulatum ut, si quispiam ex subiectis suis, tam regibus et principibus quamque uniuerso populo, transgressus fuerit Dominica mandata, excommunicet eum usque peniteat et, si impenitens fuerit, sit uobis sicut ethnicus et publi-
6 canus. De uero Ethelardo iam factoᶜ archiepiscopo Dorobernensis aecclesiae, sicut aᵈ nobis poposcit uestrorum presulum excellentia ut ei iustitiam faceremusᵉ de ipsis diocesibus suis tam episcoporum quamqueᶠ monasteriorumᵍ quibus illicite, ut uosʰ cognouistis, expoliatus est, et a uenerabili sede eius quas dudum tenuit ablatae sunt, nos per omnia enucleatius trutinantes in sacro scrinio nostro repperimus sanctum Gregorium predecessorem nostrumⁱ in integro ipsam parrochiam numero duodecim beato Augustino sincello suo archiepiscopo tradidisse et confirmasse episcopos consecrandi. Vnde et nos, ueritate ipsa reperta, ordinatione seu confirmationeʲ nostra apostolica auctoritate eas illi in integro, sicut antiquitus fuerunt, constituentes reddidimus, et priuilegium confirmationis secundum sacrorum canonum censuram aecclesiae suae obseruandum tradidimus.'

90. Offa interea, ne sibi fraudi forent dure in prouintiales admissa, undique amicos reges uenans pacemque concilians, Brihtrico regi Westsaxonum filiam Edelburgamᵏ nuptum dedit. Karolum Magnum

ᵃ⁻ᵃ om. CB (but cf. GP p.19)   ᵇ *B adds* et   ᶜ *fato AlCsBk, perhaps rightly*   ᵈ *om. A*   ᵉ *om. T⁺*   ᶠ *quam T⁺Bc*   ᵍ *monachorum T⁺*   ʰ *om. A*   ⁱ *T⁺A add* in ipsa sancta sede omnia. *The following words seem corrupt.*   ʲ *ordinationem seu confirmationem B*   ᵏ *Properly* Edburgam

more for the sake of the archbishop himself, whom you have so warmly commended to us as a man of great distinction, worth, amiability, and experience (which indeed he is), and one whom you know to be prudent and of high character, and pleasing to God and man: behold, my most dear and beloved and distinguished son, excellent king, in respect of these your asseverations we praise almighty God who has vouchsafed you such a prelate, who like a true shepherd is able to declare unto you by his words in accordance with the doctrine of the Holy Scriptures a proper penitence, and to save the souls of those who are set beneath his priestly regimen from the nethermost hell and from the fire that is not quenched, bringing them safe into the harbour of salvation, and to offer for them to almighty God a sacrifice worthy and unspotted in the sight of the divine Majesty.

'And inasmuch as the aforesaid archbishop in all his holiness and religious way of life has been in every way most pleasing to us, we, reposing great trust in him, have by the authority of St Peter prince of the Apostles, whose vicegerent albeit unworthy we are, granted unto him the episcopal power following: that if any of those who are subject unto him, be they kings and princes or the people as a whole, transgress the commandment of God, the archbishop should excommunicate him until he repents, and if he remain impenitent, he should be to you as a gentile and a publican. As for Æthelheard the archbishop of the church of Canterbury that now is, whereas your excellent bishops have demanded of us that we should see justice done him in respect of those jurisdictions, be they over bishops or monasteries, of which he has, as you know, been unlawfully despoiled, and which have been taken away from his venerable see, by which they have long been held; now therefore we, having thoroughly weighed the whole question, have discovered in our sacred registry that our predecessor St Gregory delivered and confirmed to the blessed Archbishop Augustine, his associate, the entire province with twelve suffragans, and the right to consecrate them(?). For which cause we too, having discovered the truth, by this our confirmation of privilege by Apostolic authority have restored them to him in their entirety as they were of old, and delivered this privilege and confirmation to his church to be observed according to the verdict of the sacred canons(?).'

90. Offa meanwhile went seeking friendly princes everywhere and concluding treaties of peace, in order to escape the consequences of his harsh treatment of his subjects. He gave his daughter Eadburh in

regem Francorum frequentibus legationibus amicum parauit, quanuis non facile quod suis artibus conduceret in Karoli animo inuenerit; discordarant antea, adeo ut magnis motibus utrobique concurrentibus etiam negotiatorum commeatus prohiberentur. Est epistola Albini huiusce rei index, cuius partem hic apponam, documentum ingens magnanimitatis et fortitudinis Karoli, qui omnem aetatem triuerit in bellis contra paganos Deo rebelles.

91. 'Antiqui' inquit 'Saxones et omnes Fresonum populi instante rege Karolo, alios premiis et alios minis sollicitante, ad fidem Christi conuersi sunt; sed anno transacto idem rex cum exercitu irruit super Sclauos, eosque subegit suae ditioni. Auares, quos nos Hunos dicimus, exarserunt in Italiam et, a ducibus prefati regis Christianis[a] superati, domum cum obprobrio reuersi sunt. Similiter et super Baugariam irruerunt, qui et ipsi ab exercitu Christiano superati et dispersi sunt. Etiam et eiusdem Christianissimi regis duces et tribuni multam partem Hispaniae tulerunt a Saracenis quasi trecenta milia in longum per maritima. Sed heu proh dolor, quod idem maledicti Saraceni, qui et Agareni, tota dominantur Affrica et Asia Maiori maxima ex parte. Nescio quid de nobis uenturum sit: aliquid enim dissensionis, diabolico fomento inflammante, nuper inter regem Karolum et regem Offam exortum est, ita ut utrimque nauigatio interdicta negotiantibus cesset. Sunt qui dicant nos pro pace esse in illas partes mittendos.'[1]

92. In his uerbis, preter illa quae superius notaui,[2] poterit curiosus animaduertere quantum iam annorum effluxerit ex quo Saraceni Affricam et Asiam Maiorem inuaserint.[b] Et profecto, nisi Dei clementia ingenitum robur Francorum imperatorum animasset, pridem Europam etiam[c] subiugassent: adeo contemptis imperatoribus Constantinopolitanis Siciliam et Sardiniam et Baleares insulas et pene omnes terras quae pelago cinguntur, preter Cretam et Rodum[d] et Ciprum, occupauerant. Sed nostris diebus per Normannos Siciliam, per Pisanos Corsicam et Sardiniam, per Francos et omnis generis ex Europa Christianos magnam partem Asiae et ipsam Ierusalem relinquere coacti

---

[a] Christiani *Aac; but William seems to merge two phrases of Alcuin,* a ducibus regis praefati *and* a Christianis   [b] inuaserunt *TpTcB*   [c] om. *A*   [d] Rodum et Cretam *C*

[1] Alcuin, *Ep.* vii (p. 32. 7–11, 14–20, and 25–8).

marriage to Brihtric king of the West Saxons. He also secured by frequent embassies the friendship of Charlemagne king of the Franks, although he could not easily find in Charles's character anything sympathetic to his own mode of proceeding. They had previously disagreed so sharply that there was much disturbance on both sides, and even the passage of merchants was suspended. There is a letter from Alcuin which shows this, and I will add part of it here, for it is a remarkable tribute to the greatness of mind and the courage of Charles, who spent his whole life in fighting pagans rebelling against God.

91. 'The Old Saxons', he says, 'and all the Frisian tribes, under pressure from King Charles, who approached some with presents and some with threats, have been converted to the faith of Christ; and last year he also invaded the Slavs and brought them under his rule. The Avars, whom we call Huns, flared up against Italy, but were defeated by the Christian generals of that same king, and returned home in disgrace. In the same way they invaded Bavaria, and there too they were defeated and scattered by the army of the Christians. Furthermore, the generals and captains of that same most Christian king freed a great part of Spain from the Saracens, in length about three hundred miles along the sea coast; but, to our shame be it said, those accursed Saracens, who are also called Hagarenes, still rule the whole of Africa and a great part of Asia Major. I know not what will become of us, for strife, inflamed by the devil, has lately broken out between King Charles and King Offa, to such an extent that the passage of merchants on both sides is forbidden and has come to a stop. Some people say that I am likely to be sent into those parts on a mission of peace.'[1]

92. In these words, besides the points I have already touched on,[2] the curious reader will be able to notice also how many years have now elapsed since the Saracens invaded Africa and Asia Major. Indeed, had not the Divine Mercy aroused the native might of the Frankish emperors, they would long ago have overrun Europe as well; for they thought little of the emperors of Constantinople and had occupied Sicily, Sardinia, and the Balearic Islands, and almost all the sea-girt territories except Crete, Rhodes, and Cyprus. In our time, however, they have been forced to abandon Sicily by the Normans, Corsica and Sardinia by the Pisans, and the great part of Asia, with Jerusalem itself, by the

---

[2] An allusion to the last sentence of c. 90.

sunt; de quibus quia in sequentibus*[a] [1] amplior erit narrandi locus, nunc ex uerbis Karoli fedus firmum inter eum et Offam compactum subitiam.

93. 'Karolus, gratia Dei[b] rex Francorum et Longobardorum et patritius Romanorum, uiro uenerando et fratri carissimo Offae regi Mertiorum salutem.

'Primo gratias agimus omnipotenti Deo[c] de catholicae fidei sinceritate quam in uestris laudabiliter paginis reperimus exaratam. De peregrinis uero, qui pro amore Dei et salute animarum suarum beatorum apostolorum limina desiderant adire, cum pace sine omni perturbatione[d] uadant; sed si aliqui non religioni seruientes sed lucra sectantes inueniantur inter eos, locis oportunis statuta soluant thelonea. Negotiatores quoque uolumus ut ex mandato nostro patrocinium habeant in regno nostro legitime; et si in aliquo loco iniusta affligantur oppressione, reclament se ad nos uel nostros iudices, et plenam iubebimus iustitiam fieri. Cognoscat quoque dilectio uestra quod aliquam benignitatem de dalmaticis nostris uel palliis ad singulas sedes episcopales regni uestri uel Ethelredi direximus in elemosinam domni apostolici Adriani, deprecantes ut pro eo intercedi iubeatis, nullam habentes dubitationem beatam illius animam in requie esse, sed ut fidem et dilectionem ostendamus in amicum nobis carissimum. Sed et de thesauro humanarum rerum, quem Dominus Iesus nobis gratuita pietate concessit, aliquid per metropolitanas ciuitates direximus, uestrae quoque dilectioni unum balteum et unum gladium Huniscum et duo pallia serica.'[2]

94. Haec saltuatim uerba epistolae decerpens iccirco apposui, ut posteris elucescat amicitia Offae et Karoli; cuius familiaritate fretus, licet multorum impeteretur odio, dulci tamen uitam consumpsit otio, et Egferthum filium, ante mortem suam in regem inunctum, successorem dimisit. Ille, sedulo paternae immanitatis uestigia declinans, priuilegia omnium aecclesiarum quae seculo suo genitor attenuauerat prona deuotione reuocauit. Predium quoque, quod pater Malmesberiae abstulerat, reddidit in manu Cuthberti, tunc illius loci abbatis, hortatu

---

[a] consequentibus *A* [b] gratia Dei *om. A* [c] *Tp adds* et salute animarum *(from below); hence* et saluatori animarum *Tt, de* salute animarum *Tc* [d] turbatione *A*

[1] cc. 343–89.
[2] Alcuin, *Ep.* c (pp. 145. 1–3, 12–13, 16–25; 146. 1–12), with some adaptation and abbreviation.

Franks and European Christians of every kind. As there will be more room to tell of this in what follows,[1] I will now subjoin in Charles's own words the firm treaty made between himself and Offa.

93. 'Charles, by the grace of God king of the Franks and Lombards and patrician of the Romans, to the venerable Offa, his dearest brother, king of the Mercians, greeting.

'We give thanks to almighty God first of all for the sincerity of the Catholic faith which we find so admirably expressed in your letter. As for the pilgrims, who for the love of God and the salvation of their souls desire to approach the threshold of the blessed Apostles, let them make their way in peace without let or hindrance; but if any are found among them who are not in the service of religion but pursue their own profit, let them pay the appointed tolls at the appropriate places. Merchants also we wish to have lawful protection in this our realm in accordance with our command; and if in any place they are unjustly oppressed and afflicted, let them make their complaint to us or to our judges, and we will give orders that full justice be done them. We would have you know, dear brother, that we have sent some offering in the way of our dalmatics and palls to all the episcopal sees in your kingdom and that of Æthelred as alms for our lord Pope Hadrian, begging you to ordain intercession to be made for him; not that we have any doubts that his blessed soul is at rest, but we wish to show our love and loyalty towards our dearest friend. Moreover, from the treasure of wealth in this world vouchsafed to us of His free generosity by our Lord Jesus, we have sent something for the metropolitan cities; and to you, our brother, a baldric and a Hunnish sword and two robes of silk.'[2]

94. I have extracted these words from the letter, with some omissions, and have set them down here, in order to make clear to posterity the friendship between Offa and Charles. Relying on this relationship, Offa, although the object of many men's hatred, ended his days in peace and comfort, had his son Ecgfrith anointed king before his own death, and left him as his heir. Ecgfrith was careful to desert the path of cruelty trodden by his father, and with humble devotion reinstated all the privileges of the churches, which his father in his time had whittled down. The estate which his father had taken from Malmesbury he gave back into the hand of Cuthbert, the then abbot,

Ethelardi archiepiscopi Cantuariae, strenui sane et Deo digni uiri, quem abbatem*ᵃ* ibi fuisse ante Cuthbertum*ᵇ* constans opinio asseuerat.*ᶜ* Itaque cum spes egregiae indolis primis annis Egferthi adoleret, seua mors uernantis aetatis florem messuit, unde Osberto patritio Albinus: 'Non arbitror quod nobilissimus iuuenis Egferthus propter peccata sua mortuus sit, sed quia pater suus pro confirmatione regni eius multum sanguinem effudit.'[1] Post quattuor ergo menses regni excedens, Kenulfum, quinto genu nepotem Pendae ex fratre Kenwalkio, regem constituit.

95. Kenulfus, inprimis magnus uir et uirtutibus famam supergrediens, nichil quod liuor digne carperet umquam admisit,*ᵈ* domi religiosus, in bello uictoriosus; *ᵉ*uir cuius laudes merito nitentur in altum,[2] quam diu aequus arbiter in Anglia inuenietur, laudandus cum regni sullimitate, tum mentis humilitate, qua enituit amplissime quando (ut supra diximus)[3] dignitatem Cantuariae labefactatam*ᶠ* refecit, parum fatiens rex mundanum in sua prouintia supercilium, dummodo anti-
2 quitus statutum non transgrederetur tramitem canonum.*ᵉ* Contra Cantuaritas successiuum ab Offa suscipiens odium, regionem illam ualide afflixit, regemque*ᵍ* eorum Edbrihtum cognomine Pren uinctum abduxit; sed non multo post, humana miseratione mollitus, soluendum curauit. Nam apud Wincelcumbam, ubi aecclesiam, quae adhuc superest, Deo exedificauerat,*ʰ* ipsa dedicationis*ⁱ* die regem captiuum ad altare*ʲ* manumittens libertate palpauit, memorabile clementiae suae spectaculum exhibens. Aderat ibidem munificentiae regiae applausor
3 Cuthredus, quem ille Cantuaritis regem prefecerat. Sonabat basilica plausibus, platea fremebat discursibus, quod ibi in conuentu tredecim episcoporum, decem ducum, nullus largitatis pateretur repulsam, omnes suffarcinatis marsupiis abirent; nam preter illa xenia quae magnates susceperant, inestimabilis scilicet pretii et numeri in utensilibus, uestibus, equis electissimis,*ᵏ* omnibus qui agros non habebant libram argenti, presbiteris mancam auri, monachis solidum unum, postremo toti populo multa erogauit. Idem monasterium*ˡ* cum magnis redditibus, quantum hoc tempore incredibile uideatur, ampliasset, uicesimo quarto regni anno funere suo honorauit. Filius eius Kenelmus, puer

ᵃ om. B   *ᵇ* om. T⁺   *ᶜ* T⁺A add hoc argumenti assumens, quod defunctum se eo loci tumulari fecerit   *ᵈ* T⁺ adds dum   *ᵉ⁻ᵉ* om. T⁺   *ᶠ* labefactam B   *ᵍ* regem B   *ʰ* edificauerat T⁺AaBk, perhaps rightly   *ⁱ* edificationis B   *ʲ* ad altare om. T⁺   *ᵏ* dilectissimis B   *ˡ* monasteriorum T⁺

[1] Alcuin, Ep. cxxii (p. 179. 16–18).   [2] Unidentified.   [3] Cf. cc. 87–9.

encouraged by Æthelheard archbishop of Canterbury, an energetic and holy man whom tradition uniformly asserts to have been abbot there before Cuthbert [T⁺A *add* using as proof the fact that he had himself buried there on his death]. So in Ecgfrith's early years great hopes were entertained of his noble nature, and it was a cruel death that plucked this flower in the springtide of his youth; as Alcuin says in a letter to Osberht the patrician: 'I do not think that noble young man Ecgfrith has died on account of his own sins, but because his father for the establishment of his kingdom shed so much blood.'[1] Dying thus after a reign of four months, he made Cenwulf king, who was Penda's nephew in the fifth generation through his brother Cenwealh.

95. Cenwulf was a man of outstanding distinction, whose merits were greater even than his reputation, and never exposed himself to carping by any lapse; pious at home and victorious in the field, 'his praise deservedly shall upward swell'[2] as long as an impartial judge is to be found in this country. This praise he earned not only by the splendour of his reign, but also by his personal humility, never seen more clearly than in his restoration of the shaken dignity of Canterbury, of which we have told above;[3] king as he was, he made light of his own worldly eminence in his kingdom, provided he did not transgress the old-established precepts of the canons. Inheriting from Offa a traditional hostility towards the men of Kent, he made that province suffer, carrying off in chains their king, Eadberht Præn. Not long after, however, pitying a fellow creature, he had him released; for on the actual dedication-day of the church he had built at Winchcombe, which still exists, he gave the king his liberty, manumitting him at the high altar—it was a wonderful exhibition of his natural clemency. Cuthred, whom he had set up as king of Kent, was there to applaud this act of regal generosity. The church resounded with applause, and great was the to-and-fro in the streets; for there, in the presence of thirteen bishops and ten thegns, no man met with a denial of Cenwulf's generosity, but all went home with full purses. Besides his gifts to the magnates, of inestimable number and value—dishes, raiment, horses of the choicest breeds,—each landless man received a pound of silver, each priest a mancus of gold, each monk a shilling, and many presents were given to the whole people. Having enriched that monastery with great revenues, on a scale that now seems incredible, in the twenty-fourth year of his reign he paid it the final honour of being buried there. His son Kenelm, who, when still a

admodum a sorore Quendrida innocue cesus nomenque et decus martirii adeptus, ibidem pausat.

96. Post illum regnum Mertiorum nutabundum*a* et (ut ita dicam) exsangue nichil quod littera dignetur comminisci habuit;*b* sed ne quis nos arguat semimutilatam historiam interrumpere, regum succedentium nomina transcurram. Celwlfus frater Kenulfi uno anno regnans, altero a Bernulfo*c* expulsus est. Bernulfus, tertio regni anno ab Egbirhto rege Westsaxonum uictus et fugatus, mox ab Orientalibus Anglis occisus est, quod ille Orientalem Angliam, ut debitum Mertiis*d* regnum *e*a tempore Offae, inuadere temptasset.*e* Ludekanius ab eisdem Anglis post biennem potestatem ultionem antecessoris animo intendens 2 oppressus est. Wihtlafius, in initio regni ab eodem Egbirhto sub iugum missus, regnauit annis tredecim, et illi et filio capitis et pecuniarum tributa persoluens. Eadem sorte Berhtwlfus tredecim regnans annis, nouissime a piratis Danorum ultra mare fugatus est. Burhredus, accepta Ethelswida filia regis Adulfi filii Egbirhti, affinitate illius et uectigalium pensionem et hostium depredationem consolatus est; sed post uiginti duos annos*f* ab eisdem patria deturbatus Romam diffugit, ibique apud Scolam Anglorum in aecclesia sanctae Mariae tumulatus 3 est. Vxor eius tunc quidem in patria residens, sed postea uirum secuta, apud Papiam extremam sortem incurrit. Tunc regnum illud a Danis cuidam Celwlfo Burhredi ministro traditum, et ne ultra placitum retineret sacramento firmatum, post paucos annos Elfredus nepos Egbirhti obtinuit. Ita principatus Mertiorum, qui per tumidam gentilis uiri insaniam subito effloruit, tunc per miseram semiuiri regis ignauiam omnino emarcuit, anno Dominicae incarnationis octingentesimo septuagesimo quinto.

97. *g*Sed quia quattuor potentissima regna huc usque non exiliter (ut arbitror), quantum lectio maiorum suggessit, perarauit stilus, nunc, ut in proemio dixi,[1] Orientalium Anglorum et Orientalium Saxonum principatum idem post aliorum terga percurret. Namque posterius regno Cantuaritarum sed prius regno Westsaxonum pullulauit regnum Orientalium Anglorum. Primus ergo, idemque maximus,

---

a mutabundum *CsBkBc²*　　*b* meruit *B*　　*c* ab Ernulfo *Tc(corr. to* ab Ber-*)AlBk;* ab Arnulfo *Bc*　　*d* Mercii *T*⁺　　*e-e* om. *Tt(s.l.* repeteret*)Tp;* inuaserit *Tc*　　*f* post uicesimo secundo anno *T*⁺　　*g-g* (p. 148) om. *T*⁺

[1] i pr. 5.

small child, was killed without cause on his part by his sister Cwenthryth and was rewarded with the name and glory of a martyr, is also buried there.

96. After him the kingdom of the Mercians, tottering and as if deprived of its life-blood, offers no features worthy of record; only, to escape the charge of leaving my history half mutilated, I will run through the names of succeeding kings. Cenwulf's brother Ceolwulf reigned for one year and in the next was driven out by Beornwulf. Beornwulf in the third year of his reign was defeated and driven out by Ecgberht king of the West Saxons, and shortly after was killed by the East Angles, having attempted to invade their territory as dependent, since Offa's time, on the Mercians. Ludeca reigned for two years, and then attempted to avenge his predecessor, and like him was defeated by the East Angles. Wiglaf, who at the beginning of his reign had been similarly humiliated by Ecgberht, ruled for thirteen years, paying tribute in men(?) and cattle(?) to him and to his son. Berhtwulf ruled in similar conditions for thirteen years, and finally was driven overseas by Danish pirates. Burgred married Æthelswith, daughter of King Æthelwulf the son of Ecgberht, and by this alliance found relief both from the payment of tribute and from the depredations of the enemy; but after twenty-two years the same enemies drove him from his country, and he fled to Rome, where he was buried in the church of St Mary in the Schola Anglorum. His wife remained for the time in her native land, but later followed her husband, and met her end at Pavia. The Danes then handed over the kingdom to a certain Ceolwulf, one of Burgred's servants, exacting an oath that he would not hold it longer than their good pleasure; but a few years later it was seized by Ecgberht's grandson Alfred. Thus the principate of the Mercians, having burst into sudden blossom through the vaunting madness of an heroic pagan, now withered and died through the pitiful weakness of a king who was less than a man, in the year of our Lord 875.

97. Hitherto I have described, in some fullness I think, as far as the study of my predecessors allowed, the four most powerful kingdoms; and now, as I said in my preface,[1] I will, to bring up the rear, review the princedoms of the East Angles and East Saxons; for the kingdom of the East Angles grew up later than the kingdom of Kent, but earlier than that of the West Saxons. The first and greatest king,

apud Orientales Anglos rex fuit Redwaldus, a Wodenio (ut scribunt) decimum genu nactus: omnes quippe australes Anglorum et Saxonum prouintiae citra Humbram fluuium cum suis regibus eius nutum spec-
2 tabant. Hic est ille quem superior relatio non tacuit[1] Ethelfridum regem Northanimbrorum pro Eduini fauore trucidasse. Idem suadente eodem Eduino baptizatus, consilio uxorio postmodum a fide desciuit. At uero filius eius Eorpwaldus, incorruptam Christianitatem complexus, inuiolatum spiritum Deo effudit, a Ricberto gentili innocenter peremptus. Huic Sigbertus successit, uir Deo dignus, frater eius ex matre omnemque barbariem pro Francorum nutritura exutus; namque a[a] Redwaldo in exilium actus, eorumque diu contubernio frui-
3 tus, sacramenta Christianitatis assumpserat. Quae potestate initiatus regno suo toti dignanter infudit, scolasque etiam litterarum per loca instituit; quod pro magno certe debet predicari, ut litterarum dulcedinem per eum experirentur homines agrestes antea et fanatici. Adiutor religionis fuit et studiorum incentor Felix episcopus, Burgundiae oriundus, qui nunc Ramesiae requiescit. Porro Sigbertus, seculo renuntians monachicaeque tonsurae compos, Egrico cognato thronum reliquit; cum quo a Penda rege Mertiorum sotiali bello appetitus mortem oppetiit, cum fortior ipse malis et professionis non immemor
4 uirgam tantum manu gestaret. Successor Egrici Anna, filius Eni[b] fratris Redwaldi, eodem furente Penda simili inuolutus exitio, gloriosae propaginis numerositate felix eminuit, sicut secundus liber suo loco insinuabit.[2] Successit[c] Annae frater eius Ethelhere, occisusque[d] est a rege Northanimbrorum Oswio cum Penda merito, quod ei concurreret in auxilium et fulciret exercitum qui pessumdedisset fratrem et cognatum. Huius successor frater Ethelwaldus continuatis successionibus
5 regnum reliquit eiusdem Ethelherii filiis Aldulfo et Elcwoldo.[e][3] His Beorna, huic quoque Ethelredus successit; huius fuit filius sanctus Ethelbrihtus, quem Offa rex Mertiorum dolose interemit, ut dictum est et dicetur posterius.[4] Pauci post eum in Orientali Anglia regnauerunt potentes usque ad sanctum Edmundum pro uiolentia Mertiorum, qui anno regni sui sexto decimo ab Hinguar pagano peremptus est. Ex quo in Orientali Anglia desiere regnare Angli annis quinquaginta: nouennio enim sine rege paganis uastantibus prouintia subiacuit, post

[a] ad *Aap*, om. *Al* [b] om. *CBk* [c] sucsit *Al*, successor *Aa* [d] occisus *A* [e] Elsewhere Ælfwold(us)

[1] 47. 5.
[2] 214. 1–2.
[3] i.e. Ælfwald.
[4] cc. 86, 210.

then, among the East Angles was Rædwald, who is recorded to have been tenth in descent from Woden; for all the southern provinces of the Angles and Saxons on this side the Humber, with their kings, looked to him as overlord. It was he who, as I have already recounted,[1] killed Æthelfrith king of the Northumbrians for Edwin's benefit. Edwin persuaded him to be baptized, but later he was won over by his wife to desert the faith. His son Earpwald embraced Christianity without blemish, and breathed out his soul to God unspotted, being killed in his innocence by a pagan called Ricberht. He was succeeded by Sigeberht, his half-brother on his mother's side, a devout Christian who had lost all traces of barbarism through being brought up in France; for having been driven into exile by Rædwald and spent a long time among the Franks, he had adopted the principles of the Christian religion; which on coming into power he duly diffused throughout his kingdom, also establishing schools in many places. This must certainly be accounted a great benefit, that through him the charms of literature should be brought within reach of men who were previously boorish and idolaters. He was helped in his religious work, and encouraged in his studies, by Bishop Felix, a native of Burgundy, who now rests at Ramsey. Eventually Sigeberht renounced the world and took the monastic tonsure, leaving the throne to his kinsman Ecgric. Then he was attacked in civil conflict by Penda king of the Mercians, and he and Ecgric both met their ends, though he was emboldened by his misfortunes and, mindful of his vows, carried no weapon but a staff. Ecgric's successor Anna, son of Rædwald's brother Eni, was similarly entangled in destruction by the rage of Penda, but was distinguished by the number and glory of his children as my second book shall tell in the proper place.[2] Anna was succeeded by his brother Æthelhere, who was deservedly killed by Oswiu king of the Northumbrians in company with Penda, because he had gone to Penda's assistance and was supporting the force that had killed his own brother and kinsman. His brother and successor Æthelwald left the kingdom in unbroken succession to Æthelhere's sons Aldwulf and Elcwold;[3] they were followed by Beonna, and Beonna by Æthelred. His son was St Æthelberht, who was treacherously killed by Offa king of the Mercians, as I have said before and shall have occasion to say again.[4] After him few men of any authority ruled in East Anglia on account of the violence of the Mercians, until King Edmund, who in the sixteenth year of his reign was killed by Hinguar, a pagan. Thereafter the Angles ceased to reign in East Anglia for fifty years: for nine years they were without a king, while the pagans dominated and laid waste

in ea et*a* in Orientali Saxonia Guthrum rex Danus regnauit annis duo-
6 decim tempore regis Elfredi. Guthrum habuit successorem aeque
Danum nomine Eohric, qui cum regnasset annis quattuordecim, peremptus est ab Anglis quod inciuiliter in eos egisset. Nec tamen libertas
eis assurrexit, Danorum*b* comitibus uel eos prementibus uel in Westsaxonum reges acuentibus, donec Eduardus filius Elfredi ambas
prouintias expulsis Danis, liberatis Anglis suo, id est Westsaxonico,
imperio adiecit, anno post occisionem sancti Edmundi quinquagesimo,
regni sui quinto decimo.

98. Eodem fere tempore quo cepit regnum Orientalium Anglorum,
surrexit*c* regnum Orientalium Saxonum; et habuere quidem Orientales
Saxones reges per successionem multos, sed aliis regibus et maxime
Mertiis subiectos. Primus igitur apud eos regnauit Sledda, a Wodenio
decimus. Eius filius Sebirhtus, nepos Ethelbirhti regis Cantuariorum
ex sorore Ricula, fidem Christi suscepit predicante Mellito, qui
primus Lundoniae fuit episcopus; ea enim urbs ad Orientales Saxones
spectat. Sebirhto mortuo, filii eius Sexredus et Sewardus Mellitum
expulerunt; nec multo post, a Westsaxonibus occisi, tirannidis in
Christum penas pependere. Succedens eis Sigbertus cognomento
Paruus, Sewardi filius, reliquit regnum Sigeberto, Sigebaldi filio, qui
2 fuerat frater Sebirhti. Is Sigebertus, hortatu regis Oswii in Northanimbria a Finano episcopo baptizatus, gentem suam ad fidem quam cum
Mellito abiecerant per episcopum Ceddum*d* reduxit, quique post gloriose amministratum regnum gloriosius reliquit, a propinquis interemptus quod, euangelici precepti sequax, hostibus serenus parceret, nec
delinquentes, si peniterent, rugato et duro uultu suspenderet. Post
eum frater Swithelmus regnauit, ab eodem Ceddo in Orientali Anglia
baptizatus. Eo mortuo, Sigherius filius Sigberti Parui et Sebbi filius
Sewardi regnum tenuerunt. Veruntamen Sebbi, sotio ante se defuncto,
ipse quoque tricesimo anno uoluntarie regno decessit, monachus, ut
Beda refert,[1] factus; filii eius Sigehardus et Seufredus*e* regnauerunt.
3 Illis defunctis, pauco tempore regnum moderatus est Offa filius
Sigherii, iuuenis iocundi uultus et animi, aetatis floridae, maximi apud
ciues amoris, qui hortatu Kineswidae Pendae filiae, cuius nuptias

a om. B   *b* B adds a   *c* successit C   *d* c(h)eddum C (cf. Ceddo below);
-dam AB   *e* Rightly Suefredus

[1] HE iv. 11.

the province; then Guthrum the Danish king ruled in both East Anglia and Essex for twelve years in King Alfred's time. Guthrum had as successor a Dane like himself, by name Eohric, who after a reign of fourteen years was killed by the Angles for his barbarous treatment of them; yet even so their freedom did not lift up its head, for the Danish jarls either oppressed them or made them fight against the kings of the West Saxons, until Alfred's son Edward, driving out the Danes and setting the English free, added both provinces to his own, that is, the West Saxon kingdom, in the fiftieth year after the martyrdom of St Edmund, which was the fifteenth of his own reign.

98. About the same time as the kingdom of the East Angles, arose also the kingdom of the East Saxons, and they had many kings in succession, though in subjection to other, mostly Mercian, kings. Sledd, tenth in descent from Woden, was the first to bear rule among them; his son Sæberht, nephew of Æthelberht king of Kent by his sister Ricula, adopted the Christian faith from the preaching of Mellitus, who was the first bishop of London; for London belongs to the East Saxons. On Sæberht's death, his sons Seaxred and Sæweard drove out Mellitus, and not long afterwards were killed by the West Saxons, thus paying the penalty for their violence against Christ. They were succeeded by Sæweard's son, Sigeberht called the Little, and he left the kingship to Sigeberht, son of Sæberht's brother Sigebald. This Sigeberht with encouragement from King Oswiu was baptized in Northumbria by Bishop Finan, and brought his people back by the hand of Bishop Cedd to the faith which they had driven out together with Mellitus. After a glorious reign, he won yet more glory by his death, being killed by his kinsmen because in obedience to the Gospel command he mildly forgave his enemies, and refused, so long as they repented, to regard sinners with harsh and frowning countenance. After him reigned his brother Swithhelm, who was baptized by the same Cedd in East Anglia, and on his death the throne passed to Sigehere son of Sigeberht the Little and Sebbi son of Sæweard. Sebbi, however, his partner having died before him, himself abdicated of his own accord, in his thirtieth year, and became a monk, as Bede records;[1] his sons Sigeheard and Swæfred reigned in his stead. On their deaths, the kingdom was governed for a short time by Sigehere's son Offa, a young man delightful in countenance and character, and in the flower of his youth, who was greatly loved by his subjects. He had hoped to marry Penda's daughter Cyneswith, but she taught him to set his

sperauerat, caelestes suspirare doctus amores, Romam cum Kenredo rege Mertiorum et beato Eguino episcopo Wicciorum[a] iuit, ibique attonsus caelica regna suo tempore subiuit. Illi successit Selredus, Sigeberti boni filius, triginta octo annis; quo perempto, principatus est Orientalibus Saxonibus Swithedus,[b] qui, eodem anno quo Cantuaritas Egbirhtus rex Westsaxonum debellauit, ab eodem expulsus regnum uacuefecit. Lundonia tamen cum circumiacentibus[c] regionibus Mertiorum regibus, quam diu ipsi imperitauerunt, paruit.

99. Dominabantur ergo reges Cantuaritarum proprie in Cantia, in qua[d] sunt hi episcopatus: archiepiscopatus Cantuariae, episcopatus Rofensis.

100. Reges Westsaxonum dominabantur in Wiltescire et Berkensi et Dorsatensi pagis, quibus est episcopus unus, cuius est modo sedes Salesberiae, quondam erat uel Ramesberiae uel Scireburnae. Et in Suthsexa, quae aliquanto tempore habuit proprium regem, eratque sedes episcopalis eius pagi antiquitus in Seleseo, quae est insula circumflua ponto, ut Beda narrat,[1] ubi etiam beatus Wilfridus monasterium construxit; nunc habitat episcopus apud Cicestram. Et in pagis Suthamtunensi et Sudreiensi, quibus est episcopus qui habet sedem Wintoniae. Et in pago Sumersetensi, qui habebat olim apud Wellas episcopum, qui nunc est Bathoniae. Et in Domnonia quae Deuenescire dicitur et in Cornubia quae nunc Cornugalliae dicitur, erantque tunc duo episcopatus, unus in Cridintune,[e] alter apud Sanctum Germanum; nunc est unus, et est sedes eius Exoniae.

101. Porro reges Mertiorum dominabantur in pagis his, Gloecestrensi Wigorniensi Warwicensi; in his est episcopus unus, cuius sedes est Wigorniae. Et in Cestrensi et in Derbensi,[f] Statfordensi; in his est episcopus unus, et habet partem Warwicensis et Scrobbesberiensis pagi, et est sedes apud Ciuitatem Legionum uel Couentreiam; quondam erat Licitfeldae. Et in Herefordensi, habeturque ibi[g] episcopus habens dimidium pagum Scrobbesberiae et partem Warwicensis et Gloecestrensis,[h] possidens sedem in Herefordo. Et in Oxenefordensi,

---

[a] Wiccio B   [b] Also known as Swithredus (cf. JW s.a. 758 and i. 263 Thorpe; but contrast i. 250 Thorpe)   [c] circa iacentibus B   [d] C; quo AB   [e] B adds et   [f] Bc adds et in   [g] om. B   [h] Bk(and Bc²ᵖ·ᶜ·), -ensi Bc; Gloecestr(a)e A; Gloeē Ce(and CpCdCr; what the scribe of Cs intended is unclear)

affections on things in Heaven, and he went to Rome with Cenred king of the Mercians and the saintly Ecgwine bishop of the Hwicce; there he took the tonsure and when his time was come entered the heavenly kingdom. His successor was Selred, son of Sigeberht the Good, who reigned for thirty-eight years; on his death Swithred became king of the East Saxons, but he was driven out by Ecgberht king of the West Saxons, in the year of Ecgberht's conquest of Kent, and left the throne vacant. London, however, with the country round remained obedient to the kings of the Mercians, as long as they themselves remained on the throne.

99. The kings of Kent, therefore, ruled peculiarly in Kent, in which are the following sees: the archbishopric of Canterbury and the bishopric of Rochester.

100. The kings of the West Saxons ruled in Wiltshire, Berkshire, and Dorset, having one bishop, whose seat is now at Salisbury, but was formerly at Ramsbury or Sherborne. Also in Sussex, which for some time had its own king. The episcopal seat of that county was of old at Selsey, an island surrounded by the sea, as Bede describes,[1] where St Wilfrid built a monastery; but the bishop now lives at Chichester. Also in Hampshire and Surrey, which have a bishop with his seat at Winchester. Also in Somerset, which once had a bishop at Wells, but now he lives at Bath. Also in Dumnonia, now called Devonshire, and Cornubia, now Cornwall. There were then two bishoprics there, one at Crediton and the other at St Germans; there is now one, with its seat at Exeter.

101. Further, the kings of the Mercians ruled in the following counties: Gloucestershire, Worcestershire, and Warwickshire. In these there is one bishop, with his seat at Worcester. Also in Cheshire, Derbyshire, and Staffordshire. In these there is one bishop, who has part of Warwickshire and Shropshire, and his seat is at the City of Legions or at Coventry, but was formerly at Lichfield. Also in Herefordshire, and there is a bishop there who has half Shropshire and part of Warwickshire and Gloucestershire, with his seat at Hereford. Also in Oxfordshire,

---

[1] *HE* iv. 13.

Buchingensi, Hurthfordensi, Huntendunensi, dimidia[a] Bedefordensi, Northamtunensi, Legecestrensi, Lincoliensi, quos regit episcopus qui modo habet sedem Lincoliae, quondam habebat apud Dorcecestram. Et in Legecestrensi Snotingensi, quorum Christianitas ad archiepiscopum Eboracensem spectat, habebaturque ibi olim proprius episcopus, cuius sedes erat apud Legecestram.

102. Reges Orientalium Anglorum dominabantur in pago Grantebrigensi, et est ibi episcopus cuius sedes est apud Heli. Et in Northfolke et Suthfolke, et est ibi episcopus, cuius sedes est apud Norwic, quondam erat apud Helman uel Tetford.

103. Reges Orientalium Saxonum dominabantur in Eastsexa et dimidia Hurthfordensi, habebaturque[b] ibi et habetur[c] episcopus Lundoniensis.

104. Reges Northanimbrorum dominabantur in omni regione quae est ultra Humbram fluuium usque ad Scottiam, erantque ibi archiepiscopus Eboracensis, episcopus Haugustaldensis et Ripensis, Lindisfarnensis, de Candida Casa; Haugustaldensis et Ripensis defecerunt, Lindisfarnensis translatus est in Dunelmum.

105. Hae erant partitiones regnorum, quanuis reges pro uicissitudine temporum modo hi modo illi terminos pretergrederentur pro fortitudine uel pro ignauia amitterent. Sed has omnes regnorum uarietates Egbirhtus animi magnitudine compescuit, et ea uni conquadrans[d] imperio ad uniforme dominium, seruans unicuique proprias leges, uocauit.[g] Quocirca quia, de recensitione[e] temporum fidem placitam absoluens,[1] ultra eius tempora excurri, hic figam metam primo uolumini, ut multifidus trames regnorum in unius Westsaxonici terminetur compendium.

[a] *One expects* dimidio. *But cf.* 103 Bc¹   [d] quadrans B   recenstuone
[b] *om.* A   [g] *See above, p.* 140 (sic)
[c] ibi habeturque BkBc², *om.*
[e] recensione TtTc(*and* Bc¹), Tp

[1] i   pr.   5.

Buckinghamshire, Hertfordshire, Huntingdonshire, half Bedfordshire, Northamptonshire, Leicestershire, and Lincolnshire. These are ruled by a bishop, whose seat is now at Lincoln, but was formerly at Dorchester. Also in Leicestershire and Nottinghamshire, in which the Church is subject to the archbishop of York; and they once had their own bishop, whose seat was at Leicester.

102. The kings of the East Angles ruled in the county of Cambridge; and there is a bishop there with his seat at Ely. Also in Norfolk and Suffolk; and there is a bishop there with his seat at Norwich, which once was at Elmham or Thetford.

103. The kings of the East Saxons ruled in Essex and half Hertfordshire; and there was there, and still is, a bishop at London.

104. The kings of the Northumbrians ruled over the whole region beyond the river Humber as far as Scotland. There were there the archbishop of York, and the bishops of Hexham and Ripon, Lindisfarne, Whithorn; those of Hexham and Ripon have come to an end, and the see of Lindisfarne is translated to Durham.

105. These were the divisions of the various kingdoms, although this king or that, as circumstances changed, overstepped their own boundaries if they were warlike, or losmbbbbt some of their territory if they were not. All these differences, however, between kingdom and kingdom were brought to an end by the great ability of Ecgberht; while preserving the laws proper to each kingdom, he fitted them all into a single monarchy, and brought them under uniform government. Now therefore, as in fulfilling my promise[1] to review the different periods I have run on beyond the days of Ecgberht, I will here fix the terminus of my first book, and bring the complex story of the kingdoms to a convenient end in the sole monarchy of the West Saxons.

LIBER SECVNDVS

Prologus libri secundi

DIV est quod et parentum cura et meapte diligentia libris insueui. Haec me uoluptas iam inde a pueritia cepit, haec illecebra mecum parilibus adoleuit annis; nam et*^a* ita a patre institutus eram ut, si ad diuersa declinarem studia, esset animae dispendium et famae periculum. Quocirca*^b* memor sententiae 'cupias quodcumque necesse est',[1] extorsi iuuentuti meae ut libenter uellem quod non uelle honeste non possem. Et multis quidem litteris impendi operam, sed aliis aliam. Logicam enim, quae armat eloquium, solo libaui auditu; phisicam, quae medetur ualitudini corporum, aliquanto pressius concepi; iam uero ethicae partes medullitus rimatus, illius maiestati assurgo, quod per se studentibus pateat et animos ad bene uiuendum componat; historiam precipue, quae iocunda quadam gestorum notitia mores condiens, ad bona sequenda uel mala cauenda legentes exemplis irritat. Itaque, cum domesticis sumptibus nonnullos exterarum gentium historicos conflassem, familiari otio querere perrexi si quid de nostra gente memorabile posteris posset reperiri. Hinc est quod, ab antiquo scriptis non contentus,*^c* ipse quoque scripturire incepi, non ut scientiam meam (quae pene nulla est) proponerem, sed ut res absconditas, quae in strue uetustatis latebant, conuellerem in lucem. Quapropter opiniones uolaticas despuens, cronica longe lateque corrogaui, sed nichil propemodum hac, fateor, profeci industria; omnibus enim decursis inops remansi scientiae, quippe ante non inueniens quod legerem quam lecturire desinerem.

2

3 Quaecumque uero de quattuor regnis ad liquidum edidici, primo libro indidi; in quibus, ut spero, non erubescet ueritas, etsi forte alicui suboriatur dubietas. Nunc usque ad aduentum Normannorum regni Westsaxonici monarchiam per succedentium inuicem regum genesim deducam. Quae si quis oculo bono uidere dignabitur, hanc sub fraterna caritate regulam teneat: si ista tantum ante nouerit, non fastidiat quod

---

^a om. Tt (ita et Tp), not unreasonably   *^b quod circa A*   *^c contemptus T'*

[1] Lucan iv. 487.

BOOK TWO

Prologue

IT IS many years since I formed the habit of reading, thanks to my parents' encouragement and my own bent for study. It has been a source of pleasure to me ever since I was a boy, and its charm grew as I grew. Indeed I had been brought up by my father to regard it as damaging to my soul and my good repute if I turned my attention in any other direction. I took good heed of the maxim 'Desire what you cannot avoid',[1] and made myself as a young man positively want what I could not properly help but want. I studied many kinds of literature, though in different degrees. To Logic, the armourer of speech, I no more than lent an ear. Physic, which cures the sick body, I went deeper into. As for Ethics, I explored parts in depth, revering its high status as a subject inherently accessible to the student and able to form good character; in particular I studied History, which adds flavour to moral instruction by imparting a pleasurable knowledge of past events, spurring the reader by the accumulation of examples to follow the good and shun the bad. So after I had spent a good deal of my own money on getting together a library of foreign historians, I proceeded in my leisure moments to inquire if anything could be discovered concerning England worth the attention of posterity. Not content with ancient works, I began to get the itch to write myself, not to show off my more or less non-existent erudition but in order to bring forcibly into the light things lost in the rubbish-heap of the past. Feeling an aversion to fleeting opinion, I collected chronicles from far and wide—almost, I confess, to no purpose: for when I had gone through them all I remained ignorant, not finding anything to read before I ceased to feel the urge to read it.

Still, whatever I could reliably learn of the four kingdoms I placed in Book 1: Truth, I hope, will not blush there, though Doubt may at times raise its head. Now I propose to take the story of the West Saxon monarchy down the generations of kings till I come to the arrival of the Normans. If there is anyone who will look favourably on my work, his brotherly charity should cleave to this principle: if he previously knew these things and no more, let him not scorn me for

scripserim; si plura didicerit, non succenseat quod non*a* dixerim; immo, dum uiuo, michi cognoscenda communicet, ut meo stilo apponantur saltem in margine quae non occurrerunt in ordine.

106. Superiori uolumini hic terminus obuenit, qui quattuor regna Britanniae in unum coartaret. Cuius potentiae auctor Egbirhtus, regis Inae de fratre Inigildo abnepos, amplo apud suos loco natus et ingenue educatus a pueritia inter Westsaxones emicuit. Continuatio uirtutum incendit inuidiam; et, quod fere a natura comparatum est ut reges iniquo intuitu aspitiant si quos in spem regni adolescere uideant, Brihtricus, ut predictum est,[1] suspectum habens memorandae indolis iuuenem, e medio tollere cogitabat. Quod Egbirhtus presentiens, ad Offam regem Mertiorum fuga lapsus est; quem dum ille sedula diligentia obumbraret, consecuti sunt Brihtrici nuntii, qui perfugam ad suplitium repeterent, habentes in manibus traditionis pretium. Accedebat quod suo regi filiae ipsius postulabant nuptias, ut genialis thori fedus perpetuas inter eos contineret amicitias. Ita Offa, qui bellicis minis non cederet, ad blanditias coniuente, Egbirhtus transnauigato mari Frantiam uenit. Quod Dei consilio factum intelligo, ut uir ille, ad tantum regnum electus, regnandi disciplinam a Francis acciperet. Est enim gens illa et exercitatione uirium et comitate morum cunctarum occidentalium facile princeps. Hac igitur contumelia*b* Egbirhtus ut cote usus est, qua detrita inertiae rubigine atiem mentis expediret et mores longe a gentilitia barbarie alienos indueret. Itaque defuncto Brihtrico, frequentibus suorum nuntiis Britanniam reuersus moxque imperare iussus, patriae desideriis satisfecit*c* anno Dominicae incarnationis octingentesimo, regnante in Frantia Karolo Magno anno tricesimo quarto, qui etiam duodecim annis superuixit. Interea Egbirhtus, cum clementia et mansuetudine subiectorum amorem redemisset, prima uirium documenta in Britannos qui eam insulae partem inhabitant*d* quae Cornugalliae dicitur dedit; quibus subiugatis, Aquilonales Britannos, qui a predictis brachio maris diuiduntur, tributarios fecit. Harum uictoriarum

---

a om. B   *b* contumatia A   *c* patefecit T'   *d* habitant C

[1] 43. 1.

writing them down; if he comes to know more, let him not be angry with me for not including it. Rather, let him share his information with me, while I yet live, so that my pen can at least add in the margin details that did not find a place in the text.

106. My first book found a natural end with the union of the four kingdoms of Britain into one. This powerful grouping was the work of Ecgberht, a great-great-nephew of King Ine as a descendant of his brother Ingild, who, being born to high rank among his own people and brought up as his birth required, came into prominence in Wessex from his boyhood. Unfailing excellence kindles the fire of jealousy, and it is almost a law of nature that kings should look askance at the rise of possible claimants to the throne; so Brihtric, as I have said already,[1] was suspicious of this young man's outstanding gifts, and was planning to get rid of him. Ecgberht, getting wind of this, made good his escape to the court of Offa king of the Mercians; but though Offa was at pains to give him shelter, a mission soon arrived from Brihtric, demanding that the fugitive should be handed over for punishment and tendering the price set on his head. In addition they asked the hand of Offa's daughter for their own king, that lasting friendship between them might be cemented in the bond of wedlock. Offa, who was not a man to yield to warlike threats, succumbed to their blandishments, and Ecgberht had to cross the sea into France. And in this, as I understand it, we have a stroke of divine Providence—that the destined ruler of this great kingdom should learn the art of government from the Franks; for both in martial exercises and in polish of manners the men of France are easily first among the nations of the West. Ecgberht therefore used this period of disgrace as a whetstone with which to sharpen the edge of his mind by clearing away the rust of indolence, and to acquire a civility of manners very different from the barbarity of his native land. On Brihtric's death he returned to Britain in response to many invitations from his friends, and being soon told to assume the throne, he fulfilled the dearest wishes of his countrymen in the year of our Lord 800, which was the thirty-fourth year of Charlemagne, king in France, who had yet twelve years to reign. Ecgberht meantime, having won the love of his subjects by his clemency and moderation, displayed his strength for the first time against the British who live in that part of the island known as Cornwall; and having conquered them, proceeded to exact tribute from the North British, who are divided from them by an arm of the sea. The news of

fama cum reliquos territaret, Bernulfus rex Mertiorum, tumidum quid spirans gloriosumque arbitratus si audatia sua ceterorum metum demeret, bellum Egbirhto indixit. Ille, gloriae dampnum ducens si cederet, occurrit alacriter, consertaque pugna fugit Bernulfus uictus miserabiliter. *Factum est hoc bellum apud Hellendune anno Domini octingentesimo uicesimo sexto.* Hoc euentu Westsaxo elatus animumque[b] ad altiora extendens, feruente adhuc uictoria Ethelwlfum filium cum Alhstano episcopo Scireburniae et electa manu Cantiam misit, qui prouintiam, seu longo sopitam otio seu uirtutum suarum exanimatam[c] nuntio, dominatui Westsaxonico adicerent.

107. Missi efficaciter imperatis institerunt, regionemque quaquauersum[d] finibus suis cingitur peruagati minimoque labore Baldredo rege ultra Tamensem fluuium expulso, Cantiam, Sudreiam, Australes et Orientales Saxones, qui quondam ad antecessorum suorum ius pertinebant, suae parti subdidere[e] anno regni eius uicesimo quarto. Nec multo post Orientales Angli auxilio Egbirhti animati reges Mertiorum Bernulfum et Ludekanium continuatis exceptos insidiis trucidarunt. Causa cedis fuit quod ipsi solita contumatia fines externos inquietarent. Eorum successor Wihtlafius, primo ab Egbirhto regno fugatus, mox in fidem tributariam acceptus, principatum Westsaxonum 2 ampliauit. Eodem anno Northanimbri, qui se solos remansisse et omnium digito notari cernerent, timentes ne diu conceptam iram in ipsos effunderet, tandem uel sero datis obsidibus fauerunt deditioni. Ita tota Britannia potitus, reliquum uitae per annos nouem tranquille cucurrit, nisi quod extremis fere diebus manus Danorum piratica littoribus eius appulsa otium regni fedauit. Ita uersatur humanarum rerum alea ut, primus omnibus Anglis imperitans cognatorum obsequium posset paruipendere, dum externus hostis se suosque heredes non desi-3 neret[f] incessere. Contra quos cum copiae Anglorum constitissent, non solito lenocinio Fortuna regem adulata in ipso conatu destituit; siquidem cum meliore diei parte uictoriam pene occupasset, iam prono in oceanum sole palmam amisit, sed tamen benefitio tenebrarum adiutus

---

[a–a] *om.* T¹ [b] TpCB; animum TtAl; et animum Aa [c] examinatam T¹Cs [d] quaqueuersum A [e] subdicere T¹ [f] sineret A

these victories struck fear into the other princes; only Beornwulf king of the Mercians, who was ambitious and thought it would be a glorious thing to free the others from their fears by his own daring, declared war on him. Ecgberht, knowing he would lose face if he gave way, advanced against him without hesitation; Beornwulf was ignominiously defeated in a pitched battle, and took to flight. The battle was fought at *Hellendune* in the year 826. Elated by this success, the West Saxon king conceived greater ambitions, and in the first flush of victory sent his son Æthelwulf, together with Ealhstan bishop of Sherborne and a picked force, into Kent, with instructions that the province, which was either lulled to sleep by a long period of peace or dispirited by the news of his achievements, was to come under West Saxon rule.

107. His legates set about their instructions to some purpose, and swept through the province from end to end. It was an easy task to drive King Baldred across the Thames, and add to Ecgberht's dominions Kent and Surrey, Sussex and Essex, which were at one time subject to his predecessors. This was in the twenty-fourth year of his reign. Not long afterwards, the East Angles, encouraged by assistance from Ecgberht, ambushed two kings of the Mercians, Beornwulf and Ludeca, in rapid succession and put them to death, the reason for this bloodshed being the obstinate persistence with which they harassed their neighbours' territory. Wiglaf their successor was at first driven from his kingdom by Ecgberht, then accepted as tributary, and thus further enlarged West Saxon power. In the same year the Northumbrians, conscious that they were now isolated and an obvious target, and afraid that they would soon feel the force of his long-matured hostility, at length, late though it was, submitted hostages, and decided to give in. Having thus become master of the whole of Britain, Ecgberht passed the last nine years of his life in tranquillity, except that near the end of his time a band of Danish pirates landed on his shores and disturbed the public peace. Such is the play of chance in human affairs; he who was the first to rule over the English as a whole, could derive but little satisfaction from the obedience of his countrymen while a foreign foe was ceaselessly harassing him and his heirs. The English forces took their stand against them; but this time Fortune, jade that she is, withheld her wonted favours and deserted the king in the hour of crisis. During the better part of the day victory had been within his grasp; and then, when the sun was already sinking towards the western sea, he lost the prize. None the less, he escaped defeat and disgrace by

uicti dedecus euasit. Sequenti plane prelio ingentem multitudinem parua manu fudit. Postremo post annos triginta[a] septem et menses septem decessit, sepultusque est Wintoniae,[b] magnas laudum occasiones filio relinquens felicemque fore pronuntians[c] si regnum, quod multa texuerat industria, ille consueta genti illi non interrumperet ignauia.

108. Anno Dominicae incarnationis octingentesimo tricesimo septimo[d] Ethelwlfus, quem quidam[e] Adulfum uocant, filius Egbirhti[f] regnauit annis uiginti et mensibus quinque, natura lenis et qui sub quiete degere quam multis prouintiis imperitare mallet; denique auito Westsaxonum regno contentus cetera quae pater subiugauerat appenditia filio Ethelstano contradidit, qui quando et quo fine defecerit incertum. Burhredum regem Mertiorum et[g] additamento exercitus contra Britones iuuit et filiae nuptiis [h]immane quantum[h] exaltauit. Piratas Danorum per totam insulam uagantes et inopinatis appulsionibus littora omnia infestantes, non[i] semel per se [j]et duces[j] suos contudit, quanuis (ut est tessera bellorum) ipse in eisdem frequentes[k] et insignes 2 calamitates acceperit, Lundonia et omni pene Cantia uastata. Obsistebat[l] tamen semper erumnis consiliariorum regis uiuacitas, qui nichil umquam hostes impune delinquere paterentur, quin communi umbone in eos ulciscerentur. Habebat enim duos suo tempore precellentes presules, beatum Swithunum dico Wintoniae et Alhstanum Scireburniae; hi, uidentes regem crassioris et hebetis ingenii, sedulis ammonitionibus ad scientiam regnandi[m] stimulabant. Swithunus, in terrenis nausians, dominum ad caelestia informabat; Alhstanus, forensia quoque non negligenda ratus, eundem contra Danos animabat, 3 ipse pecunias fisco suffitiens, ipse exercitum componens. Multa per illum in talibus et inchoata constanter et terminata feliciter, qui annales[1] legerit, inueniet. Vixit in episcopatu annis quinquaginta, beatus qui tanto tempore in procinctu bonorum operum fuerit;[n] quem libenter laudarem, nisi quod humana cupiditate raptatus[o] indebita usurpauit, quando monasterium Malmesberiense suis negotiis substrauit. Sentimus ad hunc diem impudentiae illius calumniam, licet

---

[a] *ABc¹C add* et, *against William's practice*   [b] sep. est Wint. *om.* T¹   [c] prenuntians T¹*   [d] octauo T¹   [e] quidem A   [f] B† *adds* regnum sortitus (*but cf.* 141. 1 anno . . . tenuit regnum annis . . .)   [g] *om.* C   [h-h] non mediocriter B† (*cf.* 388. 2 n.)   [i] plusquam B†   [j-j] ducesque B   [k] et frequentes B   [l] obsidebat T¹   [m] regni B, GP *p.* 176   [n] fuit B   [o] raptus C

[1] *ASC* s.aa. 823 (825), 845.

the timely help of darkness, and in an engagement which followed soon after routed an immense host of the enemy with a small force. At length, after a reign of thirty-seven years and seven months, he died, and was buried in Winchester, bequeathing to his son great opportunities to win renown, and foretelling that he would prosper, if only he did not, with the indolence native to his countrymen, dissipate the kingdom which his father's energy had knitted together.

108. In the year of our Lord 837 Ecgberht's son Æthelwulf, whom some call Athulf, succeeded, and he reigned for twenty years and five months. By nature gentle, he was a man to prefer a quiet life rather than the lordship over many provinces; being content, for instance, with his hereditary rule over the West Saxons, he transferred all the conquests added by his father to his son Æthelstan, the date and manner of whose death are alike uncertain. He assisted Burgred king of the Mercians against the Britons by sending additional troops, and immensely enhanced his prestige by giving him his daughter's hand. The Danish pirates, who were at large all over the island, and made the whole coast dangerous by their unexpected descents, were crushed more than once by himself and his generals, although, the chances of war being what they are, he suffered frequent and heavy losses as a result, London and almost all Kent being devastated. But these misfortunes were always countered by the vigour of the king's advisers, who were not the sort to let an enemy outrage go unpunished without forming a common front to exact reprisals. For he had two prelates outstanding in their time, St Swithhun bishop of Winchester and Ealhstan bishop of Sherborne; and these two, seeing that the king was dull and slow by nature, roused him by their constant warnings to some knowledge of his royal duties. Swithhun, sickened by the affairs of this world, put his master on the road to heavenly things; Ealhstan, who thought that worldly business too should not be neglected, spurred him on to attack the Danes, himself supplying the treasury with money and setting the army in array. In this field, any reader of the Chronicle[1] will find many examples of his bold initiative and ultimate success. Fifty years a bishop, he was fortunate in enjoying for so long the active power of doing good, and I would gladly praise him, had he not been carried away by human greed to lay hands on what was not his, in subjecting to his own purposes the abbey of Malmesbury. To this day we feel the grievance of his outrageous behaviour, although on his death the

locus idem statim eo mortuo omnem illam eluctatus fuerit uiolentiam usque ad nostrum tempus, quando in idem discrimen recidit. Ita sacra fames auaritiae mortalia pectora exedit,[1] ita magnificos et illustres in ceteris uiros in Tartara trudit.

109. Ethelwlfus, his[a] duobus sustentatoribus fretus, et [b]exteriora bene prouidere et interiora non despuere.[b] Post triumphatos scilicet hostes ad Dei cultum uersus,[c] decimam omnium hidarum infra[d] regnum suum Christi famulis[e] concessit, liberam ab omnibus functionibus, absolutam ab omnibus inquietudinibus. Sed quantula est haec eius gloria! Romam composito regno abiit, ibique tributum, quod Anglia hodieque pensitat, sancto Petro obtulit coram quarto Leone papa,[f] qui etiam antea Elfredum filium eius ad se missum honorifice susceperat et regem inunxerat. [g]Ibi ergo[g] anno integro moratus Scolam Anglorum, quae (ut fertur) ab Offa rege Mertiorum primitus instituta proximo anno conflagrauerat, reparauit egregie. Inde domum per Gallias repatrians Iudith filiam Karoli regis Francorum in coniugium sumpsit.

110. Siquidem Ludouicus Pius, Karoli Magni filius, quattuor filios habuit, Lotharium, Pipinum, Ludouicum, Karolum cognomento Caluum; quorum Lotharius, etiam patre uiuente nomen imperatoris usurpans, regnauit annis quindecim in [h]ea quae iacet iuxta[i] Alpes[h] parte Germaniae et nunc Lotharingia, quasi regnum Lotharii, dicitur, et in tota Italia cum Roma. In extremo uitae aduersa ualitudine uexatus seculo renuntiauit, uir omnium ante se longe[j] immanissimus, quippe qui proprium patrem crebro captiuatum in ergastulis[k] uinxerit. Erat sane ille mansueti animi et simplicis, sed quia mortua Ermengarde, de qua priores[l] liberos tulerat, Karolum ex[m] Iudith uxore natum arctius exosculabatur, a Lothario inclementer exagitatus. Pipinus, alter filius Ludouici, regnauit in Aquitania et Wasconia. Ludouicus, tertius filius Ludouici, preter Noricam quam habebat tenuit regna quae pater suus illi dederat, id est Alemanniam, Turingiam, Austrasiam, Saxoniam,[n] et Auarorum id est Hunorum regnum. Karolus uero medietatem Frantiae ab occidente et totam Neustriam, Britanniam et maximam partem

---

[a] om. AC   [b–b] interiora non despicere et exteriora prouidere B   [c] conuersus B   [d] intra B   [e] famulus TpB   [f] *The word order is odd (cf. 121. 1, where only C has* quarto*); the ordinal was perhaps added above the line in an ambiguous position*   [g–g] ibique T¹   [h–h] om. T⁺   [i] prope B† (cf. 112. 2, 126. 2)   [j] om. T⁺   [k] ergastulo Bc (cf. GP p. 13 ergastulum)   [l] primos B   [m] rex T⁺   [n] Saxonum A

monastery at once recovered completely from his violence, and so remained until our own time, when it has again undergone the same ordeal. Thus does Avarice 'with her curst appetite gnaw mortal hearts';[1] thus are men great and illustrious in other respects plunged by her into the pit.

109. Æthelwulf, relying on his two supporters, took due thought for external affairs without despising internal. First he defeated his enemies; then turned to the worship of God, and granted to Christ's servants a tenth of every hide in his kingdom, free from all services and quit of every interference. But this is only a small part of his glory. Once his kingdom was at peace, he set off for Rome, and there offered to St Peter the tribute which England still pays, in the presence of Pope Leo IV, who had previously received his son Alfred with honour and had anointed him king. In Rome he spent a whole year, and lavishly restored the Schola Anglorum, reputed in origin a foundation of Offa king of the Mercians, which had been burnt down the year before. Then, on his way home through Gaul, he took to wife Judith, daughter of Charles king of the Franks.

110. For Charlemagne's son Louis the Pious had four sons, Lothar, Pippin, Louis, and Charles, surnamed the Bald. Of these, Lothar usurped the title of emperor even in his father's lifetime, and reigned for fifteen years in the part of Germany that lies near the Alps and is now called Lotharingia, 'Lothar's realm', and in the whole of Italy including Rome. At the end of his life he fell seriously ill and renounced the world, having been a man of hitherto unexampled cruelty, who had often taken his own father prisoner and kept him in dungeons. Louis was indeed a mild and simple-hearted prince; but on the death of Ermengard, the mother of his elder children, he showed excessive favour to Charles, the son of Judith his second wife, and for this was persecuted without mercy by Lothar. Pippin, Louis's second son, was king in Aquitaine and Gascony. The third son, Louis, beside Norica which belonged to him, held the kingdoms given to him by his father: Alemannia, Thuringia, Austrasia, Saxony, and the kingdom of the Avars or Huns. Charles had the western half of France and all Neustria, Brittany and the greater part of Burgundy,

[1] Cf. Virgil, *Aen.* iii. 56–7.

Burgundiae, Gothiam, Wasconiam, Aquitaniam, summoto inde Pipino filio Pipini et in monasterio sancti Medardi attonso. Qui postea inde per fugam elapsus*ᵃ* et*ᵇ* Aquitaniam regressus, multo tempore fugiendo ibi latuit, iterumque*ᶜ* a Rannulfo prefecto per fidem deceptus comprehensus est,*ᵈ* et ad Karolum adductus Siluanecto perpetuo est exilio detrusus.*ᵉ*

3   Post mortem uero*ᶠ* Ludouici piissimi imperatoris Lotharius, ante obitum patris decem et octo annis unctus ad imperatorem, contra fratres suos, id est Ludouicum piissimum regem Baioariorum et Karolum, exercitum duxit, adiuncto sibi Pipino cum Aquitanorum populo in pago Autisiodorensi in loco qui uocatur Fontanetum; in quo loco cum Franci cum omnibus nationibus sibi subiectis mutua se cede prosternerent, ad ultimum Ludouicus et Karolus Lothario fugato *ᵍ*triumphum adepti sunt.*ᵍ* Post cruentissimum uero*ʰ* prelium pace inter eos facta diui-
4   serunt inter se Francorum imperium,*ⁱ* ut supra diximus.¹ Lotharius uero ex Ermengarda filia Hugonis tres filios habuit, id est Ludouicum, cui regnum Romanorum et Italiam tradidit; alterum autem Lotharium, cui sedem imperialem reliquit; tertium uero Karolum, cui Prouintiam gubernandam dimisit.*ʲ* Decessit *ᵏ*quoque Lotharius*ᵏ* anno incarnationis Domini nostri Iesu Christi*ˡ* octingentesimo quinquagesimo quinto, imperii siue regni*ᵐ* sui tricesimo tertio. Post cuius obitum Karolus filius eius, qui Prouintiam gubernabat, octauo anno moritur. Dehinc*ⁿ* Ludouicus imperator Romanorum et Lotharius fratres*ᵒ* regnum eius,
5   hoc est Prouintiam, inter se dispertiunt. Ludouicus autem rex Noricorum, id est Baioariorum, Ludouici imperatoris filius, anno incarnationis Domini octingentesimo sexagesimo quinto post festiuitatem Paschalem regnum suum inter filios suos diuisit, et Karlomanno quidem dedit Noricam, id est Baioariam, et marcas contra Sclauos et Longobardos; Ludouico uero Turingiam, Austrasios Francos et Saxoniam dimisit;*ᵖ* Karolo quoque*ᵠ* Alemanniam et Curwalam, id est comitatum Cornugalliae,*ʳ* reliquit. Ipse 'tamen Ludouicus*ˢ* super filios suos feliciter regnauit in omni potestate sua annis decem. Et post haec*ᵗ* obiit Ludouicus rex*ᵘ* anno Dominicae*ᵛ* incarnationis*ʷ* octingentesimo septuagesimo sexto, cum regnasset annis quinquaginta quattuor.
6   Karolus autem rex Occidentalium Francorum anno tricesimo sexto regni sui in Italiam pergens orandi causa*ˣ* ad limina apostolorum

ᵃ lapsus B   *ᵇ* om. T⁺, Cont. Adon. (MGH SS ii) p. 324   *ᶜ* deliluit itemque (interimque Bc) B   *ᵈ* comp. est om. B   *ᵉ* deportatus B   *ᶠ* om. A
ᵍ⁻ᵍ triumphati sunt Al, triumphauerunt Aa   *ʰ* om. A   *ⁱ* regnum T⁺

Gothia, Gascony, and Aquitaine, from which he ejected Pippin's son the younger Pippin and forced him to become a monk at Saint-Médard. This Pippin later escaped and returned to Aquitaine, where he lay long in hiding as a fugitive, but was betrayed by its governor Ranulf, seized a second time, and brought before Charles at Senlis, who sentenced him to exile for life.

After the death of the Emperor Louis the Pious, Lothar, who had been anointed emperor eighteen years before his father's death, took the field against his brothers, Louis the most pious king of Bavaria, and Charles, and joined forces with Pippin and the people of Aquitaine at a place called Fontenay in the region of Auxerre. There the Franks and all their subject peoples laid each other low with heavy losses on both sides, until at length Louis and Charles routed Lothar and won the day. After this very bloody battle they made peace and divided the Frankish empire between them, as I have described above.[1] Lothar had three sons by Hugh's daughter Ermengard: Louis, to whom he gave the kingdom of the Romans and Italy, another Lothar, to whom he left the imperial throne, and a third, Charles, to whom he entrusted the government of Provence. Lothar in his turn died in the year of our Lord 855 and the thirty-third of his own reign as emperor or king. In the eighth year after his death, his son Charles, the ruler of Provence, also died; whereupon his brothers, Louis emperor of the Romans and Lothar, divided his kingdom of Provence between themselves. Then in the year 865, after Easter, King Louis of Norica (otherwise Bavaria), son of the emperor Louis, divided his kingdom among his sons: to Carloman he gave Norica (otherwise Bavaria) and the marches against the Slavs and Lombards, to Louis he handed over Thuringia with the Austrasian Franks and Saxony, and to Charles he left Alemannia and Chur (otherwise the county of the *Churwelsch*). Louis himself, however, reigned prosperously over his sons in full possession of his power for ten years. King Louis then died, in the year of our Lord 876, after fifty-four years on the throne.

Charles king of the West Franks, in the thirty-sixth year of his reign, set off for Italy to pay his devotions and arrived at the threshold of the

---

j commisit *B*   *k–k* autem *B*   *l* nostri I. C. *om. B*   *m* siue regni *om. B†*   *n* et dehinc *B*   *o* B *adds* eius   *p* diuisit *B*   *q* autem *B*   *r* Gallie *B*   *s–s* uero *B*   *t* om. *T*⁺   *u* om. *B†*   *v* Domini *B*   *w* anno D. inc. *om. A*   *x* orationis gratia *B*

---

[1] 110. 1–2.

peruenit, ibique a cuncto populo Romano imperator eligitur et a
Iohanne papa in imperatorem consecratur, octauo kalendas Ianuarii
anno Dominicae incarnationis octingentesimo septuagesimo quinto.
Inde in*a* Galliam prospere ingressus*b* est. Anno quoque*c* regni sui*d*
tricesimo octauo et imperii tertio inchoante in Italiam iterum perrexit,
et colloquio Iohannis papae usus in Galliam reuertens,*e* transcenso
Ciniso monte presentis luminis caruit uisu tertio nonas Octobris,
indictione decima, anno Domini nostri*f* octingentesimo septuagesimo
7 septimo; cui successit in regno filius eius Ludouicus. Deinde, anno
regni sui secundo necdum expleto, idem Ludouicus obiit Compendio
palatio, sexto idus Aprilis, indictione duodecima, anno Domini
octingentesimo septuagesimo nono. Deinde filii eius Ludouicus et
Karlomannus regnum eius inter se dispertiunt. Predictus uero rex*g*
Ludouicus in pago Viminaco cum Normannis bellum gerens triumphum adeptus est, et non multo post obiit, pridie nonas Augustas,
anno*h* Domini octingentesimo octogesimo primo, indictione quinta
8 decima. Regnauit annos duos, menses tres, dies uiginti quattuor. Cui
successit in regno frater eius Karlomannus. Regnauit annis tribus et
diebus sex; deinde in Euuelino saltu in monte Aerico a fero singulari
percussus est. Obiit anno Dominicae incarnationis octingentesimo
octogesimo quarto, indictione secunda, octauo idus Decembris.
Deinde Karolus rex Suauorum, filius Ludouici regis Noricorum, monarchiam totius imperii Francorum*i* et Romanorum assumit, anno
Verbi incarnati octingentesimo octogesimo quinto, indictione tertia.
Cuius uisionem quia memorabilem puto, hic dignum duco intexere.

111. *j*"In nomine Dei*k* summi Regis regum. Ego Karolus imperator,
gratuito Dei dono rex Germanorum et patritius Romanorum atque
imperator Francorum, sacra nocte Dominici diei post celebratum
nocturnarum horarum diuinum offitium, dum irem repausationis cubi-
tum et uellem dormitionis carpere*l* somnum, uenit uox ad me terribiliter dicens: "Karole, exiet a te modo spiritus tuus in hora non
modica;" statimque fui raptus in spiritu, et qui me sustulit in spiritu
fuit candidissimus, tenuitque in manu sua glomerem lineum clarissime*m* iubar luminis emittentem, sicut solent cometae facere quando
apparent; cepitque illum dissoluere, et dixit ad me: "Accipe filum

a om. C   *b* reuersus TcB, Cont. Adon. p. 325, more appropriately   *c* autem
B   *d* om. B   *e* reuersus B   *f* Dominice incarnationis B (so too for the first
Domini in 7 below)   *g* om. B†   *h* B adds incarnacionis (cf. Cont. Adon.
p. 325 anno Dominicae incarnationis)   *i* regni Fr. simul B†   *j* The Visio is also

Apostles; where he was elected emperor by the whole population of Rome, and was consecrated by Pope John on 25 December in the year of our Lord 875. From there he made a prosperous entry into Gaul; but in the thirty-eighth year of his reign and early in his third year as emperor, he paid a second visit to Italy for talks with Pope John, and was on his way back to Gaul when, after crossing the Mont Cenis, he left the light of this present world on 5 October in the tenth indiction and the year of our Lord 877. He was succeeded 7 as king by his son Louis; but before completing two years on the throne this Louis also died, in his palace at Compiègne on 8 April in the twelfth indiction and the year of our Lord 879. His sons Louis and Carloman thereupon divided his kingdom between them. This King Louis fought a battle with the Northmen in the district of Vimeu, and defeated them; but not long after it he died, on 4 August in the year of our Lord 881, the fifteenth indiction, having reigned two years, three months, and twenty-four days. He was succeeded as 8 king by his brother Carloman, who reigned three years and six days, and was then gored by a wild boar at Montlhéry in the forest of Yvelines. He died in the year of our Lord 884, the second indiction, on 6 December. Whereupon Charles king of Swabia, son of Louis king of Norica, assumed sole rule over the whole empire of the Franks and Romans, in the year of the Incarnation 885, the third indiction. He saw a vision which I find memorable, and so I think proper to introduce it here.

111. 'In the name of the most high God, the King of kings. I Charles the emperor, by God's free gift king of the Germans, patrician of the Romans and emperor of the Franks, on the sacred night of the Lord's day, after the holy office of Nocturns had been sung, was going to my bed of rest as one that had it in mind to sleep, when there came to me a voice which uttered these terrifying words: "Charles, thy spirit shall now leave thee for some considerable time." Whereupon I was carried away in the spirit; and he that bore me in the spirit was glistening white, and in his hand he held a ball of flaxen thread that shone with a very bright radiance as comets commonly do when they appear; and he began to unroll the ball, and said to me: "Take the thread from this shining ball, and tie it

given in β (150^r–152^r): see Thomson, William of Malmesbury, pp. 148–9 B   [k] Domini

[l] capere $T^+A,\beta^{a.c.}$ [m] clarissimi C

glomeris micantis, et liga ac noda firmiter in pollice tuae dextrae
2 manus,*a* quia per illum duceris in laberintheas*b* infernorum penas." Et
hoc dicto precessit me uelociter, distorquens filum luciflui glomeris,
duxitque me in profundissimas ualles et igneas, quae erant plenae
puteis ardentibus pice et sulfure plumboque et cera et adipe. Ibi
inueni pontifices patris mei et auunculorum meorum; quos cum
pauens interrogarem quid tam grauia paterentur tormenta, responderunt michi: "Fuimus episcopi patris tui et auunculorum tuorum, et
dum debuimus illos et populum illorum de pace et concordia
ammonere et predicare, seminauimus discordias et incentores malorum
fuimus; unde nunc incendimur in istis tartareis suplitiis et nos et alii
homicidiorum et rapinarum amatores. Huc etiam tui episcopi et satel-
3 lites uenient, qui similiter amant nunc facere." Et dum haec tremebundus auscultarem, ecce nigerrimi demones aduolantes*c* cum uncis igneis
uolebant apprehendere filum glomeris quem in manu tenebam, et ad
se attrahere; sed reuerberantibus radiis illius glomeris non ualebant
filum contingere.*d* Deinde post tergum meum currentes uoluerunt me
aduncinare et in ipsos puteos sulfureos precipitare; sed ductor meus,
qui portabat glomerem, iactauit super scapulas*e* filum glomeris et
duplicauit illum traxitque post se fortiter, sicque ascendimus super
montes altissimos igneos, de quibus oriebantur paludes et flumina
feruentia et omnia metallorum genera bullientia, ubi repperi innumeras
animas hominum et principum patris mei et fratrum meorum et meorum*f* precipitatas, alias usque ad capillos, alias usque ad mentum, alias
usque ad umbilicum; clamaueruntque ad me eiulando: "Dum
4 uiximus, amauimus tecum et cum patre tuo et cum fratribus tuis et
cum auunculis tuis facere prelia et homicidia et rapinas pro cupiditate
terrena. Ideo in ista bullientia flumina et metallorum diuersa genera
sustinemus tormenta." Et cum ad haec timidus intenderem,*g* audiui
retro me animas clamare: "Potentes potenter tormenta patientur."[1] Et
respexi et uidi super ripas fluminis bullientis fornaces piceas et sulfureas, plenas magnis draconibus et scorpionibus et serpentibus diuersi
generis; ubi etiam uidi aliquos patris mei principes et meos et fratrum
meorum necnon et auunculorum meorum, dicentes michi: "Heu
nobis, Karole! Vides quam grauia habemus tormenta propter nostram

---

a manus dextere *T¹*, β (manus tue dextere *Tc*)   *b* laberinthicas *B*
c Ttᵖ·ᶜTcCs; auolantes *T¹ACeB*, β   *d* attingere *B*   *e B adds* suas   *f* et
meorum *TtTc(et Tp)AB; om. C,* β; et meorum cognatorum *Alᵖ·ᶜ*; et auunculorum meorum
in effect Hardy, no doubt rightly (but et meorum *must have fallen out before* et fratrum; *cf.
below* et meos ... et auunculorum meorum*)*   *g* accederem *T⁺*; attenderem *B*

firmly in a knot on your right thumb, for by this you shall be led in the labyrinth of infernal punishment." So saying he set off rapidly in front of me, unrolling the thread from his ball that streamed with light, and led me into valleys very deep and fiery which were full of pits blazing with pitch and sulphur and molten lead and wax and tallow. There I found prelates who served my father and my uncles; and when I asked them in terror why they suffered such grievous torments, they replied: "We were bishops of your father and your uncles, and while it was our duty to teach and to preach peace and concord both to them and to their people, we sowed discord instead and fomented evil. For this we are now consumed in these hellish punishments, and with us others who loved murder and robbery. Here too will come your bishops and your courtiers, who now love to do as we did." As I listened trembling, lo, pitch-black demons came flying with fiery hooks, and tried to catch the thread from the ball which I had in my hand and drag it to them; but the radiance from that ball beat them back, and they could not reach the thread. Then they ran behind my back and tried to get their hooks into me and plunge me headlong straight into those same sulphurous pits; but my guide, who was carrying the ball, cast the thread from it over my shoulders and doubled it and dragged me after him by force, and in this way we climbed up very high and fiery hills, from which sprang boiling marshes and rivers and all kinds of molten metals bubbling. In them I found countless souls of tenants and magnates of my father and my brothers and myself plunged in, some of them up to their hair, some to the chin, some to the navel, and they cried out to me with weeping and wailing: "While we lived, we loved, as you do and your father and your brothers and your uncles, battles and murder and robbery, from desire of earthly gain. That is why we are plunged in these boiling rivers and divers molten metals, and suffer torments." And as I listened quaking with fear to what they said, I heard the souls behind me crying: "A sore trial shall come upon the mighty."[1] And I turned round and saw on the banks of the boiling river furnaces burning with pitch and sulphur, full of great dragons and scorpions and serpents of divers kinds; and there too I saw some of my father's magnates and mine and my brothers' and my uncles', and they said to me: "Woe, woe is ours! Do you see, Charles, what heavy torments we suffer because of our

[1] Wisd. 6: 7.

malitiam et superbiam et mala consilia quae regibus nostris et tibi
dedimus propter cupiditatem?" Cumque haec*a* dolendo congemiscerem, cucurrerunt ad me dracones apertis et plenis faucibus igne et sulfure et pice, uolentes me inglutire; at ductor meus triplicauit super me filum, a cuius radiis claritatis superata sunt ora illorum ignea, et protraxit me ualidius. Et descendimus in unam uallem, quae erat ex una parte tenebrosa, ardens uelut clibanus ignis, ex alia uero parte tam amenissima et splendidissima ut nulla ratione dicere ualeam. Vertique me contra tenebrosam et flammiuomam partem, uidique ibi*b* aliquos reges mei generis in magnis suplitiis. Et tunc, nimis*c* constrictus angustia, putaui me statim in ipsis demergi suplitiis a gigantibus nigerrimis, qui ipsam uallem inflammabant cunctis generibus ignium, et ualde tremens, glomeris filo illuminante oculos meos, uidi e latere uallis paulisper albescere lumen, ibique duos fontes fluere. Vnus erat nimium calidus, alter uero clarus et tepidus; et erant ibi duo dolia. Cumque illuc irem, filo glomeris regente gressus meos, intuitus super unum ubi erat feruens aqua, uidi ibi*d* genitorem meum Ludouicum stare usque ad femora; et nimis dolore aggrauatus et angore perculsus,*e* dixit ad me: "Domine meus Karole, noli timere. Scio quia reuertetur rursus spiritus tuus ad corpus tuum; et permisit te Deus huc uenire ut uideres propter quae peccata ego et omnes quos uidisti talia toleramus suplitia. Vno enim die sum in isto feruentis dolii balneo, et altero die transmutor in isto suauissimo altero aquae dolio; et hoc fit precibus sancti Petri et sancti Remigii, cuius patrociniis hactenus genus nostrum regale regnauit. Sed si michi subueneris cito, tu et mei fideles episcopi et abbates et omnis ordo aecclesiasticus, missis oblationibus psalmodiis uigiliis elemosinis, uelociter liberatus ero de isto aquae bullientis dolio; nam frater meus Lotharius et eius filius Ludouicus sancti Petri sanctique Remigii precibus exempti sunt de istis penis, et iam ducti sunt in gaudium paradisi Dei." Dixitque ad me: "Respice sinistrorsum"; cumque respexissem, uidi ibi duo dolia altissima bullientia. "Ista" inquit "sunt tibi preparata, nisi te emendaueris et penitentiam egeris de tuis nefandis delictis"; cepique tunc grauiter horrere. Cumque cerneret comes meus in tanto pauore esse spiritum meum, dixit ad me: "Sequere me ad dexteram luculentissimae uallis

---

a hoc *A*   *b* T+ACs, β, om. CeB   *c* B adds perterritus et   *d* om. B   *e* percussus TcB

wickedness and pride and the evil counsel that we gave to our royal masters and to you, for the sake of gain?" And as I groaned at the sight of these things, dragons came running at me with open mouths, which were full of fire and sulphur and pitch, and tried to swallow me up; but my guide laid the thread over me threefold, so that its bright rays overcame their fiery jaws, and he drew me forward more firmly. And we descended into a valley which on one side was quite dark, and burning like an oven, but on the other side was so exceeding beautiful and bright that I can by no means describe it. I turned towards the dark side, which was shooting out flames, and there I saw several kings of my own family undergoing extreme torture. Then, overcome by anguish, I thought I was to be plunged forthwith in those same punishments by pitch-black giants who were setting that same valley on fire with flames of every kind; and I trembled violently, and the thread from the ball gave light to my eyes, and I saw that on the opposite side of the valley it was gradually growing lighter, and there were two springs there. One of these was very hot, and the other clear and lukewarm; and there were also two great tuns. And when I went towards them (for the thread from the ball guided my steps), I looked into the one where the boiling water was, and there I saw my father Louis, standing in it up to his thighs. In great pain and smitten with anguish, he said to me: "Be not afraid, my lord Charles. I know that your spirit will return again into your body; and God has permitted you to come hither, that you might behold the sins for which I and all those whom you have seen endure such punishments. One day I am plunged into this boiling tun as if it were a bath, and the next I am removed into that second tun of most refreshing water; and this happens through the prayers of St Peter and St Remigius, under whose patronage our royal family has reigned hitherto. But if you will help me quickly, you and the bishops and abbots who were loyal to me and the whole estate of the clergy, with masses and offerings and psalm-singing and vigils and alms, I shall swiftly be set free from this tun of boiling water; for my brother Lothar and his son Louis have been freed from these penalties by the prayers of St Peter and St Remigius, and have already entered into the joy of the Paradise of God." And he said to me: "Look to your left", and when I looked, I saw there were two very deep and boiling tuns. "These", he said, "are made ready for you, unless you mend your ways and do penance for your outrageous offences"; and I began then to shake with terror. And when my companion saw that my spirit was in such distress, he said to me: "Follow me to the right-hand side of the

paradisi." Et cum graderemur, contemplatus sum*a* ingenti claritate cum gloriosis regibus sedere Lotharium auunculum meum super lapidem topazium mirae magnitudinis, coronatum diademate pretioso, et iuxta eum filium eius Ludouicum similiter *b*corona ornatum.*b*

9 Videns*c* me comminus accersiuit*d* blanda uoce, dicens: "Karole, successor meus nunc tertius in imperio Romanorum, ueni ad me. Scio quod*e* per penalem locum uenisti, ubi est pater tuus, frater meus, positus in termis sibi destinatis; sed per misericordiam Dei citissime de illis liberabitur penis, sicut et nos liberati sumus, meritis sancti Petri sanctique precibus Remigii, cui Deus magnum apostolatum dedit super reges et super gentes*f* Francorum, qui nisi quisquiliis nostrae propaginis suffragatus fuerit et adiuuerit, iam deficiet genealogia nostra*g* regnando et imperando. Vnde scito quoniam tolletur otius potestas imperii de manu tua, et postea paruissimo*h* uiues tempore."

10 Tunc conuersus contra*i* me Ludouicus dixit michi: "Imperium quod hactenus tenuisti iure hereditario debet recipere Ludouicus filius filiae meae"; et hoc dicto, uisum est michi affore in presentiarum*j* infantulum. Tunc intuens eum Lotharius auus eius dixit michi: "Talis uidetur esse infans*k* qualis ille puer fuit quem statuit Dominus in medio discipulorum, et dixit: Talium est*l* regnum caelorum; dico uobis quia angeli eorum uident*m* fatiem Patris mei qui in caelis est.[1] Tu uero redde illi*n* potestatem imperii per illud filum glomeris quod

11 in manu tenes." Disnodans ergo filum de pollice dextrae meae, donabam illi monarchiam omnem imperii per ipsum*o* filium; statimque ipsum glomus fulgidum sicut iubar solis coadunatum est totum in manu illius.*p* Sicque post hoc factum mirabile reuersus est spiritus meus in corpore meo ualde fessus et conterritus. Denique sciant omnes, uelint an nolint, quoniam secundum destinationem Dei in manu*q* illius reuertetur totum imperium Romanorum, et quod super ipsum non preualeo agere, preripiente me articulo uocationis meae. Deus, qui uiuorum dominatur et mortuorum, illud perfitiet et confirmabit; cuius aeternum et*r* sempiternum regnum*s* permanet sine fine*t* in secula seculorum. Amen.'*u*

a *B adds* cum *b–b* coronatum *A* *c* uidensque *T*+, *β** *d* *B adds* me *e* quoniam *Tt(not Tp), β;* quia *Tc* *f* gentem *(om.* super) *B* *g* gen. nostra *om. B (adding* progenies nostra *after* imperando*)* *h* paucissimo *B* *i* ad *B* *j* *T*+, *β** *add* Ludouicum *k* infans esse *A* *l* est enim *Tt(not TpTc)B, Vulg.* *m* semper uident *B, Vulg.* *n* ei *B* *o* illud *B* *p* eius *T*+*Al*a.c.*Bk* *q* manus *B* *r* aeternum et *om. B* *s* et semp. regnum] regnum et sempiternum imperium *T*+, *β** *t* sine fine *om. TcB* *u* *om. B*

most lovely valley of Paradise." And as we went, I beheld a brilliant light, and in it among renowned kings was my uncle Lothar, seated upon a topaz of wondrous size and crowned with a precious diadem; and beside him was his son Louis, like him wearing a crown. Seeing me, he called me to him in a friendly voice and said: "Charles, my third successor, as you are now, in the empire of the Romans, come hither. I know that you have come through the place of torment, where your father, my brother, is placed in the hot bath designed for him; but by God's mercy he will very shortly be released from those punishments, as we too have been released, by the merits of St Peter and the prayers of St Remigius, to whom God granted that he should be a great apostle over the kings and nations of the Franks; and unless he supports and aids the worthless remnants of our race, our lineage will soon be unequal to its task of ruling kingdom and empire. And so you may be sure that the imperial power will quickly be taken out of your hands; and after that you will have only a very short time to live." Then Louis turned towards me and said: "The empire which you have held hitherto ought to pass by right of inheritance to my daughter's son Louis." As he said this, it seemed that a child appeared at that moment before my eyes. Then his grandfather Lothar looked upon him and said to me: "This infant looks very like that little child whom the Lord set in the midst of His disciples, and said 'Of such is the kingdom of Heaven: I say unto you that their angels behold the face of my Father who is in Heaven.'[1] You then must hand over to him the power of the empire by way of that thread from the ball which you hold in your hand." And so I undid the knot in the thread that was upon my right thumb, and gave him absolute rule over the empire by means of that same thread; and at once the whole ball, shining like the sun, was rolled up in his hand. And so after these wonderful doings my spirit returned into my body, greatly exhausted and terrified. Let it therefore be known unto all men, whether they will or no, that in accordance with God's purpose the empire of the Romans shall return entirely into his hand, and that against him I have no power to act, for the conditions of my calling forestall me. God, who is Lord of the living and the dead, shall perform and establish this, whose eternal and everlasting kingdom endureth without end for ever and ever. Amen.'

---

[1] Matt. 19: 14, 18: 10.

112. Visionem istam et regnorum partitionem uerbis quibus scripta inueni hic apposui. Hoc ergo Karolo uix duobus annis potestate integra imperii et regni*a* functo, successit in regno Karolus, filius illius Ludouici qui apud Compendium obiit. Hic est Karolus qui filiam Eduardi regis Anglorum uxorem duxit, deditque Normanniam Rolloni cum filia sua Gisla, quae esset*b* uas pacis, pigneratrix federis. At uero in imperio successit Karolo isti Arnulfus rex, de genere imperatorio, tutor Ludouici pueri de quo uisio superior narrat. Arnulfo ergo post quindecim annos defuncto, successit Ludouicus idem; quo mortuo Conradus quidam, 2 rex Teutonicorum, imperauit. Huic successit 'filius Henricus,'*c* qui misit ad Ethelstanum regem Anglorum pro duabus sororibus suis Aldgitha et Edgitha; quarum posteriorem filio suo*d* Ottoni collocauit, alteram cuidam duci iuxta*e* Alpes nuptum dedit. Ita hodieque imperium Romanorum et regnum Francorum ab antiqua unione scissum alterum imperatores, alterum reges habet.*f* Sed quia multum a proposito excessi, dum me iuuat illustrium Francorum seriem lineatim*g* protendere, nunc iam inceptam uiam repetens ad Ethelwlfum regrediar.[1]

113. Ille, ubi post annuam peregrinationem domum uenit, filia Karoli Calui*h* in matrimonium ducta, aliter quam putabat animos quorundam offendit: siquidem Ethelbaldus filius eius et Scireburnensis*i* episcopus Alhstanus et Enulfus Sumersetensis pagi*j* comes, in eius contumeliam coniurati, regno eum proturbare nitebantur.*k* *l*Sed maturiori*m* mediante consilio regnum inter parentem et prolem diuisum. Iniusta ea fuit partitio: adeo malignitas obtinuerat ut pars occidentalis melior filio, deterior orientalis patri daretur. Veruntamen ille incredibili clementia, plusquam ciuile bellum[2] formidans, aequanimiter filio cessit, prouintiales, qui dignitatem eius asserturi conuenerant, leni*n* 2 oratione cohibens. Ita quanuis omnis controuersia pro alienigena uxore fuerit, magna illam dignatione habitam throno etiam, contra morem Westsaxonum, iuxta se locabat; non enim Westsaxones reginam uel*o* iuxta regem sedere uel reginae appellatione insigniri patiuntur, propter malitiam Edburgae filiae Offae regis Mertiorum. Ea,

a regno *A*   *b* foret *B*   *c-c* rex Henricus eius filius *B*   *d* om. *T*⁺
e prope *B†(cf. 110.1, 126. 2)*   *f* *T*⁺*Ce*; habent *ACsB*   *g* seriatim lineam
B   *h* *B†* adds ut dixi *(cf. 109)*   *i* Scireburni(a)e *T*ꞌ   *j* om. *T*ꞌ
k conabantur *T*ꞌ*Bc*   *l-l* *(p. 174)* om. *T*ꞌ   *m* maturior *BkBc*²(-ore *Bc*ꞌ)
n leui *B*   *o* om. *B*

[1] Cf. c. 109.   [2] Cf. Lucan i. 1.

112. This vision, and the separation of the kingdoms, I have added here in the language in which I found them described. And so when this Charles had enjoyed his imperial and royal power in its entirety for barely two years, he was succeeded in his kingdom by Charles, son of the Louis who died at Compiègne. It is this Charles who married a daughter of Edward king of the English, and gave Rollo Normandy, with his daughter Gisela to be a pledge of peace and guarantee of the agreement. In the empire that Charles's successor was King Arnulf, a member of the imperial house who was guardian of Louis, the child told of in the vision above related. When Arnulf therefore died after fifteen years, that same Louis succeeded him; and on Louis's death a certain Conrad, king of the Teutons, became emperor. Conrad was followed by his son Henry, who sent to Æthelstan, king of the English, for the hand of his sisters Ealdgyth and Eadgyth, the latter of whom he betrothed to his son Otto, and gave the other in marriage to a certain duke near the Alps. Thus it is that to this day the empire of the Romans and the kingdom of the French are severed from their ancient union, and one is ruled by emperors, the other by kings. But I have wandered far from my subject in the agreeable task of recalling the illustrious lineage of the Franks; I must now resume to the course upon which I had already started, and return[1] to Æthelwulf.

113. After his return home from his year of pilgrimage, and his marriage to the daughter of Charles the Bald, Æthelwulf met an unexpected reception in some quarters; for his son Æthelbald, with Ealhstan bishop of Sherborne and Eanwulf ealdorman of Somerset, conspired against him and tried to drive him from his throne. Wiser counsels however intervened, and the kingdom was divided between parent and child. It was not a fair division: jealousy had been so successful that the better half to the westward was given to the son and the eastern and inferior half to the father. None the less, the king with astonishing mildness yielded to his son with a good grace, fearing 'war worse than civil',[2] and restraining by the moderation of his language those of his subjects who had gathered to defend his rightful position. Although the whole dispute was on account of his foreign wife, he treated her with the greatest deference, and even defied the tradition of the West Saxons and set her beside himself on the throne; for the West Saxons permit no consort either to take her seat beside the king or to be called queen, in memory of the wickedness of Eadburh, daughter of Offa king of the Mercians. This

ut prediximus,[1] Brihtrico regi Westsaxonum nupta, benignum (ut aiunt) uirum in pernitiem[a] insontum nequam consiliis armare; quos uero insimulare nequibat, potionibus noxiis intercipere. Compertum in quodam adolescentulo regi dilectissimo, quem illa ueneno sustulit; confestimque Brihtricus decubuit et decessit, quod ex potu sine reginae nimirum con-
3 scientia pregustauerat. Effusus ergo rumor in uulgus ueneficam regno excedere coegit. Illa ad Karolum Magnum profecta, forte cum uno filiorum stantem inuenit. Oblatis xeniis imperator, ludibundus et ioci plenus, eam quem mallet, uel se uel filium, eligere precepit. Tum[b] Edburga contuitu uiridis pulchritudinis ephebum eligente, Karolus nonnichil motus respondit: 'Si me elegisses, filium meum haberes; sed quia filium meum elegisti, nec me nec illum habebis.' Itaque in monasterio locatam, quo uitam opulenter transigere posset, non multo post depulit stupri ream. Huius malignitate perculsi Saxones decretum quod dixi protulerunt; sed id Ethelwlfus benignitate sua infirmauit.
4 Paucis uero ante mortem mensibus testamentum fecit, in quo, post diuisionem regni inter Ethelbaldum et Ethelbirhtum filios, filiae quoque dotem emancipauit, semperque ad finem seculi in omni[c] suae hereditatis decima hida pauperem uestiri et cibari precepit, omnique anno trecentas auri mancas Romam mitti, quarum[d] centum beato Petro et centum beato Paulo ad luminaria, centum Apostolico ad donaria expenderentur. Biennio ergo postquam a Roma uenerat superuiuens defungitur, et Wintoniae in episcopatu sepelitur. Ego uero, ut ad seriem postliminio reuertar, apponam scriptum libertatis aecclesiarum quod toti concessit Angliae.

114. [e]'Regnante Domino[f] nostro in perpetuum: dum[g] in nostris temporibus bellorum incendia et direptiones opum nostrarum necnon et uastantium crudelissimas depredationes hostium, barbararum paganarumque gentium multiplices tribulationes, ad affligendum usque ad internitionem tempora cernimus incumbere periculosa: quamobrem ego Ethelwlfus rex Occidentalium Saxonum cum consilio episcoporum ac principum meorum consilium salubre atque uniforme
2 remedium affirmaui, ut aliquam portionem terrarum hereditariam

---

[a] persontem *B*   [b] tunc *ACsBc*   [c] *C;* omnis *AB*   [d] *Ce;* quorum *ACsB*   [e] *This charter (the first part of Sawyer 322, there misdated) is also preserved in* ελπ   [f] Deo *B*   [g] om. *B*

---

[1] 43. 1.

Eadburh, as we have said,[1] was the wife of Brihtric king of the West Saxons, and by her evil counsels impelled her husband, by repute a kindly man, to shed innocent blood, while those whom she could not accuse successfully she carried off by poison. This came to light in the case of a young man to whom the king was much attached, whom she poisoned; and Brihtric promptly took to his bed and died, having drunk first from the poisoned cup, no doubt without his wife's knowledge. So, as the news spread, public feeling forced the poisoner to leave the kingdom. Making her way to the court of Charlemagne, she found him, as it happened, standing with one of his sons. The emperor offered her presents and, being in humorous mood, told her to make her choice between him and his son. Eadburh chose the young man, with an eye to his fresh good looks; whereat Charles was more than a little indignant, and retorted: 'Had you chosen me, you should have had my son; as you chose him, you shall have neither of us.' He therefore established her in a convent where she could live in comfort; but not long after he drove her out on a charge of unchastity. This was the woman whose wickedness provoked the Saxons to make the rule of which I spoke; but Æthelwulf with his generous nature did not enforce it. A few months before his death, he made a will in which, after dividing his kingdom between his sons Æthelbald and Æthelberht, he also made an exception of his daughter's dowry, and left instructions that to the end of time every tenth hide of his whole patrimony should be used to clothe and feed one poor man, and every year three hundred mancuses of gold should be sent to Rome, one hundred to St Peter and one hundred to St Paul for lights and one hundred to the pope for distribution. Having thus lived on for two years after his return from Rome, he died and was buried in the cathedral at Winchester. But with the intention of returning later to my narrative I will now set down the grant of church liberties which he made for the whole of England.

114. 'In the reign of our Lord the eternal King. Whereas in our own days we behold the fires of war, the pillage of our wealth, the most cruel depredations and devastation by our enemies, manifold tribulations caused by barbarous and pagan tribes, and the onset of a time of perils which may afflict us even to extinction: now therefore I Æthelwulf king of the West Saxons with the advice of my bishops and magnates have established a remedial policy and universal medicine, to wit, I have determined that a certain hereditary portion of the

antea possidentibus omnibus gradibus, siue famulis et famulabus Dei Deo seruientibus siue laicis, semper decimam mansionem (ubi minimum sit, tamen decimam partem) in libertatem perpetuam perdonari diiudicaui, ut sit tuta atque munita ab omnibus secularibus seruitutibus necnon regalibus tributis maioribus et minoribus, siue taxationibus quod nos dicimus witereden; sitque libera omnium rerum, pro remissione animarum et peccatorum nostrorum, Deo soli ad seruiendum, sine expeditione et pontis instructione[a] et arcis munitione; ut eo diligentius pro nobis ad Deum preces sine cessatione fundant quo eorum seruitutem in aliqua parte leuigamus. Placuit autem tunc postea[b] episcopis Alhstano Scireburnensis aecclesiae et Swithuno Wintancestrensis[c] aecclesiae cum suis abbatibus et seruis Dei consilium inire, ut omnes fratres et sorores nostrae ad unamquamque aecclesiam omni ebdomada Mercurii die, hoc est Wodnesdeg, omnis congregatio[d] cantet[e] quinquaginta psalmos, et unusquisque presbiter duas missas, unam pro rege Ethelwlfo et aliam pro ducibus eius huic[f] dono consentientibus pro mercede et refrigerio delictorum suorum, pro rege uiuente *Deus qui iustificas*, pro ducibus uiuentibus[g] *Pretende Domine*; postquam autem defuncti fuerint, pro rege defuncto singulariter, pro principibus defunctis communiter; et hoc sit tam firmiter constitutum omnibus Christianitatis diebus sicut libertas illa[h] constituta est, quam diu fides crescit in gente Anglorum.

4 'Scripta est autem haec donationis cartula anno Dominicae incarnationis octingentesimo [i]quadragesimo quarto,[i] indictione quarta, die quinto[j] nonas Nouembris, in ciuitate Wentana in aecclesia sancti Petri ante altare capitale; et hoc fecerunt pro honore sancti Michahelis archangeli et sanctae Mariae reginae gloriosae Dei genetricis, simulque[k] et beati Petri apostolorum principis necnon et sancti patris nostri Gregorii papae atque omnium sanctorum. Et tunc pro ampliore[l] firmitate rex Ethelwlfus posuit cartulam supra[m] altare sancti Petri, et episcopi pro fide Dei acceperunt et postea per omnes aecclesias transmiserunt in suis parrochiis, secundum quod predictum[n] est.'[1]

115. Ab hoc[o] Anglorum Cronica sursum uersus usque ad Adam lineam generationis regum texunt,[p] sicut Lucam euangelistam a Domino Iesu factitasse cognouimus. Quod si etiam ego fecero, fortasse

---

[a] constructione *B* [b] tunc postea *om. B (postea om. Aa)* [c] Wintoniensis *B* [d] omnis congregatio *om. B* [e] cantent *B*, λπ [f] *Ce*, ελπ; hoc *ACs*; in hoc *B*† *(cf. GP p. 390 n. 4)* [g] *om. B* [h] *om. B*, ελπ [i-i] XIIII° *C* [j] quoque *ACs*, ελπ [k] *om. B* [l] ampliori *AaBk*, ελπ; ampliorie *Al*

lands heretofore possessed by all ranks, whether servants of God male or female engaged on His service or lay persons, being every tenth hide or at the least every tenth part, shall be consigned to perpetual immunity, so as to be protected and defended from all lay services and from royal tribute greater and less or the assessments which we call *witeræden*, and shall be in all respects free, to the purging of souls and remission of our sins, for the service of God alone, without expeditions overseas and the building of bridges and fortifying of strongholds, that they may with the more diligence offer prayers to God without ceasing on my behalf, inasmuch as we relieve them to some extent of their burdens. It seemed good then to Ealhstan bishop of Sherborne and Swithhun bishop of Winchester to institute a plan, with their abbots and the servants of God, by which all our brethren and sisters should come together in every church on Mercury's day (that is, Wednesday) in each week, and the whole company should there chant fifty psalms and every priest sing two masses, one for King Æthelwulf and the other for his magnates who concur in this deed of gift, to win satisfaction and pardon for their sins: for the king in his lifetime *Deus qui iustificas* and for the magnates in their lifetimes *Praetende Domine*, and after their deaths for the late king by himself and for the deceased magnates in common; and let this be established for all the days of Christianity as firmly as that immunity, as long as the faith increases among the English people.

'This deed of gift was drawn up in the year of our Lord 844, the fourth indiction, on the first day of November in the city of Winchester in St Peter's church before the high altar; and this they did in honour of St Michael the archangel and St Mary queen of glory, the Mother of God, and also of St Peter prince of the Apostles and our holy father Pope Gregory and of all saints. And at the same time for greater security King Æthelwulf laid the deed on the altar of St Peter, and the bishops received it for the faith of God, and thereafter sent it to every church in their dioceses, as aforesaid.'

115. From Æthelwulf the English Chronicles gave the line of royal descent upwards as far as Adam, as the Evangelist Luke is known to have done from the Lord Jesus. If I too do the same, it may perhaps

---

m super *B*   *n* dictum *B*   *l* See above, p. *170*   *o* ad hoc *Tt*, adhuc *Tp;* ab hoc rege *B*   *p* texuit *TpB*

non erit superuacaneum, quamquam timendum sit ne barbaricorum nominum hiatus uulneret aures desuetorum in talibus.

116. Ethelwlfus fuit filius Egbirhti; Egbirhtus Elmundi; Elmundus Eafae; Eafa Eoppae; Eoppa*a* Ingildi fratris Inae regis, qui ambo filii fuere Kenredi; Kenredus Celwaldi; Celwaldus Cudae; Cuda Cudwini; Cudwinus Ceaulini; Ceaulinus Cinritii; Cinritius*b* Cerditii, qui fuit primus rex Westsaxonum; Cerditius*c* Elesii; Elesius Eslii; Eslius Giwii; Giwius Wigii; Wigius Frewini; Frewinus Fridegarii; Fridegarius Brondii; Brondius Beldegii; Beldegius Wodenii (de isto, ut sepe diximus,[1] processere reges multarum gentium); Wodenius fuit filius Fridewaldi; Fridewaldus Frelafii; Frelafius Finni; Finnus *d*Godulfi; Godulfus*d* Getii; Getius Tettii; Tettius Beowii; Beowius Sceldii; Sceldius Sceaf. Iste, ut ferunt, in quandam insulam Germaniae Scandzam,*e* de qua Iordanes historiographus Gothorum loquitur,[2] appulsus naui sine remige puerulus, posito ad caput frumenti manipulo dormiens, ideoque Sceaf nuncupatus, ab hominibus regionis illius pro miraculo exceptus et sedulo nutritus, adulta aetate regnauit in oppido quod tunc Slaswic, nunc uero*f* Haithebi appellatur. Est autem regio illa Anglia Vetus dicta,*g* unde Angli uenerunt in Britanniam, inter Saxones et Gothos constituta. Sceaf fuit*h* filius Heremodii; Heremodius Stermonii; Stermonius Hadrae;*i* Hadra*j* Gwalae;*k* Gwala Bedwegii; Bedwegius Strefii (hic, ut dicitur, fuit filius Noe in archa natus).

117. Anno Dominicae incarnationis octingentesimo quinquagesimo septimo duo filii Ethelwlfi regnum paternum partientes Ethelbaldus in Westsaxonia, Ethelbirhtus in Cantia regnauerunt. *l*Ethelbaldus ignauus et perfidus patri, eius thorum polluit, in coniugium Iudith nouercae post parentis obitum deuolutus;*l* sed post quinquennium eo defuncto et Scireburniae condito, totum regnum ad alterum deriuatum.*m* Huius tempore manus piratarum, appulsa Hamtunam, Wintoniam urbem populosam direptioni dedit; sed mox a ducibus regiis impigre fugata, multis suorum amissis, ultra mare ueliuolauit et pelago circumgirato Tanatum insulam, quae in Cantia est, elegit ad hiemandum. Cantuaritae datis obsidibus pecuniaque promissa quieti

---

a B adds fuit filius   *b* A (Al above the line) adds Creodingi(i) Creodingus; v. Asser, c. 1 (p. 2 Stevenson)   *c* T¹ adds fuit filius   *d–d* Godwini Godwinus (Eod- Aap) A   *e* B adds nomine (cf. Jordanes, Getica 9)   *f* om. B   *g* nuncupata B   *h* om. A   *i* Hadra A   *j* Stermonii ... Hadra om. T¹   *k* Gwala A   *l–l* om. T¹   *m* deuolutum T¹

be not without its uses, although it is to be feared that the uncouth barbarous names will wound the ear of those to whom such things are unfamiliar.

116. Æthelwulf was the son of Ecgberht; Ecgberht of Ealhmund; Ealhmund of Eafa; Eafa of Eoppa; Eoppa of Ingild brother of King Ine and both of them sons of Cenred; Cenred of Ceolwald; Ceolwald of Cutha; Cutha of Cuthwine; Cuthwine of Ceawlin; Ceawlin of Cynric; Cynric [A *adds* of Creoding; Creoding] of Cerdic, who was the first king of the West Saxons; Cerdic of Elesa; Elesa of Esla; Esla of Gewis; Gewis of Wig; Wig of Freawine; Freawine of Fredegar; Fredegar of Brond; Brond of Bældæg; Bældæg of Woden, from whom, as I have often said,[1] are descended the kings of many nations; Woden was the son of Fridewald; Fridewald of Frealaf; Frealaf of Finn; Finn of Godwulf; Godwulf of Geat; Geat of Tetti; Tetti of Beow; Beow of Sceld; Sceld of Sceaf. (This Sceaf, they say, landed on an island in Germany called Scandza mentioned by Jordanes the historian of the Goths,[2] as a small child in a ship without a crew, sleeping with a sheaf of wheat laid by his head, and hence was called Sheaf. The men of that country welcomed him as something miraculous and brought him up carefully, and on reaching manhood he ruled a town then called *Slaswic* but now Hedeby. The name of that region is Old Anglia, and it was from there that the Angles came to Britain; it lies between the Saxons and the Goths.) Sceaf was the son of Heremod; Heremod of Stermon; Stermon of Hathra; Hathra of Gwala; Gwala of Bedwig; Bedwig of Streph who was, they say, a son of Noah, born in the Ark.

117. In the year of our Lord 857 Æthelwulf's two sons divided their father's kingdom, and Æthelbald became king in Wessex, Æthelberht in Kent. Æthelbald, who was worthless and disloyal to his father, defiled his father's marriage-bed, for after his father's death he sank so low as to marry his stepmother Judith. After five years however he died, and was buried at Sherborne, and the whole kingdom passed to his brother. It was in this time that a band of pirates landed at Southampton and sacked the populous city of Winchester; but being soon put to flight by the energy of the king's magnates with heavy losses, they put to sea, and coasting round, chose the Isle of Thanet, which is in Kent, as their winter quarters. The men of Kent would have secured

---

[1] 5. 3, 16. 1, 44. 3, 45. 1, 74. 1, 97. 1, 98. 1.   [2] *Get.* 9, 16 seq., 25.

indulsissent, nisi fracto federe nocturnis excursionibus piratae totam regionem popularentur; quapropter coacto cetu fedifragos expulere. Ethelbirhtus, strenue dulciterque regnum moderatus, naturae debitum soluit post regni quinquennium, Scireburniae sepultus.

118. Anno Dominicae incarnationis octingentesimo sexagesimo septimo Ethelredus filius Ethelwlfi regnum patrium obtinuit, eodem numero annorum*a* quo fratres; miserabili et prorsus dolenda sorte ut immatura omnes occumberent*b* morte, nisi quod tantis malis obstrepentibus regii pueri magis*c* optarent honestum exitum quam acerbum imperium. Adeo animose*d* pro patria se certamini dabant ut non illis imputari debeat si minus cedebat*e* ex sententia quod intendebat audatia. Denique memoriae proditum*f* quod iste rex nouies anno uno*g* collatis et infestis signis contra hostes conflixerit, uaria licet fortuna, sepius tamen uictor, preter subitos excursus, quibus bellicae artis gnarus populatores palantes crebro afflixit. Interfecti a parte Danorum comites nouem, rex unus, preterea populus sine compoto.

119. *h*Memorabilis pre ceteris pugna fuit quam apud Escendune fecit; congregato*i* namque eo loci Danorum exercitu et in partes diuiso, hinc duobus regibus, illinc omnibus ducibus, rex cum fratre Elfredo aduentauit. Itaque sortito par pari retulere ut Ethelredus contra reges, Elfredus contra duces consisteret. Vtrorumque exercituum animis erectis, uesper iam occiduus bellum in crastinum protelauit. Vix ergo repente diluculo Elfredus paratus aderat; frater diuino intentus offitio remanserat in tentorio, stimulatusque nuntio paganos efferatis mentibus irruere, negauit se quoquam progredi quoad esset finis offitii. Quae fides regis multum fratrem adiuuit, immaturitate*j* iuuentae preproperum et iam progressum; namque iam aties Anglorum declinabant et urgentibus ex alto aduersariis fugam meditabantur, quod iniquo*k* Christianis loco pugnaretur, cum ille Dei cruce consignatus ex insperato aduolat, hostem proturbans, ciuem in arma ciens, cuius uirtute simul et Dei miraculo Dani territi pedibus salutem committentes fugere. Cesus ibi rex Osecg, comites quinque, uulgus innumerum.*h*

---

a om. *ABc*   *b* occurrerent *B*   *c* om. *T¹*   *d* *B adds* et fortiter   *e* sedebat *C*   *f* traditum *B*   *g* uno anno *T¹*   *h-h* om. *T¹*   *i* congregata *ACe*   *j* temeritate *B*   *k* *B adds* a

peace by the surrender of hostages and the promise of money, had not the pirates broken their agreement and ravaged the whole region by raiding at night. They therefore mustered their forces and drove out the treaty-breakers. Æthelberht, who was a vigorous but kindly ruler, paid the debt of nature after a reign of five years, and was buried at Sherborne.

118. In the year of our Lord 867 Æthelwulf's son Æthelred succeeded to his father's throne, and held it for as many years as his brothers. It was a sad and truly lamentable fate that carried them all off so early, were it not that, beset as they were by such adversities, the king's sons might well prefer death with honour to the miseries of power. They threw themselves with such spirit into their country's cause that we ought not to blame them if brave intentions fell short of the desired result. It is recorded, for example, that nine times in one year this king met the enemy in pitched battle, with varying result, it is true, but often successfully, not to mention the sudden forays in which his tactical experience often inflicted loss on the roving raiders. The losses on the Danish side were nine jarls, one king, and common folk without number.

119. Most memorable of all the battles was the fight at Ashdown, where the Danish army gathered and was divided into two halves, one commanded by two kings and the other by all the magnates, when the king and his brother Alfred arrived on the scene. They cast lots for a fair division, with the result that Æthelred took his stand against the kings and Alfred against the magnates. Both armies were eager for the fray, but the approach of evening postponed the battle till next day. So almost before daybreak Alfred was ready on the instant, while his brother had remained in his tent, absorbed in his devotions, and though spurred on by the news of a ferocious attack by the pagans, refused to budge until the office was finished. The king's devoutness did a great service to his young and headstrong brother, who had already advanced; for the English line was by now yielding, and under pressure from higher ground they were ready to break, the advantage of the ground being against the Christians. At that moment the king, with the holy Cross as his standard, unexpectedly charged, throwing the enemy into confusion, and roused the ardour of his countrymen. The combination of his prowess and God's miraculous power terrified the Danes, who sought safety in flight. Their losses were King Osecg, five jarls, and numberless common soldiers.

120. Meminerit interea lector quod interim*a* reges Mertiorum et Northanimbrorum, captata occasione aduentus Danorum, quorum bellis Ethelredus insudabat, a seruitio Westsaxonum respirantes, dominationem pene suam asseruerant.*b* Ardebant ergo cunctae seuis populatibus prouintiae; unusquisque regum inimicos magis*c* in suis sedibus sustinere quam compatriotis laborantibus opem porrigere curabat. Ita, dum malunt uindicare quam preuenire iniuriam, socordia sua exsanguem reddidere patriam. Dani sine obstaculo succrescere, dum et prouintialibus timor incresceret et proxima quaeque uictoria per additamentum captiuorum instrumentum*d* sequentis fieret. Orientalium Anglorum pagi cum urbibus et uicis a predonibus possessi; rex eorum sanctus Edmundus, ab eisdem interemptus, temporaneae mortis compendio regnum emit aeternum. Mertii, non semel obtriti,*e* obsidatu miserias suas leuauerunt; Northanimbri, iam dudum ciuilibus dissensionibus fluctuantes, aduentante hoste correxerunt discordiam. Itaque Osbirhtum regem, quem expulerant, in solium reformantes magnosque moliti paratus obuiam prodeunt, sed facile pulsi intra urbem Eboracum se includunt; qua mox a uictoribus succensa, cum laxos crines effusior flamma produceret, tota depascens menia, ipsi quoque conflagrati patriam ossibus texere*f* suis. Sic Northanimbria, bellico iure*g* obtenta, barbarorum dominium multo post tempore pro conscientia libertatis ingemuit. At uero rex Ethelredus multis laboribus infractus obiit, et Winburnae sepultus est.

121. Anno Dominicae incarnationis octingentesimo septuagesimo secundo Elfredus filius Ethelwlfi iunior, qui unctionem regiam et coronam a papa Leone*h* olim Romae susceperat, ut prediximus,[1] regnum accepit,*i* et uiginti octo et semis annos laboriosissime sed fortissime tenuit. Laborum eius inextricabiles laberinthos singillatim euoluere non fuit consilium, propterea quod sit legentium quaedam confusio gestorum per omnes annos recensitio; nam quia exercitus hostilis per eum uel satellites eius ab una parte regionis fugatus in alteram secedebat, rursusque inde pulsus alia loca petebat, omnia rapinis et cedibus complens, eum*j* quoque scripto sequi et, ut ita dicam, cum eo insulam

---

a om. B†   *b* asseuerant T¹   *c* Repeated by T¹   *d* incrementum B   *e* attriti B   *f* contexere T¹   *g* uiro T¹   *h* primus a papa L. quarto C   *i* suscepit CsB   *j* B; eam T⁺AC

[1] c. 109.

120. Meanwhile the reader should remember that all this time the kings of the Mercians and Northumbrians had seized their opportunity on the arrival of the Danes, whom Æthelred was busily confronting in battle, to seek a relief from subjection to the West Saxons, and had almost asserted their own independence. Thus whole provinces were ablaze with pitiless devastation, and each of the kings was more set on resisting the enemy in his own domains than assisting his compatriots in their hour of need. Thus, preferring to avenge injury rather than to prevent it, they drained by their folly the country's lifeblood. The Danes acquired strength without hindrance, as fear increased its hold on the inhabitants, and each successive victory, by adding to the tale of prisoners, contributed to the next. Whole districts of East Anglia with their towns and villages were taken by the invaders, who put to death its saintly King Edmund, so that at the bargain price of death in time he bought a kingdom in eternity. The Mercians after more than one crushing defeat secured a respite from their sufferings by giving hostages. As for the Northumbrians, they had long been embroiled in civil strife, but on the enemy's approach made up their quarrels. And so they restored to the throne their king Osberht, whom they had driven into exile, and after great preparations advanced against the invader. Defeated with ease, they took refuge in the city of York; but the victorious enemy soon set it on fire, and as the growing flames spread like streaming hair and devoured all the city walls, the defenders too were burnt to death and covered their native country with their bones. So Northumbria, won by right of conquest, long lay under barbarian rule, groaning as she recalled her former liberty. But King Æthelred died, broken by all his efforts, and was buried at Wimborne.

121. In the year of our Lord 872 Æthelwulf's younger son Alfred succeeded to the throne, who had been anointed and crowned king long before by Pope Leo in Rome, as we have told already,[1] and for twenty-eight and a half years he held the kingship, with great labour but great courage. His labours form an impenetrable labyrinth, which it is not my purpose to thread in detail, for to recount all his achievements year by year might somewhat confuse my reader. The enemy forces, driven by him or his subordinates out of one part of his dominions, used to take refuge in another, and again when driven from there would seek somewhere else, filling everywhere with robbery and bloodshed; and to follow him in my narrative, making the circuit of the island (if I may so put it) in his company,

circuire forsitan quis dixerit extremae esse dementiae. Summatim igitur omnia exponam.

2   Continuis nouem annis cum hostibus compugnans, modo incertis federibus illusus, modo in illudentes ultus, ad hoc tandem inopiae coactus est ut, uix tribus pagis*a* in fide rigentibus, id est Hamtescire Wiltescire Sumerseta, etiam in insulam quandam palustri uligine uix accessibilem, uocabulo Adelingeam,*b* refugerit. Solebat ipse postea, in tempora felitiora reductus, casus suos iocunda hilarique comitate familiaribus exponere, qualiterque per beati Cuthberti meritum eos euaserit, sicut plerumque mos est mortalibus ut eos illa iuuet meminisse quae olim horruerint excepisse.

3   Nam cum quadam die in insula inclusus solus domi esset, sotiis per oram fluminis ad piscandum dispersis, corpus curis egrum sopori commisit; et ecce Cuthbertus, Lindisfarnensis quondam episcopus, his dormientem alloquitur: 'Ego sum Cuthbertus, si audisti. Misit me Dominus ut tibi prospera annuntiem: quia enim Anglia iam dudum peccatorum penas enormiter luit, modo tandem, indigenarum sanctorum meritis, super eam misericordiae suae oculo*c* respicit. Tu quoque, tam miserabiliter regno extorris, gloriose post paucum tempus in solio*d* reponeris, atque adeo*e* signum eximium tibi dabo. Venient hodie piscatores tui magnam uim grandium piscium corbibus euehentes, quod eo erit mirabilius quia his diebus gelante aqua fluuius asperatus nichil tale sperari permittit; super haec, hodie gelido rore stillans aer omnem piscantium artem eludit. Verum tu, fortunae secundae compos, regaliter feceris si adiutorem tuum Deum et me eius*f* nun-
4   tium competenti deuotione demerueris.' Haec dicens sanctus regem soporatum sollicitudinibus exuit; matremque etiam*g* prope cubantem tenuesque somnos propter leuamen curarum ad durum cubile inuitantem eiusdem nuntii laetitia confortauit.*h* Experrecti ambo unum et idem se somniasse frequenti uerborum recursu iterabant, cum piscatores ingressi tantam piscium copiam exhibuere ut cuiusuis magni exercitus ingluuiem exsaturare*i* posse uideretur.

5   Nec multo post, ergastulum exire ausus, magnae astutiae periculum fecit. Regis enim Danorum sub spetie mimi subiens tentoria, unius tantum fidelissimi fruebatur conscientia. Ibi ut ioculatoriae professor

a plagis *A*   *b* Adelingeam *B;* -gea *T*⁺*AC*   *c* oc(c)ulis *C*   *d* solium *B*   *e* inde *C*   *f* ipsius *B*   *g* om.*T*⁺, *GP p.* 269   *h* conf. let. *T*   *i* saturare *C*

might seem to some perhaps the height of folly. I shall therefore give the salient points of the whole story.

Nine years without a break he battled with the enemy. Sometimes they deceived him with an uncertain truce; sometimes he took vengeance on the deceivers. At length he was reduced to such straits that, with scarcely three counties, Hampshire, Wiltshire, and Somerset, remaining stubbornly in their allegiance, he was actually forced to take refuge in an island called Athelney, which from its marshy situation was hardly accessible. Years afterwards, when happier times returned, he himself would tell his friends in cheerful intimacy the story of his adventures, and how he had survived them by the merits of St Cuthbert—so common is it among mortal men to recall with pleasure experiences that were fearful at the time.

One day, when he was penned up in the island, and had been left alone in the house while his companions spread out along the river bank to fish, he sought relief from his anxieties in sleep; and lo, as he slept, Cuthbert, sometime bishop of Lindisfarne, addressed him in these words: 'I am Cuthbert, of whom you may have heard. The Lord has sent me to bring you good tidings, for since England has long been paying very heavy penalties for all her sins, He now at length through the merits of her native saints looks on her with an eye of mercy. You too, who are now so pitifully driven from your kingdom, shall in a short time be restored in glory to your throne, and of this I will give you a striking token. Your fishermen will return today with a great catch of big fish in their creels, and this will be all the more remarkable, inasmuch as the wintry river, covered these days with ice, offers no hope of anything of the kind; besides which, the icy drizzle that drops from the air today defeats all the fishermen's skill. But you, when you are restored to prosperity, will act as a king should, if you show your gratitude to God who helps you and to me His messenger by suitable devotion.' With these words the saint relieved the sleeping king of all his cares; and with the same glad tidings he cheered the king's mother who lay nearby, wooing elusive sleep to come and relieve her anxieties on her hard bed. They both awoke, and finding they had had the selfsame dream were telling the story over and over, when the fishermen entered and displayed such a huge catch of fish as might seem enough to glut the appetite of any great army.

Not long after that, he took the risk of leaving his prison, and hazarded a most cunning trick. Dressed as a minstrel he entered the Danish king's camp, supported by one most faithful companion who

artis etiam in secretiora triclinii admissus, nichil fuit archanum quod non exciperet cum oculis tum[a] auribus; pluresque dies ibi moratus, cum ex[b] omnibus quae nosse desiderarat animo satisfecisset suo, Adelingeam rediit, congregatisque[c] comitibus exponit inimicorum otium, leue uincendi negotium. Cunctis ad audendum[d] erectis ipse, contractis undecumque auxiliis, exploratoribusque premissis de sede barbarorum certior redditus, eosque repente adorsus incredibili strage cecidit; residui[e] cum rege suo dederunt obsides quod Christianitatem susciperent
6 et ab Anglia discederent. Quod et factum est; namque[f] rex eorum[g] Guthrum, quem nostri Gurmundum uocant, cum triginta proceribus et omni pene populo baptizatus et in filium a rege Elfredo susceptus est. Datae ei[h] prouintiae Orientalium Anglorum et Northanimbrorum, ut eas sub fidelitate regis iure foueret hereditario quas peruaserat latrocinio. Verum, quia non mutabit Ethiops pellem suam, datas ille terras tirannico fastu undecim annis proterens, duodecimo uitam finiuit, posteris quoque perfidiae successionem transmittens,[i] donec a nepote istius Elfredi Ethelstano subiugati, regem unum Angliae fieri[j] uel inuiti concesserint,[k] sicut hic dies inuenit.
7 Ceteri ex Danis, qui Christiani esse recusassent, cum Hastengo mare transfretauerunt, ubi quae mala fecerint indigenae norunt; tota enim ora maritima usque ad mare Tirrenum grassati, Parisius et Turonis et multas alias urbes, quae uel super Sequanam uel Ligerim, nobiles Galliae fluuios, sitae sunt, ciuibus uacuarunt. Tunc corpora multorum sanctorum, ab antiquae requietionis sedibus[l] eruta et ad tutiora loca delata, peregrinas aecclesias usque ad hoc tempus cineribus nobilitarunt suis. Tunc et beati Martini corpus, ut Sidonius ait, 'totis uenerabile terris, in quo post uitae tempora uiuit honos,'[1] Autisiodorum a clericis suis portatum[m] et in aecclesia beati Germani locatum, inauditis signis
8 circumiacentium regionum homines excitabat. Cumque aduentantes pro remediorum gratia plurima conferrent quae baiulorum onera palparent, ut fieri solet, ex pecuniae partitione lis commissa, Turonicis totam uendicantibus quod eorum herus oblatores mirabilibus inuitasset, indigenis contra referentibus Germanum non disparem

[a] cum *AaB*   [b] om. *Tt(not Tc)A*   [c] -que om. *A*; *B* adds omnibus   [d] *A*; audiendum *TCB*   [e] reliqui *B*   [f] nam *ABk*   [g] eorum rex *A*   [h] sibi *B*   [i] mittens *T*   [j] om. *B*   [k] concesserunt *TcB*   [l] om. *A*   [m] deportatum *B*

---

[1] Sidonius, *Ep.* iv. 18. 5.

knew the secret. There, gaining entry as a professional entertainer, even to the innermost quarters, there was no secret that he did not learn with both eyes and ears. After spending several days there and finding out to his heart's content all that he wanted to know, he returned to Athelney, collected his chief men together, and explained how idle the enemy were and how easy it would be to defeat them. Having roused the courage of them all, the king himself gathered forces in support from every quarter, and having learnt the barbarians' position more exactly by sending scouts on ahead, fell upon them suddenly and cut them to pieces with incredible slaughter. The survivors, with their king, gave hostages for their conversion to Christianity and for their leaving England. And so it came to pass: for Guthrum their king, who we call Gurmund, was baptised with thirty nobles and almost all his people, and King Alfred was his godfather. He was given the provinces of East Anglians and Northumbrians, that in fealty to the king he should govern well by hereditary right what he had ravaged as an invader. But the Ethiopian will not change his skin, and for eleven years he was a proud tyrant oppressing the lands entrusted to him; in the twelfth year he met his end, leaving to his successors a tradition of perfidy which lasted till their subjugation by Alfred's grandson Æthelstan, when even against their will they had to accept that there should be one king over the whole of England, as is so today.

The remnant of the Danes, who had refused to become Christians, crossed the sea with Hæsten, and the damage they did there is well-known to the inhabitants; they descended upon the whole sea-coast as far as the Tyrrhenian sea, and emptied of their inhabitants Paris and Tours and many other cities situated on those noble rivers of Gaul, the Seine and the Loire. It was then that the bodies of many saints were lifted from their ancient resting-places and removed to greater safety, thus enriching with their relics churches to which they were strangers, as they do to this day. It was then that St Martin's body which, as Sidonius says, 'in every land revered, preserves his honour though his life is o'er',[1] was carried by his clergy to Auxerre, and lodged in the church of St Germanus, where it raised the fervour of the surrounding regions by unheard-of miracles. Those who flocked to the shrine made many offerings in gratitude for their healing, to recompense the bearers of it for the burden they carried; but, as often happens, the division of the money gave rise to disputes. The men from Tours claimed the whole sum, saying that it was their patron who had attracted the donors by his miracles; the local people, on the

merito, aequalem offitio, et uideri quidem amborum esse potentiae,[a] sed preponderare prerogatiuam aecclesiae. Ad laxandum dubietatis nodum queritur et ponitur inter duorum sanctorum corpora leprosus, uix solo anhelitu palpitans, cetera tabidus et in uiuo cadauere iam

9 premortuus. Arcetur tota nocte humana custodia; uigilat tantum Martini gloria. Nam postera die apparuit cutis hominis a parte [b]illius splendida, a parte[b] Germani solita deformitate lurida. Et ne darent euentui miraculum, obuertunt Martino latus morbidum; iam uero cum prima[c] aurora in lucem proreperet,[d] a festinantibus ministris inuenitur uir tota cute integer, tota incolumis, predicans beni-

10 uolentiam domestici presulis, qua cessit honori gratissimi hospitis. Ita Turonici ex tunc[e] et deinceps per patroni suffragium tuto familiare cumulabant marsupium, donec pacis aura clementior propriis eos penatibus inuexit. Latrunculi enim, tredecim annis Gallias infestantes, ad extremum ab Ernulfo imperatore et Britannis multis preliis uicti in Angliam, oportunum scilicet tirannidis suffugium, conuolauere.

Quo spatio Elfredus totam insulam, preter[f] quod Dani habebant, animo subdiderat suo; uolentes enim[g] Angli in eius potestatem concesserant, gaudentes se talem uirum edidisse, qui posset illos in libertatem euehere. Lundoniam, caput regni Mertiorum, cuidam primario Etheredo in fidelitatem suam cum filia Ethelfleda concessit.

11 Ille magna uirtute et fide agere, commissa tutari sedulo; Orientales et Northanimbros, iam dudum discessionem a rege parturientes, in statu continuit, obsides prebere compellens. Quod quantum profecerit, sequens occasio probauit. Nam, cum illis tredecim[h] annis pacis serenitate et glebae ubertate Anglia gauderet, rediit aquilonalis lues illa barbarorum. Iterum bella, iterum cedes, denuo Northanimbrorum et Orientalium Anglorum coniurationes; sed nec[i] aduenae nec indigenae pari qua[j] superioribus annis sorte perfuncti. Illi, transmarinis preliis imminuti, segniores erant ad inuadendum; isti, usu bellorum et hortamentis regis animati, promptiores erant non solum ad

12 resistendum sed [k]et ad[k] lacessendum. Rex ipse impigre in omnibus

---

[a] *One expects* potentiam rumperet *T (cf. 159. 1)* etiam *TtAB* [b-b] *om. C; B adds* uero [c] *et tunc* B† *(cf. 7. 3 n.o)* [c] primo *C* [d] prorumperet *T (cf. 159. 1)* [f] *B adds* id [g] *C;* etiam *TtAB* [h] XIIII *C (but cf. 10 above)* [i] *om. B* [j] quam *B* [k-k] et *C;* ad *B*

other hand, maintained that Germanus deserved no less, and had in fact done as much, so that they thought the miraculous power to belong to both, but the church where the miracles happened had the prior claim. To solve the problem, they sent for a leper, and set him between the bodies of the two saints; his gasping breath was the only sign of life and in all other respects he was moribund, and virtually dead while his corpse was still alive. All that night no human eye was allowed near, and the glory of St Martin alone kept watch. Next day the man's skin on the side turned towards St Martin was quite clear, while on St Germanus' side it was as ghastly and hideous as ever. And that the miracle might not be ascribed to chance, they turned the infected side towards Martin; as soon as dawn began to move slowly towards the day, the servants hastened to the church and found the man's skin entirely restored and cured—a great proof of the good will of the bishop of that place, which had moved him to yield to the prestige of a most welcome guest. Thereafter the men from Tours, thanks to the support of their patron saint, filled their own coffers without risk, until the more kindly air of peace restored them to their homes. For the pirates, after infesting Gaul for thirteen years, were at length overcome in a series of battles by the Emperor Arnulf and the Bretons, and departed for England, thinking this no doubt a suitable refuge for the rule of violence.

During this space of time Alfred had subjected to his will the whole island except what was held by the Danes; for the English had willingly submitted to his rule, rejoicing to think that they had produced a man capable of restoring their liberties. London, the capital of the kingdom of the Mercians, he gave to a leading noble called Æthelred in fealty to himself, together with his daughter Æthelflæd. Æthelred showed himself brave and loyal, and governed diligently what was entrusted to him; the East Anglians and Northumbrians, who had long been planning to desert the king, he retained in their allegiance by compelling them to provide hostages. The effectiveness of this policy was tested by the sequel; for when England was rejoicing in those thirteen years of peace and good harvests, the plague of the northern barbarians returned once more. Battle and carnage resumed, conspiracy revived among the Northumbrians and East Angles. But neither invaders nor natives enjoyed the same fortune as in previous years. The barbarians, having suffered losses in battles overseas, pursued the invasion with less energy, while the English, inspired by experience in fighting and the encouragement of their king, were readier not only to resist but to take the offensive. The king himself

necessitatibus aderat, nota suae uirtutis spetie alienos territans et suos corroborans; solus aduersum pectus hostibus inferre, solus inclinatam atiem restituere. Ostenduntur ab accolis loca singula in quibus uel malae fortunae copiam uel bonae persensit inopiam. Cum Elfredo enim etiam uicto, etiam iacente luctandum erat: adeo, cum omnino contritum putares, uelut anguis lubricus de manu tenentis elapsus, e cauernis subitus emergebat, sponte insultantes[a] inimicos adoriens, plerumque post fugam importabilis, et memoria repulsae circumspectior et ardore uindictae audatior.

13 [b]Ex Egelswitha[c] filia Egelredi comitis tulit liberos Ethelswidam et Eduardum, qui post se regnauit; Ethelfledam, quae nupta fuit Etheredo comiti Mertiorum; Ethelwerdum, quem litteratissimum perhibent; Elfledam[d] et Elfgifam uirgines. Valitudinis aduersae, ut qui semper uel fico uel aliquo interaneorum morbo agitaretur;[e] sed hoc eum a Deo precibus exegisse aiunt, ut incommodorum ammonitu[f] segnius illecebras mundanas amplecteretur.[g][b]

122. Verum inter haec miranda et insigni preconio prosequenda uita regis interior. Licet enim, ut quidam[1] ait, leges inter arma sileant, ille inter [h]stridores lituorum, inter[h] fremitus armorum[i] leges tulit, quibus sui et diuino cultui et disciplinae militari assuescerent. Et quia occasione barbarorum etiam indigenae in rapinas anhelauerant, adeo ut nulli tutus commeatus esset sine armorum presidio, centurias quas dicunt hundrez et decimas quas tithingas uocant instituit, ut omnis Anglus legaliter dumtaxat uiuens haberet et centuriam et decimam. Quod si quis alicuius delicti insimularetur, statim ex centuria et decima exhiberet qui eum uadarentur; qui uero huiusmodi uadem non reperiret,[j] seueritatem legum horreret. Si quis autem[k] reus uel ante uadationem uel post transfugeret, omnes ex centuria et decima

2 regis multam incurrerent. Hoc commento pacem infudit prouintiae, ut etiam per publicos aggeres, ubi semitae in[l] quadruuium finduntur,[m]

[a] insistentes *B*   [b-b] om. *Tt*   [c] Egelfleda *B†*   [d] *CsB;* Elfredam *ACe*   [e] agitarentur *C*   [f] admonite *Ce,* -iti *Cs(and CpCr)*   [g] amplecterentur *C*   [h-h] om. *C*   [i] armatorum *Tt*   [j] uadem huiusmodi non reciperet *Tt*   [k] uero *B*   [l] per *B*   [m] funduntur *ACs*[a.c.] *Bc[l]*

[1] Cicero, *Pro Milone* 11 (cited by Jerome, *Ep.* cxxvi. 2).

was actively engaged in every emergency, his mere appearance with his well-known prowess being enough to terrify the other side and reinforce his own; single-handed he would lead a charge against the enemy, and single-handed stiffen a wavering battle-line. Particular places are pointed out by the local people where he experienced an excess of bad fortune or a shortage of good. For Alfred, even when beaten, even when lying prostrate, was a force to be reckoned with; with such skill, when you might suppose him entirely crushed, did he emerge suddenly from his hiding-places, like a slippery snake that slithers from the hand that held it, launching on his triumphant enemies an attack of his own choosing. After flight he was generally irresistible, for he became more circumspect from the recollection of defeat, more bold from the thirst for vengeance.

By Æthelswith, daughter of Ealdorman Æthelred, he had children: Æthelswith and Edward, who succeeded him, Æthelflæd, who married Æthelred ealdorman of the Mercians, Æthelweard, who is said to have been a man of great learning, Ælfflæd and Ælfgifu who never married. His health was a handicap, for he always suffered from piles or some internal complaint; but this he is said to have obtained from God by prayer, in hopes that the warnings of sickness might make him less ready to embrace worldly temptations.

122. All this time, the king's inner life was remarkable and deserves high praise. It may be true, as someone says,[1] that 'laws are silent amid the clash of arms'; nonetheless, amid the braying of trumpets and the roar of battle Alfred made laws to familiarize his subjects equally with religious practices and military discipline. The barbarian invasions had given the natives too an appetite for plunder, such that no man's journey was safe without armed protection; and so he instituted the centuries which they call hundreds and the division into tenths called tithings, so that every Englishman, or those at least who lived a law-abiding life, should have his century and his tenth. If any man were accused of some misdemeanour, he had at once to produce men from his century and tenth to stand surety for him; and he who could not find any surety of this sort had to fear the full rigour of the law. If, however, any accused person, either before or after his provision of sureties, made good his escape, then all the members of his century and tenth were liable to pay a fine to the king. By this new system he spread peace throughout the province, so that even on public highways he would order bracelets of gold to be hung

armillas aureas iuberet suspendi, quae uiantum auiditatem riderent, dum non essent qui eas abriperent. Elemosinis intentus priuilegia aecclesiarum, sicut pater statuerat, roborauit, et trans mare Romam et ad sanctum Thomam in India*ª* multa munera misit. Legatus in hoc missus Sigelmus Scireburnensis episcopus, cum magna prosperitate, quod quiuis*ᵇ* hoc seculo*ᶜ* miretur, Indiam penetrauit; inde rediens exoticos splendores gemmarum et liquores aromatum, quorum illa humus ferax est, reportauit; preterea munus omni obrizo pretiosius,
3 partem Dominici ligni a papa Marino regi missam. Monasteria ubi oportunum uidebat*ᵈ* construxit: unum in Adelingea, ubi eum latuisse superior relatio meminit,[1] ibique*ᵉ* abbatem Iohannem constituit, ex antiqua Saxonia oriundum; alterum in*ᶠ* Wintonia, quod dicitur Nouum Monasterium, ubi Grimbaldum abbatem constituit, qui se euocante et archiepiscopo Remensi mittente Angliam uenerat, cognitus quod se puerum olim, ut ferunt,*ᵍ* Romam euntem benigno hospitio confouerat. Causa euocationis*ʰ* ut litteraturae studium, in Anglia sopitum et pene emortuum,*ⁱ* sua suscitaret industria. *ʲ*Sceftoniense*ᵏ* etiam monasterium sanctimonialibus compleuit, ubi et abbatissam filiam
4 suam Elfgiuam instituit.*ʲ* Habebat ex Sancto Dewi Asserionem quendam, scientia non ignobili instructum, quem Scireburniae fecit episcopum. Hic sensum*ˡ* librorum Boetii De Consolatione*ᵐ* planioribus uerbis enodauit, quos rex ipse in Anglicam linguam uertit. *ⁿ*Preterea, quia nullus in suo regno litterarum erat peritus, euocauit ex Mertia Wicciorum episcopum Werefrithum, qui iussu regis Dialogorum libros in Anglicum sermonem conuertit.*ⁿ*
5 Hoc tempore creditur fuisse Iohannes Scottus, uir perspicacis ingenii et multae facundiae, qui dudum concrepantibus undique bellorum fragoribus in Frantiam ad Karolum Caluum transierat; cuius rogatu Ierarchiam Dionisii Ariopagitae in Latinum de Greco uerbum e uerbo*ᵒ* transtulit. Composuit etiam librum quem ΠΗΡΙ ΦΙCΙΟΝ ΜΗΡΙΜΝΟΙ,*ᵖ* id est De Naturae Diuisione titulauit, propter perplexitatem necessariarum questionum soluendam bene utilem, si tamen ignoscatur ei in aliquibus, in quibus a Latinorum tramite
6 deuiauit, dum in Grecos acriter oculos intendit. Succedentibus annis

ª Indiam *B†, GP p. 177 (idiomatically)*   *ʰ* *TtB add* in   *ᶜ* tempore *B (cf. 19. 2 n. h)*   *ᵈ* uidebatur *B*   *ᵉ* asseruit sibique *B*   *ᶠ* uero in *B*   *ᵍ* fertur *Tt*   *ʰ* euocationum *B*   *ⁱ* sepultum *B*   *ʲ⁻ʲ om. Tt*   *ᵏ* *B adds* quin   *ˡ* sensus *A*   *ᵐ* *B† adds* philosophie *(so 123. 1 and GP p. 177)*   *ⁿ⁻ⁿ om. Tt*   *ᵒ* e uerbo *om. T*   *ᵖ* peri fision merimnoi *added above the line in AlC (cf. GP p. 393)*

up at crossroads, to mock the greed of passers-by, for no one dared steal them. Being devoted to almsgiving, he confirmed the privileges of churches as laid down by his father, and sent many gifts overseas to Rome and to St Thomas in India. For this purpose he despatched an envoy, Sigehelm bishop of Sherborne, who made his way to India with great success, an astonishing feat even today, and brought with him on his return gems of exotic splendour and the liquid perfumes of which the soil there is productive, and besides them a gift more to be desired than much fine gold, a portion of our Lord's Cross sent to the king by Pope Marinus. He built monasteries where he thought 3 suitable, one in Athelney where, as I have told above,[1] he had lain in hiding, and appointed John, who came from Old Saxony, to be its abbot. Another was in Winchester, called New Minster, and there he made Grimbald abbot, who had come to England at his invitation and sent by the archbishop of Reims, and whom he knew because, as the story goes, Grimbald had received him kindly long ago, when he was a boy, on his way to Rome. The motive for this invitation was the hope that his efforts might foster the pursuit of learning, which had fallen asleep in England and was almost dead. He also filled with nuns the convent at Shaftesbury, and installed his daughter Ælfgifu as abbess. He secured from St David's a man called Asser who was no 4 mean scholar, and made him bishop of Sherborne; Asser expounded with greater lucidity the meaning of Boethius' books *On Consolation*, which the king himself translated into English. Besides which, having no scholar in his kingdom, he summoned Wærferth, bishop of the Hwicce, out of Mercia, who at the king's command translated into English the books of *Dialogues*.

This is thought to have been the time when John the Scot flour- 5 ished, a man of piercing intellect and great gifts of style, who long before, when the thunders of war were rumbling everywhere, had taken refuge in France with Charles the Bald, and at his request made a word-for-word version from Greek into Latin of the *Hierarchy* of Dionysius the Areopagite. He also wrote a book which he called *Peri fision merimnoi, On the Division of Nature*, which is a valuable help to the solution of several complicated and fundamental problems, provided we excuse some deviations from the straight path of Latin opinion caused by his concentration on the Greeks. In later years Alfred's 6

---

[1] 121. 2.

munificentia Elfredi allectus uenit Angliam, et apud monasterium nostrum a pueris quos docebat grafiis, ut fertur, perforatus etiam martir estimatus est; quod sub ambiguo ad iniuriam sanctae animae non dixerim, cum celebrem eius memoriam sepulchrum in sinistro latere altaris et epitaphii prodant uersus, *a*scabri quidem et moderni temporis lima carentes, sed ab antiquo non adeo deformes:*a*

> Clauditur in tumulo sanctus sophista Iohannes,
> qui ditatus erat iam uiuens dogmate miro.
> Martirio tandem Christi conscendere regnum
> quo meruit regnant sancti*b* per secula cuncti.[1]

123. His collateralibus*c* rex fretus liberales artes totis medullis indidit, in tantum ut nullus Anglorum fuerit uel in intelligendo acutior uel in interpretando elegantior. *d*Quod eo magis erat mirum, quia iam duodennis omnis litteraturae expers fuit; tunc uero ludo benignae matris inuitatus ut pro munere libellum quem pre manibus tenebat acciperet,*e* si cito addisceret, ioco litteras ingressus auiditate siticulosa combibit.*d* Denique plurimam partem Romanae bibliothecae Anglorum auribus dedit, opimam predam*f* peregrinarum mertium ciuium usibus conuectans; cuius precipui sunt libri Orosius, Pastoralis Gregorii, Gesta Anglorum Bedae, Boetius De Consolatione Philosophiae, liber proprius quem patria lingua Enchiridion,*g* id est Manualem librum appellauit. *h*Quin et prouintialibus grandem amorem studiorum infudit, hos premiis illos*i* iniuriis hortando, neminem illiteratum ad quamlibet curiae*j* dignitatem aspirare permittens.*h* Psalterium transferre aggressus, uix prima parte explicata*k* uiuendi finem fecit. In prologo Pastoralis dicit se iccirco ad interpretandos Anglice libros animatum, quod aecclesiae, in quibus numerosae a prisco bibliothecae continebantur, cum libris a Danis incensae sint; propterea in tota insula studium litterarum abolitum, quod quisque magis uereretur capitis*l* periculum quam sequeretur librorum exercitium. Quapropter se in hoc Anglis suis consulere, ut nunc prelibarent tumultuarie quod postea, si forte pax rediret, Latino ediscerent sermone; ad omnes principales sedes librum hunc suo iussu conscriptum*m* uelle transmittere,

a–a om. B. The poem is also preserved in GP p. 394 and the Letter to Peter (Stubbs i. cxlvi)   *b* seculi A(?)   *c* lateralibus B   *d–d* om. Tt   *e* susciperet B   *f* partem Tt   *g* handboc(h) B   *h–h* om. Tt   *i* om. B   *j* om. B   *k* explicita Tt* (cf. VW iii. 28)   *l* om. B   *m* B adds se

[1] SK 2573.

generosity attracted him to England, and there he met his death in our monastery, as the story goes, when the boys whom he was teaching pierced him with their pens; for which he has been accounted a martyr. I do not say this so ambiguously in order to harm his soul; for his memory is kept warm by a tomb on the left side of the altar and an epitaph in verse—rough verse, and lacking the finish of our modern day, but not too much distorted from the ancient pattern:

> Here lieth John, that saintly was and wise,
> Who while he lived was rich in learning rare,
> A martyr worthy to Christ's realm to rise
> Among the saints, who reign for ever there.[1]

123. Relying on these supporters the king absorbed the liberal arts into his very life-blood, so much so that no Englishman had a keener understanding or could translate with greater elegance. This was the more surprising, as at the age of twelve he still had no education; but his affectionate mother then found a ruse to encourage him: he should have the book she held in her hand as a present, if he learnt it quickly. So he began to learn reading as a game, and soaked it up like a sponge. He made a great part of Latin literature accessible to English ears, bringing together a rich cargo of foreign merchandise for the benefit of his countrymen. The chief titles are Orosius, Gregory's *Pastoral Care*, Bede's *History of the English*, Boethius *On the Consolation of Philosophy*, and a book of his own which he called in his native tongue *Enchiridion*, that is *Hand-book*. He also inspired his subjects with a great love of study, encouraging some by rewards and some by penalties, for he allowed no uneducated person to hope for any position at his court. He began to translate the Psalter, but reached the end of his life when he had barely completed the first part. In the prologue to the *Pastoral Care* he tells us that he was moved to undertake English versions because the churches in which well-stocked libraries were to be found from early times had, together with their books, been burnt by the Danes; with the result that in the whole island literary studies had been done away with; for everyone had to put fear for his life above zeal for book-learning. And so, he says, he did this for the benefit of his English subjects, that they might now secure a rapid foretaste of something which later on, should peace return, they might learn properly in Latin; and he was proposing to send this book, written on his instructions, to all the principal sees, together with a golden tablet

cum pugillari aureo in quo esset manca auri. Nichil in ista uel*a* aliis interpretationibus ex suo dicere, sed omnia a spectabilibus uiris Pleimundo archiepiscopo,*b* Asserione episcopo, Grimbaldo et Iohanne presbiteris hausisse.

4 Postremo, ut omnem uitam eius breuiter elucidem, uiginti quattuor horas quae inter diem et noctem iugiter rotantur ita diuidebat, ut octo horas in scribendo et legendo et orando, octo in cura corporis, octo in expediendo regni negotia transigeret. Erat in capella sua candela uiginti quattuor partium edituusque, cui haec delegabatur prouintia,*c* ut per combustionem candelae regem de singulis ammoneret offitiis. *d*Dimidiam portionem omnium censuum, iuste dumtaxat adquisitorum, monasteriis suis delegauit. Cunctos preterea redditus in aequas duas partes diuidebat, rursusque primam in tres: quarum primam ministris suis curialibus, secundam operatoribus quos iugiter in nouarum edium extructionibus*e* mirabili et ignoto

5 Anglis modo habebat, tertiam aduenis. Secunda pars reddituum ita diuidebatur, ut prima portio daretur pauperibus regionis suae, secunda monasteriis, tertia scolasticis, quarta transmarinis aecclesiis. Iuditiorum a suis hominibus factorum inquisitor, perperam actorum asperrimus corrector. Illud insolens et inauditum, quod semper sinu gestabat libellum in quo diurni cursus psalmi continebantur, ut, si quando uacaret, arriperet et uigilanti oculo percurreret.*d* Ita uitam egit magna cum finitimis gratia, et Balduino comiti Flandriae Ethelswida filia in coniugium data, ex qua ille genuit Ernulfum et Adulfum. Iste a patre comitatum Bononiae suscepit; ex altero sunt hodie*f* comites Flandriae.

124. Elfredus *g*naturae functus munere*g* sepultus est Wintoniae in monasterio suo. Ad cuius officinas instruendas, suffitiens spatium terrae ab episcopo et canonicis tunc temporis nundinatus, ad unumquemque pedem mancam auri publico pondere pensitauit. Stupenda profecto regis abstinentia, ut tanta se pateretur emungi pecunia, nolens scilicet de rapina pauperum offerre Deo sacrifitium. Et erant ambae aecclesiae sic uicinae parietibus contiguis ut uoces canentium aliae obstreperent aliis; unde cum propter hoc, tum propter cetera plurimas infelix liuor effodiebat causas, quibus non modicas

---

a B adds in 2) *b* B adds Cantuariensi *c* prouidentia *TtCe* (but see iii pr. *d–d* om. *Tt* *e* constructionibus *Bc*, instructionibus *Bk(and Bp)* *f* om. B *g–g* morte obita *Tt*

containing a mancus of gold. Nothing, he adds, in this or the other translations is said on his own responsibility, but he has derived everything from men of high reputation, Archbishop Plegmund, Bishop Asser, and the priests Grimbald and John.

Lastly, that I may give a brief picture of his whole way of life, he 4 divided the twenty-four hours that alternate continually between day and night in such a way that eight hours were spent in writing, reading, and prayer, eight in the care of his body, and eight in despatching the business of the realm. There stood in his chapel a candle divided into twenty-four parts, and an attendant whose appointed task it was to keep the king informed, by the burning of the candle, of his various commitments. The half of all his revenues, such at least as were justly come by, he assigned to his monasteries. The rest of his income he used to divide into two equal parts, and the first of these again into three, of which the first was for his own servants at court, the second for the builders whom he employed continuously on new construction in a remarkable style never seen in England before, and the third for strangers. The second half of his income was divided so that the first 5 portion was given to the poor of his kingdom, the second to monasteries, the third to teachers, and the fourth to churches overseas. He used to review the judicial decisions made by his tenants, and if he found anything wrong, corrected it sharply. One thing was exceptional and unheard-of; he always carried in his pocket a small book containing the daily order of the psalms, so that, if he had an idle moment, he could snatch it up and read it with attention. So he passed his life in high esteem with his neighbours, and married his daughter Æthelswith to Baldwin, count of Flanders, who had by her Arnulf and Adulf. Adulf received from his father the county of Boulogne; and from the other descend the modern counts of Flanders.

124. Alfred, having paid the debt of nature, was buried at Winchester in his own monastery. To construct its buildings, he purchased a sufficient space of ground from the bishop and canons of the day, paying for every foot a mancus of gold by the public weight. The king's self-denial was really extraordinary—to be willing to be milked of so much money! No doubt he meant not to offer God a sacrifice derived from the robbery of the poor. And the two churches were so close, the walls actually touching, that the voices of those chanting in either interfered with the other. For this and many other reasons bad feeling unfortunately arose, and many pretexts were brought to the

inuicem exculperent offensas. Quapropter nuper illud cenobium extra
2 urbem translatum sanius incolitur, liberius insignitur. Aiunt Elfredum
prius in episcopatu sepultum, quod suum monasterium esset imperfectum; mox pro deliramento canonicorum, dicentium regios manes resumpto cadauere noctibus per domos oberrare, filium successorem genitoris[a] tulisse exuuias et in nouo monasterio quieta sede composuisse. Has sane nenias sicut ceteras, ut credant nequam hominis cadauer post mortem demone agente discurrere, Angli pene innata[b] credulitate tenent, a gentilibus nimirum mutuantes, sicut[c] ait Virgilius: 'Morte obita quales fama est uolitare figuras.'[1]

125. Anno Dominicae incarnationis nongentesimo[d] primo regnum obtinuit Eduardus filius Elfredi, et tenuit annis uiginti tribus,[e] litterarum scientia multum patre inferior, sed regni potestate incomparabiliter gloriosior, siquidem ille duo regna Mertiorum et Westsaxonum coniunxerit, Mertiorum nominetenus, quippe commendatum duci Etheredo, tenens; iste primum mortuo[f] Etheredo Mertios omnifariam, mox Occidentales et Orientales Anglos et Northanimbros qui cum Danis iam in unam gentem coaluerant, et Scottos qui aquilonalem insulae partem inhabitant, et Britones omnes, quos nos Walenses dicimus, bellis profligatos[g] suae ditioni subegerit, nec umquam in aliqua
2 pugna humiliorem manum habuerit. Inuenit ingenium quo excursus falleret Danorum; urbibus enim per loca oportuna multis uel ueteribus reparatis uel nouis excogitatis, repleuit eas manu militari, quae incolas protegeret, hostes repelleret. Nec frustra: adeo uirtutes prouintialium in preliis occaluerant ut, si audirent inimicos aduentantes, rege etiam et ducibus inconsultis in certamen[h] ruerent eisque semper numero et preliari[i] scientia prestarent. Ita hostes militibus contemptui, regi risui erant. Denique noui, qui ductu cuiusdam Athelwoldi filii patrui regis aduenerant, omnes ad unum cum eo interfecti; ueteres uel perempti
3 uel sub nomine Anglorum reseruati. Athelwoldus sane, primis diebus huius regis multa molitus, eius dominium dedignabatur, asserens se non inferiorem uel genere uel uirtute; sed a proceribus, qui fide

[a] patris B   [b] ingenita B   [c] ut B   [d] DCCC B   [e] annos uiginti tres T   [f] Tt adds eodem   [g] profugatos Tt   [h] in certamen om. B   [i] preliali Tt; preliandi B

[1] Aen. x. 641.

surface which could be developed into serious trouble. This monastery has therefore been moved lately to a site outside the city, and has become a more healthy, as well as a more conspicuous, residence. They say that Alfred was buried first in the cathedral, because his own monastery was still unfinished; but that not long after, the deluded canons maintained that the king's ghost returned to his dead body and wandered at night through their lodgings, and so his son and successor took up his father's remains and laid them in peace in the new monastery. This nonsense and the like (it is believed, for example, that the corpse of a criminal after death is possessed by a demon, and walks) wins credit among the English from a sort of inborn credulity; they borrow it, no doubt, from the pagans, as in Virgil's line: 'Such shapes are said to wander after death.'[1]

125. In the year of our Lord 901 Alfred's son Edward ascended the throne, which he held for twenty-three years. He was much inferior to his father in book-learning, but in his power and glory as a king there was no comparison, for one united the two kingdoms of the Mercians and West Saxons, holding the former in name only, because it was entrusted to Ealdorman Æthelred; the other first took full control of the Mercians after Æthelred's death; then he defeated in battle and subjected the West and East Angles and the Northumbrians, who had already grown into one nation with the Danes, the Scots who dwell in the northern part of the island, and the Britons (whom we call Welsh); nor did he himself ever come off second best in any contest. He thought of a plan by which he could frustrate Danish raids: he provided many cities in suitable sites, either by repairing old ones or by designing new, and filled each with a garrison to protect the inhabitants and repel the enemy. And not in vain: the courage of the local people had been so steeled in constant battles that, if they heard that the enemy was approaching, they flung themselves into the fray even without taking advice from the king and his captains, and were always superior in both numbers and fighting skill. Thus enemies came to be despised by the soldiers and not taken seriously by the king. New ones, for example, had arrived under the leadership of a certain Æthelwald, son of an uncle of the king, but they were all killed to a man, and he with them; the old ones were either wiped out or spared and called English. Æthelwald in fact had made much trouble in the early days of the new king, and had rejected his sovereignty, asserting that he himself was not his inferior in either birth or prowess; but after being forced into

obstricti fuerant, in exilium trusus piratas adduxerat, cum quibus, ut dixi, cesus fecit documentum stultum esse contra potentiores recalcitrare. De his licet merito Eduardus laudetur, palma tamen potissima debetur patri per meum arbitrium, qui tantae potentiae
4 fecit auspitium. Inter haec non pretermittatur soror regis Ethelfleda Etheredi relicta, non mediocre momentum partium, fauor ciuium, pauor hostium, *a*immodici cordis femina, quae pro experta difficultate primi partus, uel potius unius, perpetuo uiri complexum horruerit,*b* protestans non conuenire regis filiae ut illi se uoluptati innecteret quam tale incommodum post tempus urgeret.*a* Virago potentissima multum fratrem consiliis iuuare, in urbibus extruendis non minus ualere; non discernas potiore*c* fortuna an*d* uirtute ut mulier uiros
5 domesticos protegeret, alienos*e* terreret. Decessit ante germanum quinquennio sepultaque*f* in monasterio sancti Petri Gloecestrae, *g*quod ipsa cum uiro Etheredo ingenti cura extruxerat, eoque ossa beati Oswaldi*h* ex Bardenia transtulerat, sed illo tempore*i* Danorum destructo, aliud, quod nunc in eadem ciuitate precipuum habetur, Aldredus archiepiscopus Eboracensis instaurauit.*j g*

126. Rex, quia multas filias habebat, dedit Edgifam*k* Karolo regi Francorum, filio Ludouici filii Karoli Calui, cuius filiam, ut sepe*l* dixi,[1] Ethelwlfus rex*m* Roma rediens acceperat; *n*et quia se occasio ingessit,*o* uxores eius et liberos nominatim persequi non indignum ducet benignus auditor. Primogenitum Ethelstanum habuit ex Egwinna illustri femina, et filiam cuius nomen scriptum non in promptu habeo; hanc ipse frater Sihtritio Northanimbrorum regi nuptum dedit. Secundus filius Eduardi fuit Ethelwardus*p* ex Elfleda filia Ethelmi*q* comitis, litteris apprime institutus multumque Elfredum auum uultu et moribus preferens, sed cita post genitorem
2 morte subtractus. Ex eadem uxore habuit Eduinum, cuius interitus quae opinio sit, posterius non constanter sed titubanter efferam.[2] Tulit quoque ex illa sex filias, Edfledam Edgifam Ethelhildam Ethildam Edgitham Elfgiuam. Prima et tertia celibatum Deo uouentes,

a-a om. Tt   *b* horruit A   *c* potentiore Tt   *d* uel B   *e* alios Tt   *f* B adds est   *g-g* om. Tt   *h* B adds regis   *i* B adds sequenti   *j* restaurauit B   *k* Eduam T; Editham B   *l* om. B†
m om. B   *n-n* (p. 200) nec liberos pro uelocitate mortis ex ea susceperat Tt
o dedit B   *p* Properly Elfwardus   *q* Elfelmi B

[1] 109, 113. 1.   [2] 139. 4.

exile by nobles who had been bound by ties of loyalty to the king, he had brought pirates back with him, and being cut down with them, as I have said, illustrated once again the folly of kicking against the more powerful side. All this might rightly be set to Edward's credit, but the chief prize of victory, in my judgement, is due to his father, who showed the way to such great power. At the same time we must not 4 overlook the king's sister Æthelflæd, Æthelred's widow, who carried no small weight in party strife, being popular with the citizens and a terror to the enemy. She was a woman of great determination who, after having difficulties with the birth of her first, or rather her only, child, abhorred her husband's embraces ever after, declaring that it was beneath the dignity of a king's daughter to involve herself in pleasures which would be followed in time by such ill effects. She was a virago, a very powerful influence and help in her brother's policy and no less effective as a builder of cities; it would be hard to say whether it was luck or character that made a woman such a tower of strength for the men of her own side and such a terror to the rest. She died 5 five years before her brother, and was buried in the monastery of St Peter at Gloucester which she herself and her husband Æthelred had built with great exertions, translating to it the bones of St Oswald from Bardney; but that having been destroyed at the time of the Danes, another, now regarded as the chief church in that city, was put in its place by Ealdred, archbishop of York.

126. The king, having many daughters, gave Eadgifu in marriage to Charles king of the Franks, son of Louis who was son of Charles the Bald; whose daughter, as I have said more than once,[1] King Æthelwulf had married on his way back from Rome. And since the opportunity offers, the kind reader will not think it out of place if I list his wives and children by name. His first-born son was Æthelstan, born of a noble lady called Ecgwynn, together with a daughter whose name I do not find accessible in written record; she was given in marriage by that same brother to Sihtric king of the Northumbrians. Edward's second son was Æthelweard by Ælfflæd daughter of Ealdorman Æthelhelm; he had a very good education and recalled Alfred his grandfather in both looks and character, but was removed by an early death soon after his father. By the same wife he had Edwin; I shall later give a hes- 2 itating rather than confident account of the popular belief about his death.[2] He also had by the same wife six daughters: Eadflæd, Eadgifu, Æthelhild, Eadhild, Eadgyth, Ælfgifu. The first and third took a vow

Edfleda in sacrato Ethelhilda in laico tegmine, terrenarum nuptiarum uoluptatem fastidiere; iacent ambae Wiltoniae iuxta matrem tumulatae. Edgifam dedit pater Karolo regi, ut dixi, Ethildam*a* frater Ethelstanus Hugoni; Edgitham et Elfgiuam idem germanus misit Henrico Alemannorum imperatori, quarum secundam Ottoni filio ille locauit, alteram
3 cuidam duci iuxta*b* Alpes. Suscepit etiam ex tertia uxore Edgiua uocabulo*c* filios duos, Edmundum et Edredum, qui ambo post Ethelstanum regnarunt; filias duas, Edburgam et Edgiuam. Edburga, sacrata Christo uirgo, Wintoniae quiescit;*d* Edgiuam, spetiositatis eximiae mulierem, coniunxit frater Ethelstanus Ludouico Aquitanorum principi. Filias suas ita instituerat ut litteris omnes in infantia maxime uacarent, mox etiam colum et acum exercere consuescerent, ut his artibus pudice impubem uirginitatem transigerent; filios ita*e* ut primum eruditio plena litterarum in eos*f* conflueret et deinde quasi philosophi ad gubernandam rempublicam non iam rudes procederent."

127. At uero Karolus iste gener Eduardi, multis calamitatibus a Rollone coactus, partem illi Galliae quae nunc Normannia uocatur*g* concessit. Longum est persequi quot annis et quanta audatia omnia inquietauerint Northmanni ab oceano Britannico, ut ante commemoraui,*h*[1] usque ad Tirrenum mare. Primo Hasteng, mox Rollo, qui nobili sed per uetustatem obsoleta prosapia Noricorum ortus, regis precepto patria carens, multos, quos uel es alienum uel conscientia scelerum exagitabat, magnis spebus sollicitatos secum abduxit.
2 Itaque piraticam aggressus, cum ubique libera spatiaretur insania, apud Carnotum*i* hesit; siquidem ciues nec armis nec muris confisi beatae dominae Mariae suffragium*j* adorant. Camisiam*k* quoque eiusdem uirginis, quam Karolus Caluus cum aliis reliquiis a Constantinopoli aduexerat,*l* in modum uexilli super propugnacula, custodum trita pectoribus, uentis exponunt. Hostes uisam ridere et in eam per inane sagittas dirigere, non impune; nam mox oculis obnubilatis nec retro regredi nec ante tendere ualuere. Id oppidani laetis animis conspicati multa eorum cede, quantum fortuna aspirabat,*m* gaudium
3 suum satiarunt. Euasit tamen Rollo, quem suae fidei Deus reseruabat.

a Ethel(h)ildam *CsB* *b* prope *B†* (*cf. 110. 1, 112. 2*) *c* Ethelsu(u)itha nomine *B* *d* requiescit *B* *e* om. *C* *f* in eos *om. B* *n* See above, p. 198 *g* dicitur *B* *h* memoraui *T;* ut ante comm. *om. B†* (*see 138B. 5*) *i* Carnoti (*om.* apud) *B* *j* suffr. Mari(a)e *T* *k* camisia *B* *l* aduehi fecerat *B* *m* spirabat *B*

[1] 121. 7.

of virginity and spurned the pleasures of earthly marriage, Eadflæd taking the veil and Æthelhild in lay attire; both lie at Wilton, buried next to their mother. Eadgifu was given in marriage by her father to King Charles, as I have said, Eadhild by her brother Æthelstan to Hugh; Eadgyth and Ælfgifu were sent by the same brother to Henry emperor of Germany, who married the second of them to his son Otto and the other to a certain duke near the Alps. He also had by a third wife called Eadgifu two sons Edmund and Eadred, who both reigned after Æthelstan, and two daughters Eadburh and Eadgifu. Eadburh became a nun and lies at Winchester; Eadgifu was a famous beauty, and was given in marriage by her brother Æthelstan to Louis prince of Aquitaine. All the daughters had been brought up to devote most time in their childhood to letters, and thereafter to acquire further skill with distaff and needle, that with the support of these arts they might pass their girlhood in chastity; the sons had been educated so that having first received a thorough immersion in book-learning, they could then proceed no longer like rustics but like philosophers to govern the commonwealth.

127. Now it was this Charles, Edward's son-in-law, who, being disastrously hard-pressed by Rollo, granted him the part of Gaul we now call Normandy. It would be a long story to recount for how many years and with what daring deeds the Northmen set everything in turmoil from the British ocean, as I have described already,[1] to the Tyrrhenian Sea. Hæsten was the first; then came Rollo, the offspring of a noble family of Norway which had lost its eminence by lapse of time. He left his own country at the king's command, taking with him many men made restless by debt or a criminal record, whom he had suborned by lavish expectations. Taking to piracy, he ranged everywhere with unbridled ferocity. Only Chartres was too much for him; the citizens put no trust in weapons or in walls, but sought the assistance of the blessed Virgin Mary. They even took our Lady's shift, which Charles the Bald had brought with other relics from Constantinople, and let it float in the breeze like a pennon over the battlements, worn smooth by the breasts of their defenders. The enemy greeted the sight with ridicule and showered arrows on it through the empty air, but not with impunity; they were smitten with blindness, and could neither retreat nor advance. This sight filled the townsmen with joy, and they gladly made full use of Fortune's favour in heavy slaughter. Rollo, however, got away, for God spared him to bring him to the

Nec multo post Rotomagum et confines urbes armis[a] obtinuit, anno Domini octingentesimo septuagesimo[b] sexto, anno uno ante obitum Karoli Calui; cuius filii[c] filius Ludouicus, ut supra lectum est,[1] Northmannos uicit quidem sed non expulit. At uero Karolus frater istius Ludouici, nepos Karoli Calui ex filio Ludouico, ut prius tetigi,[2] multotiens aduersis bellis expertus nichil sibi Fortunam restituere quod aliis[d] abstulisset, cum magnatibus librato consilio bonum esse liberalitatem ostentare regiam cum non posset propulsare iniuriam, 4 Rollonem pacifice accersiuit. Erat ille iam grandaeuus, et[e] facile ad concordiam inclinatus est. Ita fedus ictum est ut baptisma susciperet, et terram illam de rege sicut de domino suo cognosceret. Vbi considerari potuit ingenita et effrenis barbaries uiri; siquidem cum, dono concesso,[f] astantes suggererent ut pedem largitoris oscularetur, dedignatus genibus aduolui, apprehensum pedem regis ad os suum stans attraxit. Illo resupinato secutus risus Northmannorum; Francis reprehendentibus factum, excusat Rollo impudentiam, allegans prouintiae suae morem. Ita rebus compositis Rotomagum rediit, ibique diem clausit.[g]

128. Filius huius Karoli fuit Ludouicus. Is a quodam Isambardo, qui ad paganismum uersus fidem luserat, irritatus proceres suos de suffragio conuenit; quibus nec responsum referentibus Hugo quidam, non magni nominis tiro, filius Rotberti comitis Montis Desiderii,[h] ultro pro domino duellum expetiit, et prouocatorem interemit. Ludouicus, cum toto exercitu apud Pontiuum[i] subsecutus, omnibus barbaris quos ille adduxerat uel occisis uel elapsis, opimam lauream obtinuit. Sed non multo post, pro labore illius expeditionis extrema ualitudine debilitatus, heredem regni Hugonem illum instituit, 2 predicandae fidei et uirtutis iuuenem. Ita prosapia Karoli Magni in illo cessauit, seu quod uxor eius sterilis fuerat seu quod pro breuitate uitae absque prole decesserat. Hugo alteram[j] filiam Eduardi duxit uxorem, et genuit Rotbertum; Rotbertus Henricum; Henricus Philippum; Philippus Ludouicum qui nunc in Frantia regnat. Sed, ut ad nostrum Eduardum reuertar, quid eius tempore de renouandis

[a] *om.* B [b] *om.* C [c] *om.* TBk [d] *om.* B [e] B *adds* ideo [f] concessa B [g] T *adds* anno ducatus quadragesimo secundo [h] *om.* T [i] Ponte(i)um B [j] *om.* B; indeed alteram *makes no sense, and the translation glosses over it*

[1] 110.7. [2] 110.7, 112.1.

faith. Not long after that, he took Rouen and the neighbouring cities by force, in the year of our Lord 876, one year before the death of Charles the Bald, whose grandson Louis, as we have already seen,[1] defeated the Northmen but failed to drive them out. But that Louis's brother Charles, grandson of Charles the Bald by his son Louis, as I have already indicated,[2] learnt after many reverses that Fortune would not restore to him what she had taken from others; he therefore decided after taking counsel with his magnates that, as he could not drive off his persecutors, a display of kingly generosity would be a good idea, and made peaceful overtures to Rollo. Rollo was already old, and was easily induced to make peace, so agreement was reached that he should be baptized, and acknowledge that he held that land from the king as his lord. This provided an exhibition of his innate and uncontrollable barbarity; for when this concession had been granted to him, and the bystanders suggested that he should kiss the foot of his benefactor, he scorned the idea of approaching the king on his knees, and seizing the king's foot put it to his mouth as he stood there. The king fell backward, and the Northmen roared with laughter. When the Franks protested, Rollo excused his impertinence by appealing to the custom of his own country. So they made it up, and he returned to Rouen, and died there [T *adds* in the forty-second year of his dukedom].

128. The son of this Charles was Louis. Provoked by one Isembard, who had turned to paganism and treated his allegiance with contempt, he appealed to his magnates for their support, and when they did not even reply, one Hugh son of Robert count of Montdidier, a man of no great experience or reputation, volunteered to fight a duel on behalf of his lord and killed the challenger. Louis and his whole army caught up with them in Ponthieu, and all the barbarians whom the other man had brought with him having been killed or made their escape, he won a complete victory. Not long after, however, the fatigues of this expedition having brought on a severe and exhausting illness, he made this Hugh, a young man of notable loyalty and courage, heir to his kingdom. Thus the lineage of Charlemagne came to an end with him, either because his wife could bear no children or because his life was so short that he had died without issue. Hugh married one of Edward's daughters and had a son Robert; Robert had a son Henry, Henry a son Philip, Philip a son Louis who is now king in France. But to return to our Edward, the instructions issued in his

episcopatibus a papa Formoso preceptum sit iocundum puto memoratu; itaque uerbis eisdem quibus inueni*ᵃ* scripta interseram.

129. 'Anno quo a Natiuitate Domini transacti sunt anni nongenti*ᵇ* quattuor misit papa Formosus in*ᶜ* Angliam epistolas, quibus dabat excommunicationem et maledictionem regi Eduardo et omnibus subiectis eius pro benedictione quam *ᵈ*beatus Gregorius genti Anglorum per sanctum Augustinum miserat olim, nisi cum episcopis instituisset destitutas parrochias episcoporum secundum antiquam traditionem, quae tradita est*ᵈ* genti Anglorum a*ᵉ* sede sancti Petri; nam per septem annos plenos destituta fuerat episcopis omnis regio Gewisorum, id est Westsaxonum. Quo audito, congregauit rex Eduardus sinodum senatorum gentis Anglorum, cui presidebat Pleimundus archiepiscopus interpretans districta uerba apostolicae legationis. Tunc rex et episcopi elegere sibi suisque salubre*ᶠ* consilium, et iuxta uocem Dominicam "messis quidem multa, operarii autem *ᵍ* pauci"[1] elegerunt et constituerunt singulos episcopos singulis prouintiis Gewisorum, et quod olim duo habuerunt in quinque diuiserunt. Acto concilio,*ʰ* archiepiscopus Romam cum honorificis muneribus adiit, papam magna humilitate placauit, decreta regis recitauit: quod Apostolico maxime placuit. Rediens ad patriam, in urbe Cantuariae uno die septem episcopos septem aecclesiis ordinauit: Fridestanum ad aecclesiam Wintoniensem, Adelstanum ad Cornubiensem, Werstanum ad Scireburnensem, Adelelmum*ⁱ* ad Wellensem,*ʲ* Edulfum ad Cridiensem. Sed et aliis prouintiis constituit duos episcopos, Australibus Saxonibus uirum idoneum Bernegum et Mertiis Cenulfum *ᵏ* ad ciuitatem Dorcestre. Hoc autem totum papa firmauit, ut dampnaretur in perpetuum qui hoc infirmaret decretum.'*ˡ*

130. Eduardus, uniuersae carnis uiam ingressus, quiescit in eodem monasterio quo pater, quod ipse quoque magnis redditibus ampliauerat; in quo et ante quadriennium fratrem Ethelwerdum sepelierat.

ᵃ *William had access to a 'south-western' version of this document (Thomson, William of Malmesbury, p. 135) which may be called* Γ *(edited by W. De Gray Birch, Cartularium Saxonicum no. 614; also found in* θκ)   *ᵇ* octingenti *Tt*   *ᶜ* om. *C*   *ᵈ⁻ᵈ* *Tt (and in essentials* Γ): dederat beatus Gregorius *ACB*   *ᵉ* in *Tt*   *ᶠ* om. *A*   *ᵍ* om. *Tt*   *ʰ* consilio *Tt,* Γ *(conscilio Al)*   *ⁱ* Elsewhere Athelmus *(see 184. 2 and four times in GP)*   *ʲ* Wal(l)ensem *ABcʹ* (Will- *Bk*)   *ᵏ* *GP p. 312 gives the name as* Celuulf   *ˡ* edictum *B (consilium* Γ)

time by Pope Formosus for the renewal of episcopal sees will, I think, make pleasant reading, and I shall therefore insert them here in the words of my source.

129. 'In the year which saw the completion of 904 years from our Lord's birth, Pope Formosus sent a letter to England, in which he laid excommunication and anathema upon King Edward and all his subjects in place of the blessing which St Gregory had sent to the English people through St Augustine, unless he restored together with their bishops the abandoned episcopal sees in accordance with the ancient tradition handed on to the English people by the see of St Peter; for the whole region of the Gewisse, that is the West Saxons, had for seven full years been deprived of bishops. On hearing this, King Edward summoned a synod of elder statesmen of the English people under the presidency of Archbishop Plegmund, who gave a precise exposition of the message from the Holy See. Thereupon the king and the bishops adopted a policy which was for the good of themselves and their people, and in accordance with our Lord's words "The harvest truly is great, but the labourers are few",[1] chose and appointed a suitable bishop for each individual province of the Gewisse, dividing among five what had been held by two. After the council, the archbishop set off for Rome with offerings that were a mark of respect, pacified the pope by the humility of his approach, and recounted the king's decisions, which gave great satisfaction to the Holy See. Returning home, on one day in the city of Canterbury he consecrated seven bishops for seven sees: Frithestan for Winchester, Æthelstan for Cornwall, Wærstan for Sherborne, Athelm for Wells, Eadwulf for Crediton. He also appointed two bishops for other provinces, Beornheah, a suitable man, for the South Saxons, and for the Mercians Cenwulf to Dorchester. All this was approved by the pope, with perpetual damnation threatened for any who might undermine this decision.'

130. Edward went the way of all flesh, and rests in the same monastery as his father, which he too had enriched with great revenues, and in which he had also buried his brother Æthelweard four years before.

---

[1] Matt. 9: 37 = Luke 10: 2.

131. Anno Dominicae incarnationis nongentesimo uicesimo quarto Ethelstanus filius Eduardi regnare coepit, tenuitque regnum annis sedecim. Frater eius Elwardus, paucis diebus post patrem uita decedens, sepulturam cum eodem Wintoniae meruerat. Itaque magno consensu optimatum ibidem Ethelstanus electus, apud regiam uillam quae uocatur Kingestune coronatus est; quamuis quidam Elfredus*a* cum factiosis suis, quia seditio*b* semper inuenit complices, obuiare temptasset,
2 cuius qui fuerit finis posterius uerbis ipsius regis referemus.[1] Occasio contradictionis, ut ferunt, quod Ethelstanus ex concubina natus esset; sed ipse preter hanc notam, si tamen uera est, nichil ignobile habens omnes antecessores*c* deuotione mentis, omnes eorum adoreas triumphorum suorum splendore obscurauit. Adeo prestat ex te quam ex maioribus habere quo polleas, quia illud tuum, istud*d* reputabitur alienum. Noua monasteria quot et quanta fecerit, scribere dissimulo; illud non transiliam, quod uix aliquod in tota Anglia uetustum fuerit quod non uel edifitiis uel ornamentis aut*e* libris aut prediis decorauit.*f* Ita recentia*g* ex professo, uetusta quasi aliud*h* agens artifici benignitate
3 insignibat. Cum Sihtrico rege Northanimbrorum, data ei in matrimonium una ex sororibus, uicturum fedus perculit;*i* quo post annum mortuo, prouintiam illam sibi subegit, expulso quodam Aldulfo qui rebellabat. Et quia nobilis animus semel incitatus in ampliora conatur, Iudualum regem omnium Walensium, Constantinum regem Scottorum cedere regnis compulit. Quos tamen non multo post, miseratione infractus, in antiquum statum sub se regnaturos constituit,*j* gloriosius esse pronuntians regem facere quam regem esse.
4 Postremum illi bellum cum Analauo fuit, Sihtrici filio, qui spe inuadendi regni cum supradicto Constantino iterum rebellante terminos transierat. Et Ethelstano ex consulto cedente, ut gloriosius iam insultantem uinceret, multum in Angliam processerat iuuenis audacissimus et illicita spirans animo, cui tandem magnis artibus ducum, magnis uiribus militum apud*k* Brunefeld*l* occursum. Ille, qui tantum periculum imminere cerneret, astu exploratoris munus aggressus, depositis regiis insignibus assumptaque in manibus*m* cithara ad tentorium regis nostri*n*

a Eluredus *Ce(and Cp)*, Elwerdus *Cs*   *b* factio *B*   *c* *B adds* suos
d illud *TtBc*   *e* uel *B*   *f* decorauerit *AlBc, perhaps rightly;* -erat *Aap*
g *B adds* quasi   *h* aliquid *A*   *i* *Properly* percussit *(as at 180. 9)*   *j* restituit *B*   *k* *om. Tt*   *l* *Variously represented in the MSS* (Brunef(r)ord *A*)
m manu *A*   *n* *om. Tt*

[1] c. 137.

131. In the year of our Lord 924 Edward's son Æthelstan began to reign, and held the throne for sixteen years. His brother Æthelweard, who died a few days after his father, had been thought worthy of a burial-place with him at Winchester; so Æthelstan was elected there with the overwhelming support of the nobles, and crowned in a royal town called Kingston, despite the opposition of a certain Alfred and his supporters (for sedition is never in want of support), whose end I shall report later in the king's own words.[1] The ground of this opposition, it is said, was Æthelstan's origin as the son of a concubine; but apart from this blemish (if indeed there is any truth in it), there was nothing ignoble about the man himself, who outdid all his predecessors in religious devotion, while the splendour of his victories put all their triumphs in the shade. So much more excellent is it that that for which we are renowned should be inherent, rather than derived from our ancestors; because the former will be judged exclusively our own, the latter to belong to others. As for his monastic foundations, their number and size I forbear to describe; one point I will not pass over, that there was scarcely any ancient house in all England that he did not adorn with buildings or ornaments, books or estates. Thus he distinguished them with his cunning beneficence, the new ones expressly, the old as though inadvertently. With Sihtric, king of the Northumbrians, he made a lasting peace, giving him one of his sisters in marriage; but on Sihtric's death a year later he subdued the whole province, after driving out a certain Ealdwulf who was in revolt. And because a noble spirit, once roused, seeks wider fields, he compelled Idwal, king of all the Welsh, and Constantine, king of the Scots, to abdicate. Not long after, however, yielding to pity, he restored them to their former status, to reign under his lordship, declaring it more glorious to make kings than to be one.

His last battle was with Sihtric's son Anlaf, who had crossed his boundaries in hopes of invading the kingdom in concert with the Constantine of whom I spoke, who was rebelling for the second time. And as Æthelstan deliberately gave way, in order to secure a more glorious victory over an already scoffing adversary, Anlaf had advanced some distance into England, for he was a young man and very daring, with a head full of impossible ideas. At length, however, great skill in generalship and great numbers of troops confronted him at *Brunefeld*. Anlaf, perceiving the impending danger, cunningly assumed the office of a spy and, laying aside his royal garments, equipped himself with a harp and made his way to our king's tent.

progreditur; ubi cum, pro foribus cantitans, interdum quoque quateret dulci resonantia fila tumultu,[1] facile admissus est,[a] professus mimum qui huiusmodi arte stipem cotidianam mercaretur. Regem et conuiuas musico acromate aliquantisper deliniuit, cum inter psallendum omnia oculis scrutaretur. Postquam satietas edendi finem delitiis imposuisset, et seueritas amministrandi belli in colloquio procerum recrudesceret, abire iussus pretium cantus[b] accepit; quod asportare nausians sub se in terra defodit. Notatum id a quodam, qui olim illi militasset, et confestim Ethelstano dictum. Ipse hominem incusans quod hostem[c] pre oculis positum non prodidisset, hoc responsum accepit: 'Idem sacramentum quod tibi nuper, o rex, feci, quondam Analauo dedi; quod si in ipso me[d] uidisses uiolare,[e] de te quoque posses exemplum simile cauere. Sed dignare famuli audire consilium, ut hinc tentorium amoueas, alioque loco, usque dum partes relictae[f] ueniant, manens inimicum petulanter insultantem modesta cunctatione frangas.' Dicto probato, discessum est illinc. Analauus, nocte paratus adueniens,[g] episcopum quendam, qui uespere ad exercitum uenerat, nesciusque rerum gestarum pro uiridantis campi aequore[h] ibi tabernaculum tetenderat, cum tota[i] familia occidit.[j] Tum ultra progrediens regem ipsum imparatum offendit, quippe qui nichil tale hostem ausurum timens largae quieti indulserat. Sed cum tanto fremitu stratis excussus suos, quantum per id noctis poterat, ad bellum acueret, gladius eius fortuitu uagina excidit. Quocirca, cum omnia formidinis et ceci tumultus plena essent, inclamato Deo et sancto Aldelmo[k] reductaque ad uaginam manu inuenit ensem, qui hodieque pro miraculo in thesauro regum seruatur. Est sane, ut aiunt,[l] una parte sectilis, nec umquam auri aut[m] argenti receptibilis. Hoc Dei dono fretus simulque quia iam illucescebat Noricum adorsus, tota die ["usque ad"] uesperam indefessus fugauit cum exercitu. Cecidit ibi rex Scottorum Constantinus, perfidae animositatis et uiuacis senectae homo, aliique reges quinque, comites duodecim, omnisque pene[o] barbarorum congeries; pauci qui euaserant pro fide Christi suscipienda conseruati.

---

[a] *om. Tt* [b] cautus *Tt* [c] *om. Tt* [d] me in ipso *Tt* [e] uiolasse *Tt* [f] relique *Tt, not badly* [g] *om. A* [h] planitie *B* [i] omni *B* [j] cecidit *B* [k] *Bt adds* erat enim ei ex antiquis progenitoribus consanguineus [l] ut aiunt *om. Bt* [m] uel *TtA* [n-n] adusque *AB* [o] *om. A*

---

[1] Reminiscent of Statius, *Achill.* ii. 157–8. Cf. also *VD* p. 257.

There he stood singing at the door and from time to time 'in sweet confusion struck the vocal strings',[1] and easily secured admission, pretending to be an entertainer who won his daily bread by this kind of skill. For some time he entertained the king and his guests with tuneful music, and while playing surveyed the whole scene. When they had eaten their fill, the entertainment was brought to an end, and the serious business of running a war was resumed in discussion between the nobles, at which point Anlaf was told to leave and given what he had earned by his music; but scorning to carry this away, he buried it in the ground where he stood. This was observed by a man who had once fought in his army, and at once reported to Æthelstan. Æthelstan upbraided the man for not denouncing an enemy while he was in full view, and received this reply: 'I once swore to Anlaf, O king, the same oath that I have lately sworn to you; and if you had seen me break my oath to him, you might well be on your guard against similar behaviour towards yourself. Deign to listen to the advice of a servant; move your tent away from here, pitch it in another place until the units you have left behind arrive, and use restraint and delay to break the enemy despite his impudent insults.' His suggestion was accepted, and they moved camp. Anlaf arrived by night ready for the fray. A bishop, who had come to join the army that evening not knowing what had happened, had seen a green and level field and had pitched his own tent there. Anlaf cut him and his whole household to pieces. He then went on and found the king himself unprepared, for, not fearing that the enemy would attempt anything of the kind, he was sound asleep. Aroused by the uproar, he leapt from his couch and encouraged his men to battle as far as was possible at that time of night, when his sword by chance fell from its scabbard. At this moment of universal fear and blind confusion, he called upon God and St Aldhelm [B *adds* for he was related to him by blood a long way back], reached again to his scabbard, and there found the sword, which is still preserved among the royal treasures as evidence of the miracle. It is, they say, chased on one side, but can never be inlaid with either gold or silver. Encouraged by this gift of God, and also because day was now breaking, he attacked the Norwegian, fought tirelessly all day long until evening, and put him and his army to flight. There fell that day Constantine king of the Scots, a man of treacherous ferocity and green old age, and five other kings, twelve jarls, and almost the whole horde of barbarians; the few who escaped alive were taken prisoner with a view to their conversion to Christianity.

132. De hoc rege non inualida apud*ᵃ* Anglos fama seritur, quod nemo legalius*ᵇ* uel litteratius rempublicam amministrauerit. Quamquam litteras illum scisse pauci admodum dies sunt quod didicerim, in quodam sane uolumine uetusto, in quo scriptor cum difficultate materiae luctabatur, iuditium*ᶜ* animi sui non ualens pro uoto proferre. Cuius hic uerba pro compendio subicerem,*ᵈ* nisi quia ultra opinionem in laudibus principis uagatur, eo dicendi genere quod suffultum rex facundiae Romanae Tullius in rethoricis appellat.[1] Eloquium excusat consuetudo illius temporis, laudum nimietatem adornat fauor Ethelstani adhuc uiuentis. Pauca igitur familiari stilo subnectam, quae uideantur aliquod conferre*ᵉ* emolumentum ad dignitatis eius documentum.

133. Rex Eduardus, post multa et in bello et*ᶠ* in toga nobiliter consummata, paucis ante obitum diebus Vrbem Legionum fidutia Britonum rebellantem a contumatia compescuit; ibique presidio militum imposito*ᵍ* apud Ferdunam*ʰ* uillam tactus ualitudine uitam presentem exiuit,*ⁱ* et Wintoniae, ut predixi,*ʲ*[2] humatus est. Tunc iussu patris et testamento*ᵏ* Ethelstanus in regem acclamatus est, quem iam tricennalis
2 aetas et sapientiae maturitas commendabant.*ˡ* Nam et auus Elfredus prosperum ei regnum olim imprecatus fuerat, uidens et gratiose complexus spectatae spetiei puerum et gestuum elegantium; quem etiam premature militem fecerat, donatum clamide coccinea, gemmato balteo, ense Saxonico cum uagina aurea. Post haec in curia filiae Ethelfledae et generi Etheredi educandum curauerat; ubi multo studio amitae*ᵐ* et preclarissimi ducis ad omen regni altus, gloria uirtutum calcauit et pressit inuidiam, post mortem patris et interitum fratris in regem apud Kingestune coronatus. Vnde pro tantorum successuum gloria et illius diei laetitia non iniuria uersificus exclamat:

3   Regia progenies produxit nobile stemma,
    cum tenebris nostris illuxit splendida gemma,
    magnus Adelstanus, patriae decus, orbita recti,
    illustris probitas de uero nescia flecti.

ᵃ penes *B*   *ᵇ* regalius *Tt*   *ᶜ* indicium *B*   *ᵈ* subtexam *Tt*   *ᵉ* om.
B   *ᶠ* in bello et om. *A*   *ᵍ* posito *(sic)* pres. mil. *Tt*   *ʰ* Ferendunam
AaB   *ⁱ* exuit *Tt (and Cs, perhaps after corr.)*   *ʲ* dixi *B*   *ᵏ* tunc testamento
patris *B*   *ˡ* commendabat *B*   *ᵐ* om. *B*

[1] *Rhetorica ad Herennium* iv. 15 (where editors now read *sufflata*).
[2] c. 130.

132. Concerning this king there is a vigorous tradition in England that he was the most law-abiding and best-educated ruler they have ever had; though it is only a very short time since I learnt the extent of his education, from an ancient volume in which the writer was at odds with the difficulty of his material, finding it hard to express his opinions as he would have wished. I would add his words here in an abbreviated form, except that in the praises of his prince he rambles beyond reason, in the style which Cicero, king of Roman eloquence, calls in his *Rhetoric* 'bombastic'.[1] His manner is excused by the practice of his time, and the excess of panegyric is countenanced by his enthusiasm for Æthelstan, who was then still living. I will therefore subjoin a few points in ordinary language which may perhaps make some contribution to the evidence for his good qualities.

133. King Edward, after many famous achievements in both war and peace, a few days before his death suppressed the rebellious spirit of the City of Legions, which was in revolt, relying on the support of the Britons, and installed a garrison there; then he fell ill at Farndon and departed this life and, as I have already said,[2] was buried at Winchester. Then, on his father's instructions and by the terms of his will, Æthelstan was chosen king by acclamation, recommended as he was by his age—he was now thirty—and his mature wisdom. For his grandfather Alfred too had long before wished him a prosperous reign, observing and welcoming the child's notable good looks and graceful movements, and had knighted him at an early age with the gift of a scarlet cloak, a belt set with gems, and a Saxon sword with a gilded scabbard. After that, he arranged for the boy's education at the court of his daughter Æthelflæd and Æthelred his son-in-law, where he was brought up with great care by his aunt and the eminent ealdorman for the throne that seemed to await him. There too, with the reputation won by his high qualities, he trod envy under foot and quite suppressed it; and after his father's death and the loss of his brother he was crowned king at Kingston. Such was the reputation won by those great successes, such was the happiness of the day, that the poet not unfairly breaks out in these words:

> Noble was the scion put forth by our royal stock, when on our darkness dawned the radiance of that splendid jewel, great Æthelstan, glory of his native country, the narrow path of virtue, shining integrity that knew not how to deviate from the truth. By

Ad patris edictum datus in documenta scolarum,
extimuit rigidos ferula crepitante magistros,
et potans*a* auidis doctrinae mella medullis
decurrit teneros, sed non pueriliter, annos.
Mox adolescentis uestitus flore iuuentae
armorum studium tractabat patre iubente.

4 Sed nec in hoc segnem senserunt bellica iura;
id quoque*b* posterius cognouit*c* publica cura.
Functus erat fato pater omni precluus aeuo,
perpetua fama uicturus secula cuncta;
tunc iuuenis nomen regni clamatur in omen,*d*
ut fausto patrias titulo moderetur habenas.
Conueniunt proceres et componunt diadema,
pontifices pariter dant infidis anathema;
emicat in populis solito festiuior ignis,
et produnt uariis animi penetralia signis.

5 Ardet quisque suum regi monstrare fauorem;
hic timet hic sperat, pellit spes ampla pauorem.*e*
Feruet et exundat regali regia luxu,
spumat ubique merum, fremit ingens aula tumultu,
discurrunt pueri, celerant iniuncta ministri.
Delitiis uentres cumulantur, carmine mentes;
ille strepit cithara, decertat plausibus*f* iste,
in commune sonat 'Tibi laus, tibi gloria,*g* Christe.'
Rex non inuitis oculis hunc haurit honorem,
omnibus indulgens proprium dignanter amorem.

134. Transacta consecrationis celebritate, Ethelstanus, ne spem ciuium falleret et inferius opinione se ageret, omnem omnino Angliam solo*h* nominis terrore subiugauit, preter solos Northanimbros. Nam preerat illis Sihtritius quidam, gente et animo barbarus, cognatus illius*i* Gurmundi de quo in gestis Elfredi regis legitur,[1] qui, cum antecessorum regum potentiam rugatis naribus derisisset, huius affinitatem ultro suplicibus nuntiis expetiit. Ipse quoque, festino pede subsecutus, uerba legatorum asseruit; quare et sororis copula et multiplicibus xeniis muneratus perpetui federis fundamenta iecit. Sed, ut predictum recolo,[2] post annum uita deturbatus occasionem Ethelstano

a portans *TtAl*   *b* quod *Tt**   *c* iurauit *ACs*   *d* omni *B*
e timorem *B*   *f* laudibus *B*   *g* gratia *TtACsBk, perhaps rightly*
h sui *Tt*   *i* om. *A*

his father's orders he was handed over to be taught at school, and feared stern masters and the swish of the cane; there he absorbed into his thirsty veins the honey of instruction, and so he passed his childish years, but as no ordinary child. Then, once clothed with the bloom of adolescence, he practised the pursuit of arms at his father's bidding, and in him too the laws of war did not find a laggard. This too became well known later to the public as they watched him. His father, famous for all time, had met his destined end and will live to all the ages in perpetual glory. Then was the young man loudly acclaimed as successor to the throne, that with happy omen he might hold the reins his father held. The nobles gather, and together place on him a crown; the bishops likewise issue their anathema against unbelievers; among the crowds fires leap up that mark a festival out of the ordinary, and various tokens betray a people's inmost thoughts. Every man burns to show the king how keenly he supports him; one fears, another hopes, and hope's fullness drive out fear. The palace seethes, it overflows with the rich living that befits a king. Everywhere foaming wine, and in the great hall a busy tumult; lackeys run to and fro, and servants hurry to their tasks. Food fills their stomachs, music fills their minds; one man plucks the strings, another rivals him as he beats time, all sing one burden: "Thine, O Christ, be the praise, Thine the glory." The king with welcome in his eye accepts this show of loyalty, and deigns to grant them all a share in his affections.

134. When the ceremony of his consecration was completed, Æthelstan, intent on not disappointing the hopes of his countrymen and falling below their expectations, brought the whole of England entirely under his rule by the mere terror of his name, with the sole exception of the Northumbrians. Their ruler was a certain Sihtric, a barbarian alike in blood and behaviour, a kinsman of the Gurmund of whom we read in the history of King Alfred.[1] Sihtric, though he had turned up his nose at the authority of previous monarchs, sent an embassy on his own initiative humbly requesting some closer relationship, and rapidly followed this up in person and confirmed the proposals of his envoys. Rewarded with the hand of Æthelstan's sister and gifts of many kinds, he laid the foundations of a lasting agreement. But, as I remember having said before,[2] a year later his life came to a violent end, and this gave Æthelstan the opportunity to add

[1] 121. 6.   [2] 131. 3.

exhibuit ut Northanimbriam suae parti iungeret, quae sibi et antiquo iure et noua necessitudine competeret. Fugit tunc Analauus filius Sihtrici Hiberniam, et Godefridus frater eius Scottiam; subsecuti sunt e uestigio regales missi ad Constantinum regem Scottorum et Eugenium regem Cumbrorum transfugam cum denuntiatione belli repetentes. Nec fuit animus barbaris ut contra mutirent; quin potius sine retractatione, ad locum qui Dacor uocatur uenientes, se cum suis regnis Anglorum regi dedidere.*a* In cuius pacti gratia filium Constantini baptizari iussum ipse de sacro fonte suscepit. Euasit tamen Godefridus inter apparatus itinerantium fuga cum quodam Turfrido, diuersarum partium duce, lapsus; moxque Eboracum obsidens oppidanosque nunc precibus nunc minis ad defectionem*b* sollicitans, et neutrum pro uoto expediens, abscessit. Nec multo post, in quodam castro ambo conclusi, custodientium perspicatiam*c* fugiendo luserunt; quorum Turfridus mature diem*d* obiit in pelago naufragus preda piscibus expositus, Godefridus multis miseriis terra marique iactatus ad postremum suplex curiam uenit. Ibi pacifice a rege susceptus quattuorque diebus profusissime cum eo conuiuatus, naues suas repetiit, pirata uetus et in aqua sicut piscis uiuere assuetus.*e*

Ethelstanus interea castrum, quod olim Dani in Eboraco offirmauerant, ad solum diruit, ne esset*f* quo se tutari perfidia posset; preda quae in castro reperta fuerat, et ea quidem amplissima, magnifice *g* et uiritim*g* diuisa. Hoc enim uir ille animo imperauerat suo, ut nichil opum ad crumenas corraderet, sed omnia conquisita uel monasteriis uel fidelibus suis munificus expenderet. In hoc thesauros paternos, in hoc uictoriarum suarum titulos tota uita euacuabat.

Deo famulantibus pronus et dulcis, laicis iocundus et comis, magnatibus pro contuitu maiestatis serius, minoribus pro condescensione paupertatis*h* deposito regni supercilio affabiliter sobrius. Statura, ut accepimus, quae iustam non excelleret; corpore deducto; capillo, ut ipsi ex reliquiis uidimus, flauo, filis aureis pulchre intorto. Ciuibus ammiratione fortitudinis et humilitatis percarus, rebellibus inuicta constantia fulmineus. Northwalensium, id est Britonum Aquilonalium, regulos apud Herefordensem urbem coegit occurrere, et aliquandiu

---

a dedere *Tt*   *b* dedi(c)tionem *B*   *c* diligentiam *B*   *d* om. *B*
e assuetus uiuere *Tt*   *f* foret *B*   *g–g* utrumque *BkBc²(and Bp),* utrumque *Bc¹*   *h* pietatis *B*

Northumbria to his own share, for it was his by ancient right no less than by modern connection. Sihtric's son Anlaf fled to Ireland and his brother Guthfrith to Scotland, and they were promptly followed by envoys from the king, who went to Constantine king of the Scots and Owain king of the Cumbrians to demand return of the fugitive with the alternative of war. The barbarians had no spirit to utter a word of protest; they preferred to gather without reluctance at a place called Dacre and put themselves and their kingdoms in the hands of the English king. In response to this agreement Æthelstan himself stood godfather to Constantine's son, whose baptism he had ordered. Guthfrith, however, during the preparations for the journey slipped away with a certain Turfrith, one of the captains of the other side, and shortly afterwards laid siege to York, where, after urging the townsfolk to revolt first by appeals and then by threats and getting his way with neither, he retired. Not long afterwards, when the two of them were besieged in a certain fortress, they gave the slip to those who were watching them, and escaped: Turfrith soon met his death at sea, consigned by shipwreck to be food for fishes, and Guthfrith, pursued by many misfortunes by land and sea, came at length to the king's court to surrender. There he was given a peaceable reception by the king and richly entertained for four days before returning to his ships, being a pirate of long experience and schooled to live in water like a fish. Æthelstan meanwhile levelled with the ground the fortress which the Danes had built long ago in York, in order to leave disloyalty no place of refuge; the booty found in the fortress—and very plentiful it was—he generously distributed to individuals. He had made it a principle to accumulate no wealth for his own pocket, but to spend all that he got generously on monasteries or on his loyal followers: these were the objects on which he used throughout his life to lavish his inherited treasure and the proceeds of his victories.

To professed servants of God he was well-disposed and gracious, to laymen cheerful and courteous; to magnates he was serious in consideration of his own position, for lesser folk, condescending to their humble status, he laid aside the haughty air of royalty and was mild and affable. In stature, from what I have heard, not above the average in height, slim in build, with fair hair, as I have seen for myself in his remains, beautifully intertwined with gold threads. His subjects, who admired his courage and modesty, loved him dearly; on rebels, invincible and unsleeping, he descended like a flash of lightning. The princes of the Northwalians, that is, the Northern Britons, he compelled to meet him in the city of Hereford and, after a spell of

calcitrantes in deditionem transire; ita quod nullus ante eum rex uel cogitare presumpserat, ipse in effectum formauit, ut ei nomine uectigalis annuatim uiginti libras auri, trecentas argenti penderent, boues uiginti quinque milia annumerarent, preterea quot liberet canes qui odorisequo nare spelea et diuerticula ferarum deprehenderent,[a]
6 uolucres quae aliarum auium predam per inane uenari nossent. Inde digressus in Occidentales[b] Britones se conuertit, qui Cornewalenses uocantur quod[c] in occidente Britanniae siti cornu Galliae ex obliquo respitiant.[d] Illos quoque impigre adorsus, ab Execestra, quam ad id temporis aequo cum Anglis iure inhabitarant, cedere compulit, terminum prouintiae suae citra Tambram fluuium constituens, sicut[e] Aquilonalibus Britannis amnem Waiam limitem posuerat. Vrbem igitur illam, quam contaminatae gentis repurgio defecauerat, turribus
7 muniuit, muro ex quadratis lapidibus cinxit. Et licet solum illud ieiunum et squalidum uix steriles auenas et plerumque folliculum inanem sine grano producat, tamen pro ciuitatis magnificentia et incolarum opulentia, tum etiam conuenarum frequentia, omne ibi adeo habundat mercimonium, ut nichil[f] frustra[g] desideres quod humano usui conducibile existimes. Plurima eius insignia tam in urbe illa quam in finitima regione uisuntur, quae melius indigenarum ore quam nostro stilo pinguntur.[h]

135. Propter haec[i] tota Europa laudes eius predicabat, uirtutem in caelum ferebat; felices se reges alienigenae non falso putabant si uel affinitate uel muneribus eius amicitias mercarentur. Haroldus quidam, rex Noricorum, misit ei nauem rostra aurea et uelum purpureum habentem, densa testudine clipeorum inauratorum intrinsecus circumgiratam. Missorum nomina fuere Helgrim et Osfrid, qui, regaliter in urbe Eboraca suscepti, sudorem peregrinationis[j] premiis decentibus extersere.[k] Henricus primus[l] filius Conradi (multi enim huius[m] nominis fuere), rex Teutonicorum et imperator Romanorum, sororem eius filio Ottoni expostulauit, tot in circuitu regibus pretermissis, progeniei generositatem et animi magnitudinem in Ethelstano e long-
2 inquo conspicatus. Adeo enim haec duo in eo consentiens habitaculum effecerant ut nullus esset uel genere clarior et illustrior uel animo

[a] *Tt* adds* et Tt [b] Orientales *Tt* [c] qui *CB* [d] respiciunt *C* [e] et Tt
[f] *B* adds ibi [g] ultra *Tt* [h] pingentur *TtAa* (pingetur *Al*)
[i] hoc *A* [j] sudorum peregrinationes *(Ce*[p.c.]*)C* [k] abstersere *B* [l] om. *B* [m] eius *B*

reluctance, to change their minds and surrender. He thus brought into effect what no king before him had presumed even to contemplate: they were to pay him by way of annual tribute twenty pounds of gold and three hundred pounds of silver, and to hand over by the count 25,000 oxen, besides as many as he might wish of hounds that with their keen scent could track down the lairs and lurking-places of wild beasts, and birds of prey skilled in pursuing other birds through empty air. Passing 6 on from there he turned towards the Western Britons who are called Cornish, because they live in western Britain and look across aslant towards the horn (*cornu*) of Gaul. They too were attacked vigorously and forced to leave Exeter, where they had lived until then on an equal footing with the English; and he fixed the boundary of their territory at the river Tamar, just as he had fixed the boundary of the Northern British at the river Wye. Having thus purged that city by sweeping out an infected race, he fortified it with towers and surrounded it with a wall of squared stone. And although the soil in those parts is thin and stony, producing 7 with reluctance barren oats and for the most part empty ears without their grain, yet to judge by the splendour of the city, the wealth of the inhabitants, and the number of visiting strangers, every form of merchandise is so plentiful there that you would not search in vain for anything that would contribute in your view to a civilized life. Numerous reminders of Æthelstan are to be seen both in the city and in the country round, of which the native gives a better account by word of mouth than I can with my pen.

135. This explains why the whole of Europe sang his praises and extolled his merits to the sky; kings of other nations, not without reason, thought themselves fortunate if they could buy his friendship either by family alliances or by gifts. A certain Harold, king of the Norwegians, sent him a ship with gilded beak and a scarlet sail, the inside of which was hung round with a close-set row of gilded shields. The names of the envoys were Helgrim and Osfrith, and after a royal reception in the city of York they wiped off the sweat of their journey with suitable rewards. Henry I, Conrad's son (for there were many men of that name), king of the Teutons and emperor of the Romans, asked for the hand of the king's sister for his son Otto, passing over many neighbouring kings because he had detected from a distance Æthelstan's noble ancestry and greatness of spirit. To such an extent 2 had these two qualities made in him a congenial home, that there was no one either of lineage more high-born and illustrious or of a spirit

audatior et efficatior. Quare perpenso consilio, quod quattuor sorores haberet in quibus preter aetatis discrimen nichil de formae gratia*ᵃ* dissideret,*ᵇ* duas postulanti Cesari misit, quas ille quomodo nuptum locauerit iam sermo preoccupauit.[1] Tertiam legitima copula sortitus est comparem Ludouicus Aquitanorum princeps, de genere Karoli Magni superstes. Quartam, in qua omne coagulum pulchritudinis, quod ceterae pro parte habent, naturaliter confluxerat, Hugo rex Francorum per nuntios a germano expetiit.

3   Princeps huiusce*ᶜ* legationis fuit Adulfus, filius Balduini comitis Flandriae, ex filia regis Eduardi Ethelswida.*ᵈ* Is, cum in conuentu procerum apud Abbandunam proci postulata exposuisset, protulit munera sane amplissima, et quae cuiuslibet auarissimi cupiditatem incunctanter explerent: odores aromatum qualia numquam antea in Anglia uisa fuerant; honores gemmarum, presertim smaragdorum, in quorum uiridate sol repercussus oculos astantium gratiosa luce animaret; equos cursores plurimos cum faleris, fuluum (ut Maro ait)[2]
4   mandentes sub dentibus aurum; uas quoddam ex onichino, ita subtili celatoris arte sculptum ut uere fluctuare segetes, uere gemmare*ᵉ* uites, uere moueri hominum imagines uiderentur, ita lucidum et politum ut uice speculi uultus intuentium emularetur; ensem Constantini Magni, in quo litteris aureis nomen antiqui possessoris legebatur, in capulo quoque super crassas auri laminas clauum ferreum affixum cerneres, unum ex quattuor quos Iudaica factio Dominici corporis aptarat suplitio; lanceam Karoli Magni, quam imperator inuictissimus, contra Saracenos exercitum ducens, si quando in hostem uibrabat, numquam*ᶠ* nisi uictor abibat[3] (ferebatur eadem esse quae, Dominico lateri centurionis manu impacta, pretiosi uulneris hiatu Paradisum miseris
5   mortalibus aperuit); uexillum Mauritii beatissimi martiris et Thebeae legionis principis, quo idem rex[4] in bello Hispano quamlibet infestos et confertos inimicorum cuneos dirumpere et in fugam solitus erat cogere; diadema ex auro quidem multo, sed magis gemmis pretiosum, quarum splendor ita in intuentes faculas luminis iaculabatur ut quanto quis certaret uisum intendere, tanto magis reuerberatus cogeretur cedere; particulam sanctae et adorandae crucis cristallo inclusam, ubi soliditatem lapidis oculus penetrans potest discernere qualis sit ligni

ᵃ qualitate *B*   *ᵇ* desideret *Tt*, desiderares *Tc*   *ᶜ* huius *T*   *ᵈ* B† adds sorore ipsius Ethelstani ex patre   *ᵉ* germinare *T*   *ᶠ* non *B*

[1] 112. 2, 126. 2.
[2] Virgil, *Aen.* vii. 279.
[3] Cf. Virgil, *Aen.* x. 859–60.
[4] i.e. Charlemagne.

bolder and more successful. After much thought therefore—for he had four sisters in whom, apart from their difference in age, there was nothing to choose in beauty or charm,—he sent two in answer to the emperor's request; and how he disposed of these in marriage I have already had occasion to tell.[1] The third found a good match in lawful wedlock in Louis prince of Aquitaine, a survivor of the lineage of Charlemagne. The fourth, in whom the whole mass of beauty, of which other women have only a share, had flowed into one by nature, was demanded in marriage from her brother through envoys by Hugh king of the Franks.

The leader of this mission was Adulf, son of Baldwin count of Flanders by Æthelswith daughter of King Edward [B *adds* the sister of Æthelstan himself by the same father]. After expounding the suitor's requests in a gathering of nobles at Abingdon, he produced gifts on a truly munificent scale, such as might instantly satisfy the desires of a recipient however greedy: the fragrance of spices that had never before been seen in England; noble jewels (emeralds especially, from whose green depths reflected sunlight lit up the eyes of the bystanders with their enchanting radiance); many swift horses with their trappings, 'champing between their teeth', as Virgil says,[2] 'the tawny gold'; an onyx vessel so modelled by the engraver with his subtle art that one seemed to see real ripples in the standing grain, buds really swelling on the vines, men's figures really moving, shining with such a polish that it reflected the face of the beholder like a mirror; the sword of Constantine the Great, with the ancient owner's name in gold letters, while on the scabbard over stout plates of gold you could see fixed an iron nail, one of four which the Jewish rabble had got ready for the tormenting of our Lord's body; Charlemagne's lance which, if the invincible emperor brandished it as he led the army against the Saracens, 'brought him the victory and never failed'[3] (it was said to be that same lance which, when driven by the centurion's hand into our Lord's side, opened Paradise to hapless mortals by the precious wound it made); the banner of Maurice, blessed martyr and general of the Theban legion, with which that same king[4] in his Spanish war was wont to break and put to flight the enemy squadrons however fierce and closely packed; a precious crown of solid gold, and yet more precious from its gems, of which the brilliance shot such flashing darts of light at the beholders that the more anyone strove to strain his eyes, the more he was dazzled and obliged to give up; a small piece of the holy and wonderful Cross enclosed in crystal, which the eye can penetrate, solid rock though it is, and discern the wood, its

color et quae quantitas; portiunculam quoque coronae spineae eodem
modo inclusam, quam ad derisionem regni militaris rabies sacrosancto
6 imposuit capiti. His tantis et tam elaboratis donis magnificentissimus
rex gauisus, non minoribus pene respondit benefitiis, quin et*a*
anhelantis animum nuptiis sororis refecit. Et ceteris quidem successores reges dotauit;*b* partem uero crucis et coronae Malmesberiae delegauit, quorum*c* sustentaculo adhuc credo uigere locum illum,*d* tot
libertatis naufragia, tot calumniatorum iniurias passum. Nam et
ibidem Elwinum et Ethelwinum filios patrui sui Ethelwerdi, quos in
bello contra Analauum amiserat, humari honorifice iussit,*e* sui quoque
corporis requiem ibidem futuram*f* denuntians.

De quo bello tempus est ut illius uersifici, de quo omnia*g* haec
excerpsimus, sententiam ponamus.

7   Transierat quinos et tres et quattuor annos
    iure regens ciues, subigens uirtute tirannos,
    *h*iure fideque regens hinc Anglos inde Britannos,*h*
    cum redit illa lues, Europae noxia labes.
    Iam cubat in terris fera barbaries aquilonis,
    iam iacet in campo pelago pirata relicto,
    illicitas toruasque minas Analauus anhelans.
    Bacchanti furiae,*i* Scottorum rege uolente,
    commodat assensum borealis terra serenum.
    Et iam grande tument, iam terrent aera uerbis;
    cedunt indigenae, cedit plaga tota superbis.

8   Nam quia rex noster, fidens alacrisque iuuenta,
    emeritus pridem detriuerat otia lenta,
    illi continuis fedabant omnia predis,
    urgentes miseros iniectis ignibus agros.
    Marcuerant totis uiridantia gramina campis,
    egra seges uotum deriserat agricolarum;
    tanta fuit peditum, tam barbara uis equitantum,
    innumerabilium concursus quadrupedantum.
    Exciuit tandem famae querimonia regem,
    ne se cauterio tali pateretur inuri,
    quod sua barbaricae cessissent arma securi.

9   Nec*j* mora: uictrices ducentia signa cohortes
    explicat in uentum, uexilla ferotia centum;
    cruda uirum uirtus decies bis milia quina
    ad stadium belli comitantur preuia signa.

colour and its size; a small portion too, mounted in the same fashion, of the crown of thorns, which the raving soldiers set upon that sacred head in mockery of His kingship. Delighted with presents of such 6 importance and such workmanship, the magnificent king responded with gifts that were scarcely less, and comforted the passionate suitor with the hand of his sister. With the rest of the gifts he endowed his successors on the throne; but the pieces of the Cross and the crown he entrusted to Malmesbury, and their support still, I believe, gives that place fresh life, after the shipwreck of its liberty and all the unjust claims it has to meet. For he also honoured it with instructions that Ælfwine and Æthelwine, sons of his uncle Æthelweard, whom he had lost in battle against Anlaf, should be buried there, announcing that his own body should rest there also.

On the subject of that battle, this is the moment to set down the opinions of the versifier from whom all this has been extracted.

Twelve years had he now spent ruling his subjects in justice and sub- 7 duing tyrants by his valour, ruling English and British alike with law and faith, when that plague, Europe's poisonous pest, returned. The fierce barbarians of the North now sleep on land; the pirate leaves the sea and lies on solid ground, Anlaf fiercely breathing grim, unlawful threats. To this raging fury, with the consent of the king of the Scots, the northern land lends its support with no misgivings; and now they are swollen with pride, they frighten with their words the very air; the natives, the whole region yields to their presumption. For because our king, though young and self-confident, had long 8 ago given up war and passed his time in indolent leisure, they ruined everything by continual raids, and laid waste the sad fields by spreading fire; in every meadow the green grass had withered, and the sickly grain had mocked the prayers of the husbandman; so great and so barbarous was the great mass of men both foot and horse, the concourse of innumerable steeds. Rumour's complaints at length aroused the king not to allow himself to be branded by the disgrace of yielding to the barbarian axe. Without delay he opens to the 9 breeze the ensigns that lead his victorious squadrons, a hundred threatening standards. The raw valour of his troops, one hundred thousand men, accompany to the battlefield the standards that show

---

^a *om.* C   ^b ditauit C *(but cf. GP p. 217)*   ^c quarum B†   ^d *om.* C   ^e fecit Tt   ^f *om.* Tt   ^g cuncta B   ^{h–h} Tt; *om.* ACB   ⁱ furies B   ^j non C

Hic strepitus mouit predatorum legiones,*a*
terruit insignis uenientum fama latrones,
ut posita preda proprias peterent regiones.
At uulgus reliquum, miseranda strage peremptum,
infecit bibulas tetris nidoribus auras.
Fugit Analauus, de tot modo milibus unus,
depositum mortis, fortunae nobile munus,
post Ethelstanum rebus momenta daturus.

136. Hic locus exigere uidetur ut interitum Elfredi, de quo superius fidem promissae narrationis obstrinxi,[1] regis sermonibus exponam. Nam quia*b* Malmesberiam corpora cognatorum deferri et ad caput sepulchri sancti Aldelmi tumulari iusserat, ita locum illum coluit in posterum ut nichil desiderabilius, nichil*c* haberet sanctius. Multa ibi largitus predia cartis quoque confirmauit, in quarum una post donationem subiecit:

137. *d*'Sciant sapientes*e* regionis nostrae nos has prefatas terras*f* non iniuste rapuisse rapinamque Deo dedisse; sed sic eas accepi quemadmodum iudicauerunt omnes optimates regni Anglorum, insuper et apostolicus papa Romanae aecclesiae Iohannes, Elfredo defuncto, qui nostrae felicitati et uitae emulus extitit*g* nequitiae inimicorum nostrorum consentiens, quando me uoluerunt patre meo defuncto cecare in ciuitate*h* Wintonia, si non me Deus sua pietate eripuisset. Sed denudatis eorum machinamentis, missus*i* est ad Romanam aecclesiam, ut ibi se coram apostolico Iohanne iureiurando defenderet. Et hoc fecit coram sancti Petri altari; sed facto iuramento cecidit coram altari, et manibus famulorum suorum portatus est ad Scolam Anglorum, et ibi tertia nocte uitam finiuit. Et tunc*j* Apostolicus ad nos remisit, et quid de eo ageretur a nobis consuluit, an cum ceteris Christianis corpus illius poneretur. His peractis et nobis renuntiatis, optimates nostrae regionis*k* cum propinquorum illius turma*l* efflagitabant omni humilitate ut corpus illius per nostram licentiam cum corporibus poneretur Christianorum; nosque*m* illorum efflagitationi consentientes Romam remisimus, et consentiente papa positus est ad ceteros Christianos, quanuis indignus. Et sic iudicata est michi tota possessio eius in

---

a *The line is written in Tt as an alternative to that following; in Ce it follows that line; in CsB it is omitted altogether. The two are certainly very similar in sense*   *b* qui C   *c* desid. nichil *om.* C   *d* *Part of Sawyer 436, given more fully in GP pp. 401–3*   *e* gentes B   *f om.* B   *g* fuit B   *h* urbe B   *i* remissus TtACs, GP p. 402   *j* nunc Tt   *k* regionis nostr(a)e A   *l* turba B   *m* nos quoque B

the way. This noise sapped the courage of the pirate legions; the report of their advance terrified those famous robbers, made them drop their booty and seek their native land. But the rest of the crowd, cut down in pitiful slaughter, fouled with revolting stench the thirsty air. Anlaf escaped, alone out of what were lately so many thousands, a deposit left by death, the noble gift of Fortune, destined to shape events after Æthelstan's time.

136. This seems the right place to recount in the king's own words the death of Alfred, of which I promised in an earlier passage to tell the story.[1] For the king, having ordered that the bodies of his kinsmen should be taken to Malmesbury and buried there at the head of St Aldhelm's tomb, had such a veneration for the place thereafter that he thought nowhere more desirable or more sacred. He gave it many estates and confirmed them with charters, in one of which after making the gift he continues as follows:

137. 'Be it known to the wise men of our country that the lands aforesaid were not seized by us unjustly and offered to God as the spoils of robbery, but I received them in accordance with the judgement of all the nobles of the English kingdom and of Pope John on the death of Alfred, who was always jealous of my prosperity and of my life and was party to the wickedness of my enemies when they tried after my father's death to blind me in the city of Winchester, though God in His mercy preserved me. So, when their evil designs were laid bare, he was sent to the Church of Rome, to defend himself there on oath in the presence of Pope John. And this he did at the altar of St Peter; but having sworn the oath, he fell down before the altar and was carried by his servants into the Schola Anglorum, where two nights later he died. Then the pope sent to us, and asked us what should be done with him and whether his body should be given Christian burial. So when this had happened and had been reported to us, the nobles of our country together with a crowd of his kinsmen most humbly urged that with our permission his body might be given Christian burial; and we granted their request and replied to Rome accordingly, and with the pope's consent he was given Christian burial, little as he deserved it. Thus it was that all his possessions both great and

[1] 131. 1.

magnis et*a* modicis. Sed et haec apicibus litterarum prenotauimus, ne quam diu Christianitas regnat aboleatur unde michi prefata possessio, quam Deo et sancto Petro dedi, donatur;*b* nec iustius noui quam Deo et sancto Petro hanc possessionem dare,*c* qui emulum meum in conspectu omnium cadere fecerunt, et michi prosperitatem regni largiti sunt.'

138. In his uerbis regis sapientiam et pietatem eius in Dei rebus suspicere par est: sapientiam, quod animaduerteret iuuenis presertim non esse Deo gratiosum de rapina holocaustum, pietatem quod munus ultione diuina collatum Deo potissimum*d* non ingratus rependeret. Preterea datur animaduertendum quod tunc basilica sancti Petri *e*primaria cenobio fuerit, quae nunc in secundis habetur, aecclesia beatae Mariae, quam monachi modo frequentant, postea regis Edgari diebus sub abbate Elfrico edificata.*e*

Et haec quidem fide integra de rege conscripsi; sequentia magis cantilenis per successiones temporum detritis quam libris ad instructiones*f* posteriorum*g* elucubratis didicerim.*h* Quae ideo apposui, non ut earum ueritatem defendam, sed ne lectorum scientiam*i* defraudem. Ac primum de natiuitate referendum.

139. Erat in quadam uilla opilionis filia, eleganti spetie*j* puella, quae quod non contulissent natales formae mercabatur gratia. Huic per uisum monstratur prodigium, lunam de suo uentre splendere,*k* et hoc lumine totam Angliam illustrari. Quod cum mane ad sodales detulisset*l* ludo, ab illis non ioculariter exceptam confestim uillicae auribus, quae regis filios nutrire solebat, insonuit. Illa rem examinans puellam intra lares suos receptam filiae loco habuit, cultioribus uestimentis cibis deli-
2 catioribus gestibus facetioribus uirgunculam informans. Non multo post, filius regis Elfredi Eduardus, itineris casu per uillam transiens, ad domum diuertit infantilium rudimentorum olim consciam (neque enim integrum famae suae rebatur si nutricem salutare*m* fastidiret), ubi uisae uirginis amore captus noctem petiit. Ipsa uno complexu grauidata, cum peperisset filium Ethelstanum, somnii fidem absoluit;

---

a B *adds* in   *b* One expects donata est   *c* donare B   *d* ipsi pot. Deo B   *e–e* For B's version at this point (numbered as 138B.1–5) see Appendix, p. 820   *f* instructionem B†   *g* posterorum T*t*B, rightly?   *h* Cf. GP p. 133

small were adjudged to me. All this I have set down in writing that so long as Christianity endures it may not be forgotten how it came about that the possessions aforesaid, which I have given to God and St Peter, were made over to me. And I know no more just course of action than to give them to God and St Peter, who caused my enemy's downfall in the sight of all men and have given me a prosperous reign.'

138. In these words we must admire both the king's wisdom and his devotion towards God: his wisdom in that he observed, young as he was, that an offering of the spoils of robbery is not acceptable to God, and his devotion in that he gratefully restored to God above all a gift which the divine vengeance had conferred upon him. Another point is also worth observing, that at the time St Peter's church, which is now of the second rank, came first in the monastery; St Mary's, which the monks now use, was built later, in King Edgar's days, under Abbot Ælfric.

What I have written of the king so far is perfectly trustworthy; what follows I have learnt more from popular songs which have suffered in transmission than from scholarly books written for the information of posterity. I have added it here not to defend its veracity, but in order not to keep any knowledge from my readers. And first I will speak of his birth.

139. There lived in a certain village a shepherd's daughter, a very beautiful girl, who redeemed by the attractions of her person the defects of her birth. One night she had a marvellous dream, an omen: her belly shone with the brightness of the moon, and all England was illuminated by its brilliance. In the morning she told her companions as a joke; but they took it seriously, and it soon reached the ears of the steward's wife, who served as wet-nurse to the king's sons. After thinking it over, she took the girl into her home and treated her as her own daughter, making her familiar with more elegant clothes, a more refined diet, and the behaviour of polite society. Not long afterwards 2 King Alfred's son Edward happened to be passing through the village on a journey, and thinking it would be a reflection on his honour if he were too proud to greet his nurse, he turned aside to visit the house which had learnt to know him as a baby. He saw the girl, fell in love with her, and asked whether he might sleep with her. That one night left her with child, and by bearing a son, who was Æthelstan, she

---

i conscientiam *B (cf. GP p. 162) Tt* *l* om. *Tt* *m* uisitare *B* *j* elegantis speciei *Tt* *k* splendescere

nam cum ille pueritia mortua in adolescentiam euaderet, magnam spem regiae indolis dabat, preclaris facinoribus approbatus. Itaque *rege Eduardo defuncto, filius eius* Elwardus, ex legitima coniuge creatus, *patrem cita* morte secutus.*c* Tunc omnium spebus in Ethelstanum erectis, solus Elfredus, magnae insolentiae homo, cum suis clam*d* restitit quoad potuit, dedignatus subdi domino quem suo non
3 delegisset*e* arbitrio. Quo, ut superius rex retulit,*f* [1] prodito et exanimato,*g* fuere qui fratrem regis Eduinum insidiarum insimularent: scelus horrendum et fedum, quod sedulitatem fraternam sinistra interpretatione turbarent. Eduinus per se et per internuntios*h* fidem germani implorans et licet sacramento delationem infirmans, in exilium actus est. Tantum quorundam mussitatio apud animum in multas curas distentum ualuit ut ephebum etiam externis miserandum oblitus consanguineae necessitudinis expelleret, inaudito sane crudelitatis modo, ut solus cum armigero nauem conscendere iuberetur remige et remi-
4 gio uacuam, preterea uetustate quassam. Diu laborauit Fortuna ut insontem terrae restitueret; sed cum tandem in medio mari*i* furorem uentorum uela non sustinerent, ille ut*j* adolescens delicatus*k* et uitae in talibus pertesus uoluntario in aquas precipitio mortem consciuit. Armiger, saniori consilio passus animam producere, modo aduersos*l* fluctus eludendo, modo pedibus subremigando domini corpus ad
5 terram detulit angusto scilicet a Dorobernia in Witsand mari. Ethelstanus, postquam ira deferbuit, animo sedato factum exhorruit septennique penitentia accepta in delatorem fratris*m* animose ultus est. Erat ille pincerna regis, et per hoc ad persuadenda*n* quae excogitasset accommodus. Itaque cum forte die sollemni uinum propinaret, in medio triclinio uno pede lapsus, altero se recollegit; tunc occasione accepta fatale sibi uerbum emisit: 'Sic frater fratrem adiuuat.' Quo rex audito perfidum obtruncari precepit, sepius auxilium germani, si uiueret, increpitans et mortem ingemiscens.

---

a–a patre defuncto B   *b–b* concita B   *c* B adds est   *d* om. Tt
e elegisset Tt   *f* protulit Bk(and Bp), om. Bc   *g* examinato CsB   *h* germanos B   *i* maris (om. in medio) Tt (Tt*p.c.* accordingly reads uentorumque)
j om. A   *k* om. B   *l* aduersus ABk   *m* For B's version here see Appendix, p. 822   *n* suadenda B

[1] c. 137.

made her dream come true; for as soon as he left boyhood behind him and reached adolescence, he gave great promise of a kingly nature and won renown by his distinguished record. When King Edward died therefore, and his son Æthelweard, born in lawful wedlock, followed him soon afterwards, the hopes of all were set on Æthelstan. Only Alfred, a man of overweening insolence, with his followers resisted in secret as long as he could, disdaining to submit to a lord who was not of his own choosing. When he was betrayed and put to death, as the king has recorded above,[1] there were some who accused the king's brother Edwin of plotting against him; and a foul and loathsome crime it was to undermine by their malevolent constructions the love of one brother for another. Edwin in person and through intermediaries besought his brother to believe him, but though he denied the charge on oath he was driven into exile. Such was the power of whispering tongues over a mind already distracted by many anxieties, that he forgot the ties of kinship and expelled a youth whom even strangers could not choose but pity. Even his cruelty took a form without parallel; for he compelled his brother, attended by a single squire, to go on board a boat without oars or oarsmen, and, what is more, rotten with age. Fortune long did her best to bear the innocent victim back to land; but at length, when they were far out to sea and the sails could no longer endure the fury of the winds, the young man, who was of delicate nurture and could no longer bear to live in such conditions, sought his own death by plunging into the waters. His squire with more prudence found courage to prolong his own life and, partly by evading the onset of the waves, partly by propelling the boat with his feet for oars, brought his master's body to land in the narrow sea that flows between Dover and Wissant. Æthelstan, once he had simmered down, was aghast at what he had done and, submitting to a seven-year penance, took passionate vengeance on the man who had informed against his brother. The culprit was the royal cup-bearer, and therefore in a favourable position to persuade the king of the truth of his inventions. It so happened that on a feast-day he was pouring wine, and he slipped in the middle of the dining-room with one foot and recovered his balance with the other. Prompted by what had happened, he uttered a phrase which was to prove his undoing: 'Thus does one brother aid another.' The monarch heard, and ordered the traitor's head to be struck off, for he often dwelt bitterly on the help his brother would have given him had he lived, and mourned his loss.

140. Haec de fratris nece, etsi ueri similia uidentur,^a eo minus corroboro quod mirabilem suae pietatis diligentiam in reliquos fratres intenderit;^b quos, cum pater puerulos admodum reliquisset, ille paruos magna dulcedine fouit et adultos regni consortes fecit.^c De sororibus^d superius lectum est,[1] quanta eas^e maiestate prouexerit quas pater et innuptas et indotatas reliquerat. Vitae termino expleto, et quidem immaturo, Ethelstanus Gloecestrae diem clausit. Exuuiae triumphales Malmesberiam delatae et sub altari tumulatae. Portata ante corpus multa in argento et auro donaria, simul et sanctorum reliquiae de transmarina Britannia emptae. In talibus enim thesauros patris, quos ille diu coaceruatos et intactos reliquerat, consumpsit, somnio (ut ferunt) ammonitus: uir qui parum aetati uixerit, multum gloriae.

141. Anno Dominicae incarnationis nongentesimo quadragesimo Edmundus frater Ethelstani, adolescens octodecim circiter annorum, tenuit regnum annis sex et semis. Huius tempore Northanimbri, rediuiua meditantes prelia, pactum quod cum Ethelstano pepigerant corrupere, et Analauum, ab Hibernia reuocatum, statuere regem. At uero Edmundus, qui existimaret iniurium si non fraternae uictoriae reliquias persequeretur, copias contra desertores ductitauit. Quibus mox loco cedentibus, omnes ciuitates citra Humbram fluuium suae

2 potentiae redegit. Analauus cum quodam regulo Reinaldo, filio illius Gurmundi de quo in gestis Elfredi tetigimus,[2] animum regis temptans, deditionem sui^f obtulit, Christianitatem obsidem fidei suae professus. Sed non diu barbaricus animus in sententia mansit, quin et sacramentum lederet et dominum irritaret; quapropter anno sequenti pulsus perpetuo exilio penas luit, prouintia quae uocatur Cumberland regi Scottorum Malcolmo sub fidelitate iurisiurandi commendata.

142. ^gInter ea^h benefitia quae diuersis aecclesiis contulit, miro affectu Glastoniensem aecclesiam magnis prediis et honoribus sullimauit, et priuilegium in haec uerba concessit:

^a uideantur *TtACs, not impossibly*   ^b intenderet *A*   ^c fatiens *B, adding* numquam eorum intuitu dare operam *(*curam *Bc)* matrimonio curauit   ^d *A adds* suis   ^e om. *A*   ^f om. *A*   ^g *cc. 142–3 are omitted in TtABc¹, but the (spurious) charter (Sawyer 499) is variously transmitted in AG pp. 116–18 and* ρστ   ^h interea *Ce(and Cd)BkBc²;* inter cetera *Cs(and CpCr)*

[1] 112. 2, 126. 2, 135. 2.   [2] 121. 6 (see p. 213 n. 1 above).

140. This story of his brother's death, plausible though it seems, I am the less ready to affirm, inasmuch as he gave practical proof of remarkable affection towards his other brothers: mere infants at his father's death, he brought them up lovingly in childhood, and when they grew up gave them a share in his kingdom [B *adds* never, out of respect for them, turning his thoughts towards marriage]. As for his sisters, the reader has already heard of the royal eminence to which he raised such of them as his father had left without husband or dowry.[1] So, having fulfilled his allotted span—and very short it was—Æthelstan died at Gloucester. His remains were borne in state to Malmesbury, and buried there beneath the high altar. Many gifts from him in silver and gold were carried before the body, and many relics of saints, bought in Brittany, for such were the objects on which he expended—warned (it is said) in a dream—the treasure accumulated and left untouched by his father. His years, though few, were full of glory.

141. In the year of our Lord 940 Æthelstan's brother Edmund, a youth about eighteen years of age, succeeded, and held the throne for six and a half years. In his time the Northumbrians, planning a fresh outbreak of hostilities, tore up the treaty they had made with Æthelstan, recalled Anlaf from Ireland, and made him king. Edmund, however, who thought it dishonourable not to pursue what remained of his brother's victory, led out his forces against the rebels, and as they soon retired before him, he made himself master of all the towns south of the river Humber. Anlaf, together with a prince called Rægnald, son of the Gurmund whom I touched on in my account of Alfred,[2] by way of trying out the king offered to surrender, and professed himself a convert to Christianity as a guarantee of good faith; but his barbarian heart soon abandoned its resolve, and did not prevent him from a breach of his oath and a challenge to his lord. Next year therefore, he was driven out and punished with perpetual exile. The province called Cumberland was entrusted under an oath of fealty to Malcolm king of the Scots.

142. Among the other benefits conferred by Edmund on various churches, he showed a wonderful affection for the church of Glastonbury, and exalted it with great estates and privileges, giving it a charter in the following terms:

143. 'In nomine Domini nostri Iesu Christi. Ego Edmundus, rex Anglorum ceterarumque gentium in circuitu persistentium gubernator et rector, cum consilio et consensu optimatum meorum, pro aeternae retributionis spe et relaxatione peccaminum meorum, concedo aecclesiae sanctae[a] Dei genitricis Mariae Glastoniae et uenerabili uiro Dunstano, quem ibidem abbatem constitui, libertatem et potestatem, iura,[b] consuetudines et omnes forisfacturas omnium terrarum suarum, id est burhgerihta et hundredsetena, athas et ordelas et infangenetheofas, hamsocne et frithbrice et forestal, et tol et team, in omni regno meo; et sint terrae suae sibi liberae et solutae ab omni calumnia, sicuti meae 2 michi habentur. Sed precipue ipsa uilla Glastoniae, in qua celeberrima Vetusta Aecclesia sanctae Dei genitricis sita est, pre ceteris sit liberior cum terminis suis. Abbati eiusdem tantummodo potestas sit tam in notis causis quam in ignotis, in modicis et in magnis, et in his etiam quae sunt super et subtus terram, in aridis et in riuis, in siluis et in planis, et eandem auctoritatem puniendi et dimittendi delinquentium in ea commissa habeat quam mea curia, quemadmodum mei antecessores concesserunt et statuendo confirmauerunt; uidelicet Eduardus pater meus et Elfredus[c] pater eius et Centwines, Ines et Cuthredus et 3 alii quam plures qui locum illum honorantes gloriosum habuerunt. Et ne quisquam mortalium seu episcopus uel dux aut princeps aut quislibet ministrorum eorum audeat eam omnino intrare causa placitandi uel rapiendi uel quippiam fatiendi quod contrarium fore possit inibi Deo seruientibus Dei interdictione prohibeo. Quisquis igitur beniuola mente meam donationem amplificare sategerit, in hoc presenti seculo 4 uita illius prospera feliciter ⟨sit et⟩[d] longiturnae uitae[e] gaudia teneat. Si quis autem propria temeritate uiolenter inuadere presumpserit, sciat se proculdubio ante tribunal districti Iudicis titubantem tremebundumque rationem redditurum, nisi prius digna satisfactione emendare maluerit.

'Acta est haec prefata donatio anno ab incarnatione Domini nostri Iesu Christi nongentesimo quadragesimo quarto, indictione secunda; scriptaque est litteris aureis in libro euangeliorum quem eidem aecclesiae obtulit eleganti satis opere compositum.'

144. Verum tantos et tam felices successus miserandus decolorauit exitus: siquidem latrunculus quidam Leof,[f] quem[g] propter latrocinia

---

[a] om. CBk(and Bp), L of AG, σ   [b] Bk, AG, σ[p.c.]τ add et   [c] Ethelfredus BkBc[2]   [d] sit et found only in AG (not MS L), στ   [e] om. BkBc[2], ρ
[f] Leua TtA   [g] quam Tt

143. 'In the name of our Lord Jesus Christ. I Edmund, king of the English, governor and ruler of all the other nations that lie round about them, with the counsel and consent of my nobles, in hope of everlasting reward and the remission of my sins, grant to the church of St Mary, Mother of God, at Glastonbury and to the venerable father Dunstan whom I have made abbot there, liberty and authority, rights, customs, and all forfeitures of all their lands, that is to say *burhgerihta and hundredsetena, athas and ordelas and infangenetheofas, hamsocne and frithbrice and forestal, and tol and team* in all my kingdom, and that they may hold their lands free and quit of all claim, as I hold my own lands. In particular, the town of Glastonbury itself, in which is situated the famous Old Church of the holy Mother of God, together with its bounds, is to be more free than the rest. The abbot of the same, and he alone, is to have power both in known cases and in unknown, in small and in great, as also in things which are above and below the earth, in dry places and in rivers, in woodland and in open country, and he is to have the same authority to punish or to pardon the offences of those who err therein that is enjoyed by my own court, as was granted by my predecessors and confirmed by their decisions, to wit Edward my father and his father Alfred, and Centwine, Ine, and Cuthred, and many others who have held that place in high honour and esteem. And I forbid, under the curse of God, that any mortal man, be he bishop or thegn or prince or any of their servants, should dare to enter that place in any way with intent to hold court or seize anything or do anything that might be to the detriment of those who serve God therein. Whosoever therefore with good intent sets himself to multiply this my gift, may his life in this present world be prosperous and may he possess the joys of the life which endures. But if any man with headstrong violence shall presume to trespass on the same, let him be warned that he shall give account in fear and trembling before the tribunal of the strict Judge, unless he first prefers to mend his ways and make due satisfaction.

'This donation aforesaid was made in the year of our Lord 944, the second indiction; and it was written in letters of gold in the book of the Gospels, of most elegant workmanship, which he presented to the church aforesaid.'

144. But these great and happy successes were overcast by a lamentable end. A thief named Liofa, whom he had banished for his

eliminauerat, post sexennium regressus in sollemnitate sancti Augustini Cantuariae archiepiscopi inopinus apud Pukelecerce inter conuiuas regios assedit, quo scilicet die Angli festiue obsoniari[a] solebant pro predicatoris sui memoria, et forte iuxta ducem recumbebat quem rex ipse partibus de cena dignatus fuerat. Id ab eo solo animaduersum, ceteris in uina spumantibus; itaque bili concitata et, ut eum fata agebant, e mensa prosiliens predoni in capillos inuolat[b] et ad terram
2 elidit. Ille latenter sicam de uagina eductam in pectus regis superiacentis quanto potest conatu infigit; quo uulnere exanimatus,[c] fabulae ianuam in omnem Angliam de interitu suo patefecit. Latro quoque mox concurrentibus satellitibus membratim dissectus prius nonnullos sautiauit. Preuiderat tam[d] infamem finem beatus Dunstanus tunc Glastoniensis abbas, demonis ante se saltantis gesticulationibus et plausibus edoctus scurrilibus, quocirca equo concito curiam properans in medio itinere gestae rei nuntium
3 [e]accepit, [e]accepit. Communi ergo decretum consilio, et funus corpusque Glastoniam delatum, ibique in aquilonali parte turris suscipiens magnifice humatum. Id eum uoluisse pro familiari abbatis Glastoniae amicitia per nonnulla claruerat inditia. Data in inferias sepeliuit.[e] uilla in qua occubuerat, ut quae semel conscia fuerat homicidii, semper in posterum pro anima eius esset adiutrix benefitii.[e]

145. Huius anno quarto, id est anno Dominicae incarnationis nongentesimo quadragesimo quarto, Willelmus filius Rollonis, dux Normannorum, dolo in Frantia[f] occisus est. Quod non immerito factum maiores tradunt: Riulfus siquidem, unus procerum Normannicae[g] gentis, in simultatem nescio qua de causa ueniens cum Willelmo, multis illum assultibus afflixit. Militabat filius eius Anschetillus comiti, qui, ut domino placeret, ausus est temerare naturam, ut patrem duello caperet et in potestatem comitis traderet, maximo tamen sacramento credulus ne quicquam iniuriae preter uincula pater-
2 etur. Sed sicut semper nequitia causas[h] malorum comminiscitur, post non multum tempus afficta occasione comes Anschetillum in

---

[a] obsonari *Aa, more correctly (cf. VW iii. 2)* *TtBk*   [b] euolat *Tt*   [c] examinatus *TtBk*   [d] tamen *Bc, om. Bk (Bp avoids error)*   [e–e] accepit... sepeliuit *TtA;* accepit... benefitii *CB (cf. VD p. 277)*   [f] Franciam *Tt*   [g] Nor(th)manni(a)e *(om. gentis) TtA*   [h] causa *BkBc²(and Bp),* causam *Bc¹*

robberies, returned after six years, and on the festival of St Augustine, archbishop of Canterbury, at Pucklechurch, unexpectedly took his seat among the royal guests. It was the day when the English were accustomed to hold a festival dinner in memory of him who preached the Gospel to them, and as it happened he was sitting next to the thegn whom the king himself had condescended to make his guest at the dinner. The king alone noticed this, for all the rest were aflame with wine; and in sudden anger, carried away by fate, he leapt up from the table, seized him by the hair, and flung him to the ground. The man drew a dagger in stealth from its sheath, and as the king lay on him plunged it with all his force into his chest. The wound was fatal, and gave an opening for rumours about his death that spread all over England. The robber too, as the servants soon came running up, was torn limb from limb, but not before he had wounded several of them. St Dunstan, then abbot of Glastonbury, had had a previous vision of this inglorious ending, when he was warned by the gestures and the loud jeers of a devil dancing before him. This made him spur his horse and hasten to the court, and when halfway there he heard news of what had happened.

TtA So, taking up the body, he buried it at Glastonbury.

CB So a decree was passed in the common council, and the body was taken to Glastonbury, and there buried with great pomp in the northern part of the tower. That this was his wish on account of his close friendship with the abbot had been clear from various indications. The village in which he had lain sick was made an offering for the dead, that the place which had once been a witness of his murder might forever offer spiritual support for the benefit of his soul.

145. In his fourth year, that is in the year of our Lord 944, William son of Rollo, Duke of Normandy, was treacherously killed in France, a fate which according to tradition was not undeserved. Riulf, one of the nobles of Norman stock, fell into a dispute with William, for some reason I do not know, and made a number of damaging attacks on him. Riulf's son Anscytel was fighting for the duke, and to win favour with his lord he dared to perpetrate a breach of the order of nature, by taking his own father prisoner in single combat and handing him over to the duke; but he put his trust in the duke's most solemn oath that he should suffer no harm except being put in chains. But wickedness is always fertile in fresh causes of evil, and it was not long before

Papiam dirigit, epistolam de sua ipsius nece ad ducem Italiae portantem. Ille permenso itinere urbem introiens magnifice susceptus est. Porrectis litteris dux fraudem miratus diriguit, quod insignis festiuitatis miles iuberetur interfici; sed quia tantae famae comiti resultare non esset consilium, Anschetillum iam ciuitatem egressum excepit insidiis mille, ut fertur, equitum; ubi ille cum sotiis, quos lectissimos ex omni Normannia adduxerat, diu uiolentiae restitit, sed tandem, mortem suam multis cesis compensans, non ignaue occubuit. Solus ex utraque parte Balzo Normannus superstes, uir exigui corporis sed immanis fortitudinis, quanuis quidam per hironiam dicant eum Curtum uocatum; solus inquam ciuitatem obsedit, solus ciues gladio suo quoad^a uisum est exterruit. Hoc incredibile non iudicabit qui cogitabit quantum^b conetur hominis audacis desperatio, et quam parum ualeant illi prouintiales in prelio. Inde repatrians querelam apud regem Francorum de domini sui perfidia deposuit; nam et Riulfum fama ferebat in uinculis cecatum. Quare ad iuditium euocatus Parisius, et ab obuio sibi^c Balzone sub spetie^d colloquii obtruncatus, in medio, ut aiunt, Sequanae perfidiae suae et irae illius satisfecit. Interitus eius diutinam inter Francos et Normannos discordiam peperit, donec per industriam Ricardi filii ipsius finem accepit uirtute sua dignum. 'Porro ueratiores litterae dicunt illum, contractis inimicitiis cum Ernulfo comite Flandriae, unum ex castellis eius peruasisse; a quo simulata uoluntate federis ad colloquium euocatum, consertoque sermone in naui per Balzonem obtruncatum; clauem ad eius cingulum inuentam, seraeque familiaris scrinii compositam, monachilium indumentorum intus inuolutorum inditium fecisse, quod semper inter bella meditaretur monachus fore apud Gimegium, quem locum, a tempore Hasteng desertum, ipse fruticosis sentibus eruderauerat^f et ad hunc statum qui modo est principali indulgentia erexerat.$^{g\,e}$

146. Anno Dominicae incarnationis nongentesimo quadragesimo sexto Edredus, tertius ex filiis Eduardi, regnum suscipiens rexit annis nouem et dimidio. Eius magnanimitas a patre et fratribus non

^{a} quod ad *Tt* ^{b} quanta *Tt* ^{c} om. *Tt* ^{d} spe *A* $^{e-e}$ om. *Tt* ^{f} eruderauerit *A* ^{g} erexerit *A*

the duke invented some excuse for sending Anscytel to Pavia, bearing a letter to the duke of Italy which was his own death-warrant. He accomplished his journey, entered the city, and was given a splendid welcome. When he produced his letter, the duke froze with amazement at such treachery, wondering how orders could be given for the death of a knight of such outstanding charm; but as it was not policy to differ from a duke of such high repute, he caught Anscytel, who had already left the city, in an ambush of (it is said) a thousand knights. There he and the companions he had brought with him, who were hand-picked from the whole of Normandy, resisted their violence for a long time, but in the end he was killed, not without glory, after slaying many to balance his own death. Balzo, a Norman, was the only survivor on either side; he was small in build, but of enormous courage, though some say that he was nicknamed Tiny only as a joke. Single-handed, I repeat, he blockaded the city, and single-handed terrified the citizens with his sword for as long as he thought fit. This will not be judged incredible by anyone who considers how much can be attempted by a brave man in desperate straits, and how little the people of that region are worth in battle. On returning home, he lodged with the king of the French a complaint touching the treachery of his lord, for report had it too that Riulf had been blinded in prison. William was therefore summoned to Paris for the hearing of the case, and on the way met Balzo who, under pretence of talking with him, struck him dead, in the middle, it is said, of the Seine. Thus he atoned for his own perfidy and satisfied Balzo's wrath. His death produced a long estrangement between the French and the Normans, until the efforts of his son Richard at length brought it to an end worthy of his high qualities. In fact, more trustworthy sources tell us that, hostility having developed between him and Arnulf count of Flanders, he had seized one of the count's castles. Under the pretext of wishing to come to an agreement, the count invited him to a discussion; and when talks had started on board ship, he was killed by Balzo. A key found in his belt fitted the lock of his private chest, and revealed a monastic habit folded up inside it, for amidst his wars he had always thought of becoming a monk at Jumièges, a place deserted since the days of Hæsten, which he himself had cleared of scrub and brambles, and raised with princely generosity to its present state.

146. In the year of our Lord 946 Eadred, Edward's third son, came to the throne, and reigned for nine and a half years. His enterprise, in

degenerans hanc summam dedit: Northanimbros et Scottos facile ad sacramentum suae fidelitatis adactos et mox fedifragos, quodam Iritio rege super se statuto, pene ex hominibus deleuit, tota prouintia fame ferroque fedata; archiepiscopum Eboraci Wlstanum, qui compatriotis*a* in transfugio coniuere diceretur, diu in uinculis tentum, postea cleri-
2 calis reuerentiae respectu uenia donatum laxauit. Ipse interea sanctorum pedibus acclinis*b* Deo et Dunstano uitam suam deuouerat, cuius monitis tortiones crebras corporis patienter ferre, orationes continuare, prorsus palatium suum gimnasium uirtutum*c* facere. Decessit magno luctu hominum sed gaudio angelorum prosecutus: siquidem Dunstanus nuntio egrotantis audito, cum illuc sonipedem calcaribus urgeret, uocem desuper tonantem audierit: 'Modo rex Edredus obdormiuit in Domino.' Requiescit Wintoniae in episcopatu.

147. Anno Dominicae incarnationis nongentesimo quinquagesimo quinto Edwius, filius Edmundi superioris regis, regno potitus tenuit annis quattuor, petulans adolescens et qui*d* spetiositate corporis in libidinibus abuteretur. Denique proxime cognatam inuadens uxorem eius forma deperibat, sapientium consilia fastidiens. Ipso quippe die quo in regem sacratus fuerat, frequentissimo consessu procerum, dum de*e* rebus seriis et regno necessariis inter eos agereturʲ e medio quasi ludibundus prorupit, in triclinium et*g* complexum ganeae deuolutus.
2 Fremere omnes facti uerecundiam, et inter se mussitare; solus Dunstanus iuxta nominis sui firmitatem nichil regale supercilium ueritus, lasciuientem iuuenculum uiolenter e cubiculo abstraxit et, per Odonem archiepiscopum pelicem repudiare coactum, perpetuum sibi inimicum fecit. Mox etenim, miserrimis satellitibus subnixus, omnes in tota Anglia monastici ordinis homines, prius nudatos facultatum auxilio, post etiam deportatos exilio, calamitatibus indignis affecit; ipsum Dunstanum monachorum primicerium in Flandriam propellit.
3 Ea tempestate faties monasteriorum feda et miserabilis erat; nam et Malmesberiense cenobium, plusquam ducentis septuaginta annis*h* a monachis inhabitatum, stabulum clericorum fecit. Sed tu, Domine Iesu, creator et recreator noster, bone artifex multumque potens

a cum patriotis *TtB*   *b* acliuis *TtBk*   *c* suum *B*   *d A adds* sub
e om. A   *f* aggrederetur *Tt*   *g* ad *Tt;* et in *Bk,* in *Bc¹* (*Bc²Bp avoid error*)   *h om. Tt*

which he did not fall short of his father and brothers, produced the following results. The Northumbrians and the Scots were easily brought to swear an oath of fealty to him, and soon afterwards, when they broke the agreement and set up a certain Eric as king over them, he almost wiped them out, and laid waste the whole province with famine and bloodshed. Archbishop Wulfstan of York, who was said to be in touch with his compatriots among the rebels, he held imprisoned for some time, but later pardoned and released out of respect for his position in the Church. He himself meanwhile, prostrate at the feet of the saints, had devoted his life to God and Dunstan, on whose advice he learnt to endure frequent bodily pain, to be constant in prayer, and in short to make his palace a school of all the virtues. His death was greeted by great grief among men but joy among the angels; for Dunstan, who on learning of his illness was spurring his horse towards him, heard a loud voice from Heaven saying: 'Now has King Eadred fallen asleep in the Lord.' He lies at Winchester in the cathedral church.

147. In the year of our Lord 955 Eadwig, son of Edmund the earlier king, came to the throne and held it for four years. He was a wanton youth, and one who misused his personal beauty in lascivious behaviour. For example, he took up with a woman to whom he was closely related, and doted on her person, in defiance of wiser men. On the very day of his consecration as king, in a very full gathering of the nobles, while serious and immediate affairs of state were under discussion, he burst out of the meeting as though he were completely at leisure, and sank on a couch into the arms of his doxy. This shameless conduct was universally resented, and there was subdued protest; only Dunstan, as the rocky element in his name would suggest, thought nothing of the king's contemptuous air, dragged the lecherous youngster by main force from the bed-chamber, and obliged him through Archbishop Oda to dismiss his concubine, thus earning for himself the king's undying enmity. For soon, with the support of his pitiful toadies, he plunged all men of the monastic order all over England into undeserved calamities, first stripping them of the support of their revenues and then driving them into exile. Dunstan himself as head of all the monks was sent packing into Flanders. That was a time when all monasteries wore an unkempt and pitiful air. Even the convent of Malmesbury, where monks had dwelt for over two hundred and seventy years, he made into a bawdy-house for clerks. But you, O Lord Jesus, our creator and re-creator, a skilled artificer well able to

formare nostra deformia, per illos homines irregulares et uagos thesaurum tuum tot annis abditum in lucem propalasti, beati Aldelmi corpus dico, quod ipsi de terra eleuatum in scrinio locarunt. Accessit clericorum gloriae regalis liberalitas, ut daret sancto predium ampli-
4 tudine et uicinitate ipsa peroportunum. Ceterum longe horret nostra memoria quam immanis fuerit in reliqua cenobia et propter aetatis lubricum et propter pelicis consilium, quae tenerum iugiter obsidebat animum. Sed ignoscat dolori meo anima iam dudum in requie collocata*a* per Dunstani interuentum; dolor, inquam, me cogit illum adiudicare, quia priuata utilitas publico dampno non preiudicat, immo commune dispendium priuato commodo preponderat. Luit ille penas ausus temerarii etiam hac in uita, maxima parte regni mutilatus. Qua iniuria percussus uiuendi finem fecit, Wintoniae in Nouo Monasterio tumulatus.

148. Anno Dominicae incarnationis nongentesimo quinquagesimo nono Edgarus, honor ac delitiae Anglorum, filius Edmundi, frater Edwii, iuuenculus annorum sedecim regnum adipiscens eodem annorum*b* numero ferme*c* tenuit. Res eius multum splendide etiam nostro celebrantur tempore. Affulsit annis illius diuinitatis amor propitius, quem ipse mercabatur sedulo deuotione animi et uiuacitate consilii. Denique uulgatum est quod eo nascente angelicam uocem Dunstanus exceperit:*d* 'Pax Angliae quam diu puer iste regnauerit et Dunstanus
2 noster uixerit.' Respondit ueritas rerum caelesti oraculo: adeo illis uiuentibus splendor aecclesiasticus effloruit et tumultus bellicus emarcuit, nec ullus fere annus in Cronicis preteritus est quo non magnum et necessarium patriae aliquid fecerit, quo non monasterium nouum fundauerit. Nullas insidias domesticorum, nullum exterminium alienorum sensit. Regem Scottorum Kinadium, Cumbrorum Malcolmum, archipiratam Mascusium omnesque reges Walensium,*e* *f* quorum nomina fuere Dufnal Giferth Huual Iacob Iudethil,*f* ad curiam coactos uno et perpetuo sacramento sibi obligauit, adeo ut apud Ciuitatem Legionum sibi occurrentes in pompam triumphi per fluuium De*g* illos deduceret. Vna enim naui impositos ipse ad*h* proram*i* sedens remigare cogebat, per hoc ostentans regalem magnificentiam,

a collata *Tt* *b* om. *TA* *c* ferme numero *T* *d* accepit *T;* excepit *ABc¹* *e* uualensium regulos *(sic) T* *f-f* om. *T* *g* om. *TB* *h* om. *B* *i* clauum *T (cf. JW s.a. 973)*

reform our deformities, used those unruly and wandering persons to bring to light and public knowledge your treasure that for so many years lay hidden—I mean the body of St Aldhelm, which they themselves raised from the ground and established in a shrine. The prestige of those clerks was further enhanced by royal generosity, which gave the saint an estate admirably adapted both by its size and by its convenient position. All the same, even at this distance, it is horrible to 4 remember how cruelly the king behaved to the other monasteries, being himself young and foolish, and moved too by the advice of his mistress, who constantly laid siege to his childish mind. But may his soul, which has long been in peace through Dunstan's intervention, forgive my grief; and grief it is, I repeat, that makes me pass judgement on him, for private profit has no priority over public loss—rather, what hurts the community weighs more than what benefits the individual. He paid the price, even in this life, for his rash daring, when stripped of the most part of his kingdom, and under the shock of this loss he died, and lies buried in New Minster at Winchester.

148. In the year of our Lord 959 Edgar, the honour and delight of Englishmen, Edmund's son and Eadwig's brother, a youth of sixteen, came to the throne, and held it for about the same number of years. His record still shines, bright and popular, in our own day. Heaven's love and favour shone upon his reign, and this he earned by his own efforts, by the devotion of his spirit and the vigour of his policy. It is widely believed, for example, that when he was born Dunstan heard the voice of an angel, saying: 'Peace be to England, as long as this child is king and our beloved Dunstan lives.' This oracle from Heaven 2 found its true answer in the outcome: such splendour blossomed in the Church during their lifetime, while war and tumult withered, and scarcely a year is passed over in the Chronicles without his doing his country some notable and necessary service and without his founding some new monastery. He suffered no treachery from his own people and no destruction from foreigners. Kenneth, king of the Scots, Malcolm king of the Cumbrians, Mascusius the pirate king, and all the Welsh kings (whose names were Dyfnwal, Giferth, Hywel, Iago, and Iudethil) he compelled to attend his court, and bound them to him by one perpetual oath, so much so that, when they all met him at the City of Legions, he took them for a triumphal procession on the river Dee. For he set them in one boat, and made them row while he sat at the prow, as a way of displaying the majesty of a king who held the

qui subiectam haberet tot regum potentiam. *"*Denique fertur dixisse tunc demum posse successores suos gloriari se reges Anglorum esse, cum tanta honorum prerogatiua fruerentur.*"* Vnde factum est ut, fama eius per ora omnium uolitante,[1] alienigenae Saxones, Flandritae, ipsi etiam Dani, huc frequenter annauigarent, Edgaro familiares effecti: quorum aduentus magnum prouintialibus detrimentum peperit, quod a Saxonibus animorum inconditam ferocitatem, a Flandritis corporum eneruem mollitiem, a Danis potationem discerent, homines antehac in talibus integri et naturali simplicitate sua defensare,*^b* aliena non mirari. Inde merito iureque culpant eum litterae; nam ceteras infamias, quas post dicam,[2] magis resperserunt cantilenae.

149. Eo tempore micuerunt per Angliam sanctorum uirorum lumina, ut crederes e caelo arridere sidera. Quorum sepe nominatus Dunstanus prius abbas Glastoniae, post episcopus Wigorniae, mox archiepiscopus Cantuariae, multae in seculo potentiae, magnae apud Deum gratiae, illic Martham istic exhibebat Mariam. Ipse artium liberalium in tota insula post regem Elfredum excitator mirificus, ipse regularium*^c* locorum reparator munificus; in reges et delinquentes duces insonare terribile,*^d* pauperes et mediocres iuste sustentare; in tantum et*^e* in friuolis pacis sequax ut, quia compatriotae in tabernis conuenientes iamque temulenti pro modo bibendi contenderent, ipse clauos argenteos uel aureos iusserit uasis affigi, ut, dum metam suam quisque cognosceret, non plus subseruiente uerecundia uel ipse appeteret uel alium appetere cogeret. Plura et non contempnenda de uiro uolentem dicere

| *^f*liber Osberni reuocat, quem de uita ipsius mira uerborum et sententiarum concinnitate edidit;*^f* | *^f*reuocat Cantuariae cantor Osbernus, qui eius uitam Romana elegantia composuit, nulli nostro tempore stilo secundus, musica certe omnium sine controuersia primus;*^f* |

simul quoniam, si gratia diuina comitetur dispositum, proposui post nomina regum omnium episcoporum Angliae cuiuscumque prouintiae

---

^{a-a} om. T *^b The construction of these infinitives is uncertain* *^c TtCe;* regalium *ACsB* *^d* terribiles *Bk,* terribiliter *Bc (Bp avoids error)* *^e* etiam *Tt** *^{f-f}* liber ... edidit *Tt;* reuocat ... primus *ACB*

[1] Cf. Virgil, *Georg.* iii. 9 (also recalled at 167. 1).
[2] cc. 157–9.

power of so many kings in subjection. Indeed, he is reported to have said that his successors would only be able to boast of being kings of England when they enjoyed so singular an honour. The result was 3 that, as his fame 'flitted o'er the lips of all men',[1] foreigners in crowds, Saxons, Flemings, even Danes, visited this country and became Edgar's friends; and their arrival had a very bad effect on its inhabitants, who learnt from the Saxons unalloyed ferocity, from the Flemings a spineless physical effeminacy, and from the Danes a love of drinking, though previously they had been immune from such failings and had maintained their own standards naturally and simply without coveting those of others. For this the texts properly and rightly blame him, while the other slanders of which I shall speak later[2] were more the aspersions of popular song.

149. In those days there were holy men who shone like lights all over England, so that one might think the stars in heaven smiled upon it. Among these was Dunstan, of whom I have often spoken, first abbot of Glastonbury, then bishop of Worcester, later archbishop of Canterbury, a man of great influence in the world and of much grace in the eyes of God, who showed himself a Martha in one field and a Mary in the other. He was himself a wonderful stimulator of the liberal arts in the whole island, second only to King Alfred; he himself was a generous restorer of places where the Rule was observed; his thunders against kings and delinquent magnates could be terrible; his relief of the poor and humble was justly measured. Such was his 2 zeal for peace even in things of no importance that, seeing how his compatriots gathered in taverns and, when already flown with wine, fought over the amount that each should drink, he ordered that pins of silver or gold should be fixed in the drinking-vessels, so that each man could recognize his own proper limit, and not forget his good manners and either demand more for himself or compel another man to do so. I would gladly add more facts, facts which should by no 3 means be overlooked, about this great man, but I am restrained

| Tt by Osbern's book about his life, written with remarkable elegance of both words and matter; | ACB by Osbern, precentor of Canterbury, who has written his life with Roman elegance, being second to none in our time as a stylist as well as leading the field without dispute in music; |

and at the same time by the intention (if Heaven's grace accompanies my plan) once I have named the kings to give at least a summary

nomina saltem transcurrere et ad scientiam nostrorum procudere,*a* si
4 quid dignum ualuero de antiquitatis moneta exculpere. Veruntamen
quantum*b* efficax fuerit, sanctitas et probitas discipulorum suorum
inditio est. Athelwoldus ex monacho Glastoniensi abbas Abbendoniensis idemque post haec episcopus Wintoniensis tot et tanta monasteria fecit quod uix modo uideatur credibile ut talia fecerit episcopus urbis unius qualia uix possit rex Angliae totius. Fallor, et precipiti sententia pecco, si non palam sit quod dico. Quantula*c* sunt cenobia Heliense Burchense Thorniense,*d* quae ille a fundamentis suscitauit et sua industria perfecit; quae, cum semper exactorum uellicet nequitia, sunt nichilo-
5 minus habitatoribus suis suffitientia. Huius uitam Wlstanus quidam cantor Wintoniensis, discipulus eius scilicet et alumnus,*e* composuit stilo mediocri. Fecit et aliud opus de tonorum armonia ualde utile, eruditi Angli inditium, homo uitae bonae et eloquentiae castigatae. Tunc quoque Oswaldus Odonis archiepiscopi, qui ante Dunstanum fuerat, nepos, ex monacho Floriacensi Wigorniae episcopus et Eboraci archiepiscopus, titulos non inferiores ceteris promeruit; nam easdem terens orbitas, monachorum regulam iure suo ampliauit, et monasterium
6 Ramesiae in quodam palustri loco edificauit. Sedem episcopalem Wigorniae, clericis non ui expulsis sed sancta arte circumuentis, repleuit monachis regularibus. Expulerat antea regali iussione Athelwoldus clericos de Wintonia, qui cum, data sibi optione ut aut regulariter uiuerent aut loco cederent, magis uitam mollem elegissent, tunc tota insula incertis uagabantur sedibus. Ita his tribus uiris agentibus, quasi triformi lumine Angliam serenante, densae uitiorum tenebrae euanuere.
7 *f*Quo factum est ut Edgarus Glastoniensem aecclesiam, quam semper pre omnibus dilexit, magnis possessionibus amplificaret, et in omnibus quae ad aecclesiae decorem siue utilitatem pertinent tam interius quam exterius inuigilaret. Priuilegium sane quod eidem aecclesiae contulit huic nostrae historiae, sicut in eorum antiqua scedula legi, non est absurdum inserere.*f*

a Rather producere *(cf. HN 503* posterorum producetur notitie*)*   *b* quanta *(om.* efficax*) Tt*   *c* For this usage cf. GP p. 24 *(*qualia *VD p. 303)*   *d* om. *Tt*   *e* Alcuinus *(!) Tt*   *f-f* om. *TtABc¹*

account of all the bishops of England of every province, and to beat out something for the instruction of our countrymen, if I prove capable of fashioning some worthy result after the model of Antiquity. But how effective he was is shown by the saintliness and the integrity of his disciples. Æthelwold, a monk of Glastonbury who afterwards became abbot of Abingdon and then bishop of Winchester, founded monasteries so many and of such importance that it seems hard to believe now that the bishop of a single city did things such as are hardly within the powers of a king of all England. I am much mistaken, and hasty judgement leads me astray, if what I say is not obvious. Think of monasteries such as Ely, Peterborough, Thorney, which he raised from their foundations and completed by his own efforts, and which, though always troubled by the tax-gatherer, are none the less adequate to support their inhabitants. His Life has been written in a middling style by one Wulfstan, precentor of Winchester, his disciple and protégé. He also wrote another work *On the Harmony of Tones* which is very useful, and shows him to be a learned Englishman—a man of good life and correct manner of writing. At that time too there was Oswald, nephew of Archbishop Oda, Dunstan's predecessor, formerly a monk of Fleury, then bishop of Worcester and archbishop of York, whose claims were no less than those of the others; for while he followed the same course as they, he enlarged the monastic Rule on his own responsibility and built the monastery of Ramsey in a place in the fens. At Worcester he removed the clerks from the cathedral church, not driving them out by force but outmanoeuvring them with pious ingenuity, and filled it with monks living under the Rule. Æthelwold, on orders from the king, had already expelled the clerks from Winchester; and when they were given the choice between living under the Rule and leaving, and had chosen for preference a life of ease, they then roamed the whole island with no certain home. Thus through the activity of these three men, as though a three-fold light had cleared the English sky, the dense clouds of wickedness disappeared.

Thus it came about that Edgar advanced the church of Glastonbury, which he always favoured above all others, with great properties, and showed his concern in everything to do with the church's beauty or convenience, inside and out. It is not improper to insert in this our history the privilege that he bestowed on the church, just as I read it in an old document of theirs.

[*For the B version of cc. 150–1 see Appendix, pp. 824–31.*]

150C. *"In nomine Domini nostri Iesu Christi. Quanuis decreta pontificum et uerba sacerdotum, uelut fundamenta montium, inconuulsis ligaminibus fixa sint, tamen plerumque tempestatibus et turbinibus secularium rerum religio sanctae Dei aecclesiae maculis reproborum dissipatur ac rumpitur. Iccirco profuturum succedentibus posteris esse decernimus, ut ea quae salubri consilio et communi assensu diffiniuntur nostris litterulis roborata firmentur. Quapropter dignum uidetur ut aecclesia beatissimae Dei genetricis semperque uirginis Mariae Glastoniae, sicut ex antiquo principalem in regno meo obtinet dignitatem, ita spetiali quadam et singulari priuilegii libertate per nos honoretur. Hoc itaque Dunstano Dorobernensi atque Oswaldo Eboracensi archiepiscopis adhortantibus, consentiente etiam et annuente Brihtelmo Fontanensi episcopo ceterisque episcopis abbatibus et primatibus meis, ego Edgar, diuina dispositione rex Anglorum ceterarumque gentium in circuitu persistentium gubernator et rector, in nomine almae Trinitatis, pro anima patris mei qui ibi requiescit et antecessorum patrum meorum,*[b]* presenti priuilegio decerno statuo confirmo ut predictum monasterium omnisque possessio eius ab omni tributo fiscalium negotiorum nunc et in perpetuum libera et quieta maneant, et habeant socam et sacam, on strande, on streame, on wude, on felde and*[c]* on grithbrice, on burhbrice, hundredsetena, morthas, athas and*[c]* ordeles, ealle hordas bufan eorthan and*[c]* beneothan, infangenetheof and*[c]* utfangenetheof and*[c]* flemeneferthe, hamsochne, frithbrice, forsteal, tol and*[c]* team, ita libere et quiete sicut ego habeo in regno meo. Eandem quoque libertatem et potestatem quam ego in curia mea habeo, tam in dimittendo quam in puniendo, in quibuslibet omnino negotiis abbas et monachi prefati monasterii in sua curia habeant. Si autem abbas uel monachus quislibet*[d]* loci illius latronem, qui ad suspendium uel ad quodlibet mortis periculum ducitur, obuium habuerit in itinere, habeant potestatem eripiendi eum ab imminenti periculo in toto regno meo. Confirmo etiam et corroboro ut, quod hactenus ab omnibus antecessoribus nostris diligenter obseruatum est, Fontanensis episcopus uel eius ministri super hoc monasterium uel super parrochiales eiusdem aecclesias, uidelicet Stret Mirelinch Budecalege Sceapwic Sowi aut super earum capellas, nec etiam super eas quae in insulis continentur, scilicet Beocherie (quae Parua Hibernia dicitur) Godenie Martinesie Patheneberge

---

[a] *cc. 150–1 (omitted by TtABc¹: Bc¹ also omits 152–3) are printed as they are found in C; for B's version see Appendix, p. 824. The charter (150C. 1–6: Sawyer 783) is also available in various*

150 C. 'In the name of our Lord Jesus Christ. Although the decrees of bishops and the words of priests are, like the foundations of mountains, fixed by unshakeable bonds, yet often, thanks to the storms and whirlwinds of this world, reverence for God's holy Church is scattered and broken by the faults of wicked men. Therefore we decree that it will be profitable to those who follow us that those things which are determined by sound counsel and common agreement should be strengthened and assured by our humble letter. Wherefore it seems right that the church of the most blessed Mother of God, the ever-virgin Mary, at Glastonbury, just as it has held from of old the foremost distinction in my kingdom, so should it be honoured by us with some special and particular privilege and liberty. So on the advice of Dunstan archbishop of Canterbury and Oswald archbishop of York, and with the consent and agreement of Byrhthelm bishop of Wells, and all my other bishops, abbots, and noblemen, I Edgar, by God's will king of the English and governor and ruler of the other nations around about, in the name of the blessed Trinity, and remembering the soul of my father who lies there in peace and of my own ancestors who preceded him, by this present privilege decree, ordain, and confirm that the aforesaid monastery and all its possessions be free and quit, now and for ever, of all payment of fiscal burdens, and have *socn and sacu, on strande, on streame, on wude, on felde, and on grithbrice, on burhbrice, hundredsetena, morthas, athas and ordeles, ealle hordas bufan eorthan and beneothan, infangenetheof and utfangenetheof, and flemeneferthe, hamsochne, frithbrice, forsteal, tol and team*, as freely and with the same immunity as I have in my kingdom. The abbot and monks of the said monastery are to have in their court the same liberty and power that I have in my own court, both in pardoning and in punishing, in absolutely every kind of business. But if the abbot or any monk of that place meets on a journey a thief being led to the gallows or any other capital punishment, he shall have the power in all my realm to snatch him from his impending peril. I also confirm and establish anew that, as has hitherto been carefully observed by all our predecessors, the bishop of Wells and his servants shall have absolutely no power over this monastery or over its parish churches, to wit Street, Moorlinch, Butleigh, Shapwick, and Zoy, or over their chapels, nor over those in the islands, namely Beckery, which is called Little Ireland, Godney, Marchey, Panborough,

forms in AG pp. 122–6 and γδρστ.   [b] patris mei *Cs;* meorum *(om.* patrum*) AG,* γδρτ
(*rightly*)   [c] σ; & *(or* et*) C, AG,* γδρτ   [d] quilibet *AG,* γδρτ

Edredesie Ferremere, nullam omnino potestatem habeant, nisi tantum cum ab abbate causa dedicandi uel ordinandi aduocati fuerint, nec eorum presbiteros ad sinodum suam uel ad capitulum uel ad quodlibet placitum conuocent, nec ab offitio diuino suspendant, et
5 omnino nullum ius in eos exercere presumant. Monachos suos et predictarum aecclesiarum clericos secundum antiquam Glastoniensis aecclesiae consuetudinem et apostolicam auctoritatem, archipresulis Dunstani et omnium episcoporum regni mei assensu, abbas a quocumque comprouintiali episcopo uoluerit ordinari fatiat; dedicationes uero earum, si ab abbate[a] rogatus fuerit, Fontanensi episcopo permittimus. In Pascha quoque crisma sanctificationis et oleum a Fontanensi episcopo ex more accipiat et per prefatas aecclesias suas distribuat. Hoc uero precipue Dei interdictione[b] et nostra auctoritate, salua tamen sanctae Romanae aecclesiae et Dorobernensis dignitate, prohibeo, ne persona cuiuscumque potestatis, siue rex siue episcopus siue dux aut princeps uel quilibet ministrorum eorum,[c] Glastoniae terminos uel supradictarum parrochiarum perscrutandi rapiendi placitandi gratia uel aliquid aliud fatiendi quod contrarium possit esse ibidem Deo seruientibus intrare presumat; abbati tantummodo et conuentui potestas sit, tam in notis causis quam in ignotis, in modicis et in magnis et omnibus omnino negotiis, sicut supra memorauimus.
6 Quisquis autem huius mei priuilegii dignitatem qualibet occasione, cuiuscumque dignitatis, cuiuscumque ordinis, cuiuscumque professionis, peruertere uel ⟨in⟩[d] irritum deducere sacrilega presumptione amodo temptauerit, sciat se proculdubio ante districtum Iudicem titubantem tremebundumque[e] rationem redditurum, nisi prius digna satisfactione emendare studuerit.'
7 Hanc priuilegii paginam predictus rex Edgarus duodecimo anno regni sui sacro scripto apud Lundoniam communi consilio optimatum suorum confirmauit; eodemque anno, qui fuit nongentesimus sexagesimus quintus Dominicae incarnationis, indictione quarta decima, papa Iohannes hanc ipsam paginam Romae in generali sinodo auctorizauit cunctosque potioris dignitatis uiros, qui prefuerunt eidem concilio, confirmare fecit, necnon epistolam Alurico duci, prefatam aecclesiam grauiter persequenti, paterna motus pietate in haec uerba direxit:

151C. [f]'Iohannes episcopus, seruus seruorum Dei, Alurico inclito

[a] ab *(om. γδ)* abbate si *(si om. Cp)* Cs Cd)   [d] in *Cd, AG,* ρτ; *om. C,* γδσ *I. i. 36) is also preserved in* ζ   [b] indictione *Cs*   [e] -que *om. Cs*   [c] meorum *Ce (and*   [f] *This letter (Counc.*

Nyland, and Meare, except only when they are summoned by the abbot to dedicate or ordain, nor are they to summon their priests to their synod or chapter or any court whatsoever, nor to suspend them from divine office, or presume to exercise any power at all over them. The abbot is to have his monks and the clerks of the said churches ordained by any bishop of the province that he wishes, according to the ancient custom of the church of Glastonbury and the Apostolic authority, with the assent of Archbishop Dunstan and all the bishops of my kingdom; but we allow their dedication to the bishop of Wells, if he is asked to act by the abbot. Also at Easter he is to accept the chrism of sanctification and the holy oil from the bishop of Wells according to custom and distribute it among his said churches. But this I especially prohibit by the interdiction of God and by our authority, saving only the dignity of the holy Roman church and that of Canterbury: no one of any rank, be he king, bishop, thegn, magnate, or any of their servants, is to presume to enter the bounds of Glastonbury or the said parishes to search, seize, hold court or do anything else that may be prejudicial to those who serve God there. Power is reserved to the abbot and convent, in known and unknown cases, in absolutely all matters, great and small, as we have mentioned above. But whosoever on any pretext, to whatever rank, order, and profession he may belong, with sacrilegious daring tries henceforth to overthrow or annul the dignity of this my privilege, should know that he will without doubt answer for it in fear and trembling before the stern Judge, unless he first takes care to amend his fault by proper penalty.'

The document containing this privilege King Edgar confirmed in London in the twelfth year of his reign, by his holy writ and on the unanimous advice of his noblemen. And in that same year 965, the fourteenth indiction, Pope John, in general synod at Rome, authorized this document, and caused all the distinguished men who controlled the council to confirm it. Further, his fatherly pity caused him to send to Ealdorman Ælfric, who was grievously persecuting the church of Glastonbury, the following letter:

151 C. 'Bishop John, servant of the servants of God, to the

duci, amantissimo filio nostro spirituali, salutem continuam et apostolicam benedictionem.

'Relatione quorundam fidelium comperimus te plurima agere mala in aecclesia sanctae Dei genitricis Mariae, quae nuncupatur Glastingaburh, quae totius Britanniae prima[a] et ab antiquis primoribus ad proprietatem et tutelam Romani pontificis pertinere dinoscitur, et predia ac uillas, sed et aecclesias de Brente de Piltune, quas Ina rege dante operam . . .,[b] cum aliis aecclesiis quas adhuc[c] iuste et canonice possidet, scilicet Soweie Stret Merlinch Budecalege Sapewice, ab eius iure tua auida cupiditate diripuisse, et propter quod eidem loco propinqua heres habitatione illi semper nocuus esse. Oportunum autem extiterat ut tuo suffragio sancta Dei aecclesia, cui propinquus habitando effectus es, perplurimum accresceret et copia tui adiutorii proprietatibus ditaretur. Sed, quod nefas est, tuo[d] decrescit impedimento tuaque humiliatur oppressione. Et quia licet indigni non dubitamus nos ⟨a⟩[e] beato Petro apostolo omnium aecclesiarum curam omniumque[f] suscepisse sollicitudinem, ideo tuam ammonemus dilectionem ut, pro amore apostolorum Petri et Pauli nostraque ueneratione, ab ipsius loci cesses direptione, nil de eius proprietatibus, aecclesiis capellis uillis et possessionibus inuadens. Quod si haec non[g] feceris, scias ⟨te⟩[h] uice apostolorum principis nostra auctoritate excommunicatum et a cetu fidelium remotum perpetuoque anathemati summissum et aeterno igni cum Iuda proditore perhenniter mancipatum.'

152. Tunc[i] ordo monasticus[j] iam dudum lapsus precipue[k] caput erexit; unde factum est ut etiam[l] monasterium nostrum denuo in pristinam libertatem euaderet. Quod conuenientius opinor ipsius regis uerbis notificare:

153. [m]'Ego Edgarus totius Albionis basileus, necnon maritimorum seu insulanorum regum circumhabitantium (adeo ut nullus progenitorum meorum) subiectione largiflua Dei gratia suppetente sullimatus, quid imperii mei potissimum Regi regum Domino darem, tanti memor honoris sollertius sepe tractaui. Piae igitur fautrix deuotionis

---

[a] Add esse or est?   [b] A verb such as possidet has dropped out   [c] om. Ce
[d] te Ce(and Cp)   [e] a Cd (in ζ); om. C   [f] ζ adds fidelium, no doubt correctly   [g] om. Ce, not absurdly   [h] This necessary word is added here by ζ, after auctoritate by Cs   [i] om. TtA   [j] monasticus ordo TtA   [k] tunc

distinguished Ealdorman Ælfric, our most beloved spiritual son, continuing health and the Apostolic blessing.

'We learn from certain of the faithful that you are doing much evil in the matter of the church of Mary, the holy Mother of God, called Glastonbury, which is first in all Britain and is known to have belonged since antiquity to the pope of Rome for him to own and protect, and that you have snatched from its control, with avaricious greed, its estates and villages: but also the churches of Brent and Pilton, which [it possesses] as the result of Ine's efforts, together with the other churches which it possesses to this day by canon law, namely Zoy, Street, Moorlinch, Butleigh, and Shapwick; and that, because you dwell near to the place, you are always harming it. Yet it was proper rather that your help should enable the holy church of God of which you are a neighbour to increase greatly and be enriched in properties by the resources of your aid. Instead, it is being disgracefully diminished thanks to your obstructiveness, and brought low by your harassment. For all our unworthiness, we do not doubt that we have received from the holy Apostle Peter the care of all churches and responsibility for all [the faithful]. We therefore admonish you, our beloved son, out of love of the Apostles Peter and Paul and reverence for me, to cease from laying the place waste, and to refrain from invasion of its properties, churches, chapels, villages and possessions. If you disobey, know that you are excommunicate by our authority, derived as it is from the prince of the Apostles, removed from the company of the faithful, placed under perpetual anathema, and handed over to eternal flames for all time alongside the traitor Judas.'

152. The monastic order, which had for so long lain low, at this point notably raised its head; and thus it came about that our monastery likewise emerged to enjoy anew its ancient liberty—a fact which it will, I think, be more fitting to set forth in the king's own words:

153. 'I Edgar, monarch of all Albion, who by the subjection of the neighbouring kings of coasts and islands am raised higher than were any of my forbears, thanks to the grace of God that supports me in such generous measure, have often considered with care what portions of my realm I could for preference give to our Lord the King of kings in memory of this great honour. So it was that my pious devotion was

TtA   *¹ om. TtA*   *ᵐ This charter (Sawyer 796) is given by GP pp. 404–5, in a longer form, and by various other manuscripts (ελπρ)*

peruigili meae studiositati superna subito insinuauit pietas quaeque in regno meo sancta restaurare monasteria,[a] quae uelut musciuis scindulis cariosisque tabulis tignotenus uisibiliter diruta, sic (quod maius est) intus a seruitio Dei ferme uacua fuerant neglecta. Idiotis nempe clericis eiectis, nullius regularis religionis disciplinae subiectis, plurimis[b] in locis sanctioris[c] seriei, scilicet monachici habitus, prefeci[d] pastores, ad ruinosa quaeque templorum redintegranda opulentos[e] eis fiscalium munerum exhibens sumptus. Quorum unum, nomine Elfricum, uirum in omnibus aecclesiasticum, famosissimi constitui custodem cenobii quod Angli bifario uocitant onomate Maldelmesburh. Cui pro commoditate animae meae,[f] ob Saluatoris nostri eiusque ΘΗΩΘΟΚΟC[g] semper uirginis Mariae, necnon apostolorum Petri et Pauli Aldelmique almi presulis, honorem, particulam terrae' (et nominat terram) 'cum pratis et siluis munifica liberalitate restitui.[h] Haec a predictis accommodata clericis a contentioso iniuste possessa est Athelnodo; sed superstitiosa subtilique eius disceptatione a sapientibus meis audita et conflictatione illius mendosa ab eisdem me presente conuicta,[i] monasteriali a me reddita est usui, anno Dominicae incarnationis nongentesimo septuagesimo quarto, [j]regni uero mei quarto decimo, regiae consecrationis primo.'[j]

154. Interea non indecens opinor si quiddam quod ei diuinitus ostensum est stilo commendem. Venerat in saltum uenationis feracem, utque fit plerumque, sotiis ad insequendas feras per deuia dispersis, solus remanserat. Itaque, continuatione cursus ad egressum nemoris peruenines, constitit sodales operiens. Nec mora, grauante nutantia lumina somno,[1] pedes efficitur, ut transacti laborem diei temperaret medicae[k] quietis uoluptas. Iacebat ergo sub malo[l] siluatica stratus, ubi penduli per circuitum rami foliatam effecerant cameram. Lassitudine itaque suadente, riuus subter scatebris loquacibus fluens soporem inuitabat, cum canis femina, cui cura ferarum uestigia insequi, pregnans et iuxta pedes accubans dormitantem[m] exterruit; namque matre tacente

---

[a] misteria *Tt* [b] pluris *C* [c] sanctiores *Ce*, sanctio *Cs (and CpCr)* [d] prefecti *BkBc²* [e] opulenta *C* [f] *om. C* [g] teotocos *(teoteos Aap)* overwritten in *TtACe (cf. GP)* [h] *om. Tt* [i] coniuncta *A* [j-j] *om. CsBkBc²* [k] medic(a)e *AlCe;* modice *TAaCsBc;* medicine *Bk* [l] mala *C* [m] dormientem *A*

---

[1] Cf. Virgil, *Georg.* iv. 496.

fostered by the divine Goodness, which suddenly suggested to my wakeful mind as I brooded on this question, that I should restore all those holy monasteries in my kingdom which had suffered neglect equally as they fell into ruin for all to see, with moss-grown shingles and planking that crumbled down to the framing beams, and no less (but it matters more) inwardly, because they were almost emptied of God's service. Thus I have cast out secular clerks not subject to the discipline of any religious rule, and over many places have appointed shepherds of a more holy sort (wearing, that is, the monastic habit), providing them with plentiful supplies in the way of financial resources with which to meet the cost of restoring the ruinous portions of their churches. One of these, Ælfric by name, in all respects what a churchman should be, I have made warden of the famous monastery called in England by the two-fold appellation of Malmesbury; and for the good of my soul and the honour of our Saviour and His mother, Mary the ever-virgin, Mother of God, as well as of the Apostles Peter and Paul and the saintly Bishop Aldhelm, I have munificently restored to it a portion of its land'—and he names the land—'with meadow and woodland. This land, which was leased out by the aforesaid clerks, was taken into possession unjustly by the contentious Æthelnoth; but his subtle and superstitious argumentation having been heard by my wise men and his defective claims rejected by them in my presence, it was given back by me for the benefit of the monastery in the year of our Lord 974, in the fourteenth year of my reign and the first of my coronation as king.'

154. Meanwhile it is not, I think, inappropriate if I commit to writing a vision which was shown him by some heavenly agency. He had gone to a forest rich in game, and there, as so often happens, his companions had scattered in different directions, following the deer, and he was left alone. When therefore, as he pursued his course, he came to the way out of the wood, he halted to wait for the others, and it was not long before, 'as sleep lay heavy on his nodding eyelids',[1] he dismounted, thinking to allay the past day's exertions by the pleasure of curative sleep. So he lay down at full length under a crab-apple tree of which the branches, hanging in a circle, made a leafy dome. Wooed there as he was by weariness, a bubbling, tinkling stream that flowed below was tempting him to sleep, when the dog lying at his feet, a bitch in whelp whose task it was to track the deer, woke him in terror. It was the puppies: their mother was silent, while they, still

catuli aluo inclusi latratus multiformes et sonoros reddidere, quodam nimirum sui carceris gaudio incitati. Hoc monstro attonitus, dum ad cacumen arboris oculos intendit, uidet poma unum et alterum delapsa in fluuium; quorum collisione bullis aquatilibus inter se crispantibus uox articulata insonuit: 'Wel is*a* the!',*b* id est 'bene est tibi!' Nec multo post, undarum uoluminibus agentibus, urceolus super aquam apparuit, et post urceolum urceus*c* exundans aqua (nam alter uacuus erat); et quanuis crebro gurgitis impulsu maior minorem*d* urgeret, ut scilicet aquas suas in illum infunderet, numquam tamen obtinere potuit quin urceolus uacuus recederet, iterumque quasi superbo gestu uictor urceum impeteret. Domum itaque regressus, ut dicit psalmista,[1] exercitabatur et scopebat spiritum suum. Sed conuenit eum mater ut serenaret frontem et animum: sibi studio futurum ut 'appellaret Deum,' qui nosset enigmata inspiratione sua patefacere. Quo ammonitu retudit*f* ille mestitiam et soluit in otia curas,[2] conscius maternae sanctitatis, cui soleret Deus multa reuelare. Erat ea uocabulo*g* Elfgiua, bonis operibus intenta, pietate et dulcedine predita, ut etiam reos quos tristis sententia iudicum palam dampnauerat ipsa occulte redimeret. Pretiosus amictus, qui plerisque mulieribus est leno soluendi pudoris, illi erat suppellex munificentiae, ut quamlibet operosam uestem conspecto statim largiretur pauperi. Spetiem corporis et artifitium manuum in ea liuor quoque laudaret, cum nichil reprehendere posset. Haec igitur, intimis medullis uaticinium combibens, postero mane filio dixit: 'Latratus catulorum quem matre quiescente dedere significat quod post obitum tuum, quiescentibus illis qui modo ualent et uiuunt, nondum nati nebulones contra Dei latrabunt aecclesiam. Sane quod unum pomum secutum est alterum, ita ut ex collisione secundi in prius uideretur uox sonuisse "Wel is the!", hoc innuit, quod ex te, qui modo arboris totam inumbras Angliam, duo procedent filii. Fautores secundi extinguent primum; tunc diuersae partis incentores dicent pueris utrisque: "Wel is the!", quia mortuus regnabit in caelo, uiuus in seculo. Iam uero,*h* quod urceus maior minorem implere non poterat,

---

a hi(i)s *CB; similarly at 4 and 5 below* *b* te *TBk; similarly at 4 and 5 below* *c* urceolus *T* *d* maiore minorem *Al,* maiore minor *Aap* *e–e* a parte Domini *CB* *f* recudit *T* *g* eius (ei *with a gap Tt*) uocabulum *T* *h* om. *A*

---

[1] Ps. 76 (77): 7.
[2] Cf. Prudentius, *Psychomachia* 729; Claudian, *Carm. min.* xxix. 23.

immured in her womb, gave tongue in wild and noisy barking, as though excited by joy at their prison. Astonished by this portent, he 2 looked up to the top of the tree, and saw two apples, first one and then another, fall into the stream, and as they knocked together and made competing bubbles in the water, he heard spoken words: 'Wel is the', which means 'It is well for thee.' Not long after a small pot appeared on the water, carried along by the curling ripples, and after the small pot a larger pot full to the brim with water; for the first one was empty, and however often, driven by the current, the larger struck the smaller as though big intended to pour the water it contained into little, it never could prevent the little pot from retreating still empty, and then, as if with a gesture of defiance, having won the encounter, returning to attack the big pot. So he went home and, as the psalmist puts it, 'communed with his own heart and sought out his spirit'.[1] But his mother urged him to clear his anxious brow and 3 mind: she herself, she said, would take pains to appeal to God, who knows how by His inspiration to make all riddles plain. On this advice he repressed his anxieties, 'and his cares melted into peace of mind',[2] for he knew his mother was a saintly person, to whom God granted many revelations. Her name was Ælfgifu, and she was devoted to good works and endowed with such piety and sweetness of temper that she would secretly redeem with her own money culprits who had been openly condemned by a strict verdict in the courts. The costly garments which most women find a temptation to relax their chastity were to her the material of generosity, so that, however expensive a dress might be, she would give it at once to a beggar at the mere sight of him. Her personal beauty and her skill in handiwork might win the 4 praise of jealousy itself, for it could find nothing in her to criticize. She it was then who drank in the prophecy in her inmost heart, and next morning addressed her son as follows: 'The barking of those whelps while their mother was asleep signifies that after your death, while those who are now alive and powerful are asleep, a set of rascals not yet born will bark like dogs against the Church of God. As for the fact that a second apple followed the first, in such a way that from the collision between the two you seemed to hear a voice saying 'Wel is the', this indicates that from you, who overshadow all England like a tree, there shall come two sons. The supporters of the second shall do 5 away with the first, and then the moving spirits of the opposite party shall say to both sons 'Wel is the' because the dead son will reign in Heaven and the living son in this world. If the larger pot could not fill

hoc designat, quod gentes aquilonales, quae numerosiores sunt quam Angli, Angliam post mortem tuam impetent et, quanuis crebro compatriotarum aduentu ruinas suas suppleant, numquam hunc angulum mundi poterunt implere; quin potius Angli nostri, cum maxime uicti uidebuntur, eas expellent, eritque sub suo et Dei arbitrio usque ad prefinitum tempus a Christo.'

155. Huius uaticinii ueritatem lectio posterior patefatiet. Considerari ergo debet parentis et prolis indubitata sanctitas, quod alter uiderit enigma uigilans sine obstaculo, et altera soluerit problema delonge porrecto prophetiae oculo.

Sanctitati quoque[a] morum communicabat seueritatis animositas, ut nullum cuiuscumque dignitatis hominem leges eludere impune permitteret. Nemo eius tempore priuatus latro, nemo popularis predo, nisi qui mallet in fortunas alienas grassari propriae uitae dispendio. Quomodo enim ausus hominum preteriret qui etiam omnis generis feras sanguinis auidas ex regno exterminare cogitarit,[b] Iudualoque[c] regi Walensium edictum imposuerit ut sibi quotannis tributum trecentorum luporum pensitaret? Quod cum tribus annis fecisset, quarto destitit, nullum se ulterius posse[d] inuenire professus.

156. Preterea licet, ut fertur, staturae fuerit[e] et corpulentiae perexilis, tantas uires in illo corpusculo dignatio naturae incluserat ut ultro ad congrediendum lacesseret quemcumque audacem nosset,[f] hoc maxime timens, ne in tali colludio timeretur. Denique in quodam conuiuio, ubi se plerumque fatuorum dicacitas liberius ostentat, fama est Kinadium regem Scottorum ludibundum dixisse mirum uideri tam uili homuntioni tot prouintias subici, idque[g] a quodam mimo sinistra aure acceptum et Edgaro postmodum sollemni conuitio[h] in os obiectum. At ille, re suis celata, Kinadium quasi magni misterii consultandi gratia accersiit longeque in siluam seducto unum ex duobus, quos secum attulerat, ensibus tradidit, et 'Nunc' inquit 'licebit uires tuas experiare, cum soli simus. Iam enim faxo ut appareat quis alteri

---

[a] *T;* sanctitatique *ACB*   [b] cogitaret *A*   [c] Woualoque *T*   [d] om. *TBk*   [e] *One expects* fuerit breuis *(cf. 279. 1, though note 263. 2)*   [f] cognosceret *T*   [g] itaque *A*   [h] conuiuio *TBc (but see GP p. 392)*

the smaller, this means that the northern peoples, who are more numerous than the English, will attack England after your death, and however frequently they make good their losses by fresh arrivals of their compatriots, they will never succeed in filling this corner of the world. On the contrary, our English people, at a moment when they seem to be most heavily defeated, will drive them out, and England will be under its own government, and God's, until the time already laid down by Christ.'

155. The truth of this prophecy will be made clear to the reader later. We ought therefore to consider the unquestioned sanctity of both mother and son: one of them as he lay awake saw the problem without impediment; the other solved the riddle by directing the eye of prophecy upon it at long range.

High-spirited severity associated in Edgar with saintliness of character to prevent any man, whatever his position in society, from evading the laws with impunity. In his time no private person was a thief, none of the common people were robbers, except those who deliberately chose to make secret attacks on other men's possessions at the cost of their own lives. How could a king overlook the criminal acts of men, if he had it in mind to exterminate from his kingdom even those beasts of every kind that shed blood, and laid on Idwal king of the Welsh an obligation to pay him an annual tribute of three hundred wolves?—which he paid for three years, and in the fourth year defaulted, saying he could find no more.

156. Besides which, although, as tradition has it, he was of short stature and slight in build, nature to make amends had equipped his small body with such strength that he would readily challenge to a contest anybody he knew to be of good courage, his principal fear being that in a friendly match of this kind the man might be afraid of *him*. Once, for example, at a party, where fools often give too free a display of careless talk, the story goes that Kenneth king of the Scots said by way of a jest that it seemed odd that so many provinces should be ruled by a poor little dwarf, and this was picked up by some jester who was out to make mischief and later used against Edgar to his face as a regular taunt. Edgar however, concealing this from his own men, sent for Kenneth as though he wished to consult him on some great state secret, and having taken him a long way into a forest, offered him one of two swords which he had brought with him. 'And now,' he said, 'you are welcome to try your strength, as we are alone. For now I shall make it quite clear which

merito supponi debeat; tu quoque ne pedem referas, quin mecum rem uentiles. Turpe est enim regem*a* in conuiuio esse dicaculum, nec esse in prelio promptulum.' Confusus ille nec uerbo mutire ausus, ad pedes domini regis procidit, simplicis ioci ueniam precatus et
2 confestim consecutus. *b*Quid illud? Omni aestate, emensa statim Paschali festiuitate, naues per omnia littora coadunari precipiebat, ad occidentalem insulae partem cum orientali classe et illa remensa*c* cum occidentali ad borealem, inde cum boreali ad orientalem remigare consuetus, pius scilicet explorator, ne quid piratae turbarent. Hieme et uere per omnes prouintias equitando iuditia potentiorum exquirebat, uiolati iuris seuerus ultor; in hoc iustitiae, in illo fortitudini studens, in utroque reipublicae utilitatibus consulens.*b*

157. Sunt qui ingenti eius gloriae neuum temptent apponere, dicentes primis temporibus fuisse crudelem in ciues, libidinosum in uirgines. Verbi gratia*d* prioris exemplum ponunt. Athelwoldus erat quidam sui temporis comes egregius et a secretis. Huic rex iniunxerat negotium ut Elfridam filiam Ordgari ducis Deuenensium, quae forma sui oculos relatorum pellexerat quatinus eam regiis auribus commendarent—huic, inquam, preceperat ut illam*e* iret speculatum, nuptias conciliaturus si ueritas famae conquadraret. Ille uiam celerans nichilque preter opinionem comperiens, celato apud parentes nuntio, suis potius
2 usibus puellam applicuit. Rediens ad regem, quae suis partibus conducerent allegat, spetiei uulgaris et cotidianae pusiolam esse nec tantae maiestati conuenire. Reducto ab his animo et aliis amoribus intento delatores nuntiant quanta illum Athelwoldus astutia emunxerit.*f* Ille clauo clauum expellens, fraude scilicet fraudem eludens,*g* frontem serenam comiti ostendere, diem quo uisitaret tam laudatam mulierem quasi ioco edicere. Qui, tam terribili ludo exanimatus,*h* precurrit ad coniugem, rogans ut suae saluti consuleret et quantum posset uestibus se deformaret, tunc primum aperiens facti sui consilium. Sed quid

a regi *TA* *b–b* om. *Tt (Tc ends this extract at* consecutus*)* *c* remissa *A, JW*
s.a. 975, *doubtless rightly* *d* causa *Tt* *e* illo *Tt (cf. 291)* *f* emunxerat *A* *g* ducens *Tt* *h* examinatus *TtBk*

of us ought rightly to be subject to the other, and you too must not retreat without discussing this question with me. It is no credit to a king to be a free talker at a drinking-party and in a fight to show a touch of reluctance.' Kenneth was covered with confusion, and not daring to say a word threw himself at the feet of his lord the king, begging forgiveness for a simple joke—which he at once obtained. And what of this?—every 2 summer, immediately after the Easter festival, he used to order a gathering of the ships on every coast, his custom being to go with the eastern fleet to the western part of the island, and when that had been patrolled, to make with the western fleet for the northern, and then with the northern fleet for the eastern, his virtuous purpose being to find out whether pirates were giving any trouble. In winter and spring he travelled on horseback through all the provinces, enquiring into the judgements handed down by the more powerful nobles and punishing severely any breaches of the law. His object in this was justice, in the other case naval strength; and in both his first thought was for the benefit of the commonwealth.

157. Some people try to identify blemishes in his immensely distinguished record, saying that in his early years he was cruel to his subjects and lecherous with young women. For instance, they give as an example of the former a certain Æthelwold, a leading noble in his day and one of his confidants. The king had given him a task respecting Ælfthryth, daughter of Ordgar, ealdorman of Devon, whose beauty had beguiled the eyes of all those who brought news of it, until through them its praises reached the king's ears—it was she whom Æthelwold, as I was saying, had been commissioned to go and inspect, with a view to arranging marriage if the reality squared with the reports. Hastening on his way, he found nothing contrary to the public opinion of her and, concealing the purpose of his mission from her parents, he diverted the young lady to his own personal advantage. Returning to 2 the king, he reported what would suit his own views: she was a girl of ordinary everyday appearance, and unworthy of his most excellent Majesty. The king took his mind off her; but while he was pursuing other loves, he heard through informers of the cunning by which Æthelwold had cleaned him out. Driving out nail with nail, undermining (that is) one fraud with another, the king greeted the ealdorman with unruffled composure, and as though it was a joke, fixed the day when he would visit this woman of whom he had heard so much. Aghast at this terrifying pleasantry, Æthelwold hastened on ahead to see his wife, begging her to think of his own survival and to dress herself to look as ugly as she could; it was then for the first time that

non presumit femina? Ausa est miseri amatoris et primi coniugis fidem fallere et speculo uultum comere, nichil omittens quod ephebi
3 et potentis lumbos pertemptaret. Nec citra propositum accidit. Visam enim adeo inarsit ut, dissimulato odio, comitem in siluam Warewellae gratia uenandi accitum iaculo*a* traiceret. Vbi cum filius occisi nothus familiari usu superuenisset, et a rege interrogatus esset qualiter ei talis uenatio placeret, respondisse fertur: 'Bene, domine rex: quod tibi placet michi displicere non debet.' Quo dicto ita tumentis animum mansuefecit ut nichil carius in uita sua post haec*b* haberet quam iuuenem illum, tirannici facti offensam in patrem sedulitate regia in filium alleuans.*c* Ob illius sceleris expiationem ibidem monasterium ab Elfrida edificatum sanctimonialium frequentia inhabitatur.

158. Huic exemplo crudelitatis adiungunt aliud libidinis. Virginis Deo dicatae audiens pulchritudinem, uiolenter eam*d* a monasterio abstraxit, abstractae pudorem rapuit et non semel thoro suo collocauit. Quod cum aures beati Dunstani offendisset, uehementer ab eo increpitus, septennem penitentiam non fastidiuit, dignatus rex affligi ieiunio simulque diademate carere septennio.

159. Subitiunt tertium in quo utrumque appareat uitium. Rex, inquiunt, Edgarus ueniens Andeueram, qui est uicus non longe a Wintonia, cuiusdam ducis filiam, cuius formae fama percrebruerat, adduci precepit. Mater puellae, quae concubinatum filiae dedignaretur, ancillam adiuta noctis tenebris cubili apposuit, uirginem sane nec inelegantem nec illepidam. Euoluta nocte, cum aurora in lucem prorumperet, mulier conata surgere, interrogataque quid festinaret, ad opus cotidianum dominae persoluendum respondit; egre licet retenta regis genibus super statu miseriarum suarum applorat: pro mercede conubii redderet ingenuitatem; decere magnanimitatem eius ut regiae uoluptatis conscia dominorum crudelium ulterius non ingemisceret

a om. Tt *b* TtA add rex *c* alleuians Cd (cf. 5. 2 n. c) *d* om. TtAap

he told her what he had done and why. But is anything beyond a woman's ambition? She found the heart to break faith with her wretched lover and her first husband, and sat down at the mirror to paint her face, leaving nothing undone that might excite the lust of a young man and a man of power. All happened as she intended. He fell in love with her at first sight so passionately that, concealing his resentment, he sent for the ealdorman to come hunting in the forest of Wherwell, and there pierced him with a javelin. When the bastard son of the dead man approached familiarly, and the king asked him how he liked this kind of hunting, he is said to have replied: 'I like it well, your Majesty; what pleases you ought not to displease me.' These words so calmed the king's anger that thereafter he had as much affection for the young man as for anyone in his whole life, lightening the guilt of his despotic action against the father by his kingly care for the son. To expiate the crime a monastery was built on the spot by Ælfthryth, which is still inhabited by a large community of nuns.

158. To this example of cruelty they add an example of lust. Hearing of the beauty of a nun under vows, he removed her by violence from her convent, and having done so violated her, and forced her more than once to sleep with him. When this reached the ears of St Dunstan, he was severely rebuked by the saint and did not refuse seven years' penance, submitting, king though he was, to be ordered to fast, and at the same time to forego wearing his crown for seven years.

159. They add a third incident, in which both these vices can be seen. King Edgar, so they say, on arriving at Andover, which is a town near Winchester, gave orders that a certain nobleman's daughter, whose reputation for beauty had become widespread, should be brought to him. The girl's mother disdained to have her daughter treated as a concubine. Assisted by the cover of darkness, she sent to sleep with him a serving-maid, who was a virgin not without some elegance and charm. When the night was over and dawn was breaking into daylight, the woman tried to get up, and when asked why she was in such a hurry, replied that she must fulfil the daily task that she owed her mistress. When restrained though with difficulty, she fell at the king's feet, bewailing the miseries of her present status and begging him, in return for their night together, to give her back her freedom; it was to be expected of his generosity, she said, that one who had shared the king's pleasures should groan no longer under the

imperia. Tunc ille, felle commoto, et formidabile ridens, cum in animo eius fluctuaret hinc de famula miseratio, hinc de domina indignatio, quasi in iocos effusus usum obsequiorum penamque remittit. Mox antiquis dominatoribus uellent nollent dominantem magna sullimauit dignatione; dilexit unice, integram lecti uni deferens fidem, quoad legitimam uxorem accepit Elfridam filiam Ordgari. De qua Edmundum, qui ante ipsum quinquennio decedens Rumesiae*a* iacet, et qui post eum regnauit Egelredum tulit. Nam de Egelfleda, cognomento Candida, filia Ordmeri ducis potentissimi, Eduardum genuit; et sanctam Edgitham de Wlfrida, quam certum est non tunc sanctimonialem fuisse, sed timore regis puellam laicam se uelauisse, moxque eandem abrepto*b* uelo lecto imperiali subactam; unde offensum beatum Dunstanum,*c* quod illam concupisset quae uel umbratice sanctimonialis fuisset, uigorem pontificalem in eum egisse.*d*

160. Sed haec quomodocumque se habeant, illud constat, quod a sexto decimo aetatis anno, quo rex constitutus est, usque ad tricesimum sine regio insigni regnauerit.*e* Tunc enim, principibus et omnis ordinis uiris*f* undique confluentibus, cum magna gloria in Pentecoste Bathoniae coronatus est; nec nisi triennio superuixit, sepultusque est Glastoniae.

2 *g*Corpus tunc*h* terra opertum, sed post scrinio argenteo et inaurato locatum pro merito personae honoratur. Namque*g*

*g*Nec illud oblitterandum quod, cum abbas Eilwardus eius tumulum anno incarnationis Domini millesimo quinquagesimo secundo effodisset, inuenit corpus nullius labis conscium. Quod cum eum ad reuerentiam debuisset inflectere, ad audaciam leuauit; nam quia locellus quem parauerat difficilem pro magnitudine corporis minabatur ingressum, regales exuuias ferro temerauit, unde continuo sanguis undatim emicans astantium corda pauore concussit. Ita regium corpus in scrinio, quod ipsi aecclesiae contulerat, super altare locatum est cum capite sancti Apollinaris et reliquiis Vincentii martiris, quae ille magno empta decori domus Dei adiecerat. Temeratorem porro sacri corporis mox animus reliquit; nec multo post aecclesia egressum

---

a Risiae *Tt* *b* arrepto *Tt* *c* offensus beatus Dunstanus *Tt* *d* effudit *Tt* *e* regnauit *Tt* *f* om. *Tt* *g-g* (p. 262) corpus ... namque *TtA (cf. VD p. 307);* nec ... ergo *CB (cf. AG p. 134)* *h* *Tt* adds* quidem *(cf. VD)*

commands of cruel masters. At that his temper flared up, and with a terrifying laugh (for his mind was in turmoil with pity for the slave-girl on the one hand and indignation against her mistress on the other), and as though breaking into jest, he excused her her regular duties and her punishment. Soon she was mistress of her ancient masters, whether they would or no: he raised her to a position of high honour, and loved her and her only, remaining faithful to her alone as his bedfellow until he took Ordgar's daughter Ælfthryth as his lawful wife. By her he had Edmund, who died five years before his father and lies buried at Romsey, and Æthelred who succeeded him. For by Æthelflæd, also called Candida, daughter of the powerful ealdorman Ordmær, he begat Edward, and St Eadgyth by Wulfthryth, who was certainly not a nun at the time but as a girl of lay status had adopted the veil out of fear of the king, but later had it snatched away and was forced into a royal marriage. It is also certain that St Dunstan was indignant at his casting eyes of desire on one who had passed even through a shadow of the religious life, and used all his powers as archbishop against him.

160. But however that may be, this fact is certain, that from his sixteenth year, when he was established as king, to his thirtieth he reigned without the royal insignia. It was then that in a gathering of princes and men of every rank from all parts he was crowned with great glory at Pentecost in Bath; nor did he survive that more than three years, and was buried at Glastonbury.

TtA His body was at that time buried in the earth; later it was placed in a silver-gilt casket, and receives the honours its occupant deserved. For

CB Nor should we forget that when Abbot Æthelweard opened his tomb in the year of our Lord 1052, he found his body clear of all stain. This should have moved him to reverence; but it made him bolder, for as the coffin that he had prepared threatened to make it hard to insert the corpse because of its size, he rashly took a knife to the king's remains, whence blood at once spurted in streams, to the terror of the bystanders. Thus the king's body was placed in a casket which he had given to the church, over the altar, with the head of St Apollinaris and relics of Vincent the martyr which he had bought for a great sum and added to the glory of God's house. He who made the rash attack on the sacred body soon lost his wits, and not long after met his death from a broken neck as he

fracta ceruice mors inuenit. Nec in his hesit regiae sanctitatis ostensio, sed in ulteriora processit, sanato ibi furioso et ceco. Merito ergo[g] non infirma inter Anglos fama est nullum nec eius nec superioris aetatis[a] regem in Anglia recto et aequilibri iuditio Edgaro comparandum: ita nichil uita eius sanctius, nichil iustitia probabilius fuit, exceptis[b] uitiis quae postea amplis uirtutibus deleuit, qui patriam suam preclara fortitudine illustrem reddiderit et rerum gestarum claritate et Deo seruientium multiplicitate. Post mortem eius res et spes Anglorum retro sublapsae.

161. Anno Dominicae incarnationis nongentesimo septuagesimo quinto Eduardus filius Edgari regnare cepit, et tribus annis et dimidio potestate potitus est. Illum Dunstanus et ceteri episcopi consentanei regali culmine sullimarunt, contra uoluntatem quorundam, ut aiunt,[c] optimatum et nouercae, quae uix dum septem annorum puerulum Egelredum[d] filium prouehere conabatur, ut ipsa potius sub eius nomine imperitaret. Ex tunc malitia hominum pullulante felicitas regni imminuta. Tunc uisa cometes, quae uel pestem prouintialium uel regni mutationem portendere pro uero asseueratur. Nec mora, secuta sterilitas arui, fames hominum, mors iumentorum. Apud uicum regium qui uocatur Calna casus insolitus. Nam defuncto Edgaro clerici quondam ab aecclesiis expulsi rediuiua prelia suscitarunt: ingens esse et miserabile dedecus ut nouus aduena ueteres colonos migrare compelleret; hoc nec Deo gratum putari, qui ueterem habitationem concessisset, nec alicui probo homini, qui sibi idem timere posset quod aliis preiuditio accidisse cerneret. Ea de re in clamores[e] et iras surrectum, et[f] ad Dunstanum perrectum, precipue proceribus, ut laicorum est, succlamantibus preiuditium, quod clerici passi fuerant iniuste, leniori[g] consilio[h] succidi debere. Nam et unus eorum Elferius omnia pene monasteria quae reuerentissimus Athelwoldus construxerat in prouintia Mertiorum magna usus insolentia euertit. Itaque frequenti sinodo coacta primo Wintoniam uentum. Quis ibi fuerit finis certaminis aliae litterae docent, Dominicam imaginem expresse locutam clericos eorumque fautores confudisse; sed adhuc non sedatis

---

[g] *See above, p. 260*   [a] *om. Tt*   [b] *Tt* adds* pauculis   [c] *om. Tt*
[d] Elearedum *Tt*   [e] clamatores *Tt(and Aap*[a.c.]*?)*   [f] *om. Tt*   [g] leuiori *TtCsBc*   [h] *Bp, VD p. 307;* concilio *TtACB*

left the church. Nor did the evidence for the king's sanctity end here: it went further with the healing there of a lunatic and a blind man. Rightly therefore there is a strong tradition among the English that neither in his own nor in any earlier age has there been a king in England who could be properly and justly compared with Edgar: nothing was more saintly than his life or more admirable than his justice, except for [Tt *adds* a very few] faults which were extinguished later by his ample virtues. He made his country famous by his courage and his distinguished exploits, and by the great increase of those who served God in religion. After his death the position and prospects of the English suffered a set-back.

161. In the year of our Lord 975 Edward, Edgar's son, began to reign, and he held the throne for three and a half years. He was raised to the royal dignity by Dunstan in agreement with the other bishops, against the wishes (so the story goes) of certain nobles and of his stepmother, who tried to promote her son Æthelred, a child barely seven years old, in order that she might reign herself in his name. From that time forward crime flourished in the population, and public prosperity sank. At that time a comet appeared, something which, as we are credibly informed, foretells either a pestilence in the kingdom or a change in the kingship. Without delay a failure of the harvest followed, bringing famine for men and death for beasts. In the royal town called Calne a strange thing happened. On Edgar's death, the clerks who some time before had been expelled from the churches revived the old feuds: it was, they claimed, a very great and pitiable disgrace that new arrivals should force old tenants to move out, and this could not be thought pleasing to God, who had granted them their ancient habitation, nor to any right-thinking man, who might fear that the same thing could happen to him which he saw had caused such loss to others. The question provoked uproar and fury, and recourse was had to Dunstan, the nobles in particular complaining, as laymen will, that the loss which they, the clerks, had unjustly suffered should be redressed by gentler measures. Indeed one of them, Ælfhere, with a great display of insolence overthrew almost all the monasteries which that holy man Æthelwold had built in the province of the Mercians. So a crowded synod was summoned, and held its first meeting at Winchester. The conclusion of the dispute arrived at there we learn from other written sources: an image of our Lord spoke out clearly and routed the clerks and their supporters. Feeling however had not yet

animis Calnae concilium indictum, ubi cum in cenaculo, absente propter aetatem rege, considentibus totius Angliae senatoribus magno conflictu et controuersia res ageretur, et ualidissimum illum aecclesiae murum, Dunstanum dico, multorum conuitiorum iacula impeterent nec quaterent, suas partes cuiusque ordinis uiris summo studio tuentibus, solarium totum repente cum axibus et trabibus dissiluit et concidit. Omnibus ad terram elisis, solus Dunstanus stans super unam trabem quae superstes erat probe euasit; reliqui uel exanimati uel perpetui languoris compede detenti. Hoc miraculum archiepiscopo exhibuit pacem de clericis, omnibus Anglis tunc et deinceps in eius sententiam concedentibus.

162. Interea rex Eduardus fratrem puerulum et nouercam pietate congrua colere, solum nomen regis habere, illis cetera permittere, paternae religionis uestigia rimari, bonis consiliis aurem et animum accommodare; at mulier, nouercali odio uipereum dolum ruminans ut nec nomen regis filio deesset, insidias priuigno struere, quas hoc modo consummauit. Lassus uenatione reuertebatur propter laborem siti anhelus; comites, *quo quemque* casus tulerat, canes consectabantur; auditoque quod illi in contigua uilla habitarent, equo concito illuc contendit iuuenculus solus, nichil propter innocentiam metuens, aliorum quippe animos ex suo ponderans. Tunc illa muliebri blanditia aduentantem allitiens, sibi fecit intendere, et post libata basia porrectum poculum auide haurientem per satellitem sica transfodit. Quo uulnere sautius, cum quantis poterat animae reliquiis sonipedem calcaribus monuisset ad suos reuerti, uno pede lapsus alteroque per deuia tractus undante cruore inditia interitus sui se querentibus dedit. Et tunc quidem sine honore apud Werham sepeliri iusserunt, inuidentes scilicet mortuo cespitem aecclesiasticum cui uiuo inuiderant decus regium. Actitabant igitur publicam et festiuam letitiam, quasi[b] cum corpore pariter infodissent memoriam. Sed affuit diuinae serenitatis assensus, qui innocenter cesum miraculorum sullimaret gloria:

[a-a] quoque quocumque *Bk*, quo quemcumque *Bc (*quo quecumque *Bp)*   [b] quia *A*

abated, and a council was called together at Calne, where, in the absence of the king on grounds of age, the elder statesmen of all England took their seats in an upper room, and the discussion was marked by much conflict and controversy, in the course of which the Church's strongest bulwark (by which I mean Dunstan) was attacked, but not shaken, by a hail of abuse, as men of every class supported their views with the utmost feeling. In the midst of this, the whole storey with its posts and beams suddenly came to pieces and collapsed; everyone was thrown down headlong and only Dunstan, standing on one beam which had remained intact, escaped safe and sound. The remainder were either killed, or handicapped for life by an incurable sickness. This miracle provided the archbishop with a solution to the problem of the clerks, for all the English, then and later, came round to his opinion.

162. Meanwhile King Edward treated his brother, who was still a boy, and his stepmother with proper warmth of feeling, keeping the royal title for himself alone, but allowing them all other privileges. He followed in the footsteps of his father's religious activity; he listened to good advice and took it to heart. The woman however, with a stepmother's hatred and a viper's guile, in her anxiety that her son should also enjoy the title of king, laid plots against her stepson's life, which she carried out as follows. He was coming back tired from hunting, breathless and thirsty from his exertions; his companions were following the hounds where chance had led each one; and hearing that they were quartered in a neighbouring village, the young man spurred his horse and hastened to join them, all by himself, too innocent to have any fears and no doubt judging other people by himself. On his arrival, his stepmother, with a woman's wiles, distracted his attention, and with a kiss of welcome offered him a drink. As he greedily drank it, she had him pierced with a dagger by one of her servants. Wounded mortally by the blow, he summoned up what breath he had left, and spurred his horse to join the rest of the party; but one foot slipped, and he was dragged through byways by the other, leaving streams of blood as a clear indication of his death to those who looked for him. At the time they ordered him to be buried without honour at Wareham, grudging him consecrated ground when he was dead, as they had grudged him the royal title while he was alive. So they enjoyed a public festival of rejoicing, as though they had buried his memory along with his corpse. But the divine Serenity acknowledged him, and did honour to the innocent victim with the glory of miracles:

3 adeo caelestia iuditia humanis preponderant. Ibi ostensa de caelo lumina, ibi claudus gressum composuit, ibi mutus organum resumpsit, ibi prorsus omnis inualitudo sanitati*a* locum fecit. Sparsus rumor per totam Angliam martiris merita predicabat. Quo excita interfectrix iter illuc adoriebatur, iamque equum inscensum*b* stimulis urgebat cum manifestam iram Dei persensit. Animal namque familiare, quo sedere consueuerat, antea uentis pernitius quod auras ipsas precurreret,*c* tunc nutu Dei stabat immobile. Instant ministri hinc flagris illinc clamoribus, ut potentem heram qua solebat alacritate eueheret: cassus labor consumitur. Mutato quoque iumento casus idem sequitur. Intellexit licet tarde brutum pectus quo portentum illud respiceret; quapropter quod ipsa*d* non meruit, per alium fieri consensit.

4 Namque Elferius*e* ille, quem supra¹ culpaui quod monasteria destruxisset, temeritatis penitens*f* multoque gemitu animum angens, sacro corpori de ignobili loco leuato iustas et egregias inferias apud Sceftoniam soluit; non tamen effugit, sed post annum uermibus quos pediculos dicimus consumptus est. Et quoniam animus indisciplinatus ipse sibi tormentum est, patiturque suos etiam hic mens anxia manes, Elfrida de illo regali supercilio inclinata dire penituit, adeo ut multis annis apud Warewellam carnem in delitiis nutritam cilitio conuolueret, noctibus solo strata sine ceruicali somnum hauriret, cruces preterea quascumque posset corpori comminiscens—spetiosa mulier et pulchre uiro sobria, sed quia tantum nefas commisit pena digna. Creditumque et celebriter uulgatum quod propter eius in Eduardum insolentiam multo post tempore tota patria seruitutem infremuisset barbaricam.

163. Certe apud Sceftoniam splendidum regiae sanctitudinis refulgurat speculum, quoniam illius meritis deputatur quod eo loci multus deuotarum Deo feminarum chorus, claritate religionis terras istas irradians, etiam ipsa prestringit*g* sidera. Illic sacrae uirgines nullius penitus corruptelae consciae, illic religiosae continentes post primi thori dampna secundi ignis nesciae, in quarum omnium moribus ita facetus pudor cum seuera consentit elegantia quod nichil supra.

a sanati *A*   *b* incensum *Bc(and Bp)*, ascensum *Bk*   *c* percurreret *B*
d per se *TA, GP p. 187*   *e* Elfredus *T*   *f* penitus *B*   *g* restringit *Tt*; perstringit *A*

¹ 161. 2.

so far do Heaven's judgements outweigh those of men. There lights 3 shone in the sky, there a lame man walked, there a dumb man regained the use of his tongue, there every kind of sickness gave way to health. The story spread through all England, and made the martyr's merits well known. Aroused by this, the murderess planned a journey to the place; she had already mounted her horse and was spurring him on, when she felt the manifest anger of God. Her familiar palfrey on which she had been used to ride, and which had before been swift as air and could outstrip the very winds, then by the will of God stood motionless. The grooms set about it with whips and shouting, to make it carry its powerful mistress with its wonted eagerness; their labour was spent in vain. She changed her mount, but with the same result. At length, though slowly, her unfeeling heart understood the purport of the portent, and what she did not deserve to do herself she agreed to get done by another hand. Ælfhere, the man I have already 4 blamed for the destruction of monasteries,[1] regretting his rash actions and heaving deep sighs of penitence, took up the saint's body from its lowly resting-place and gave it its due with a splendid funeral at Shaftesbury. Even so he did not escape, but a year later was consumed by the worms which we call lice. And since an unruly spirit is its own torment, and an anxious mind suffers its own evil genius even in this present world, Ælfthryth fell from her pride of royalty into a dire repentance, such that for many years at Wherwell she clad her delicately-nurtured limbs in haircloth and at night slept stretched on the ground without her pillow, besides inventing all the tortures she could for her body, a beautiful woman and finely faithful to her husband but worthy of punishment for the great crime she committed. It is believed, and a widely popular view, that it was through her cruelty to Edward that the whole country, for a long time after, groaned under the barbarian yoke.

163. At Shaftesbury certainly the king's sanctity is reflected as though in a gleaming mirror, for it is due to his merits that at that place there is a great throng of women devoted to God who by the brightness of their religious faith shed light over all that region and outshine the stars themselves. There one finds holy virgins with no blemish of any kind upon their consciences, and other religious women living in continence, ignorant of a second flame after the extinction of the first; and in the character of them all there is such a blend of modest liveliness and elegant severity as has no superior. You might

Denique incerto*ᵃ* hereas quid potissimum*ᵇ* predicare uelis, an assiduitatem ad Dei famulitium an affabilitatem ad hominum colloquium; unde non iniuria credulitas apponitur dicentibus quod per illarum orationes totus sustentatur orbis, qui iam pridem suis uacillat peccatis.

164. Anno Dominicae incarnationis nongentesimo septuagesimo nono Egelredus filius Edgari et Elfridae regnum adeptus obsedit potius quam rexit annis triginta septem. Eius uitae cursus seuus in principio, miser in medio, turpis*ᶜ* in exitu asseritur: ita parricidio cui coniuentiam adhibuerat immanis, ita fuga et mollitie infamis, ita morte miserabilis fuit. Ignauiam eius predixerat Dunstanus, fedo exemplo ammonitus: nam cum pusiolus in fontem baptismi mergeretur, circumstantibus episcopis alui profluuio sacramenta interpolauit, qua re ille turbatus 2 'Per Deum' inquit 'et Matrem eius, ignauus homo erit!' Vidi scriptum¹ quod, cum decennis puer fratrem necatum conclamari audiret, fletu suo furentem genitricem adeo irritauit ut, quia flagellum ad manum non habebat, arreptis candelis innocentem cederet, nec prius desisteret quam pene exanimem et ipsa lacrimis infunderet. Quapropter tota uita ita candelas exhorruit in posterum ut numquam ante se pateretur inferri lumen earum. Matris suffragio proceribus congregatis dies dicta ut Dunstanus adueniret regem iure archiepiscopi coronaturus; ille, licet infensus esset, supersedit resistere,*ᵈ* pontifex aeui maturioris 3 et in secularibus emeritus. Iam uero diadema componens non se continuit*ᵉ* quin spiritum propheticum totis medullis haustum ore pleno effunderet: 'Quia' inquit 'per mortem fratris tui aspirasti ad regnum, propterea audi uerbum Domini. Haec dicit Dominus Deus: non delebitur peccatum ignominiosae matris tuae*ᶠ* et peccatum uirorum qui interfuerunt consilio illius nequam, nisi multo sanguine miserorum prouintialium; et uenient super gentem Anglorum mala qualia non passa est ex quo Angliam uenit usque ad tempus illud.' Nec multo post, id est anno eius tertio, uenerunt Hamtunam, portum iuxta Wintoniam, septem naues piratarum, et populata ora maritima refugerunt in altum; quod ideo non preterii, quia multus sermo apud Anglos fertur de his ratibus.

ᵃ incertum *Tt; cf. Hegesippus* i. *30. 9.*   *ᵇ* om. *Tt*   *ᶜ In view of what follows, one would expect William to have written* turpis . . . miser   *ᵈ* om. *Tt*   *ᵉ* conticuit *A*   *ᶠ* matris tuae ign. *Tt*

¹ *Passio S. Eadwardi* p. 7 Fell.

wonder, for example, which to praise more highly, their devotion to God's service or their courtesy in converse with man; so that not without reason there is much support for those who say that it is their prayers which support a world that quakes long since under its own sins.

164. In the year of our Lord 979 Æthelred, son of Edgar and Ælfthryth, came to the throne, and occupied (rather than ruled) the kingdom, for thirty-seven years. His life is said to have been cruel at the outset, pitiable in mid-course, and disgraceful in its ending. He showed cruelty in the murder of his kinsman, in which he was an accomplice; his running away and his effeminacy disgraced him; and he was miserable in his death. His worthlessness had already been foretold by Dunstan, warned by a filthy token of it: when as a baby he was being plunged in the font at his christening with the bishops standing round, he interrupted the sacrament by opening his bowels, at which Dunstan was much concerned—'By God and His Mother', he said, 'he will be a wastrel when he is a man.' I have seen it stated in writing[1] that when he was ten years old he heard it noised about that his brother had been murdered, and by his own tears so irritated and enraged his mother that, having no whip handy, she snatched up the candles and beat the innocent child with them, not stopping until he was nearly dead and even she was weeping over him. As a result, for the rest of his life thereafter he had such a horror of candles that he would never allow a candle-light to be brought into his presence. At his mother's prayer, in a meeting of the nobles, a day was appointed for Dunstan to come and crown him king, by his privilege as archbishop. Dunstan hated him but he would not say no, being a bishop advanced in years and with much experience in worldly affairs. But as he put the crown on his head he could not restrain himself, and poured out in a loud voice the spirit of prophecy with which his own heart was full. 'Inasmuch', he said, 'as you aimed at the throne through the death of your own brother, now hear the word of the Lord. Thus saith the Lord God: the sin of your shameful mother and the sin of the men who shared in her wicked plot shall not be blotted out except by the shedding of much blood of your miserable subjects, and there shall come upon the people of England such evils as they have not suffered from the time when they came to England until then.' Not long after, in the third year of his reign, there came to Southampton, a harbour near Winchester, seven ships full of pirates, and having ravaged the sea-coast they retired out to sea; and I have not passed over this, because there has been much talk among the English about these ships.

165. Surrexerat inter regem et episcopum Rofensem simultas, incertum qua de causa, quocirca contra ciuitatem exercitum duxit.[a] Mandatum ei ab archiepiscopo ut furori[b] desisteret nec sanctum Andream, in cuius tutela episcopatus est, irritaret, sicut ad indulgendum facilem, ita ad ulciscendum terribilem. Verborum nuditate contempta, adornat preceptum pecunia, et mittit centum libras ut obsidionem solueret, pretio emptus abiret; quo ille accepto receptui cecinit, procinctum militum feriari permisit. Miratus Dunstanus hominis cupiditatem haec per nuntios retulit: 'Quoniam pretulisti argentum Deo, pecuniam apostolo, cupiditatem michi, uelociter uenient super te mala quae locutus est Dominus. Sed haec me uiuente non fient,
2 quia[c] et haec locutus est Dominus.' Iam uero post beati uiri obitum, qui decimo anno regni eius fuit, properant impleri predicta, festinant consummari prenuntiata. Danis enim omnes portus infestantibus et leuitate piratica ubique discurrentibus, dum nesciretur ubi eis occurri deberet, decretum a Siritio, archiepiscopo post Dunstanum secundo, ut repellerentur argento qui non poterant ferro. Ita[d] decem milia librarum soluta cupiditatem Danorum expleuere: exemplum infame[e] et uiris indignum, libertatem pecunia redimere, quam ab inuicto animo nulla uiolentia possit excutere. Et tunc quidem paulisper ab excursibus cessatum; mox, ubi uires otio resumpserunt, ad superiora
3 reditum. Tantus[f] timor Anglos incesserat ut nichil de resistendo cogitarent; si qui sane antiquae gloriae memores obuiare et signa colligere temptassent, hostium multitudine et sotiorum defectione destituebantur. Defectionis signifer fuit Elfricus quidam, quem congregatis nauibus rex prefecerat; qui, cum nauali certamine fortunam experiri debuisset, nocte qua dies pugnae illucescebat transfuga uilis ad hostes concessit, prius per nuntios monitos quid cauerent; et quanuis pro culpa perfidiae filium eius rex excecari iusserit, iterum rediit iterumque defecit. Northanimbria tota populata, hostes pugna excepti et fugati
4 sunt; Lundonia obsessa, sed a ciuibus probe defensa. Quocirca obsessores afflicti et desperantes posse capi ciuitatem discesserunt, totamque

---

[a] misit Tt [b] furorem A; furore Savile (cf. GP p. 92 itinere; but VD p. 310 confirms the dative) [c] om. Tt [d] TtA, VD p. 321; item CB [e] infamiae Tt [f] tunc CB

165. A dispute had arisen, the cause of which is not clear, between the king and the bishop of Rochester, as a result of which the king led an army against the city. The archbishop told him to abandon this crazy enterprise, and not to rouse St Andrew, the patron saint of the see, who was generous in granting favours but terrible in revenge. His bare words were met with scorn, so he gilded his instructions with money, and sent him a hundred pounds as the price of raising the siege, if he would take the money and go away. He took it and beat a retreat, allowing his armed force to go on leave. Dunstan was astonished at the man's greed, and sent emissaries with the following reply: 'Inasmuch as you have preferred silver to God, money to the Apostle, and your own greed to myself, there shall come rapidly upon you evils of which the Lord has spoken; but this will not happen in my lifetime, for this too the Lord has told me.' Soon after the saint's death, 2 which took place in the tenth year of the king's reign, these prophecies were quick to be fulfilled and what he foretold hastened to come to pass. The Danes infested every harbour, and overran everything with the rapid movements typical of pirates, while it was impossible to know where they ought to be confronted. Sigeric therefore, the archbishop next but one after Dunstan, decided that they must be driven away with silver if steel could not do it. So Danish greed was satisfied with the payment of ten thousand pounds; and it was a disgraceful precedent, unworthy of true men, to buy with money the freedom of which no violence can rob an invincible spirit. And at that point there was for a time an end to the raids; but soon, their strength refreshed by leisure, they returned to the old ways. The English were now so 3 frightened that there was no thought of resistance; if any remembered their old traditions and tried to meet them and do battle, they were left in the lurch by the great numbers of the enemy and the desertion of their own allies. The leader of this desertion was a certain Ælfric, whom the king had put in command of his assembled ships; when it was his duty to try his luck in a sea-battle, on the night before the dawn that was to usher in the battle he became a worthless turncoat and went over to the enemy, having previously informed them by messengers what to look out for. And though in return for this perfidy the king ordered his son to be blinded, he came back, and deserted a second time. When the whole of Northumbria had been ravaged, the enemy were met in battle and driven off; London was besieged, but defended bravely by the citizens. As a result the besiegers were hard 4 hit, and in despair of capturing the city departed; but by devastating

prouintiam ab oriente uastantes regem ad pecuniam sedecim milium librarum soluendam coegerunt. Quin etiam regem eorum Analauum datis obsidibus ad se uenire fecit, baptizatum de fonte suscepit, et regali munificentia donatum sacramento constrinxit ne umquam reuerteretur in Angliam. Sed non sic malum quieuit; nam semper, ut hidrae capitibus, hostibus ex Danemarkia pullulantibus nusquam
5 caueri poterat. Occidentalis prouintia, quae Deuenescire uocatur, pessumdata, euersis monasteriis et Exonia urbe incensa. Cantia depredationi data, urbs metropolis et patriarcharum sedes conflagrata; ipse patriarcha, sanctus et reuerentissimus uir Elfegus, abductus et in uinculis tentus; ad extremum cum rusticos suos expilare ad se cogeretur redimendum et abnueret, lapidatus et securi percussus anima caelum glorificauit. Occisum Deus sullimat,[a] adeo ut Dani, qui in necem eius grassati fuerant, uiso miraculo quo[b] lignum aridum sanguine ipsius litum sub nocte una reuiruerat, certatim 'in oscula defuncti ruerent,
6 certatim'[c] colla subicerent. Ita naturali ceruicositate substrata, sacrum corpus Lundoniam euehi patiuntur. Ibi glorifice sepultum, et post decem annos ab omni corruptionis labe immune leuatum, archiepiscopium suum nobilitauit. Durat ad hoc tempus et recens sanguis et illibata integritas, miraculoque ducitur posse cadauer exanimari et non posse tabefieri. Et ne longum fatiam singillatim enumeratis prouintiis quas uastauerunt, hoc sit ad summam complecti quod, cum numerentur in Anglis triginta duo pagi, illi iam sedecim inuaserant, quorum[d] nomina propter barbariem linguae scribere refugio.
7 Rex interea, strenuus et pulchre[e] ad dormiendum factus, tanta negotia postponens oscitabat, et si quando resipuerat ut uel cubito se attolleret, confestim uel grauante desidia uel aduersante fortuna in miserias recidebat. Exagitabant illum umbrae fraternae, diras exigentes inferias. Quis possit enumerare[f] quotiens exercitum congregauerit, quotiens [g]naues fabricari iusserit, quotiens[g] duces undecumque euocauerit, et nichil umquam horum processerit? Nam exercitus principe carens et disciplinae militaris ignarus aut ante congressionem
8 dilabebatur aut in ipso conflictu facile cedebat. Valet multum in bellis

[a] sublimauit *Aa*p[b.c.]*Bk Tt(?)*   [b] quod *TcA*   [c-c] om. *CB*   [d] quarum
[e] pulcher *Tt*   [f] numerare *Tt*   [g-g] om. *A*

the whole province to the eastward they forced the king to pay sixteen thousand pounds in money. He also made their king Anlaf come to him, after giving hostages, acted as godfather at his baptism and, after giving him a generous present, bound him by oath never to return to England. But the evil could not be lulled to rest like that; for enemies were always sprouting out of Denmark like a hydra's heads, and nowhere was it possible to take precautions. The western province, known as Devonshire, was ravaged, monasteries overthrown, and the city of Exeter set on fire. Kent was abandoned to pillage, and the metropolitan city and seat of the patriarchs burnt; the patriarch himself, the saintly and most reverend Ælfheah, was carried off and held in chains, and in the end, when he was pressed to plunder the country-folk in his diocese in order to collect a ransom and refused, he was stoned and struck with an axe, and his soul was added to the glories of Heaven. On his death God exalted him, so much so that the Danes who had conspired to kill him, when they saw the miracle of the dry wood which had been smeared with his blood and grown green again in a single night, hastened to kiss his corpse and to bear it on their shoulders. Their natural arrogance being thus subdued, they allowed his sacred body to be brought to London. There it was solemnly buried, and ten years later, being found free from all taint of corruption, it was taken up, and added to the nobility of his cathedral church. To this day the fresh blood and the untainted perfection of the body still survive, and it is counted a miracle that a corpse should be able to lose the breath of life and yet not be corrupted. And not to make too long a story by listing singly all the provinces the Danes devastated, this summary may suffice: there are thirty-two counties in England, and of these they had already invaded sixteen, the names of which I am loth to set down because of their barbarous forms.

The king meanwhile, active and well-built for slumber, put off such important business and lay yawning; and if he ever thought better of it to the extent of even rising on one elbow, at once either sloth was too much for him or fortune was against him, and he sank back into wretchedness. He was hounded by the shade of his brother, demanding terribly the price of blood. Who could count how often he summoned his army, how often he ordered ships to be built, how often he called his nobles together from every quarter, and nothing ever came of it? The army had no leader and no inkling of military discipline, and either melted away before facing the enemy or gave way easily when battle was joined. There is a great force in the presence of a general in

ducis presentia, ualet spectata in talibus audatia, ualet usus et maxime disciplina; quibus, ut dixi, carens exercitus prouintialibus irrecuperabili dispendio, hostibus miserabili erat ludibrio. Est*ᵃ* illud hominum genus,*ᵇ* si non coherceatur ante bellum, in rapinas promptum; si non animetur in bello, ad fugam pronum. Naues ad tutandam oram maritimam fabricatas, cum in anchoris constitissent,*ᶜ* repente coorta tempestas corripuit, et collisas inter se disiectis armamentis inutiles reddidit. Paucae de reliquiis multarum factae impetu cuiusdam Wlnodi, quem rex exlegatum eiecerat, summersae uel incensae, spem totius Angliae fefellerunt. Duces si quando ad concilium conuenissent, pars hoc pars illud eligere, uix aut numquam in bonam sententiam conuenire; magis enim de simultatibus domesticis quam de publicis necessitatibus consultabant. Iam uero si quid urgente periculo utile et archanum decreuissent, statim ad Danos per proditores deferebatur; nam preter Elfricum, Elferii qui superiorem regem occiderat successorem, erat in talibus improbe idoneus Edricus, quem rex comitatui Mertiorum prefecerat: fex hominum et dedecus Anglorum, flagitiosus helluo, uersutus nebulo, cui nobilitas opes pepererat, lingua et audatia comparauerat. Hic dissimulare catus,*ᵈ* fingere paratus, consilia regis ut fidelis uenabatur, ut proditor disseminabat. Sepe ad hostes missus pacis mediator pugnam accendit. Cuius perfidia cum crebro huius regis tempore, tum uel maxime sequentis*ᵉ* apparuit; de qua*ᶠ* posterius dicam.¹ Solus ex omnibus comes Orientalium Anglorum Vlkillus et*ᵍ* tunc impigre contra inuasores restitit, ita ut, quanuis nomen uictoriae ad hostes concessisset, multo plus afflicti qui uicerant quam qui uicti erant estimarentur. Nec sane piguit barbaros ueritatem confiteri, cum multotiens illam uictoriam deplorarent. Et emicuit precipue post mortem Egelredi uirtus comitis*ʰ* in illo bello quod omnem florem prouintiae demessuit; ubi et ipse a tergo circumuentus, dum cedere pudori ducit, audatiam regi sanguine peperit suo. Sed haec postmodum.²

Tunc uero, ne quid miseriae regi Egelredo deesset, fame per totam Angliam debachante, uulgus quod bello reliquum erat absumptum inedia. Hostes adeo libere in regione uagabantur ut per quinquaginta

---

ᵃ et *Bk(and Bph)*, est et *Bc TtBk*   *ᵇ* genus hominum *TtA*   *ᶜ* constituissent *TtBk*   *ᵈ* cautus *TtB*   *ᵉ* sequenti *Tt*   *ᶠ* quo *Tt*ᵛ*Cs*   *ᵍ* om. *Aa, not without reason*   *ʰ* om. *B*

¹ 179. 4–180.
² 180. 7.

battle, and in his visible courage in such circumstances; great force in experience, and above all in discipline. All these, as I have said, the army lacked, which was a source of irrecoverable loss to their fellow-subjects and of pity and contempt to the enemy. That sort of men, if not disciplined before the battle, quickly fall to pillaging, and if not inspirited during the battle are quickly ready to run away. The ships built to protect the sea-coast, while lying at anchor, were seized by a sudden storm, which drove them together, scattered their tackle, and rendered them useless. A few, put together out of the remains of many, were attacked by a certain Wulfnoth whom the king had sent into exile, and were either sunk or burnt, thus frustrating the hopes of the whole of England. If his nobles ever gathered for a council, different parties made different 9 choices, and rarely or never agreed on a sensible course, for they discussed their private quarrels much more than necessary public action. And if, under pressure of danger, they came to some profitable decision in secret, it was at once conveyed to the Danes by treachery; for besides Ælfric, successor of the Ælfhere who had killed the previous king, there was a man scandalously suitable for such purpose—Eadric, whom the king had promoted to be ealdorman of the Mercians: the dregs of mankind and a disgrace to his countrymen, a criminal debauchee and a cunning rascal, whose wealth owed its origin to his rank and had been increased by his skill in speech and his effrontery. A skilful deceiver with a ready invention, he sought out the king's intentions as his faithful servant, and spread them around as a common traitor. Often, when sent on a mission to the enemy to secure peace, he rekindled the war. His perfidy was often displayed in the time of this king, but most of all in that of his successor; and of that I shall say something later.[1] Among 10 them all, only Ulfcytel, ealdorman of the East Angles, resisted the invaders even then with energy such that, though he had to allow the enemy a nominal victory, the victors were reckoned to have suffered much more than the vanquished. Nor were the barbarians unwilling to confess the truth, so often did they lament that victory. And it was after Æthelred's death that the ealdorman's valour was seen at its brightest, in the battle which mowed down all the flower of the province; in which he himself had been shut in to the rear, and thinking it shameful to surrender, he purchased new confidence for the king at the price of his own life. But of this later.[2]

At that point, that King Æthelred's cup of misery might be full, 11 famine raged through the whole of England, and such of the common people as had survived the war were dying of hunger. The enemy

milia predam per terram ad naues conuectarent, nullas prouintialium insidias formidantes. His malis undique circumstrepentibus, rursus consilium uolutabatur ut pecunia bellum leuaretur. Et factum est; nam prius uiginti quattuor milia librae, mox triginta milia datae, quod quantum profecerit, sequens tempus ostendit. Veruntamen multa michi cogitanti mirum uidetur cur homo (ut a maioribus accepimus) neque multum fatuus neque nimis*ᵃ* ignauus in tam tristi pallore tot calamitatum uitam consumpserit. Cuius rei causam si quis me interroget, non facile respondeam, nisi ducum defectionem ex superbia regis prodeuntem. Illorum perfidiam sermo preoccupauit; de ipsius insolentia nunc dicam, qua adeo intolerabilis erat ut nec propriis affectibus parceret. Nam preter Anglos, quos nullis causis extantibus exheredabat uel afficto crimine opibus emungebat; preter Danos, quos leuibus suspitionibus omnes uno die in tota Anglia trucidari iusserat, ubi fuit uidere miseriam dum quisque carissimos hospites, quos etiam arctissima necessitudo dultiores effecerat, cogeretur prodere et amplexus gladio deturbare,—preter haec ergo etiam in uxorem adeo proteruus erat ut uix eam cubili dignaretur, sed cum pelicibus uolutatus*ᵇ* regiam maiestatem infamaret. Illa quoque, conscientiam alti sanguinis spirans, in maritum tumebat, quod se nec pudor ingenuus nec fecunditas commendaret; nam duobus liberis Elfredo et Eduardo penates uiri compleuerat. Ea fuerat filia Ricardi comitis Normanniae, filii Willelmi, qui post patrem quinquaginta duobus annis illi ducatui prefuit, et octauo decimo anno huius regis uitam terminauit. Iacet apud Fiscamnum cenobium, quod ipse aliquantis redditibus ampliatum regula monastica per Willelmum quendam abbatem Diuionensem insigniuerat: uir eximius, qui etiam Egelredum sepe iniuriis pulsauerit; quod cum auditum Romae esset, non passa sedes apostolica duos Christianos digladiari, misit in Angliam Leonem Treuerensem episcopum ut pacem componeret. Cuius legationis epistola haec est:

166. 'Iohannes quintus decimus sanctae Romanae aecclesiae papa omnibus fidelibus.*ᶜ*

ᵃ multum *A*   *ᵇ* om. *Tt*   *ᶜ* *TtBk* add salutem. The letter (Counc. I. i. 38) is also given by ζ and by θκ

ranged so freely over the country that they drove their booty fifty miles overland to their ships with no fear of being ambushed by the inhabitants. With evils of this magnitude raging round them, the plan was again discussed of paying money to lighten the burden of the war, and this was done: first 24,000 pounds were paid over, and then 30,000; and how much good this did, appeared in the sequel. But I have devoted much thought to this, and it seems to me extraordinary that a man who was, as we learn from our forebears, neither a great fool nor excessively cowardly should pass his life in the dismal twilight of so many calamities. If anyone were to ask me the reason for this, I should not find it easy to answer, unless it was the disloyalty of his chief nobles, arising from the pride of the king himself. Of their treachery I have already said something; of the king's insolence I will now speak, which made him so intolerable that he did not spare even his own natural affections. Apart from the English, whom he deprived of their inheritance for no reason or stripped of their property on some trumped-up charge, and apart from the Danes, all of whom in the whole of England he had ordered, on the strength of flimsy suspicions, to be murdered on the same day (and a pitiful sight it was when every man was compelled to betray his beloved guest-friends, whom he had made even more dear by close ties of relationship, and to disrupt those embraces with the sword)—apart from all this, he was so offensive even to his own wife that he would hardly deign to let her sleep with him, but brought the royal majesty into disrepute by tumbling with concubines. She on her side, well aware of her own high birth, was indignant with her husband, finding that neither her inborn virtue nor her fertility recommended her; for she had enriched her husband's house with two children, Alfred and Edward. She had been a daughter of Richard, duke of Normandy, son of William, who in succession to his father ruled the duchy for fifty-two years, and died in the eighteenth year of our king. He lies in the monastery of Fécamp, which he himself had enriched with considerable revenues and had distinguished by installing a monastic rule through the agency of a certain William, abbot of Dijon. Richard was a distinguished man, and he had often struck at Æthelred and caused him injury; but when the news of this reached Rome, the Holy See would not allow two Christian rulers to start fighting, and sent Leo, bishop of Trier, to England to make peace. His mission appears from the following letter.

166. 'John XV, pope of the Holy Roman Church, to all the faithful.

'Nouerint omnes sanctae matris nostrae aecclesiae fideles et nostri utriusque ordinis per climata seculi dilatati, qualiter nobis relatum est a compluribus de inimicitia Edelredi Saxonum Occidentalium regis necnon et Ricardi marchionis; unde nimium tristis effectus, utpote de filiis nostris spiritualibus, tandem inito salubri consilio accersiui quendam apocrisarium[a] nostrum, Leonem uidelicet episcopum sanctae Treuerensis[b] aecclesiae, et misi eum illuc cum litteris nostris exhortatoriis, ut resipiscerent ab hac superstitione. Qui, transiens uastas intercapedines terrarum, tandem marinos transmeauit fines et in die Natalis Domini peruenit ante conspectum regis prefati, moxque ex parte nostra salutato obtulit litteras quas illi[c] miseramus. Qui accersitis cunctis sui regni utriusque ordinis fidelibus sapientioribus,[d] ob[e] amorem et timorem Dei omnipotentis necnon et sancti Petri apostolorum principis, et per nostram ammonitionem paternam, firmissimam concessit pacem cum omnibus filiis suis et filiabus presentibus et futuris et cum omnibus fidelibus suis sine dolo. Qua de re misit Edelsinum sanctae Scireburnensis aecclesiae presulem, necnon et Leofstanum filium Alfwoldi atque Wistani filium Edelnodum, qui transierunt marinos fines et peruenerunt usque ad Ricardum prefatum marchionem. Qui et monita nostra pacifice suscipiens simulque audiens decretum suprafati regis, libenti animo eandem pacem firmauit, cum filiis et filiabus suis[f] presentibus et futuris et cum omnibus fidelibus suis, eo rationis tenore ut, si aliquis eorum uel ipsi iniuste aliquid contra alterum perpetrauerint,[g] digna emendatione purgetur, paxque maneat stabilis perpetualiter et inconuulsa, sacramentorum utriusque partis[h] stigmate stipulata.

'Ex parte scilicet Edelredi regis Edelsinus presul sanctae Scireburnensis aecclesiae et Leofstan Alfwoldi filius et Edelnodus Wistani filius; ex parte Ricardi Rogerus episcopus, Rodulfus Hugonis filius, Turstenc filius Turgis. Actum Rotomago kalendis Martii anno ab incarnatione Domini nongentesimo nonagesimo primo, indictione quarta. Et de hominibus regis uel inimicis suis nullum Ricardus recipiat, nec rex de suis, sine sigillo eorum.'

167. De hoc sane Iohanne, qui et Gerbertus dictus est, non absurdum erit, ut opinor, si litteris mandemus quae per omnium ora

[a] apocrisarium ζ (-crifarium *Tt*); -crisiarium *ACB*, θ(κ)   [b] *Correctly* Treuensis *(so* ζ[a.c.]*)*   [c] ei *Tt*   [d] sapientibus *Tt*   [e] ad *B*   [f] suis et filiabus *A*   [g] perpetrauerant *Tt*   [h] pacis *Tt; om. B*

'Be it known to all the faithful of our holy Mother the Church and to our people both religious and secular dispersed through every quarter of the world, how reports have reached us from many sources of enmity between Æthelred, king of the West Saxons, and Marquis Richard, by which we have been filled with grief, seeing that they are both our spiritual sons. At length therefore I adopted a plan to mend the matter, summoned a certain secretary of mine, to wit Leo, bishop of the holy church in Trier, and despatched him thither with a letter from myself, urging them to repent of this pagan behaviour. Passing vast intervening spaces of land, he at length crossed the boundary set by the sea, and on the festival of our Lord's Nativity coming into the presence of the aforesaid king, and greeting him on our behalf, gave him the letter which we had sent him. Then he, sending for all those of his faithful subjects both religious and secular who were particularly wise, on account of his love and fear of Almighty God and of St Peter prince of the Apostles and by reason of our fatherly admonition, agreed to a most lasting peace, together with all his sons and daughters present and future, and with all his faithful subjects, without deceit. For which reason he sent Æthelsige, bishop of the holy church of Sherborne, and Leofstan son of Ælfwold and Æthelnoth son of Wigstan, who passed the boundaries set by the sea and came to Richard the marquis aforesaid. Accepting our instructions in a peaceful spirit, and at the same time hearing the decision of the aforesaid king, he himself willingly confirmed the same peace, together with his sons and daughters present and future, and with all his faithful subjects, on the understanding that, should any of their subjects or they themselves be guilty of any injustice against the other party, this should be purged by due and proper emendation; and peace should abide in perpetuity firm and unshaken, supported by the binding oath of both parties.

'On the part, that is, of King Æthelred: Æthelsige, bishop of the holy church of Sherborne, and Leofstan son of Ælfwold and Æthelnoth son of Wigstan; on the part of Richard: Bishop Roger, Rudolf son of Hugh, Thurstan son of Turgis. Delivered at Rouen the first day of March in the year of our Lord 991, the fourth indiction. And of the king's men or of his enemies Richard shall receive none, nor shall the king receive any of his, without their warranty under seal.'

167. Of this John, also called Gerbert, it will not be out of place, I think, to record in writing the stories that are on all men's lips.

uolitant. Ex Gallia natus, monachus a puero apud Floriacum adoleuit. Mox cum Pitagoricum biuium attigisset, seu tedio monachatus seu gloriae cupiditate captus, nocte profugit Hispaniam, animo precipue intendens ut astrologiam et ceteras id genus artes a Saracenis edisceret. Hispania, olim multis annis a Romanis possessa, tempore Honorii imperatoris in ius Gothorum concesserat; Gothi, usque ad tempora beati Gregorii Arriani, tunc per Leandrum episcopum Hispalis[a] et per Ricaredum regem fratrem Herminigildi, quem pater nocte Paschali pro fidei confessione interfecerat, catholico choro uniti
2 sunt. Successit Leandro Isidorus, doctrina et sanctitate nobilis, cuius corpus nostra aetate Aldefonsus rex Gallitiae Toletum transtulit, ad pondus auro comparatum. Saraceni enim, qui Gothos subiugarant, ipsi quoque a Karolo Magno uicti Gallitiam et Lusitaniam, maximas Hispaniae prouintias, amiserunt; possident usque hodie superiores regiones. Et sicut Christiani Toletum, ita ipsi[b] Hispalim, quam Sibiliam uulgariter uocant, caput regni habent, diuinationibus et incantationibus more gentis familiari studentes. Ad hos igitur, ut dixi, Gerbertus perueniens desiderio satisfecit. Ibi uicit scientia Ptholomeum in astrolabio, Alhandreum in astrorum interstitio, Iulium Fir-
3 micum in fato. Ibi quid cantus et uolatus auium portendat didicit, ibi excire tenues ex inferno figuras, ibi postremo quicquid uel noxium uel salubre curiositas humana deprehendit; nam de licitis artibus, arithmetica[c] musica et astronomia et geometria,[d] nichil attinet dicere, quas ita ebibit ut inferiores ingenio suo ostenderet, et magna industria reuocaret in Galliam omnino ibi iam pridem obsoletas. Abacum certe primus a Saracenis rapiens, regulas dedit quae a sudantibus abacistis uix intelliguntur. Hospitabatur apud quendam sectae illius philosophum, quem multis primo expensis, post etiam promissis demerebatur. Nec deerat Saracenus quin scientiam uenditaret; assidere frequenter, nunc de seriis nunc de nugis colloqui,
4 libros ad scribendum prebere. Vnus erat codex totius artis conscius quem nullo modo elicere poterat. Ardebat contra Gerbertus librum quoquo modo ancillari. Semper enim in uetitum nitimur,[1] et

---

[a] Hispanis *Al*, Hispalensem *Aa (so Tt, but not Tc)*   [b] om. *A*   [c] *One expects* et to follow   [d] geometria *TcA*

[1] Cf. Ovid, *Amores* iii. 4. 17.

A native of Gaul, he grew up from boyhood as a monk at Fleury; but after reaching Pythagoras's parting of the ways, he either grew tired of the monastic life or was taken with a thirst for reputation, and made his escape one night for Spain, his chief intention being to learn astrology and other such arts from the Saracens. Spain, in old days held for many years by the Romans, had passed in the time of the emperor Honorius into the hands of the Goths; and the Goths, who were Arians down to the time of St Gregory, were then united to the Catholic communion by Leander bishop of Seville, and by King Reccared, brother of the Hermenigild who had been put to death by his father on Easter eve for confessing the true faith. Leander was succeeded by Isidore, famous for his learning and saintly life, whose body has been translated in our own days to Toledo by Alfonso, king of Galicia, who bought it for its weight in gold. For the Saracens, conquerors of the Goths, had themselves been defeated by Charlemagne and lost Galicia and Lusitania, Spain's largest provinces; though all its southern regions are still theirs to this day. The Christians have Toledo for their capital and the Saracens Hispalis, commonly called Seville; there they devote themselves to divination and witchcraft, as their national custom is. So it was to the Saracens that Gerbert went, as I have said, and there he obtained his desire. There he surpassed Ptolemy in knowledge of the astrolabe, Alhandreus in that of the relative positions of the stars, and Julius Firmicus in judicial astrology. There he learnt to interpret the song and flights of birds, to summon ghostly forms from the nether regions, everything in short, whether harmful or healthful, that has been discovered by human curiosity; for of the permitted arts, arithmetic, music, astronomy, and geometry, I need say nothing—by the way he absorbed them he made them look beneath the level of his intelligence, and re-established in Gaul through his untiring efforts subjects that had long been completely lost. He was the first to seize the abacus from the Saracens, and he handed down the rules which calculators for all their efforts hardly understand. He lodged in the house of a philosopher who was of their religion, whose esteem he earned first by lavish spending and later also by promises. And the Saracen played his part; he sold his knowledge, often sat with him discussing topics sometimes serious, sometimes trivial, and provided him with books to copy. There was, however, one volume to which he had committed all his art and which Gerbert could by no means get out of him. On his side he was passionately anxious to make the book somehow serve his turn. 'We ever strive towards what is forbidden',[1] and

quicquid negatur pretiosius putatur. Ad preces ergo conuersus orare per Deum, per amicitiam; multa offerre, plura*a* polliceri. Vbi id parum procedit, nocturnas insidias temptat. Ita hominem, coniuente etiam filia, cum qua assiduitas familiaritatem parauerat, uino inuadens uolumen sub ceruicali positum abripuit et fugit. Ille somno excussus 5 inditio stellarum, qua peritus erat arte, insequitur fugitantem. Profugus quoque respitiens eademque scientia periculum comperiens sub ponte ligneo qui proximus se occulit,*b* pendulus et pontem amplectens ut nec aquam nec terram tangeret. Ita querentis auiditas frustrata, domum reuertit.*c* Tum*d* Gerbertus uiam celerans deuenit ad mare. Ibi per incantationes diabolo accersito, perpetuum paciscitur hominium*e* si se ab illo qui denuo insequebatur defensatum ultra pelagus eueheret. Et factum est.

Sed haec uulgariter ficta crediderit aliquis, quod soleat populus litteratorum famam ledere, dicens illum loqui cum demone quem in aliquo uiderint excellentem opere. Vnde Boetius in libro de Consolatione Philosophiae queritur se*f* propter studium sapientiae de talibus notatum, quasi conscientiam suam sacrilegio polluisset ob 6 ambitum dignitatis. 'Non conueniebat' inquit 'uilissimorum me spirituum presidia captare, quem tu in hanc excellentiam componebas ut consimilem deo faceres. Atqui hoc ipso uidemur affines malefitio, quod tuis imbuti disciplinis, tuis instituti moribus sumus.'[1] Haec Boetius. Michi uero fidem facit de istius sacrilegio inaudita mortis excogitatio. Cur enim se moriens, ut postea dicemus,[2] excarnificaret ipse sui corporis horrendus lanista, nisi noui sceleris conscius esset? Vnde in uetusto uolumine quod in manus meas incidit, ubi omnium Apostolicorum nomina continebantur et anni, ita scriptum uidi: 'Iohannes, qui et Gerbertus, menses decem: hic turpiter uitam suam finiuit.'

168. Gerbertus Galliam repatrians, publicasque*g* scolas professus, arcem*h* magisterii attigit. Habebat conphilosophos et studiorum sotios Constantinum abbatem monasterii sancti Maximini, quod est iuxta

---

a plurima *A*   *b* occuluit *A*   *c* reuertitur *TCs*   *d* tunc *TAaBk*
e hominum *Tt(not Tc)AaB*   *f* se om. *A (then* se de *Aa)*   *g* publicas *T*
h *TtACeBc²* (cf. *GP p. 333);* artem *TcCsBkBc¹*

---

[1] *Cons. phil.* i. 4. 39 and 41.
[2] 172. 2.

set a higher value on what we are not allowed to have. Turning to entreaties therefore, he begged the man in God's name and in the name of their friendship; he made him handsome offers and still more handsome promises. Making no progress, one night he tried a stratagem. With the connivance of the man's daughter, intimacy with whom he had won by constant attentions, he plied him with wine, seized the book, which was kept under his pillow, and made himself scarce. The Saracen awoke with a start and, guided by the stars—for he was expert in the art—pursued the fugitive. Gerbert, looking behind him as he ran and by the same expert knowledge perceiving his danger, hid himself under a wooden bridge that was close by, and hung there, grasping the structure so that he touched neither water nor earth. Thus all his pursuer's zeal was frustrated, and he returned home. Gerbert speedily resumed his journey, and reached the coast. There he called up the Devil with incantations, and covenanted to pay him perpetual homage if he would protect him from the Saracen, who had resumed the pursuit, and convey him overseas. And so it happened.

Some people may think this mere popular fiction; for public opinion often wounds the reputation of learned men, maintaining that one whom they have seen to excel in some department converses with the Devil. Boethius in his book *On the Consolation of Philosophy* complains that his passion for wisdom has brought him criticism of this kind, as though he had laid on his conscience the stain of sacrilege in order to satisfy his ambitions. 'It could not be right', he says, 'for me to seek the support of most worthless spirits, when you were shaping me to such a degree of excellence that you would make me resemble god. And yet this is the very point at which I am thought to be akin to magic arts: that I am steeped in your teaching and trained to follow your way of life.'[1] Thus Boethius. But I am encouraged to credit the story of Gerbert's sacrilege by the thought of his strange choice of death; for why should a man at the hour of death, as I shall recount later,[2] become a frightful butcher and cut up his own body, unless he had on his conscience some unprecedented crime? This explains why, in an ancient volume which I have had in my hands, containing the names and years of all the popes, I have seen written: 'John, also called Gerbert, ten months: he put a shameful end to his own life.'

168. Gerbert, returning to his native Gaul and lecturing in the public schools, reached the peak of the teaching profession. He had as fellow philosophers and companions of his studies Constantine, abbot

Aurelianis, ad quem edidit Regulas de*a* Abaco; Adelboldum episcopum, ut dicunt, Winziburgensem, qui et ipse*b* ingenii monimenta dedit in epistola quam facit*c* ad Gerbertum de questione diametri super Macrobium, et in nonnullis aliis. Habuit discipulos predicandae indolis et prosapiae nobilis, Rotbertum filium Hugonis cognomento
2 Capet, Ottonem filium imperatoris Ottonis. Rotbertus postea rex Frantiae magistro uicem reddidit et archiepiscopum Remensem fecit. Extant*d* apud illam aecclesiam doctrinae ipsius documenta, horologium arte mechanica compositum, organa hidraulica ubi mirum in modum per aquae calefactae*e* uiolentiam uentus emergens implet concauitatem barbiti, et per multiforatiles tractus aereae fistulae modulatos clamores emittunt. Et erat ipse rex in aecclesiasticis cantibus non mediocriter doctus, et cum in hoc, tum in ceteris multum aecclesiae profuit; denique pulcherrimam sequentiam 'Sancti Spiritus assit nobis gratia' et responsorium 'O Iuda et Ierusalem' contexuit et alia
3 plura, quae non me pigeret dicere si non alios pigeret audire. Otto, post patrem imperator Italiae, Gerbertum archiepiscopum Rauennatem et mox papam Romanum creauit. Vrgebat ipse fortunas suas fautore diabolo, ut nichil quod semel excogitasset imperfectum relinqueret. Denique thesauros olim a gentilibus defossos arte nigromantiae molibus eruderatis inuentos cupiditatibus suis implicuit. Adeo improborum uilis in Deum affectus,*f* et eius abutuntur patientia, quos ipse mallet redire quam perire. Sed repperit tandem ubi magister suus hereret et, ut dici solet, quasi*g* cornix cornici oculos effoderet, dum pari arte temptamentis eius occurreret.

169. Erat iuxta Romam in campo Martio statua, aerea an ferrea incertum michi, dextrae manus indicem digitum extentum habens; scriptum quoque in capite 'Hic percute'. Quod superioris aeui homines ita intelligendum rati quasi ibi thesaurum inuenirent, multis securium ictibus innocentem statuam laniauerant. Sed illorum Gerbertus redarguit errorem, longe aliter ambiguitate absoluta; namque meridie sole in centro existente notans quo protenderetur umbra digiti ibi palum figit, mox superueniente nocte solo cubiculario laternam portante comitatus eo contendit. Ibi terra solitis artibus dehiscens latum ingre-
2 dientibus patefecit introitum. Conspicantur ingentem regiam, aureos

a regulam de *Bc(and Bph), om. Bk*   *b* ipsi *B*   *c* fecit *CsB, rightly?*
d *A adds* enim   *e* om. *T*   *f* effectus *B*   *g* quia *Al, om. Aa*

of the monastery of Saint-Mesmin near Orléans, to whom he dedicated his *Rules for the Abacus*, and Adalbold, bishop (it is said) of Utrecht, who also left evidence of his gifts in the letter which he wrote to Gerbert on the question of the diameter in Macrobius and in several other pieces. He had pupils of notable gifts and noble birth, Robert the son of Hugh called Capet, and Otto the son of the emperor Otto. Robert later as king of France repaid his teacher by making him archbishop of Reims, where the cathedral still possesses evidence of his learning: there is a clock built on mechanical principles, and a pair of hydraulic organs in which power derived from hot water drives air out to fill the windchest of the instrument in wonderful fashion, and through passages with many holes in them bronze pipes produce musical sounds. The king himself had no little knowledge of church music, and both in this and other ways did much for the Church; he composed for example a very beautiful sequence 'Sancti Spiritus assit nobis gratia' and a responsory 'O Iuda et Jerusalem', and other things of which I would gladly tell, except that others might not so gladly listen. Otto, who succeeded his father as emperor of Italy, made Gerbert archbishop of Ravenna and later pope in Rome. He kept up the pressure for his own advancement with the Devil's assistance, so that no project which he had conceived was ever left unfinished. For instance, his skill in necromancy enabled him to clear away the rubble and discover treasures buried by pagans long ago, which he used to satisfy his greed. Of so little value to the wicked is their feeling towards God; so ready are they to misuse His patience, though He Himself would rather have them return to the fold than perish. But he found a point at length at which his master called a halt and, as the saying goes, one crow pecked out another crow's eyes, foiling his attempts with skill no less than his.

169. There stood near Rome in the Field of Mars a statue, whether of bronze or iron I am uncertain, pointing with the forefinger of the right hand, and on its head were the words 'Strike here'. Men in times past had taken this to mean that they should find treasure there, and many a blow from the axe had that poor statue suffered. But Gerbert proved them wrong, finding quite another answer to the riddle. At midday with the sun high overhead, he observed the spot reached by the shadow of the pointing finger, and marked it with a stake; then at nightfall, attended by a single servant carrying a lantern, he hastened to the place. There in response to his familiar arts the earth opened, revealing a broad passage as they entered. Before their eyes lay a vast

parietes, aurea lacunaria, aurea omnia; milites aureos aureis tesseris quasi animum oblectantes; regem metallicum cum regina discumbentes,[a] apposita obsonia, astantes ministros, pateras multi ponderis et pretii, ubi naturam uincebat opus.[1] In interiori parte domus carbunculus lapis in primis nobilis et paruus inuentu tenebras noctis fugabat. In contrario angulo stabat puer, arcum tenens extento neruo et harundine intenta. Ita in omnibus, cum oculos spectantium ars pretiosa raptaret, nichil erat quod posset tangi etsi posset uideri; continuo enim ut quis manum ad contingendum aptaret, uidebantur omnes
3 illae imagines prosilire et impetum in presumptorem facere. Quo timore[b] pressus Gerbertus ambitum suum fregit; sed non abstinuit cubicularius quin mirabilis artifitii cultellum, quem mensae impositum uideret,[c] abriperet, arbitratus scilicet in tanta preda paruum latrocinium posse latere. Verum mox omnibus imaginibus cum fremitu exsurgentibus, puer quoque emissa harundine in carbunculum tenebras induxit, et nisi ille monitu domini cultellum reicere accelerasset, graues ambo penas dedissent. Sic insatiata cupiditatis uoragine laterna gressus ducente discessum.
4   Talia illum aduersis prestigiis machinatum fuisse constans uulgi est opinio. Veruntamen, si quis uerum diligenter exculpat, uidebit nec Salomonem, cui Deus ipse dederit sapientiam, huiusce inscium commenti fuisse (ut enim Iosephus[2] auctor est, thesauros multos cum patre[3] defodit in loculis qui erant, inquit, mechanico modo reconditi sub terra), nec Hircanum, prophetia et fortitudine clarum, qui ut obsidionis leuaret iniuriam de Dauid sepulchro tria milia talenta auri arte mechanica eruit, ut obsessori partem enumeraret, parte xenodochia con-
5 strueret. At uero Herodes, qui magis presumptione quam consilio idem aggredi uoluerit, multos ex satellitibus igne ex interiori parte prodeunte amiserit.[d] Preterea cum audio Dominum Iesum dicentem: 'Pater meus usque modo operatur, et ego operor,'[4] credo quod qui dederit Salomoni uirtutem super demones, ut idem historiographus testatur, adeo ut dicat etiam suo tempore fuisse uiros qui illos ab obsessis corporibus expellerent, apposito naribus patientis anulo habente

---

[a] discumbentem *AlCe; for similar plurals see nn. on 341. 1* constituerat *and 352. 6* pausat (also *Justin xiv. 6. 13* custodiendos)   [b] T adds abstinuit   [c] uiderat *TBc, perhaps rightly*   [d] amisit *Cd, no doubt rightly*

---

[1] Cf. Ovid, *Met.* ii. 5.
[2] Josephus Lat. (ed. 1534), *Bell. Iud.* i. 2; *Ant. Iud.* vii. 16, xiii. 15, xvi. 7 (also viii. 2 for the seal).
[3] i.e. David.   [4] John 5: 17.

palace, gold walls, gold ceilings, everything gold; gold knights seemed to be passing the time with golden dice, and a king and queen, all of the precious metal, sitting at dinner, with their meat before them and servants in attendance; the dishes of great weight and price, in which 'workmanship outdid nature'.[1] In the inner part of the palace hung a carbuncle, a jewel rich and rare that turned night into day; in an opposite corner stood a boy, holding a bow at full stretch with arrow at the ready. So it was with all of them: though the priceless workmanship ravished the eye of the beholder, nothing could be touched, although it could be seen; for the moment anyone put out a hand as if to touch, all those figures seemed to leap forward to repel such presumption. Fear of this repressed Gerbert and made him drop his ambitious plan; but his servant did not refrain from snatching up a knife of wonderful workmanship, which he saw lying on a table, for he supposed no doubt that in such a mass of loot a small theft would remain undetected. In a moment, however, all the figures leapt to their feet with a roar, and the boy shot his arrow at the carbuncle and plunged everything in darkness; and had not the servant, at a warning word from his master, instantly thrown back the knife, they would both have paid a grievous penalty. So they came away, with the lantern to guide their steps, leaving their bottomless appetites unsatisfied.

It is uniformly believed by the common people that Gerbert achieved such results by the black arts. But any diligent seeker after the truth will see that Solomon, to whom God Himself gave the gift of wisdom, was not without knowledge of these inventions (for, as Josephus tells us,[2] he buried with his father[3] much treasure in chests hidden, he says, underground by mechanical ingenuity); nor was Hyrcanus, a man celebrated for his prophetic gifts and his courage, who in order to relieve the damage done by a siege dug up by mechanical means three thousand talents of gold from David's tomb, in order to pay half to the besieger and spend half on lodgings for strangers. Herod, however, who wished to make the same attempt more from ambition than policy, lost many of his workpeople when fire broke out from its recesses. Besides which, when I hear the Lord Jesus saying 'My Father worketh hitherto, and I work',[4] I believe that He who gave Solomon power over demons, as the same historian affirms—so much so that he says that even in his time there were men who could drive out demons from the bodies of those possessed by them by putting to the patient's nostrils a ring bearing a seal as demonstrated by

sigillum a Salomone monstratum, credo, inquam, quod et isti hanc scientiam dare potuerit; nec tamen affirmo quod dederit.

170. Sed haec lecturis relinquens, dicam quod a quodam loci nostri monacho, genere Aquitanico, aetate prouecto, arte medico, in pueritia audisse me memini. 'Ego' aiebat 'septennis, despecta exilitate patris mei, municipis Barcinonensis admodum tenuis, transcendens niues Alpinas in Italiam ueni. Ibi, ut id aetatis pusio, summa inopia uictum queritans, ingenium potius quam uentrem colui. Adultus multa illius terrae miracula oculis hausi et memoriae mandaui; inter quae uidi montem perforatum, ultra quem accolae ab antiquo estimabant thesauros Octouiani reconditos. Ferebantur etiam multi causa scrutandi
2 ingressi per anfractus et semetra[a] uiarum intercepti perisse. Sed, quia nullus fere timor auidas mentes ab incepto reuocat, ego cum sodalibus meis, uiris circiter duodecim, seu predandi seu uidendi studio illud iter meditabar aggredi.[b] Itaque Dedali secuti ingenium, qui Theseum de laberintho filo eduxit preuio, nos quoque glomus ingens portantes paxillum in introitu fiximus. Ibi principio fili ligato, accensis laternis ne preter deuia etiam cecitate impediremur, deuoluto glomere et per unumquodque miliarium paxillo apposito, sub cauerna montis quomodocumque iter nostrum direximus. Ceca erant omnia et magni[c] horroris plena; uespertiliones de concauis egredientes oculos et ora infestabant; semita arta, et a leua precipitio et subterlabente fluuio
3 timenda. Vidimus tramitem uestitum nudis ossibus; fleuimus cadauera tabo adhuc fluentia hominum quos eadem quae nos spes raptasset, post montis[d] introitum non ualentium inuenire exitum. Sed tandem aliquando post multos timores ad egressum ulteriorem peruenientes uidimus stagnum placidum aquis crispantibus, ubi dulcibus illisa lapsibus alludebat unda littoribus. Pons aereus utramque ripam continuabat; ultra pontem uisebantur mirae magnitudinis equi aurei cum assessoribus aeque aureis, et cetera quae de Gerberto dicta sunt, in quibus die medio Phebi iubar infusum duplicato fulgore oculos

[a] semitas *Tt(corr. from -*ta?*)Tc (but cf. 180. 3)*   [b] ingredi *A*   [c] magna *A*   [d] multis *Al, om. Aa*

Solomon—I believe, I say, that He could have given Gerbert too this power. I do not assert, however, that He did so.

170. But leaving these questions to my future readers, I will repeat something I remember hearing in my boyhood from a monk of our convent who was a native of Aquitaine, a very old man and skilled as a physician. 'When I was seven years old', he used to say, 'despising my father's humble circumstances, who was a citizen of Barcelona with very little money, I crossed the Alpine snows and made my way to Italy. There, seeking a livelihood in deepest poverty as a child of that age must, I did not fill my stomach but I sharpened my wits. As I grew up, I gazed spellbound at the many wonders of that country, and committed them to memory; among which I saw a mountain with a hole in it, beyond which the local people thought that the treasures of Octavian had lain hidden since Antiquity. The story also went that many people who had entered in order to explore had lost their way in the windings and confusion of the passages and had perished. But when the mind is set on something, fear hardly ever recalls it from its purpose; and whether it was in hopes of something worth stealing or worth seeing, I with my companions, about twelve of them, began planning to attempt that expedition. So we adopted the device of Daedalus, who brought Theseus out of the labyrinth with a thread that showed him the way, and we too carried a huge ball of thread, and fixed a peg in the entrance. To this we tied the beginning of the thread, lit lanterns that we might not be hindered by darkness as well as by the intricacy of the way, and, unwinding the ball as we went and fixing a peg at the end of every mile, set off on our journey through that cavern in the mountain as best we could. All was dark, all full of great horror; bats came out of every crevice and attacked our eyes and faces; the track was narrow, and rendered frightful by a precipice on the left hand and a river that flowed below. We saw our track deep in bare bones; we shed tears at the corpses, still dank with corruption, of men whom the same hope as ours had carried off, because after entering the mountain they could not find any exit. But the time somehow came when after many terrors we reached a way out at the farther end and saw a peaceful pool with rippling water, whose wavelets broke sweetly as they fell and played upon the shore. A bridge of bronze joined the two banks, and across the bridge we gazed upon wonderful great golden horses with riders too all of gold, and the other things in Gerbert's story; the midday sun played on

intuentium hebetabat. Nos qui haec eminus uidentes propiori aspectu delectaremur, asportaturi si fors*a* sineret aliquam splendidi*b* metalli crustam, hortamine alterno animati stagnum transire paramus; sed
4 nequiquam. Dum enim quidam ceteris preruptior citeriori margini pontis pedem imponeret, continuo (quod mirum auditu sit) illo depresso ulterior eleuatus est, producens rusticum aereum cum aereo malleo, quo ille undas uerberans ita obnubilauit aera ut diem caelumque subtexeret;*c* retracto pede pax fuit. Temptatum idem a pluribus, idemque expertum. Itaque desperato transitu aliquantum ibi constitimus et, quam diu potuimus, solo saltem uisu libauimus aurum. Mox per uestigia fili regressi*d* pateram argenteam repperimus, qua in frusta desecta et minutatim partita pruritum auiditatis nostrae tantummodo irritantes, non etiam fami fecimus satis.
5 'Postero die, collato consilio, magistrum quendam illius temporis adiuimus, qui dicebatur nomen Domini ineffabile scire. Interrogatus scientiam non infitiatur, aditiens quod tanta esset eius nominis uirtus ut nulla ei magia, nulla mathesis obsistere posset. Ita multo pretio redemptus, ieiunus et confessus nos eodem modo paratos duxit ad fontem. De quo hausta aqua in fiala argentea tacens digitis litteras*e* figurabat, donec oculis intelleximus quod ore effari nequiremus. Tunc fidutialiter ad montem accessimus; sed exitum ulteriorem a demonibus credo obstipatum offendimus, inuidentibus scilicet nomini Domini,
6 quod eorum commenta refelleret. Venit mane*f* ad me nigromanticus Iudeus, quem audita gestorum fama exciuerat, percunctatusque rem, ubi socordiam nostram accepit,*g* multo cachinno bilem succutiens "Quin tu" inquit "uideas licebit quantum potentia meae artis ualeat?" Et incunctanter montem introiens, non multo post egressus est, multa quae ultra fluuium notaueram ad inditium transitus sui afferens, puluerem sane locupletissimum, quo quicquid contingeretur in aurum flauescebat, non quod ita pro uero esset, sed quia ita uideretur quoad aqua dilueretur; nichil enim quod per nigromantiam fit potest in aqua aspectum intuentium fallere. Confirmat ueritatem sermonis mei res quae tempore eodem acciderat.

a sors *TcCsB* *b* splendidam *B* *c* subtexerat *Al*, -texerit *Aa* *d* egressi *B* *e* litteris *CsB* *f* sane *T* *g* audiuit *T*

them, dazzling the eyes of the beholder with redoubled radiance. Seeing all this from a distance, we should have been delighted with a nearer view, and were minded, should we be so lucky, to carry off some fragment of the gleaming metal; so shouting encouragements to one another we prepared to cross the pool. In vain. When one of us 4 more dashing than the rest set his foot upon the near edge of the bridge, all of a sudden (strange to relate) as the near end went down up came the further end, and with it a bronze rustic with a bronze hammer with which he beat the water, filling the air with mist so that sun and sky were blotted out. He withdrew his foot and all was peace. Several of us tried the same experiment, with the same result. So as there was no hope of crossing, we waited there for a while, and feasted our eyes, and no more, on the gold. After that, as we made our way back along the track of the thread, we found a silver dish. This we cut in pieces and divided in small shares; but we merely made our itching greed more painful without satisfying our hunger.

'Next day we held council, and approached a leading authority of the 5 day, who was said to know the ineffable name of the Lord. When asked, he did not disclaim his knowledge, adding that the virtue of that name was so great that no magic and no astrology could resist it. So we bought his services at a high price, and after fasting and making his confession, he conducted us, who had undergone the same preparation, to a spring. From this he drew water in a silver jug, and silently drew letters with his fingers, until we took in with our eyes what we might not utter by word of mouth. We next went in high confidence to the mountain, but found the farther way out blocked, I suppose by demons, who were no doubt jealous of the name of the Lord which could make nonsense of all their inventions. Next morning 6 there came to me a Jewish necromancer, aroused by what he had heard of our activities, and asked us what had happened. When told of our cowardice, he relieved his feelings with a roar of laughter. "Now", he said, "you will have a chance to see what the force of my art can do." Without delay he entered the mountain and not much later came out bringing many of the things I had noticed on the other side of the river as evidence that he had crossed it, particularly a very rich kind of dust: everything touched by it turned yellow, like gold, not because it was so, but because it seemed so until it was washed in water; for nothing done by necromancy can deceive the eyes of a spectator when put into water. The truth of what I say is confirmed by something which had happened at the same time.

171. 'Erant in strata publica qua Romam itur duae aniculae,[a] quibus nichil bibatius, nichil putidius,[b] uno commorantes tugurio, uno imbutae malefitio. Hae hospitem, si quando solus superueniebat, uel equum uel suem uel quodlibet aliud uideri fatiebant et mercatoribus uenum proponebant, nummos inde acceptos ingurgitantes.[c] Et forte quadam nocte quendam ephebum, qui motibus histrionicis uictum exigeret, excipientes hospitio asinum uideri fecerunt, magnum suis commodis emolumentum habentes asinum qui transeuntium detineret oculos miraculo gestuum; quocumque enim modo precepisset anus, 2 mouebatur asinus. Nec enim[d] amiserat intelligentiam, etsi amiserat loquelam. Multum itaque questum conflauerant uetulae, undique confluente multitudine uulgi ad spectandos ludos asini. Rumor uicinum diuitem aduocauit, ut quadrupedem non pauculis nummis in usus suos[e] transferret, ammonitus ut, si perpetuum uellet habere histrionem, arceret eum aqua. Custos ergo appositus mandatum seuere exsequebatur. Preteriit plurimum tempus; asinus, quando temulentia dominum in gaudium excitasset, conuiuas iocis suis letificabat. Sed, sicut rerum omnium fastidium est, dissolutius post haec haberi cepit; quapropter incautiorem nactus custodiam, abrupto loro effugiens in proximum lacum se proiecit et, diutius in aqua uolutatus, figuram 3 sibi humanam restituit. Custos ab obuiis sciscitatus illumque[f] uestigiis insecutus, interrogat an uidisset asinum. Refert ille se asinum fuisse, modo hominem, omnemque casum exponit. Miratus famulus ad dominum detulit, dominus ad Apostolicum, Leonem dico nostro seculo sanctissimum; conuictae anus idem fatentur. Dubitantem papam confirmat Petrus Damianus, litteraturae peritus, non mirum si haec fieri possint, productoque exemplo de Simone Mago, qui Faustinianum in Simonis figura uideri et a filiis horreri fecit, instructiorem de cetero in talibus reddidit.'

172. Haec Aquitanici uerba ideo inserui, ne cui mirum uideatur quod de Gerberto fama dispersit: fudisse sibi statuae caput certa inspectione siderum, cum uidelicet omnes planetae exordia cursus sui meditarentur, quod non nisi interrogatum loqueretur, sed uerum uel

---

[a] ancillae *T* [b] pudicitius *Ce*, impudicitius *Cs(and Cr)Bc¹*; pudicius *BkBc²(and CpBpBph)* [c] abligurrientes *TA* [d] om. *A* [e] suos usus *T* [f] illum *Tt(not Tc)Al*

171. 'On the high road that leads to Rome lived two old crones, altogether filthy and given to liquor, who shared one cottage and were filled with one spirit of witchcraft. If ever a traveller came to lodge with them by himself, they used to make him take the shape of horse or hog or some other animal and offer him for sale to the dealers in such things, spending on their stomachs the coin they thus obtained. One night, as it happened, they gave lodging to a youth who earned his living as an acrobat, and made him take the shape of an ass, thinking that a donkey whose astonishing capers could hold the attention of passers-by would be a great addition to their assets; for whatever movements were dictated by one of the dames the donkey followed. He had not, you see, lost a man's intelligence, though he had lost the power of speech. In this way the old beldams had raked in a pretty penny, for crowds of common people came from everywhere to see their donkey's tricks. The news attracted a rich man in the neighbourhood, who was moved to acquire the poor beast at a considerable price for his own service, subject to the warning that if he wished his entertainer to last, he must keep him away from water. A keeper was therefore appointed to see that this precept was strictly observed. Thus passed a considerable time: when his master had been made jolly by liquor, the ass used to entertain the guests with his comic tricks. But everything goes out of fashion, and the day came when the watch kept over him became more slipshod; so, finding his keeper more careless, he broke his halter and ran away, threw himself into a pool hard by, and after prolonged rolling in the water regained his human shape. The keeper, asking everyone he met and following him by his tracks, enquired if he had seen a donkey. He replied that he himself had been a donkey, but was now a man, and told him the whole story. The servant, greatly astonished, told his master, and his master told the pope—Leo, it was, the most saintly man of our time; the old women were convicted and confessed. The pope had his doubts, but was encouraged by Peter Damiani, a great scholar, to think it not surprising if these things can happen; by citing the example of Simon Magus, who caused Faustinianus to appear in Simon's shape and frighten his children, he made the pope more knowledgeable about such things for the future.'

172. I have included these stories told by the monk from Aquitaine so that a tale about Gerbert need occasion no surprise: how, after close inspection of heavenly bodies (at a time, that is, when all the planets were proposing to begin their courses afresh) he cast for himself

affirmatiue uel negatiue pronuntiaret. Verbi gratia, diceret Gerbertus 'Ero Apostolicus?' responderet statua 'Etiam.' 'Moriar antequam cantem missam in Ierusalem?' 'Non.' Quo illum ambiguo deceptum ferunt, ut nichil excogitaret penitentiae qui animo blandiretur suo de longo tempore uitae: quando enim Ierosolimam ire deliberaret ut mortem stimularet? Nec prouidit quod est Romae aecclesia Ierusalem dicta, id est, Visio pacis, quia quicumque illuc confugerit, cuiuscumque
2 criminis obnoxius, subsidium inuenit. Hanc in ipsius urbis[a] rudimentis Asilum accepimus dictam, quod ibi Romulus, ut augeret ciuium numerum, statuisset omnium reorum refugium. Ibi cantat missam papa tribus dominicis quibus pretitulatur Statio ad[b] Ierusalem. Quocirca, cum uno illorum[c] dierum Gerbertus ad missam se pararet, ui ualitudinis ictus ingemuit, eademque crescente decubuit; consulta statua deceptionem et mortem suam cognouit. Aduocatis igitur cardinalibus diu facinora sua deplorauit; quibus inopinato stupore perculsis nec aliquid referre ualentibus, ille insaniens et pre dolore ratione hebetata minutatim se dilaniari et membratim foras proici iussit, 'Habeat' inquiens 'membrorum offitium qui eorum quesiuit hominum; namque animus meus numquam illud adamauit sacramentum, immo sacrilegium.'

173. Et quia diuerticulum feci, puto non inhonestum si dicam quod in Saxonia tempore regis istius[d] accidit, et non adeo notum, anno Dominicae incarnationis millesimo duodecimo. Melius est interim spatiari in talibus quam immorari in eius rebus et ignauis et tristibus. Quod profecto erit iocundius si ab antiquitate scriptum illius qui passus est apposuero; simul et propius uero uidebitur quam si meis texuissem litteris. Preterea non indecens estimo si multicolori stilo uarietur oratio.

174. '"Ego Otbertus peccator, et si uellem celare quod in me factum est diuinum iuditium, membrorum meorum tremor proderet; quod quemadmodum factum sit referam, ut omnibus innotescat quanta sit pena inobedientiae. Eramus ad uigilias Natalis Domini in uilla quadam Saxoniae ubi erat aecclesia Magni martiris. Presbiter nomine Rotbertus missam primam inchoauerat. Ego in cimiterio cum

[a] *om. B*   [b] *om. CB*   [c] eorum *A*   [d] istius regis *TcA*

the head of a statue which could speak, though only if spoken to, but would utter the truth in the form of either Yes or No. If, for example, Gerbert were to say: 'Shall I be pope?' the statue would reply: 'Yes.' 'Shall I die before I sing mass in Jerusalem?' 'No.' This answer, they say, was ambiguous and misled him, with the result that he gave no thought to repentance, flattering himself with the prospect of long life; for why should he go deliberately to Jerusalem to hasten his own death? He did not foresee that there is in Rome a church called Jerusalem, that is 'Vision of peace', because the man who makes his escape to it when guilty of any crime finds sanctuary. We are told that in the city's very 2 early days it was called Asylum, because Romulus, in order to increase the number of his citizens, had appointed there a refuge for guilty men of every kind. In that church the pope sings mass on the three Sundays marked in the calendar *Statio ad Ierusalem*. Consequently on one of those days, when Gerbert was preparing for mass, he began to groan at a violent stroke of sickness, and, as it increased, took to his bed; on consulting the statue, he understood the deception and his own approaching death. Sending for the cardinals, he lamented at length his own misdeeds, and when they were struck with sudden amazement and unable to reply, he lost his reason and, beside himself with pain, gave orders that he should be cut in small pieces and cast out limb by limb. 'Let him have the service of my body', he cried, 'who sought its obedience; my mind never accepted that oath, not sacrament but rather sacrilege.'

173. And since I have been digressing, it will not, I think, be found improper if I tell of an event that happened in Saxony in the time of that same king, and is not so well known, in the year of our Lord 1012. It is better for a time to digress into topics such as this than to dwell on his record of cowardice and disaster. And it will increase the reader's enjoyment if I append the original account of the sufferer; it will also seem nearer the truth than if I had rewritten it in my own words. Besides which, I think it not inappropriate to enliven what I write with various changes of style.

174. '"My name is Otbert, a sinner, and even if I wished to conceal the divine judgement that has been passed on me, my shaking limbs would make it known; but I will tell how it happened, that all men may clearly see how great is the penalty of disobedience. It was Christmas eve, and we were in a village in Saxony where there was a church of St Magnus the martyr. The priest, whose name was Robert, had

sodalibus octodecim, uiris quindecim feminis tribus, choreas ducens et cantilenas seculares perstrepens, ita sacerdotem impediebam ut ipsa uerba nostra inter*ᵃ* sacrosancta missarum sollemnia resonarent.*ᵇ* Quocirca, mandato nobis ut taceremus et neglecto, imprecatus est dicens: 'Placeat Deo et sancto Magno ut ita cantantes permaneatis usque ad
2 annum!' Verba pondus habuerunt. Filius presbiteri Iohannes sororem suam nobiscum cantantem per brachium arripuit, statimque illud a corpore auulsit, sed gutta sanguinis non exiit. Ipsa quoque toto anno nobiscum permansit choros ducens et cantans. Pluuia non cecidit super nos; frigus nec*ᶜ* calor nec fames nec sitis nec lassitudo nos affecit; indumenta nec calciamenta nostra attriuimus, sed quasi uecordes cantitabamus. Primum ad genua, mox ad femora, terrae dimersi sumus. Fabrica tecti aliquando nutu Dei super nos erigebatur, ut pluuias arceret. Tandem euoluto anno Herbertus, ciuitatis Coloniensis episcopus, a nodo quo manus nostrae ligabantur nos absoluit et ante altare sancti Magni reconciliauit. Filia presbiteri cum aliis duobus continuo efflauit, ceteri continuis tribus diebus et noctibus dormiuimus. Aliqui postea obierunt et miraculis coruscant, ceteri penam suam tremore membrorum produnt." Datae sunt nobis hae litterae a domno Peregrino, beati*ᵈ* Herberti successore, anno Dominicae incarnationis millesimo tertio decimo.'

175. In hac urbe, quae olim Agrippina ab Agrippa genero Augusti dicta, postea a Traiano imperatore Colonia denominata est, quod ibi in imperium allectus colonias ciuium Romanorum eo deduxerit,—in hac, inquam, ciuitate fuit episcopus quidam, preclarus religione quanuis turpis corpore, cuius unum miraculum, quod moriens predixit,*ᵉ* referam, si prius dixero quam insolitus casus eum in tanto culmine fastigauerit. Imperator terrae illius, dominica illa quae uocatur Quinquagesima uenatum pergens, solus ad oram siluae deuenit omnibus comitibus dispersis, iuxta quam habebat aecclesiam ille presbiter
2 agrestis, deformis sane et pene portentum naturae. Imperator, militem se mentitus, supliciter missam rogat.*ᶠ* Ille confestim parat;*ᵍ* alter interea uoluebat animo quare Deus, *ʰ*a quo formosa cuncta procedunt,*ʰ* tam deformem hominem sacramenta sua conficere sineret. Mox cum ad uersum tractus uentum esset: 'Scitote quoniam Dominus ipse est

ᵃ intra A   *ᵇ* resonaret Tt(not Tc)AlCeBk   *ᶜ* non CB   *ᵈ* om. A
ᵉ dixit B   *ᶠ* rogat missam A   *ᵍ* paret TCs   *ʰ⁻ʰ* after sineret T

begun the first mass. There was I in the churchyard with eighteen companions, fifteen of us men and three women, dancing and bawling worldly songs, interrupting the priest so effectively that our actual words could be heard through the most sacred liturgy of the mass. He told us to be quiet, and we paid no attention; so he cursed us, saying: 'Please God and St Magnus, may you sing for a whole year without a break.' There was weight in his words. John, the priest's son, seized his sister, who was dancing with us, by the arm, and at once broke it off from her body, but not a drop of blood came out. For a whole year she stayed with us dancing and singing. No rain fell upon us; no cold or heat, no hunger or thirst, no weariness troubled us at all; our clothes did not wear out nor did our shoes; but we sang as though possessed. We sank to the ground, first knee-deep, then up to our thighs. At one stage by the will of God a roof was built over us to keep off the rain. At last, when the year was up, Heribert bishop of the city of Cologne absolved us from the knot with which our hands were tied, and reconciled us to the Church before the altar of St Magnus. The priest's daughter and two others at once breathed their last; the rest of us slept for three days and nights without a break. Some died later, and are distinguished by their miracles; others betray their punishment by the shaking of their limbs." This letter was sent us by my lord Pilgrim, blessed Heribert's successor, in the year of our Lord 1013.'

175. In this city, named of old Agrippina from Agrippa, son-in-law of Augustus, and afterwards renamed Colonia by the Emperor Trajan because he was chosen emperor there and established there colonies of Roman citizens—in this city, I repeat, there was once a bishop famous for his piety although hideous to look at, one of whose miracles, foretold on his deathbed, I will relate, having first recounted the unusual chance that lodged him in such an eminent position. The emperor of that country, on the Sunday known as Quinquagesima, was on his way to hunt, and came all by himself, for his companions had scattered, to the edge of a forest, where this man had a church, being a country priest of great ugliness, almost a freak of nature. The emperor, pretending he was only a knight, begged humbly for a mass; the priest at once made ready, and meanwhile the other was turning over in his mind why God, from whom all lovely things proceed, allowed one so hideous to celebrate His sacraments. Soon afterwards, when they reached the versicle of the tract 'Be ye sure that the Lord, He is

Deus',[1] sacerdos socordiam pueri familiaris increpitans respexit et concitatiori uoce, quasi cogitanti imperatori responderet,[a] dixit: 'Ipse fecit nos et non ipsi nos.'[2] Quo dicto reperculsus imperator, propheticum uirum estimans, inuitum et renitentem sullimauit in archiepiscopium.[b] Quod tamen semel susceptum dignis moribus honestauit: bene agentes blande appellare, improbos excommunicationis stigmate inurere sine personarum[c] acceptione.

3 Multa illius acta constanter accolae predicant, quorum unum pro suscepti operis breuitate lector percurret. In monasterio sanctimonialium urbis illius erat uirgo quaedam, quae illic magis parentum offitio quam bonae uitae studio adoleuerat. Haec et spetiei lenocinio et dulci ad omnes colloquio[d] amatores inuitabat; sed cum ceteri uel timore Dei uel pro infamia seculi cupiditates suas cohiberent, unus, quem opum congeries et alta progenies in proteruiam accenderant, abrupit quod legis quod iustitiae, puellae uirginal expugnare ausus, abductamque domum[e] loco iustae coniugis habuit. Transiit multum tempus in abbatissae precibus, in propinquorum ammonitionibus, ne tam fedo facinori assuesceret; ille surdis auribus ammonentes transiens uelut pelagi 4 rupes immota resistit.[3] Ac[f] tum forte antistes aberat, curiae curis implicitus; regresso res nuntiatur. Mandat ille[g] continuo ut ouis ouili restituatur; ita, multis uerbis ultro citroque habitis, mulier monasterio redditur, sed non multo post, abscessu pontificis aucupato, abripitur. Tunc in delinquentem excommunicatio promulgatur, ita ut nullus ciuium cum eo colloqui, nullus conuiuari auderet; quam ille iniuriam paruipensans in predia iuris sui longe abiit, non ut preceptum foueret sed ut arbitrum fugeret, ibi cum excommunicata sua uitam transigens, 5 homo factiosus et potens. Sed cum Deus episcopum ad superos euocaret, et graui dolore membra depastus in lecto decumberet, conuenerunt undique compatriotae ut extremae benedictioni beati uiri communicarent. Solus ille uenire non presumens subornauit aliquos qui pro se loquerentur. Eius nomen auditum primo pontifex gemitu excepit, inde subiecit uerba (uerba ipsa dicturus sum): 'Si miser ille

[a] responderit B [b] AlCs; archiepiscopum TAaCe; episcopum BA [c] persone [d] alloquio TA, perhaps rightly [e] T adds in [f] at TCsBc [g] igitur B

[1] Ps. 99 (100): 3.
[2] Ibid.
[3] Cf. Virgil, Aen. vii. 586.

God',[1] the priest by way of rebuking the slackness of the boy who was serving, looked round at him and said in an emphatic voice as though answering the emperor's thoughts: 'It is He that hath made us and not we ourselves.'[2] Much taken aback by this, the emperor thought that the man had prophetic powers, and against strong resistance on his part exalted him to the archbishopric. Yet, once he had accepted the see, he did it credit by his high character, courteously encouraging the good and branding evildoers with the stigma of excommunication without any respect of persons.

Many of his doings are constantly on the lips of the local people, and of one of them the reader shall have a running account, as far as the brevity of my planned work permits. In a convent of nuns in that city there was a young woman who had grown up there, thanks more to the dutiful care of her parents than to her own zeal for the religious life. Her alluring person and obliging readiness to talk to everybody attracted lovers; but the rest, either from fear of God or to avoid public scandal, kept their desires in check, and only one, whose lack of shame was fired by plenty of money and by ancient lineage, broke the bonds of law and equity and boldly deflowered the girl, taking her home to live with him in place of a lawful wife. Much time passed in prayers from the abbess and objurgations from his relatives, urging him not to grow hardened in such flagrant sin; but turning a deaf ear he threw off all their warnings, 'as some sea-cliff unmoved stands firm'.[3] It so happened that the archbishop was then away, immersed in the business of the court, and the affair was reported to him on his return. He at once gave instructions that the sheep must be returned to the fold; so, after much argument on both sides, the woman was restored to her convent, from which not much later, after waiting for the archbishop's absence, she was abducted. Sentence of excommunication was then published against the delinquent, with the effect that none of his fellow-citizens dared speak or sit at table with him; but making light of these attacks, he departed for some distant estates of his, not in order to do as he was told but to escape observation, spending his life there with his outlawed paramour, for he was a powerful and turbulent man. But when God summoned the bishop to a better world, and he lay in bed racked with severe bodily pain, his fellow-countrymen came flocking together to share in his final blessing. Only the culprit did not dare to come, and put up others to speak for him. When he heard his name, the archbishop first received it with a groan, and then added words which I will quote exactly: 'If that poor wretch

maledictam mulierem deseruerit, sit absolutus; si perstiterit, posteriori anno hac eadem die et hora qua ego decedam sit ante Deum reddere rationem paratus. Videbitis autem me quando signum ad sextam insonuerit efflare.' Nec fides uerbis defuit; nam et iste hora*a* qua predixerat defunctus, et ille anno euoluto eadem die et hora cum amica fulmine ictus*b* exanimatus est.

176. At uero rex*c* Egelredus, martirizato ut prediximus[1] sancto Elfego, dedit episcopatum*d* cuidam episcopo Liuingo. Resederat autem in Anglia Turkillus Danus, qui fuerat incentor ut lapidaretur archiepiscopus, habebatque Orientales Anglos suae uoluntati parentes.*e* Nam ceteri, dato ab Anglis octo milium librarum tributo, per urbes et agros quo quisque commodius poterat dilapsi; quindecim eorum naues cum hominibus regis fidem secutae. Turkillus interea regem patriae suae Suanum nuntiis accersit ut Angliam ueniat; preclaram esse patriam et opimam, sed regem stertere;*f* illum ueneri uinoque studentem nichil minus quam bellum cogitare, quapropter odiosum suis, ridiculum alienis; duces infidos, prouintiales infirmos, primo stridore lituorum prelio cessuros.

177. Erat Suanus in sanguinem pronus, nec ei magno hortamento opus fuit.*g* Nauibus itaque paratis transitum maturauit; Sandwic uocatur portus ubi appulit,*h* ultionem precipue Gunhildis sororis intendens animo. Haec, non illepidae formae uirago, Angliam cum Pallingo marito potenti comite uenerat, et accepta Christianitate obsidem se Danicae pacis fecerat. Eam cum ceteris Danis infaustus furor Edrici decapitari*i* iusserat, pronuntiantem*j* quod sui sanguinis effusio magno toti Angliae foret dispendio. Et illa quidem mortem presenti*k* tulit animo, quia nec moritura expalluit nec mortua, consumpto etiam sanguine, uultum amisit; occiso prius ante ora marito et filio, commodae indolis puero, quattuor lanceis forato. Tunc ergo Suanus,*l* per Orientales Anglos profectus in Northanimbros, ditioni*m* eos suae*n* sine pugna subdidit, non quod in illorum mentibus genuinus ille calor et dominorum impatiens refriguerit, sed quod princeps eorum Vhtredus

a et hora iste Al*a.c.*, iste et hora Aa	*b* TcAlCsB add et *(Ce has an erasure)*	*c* om. CeB
d archiepiscopatum Tt	*e* om. Tt	*f* sternere Tt *g* erat A
h Tt adds Suanus	*i* decapitare ABc	*j* prenuntiantem Bc *(cf. 107. 3 n. c)*
k patienti Tt	*l* om. Tt	*m* Tt adds uero *n* suae eos Tt

[1] 165. 5.

leaves his cursed woman, let him be forgiven. If he persists, a year from now, the same day and hour that I pass away, let him be ready to give an account of himself before God. And when the bell rings for sext, you will see me breathe my last.' Nor did his words lack confirmation; for he himself died at the hour he had foretold, and the other man, when a year had passed, died the same day and hour, struck by lightning, together with his mistress.

176. So King Æthelred, after the martyrdom of St Ælfheah of which I have already spoken,[1] gave the see to a bishop called Lyfing. Thurkil the Dane, who had instigated the stoning of the archbishop, had settled in England and kept the East Anglians in subjection. The other Danes levied on the English eight thousand pounds of tribute, and scattered through cities and countryside as each found most convenient, while fifteen of their ships with crews transferred their allegiance to the king. Thurkil meanwhile sent to invite Swein, the king in his native land, to come to England, saying that it was a splendid rich country, with a king who was asleep and snoring; given to women and wine, he thought of nothing so little as fighting, which made him unpopular with his own people and a laughing-stock to others; his generals disloyal, his subjects weak, both liable to leave the field at the first blast of the trumpet.

177. Swein was a man of blood, and needed little persuasion; so he fitted out his ships and came hastening over. The port where he landed is called Sandwich, and his chief purpose was to avenge his sister Gunnhild. Gunnhild, who was a woman of some beauty and much character, had come to England with her husband the powerful jarl Pallig, adopted Christianity, and offered herself as a hostage for peace with the Danes. Eadric in his disastrous fury had ordered her to be beheaded with the other Danes, though she declared plainly that the shedding of her blood would cost all England dear. And for her part, she faced death with presence of mind; she never grew pale at the prospect, nor did she change expression after death, even when her body was drained of blood, though her husband had been killed before her eyes, and her son, a very likely child, pierced by four lances. So at that time Swein passed through East Anglia into Northumbria, which he subjected to his power without a battle; it was not that in men's minds that inborn fire, so impatient of servitude, had grown cold, it was their own prince Uhtred who gave the first example

primus exemplum defectionis dederit. Illis sub iugum missis, ceteri quoque*ᵃ* omnes populi qui Angliam ab aquilone inhabitant uectigal et obsides dederunt. Mox ad australes regiones ueniens, Oxenefordenses et Wintonienses leges suas adorare coegit; soli Lundonienses, regem legitimum intra menia tutantes, portas occluserunt. Dani contra ferotius assistentes spe gloriae uirtutem alebant; oppidani in mortem pro libertate ruebant, nullam sibi ueniam futuram arbitrantes si regem
3 desererent, quibus ipse uitam suam*ᵇ* commiserat. Ita cum utrimque acriter certaretur, iustior causa uictoriam habuit, ciuibus magna ope conantibus, dum unusquisque sudores suos principi ostentaret*ᶜ* et pro eo pulchrum putaret emori. Hostium pars prostrata, pars in flumine Tamensi necata, quod precipiti furore pontem non expectauissent. Lacero agmine petit Suanus Bathoniam; ibi Ethelmerus, occidentalis regionis comes, cum suis omnibus manus ei dedit. Nec adhuc flecterentur Lundonienses, tota iam Anglia in clientelam illius inclinata, nisi Egelredus presentia eos destitueret sua; quippe homo inertiae deditus et formidine meritorum nullum sibi fidelem metiens bellique et obsidionis necessitatem subterfugiens, illos fuga sua reliquit in medio.
4 Quocirca rebus extremis medentes compatriotarum exemplo se dedidere: laudandi prorsus uiri, et quos Mars ipse collata non sperneret hasta,[1] si ducem habuissent; cuius dum uel sola umbra protegerentur, totius pugnae aleam, ipsam etiam obsidionem non paucis mensibus luserant. Ille interea,*ᵈ* naturalis desidiae conscientiam excitans, ab urbe profugit, cumque clandestinis itineribus Hamtunam uenisset, inde Wehtam enauigauit.

Ibi abbates et episcopos, qui nec in tali necessitate dominum suum
5 deserendum putarent, in hanc conuenit sententiam. Viderent quam in angusto res essent suae et suorum. Se perfidia ducum auito extorrem solio et opis egentem alienae, in cuius manu aliorum solebat salus pendere, quondam monarcham et potentem, modo miserum et exulem; dolendam sibi hanc*ᵉ* commutationem, quia facilius toleres*ᶠ*

ᵃ ceterique *Tt* *ᵇ* om. *A* *ᶜ* *Tt;* ostentare *ACB* *ᵈ* interim *Tt*
ᵉ om. *A* *ᶠ* tolerasset *Tt* ('in litura' *Mynors*)

[1] Cf. Statius, *Theb.* ix. 87–8.

of surrender. After they had passed under the yoke, all the other peoples likewise who dwell in northern England handed over tribute and hostages. Next he proceeded to the southern provinces, and forced the people of Oxford and Winchester to bow before his sway; but the Londoners, who had their lawful king safe inside their walls, shut their gates. The Danes, attacking furiously, raised their spirits high with the hope of glory; the townsmen charged to their deaths in the cause of freedom, thinking that they to whom the king had himself entrusted his life would never be forgiven if they were to desert him. Thus, after fierce fighting on both sides, the just cause won the day, for the citizens put all they had into the attempt, each man showing his mettle before the eyes of his prince and thinking that to die in his cause was a noble death. Of the enemy some were laid low, some drowned in the river Thames, because in their mad haste they had not waited for a bridge. Swein with the ragged remnant of his army made for Bath, where Æthelmær, ealdorman of the western region, with all his men submitted to him. The men of London still would not have yielded, although by now the whole of England had gone over to his allegiance, had not Æthelred deprived them of his presence; for he was a man abandoned to sloth and one who, afraid of the treatment he deserved, reckoned that no one could be trusted. So he evaded the necessities of battle and siege, took to his heels, and left them in the lurch; whereupon, as the only remedy for their desperate state, they followed the example of their fellow-countrymen and surrendered, though they were admirable men to be sure, 'whom Mars himself in melée would not spurn',[1] had they had a leader; for while they had even the shadow of one to protect them, they had played the whole hazardous game of battle, and even of actual siege, for many months. Æthelred meanwhile, reviving his reputation for innate cowardice, escaped from the city, and having made his way in secret to Southampton took ship for the Isle of Wight.

There he addressed the abbots and bishops who even in such a crisis had thought it their duty not to desert their lord, to the following effect. They must consider in what a tight place he and his followers now found themselves. The treachery of his nobles had driven him from his ancestral throne, and he on whose power other men's wellbeing used at one time to depend now needed the help of others; once a ruler independent and powerful, he was now an object of pity and an exile, and had good reason to lament this change, for never to have had any resources is a lighter burden than to have had them and lost

opes non habuisse quam habitas amisisse, pudendam Anglis eo magis, quod deserti ducis exemplum processurum sit in orbem terrarum. Illos amore sui sine sumptibus uoluntariam subeuntes fugam, domos et facultates suas predonibus exposuisse; in arto esse uictum omnibus, uestitum deesse pluribus; probare se quidem fidem illorum, sed non reperire salutem; adeo iam subiugata terra obseruari litora ut nusquam
6 sine periculo sit exitus. Quapropter consulerent in medium quid censerent faciendum. Si maneant, cauendum plus a ciuibus quam ab hostibus; forsan enim crucibus suis noui domini gratiam mercarentur, et certe occidi ab hoste titulatur*a* fortunae, prodi a ciue addicitur ignauiae. Si ad exteras gentes fugiant, gloriae fore dispendium; si ad notas, metuendum ne cum fortuna colorent*b* animum; plerosque enim probos et illustres uiros hac occasione cesos. Experiendam tamen sortem et temptandum pectus Ricardi Normannorum ducis, qui si sororem et nepotes non ingrato animo susceperit, se quoque
7 non aspernanter protecturum. 'Vadabitur enim' inquit 'michi meam salutem coniugi et liberis impensus fauor. Quod si ille aduersum pedem contulerit, non deerit michi animus plane, non deerit,*c* quin malim hic gloriose occumbere quam illic ignominiose uiuere. Quocirca hoc interim mense Augusto, dum clementior aura componit pelagus, Emma ad fratrem nauiget, communia pignora apud eum depositura; sint*d* comites eorum episcopus de Dunelmo et abbas de Burgo. Ego hic usque ad Natale Domini manebo, si bona nuntiauerint subsecuturus continuo.'

178. Soluto conuentu paretur ab omnibus; nauigant illi Normanniam, ipse serenae famae auidus interim resident. Mox a transmarinis nuntiatum partibus Ricardum suscepisse sororem magna alacritate, regem quoque inuitare ut suos dignetur lares. Ita Egelredus, mense Ianuario Normanniam ueniens, miserias suas sedulitate hospitis consolatus est. Erat ille Ricardus filius Ricardi primi, qui felicitate et probitate sua patrem aequarit, certe in Dei rebus maior. Cenobium

---

a titulantur *A Tt*   *b* *ACeBc'mg.;* colerent *TtCsBk;* tolerent *Bc*   *c* non deerit *om.*
d sunt *Tt*

them. And it was a change that would bring disgrace on England; all the more so in that to desert one's lord set a bad example that would spread worldwide. His hearers out of love of him had submitted to a voluntary exile with no financial support, and by so doing had exposed their homes and property to robbers; all of them were short of food and many needed clothing. For his own part, he was grateful for their loyalty, but could find no way of ensuring their safety; so completely was the land now occupied and the coast watched, that no way out was free from danger. They must therefore consider in common what 6 they thought the best course. If they were to stay where they were, they would be in greater danger from their fellow-citizens than from the enemy, for it might be that their own shameful deaths might be used to buy the favour of a new lord; and in any case, to be killed by an enemy is labelled misfortune while to be betrayed by one's fellows is ascribed to cowardice. If they were to take refuge with foreigners, this would entail a loss of reputation; if with peoples whom they knew, there was a risk that their feelings might change colour with the change of fortune, for many valiant and distinguished men had been killed in such circumstances. All the same, they must try their luck, and sound out Duke Richard of Normandy, for 'if he receives his sister and his nephews in a not unfriendly spirit', said Æthelred, 'he will protect me too without disdain; for kindness shown to my wife 7 and children will give me assurance of my own safety. If however he takes steps against them, I shall not lack the spirit—far from it—to die a glorious death here in preference to a life of shame with him. In the mean time therefore, in this month of August in which milder winds offer a calm sea, let Emma take ship to join her brother and place her young ones in his charge, and let the bishop of Durham and the abbot of Peterborough go with them. I myself will stay here till Christmas, and then if their news is good, will follow them forthwith.'

178. The gathering broke up, and all did as they were told. One party took ship for Normandy, while the king, eager for favourable tidings, stayed for the present where he was. News soon arrived from across the sea: Duke Richard had eagerly welcomed his sister, and invited the king likewise to pay him the compliment of a visit. In the month of January therefore Æthelred crossed over to Normandy, where he was consoled for his misfortunes by his host's assiduity. Duke Richard was the son of Richard I, and in good fortune and integrity the equal of his father; in the things of God he surpassed

Fiscamnense, quod pater inchoauerat, ad summam manum euexit, orationibus et frugalitati adeo intentus ut nullum monachum nullum heremitam desiderares, humilitate cernuus ut lacessentium ceruicositates patientia sibi substerneret. Denique fertur quod noctibus, custodias famulorum fallens, incomitatus ad matutinas monachorum uenire solitus fuerit, genuflexionibus*a* usque ad lucem incumbens. Id presertim apud Fiscamnum exercens, quadam nocte maturius se agebat, cumque inuenisset hostium obseratum, excusso uiolentius pessulo soporem sacristae turbauit. Ille, miratus in tali noctis horrore pulsantis strepitum, surrexit ut uideret tam audacis facti conscium, reperiensque ut uidebatur rusticum plebeio tectum amictu non potuit animo suo imperare ut manibus temperaret, sed uehementi felle commotus crinem inuadit, multos illustri uiro colaphos infringens. Durat ille incredibili patientia nec mutire dignatus. Postero die in capitulo querelam deponit, iraque simulata monachum ad uicum Argentias sibi precepit occurrere, minitans se ulturum in eius peruicatia,*b* quod tota loqueretur Gallia. Die dicta monacho astante et pre metu pene exanimato, rem proceribus exponit, atrocitatem facti per amplificationem exaggerans; conantem reum*c* respondere callidis obiectionibus aliquandiu suspendit. Postremo, ut iocundior esset miserationis materia, ab optimatibus iudicatum clementer absoluit, totumque uicum illum, qui optimi uini ferax esse dicitur, cum appenditiis suis offitio eius addixit, pronuntians monachum esse optimum qui, bene custodiens munus iniunctum, nec percitus ira laxauerit silentium. Post uiginti octo*d* annos ducatus mortis uiam ingrediens, iubet suum corpus*e* sepeliri ad aecclesiae hostium, ubi et pedibus calcantium et stillicidiis ex alto rorantibus esset obnoxium; sed nostro tempore Willemus, illius loci*f* abbas tertius, rem deformem esse permensus longam sustulit inuidiam, et inde leuatum ante maius altare locauit. Habuit fratrem Rotbertum, quem archiepiscopum fecit Rotomagi, in hoc sane non parua macula gloriam aspergens; nam ille immaniter honore abusus multa primo facinora, multa*g* flagitia commisit, sed postea in senium uergens elemosinis largissimis haud dubie quaedam deleuit.

---

a genuflexibus *CB*   *b* One expects peruicatiam *Tt*   *c* eum *TcB*   *d* om. *CsB*
e corpus suum *Tt*   *f* loci illius *A*   *g* primo facinora multa om.

him. The monastery of Fécamp, begun by his father, he brought to completion. He was as devoted to prayer and abstinence as any monk or hermit, and his humility was so lowly that by long suffering he subdued the obstinacy of those who attacked him. It is said, for example, 2 that by night he would give the servants who guarded him the slip, and join the monks all by himself at matins, remaining on his knees till daybreak. This was his practice particularly at Fécamp. There one night he was up rather early and found the door bolted. Driving back the bolt with some violence, he woke the sacrist who, astonished by this racket at the door at such a frightful hour of the night, leapt up to see who was responsible for this outrage. Finding, as he thought, a countryman in the most common clothes, he could not restrain himself from laying hands on him, and in a passion of rage seized the hair of his distinguished visitor and beat him soundly. The duke endured this with incredible patience and uttered not a sound. Next day he laid a 3 complaint in chapter, and with a great show of anger ordered the monk to meet him at the village of Argences, threatening to exact for the man's obstinacy a revenge that would be the talk of all Gaul. On the appointed day, with the monk standing there almost dead with fear, he recounted the story to his nobles, artfully exaggerating the wickedness of it, and when the accused attempted to answer, kept him in suspense for some time with ingenious objections. At length, to increase the scope and the good humour of his forgiveness, when the nobles had passed judgement on the man, he mercifully pardoned him, and assigned to his office the whole of that village (which is said to produce an excellent wine) with all its appurtenances, declaring that it was an excellent monk who took such care of the office entrusted to him, and even when roused to anger did not break his vow of silence. After twenty-eight years in the dukedom he trod the path of death, 4 leaving orders that his body should be buried near the door of the church, where it would be exposed to the feet of passers-by and to the rain that fell from above; but in our own day William, third abbot of that house, feeling that there was something wrong in this, ended the prolonged neglect by raising the body from where it was and placing it before the high altar. He had a brother, Robert, whom he made archbishop of Rouen, thereby inflicting no small stain on his own reputation; for Robert made a monstrous misuse of his promotion and at first committed many outrages and many crimes. Later, however, when he approached old age, he undoubtedly removed some of these from his record by very liberal almsgiving.

5 Post Ricardum filius eiusdem nominis principatum sortitus uixit anno uix uno. Opinio certe incerta uagatur quod coniuentia fratris Rotberti, quem Ricardus secundus ex Iuditha,*a* filia comitis Britonum Conani, susceperat, uim iuueni uenefica consciuerit: cuius rei gemens conscientiam Ierosolimam post septem annos comitatus abierit, magnae laudis causam tunc temporis adorsus, ut iter motibus*b* suspectum barbaricis, ritibus diuersum Saracenicis, cum paucis inuaderet. Pertendit tamen, nec abstitit, totam uiam salubriter emensus, multoque auro introitum mercatus illud Christianorum decus, sepulchrum dico 6 Dominicum, nudipes et lacrimans ueneratus est. Hoc labore apud Deum, ut credimus, federata gratia, domumque reuertens, apud Niceam urbem Bithiniae dies impleuit, ueneno ut fertur interceptus, auctore ministro Radulfo cognomento Mowino, qui scelus illud spe ducatus animo suo extorserit. Sed Normanniam regressus re cognita ab omnibus quasi monstrum exsufflatus, in exilium perpetuum discessit. Successit Rotberto filius Willelmus puerulus, de quo in consequentibus dicturus[1] nunc quod instat*c* repetam.

179. Suanus interea modo quo diximus[2] inuasam Angliam repinis et cedibus urgebat; prouintialium substantiae prius abrasae, mox proscriptiones factae. Hesitabatur totis urbibus quid fieret: si pararetur rebellio assertorem non haberent, si eligeretur subiectio placido rectore carerent. Ita priuatae et publicae opes ad naues cum obsidibus deportabantur, quod non esset ille dominus*d* legitimus sed tirannus atrocissimus. Sed non diu propitia diuinitas in tanta miseria siuit fluctuare Angliam, siquidem peruasor continuo ad Purificationem sanctae Mariae, ambiguum qua morte, uitam effudit. Dicitur quod terram sancti Edmundi depopulanti martir idem per uisum apparuerit, leniterque de miseria conuentum suorum insolentiusque respondentem in capite perculerit; quo dolore tactum in proximo, ut predictum*e* est, 2 obisse. Dani Cnutonem filium Suani in regem eligunt. Angli contra, naturalem dominum cariorem sibi pronuntiantes, si regalius se quam

a inclita *Tt*   *b* moribus *Tt*^v   *c* distat *Tt*   *d* dominus ille *Tt*
e dictum *Tt*

[1] cc. 228 seq.
[2] cc. 176–7.

After Richard, his son of the same name inherited the dukedom, but 5 lived for barely one year. A very doubtful story is in currency that with the connivance of his brother Robert, son of Richard II by Judith, daughter of Conan count of the Bretons, a violent death was contrived for the young man by a poisoner, and that it was repentance for his complicity in this that made Robert go to Jerusalem after seven years in the dukedom. He was attempting an enterprise which at that time deserved high praise, to undertake with a few companions a journey made so risky by the movements of the barbarians and so strange by the customs of the Saracens. But he persevered and did not flinch, completing the whole passage successfully, and having purchased the right of entry with a large sum in gold, he worshipped barefoot and weeping at that glory of Christendom, the Holy Sepulchre. By this 6 effort, as I believe, he made his peace with God, and ended his days on the way home at the city of Nicaea in Bithynia, being carried off (it is said) by poison. The man responsible for this was his servant Ralph, surnamed Mowin, who steeled himself to commit the crime in hopes of the dukedom; but on his return to Normandy the facts became known, and he was universally rejected as a monster and departed into lifelong exile. Robert was succeeded by his son William, then a small child, of whom I will tell in the sequel;[1] but now I shall resume my story.

179. Swein meanwhile, having invaded England in the way I have described,[2] oppressed it with rapine and slaughter; first the people there had their property seized, then their persons were proscribed. Whole cities were in suspense, wondering what would happen; if they prepared to rebel, they would have no champion, and if they chose submission, a benign ruler would not be available. Thus private and public wealth was carried down to the ships, and hostages with it, because Swein was no lawful lord but a most atrocious tyrant. However, the divine Mercy did not long leave England tossing in this sea of misery, for the invader soon met his end on the Purification of St Mary, by what form of death is disputed. It is said that while he was ravaging the lands of St Edmund, the martyr himself appeared to him in a vision and complained mildly about the miseries of his community; and when he returned an insolent reply, the saint struck him on the head a blow from the pain of which he shortly afterwards died, as I have said. The Danes chose Swein's son Cnut 2 as king; the English on the other hand, declaring that they preferred

consueuerat ageret, e Normannia Egelredum accersiunt.[a] Ille primo mittit Eduardum filium, qui fidem principum, fauorem uulgi, presens specularetur; qui ubi omnium uota[b] in bonam partem uidit conuenientia, securus pro patre reuertitur. Ita rex regressus et laetis plausibus Anglorum delinitus, ut familiarem desidiam excussisse uideretur, maturauit contra Cnutonem exercitum colligere, qui tunc temporis in Lindesia, ubi eum genitor cum ratibus et obsidibus dimiserat, tirones et equos exigebat, ut pariter coactis uiribus in imparatos se
3 effunderet, grauiter, ut ipse dictitauit,[c] in desertores ulturus. Sed dolo qualem ipse machinabatur preuentus terga ostendit; tunc egre saluatus, et in altum cum reliquiis prouectus, ab oriente usque in austrum mari Britanniae circuito, ad Sandwic appulit. Ibi, humano et diuino iure contempto, obsides quos habebat, magnae nobilitatis et elegantiae pueros, naribus et auribus truncos, quosdam etiam euirauit; sic in insontes grassatus, et magnum quid egisse gloriatus, patriam petiit.

Eodem anno fluctus marinus, quem[d] Greci euripum, nos ledonem uocamus, mirum in modum excreuit, quantum nulla hominum memoria potest attingere, ita ut uillas ultra[e] multa miliaria summergeret et habitatores interceptos necaret.

4 Sequenti[f] magnum concilium congregatum est apud Oxenefordum Danorum et Anglorum, ubi rex nobilissimos Danorum, Sigeferdum et Morcardum, interfici iussit, delatione proditoris Edrici perfidiae apud se insimulatos. Is illos fauorabilibus[g] assentationibus deceptos in triclinium pellexit, largiterque potatos satellitibus ad hoc preparatis anima exuit; causa cedis ferebatur quod in bona eorum inhiauerat. Clientuli eorum, necem dominorum uindicare conantes, armis repulsi et in turrim aecclesiae sanctae Frideswidae coacti; unde dum eici nequirent, incendio conflagrati. Sed mox, regis penitentia eliminata spurcitia, sacrarium reparatum; legi ego scriptum,[1] quod in archiuo
5 eiusdem aecclesiae continetur index facti. Vxor Sigeferdi Malmesberiam in captionem est[h] abducta, spectabilis nobilitatis femina;

---

[a] accersunt *Ce (but cf. GP p. 216* accersiente)   [b] *om.* B   [c] dictitabat *TtA*   [d] quam *B*   [e] *om.* B   [f] *CsBk add the much-needed* anno   [g] fauoralibus *TtCs*   [h] *om. Tt*

---

[1] Sawyer 909.

their natural lord, if he were to behave in a more kingly manner than had been his custom, summoned Æthelred from Normandy. He first sent his son Edward to investigate on the spot the loyalty of the nobles and the feeling among the common people; and when he found that the wishes of all coincided in favour, he went back with no misgivings to fetch his father. So the king returned and, flattered by the warmth of his welcome from the English, hastened to collect an army against Cnut, in order to give the impression of having shaken off his customary indecision. Cnut was at that time in Lindsey, where his father had left him with ships and hostages; he was levying recruits and horses, in order, once he had gathered his forces, to hurl them jointly at an enemy who was still unprepared and to teach the deserters, as he himself put it, a severe lesson. He was, however, forestalled by a stratagem of the sort he was planning himself, and took to his heels; then, having escaped with difficulty, he put out to sea with what he had left, and after sailing round the British sea from east to south, landed at Sandwich. There, in defiance of law human and divine, he took the hostages whom he had with him, boys of high birth and elegant upbringing, cut off their ears and noses, and even castrated some of them. After this outrageous attack on the innocent, boasting as though he had done some great exploit, he returned to his native land.

In the same year a tidal wave, of the sort which the Greeks call *euripus* and we *ledo*, grew to an astonishing size such as the memory of man cannot parallel, so as to submerge villages many miles inland and overwhelm and drown their inhabitants.

In the following year a great council of both Danes and English gathered at Oxford, at which the king ordered the execution of two very highborn Danes, Sigeferth and Morcar, who had been accused of high treason on information supplied by the traitor Eadric. The king lured them to his dinner-table with flattering messages and there, having plied them with wine, had them killed by servants posted for the purpose; the cause of the murder was said to be greed for their estates. Their supporters, trying to avenge their lords' deaths, were defeated and driven into the tower of St Frideswide's church, where, since they could not be driven out, they were burnt to death. Later the king repented, the filth was cleared away and the shrine restored. I have read an account[1] which is contained in the archives of the church as a record of what happened. Sigeferth's wife, a lady of distinguished lineage, was removed to imprisonment at Malmesbury. This caused

quapropter Edmundus regis filius, dissimulata intentione in partes illas iter arripiens, uisam concupiuit, concupitae communionem habuit, sane patris eludens conscientiam,*a* qui domesticis ut alienis esset ridiculo. Erat iste Edmundus non ex Emma natus sed ex quadam alia, quam fama obscura recondit.[1] Preter illud*b* integer ⟨et⟩*c* in ceteris predicandae indolis iuuenis, magni roboris et animo et corpore, et propter hoc ab Anglis Ireneside, id est Ferreum latus, nuncupatus, qui patris ignauiam, matris ignobilitatem uirtute sua probe premeret, si Parcae parcere nossent.*d*[2] Nec mora, nuptae consilio comitatum Sigeferdi, qui apud Northanimbros amplissimus erat, a patre petitum nec impetratum, suapte industria uendicauit, hominibus eiusdem prouintiae in obsequium eius facile cedentibus.

180. Eadem aestate Cnuto, compositis rebus in Danemarkia, federata cum finitimis regibus amicitia, uenit Angliam, eo animo ut aut uincendum aut moriendum sibi proponeret. Itaque a Sandwico Cantiam, inde in Westsaxoniam progrediens, omnia cedibus incendiisque fedabat, rege apud Cosham morbo decumbente. Temptauit quidem Edmundus occurrere, sed ab Edrico prepeditus copias interim tuto loco continuit. At Edricus non ultra dissimulandum ratus, quin artes suas aperta*e* fronte nudaret, ad Cnutonem cum quadraginta nauibus defecit; omnis quoque Westsaxonia datis obsidibus et armis idem fecit. Mertii uero sepenumero congregati se ad resistendum offerebant: ueniret modo*f* rex et quo progrediendum esset preciperet, duceret secum proceres Lundoniae, paratos esse sanguinem suum patriae impendere. Ille solitus salutem suam muris committere, non in hostem excurrere,*g* Lundoniae degebat, propter proditores (ut aiebat) nusquam procedens. Alter interea partibus suis urbes et uicos applicare, nullo tempore feriari, noctibus consultare, diebus pugnare. Edmundus, diu deliberato consilio, in tanta rerum angustia optimum factu*h* arbitratus si urbes quae defecerant pugnando reciperet, in eundem sensum Vhtredum quendam, Transhumbranum comitem, adduxit; ceteras enim, quae adhuc dubio fauore pendebant, confirmandas putabant si de rebellantibus graues penas sumerent.

a om. *Tt*   *b* istud *TtA*   *c* Supplied by Mynors   *d* nosset *TtAl*^{*a.c.*}*Cs*   *e* apta *A*   *f* mox *Tt*   *g* occurrere *Tt*   *h* factum *Tt*

---

[1] Cf. Virgil, *Aen.* v. 302.
[2] Cf. Virgil, *Georg.* iv. 489.

the king's son Edmund, concealing his intentions, to pay a hasty visit to that part of the world; he saw her, desired her, and got what he desired, having of course avoided telling his father, who was taken no more seriously by his own family than by outsiders. This Edmund's mother was not Emma but some other woman, 'whom fame in darkness hides'.[1] Apart from this, he was in other respects an irreproachable young man of notable gifts, of great strength of body and mind, and therefore called by the English 'Ironside'. His father's sloth and his mother's low birth he would honourably have put in the shade by his own prowess, 'had Fate but learnt to spare'.[2] Nor was it long before, on his wife's advice, he asked his father for Sigeferth's earldom, which was the largest in Northumbria, and when he did not get it, he seized it by his own efforts, and had no difficulty in persuading the men of the province to accept him.

180. In that same summer Cnut, having settled affairs in Denmark and made treaties of friendship with the neighbouring kings, came to England with the intention of pursuing either victory or death. From Sandwich therefore he proceeded into Kent and thence into Wessex, defiling everything with fire and slaughter, while the king lay sick at Cosham. Edmund did indeed attempt to stand in his way, but was hampered by Eadric, and kept his forces back for the time being in a safe place. Eadric, however, thinking there was no further need for concealment and that he might as well expose his tricks openly, deserted to Cnut with forty ships, and the whole of Wessex did the same, handing over hostages and weapons. But the Mercians, after frequent meetings, offered their services for the resistance: provided only that the king would come, bringing with him the chief men of London, and tell them in which direction they ought to proceed, they were ready, they said, to shed their blood for their country. The king, whose habit it was to entrust his safety to walls and not to sally forth against the enemy, stayed on in London, and never issued out in any direction for fear, he said, of treachery. Cnut in the mean time was adding cities and towns to his own share, never at rest for a moment, taking counsel by night and fighting by day. Edmund after long deliberation decided that in such an emergency the best he could do was to recover by force of arms the cities which had deserted, and he brought over to the same opinion a certain Uhtred, an earl from across the Humber; for the other cities, whose allegiance was still doubtful, would, they thought, be confirmed in their loyalty if heavy penalties were exacted from those who rebelled.

3 Sed Cnuto, non minori preditus astutia, simili eos ingenio circumuenit; nam commendatis Westsaxonibus et Mertiorum parte quam subiecerat ducibus suis, ipse in Northanimbros profectus depopulatione locorum Vhtredum ad sua defensanda redire coegit. Itaque,[a] licet se dedidisset,[b] barbarica leuitate iussus est iugulari. Comitatus eius datus Iritio, quem postea, aequas sibi partes uendicantem, Cnuto ab Anglia expulit. Ita subiectis omnibus Edmundum, per semetra fugitantem, non prius persequi destitit quam Lundoniam ad patrem peruenisse cognosceret. Tunc usque post Pascha quieuit, ut cum omnibus copiis urbem adoriretur. Sed preuenit conatum eius mors Egelredi; nam in[c] initio Quadragesimae die sancti Gregorii animam laboribus et miseriis[d] natam efflauit. Iacet apud Sanctum Paulum Lundoniae.

4 Oppidani Edmundum in regem conclamant. Ipse mox congregato exercitu apud Pennam iuxta[e] Gilingeham Danos fugauit diebus Rogationum. Post festum sancti Iohannis ad Sceorstanum eisdem congressus aequis manibus discessit, Anglis suis initium fugae fatientibus auctore Edrico, qui in parte aduersariorum stans et gladium in manu tenens, quem in pugna quodam rustico impigre ceso cruentarat, 'Fugite,' inquit, 'miseri, fugite![f] Ecce rex uester hoc ense occisus est!' Fugissent continuo Angli, nisi rex cognita re in editum quendam collem procederet, ablata galea caput suum commilitonibus ostentans.[g] Tunc quantis poterat uiribus hastile ferreum intorquens[h] in Edricum misit; sed ab illo preuisum et uitatum in militem prope stantem pec-
5 cauit,[i] adeo ut alterum quoque affigeret. Nox prelium diremit, atiebus quasi ex coniuentia discedentibus, Anglis tamen uictoriam pene sperantibus; quo facto Westsaxonum conuersi animi dominum legitimum[j] cognouerunt. Ipse Lundoniam contendit, ut bene meritos ciues liberaret, quos pars hostium statim post discessum suum[k] incluserat; fossa etiam urbem, qua fluuio Tamensi non alluitur, foris totam cinxerat, multaque uulnera fecerat et acceperat. Itaque audito regis aduentu fugam per prona inuadunt; subsecutus eos e uestigio, et transito uado quod Brentford dicitur, uictoriosa strage deleuit. Reliqua

[a] *One expects* isque *Tt*   [b] dedisset *CsB*   [c] om. *ACeBc*   [d] et miseriis *om. Tt*
[e] et *CB (but see ASC (DE) s.a. 1016)*   [f] om. *Tt*   [g] ostendans *Al*[a.c.],
-dens *Aap*   [h] om. *Tt*   [i] deliquit *Tt*   [j] om. *A*   [k] om. *Tt*

But Cnut, whose cunning was no less than theirs, outwitted them with a similar trick: entrusting to his nobles Wessex and that part of Mercia which he had subdued, he himself set off for Northumbria, and by his ravaging of the country forced Uhtred to return to defend his own territory. Thus Uhtred, although he had surrendered, was sentenced with typical barbarian lack of principle to have his throat cut, and his earldom was given to Eric, who later on, when he demanded parity for himself, was expelled from England by Cnut. Having thus got all into his power, he pursued Edmund, who was making his escape on by-roads, and did not give up until he heard that he had reached London and joined his father. He then rested until after Easter, intending to attack the city with all his forces. But his attempt was forestalled by Æthelred's death; for at the beginning of Lent on St Gregory's day he departed this life, a life made for trouble and misery, and lies buried in St Paul's in London.

The citizens chose Edmund as king by acclamation, and he soon got together an army and at Rogationtide put the Danes to flight at Penselwood near Gillingham. After St John's day he joined battle with them again at Sherston, but it was broken off with the two sides equal, his English troops taking the first steps towards retreat under the influence of Eadric, who stood on the enemy's side brandishing a sword which he had blooded in the battle by the bold slaughter of some country fellow, and shouting: 'Flee, flee, poor wretches! Look, this is the sword which has killed your king!' And the English would have fled immediately, had not the king heard of this and made for a prominent hill, where he took off his helmet and displayed his bare head to his fellow-soldiers. He then brandished an iron spear with all the force he could muster and hurled it at Eadric; but he saw it coming and dodged it, and it went astray and pierced the soldier who was standing next to him with such violence that it transfixed a second man as well. Night broke off the battle, the two sides separating as though by prior agreement, but the English had good hope of victory, as a result of which the West Saxons changed their minds and recognized their lawful lord. Edmund himself hastened to London in order to free the citizens to whom he owed so much; for immediately after his departure part of the enemy had invested the city, and had also surrounded with a moat on the outside all that part of it which is not washed by the Thames, causing and receiving many casualties. When therefore they heard of the king's approach, they retreated at top speed, and he followed close behind them, crossed at the ford called Brentford, and destroyed them with heavy loss. The

multitudo, quae cum Cnutone remanserat, Edmundo aliquantum feriato et partes suas componente, Lundoniam iterum terra flumineque obsidet; sed ab oppidanis magnanimiter pugnantibus repulsa, iram in collimitaneam Mertiam effundit,*a* uicos et uillas rapinis incendiis cedi-
6 busque*b* depopulans. Opima preda ad naues conuecta quas in amne Medeguaia congregauerat; fluuius ille Rofensem urbem preterfluens, uiolentus et rapaci gurgite minax, menia pulchra lauat.[1] Inde quoque rege pugnante fugata, preoccupatoque uado quod superius nominaui Brentford, insigni cede profligata. Conantem ulterius tendere Edmundum, ut reliquias predonum persequeretur ad internitionem, uafer ille et pessimus Edricus reuocauit, ficto iam dudum animo in gratiam reuersus; consilio enim Cnutonis cum Edmundo erat, ut eius medita-
7 tiones renuntiaret. Vltimus ille dies Danis profecto fuisset, si perseuerandum rex putasset; sed preuentus, ut dixi, susurro proditoris, qui hostes nichil ultra ausuros affirmaret, maturum sibi exitium et Angliae toti parauit. Namque illi data uia fugiendi iterum in unum coaluere, Orientales Anglos bello infestantes; ipsum quoque regem suppetias ferentem apud Assandunam cedere coegerunt. Auspitium fugae fuit ille ex consulto quem totiens nominare pudet. Pauci qui gloriae suae non immemores et alterutros excitantes cuneum fecerant, ad unum interempti. Ibi Cnuto regnum expugnauit, ibi omne decus Angliae occubuit, ibi flos patriae totus emarcuit; inter quos Vlkillus Estanglorum comes, perpetuam iam famam meritus tempore Suani, quando primus omnium piratas adorsus spem dedit posse illos superari, et precipui tunc uiri, abbates et episcopi.
8 Edmundus inde pene solus pedem*c* referens Gloecestram uenit, ut ibi recollectis uiribus hostes recenti uictoria otiosos, sicut putabat, aggrederetur; nec Cnutoni audatia defuit quin fugientem insequeretur. Ita cum infestis signis constitissent, Edmundus singularem pugnam petiit, ne duo homunculi propter ambitionem regnandi tot subiectorum sanguine culparentur, cum possent sine dispendio

---

a effudit *TtBk* *b* rebusque *CsB* *c* pedes *(om. referens) Tt*

[1] Cf. Prudentius, *Perist.* iii. 189–90.

remainder of the host that had stayed with Cnut, while Edmund was taking a short break and regrouping his forces, again laid siege to London by land and river, but being driven off by the citizens, who fought heroically, they vented their resentment on neighbouring Mercia, ravaging villages and towns with rapine, fire, and slaughter. Rich booty was conveyed to the ships, which had gathered in the river 6 Medway, the stream which with great force and dangerous whirlpools flows past the city of Rochester and 'laves its lovely walls'.[1] From there too they were driven when the king joined battle, for, having previously seized the ford at Brentford of which I have already spoken, he crushed them with heavy casualties. When, however, Edmund attempted to go further, in order to pursue what was left of the pirates until he had destroyed them, he was recalled by that cunning scoundrel Eadric, who had long since returned to favour by concealing his true sentiments; it was Cnut's plan that he should stay with Edmund, so that he could report all the king's intentions. That would have been absolutely the 7 Danes' last day, had the king thought it right to persevere; but being forestalled, as I have said, by a hint from the traitor, who assured him that the enemy would not dare go any further, he cleared the way for an early disaster for himself and all England. The Danes, given a way of escape, again reunited and harassed the East Angles in battle, and obliged the king himself as well, who was coming to their assistance, to yield at *Assandun*. Here again, the person I am ashamed to mention so often deliberately gave the first example of flight. The few who did not forget their reputation, and with mutual encouragement had adopted a battle-formation, were killed to a man. On that field Cnut destroyed a kingdom, there England's glory fell, there the whole flower of our country withered; among them Ulfcytel, ealdorman of the East Anglians, who had already earned a lasting reputation in Swein's time when, as the first who ever attacked the pirates, he gave men hope that they might be overcome, and with him the leading men of the time, abbots and bishops.

Edmund, almost the only one to get away, came to Gloucester, in 8 hopes of there pulling his forces together and attacking the enemy, who would, he supposed, be off their guard after their recent victory. Nor did Cnut lack the courage to pursue him in his retreat, and the two sides took their stand in line of battle. Edmund then asked for single combat, rather than have two mortal men moved by ambition to be king carry the guilt for the blood of so many of their subjects, when it was possible to put fortune to the test without the loss of any

fidelium suorum^a fortunam experiri; magnam utrilibet laudem futuram,^b qui suo potissimum periculo tantum regnum nancisceretur. Haec cum Cnutoni renuntiarentur, abnuit prorsus, pronuntians animo se quidem excellere, sed contra tam ingentis molis hominem corpusculo diffidere; uerum quia ambo non indebite regnum efflagitent quod patres amborum tenuerint, conuenire prudentiae ut deposlitis animositatibus Angliam partiantur. Susceptum est hoc dictum ab utroque exercitu magnoque^c assensu firmatum, quod et aequitati conquadraret, et mortalium paci tot miseriis defatigatorum placide consuleret. Ita Edmundus unanimi clamore omnium superatus concordiae indulsit, fedusque cum Cnutone percussit, sibi Westsaxoniam, illi concedens Mertiam. Nec multo post, in festo sancti Andreae ambiguum quo casu extinctus, Glastoniae iuxta Edgarum auum suum sepultus est. Fama Edricum infamat, quod fauore alterius mortem ei per ministros porrexerit:^d cubicularios regis fuisse duos, quibus omnem uitam suam commiserat, quos pollicitationibus illectos et primo immanitatem flagitii exhorrentes, breui complices suos effecisse; eius consilio ferreum uncum ad naturae requisita sedenti in locis posterioribus adegisse.

10 'Frater eius ex matre Edwius, non aspernandae probitatis adolescens, per proditorem Edricum Anglia iubente Cnutone cessit; diu^f terris iactatus et alto,¹ angore animi (ut fit) corpus infectus, dum furtiuo reditu apud Anglos delitescit, defungitur et apud Tauistokium tumulatur.^e Filii eius Edwius et Eduardus, missi ad regem Sweuorum ut perimerentur, sed, miseratione eius conseruati, Hunorum regem petierunt; ubi dum benigne aliquo tempore habiti essent, maior diem obiit, minor Agatham reginae sororem in matrimonium accepit. Fratres ex Emma, Elfredus et Eduardus, toto tempore quo Cnuto uixit in 11 Normannia tutas fouere latebras. De illorum in patriam^g restitutione Ricardum auunculum nichil egisse comperimus, quin et sororem suam Emmam hosti et inuasori nuptum collocauit: ignores maiore illius^h dedecore qui dederit, an feminae quae consenseritⁱ ut thalamo illius caleret qui uirum infestauerit, filios effugauerit. Porro Rotbertus,

^a om. B   ^b Tt repeats experiri here   ^c magno Al, et magno Aa   ^d porrexit TtBk; perrexerit A   ^{e-e} om. Tt   ^f diuque A   ^g patria A
^h om. ABc   ⁱ senserit B

¹ Virgil, Aen. i. 3.

of their faithful dependants; great credit would be due to whichever of them should acquire so great a kingdom at his own private risk and no one else's. When this was reported to Cnut, he rejected it out of hand, declaring that in spirit he was a match for anyone, but did not trust his tiny frame if matched against a man of such enormous might. Surely, since both not without reason were demanding a kingdom which had been held by the parents of both, it would be sensible to lay aside their enmity and divide England between them. This remark was taken up by both armies and ratified with massive agreement, as both consonant with justice and a benign step towards peace among mortals who were already exhausted by so much misery. Edmund, overwhelmed by the unanimous and universal shouts of approval, gave peace its chance, and made a treaty with Cnut which assigned himself Wessex, and the other Mercia. Not long afterwards, on St Andrew's day, he met his end (by what accident, is an open question), and was buried at Glastonbury near Edgar his grandfather. Rumour implicates Eadric as having, in support of Cnut, contrived his death by means of servants. There were, it was said, two of the king's chamberlains to whom he had entrusted his entire life. Eadric won them over with promises, and though at first they were horrified at such a monstrous crime, he soon made them his accomplices, and, as he had planned, when the king took his seat for the requirements of nature, they drove an iron hook into his hinder parts.

Eadwig, his brother by the same mother, a youth who deserved respect for his high character, was driven out of England by the traitor Eadric on Cnut's orders; long 'tossed on land and sea',[1] he suffered in body, as sometimes happens, from unhappiness of mind, returned surreptitiously to England, died while in hiding, and was buried at Tavistock. Edmund's sons Eadwig and Edward were despatched to the king of the Swedes to be put to death; but he took pity on them and spared their lives, and they took refuge with the king of the Huns. There they were for some time well treated; then the elder died, and the younger married Agatha, the queen's sister. His brothers by Emma, Alfred and Edward, remained safely in hiding in Normandy, as long as Cnut lived. For their restoration to their own country their uncle Richard took, I find, no steps; in fact, he married his sister Emma to the enemy and the invader, and you would not know which incurred the greater disgrace, the man who gave her away or the woman who agreed to share the bed of one who had harassed her husband and exiled her sons. Robert, indeed, of whose journey to

quem superius diximus[1] Ierosolimam iuisse, multotiens congregatis nauibus et impositis militibus profectionem parauit, subinde iactitans se pronepotes suos coronaturum; et proculdubio fidem dictis explesset, nisi quia, ut a maioribus accepimus, semper ei uentus aduersabatur contrarius, per occultum scilicet Dei iuditium, in cuius uoluntate sunt potestates regnorum omnium. Reliquiae ratium, multo tempore dissolutarum, Rotomagi adhuc nostra aetate uisebantur.

181. Anno[a] incarnationis Dominicae millesimo septimo decimo Cnuto regnare cepit, et uiginti annis regnauit, iniuste quidem regnum ingressus sed magna ciuilitate et fortitudine uitam componens; primis diebus regnum in quattuor partitus,[b] sibi Westsaxones, Edrico Mertios, Turkillo Orientales Anglos, Iritio Northanimbros. Ac primo interfectores Edmundi, qui ultro spe ingentis premii rem detulerant, apud se interim celatos magna frequentia populi produxit in medium, palamque genus insidiarum professos suplitio affecit. Eodemque anno Edricus, quem digne infamare non possum, iussu regis arte qua multos frequenter circumuenerat ipse quoque conuentus,[c] putidum spiritum
2 transmisit ad inferos. Nam nescio qua simultate orta,[d] dum asperius colloquerentur,[e] ille fidutia meritorum benefitia regi sua quasi amicabiliter improperans ait: 'Edmundum pro te primo deserui, post etiam ob fidelitatem tui extinxi.' Quo dicto Cnutoni faties immutata iram rubore prodidit, et continuo prolata sententia 'Merito ergo' inquit 'et tu moriere, cum sis lesae maiestatis reus in Deum et in me, qui dominum proprium et fratrem michi federatum occideris. Sanguis tuus super caput tuum, quia os tuum locutum est contra te quod misisti manus in christum Domini.'[2] Mox, ne tumultus fieret, in eodem cubiculo proditor fauces elisus[f] et per fenestram in Tamensem precipitatus perfidiae meritum habuit.
3 Succedente tempore Turkillus et Iritius, ab Anglia captatis occasionibus eliminati, natale solum petierunt; quorum primus, qui incentor necis beati Elfegi fuerat, statim ut Danemarkiae littus attigit

[a] B adds ab [b] partiens Tt [c] circumuentus Bk, as one might expect [d] orati Bk, om. Bc (Bp avoids error) [e] loquerentur Tt [f] elisus fauces Tt

[1] 178. 5.
[2] Cf. 2 Kgs. (2 Sam.) 1: 16.

Jerusalem I have already spoken,[1] many times set an expedition on foot, gathering ships and filling them with soldiers, from time to time boasting that he would crown his great-nephews; and no doubt he would have been as good as his word, except that (as I have heard from my elders) a contrary wind was always against him, no doubt by the hidden purposes of God, whose will controls all kingdoms. The remains of the ships, much damaged by long lapse of time, were still to be seen at Rouen in our own day.

181. In the year of our Lord 1017 Cnut began to reign, and he reigned for twenty years. There was no justice in his succession to the throne, but he arranged his life with great statesmanship and courage. In his early days he divided his kingdom into four: the West Saxons for himself, the Mercians for Eadric, the East Anglians for Thurkil, and the Northumbrians for Eric. Edmund's murderers, who had themselves reported the fact in hopes of a large reward, he first kept for a while at his court in concealment, and then produced them before a large public gathering, and after they had openly admitted the treacherous methods they had used, they were duly executed. In the same year Eadric, to whose infamy I cannot do justice, was by the king's command entrapped in his turn by the same trick that he had frequently used in the past to entrap many others, and his disgusting spirit was transferred to hell. High words had arisen as a result of 2 some dispute or other, and Eadric, emboldened by the services he had rendered, reminded the king as though in a friendly fashion of his deserts: 'First I abandoned Edmund for you,' he said, 'and then also put him to death out of loyalty to you.' At these words Cnut's expression changed; his face flushed with anger, and he delivered sentence forthwith. 'Then you too,' he said, 'will deserve to die, if you are guilty of high treason against God and myself by killing your own lord and a brother who was in alliance with me. Thy blood be upon thy head; for thy mouth hath testified against thee, saying that thou hast lifted up thy hand against the Lord's anointed.'[2] And then, to avoid a public disturbance, the traitor was strangled in that same chamber and thrown out of the window into the Thames, thus paying the due penalty for his perfidy.

As time went on, Thurkil and Eric were turned out by the English, 3 who were watching their opportunity, and returned to their native land; the first of them, who had provoked the murder of St Ælfheah, was eliminated by the nobles as soon as he set foot on the coast of

a ducibus oppressus est. Ita cum omnis Anglia pareret uni, ille ingenti studio Anglos sibi conciliare, aequum illis ius cum Danis suis in consessu*a* in concilio in prelio concedere. Qua de re, ut predixi,[1] uxorem superioris regis e Normannia accersiit, ut, dum consuetae dominae deferrent obsequium, minus Danorum suspirarent*b* imperium; simul eo facto Ricardi allitiens gratiam, ut parum de nepotibus cogitaret, qui alios ex Cnutone se suscepturum speraret. Monasteria per Angliam suis et patris excursionibus partim fedata partim eruta reparauit; loca omnia in quibus pugnauerat, et precipue Assandunam, aecclesiis insigniuit, ministros instituit qui per succidua seculorum uolumina Deo suplicarent pro animabus ibi*c* occisorum. Ad consecrationem illius basilicae et ipse affuit, et optimates Anglorum et Danorum donaria porrexerunt; nunc, ut ferunt, modica est aecclesia presbitero parrochiano delegata. Supra corpus beatissimi Edmundi, quem antiquiores*d* Dani interfecerant,*e* basilicam animositate regia construxit, abbatem et monachos instituit, predia multa et magna contulit; prestat*f* hodieque donorum eius amplitudo integra quod locus ille infra se aspitiat omnia pene Angliae cenobia. Corpus beati Elfegi, apud Sanctum Paulum Lundoniae tumulatum, ipse suis manibus inde leuauit, et ad propria remissum dignis assentationibus ueneratus est. Ita omnia quae ipse et antecessores sui deliquerant corrigere satagens, prioris iniustitiae neuum apud Deum fortassis, apud homines certe abstersit. Wintoniae maxime munificentiae suae magnificentiam ostendit, ubi tanta intulit ut moles metallorum terreat aduenarum animos, splendor gemmarum reuerberet intuentium oculos; Emmae suggestu, quae in talibus thesauros dilapidabat sanctitate prodiga, dum ille in exteris terris dura meditaretur prelia. Nam nescia uirtus eius stare loco,[2] nec contenta Danemarkia quam auito et Anglia quam bellico iure obtinebat, martem in Sweuos transtulit. Sunt illi Danis contermini, pertinatioribus studiis iram Cnutonis emeriti. Sed primo exceptus insidiis multos ex*g* suis*h* amisit; postremo reparatis uiribus insistentes*i* in fugam uertit, reges gentis Vlf et Eiglaf ad deditiones*j*

---

a consensu *A* *b* suspirassent *Tt* *c* om. *B* *d* om. *Tt* *e* interfecerunt *CsB* *f* *ACsBk*; perstat *TtCeBc, GP p. 155* *g* e *Tt* *h* suos *A* *i* resistentes *TtA, perhaps rightly* *j* *Perhaps read* conditiones *(cf. 231. 1, 387. 3)*

---

[1] 180. 11.
[2] Cf. Lucan i. 144–5.

Denmark. Thus all England obeyed a single master, and he took great pains to conciliate the English, allowing them the same rights as his own Danes in order of seating, in council, and in battle. For the same reason, as I have said already,[1] he sent to Normandy for the wife of the former king, in hopes that if his subjects owed allegiance to a mistress with whom they were familiar, they would be less disposed to repine at being ruled by Danes, while at the same time by so doing he courted Duke Richard's favour, who might think less about his nephews if he had the prospect of a further supply begotten by Cnut. Monasteries all over England which had been desecrated or destroyed 4 by his invasions and his father's were restored, and he marked out by building churches every place where he had fought a battle, and particularly *Assandun*, installing clergy who, as succeeding centuries unrolled, would pray to God for the souls of those who had fallen there. At the consecration of that minster he was present in person, and the nobles, both English and Danes, offered gifts; now it is, they say, a modest church, entrusted to a parish priest. Over the body of the most blessed Edmund, who had been killed by earlier Danes, he erected a minster of royal magnificence, installed an abbot and monks, and contributed many and great estates; the generosity of his gifts, which remain intact to this day, ensures that that place can regard almost all the monasteries in England as beneath it. The body of 5 St Ælfheah, buried in St Paul's in London, he lifted with his own hands and transferred back to Canterbury, venerating it with due marks of respect. Thus he did his best to correct all the misdoings of himself and his predecessors, and wiped away the stain of earlier injustice, perhaps before God and certainly in the eyes of men. At Winchester especially he exhibited the munificence of his generosity, where his offerings were such that strangers are alarmed by the masses of precious metal and their eyes dazzled as they look at the flashing gems. This was prompted by Emma, who lavished her treasure on such things with holy prodigality, while her husband was planning hard campaigns in foreign lands; for his was 'the valour that knows not how to stand still',[2] and not content with Denmark which he held by inheritance and England which was his by right of war, he set upon the Swedes. They are neighbours of the Danes, and had roused 6 Cnut's resentment by their obstinate ambitions. At first however he was caught in an ambush and lost many of his troops; but in the end, having recouped his losses, he put his opponents to flight, and drove their kings Ulf and Eilaf to accept terms for peace. The greatest

pacis adduxit; promptissimis ea pugna Anglis, hortante Goduino comite ut pristinae gloriae memores robur suum oculis noui domini assererent: illud fuisse fortunae quod ab eo quondam uicti fuissent, istud^a uirtutis quod illos premerent qui eum uicissent. Incubuere igitur uiribus Angli, et uictoriam consummantes comitatum duci, sibi laudem pararunt. Rediens inde domum, totum regnum Noricorum subegit, effugato rege Olauo; qui posteriori anno, ut animos prouintialium suorum temptaret, cum parua manu in regnum regressus infidos sibi sensit, cum suis cesus.

182. Cnuto quinto decimo anno regni[b] Romam profectus est. Ibi aliquantis diebus commoratus et elemosinis per aecclesias peccata redimens,[c] nauigio Angliam rediit, et mox Scottiam rebellantem regemque Malcolmum expeditione illuc ducta paruo subegit negotio. [d]Veruntamen non inoperosum uidebitur si epistolam, quam Roma digrediens Anglis suis per Liuingum Tauistokiensem abbatem, mox episcopum Cridintunensem misit, apponam ad documentum emendatioris uitae et regalis magnificentiae.

183. 'Cnuto rex totius Angliae et Danemarkiae et Norregiae et partis Swauorum Ailnotho metropolitano et Alfrico Eboracensi omnibusque episcopis et primatibus et toti genti Anglorum, tam nobilibus quam plebeiis, salutem.

'Notifico uobis me nouiter isse Romam, oratum pro redemptione peccaminum meorum et pro salute regnorum quique meo subiacent regimini populorum. Hanc quidem profectionem Deo iam olim deuoueram, sed pro negotiis regni et causis impedientibus huc usque non poteram perficere. Nunc autem ipsi Deo meo omnipotenti ualde humiliter gratias ago, quod[e] concessit in uita mea beatos apostolos Petrum et Paulum et omne sanctuarium quod intra urbem Romam aut extra addiscere potui expetere et secundum desiderium meum presentialiter uenerari et adorare. Et ideo maxime hoc patraui, quia a sapientibus didici sanctum Petrum apostolum magnam potestatem accepisse a Domino ligandi et soluendi clauigerumque esse caelestis regni; et ideo spetialiter eius patrocinium apud Deum expetere ualde

---

^a illud *A*   ^b *ABc add* sui *(cf. e.g. 150C. 7)*   ^c *Aac adds* erogatis, *and* per aecclesias *certainly seems to need support*   ^{d-d} *(p. 330) om. Tt. The letter (Counc. I. i. 65) is also given by JW s.a. 1031*   ^e *Aa adds* michi *(qui mihi JW)*

readiness in this battle was shown by the English, who were encouraged by Earl Godwine to remember their former glory and display their courage before the eyes of their new lord: they owed it to fortune, he said, that they had once been beaten by Cnut; they would owe it to their own valour that they were too much for those who had beaten him. The English therefore exerted all their strength, and by completing their victory secured an earldom for their leader and renown for themselves. On his way home Cnut subdued the whole realm of the Norwegians, driving out King Olaf, who, returning to his kingdom the following year with a small force in order to test the sentiments of his subjects, proved their disloyalty when he and his men were cut to pieces.

182. In the fifteenth year of his reign Cnut set off for Rome, and spent some days there; then, after redeeming his sins by distributing alms among the churches, returned to England by sea. Soon after, he led an expedition to Scotland, and had little difficulty in subduing the Scots, who were in revolt, and their king Malcolm. But it will not seem unhelpful if I append the letter which on his departure from Rome he sent to his English subjects by the hand of Lyfing abbot of Tavistock, later bishop of Crediton, as evidence of his amended life and royal generosity.

183. 'Cnut, king of all England, Denmark, and Norway, and of part of the Swedes, to Æthelnoth the metropolitan and Ælfric of York, and to all his bishops and chief men, and to all the people of the English both noble and plebeian, greeting.

'I give you notice that I have lately gone to Rome to pray for the redemption of my sins and for the salvation of my kingdoms and of the peoples who are subject to my rule. This journey I had vowed to God long ago, but because of the business of the realm and other impediments I had not hitherto been able to perform it. Now, however, I render most humble thanks to almighty God, my God, that He has allowed me in my lifetime to seek out the blessed Apostles Peter and Paul and every sanctuary that I could learn of within the city of Rome or outside it, and there according to my desire to venerate and adore them in my own person. And my reason for doing so was above all this, that I have learnt from wise men of the great power which the holy Apostle Peter had received from our Lord of binding and loosing, and that it is he who bears the keys of the kingdom of Heaven; and for this I thought it very profitable to seek his advocacy in particular

utile duxi. Sit autem uobis notum quia magna congregatio nobilium in ipsa Paschali sollemnitate ibi cum domno papa Iohanne et imperatore Conrado erat, scilicet omnes principes gentium a Monte Gargano usque ad istud proximum mare; qui omnes me et honorifice suscepere et magnificis donis honorauere. Maxime autem ab imperatore donis uariis et muneribus pretiosis honoratus sum, tam in uasis aureis et
3 argenteis quam in palliis et uestibus ualde pretiosis. Locutus sum igitur cum ipso imperatore et domno papa et principibus qui ibi erant de necessitatibus totius populi mei tam Angli quam Dani, ut eis concederetur lex aequior et pax securior in uia[a] Romam adeundi, et ne tot clausuris per uiam arctentur, et propter iniustum theloneum fatigentur; annuitque postulatis imperator et Rodulfus rex qui maxime ipsarum clausurarum dominatur cunctique principes, edictisque firmarunt ut homines mei, tam mercatores quam alii orandi gratia uiatores, absque omni angaria clausurarum et theloneariorum cum firma pace Romam
4 eant et redeant. Conquestus sum iterum coram domno papa, et michi ualde displicere dixi quod mei archiepiscopi in tantum angariabantur immensitate pecuniarum quae ab eis expetebatur, dum pro pallio accipiendo secundum morem apostolicam sedem expeterent; decretumque est ne id deinceps fiat. Cuncta enim quae a domno papa et ab imperatore et a rege Rodulfo ceterisque principibus per quorum terras nobis transitus est ad Romam pro meae gentis utilitate postulabam, libenter annuerunt, et concessa etiam sacramento firmarunt sub testimonio quattuor archiepiscoporum et uiginti episcoporum et innumerae multitudinis ducum et nobilium quae aderat.
5 'Quapropter Deo omnipotenti gratias magnificas reddo, quia omnia quae desideraueram, prout mente decreueram, prospere perfeci, uotisque meis ad uelle satisfeci. Nunc itaque sit notum quia ipsi Deo suplex deuoui uitam meam amodo in omnibus iustificare et regna michi subdita populosque iuste et pie regere aequumque iuditium per omnes[b] obseruare; et si quid per meae iuuentutis intemperantiam aut negligentiam hactenus preter id quod iustum erat actum est, totum
6 Deo auxiliante dispono emendare. Iccirco obtestor et precipio meis consiliariis quibus regni consilia credidi ne ullo modo aut propter meum timorem aut alicuius potentis personae fauorem aliquam

[a] uiam *CsB*   [b] omnes *CB, JW*; omnia *A, probably rightly (and so translated)*

with God. And I would have you know that there was a great gathering of nobles there at the Easter solemnity with our lord Pope John and the Emperor Conrad, to wit, all the princes of the peoples from Monte Gargano to this the nearest sea, who all gave me a respectful welcome and honoured me with magnificent gifts. In particular I was honoured by the emperor with sundry gifts and precious presents: vessels of gold and silver and very precious fabrics and robes. I spoke 3 therefore with the emperor himself and with my lord the pope and the princes who were there about the needs of all my people, both English and Danes, that they should be granted more equitable law and more secure peace on the road to Rome, and not be harassed by so many barriers on the way and afflicted by unjust transit-dues; and the emperor consented to my requests, and so did King Rudolf who is especially in control of those same barriers, and all the princes; and they confirmed by proclamations that all my subjects, both merchants and others who travel in order to say their prayers, should be allowed to go to and return from Rome in unbroken peace with no constraint of barriers or tax-collectors. I complained on another occasion to my 4 lord the pope, and said I was much dissatisfied that my archbishops should be so much constrained by the immense sums of money that were demanded from them when according to custom they made their way to the seat of the Apostles to receive the pallium; and it was decided that this should not happen in future. For all the requests which I made of my lord the pope and of the emperor and of King Rudolf and the other princes through whose territories we have to pass on the way to Rome, for the benefit of my own people, were readily granted, and the concessions confirmed on oath, on the testimony of four archbishops and twenty bishops and an immense multitude of dukes and nobles who were present.

'For this reason I give abundant thanks to almighty God, because I 5 successfully achieved all my desires just as I had intended and fulfilled my vows as I wished. Now therefore be it known that I have humbly vowed to God that henceforward I will lead a godly life in all respects, and will rule in justice and piety the kingdoms and peoples committed to me and observe a right judgement in all things; and if in the impatience or negligence of my youth I have hitherto done anything beyond what is right, I intend with God's help to correct it all. For 6 this purpose I enjoin upon and command my councillors to whom I have committed the counsels of my realm, that on no account either from fear of me or to secure the favour of any powerful person shall

iniustitiam amodo consentiant uel fatiant pullulare in omni regno meo. Precipio etiam omnibus uicecomitibus et prepositis uniuersi regni mei, sicut meam uolunt habere amicitiam aut suam salutem, ut nulli homini nec diuiti nec pauperi uim iniustam inferant, sed omnibus tam nobilibus quam ignobilibus sit fas iusta lege potiundi, a qua nec propter fauorem regium*a* nec propter *b*alicuius potentis personam nec propter*b* michi congerendam pecuniam ullo modo deuient, quia nulla michi necessitas est ut iniqua exactione pecunia michi congeratur.

7 'Ego itaque notum uobis fieri uolo quod, eadem uia qua exiui regrediens, Danemarkiam uado, pacem et firmum pactum omnium Danorum consilio compositurus cum eis gentibus quae nos et uita et regno priuare, si eis esset possibile, uolebant, sed non potuerunt, Deo scilicet uirtutem eorum destruente, qui nos sua benignitate in regno et honore conseruet omniumque inimicorum nostrorum potentiam annichilet. Composita denique pace cum gentibus quae in circuitu nostro sunt, dispositoque et pacato*c* omni regno nostro hic in oriente, ita ut a nulla parte bellum aut inimicitias aliquorum timere habeamus, quamcitius hac aestate apparatum nauigii habere potero, Angliam uenire

8 dispono. Hanc autem epistolam iam premisi, ut de mea prosperitate omnis populus regni mei laetificetur, quia (ut uos ipsi scitis) numquam memet ipsum nec meum laborem abstinui nec adhuc abstinebo impendere pro omnis populi mei necessaria utilitate.

'Nunc igitur obtestor omnes episcopos meos et regni prepositos per fidem quam michi debetis et Deo,*d* quatinus fatiatis ut, antequam Angliam ueniam, omnium debita quae secundum legem antiquam debemus sint persoluta, scilicet elemosina pro aratris, et decimae animalium ipso anno procreatorum, et denarii quos Romam ad sanctum Petrum debetis siue ex urbibus siue ex uillis, et mediante Augusto decima*e* frugum, et in festiuitate sancti Martini primitiae seminum ad aecclesiam sub cuius parrochia quisque degit, quae Anglice cyrcscet nominatur. Haec et alia si cum uenero non erunt persoluta, regia exactione secundum leges in quem culpa cadit districte absque uenia comparabit.'

9 Nec dicto deterius fuit factum. Omnes enim leges ab antiquis regibus et maxime ab antecessore suo Egelredo latas sub interminatione regiae multae perpetuis temporibus obseruari precepit; in quarum

---

a regni *A* *b-b* om. *B* *c* *Al*^*p.c.*^*Ce, JW;* parato *ACsB* *d* Deo et michi debetis *Cs, JW* *e* decime *Bc, JW;* -mas *Bk (BpBph avoid error)*

they henceforward consent to any injustice or cause it to arise throughout my realm. I also command all the sheriffs and reeves throughout my realm, as they wish to enjoy my goodwill or their own prosperity, to use no unjust violence against any man be he rich or poor, but that all men as well noble as simple shall have the right to secure justice under the law, from which they shall in no way deviate either to obtain the king's favour or out of respect for any powerful person or for the sake of heaping up money for myself, because I have no need that money should be accumulated for me by unjust exactions.

'I therefore wish it to be known to you that, returning by the same road by which I came out, I am making my way to Denmark, with the intention of establishing peace and lasting agreement, on the advice of all the Danes, with those nations who wished to deprive us, had it been possible, of our life and kingdom; but they could not do it because God destroyed their power, for He preserves us by His goodness in our realm and honour and brings to nothing the power of all our enemies. Then, having established peace with those nations which live round about us and having set in order and in concord my whole realm here in the east, so that we have to fear no war from any quarter nor any persons' hostile acts, I intend, as soon this summer as I can have a fleet ready, to come to England. I have now sent on this letter in advance, that all the people in my realm may rejoice in my prosperity, because, as you yourselves well know, I have never refrained, nor will I ever refrain in future, from expending myself and all my energies on behalf of the necessary advancement of my whole people.

'Now therefore I request all my bishops and the chief men of the realm, by the fealty which you owe to me and to God, to ensure that before my arrival in England the debts of all men which we owe under ancient laws are paid, namely plough-alms and tithes of animals born in that year and the pence which you owe to St Peter at Rome, whether from towns or villages, and in mid-August a tithe of the produce of the earth, and at Martinmas first-fruits of seed owed by each man to his parish church, which is called in English "church-scot". If these and other sums have not been paid by the time I arrive, the person responsible will be forced to pay up by the king's servants, in accordance with the law, without hope of pardon'.

He was as good as his word. He gave orders that all the laws enacted by the ancient kings, and particularly by his predecessor Æthelred, should be observed in perpetuity under threat of a royal fine; and for the observance of these laws, even now that times have improved, an

custodiam[a] etiam nunc tempore bonorum sub nomine regis Eduardi iuratur, non quod ille statuerit sed quod obseruarit.[d]

184. Erant tunc in Anglia summi et sapientissimi uiri, quorum precipuus Egelnodus, archiepiscopus post Liuingum. Hic, ex decano summus sacerdos, multa opera predicabili memoria digna[b] fecit, regem ipsum auctoritate sanctitudinis in bonis actibus mulcens, in excessibus terrens. Sedem archiepiscopatus et prius presentia corporis sancti Elfegi sullimauit, et postea Romae presens in pristinam dignitatem reparauit. Domum rediens apud Papiam brachium sancti Augustini doctoris centum talentis argenti et talento auri comparatum apud Couentreiam misit.

2 'Porro Cnuto Glastoniensem aecclesiam, ut fratris sui Edmundi manes inuiseret (sic enim eum uocare solitus fuerat), festinauit, factaque oratione super sepulchrum pallium misit uersicoloribus figuris pauonum, ut uidetur, intextum. Astabat regio lateri supradictus Egelnodus, qui septimus ex monachis[d] Glastoniensis cenobii presidebat cathedrae Cantuariensi. Primus Berhtwaldus; secundus Athelmus, qui primus Wellis episcopus; tertius nepos eius Dunstanus; quartus Ethelgarus, qui Noui Monasterii Wintoniae abbas primus, deinde Cicestrensis episcopus; quintus Siritius, qui factus archiepiscopus nutriculae suae septem dedit pallia, de quibus in anniuersario eius tota antiqua ornatur aecclesia; sextus Elfegus, qui ex prioratu Glastoniae primus factus est abbas Bathoniae, deinde episcopus Wintoniae; septimus Egelnodus, qui, cum regi antecessorum suorum priuilegia ostendisset, rogauit et rogando obtinuit ut scripto regio in haec uerba confirmaret:

185. [c] 'Regnante in perpetuum Domino, qui sua ineffabili potentia omnia disponit atque gubernat, uicesque temporum hominumque mirabiliter discernens terminumque incertum prout uult aequanimiter imponens, et de secretis naturae misteriis misericorditer docet ut de fugitiuis et sine dubio transitoriis mansura regna Dei suffragio adipiscenda sunt: quapropter ego Cnut, rex Anglorum ceterarumque gentium in circuitu persistentium gubernator et rector, cum consilio et decreto archipresulis nostri Ethelnothi simulque cunctorum Dei

---

[a] custodia B   [d] See above, p. 324   [b] om. A   [c-c] (p. 332) CB (cf. AG pp. 136, 132); om. TtA   [d] ex monachis om. CsB   [e] This document (Sawyer 966) appears also in AG p. 132 and in e.g. ξρστ

oath is taken in the name of King Edward, not because he established them, but because he kept them.

184. In those days there were in England men of high quality and wisdom, chief among whom was Æthelnoth, who succeeded Lyfing as archbishop. He had been dean before becoming primate, and carried through many works which deserve an eloquent memorial; with the authority which his holiness gave him he could compliment the king himself when he did well and put the fear of God into him when he erred. The church of his see as archbishop he had already exalted with the actual body of St Ælfheah, and later when in Rome in person he restored it to its pristine dignity. On his way home, at Pavia, he bought for one hundred talents of silver and a talent of gold an arm of St Augustine, doctor of the Church, and despatched it to Coventry.

Cnut, moreover, hastened to the church of Glastonbury to visit the remains of his brother Edmund (for so he used to call him), and having offered prayers he placed over his tomb a pall woven with figures apparently of peacocks in various colours. There stood at the king's side Æthelnoth, of whom I was speaking, who was the seventh from the monastery of Glastonbury to preside over the see of Canterbury. The first was Berhtwald; the second Athelm, first bishop of Wells; the third Dunstan, his nephew; the fourth Æthelgar, the first abbot of New Minster at Winchester and after that bishop of Chichester; the fifth Sigeric, who on being made archbishop gave his mother church seven hangings with which the whole of the ancient church is decorated on his anniversary; the sixth Ælfheah, who from being prior of Glastonbury was made the first abbot of Bath and then bishop of Winchester; the seventh Æthelnoth who, after showing the king the privileges of his predecessors, asked him for a royal charter to confirm them, and obtained the confirmation he sought in the following words:

185. 'In the everlasting reign of the Lord who disposes and governs all things by His ineffable might, determining in a wonderful way the alternations of times and of men and calmly fixing their uncertain end as pleases Him, and in His mercy teaches us from the secret mysteries of nature how out of things which are fugitive and beyond question transitory an everlasting kingdom can with God's help be obtained: now therefore I Cnut, king of the English and governor and ruler of all surrounding nations, with the counsel and determination of Æthelnoth our archbishop, and with him of all God's priests, and the

sacerdotum et consensu optimatum meorum, ob amorem caelestis regni et indulgentiam criminum meorum et relaxationem*a* peccaminum fratris mei regis Edmundi, concedo aecclesiae sanctae Dei genitricis semperque uirginis*b* Mariae Glastoniae iura et consuetudines in omni regno meo et omnes forisfacturas omnium terrarum suarum; et sint terrae eius sibi liberae et solutae ab omni calumnia et inquietatione,
2 sicuti meae michi habentur. Verum illud precipue ex omnipotentis Patris et Filii et Spiritus sancti auctoritate et perpetuae Virginis interdictione prohibeo, et uniuersis regni mei prepositis et primatibus super suam salutem precipio, ut nullus omnino illam insulam intrare audeat, cuiuscumque ordinis aut dignitatis sit, sed omnia tam in aecclesiasticis quam in secularibus causis tantummodo abbatis iuditium et conuentus expectent, sicuti predecessores mei sanxerunt et priuilegiis confirmauerunt Centwines Ines Cuthredus Elfredus Eduardus Ethel-
3 stanus et gloriosissimus*c* Edmundus et incomparabilis Edgarus. Si quis autem quouis deinceps tempore sub aliqua occasione interrumpere atque irritum facere huius priuilegii testamentum nisus fuerit, sit a consortio piorum ultimi examinis uentilabro dispertitus. Si quis uero beniuola intentione haec facere probare et defensare studuerit, beatissimae Dei genitricis*d* et omnium sanctorum intercessione amplificet Deus portionem eius in terra uiuentium.'
4   Scripta est huius priuilegii donatio et promulgata in lignea basilica sub presentia regis Cnutonis anno ab incarnatione Domini millesimo tricesimo secundo, indictione quinta decima.*e c*

186. *f* Eiusdem etiam archipresulis monitu rex*f* ad transmarinas aecclesias pecunias mittens maxime Carnotum ditauit, ubi tunc florebat Fulbertus episcopus in sanctitate et philosophia nominatissimus. Qui inter cetera industriae suae documenta aecclesiae dominae nostrae sanctae Mariae, cuius fundamenta iecerat, summam manum mirifico effectu imposuit; quam etiam pro posse honorificare studens musicis modulationibus crebro extulit. Quanto enim amore in honorem Virginis anhelauerit, poterit conicere qui cantus audierit caelestia uota sonantes. Extat inter cetera opuscula eius epistolarum uolumen, in

---

a relaxationem *Cd*, ρ; -one *CB*, σ; remissionem τ (*the MSS of AG vary between this and* remissione (*so* ξ))   *b* semperque uirginis *om. Bk*, ρτ   *c* Athelstanus et gloriosissimus *C(A. et gloriosus ξ); Ethelredus Ailstanus et gloriosissimus Bk(and similarly BpBph)*, ρ; *om. Bc, AG*, ξτ   *d* B adds Marie (*so AG*, ξρτ), *rightly?*   *e* quintadecima *Cs (correctly), secunda Ce(and Cr; prima Cd), σ; om. B(and Cp)*, ξρτ   *f See above, p. 330*   *f-f CB; eius monitu rex etiam TtA*

agreement of my nobles, on account of my love for the kingdom of Heaven and to secure indulgence for my misdeeds and remission of the sins of my brother King Edmund, do hereby grant to the church of the holy Mother of God, the ever-virgin Mary, in Glastonbury their rights and customs in all this realm of mine and all forfeitures in all their lands, and its lands are to be free and immune from all claim and interference, as I hold my own lands. But this in particular I forbid on the authority of the almighty Father, Son, and Holy Spirit and on the prohibition of the ever-Virgin, and make it an ordinance for all the magnates and chief men of my whole realm as they value their own salvation: that no person whatsoever dare intrude into that island, whatever his rank and dignity; but all things, in causes both ecclesiastical and secular, shall await solely the decision of the abbot and convent, as was authorized and confirmed in charters of privilege by my predecessors Centwine, Ine, Cuthred, Alfred, Edward, Æthelstan, the right glorious Edmund, and the incomparable Edgar. But if any man at any time hereafter and on any excuse shall attempt to breach the provisions of this privilege or make them null and void, may he be separated from the company of the faithful by the winnowing fan of the last Judgement. But if any well-intentioned person does his best to carry out these provisions and to confirm and defend them, may the most blessed Mother of God and all the saints intercede for him and may God grant him a larger portion in the land of the living.'

This grant of privilege was put in writing and published in the timber-built minster in the presence of King Cnut, the year of our Lord 1032, the fifteenth indiction.

186. On the advice of the same archbishop the king also sent money to churches overseas, and particularly enriched Chartres, where at that time Bishop Fulbert was flourishing and enjoyed a great name for holiness and philosophy. Among other evidence of his energy, he put the finishing touches with marvellous success to the church of our lady St Mary, of which he had laid the foundations, and also, in his anxiety to honour it to the utmost of his power, he frequently brought it fame by the music that he wrote for it. The depth of the love with which he strove to honour the Virgin anyone will be able to imagine who hears the songs that voice his prayers to Heaven. Among his other works is to be found a volume of letters, in one of which he expresses

quarum una gratias agit Cnutoni magnificentissimo regi, quod largitatis suae uiscera in expensas*ᵃ* aecclesiae Carnotensis effuderit.[1]

187. Eius anno quinto decimo Rotbertus rex Francorum, de quo supra prelibauimus,[2] uitam clausit, uir elemosinis deditus adeo ut festis diebus, cum amiciretur et exueretur regiis insignibus, si non aliud haberet ad manum, ipsa uestimenta pauperibus distribueret, nisi ex industria uestiarii egenos importune petentes arcerent. Habebat*ᵇ* duos filios, Odonem et Henricum; Odo maior natu hebes, alter astutus et uehemens. Diuiserat in amorem prolem utramque parens uterque: pater primogenitum amplectebatur, dictitans successurum; mater minorem fouebat, cui, etsi non per aetatem, per prudentiam certe regnum
2 deberetur. Ita, ut sunt feminae in incepto pertinaces, non prius abstitit quam omnes duces qui regno Francorum famulantur premiis et pollicitis ingentibus in sua uota transduceret. Henricus ergo, maxime annitente Rotberto Normanno, coronatus est priusquam plane pater*ᶜ* expiraret. Cuius benefitii obnoxius, cum ille, ut superius dixi,[3] Ierosolimam iret, Willelmum filium eius puerulum contra desertores enixissime iuuit. At Cnuto, transcursa uitae meta, Sceftoniae defunctus et Wintoniae sepultus est.

188. Anno Dominicae incarnationis millesimo tricesimo sexto Haroldus, quem fama filium Cnutonis ex filia Elfelmi comitis loquebatur, regnauit annis quattuor et mensibus totidem. Elegerunt eum Dani et Lundoniae ciues, qui iam pene in barbarorum mores propter frequentem conuictum transierant. Angli diu obstiterunt, magis unum ex filiis Egelredi, qui in Normannia morabantur, uel Hardacnutum filium Cnutonis ex Emma, qui tunc in Danemarkia erat, regem habere uolentes. Maximus tum*ᵈ* iustitiae propugnator fuit Goduinus comes, qui etiam pupillorum se tutorem professus reginam Emmam et regias gazas custodiens resistentes umbone nominis sui aliquandiu dispulit;
2 sed tandem, ui et numero impar, cessit uiolentiae. Haroldus sceptro confirmato nouercam exiliauit. Illa in Normannia nichil sibi tutum arbitrata, ubi defunctis fratre et nepotibus recens deserti orphani

---

ᵃ expensis *B*   *ᵇ* habuit *A*   *ᶜ* pater plan(a)e *T*   *ᵈ* tunc *TBc'*

[1] *Ep.* xxxvii.
[2] 168. 1–2.
[3] 178. 5.

his thanks for the great generosity of King Cnut, in lavishing the bounty of his munificence on the costs of Chartres cathedral.[1]

187. In his fifteenth year Robert, king of the French, on whom I have touched already,[2] ended his days, a man so devoted to almsgiving that on festivals, when he wore and then put off his royal insignia, if he had nothing else handy he would have given his actual robes to the poor, had not the keepers of his wardrobe deliberately held at a safe distance the needy who begged at such an ill-chosen moment. He had two sons, Odo and Henry; Odo, the elder, was slow-witted, his brother clever and impetuous. The parents' affection was divided, each of them preferring one of their offspring: the father supported the elder and insisted that he should succeed, the mother's favourite was the younger, to whom (she said) the crown was owing in view of his judgement if not by right of seniority. So, being obstinate as women are once they have started something, she did not cease until by bribes and large promises she had brought all the magnates in the service of the French monarchy over to her way of thinking. So Henry, with the aid in particular of Robert of Normandy, was crowned before his father had finally expired; and in gratitude for this service, when Duke Robert, as I have said above,[3] went to Jerusalem, Henry supported his young son William most vigorously against traitors. Cnut, however, reaching the end of his life, died at Shaftesbury, and was buried at Winchester.

188. In the year of our Lord 1036 Harold [Harefoot], who according to report was the son of Cnut by the daughter of Earl Ælfhelm, held the throne for four years and four months. He was elected by the Danes and the citizens of London, who from frequent contacts had by now almost adopted barbarian ways. The English put up a prolonged resistance, preferring as their king one of Æthelred's sons who were living in Normandy or Harthacnut, Cnut's son by Emma, who was at that time in Denmark. The principal champion of justice at that time was, however, Earl Godwine, who maintaining also that he was guardian of the children in their minority and keeping Queen Emma and the royal treasure under his protection, held the opposition for some time at bay by the power of his name, but at length, outclassed in power and in numbers, yielded to brute force. Harold, once established on the throne, sent his stepmother into exile. She, thinking there was no safety for her in Normandy where, her brother and nephews being now dead, there was a fresh outbreak of hostility to the deserted

feruebat inuidia, in Flandriam transiit ad Balduinum comitem, expertum probitate uirum; qui postea, defuncto rege Henrico qui Philippum paruum reliquerat filium, regnum Francorum nobiliter aliquantis annis rexit fideliterque adulto (nam eius amitam uxorem habebat) restituit. Huius sub umbra Emma securum triennium egit; quo peracto, Haroldus, apud Oxenefordam mense Aprili defunctus, Westmonasterio tumulum habet.

3 Tunc Anglis et Danis in unam sententiam conuenientibus, propter Hardacnutum missum. Ille per Normanniam in Angliam mense Augusto uenit; nam filii Egelredi iam fere omnibus despectui erant, magis propter paternae socordiae memoriam quam propter Danorum potentiam. Hardacnutus, biennio preter decem dies regnans, spiritum inter pocula apud Lamudam iuxta Lundoniam amisit, et Wintoniae iuxta patrem sepultus est, iuuenis qui egregiam pietatem animi in fratrem et sororem ostenderit: germanum enim[a] Eduardum, annosae peregrinationis tedio et spe fraternae necessitudinis natale solum reuisentem, obuiis ut aiunt manibus excipiens indulgentissime retinuit.

4 [b]Veruntamen immaturus in ceteris, per Elfricum Eboracensem episcopum et alios quos nominare piget Haroldi cadauere defosso caput truncari et miserando mortalibus exemplo in Tamensem proici iussit. Id a quodam piscatore exceptum sagena in cimiterio Danorum Lundoniae tumulatur. Tributum inexorabile et importabile Angliae imposuit, ut classiariis suis per singulas naues uiginti marcas ex pollicito pensitaret. Quod dum importune per Angliam exigitur, duo infestius hoc munus exsequentes a Wigorniae ciuibus extincti sunt; quapropter per comites suos urbe incensa et depopulata fortunisque ciuium abrasis, contumeliam famae et amori suo detrimentum ingessit.[b]

5 Sane ne silentio premam quod de primogenito Egelredi[c] Elfredo rumigeruli spargunt, ille inter mortem Haroldi et expectationem Hardacnuti fluctuans,[d] regnum ingressus, compatriotarum perfidia et maxime Goduini luminibus orbatus est apud Gilingeham; inde ad Heliense cenobium directus, miseram uitam pauco tempore pane cibario sustentauit, omnibus comitibus preter decimos decapitatis; nam sors decimum quemque morti exemerat. Haec, quia fama serit,
6 non omisi; sed, quia Cronica tacet,[e] pro solido non asserui. Hac de

[a] om. T [b-b] om. T [c] om. TA [d] fluctiuagans T [e] tacent Tt(not Tc)Cs, rightly?

orphan, moved across to Flanders to Count Baldwin, a man of well-tried integrity who later, when King Henry died leaving his son Philip still a child, ruled the French kingdom with distinction for some years and loyally gave it back to the boy (whose aunt was his wife) when he grew up. Under his shadow Emma spent three years in security; at the end of which Harold died at Oxford in the month of April, and lies buried at Westminster.

Thereupon the English and the Danes, having come to an agreement, sent for Harthacnut. He came to England by way of Normandy in August; for Æthelred's sons were now despised by almost everyone, more from memories of their father's indolence than from Danish influence. Harthacnut, after a reign of two years less ten days, died in his cups at Lambeth near London, and was buried at Winchester next to his father. He was a young man who showed an outstandingly affectionate disposition towards his brother and sister; for when his brother Edward was weary of his years of wandering and revisited his native land in hope of a closer relationship with his brother, he received him, as the saying goes, with open arms and kept him as his guest with the greatest kindness. He was, however, immature in other respects, and through the agency of Ælfric archbishop of York and others whom I would rather not name he ordered that Harold's corpse should be exhumed and beheaded, and his head (a pitiable spectacle to men) thrown into the Thames. This was taken in his net by a fisherman, and buried in the Danish cemetery in London. He also imposed on England a pitiless and unbearable tax, that he might pay, as he had promised, twenty marks to the captains of each of his vessels. While this was being over-zealously collected all over England, two officers who were performing this duty with excessive brutality were put to death by the citizens of Worcester. As a result, the city was set on fire by his earls, its people driven out, and their fortunes pillaged; and he suffered a slur on his reputation and a loss to his popularity.

I should clearly not pass over in silence the tales told by rumour-mongers about Alfred, Æthelred's eldest son. Being in suspense, between Harold's death and the expected arrival of Harthacnut, he returned to the kingdom, but through the treachery of his compatriots and of Godwine especially was blinded at Gillingham and sent from there to the monastery of Ely, where for a short time he supported a pitiable life on coarse bread, nine-tenths of his companions having been beheaded, for the lot had saved every tenth man from death. This I have not omitted, because it is a well-known story; but, since the Chronicle is silent, I do not affirm it as certain. This made Harthacnut very

causa Hardacnutus Liuingo Cridintunensi episcopo, quem fama facti auctorem asserebat, infensus illum episcopatu expulit; sed post annum pecunia serenatus restituit. Goduinum quoque obliquis oculis intuitus ad sacramentum purgationis compulit. Apposuit ille fidei iuratae xenium, ut gratiam plenam redimeret, locupletissimum sane et pulcherrimum, ratem auro rostratam, habentem octoginta milites qui haberent in brachiis singulis*a* armillas duas, unamquamque sedecim unciarum auri, in capitibus cassides deauratas, securim Danicam in humero sinistro, hastile ferreum dextra manu gestantes et, ne singula enumerem, armis omnibus instructos, in quibus fulgor cum terrore certans sub auro ferrum occuleret.

7 Ceterum, ut dicere ceperam,[1] Hardacnutus Gunhildem sororem suam,*b* filiam*c* Cnutonis ex Emma, spectatissimae*d* spetiei puellam, a multis procis tempore patris suspiratam nec impetratam, Henrico imperatori Alemannorum nuptum misit. Celebris illa pompa nuptialis fuit, et nostro adhuc seculo etiam in triuiis cantitata, dum tanti nominis uirgo ad nauem duceretur, stipantibus omnibus Angliae proceribus et in expensas conferentibus quicquid absconderat uel marsupium 8 publicum uel aerarium regium.[2] Ita ad sponsum perueniens multo tempore fedus coniugale fouit; postremo, adulterii accusata, puerulum quendam sturni sui alumnum, quem secum ex Anglia duxerat, delatori, giganteae molis homini, ad monomachiam opposuit,*e* ceteris clientibus inerti timore refugientibus. Itaque conserto duello per miraculum Dei insimulator succiso poplite eneruatur. Gunhildis, insperato triumpho tripudians, uiro repudium dedit, nec ultra minis aut delinimentis adduci potuit ut thalamo illius consentiret, sed uelum sanctimonialium suscipiens in Dei seruitio placido consenuit otio.

189. Erat imperator multis et magnis uirtutibus preditus et omnium pene ante se bellicosissimus, quippe qui etiam Vindelicos et Leutitios subegerit ceterosque populos Sueuis conterminos, qui usque ad hanc diem soli omnium mortalium paganas superstitiones anhelant. Nam Saraceni et Turchi deum creatorem colunt, Mahumet non deum sed

---

a singuli *T** (*cf. JW s.a. 1040* unusquisque*)*   *b* om. *Tt(not Tc)A*   *c* filiam *TA* (filia *after* Emma *Ce*); om. *CsB*   *d* spectatissimam *A*   *e* apposuit *CeB*

[1] 188. 3.

angry with Lyfing bishop of Crediton, who was said by common report to be responsible, and he turned him out of his see; but a year later, pacified by money, he reinstated him. He also looked askance at Godwine, and compelled him to purge himself on oath. Godwine swore the oath, and added a present in order to win back his favour in full, an object very expensive and very beautiful. It was a ship with a beak of gold, containing eighty soldiers, each of whom had two bracelets on each arm, each bracelet containing sixteen ounces of gold; on each man's head was a gilded helmet, on his left shoulder a Danish axe, in his right hand an iron spear; in fact, not to list every detail, they were fully equipped with arms of every kind, in which brilliance competing with terror was meant to hide iron in a blaze of gold.

For the rest Harthacnut, as I began to tell,[1] sent his sister Gunnhild, Cnut's daughter by Emma (a girl of the greatest beauty for whom many suitors had sighed in her father's time but never won her), to be married to Henry emperor of Germany. The wedding ceremony was thronged, and even in our own day is still the subject of popular song, such was the eminence of the bride who was being led to the ship, attended by all the nobles of England, who contributed to the outlay whatever had lain hid in public purse or royal treasury.[2] Being thus brought to her husband, she for a long time kept her matrimonial vows; but at length was accused of adultery. To do battle with her accuser, a man of gigantic bulk, she put up a page-boy, the keeper of her pet starling, whom she had brought with her from England, the rest of her household being so lazy and so frightened that they refused. They joined therefore in single combat, and by a divine miracle the informer was hamstrung and collapsed. Gunnhild, rejoicing at this unexpected triumph, gave her husband notice of divorce, and could never thereafter by threats or blandishments be brought to agree to enter his bed again. Instead, she took the veil as a nun, and spent a peaceful and leisurely old age in the service of God.

189. The emperor was a man of great and various gifts, and perhaps more skilled in war than any of his predecessors, for he subdued even the Wends and Liuticii, and all the other peoples bordering the Swedes, who alone among mankind are to this day devoted to pagan superstitions; for the Saracens and Turks believe in a divine Creator,

---

[2] A strange phrase. William probably meant '*private* purse' (cf. 337. 3). As for the 'treasury', are the magnates thought of as contributing from it because they had originally paid into it?

dei prophetam estimantes; Vindelici uero Fortunam adorant, cuius idolum loco nominatissimo ponentes, cornu dextrae illius componunt plenum potu illo quod Greco uocabulo, ex aqua et melle, idromellum uocamus. *"*Idem sanctus Hieronimus Egiptios et omnes pene Orientales fecisse in octauo decimo super Isaiam libro confirmat.*"*[1] Vnde ultimo die Nouembris mensis in circuitu sedentes, in commune pregustant; et si cornu plenum inuenerint, magno strepitu applaudunt, quod eis futuro anno pleno copia cornu[2] responsura sit in omnibus; si contra, gemunt. Hos ergo*[b]* ita Henricus tributarios effecerat, ut omnibus sollemnitatibus quibus coronabatur reges eorum quattuor lebetem quo carnes condiebantur in humeris suis per anulos quattuor uectibus ad coquinam uectitarent.

190. Preterea crebro tumultibus regni expeditus, cum se communioni et hilaritati dedisset, ioci plenus, ut sat erit duobus probare exemplis. Sororem sanctimonialem unice diligebat, ut suo eam lateri deesse non pateretur, sed semper triclinium eius suo coniungeret. Dum igitur quadam hieme, quae niuibus et pruinis aspera inhorruerat, uno diu loco detineretur, clericus quidam curialis, familiarior iusto puellae effectus, crebro nocturnas in cubiculo eius protelabat uigilias; et quamlibet multimodis tergiuersationibus nequitiam palliaret, aduertit illud aliquis, quod difficile sit crimen non prodere uultu uel gestu. Et iam uulgo rem uentilante, solus nesciebat imperator, et sororem suam pudicam credere audebat. Sed cum quadam nocte cupitis fruerentur amplexibus, et diutius se uoluptas protenderet, illuxit mane, et ecce omnem terram nix operuerat. Tum*[c]* clericus, qui se deprehendendum per uestigia in niue timeret, persuadet amicae ut dorso eius impositus angustias illas euaderet. Illa, non refutans impudentiam dum modo uitaret uerecundiam, leuat tergo amasium et extra curiam effert. Et forte tum imperator minctum surrexerat, et per fenestram cenaculi despiciens uidit clericum equitantem; primo quidem uisu hebetatus, sed re diligentius explorata pudore et indignatione obmutuit. Interea hesitanti utrum peccatum impunitum dimitteret uel peccantes honeste

a–a om. *T*   *b* igitur *A*   *c* tunc *TA*

[1] xviii. 65. 11–12 (*PL* xxiv. 639).
[2] Horace, *Carm. saec.* 59–60; *Ep.* i. 12. 29.

accounting Mahomet not God but His prophet. But the Wends worship Fortune, whose idol they set in a very prominent place, putting in its right hand a drinking-horn full of the drink which we call by its Greek name 'hydromel', a compound of water and honey. St Jerome too in Book XVIII of his commentary on Isaiah,[1] confirms that the Egyptians and nearly all the peoples of the East did the same. From this on the last day of November, sitting round in a circle, they make a public tasting; if they find the horn full, there are great shouts of glee, because in the year to come 'Plenty with her brimming horn'[2] will answer to all their prayers, but if not, there is weeping and wailing. These then were the peoples whom Henry had forced to pay tribute, on terms that, on all the high festivals on which he wore his crown, the pot in which his meat was dressed, hanging from poles by four rings, should be carried shoulder-high to the kitchen by their four kings.

190. Often too when, freed from the turmoil of state affairs, he had given himself up to friendly merriment, he was full of humour, as two examples will suffice to show. He was much devoted to his sister, who was a nun, so much so that he never allowed her to leave his side, and had her sleep in the chamber next his own. One winter of heavy snow and bitter frost, he was detained for a long time in one place, and a certain clerk belonging to the court, who became more intimate with the lady than he should have been, often spent long nightly vigils in her room. However many shifts he tried to conceal his bad behaviour, someone noticed, for it is hard not to betray one's guilt by face or bearing: and they soon became the talk of the town. Everybody knew except the emperor, and he was the only man who still dared to suppose his sister chaste. But one night they were enjoying each other's embraces, and prolonged their pleasures until daybreak, when lo and behold the ground was all covered with snow. So the clerk, afraid that his footprints would give him away, persuaded his lady to let him escape from this tight spot by riding on her back. The princess accepted this shameless proposal, rather than be put to shame herself, lifted her lover on her shoulders, and carried him out of the royal precinct. It so happened that at that moment the emperor had risen to relieve himself, and looking out of the closet window he saw the clerk on his mount. At first he was stupefied by the sight; then, when he went into the matter, shame and resentment kept him silent. While he was still hesitating whether to let the offence go unpunished, or to clear his honour by the exposure of the guilty parties, the chance

redargueret, obuenit occasio ut episcopatum uacantem daret clerico, haec uerba auribus insusurrans: 'Accipe' inquit 'episcopatum, et uide ne ulterius inequites mulierem.' Item dans abbatiam sanctimonialium germanae, 'Esto' ait 'abbatissa, nec ultra patiaris*a* clericum equitem.' Confusi illi, qui tam graui dicto se sentirent lapidatos, desciuerunt a flagitio quod diuinitus inspiratum putabant*b* domino.

191. Item habebat clericum in curia qui et litterarum peritiam et uocis elegantiam uitio corporis deformabat, quod meretriculam uillae dementer ardebat; cum qua nocte quadam sollemni uolutatus, mane ad missam imperatoris aperta fronte astabat. Dissimulata scientia, mandat ei Cesar ut se paret ad euangelium, quod eius melodia delectaretur; erat enim diaconus. Ille pro peccati conscientia multis prestigiis subterfugere, imperator contra nuntiis urgere, ut probaret constantiam; ad extremum prorsus abnuenti, 'Quia' inquit 'non uis michi*c* parere in tam facili obsequio, ego te extorrem totius terrae meae esse*d* precipio.'
2 Clericus amplexus sententiam abscessit continuo; missi pedisequi qui eum persequerentur ut, si perseuerandum putaret, iam urbem egressum reuocarent. Ita incunctanter compilatis omnibus suis et in sarcinulas compositis, iam profectum magnaque uiolentia retractum Henrici presentiae sistunt. Qui laetum subridens 'Probe' ait 'fecisti, et gratulor probitati tuae, quod pluripenderis Dei timorem quam patriam, respectum caelestis irae quam meas minas. Quapropter habeto episcopatum qui primus in imperio meo uacauerit: tantum indecenti amori renunties.'

192. At, quia nichil constans est in humanis gaudiis, quoddam triste portentum tempore eius accidit, quod non tacebo. Fuldense cenobium est in Saxonia, sancti Galli corpore insigne et prediis ditatum permagnificis. Eius loci abbas sexaginta milia bellatorum imperatori prebet in hostem, habetque ex antiquo priuilegium ut in precellentibus festiuitatibus ad dextram eius consideat. Hic ergo Henricus Pentecosten apud Mogontium celebrabat. Paulo ante missam, cum sedilia pararentur in aecclesia, inter cubicularios archiepiscopi et abbatis

a patieris *A*   *b* put. insp. *T*   *c* michi non uis *T*   *d* om. *A*

arose to give the clerk a vacant bishopric; and so he did, whispering in his ear: 'The see is yours, and let us have no more of this mounting a woman.' In the same way he gave his sister charge of a nunnery, saying: 'You shall be an abbess, only never again let your chaplain ride you.' They were covered with confusion, feeling themselves stunned by such a rebuke, and ended the misconduct, of which they supposed their lord must have learnt by some divine inspiration.

191. He had at court another clerk, whose literary gifts and cultivated voice were marred by a fault of the flesh, for he was madly in love with a light wench in the town. Having spent the night with her on the eve of some festival, he appeared next morning as bold as brass at the emperor's mass. Concealing that he knew all about it, the monarch bade him prepare to intone the Gospel, because he delighted in the man's lovely voice, and he was a deacon. The clerk, with this sin on his conscience, used every shift to get out of it, while the emperor pressed him with one message after another, to see how long he would hold out. At length, as the clerk still refused, 'Very well', he said: 'as you will not obey me in the simplest service, I will banish you from the whole of my dominions.' The clerk accepted the sentence and made off at once, followed by servants who had orders to keep after him and, if he should think it his duty to persist, to bring him back as soon as he had left the city. Having put all his things together and packed them without delay, off he went, only to be dragged back by main force and brought into Henry's presence. The emperor laughed. 'You're an honest fellow,' he said, 'and I am glad to see you setting the fear of God above your country, and more afraid of the wrath of Heaven than of any threats of mine. You shall have the next bishopric that falls vacant in my empire; only you must give up your unseemly amour.'

192. But in human happiness nothing endures, and in his time a sinister portent happened, of which I must tell. There is in Saxony a monastery called Fulda, famous for the body of St Gall and endowed with magnificent estates. The abbot of Fulda finds sixty thousand men-at-arms for the emperor's wars, and enjoys the time-honoured privilege at the chief festivals of sitting on his right. Our Henry then was keeping Whitsuntide at Mainz. Shortly before mass, when the seats were being got ready in the cathedral, a dispute arose between the archbishop's servants and the abbot's, as to which party should

iurgium agitatum, utrorum dominus iuxta Cesarem sederet, illis pre-
2 rogatiuam antistitis, istis priscum morem referentibus. Vbi uerbis
parum ad concordiam proceditur, ut habent Germani idemque
Teutones indomitum animum, ad pugnam uentum. Itaque pars
sudes arripere, pars saxa iacere, pars enses euaginare, postremo quicquid primum ira inuenisset eo pro armis uti; ita furore per aecclesiam
grassante, pauimentum sanguine inundauit. Sed statim episcopis
conuolantibus pace inter reliquias dissidentium statuta, templum
purgatum, missa festiuis clamoribus acta. Cum uero (mira subitiam)
sequentia cantata,*a* et uersu 'Hunc diem gloriosum fecisti' chori conti-
cuissent, uox ab aere lapsa late insonuit: 'Hunc diem bellicosum ego
3 feci.' Rigentibus ceteris imperator, diligentius intendens muneri laeti-
tiamque intelligens inimici, 'Tu,' inquit, 'omnis malitiae inuentor
simul et incentor, diem bellicosum et arrogantibus luctuosum fecisti;
sed nos per Dei gratiam, qui illum gloriosum fecit, pauperibus gratiosum reddemus.' Et mox reincepta sequentia sollemni ploratu Spiritus
sancti gratiam inuitabat; intelligeres*b* illum aduentasse, illis cantanti-
bus, istis lacrimantibus, omnibus pectora tundentibus. Finita missa,
egenis per precones conclamatis, omnes dapes quae sibi et curialibus
parabantur in usus eorum exhausit, ipse obsonia apponens, ipse
iuxta disciplinam ministrorum delonge consistens, ipse superflua
ciborum abstergens.

193. Tempore Conradi patris a quodam clerico fistulam tulerat
argenteam qua pueri ludo aquam iaculantur, pactus episcopatum cum
foret imperator. Adultus repetenti pollicitum impigre dederat; nec
multo post aspera ualitudine correptus decubuit. Morbo crescente,
triduo exsensis et mutus iacuit, cum in solo pectore uitalis halitus palpitaret; nec aliud uitae inditium erat quam quod manu ad nares apposita
quantuluscumque sentiebatur anhelitus. Episcopi presentes, triduano
indicto ieiunio, lacrimis et uotis pro uita regis superos pulsabant.
2 Quibus, ut credi fas est, remediis conualescens, accitum episcopum

---

a cantitata *C; understand* esset   *b* intelligens *TCs*

have their master sit next the emperor; the archbishop's men maintained the privileges of the diocesan, the abbot's claimed ancient custom. When words failed to bring them to agreement, for Germans and Teutons are an obstinate lot, they came to blows; some snatching up pieces of wood, some throwing stones, some drawing their swords, each took as his weapon the first thing his anger found, and as their frenzy spread through the cathedral, the floor became deep in blood. The prelates quickly made their way to the scene, and peace having been established between what was left of the combatants, the cathedral was cleansed and mass celebrated with festival honours. But when—and this is the wonderful part of my story—when the sequence had been sung and the choirs had paused at the versicle 'This day hast thou made a day of glory', a voice was heard widely echoing from the air: 'This day have *I* made a day of battle.' All froze with horror except the emperor, who attended to the office with the more concentration, and understanding the rejoicing of the Evil One, replied: 'O source and stimulus of all wickedness, you may have made this a day of battle and of sorrow for the proud; but we, by the grace of God who made it a day of glory, will make it also a day of comfort for the poor.' The sequence was re-started, and with solemn lamentation Henry besought the grace of the Holy Spirit; and you might have taken it that the Spirit had come upon them as some sang, some wept, and all beat their breasts. When mass was over, he summoned the poor by proclamation, and lavished upon their needs all the feast that was being made ready for himself and his courtiers, in person serving the dishes, waiting at a distance as the practice of servants is, and clearing up the broken meats that remained.

193. In the time of his father Conrad, he had received from a certain clerk a silver pipe of the kind that children use for squirting water in play, promising a bishopric in return when he should become emperor. When he grew up and the man claimed his reward, it had been given him without hesitation, and shortly after Henry fell seriously ill and took to his bed. As his distemper increased, he lay for three days senseless and speechless, while the breath of life just flickered in his chest and nowhere else, nor was there any other sign of life, except that a hand held to his nostrils felt just a trace of respiration. The bishops who were present ordered a fast for three days, and bombarded Heaven with tears and prayers for the king's life. With this treatment, as it is proper to believe, he recovered and, sending

quem iniuste fecerat sententia concilii deposuit, professus se toto triduo demones infestos uidisse flammam in se per fistulam iaculantes, flammam adeo pertinacem ut noster ignis in comparatione illius iocus putetur et nichil calere; iuuenem inter haec semiustulatum aduentasse, ferentem immensae magnitudinis calicem aureum aqua plenum, cuius uisione et laticis aspergine delinitum, extinctis ardoribus, in sanitatem euasisse; ephebum illum beatum fuisse Laurentium, cuius aecclesiae tectum longa carie dissolutum compaginarit, et preter alia xenia calice aureo honorificarit.

194. Occurrunt hoc loco quae de illo uiro feruntur magna miracula, ut de cerua quae illum inimicos[a] fugitantem ultra inuadabilem fluuium dorso euexerit, et quibusdam aliis, quibus ideo supersedeo quia estimationem lectoris supergredi nolo. Obiit octauo decimo anno imperii emenso, et apud Spiram conditus est, quam ipse ex antiquissima et
2 diruta Nemeto ita nominatam nouauit.[b] [c]Epitaphium eius hoc est:[c] [1]

> Cesar, tantus eras quantus et orbis,
> at nunc in modico clauderis antro:
> post haec quisque sciat se ruiturum,
> et quod nulla mori gloria tollat.[d]
>
> Florens imperii gloria quondam
> desolata suo Cesare marcet,
> hanc ultra spetiem[e] non habitura
> quam tecum moriens occuluisti.
>
> Leges a senibus patribus auctas,[f]
> quas lassata diu raserat aetas,
> omnes ut fuerant ipse reformans
> Romanis studuit reddere causis.
>
> Tu longinqua satis regna locosque
> quos nullus potuit flectere, Cesar,
> Romanis onerans uiribus artus[g]
> ad[h] ciuile decus excoluisti.
>
3 > O quanto[i] premitur Roma dolore
> desolata prius morte Leonis!
> Nunc, Auguste, tuo funere languens
> bino se uiduam lumine plangit.

[a] om. T   [b] nom. nominauit Tt   [c-c] om. B. The poem is also found in this version in β; see Thomson, William of Malmesbury, p. 141.   [d] tollit β (and some MSS of the poem)   [e] spem T   [f] The poet wrote actas   [g] arcus TACs, β   [h] ac T, β   [i] quanta ACsBk

for the man whom he had unjustly made a bishop, had him degraded by the verdict of a council, declaring that for the whole three days he had seen hostile demons blowing flames at him through a pipe, flames so penetrating that in comparison our ordinary fire would be thought a mere trifle and not hot at all. Meanwhile, he said, a young man, half burnt, came to him, carrying an enormous gold chalice, full of water. It was the sight of him, and the relief from being sprinkled with the water, which put out the flames, that restored him to health; and the young man was St Laurence, whose church he had re-roofed after long years of decay and had honoured with many gifts, including a golden chalice.

194. At this point other miraculous stories present themselves which are told about that great man: for example, of the hind which, when he was fleeing from his enemies, carried him on its back across an unfordable river, and several others which I omit, not wishing to overtax my credit with the reader. After reigning as emperor for eighteen years, he died and was buried at Speyer, which he himself restored under that name on the site of the very ancient and now ruined city of Nemetum. His epitaph runs as follows:[1]

> Caesar, once you were as great as the whole world, but now in a small and strait space you are confined: henceforth let every man know that his end must come, and that no glory does away with death.
>
> The empire, once in the flower of glory, robbed of its Caesar is now wilting: no longer will it display that beauty which you have hidden with you in the grave.
>
> The laws authorized by senators of old, long since erased by weary time: all these he himself renewed as they had been, and zealously restored them to the Roman courts.
>
> Far distant realms and regions which no one could subject, Caesar: these you raised to the honour of civilization, burdening their limbs with the power of Rome.
>
> Alas for the grief that now lies heavy on Rome, already desolate since the death of Leo: now she is stricken by the death of her Augustus, and mourns the loss of her two luminaries.

---

[1] *MGH Poetae* iv (2). 1074–5.

Quae te non timuit patria uiuum?
Vel quae non doluit, Cesar, obisse?
Nam sic laetus*a* eras iam superatis
et sic indomitis gentibus asper,
ut quae non timuit iure doleret
et quae non doluit iure timeret.
Luge, Roma, tuum nomen in umbris,
et defecta duo lumina*b* luge.

195. Sane iste Leo, de quo epitaphium loquitur, fuerat Romae Apostolicus, ex Brunone Spirensi episcopo ita uocatus et prouectus, magnae et mirabilis sanctitatis, cuius Romani multa miracula per orbem serunt. Obierat ante Henricum post quinque annos apostolatus.

196. Anno ab incarnatione Domini millesimo quadragesimo secundo Eduardus filius Egelredi suscepit regnum, mansitque in eo annis uiginti quattuor non plenis, uir propter morum simplicitatem parum imperio idoneus, sed Deo deuotus ideoque ab eo directus. Denique eo regnante nullus tumultus domesticus qui non cito comprimeretur, nullum bellum forinsecus, omnia domi forisque quieta, omnia tranquilla; quod eo magis stupendum, quia ita se mansuete ageret ut nec uiles homunculos uerbo ledere nosset. Nam dum quadam uice uenatum isset, et agrestis quidam stabulata illa quibus in casses cerui urgentur confudisset, ille sua nobili percitus ira 'Per Deum' inquit 'et Matrem eius, tantundem tibi nocebo, si potero.' Egregius animus, qui se regem in talibus non meminisset, nec abiectae con-
2 ditionis homini se posse nocere putaret. Erat interea eius apud domesticos reuerentia uehemens, apud exteros metus ingens; fouebat profecto eius simplicitatem Deus, ut posset timeri qui nesciret irasci. 'Sed quanuis uel deses uel simplex putaretur, habebat comites qui eum ex humili in altum conantem erigerent: Siwardum Northimbrensium, qui iussu eius cum Scottorum rege Macbetha congressus uita regnoque spoliauit, ibidemque Malcolmum filium regis Cumbrorum regem instituit; Lefricum Herefordensium, qui eum contra simultates Goduini fauore magnifico tutabatur, quod ille fidente conscientia meritorum minus regem reuereretur*d* (Lefricus cum coniuge Godifa

a lenis β, *rightly* *b* numina TcAlCsB, β *c-c* (p. 350) om. Tt *d* ueretur Bk, reueretur Bc (and Aa; BpBph avoid error)

What country did not fear you while you lived, and mourn you, Caesar, when you died?—such a glad sight you were to people you had conquered, so fierce towards those as yet untamed.

Thus every region that had lost its fear of you had reason to lament you, and any which did not lament had cause to fear: lament, O Rome, for your name cast in the shade, lament for your two luminaries now eclipsed.'

195. This Leo, of whom the epitaph speaks, had of course been pope in Rome, having been Bruno bishop of Speyer before he took that name on his promotion. He was a man of great and wonderful sanctity, and many of his miracles are reported world-wide by the people of Rome. He had died before Henry, after five years on the papal throne.

196. In the year of our Lord 1042 Edward the son of Æthelred came to the throne, and held it just short of twenty-four years. The simplicity of his character made him hardly fit to govern, but he was devoted to God and therefore guided by Him. Thus during his reign there was no civil strife that was not soon suppressed, no foreign war; at home and abroad all was peace and quiet, a result all the more surprising in that he was so gentle, and could not bring himself to utter a harsh word against even the lowest of mankind. On one occasion, when he had gone hunting, and some country fellow had overset the usual shewels that direct the stags into the nets, with that generous anger that was typical of him he said merely: 'By God and His Mother, I will do the same to you if I get the chance.' There spoke a noble spirit, which could forget at such a moment that he was a king, and think of himself as unable to hurt a man of base condition. At the same time he was idolized by his court, and much feared by foreign princes; it was God who protected his singleness of heart and thus, though never angry, he could still inspire respect. Yet, idle or innocent though he might appear, he had ministers who could second his efforts to rise higher in the world. Siward, earl of Northumbria, on his instructions attacked Macbeth, king of the Scots, deprived him of his life and throne, and installed Malcolm, son of the king of the Cumbrians, in his place. The generous support of Leofric earl of Hereford was his defence against the hostility of Godwine, whose belief in his own deserts led him to underestimate the king. Leofric, with his wife

in Dei rebus munificus monasteria multa constituit, Couentreiae, Sanctae Mariae Stou, Weneloch, Leonense et nonnulla alia; ceteris ornamenta et predia, Couentreiae corpus suum cum maximo apparatu
3 auri et argenti delegauit); Haroldum Westsaxonum filium Goduini, qui duos fratres reges Walensium Ris et Griffinum sollertia sua in mortem egerit, omnemque illam barbariem ad statum prouintiae sub regis fide redegerit.[c] Fuerunt tamen nonnulla quae gloriam temporum deturparent: monasteria tunc monachis uiduata, praua iuditia a peruersis hominibus commissa, supellex matris eius precipiente illo penitus abrasa. Sed harum rerum inuidiam amatores ipsius ita extenuare conantur: monasteriorum destructio, peruersitas iuditiorum non eius scientia sed per Goduini filiorumque eius sunt commissa[a] uiolentiam, qui regis ridebant indulgentiam; postea tamen [b]ad eum[b]
4 delata acriter illorum exilio uindicata. Mater angustos[c] filii iam dudum riserat annos,[1] nichil umquam de suo largita, hereditario scilicet odio parentis in prolem; nam magis Cnutonem et amauerat uiuum et laudabat defunctum. Preterea congestis undecumque talentis crumenas infecerat,[d] pauperum oblita, quibus non patiebatur dari nummum ne diminueret numerum. Itaque quod iniuste coaceruarat, non inhoneste ablatum, ut egenorum proficeret compendio et fisco sufficeret regio. Haec referentibus etsi plurimum fides haberi debeat, sanctam tamen mulierem fuisse comperio, et thesauros suos in ornamenta aecclesiae Wintoniae et aliarum fortassis expendisse.
5 Sed ut ad superiora redeam: Hardacnuto mortuo, Eduardus tam tristi nuntio accepto, incertumque fluctuans quid ageret, quo se uerteret nesciebat. Multa uoluenti[e] potior sententia uisa ut Goduini consilio fortunas suas trutinaret. Conuentus ille per legatarios ut pace prefata colloquerentur, diu hesitabundus et cogitans tandem annuit;[f] uenientem ad se et conantem[g] ad genua procumbere alleuat; Hardacnuti mortem exponentem orantemque in Normanniam reditus
6 auxilium ingentibus promissis onerat. Melius esse ut uiuat gloriosus[h] in[i] imperio quam ignominiosus moriatur in exilio; illum Egelredi

---

[c] See above, p. 348   [a] commissa sunt Tt   [b-b] delenni (sic) Tt   [c] augustos A   [d] infarserat suggested by Howlett (cf. 277. 2, VD p. 300, VW i. 7)   [e] uolenti TtAapBk   [f] non abnuit TtA   [g] conantemque (om. et) TtA   [h] gloriosius A   [i] om. AaB

---

[1] Unidentified.

Godgifu, was a lavish supporter of God's service and founded many monasteries, Coventry, St Mary's Stow, Wenlock, Leominster, and others, giving to the rest ornaments and estates and to Coventry his body, with very great store of gold and silver. Harold earl of the West Saxons, son of Godwine, by his skilful tactics brought to their deaths two brothers who were kings of the Welsh, Rhys and Gruffydd, and reduced the whole of that barbarous country to the status of a province owing allegiance to the king. There were, however, a few blemishes on the glory of those days: the monasteries at that time were emptied of monks; crooked judgements were handed down by wicked men; his mother's property on his instructions was entirely taken from her. But his supporters try to minimize the unpopularity resulting from these conditions by saying that the destruction of monasteries and the corruption of the law-courts came about without his knowledge through the violence of Godwine and his sons, who laughed at the king's mildness, and that later, when they were reported to him, he punished them severely and exiled the culprits. As for his mother, 'long had she mocked her offspring's years of need'.[1] She never contributed anything out of her own resources, passing down her hatred of the father to the child; for she had loved Cnut more while he was alive and dwelt more on his praises after his death. Besides which, she had stuffed her money bags with bullion gathered from every source, with no thought for the poor, to whom she would not allow a penny to be given for fear of diminishing her pile; so it was not dishonourable to take away what she had unjustly accumulated, that it might be a blessing to the needy and replenish the royal treasure. Although those who use such arguments fully deserve our confidence, I find that she was a saintly woman, and expended her treasure on the adornment of Winchester and perhaps other churches.

But I must resume my previous topic. When Edward received the sad news of Harthacnut's death, he was in a quandary, and did not know what to do or which way to turn. After deep thought, it seemed the best plan to assess his future with help from the advice of Godwine. Invited by emissaries to a conference, under a prior agreement to keep the peace, Godwine hesitated and thought it over for a long time, but at length agreed. When Edward came to him and attempted to throw himself at his feet, he raised him; and when he told the story of Harthacnut's death, and begged for assistance in returning to Normandy, Godwine loaded him with copious promises: he would do better to live in glory on his throne than to die in obscurity in exile; as the son of Æthelred

filium, Edgari nepotem; iure ei competere regnum aeui[a] maturo, laboribus defecato, scienti amministrare principatum per aetatem seuere, miserias prouintialium pro pristina egestate temperare; id quo minus fiat nichil obstare, si sibi credendum putet; suam auctoritatem plurimum in Anglia[b] ponderare;[c] quo se pronior inclinauerit, eo fortunam uergere; si auxilietur, neminem ausurum obstrepere, et e conuerso; paciscatur ergo sibi amicitiam solidam, filiis honores integros, filiae matrimonium; breui futurum ut se regem uideat qui nunc uitae naufragus, exul spei, alterius opem implorat.

197. Nichil erat quod Eduardus pro necessitate temporis non polliceretur; ita utrimque fide data, quicquid petebatur sacramento firmauit. Nec mora, Gilingeham[d] congregato concilio, rationibus suis explicitis regem effecit, hominio palam omnibus[e] dato: homo affectati leporis et ingenue gentilitia lingua eloquens, mirus dicere, mirus populo persuadere quae placerent. Quidam auctoritatem eius secuti, quidam muneribus flexi, quidam etiam debitum Eduardi amplexi; pauci qui preter aequum et bonum restitere et tunc censorie notati
2 et postmodum ab Anglia expulsi. Eduardus die sollemni Paschae magna pompa apud Wintoniam[f] coronatus, et ab Edsio archiepiscopo sacra regnandi precepta edoctus, quae ille tunc memoria libenter recondidit et postea sancte factis propalauit. Idem Edsius, posteriori anno in incurabilem morbum incidens, successorem sibi abbatem Abbendoniae Siwardum statuit, ante cum rege tantum et comite communicato consilio, ne quis ad tantum fastigium aspiraret indignus uel prece uel pretio. Non multo post Edgitham filiam Goduini rex in conubium accepit, feminam in cuius pectore omnium liberalium artium esset gimnasium sed prauum in mundanis rebus ingenium; quam cum uideres, si litteras stuperes, modestiam certe animi et
3 spetiem corporis desiderares. Haec, et uiuo marito et mortuo, probri suspitione non caruit; sed, moriens tempore[g] Willelmi, iureiurando astantibus de perpetua integritate ultro satisfecit. Nuptam sibi rex hac arte tractabat, ut nec thoro amoueret nec uirili more cognosceret;

[a] (a)euo T*t*ACs, cf. 225. 6; but contrast 407. 3, GP p. 73   [b] Angliam B   [c] ponderari T*t*ACe   [d] Lundoniam B†   [e] One might expect ab omnibus   [f] Lundoniam B†   [g] A adds regis

and grandson of Edgar, the kingdom was his by right; he was now of full age; disciplined by difficulty, he had learnt from length of years how to rule a kingdom strictly and from his early privations how to moderate the hardships of his subjects. 'There is nothing in the way,' said Godwine, 'if you are willing to trust me. My authority carries very great weight in England, and on the side which I incline to, fortune smiles. If you have my support no one will dare oppose you, and conversely. Agree with me therefore for true friendship between us, undiminished honours for my sons, and my daughter's hand. As a result you will soon see yourself a king, who are now shipwrecked on the sea of life, exiled from the world of hope, and a suitor for the help of others.'

197. In the need of the moment there was nothing Edward would not promise; loyalty was pledged on each side, and he confirmed on oath whatever was asked of him. Soon after, convening an assembly at Gillingham, Godwine unfolded his reasons and made him king, and homage was paid to him publicly by everyone. Godwine was a man of assumed charm and natural eloquence in his mother tongue, with remarkable skill in speaking and in persuading the public to accept his decisions. Some people followed his authority, some had been won over by gifts, some even accepted that Edward had the right; a few, who resisted beyond what was fair and just, received a black mark at the time and later were banished from England. Edward was crowned on Easter Day with great pomp at Winchester, and was taught by Archbishop Eadsige the sacred principles of kingship, which he gladly stored at that time in his memory and later made well known in his saintly conduct. That same Eadsige the next year contracted an incurable illness, and appointed Siward abbot of Abingdon as his successor, having previously imparted his design to the king and the earl only, for fear that some unworthy candidate might aspire to such a high dignity either by prayer or by price. Not long after, the king took Godwine's daughter Eadgyth as his wife, a woman in whose bosom there was a school of all the liberal arts, though she had a bad judgement in worldly matters; when you saw her, if you were astonished by her learning, you would at the same time feel a certain lack of intellectual humility and of personal beauty. During her husband's life and after his death, she was not free from suspicions of misconduct, but on her deathbed, in William's time, she satisfied those who stood round on oath, at her own suggestion, of her perpetual virginity. After her marriage to him, the king's policy with her was neither to keep her at

quod an familiae*a* illius odio, quod prudenter dissimulabat pro tempore, an amore castitatis fecerit, pro certo compertum non habeo. Illud celeberrime fertur, numquam illum cuiusquam mulieris contubernio pudicitiam lesisse.

4 Sed quia ad id locorum uentum est, lectorem premonitum uolo quod hic quasi ancipitem uiam narrationis uideo, quia ueritas factorum pendet in dubio. Siquidem aliquantos Normannos rex accersierat, qui olim inopiam exulis pauculis benefitiis leuarant; inter quos Rotbertum, quem ex monacho Gemmeticensi episcopum Lundoniae et post 5 archiepiscopum Cantuariae statuerat. Hunc cum reliquis Angli moderni uituperant delatorem Goduini et filiorum eius, hunc discordiae seminatorem, hunc archiepiscopii emptorem; Goduinum et natos magnanimos uiros et industrios, auctores et tutores regni Eduardi; non mirum si succensuerint quod nouos homines et aduenas sibi preferri uiderent; numquam tamen contra regem, quem semel fastigauerint,*b* asperum etiam uerbum locutos. Contra Normanni sic se defensitant, ut dicant et eum et filios magna arrogantia et infidelitate in regem et in*c* familiares eius egisse, aequas sibi partes in imperio uendicantes; sepe de eius simplicitate solitos nugari, sepe insignes facetias in illum iaculari; id Normannos perpeti nequisse, quin illorum potentiam quantum possent eneruarent; denique Deum monstrasse quam sancto 6 animo Goduinus seruierit. Nam cum post piraticas rapinas, unde dicemus inferius,[1] priori gratiae redditus esset, et in conuiuio cum rege discumberet, orto sermone de Elfredo regis fratre, 'Tu,' inquit, 'rex, ad omnem memoriam germani rugato me uultu uideo quod aspitias; sed non patiatur Deus ut istam offam transglutiam, si fui conscius alicuius rei quae spectaret ad eius periculum uel tuum incommodum.' Hoc dicto, offa quam in os miserat suffocatus, oculos ad mortem inuertit. Inde ab ipso filio eius Haroldo, qui regi astabat, sub mensa extractus, in episcopatu Wintoniae sepultus est.

198. Propter istas, ut dixi, altercationes periclitatur oratio, dum quod ex asse uerum diffiniam non habeo, uel propter naturale

---

a facile *CsB*   *b* fatigauerint *Bk*, fastigauerant *Bc (BpBph avoid error)*   *c* om. *TtCBk, perhaps rightly*

---

[1] 199. 8.

a distance from his bed nor to know her as a man would; whether he did this out of hatred for her family which he prudently concealed to suit the time, or whether from a love of chastity, I have not discovered for certain. One thing is very widely reported, that he never broke the rule of chastity by sleeping with any woman.

But since we have reached this point, I should like to warn the reader that here I perceive the course of my narrative to be somewhat in doubt because the truth of the facts is in suspense and uncertain. For the king had invited a certain number of Normans, who had previously relieved his necessities when he was in exile with a few small benefactions, among them Robert, a former monk of Jumièges, whom he had appointed bishop of London and later archbishop of Canterbury. He, with the rest of them, is much blamed by the modern English as the accuser of Godwine and his sons, as a sower of discord, and as the purchaser of his archbishopric. Godwine and his sons, they say, were men of noble spirit and great energy, founders and pillars of Edward's reign as king; it was not surprising if they were indignant when they saw new men and foreigners promoted over their heads, but they had never so much as spoken a harsh word against the king, whom they had raised to his high position once and for all. The Normans on the other hand defend themselves by saying that he and his sons were both arrogant and disloyal in their behaviour towards the king and his friends, claiming equal shares for themselves in his royal power, habitually making fun of his simple ways and often making jokes about him that could not be overlooked. This, they say, the Normans could not endure without taking such steps as they could to reduce their influence, and in the end it was God who showed with what integrity Godwine served his king. When his pirate-raids, of which I shall speak below,[1] were over and when he had resumed his former position in the king's favour, he was sitting with the king at dinner, and the conversation turned on the king's brother Alfred. 'I notice, your Majesty,' he said, 'that at every mention of your brother you look at me with a frown on your brow: may God not permit me to swallow this mouthful, if I was ever aware of having done anything designed to endanger him or hurt you.' With these words, he was choked by the food he had just put into his mouth, and turned up his eyes in death. Then his son Harold, who was standing by the king, pulled him with his own hands from beneath the table, and he was buried in Winchester cathedral.

198. It is these differences of opinion which, as I have said, put my narrative at risk, since I cannot decide what precisely is the truth,

utrarumque gentium discidium, uel quia ita se res habet quod Angli aspernanter ferant*a* superiorem, Normanni nequeant*b* pati parem. Sed de moribus eorum in sequenti libro pergam dicere,[1] cum de aduentu Normannorum in Angliam occasio se obtulerit. Nunc, quanta ueritate potuero, perstringam de simultate regis in Goduinum et filios eius.

199. Eustachius erat comes*c* Bononiae, pater Godefridi et Balduini qui nostro tempore reges *d*apud Ierosolimam*d* fuerunt, *e*habebatque sororem regis Godam legitimis nuptiis desponsatam. Quae ex altero uiro, Waltero Medantino, filium tulerat Radulfum, qui eo tempore erat comes Herefordensis, ignauus et timidus, qui Walensibus pugna cesserit, comitatumque suum et urbem cum episcopo ignibus eorum consumendum reliquerit; cuius rei infamiam mature ueniens Haroldus uirtutibus suis abstersit.*e* *f*Eustachius ergo*f* transfretato mari de Witsand in Doueram regem Eduardum, nescio qua de causa, adiit. Collocutus cum eo et re impetrata quam petierat, per Doroberniam redibat.

2 Vnus antecursorum eius ferotius cum ciue agens, et uulnere magis quam prece hospitium exigens, illum in sui excidium inuitauit. Quo cognito Eustachius,*g* ad ulciscendam necem serui cum toto comitatu profectus, homicidam quidem cum aliis decem et octo interemit; sed ciuibus ad arma conuolantibus uiginti ex suis amisit innumeris uulneratis, ipse uix cum altero in ipso tumultu subterfugit. Inde ad curiam pedem referens, nactusque secretum, suae partis patronus assistens*h* iram regis in Anglos exacuit. Goduinus per nuntios ad curiam*i* accitus uenit. Exposita causa, et precipue rege insolentiam Dorobernensium accumulante, intellexit uir acrioris ingenii unius tantum partis auditis

3 allegationibus non debere*j* proferri sententiam. Itaque quanuis rex iussisset illum continuo cum exercitu in Cantiam proficisci in Dorobernenses grauiter ulturum, restitit,*k* et quod omnes alienigenas apud regis gratiam inualescere inuideret et quod compatriotis amicitiam prestare uellet. Preterea uidebatur eius*l* responsio in rectitudinem propensior, ut magnates illius castelli blande in curia regis de seditione

---

a ferunt *TtA*   *b* nequeunt *Tt (before corr.?)*   *c* comes erat *A*   *d–d* Ierosolimorum *TtA*   *e–e* om. *Tt*   *f–f* hic *Tt*   *g* om. *Tt*   *h* existens *Tt*   *i* ad curiam om. *Tt*   *j* deberi *B*   *k* resistit *Tt*   *l* om. *CsB*

---

[1] cc. 245–6.

either from the natural division between the two nations or because the fact is that the English are scornful of any superior and the Normans cannot endure an equal. But I shall have more to say of these differences of character in my next book,[1] when the arrival of the Normans in England provides me with an opportunity. I will now sketch with such truth as I can attain the king's quarrel with Godwine and his sons.

199. Eustace was count of Boulogne; he was father of Godfrey and Baldwin who in our time have been kings of Jerusalem, and was joined in lawful wedlock to the king's sister Godgifu; she, by her first husband Walter of Mantes, had a son Ralph, at that time earl of Hereford, an idler and a coward, the man who yielded to the Welsh in battle and abandoned his county and the city with its bishop for them to burn, a disgraceful act wiped out by the prompt arrival and martial gifts of Harold. This Eustace it was, then, who crossed the sea from Wissant to Dover and visited King Edward, for some reason which I do not know. Having spoken with him and secured whatever it was that he had come to seek, he was returning by way of Canterbury, when one of his advance-guard, treating a townsman brutally and demanding lodgings with blows rather than polite entreaty, provoked the townsman to kill him. When Eustace heard of this, he set off with his whole party to avenge his servant's death, and killed the murderer and eighteen others; but the townspeople flew to arms and he lost twenty of his own men and countless wounded, he himself and one other escaping with difficulty at the height of the tumult. From there he returned to court, and having obtained a secret interview became an advocate for his own side and roused the king's anger against the English. Godwine was summoned to court by messengers and arrived. The case was expounded, and the king in particular dwelt on the wickedness of the Canterbury people. Godwine, however, being a more clear-headed man, perceived that one ought not to pronounce a verdict after hearing the charges of one side only, and so, though the king had ordered him to set off instantly for Kent with an armed force, to take heavy vengeance on the townsfolk of Canterbury, he resisted, grudging the increasing influence of all foreigners with the king and wishing to show friendship to his own compatriots. Besides which, his reply seemed much more consistent with the administration of justice: the leaders of that stronghold ought to be calmly charged with sedition in the king's court, and if they could clear themselves, they should leave the court

conuenirentur: si se possent explacitare, illesi abirent; si nequirent, pecunia uel corporum suorum dispendio regi cuius pacem infregerant et comiti quem leserant satisfacerent; iniquum uideri ut quos tutari debeas, eos ipse potissimum inauditos adiudices. Ita tunc discessum, Goduino paruipendente regis furorem quasi momentaneum.

Quocirca totius regni proceres iussi Gloecestram conuenire, ut ibi magno conuentu res uentilaretur.[a] Venerunt eo etiam Northanimbri comites tunc famosissimi, Siwardus et Lefricus, omnisque Anglorum nobilitas. Soli Goduinus eiusque filii,[b] qui se suspectos scirent, sine presidio armorum ueniendum non arbitrati, cum manu ualida Beuerstane restiterunt, famam serentes in uulgus quod ideo exercitum adunassent ut Walenses compescerent, qui tirannidem in regem meditantes oppidum in pago Herefordensi offirmauerant, ubi tunc Suanus, unus ex filiis Goduini, militiae pretendebat excubias. Sed Walenses iam audientiam[c] preuenerant, et conspirationis accusatos inuisos curiae toti fecerant, adeo ut rumor spargeretur quod in eodem loco regius exercitus eos adoriretur. Quo accepto, Goduinus ad coniuratos classicum cecinit ut ultro domino regi non resisterent, sed si conuenti fuissent, quin se ulciscerentur loco non cederent. Et profecto facinus miserabile et plusquam ciuile bellum[1] fuisset, nisi maturiora[d] consilia intercessissent.

Ita quantulacumque[e] concordia interim inita, iterum preceptum ut Lundoniam concilium congregaretur; mandatum Suano filio Goduini ut fuga sua regis iram mitigaret; Goduinus et Haroldus quamtotius ad concilium hac conuentione uenirent,[f] inermes duodecim solum homines adducerent, seruitium militum quos per Angliam habebant regi contraderent. Contra illi negare: non posse se ad conuenticulum factiosorum sine uadibus et obsidibus pergere; domino suo in militum deditione parituros, tum preterea in omnibus preter gloriae et salutis periculum; si ueniant inermes, uitae timere[g] dispendium; si paucos stipatores habeant, gloriae fore obprobrium. Obstinatius offirmarat rex animum ne adquiesceret precibus suplicantium; itaque prolatum edictum ut intra quinque dies Anglia excederent. Goduinus et

---

[a] agitaretur *Tt* [b] eius filiique *Bk*, et eius filii *Bc (BpBph avoid error)* [c] audaciam *Tt* [d] maiora *Tt* [e] quantumcumque *Tt* [f] One expects ut (or quod) essent *to follow (so translated)* [g] timeri *TtA*

---

[1] Cf. Lucan i. 1.

unscathed; if they could not, they should make satisfaction to the king whose peace they had broken and the count to whom they had done harm, either financially or physically; it is clearly unjust to condemn personally, and especially to condemn unheard, those whom it is your duty to protect. At that point they separated, Godwine making 4 light of the king's fury, which he thought would not last.

The nobles of the whole realm were therefore summoned to meet at Gloucester, so that the business might be discussed there at a great council. This was also attended by two Northumbrian earls who at that time had a great reputation, Siward and Leofric, and all the nobility of England. Only Godwine and his sons, knowing they were under suspicion, did not think it safe to come without armed protection, and halted at Beverstone with a large force. They put it about that they had got an army together in order to suppress the Welsh, who were plotting a rising against the king, and had fortified a town in the county of Hereford, where at that time Swein, one of Godwine's sons, was on the watch. But the Welsh had come beforehand to the 5 hearing, and, accusing them of conspiracy, had made them unpopular with the whole council, so much so that a rumour spread that the king's army would attack them where they were. On hearing this Godwine sent a signal to his supporters, telling them not to take the initiative in resisting their lord the king, but if they had been summonsed, they should not retreat without defending themselves. And indeed this would have been a disastrous business, a 'war worse than civil',[1] had not riper counsels prevailed.

So, some small degree of agreement having meanwhile appeared, it 6 was ordered that the council should reconvene, this time in London; Godwine's son Swein was told to appease the king's anger by leaving the country; Godwine and Harold were to come to the council promptly, with stipulations that they should be unarmed and bring only twelve men with them; the soldiers in their service, whom they held all over England, were to be handed over to the king. In reply, they refused; it was not possible, they said, for them to attend a meeting of hostile parties without sureties and hostages; in the matter of surrendering their troops, they would obey their lord, and in all else besides where there was no peril to reputation and to life. If they were to come unarmed, they feared for their lives, and if they brought few men in their train, this would be a stain on their honour. The king had even 7 more firmly made up his mind not to yield to any suppliant's prayers, and so the decision was handed down that they must leave England

Suanus Flandriam, Haroldus concessit Hiberniam. Comitatus eius attributus Elgaro Lefrici filio, uiro industrio. Quem ille suscipiens tunc rexit nobiliter, reuerso restituit libenter; et postea Goduino mortuo, cum Haroldus parentis ducatum impetrasset, repetiit audacter, aliquanto tamen tempore inimicorum accusatione exiliatus. Omnis reginae substantia ad unum nummum emuncta; ipsa regis sorori apud Warewellam in custodiam data, ne scilicet omnibus suis parentibus patriam suspirantibus sola sterteret in pluma.

8   Posteriori anno exulum quisque de loco suo egressi Britannicum mare circumuagari, littora piraticis latrociniis infestare, de cognati populi opibus predas eximias conuectare. Contra quos a regis parte plusquam sexaginta naues in anchoris constiterunt; prefecti classi Odo et Radulfus comites et regis cognati. Nec segnem sensit regem illa necessitas, quin ipse in naui pernoctaret et latronum exitus specularetur, sedulo explens consilio quod manu nequibat pre senio. Sed cum comminus uentum esset et iam pene manus consererentur, nebula densissima repente coorta furentum obtutus confudit, miseramque mortalium audatiam compescuit; denique Goduinus eiusque comites eo unde uenerant uento cogente reducti.[1]

9   Non multo post pacifico animo repatriantes regem apud Lundoniam offenderunt. Orantes ueniam admissi sunt. Senex ille[2] et lingua potens ad flectendos animos audientium probe se de omnibus quae obiectabantur expurgauit, tantumque breui ualuit ut sibi liberisque suis honores integros restitueret, Normannos omnes ignominiae notatos ab Anglia effugaret, prolata sententia in Rotbertum archiepiscopum eiusque complices quod statum regni conturbarent animum regium in prouintiales agitantes. Verum ille, non expectata uiolentia, sponte profugerat cum sermo pacis componeretur, Romamque profectus et de causa sua sedem apostolicam appellans, cum per Gemmeticum reuerteretur, defunctus ibique sepultus est in aecclesia sanctae Mariae,

10 quam ipse precipuo et sumptuoso opere construxerat. Inuasit continuo, illo uiuente, Stigandus, qui erat episcopus Wintoniae, archiepiscopatum Cantuariensem, infamis ambitus pontifex et honorum[a]

---

[a] bonorum A

---

[1] Unidentified, if a quotation at all.   [2] i.e. Godwine.

within five days. Godwine and Swein retired to Flanders, Harold to Ireland. Harold's earldom was assigned to Leofric's son Ælfgar, a man of great energy; he held it and ruled it at that time with distinction, then readily gave it up on Harold's return. Later, after Godwine's death, when Harold had secured his father's earldom, Ælfgar boldly asked for it back, though he had for some time been kept in exile after accusations by his enemies. The whole of the queen's resources were confiscated to the last penny; she herself was despatched to the king's sister at Wherwell for safe custody, for fear no doubt that, while all her kinsfolk were sighing for loss of their country, she might be the only one left snoring on a feather-bed.

In the following year each of the exiles left his place of refuge and roamed the sea round Britain, harassing the coasts with pirate raids and amassing valuable booty from the wealth of the inhabitants, who were their kin. Against them on the king's side more than sixty ships had taken position, riding at anchor; commanders of the fleet were Odda and Ralph, earls and kinsmen of the king. Nor did that crisis find the king slow to move: nothing stopped him spending all night in a ship and watching the movements of the pirates with his own eyes, diligently compensating, by the wisdom of his counsel, for that personal service which age denied. When, however, they had come to close quarters and it was almost the moment for a hand-to-hand engagement, the sudden onset of a thick fog confounded their ardour for battle by making them invisible to each other, and brought to naught the piteous heroism of mortal men. Godwine and his companions eventually returned whence they had come, 'driven back by wind adverse'.[1]

Not long afterwards they returned to their country with peaceful intentions, and found the king in London; they asked for pardon, and were received. That aged man,[2] master of language that would move the hearts of his audience, cleared himself successfully of all the charges brought against him, and in a short time regained so much power that he got back for himself and his children their honours unimpaired; all the Normans were branded with infamy and ejected from England. Sentence was passed on Archbishop Robert and his accomplices for disturbing the peace of the realm by exciting the king's resentment against his subjects. The archbishop, however, not waiting for force to be exerted, had fled the country while terms of peace were being put together. He made for Rome and appealed to the Apostolic See in his defence. Returning by way of Jumièges, he died and was buried there in St Mary's church, the noble and sumptuous building which he himself had constructed. While he was still alive, the archiepiscopal see of Canterbury was promptly seized by Stigand bishop of Winchester, a prelate with a bad name for ambition and one who sought promotion

ultra debitum appetitor, qui, spe throni excelsioris episcopatum Saxonum Australium deserens, Wintoniam insederit,*a* illam quoque cum archiepiscopatu tenuerit; quapropter numquam ab apostolica sede pallium meruerit,*b* nisi quod Benedictus quidam peruasor apostolatus misit, pecunia scilicet ad concedendum*c* corruptus, uel quod mali

11 gratificantur similibus. Sed ille mox a Nicholao, qui ex episcopo Florentiae legitime papatum susceperat, expulsus zelo fidelium indebitum nomen exuit. Stigandus quoque tempore regis Willelmi per cardinales Romae degradatus perpetuisque uinculis innodatus, inexplebilis auiditatis nec moriens finem fecit. Siquidem eo mortuo clauicula in secretis reperta quae, serae cubicularis scrinii apposita, innumerabilium thesaurorum dedit inditium, cartas in quibus notata erat et metallorum qualitas et ponderum quantitas quae per omnia predia compilator auarus defoderat. Sed haec postmodum;[1] nunc de Goduino quod inchoaueram terminabo.

200. Habuit primis annis uxorem Cnutonis sororem, ex qua puerum genuerat; qui primis pueritiae annis emensis, dum equo quem ab auo acceperat puerili iactantia superbiret, ab eodem in Tamensem portatus uoragine aquae suffocatus interiit. Mater quoque ictu fulminis exanimata*d* seuitiae penas soluit, quod dicebatur agmina mancipiorum in Anglia coempta Danemarkiam solere mittere, puellas presertim quas decus et aetas pretiosiores facerent, ut earum deformi commertio cumulos opum aggeraret. Post eius obitum aliam duxit, cuius genus non comperi, de qua liberos tulit Haroldum Suanum Tostinum Wlnodum Girtham Leofwinum. Haroldus post Eduardum rex aliquot mensibus fuit, et a Willelmo apud Hastingas uictus uitam et regnum cum fratribus duobus iunioribus amisit. Wlnodus a rege Eduardo Normanniam missus, quod eum pater*e* obsidem dederat, ibi toto tempore Eduardi inextricabili captione irretitus, regnante Willelmo

2 in Angliam remissus, in uinculis Salesberiae consenuit. Suanus, peruersi ingenii et infidi in regem, multotiens a patre et fratre Haroldo desciuit, et pirata factus predis marinis uirtutes maiorum polluit. Postremo pro conscientia Brunonis cognati interempti et, ut quidam

---

a insederit *Ce(and CdCr);* -dit *TtACsB*   *b* meruit *TtA**   *c* persuadendum *TtACs*   *d* examinata *Tt*   *e* pater eum *A*

---

[1] See 269. 1; but the reference is perhaps to *GP* p. 35, where Stigand's rapacity is again mentioned.

beyond his due. In hopes of a more lofty see he had deserted the bishopric of the South Saxons and seated himself at Winchester, which he held with the archbishopric. That was why he was never thought by the Apostolic See to be worthy of the pallium, except that he was sent one by a certain Benedict, a usurping pope, who had been bribed no doubt to make the grant, or because bad men make gifts to others like themselves. However, he was soon expelled by Nicholas, who from being bishop of Florence had lawfully assumed the papacy, and by the zeal of the faithful lost the title to which he had no right. Stigand also was degraded in the time of King William by the Roman cardinals, and put in chains for life. Not even his death put an end to his insatiable avarice; for after it a small key was found in a secret place which, when inserted in the lock of a cupboard in his chamber, produced the evidence for treasures without number, in the form of parchments on which were recorded the quality of precious metals and their quantity by weight, which this miserly hoarder had buried all over his estates. But of that later;[1] I must now complete what I had begun to say of Godwine.

200. In his early years he was married to a sister of Cnut, by whom he had had a son. The child, when he had passed his early boyhood, was riding one day with boyish glee a horse given him by his grandfather, when the animal plunged with him into the Thames, and he sank into the eddying river and was drowned. His mother too was struck by lightning, and so paid the penalty for her cruel acts; she was said to buy parties of slaves in England and ship them to Denmark, young girls especially, whose beauty and youth would enhance their price, so that by this hideous traffic she could accumulate vast wealth. After her death Godwine took another wife, of whose origin I am ignorant, by whom he had Harold, Swein, Tostig, Wulfnoth, Gyrth, and Leofwine. Harold succeeded Edward as king for a few months, and then was defeated by William at Hastings, and lost life and throne, together with two younger brothers. Wulfnoth, sent by King Edward into Normandy because his father had handed him over as a hostage, remained there, held in close custody, all Edward's time; under William's rule he was sent back to England and grew old in chains at Salisbury. Swein, who was cross-grained and disloyal to the king, revolted from his father and his brother Harold many times, turned pirate, and brought disgrace on his distinguished ancestry by robbery at sea. At length, burdened with guilt for the death of his kinsman Beorn and, as some say, of his brother, he set off for

dicunt, fratris Ierosolimam abiit, indeque rediens a Saracenis circumuentus et ad mortem cesus est. Tostinus a rege Eduardo post mortem Siwardi Northanimbriae comitatui prelatus, pene decennio prouintiae prefuit; quo exacto, asperitate morum Northanimbros[a] in rebellionem excitauit. Solitarium enim repertum ex regione fugarunt, pro contuitu ducatus occidendum non arbitrati; homines eius et Anglos et Danos obtruncarunt, equos et arma et supellectilem omnem corradentes.[b] Rumore ad regem delato turbataque patria, Haroldus iuit obuiam ut
3 propulsaret iniuriam. Northanimbri, licet non inferiores numero essent, tamen quieti consulentes factum apud eum excusant: se homines libere natos, libere educatos, nullius ducis ferotiam pati posse; a maioribus didicisse aut libertatem aut mortem; proinde, si subditos uelit, Marcherium filium Elgari eis prefitiat; re experturum quam dulciter sciant obedire si dulciter tractati fuerint. Haec Haroldus audiens, qui magis quietem patriae quam fratris commodum attenderet, reuocauit exercitum, et adito rege firmum ducatum Marcherio statuit. Tostinus infensus omnibus cum uxore et liberis Flandriam abiit, ibique usque ad Eduardi fuit obitum; qui nostris litteris differetur interim,[1] dum dixero quod eius tempore Romae accidisse a senioribus didicimus.

201. Erat papa Gregorius sextus, ante dictus Gratianus, magnae religionis et seueritatis. Is ita Romani apostolatus statum per incuriam antecessorum diminutum inuenit ut preter pauca oppida urbi uicina et oblationes fidelium pene nichil haberet quo[c] se sustentaret. Ciuitates et possessiones in longinquo positae, quae ad ius aecclesiae pertinebant, a predonibus ablatae; tramites publici et strata uiarum per totam Italiam[d] a latronibus stipabantur, ut nullus peregrinus nisi cum maiori manu impune transiret. Feruebant totis semitis insidiatorum examina, nec inueniebat uiator quo colludio euaderet; ita in uacuum sicut in pecuniosum furebatur, nec suplex habere gratiam nec resistens pati
2 poterat uiolentiam. Cessatum est ab omni prouintia Romam iter aggredi, quod mallet quislibet[e] per domesticas aecclesias nummos suos diuidere quam latrunculos propriis laboribus pascere. Quid in urbe, unico olim habitaculo sanctitatis? Ibi medio foro uagabantur

[a] Northanimbriam *Tt*   [b] corrodentes *Tt*   [c] quod *AlCBc*   [d] Italiam totam *A*   [e] quilibet *T**

[1] Till 228. 6.

Jerusalem, and on the way back was ambushed by the Saracens and mortally wounded. Tostig was advanced by King Edward after Siward's death to the earldom of Northumbria, and ruled the province for nearly ten years, at the end of which time his habitual ferocity roused the Northumbrians to revolt. Tostig himself they found unsupported, and drove him from the province, not liking to kill him out of respect for his earldom; his men, both Englishmen and Danes, they cut to pieces, appropriating their horses and armour and all their gear. When news reached the king, and the country was in an uproar, Harold went north to put a stop to the mischief. The Northumbrians, 3 though not outnumbered, were conciliatory, and defended what they had done before him, maintaining that, being born and bred as free men, they could not brook harsh treatment from any superior; freedom or death was their tradition. 'If you wish to keep us in subjection,' they said, 'set Morcar son of Ælfgar over us; you will find by experience how mildly we have learnt to obey, if we are mildly treated.' Hearing this, Harold, who was a man to consider his country's tranquillity in preference to his brother's personal advantage, recalled his forces and, after approaching the king, firmly established Morcar as earl. Tostig, embittered towards all, retired with his wife and children to Flanders, and remained there until Edward's death. That event I will postpone for the time being,[1] until I have described what happened in Rome in his day, as I have heard from my elders.

201. Pope Gregory VI, formerly Gratian, was a man of holy life and high standards. He found the Apostolic See brought so low by the neglect of his predecessors that, apart from a few townships near the City and the offerings of the faithful, it had almost no resources for its support. The more distant towns and estates belonging to the Church had been seized by freebooters, and the public roads and highways all over Italy were so thick beset with robbers that no pilgrims could pass unscathed unless under escort. Not a track but swarmed with ruffians in ambush, and there was no scheme by which the traveller could escape. The empty-handed and the rich were equally objects of their fury; surrender could not win their mercy, nor resistance keep their violence at bay. In every province the pilgrimage to Rome fell into 2 abeyance, for men would rather share out their wealth among the churches of their own country than fatten malefactors with the produce of their labours. As for the City, once the peerless abode of holy religion, there a treacherous and cunning tribe of cut-throats roved at

sicarii, genus hominum infidum et uersutum. Si quis semitarum obseruatores aliquo transisset artifitio, capitis scilicet periculo Apostoli aecclesiam uidere cupiens, in sicarios incidens nullo modo sine substantiae uel salutis dampno domum reuerteretur. Super ipsa sanctorum apostolorum et martirum corpora,[a] super[b] sacra altaria gladii nudabantur; oblationes accedentium uix dum appositae de manibus abripiebantur, abreptae in comesationes et scortorum abusiones consumebantur.

3 Tantorum malorum turbo Gregorii papatum offendit. Ille primo leniter et, ut pontificem decet, magis amore quam terrore cum subiectis agere, delinquentes plus uerbis quam uerberibus premere: urbani a[c] peregrinorum infestatione, a rapina sacrorum cessarent; alterum esse contra naturam, ut ille qui communi uesceretur aere non communi frueretur pace; Christiano inter Christianos libere quo liberet progrediendum, dum omnes sint ex uno famulitio, omnes unius sanguinis coniuncti coagulo, redempti pretio; alterum contra Dei mandata, qui[d] preceperit[e] ut qui altario deseruiunt de altario uiuant;[1] preterea domum Dei decere esse domum orationis, non speluncam latronum, non gladiatorum conuenticulum; permitterent[f] oblationes in usus transire sacerdotum uel in expensas pauperum; prouisurum se illis quos egestas ad rapinas compelleret, ut aliquo honesto offitio stipem haberent; quos cupiditas exagitabat, ipsi sibi pro Dei timore et seculi honest-
4 ate modum ponerent. Inuasores aecclesiastici patrimonii mandatis et epistolis inuitauit ut aut indebita redderent aut se iure illa tenere in senatu Romano probarent; si neutrum facerent, aecclesiae membra se non esse cognoscerent, qui capiti aecclesiae beato Petro et eius uicario resultarent.

Talia frequenter contionatus aut[g] parum aut nichil profitiens, seuerioribus remediis inueterato morbo temptauit occurrere. Cauterio itaque excommunicationis omnes ab aecclesiae corpore remouit uel qui talia facerent uel qui agentibus conuiuio uel etiam colloquio participarent. Haec ille pro suo offitio satis agebat, sed pene in pernitiem uersa sedulitas; nam ut ille dicit: 'Qui arguit derisorem, ipse sibi iniuriam facit',[2] maligni illi leui[h] ammonitione perstricti contra furere, minis auras territare, muros urbis armis circumsonare, adeo ut pene

---

[a] corpora *after* ipsa A   [b] supra ABc   [c] om. CB   [d] TtBc¹; qu(a)e TcACBkBc²   [e] precepit A   [f] premitterent A   [g] et T (et aut Aa)   [h] leni Cd (cf. GP p. 155 and esp. p. 425)

---

[1] 1 Cor. 9: 13.   [2] Prov. 9: 7.

large in the Forum. If a man by some trick had made his way through those who kept watch on the road, desiring to see the church of the Apostle even at the risk of his life, he would fall into the hands of these gangs, and by no means return home without heavy loss in property or person. Over the very bodies of the holy apostles and martyrs, over the sacred altars swords were drawn; the offerings of pilgrims, scarcely made, were snatched from their hands, and spent on revelling and lechery.

Such was the sink of all iniquity that confronted Gregory as pope. He dealt with his subjects gently at first, and as a pontiff should more by charity than terror, putting pressure on evildoers with words rather than blows, calling on the Romans to desist from the persecution of pilgrims and the plundering of holy things. On the first point, it was against nature, he argued, that those who breathed the same air should not share a common peace: a Christian among Christians should be free to go where he would, for all were bound to the same service, united in the bond and redeemed by the price of the one Blood. The second offence was against God's commandment, who has laid down that those who minister to the altar should live of the altar;[1] God's house should be a house of prayer, not a den of thieves and assassins' trysting-place. 'Let the offerings go', he said, 'to the benefit of the priests and the needs of the poor. I will take steps to see that those who are driven to robbery by destitution have some honest employment by which to earn their bread; those who are hounded on by greed must restrain themselves for fear of God and respect for honour in this present world.' By mandates and letters he urged those who had despoiled the Church's patrimony to restore that to which they had no right, or prove their right to hold it before the Roman senate, warning those who did neither that they would no longer be members of the Church, for they would be rebels against St Peter the Church's head, and against his vicar.

When by frequent exhortations on this theme he had made little or no progress, he tried to meet the chronic disease with more stringent remedies. With the red-hot iron of excommunication he eliminated from the body of the Church all who were guilty of such practices, or who ate in common or even conversed with the guilty. In this way he for his part performed his duty; but his energy almost turned to his destruction, for (as has been well said) 'He that reproveth a scorner, getteth to himself shame',[2] and those evil men, when lightly smitten by his rebuke, reacted violently, made the air quake with their threats,

5 papam interimerent. Itaque ferro abscisionis utendum iudicans, arma undecumque et equos conquisiuit, milites et equites adornauit, ac primum basilicam beati Petri preoccupans raptores oblationum uel extinxit uel effugauit. Inde Fortunam sibi aspirare uidens longius progreditur et, si qui resisterent occisis, predia omnia et*a* oppida multis temporibus amissa in antiquum ius reformauit. Ita pax, per multorum segnitiem exulans, per unum hominem in patriam rediit. Securi peregrini insuetas uiarum terebant orbitas, leti per urbem antiquis oculos
6 pascebant miraculis, cantitantes donis factis repatriabant. Quirites interea, rapto uiuere assueti, sanguinarium illum uocabant; indignum esse qui Deo offerret sacrifitium tot cedium conscius; et ut fieri solet quod morbus obliquii ab uno serpat in omnes, ipsi etiam cardinales argumenta populi probabant, adeo ut, cum beatus ille ualitudine qua defunctus est decumberet, consilio inter se prius*b* habito, ausu temerario ammonerent ne se in aecclesia sancti Petri cum ceteris Apostolicis tumulari preciperet, qui tot hominum mortibus offitium fedasset. Tum ille recollecto spiritu toruisque luminibus minax hanc orationem habuit:

202. 'Si in uobis uel scintilla humanae rationis uel scientia diuinae auctoritatis esset, tam precipiti suasione non conueniretis pontificem uestrum; qui, quantum uixi, et patrimonium meum in uestra commoda effudi et postremo famam mundi pro uestra liberatione neglexi. Et si alii haec quae proscinditis attexerent, par erat uos obsistere, opiniones stultorum melioribus interpretationibus lenientes. Cui, queso, thesaurizaui? Forsitan michi: at thesauros antecessorum meorum habebam, qui cuiuslibet auaritiae sufficerent. Quibus salutem, quibus libertatem restitui? Referetis quod michi: at adorabar a populo et libere quae uolebam actitabam; applaudebatur michi totis
2 orationibus, acclamabatur in laudes meas totis diebus. Has laudes, hos plausus abstulit michi uestrae tenuitatis contuitus: ad uos flexi animum, et seuerius agendum estimaui. Fortunarum uestrarum titulos predo impius abliguriebat, uos inopem uitam diurno pane agebatis.

a et omnia *T* *b* om. *T*

and surrounded the city walls with the din of arms, until they nearly killed the pope. So he judged it time to use the surgeon's knife; collecting munitions and horses wherever he could, he fitted out knights and cavalry, and descending first on the basilica of St Peter, he either drove out, or wiped out, those who battened on the offerings. Next, as he saw Fortune favourable, he went further, and, killing any who resisted, reclaimed into their ancient obedience all the estates and towns that had been lost over many years. So peace, which the sloth of many men had driven into exile, through one man's energy returned to her own country. Without a care the pilgrims thronged the unfamiliar roads; lightheartedly they roamed the city, feasting their eyes on its historic wonders; and having made their offerings, they went home singing. The Romans meanwhile, accustomed to living by rapine, called him a man of blood, unworthy to offer God sacrifice with so much slaughter on his conscience; and even the cardinals themselves (for the disease of evil-speaking is, as we know, highly infectious) endorsed the protests of the people and actually, when the saintly man lay sick of his last illness, held counsel first among themselves, and then with rash presumption warned him not to give orders for his burial in St Peter's with the other popes, because he had defiled his office with the deaths of so many men. Whereat he gathered himself together, and, glowering with blazing eyes upon them, spoke as follows:

202. 'If there were a spark of human reason in you, or any knowledge of the divine commandment, you would not have set upon your pontiff with such hastily-conceived advice. All my life long I have lavished my patrimony for your advantage, and in the end I have neglected my reputation in the world to win your freedom. If anyone else were to fabricate the slanders you bring against me, it would be your duty to resist them, moderating the opinions of the foolish by more charitable interpretations. For whose benefit, pray, have I been hoarding money? For my own, perhaps? Why, I had all the treasures of my forerunners, enough to satisfy the greed of any man. For whose benefit did I restore security and freedom? You will say, my own. But I was adored by the people, and was free to do as I would; they blessed me in all their prayers, and every day were clamorous in my praise. This praise and popularity were taken from me by consideration of your parlous state; I turned my attention to you, and found it necessary to take a stronger line. The foundations of your well-being were the prey of godless ruffians, while you lived a life of poverty on a crust of

Ille de oblationibus uestris pretiosa sibi serica mercabatur, uos populari et dissuto amictu oculos mouebatis meos. Itaque, cum haec nequirem pati, bellum aliis indixi, ut dampno ciuium emerem gratiam clericorum. Sed, ut modo experior, in ingratos benefitia collata perdidi; 3 quod alii per angulos mussitant, uos euomitis in publico. Et libertatem quidem probo, sed pietatem requiro. Morientem patrem filii de sepultura sua exagitant;[a] communem mortalium domum michi negabitis? Non arcetur ab introitu aecclesiae meretricula, non usurarius, non latro; et uos papam ingredi prohibetis? Quid refert an mortuus an uiuus sacrarium introeat, nisi quod uiuus multis temptatur[b] illecebris, ut nec in aecclesia macularum subsistat immunis, ibi sepe peccandi reperiens materiam ubi uenerat diluere culpam; mortuus peccare nesciat, immo peccare non possit, supremo carens uiatico?[1] Quam immanis igitur barbaries ut hunc a domo Dei excludas cui peccandi desit et 4 uoluntas et facultas! Quapropter, filii, tam preruptae audatiae penitentiam agite, si forte uobis remittat[c] Deus hanc noxam. Stulte enim et amare locuti estis ad hanc horam.

'Sed, ne putetis me sola niti auctoritate, rationem accipite. Omnis actus hominis secundum cordis intentionem debet examinari, ut eo uergat facti iuditium unde processit fatiendi consilium. Fallor si non idem Veritas dicit: "Si oculus tuus fuerit simplex, totum corpus tuum lucidum erit; si uero nequam fuerit, totum corpus tuum tenebrosum 5 erit."[2] Crebro me miserabilis conuenit egenus ut eius leuarem inopiam; ego futurorum inscius non abnui, sed diuersis monetis onustatum dimisi. Discedens ille in publico aggere latronem offendit; incautus cum eo sermonem conseruit, predicans sedis apostolicae indulgentiam, et ut fidem dictorum probaret marsupium protulit. Interim dum itur multaque confabulatione uia fallitur, dolosus ille paulisper remoratus caputque peregrini claua quam ferebat affligens nec mora extinxit, surreptisque denariis gloriatus est de homicidio quod persuaserat pecuniae cupido. Numquid ergo me inde recte iudicabitis, qui peregrino dederam unde causam mortis incurreret?

[a] eiciunt *T*   [b] *One expects* temptetur *(cf.* nesciat *below)*   [c] remit(t)at uobis *T*

---

[1] Point uncertain.
[2] Luke 11: 34 (cf. Matt. 6: 22).

bread a day; they bought themselves rich silken garments with the offerings that were really yours, and my pity was aroused by the sight of you in your lowly ragged garb. Unable to endure this, I declared war on the other party, thinking to win the gratitude of the clergy at the citizens' expense. But, as I now find, I wasted all my kindness by expending it upon ungrateful men. Others grumble in corners; you voice the same poison in public. Your frankness I approve; but where 3 is your sense of decency? The father on his deathbed is hounded by his children from the place of burial; will you deny me the common haven of all mortal men? The prostitute, the usurer, and the thief are not debarred from entering the church; and do you forbid the pope to enter? What difference does it make, whether a man has access to the holy place dead or alive, except that the living is exposed to many temptations, so that even in church he cannot be free from stain, often finding incentive to sin in that very place to which he had gone to wash away his faults; while the dead man knows not how to sin, and indeed cannot sin, being without the last sacrament?[1] What monstrous cruelty it is, then, to debar from the house of God a man who has neither the will nor the power to do evil! Repent, therefore, my 4 children, of this outrageous conduct, in hope that God may forgive you the guilt of it. Foolish indeed and bitter have your words been up till now.

'Do not imagine, however, that I have nothing but authority on my side; hear the words of reason. Every human action should be judged according to the motive of the heart, that the judgement of the thing done may be directed to the same quarter whence came the intention of doing it. Unless I am much mistaken, the Truth says the same: "If thine eye is single, thy whole body will be full of light: but if it is evil, thy whole body will be full of darkness."[2] Often did a poor man 5 in sorry case appeal to me for the relief of his distress; and I, not foreseeing the future, did not refuse, but sent him away loaded with coin of different kinds. On his way home he fell in with a robber on the highroad; rashly he began a conversation with him, praising the generosity of the Holy See, and to prove the truth of his words produced his purse. As they went along meanwhile, beguiling the journey with plenty of talk, the rascal lagged behind for a moment, brought down the cudgel he was carrying on the pilgrim's head, and killed him on the spot; then took his money and went off, boasting of the murder which greed had inspired. Will you then properly pass judgement on me, who gave the pilgrim that which caused his death?

Neque enim ille, quanuis crudelissimus, hominem pessumdaret, nisi
auidis sinibus nummos infarcire speraret. Quid dicam de legibus forensibus et aecclesiasticis? Nonne in eis unum idemque factum diuerso respectu et punitur et laudatur? Animaduertitur in latronem quod occiderit hominem in occulto, probatur in milite si fuderit hostem in bello; ita homicidium et in illo uituperabile et in isto laudabile censetur, quia iste pro salute patriae, ille occiderit pro auiditatis ingluuie. Laudatus est olim predicandae memoriae predecessor noster Adrianus primus, quod inuestituras aecclesiarum Karolo Magno concesserit, ita ut nullus electus consecraretur ab episcopo nisi prius a rege insigniretur et anulo et baculo; contra laudatur in nostri seculi pontificibus quod has donationes tulerunt principibus. Poterat tunc rationabiliter concedi quod nunc rationabiliter*a* debet auferri. Cur ita? Quia erat animus Magni*b* aduersus auaritiam inuictus, nec facile inuenisset aditum aliquis nisi intrasset per hostium. Preterea per tot terrarum interstitia nequibat requiri sedes apostolica ut unicuique electo assensum commodaret*c* suum, dum esset prope rex qui nichil per auaritiam disponeret, sed iuxta sacra canonum scita religiosas personas aecclesiis introduceret. Nunc omnia palatia regum luxus et ambitus occupauit; quare merito libertatem suam sponsa Christi asseuerat, ne illam tirannus ambitioso usurpatori prostituat.

'Ita in utranuis partem potest causa mea infirmari uel allegari. Non est episcopi offitium ut ipse committat uel*d* committi iubeat prelium; ceterum spectat ad munus episcopi ut, si uideat naufragari innocentiam, et manu et lingua occurrat. Sacerdotes Ezechiel accusat quod non steterint ex aduerso, nec opposuerint*e* clipeum pro domo Israel in die Domini.[1] Duae sunt scilicet personae in aecclesia Dei ad resecanda uitia constitutae, una quae exacuat eloquium, altera quae portet gladium. Ego, ut uos michi testes esse potestis, non neglexi meas partes. Quoad speraui proficere, armaui linguam; illum cuius interest rem agere gladio, certiorem feci nuntio. Occupatum se rescripsit bello Vindelicorum, rogans ut meis laboribus suis expensis non grauarer deturbare latronum conciliabula. Si renuissem, quam excusationem*f*

---

a laudabiliter *TA*   *b* magni Karoli *Tt*; Karoli Magni *TcCs*   *c* *Aap* (accommodaret *Tc*), *cf. GP p. 110*; com(m)endaret *TtAlCB*   *d* committat uel *om. CB*
e opposuerint *TAl*; app- *AaCB*   *f* accusationem *A*

---

[1] Ezek. 13: 5.

Cruel as he was, the ruffian would not have finished off his victim, if he had not hoped to stuff his greedy pockets with coin. Look at our laws both civil and ecclesiastical: do they not praise and punish the one identical action, seen from different points of view? The robber is punished for killing his man in secret, the soldier praised for laying low an enemy in battle. Manslaughter is reckoned worthy of blame in the one and of praise in the other, because one killed in defence of his country, the other to satisfy his greed. My predecessor of renowned memory, Hadrian I, was praised at one time for granting the investiture of churches to Charlemagne, on terms that no candidate after election should be consecrated by a bishop, unless he were first invested by the king with ring and staff; in our own day, on the other hand, the popes are praised for having withdrawn from princes the making of these grants. It was reasonable at one time to confer powers which it is reasonable at another to take away. How can this be? The heart of Charlemagne was immune from desire of gain, and no man could easily have secured admission unless he had entered by the door; besides which, over such great distances it was in those days impractical to ask the Holy See to lend its approval to every single elected candidate, while there was a prince at hand, known to do nothing for love of gain, but to install religious persons in his churches in accordance with canon law. But now every palace is dominated by the luxury and the greed of kings, and rightly does the Bride of Christ assert her freedom, refusing to be prostituted by a tyrant to the ambitions of some interloper.

'Similarly in my own case, arguments for or against can be produced by either side. It is no part of a bishop's duty to join battle himself, or command that it be joined; but it is certainly a bishop's business, if he sees innocence in trouble, to bring it aid in deed and word. Ezekiel accuses the priests, because they "did not stand face to face or hold their shields in the way on behalf of the house of Israel in the day of the Lord."[1] There are of course two persons in the Church of God appointed to cut back the growth of wickedness, of whom the one is charged to sharpen the weapon of words, the other to bear the sword. As for me, you can bear witness for me that I have done my share; as long as I hoped to do any good, I fought with words; I warned him whose business it is to use the sword, and he replied that his hands were full with the war against the Wends, and asked me not to hesitate to root out the nests of robbers by my own efforts and at his expense. Had I refused, what excuse could I offer before God, once the emperor

Deo afferrem, cum imperator suas in me partes refudisset? Viderem cedem ciuium, dampnum peregrinorum, et dormitarem? Atqui*ᵃ* qui parcit latroni, occidit innocentem.¹ Sed obicietur non esse sacerdotis ut se cede cuiuslibet immaculet, et ego concedo, si ille se inquinat qui, sontem premens, insontem liberat; immo uero, immo "beati qui custodiunt iuditium et fatiunt iustitiam in omni tempore".² Sacerdotes fuerunt amplissima laude famosi, Finees et Mathathias, ambo sacra thiara frontem insigniti, ambo sacerdotalibus stolis amicti; ambo tamen in delinquentes manu ulti sunt. Alter uenerios amplexus pugione confodit; alter immolantem immolatitio cruori commiscuit.³ Si ipsi, quasi spissas legis tenebras palpantes, pro ipsis umbraticis misteriis zelo diuino efferati sunt, nos aperta fronte ueritatem contuentes patiemur sacra nostra profanari? Azarias*ᵇ* sacerdos regem Oziam thurificantem expulit, et proculdubio non dubitasset occidere, nisi ille accelerasset cedere. Preuenit episcopalem manum plaga diuina, ut lepra depasceretur illius cadauer cuius animus anhelasset*ᶜ* illicita.⁴ Deturbata fuit regis deuotio, et non deturbabitur latronis ambitio?

11 'Parum est quod excuso, si non et laudem factum meum. Contuli enim illis benefitium quibus uideor contulisse exitium; penam minui qui mortem acceleraui. Sceleratus enim, quanto plus uixerit, tanto plus peccabit, nisi forte aliquis*ᵈ* quem Deus singulari exemplo respexerit. Mors in commune bona est omnibus: per eam iustus reponitur in celestibus, iniustus ponit ferias sceleribus; malus dat flagitiis terminum, bonus pertendit ad brauium; sanctus propinquat ad palmam, peccator spectat ad ueniam, quod figit flagitiis metam. Gratiae igitur michi habendae sunt illorum uice qui tantis miseriis exempti sunt meo munere.

12 Haec habui quae pro me dicerem, ut uestras assertiones euacuarem. Sed quoniam et meae et uestrae ratiocinationes falli possunt, committamus omnia diuino examini. Corpus meum, antecessorum more compositum, ante ianuas aecclesiae sistite; ianuae seris et repagulis dampnentur.

ᵃ at *TcCsB* T   *ᵇ* Zacharias *Bk*, at Zacharias *Bc* (Azacharias *Bp*)   *ᶜ* depredasset
ᵈ om. *A*

¹ Perhaps not a quotation.
² Ps. 105 (106): 3.
³ Num. 25: 7–8; 1 Macc. 2: 24.
⁴ 2 Chr. 26: 17–21.

had delegated his role to me? Was I to contemplate the massacre of citizens and robbing of pilgrims, and sleep through it all? Yet "he that spares a robber, kills an innocent man".[1] It will be objected that it is not right for the priest to defile himself with the blood of any man, and I agree—if indeed he does defile himself who puts down the guilty and sets the innocent free. But in fact "blessed are they that keep judgement, and do righteousness at all times".[2] There were two priests of most honourable reputation, Phinehas and Mattathias; both wore the sacred ephod on their foreheads and both were clad in priestly robes, yet both took violent action against offenders. One stabbed a pair locked in adulterous embraces, the other mixed the blood of a man who was sacrificing with the blood of his own sacrifice.[3] If they, who had to feel their way through the thick darkness of the Law, were carried away by holy zeal on behalf of mysteries which were but a shadow of reality, shall we, who behold the truth in all clarity, allow our holy things to be profaned without protest? Azariah the priest drove out King Uzziah when he was offering incense, and no doubt would have killed him without hesitation, had he not made haste to leave. Such action by the bishop was forestalled by the stroke of divine punishment, which ordained that, as his mind had lusted for that which is unlawful, his body should be devoured by leprosy.[4] If a king has been driven from his religious observance, shall not a robber be driven from his rapacity?

'But to defend what I have done is not enough: I must claim credit for it too. I am the benefactor of those whom I seem to have destroyed, and I have reduced their punishment by hastening their deaths. The longer he lives, the more sins a criminal will commit, with rare exceptions upon whom God has looked graciously to provide a striking example. Death is in general a good thing for all men; it gives the just rest in heaven, and makes the unjust call a halt to their wrongdoing. The wicked man puts a stop to his crimes, the good attains to his reward; the saint draws near his crown, the sinner turns his thoughts towards mercy, because he makes an end of sinning. I ought therefore to be thanked on behalf of those who by my service have been rescued from such misery.

'So much I wished to say in my own defence, that I might show the falsity of your accusations. But since both your reasoning and mine may be proved wrong, let us entrust the whole question to the arbitrament of Heaven. Prepare my body for burial after the fashion of my predecessors, and lay it before the church door; then make the doors fast with bolt and

Si Deus uoluerit ut ingrediar, applaudetis miraculo; sin minus, de cadauere meo facite quod potius uestris insederit animis.'

203. Hac permoti oratione, cum ille extremum efflasset,[a] ante portas seris occlusas exanimis presulis exuuias deportant; sed mox diuinitus turbo emissus omnia repagulorum obstacula dirumpens ualuas etiam ipsas, uehementi patefactas impetu, ad parietem impulit. Populus astans[b] acclamat in gaudium; pontificis corpus cum patribus[c] celebri ueneratione locatum.

204. Isdem diebus simile huic in Anglia contigit, non superno miraculo sed inferno prestigio; quod cum retulero, non uacillabit fides historiae etsi mentes auditorum sint incredulae. Ego illud a tali uiro audiui qui se uidisse iuraret, cui erubescerem non credere. Mulier in Berkeleia mansitabat malefitiis, ut post patuit, ⟨non⟩[d] insueta, auguriorum ueterum non inscia, gulae patrona, petulantiae arbitra, flagitiis non ponens modum, quod esset adhuc citra senium, uicino licet pede pulsans senectutis aditum. Haec cum quadam die conuiuaretur, cornicula quam in delitiis habebat uocalius solito nescio quid cornicata est. Quo audito, dominae cultellus de manu[e] excidit, simul et uultus expalluit, et producto gemitu 'Hodie' ait 'ad ultimum sulcum meum peruenit aratrum. Hodie audiam et accipiam grande incommodum.' Cum dicto nuntius miseriarum intrauit. Percunctatus quid ita uultuosus aduentaret, 'Affero' inquit 'tibi ex uilla illa' (et nominauit locum) 'filii obitum et totius familiae ex subita ruina interitum.' Hoc dolore femina pectus sautia continuo decubuit, sentiensque morbum perrepere ad uitalia superstites liberos, monachum et monacham, pernicibus inuitauit epistolis. Aduenientes uoce singultiente alloquitur: 'Ego, filii, quodam meo miserabili fato demonicis semper artibus inseruii; ego uitiorum omnium sentina, ego illecebrarum magistra fui. Erat tamen inter haec mala spes uestrae religionis quae miseram palparet animam; de me desperata in uobis reclinabar; uos proponebam propugnatores aduersus demones, tutores contra seuissimos hostes. Nunc igitur, quia ad finem uitae accessi,

---

[a] T adds spiritum (eff. spir. Cs); contrast GP pp. 123 and 201   [b] clamans T
[c] presbiteris Al, predecessoribus Aa   [d] Supplied by Winterbottom (cf. GP p. 175)
(assueta Aac)   [e] de manu om. A

bar. If it is God's will that I should enter, there will be a miracle for you to acclaim; if not, you may do with my corpse whatever you have a mind to.'

203. They were much moved by this speech, and when he had breathed his last, they brought the mortal remains of their deceased pontiff, and set them before the church doors, which were bolted fast. Soon, however, a whirlwind sent by heavenly agency broke through all hindrance of bolts and bars, and by the force of its impact flung open the doors themselves and drove them back against the wall. The common people who were standing by shouted for joy, and the pope's body was laid with full ceremonial among those of his predecessors.

204. About the same time, something of the same sort occurred in England—no heavenly miracle this, but a portent from Hell. As I tell the story, the truth of my narrative shall remain unshaken, let my hearers doubt it if they will. I have it from the sort of man who would swear he has seen it, and whose word I should be ashamed to impugn. There lived in Berkeley a woman of great skill in witchcraft (as appeared later), versed in the ancient arts of soothsaying, greedy and lascivious, one who put no limits on her misdoings, for she had not yet reached old age, although her foot was now set upon its threshold. One day as she sat at dinner, a tame raven that she kept uttered some 2 croaking message more articulate than its wont; at which the knife fell from her nerveless hand, and she turned white as a sheet. 'Today', she said with a deep groan, 'my plough has come to its last furrow, today I shall hear and receive some great misfortune.' As she said these words, there entered the bearer of bad news. Asked why he came with such a face of woe, he answered: 'I bring you tidings from such-and-such a village', and he named the place. 'Your son is dead; the house has fallen and killed the whole family.' It was a mortal blow; she took to her bed on the instant, and, feeling the sickness make its way into her vitals, hastily wrote to summon her two surviving children, who were monk and nun. When they came to the bedside, she addressed 3 them in a voice shaken with sobs: 'My children, such was my hapless fate, I have ever been the slave of devilish arts; I have been a sink of all iniquity, and past mistress of every means of allurement. Amid these crimes, your holy lives were the one hope that comforted my wretched heart; in despair of myself, I found rest in you; you were my champions against the devils, my shield against my cruel foes. So now—now that I am come to the end of my life, and they who

et illos habebo*a* exactores in pena quos habui suasores in culpa, rogo uos per materna ubera, si qua fides, si qua pietas, ut mea saltem temptetis
4 alleuiare tormenta. Et de*b* anima quidem sententiam prolatam non reuocabitis; corpus uero forsitan hoc modo seruabitis. Insuite me*c* corio ceruino, deinde in sarcofago lapideo supinate, operculum plumbo et ferro constringite; super haec lapidem tribus catenis ferreis, magni scilicet ponderis, circumdate; psalmicines quinquaginta*d* sint noctibus, eiusdemque numeri missae diebus,[1] qui aduersariorum excursus feroces leuigent. Ita, si tribus noctibus secure iacuero, quarto die infodite matrem uestram humo; quamquam uerear ne fugiat terra sinibus me recipere et fouere suis, quae totiens grauata est malitiis meis.' Factum
5 est ut preceperat, illis magno studio incumbentibus. Sed proh nefas! nil lacrimae ualuere piae,[2] nil uota, nil preces: tanta erat mulierculae malitia, tanta diaboli uiolentia. Primis enim duabus noctibus, cum chori clericorum psalmos circa corpus concreparent, singuli demones hostium aecclesiae, immani obice clausum, leui negotio defringentes extremas catenas diruperunt; media, quae operosius elaborata erat, illibata durauit.*e* Tertia nocte circa gallicinium strepitu aduenientium hostium omne monasterium a fundamentis moueri*f* uisum.*g* Vnus, ceteris et uultu terribilior et statura eminentior, ianuas maiori ui concussas in
6 fragmenta deiecit. Diriguere clerici metu, 'steteruntque comae et uox faucibus hesit'.[3] Ille arroganti, ut uidebatur, gestu ad sarcofagum accessit, inclamatoque*h* nomine ut surgeret imperauit. Qua respondente quod nequiret pro uinculis, 'Solueris,' inquit, 'et malo tuo'; statimque catenam, quae ceterorum ferotiam eluserat, nullo conamine ut stuppeum uinculum dirupit. Operculum etiam tumbae pede depulit, apprehensamque manu palam omnibus ab aecclesia extraxit; ubi pro foribus equus niger et superbum hinniens uidebatur, uncis ferreis per totum tergum protuberantibus, super quos misera imposita mox ab oculis intuentium cum toto sodalitio disparuit. Audiebantur tamen clamores per quattuor fere miliaria miserabiles suppetias*i* orantis.
7   Ista incredibilia non iudicabit qui legerit beati Gregorii Dialogum, qui refert in quarto libro[4] nequam hominem, in aecclesia sepultum, a

a habeo *TCsBk*   *b* om. *A*   *c* om. *A*   *d* tribus *Tt (but not Tc), rightly?*   *e* ill. durauit om. *A*   *f* om. *A*   *g* *T* adds est   *h* inclamat(a)eque *ACBk (but cf. GP p. 29)*   *i* sub specie *T*

[1] The expression is mysterious (not least because *psalmicines* means 'singers of psalms') and Tt's *tribus* does not completely mend matters. What one expects is the sense: let fifty psalms a night be sung for three nights (thus completing the psalter), and three masses be said a day for three days.

encouraged my errors will be my executioners,—I beseech you, by the breasts that you have sucked, if you have any gratitude, if you have any pity, try at least to lighten the burden of my torments. The sentence passed upon my soul you will not undo; my body you might perhaps protect in the following way. Sew me in a deerskin, lay me on my back in a stone coffin, fasten the lid with iron and lead, then bind the stone with three iron chains of massy weight. Let there be fifty psalms by night and the same number of masses by day,[1] to relieve the bitter onslaught of my adversaries. If I can thus lie in peace for three nights, on the fourth day commit your mother to the ground, although I fear that earth itself, which I have so often burdened by my wickedness, may refuse to take and hold me in its bosom.' The children set to with a will, and her orders were carried out. But 'ah! what availed their pious tears',[2] their vows and prayers?—such was the woman's wickedness, and such was the Devil's fury. For the first two nights, as clerks in choir were singing psalms round the body, a demon came each night, and with the greatest ease burst open the church door, fastened as it was with a huge bar, and broke the outside chains; the inner one, more cunningly wrought, remained inviolate. On the third night, about cockcrow, the whole convent seemed to shake from the foundations at the roar of an advancing foe; one of them, taller and more frightful than the rest, smote the door with great force and sent the splinters flying. The clerks were paralysed with fright; 'stood hair on head, and voice in throat did freeze.'[3] With haughty mien, it seemed, he strode up to the coffin, and calling the dead woman by name, commanded her to arise. She said she could not because of the chains. 'You are loosed' he said; 'much good may it do you,' and as he spoke, he snapped without effort like a piece of string the chain that had defeated the others for all their fury, kicked off the coffin lid, and seizing her by the hand dragged her out of the church before them all. Outside the door appeared a stallion, black, whinnying proudly, with iron barbs set point upwards all down its back. On those they set her, poor wretch, and soon with the whole company she vanished from their sight, only her piteous cries being heard, for a distance of some four miles, as she begged for help.

These things no man will deem incredible who reads St Gregory's *Dialogues*; he tells in his fourth book[4] of a wicked wretch who was

[2] Unidentified. [3] Virgil, *Aen.* iii. 48.
[4] iv. 53.

demonibus foras eiectum. Apud Francos quoque non semel auditum est quod dicam: Karolum Martellum, insignis fortitudinis uirum, qui Saracenos Gallias ingressos Hispaniam redire compulit, exactis diebus suis in aecclesia sancti Dionisii sepultum; sed quia patrimonia omnium pene monasteriorum Galliae pro mercede commilitonum mutilauerat, uisibiliter a malignis spiritibus e sepulchro abreptum, ad hanc diem nusquam uisum. Denique illud reuelatum Aurelianensi episcopo, et per eum in uulgus seminatum.

205. Verum ut Romam reuertar: eiusdem urbis ciuis ephebus aetate, locuples opibus, genere senatorio sullimis uxorem nouiter duxerat, sodalibus suis accitis conuiuium frequens parauerat. Post cibum, cum minutioribus poculis hilaritatem inuitassent,[a] in Campum[1] prodeunt, ut oneratos dapibus stomachos uel saltu uel[b] iactu uel aliquo exercitio attenuarent. Ipse rex conuiuii, ludi signifer, pilam poposcit; interim anulum sponsalitium digito extento statuae aereae, quae proxime astabat, composuit. Sed cum pene omnes solum impeterent, suspiriosus[c] extis incalescentibus primus se a lusu remouit; anulum
2 repetens inuenit statuae digitum usque ad uolam curuatum. Diu ibi luctatus, quod nec anulum eicere nec digitum ualeret frangere, tacite discessit, re sodalibus celata, ne uel presentem riderent uel absentem anulo priuarent. Ita nocte intempesta cum famulis rediens, digitum iterum[d] extentum et anulum surreptum miratus est. Dissimulato dampno, nouae nuptae blanditiis[e] delinitus est. Cumque hora cubandi uenisset seque iuxta uxorem collocasset, sensit quiddam nebulosum et densum inter se et illam uolutari, quod posset sentiri nec posset uideri. Hoc obstaculo ab amplexu prohibitus, uocem etiam audiuit: 'Mecum concumbe, quia hodie me desponsasti. Ego sum Venus,
3 cuius digito apposuisti anulum; habeo illum, nec reddam.' Territus ille tanto prodigio nichil referre ausus est nec potuit;[f] insomnem illam noctem duxit, tacito iuditio rem examinans. Elapsum est in hoc multum tempus, ut quacumque ille hora gremio uellet coniugis incumbere, illud idem sentiret et audiret, alias sane ualens et domi

---

[a] inuitasset *Bk*, ministrassent *Bc (Bp avoids error)* [b] saltu uel *om. T* [c] suspiriosis *T* [d] *om. T* [e] deliciis *T* [f] ualuit *T*

[1] Apparently the Campus Martius.

buried in church, and cast out of doors by demons. In France too, what I am about to relate has been heard of more than once: Charles Martel, the brave captain who drove back into Spain the Saracen invaders of Gaul, when his life ended was buried in the church of Saint-Denis; but inasmuch as he had dismembered the estates of nearly every monastery in Gaul to pay his troops, he was snatched from his grave before men's eyes by evil spirits, and from that day to this has never been seen again. Eventually this was revealed to the bishop of Orléans, and so the truth got out.

205. But to return to Rome. There was a young Roman citizen, rich, and of high senatorial family, who, having lately married, had arranged a large dinner-party and invited all his friends. After dinner, when they had made merry with moderate draughts of liquor, they went out into the Campus[1] to relieve the repletion of the feast by jumping, throwing the javelin, or exercise of other kinds. The host of the party, as leader in the sport, called for a game of ball, and in the meantime placed his engagement-ring on the outstretched finger of a bronze statue that stood nearby. But since he was the target of nearly every attack, panting and feverish, he was the first to quit the field of play; and on going to reclaim his ring, he found the finger of the statue curved right down into the palm of its hand. After a long struggle, finding he could neither get the ring off nor break the statue's finger, he went away without saying anything, concealing the fact from his companions for fear they would laugh at him to his face, or rob him of his ring when his back was turned. When he came back at dead of night with his servants, there to his surprise was the finger again outstretched, and the ring removed. Saying nothing of his loss, he consoled himself with the caresses of his bride. But when bedtime came, and he lay down beside his wife, he was aware of some thick, murky substance that rolled between himself and her, which could be felt but not seen. Prevented by this barrier from embracing his bride, he further heard a voice, which said: 'It is with me that you must sleep, for you have betrothed yourself to me this day. My name is Venus, and it was upon my finger that you placed your ring. I have it and I will not give it up.' The poor young man was terrified by these alarming words; he found neither spirit nor voice to reply, and spent a sleepless night, silently pondering his problem. So passed a considerable time: whenever he sought his wife's embraces, he felt the same barrier and heard the same words, though in every other respect he was in the best of

aptus et militiae. Tandem querelis uxoriis[a] commonitus, rem parentibus detulit; illi habito consilio Palumbo cuidam suburbano presbitero negotium pandunt. Erat is nigromanticis artibus instructus magicas excitare figuras, demones territare et ad quodlibet offitium impellere.

4 Pactus ergo grande mercimonium ut, si amantes coniungeret, multo aere fulciret marsupium, in omne se ingenium notis artibus excitauit, compositamque epistolam iuueni dedit, 'Vade' inquiens 'illa[b] hora noctis ad compitum, ubi se findit in quadruuium, et stans tacite considera. Transient ibi figurae hominum utriusque sexus, omnis aetatis, omnis gradus, omnis postremo conditionis; [c]quidam equites, quidam pedites; alii uultum in terram deiecti, alii tumido supercilio elati; et prorsus quicquid ad laetitiam uel tristitiam pertinet, in illorum uidebis et uultibus et gestibus.[c] Nullum eorum compellabis, etsi loquantur tecum. Sequetur illam turbam quidam, reliquis statura procerior, forma corpulentior, curru sedens; huic tacitus epistolam trades legendam. Fiet e uestigio quod uoles; fac tantum presenti animo sis.'

5 Aggreditur ille iter preceptum, et nocte sub diuo astans fidem dictorum presbiteri uisu explorat; nichil enim fuit quod minus promissis desideraret.[d] Inter ceteros quoque transeuntes uidit mulierem ornatu meretritio mulam inequitantem; crinis solutus humeris inuolitabat, quem uitta aurea superne constrinxerat; in manibus aurea uirga qua equitaturam regebat; ipsa pre tenuitate uestium pene nuda gestus impudicos exsequebatur. Quid plura? Vltimus, qui dominus uidebatur, oculos terribiles in iuuenem exacuens, ab axe superbo smaragdis et

6 unionibus composito causas aduentus exquirit. Nichil ille contra, sed protenta manu porrigit epistolam. Demon, notum sigillum[e] non ausus contempnere, legit scriptum, moxque brachiis in caelum elatis 'Deus' inquit 'omnipotens, quam diu patieris nequitias Palumbi presbiteri?' Nec mora, satellites a latere suo misit, qui anulum extorquerent a Venere; illa, multum tergiuersata, uix tandem reddidit. Ita iuuenis uoti compos sine obstaculo potitus est diu suspiratis amoribus. Sed Palumbus, ubi demonis clamorem ad Deum de se audiuit, finem

[a] uxoris TcB   [b] in illa T   [c-c] after animo sis (below) T   [d] desideraret TAl[p.c.]Ce; -ares ACsB, perhaps rightly   [e] om. T

health, and fit for both peace and war. At length, driven by his wife's complaints, he made a clean breast of it all to the family, and they, after taking counsel, told the whole story to a certain Palumbus, a priest who lived near the city. Palumbus was skilled in the black arts; he knew how to raise up magic figures, and how to terrify demons and make them work for him as he pleased. He demanded a rich 4 reward, stipulating that, if he brought that loving pair together, his purse should be well lined with gold; then he bestirred himself with his familiar arts to every trick he knew, and gave the young man a letter which he had prepared. 'Go', he said, 'at such-and-such an hour of night to the crossroads where four ways meet; there take your stand, and watch in silence. Shapes will pass by of people of either sex, of every age and every degree and every class; some on horseback, some on foot; some with their faces cast down to the ground, some proud and jaunty. Every aspect of joy or sorrow will be visible in their face and mien; you will not address a word to any of them, even if they speak to you. After this throng will follow one taller than the rest and of more swelling port, seated in a carriage. Give him the letter to read, without a word, and what you wish will be instantly performed; only be sure to keep your wits about you.' The young man set off to 5 the place indicated and, standing there under the night sky, peered this way and that to see if the priest spoke truth. There was nothing he could find missing; all that he had been promised took place. Among those who passed by, he saw a woman in wanton dress riding on a mule; her long hair floated down over her shoulders, and was bound above by a golden riband. In her hands was a golden switch, with which she managed her mount. She herself was almost naked, so thin was her raiment, and she was making lewd gestures all the time. To cut a long story short, the last of them, who seemed to be their master, turned his terrible piercing eyes on the young man, from his proud chariot framed of emerald and pearl, and asked him why he had come. In reply, he said not a word, but held out his hand and 6 offered him the letter. The demon, who knew the seal and dared not treat it lightly, read what was written in it, and raising his arms to heaven burst out: 'O God Almighty, how long wilt Thou endure the wickedness of this priest Palumbus?' Without hesitation he despatched some servants of his train to exact the ring from Venus, and, after trying many a shift, she had at last reluctantly to give it up. So the young man's prayer was heard, and he found himself in undisturbed enjoyment of the love he had sighed for so long. As for Palumbus,

dierum sibi presignari intellexit. Quocirca omnibus membris ultro truncatis miserabili defunctus est penitentia, confessus papae coram populo Romano inaudita flagitia.

206. Tunc corpus Pallantis, filii Euandri, de quo Virgilius narrat,[1] Romae repertum est illibatum, ingenti stupore omnium quod tot secula incorruptione*a* sui superauit; quod ea sit natura conditorum corporum, ut carne tabescente cutis exterior neruos, nerui ossa contineant. Hiatus uulneris quod in medio pectore Turnus fecerat quattuor pedibus et semis mensuratum est. Epitaphium huiusmodi repertum:

> Filius Euandri Pallas, quem lancea Turni
> militis occidit more suo, iacet hic.

2 Quod non tunc crediderim factum, licet dicatur Carmentis mater Euandri Latinas litteras inuenisse, sed ab Ennio uel alio aliquo antiquo poeta compositum. Ardens lucerna ad caput inuenta arte mecanica, ut nullius flatus uiolentia, nullius liquoris aspergine ualeret extingui. Quod cum multi mirarentur, unus, ut semper aliqui sollertius ingenium in malis habent, stilo subtus flammam foramen fecit; ita introducto aere ignis euanuit. Corpus muro applicitum uastitate sui menium altitudinem uicit; sed procedentibus diebus, stillicidiis rorulentis infusum, communem mortalium corruptionem agnouit, cute soluta et neruis fluentibus.

207. Tunc quoque in confinio Britanniae et Normanniae portentum uisum est.*b* In una uel potius duabus mulieribus duo erant capita, quattuor brachia, et cetera gemina omnia usque ad umbilicum; inferius duo crura, duo pedes et cetera omnia singula. Ridebat comedebat loquebatur una, flebat esuriebat tacebat altera; ore gemino manducabatur, sed uno meatu digerebatur. Postremo una defuncta superuixit altera; portauit pene triennio uiua mortuam, donec et mole ponderis 2 et nidore cadaueris ipsa quoque defecit. Putatum est a quibusdam,*c* et litteris etiam traditum, quod hae mulieres Angliam et Normanniam significauerint, quae, licet spatiis terrarum sint diuisae, sunt tamen

---

a illibatione *B*   *b* uisum est portentum *T*   *c* quibus *T*

[1] *Aen.* x. 474–87. The 'epitaph' is registered as SK 5130.

when he heard the demon cry to Heaven against him, he knew that the end of his days was foretold. So he deliberately cut off all his own limbs, and expired of this lamentable penance, after confessing unheard-of crimes to the pope before all the people of Rome.

206. It was at that time that the body of Pallas son of Evander, of whom Virgil tells,[1] was discovered intact in Rome. The way it had lasted for so many centuries incorrupt caused universal astonishment; for the nature of embalmed corpses is such that, while the flesh decays, the outer skin holds together the sinews, and the sinews hold together the bones. The great gaping wound made in his breast by Turnus measured four feet six inches by the rule. An epitaph was also found, that ran somewhat as follows:

> Here Pallas lies, Evander's son;
> By Turnus' lance he was undone.

I cannot suppose that this was written at the time, although Evander's mother Carmentis is said to have invented the Latin alphabet, but rather that it is the work of Ennius or some other ancient poet. By his head a lamp was found burning, so artfully contrived that no violent blast of wind and no sprinkling of water could put it out. While many were wondering at this, one man, with the ingenious cunning some people always show when they are up to mischief, made a hole with a bodkin below the flame; and when he thus let in the air, the flame went out. The body was leant against the wall, and was so huge that it overtopped the battlements; but as time went on, and it absorbed the drips that came down like dew, it acknowledged the common law of our mortality, the skin gave way, and the sinews disintegrated.

207. It was then too that a portent appeared on the borders of Brittany and Normandy: a woman, or rather a pair of women, with two heads, four arms, and everything else double down to the navel; below that two legs, two feet, and everything else single. One of them laughed, ate, and talked; the other cried, fasted, and said nothing. There were two mouths to eat with, but only one channel for digestion. In the end one died, and the other lived; the survivor carried round her dead partner for nearly three years, until the heavy weight and the smell of the corpse were too much for her also. Some people thought, and the idea was even published, that these women signified England and Normandy which, although geographically divided, are yet united

sub uno dominio unitae. Hae quicquid pecuniarum auidis faucibus insorbuerint, in unam lacunam defluit, quae sit uel principum auaritia uel circumpositarum gentium ferotia. Mortuam et pene exhaustam Normanniam uigens*a* pecuniis sustentat Anglia, donec et ipsa fortassis succumbat exactorum uiolentia; felix si umquam in libertatem respirare poterit, cuius inanem iam dudum persequitur umbram. Nunc gemit calamitatibus afflicta, pensionibus addicta, *b*et omni nobilitate antiquorum extincta.*b*

3 Causam huiusce calamitatis describam,[1] si prius quaedam dixero ad rem pertinentia. Quia enim forensia gesta et negotia bellica regum Anglorum huc usque contexui, libet aliquantisper in sanctitate quorundam spatiari; simulque considerandum quatinus*c* diuinae pietatis fulgor ab initio fidei populum illum circumfulserit, quod nusquam gentium, ut opinor, reperies tot sanctorum illibata post mortem corpora, incorruptionis illius extremae simulacrum preferentia. Quod ideo fieri credo caelitus, ut natio pene extra orbem posita, ex consideratione incorruptelae sanctorum, fidentius ad spem resurrectionis ani-
4 maretur. Et sunt sane quinque omnino quos nouerim, ceterum plures accolae predicant sui: sancta Etheldrida et Wiburga uirgines, rex Edmundus, archiepiscopus Elfegus, Cuthbertus antiquus pater, omnes inuiolatis cute et carne, flexibilibus articulis, extremus uitali quodam tepore,*d* spetiem dormientium meditantes. Quis enumeret ceteros omnifariae conditionis et professionis sanctos? Quorum nuncupatim nomina*e* et uitas persequi nec propositum est nec otium, quamquam o si tempus olim*f* fuerit super! Sed tacebo, ne maiora uiribus uidear polliceri. Atque adeo nullum de plebe necesse est nominare, sed tantum regiae stirpis pueros puellasue, ut ceptae materiae orbitas ducam; plerosque innocenter cesos, quos non humana coniectura sed diuina ratio martires consecrauit, unde datur cognosci quantam fecerint licentiae uoluptatum parsimoniam, qui tam facilis necis compendio caelestem occuparint gloriam.

208. *g*In laudibus beatissimi Oswaldi regis et martiris in superiori libro aliquandiu uersata est oratio.[2] Cuius sanctitatis fuere inditia cum

---

a ingens *TCsBc*   *b-b* *T; om. ACB*   *c* quantus *TCs(and CpCd);* qualiter *Ce*   *d* tempore *AapB*   *e* omnia *A*   *f* om. *T*   *g* *T omits this chapter*

[1] cc. 227 seq.   [2] c. 49.

under one rule. Whatever money these two engulf in their greedy jaws descends into a single maw, which may be either the greed of princes or the ferocity of neighbouring nations. Normandy, dead and nearly sucked dry, is supported by the financial strength of England, until maybe she herself is overwhelmed by the violence of her oppressors. O happy England, if the moment ever comes when she can breathe the air of that freedom whose empty shadow she has pursued so long! As it is, she bewails her lot, worn by calamity and wasted by taxation, with all the nobility of ancient days extinct.

Of the cause of this misfortune I will say something;[1] but first I must touch on several relevant points. Hitherto, I have woven into my narrative the public acts and military exploits of the English kings; let me now dwell for a short space on the merits of some English saints. At the same time we must consider how the bright light of divine love has shone upon this people from the first days of their conversion, so that nowhere else on earth, in my opinion, will you find so many bodies of saints that are incorrupt after death, and offer an image of the incorruption that is to come at the last. I believe Heaven's purpose in this was that our nation, situate almost beyond the world, might by considering the incorruption of the saints be kindled to a more confident hope in the resurrection. Five are certainly known to me (and there are more than five whose praises are sung by those who live near them): the virgin saints Æthelthryth and Wihtburh, King Edmund, Archbishop Ælfheah, and the patriarch St Cuthbert—all with skin and flesh inviolate and joints yet supple, the last of them even with something of the warmth of life, as though they meant only to seem asleep. The other saints, of every rank and all professions, who shall number? It is not my purpose to recount their individual names and lives, nor have I the leisure; although, if only one day I have time to spare . . . ! But I will say no more, for fear of seeming to promise what is beyond my strength. And indeed I need name none of lowly birth, but only (to keep to the main line of my chosen subject) young men and maidens of the blood royal, most of them put to death in their innocence, consecrated as martyrs by heavenly providence and not by human speculation. We can see from this how sparingly they must have used their opportunities of worldly pleasure, who by the short road of a death so easy have claimed their share of heavenly glory.

208. The praise of the most blessed Oswald, king and martyr, has already occupied my pen for a space in the last book.[2] To other

cetera, tum illud quod secundum quaedam exemplaria in Gestis Anglorum asseritur:[1] in Selesiensi cenobio, quod sanctae religionis Wilfridus monachis Northanimbris repleuerat, exitialem morbum exortum multos necasse; reliquos triduano indicto ieiunio pestem*a* pellere temptasse; secunda ieiunii die beatos apostolos Petrum et Paulum puero
2 eadem ualitudine decumbenti apparentes his illum animasse: non eum debere metuere mortem imminentem, quae sit et presentis languoris exitus et uitae perhennis introitus; ceterum neminem de illo monasterio hac pestilentia moriturum, quod Deus preclari regis Oswaldi concesserit meritis pro compatriotis eadem die suplicantis; hunc enim esse diem quo idem rex peremptus a perfidis stellatum in momento tribunal conscenderit; quererent ergo in albo quo mortuorum scribebantur nomina, et, si ita inuenirent, soluto ieiunio securitati et laetitiae
3 indulgentes missarum sollemnia Deo et sancto regi concinerent. Huic uisioni pueri mors e uestigio subsecuta, martirisque dies in martirologio inuenta, simul et expulsio morbi ab omni prouintia adeo sunt attestata ut nomen Oswaldi ex tunc inter martires notaretur, quod pro recenti funere fidelium antea numero sotiabatur. Merito ergo, merito inquam laudandus, cuius gloriam diuinus assensus approbato extulit inditio, ut eum missarum preciperet celebrari preconio, inusitato (ut opinor) mortalibus exemplo. Ne*b* autem haec uideantur friuola prohibet indubitata historici auctoritas, simulque beatus episcopus Acca relatoris simmistes.

209. Egberhtus rex Cantuariorum, filius Ercomberhti, de quibus supra dixi,[2] habuit cognatos iuuenes, uicino consanguinitatis gradu lineam regum contingentes, Egelredum et Egelbrihtum, filios scilicet Ermenredi patrui sui. Hos ille in spem regni adolescere metuens, salutique suae timens, egro et miserabili uictu circa se aliquandiu habitos,*c* tandem contuitum suum eis inuidens ab aulae frequentia remouit; moxque per ministrum nomine Thunre, quod tonitruum sonat, occulte interemptos scrobi*d* profundae immersit, arbitratus posse latere

a om. CsB   *b* nec B   *c* hab. aliqu. T   *d* TBc¹*p.c.*, GP p. 318; scobi ACB

[1] Bede, HE iv. 14.
[2] cc. 11–12.

evidence for his sanctity we made add a story told in some copies of the *History of the English*.[1] In the monastery of Selsey, which had been filled by Wilfred of blessed memory with Northumbrian monks, a severe attack of pestilence had broken out, causing many deaths, and the survivors were trying to drive away the plague by a three-day fast. On the second day, the holy Apostles Peter and Paul appeared to a boy who was lying sick of the disease and encouraged him, saying that he ought not to fear the approach of death, which would put an end to his present sickness and also give him entrance into everlasting life. In any case, they said, no [other] person in the monastery would die of this pestilence, for so God had granted to the merits of the noble King Oswald, who was making supplication for his fellow-countrymen on that very day; for it was the day on which the king was done to death by traitors, and ascended in a moment to the starry throne. The monks therefore were bidden to look in the register in which the names of their dead were recorded, and if they found this to be the day, they must break off their fast, making way for confidence and joy, and sing solemn masses in the honour of God and the royal saint. Shortly after the vision the boy died; the martyr's obit was found in the martyrology; and the plague was expelled—all facts so well known in the whole region that Oswald's name was entered thenceforward among the martyrs, though from his recent death it was previously classed in the general mass of the faithful. Well and truly therefore, well and truly, I repeat, does he deserve our praise, whose glory has been exalted by the favour of Heaven with such a sign of approval, commanding that honour should be paid to him in the ceremony of the mass—an honour to which few mortals, I suppose, can provide a parallel. The unquestioned authority of the historian, and the saintly bishop Acca, who was a colleague of the narrator, forbid us to consider this an idle tale.

209. Ecgberht king of Kent, son of Earconberht, both of whom I have mentioned above,[2] had two young kinsmen Æthelred and Æthelberht, who were closely connected in blood with the royal line, being sons of his uncle Eormenred. The king was afraid that they might grow up to aspire to the throne and, fearing for his own safety, kept them near him for some time in poor and pitiful circumstances; but at length, grudging them the sight of himself, he banished them from his court, and then had them covertly put to death by a servant called Thunor (which means 'thunder'), and buried in a deep pit, thinking that a murder which he had committed out of sight of all

2 homicidium quod commisisset clam uisibus hominum. Sed diuinus ille oculus, quem archana cordium non fallunt, tulit in lucem insontes, multas ibi largitus sanitatum gratias; quoad uicini commoti, rudera illa tumultuario cespite corporibus coniecta*ᵃ* effodientes, fossam ad spetiem sepulchri dirigunt, aecclesiola superedificata. Iacuere ibi usque ad tempus regis Edgari; tunc enim a beato Oswaldo archiepiscopo*ᵇ* Wigorniensi leuata et ad cenobium Ramesiae deportata sunt, ex qua die multis se miraculis manifestarunt suplicum uotis exorabiles.

210. Offa rex Mertiorum pro confirmatione, ut putabat, regni sine ullo delectu amici uel inimici multos potentes trucidauit, inter quos Ethelbrihtum regem, nefariam rem in procum filiae operatus. Verum illius mors innocua breui regno filii Offae creditur, ut supra dixi,[1] uindicata; quin et Deus adeo euidentibus signis sanctitatem eius prodidit ut hodieque sedes episcopalis Herefordi sub ipsius nomine consecretur. Nec ineptum debet uideri aut incongruum quod antecessores nostri, probi et religiosi uiri, uel taciturnitate tolerauerunt uel auctoritate roborauerunt.

211. Quid de sancto Kenelmo, tenerae aetatulae*ᶜ* puero, stilus hic comminiscetur dignum? Hunc pater Kenulfus rex Mertiorum septennem Quendridae sororis fidei educandum reliquit; sed illa, falso sibi regnum presagiens, fraterculum tollendum e medio satelliti qui alumnus erat commendauit. Is insontem causa remittendi animum quasi uenatum ducens, inter frutecta obtruncatum occuluit. Et mirum dictu quod fraus, tam celate in Anglia commissa, Romae diuinitus innotuit: siquidem membrana super altare sancti Petri superne columba ferente
2 delapsa necis et sepulchralis loci per ordinem index.*ᵈ* Quae quia elementis Anglicis erat conscripta, a Romanis et aliarum gentium hominibus qui aderant frustra legi*ᵉ* temptata. Sed salubriter et in tempore astitit Anglus, et linguae inuolucrum Latialiter Quiritibus euoluens effecit ut Apostolici epistola regibus Anglis compatriotam martirem indicaret; quapropter frequenti cetu innocentis corpus leuatum Wincelcumbam

---

ᵃ iniecta *TA*; cf. *GP p. 319* *ᵇ* episcopo *Cd* *ᶜ* aetate *Al*, etatis *Aa*
ᵈ index fuit *Aa, GP p. 294 (MS A*ᵖ·ᶜ·*); cf. c. 276 below* *ᵉ* om. *T*

---

[1] 94. 2.

men could remain hid. But that divine Eye from which the secrets of the heart are not concealed brought his innocent victims into the light of day, by vouchsafing many miracles of healing at the place; until the neighbours, much concerned, shovelled away the stones and turf that had been hastily piled over the bodies, and dug a pit in the shape of a proper grave, with a little chapel built over it. There they lay until the time of King Edgar; for they were then taken up by St Oswald archbishop of Worcester, and carried to Ramsey abbey, since when they have shown by many miracles their readiness to listen to the prayers of suppliants.

210. Offa, king of the Mercians, for the better establishment, as he supposed, of his own kingdom put many leading men to death without distinction between friend and foe, and among them King Æthelberht, a monstrous outrage against one who sought his daughter's hand. But the death of that innocent man was avenged, it is believed, by the brevity of the reign of Offa's son, as I have said above;[1] and what is more, God made known his holiness by such evident signs that even now the cathedral church of Hereford is dedicated to him. Nor should anything seem pointless or inappropriate which our predecessors, worthy and devout men as they were, either failed to controvert or confirmed by their authority.

211. What can my pen find to write that is worthy of St Kenelm, a child of tender years? When he was seven, his father Cenwulf, king of the Mercians, entrusted him to his sister Cwenthryth to be educated, and she, wrongly expecting to get the kingdom for herself, handed over her little brother to the page who had brought him up, to be put out of the way. He took the poor innocent out hunting (as he pretended) by way of recreation, killed him, and hid the body among some bushes. And wonderful to relate, the crime so secretly committed in England came to light by divine agency in Rome. A parchment carried by a dove fluttered down upon the altar of St Peter's with precise details of his death and burial-place which, being written in English characters, the Romans and men of other nationalities who were there tried in vain to read. By good luck an Englishman appeared in the nick of time, who untied the knot of language, speaking good Latin to those men of Rome, and ensured that a letter from the pope should make known to the English kings this martyr of their own nation. As a result, the innocent child's body was taken up and conveyed with an

uehebatur. Ita clericorum uocali cantu et laicorum alacri plausu parricidalis femina commota e*ᵃ* fenestra cenaculi in quo stabat caput extulit; et forte psalterium pre manibus habens, continuatione lectionis ad psalmum peruenerat 'Deus laudem meam',*ᵇ*[1] quem a fine nescio quo prestigio retrograde dicens,*ᶜ* nitebatur laetitiam cantantium infirmare.

3 Tum uero ui diuina lumina ueneficae cauis orbibus euulsa cruore uersum polluerunt 'Hoc opus eorum qui detrahunt michi apud Dominum, et qui loquuntur mala aduersus animam meam'. Cruoris signa extant hodie, immanitatem mulierculae et Dei ultionem spirantia. Corpusculum sancti celebriter colitur, nec ullus fere locus in Anglia maiori ad festum aduentantium ueneratur frequentia. Exigit hoc et antiqua sanctitatis persuasio et miraculorum crebra exhibitio.

212. Nec uacabunt laude tua paginae nostrae, felix puer Wistane fili Wimundi, filii Wihtlafii regis Mertiorum, et Ethelfledae filiae Celwlfi, qui fuit patruus Kenelmi; te, inquam, non tacebo, quem Berferthus cognatus nefarie interemit. Norintque posteri, si qui has litteras cognitione dignas duxerint, nichil in seculo indolis tuae nobilitate gloriosius, qua irritatus infestus lanio te mortificauerit, nichil in Deo puritate tua innocentius, qua inuitatus internus arbiter te honorificauerit. Nam caelo demissa columna lucifera, densaeque noctis dirumpens pallia, profundae caueae scelus detexit, carnificis nequitiam arguit. Quapropter uenerandae reliquiae, leuatae parentum offitio, Rapendune locatae sunt, tunc temporis famoso monasterio; nunc est uilla comitis Cestrensis, cuius gloria pro situ uetustatis exoleta. Nunc Eueshamum inhabitas, dignus qui fauentum uotis serenus indulgeas.

213. De sanctitate regum Orientalium*ᵈ* Saxonum et Orientalium Anglorum Beda multa retulit, quorum regnorum genealogiam huius operis primo libro breuiter intexui,[2] quia plena gesta regum nusquam potui reperire. Veruntamen de sancto Edmundo, quem seculum Bedae non attigit, amplior procudetur oratio, qui in Orientali Anglia

---

ᵃ est *ABk*   *ᵇ* *TCs add* ne tacueris   *ᶜ* ducens *GP p. 295*   *ᵈ* Australium *T*

[1] Ps. 108 (109): 2 (and then 20).
[2] cc. 97–8.

immense concourse to Winchcombe. Roused by the sonorous chanting of the clergy and the laity's enthusiastic cheers, the murderess put her head out of the window of the chamber in which she was standing; she happened to have a psalter in her hands, and in the course of her reading had reached the psalm 'Hold not thy tongue, O God, of my praise.'[1] This she recited backwards, hoping by some nefarious trick to mar the singers' rejoicing. Then Heaven showed its power: the eyeballs of that witch were wrenched from their hollow sockets, and polluted with blood the verse 'This is the work of those who slander me before the Lord, and who speak evil against my soul.' The bloodstains can still be seen today, a vivid witness to that woman's cruelty and to the vengeance of God. The saint's tiny body is held in high esteem, and hardly any place in England is honoured by larger crowds of people coming to the saint's festival. This is demanded both by the ancient belief in his sanctity and by the frequent display of miracles.

212. Nor shall your praise, O blessed child, be lacking in my pages—Wigstan, the son of Wigmund (son of Wiglaf king of the Mercians) and Æthelflæd, daughter of Ceolwulf who was Kenelm's uncle. Of you, I say, I will not keep silence, whom your kinsman Berhtfrith so wickedly put to death; and posterity, if any of them think these lines worthy of perusal, may learn that there was nothing in the world more glorious than your noble nature, which provoked that hostile cutthroat to murder you, and nothing under God more innocent than your purity, by which the Judge of all hearts was moved to do you honour. For a column of light, descending from the sky and cleaving the deep pall of night, disclosed the crime within its deep cave and displayed the wickedness of the murderer. His venerable remains were therefore taken up by his dutiful kinsfolk and buried at Repton, which was in those days a famous monastery and is now a manor of the earl of Chester, its glory dimmed by neglect and age. Now you dwell in Evesham, and are a fit and proper person to look with a placid and indulgent eye upon the prayers of your supporters.

213. On the sanctity of the kings of the East Saxons and East Angles Bede had much to say. I have incorporated a brief genealogy of those kingdoms in the first book of this work,[2] because I have never been able to find a full history of the kings. Of St Edmund, however, whom Bede's span of time did not reach, I will fashion a fuller account. He ruled in East Anglia. That region is bounded on the south and

principatum tenuit. Prouintia illa ab austro et oriente cingitur oceano; ab aquilone paludum uligine et stagnorum rapaci uoragine, quae trium uel duum milium spatio latitudine infinitaque longitudine protensa, incolarum usui piscosam prebent exuberantiam; ab occidente reliquae insulae continua, sed defossa humo ad instar muri aggere promunita. Pecorum pabulis, ferarum capturis humus egregia, cenobiis referta, congregationibus monachorum numerosissimis intra ipsas stagnorum insulas institutis; gens laeta et lepida facetaque fes-
2 tiuitate iocorum ad petulantiam pronior. Hic regnauit Edmundus, uir Deo deuotus, auita prosapia regum excellens. Qui cum aliquot annis pacifice prouintiae prefuisset, nulla temporum mollitie uirtutem euirare impulsus, Danorum duces Hinguar et Hubba Northanimbrorum et Orientalium Anglorum depopulaturi prouintias uenere; quorum primus regem non resistentem sed armis proiectis solo pronum et orantem cepit et post nonnulla tormenta decapitauit. Emicuit post necem beati uiri transactae uitae puritas miraculis inauditis. Caput, a corpore lictoris seuitia diuisum, dumeta proicientibus Danis
3 occuluerant. Quod dum ciues quererent hostem abeuntem uestigiis insecuti, funeri regio iustas soluturi inferias, iocunda Dei munera hausere: exanimati capitis uocem expressam, omnes ad se lustratores inuitantis; lupum, feram cadaueri assuetam, lacertis illud circumplexum innoxiam pretendere custodiam; eundem more domestici animalis baiulos post tergum modeste ad tumbam secutum nullum lesisse, a nullo lesum esse.

Tunc pro tempore humi traditum corpus uenerabile, terrea gleba
4 superiecta, et exilis pretii lignea capella superstructa. Sed aderat oscitantibus prouintialibus uirtus martiris, semisopitas mentes eorum ad sui reuerentiam signis excitans; et leue quidem ac frigidum sit, sed primum uirtutum eius experimentum, quod subitiam. Latrunculos, noctu sacram edem expilare aggressos, inuisis loris in ipsis conatibus irretiuit; formoso admodum spectaculo, quod preda predones tenuit, ut nec cepto desistere nec inchoata ualerent perficere. Quapropter Theodredus Lundoniae presul, qui apud Sanctum Paulum iacet,

east by the ocean, on the north by peat-marshes, lagoons and quicksands, stretching for two or three miles in width over an infinite length, and giving the inhabitants an unlimited supply of fish; on the west, it is continuous with the rest of the island, but is defended by a moat, the earth being thrown up in the form of a rampart. The soil provides good pasture for sheep and capital hunting, and is filled with convents, very populous communities of monks having been founded right among the islands of the fen; the people are cheerful and agreeable, and so much disposed to a merry jest that they verge on insolence. Here Edmund was king, a devout Christian distinguished by ancient and royal lineage. After he had reigned over the region in peace for a number of years without allowing the effeminacy of the times to sap his manhood, the Danish leaders, Hinguar and Hubba, arrived with intent to ravage the regions of the Northumbrians and the East Angles; the first of whom, finding the king not resisting but prostrate on the ground, having thrown away his arms, and saying his prayers, took him prisoner and, after sundry tortures, beheaded him. After his death the purity of the life led by that blessed man was rendered conspicuous by unheard-of miracles. His head, severed from his body by the cruelty of the executioner, lay hidden in the thickets into which the Danes had thrown it; and while the local people, following the footsteps of the departing enemy, were hunting for it in order to pay proper funeral rites to the royal corpse, they received a gift of God that filled them with joy. They heard a noise coming from the lifeless head that summoned all the search-party towards it, and they saw a wolf, a wild animal accustomed to prey upon corpses, with the head between its forelegs, keeping watch over it without harming it at all. This wolf, like a domestic animal, followed modestly behind them as they carried the head to the grave; it harmed no one, and no one did it any harm.

At that time as a temporary measure the venerable body was consigned to the ground and covered with clods of earth, and a cheap chapel of timber built over the place. But the sleepy local people were exposed to the martyr's power, and by working miracles he roused their half-slumbrous minds to do him proper reverence. I shall add here what may be a trifle of little interest, but it is the first evidence of his miracle-working. Thieves who were trying to rob the church by night he bound by invisible thongs in mid attempt; and a very pretty sight it was to see the hunters held fast by their quarry, so that they could neither give up their attempt nor complete what they had started. As a consequence, Theodred bishop of London, who lies in

plebeiae machinae diuturnam *amolitus est iniuriam,* augustius edifitium super ueneranda membra molitus; quae et miranda incorruptione
5 et lacteo quodam candore gloriam sanctae animae predicabant. Caput, olim a ceruice reuulsum,¹ nunc reliquo corpori compaginatum, signum tamen*b* martirii coccinea cicatrice pretendens. Porro illud humana miracula excedit, hominis mortui crines et ungues sensim pullulare; quos Oswen quaedam sancta mulier quotannis hos tonderet illos desecaret, sacra ueneratione posteris futuros, sanctae temeritatis femina quae coram cerneret et contrectaret artus quibus omnis inferior hic est mundus. At non ita Lefstanus, precipitis et effrenatae audatiae adolescens, qui sibi corpus martiris minis inflatioribus ostendi exegerat, famae (ut dicebat) incertum fide oculorum ponderare deliberans.*c* Ideoque prerupti ausus penam tulit, amens effectus, et post modicum
6 scaturiens uermibus et mortuus. Nouit profecto quod olim consueuerat, nouit Edmundus modo facere, 'parcere subiectis et debellare superbos'.² Quibus artibus ita sibi omnis Britanniae deuinxit incolas ut beatum se in primis astruat qui cenobium illius uel nummo uel ualenti illustrat. Ipsi quoque reges, aliorum domini, seruos se illius gloriantur et coronam ei regiam missitant, magno si uti uolunt redimentes commertio. Exactores uectigalium, qui alias bachantur fas nefasque iuxta metientes, ibi suplices citra fossatum sancti Edmundi litigationes sistunt, experti multorum penam qui perseuerandum putarunt.

214. Nomina quoque puellarum regii generis aliquarum oris mei perstringet preconium, prefata breuitatis uenia quam non fastidii nausia sed miraculorum facit inscitia. Anna rex Orientalium Anglorum habuit filias tres, Etheldridam Ethelburgam Sexburgam. Etheldrida duobus uiris nupta felici, ut Beda auctor est,³ continentia, sine ulla pudoris iactura, sine ulla libidinis urtica perpetuae uirginitatis lauream
2 caelo uictrix exhibuit. Ethelburga in monasterio Galliae quod dicitur Brigis sanctimonialis primum, dehinc abbatissa, illibatae integritatis signaculo floruit. Et spetiosum certe quod ambae sorores, sicut concupiscentiam carnis in se uiuae domuerant, ita defunctae

a–a sustulit inuidiam *TA, GP p. 154*   *b* om. *B (adding* cum *after* mart.*)*   *c* desiderans *A*

¹ Cf. Virgil, *Georg.* iv. 523.
² Virgil, *Aen.* vi. 853.
³ *HE* iv. 19–20.

St Paul's, removed the lasting disgrace of so mean a structure, and erected a more distinguished building over his venerable remains, which by their marvellous incorruption and by a sort of milk-white radiance proclaimed the glory of that holy soul. The head, once 'from his shoulders torn',[1] was now reunited with his body, but none the less showed as evidence of his martyrdom a scarlet scar. Another thing moreover transcends all marvels known to man: the dead man's hair and nails slowly grew, and a holy woman called Oswen cut his hair every year and clipped his nails, that they might be an object of veneration to posterity. Such was the daring of her devotion, to see at close quarters and even handle the limbs worth more than all this world affords. It was not so with Leofstan, a daring young man, rash and headstrong, who demanded with bombastic threats that he should be shown the martyr's body, his plan being, so he said, to balance the uncertainties of rumour with the evidence of his own eyes. In consequence he paid the penalty for his audacity by going out of his mind, and soon he was eaten by worms and died. Well indeed does Edmund know how to put into practice now what was his custom in the old days: 'to spare the lowly and beat down the proud'.[2] By these arts he has so engaged the loyalty of all the inhabitants of Britain that anyone thinks it a privilege to enrich his monastery by even a penny. Even kings, the lords of other men, rejoice to call themselves his servants, and place their royal crown at his service, redeeming it at a great price if they wish to use it. The tax-collectors who run riot in other places, making no distinction between right and wrong, are on their knees before St Edmund, and stay their legal process at his boundary-ditch, knowing from experience how many have suffered who have thought fit to persist.

214. There are some virgins too of royal lineage on whose names I will touch with words of praise, having first begged pardon for my brevity, which is the fruit of ignorance of their miracles and not lack of interest. Anna king of the East Angles had three daughters, Æthelthryth, Æthelburh, and Seaxburh. Æthelthryth, married to two husbands, but happily (as Bede tells)[3] maintaining her chastity, with no loss of modesty and none of the pricking of fleshly desire, displayed to Heaven her victor's palm of perpetual virginity. Æthelburh, at first a nun and afterwards abbess of the convent in Gaul that is called Brie, flourished with the seal of her virginity unbroken; and it is a beautiful thought that both sisters, who had tamed the desires of the flesh in themselves during life, preserve that same flesh incorrupt after death,

incorruptam eandem preferunt, illa in Anglia, ista in Gallia, ut earum sanctitas, quae habunde fulgurat, 'suffitiat geminos irradiare polos'.[1] Sexburga, Ercomberhto*a* regi Cantuariorum in matrimonium data, et post eius mortem*b* uelata in eodem monasterio quo soror Etheldrida 3 predicatur sancta. Habuit ex illo rege filias Ercongotam et Ermenhildam. De Ercongota scire uolentes lectio Bedae informabit.[2] Ermenhilda Wlferio regi Mertiorum locata habuit filiam Werburgam, uirginem sanctissimam. Vtraeque sanctae,*c* mater *d*apud Heli, ubi post matrem Sexburgam abbatissa fuit,*d* filia*e* apud Ciuitatem Legionum pausant, in monasterio eiusdem urbis quod construxit nouiter Hugo comes Cestrensis, eiectis inde pauculis clericis qui ibidem fedo et paupere uictu uitam transigebant. Earum, et precipue iunioris, ibi laudantur merita, extolluntur miracula, cumque omnium petitionibus sint incunctanter fauorabiles, tum*f* maxime orationes feminarum et puerorum uicino et contiguo auxilii pede attingunt.

215. Frater Wlferii Merewaldus ex Ermenberga filia Ermenredi fratris Ercomberhti tulit filias Mildritham et Milburgam. Mildritha in Tanato insula Cantiae, *g*quam matri suae in solutione necis fratrum suorum Egelredi et Egelbrihti dederat rex Egberhtus,*g* celibatui dans operam, ibidem uitae metam incurrit. Sequenti tempore ad cenobium sancti Augustini Cantuariam translata, eximia monachorum sedulitate honoratur, pietatis fama et dulcedinis iuxta uocabulum suum[3] in cunctos aeque predicabilis. Et quanuis ibi pene omnes monasterii anfractus pleni sint sanctorum corporibus, nec eorum parui nominis aut meriti, sed quorum *h*singula per se possent*h* illustrare Angliam, nullo*i* tamen illa colitur*j* inferius, quin immo amatur et commemoratur dultius. Adest illa se diligentibus, nullos surda transiens aure saluti consulentes*k* animae.

216. Milburga apud Weneloch requiescit, olim ab accolis nota, sed post aduentum Normannorum dum nescitur locus sepulchri aliquandiu obliuioni data; nuper uero adunato ibi conuentu monachorum Cluniacensium, dum inchoata noui templi machina quidam puer per

---

a Ercomberti *A*   *b* mortem eius *A*   *c* om. *T*; before utraeque *ACs*
d–d om. *T*   *e* et filia *TA*   *f* tunc *A*   *g–g* om. *T*   *h–h* unus per se posset *Tt*, unus posset per se *Tc*   *i* in illo *Tt*, in nullo *Tc*   *j* colitur illa *T*
k consulens *CB*

---

[1] Unidentified.   [2] *HE* iii. 8.

one in England and the other in Gaul, so that their holiness with its abundant radiance 'illuminates at once two separate skies'.[1] Seaxburh was married to Earconberht king of Kent, but after his death took the veil in the same convent as her sister Æthelthryth, and has a reputation for sanctity. By that king she had two daughters, Earcongota and Eormenhild. Those wishing to know more of Earcongota will learn from the pages of Bede.[2] Eormenhild, married to Wulfhere king of the Mercians, had a daughter Wærburh, a virgin of great sanctity. Both saints lie, the mother at Ely where after her mother Seaxburh she was abbess, the daughter in the City of Legions, in the monastery in that city recently constructed by Hugh earl of Chester, after the expulsion of a few clerks who were living there in dirt and poverty. Both of them, and especially the younger, are praised there for their virtues and extolled for their miracles, and while their replies to all prayers are prompt and favourable, it is women and children whom they are most close at hand to help.

215. Wulfhere's brother Merewald had by Eormenburh, daughter of Earconberht's brother Eormenred, two daughters, Mildred and Mildburh. Mildred devoted herself to a celibate life in the Isle of Thanet in Kent, which King Ecgberht had given to her mother in compensation for the death of her brothers Æthelred and Æthelberht, and there she ended her days. At a later date she was translated to St Augustine's monastery at Canterbury, where she is honoured with exceptional assiduity by the monks, and celebrated equally for her piety and kindliness to all, as her name implies.[3] And although almost every nook and cranny of that monastery is filled with the bodies of saints, and those of no small reputation or merit but such that any single one might shed light on the whole of England, yet she receives no less honour than the best of them and in fact is loved and celebrated with more affection. She is at hand to help those who love her, turning a deaf ear to none who take thought for the salvation of their souls.

216. Mildburh lies at Wenlock, where she was once well known to the local people, but after the arrival of the Normans, the place of her burial being unknown, she fell for some time into oblivion. Lately, however, after the gathering in that place of a community of Cluniac monks, they had started to build a new church, and a boy, running

---

[3] *Mild* = mild; *ræd* = counsel.

pauimentum concitatius cursitaret, effracta mausolei fouea propalam corpus uirginis fecit. Tunc balsamiti odoris aura per aecclesiam spirante,*a* altius leuatum[1] tot miracula prebuit ut cateruatim eo populorum undae confluerent; uix patuli campi capiebant uiatorum*b* agmina, dum aequis umbonibus diues et mendicus se agerent, cunctos in commune precipitante fide. Nec cassum euentum res habuit, adeo ut nullus inde nisi extincta uel mitigata ualitudine discederet, nonnullosque regius morbus, medicis sane incurabilis, per merita uirginis relinqueret.

217. Eduardus senior, de quo superius multa retuli,[2] suscepit ex uxore Edgiua*c* filias multas, inter quas et Edburgam, quae uix dum*d* trima esset spectabile futurae sanctitatis dedit periculum. Explorare uolebat pater utrum ad Deum an ad seculum declinatura esset pusiola, posueratque in triclinio diuersarum professionum ornamenta, hinc calicem et euangelia, inde armillas et monilia. Illuc uirguncula ulnis nutritiae blandientis allata genibus parentis assedit, iussaque utrum uellet eligere, toruo aspectu secularia despuens prompteque manibus reptans, euangelia et calicem puellari adorauit innocentia. Exclamat cetus assidentium, auspitium futurae sanctitatis in puella exosculatus; pater ipse, arctioribus basiis dignatus sobolem, 'Vade' inquit 'quo te uocat diuinitas, sequere fausto pede quem elegisti Sponsum, et profecto et ego et coniunx felices erimus si a filia religione uicti fueri-
2 mus.' Ita sanctimonialium habitum induta, cunctas sodales ad amorem sui in urbe Wintoniae sedulitate obsequii inuitabat, nec resupinabat eam alta prosapiae magnitudo, quod generosum putaret in Christi inclinari*e* seruitio. Crescebat cum aetate sanctitas, adolescebat cum adulta humilitas, in tantum ut singularum soccos furtim noctu surriperet, et diligenter lotos et inunctos lectis rursus*f* apponeret. Quapropter, licet multis miraculis Deus uiuentem insignierit, istud exemplum magis in*g* causa predico, quod omnia opera eius inchoabat caritas et consummabat humilitas. Denique deuotionem pectoris et integritatem corporis eius miracula in uita et post mortem commen

---

a spirante T*Al(-tem Aap), GP p. 306 (cf. esp. 348. 2); properante CB* *b* populorum T, GP p. 306   *c* Ce; Elfguia Tt; Elfgiua TcA; Ethelswitha (or sim.) CsB *d* dum uix Bk(and Bp), cum uix Bc (but cf. GP p. 174)   *e* inclinare A   *f* rursum ABc   *g* One expects ea or the like

---

[1] i.e. translated.
[2] From c. 125 (see Index).

with some vigour over the floor-area, put his foot through into a hollow grave, and brought the virgin's body to light. At that moment the fragrance of balsam breathed through the church, and the corpse, raised on high,[1] performed so many miracles that throngs of people came flooding to the place. Scarcely did spacious fields contain the columns of pilgrims, as the rich man and the beggar pressed on side by side, all driven to one common object by their faith. Nor did the result prove vain, so much so that no one went away without a cure or great improvement of his complaint; some even, by this virgin's merits, obtained relief from the king's evil, which physicians cannot cure.

217. Edward the Elder, of whom I have had much to say already,[2] had by his wife Eadgifu many daughters, among them Eadburh, who, while she was scarcely three years old, gave remarkable evidence of her future sanctity. Her father wished to test whether the little maid was likely to tend towards God or the world, and had laid out in his chamber symbols of different professions, a chalice and a gospel-book on one side and on the other bracelets and necklaces. The little girl was brought in in the arms of her fond nurse, and sat on her father's knee. Told to choose what she wanted, she scorned the secular objects with a severe frown and, crawling quickly towards them on hands and knees, adored in her childish innocence the Gospels and the chalice. The company who sat round received this evidence of future sanctity in a small girl with cries of welcome; and her father himself, embracing his offspring yet more closely, said: 'Go whither Providence calls you; follow the spouse of your choice, and a blessing be upon your going. You may be sure my wife and I shall be happy if we are outdone in religion by our daughter.' So, taking the habit of a nun, she persuaded all 2 her companions in the city of Winchester to love her, by her unfailing service to them; nor was she puffed up by the grandeur of her lineage, because she thought that true nobility lay in abasing oneself in the service of Christ. Her holiness increased with her years, and her humility grew as she grew, so much so that at night-time she would secretly steal away the socks of the individual sisters, wash them carefully and anoint them, and put them back again on their beds. And so, although God marked her out, while she was still alive, by many miracles, I give greater prominence to this instance in order to show that, whatever she did, charity began it and it was perfected in humility. In sum, her heart's devotion and her body's purity are vouched for by the numerous miracles in life and after death, which the sacristans of

dant plurima, quae templorum eius editui Wintoniae et Perscorae nescientibus uiua uoce pronuntiant.

218. Edgari regis filia, beata Edgitha, Wiltunense cenobium, sedem ossuum suorum, 'dulcibus exuuiis ornat, amore fouet,'[1] ubi ab infantia scolae Dominicae tradita incorrupta semper uirginitate et frequentibus excubiis Dei gratiam demerebatur, natalium tumorem mentis ingenuitate premens. Vnum a maioribus accepi quo non mediocriter iuditium offendebat hominum, fallens uidelicet oculos eorum auratarum apparatu uestium; siquidem cultioribus indumentis iugiter ornata procederet quam illius professionis sanctitudo exposceret. Vnde a sancto Athelwoldo palam increpita[a] respondisse fertur, nec inepte nec infacete: 'Verax et irrefragabile iuditium Dei, sola mortalium operitur conscientia;[2] nam et in sordibus luctuosis potest esse iactantia. Quapropter puto quod tam incorrupta mens potest esse sub istis uestibus quam sub tuis discissis pellibus.' Hoc dicto repercussus pontifex et ueritatem dicti approbans taciturnitate sua, laetumque erubescens quod scintillante puellae sententia fuerit[b] inustus, siluit. Viderat illam sanctus Dunstanus in consecratione basilicae beati[c] Dionisii, quam illa in amorem martiris edificauerat, pollicem dextrum frequenter protendere et signum crucis fronti e regione pingere, delectatusque admodum 'Numquam' inquit 'putrescat hic digitus.' Continuoque intra[d] missarum agenda prorupit in lacrimas, lacrimas[e] adeo profluas ut singultiente uoce discipulum prope[f] astantem concuteret; reique causam quesitus, 'Cito' ait 'haec florida rosa marcescet, cito auis dilecta Deo[g] auolabit, post sex ab hoc die septimanas.' Consecuta est e uestigio rerum ueritas pontificale uaticinium; namque illa, nobilis propositi tenax, predicta die citra iuuentae terminum efflauit, cum esset annorum uiginti trium. Nec multo post idem beatus uidit somnii[h] uisione sanctum Dionisium uirginem amicabiliter manu tenentem, et ex oraculo diuino constanter iubentem ut a famulis honorificaretur in terris, sicut a Sponso et Domino uenerabatur in caelis. Ita crebrescentibus ad tumbam miraculis, edictum ut corpus uirgineum leuaretur et altius

[a] increpata *ACs, GP p. 189* [b] fuit *T* [c] sancti *A, VD p. 310* [d] infra *T* [e] lacrimas *once in TAap, VD p. 310 (contrast GP p. 189)* [f] Ce, *GP p. 189;* propter *TACsB, VD p. 311* [g] Deo dilecta *T, GP p. 189 (contrast VD p. 311)* [h] somni *A, VD p. 311 (contrast GP p. 189)*

[1] Cf. Prudentius, *Perist.* iii. 5.
[2] The *GP* version (p. 189) punctuates after 'Dei', and we have translated this sentence accordingly; an obscure contrast is made between the clear judgement of God and the hidden purposes of men.

her churches at Winchester and Pershore proclaim aloud to those who do not know them.

218. King Edgar's daughter, the blessed Eadgyth, 'decks with her remains, fosters with her love'[1] the convent of Wilton, resting-place of her bones, where, having been bound to the Lord's service from infancy, she earned God's favour by ever-incorrupt virginity and constant vigils, repressing the pride of her lineage by the simplicity of her mind. In one thing, so I have heard from my elders, she used to give no small offence to public opinion (deceiving it, no doubt, by appearances), the splendour of her gold-embroidered garments; for she always went about in more elegant clothes than were called for by the sanctity of her profession. For this she was openly rebuked by 2 St Æthelwold, and her reply, according to the story, was neither irrelevant nor without point: 'The judgement of God is true and irrefutable, while man's conscience, alone, is hidden;[2] for even in dismal mourning garb there can be an element of display. This makes me think that a pure heart may lie hid beneath these garments as easily as under your ragged sheepskin.' At these words the bishop was abashed and, showing by his silence that he felt the force of what she said, blushed (but not without pleasure) to find himself the target of a sparkling moral maxim from a young woman, and held his peace. St Dunstan had 3 seen her at the consecration of the church of St Dionysius, which she had built for love of the martyr, frequently extending her right thumb and making the sign of the cross full on her forehead, and being greatly delighted with this, he said: 'May that finger never decay.' And immediately, during the celebration of the mass, he burst into tears, such a flood of tears that the sobs in his voice shocked the assistant who was standing by him; and when asked the reason, he replied: 'Soon this rose in flower will wither, soon will the bird that God loves fly away, this day six weeks.' The truth closely followed what the bishop had foretold, for, holding to her noble purpose, on the appointed day she breathed her last before she reached the limit of her youth, being then but twenty-three years old. Not long after, 4 the saintly bishop in a dream saw a vision of St Dionysius clasping the virgin's hand in a friendly fashion, and by divine command giving strict instructions that she should be honoured by her servants on earth, just as she was respected by her Spouse and Lord in Heaven. So, as the number of miracles at her tomb increased it was decided that her virgin body should be lifted up and translated to a higher

efferretur; inuentumque totum in cineres solutum preter digitum et aluum et aluo subiecta. Vnde disputantibus nonnullis, uni ex his qui uiderant dormienti uirgo ipsa astitit, dicens non mirum esse si partes illae corporis putruerint, quod usus habeat exanimata corpora in quosdam archanos naturae sinus defluere, et ipsa utpote puella membris illis peccauerit; ceterum iuste uentrem nulla corrumpi putredine, qui nulla sit aculeatus umquam*a* libidine; immunem se fuisse crapulae et carnalis copulae.

219. Sane ambae istae uirgines meritis suis singula fulciunt cenobia, adunatis in utroque multarum sanctimonialium cetibus, quae dominabus et magistris suis uocantibus ad gratiam respondent per obedientiam. Fortunatus qui uirginalium orationum particeps fuerit, quarum deuotioni se Dominus Iesus placido indulget assensu. Nam, ut de Sceftoniensibus dixi,[1] omnes iam dudum uirtutes terris relictis caelum petiere; in solis fere sanctimonialium mentibus, si uspiam sunt terrarum, illas*b* reperies. Quod michi sanctorum uirorum pace dixisse licuerit, quia multum laudandae sunt feminae quae, dissimulata sexus infirmitate, certantibus studiis seruantes continentiam opimam ad superos euehunt uictoriam.

220. Plures e familia regia utriusque sexus cognouisse ad rem referre arbitror, ut sciatur quod a uirtutibus maiorum rex Eduardus, de quo ante digressionem dicebam,[2] minime degenerauerit. Denique miraculis et prophetiae spiritu, sicut deinceps dicam,[3] claruit. In exactionibus uectigalium parcus, quippe qui et exactores execraretur; in cibis et potibus regalis luxus immunis; in precipuis festiuitatibus, quanuis amiciretur uestibus auro intextis*c* quas regina sumptuosissime elaborauerat, ita temperans erat ut nec maiestati suae deesset nec tamen supercilium attolleret, magis Dei*d* de his munificentiam quam mundialem gloriam mente uersans. Vnum erat quo in*e* seculo animum oblectaret suum, cursus canum uelocium quorum*f* circa saltus latratibus solebat laetus applaudere, uolatus uolucrum quorum natura est de cognatis auibus predas agere. Ad haec exercitia continuis diebus post

a unquam *after* libidine *Tt*^{*a.c.*}, *after* nulla *Tc, GP p. 190*   *b* eas *T*   *c* textis *T*   *d* *om.* CB   *e* *A adds* hoc   *f* quibus *T*

[1] c. 163.
[2] That is, before c. 201.
[3] cc. 222–7.

place; and it was found all fallen into dust except the finger and the belly and the parts beneath it. This caused some discussion; and one of those who had seen it, while asleep, found the virgin herself standing there, saying it was not strange if those parts of the body had decayed, because it is normal for dead bodies to fall away and disappear into some hidden recesses of nature, and she herself, being only a girl, had sinned with those parts; but it was right that her belly should suffer no corruption, because it had never felt the prick of any lust, she always having been free from gluttony and carnal connection.

219. Of these two virgins each, of course, forms by her merits the cornerstone of a convent, and in both places are gathered together large communities of nuns who, when their abbesses and those with authority over them call them to virtue, reply by their obedience. Happy the man who finds a place in the prayers of virgins, to whose devotion the Lord Jesus lends Himself with a placid and indulgent ear. For, as I said of the nuns of Shaftesbury,[1] all the virtues have long since abandoned earth and retired to Heaven; only, perhaps, in the mind of nuns will you find them, if anywhere on earth (let me say this without offence to holy monks), for great praise is due to those women who, ignoring their sex's weakness, with competing zeal preserve their chastity, and carry a glorious victory with them to Heaven.

220. I think a knowledge of several members of the royal house of either sex is relevant, to establish that King Edward, of whom I was speaking before this digression,[2] fell by no means short of the virtues of his ancestors. He was, for instance, distinguished by miracles and a spirit of prophecy, as I shall tell in due course.[3] In the exacting of taxes he was moderate, because he execrated those who collected them. In eating and drinking he was untouched by royal luxury. On high festivals, although he wore robes interwoven with gold which the queen had worked for him at very great expense, he showed moderation, neither falling short of his royal majesty nor yet displaying pride, his mind being set much more on God's generosity in this regard than on worldly glory. There was one thing in this world which gave him great pleasure, the running of swift hounds, whose baying round his forests he would respond to with great delight, and the flying of those birds whose nature it is to pray upon their kindred. To these sports he would devote himself for days on end, once he had heard

audita mane diuina offitia intendebat. Cetera uir Deo uoluntarie deditus inter regni negotia uiuebat angelum, pauperibus hospitibusque, maxime transmarinis et religiosis, benignus appellando, munificus dando, et ad illorum sanctitatem monachos suae patriae inuitando. Erat discretae proceritatis, barba et capillis cigneus, fatie roseus, toto corpore lacteus, membrorum habitudine commoda peridoneus.

221. Viderat quondam somnii reuelatione seculi illius felicitatem Brihtwoldus Wiltunensis episcopus, uiderat et annuntiauerat. Nam dum tempore regis Cnutonis caelestibus apud Glastoniam lucubraret excubiis, subissetque illum cogitatio, quae frequenter angebat, de regia stirpe Anglorum pene deleta, haec meditanti sopor irrepsit: et ecce in superna raptus uidet apostolorum principem Petrum ipsum Eduardum, qui tunc in Normannia exulabat, in regem consecrare, celibe designata uita et[a] certo[b] uiginti quattuor annorum numero regni computato; eidemque conquerenti de posteritate respondere: 'Regnum Anglorum est Dei; post te prouidit regem ad placitum sui.'

222. Porro ut iam de miraculis dicam: adolescentula iuxta parilitatem natalium uirum habens, sed fructu coniugii carens, luxuriantibus circa collum humoribus turpem ualitudinem contraxerat, glandulis protuberantibus horrenda. Iussa somnio lauaturam manuum regis exquirere curiam ingreditur. Rex ipse per se opus pietatis adimplens digitis aqua intinctis collum pertractat mulieris; medicam dextram sanitas festina prosequitur, letalis crusta dissoluitur, ita ut uermibus cum sanie profluentibus omnis ille noxius tumor resideret. Sed quia hiatus ulcerum fedus et patulus erat, precipit eam usque ad integram sanitatem curialibus stipendiis sustentari. Verum[c] ante septimanam exactam ita obductis cicatricibus uenusta cutis rediit ut nichil preteriti morbi discerneres; post annum quoque geminam prolem enixa sanctitatis Eduardi miraculum auxit. Multotiens eum hanc pestem in Normannia sedasse ferunt qui interius eius uitam nouerunt; unde nostro tempore quidam falsam insumunt operam, qui asseuerant istius

[a] om. T [b] certe A [c] ueruntamen A

the morning service. For the rest, being a man devoted to God with all his heart, he lived amid the business of the realm an angel's life: to the poor, to guests, especially those from overseas and of a religious order, he was easy of address and generous, and he was always ready to encourage the monks of his own country to follow their holy example. He was of reasonable height, with snow-white beard and hair and rosy complexion; his whole body pallid, and with supple limbs very well proportioned.

221. The felicity of that generation had once been revealed in a dream to Brihtwold bishop of Wiltshire; he had seen it and spread the news. For in the days of King Cnut, at Glastonbury, as he was lying awake immersed in heavenly meditation, he was beset by the thought, which frequently distressed him, of the royal line of England and how it was almost completely destroyed. During these thoughts sleep overcame him, and lo, he was rapt up to Heaven and saw Peter himself, prince of the Apostles, consecrating Edward, who was at that time an exile in Normandy, as king, laying down a celibate life for him and allotting him a definite span of twenty-four years on the throne; and when he complained of his lack of posterity, the reply was: 'The English kingdom is in the hand of God, and after you He has provided a king as pleases Him.'

222. And now to speak of his miracles. A young woman with a husband much of her own age, but lacking any offspring of the marriage, had contracted an unsightly complaint; her glands became horribly prominent, for fluids had collected around her neck. Advised by a dream to try the water in which the king had washed his hands, she came to court. The king of his own free will performed a work of mercy: he dipped his fingers in water and stroked the woman's neck, and health hastened to follow his healing hand; the deadly crust melted away, so that, once worms and corrupt matter had come out of it, the whole toxic swelling subsided. Since, however, the site of the ulcers was an ugly and open wound, he gave orders that she should be kept at the expense of the court until her health was fully restored; but before a week was up, her scars were healed over and fresh skin growing so well that one could discern no trace of her trouble. A year later the birth of twins increased the miracle of Edward's sanctity. Those who knew his life intimately report that he cured this disease in Normandy many times; which shows that some people in our own day are wasting their time, when they wrongly assert that the cure of

morbi curationem non ex sanctitate sed ex regalis prosapiae hereditate fluxisse.

223. Cecatus quidam, quo incommodo incertum, rumorem frequentem in curia seuerat sanitatem se recepturum si aqua ex ablutione manuum regis oculos tangeretur. Id ad se delatum non paucis nuntiis ille riserat, referentes rugato aspectu insectatus:[a] peccatorem se esse, opera sanctorum uirorum sibi non conuenire. Verum ministri non negligendum arbitrati, eo nesciente sed in aecclesia orante, somnio credulitatem fatiunt; namque confestim ut lotus est aqua, diuturnis tenebris exulantibus, lux tempestiua orbes[b] impleuit. Laeto fragore plaudentium suscitato, rex causam percunctatus edidicit; moxque certitudine uisus eius comperta, quod scilicet digitos suos in oculos sanati intentans illum reducto capite cauere cerneret, gratias Deo porrectis in caelum manibus egit. Eodem modo sanauit cecum quendam Lincoliae, qui multis annis superuixit, regalis index miraculi.

224. Et ut perfectam uiri uirtutem[c] in hac presertim potentia cognoscas, subitiam quod mireris. Wlwinus quidam cognomento Spillecorn, filius Wlmari de Nutegareshale, quadam die in silua Bruhelle ligna cedens, dum diuturno[d] post laborem sopori indulsisset, sanguine (ut credo) circa oculos coagulato uisum decem et septem annis amisit.[e] Quibus euolutis, somnio[f] edoctus octoginta septem aecclesias circuiuit, remedium cecitatis a sanctis efflagitans. Postremo ad regis curiam ueniens, uestibulum camerae aduersantibus cubiculariis frustra diu triuit; sed perstitit improbus pulsator, donec egre admodum rege ipso
2 iubente admissus est. Audiens quippe somnium innocue responderat: 'Per dominam meam sanctam Mariam, multum grate[g] feram si Deus uoluerit per me misero misereri.' Itaque, quamquam nichil de miraculis auderet, coactus a ministris cum aqua ceco manum imposuit, confestimque[h] sanguine ex oculis ubertim stillante,[i] clamorem alacrem sanatus produxit: 'Video te, rex! Video te, rex!' Ita uidens regali palatio multis temporibus apud Windlesores (nam ibi curatus fuerat) prefuit,

---

[a] *T (cf. 239. 1 insecutus);* inspectatus *ACB error)*   [c] om. *T*   [d] diutino *T*   [b] urbes *Bk,* oculos *Bc (Bp avoids* [e] amiserat *T*   [f] sompno *B*   [g] graue *T*   [h] -que om. *A*   [i] fluente *T*

this complaint proceeded not from personal sanctity but from hereditary virtue in the royal blood.

223. A man who had been blinded, by what misfortune is uncertain, had put around frequent rumours at court that, if his eyes could be touched with water in which the king had washed his hands, his health would be restored. This had reached the king from many sources, and he had laughed it off, subjecting those who reported it to a frown: he was a sinner, he said, and saints and their doings were not for him. But the servants thought they ought not to lose the opportunity, and one day, without his knowledge, when he was praying in church, they made the dream come true; for the moment the blind man was washed with the water, the long-standing darkness fled, and the welcome light filled his eyes once more, rousing the joyful plaudits of spectators. The king asked, and was told, the reason for the noise; and soon, having established that the cured man certainly could see by bringing his fingers close to his eyes and seeing him draw his head back to protect them, he raised his hands to heaven and gave thanks to God. In the same way he cured a blind man at Lincoln, who lived on for many years as evidence of the royal miracle.

224. And to show you the perfection of his virtue, especially in this miraculous power, I will add something that will surprise you. A certain Wulfwine surnamed Spillecorn, son of Wulfmær of Ludgershall, was cutting wood one day in the forest of Brill, and had fallen into a prolonged sleep after his work was over, when the blood congealed (as I suppose) around his eyes, and he lost his sight for seventeen years. At the end of that time, instructed by a dream, he went round eighty-seven churches, seeking a remedy for his blindness from the saints. At length he came to the king's court, and there wasted a lot of time in the vestibule of the king's chamber, from which he was barred by the attendants; but he persisted, this obstinate petitioner, until he was admitted most reluctantly on the king's own orders. On hearing of the dream, the king had replied benignly: 'By my lady St Mary, I shall take it very kindly if God through me is willing to have mercy on a miserable creature.' And so, though he had no confidence in his powers, under pressure from his servants he laid his hand, dipped in water, upon the blind man. At once the blood flowed copiously from his eyes, and he was cured and cried out joyfully: 'I see you, your Majesty; I see you, your Majesty.' So, having recovered his sight, he had for a long time charge of the royal palace at Windsor

sanatoris annos longeuitate uitae transcendens. Ipso die ex eadem aqua tres ceci et unus monoculus, qui regali elemosina pascebantur, sanati sunt, ministris plena fide liquorem salutiferum largientibus.

225. Die sancti Paschae ad mensam apud Westmonasterium assederat, diademate fastigatus et optimatum turma circumuallatus. Cumque alii, longam Quadragesimae inediam recentibus cibis compensantes, acriter comederent, ille, a terrenis auocato animo diuinum quiddam speculatus, mentes conuiuantium permouit ampliorem effusus[a] in risum; nulloque causam laetitiae perquirere presumente, tunc quidem ita tacitum, donec edendi satietas obsoniis finem imposuit. Sed remotis mensis, cum in triclinio regalibus exueretur, tres optimates eum prosecuti, quorum unus erat[b] Haroldus, secundus abbas, tertius episcopus, familiaritatis ausu interrogant quare riserit: mirum omnibus, nec immerito, uideri quare in tanta serietate diei et negotii, 2 tacentibus ceteris, scurrilem cachinnum eiecerit. 'Stupenda' inquit 'uidi, nec ideo sine causa risi.' Tum illi, ut moris est humani ingenii, sciscitari et querere causam ardentius, ut suplicibus dignanter rem impertiatur. Ille, multum cunctatus, tandem instantibus mira respondit: septem dormientes in Celio monte requiescere, iam ducentis annis in dextro iacentes latere; sed tunc in ipsa hora risus sui latus inuertisse sinistrum; futurum ut septuaginta quattuor annis ita iaceant, dirum nimirum miseris mortalibus omen.[1] Nam omnia uentura in his septuaginta quattuor annis quae Dominus circa finem mundi predixit discipulis suis, gentem contra gentem surrecturam et regnum aduersus regnum, terrae motus per loca, pestilentiam et famem, terrores de caelo et signa magna,[2] regnorum mutationes, gentilium in Christianos 3 bella, item Christicolarum in paganos uictorias.' Talia mirantibus inculcans passionem septem dormientium et habitudines corporum singulorum, quas nulla docet littera, ita prompte disseruit ac si cum eis cotidiano uictitaret contubernio. His auditis, comes militem,

---

[a] perfusus TcA [b] Tt(not Tc)A add comes (one expects that, without Haroldus, cf. below 3)

[1] Cf. Virgil, Aen. xi. 182.
[2] Luke 21: 10–11 (cf. Matt. 24: 7, Mark 13: 8).

(for that is where he was cured), outliving by many years the man who had cured him. That same day, and with the same water, three blind men and one who had sight in only one eye, recipients of the royal alms, were healed, the servants giving them plenty of the healing liquid in perfect confidence.

225. One Easter Day he had taken his seat at table at Westminster, wearing his crown and surrounded by a throng of nobles. While the others were eating greedily, making up with fresh food for the long fast of Lent, the king's mind was turned away from earthly things and his thoughts concentrated on something divine, when he suddenly astonished his guests by breaking out into a roar of laughter. No one presumed to ask the reason for this merriment, and so for the moment nothing was said, until they had eaten their fill and the feast was ended. But when the tables were cleared, and he was in his chamber being relieved of his royal insignia, three leading nobles who had accompanied him (one of whom was Harold, the second an abbot, and the third a bishop), presuming on their friendship, asked him why he had laughed; everyone was surprised, they said, naturally enough, when, the day and the business being so serious and everyone else silent, he let out a great coarse laugh. 'I have seen stupendous sights,' he said, 'and so I did not laugh without good reason.' Then, as is the way of human nature, they begged and prayed him with the more warmth to explain, if only he would deign to share the story with his humble servants. After much hesitation, he at length replied to their pressure with a strange tale. 'The Seven Sleepers on Mount Cheilaion', he said, 'have now been resting on their right side for two hundred years, and at that moment, at the very instant when I laughed, they changed to their left side; in this way they will lie for seventy-four years, "a portent dire indeed for hapless men".[1] For everything will come to pass in these seventy-four years which the Lord foretold to His disciples concerning the end of the world: "Nation shall rise against nation, and kingdom against kingdom, and there shall be earthquakes in diverse places, pestilence and famine, fearful sights from heaven and great signs",[2] changes of kingdoms, wars of the Gentiles against Christians and also victories of Christians over pagans.' In recounting all this to his astonished audience, he gave as ready an account of the passion of the Seven Sleepers and personal details of them individually, which cannot be learnt from any written source, as if he lived in daily contact with them. After hearing the story, the earl sent

episcopus clericum, abbas monachum ad ueritatem uerborum exculpendam Manicheti Constantinopolitano imperatori misere, adiectis regis sui litteris et muneribus. Eos ille, benigne secum habitos, episcopo Ephesi destinauit, epistola pariter quam sacram uocant comitante, ut ostenderentur legatis regis*a* Angliae septem dormientium martiriales*b* exuuiae. Factumque est, et uaticinium regis Eduardi Grecis omnibus comprobatum, qui se a patribus accepisse iurarent super dextrum illos latus quiescere, sed, post introitum Anglorum in speluncam, ueritatem peregrinae prophetiae contubernalibus suis predicarent.

4 Nec moram festinatio malorum fecit quin Agareni et Arabes et Turchi, alienae scilicet a Christo gentes, Siriam et Litiam et Minorem Asiam omnino et Maioris multas urbes, inter quas et Ephesum, ipsam etiam Ierosolimam depopulati super Christianos inuaderent. Tunc etiam mortuo Manichete Constantinopolis imperatore Diogenes et Michaelius ac Butinatius et Alexius uicissim se de imperio precipitarunt. Quorum ultimus, ad nostra tempora usque*c* durans, Iohannem filium reliquit heredem, astutia et fraudibus quam probitate notior, multa noxia in peregrinos sacri itineris machinatus; Anglorum tamen fidem suspitiens, precipuis familiaritatibus suis eos applicabat,
5 amorem eorum filio transcribens. His septem annis proximis tres papae, Victor Stephanus Nicholaus, apostolatus uigorem continuis mortibus labefactarunt. E uestigio quoque Henricus, pius Romanorum imperator, defunctus successorem Henricum filium habuit, qui multas oppressiones orbi Romano fatuitate nequitiaque sua intulit. Eodem anno Henricus rex Francorum, miles strenuus et bonus, potionis haustu interiit. Non multo post, cometes stella, ut ferunt, mutationem regnorum*d* pretendens*e* longos et flammeos crines per inane ducens
6 apparuit; unde pulchre quidam nostri monasterii monachus, Eielmerus nomine, uiso coruscantis astri terrore conquiniscens,*f* 'Venisti,' inquit, 'uenisti, multis matribus lugende. Dudum est quod te uidi, *g*sed nunc multo terribiliorem te intueor, patriae huius excidium*g* uibrantem.' Is erat litteris, quantum ad id temporis, bene imbutus, aeuo maturus, immanem audatiam prima iuuentute conatus: nam pennas manibus et pedibus haud scio qua innexuerat arte, ut Dedali more uolaret, fabulam

a om. T *b* materiales T, rightly? *c* usque before ad ABc *d* regni T *e* portendens T (cf. e.g. 161.1) *f* congemiscens T *g-g* om. T

a knight, the bishop a clerk, and the abbot a monk to Maniches, emperor of Constantinople, to get at the truth, together with a letter and gifts from their king. The emperor received them kindly, and sent them on to the bishop of Ephesus, accompanied by what they call a sacred letter, to the effect that the martyred remains of the Seven Sleepers were to be shown to the envoys of the king of England. This was done, and King Edward's prophecy was confirmed by all the Greeks, who swore they had heard from their fathers that the Sleepers lay on their right side, but, after the Englishmen's entry into the cave, made public among their colleagues the truth of this prophecy from a foreign land.

The evil hour approached with speed, and made no delay. Hagarenes, Arabs, Turks, nations hostile to Christ, ravaged Syria and Lycia and Asia Minor as a whole, with many cities of Asia Major including Ephesus and Jerusalem itself, and invaded them at the expense of the Christians. At that time too, on the death of Maniches emperor of Constantinople, Diogenes and Michael Ducas, Botaniates and Alexius toppled one another in turn from the imperial throne; of whom the last endured to our own day and left as his heir a son, John. Alexius, better known for cunning and treachery than for honest dealing, contrived much hurt for the pilgrims on their sacred journey. He respected none the less the faith of the English, numbered them among his special friends, and bequeathed this affection for them to his son. In the next seven years three popes, Victor, Stephen, and Nicholas, weakened the vigour of the Holy See by their successive deaths. Promptly too Henry, the pious emperor of the Romans, died, and left as his successor a son Henry who inflicted much oppression on the Roman world by his folly and wickedness. That same year Henry king of the French, an active and skilful soldier, died of a draught of poison. Not long after, a comet, portending (they say) a change in governments, appeared, trailing its long flaming hair through the empty sky: concerning which there was a fine saying of a monk of our monastery called Æthelmær. Crouching in terror at the sight of the gleaming star, 'You've come, have you?', he said. 'You've come, you source of tears to many mothers. It is long since I saw you; but as I see you now you are much more terrible, for I see you brandishing the downfall of my mother-country.' By the standards of those days he was a good scholar, advanced in years by now, though in his first youth he had taken a terrible risk: by some art, I know not what, he had fixed wings to his hands and feet, hoping to fly like Daedalus, whose fable he took

pro uero amplexus, collectaque e summo turris aura spatio stadii et plus uolauit. Sed uenti et turbinis uiolentia, simul et temerarii facti conscientia, tremulus cecidit, perpetuo post haec debilis et crura effractus. Ipse ferebat causam ruinae quod caudam in posteriori parte oblitus fuerit.

226. Similem huic prophetiam Eduardus moriens exhibuit, quam hic per anticipationem dicam. Cum enim biduo elinguis iacuisset, die tertio post soporem grauiter et profunde suspirans 'Deus' inquit 'omnipotens, si non est fantastica illusio sed uerax uisio quam uidi, da michi facultatem eam astantibus exponendi, aut e conuerso.' Ita mox expedita loquela 'Duos' inquit 'modo monachos uidi michi assistere, quos adolescens olim in Normannia uideram religiosissime uixisse et Christianissime obisse. Hi, se Dei nuntios prefati, talia ingessere: "Quoniam primores Angliae, duces episcopi et abbates, non sunt ministri Dei sed diaboli, tradidit Deus hoc regnum post obitum tuum anno uno et die uno in manu inimici, peruagabunturque demones totam hanc terram." 2 Cumque ego haec me ostensurum populo dicerem, illumque[a] penitentia facta liberandum, premisso exemplo Niniuitarum, promitterem, "Neutrum" aiunt "erit, quia nec ipsi penitebunt nec Deus eis miserebitur". "Et quando" inquam "tantarum calamitatum remissio sperari poterit?" "Tunc" inquiunt "quasi si arbor uiridis succidatur in medio, et pars abscisa deportetur a stipite trium iugerum spatio, cum sine quolibet amminiculo suo iterum conexa trunco ceperit et floribus pubescere et fructus protrudere[b] ex coalescentis suci amore pristino, tunc demum poterit sperari talium malorum remissio."'

227. Huius uaticinii ueritatem, quanuis ceteris timentibus tunc Stigandi archiepiscopi risus excepisset, dicentis uetulum accedente morbo nugas delirare: huius ergo uaticinii ueritatem nos experimur, quod scilicet Anglia exterorum facta est habitatio et alienigenarum dominatio. Nullus hodie Anglus uel dux uel pontifex uel abbas; aduenae quique diuitias et uiscera corrodunt Angliae, nec ulla spes est

[a] -que om. T   [b] protudere B

to be true. Catching the breeze from the top of a tower, he flew for the space of a stade and more; but what with the violence of the wind and the eddies, and at the same time his consciousness of the temerity of his attempt, he faltered and fell, and ever thereafter he was an invalid and his legs were crippled. He himself used to give as a reason for his fall, that he forgot to fit a tail on his hinder parts.

226. A prophecy similar to this was uttered by Edward on his deathbed, which I will relate at this point by anticipation. He had lain for two days speechless; waking on the third day, he said, sighing heavily and deeply: 'Almighty God, if what I have seen is not a baseless illusion but a truthful vision, give me the power of telling it to those who stand around; or the reverse.' So his speech soon cleared, and he began: 'I saw just now two monks standing by me, whom as a young man long ago in Normandy I had seen living most holy lives and dying Christian deaths. They announced that they were sent from God, and gave me the following message: "Since the leading men in England, earls, bishops, and abbots, are servants not of God but of the Devil, God has given this kingdom after your death for a year and a day into the hand of the enemy, and demons will roam at large over the whole of this land." And when I said that I would show the people this, and promised that they would do penance and earn their freedom, instancing the example of the people of Nineveh, "Neither part of this", they said, "will come to pass: for they will not repent themselves, nor will God have pity on them." "And when", said I, "will it be possible to hope for an end to such great calamities?" "It will be", was the reply, "as though a green tree were cut through the middle of the trunk and the part cut off carried away for the space of three furlongs: when without support of any kind that part is again joined to its trunk and begins to bloom and produce fruit, as the sap of each runs together with the affection there was of old between them, then and not till then will it be possible to hope for an end to such evils."'

227. The truth of this prophecy, although while all other men trembled it had at that time been received with a laugh by Archbishop Stigand, who said that the poor old man was getting worse and talking nonsense,—the truth of this, I say, we now experience, now that England has become a dwelling-place of foreigners and a playground for lords of alien blood. No Englishman today is an earl, a bishop, or an abbot; new faces everywhere enjoy England's riches and gnaw her

finiendae miseriae. Cuius mali causam tempus est, sicut dudum spopondi,[1] ut sermo noster paucis absoluere temptet.

228. Rex Eduardus pronus in senium, quod ipse non susceperat liberos[a] et Goduini uideret inualescere filios, misit ad regem Hunorum ut filium fratris Edmundi Eduardum cum omni familia sua mitteret: futurum ut aut ille aut filii sui succedant regno hereditario Angliae; orbitatem suam cognatorum suffragio sustentari debere. Ita uenit Eduardus, sed continuo apud Sanctum Paulum Lundoniae fato functus est, tribus liberis superstitibus, uir neque promptus manu neque probus ingenio:[b] Edgaro, qui post occisionem Haroldi a quibusdam in regem electus et uario lusu Fortunae rotatus[c] pene decrepitum diem ignobilis ruri agit; Christina, quae sanctimoniali[d] habitu apud Rumesiam consenuit; Margareta, quam Malcolmus rex Scottorum legitimo matrimonio duxit. Haec, numerosa prole fecunda, habuit filios Edgarum et Alexandrum, qui post patrem regnauerunt in Scottia successione continua (nam senior Eduardus in bello cum patre occubuit, iunior Dauid mansuetudine et sapientia celebris rex Scottiae modo habetur); filias Mathildem quam nostro seculo rex Henricus, Mariam quam Eustachius iunior comes Bononiae[e] uxores duxerunt. Rex itaque defuncto cognato, quia spes prioris erat soluta suffragii, Willelmo comiti Normanniae successionem Angliae dedit. Erat ille hoc munere dignus, prestans[f] animi iuuenis et qui in supremum fastigium alacri robore excreuerat; preterea proxime consanguineus, filius Rotberti filii Ricardi secundi, quem fratrem fuisse Emmae matris Eduardi non semel est quod diximus.[2]

Ferunt quidam ipsum Haroldum a rege in hoc Normanniam missum; alii, secretioris consilii conscii,[g] inuitum uenti uiolentia illuc actum, quo se tueretur inuenisse commentum. Quod, quia propius uero uidetur, exponam. Haroldus in predium iuris sui Boseham uenerat. Ibi, ut animum oblectaret suum, piscatorium conscendit nauigium, et interim quidem longiusculo ludo in altum proceditur; sed subito aduersa tempestate coorta, ipse cum sodalibus in Pontiuum pagum compellitur. Homines illius regionis pro more gentis insito

---

[a] filios *Tt* [b] *Tt adds* scilicet [c] *TtA* add* nunc [d] sanctimonialium *Tt* [e] Beloniae *Tt (*Ben-*Al)* [f] prestantis *Tt* [g] conscium *Tt*

---

[1] c. 207.
[2] 177. 6–7, 180. 11.

vitals, nor is there any hope of ending this miserable state of affairs. The time has come for my pen to attempt, as I promised long ago,[1] a brief account of the cause of these disasters.

228. King Edward, now advanced in years, having no children of his own and seeing Godwine's sons growing more powerful, sent to the king of the Huns, asking him to send Edward, his brother Edmund's son, with all his household: either he or his sons, he said, should succeed to the hereditary throne of England, for his own lack of offspring ought to be made good by the support of his kinsfolk. So Edward came; but he promptly died at St Paul's in London, leaving three surviving children; he was a man of no energy in action and no personal integrity. The children were Edgar, who after Harold's death was elected king by some people, but after many turns of Fortune's wheel is now almost decrepit and lives ingloriously in the country; Christina who grew old as a nun at Romsey; and Margaret, whom Malcolm, king of the Scots, took in lawful wedlock. Margaret had a large 2 family. The sons were Edgar and Alexander, who reigned successively in Scotland after their father; for an elder son, Edward, died along with his father in battle, and a younger, David, notable for his mildness and wisdom, is king of Scotland now. The daughters were Matilda, who in our own day married King Henry, and Mary, who married the younger Eustace, count of Boulogne. So the king, having by his kinsman's death lost the hope of his first choice, gave the succession in England to William duke of Normandy. The duke was well worthy of this gift, being a young man of high spirit, who had reached his high dignity by energy and strength of character; besides which, he was nearest by blood, as the son of Robert, son of the second Richard who, as I have said more than once,[2] was the brother of Edward's mother Emma.

Some say that Harold himself was sent to Normandy for this 3 purpose by the king; others, more familiar with his secret intentions, maintain that he was driven there against his will by the violence of the wind, and to protect himself invented a story which, since it looks very close to the truth, I will now tell. Harold had gone to an estate of his at Bosham, and there, by way of pastime, he boarded a fishing-boat and for a time, pressing his entertainment rather far, proceeded out to sea; but a storm blew up suddenly from the wrong quarter, and he and his companions were driven to the county of Ponthieu. The men of that country, as is their national habit, flocked together

repente ex omni parte conuolauere; inermes ab armatis, pauci a pluribus, *"quod facile fuit, oppressi manus manicis,"* pedes compedibus
4 prebuere. Haroldus, astuto pectore uoluens casus remedium, hominem promissis ingentibus sollicitatum ad Willelmum mittit: missum se Normanniam a rege, ut quod minores nuntii balbutierant, ipse potissimum sua confirmaret presentia; in uinculis a Guidone Pontiui comite*[b]* detineri quo minus mandata exsequatur; barbarum et effrenatum morem regionis esse ut qui euaserant in mari naufragium in terra inuenirent periculum; conuenire tanti nominis uiro ne impunitum dimittat, quod fidem eius appellantibus uincula iniecta nonnichil de maiestate ipsius diminuerint; si pecuniis exuenda*[c]* captiuitas esset,
5 libens daret Willelmo comiti, non semiuiro Guidoni.*[d]* Ita Haroldus Willelmo mandante liberatus et ab ipso Guidone*[d]* Normanniam ductus est. Comes eum magna dignatione*[e]* gentilitio ornatu in cibis et uestibus coluit, et ut notiorem faceret, simul et uirtutem experiretur, Britannica expeditione,*[f]* quam tunc forte susceperat, secum habuit. Ibi Haroldus, et ingenio et manu probatus, Normannum in sui amorem conuertit atque, ut se magis commendaret, ultro illi tunc quidem castellum Doroberniae, quod ad ius suum pertineret, et post mortem Eduardi regnum Anglicum sacramento firmauit; quare et filiae adhuc impubis desponsione et totius patrimonii amplitudine
6 donatus, familiarium partium habebatur. Nec multum temporis intercessit quod, illo domum reuerso, rex in Natali*[g]* Domini apud Lundoniam coronatus est; ibidemque morbo ictus quo*[h]* se moriturum sciret, aecclesiam Westmonasterii die Innocentum dedicari precepit. Ita aeui plenus et gloriae simplicem spiritum caelesti regno exhibuit, et in eadem aecclesia die Theophaniae sepultus est, quam ipse illo compositionis genere primus in Anglia edificauerat quod nunc pene cuncti sumptuosis emulantur expensis.
7 Progenies Westsaxonum, quae in Britannia a Cerditio quingentis et septuaginta*[i]* uno annis, ab Egbirhto ducentis et sexaginta uno regnauerat, in illo ad regnandum omnino*[j]* defecit; nam recenti adhuc regalis funeris luctu, Haroldus ipso Theophaniae die extorta a principibus fide arripuit diadema, quanuis Angli dicant a rege concessum.

[a-a] om. B *[b]* comite Pontiui Tt *[c]* exeunda B *[d]* Godwini... Godwine A *[e]* Tt* adds complexus (so translated) *[f]* Britannicam expeditionem Tt *[g]* TtAa (cf. GP p. 427); natale AlCB *[h]* quod CeB *[i]* sexaginta Tt *[j]* ibidem Tt

suddenly from all directions, and the party, being few and unarmed, were easily overwhelmed by a larger force of armed men; their hands were bound and their feet shackled. Harold, pondering with all his 4 ingenuity how to mend the situation, suborned a man with large promises and sent him to William. He had been sent to Normandy by the king, he said, as the best man to confirm by his presence the message haltingly conveyed by lesser envoys; he was being held in chains by Guy count of Ponthieu, to prevent him carrying out his mission. It was a barbarous and outrageous custom of the region that those who had escaped shipwreck and sea must find peril waiting on land, and proper for a man of William's reputation not to let it go unpunished, for the putting in chains of those who sought his protection did some damage to his own position. If ransom was the only way out of his captivity, he would gladly pay it to Duke William, but not to an effeminate like Guy. So Harold was freed on William's orders, and taken person- 5 ally to Normandy by Guy. The duke received him with great respect, and fed and clothed him splendidly, according to the custom of his country; and that he might increase his reputation, as well as to test his valour, took him with him on an expedition to Brittany which he happened to have undertaken at that moment. There Harold, gaining approval both for his character and in the field, won the duke's affections and, to commend himself still more, voluntarily confirmed to him on oath at that time the castle of Dover, which was in his fief, and after Edward's death the kingdom of England. For this he was given the hand of the duke's daughter, who was not yet of age, and the whole of her inheritance, and was reckoned one of his intimates. Not much later, after his return home, the king wore his crown on 6 Christmas Day in London; and there too, being struck by the illness of which he knew he would die, he gave orders for the church of Westminster to be consecrated on Holy Innocents' Day. So, full of years and glory as he was, he returned his simple spirit to the kingdom of Heaven, and was buried on the feast of the Epiphany in the church aforesaid, which he himself had built, using for the first time in England the style which almost everyone now tries to rival at great expense.

The West Saxon line, which had reigned in Britain for 571 years 7 since Cerdic and 261 since Ecgberht, came with him, as concerns the throne, entirely to an end, for while grief for the king's death was still fresh, on that same feast of the Epiphany Harold, who had exacted an oath of loyalty from the chief nobles, seized the crown, though the English say that it was granted to him by the king. This claim,

Quod tamen magis beniuolentia quam iuditio allegari existimo,ᵃ ut illi hereditatem transfunderet suam cuius semper suspectam habuerat
8 potentiam: quanuis, ut non celetur ueritas, pro persona quam gerebat regnum prudentia et fortitudine gubernaret, si legitime suscepisset; denique uiuente Eduardo quaecumque contra eum bella incensa sunt, uirtute sua compressit, cupiens se prouintialibus ostentare, in regnum scilicet spe prurienti anhelans. Griffinum, ut supra dixi,[1] regem Walensium et prius bello uicit et postmodum multis nisibus resurgere conantem capite priuauit, successores duos ex satellitibus suis, fratres eiusdem Griffini Blegent et Riuallonem, qui eum obsequio demeruerant, constituens.
9 Eodem anno Tostinus, a Flandria in Humbram nauigio sexaginta nauium delatus, ea quae circa oram fluminis erant piraticis excursionibus infestabat; sed ab Eduino et Morcardo concordis potentiae fratribus impigre de prouintia pulsus uersus Scottiam uela conuertit; ibi regi Noricorum Haroldo Haruagrae obuio manus dedit, qui cum trecentis nauibus Angliam aggredi meditabatur. Ambo ergo consertis umbonibus terram Transhumbranam populabantur; germanos recenti uictoria feriatos, qui nichil minus quam talia latrocinia metuerent, aggressi uictos intra Eboracum includunt. Haroldus nuntio accepto cunctis uiribus regniᵇ eo contendit; pugna ingens commissa, utrisque
10 gentibus extrema ui nitentibus. Angli superiorem manum nacti Noricos in fugam egerunt, sed tantorum et tot uirorum uictoriam, quod forsitan posteritas difficileᶜ credat, unus Noricus multa hora interpolauit; siquidem in ingressu pontis qui Stanfordbrigge dicitur consistens, uno et altero et pluribus nostrae partis interemptis, omnes ab transitu arcuit. Inuitatus ad deditionem, ut tanti roboris homo largam clementiam Anglorum experiretur, inuitantes ridebat, subinde rugatoᵈ uultu increpitans imbecillis animi homines esse qui nequirent uni resistere. Nemine itaque propius accedente, quod inconsultum estimarent cum illo comminus congredi qui salutis omne uiaticum desperatus effunderet, unus ex collateralibus regis iaculum ferreum in eum eminus uibrat, quo ille, dum gloriabundus proludit ipsa securitate incautior,
11 terebratus uictoriam Anglis concessit. Continuo enim libero transitu

ᵃ estimo *Tt*   ᵇ om. *A*   ᶜ om. *Tt*   ᵈ rugante *Tt*

[1] 196.

3.

however, rests, I think, more on good will than judgement, for it makes him pass on his inheritance to a man of whose influence he had always been suspicious; although, not to conceal the truth, he might 8 well have ruled the kingdom, to judge by the figure he cut in public, with prudence and fortitude, had it come to him lawfully. For example, during Edward's life, whatever wars were kindled against him, it was Harold's valour that extinguished them, for he was always trying to impress public opinion, being of course consumed with ambition to be king. Gruffydd, king of the Welsh, as I have said above,[1] he first defeated in battle and later, after his many attempts to rise again, beheaded, setting up two successors from among his own followers, Gruffydd's brothers Bleddyn and Rhiwallon, who had earned his approval by their service.

In the same year Tostig sailed with a fleet of sixty ships from Flan- 9 ders to the Humber and despoiled everything near the mouth of the river with piratical raids; but by Edwin and Morcar, two brothers who used their power as one, he was vigorously driven out of the province, and turned his sails towards Scotland. There he met Harold Fairhair, king of the Norwegians, who was preparing an attack on England with three hundred ships, and gave him his fealty. Both therefore, joining forces, ravaged the land north of the Humber; the two brothers, who were resting after their recent victory and fearing nothing less than such brigandage, they attacked, defeated, and besieged in York. Harold, hearing the news, hastened north with all the forces in the kingdom, and an immense battle was fought in which both nations did their utmost. The English won the day and put the Norwegians 10 to flight; but the victory of such large and powerful forces was interrupted for many an hour (a thing posterity may hardly believe) by a single Norwegian, who is recorded to have taken his stand at the entry to the bridge called Stamford Bridge, and by killing two or three and then more of our side to have prevented them all from crossing. Called upon to surrender, that a man of such physical strength might receive generous treatment from the English, he spurned the invitation with a frown and kept taunting the enemy, saying they were a poor lot if they could not deal with a single man. So no one went near him, for it seemed unwise to attack at close quarters a desperate man who rejected all offers of safe-conduct; but one of the king's bodyguard hurled an iron javelin at him from a distance, and as he was demonstrating boastfully, rendered more incautious by justified confidence, this pierced him through and he yielded the day to the English. Given free passage, 11

exercitus traiectus Noricos palantes a tergo cecidit. Rex Haruagra et Tostinus interempti, regis filius cum omnibus nauibus domum clementer remissus. Haroldus, triumphali euentu superbus, nullis partibus predae commilitones dignatus est; quapropter multi, quo quisque poterat dilapsi, regem ad bellum Hastingense proficiscentem destituere; nam preter stipendiarios et mercennarios milites paucos admodum ex prouintialibus habuit. Vnde cum suis quos ductabat post nouem menses et aliquot dies accepti regni, astutia Willelmi circumuentus, fusus est; leui[a] uidelicet belli negotio sed occulto et stupendo Dei consilio, quod numquam postea Angli communi prelio in libertatem spirauerint, quasi cum Haroldo omne robur deciderit Angliae, qui certe potuit et debuit etiam[b] per inertissimos soluere penas perfidiae. Nec hoc dicens uirtuti Normannorum derogo, quibus cum pro genere tum pro benefitiis fidem habeo. Sed michi uidentur errare qui Anglorum numerum accumulant et fortitudinem extenuant; ita Normannos, dum laudare intendunt, infamia respergunt. Insignis enim plane laus gentis inuictissimae, ut illos uicerit quos multitudo impeditos, ignauia fecerit timidos! Immo uero pauci et manu promptissimi fuere qui, caritati corporum renuntiantes, pro patria animas posuere.

Sed quia haec diligentiorem relationem expectant, nunc dabo secundo libello[c] terminum, ut et[d] michi dictandi et aliis lectitandi studium.
reuirescat

[a] *Cs (cf. 121.5, 204.5);* leni *TtACeB*   [b] et *TtCs*   [c] libro *Tt*   [d] et ut *B*

the army crossed immediately and cut down the Norwegians, who were straying at random, from the rear. King Fairhair and Tostig were killed; the king's son with all the ships was mercifully sent home. Harold, inflated by this triumphant result, did not deign to share any part of the booty with his fellow-soldiers, with the result that many, slipping away as each best could, abandoned their king as he set off for the battle of Hastings; for apart from stipendiary knights and mercenaries he had very few Englishmen with him. Thus he, together with his men, whose leader he was, nine months and a few days after his acceptance of the throne was outwitted by William's cunning and put to rout. The war itself was a mere trifle; it was God's hidden and stupendous purpose that never again should Englishmen feel together and fight together in defence of their liberties, as though all the strength of England had fallen away with Harold, who could and should have paid the penalty for his perfidy even through the agency of utter cowards. In so saying I make no reflections on the valour of the Normans; they have my loyalty, both for my own origins and for what I owe them. But those men seem to me wrong who exaggerate the number of the English and diminish their courage, thus bringing discredit on the Normans whom they mean to praise. A mighty commendation indeed! that a most warlike nation should conquer a set of people who were disorganized because of their numbers, and fearful through cowardice! On the contrary, they were few in number and brave in the extreme, who disregarded the love of their own bodies and laid down their lives for their country.

But since these things require a more detailed treatment, I will now bring my second book to an end, that I may return to my writing, and others to their reading, with fresh zest.

LIBER TERTIVS

Prefatio libri tertii

DE WILLELMO rege scripserunt, diuersis incitati causis, et Normanni et Angli. Illi ad nimias efferati sunt laudes, bona malaque iuxta in caelum predicantes; isti pro gentilibus inimicitiis fedis dominum suum proscidere conuitiis. Ego autem, quia utriusque gentis sanguinem traho, dicendi tale temperamentum seruabo: bene gesta, quantum cognoscere potui, sine fuco palam efferam; perperam acta, quantum *ᵃ*suffitiat scientiae,*ᵃ* leuiter et quasi transeunter attingam, ut nec mendax culpetur historia, nec illum nota inuram censoria cuius cuncta pene, etsi non laudari, excusari certe possunt opera. Itaque de illo talia narrabo libenter et morose*ᵇ* quae sint inertibus incitamento, promptis exemplo, usui presentibus, iocunditati sequentibus. Verum in his protrahendis non multum temporis expendam impendium quae nulli emolumentum, immo legenti fastidium, scribenti*ᶜ* pariant odium. Satis superque suffitiunt qui genuino molari facta bonorum lacerent.*ᵈ* Michi haec placet prouintia, ut mala*ᵉ* quantum queo sine ueritatis dispendio extenuem, bona non nimis uentose collaudem. De qua moderatione, ut estimo, ueri qui erunt arbitri me nec timidum nec inelegantem pronuntiabunt. Hoc itaque non solum de Willelmo sed et de duobus filiis eius stilus obseruabit, ut nichil nimie, nichil nisi uere dicatur; quorum primus parum quod laudetur egit preter primos regni dies, tota uita dampno prouintialium comparans fauorem*ᶠ* militum. Secundus, patri quam fratri morigeratior,[1] inuictum animum inter aduersa et prospera rexit, cuius si expeditiones attendas ignores cautior an audatior fuerit, si fortunas aspitias hesites beatior aut boni euentus indigentior fuerit. Sed de talibus tempus erit cum lector arbitretur. Nunc, tertium uolumen incepturus, satis reor egisse ut attentum et docilem facerem; ipse sibi benigne persuadebit ut beniuolus sit.

ᵃ⁻ᵃ sciri necessarium erit *TtTc*, necessarium erit sciri *Tp*   *ᵇ* libenter et morosius narrabo *Tʳ*, libenter narrabo *Tc*   *ᶜ* scribendi *TpA*   *ᵈ* lacerant *A*   *ᵉ* malum *A*   *ᶠ* om. *T⁺*

---

[1] The context suggests this meaning, though the word *morigeratior* should = 'more virtuous'.

BOOK THREE

Preface

KING WILLIAM has been taken as their subject, under the spur of differing motives, by authors both Norman and English. The Normans in their enthusiasm have overpraised him, and his good and bad deeds alike have been lauded to the sky; the English, inspired by national enmities, have savaged their lord with foul calumnies. For my part, having the blood of both nations in my veins, I propose in my narrative to keep a middle path: his good deeds, so far as they have come within my knowledge, I will publish unadorned; his misdeeds I will touch on lightly and as it were in passing, so far as is needed to make them known. Thus my history will not be accused of falsehood, nor shall I be passing sentence on a man whose actions, even when they do not merit praise, at least almost always admit of excuse. Willingly therefore and with due care I will recount such incidents in his life as may provide a stimulus for the indolent or an example for the active, profitable for our own day and of interest to later generations. I shall not, however, waste much time in telling of things of no practical value, which are indeed tedious to the reader and make the writer unpopular. There are quite enough people already to tear a good man's record to pieces with the tooth of envy. My chosen province is to extenuate faults, so far as I can without sacrificing truth, and to praise good actions without undue verbiage. Good judges, I believe, will acquit me both of cowardice and of bad taste in taking this middle course. The same principle shall be observed not only for William but for his two sons: nothing to excess, nothing that is not true. The first of the sons did little worthy of praise, save in the first days of his reign; all his life long he despoiled his subjects to buy the support of his knights. The second son, who in character resembled his father rather than his brother,[1] maintained an invincible spirit in bad times and in good. If one looks at his campaigns, it would be hard to say whether caution or audacity predominated; if one considers the outcome, one wonders whether he was more fortunate or unsuccessful. But the time will come when the reader may judge for himself. Now, on the threshold of my third book, I trust I have said enough to make him attentive and receptive, and he with his usual kindness will bring himself to be well-disposed.

229. Rotbertus, alter filius Ricardi secundi, postquam septem annis gloriose ducatum Normanniae tenuit, Ierosolimam pergere mentem appulit. Habebat tunc filium septennem, ex concubina susceptum, cuius spetiem in choreis saltitantis forte conspicatus non abstinuit quin sibi nocte coniungeret, deinceps unice dilexit et aliquandiu iustae uxoris loco habuit. Puer ex ea editus Willelmus a nomine abaui dictus, cuius magnitudinem futuram matris somnium portendebat, quo intestina sua per totam Normanniam et Angliam extendi et dilatari uiderat. Ipso quoque momento quo, partu laxato, in uitam effusus pusio humum attigit, ambas manus iunco quo pauimenti puluis cauebatur impleuit, stricte quod corripuerat compugnans. Ostentum[a] uisum mulierculis laeto plausu gannientibus; obstetrix quoque fausto omine acclamat puerum regem futurum.

230. Paratis ergo omnibus quae Ierosolimitani itineris uiaticum informarent, apud Fiscamnum concilium proceribus indicitur. Ibi iubente patre in nomen et fidem Willelmi ab omnibus iuratur; Gislebertus comes tutor pupilli constituitur; tutela tutoris regi Francorum Henrico assignatur. Rotberto ceptam uiam expediente, Normanni omnes communi umbone patriam per sua quisque munimenta tutari, paruum herum ex amore uenerari. Stetit haec fides usque ad famam obitus eius, qua ubique gentium disseminata, cum fato mutatus amor:[1] mox quisque sua munire oppida, turres agere, frumenta comportare, causas aucupari quibus quamprimum a puero discidium
2 meditarentur. Inter haec ille, haud equidem reor sine Dei auxilio,[2] qui eum tanto principaturum preuiderat imperio, tutus adolescebat, cum solus pene Gislebertus aequum et bonum armis defensitaret suis; ceteri studiis partium agebantur. Iam uero interfecto Gisleberto a Radulfo patruele suo, ubique cedes, ubique ignes uersabantur. Clarissima olim patria, intestinis dissensionibus exulcerata, pro latronum libito diuidebatur, ut merito posset querimoniam facere: 'Ve terrae cuius rex puer est!'[3] At ille, ubi primum per aetatem potuit, militiae insignia a rege Francorum accipiens, prouintiales in spem quietis
3 erexit. Sator discordiarum erat Guido quidam, Burgundus a patre,

[a] ostensum T^+A

---

[1] Cf. Lucan ii. 705; vi. 453.
[2] Cf. Virgil, *Aen.* v. 56.
[3] Eccles. 10: 16.

229. Robert, the second son of Duke Richard II, after holding the duchy of Normandy with distinction for seven years, set his mind on a journey to Jerusalem. He had at that time a seven-year-old son, the child of a mistress. Her beauty had once caught his eye as she was dancing, and he could not refrain from sleeping with her; and henceforward he loved her above all others, and for some time kept her in the position of a lawful wife. The son she bore him was called William after his great-great-grandfather; his future eminence was foretold to his mother by a dream in which she saw her own inward parts extend and spread over all Normandy and England. The child himself too as a new-born baby, when at the very moment of his coming into the world he first touched the ground, filled both his hands with the rushes with which the floor was covered against dirt, and tightly clutched what he had seized. The gossiping women received this as a portent with cries of joy, and the midwife, greeting the good omen, acclaimed a baby born to be king.

230. So, having made all provision for his journey to Jerusalem, Robert summoned his magnates to a council at Fécamp, and there, at the father's bidding, all took the oath of fealty to his son William; Count Gilbert was appointed guardian to the child in his minority, and Henry king of the French invited to act as overseer of the guardian. As Robert went on his way, the Normans made common cause, each in his own stronghold, to defend their country and regard their young master with affection and respect. And faithful they remained, until the report of their lord's death; but when that news spread far and wide, 'love did with fortune change',[1] and soon everyone was fortifying his own towns, building his towers, collecting stores of grain, and on the lookout for pretexts to plan a break with the child as soon as possible. All this time, William was growing up in safety, 'not, I do think, without'[2] God's help, who had foreseen that he should be ruler over a great kingdom, though Gilbert was almost the only one to take up arms in defence of the right and good; all the others followed the lead of party passions. When, however, Gilbert was killed by his cousin Ralph, it was fire and sword everywhere. That country once so famous but now plagued by internal strife was parted by robbers among themselves at their good pleasure, and might lament with good reason. 'Woe to the land whose king is a child!'[3] William, however, as soon as he was old enough, was knighted by the king of the French, and inspired the people of the duchy with some hope of peace. The seeds of discord were sown by a certain Guy,

nepos Ricardi secundi e filia. Infantiam cum Willelmo cucurrerat, tunc quoque ianuas adolescentiae pariter urgebant; conuictus familiaritatem, familiaritas amicitias parauerat. Huc accedebat quod ei Brionium et Vernonium castella dederat, nichil pro consanguinitate negandum putans. Horum Burgundus immemor, affictis criminibus quibus id merito facere uideretur, abalienauit se a comite.

4 Longum est et non necessarium si persequar quae hinc inde acta, quae castella capta; reppererat enim perfidia sotios Nigellum uicecomitem Constantini, Rannulfum uicecomitem Baiocensem, Haimonem Dentatum, auum Rotberti qui nostro tempore in Anglia multarum possessionum incubator extitit. Cum his per totam Normanniam grassabatur predo improbissimus, inani spe ad comitatum illectus. Necessitas regem tutorem exciuit ut desperatis partibus pupilli succurreret. Itaque paternae beniuolentiae recordatus, quod eum fauore suo in regnum sullimauerat, apud Walesdunas in defectores irruit; cesa illic multa eorum milia, multi fluminis Olnae*a* rapacitate intercepti, quod

5 in arcto locati equos ad transuadandos*b* uortices instimularent. Guido uix elapsus Brionio se recepit; inde per Willelmum expulsus, non ferens probri famam, ultro Burgundiam, natiuum scilicet solum, contendit. Nec ibi inquietus animus quietem inuenit: nam a comite illius prouintiae, fratre suo Willelmo, quem insidiis impetiuerat, fugatus incompertum quem finem habuit. Nigellus et Rannulfus*c* in fidem recepti. Haimo in atie cesus, cuius insignis uiolentia laudatur quod ipsum regem equo deiecerit; quare a concurrentibus stipatoribus interemptus, pro fortitudinis miraculo regis iussu tumulatus est

6 egregie. Tulit huius gratiae stipendium rex Henricus, a Normanno domino contra Gaufredum Martellum apud Molendinum Herlae, quod castrum in Andegauensi regione est, summa ui adiutus; nam iam in*d* uirile robur excreuerat, maioribus natu et pluribus solus metuendus. Solus caput*e* discriminibus inferre, solus uel cum paucis in confertissimos diuersae partis insilire. Quapropter ab illa expeditione laudatae fortitudinis specimen et amicitiarum apud regem culmen retulit; adeo ut quasi paterno consilio sepe ammoneret ne ad pericula promptus uitam suam despiceret, quae esset Francis decori, Normanniae tutamento, utrisque*f* exemplo.

a Oll(a)e *A*   *b* transuadendos *A*   *c* Radulfus *CB (but cf. 4 above)*
d om. *T¹*   *e* B adds in   *f* utrique *T¹*

a Burgundian on his father's side and on his mother's the grandson of Richard II; he and William had run the course of childhood together and were now both on the threshold of adult life. Their common upbringing had made them acquainted, and acquaintance had given place to friendship; besides which William had given Guy the castles of Brionne and Vernon, thinking that a kinsman should have all he asked. All this Guy of Burgundy forgot and, inventing grievances to justify his conduct, abandoned the duke.

It would be tedious and pointless to recount the moves made on each 4 side and the castles taken; for treachery had found accomplices in Nigel viscount of the Cotentin, Ranulf viscount of Bayeux, and Haimo Longtooth, grandfather of the Robert who in our day accumulated such great possessions in England. With these supporters the infamous marauder ranged all over Normandy, led on by the empty hope of making himself duke. William's guardian, the king, was roused by the emergency to come to the help of his ward in these desperate straits; and, remembering the father's friendship, whose support had raised him to the throne, he fell upon those traitors to the son at Val-ès-Dunes. Many thousands died on the field; many men, while trying to escape from a tight place by urging their horses to ford the rapids of the river Orne, were swept away by its swift course. Guy made his escape with difficulty 5 and took refuge in Brionne, but was driven out by William and, overcome with disgrace, beat a rapid retreat to Burgundy, his native soil. Even there his restless mind found no peace, for he was driven out by the count of the province, his own brother William, against whom he had intrigued, and what his end was no one knows. Nigel and Ranulf were admitted to do homage; Haimo fell in the battle, but won great praise for his valour by unhorsing the king himself, and after the bodyguard had rallied and cut him down, his astonishing courage was rewarded at the king's command with a splendid funeral. King Henry was requited for this service 6 by the lord of Normandy, who aided him with might and main against Geoffrey Martel at Mouliherne, a castle in Anjou. For he had now come to a man's strength. He was an object of fear to older men and, even when single-handed, to numbers; alone he would expose himself to dangers and alone or with few companions rush into the thickest of the opposing side. Thus he returned from this expedition with a reputation for the valour all had admired, and the highest place in the king's esteem, so that the king often warned him like a father not to plunge headlong into danger and make too little of his own life, which was a credit to the French, a tower of strength to Normandy, and an example to both alike.

231. Eo tempore erat comes Andegauorum Gaufredus cognomento Martellus; quod ipse sibi usurpauerat, quia uidebatur sibi felicitate quadam omnes obsistentes contundere. Denique dominum suum, comitem Pictauensem, aperto marte cepit ferreisque uinculis innodatum ad ignobilis pacis conditiones adduxit: Burdegala et confinibus urbibus[a] cederet, de ceteris annuum uectigal pensitaret. Sed ille, ut creditur, pro ferri iniuria et ciborum inedia benefitio oportunae mortis post triduum perpetuae ignominiae exemptus est. Tum Martellus, ne quid deesset impudentiae, nouercam defuncti matrimonio sibi copulauit, fratres in tutelam recipiens quoad possent principatui regendo
2 sufficere. Mox Teodbaldi Blesensis comitis ingressus limites, urbem Turonicam obsedit, ipsum ciuibus suis auxilium ferre uolentem consortio erumnae implicuit; siquidem captus Teodbaldus[b] et in ergastulo reclusus urbem sibi omnibusque suis heredibus in posterum abiurauit.[c] Pudendam miseriam hominis quis dixerit, ut, pro ambitione quantulaecumque uitae, tantae urbis dominio successores suos perpetuo fraudaret, licet seueriores plerumque aliorum[d] arbitri simus quam ipsi
3 nobis consulere nouerimus, si forte in talibus deprehensi fuerimus. Ita Martellus, tantarum uirium augmento turgidus, etiam Normannum comitem Alentii castelli possessione uellicauit, pronis in perfidiam habitatoribus. Qua is irritatus iniuria par pari retulit, et Danfrontum, quod erat tunc comitis Andegauorum, obsidione coronauit. Nec mora, obsessorum querelis commonitus Gaufredus non segnis[e] aduolat innumero stipatus milite. Nuntio aduenientis accepto, Willelmus Rogerium de Monte Gomerico et Willelmum filium Osberni exploratum mittit; illi, pro alacritate iuuentae breui multa miliaria progressi, equitantemque[f] Martellum conspicati, certiorem de domini sui auda-
4 tia fatiunt. Ille contra fremere, immania minari, post tridie se illuc uenturum, ostensurum mundo quam[g] prestet in armis Andegauensis Normanno; simul eximia arrogantia colorem equi sui et armorum insignia quae habiturus sit insinuat. At exploratores non minori fastu eadem de Willelmo denuntiantes regrediuntur,[h] et suos in certamen accendunt. Haec ideo seriatim retuli, ut Martelli tumor legentibus elucesceret. Ceterum nichil tunc de solita magnanimitate ausus,

---

[a] eius T^+ plerumque T^+ [b] om. T^+A [c] obiurauit CeB [d] aliorum (alio et Tp) [e] segni A [f] -que om. A [g] quod A [h] ingrediuntur B

231. The count of Anjou at this time was Geoffrey surnamed Martel, 'the Hammer', a style that he had himself adopted in the belief that by some special fortune he was able to beat down all opposition. For example, he took his own lord, the count of Poitou, prisoner in pitched battle, put him in irons, and forced him to make peace on shameful terms, the surrender of Bordeaux and neighbouring cities and the payment of an annual tribute for the rest. Three days later, however, the count was rescued from lifelong disgrace by a well-timed death, brought on, it is supposed, by the chafing chains and lack of food. Thereupon Martel, to complete his effrontery, married the dead man's stepmother, and took his brothers into wardship until they should be capable of ruling their own inheritance. Next, invading the territory of 2 Count Theobald of Blois, he laid siege to the city of Tours, and Theobald, trying to bring help to his citizens, was caught up in their misfortunes; after being taken prisoner and confined in a dungeon, he resigned all rights in the city for himself and all his heirs in perpetuity. Anyone would cry shame on such a pitiful performance, to deprive his successors for all time of the lordship of that great city, in hopes of recovering a few years of his own life; though we are generally more severe judges of other people than we shall be of ourselves, if we are ever caught in such a plight. So Martel, inflated by this great accession 3 of strength, went on to provoke the Norman duke by seizing the castle of Alençon, its inhabitants being all too prone to treachery. Aroused by this insult, William paid him in the same coin, and invested Domfront, which in those days belonged to the count of Anjou. Geoffrey was soon aroused by the appeals of the besieged, and hastened to the spot with a large force. On hearing news of his approach, William despatched Roger of Montgomery and William Fitz Osbern to reconnoitre, who, with all the energy of youth, covered many miles in a short time and, having espied Martel on the move, informed him of the bold intentions of their own lord. In reply Geoffrey stormed at them with tremendous 4 threats: he would be at Domfront next day, and show the world that an Angevin in arms was more than a match for any Norman. At the same time, with exceptional arrogance, he let them know the colour of his horse and the bearings he would be displaying on his armour. The scouting-party, not to be outdone, replied with the same information about William, and then returned and made their own side eager for the fray. This story I have told in some detail, in order to give my readers a clear picture of the boastful nature of Geoffrey Martel. As it was, he displayed on that occasion none of his usual courage, and turned tail

antequam in manus ueniretur terga ostendit. Quo audito, Alentini se dedidere, pacti membrorum salutem; post etiam Danfrontini felitiora signa secuti.*a*

232. Posterioribus annis rebellauit Willelmus comes de Archis, patruus eius sed nothus, a primis auspitiis ducatus infidus et uersipellis; nam et in obsidione Danfronti clam profugerat, et multis sepe animi sui latebras aperuerat. Quapropter Willelmus quibusdam,*b* quos fideles falso arbitrabatur, firmitatem castelli commiserat; uerum ille astu quo callebat, multa largiendo, plura pollicendo, in suas partes eosdem traduxit. Munitione igitur potitus, bellum domino suo denuntiauit. Ille solito more alacerrime Archas obsedit, dissuadentibus amicis, palam professus nichil latrones ausuros si in conspectum eius uenissent. Nec promissio fide caruit: namque plusquam trecenti milites, qui pabulatum et populatum processerant, eo pene solo conspecto intra munitiones refugere. Dux sine sanguine rem peragere uolens, offirmato contra Archas castello, ad alia quae magis urgebant bella conuersus est, simul quia sciebat regem Francorum, iam pridem nescio qua simultate sibi infensum, ad opem obsesso ferendam aduentare; namque predicandi moderaminis consilio, quanuis iustiorem causam habere uideretur, cum eo decernere ferro cauebat cui et pro sacramento et pro suffragio obnoxius erat. Reliquit tamen primates aliquos qui impetum regium tardarent; quorum astutia insidiis exceptus, Isembardum Pontiui comitem coram se obtruncari, Hugonem Pardulfum capi merito ingemuit. Nec multo post eo dulcem Frantiam, quia res male cesserat, repetente, comes Arcensis fame tabidus et uix ossibus herens deditioni consensit, ad exemplum clementiae, ad inditium industriae uitae et membris reseruatus. Huiusce obsidionis interuallo populus castri quod Molendinis dicitur exsolescens ad partes regis incentore quodam Galterio transiit. Imponitur ibi non segnis militum manus, prefecto Guidone fratre comitis Pictauensis. Is aliquantis diebus sedulo militiae munia exsecutus est; uerum crebrescente fama Arcensis uictoriae Frantiam elapsus, non leue incrementum accessit ducalis gloriae.

a T*+* adds sunt   *b* quidam B

before they came to grips. When this news reached them, his men in Alençon surrendered, stipulating for their personal safety, and thereafter the people of Domfront likewise joined the winning side.

232. In later years came a rebellion of William count of Arques, his uncle but born out of wedlock, who from the first beginnings of the dukedom had been treacherous and fickle; even during the siege of Domfront he had secretly deserted, and had often revealed to many the duke's inmost secrets. Duke William had therefore entrusted the security of the fortress to certain other persons, wrongly supposed by him to be trustworthy; but the count with his usual cunning, by lavish gifts and still more lavish promises, brought them over to his side. Having thus got possession of the castle, he declared war on his own lord. The duke with all his wonted energy laid siege to Arques against the advice of his friends, declaring openly that the rascals would dare do nothing if once they came within sight of him. And he was quite right, for more than three hundred knights, who had sallied forth in search of forage and plunder, had scarcely caught sight of his unattended person when they took refuge within the walls. The duke, hoping to settle things without bloodshed, established a fort in front of Arques, and turned to other and more urgent conflicts, being aware at the same time that the king of the French, who had long for some unknown reason been out of temper with him, was approaching to bring help to the besieged; for with commendable prudence, although he seemed to have more justice on his side, the duke was reluctant to force a decision in the field upon a prince to whom he was bound by an oath of fealty and by gratitude for his support. However, he left some of his nobles to delay the king's advance; and by their cunning the king was ambushed, and had to mourn not undeservedly the loss of Isembard count of Ponthieu, killed before his eyes, and Hugh Bardulf, taken prisoner. Before long the king, whose expedition had gone none too well, retired to his beloved France, and the count of Arques, stricken with famine and mere skin and bone, agreed to surrender, being spared in life and limb to be an example of clemency and show what energy can do. During the siege the people of a walled town called Moulins went to the bad and crossed over to the king's side at the instigation of a certain Walter. An active garrison was installed there, commanded by Guy, brother of the count of Poitou, who for some days was vigorously engaged on operations; but when news spread of the victory at Arques, he escaped to France, thereby considerably increasing the duke's reputation.

233. Nec rex Henricus otio indulsit, quin*a* grunniret exercitus suos ludibrio fuisse Willelmo. Coactis itaque omnibus uiribus et copiis bipertitis, totam inundauit Normanniam, ipse de parte Galliae*b* Celticae,*c* quae inter Garunnam et Sequanam fluuios iacet, quicquid militum erat suo ductu trahens, Odonem fratrem populo Galliae Belgicae, 2 quae est inter Renum et Sequanam, prefitiens. Eodem modo Willelmus suos qua poterat animositate diuisit, iuxta regis castra sensim obambulans, quae iam in Ebroicensi pago metabatur, ut nec comminus pugnandi copiam faceret nec prouintiam coram se uastari sineret. Duces eius Rotbertus comes Aucensis, Hugo Gornacensis, Hugo Montis Fortis, Willelmus Crispinus ad castellum quod Mortuum Mare uocatur infestis signis contra Odonem constitere. Nec ille pro numero militum, quo tumebat, moram pugnae fecit, sed parumper resistere ausus, mox impetum Normannorum non ferens terga nudauit, omen fugae 3 primus auspicatus. Ibi dum Guido Pontiui comes studiosius ultioni fratris intendit, captus fatalem familiae suae manum exhorruit; preterea plures alii precellentes opibus,*d* turgentes maiorum natalibus. Hunc successum, ex aduenientibus*e* cognitum, Willelmus circum regis tentoria nocte intempesta preconari curauit; quo audito, post aliquot dies quos in Normannia egit, refugit in Frantiam. Nec multo post tempore, discurrentibus utrobique nuntiis, pacifice conuentum ut regii captiui absoluerentur, comes erepta uel eripienda Martello iure uendicaret legitimo.

234. Longum est et non necessarium referre quantae inter eos contentiones uersatae sint, quomodo Willelmus semper superiorem manum retulerit. Quid quod inestimabili presumptione fortitudinis numquam subito, nec nisi prenuntiata die, illum aggredi dignatus, nostri temporis morem animi magnitudine contempserit? Illud quoque pretereo, quod iterum ruptis*f* amicitiis rex Henricus, Normanniam ingressus, per pagum Oximensem usque ad fluuium Diuae peruenerit, iactitans*g* solum oceanum progressioni suae esse obstaculum. Verum Willelmus, qui se uideret propter fidei dissimulationem immoderate premi, tunc tandem consciae uirtutis arma concutiens regias copias quae citra*h* flumen erant*i* (nam pars paulo ante eius

---

a T^+Cs *(cf. 16. 2);* qui *ACeB*   *b* Galliti(a)e *A*   *c* Celtica T^+ *d* operibus *CB*   *e* aduentantibus T^+A *f* raptis *A*   *g* iactans T^+
h T^+ *(cf. William of Poitiers p. 82 Foreville);* circa *ACB*   *i* om. T^+

233. Nor did King Henry remain idle. It rankled that William should have made a laughing-stock of his armies, and so he collected all his strength and, dividing his forces in two, swept over the whole of Normandy. All the knights from Celtic Gaul, which lies between the rivers Garonne and Seine, he led in person, while he put his brother Odo at the head of the men from Belgian Gaul, which lies between Rhine and Seine. William made a similar division of his own 2 forces with all his usual élan, and moved slowly back and forth not far from the king's camp, which by this time was pitched in the region of Évreux, so that he gave the king no opportunity for a hand-to-hand engagement, and yet did not allow the province to be ravaged before his eyes. His chief captains, Robert count of Eu, Hugh of Gournay, Hugh of Montfort, and William Crispin, took up a threatening position against Odo at a castle called Mortemer. Nor did Odo delay battle, in view of the large force of knights of which he was so proud; but soon, after a brief resistance, the onset of the Normans proved too much for him, and he took to his heels, thus giving a foretaste of the rout that was to follow. Guy count of Ponthieu did his best to avenge 3 Odo's brother, but was taken prisoner, and had good cause to dread an enemy so fatal for his family; with him, many others of outstanding wealth and lordly lineage. When apprised of this success by new arrivals, William had it proclaimed at dead of night round the king's camp, and on hearing the news the king, after a few days spent in Normandy, retired to France. It was not long before an interchange of emissaries was followed by amicable agreement: the king's men who had been taken were to be released, and the duke could legitimately claim any territory he had taken or might thereafter take from Martel.

234. It would be tedious and unnecessary to recount all the contests waged between them, and how William always got the upper hand. How can I do justice to the incredible courage and self-confidence he showed in never stooping to a surprise attack, always naming the day beforehand, as though his proud spirit disdained the normal practice of our times? Another point too I must pass over: how, when friendly relations were again broken off, King Henry invaded Normandy and progressed through the region of Exmes as far as the river Dives, boasting that nothing but the ocean could stop him. Whereupon William, who found himself unduly hard-pressed by breaches of loyalty, at length with a display of deliberate valour fell upon those of the royal forces who were on his side of the river (for some of them had forded

aduentu audito transuadauerat) tanta internitie cecidit ut nichil postea
2 Frantia plus metueret quam Normannorum ferotiam irritare. Terminum discordiarum fecit properata mors Henrici, nec*a* multo post Martelli. Rex moriens Balduino comiti Flandriae tutelam admodum paruuli Philippi filii delegauit. Is erat fide et sapientia aeque mirandus, preuiridantibus membris*b* incanus, preterea regiae sororis conubio sullimis; filia eius Mathildis Willelmo iam dudum nupserat, femina nostro tempore singulare prudentiae speculum,*c* pudoris culmen. Hinc factum est ut pupilli et generi mediator tumores ducum et prouintialium salubri proposito compesceret.

235. Sed quia totiens Martelli se occasio ingessit, genealogiam*d* comitum Andegauensium, quantum*e* relatoris nostri memoria attigit, transcurram, prefata diuerticuli uenia. Fulco antiquior, pluribus annis usque ad senium illum moderatus comitatum, multa fecit industrie, multa egregie. Vnum omnino est quo eum notari audierim, quod Herbertum comitem Cinomannensem, Sanctonas sponsione urbis illectum, in medio colloquio ab apparitoribus arctari et quibus placuit conditionibus irretiri fecit; cetera sanctus et integer, extremis fere
2 annis filio sepe dicto[1] Gaufredo principatu uiuens cessit. Ille in prouintiales immane quam dure, in ipsum collatorem honoris quam superbe actitans, iussusque*f* magistratum et fasces deponere, adeo sibi arrogauit ut contra patrem arma sumeret. Tunc senis frigidus iam et effetus sanguis ira incaluit, filiumque iuueniliter insultantem paucis diebus maturiori consilio adeo infregit ut per aliquot miliaria sellam dorso uehens*g* pronum se cum sarcina ante pedes patris exponeret. Ille, cui uetus animositas adhuc palpitaret, assurgens et pede iacentem pulsans, 'Victus es tandem, uictus' ter quaterque ingeminat. Superfuit uicto spiritus, et quidem egregius, ut responderet: 'Tibi, pater, soli,*h* quia pater es, uictus, ceteris omnibus inuictus sum.' Hoc relatu tumentis animus emollitus, patriaque pietate uerecundiam prolis consolatus principatui restituit, monitum ut maturius se ageret: prouintialium

a ne *Bk*, non *Bc¹* (but *Bc²Bph avoid error*)   *b* memb. preu. *T⁺*   *c* specimen *T⁺*   *d* genealogia *B*   *e* quam *CB*   *f* iussuque *CsBk (and Bph)*, iussumque *Bc*   *g* euehens *T⁺A*   *h* om. *B*

[1] Since 230. 6.

it shortly before, on hearing the news of his arrival), and cut them to pieces with such slaughter that France for the future was to fear nothing more than rousing the fury of the Normans. The conflict was 2 brought to an end by Henry's untimely death, soon followed by the death of Martel. On his deathbed the king appointed as guardian of his young son Philip Baldwin count of Flanders, a man admirable alike for loyalty and wisdom, grey-haired yet with the vigour of youth, and of exalted position as husband of the king's sister. His daughter Matilda had long been married to William, and was a model of wisdom and exemplar of modesty without parallel in our time. Being thus placed as mediator between his ward and son-in-law, he was able by a policy of common sense to restrain the ambitions of both nobles and common people in the province.

235. Having had occasion so often to speak of Martel, let me now (if a digression is forgiven me) sketch the descent of the counts of Anjou, as far as my informant's memory ran. The elder Fulk, who ruled that county for many years until he reached an advanced age, was active, vigorous and successful. All in all, there is only one action for which I have heard him criticized: he lured Herbert count of Maine to Saintes by promising him the city, and in the middle of their discussion had him arrested by the sergeants and bound him by such conditions as he thought fit. In other respects he was upright and honourable, and near the end of his life resigned his position, while still living, to his son Geoffrey whom I have so often mentioned.[1] Geoffrey treated the people of the province with great severity and the 2 man who had promoted him with overweening arrogance, and when ordered to lay aside his rank and emblems of power, he went so far as to take up arms against his own father. In the old man's cold and enfeebled veins the blood flowed hot with anger, and in a few days his riper wisdom so crushed his rash and headstrong son that, after carrying a saddle on his back for several miles, he exhibited himself, prone beneath the burden, at his father's feet. Fulk's breast still heaved with his old passion; he rose and kicked his prostrate son. 'That's beaten you at last', he said, three or four times. But there was spirit, noble spirit left in the beaten man. 'Beaten in your eyes alone, father', he replied, 'because you are my father; but to all men else unbeaten.' At this answer his proud heart relented; with fatherly affection he consoled his crestfallen son, and restored him to power with the warning that he should conduct himself in a less childish way in future, remembering

fortunas et pacem suum esse decus ad extraneos, commodum ad domesticos. Eodem anno ueteranus et secularibus stipendiis emeritus, iam de animae uiatico cogitans, Ierosolimam adiit. Ibi a duobus seruis, sacramento adactis ut quod iuberet facerent, per publicum ad sepulchrum Domini nudus inspectantibus Turchis tractus est; alter restem*a* ligneum*b* collo eius intorserat, alter flagris terga expoliati urgebat. Inter haec ille*c* clamabat: 'Accipe, Domine, miserum Fulconem, periurum tuum, fugitiuum tuum; confessam dignare animam, Domine Iesu Christe.' Nec tamen quod desiderabat tunc impetrauit, sed domum placide regressus post aliquot annos obiit.

4 Filii eius Gaufredi preruptam audatiam superior narratio patefecit.[1] Is moriens Gaufredo, sororis filio, hereditatem suam contradidit, sed industriam seculi transfundere non potuit. Nam ille, simplicium morum iuuenis, magis in aecclesiis orare quam arma tractare consuetus, homines regionis illius, qui quiete uictitare nescirent, in contemptum sui excitauit; quare, tota terra predonibus exposita, Fulco frater illius 5 ultro ducatum corripuit. Fulco, Rechin dictus quod[2] germani simplicitati crebro infrendens ad ultimum honore spoliatum perpetua custodia coercuerit, habuit uxorem quae, pruritu altioris nominis allecta, illo relicto Philippo regi Francorum nupsit. Quam is, immemor dicti 'non bene conueniunt nec in una sede morantur maiestas et amor',[3] tanta uenere ardebat ut, cum imperare aliis omnibus cuperet, ab ea sibi imperari aequanimiter ferret. Denique omnium digitis quasi fatuus notari, ab omni orbe Christiano excommunicari propter eius 6 libidinem aliquantis annis sustinuit. Filii Fulconis fuerunt Gesfridus et Fulco. Gesfridus, cognomen Martelli hereditarium sortitus, suis sudoribus ampliauit, tanta pace et quiete per terras illas parta quantam nemo uiderit, nemo*d* uisurus sit; quapropter suorum insidiis necatus, egregiae probitatis decus luit. Fulco, in regimine succedens, adhuc in rebus humanis uersatur; de quo forsitan tempore regis Henrici dicturus,[4] nunc de Willelmo explanabo quod restat.

236. Ille, ubi ciuile discidium multo exercitio composuit, rem maioris gloriae animo sequens, terras olim Normanniae appendices,

a uectem *CsB* *b* lineam *Tc, correcting gender and (cf. e.g. 336. 1) form* *c* om. *B* *d* uiderit nemo *om. CB*

[1] Since 230. 6.
[2] 'Rechin' being derived from Anglo-Norman French *rechiner*, 'bare one's teeth'.
[3] Ovid, *Met.* ii. 846–7.
[4] 405. 4, 419. 1 and 8.

that the prosperity and peace of his subjects meant glory for himself abroad and happiness at home. In the same year, his earthly campaigns now over, the veteran warrior, thinking now about provision for his soul's long journey, set off for Jerusalem. There two servants, whom he had bound by oath to do exactly as they were told, dragged him naked through the public streets to the Holy Sepulchre while the Turks looked on; one had twisted a flaxen cord round his neck, the other plied a scourge on his bare back. All the while he was crying: 'Reject not, O Lord, Thy piteous servant Fulk, Thy perjurer, Thy renegade. Accept a penitent soul, Lord Jesus Christ.' He did not at that time obtain what he longed for, but returned home in peace, and died some years later.

The sheer audacity of his son Geoffrey has appeared from my previous narrative.[1] On his death, he made over his inheritance to Geoffrey, his sister's son, but his worldly ability he could not transfer. The nephew was a simple-hearted young man, more used to praying in church than to handling weapons, and he aroused contempt among the men of that region, who were incapable of a quiet life. The whole country being thus left a prey to marauders, his brother Fulk set to, and seized the county. This Fulk, named Rechin because[2] after much gnashing of his teeth at his brother's folly he finally deprived him of his power and kept permanently in custody, had a wife, who was enticed by the itch for a grander title to abandon him and marry Philip king of the French. The king, forgetting that, as the poet says,[3] 'Kingship and love make sorry bedfellows and sort but ill together', loved her with such passion that, while aiming at universal dominion himself, he was quite content to be dominated by her. In the end he became the object of general ridicule as a man besotted, and was cut off by excommunication from the whole of Christendom on account of his criminal passion; and this he put up with for some years. Fulk's sons were Geoffrey and another Fulk. The hereditary surname Martel fell to Geoffrey's lot, and he enhanced it by his own efforts; the peace and quiet he brought about in that country were such as no man has ever seen or will ever see again. As a result he was put to death by the treachery of his own men, and paid the price for his outstanding integrity. Fulk, his successor, is still in the land of the living; of him I will perhaps say more when I reach King Henry's time,[4] but first I must finish the story of William.

236. After quelling the internal disturbances with a practised hand, William aspired to greater feats, and set himself to recover the

quae longo usu insoleuerant,[a] restituere intendit, Cinomannicum dico comitatum et Britanniam. Quorum Cinomannis, dudum a Martello succensa et domino suo Hugone priuata, tunc nuper aliquantum sub Herberto Hugonis filio respirauerat. Qui, ut tutior contra Andegauensem esset, Willelmo se manibus dediderat, in eius fidelitatem sacramento iuratus. Preterea filiam ipsius petierat et desponderat; quae priusquam nubilibus annis matura coniugio fieret, ille morbo decessit, heredem sibi Willelmum pronuntians, adiuratis ciuibus ne alium susciperent, habituri si uellent lenem et probum dominum, si 2 nollent recti sui exactorem immodicum. Quo defuncto, Cinomannenses magis ad Gualterium Medantinum declinantes, cui soror Hugonis nupserat, sero tandem ut Willelmum susciperent resipuere, grauibus sepe dampnis ammoniti. Illud fuit tempus quo Haroldus inuitus Normanniam importuna sibi aura euectus est; quem, sicut supra dictum est,[1] Willelmus in Britannicam expeditionem duxit, uolens eius manum explorare, simul et strictiori consilio apparatum ostentans suum, conspicaturo quantum prestaret Anglicis bipennibus 3 ensis Normannicus. Alanus tunc ibi comes, uiridis iuuenta et precellens robore, Eudonem patruum uinxerat, multa egregie fecerat, Willelmum non solum non timebat sed et irritabat. At ille Britanniam ut hereditarium solum calumnians, quod eam Karolus[2] Rolloni cum filia Gisla dederat, breui effecit ut ultro Alanus adueniens supliciter se suaque[b] dederet. Sed quia de Britannia parum alias dicturus sum, hic quoddam miraculum, quod illis ferme diebus in Namnetis ciuitate contigit, paucis inseram.

237. Erant in urbe illa[c] duo clerici, nondum patientibus annis presbiteri; id offitium magis precario quam bonae uitae merito ab episcopo loci exegerant; denique alterius miserandus exitus superstitem instruxit quam fuerint antea in inferni lapsum ambo precipites. Ceterum quod ad scientiam litterarum tendit ita edocti ut aut parum aut nichil ipsis deberent artibus; a reptantibus infantiae rudimentis adeo iocundis amicitiae offitiis emuli ut iuxta comici dictum[3] manibus pedibusque conando periculum etiam, si necesse esset, capitis pro

[a] insoluerant *TtTcB;* insoluerent *Tp* [b] se sua *Al,* se et sua *Aa* [c] om. *T*⁺

---

[1] 228. 5.
[2] i.e. Charles the Simple.
[3] Cf. Terence, *Andria* 676–7.

territories that had formerly belonged to Normandy but had grown arrogant by long custom—the county of Maine, that is, and Brittany. Le Mans had been burnt some time before by Martel and deprived of Hugh its lord, but at that time had recently made some recovery under Hugh's son Herbert, who, to strengthen his position against the count of Anjou, had put his hands in William's and sworn fealty to him. He had also asked for the hand of a daughter of William's, and had been betrothed to her; but before she was of marriageable age and ready for wedlock, he fell sick and died, nominating William as his heir and adjuring his subjects to accept no one else. William, he said, if they would have him, would be a mild and honourable lord; otherwise they would find him pitiless in the exaction of his rights. On his death, the people of Maine inclined more to Walter of Mantes, Hugh's sister's husband, but after frequent and severe losses they learnt their lesson, and belatedly accepted William. It was at this time that Harold was reluctantly obliged to land in Normandy by a contrary wind and, as I have said above,[1] was carried by William on his expedition into Brittany in order to test Harold's strength, and with the deeper design of showing him William's warlike preparations, so that he could see how much Norman swords were superior to English axes. Alan, at that time count of Brittany, a man in the prime of life and of exceptional physique, had put his uncle Eudo in chains, and had many brilliant actions to his credit. So far from fearing William, he actually provoked him; but William, claiming the land of Brittany as his inheritance on the ground that Charles[2] had given it to Rollo with his daughter Gisela, soon forced Alan to come of his own accord and humbly surrender himself and his possessions. But now, since I shall have few other opportunities to speak of Brittany, let me briefly insert the story of a miracle which befell there about that time in the town of Nantes.

237. There were in that city two clerks, in priest's orders though not yet of proper age; for they had obtained that office from the local bishop more as a favour than through any holiness of life. In fact it was the pitiful end of one of them that taught the survivor how both had previously been hanging precariously over the abyss. In knowledge of literature their accomplishments were such as owed little or nothing to schooling in the proper sense, and since their earliest childhood they were such merry and devoted friends that, as it says in the play,[3] they would 'strive hand and foot and, should occasion call, each for

2 inuicem facerent. Quare die quadam liberiorem animum a curis forinsecis nacti, in secreto conclaui huiuscemodi sententias fudere: pluribus se*a* annis nunc litteris nunc seculi lucris mentes exercuisse, nec satiasse magis ad distortum quam ad rectum intentas; inter haec illum acerbum diem sensim appropinquare qui sotietatis suae inextricabile in uita uinculum dirumperet; unde preueniendum mature ut fides, quae conglu-
3 tinarat uiuentes, primo mortuum comitaretur ad manes. Paciscuntur ergo ut, quisquis eorum ante obiret, superstiti uel dormienti uel uigilanti appareret infra triginta proculdubio dies; si fiat, edocturus quod secundum Platonicos mors spiritum non extinguat sed ad principium sui Deum tamquam e carcere emittat; sin minus, Epicureorum sectae concedendum, qui opinantur animam corpore solutam in aerem euanescere, in auras effluere. Ita data acceptaque fide, cotidianis colloquiis sacramentum frequentabant.
4 Nec multum in medio, et ecce mors repentine*b* imminens indignantem halitum uni eorum uiolenter extraxit. Remansit alter, et serio de sotii sponsione cogitans et iam iamque affuturum prestolans, cassa opinione triginta diebus uentos pauit. Quibus elapsis, cum desperans aliis negotiis auocasset otium, astitit subito uigilanti et quiddam operis molienti, uultu qualis solet esse morientium anima fugiente exsanguis. Tum tacentem uiuum prior mortuus compellans, 'Agnoscis me?'
5 inquit. 'Agnosco' respondit, 'et non tantum de insolita tua turbor presentia quantum de diuturna miror absentia.' At ille, ubi tarditatem aduentus excusauit, 'Tandem' ait, 'tandem expeditis morarum nexibus uenio; sed aduentus iste tibi, si uoles, amice, erit commodus, michi omnino infructuosus, quippe qui pronuntiata et acclamata sententia sempiternis sim deputatus suplitiis.' Cumque uiuus ad ereptionem mortui omnia sua monasteriis et egenis expensurum, seque dies et
6 noctes ieiuniis et orationibus continuaturum promitteret, 'Fixum est' inquit 'quod dixi, quia sine penitentia sunt iuditia Dei, quibus in sulfuream uoraginem inferni demersus sum. Ibi "dum rotat astra polus, dum pulsat littora pontus"[1] pro criminibus meis uoluar. Inflexibilis

---

a om. A (erasure in Al)   *b* repentina T+A

[1] Cf. Claudian v [*In Rufinum* ii]. 527.

the other challenge Death himself'. One day, when their minds were free from outward cares, their conversation, as they chatted privately together, ran on these lines: 'For many years now we have employed our minds sometimes on books and sometimes on worldly gain, and never been satisfied, for we have preferred the crooked to the straight; and all the time that cruel day is gradually approaching which will snap the links of our mutual attachment, which nothing in life can part. We must take steps in good time to ensure that whichever dies first takes with him to the shades the loyalty that has bound us together during life.' They therefore agreed that the first to die should appear to the survivor, sleeping or waking, within thirty days without fail. If he succeeded, he would demonstrate that, as the school of Plato hold, death does not quench the spirit, but returns it as though released from prison unto God its author; otherwise, it would be necessary to fall in with the Epicureans, who believe that the soul, once freed from the body, evaporates and vanishes into thin air. They made their compact accordingly, and recalled their oath in daily conversation.

Nor was it long before Death suddenly appeared, and put a violent and unwelcome end to one of them. The other was left; and as he pondered soberly on his friend's promise and looked for him to reappear at any moment, he fed the light winds for thirty days with fruitless expectation. At the end of that time he had given up hope and began to occupy his leisure with other concerns, when suddenly, while he was awake and busy with some matter, his friend stood by him, in his face the ghastly pallor of those at the hour of death. The silence of the living man was broken by the dead man's voice. 'Do you know me?', he said. 'I do indeed' was the reply; 'and I am not so much moved by your coming, unusual though it is, as surprised that you have stayed away so long.' 'At last,' said the other, after apologizing for his late arrival, 'at last I have broken through all delays, and here I am. And this visit of mine, my friend, will be a blessing to you, if you so please, though it can do me no good at all; for judgement on me has been passed and ratified, and I am sentenced to eternal torment.' The living man offered to give all he had to monasteries and to the poor to buy an amnesty for his old friend, and to spend his own nights and days in continual fasting and prayer. 'What I have said is final', he replied; 'there is no place for repentance in the judgements of God, by which I have been plunged into the sulphurous gulfs of Hell. There, "long as the starry heavens revolve, long as the waves beat on the shore",[1] I shall be whirled round in recompense for my crimes.

sententiae manet rigor, aeterna et innumera penarum genera comminiscens, totus modo mundus ualitura remedia exquirat. Et ut aliquam*a* experiaris ex meis innumerabilibus penis,' protendit manum sanioso ulcere stillantem, et 'en' ait 'unam*b* ex minimis. Videturne tibi leuis?'
7 Cum leuem sibi uideri referret, ille, curuatis in uolam digitis, tres guttas defluentis tabi*c* super eum iaculatus est; quarum duae timpora, una frontem contingentes cutem et carnem sicut ignito cauterio penetrarunt, foramen nucis capax effitientes. Illo magnitudinem doloris clamore testante, 'Hoc' inquit mortuus 'erit tibi, quantum uixeris, et penarum mearum graue documentum et, nisi neglexeris, salutis tuae singulare monimentum. Quapropter dum licet, dum nutat ira, dum pendula Deus te*d* operitur clementia, muta habitum, muta animum,
8 Redonis monachus effectus apud Sanctum Melanium.' Ad haec uerba uiuo respondere nolente, alter eum oculi uigore perstringens, 'Si dubitas' inquit 'conuerti, miser, lege litteras istas.' Et simul cum dicto manum expandit tetricis notis inscriptam, in quibus Sathanas et omne inferorum*e* satellitium gratias omni aecclesiastico cetui de Tartaro emittebant, quod cum ipsi in nullo suis uoluptatibus deessent, tum tantum numerum subditarum animarum paterentur ad inferna descendere predicationis incuria quantum numquam retroacta uiderunt secula. His dictis loquentis aspectus disparuit, et audiens, omnibus suis per aecclesias et egenos distributis, Sanctum Melanium adiit, omnes audientes et uidentes de subita conuersione et illustri conuersatione*f* ammonens ut dicerent: 'Haec est mutatio dexterae Excelsi.'[1]

238. Ista pro utilitate legentium me inseruisse non piguit; nunc de Willelmo loquar. Nam quia breuiter, nec ut puto inutiliter, res eius*g* quas dumtaxat comes in Normannia annis triginta actitauit percurri, modo aliud narrandi exordium ordo temporum flagitat, ut de regno eius, quantum nostra sciscitatio penetrare potuit, mendatium arguam, ueritatem pronuntiem.

Rex Eduardus fato functus fuerat; Anglia dubio fauore nutabat, cui se rectori committeret incerta, an Haroldo an Willelmo an Edgaro (nam et illum, pro genere proximum regno, proceribus rex commendauerat, tacito scilicet mentis iuditio, sed prono in clementiam
2 animo). Quare, ut predixi, Angli diuersis uotis ferebantur, quanuis

a aliquem *A*   *b* una *A*   *c* Properly tabis *(cf. 444. 2)*   *d* om. *CB*
e inferiorum *A*   *f* et ill. conu. om. *CB*   *g* om. *T*⁺

[1] Ps. 76 (77): 11.

iii. 238. 2   THE HISTORY OF THE ENGLISH KINGS   445

My doom remains fixed and immutable, fertile in countless forms of everlasting torment, though the whole world be set to find an effective remedy. And to give you a taste of one of my unnumbered punishments, here,' he said, holding out a hand from which oozed the noisome filth of a running sore, 'here is one of the least of them. Do you think it a trifle?' Then, when the other replied that he did think that, he clenched his fingers and threw at him three drops of that poisonous ooze. Two of them struck his temples, one his forehead, where they pierced skin and flesh like red-hot iron and left a hole as big as a walnut. As he screamed in agony, 'Take that!', said the dead man; it shall be, all your life long, terrible evidence of my damnation, and a powerful reminder of how you can win salvation for yourself, unless you ignore it. Before it is too late, while wrath hangs in the balance, while God's mercy is still in suspense, change your way of life and change your heart. Become a monk of Saint-Melaine at Rennes.' To these words the living man vouchsafed no reply. 'If you hesitate to repent, poor wretch', cried the other, glaring at him with blazing eyes, 'read that!', and he opened his hand. In the palm was etched a hideous missive, addressed by Satan and his hellish court to the whole body of the clergy, thanking them from Tartarus for the way in which, while giving free rein to their own appetites, they allowed more of the souls entrusted to them to go down to Hell, by their own negligence in preaching, than ages past had ever seen. With these words the speaker vanished, and his hearer, after distributing all he had to churches and to the poor, made his way to Saint-Melaine's, giving all who heard of and saw his sudden conversion and distinguished holiness as a monk good reason to say: 'This change is the work of the right hand of the Most High.'[1]

238. This story I have included without regret, for the profit of my readers; but now I must return to William. So far I have recounted, briefly but not I trust unprofitably, his doings during thirty years when he was only a duke in Normandy. The order of events now calls for a fresh start, for I must give the result of my enquiries into his reign as king, refuting falsehood, setting forth the truth.

King Edward had finished his allotted span, and England was in suspense, wondering whom to accept as her ruler, Harold or William or Edgar; for Edgar too, as being the nearest to the throne by birth, had been commended to his magnates by the king, who expressed no judgement but showed a disposition to be kind to him. And so, as I

palam cuncti bona Haroldo imprecarentur. Et ille quidem, diademate fastigatus, nichil de pactis inter se et Willelmum cogitabat, liberatum se sacramento asserens quod filia eius quam desponderat citra nubiles annos obierat. Fertur enim uir ille, non paucis uirtutibus preditus, parum aduersus perfidiam sibi consuluisse, dummodo posset quibuscumque prestigiis hominum ratiocinationes suspendere. Preterea, qui putaret minas Willelmi numquam ad factum erupturas quod ille conterminorum ducum bellis implicaretur, totum animum otio cum subiectis indulserat; nam profecto, nisi quod Noricorum regem aduentare didicit, nec militem conuocare nec atiem dirigere dignatus fuisset.

3 Alter interea illum per nuntios leniter conuenire, de rupto federe expostulare, precibus minas insuere: sciret se ante annum emensum ferro debitum uendicaturum, illuc iturum quo[a] Haroldus tutiores se pedes habere putaret. Contra ille, quae dixi[1] de puellae nuptiis referens, de regno addebat presumptuosum fuisse quod absque generali senatus et populi conuentu et edicto alienam illi[b][2] hereditatem iurauerit;

4 proinde stultum sacramentum frangendum. Nam si iusiurandum uel[c] uotum quod puella in domo patris nesciis parentibus de suo corpore uolens fecerit iudicatur irritum, quanto magis quod ille, sub regis uirga constitutus, nesciente[d] omni Anglia, de toto regno necessitate temporis coactus impegerit[e] uideatur non esse ratum? Preterea iniquum postulatu ut imperio decedat quod tanto fauore ciuium regendum susceperit; hoc nec prouintialibus gratum nec militibus tutum. Ita reuertebantur inanes nuntii, uel ueris uel ueri similibus argumentis prestricti.

5 Sed comes toto illo anno bello necessaria expediebat, largis sumptibus milites suos continebat, alienos inuitabat; ordines atiesque ita instituebat ut milites proceri corpore precellentes robore essent, duces et antesignani preter scientiam rei militaris etiam consilii et aetatis maturitate pollerent, ut, si singulos uel in atie uel alibi cerneres, non proceres sed

---

[a] iterum quod *B*   [b] sibi *T*⁺*   [c] et *T*⁺   [d] nescienti *B*   [e] impigeret *Al*, pepigerat *Aa; the reading is not certain*

---

[1] 238. 2 (cf. 228. 5).
[2] The *T* reading implies that it was not Harold's to give, the *ACB* version that William had no claim to it.

have said, Englishmen's wishes were divided, though openly all wished Harold well. Harold, once crowned, did not spare a thought for the agreement between himself and William, declaring himself released from his oath because William's daughter, to whom he had been betrothed, had died before she was old enough to marry. Endowed as he was with many good qualities, he was too careless, it is said, in breaking faith, so long as he could hold men's judgements in suspense by some piece of legerdemain. Besides which, as though he expected that William's threats would never be put into practice, involved as he was in fighting with neighbouring magnates, he had abandoned himself and his subjects to complete inactivity; in fact, had he not learned that the king of Norway was approaching, he would never have troubled to call out his knights or order a battle-line. William meanwhile was sending messages of mild remonstrance, complaining of the breach of faith, and mingling threats with his entreaties; for he warned Harold that before the year was out, he would claim what was his due by force of arms, and come to a place where Harold supposed his footing secure. Harold in reply made the point, of which I spoke,[1] about his engagement to William's daughter, and added with regard to the kingdom that it had been presumptuous to promise on oath a succession that was not his,[2] without the general assembly and decision of his council and his folk; and so a foolish oath deserved to be broken. If an oath or vow disposing of her hand taken voluntarily by a maiden in her father's house without her parents' knowledge is held to be null and void, how much less weight should be given to the oath by which he had disposed of the whole kingdom, while under the king's authority, without the knowledge of all England and compelled by circumstances! It was moreover unfair to demand that he should resign the authority conferred upon him with such popular support; this would be unwelcome to his countrymen and perilous for his knights. So the mission made its way home again empty-handed, put down by arguments that either had, or seemed to have, some force.

Duke William, however, spent the whole of that year in warlike preparations, using lavish expenditure to keep his own knights in readiness and to attract those of others. The troops of his battle-line he organized in such a way as to have knights of outstanding stature and strength, with captains and commanders remarkable no less for their maturity of years and judgement than for skill in arms, so that if you had seen any one of them in the field or elsewhere, you would have thought him no mere magnate but of royal blood. Such was at that time the

reges putares. Ita episcopi et abbates illius temporis religione, ita optimates magnanima liberalitate certabant ut mirum sit quod
6 *ᵃnondum sexaginta annis euolutis utraque turba, abortiuum bonitatis effecti, iurata bella contra iustitiam susceperint: illi pro ambitione sacrorum magis distortum quam aequum et bonum amplectentes, isti reiecto pudore undecumque captatis occasionibus compendia pecuniarum uelut cotidianam stipem emendicantes.ᵃ* / *ᵃpaucissimis annis euolutis pleraque et pene omnia in utrisque ordinibus mutata uideas: illi in quibusdam hebatiores, sed largiores; isti in omnibus prudentiores, sed tenatiores; utrique tamen in defensanda patria manu ualidi, consilio prouidi, fortunas suas euehere, inimicorum deprimere parati.ᵃ*

7 Verum tunc Willelmi industria, cum prouidentia Dei[b] consentiens, iam spe Angliam inuadebat et, ne iustam causam temeritas decoloraret, ad Apostolicum, qui ex Anselmo Lucensi episcopo Alexander dicebatur, misit, iustitiam suscepti[c] belli quantis poterat facundiae neruis allegans. Haroldus id facere supersedit, uel quod turgidus natura esset, uel quod causae diffideret, uel quod nuntios suos a Willelmo et eius complicibus, qui omnes portus obsidebant, impediri timeret. Quare, perpensis apud se utrimque partibus, papa uexillum in omen regni
8 Willelmo contradidit. Quo ille accepto conuentum magnatum apud Lillebonam[d] fecit, super negotio singulorum sententias sciscitatus;[e] cumque omnes eius uoluntatem plausibus excipientes magnificis promissis animasset,[f] commeatum nauium omnibus pro quantitate possessionum indixit.

Ita tunc discessum, et mense Augusto ad Sanctum Walericum in commune uentum (portus ita per metonomiam[1] dicitur). Congregatis undecumque nauibus, felix expectabatur aura quae illas ad destinatum
9 eueheret. Qua multis diebus remorante, uulgus militum, ut fieri solet, per tabernacula mussitabat: insanire hominem qui uellet alienum solum in ius suum refundere; Deum contra tendere, qui uentum arceret; idem patrem uoluisse eodemque modo inhibitum; fatale illi familiae esse ut, altiora uiribus spirans, Deum aduersantem experiatur. Ista per publicum serebantur, quae possent fortium robur eneruare.

ᵃ⁻ᵃ nondum ... emendicantes *T⁺A*; paucissimis ... parati *CB*   *ᵇ* Dei prou. cum Will. ind. *T⁺*   *ᶜ* om. *T⁺*   *ᵈ* Lillebonam (Lilli-) *T⁺A*; -bona *CB*   *ᵉ* One expects sciscitaturus (so translated)   *ᶠ* Savile; -ent *MSS*

---

[1] i.e. after the local saint.

competition in religious fervour between bishops and abbots and between nobles in high-minded generosity, that it is astonishing

T⁺A that before sixty years have passed both parties have become sterile in good works and have bound themselves by oath to fight wars against justice: the clergy in their ambition for ecclesiastical office embracing wrong rather than what is right and good, the others with no thought for shame seizing every opportunity to beg some pecuniary gain as though it were their daily alms.

CB to see how after the lapse of so few years, almost everything in both estates has changed: the churchmen in some things more lukewarm, yet more open-handed, the laymen wiser in every way, yet more close-fisted; but in the defence of their native land both parties valiant in action, prudent in counsel, determined to advance their own fortunes and depress those of their enemies.

But at that time William, his energy allied with the providence of God, was already in full expectation of invading England, and for fear that by acting rashly he might throw doubt on a just cause, he sent to the pope, the former Anselm bishop of Lucca who had taken the name Alexander, to urge the justice of his campaign with all the eloquence at his command. Harold thought such a step unnecessary, either because he was too proud by nature, or because he did not believe in his own case, or feared that his emissaries might be interfered with by William and his allies, who blockaded all the ports. And so, after weighing the arguments on both sides, the pope gave William a banner as a token of kingship; on receipt of which he summoned a council of his magnates at Lillebonne, in order to ascertain the views of individuals on the project. All received his intentions with enthusiasm; he encouraged them with lavish promises, and levied a demand on all of them for ships in proportion to their possessions.

So they separated for the time, and in August reassembled at Saint-Valery (as the port is called by metonomy).[1] The ships having been got together from all parts, they waited for a favourable wind to carry them to their destination. This was many days in coming, and the generality of soldiers, as usually happens, grumbled in their tents. A man must be mad, they said, who wants us to take over land rightfully belonging to others; God is against us, for He denies us a wind; his father had the same idea, and was prevented in the same way; there is a curse on this family—it always conceives more than it can perform and finds God in opposition to it. Such sentiments were spreading publicly, and might well weaken the resolution of brave men. So the

Dux itaque, facto cum senioribus concilio,[a] corpus sancti Walerici foras efferri et pro uento deprecando sub diuo exponi iussit; nec mora intercessit, quin prosper flatus carbasa impleret. Tunc laetus clamor exortus omnes ad naues inuitauit; comes ipse, a continenti primus in[b] altum prouectus, ceteros in medio fere mari anchoris iactis sustinuit. Omnibus itaque ad pretoriae puppis uermiculatum uelum conuolantibus, post cibum sumptum placido cursu Hastingas appulerunt. In egressu nauis pede lapsus euentum in melius commutauit, acclamante sibi proximo milite: 'Tenes' inquit 'Angliam, comes, rex futurus.' Omnem exercitum a preda continuit, parcendum rebus quae suae forent prelocutus, continuisque quindecim diebus adeo se quiete agens ut nichil minus quam bellum cogitare uideretur.

239. Interea Haroldus de pugna Noricorum reuertebatur, sua estimatione felix quod uicerat (meo iuditio contra, quod parricidio uictoriam compararat); allatoque ad se nuntio aduentus Normannici, sicut erat cruentus in armis, paucissimo stipatus milite Hastingas pertendit.[c] Precipitabant eum nimirum fata, ut nec auxilia conuocare uellet nec, si uellet, multos parituros inueniret; ita, ut ante dixi,[1] omnes illi erant infensi, quod solus manubiis borealibus incubuerat. Premisit tamen qui numerum hostium et uires specularentur; quos intra castra deprehensos Willelmus circum tentoria duci moxque largis eduliis pastos
2 domino incolumes remitti iubet. Redeuntes percunctatur Haroldus quid rerum apportent; illi, uerbis amplissimis ductoris magnificam confidentiam prosecuti, serio addiderunt pene omnes in exercitu illo presbiteros uideri, quod totam fatiem cum utroque labio rasam haberent. Angli enim superius labrum pilis incessanter fruticantibus intonsum dimittunt, quod etiam gentilitium antiquis Britonibus fuisse Iulius Cesar asseuerat in libro Belli Gallici.[2] Subrisit rex fatuitatem referentium, lepido insecutus cachinno quia[d] non essent presbiteri sed
3 milites armis ualidi, animis inuicti. Rapuit ergo ex ore ipsius sermonem Gurtha frater, plus puero adultus et magnae ultra aetatem uirtutis et

---

[a] consilio T<i>c</i>B   [b] T⁺A (cf. e.g. 179. 3); ad CB   [c] T⁺A (cf. e.g. 357. 1); protendit CB   [d] qui C<i>s</i>B

[1] 228. 11.
[2] v. 14. 3.

duke, after consulting his older captains, gave orders to bring out the body of St Walaric and expose it under the open sky to support prayers for a wind; and without delay their sails were filled with a favouring breeze. The shouts of joy that followed summoned them all to their ships. The duke himself, putting out first from land into deep water, made the rest heave to some way out to sea, and cast anchor. So all gathered round their admiral's ship with its scarlet sail, and having eaten their dinner they made a smooth passage and landed at Hastings. As he left the vessel, he slipped, but turned the mishap into a good omen, for the knight who was nearest cried: 'You have England in your hand, duke, and you shall be king!' He restrained his whole army from plunder, warning them in advance to spare what would soon be their own property; and for the next fortnight lay there so quietly that fighting might have been the last thing that crossed his mind.

239. Meanwhile Harold was returning from his battle with the Norwegians, blessed in his own opinion with success, though I take the opposite view, since his victory was gained by parricide; and on receiving news of the Norman landing, just as he was, with the blood still on his armour, and accompanied by very few knights, he made straight for Hastings. Fate surely was hurrying him to his doom, unwilling as he was to get together any reinforcements and unlikely, had he been willing, to find many to respond, such was the general hostility aroused, as I said above,[1] by his monopoly of the spoils of the northern war. He did, however, send scouts on ahead to spy out the numbers and strength of the enemy. When they were caught inside his camp, William gave orders that they should be conducted round the lines, given a substantial dinner, and then sent back to their master unharmed. On their return Harold asked them what tidings they brought with them. After enlarging at great length on the leader's superb self-confidence, they added in all seriousness that almost every man in William's army seemed to be a priest, all their faces including both lips being clean-shaven; for the English leave the upper lip, with its unceasing growth of hair, unshorn, which Julius Caesar describes as a national custom of the ancient Britons too in his book on the Gallic War.[2] The king smiled at the folly of his informants, adding with a merry laugh that they were no priests, but knights as valiant in battle as they were invincible in spirit. His brother Gyrth, who was now grown out of boyhood, and of courage and understanding

scientiae. 'Cum' inquit 'tantam fortitudinem Normanni predices, indeliberatum existimo cum illo confligere, quo*a* inferior robore et merito habearis. Nec enim ibis in infitias quin illi sacramentum uel inuitus uel uoluntarius feceris. Proinde consultius ages si, instanti necessitati te subtrahens, nostro periculo colludium pugnae temptaueris; nos, omni iuramento expediti, iuste ferrum pro patria stringemus. Timendum ne, si ipse decernas, uel fugam uel mortem oppetas;*b* sed nobis solis preliantibus causa tua utrobique in portu nauigabit, quia et fugientes restituere et mortuos ulcisci poteris.'

240. Noluit effrenata temeritas aurem placidam monenti commodare, existimans inglorium et anteactae uitae obprobrium cuicumque discrimini terga nudare, eademque impudentia uel, ut indulgentius dicam, imprudentia monachum Willelmi legatum nec bono uultu dignatus turbide abegit, hoc tantum imprecans, ut Deus inter eum et Willelmum iudicaret. Afferebat ille tria, ut uel regno secundum conditiones descenderet, uel sub eo regnaturus teneret, uel 2 certe spectante utroque exercitu gladio rem uentilarent. Calumniabatur enim Willelmus regnum, quod rex illi Eduardus concesserat consilio Stigandi archiepiscopi et Goduini et Siwardi comitum, eiusque doni obsides filium et nepotem Goduini Normanniam miserat. Si id negare uelit Haroldus, iuditio se sedis apostolicae uel prelio acturum. Quibus omnibus solo quod dixi nuntius frustratus responso discessit, suisque ad dimicandum uiuatiores animos dedit.

241. Ita*c* utrimque animosi duces disponunt aties, patrio quisque ritu. Angli, ut accepimus, totam noctem insomnem cantibus potibusque ducentes, mane incunctanter in hostem procedunt; pedites omnes cum bipennibus, conserta ante se scutorum testudine, impenetrabilem cuneum fatiunt; quod profecto illis ea die saluti fuisset, nisi Normanni simulata fuga more suo confertos manipulos laxassent. Rex ipse pedes

a qui *CsB*   *b* ineas *T*+   *c* itaque *C*

beyond his years, took him up at once. 'If the Norman duke is as strong as you maintain', he said, 'I think it most unwise to struggle against him, when you are thought to have both weaker forces and a weaker cause. For you will not deny that you have taken an oath to him, whether unwillingly or of your own free will. It will be more prudent to withdraw from the emergency that faces you now, and try a throw with him at *our* expense: we, who are not restrained by any oath, shall draw our swords to defend our country with perfect justice. We are bound to fear that, if you enter the lists yourself, you may be put to flight or killed, whereas, if we alone fight, you will be in calm water on both counts: you will be able to restore the situation if we flee, and avenge us if we fall.'

240. But there was no holding Harold. Rash as he was, he refused to lend a patient ear to good advice, thinking it discreditable and a blot upon his record to turn tail in the face of any danger. With the same impudence, or—to put it more kindly—imprudence, he sent packing the monk who had come as an emissary from William, refusing in his passion even to receive him with civility; he merely expressed the wish that God might judge between himself and William. The man brought three proposals: that Harold should abdicate on conditions, or that he should continue to reign under William as suzerain, or at least that they should air the question in single combat while the two armies looked on. For William laid claim to the kingdom on the ground that King Edward had conveyed it to him on the advice of Archbishop Stigand and Earls Godwine and Siward, and had sent Godwine's son and grandson over to Normandy as security for the gift. If Harold wished to deny this, he would submit himself to the decision of the Holy See or to ordeal by battle. To all this the emissary received no reply beyond what I have related, and departed, thus making his own side more eager for the fray.

241. So the leaders on both sides, in high spirits, drew up their lines of battle, each in the traditional manner. The English—so I have heard—spent a sleepless night in song and wassail, and in the morning moved without delay against the enemy. All the foot-soldiers with their axes, joining their shields into a wall in front of them, formed an impenetrable mass; and this would surely that day have been their salvation, had not the Normans in their usual way loosened the close-packed ranks by pretending to retreat. The king himself on foot stood

iuxta uexillum stabat cum fratribus ut, in commune periculo aequato, nemo de fuga cogitaret. Vexillum illud post uictoriam papae misit Willelmus, quod erat in hominis pugnantis figura, auro et lapidibus arte sumptuosa intextum.[a]

242. Contra Normanni, nocte tota[b] confessioni peccatorum uacantes, mane Dominico corpori communicarunt. Pedites cum arcubus et sagittis primam frontem muniunt, equites retro diuisis alis consistunt. Comes uultu serenus, et clara uoce suae parti utpote iustiori Deum affuturum pronuntians, arma poposcit; moxque ministrorum tumultu loricam inuersam indutus, casum risu correxit, 'Vertetur'
2 inquiens 'fortitudo comitatus mei in regnum'. Tunc cantilena Rollandi inchoata, ut martium uiri exemplum pugnaturos accenderet, inclamatoque Dei auxilio prelium consertum bellatumque acriter, neutris in multam diei horam cedentibus. Quo comperto, Willelmus innuit suis ut ficta fuga campo se subtraherent. Hoc commento Anglorum cuneus solutus, quasi palantes hostes a tergo cesurus, exitium sibi maturauit; Normanni enim, conuersis ordinibus reuersi, dispersos adoriuntur et in fugam cogunt. Ita ingenio circumuenti pulchram mortem pro patriae ultione meruere, nec tamen ultioni suae defuere, quin crebro consistentes de insequentibus insignes cladis aceruos facer-
3 ent. Nam occupato tumulo Normannos, calore successus[c] acriter ad superiora nitentes, in uallem deiciunt, leuique negotio in subiectos tela torquentes, lapides rotantes, omnes ad unum fundunt. Item fossatum quoddam preruptum compendiario et noto sibi transitu euadentes, tot ibi inimicorum conculcauere ut cumulo cadauerum planitiem campi aequarent. Valuit haec uicissitudo, modo illis modo istis uincentibus, quantum Haroldi uita moram fecit; at ubi iactu sagittae uiolato cerebro procubuit, fuga Anglorum perhennis in noctem[d] fuit.

243. Emicuit ibi uirtus amborum ducum. Haroldus, non contentus munere imperatorio ut hortaretur alios, militis offitium sedulo exsequebatur; sepe hostem comminus uenientem ferire, ut nullus impune

---

[a] contextum T^+A [b] tota nocte T^+*   [c] successus *Al(and Tp;* -sos *TcCs),* successo *Aap*   [d] nocte *CB*

by the standard with his brothers, that the danger might be the same for all alike, and no one think of flight. That same standard, after his victory, was sent by William to the pope; it bore the figure of a warrior, richly embroidered with gold and gems.

242. The Normans on the other hand spent the whole night confessing their sins, and in the morning made their communion. Their foot-soldiers with bows and arrows held the front line; the cavalry, divided into squadrons, took up their station behind. The duke, with a confident air and loudly affirming that God would be on their side because their cause was just, called for his armour, and when, by some confusion among his squires, his corselet was put on him the wrong way round, he made the best of this mischance with a jest: 'We shall turn the strength of my duchy', he said, 'into a kingdom.' Then they struck up the song of Roland to fire them as they went into battle with the example of a heroic warrior, and calling on God's help came to grips and fought furiously, neither side giving way till a late hour. Seeing this, William gave his men the signal for simulating flight and withdrawing from the field. By this stratagem the close battle-order of the English was broken up, in hopes of cutting down the enemy from behind as they fled at random, and thereby they hastened their own doom; for the Normans turned about and came back, to fall upon them in their disorder and put them to flight. So they were undone by a trick, and earned a glorious death in avenging their country, nor did they fail in spite of that to avenge themselves: repeatedly they made a stand, and piled the bodies of their pursuers in great heaps of slaughter. Seizing a knoll, they hurled the Normans down to the lower ground as, fired by success, they struggled fiercely up the slope, and finding it an easy task to rain missiles and roll down stones on those below them, routed them all to a man. Again, making their way round a precipitous ditch by a short cut known only to themselves, they trampled down so many of their foes on the spot that they filled it level to the brim with a pile of bodies. This alternation of fortune, now one side prevailing and now the other, held as long as Harold lived; but when his brain was pierced by an arrow and he fell, the English fled without respite till the night.

243. On that field both leaders were distinguished by their valour. Harold, not content with the commander's task of urging others on, vigorously performed the duty of a soldier. Often he would strike an

accederet quin statim uno ictu equus et eques prociderent; quapropter, ut dixi, eminus letali harundine¹ ictus mortem impleuit. Iacentis femur unus militum gladio proscidit;*a* unde a Willelmo ignominiae notatus, quod rem ignauam et pudendam fecisset, militia pulsus est.

244. Item Willelmus suos clamore et presentia hortari, ipse primus procurrere, confertos hostes inuadere; ideo, dum ubique seuit, ubique infrendet, tres equos lectissimos sub se confossos ea*b* die amisit. Perstitit tamen magnanimi ducis et corpus et animus, quanuis familiari susurro a custodibus corporis reuocaretur; perstitit, inquam, donec uictoriam plenam superueniens nox infunderet. Et proculdubio diuina illum manus protexit, ut nichil sanguinis ex eius corpore hostis hauriret, quamquam illum tot iaculis impeteret.

245. Illa fuit dies fatalis Angliae, funestum excidium dulcis patriae, pro nouorum dominorum commutatione. Iam enim pridem moribus Anglorum insueuerat, qui uarii admodum pro temporibus fuere. Nam primis aduentus sui annis uultu et gestu barbarico, usu bellico, ritu fanatico uiuebant; sed postmodum, Christi fide suscepta, paulatim et per incrementa temporis, pro otio quod actitabant exercitium armorum 2 in secundis ponentes, omnem in religione operam insumpsere. Taceo de pauperibus, quos fortunarum tenuitas plerumque continet ne cancellos iustitiae transgrediantur; pretermitto graduum aecclesiasticorum uiros, quos nonnumquam professionis contuitus, sed et infamiae metus, a uero deuiare non sinit. De regibus dico, qui pro amplitudine potestatis licenter indulgere uoluptatibus possent; quorum quidam in patria, quidam Romae mutato habitu caeleste lucrati sunt regnum, beatum nacti commertium, multi spetietenus tota uita mundum amplexi, ut thesauros egenis effunderent, monasteriis diuiderent. Quid dicam de tot episcopis, heremitis, abbatibus? Nonne tota insula tantis*c* reliquiis indigenarum fulgurat ut uix aliquem

---

a procidit *CBk*   *b* eo *A*   *c* sanctis *T*⁺

¹ Virgil, *Aen.* iv. 73.

enemy who came within range, so that no one could approach unscathed, but horse and rider were at once laid low with a single stroke; and hence, as I said, it was a 'death-dealing shaft'[1] from a distance that gave him the mortal wound. One of the knights hacked at his thigh with a sword as he lay on the ground; for which he was branded with disgrace by William for a dastardly and shameful act and degraded from his knighthood.

244. William too encouraged his men by his shouts and by his presence, leading the charge in person and plunging into the thick of the enemy; so that while he carried rage and fury everywhere, three splendid horses were cut down under him as he rode that day. But the brave duke never flinched in body or in spirit, however much his bodyguard tried to recall him by murmuring friendly remonstrance; he never flinched, I repeat, until night supervened and made the victory complete. And without doubt it was God's hand that protected him, so that though the enemy beset him with a hail of missiles, not a drop of his blood was spilt.

245. That was a day of destiny for England, a fatal disaster for our dear country as she exchanged old masters for new. Long since had it grown used to the character of the English—though that changed greatly with the passage of time. In the early years after their arrival, their appearance and bearing were barbaric, their habits warlike, their religion heathen. Later, when they had once accepted Christianity, little by little, as time went on, thanks to the peace they enjoyed, the practice of arms took second place and they devoted all their efforts to religion. I speak not of the poor, whose modest resources restrain them as a rule from overstepping the bounds of what is right; I say nothing of the men in holy orders, who are prevented from straying from the true path, sometimes by a regard for their calling but also by fear of disgrace. It is the kings of whom I speak, whose ample power would permit them to indulge freely in pleasures. Some of these in their native country and some in Rome adopted the religious life and were rewarded with a heavenly kingdom, and a blessed exchange they made; many of them spent their whole lives to all appearances in the world, in order to lavish their treasure on the poor and divide it between monasteries. What shall I say of all those bishops, anchorites and abbots? Does not the whole island gleam with so many relics of its own natives, that you can scarcely pass through any town of note

uicum insignem pretereas ubi noui sancti nomen non audias? Quam multorum etiam periit memoria pro scriptorum inopia!

3 Veruntamen litterarum et religionis studia aetate procedente obsoleuerunt, non paucis ante aduentum Normannorum annis. Clerici litteratura tumultuaria contenti uix sacramentorum uerba balbutiebant; stupori erat et miraculo ceteris qui grammaticam nosset. Monachi subtilibus indumentis et indifferenti genere ciborum regulam ludificabant. Optimates gulae et ueneri dediti aecclesiam more Christiano mane non adibant, sed in cubiculo et inter uxorios amplexus matutinarum sollemnia et missarum a festinante presbitero auribus tantum libabant.

4 Vulgus in medio expositum preda erat potentioribus, ut, uel eorum substantiis exhaustis uel etiam*a* corporibus in longinquas terras distractis, aceruos thesaurorum congererent, quamquam*b* magis ingenitum sit illi genti commesationibus quam opibus inhiare. Illud erat a natura abhorrens, quod multi ancillas suas ex se grauidas, ubi libidini satisfecissent, aut ad publicum prostibulum aut ad externum obsequium uenditabant. Potabatur in commune ab omnibus, in hoc studio noctes

5 perinde ut dies perpetuantibus. Paruis et abiectis domibus totos absumebant*c* sumptus, Francis et Normannis absimiles, qui amplis et superbis edifitiis modicas expensas agunt. Sequebantur uitia ebrietatis sotia, quae uirorum animos effeminant. Hinc factum est ut, magis temeritate et furore precipiti quam scientia militari*d* Willelmo congressi, uno prelio et ipso perfacili seruituti se patriamque pessumdederint. Nichil enim temeritate leuius, sed quicquid cum impetu inchoat, cito desinit uel compescitur.*e* Ad summam, tunc erant Angli uestibus ad medium genu expediti, crines tonsi, barbas rasi, armillis aureis brachia onerati, picturatis stigmatibus cutem insigniti; in cibis urgentes

6 crapulam, in potibus irritantes uomicam.*f* Et haec quidem extrema iam uictoribus suis participarunt, de ceteris in eorum mores transeuntes. Sed haec mala de omnibus generaliter Anglis dicta intelligi nolim: scio clericos multos tunc temporis simplici uia semitam sanctitatis triuisse, scio multos laicos omnis generis et conditionis Deo in eadem gente placuisse. Facessat ab hac relatione inuidia, non cunctos pariter haec inuoluit calumnia; uerum sicut*g* in tranquillitate malos

---

a om. B *b* quamuis *T*⁺ *c* abligur(r)iebant *T*⁺*Al* (insumebant *Aa*), cf. 4. 1
d *T*⁺ adds cum *e* consumitur *T*⁺ *f* Mynors conjectured uomitum, but cf. VD p. 300 *g* ut *Bc¹*, om. *BkBc²* (and *Bph*)

without hearing the name of a new saint? And think of the many whose memory has perished for want of historians!

But zeal both for learning and for religion cooled as time went on, not many years before the coming of the Normans. The clergy, content with a mere smattering of knowledge, scarce mumbled the words of the sacraments; a man who knew any grammar was a marvel and a portent to his colleagues. Monks, with their finely-woven garments and their undiscriminating diet, made nonsense of their Rule. The nobles, abandoned to gluttony and lechery, never went to church of a morning as a Christian should; but in his chamber, in his wife's embrace, a man would lend a careless ear to some priest galloping through the solemn words of matins and the mass. The common people, vulnerable from every quarter, were the prey of their more powerful neighbours, who drained away their resources or even sold their persons off to distant parts, in order to pile up treasure for themselves, although it is ingrained in that nation to dote on wassail rather than wealth. One practice in particular was perfectly inhuman: many of them got their own serving-maids with child and, when they had sated their lust on the girls, sold them to a public brothel or to service in a foreign country. Drinking in company was a universal practice, and in this passion they made no distinction between night and day. In small, mean houses they wasted their entire substance, unlike the French and the Normans, who in proud great buildings live a life of moderate expense. There followed the vices that keep company with drunkenness, and sap the virility of a man's spirit. As a result there was more rashness and headlong fury than military skill in their conflict with William, so that in one battle—and a very easy one—they abandoned themselves and their country to servitude. For hot blood has no staying power; whatever it starts with a rush fails or is suppressed. In brief, the English of those days wore garments half way to the knee, which left them unimpeded; hair short, chin shaven, arms loaded with gold bracelets, skin tattooed with coloured patterns, eating till they were sick and drinking till they spewed. These last two habits they have passed on to their conquerors, whose ways in other things they have adopted. But I should not wish these strictures to be understood as aimed at the English in general: I know that many clerics in those days trod the narrow path of holiness in simplicity of life, that many laymen in this country of all sorts and conditions led lives pleasing to God. Far from my narrative be any censoriousness; these charges do not apply to all alike. But as in tranquil times God's serene kindness often fosters bad

cum bonis fouet plerumque Dei serenitas, ita in captiuitate bonos cum malis nonnumquam eiusdem constringit seueritas.

246. Porro Normanni, ut de eis quoque dicamus, erant tunc, et sunt adhuc, uestibus ad inuidiam culti, cibis citra ullam nimietatem delicati. Gens militiae assueta et sine bello pene uiuere nescia, in hostem impigre procurrere, et ubi uires non successissent, non minus dolo et pecunia corrumpere. Domi ingentia, ut dixi,[1] edifitia, moderatos sumptus moliri; paribus inuidere, superiores pretergredi uelle; subiectos ipsi uellicantes ab alienis tutari; dominis fideles, moxque leui offensa infideles.
2 Cum fato ponderare perfidiam, cum nummo mutare sententiam. Ceterum omnium gentium benignissimi aduenas aequali secum honore colunt; matrimonia quoque cum subditis iungunt. Religionis normam, usquequaque in Anglia emortuam, aduentu suo suscitarunt; uideas ubique in uillis aecclesias, in uicis et urbibus monasteria nouo edificandi genere consurgere, recenti ritu patriam florere, ita ut sibi perisse diem quisque[a] opulentus existimet quem non aliqua preclara magnificentia illustret. Sed, quia de his satis dictum, Willelmi gesta prosequamur.

247. Ille, ubi perfecta uictoria potitus est, suos sepeliendos mirifice curauit; hostibus quoque, si qui uellent, idem exsequendi licentiam prebuit. Corpus Haroldi matri repetenti sine pretio misit, licet illa multum per legatos obtulisset; acceptum itaque apud Waltham sepeliuit, quam ipse aecclesiam ex proprio constructam in honore sanctae Crucis canonicis impleuerat. Sensim ergo Willelmus, ut triumphatorem decebat, cum exercitu non hostili sed regali modo progrediens, urbem regni maximam Lundoniam petit, moxque cum gratulatione ciues omnes effusi
2 obuiam uadunt. Prorupit omnibus portis unda[b] salutantium, auctoribus magnatibus, precipue Stigando archiepiscopo Cantuariensi et[c] Aldredo Eboracensi. Nam precedentibus diebus Eduinus et Morcardus, amplae spei fratres, apud Lundoniam audito interitus Haroldi nuntio, urbanos sollicitauerant ut alterutrum in regnum sulleuarent; quod frustra

[a] quique A   [b] turba T+   [c] om. B

[1] 245. 5.

and good men equally, so in the hour of captivity His stern judgement sometimes grips good as well as bad.

246. The Normans on the other hand (to say a word about them too) were then, as they still are, well-dressed to a fault, and particular about their food, but this side of any excess. The whole nation is familiar with war, and hardly knows how to live without fighting. They charge the enemy with spirit, and if force has not succeeded, are equally ready to corrupt him with craft and coin. At home the programme is great buildings, as I have said,[1] and low expenses. They look askance at their equals and wish to overtake their superiors; they fleece their underlings themselves but protect them from outsiders; loyal to their lords, and then on some slight cause of offence disloyal. Fortune changes, and fidelity is in the balance too; coin changes hands, conviction changes with it. For all that, they are of all nations the most hospitable, they treat strangers with the same respect as each other, and in marriage too they wed their inferiors. The standard of religion, dead everywhere in England, has been raised by their arrival: you may see everywhere churches in villages, in towns and cities monasteries rising in a new style of architecture; and with new devotion our country flourishes, so that every rich man thinks a day wasted if he does not make it remarkable with some great stroke of generosity. But of this I have said enough; let us pursue the story of William.

247. Having secured a complete victory, he saw his dead splendidly buried, and gave the enemy too permission to do the same if they wished. When Harold's mother asked for his body, he sent it to her without ransom, although she through her emissaries had offered a large sum. And so on receipt of it she buried it at Waltham, a church which he himself had built with his own money in honour of the Holy Cross, and had filled with canons. So William went forward with his army slowly, as a victorious general should—a royal progress rather than an enemy advance—and made for London, the largest city in his kingdom, where all the citizens soon poured out to meet him with rejoicing. They burst out in waves from every gate to welcome him, encouraged by the magnates, especially Archbishops Stigand of Canterbury and Ealdred of York; for in the days preceding, Edwin and Morcar, two brothers of great ambition, having heard in London the news of Harold's death, had tried to persuade the city folk to make one of them king, and on the failure of the attempt had left for

conati, Northanimbriam discesserant, ex suo coniectantes ingenio^a numquam illuc Willelmum esse uenturum. Ceteri proceres Edgarum eligerent, si episcopos assertores haberent; sed proximo urgente periculo
3 et domesticae litis discidio, nec illud quidem effectum. Ita Angli, qui in unam coeuntes sententiam potuissent patriae reformare ruinam, dum nullum ex suis uolunt, alienum induxerunt. Tunc ille, haud dubie rex conclamatus, die Natalis Domini coronatus est ab Aldredo archiepiscopo; cauebat enim id munus a Stigando suscipere, quod esset is archiepiscopus non legitime.

248. Omnium deinde bellorum quae gessit haec summa est. Vrbem Exoniam rebellantem leuiter subegit, diuino scilicet iutus auxilio, quod pars muralis ultro decidens ingressum illi patefecerit; nam et ipse audatius eam assilierat, protestans homines irreuerentes Dei destituendos suffragio, quia unus eorum supra murum stans nudato inguine auras sonitu inferioris partis turbauerat, pro contemptu uidelicet Nor-
2 mannorum. Eboracum,^b unicum rebellionum suffugium, ciuibus pene deleuit fame et ferro necatis. Ibi enim rex Scottorum Malcolmus cum suis, ibi Edgarus et Marcherius et Waldefus cum Anglis et Danis nidum tirannidis sepe fouebant, sepe duces illius trucidabant; quorum singillatim exitus si commemorauero, fortasse superfluus non ero, licet fastidii discrimen immineat, dum relatori, si forte secundum dictores suos mentiatur, difficilis sit regressus ad ueniam.

249. Malcolmus omnes^c Anglorum perfugas libenter recipiebat, tutamentum singulis quantum poterat impendens; Edgarum precipue, cuius sororem pro antiqua memoria nobilitatis iugalem sibi fecerat. Eius causa conterminas Angliae prouintias rapinis et incendiis infestabat, non quod aliquid ad regnum illi profuturum arbitraretur, sed ut Willelmi animum contristaret, qui Scotticis predis terras suas obnoxias indignaretur. Quapropter Willelmus,^d coacta peditum et militum^e
2 manu, aquilonales^f insulae partes petiit. Et primo urbem metropolim, quam Angli cum Danis et Scottis obstinate tenebant, in deditionem

^a om. CsB   ^b T⁺A add ciuitatem   ^c comes T⁺   ^d om. T⁺A
^e militum et peditum T⁺*(cf. GP p. 116)   ^f aquilonales A; -nares T'; -nalis TcCB

Northumbria, supposing on the basis of their own capacities that William would never get so far. The other nobles would have chosen Edgar if they had had the bishops on their side; but in the face of immediate danger and as they were divided by internal quarrels, this too came to nothing. Thus the English who, had they agreed on one course of action, could have rebuilt the ruins of their country, through reluctance to accept one of their own number gave an outsider his chance. Then William, chosen king by acclamation beyond all doubt, was crowned on Christmas Day by Archbishop Ealdred; for he was careful not to receive this office from Stigand, because he was not legally archbishop.

248. All the campaigns which he then fought can be summarized as follows. The city of Exeter, which was in revolt, he easily subdued, aided as he was by the help of Heaven, when part of the walls collapsed of its own accord and gave him admittance; indeed he himself had assaulted it with particular ferocity, protesting that such irreverent men must surely be deprived of divine support, after one of them, standing on the wall, had bared his breech and made the welkin re-echo with the noise of his nether parts, to show his contempt for Normans. York, the only remaining refuge for rebels, he almost wiped out, so many of the citizens perished by famine or sword; for that was where Malcolm king of the Scots with his forces, where Edgar and Morcar and Waltheof with English and Danish troops often made a snug nest for tyranny, and often cut to pieces William's generals. If I record the ends of these men one by one, I shall perhaps not go too far, though there is some risk of becoming tedious, and the narrator who by chance in following his authorities tells an untruth has a hard path back to his reader's good graces.

249. Malcolm had a warm welcome for all runaways on the English side, and gave them each as much protection as he could, Edgar especially, whose sister, in the light of the ancient tradition of her noble blood, he had married. For his sake he ravaged the neighbouring provinces of England with robbery and arson, not that he thought it would forward Edgar's hopes of becoming king, but to annoy William, and make him angry at the sight of his own lands exposed to Scottish forays. William therefore got together a force of infantry and knights and made for the northern parts of the island. First he accepted the surrender of the metropolitan city, which was held tenaciously by

accepit, ciuibus longa inedia consumptis; maximum quoque hostium numerum, qui obsessis in auxilium conuenerant, ingenti et graui prelio fudit, non incruenta sibi uictoria multos suorum amittens. Tunc totius regionis uicos et agros corrumpi, fructus et*a* fruges igne uel aqua labefactari iubet, maritima maxime, cum propter recentem iram, tum quia Cnutonem Danorum regem, filium Suani, aduentare rumor
3 sparserat. Ea precepti ratio, ut nichil circa oram maritimam predo piraticus inueniret, secum asportaturus si citius remeandum, uel fami consulturus si diutius manendum putaret. Itaque prouintiae quondam fertilis et tirannorum nutriculae incendio, preda, sanguine nerui succisi; humus per sexaginta et eo amplius miliaria omnifariam inculta; nudum omnium solum usque ad hoc etiam tempus. Vrbes olim preclaras, turres proceritate sua in caelum minantes, agros laetos pascuis irriguos fluuiis, si quis modo uidet peregrinus, ingemit; si quis superest uetus incola, non agnoscit.

250. Malcolmus, antequam ad manus ueniretur, se dedidit, totoque Willelmi tempore incertis et sepe fractis federibus aeuum*b* egit; sed filio Willelmi Willelmo regnante simili modo impetitus, falso sacramento insequentem abegit. Nec multo post, dum fidei immemor superbius prouintiam inequitaret,*c* a Rotberto de Molbreia, comite Northanimbriae, cum filio cesus est, humatusque multis annis apud Tinemuthe, nuper ab Alexandro filio Scottiam ad Dunfermelin portatus est.

251. Edgarus, cum Stigando et Aldredo archiepiscopis regis*d* dedititius,*e* sequenti anno facto ad Scottum transfugio iusiurandum maculauit; sed cum ibi aliquot annis*f* degens nichil ad presens commodi, nichil ad futurum spei preter cotidianam stipem nactus esset, Normanni liberalitatem experiri pergens, ad eum tunc ultra mare degentem nauigauit. Quod regi gratissimum fuisse*g* ferunt, ut incentore bellorum Anglia uacaret; nam et ultro solitus erat quoscumque Anglos suspectos habebat quasi honoris causa Normanniam

a uel *T*⁺   *b* eum *CB*   *c* inquietaret *T*⁺   *d* om. *T*⁺   *e* dediti us *CBc* (deductus *Bk*)   *f* annos *TcA*   *g* om. *T*⁺*A*

English with Danes and Scots, after exhausting the citizens by a lengthy famine. He also routed a very large enemy force which had gathered to aid the besieged, in a massive and severe conflict, a victory far from bloodless, for he lost many of his own men. He then gave orders for the towns and fields of the whole region to be devastated, and the fruit and grain to be ruined by fire or water, especially near the sea, partly because of his recent anger, but also since a rumour had spread that Cnut king of the Danes, son of Swein, was approaching, the purpose of this order being to leave nothing near the seashore which a raiding pirate could find and carry off if he had to make a rapid return home, or use for food if he thought he could stay longer. Thus a province once fertile and a nurse of tyrants was hamstrung by fire, rapine, and bloodshed; the ground for sixty miles and more left entirely uncultivated, the soil quite bare even down to this day. As for the cities once so famous, the towers whose tops threatened the sky, the fields rich in pasture and watered by rivers, if any one sees them now, he sighs if he is a stranger, and if he is a native surviving from the past, he does not recognize them.

250. Malcolm surrendered before they came to grips, and for the rest of William's time lived under unreliable agreements, often broken. When William's son William came to the throne, he was attacked in the same fashion, and shook off his pursuer by swearing an oath which he did not keep. Not long afterwards, while in an overweening breach of faith he was making a foray into the province, he was killed by Robert of Mowbray, earl of Northumberland, and his son with him; he lay buried for many years at Tynemouth, but was recently moved by his son Alexander to Dunfermline in Scotland.

251. Edgar, who had surrendered to the king with Archbishops Stigand and Ealdred, stained the honour of his oath in the following years by escaping to join the king of the Scots; but as, after spending several years there, he had been offered, apart from his daily allowance, no privileges for the present and no hope for the future, he went on to test the liberality of the Norman duke, and took ship to join him, for at that time he was living overseas. The king is said to have been delighted at this removal from England of a man who might stir up trouble; for it was in any case his practice, if he had his suspicions of any Englishmen, to take them with him to Normandy as though this were a mark of distinction, to prevent any disturbance in the kingdom

2 ducere, ne quicquam se absente in regno turbarent. Receptus ergo Edgarus et magno donatiuo donatus est, pluribusque annis in curia manens pedetemptim pro ignauia et, ut mitius dictum sit, pro simplicitate contemptui haberi cepit. Quantula enim simplicitas ut libram argenti, quam cotidie in stipendio accipiebat, regi pro uno equo perdonaret! Subsequenti tempore cum Rotberto filio Goduini, milite audacissimo, Ierosolimam pertendit. Illud fuit tempus quo Turchi Balduinum regem apud Ramas obsederunt; qui cum obsidionis iniuriam ferre nequiret, per medias hostium aties effugit, solius Rotberti opera liberatus preeuntis et euaginato gladio dextra leuaque Turchos cedentis; sed cum, successu ipso truculentior,[1] alacritate nimia procurreret, ensis manu excidit, ad quem recolligendum cum se inclinasset, omnium incursu[a] oppressus uinculis palmas dedit.
3 Inde Babilonem[2] ut aiunt ductus, cum Christum abnegare nollet, in medio foro ad signum positus et sagittis terebratus martirium sacrauit. Edgarus amisso milite regressus, multaque beneficia ab imperatoribus Grecorum et Alemannorum adeptus, quippe qui etiam eum retinere pro generis amplitudine temptassent, omnia pro natalis soli desiderio spreuit; quosdam enim profecto fallit amor patriae, ut nichil eis uideatur iocundum nisi consuetum hauserint caelum. Vnde Edgarus fatua cupidine illusus Angliam rediit; ubi,[b] ut superius dixi,[3] diuerso fortunae ludicro rotatus, nunc remotus et tacitus canos suos in agro consumit.

252. Eduinus et Morcardus erant fratres, filii Elfgari filii Lefrici. Hi comitatum Northanimbrorum susceperant, et communi umbone pacifice tuebantur; nam, ut predixi,[4] paucis diebus ante mortem regis Eduardi prouinciales aquilonis in rebellionem surrexerant et Tostinum comitem suum expulerant, petierantque et acceperant unum e fratribus dominum, annitente Haroldo. Fiebant ista, ut a consciis accepimus, infenso rege, quia Tostinum diligeret; sed morbo inualidus, senio grauis, pene iam despectui haberi ceperat, ut dilecto auxiliari non posset; quare ex animi egritudine maiorem ualitudinem corporis

---

[a] occursu *TtTc*, occursi *Tp* [b] unde *CB*

[1] i.e. Robert.
[2] i.e. Cairo.
[3] 228. 1.
[4] 200. 2–3, 228. 9.

during his absence. Edgar was kindly received therefore, and given a 2
large sum of money; and at the court he remained for some years,
coming by degrees to be despised for his indolence or, to use a kinder
word, his simplicity. Indeed, what simplicity it shows to let the king
off the payment of a pound of silver, which was his daily allowance, in
return for one horse! Later he set off for Jerusalem with Robert son of
Godwine, a most valiant knight. That was the time when the Turks
were besieging King Baldwin in Ramlah, and since he could not
endure the disgrace of being besieged, he broke out through the thick
of the enemy lines, owing his freedom to Robert alone, who went in
front with drawn sword mowing down the Turks to right and left. Success however made him[1] too ferocious, and as he pressed forward with
excess of zeal the sword slipped from his hand. He stooped down to
pick it up, and they all fell upon him and overwhelmed him, and he
was put in chains. From there he was taken, so the story goes, to Baby- 3
lon,[2] and when he refused to deny Christ, he was set up as a target in
the middle of the market-place and there, pierced through and through
with arrows, achieved a martyr's death. After the loss of the knight,
Edgar made his way back and, after receiving many acts of kindness
from the Greek and German emperors—for they had even tried to
retain him in view of his distinguished lineage—he spurned all their
offers in his longing for his native land; for some people are simply
misled by the love of their country, so that they can enjoy nothing
unless they can breath familiar air. Thus it was that Edgar, deceived
by this foolish longing, returned to England where, as I have said
above,[3] he suffered a turn of Fortune's wheel, and now, in solitude
and silence, wears out his gray hairs in the depths of the country.

252. Edwin and Morcar were brothers, sons of Leofric's son Ælfgar.
They had taken over the earldom of the Northumbrians, and kept it
in peace with a defence force which they shared; for, as I have said
already,[4] a few days before King Edward's death the inhabitants of the
northern province had risen in revolt, and after driving out Tostig,
their earl, had asked for one of the brothers as their lord, and had
been given him with Harold's support. This proceeding, as I have
heard from those in a position to know, angered the king, who was
much attached to Tostig; but he was handicapped by illness and burdened with old age, and had almost become an object of contempt
already, so that he could do nothing for his favourite. As a result, his
low spirits brought on a more serious physical illness, and he died not

2 contrahens, non multo post decessit. Perstitit in incepto Haroldus ut fratrem exlegaret; quocirca ille, prius piraticis excursibus auitos triumphos polluens, mox cum rege Noricorum, ut supra scripsi,[1] cesus est. Cadauer eius, inditio uerrucae inter duas scapulas agnitum, sepulturam Eboraci meruit. Tunc Eduinus et Morcardus Haroldo iubente manubiales predas Lundoniam tulere; nam ipse ad Hastingensem pugnam
3 festinabat, unde[a] iam partam uictoriam falso presagus somniabat. At eo interempto germani, ad terras suae potestatis profugientes,[b] aliquot annis pacem Willelmi turbauerunt, clandestinis latrociniis siluas infestantes nec umquam comminus et aperte martem agentes; sepe etiam capti, plerumque se dedidere, sed miseratione iuuenilis decoris et gratia nobilitatis impune dimissi. Postremo nec ui nec dolo hostium sed suorum perfidia trucidati, regem ad lacrimas flexere; quibus ipse et coniugia cognatarum et amicitiae dignationem iam pridem indulsisset, si quieti adquiescere uellent.

253. Waldefus, amplae prosapiae comes, multam familiaritatem noui regis nactus fuerat, quod ille, preteritarum offensarum immemor, magis illas uirtuti quam perfidiae attribuebat.[c] Siquidem Waldefus in Eboracensi pugna plures Normannorum solus obtruncauerat, unos et unos per portam egredientes decapitans; neruosus lacertis, thorosus pectore, robustus et procerus toto corpore, filius Siwardi magnificentissimi comitis, quem Digera Danico uocabulo, id est fortem, cognomina-
2 bant. Postmodum uero, uictis partibus sese sponte dedens, et Iudithae neptis[d] regis conubio priuataque amicitia donatus, non permansit in fide, prauum[e] ingenium cohibere impotens. Compatriotis enim omnibus qui existimarant resistendum cesis uel subiectis, etiam in Radulfi de Waher[f] perfidia se immiscuit; sed coniuratione detecta comprehensus diuque[g] in uinculis tentus, ultimo spoliatus capite Crolando sepultus est; quanuis quidam dicant necessitate interceptum, non uoluntate addictum, infidelitatis sacramentum agitasse. Anglorum est ista excusatio (nam cetera Normanni afferunt),[h] Anglorum qui plurimum ueritate[i] prestent. Quorum astipulationi Diuinitas suffragari

[a] inde *Al*, indeque *Aa*   [b] profugientes *(-gentes Tp)* T^+; per- *ACB*   [c] attribuerat *A*   [d] om. T^+ [e] primum T^+ [f] Waber T^+; *Orderic calls him* Guader   [g] diu *A*   [h] asserunt T^+ *(but cf. GP p. 322)*   [i] T^+, *GP p. 322;* om. *ACB*

[1] 228. II.

long after. Harold persisted in the attempt to outlaw his brother 2 [Tostig], who as a result, having first brought dishonour on the triumphs of his ancestors by turning pirate, was then killed together with the king of the Norwegians, as I have already recounted.[1] His body, recognized by the evidence of a wart between the shoulder-blades, received the honour of burial at York. Then Edwin and Morcar, on Harold's instructions, took the booty to London, for he himself was hurrying to battle at Hastings where, he dreamed with foolish optimism, victory was already won. When he was killed, how- 3 ever, the brothers escaped to regions which were under their own control, and there disturbed William's peace for some years by infesting the forests with covert brigandage and never fighting openly and at close quarters. Often too they were captured, often did they surrender; but sympathy for their youth and good looks and respect for their high birth secured their release without penalty. At length they were cut down, not by the force or fraud of their enemies but by the treachery of their own men, and the king was moved to tears. He himself would long ago have married them to his own kinswomen and honoured them with his friendship, had they been content to remain at peace.

253. Waltheof, an earl of noble lineage, had been a great friend of the new king, who was prepared to forget his past offences and ascribe them to a high spirit rather than disloyalty. For in the battle of York Waltheof had laid low many of the Normans single-handed, beheading them one by one as they issued from the gate; he had great strength of arm, powerful chest muscles, his whole frame tough and tall. He was a son of Siward, the very grand earl called Digera in Danish, which means 'the Mighty'. At length however his 2 party was defeated, and after a voluntary surrender he was granted the king's niece Judith in marriage and honoured with his personal friendship. Even so he did not remain loyal, being unable to control his natural perversity. When all his compatriots who had decided to fight on had been killed or overcome, he actually plunged into the conspiracy of Ralph of Gael; and when the plot was detected, he was seized, was kept for a long time in chains, and eventually lost his head and was buried at Crowland. Some, however, say it was the force of necessity and not inclination that made him join the traitors. Such is the excuse put forward by the English, for the rest of the story is Norman; but they are Englishmen of the highest credit. And their assertion seems to be supported by divine authority, which

uidetur, miracula multa, et ea permaxima, ad tumbam illius ostendens. Aiunt enim in catenas coniectum cotidianis singultibus perperam commissa diluisse.

254. Inde*a* propositum regis fortassis merito excusatur, si aliquanto durior in Anglos fuerit, quod pene nullum eorum fidelem inuenerit. Quae res ita ferocem animum exasperabat*b* ut potentiores primum pecuniis, mox terris, nonnullos etiam uita exueret. Quin etiam Cesarianum[1] secutus ingenium, qui Germanos in Ardenna maxima silua abditos, et inde crebris eruptionibus exercitum suum affligentes, non per Romanos suos sed per Gallos federatos expulit, ut, dum alienigenae alterutros transfoderent, ipse sine sanguine triumphum duceret—idem, inquam, Willelmus in Anglos egit. Nam contra quosdam, qui post primam infelicis ominis*c* pugnam Danemarkiam et Hiberniam profugerant, et ualida congregata manu tertio anno redierant, Angligenam exercitum et ducem obiecit, Normannos feriari permittens, ingens sibi leuamen prouidens, utrilibet uincerent. Nec eum cogitatio lusit; nam utrique Angli, aliquandiu digladiati inter se, palmam otiosam*d* regi refudere:*e* aduenae Hiberniam fugati, regii maxima sui clade nomen inane uictoriae amisso duce mercati. Vocabatur is Ednodus, domi belloque Anglorum temporibus iuxta*f* insignis, pater Hardingi qui adhuc superest, magis consuetus linguam in lites acuere quam arma in bello concutere. Ita laicorum potentia subruta, stabili quoque offirmauit edicto ut nullum eius gentis*g* monachum uel clericum ad aliquam dignitatem conari pateretur, a Cnutonis quondam regis facilitate immaniter abhorrens, qui uictis honores integros exhibuit; unde factum est ut eo defuncto indigenae aduenas leuiter expellerent sibique antiquum ius uendicarent. At iste certis de causis uiuentes quosdam canonice deposuit, et in locum illorum qui morerentur cuiuscumque gentis industrium*h* preter Angligenam imposuit. Exigebat hoc, nisi fallor, indurata in regem peruicatia, cum sint Normanni, ut ante dixi,[2] in conuiuentes aduenas naturali benignitate procliues.*i*

---

a unde *T*⁺   *b* *Tc;* -bant *T'ACB*   *c* *TpTcAap*^{p.c.} *Bc'*^{p.c.} *Bc²;* hominis *ACBk;* omnis *TtBc'*   *d* otioso *T*⁺*A*   *e* retulere *T*⁺ (*cf. 389. 5*)   *f* uita *T*⁺   *g* gentis eius *A*   *h* *T*⁺*A add* hominem   *i* percliues *Bk,* proclues *Bc* (*Bph avoids error*)

---

[1] *Bell. Gall.* v. 3. 4 (Ardennes), vi. 34. 8 (use of Gauls).
[2] 246. 2.

manifested many miracles at his tomb, and those of great importance; for they say that while in chains he purged his misdeeds by daily tears.

254. It perhaps provides some proper justification for the king's policy if he was somewhat too harsh towards the English, that he found almost none of them trustworthy—behaviour which so exasperated his ferocity that he deprived the more powerful among them first of their revenues, then of their lands, and some even of their lives. He followed moreover the ingenious practice of Caesar's[1] in his campaign against the Germans hidden in the vast forest of the Ardennes, from which they used to harass his troops with frequent sallies: he drove them out, by using not his own Romans but his Gaulish allies, so that, while the two sets of aliens cut each other to pieces, he himself enjoyed a triumph without bloodshed. This, as I was saying, was the method William used against the English. Some of them, who after the first fatal encounter had fled to Denmark and Ireland, and two years later had collected a powerful force and returned, he confronted with an army and a general of English blood, while he allowed his Normans to take a holiday, foreseeing an immense relief for himself, whichever side won. Nor did his strategy mislead him; for the English on both sides, after fighting it out for some time between themselves, presented the king with an effortless victory: the new arrivals were sent packing to Ireland, and the king's side bought the empty name of victory at the price of very heavy casualties and the loss of their general. His name was Eadnoth, and under the English regime he had enjoyed a high reputation equally at home and in the field; he was the father of Harding, who still survives, and is more familiar with the sharp tongue as a weapon of dispute than with the clash of arms on the battlefield. Having thus undermined the influence of the laity, he further established it as a regular practice by proclamation that he would allow no one of English nationality, whether monk or cleric, to aspire to any dignity—a savage change from the easy ways of his predecessor King Cnut, who let the vanquished keep all their privileges. As a result, on his death the natives easily drove out all the newcomers and reclaimed their ancient rights. But for specific reasons William deposed some of the clergy in their lifetime legally, and in the place of those who died put a competent man of any nationality except English. He was driven to this, unless I am mistaken, by their ingrained prejudice against the king, for the Normans, as I said before,[2] have a natural kindliness which predisposes them to foreigners living in their midst.

255. Radulfus, de quo prius tetigi,[1] erat per donum regis comes Northfolki et Suthfolki, Brito ex patre, distorti ad omne bonum animi. Is quod cognatam regis, filiam Willelmi filii Osberni, desponderat maiora iusto mente metiens, tirannidem adoriri meditabatur. Itaque ipso nuptiarum die magnis apparatibus conuiuium agitatum, quod Normannorum gulae iam Anglorum luxus influxerat. Ebriis conuiuis et uino tumentibus, amplo uerborum ambitu propositum suum aperit; illi, quia in eorum animo pro potu omnis ratio caligabat, ingenti
2 plausu dicenti acclamant. Ibi Rogerius comes Herefordensis uxoris Radulfi frater, ibi Waldefus, ibi preterea quamplurimi in necem regis coniurant; sed postero die, cum digesto calore uini temperatior aura corda quorundam afflasset, maior pars facti penitens a conuiuio dilapsa. Vnus eorum Waldeof fertur, qui consilio Lanfranci archiepiscopi Normanniam ultro enauigans rem regi, causa sua dumtaxat celata, detulit; at comites in incepto persistere, prouintiales suos quisque in
3 tumultum excitare. Sed obsistebat eis Deus, omnes conatus eorum in irritum deducens. Mox enim re comperta, duces regis, qui custodiam pretendebant, Radulfum ad hoc calamitatis compulere ut arrepta naue apud Norwic mari se committeret; uxor eius, pacta membrorum salutem[a] traditoque castello,[b] maritum secuta. Rogerius, a rege uinculis irretitus, tota uita carcerem frequentauit uel potius incoluit, detestandae perfidiae[c] iuuenis nec moribus patrissans.

256. Siquidem genitor eius, Willelmus filius Osberni, principibus optimis comparandus fuerit, haud scio an etiam preponendus. Eius consilio rex Willelmus primo animatus ad inuadendam Angliam, mox uirtute adiutus ad manutenendam. Erat in eo mentis animositas quam commendabat manus pene[d] prodiga liberalitas, unde factum est ut militum multitudine, quibus larga stipendia dabat, hostium auiditatem arceret, ciuium sedulitatem haberet; quare pro effusis sumptibus asperrimam regis offensam incurrit, quod gazas suas improuide dilapi-
2 daret. Manet ad hanc diem in comitatu eius apud Herefordum legum quas statuit inconcussa firmitas, ut nullus miles pro qualicumque

---

[a] salute C [b] marito T' [c] malici(a)e T' [d] om. T'

---

[1] 253. 2.

255. Ralph, whom I have touched on previously,[1] was by the king's gift earl of Norfolk and Suffolk, a Breton on his father's side, and a man of warped mind as regards every good action. Betrothed as he was to a kinswoman of the king, a daughter of William Fitz Osbern, he conceived ambitions beyond what was right, and planned to usurp the throne. And so, precisely on his wedding-day, a feast was held on the most lavish scale (for English luxury had now influenced Norman appetites); and when the guests were intoxicated and flown with wine, he laid his plans before them in a lengthy speech. In the minds of his audience all reasons had been darkened by drink, and they received his remarks with prolonged applause. There was Roger earl of Hereford, Ralph's brother-in-law, there was Waltheof, there were many, many more, forming a conspiracy to kill their king. Next day, when the heat of the wine had been dissipated and a milder breeze blew in the hearts of some of them, the majority repented of what they had done, and slipped away from the party. One of them is said to have been Waltheof who, on the advice of Archbishop Lanfranc crossed to Normandy, and told the king what had happened, merely concealing his own part in it. The earls none the less proceeded with their undertaking, each of them rousing the people of his own province to revolt. But God withstood them and brought all their attempts to nought. For the story soon got out; the king's earls, who were keeping watch, reduced Ralph to such straits that he had to take a ship at Norwich and entrust himself to the sea; his wife, after securing a promise of her physical safety and handing over the castle, followed her husband. Roger was put in irons by the king, and spent the rest of his life as a sojourner, or rather an inmate, in prison. He was a young man of abominable disloyalty, who in character did not take after his father.

256. For his father, William Fitz Osbern, might well be compared with the best of princes, and perhaps even placed above them. It was on his advice that King William first aspired to the invasion of England, and by his courage that he was later enabled to retain it. He was a man of great determination, seconded by a generosity that was almost spendthrift, so that with the large number of knights to whom he paid generous fees he kept at bay the greed of enemies, and enjoyed the devotion of his own people; and hence his generous spending earned very severe disapproval from the king, who considered that he was thoughtlessly wasting the royal resources. To this day the laws which he made for his earldom of Hereford remain valid and unshaken:

commisso plus septem solidis soluat, cum in aliis prouintiis ob paruam occasiunculam in transgressione precepti herilis uiginti uel*ᵃ* uiginti quinque pendantur. Sed tam secundos euentus turpi fine fortuna conclusit, dum tanti regni sustentator, Angliae et Normanniae consiliarius, pro feminea cupidine Flandriam pergens ab insidiatoribus impetitus
3 interiit. Nam Balduinus antiquus ille, de quo superius dixi,[1] pater Mathildis, duos habuit filios,*ᵇ* Rotbertum, qui patre superstite comitissam Frisiae uxorem nactus Frisonis cognomen*ᶜ* accepit,*ᵈ* Balduinum, qui post patrem aliquot annis Flandriae prefuit immatureque fato functus est, superstitibus duobus liberis Arnulfo et Balduino de Richelde uxore, quorum tutelam regi Francorum Philippo, cuius amitae filius erat, et Willelmo filio Osberni commendauerat. Libens id munus suscepit Willelmus, ut federatis cum Richelde nuptiis altius nomen sibi
4 pararet. At illa, femineo fastu altiora*ᵉ* sexu spirans nouaque a prouintialibus tributa exigens, in perfidiam illos excitauit; misso quippe propter Rotbertum Frisonem nuntio, ut suplicantis patriae habenas acciperet, omnem fidelitatem Arnulfo, qui iam comes dicebatur, abiurant. Nec
5 uero defuere qui pupilli partes fulcirent. Ita multis diebus Flandria intestinis dissensionibus conturbata. Id filius Osberni, qui totus in amorem mulieris concesserat, pati nequiuit, quin militari manu coacta Flandriam intraret; susceptusque primo ab his quos tutari uenerat, post paucos dies securus de*ᶠ* castello in aliud equitabat expeditus cum paucis. Contra Friso, quem huiusmodi fatuitas non latebat, occultatis insidiis inopinum excepit, et nequiquam fortiter agentem ipsum et nepotem suum Arnulfum cecidit.

257. Ita Flandria potitus, sepe Willelmum regem Normannicis predis irritauit. Filia eius Cnutoni regi Danorum nupsit, de qua genitus est Karolus qui modo principatur in Flandria. Pacem cum Philippo rege comparauit, data sibi in uxorem priuigna, de qua ille Ludouicum tulit qui modo regnat in Frantia; nec multo post pertesus conubii, quod illa prepinguis corpulentiae esset, a lecto remouit, uxoremque Andegauensis comitis*ᵍ* contra fas et ius sibi coniunxit. Eorum affinitate tutus, Rotbertus nichil quod deploraret suo tempore uidit, licet

ᵃ uiginti uel *om. T¹*   *ᵇ* filios habuit *T¹Bc¹*   *ᶜ* nomen *T¹Bc*   *ᵈ* One expects et *to follow*   *ᵉ* ampliora *Cᵉᵛ B*   *ᶠ* One expects alio (*or* uno, *cf. 378.2*) *to follow*   *ᵍ* com. And. *T¹*

[1] 188. 2, 234. 2.

no knight is to pay more than seven shillings for any offence, while in other provinces even a tiny transgression of the lord's instructions incurs a fine of twenty or twenty-five. But to this record of successes fortune set a discreditable end when, to satisfy his passion for a woman, the pillar of that great kingdom, wise counsellor of both England and Normandy, went off to Flanders and met his death in an ambush. For Baldwin the elder whom I mentioned previously,[1] Matilda's father, had two sons, Robert who during his father's lifetime married the countess of Frisia and was nicknamed 'the Frisian', and Baldwin, who ruled Flanders for some years after his father, and died young. He left, by his wife Richildis, two children, Arnulf and Baldwin, and appointed as their guardians Philip king of the French (his mother was the king's aunt) and William Fitz Osbern. William gladly took up the position in hopes, by undertaking to marry Richildis, of winning a more distinguished name for himself. But she, with a woman's ambition, was forming plans beyond her sex, and by exacting new taxes from the people of the province she roused them to revolt. They sent a message for Robert the Frisian, urging him to answer the appeal of his native country and seize the reins of power, while they renounced any loyalty to Arnulf, who was now called count. Nor indeed was there any lack of support for the party of the ward. Thus Flanders was for some time a prey to internal dissensions, and Fitz Osbern, who had surrendered entirely to his passion for the woman, found this intolerable; in fact, he got together a band of knights, and entered Flanders. There he was warmly received at first by those whom he had come to protect, and in a few days' time was riding confidently from one castle to another, lightly armed and with few companions. Robert the Frisian on the other hand, who did not fail to notice his folly, laid an ambush and caught him off his guard. In vain he fought bravely; he and Robert's nephew Arnulf were killed.

257. Having thus got possession of Flanders, Robert often provoked King William by his raids on Normandy. His daughter married Cnut king of the Danes, and was mother of Charles who now rules in Flanders. He secured peace with King Philip, giving him his step-daughter as his wife, by whom he had the Louis who now reigns in France; but not long afterwards, growing tired of this marriage because his wife was inordinately stout, he sent her away and, contrary to law divine and human, took the wife of the count of Anjou to live with him. Protected by these relationships, Robert saw nothing in his time that he might regret,

Balduinus frater Arnulfi, qui in Hanoea prouintia et castello Valentianis comitatum habuit, regis Willelmi auxilio plures assultus faceret.

2 Tribus ante mortem annis, iam canis sparsus caput, Ierosolimam contendit pro peccatorum alleuiamento; regressus mundanis inuolucris renuntiauit, finem uitae quietus a negotiis Christiana sollicitudine operiens. Filius eius Rotbertus ille fuit qui in expeditione Asiatica quam nostris diebus Europa contra Turchos mouit mirandus innotuit; sed nescio quo infortunio, postquam domum reuersus est, nobilem illum laborem decolorauit, in quodam quod uocant torniamento ad mortem Iesus. Nec filium eius Balduinum fortuna excepit felitior, qui, ultro in Normannia regis Anglorum Henrici uires lacessens, iuuenilis audatiae temeritatem luit; namque conto in capite percussus, multorumque medicorum promissis illusus, metam uitae abrupit, Karolo illi, de quo supra diximus, principatu tradito.

258. At uero rex Willelmus in subiectos leniter, turbide in rebelles agens feliciter omni Anglia potiebatur, Walenses omnes tributarios habens. Iam uero trans mare numquam otiosus Cinomannico solo pene exterminium indixit, ducta expeditione illuc de Anglis, qui sicut facile in solo suo potuerunt opprimi, ita in alieno semper apparuere inuicti. Apud Dolum, castellum transmarinae Britanniae, dum nescio qua simultate irritatus manum illuc militarem duxisset, innumeros ex suis desiderauit. Philippum regem Francorum, cuius amitae filiam uxorem duxerat, semper infidum habuit, quod scilicet ille tantam gloriam uiro inuideret quem et patris sui et suum hominem esse constaret.

2 Sed Willelmus nichilo setius eius conatibus improbe obuiabat,[a] quanuis primogenitus filius eius Rotbertus fatuo consilio conatibus eius assisteret;[b] unde contigit ut in quodam assultu apud Gibboracum filius patri resultans eo uulnerato equum ipsius[c] confoderet, Willelmus medius filiorum sautius abiret, multi ex regiis caderent. Ceterum tota uita ita fortunatus fuit ut exterae et remotae gentes nichil magis quam nomen eius timerent. Prouintiales adeo nutui suo substrauerat ut sine ulla contradictione primus censum omnium capitum ageret, omnium prediorum redditus[d] in tota Anglia notitiae suae per scriptum adiceret, omnes liberos homines, cuiuscumque essent,[e] suae fidelitati sacramento

---

[a] obu. imp. T   [b] obsisteret T; *the sentence is clumsy (Aa rewrites:* contra patrem illi assisteret)   [c] eius T   [d] reditus TA   [e] cuius. essent *om.* T

though Arnulf's brother Baldwin, who had his county in the province of Hainault and the castle of Valenciennes, made several attacks on him with King William's help. Three years before his death, when his hair 2 was already sprinkled with white, he set off to Jerusalem for the remission of his sins, and on his return renounced the ties of this world, and awaited the end of life, quit of all business, intent on the cares that befit a Christian. His son was the Robert who gained a wonderful reputation on the expedition to Asia mounted in our own days by Europe against the Turks; but by some misfortune, after returning home, he brought discredit on that noble endeavour, and was mortally wounded in what they call a tournament. Nor did a happier future await his son Baldwin, who deliberately attacked the power of the English king Henry in Normandy, and paid for his youthful rashness; he was struck on the head with a pike, and after being deceived by the promises of many physicians lost his life, leaving his princely position to the Charles of whom I have spoken above.

258. Meanwhile King William, by a mixture of mildness towards the submissive and severity towards rebels, was successfully holding the whole of England in his power, while he had all the Welsh as tributaries. By now he was in continual action overseas, and threatened Maine with reduction virtually to a desert, leading an invasion of English troops, who, though they could be so easily defeated in their own country, always showed themselves invincible on foreign soil. At Dol, a walled town in Brittany against which on some provocation or other he had led a force of knights, he lost a large proportion of his troops. King Philip, whose aunt's daughter he had married, he always found untrustworthy, no doubt because Philip took it amiss that so much glory should be achieved by someone who was known to have been his father's man and his own. None the less, however, William 2 obstinately blocked his initiatives, although Robert, his eldest son, was so foolish as to support the French king. Hence it came about that in an assault on Gerberoi the son clashed with the father, wounded him and cut down his horse; William, his middle son, got away wounded; and the royal troops suffered heavy casualties. For all that, he enjoyed such good fortune life long that nations foreign and far-distant feared nothing so much as his name. His subjects he had made so subservient to his lightest wish that there was no opposition when he made the first census by counting heads, adding to his records in writing the rents of all properties in the whole of England, and bound all those of free birth, no matter whose man each of them was, by an oath of

3 adigeret. Solus eius maiestatem concutiebat Cnuto rex Danorum, qui et affinitate Rotberti Frisonis et suapte potentia in immensum extollebatur, rumore in populos sato quod Angliam inuaderet, debitum sibi pro affinitate antiqui Cnutonis solum; et profecto fecisset, nisi Deus eius audatiam uento contrario infirmasset. Quae res ammonuit ut genealogiam regum Danorum qui post nostrum Cnutonem fuere strictim abbreuiem, de Noricis quoque pauca inserturus.

259. Ei, ut ante dictum est,[1] successit Haroldus in Anglia, Hardacnutus in Danemarkia, filii eius; nam Noricam, quam subegerat, recuperauit Magnus, filius Olaui, quem in gestis Cnutonis dixi[2] a prouintialibus suis necatum fuisse.*a* Haroldo in Anglia defuncto, ambo regna tenuit Hardacnutus pauco tempore; quo mortuo successit Eduardus simplex, auitoque regno contentus transmarinum imperium ut laboriosum et barbarum despuit. Tunc rex Danorum leuatus est Suanus quidam, haud dubie nobilissimus; cuius cum regnum aliquot annis prosperaretur, Magnus rex Noricorum consentientibus Danis 2 quibusdam illum ui bellica expellens suo animo terram subiecit. Eiectus Suanus regem Sueuorum adiit, eiusque auxilio, cum Sueuos et Vindelicos et Gothos corrasisset, rediit ut regnum reformaret; sed conspirantibus Danis qui potestatem Magni diligerent, prioris fortunae calamitatem expertus est. Ingens illud et memorabile in ea barbarie prelium fuit, quo*b* numquam uel discrimen formidabilius uel omen laetius Dani uiderunt. Denique ad hoc tempus uotum illibatum custodiunt quo se ante pugnam constrinxerunt, ut uigiliam sancti Laurentii cunctis in posterum seculis ieiunio et elemosinis sacrarent.*c* Eo enim die certatum, et tunc quidem Suanus fugit; sed non multo post, mortuo Magno, regnum suum integre recepit.

260. Successit Magno in Norica Suanus quidam, Herdhand*d* cognominatus, non de regia progenie sed manu et calliditate prouectus; illi Olauus, patruus Magni, quem sanctum ferunt; Olauo Haroldus Haruagra, frater Olaui, qui etiam imperatori Constantinopolitano

---

a fuisse necatum *Tt;* necatum esse *A*   *b* *Savile;* quod *MSS*   *c* consecrarent *B*   *d* Herdanus *Tt*

[1] 188. 1.
[2] 181. 6.

fealty to himself. The only person who shook his royal state was Cnut 3
king of the Danes, who was rising to very great heights as a result of
his kinship with Robert the Frisian and his personal resources. A popular rumour was put about that he would invade England, the soil of
which was rightly his as a relative of the elder Cnut; and indeed he
would have done so, had not God taken the drive out of his rash
attempt with a contrary wind. This event has suggested to me that I
should give a very brief summary of the genealogy of the Danish
kings who reigned after our Cnut; and I will also insert a few remarks
about the Norwegians.

259. Cnut, as I have said before,[1] was succeeded by his sons, Harold
[Harefoot] in England and Harthacnut in Denmark; for Norway,
which he had conquered, was recovered by Magnus, son of that Olaf
of whose murder by his subjects I have told in my account of Cnut.[2]
After Harold's death in England, Harthacnut held both kingdoms for
a short time. Edward the Simple, who succeeded him on his death,
was content with the kingdom of his forefathers, and rejected the rule
of land across the sea as toilsome and barbarous. Then a man called
Swein, of high birth without doubt, was promoted to be king of the
Danes; but though he ruled prosperously for several years, Magnus
king of the Norwegians, supported by a number of Danes, then threw
him out by force of arms and subjected the country to his own will.
On his expulsion Swein approached the king of the Swedes, and 2
having with his help scraped together a force of Swedes, Wends, and
Gauts, returned in hopes of re-establishing his rule; those Danes, however, who preferred to be ruled by Magnus, conspired against him,
and his former disastrous experience was repeated. That was an
immense battle, and in those barbarous days unforgettable, the most
formidable crisis and the most promising omen the Danes ever saw.
To this day, for instance, they keep inviolate the oath by which they
bound themselves before the fight, that for all ages to come they
would consecrate St Laurence's eve to fasting and almsgiving. That
was the day of the battle, and it was then that Swein fled; but not
long after, on Magnus's death, he regained his kingdom intact.

260. Magnus was succeeded in Norway by another Swein, nicknamed Hardhand, not of royal lineage, but owing his elevation to boldness and cunning; after him Olaf, Magnus's uncle, whom they call
St Olaf; after Olaf his brother Harold Fairhair, who as a young man

dudum iuuenis militauerat, cuius iussu pro stupro illustris feminae leoni obiectus, beluam immanem nudo lacertorum nisu suffocauit. Hic in Anglia ab Haroldo filio Goduini cesus.*a* Filii eius Olauus et Magnus regnum paternum partiti, sed Magno premature mortuo Olauus totum occupauit. Illi successit filius Magnus, qui nuper in Hibernia, dum temere illuc*b* appulisset, miserabiliter occisus est.

2 Ferunt Magnum superiorem, filium Haroldi, post mortem patris ab Haroldo rege Angliae clementer domum dimissum, illius benefitii memoria Haroldum filium Haroldi, post uictoriam Willelmi ad se uenientem, benigne tractasse, eundemque in expeditione sotium habuisse quam in Angliam tempore Willelmi iunioris duxit, quando et Orcadas et Meuanias insulas sibi subiecit,*c* et occurrentes comites Hugonem Cestrensem et Hugonem Salopesberiensem priorem fugauit,*d* secundum interemit. Filii ultimi Magni, Hasten et Siwardus, regno adhuc diuiso imperitant; quorum posterior, adolescens spetiosus et audax, non multum est quod Ierosolimam per Angliam nauigauit, innumera et preclara facinora contra Saracenos consummans, presertim in obsessione*e* Sidonis, quae pro conscientia Turchorum immania in Christianos fremebat.

261. Sed Suanus in regno Danorum, ut dixi,[1] restitutus, egre quietem ferens in Angliam bis Cnutonem filium misit, primo cum trecentis, secundo cum ducentis nauibus. Prioris classis sotius fuit Osbernus frater Suani, sequentis Hacco; utrique accepta pecunia conatus adolescentis fregere, domum sine effectu repatriantes, quare a Suano rege, graui contumelia inusti quod fidem pecunia lesissent, in exilium acti*f* sunt. Suanus, ad mortem ueniens, omnes iuramento prouintiales constrinxit ut, quia quattuordecim filios habebat, omnibus per ordinem 2 regnum delegarent, quantum ipsa soboles durare posset. Eo ergo defuncto, successit filius Haroldus annis tribus; illi Cnuto, quem pater in Angliam miserat. Is ueteris repulsae memor classem, ut accepimus, mille et eo amplius nauium in Angliam parat. Auxilio ei erat socer Rotbertus Friso, sexcentarum ratium dominus; sed duobus pene annis uenti aduersitate coercitus, uoluntatem mutauit, pronuntians non sine Dei nutu esse quod transfretare nequiret. Verum *g*post modicum*g*

a T*t*AB*c'* *add* est *b* *om.* T*t* *c* subegit T*t* (*cf. 131. 3*) *d* fugit A*l*C*e*B *e* obsidione T*t* *f* aucti T*t* *g–g* postmodum *A*

[1] 259. 2.

had done long service in the forces of the emperor of Constantinople, and in return for debauching a lady of distinguished family had on his orders been thrown to a lion, whereupon he strangled the raging beast with his bare hands. This king was killed in England by Harold son of Godwine. His sons, Olaf and Magnus, divided their father's kingdom, but Magnus died young, and Olaf took over the whole. He was succeeded by his son Magnus, who was killed wretchedly not long ago in Ireland, after making a rash landing. The story goes that the elder 2 Magnus, Harold's son, was mercifully sent home by Harold king of England after his father's death; and that it was in memory of this kindness that he treated Harold's son Harold so kindly when he came to him after William's victory, and took him with him on the expedition to England in the younger William's time, on which he conquered the Orkneys and the Mevanian Isles, and of the earls who came against him, Hugh of Chester and Hugh of Shrewsbury, put the first to flight and killed the second. The sons of the last Magnus, Eystein and Sigurd, rule over a kingdom that is still divided. The latter of them, a good-looking and brave young man, sailed not long ago to Jerusalem by way of England, and there performed countless brave feats against the Saracens, especially at the siege of Sidon, which in defence of the Turkish cause was raging madly against the Christians.

261. But Swein, restored, as I have said,[1] to the throne of the Danes, and finding peace intolerable, sent his son Cnut twice to England, first with three hundred ships and then with two hundred. Swein's brother Osbjorn was a partner in the first fleet, and Hakon in the second; both took money to bring the young man's efforts to nothing, and returned home without result, whereupon they were severely disgraced by King Swein for accepting bribes to turn traitor, and driven into exile. When Swein was on his deathbed, he bound all his subjects by an oath that, as he had fourteen sons, they would offer the kingdom to them all in turn as long as his descendants lasted. When 2 he died therefore, he was succeeded by his son Harold for three years, and after Harold came the Cnut whom his father had sent into England. With his former failure in mind, Cnut prepared a fleet of a thousand ships and more (so I have heard) for the invasion of England, assisted by his father-in-law Robert the Frisian, who was lord of six hundred ships; but after being held up by contrary winds for nearly two years, he changed his mind, declaring that his inability to cross the sea must reflect the will of God. After a short time, however,

quorundam colloquiis deprauatus, qui difficultatem transitus anicularum malefitiis imputabant, optimatibus quorum*a* feminae de hoc insimulabantur pensiones importabiles indixit; Olauum quoque fratrem, factionis eiusdem principem accusatum, uinculis irretiuit et
3 socero in exilium misit; quapropter barbari, libertatis suae iniuriam non ferentes, intra aecclesiam quandam altare amplexum et emendationem facti promittentem trucidarunt. Aiunt eo loci multa miracula caelitus ostensa, quod fuerit uir ille ieiuniis et elemosinis deditus, et qui in legum transgressores magis diuinas quam suas persequeretur contumelias; unde et ei martiris honor consecratus est a papa Romano. Post eum homicidae, ut inuidiam facti aliquo bono compensarent, Olauum a uinculis decem milibus marcarum argenti redemerunt. Hic octo annis ignaue imperitans regnum fratri Henrico reliquit. Is, uiginti nouem annis modeste uiuens, Ierosolimam abiit, medioque mari spiritum euomuit. Quintus nunc Nicholaus in regno subsistit.

262. Rex igitur Danorum, ut dixi,[1] solus erat obstaculum ne Willelmus continua feriaretur laetitia; cuius respectu tantam multitudinem stipendiariorum conducebat militum ex omni quae citra montes est prouintia ut eorum copia regnum grauaret. Sed ipse pro magnanimitate sua dispendium expensarum non sentiens, etiam Hugonem Magnum, regis Francorum fratrem, cum illius commilitio inter militares numeros sibi seruiturum redegerat. Animabat et excitabat ipse uirtutem suam propter Rotberti Guiscardi memoriam, pronuntians
2 pudendum si illi fortitudine cederet quem nobilitate preiret; siquidem Rotbertus mediocri parentela in Normannia ortus, quae nec humi reperet[2] nec altum quid tumeret, paucis ante aduentum Willelmi in Angliam annis cum quindecim militibus abierat*b* Apuliam, penuriam necessariorum gentis illius ignauae stipendiis correcturus. Nec multi fluxerunt anni quod stupendo Dei munere totam terram in potestatem accepit; nam ubi uiribus destituebatur, ingenio callebat, oppida primo, mox ciuitates suae ditioni assotians. Ita ergo profecit ut se ducem Apuliae et Calabriae, fratrem Ricardum principem*c* Capuae, alterum
3 Rogerum comitem Siciliae faceret. Postremo, data Apulia filio Rogero, cum altero filio Boamundo Adriaticum pelagus transiuit, statimque

a quarum *TtACeBk* *b* adierat *T* *c* om. *TAl*

[1] 258. 3.
[2] Cf. Horace, *Ep.* ii. 1. 251.

misled by some men's talk who were attributing the problems of his crossing to witchcraft, he demanded intolerable fines from the nobles whose womenfolk were held responsible; and his brother Olaf, who was accused of being a leader of the same conspiracy, he put in chains and banished to live with his father-in-law. As a result the barbarians, finding these 3 restraints on their liberty intolerable, murdered him in a church as he was clasping the altar and promising reparation. They say that on the spot Heaven has vouchsafed many miracles, for he was a man devoted to fasting and almsgiving, who when dealing with law-breakers pursued the claims of the Church rather than his own; and so he was honoured with consecration as a martyr by the Roman pontiff. To succeed him the murderers, in hopes of making up for their detestable crime by some good action, ransomed Olaf from his chains for ten thousand marks of silver. He ruled ingloriously for eight years, and left the kingdom to his brother Eric, who, after living a retired life for twenty-nine years, set off to Jerusalem, but died on the high seas. A fifth son, Niels, is now on the throne.

262. So the king of the Danes was, as I said,[1] the only obstacle between William and continual peace and happiness, and it was with him in mind that he hired such a great multitude of knights serving for pay, from every province this side of the Alps, that their numbers were a burden on the kingdom. However he himself, in his expansive way, did not feel the outlay, and had even hired Hugh the Great, the French king's brother, with his retinue of knights, and ranked him among his own knights, to serve him in future. The spirit and energy of his activities were increased by the example of Robert Guiscard, for he used to declare that it would be disgraceful if he yielded in enterprise to a man he surpassed in birth. Robert came from a modest 2 family in Normandy, which neither 'crept along the ground'[2] nor indulged in great ambitions, and a few years before William's arrival in England he had set off for Apulia with fifteen knights, hoping to redress his shortage of necessities by taking the pay of that unenterprising people. Before many years had passed, he had, by the marvellous gift of God, made himself master of the whole country, for where his strength proved inadequate, he showed a practised cunning in gathering first towns and then cities under his rule. He was thus so successful that he made himself duke of Apulia and Calabria, his brother Richard prince of Capua, and a second brother Roger count of Sicily. Eventually he gave Apulia to his son Roger, and with his 3 other son Bohemond crossed the Adriatic Sea, captured Durazzo

Dirachio capto super Alexium imperatorem Constantinopolitanum ulterius progrediebatur; seuientem retinuit nuntius Hildebrandi apostolici. Imperator enim Alemannorum Henricus, filius Henrici de quo supra memorauimus,[1] iratus contra papam quod excommunicationem in eum propter inuestituras aecclesiarum promulgauerat, cum exercitu ueniens Romam obsedit, Hildebrandum expulit, Wibertum Rauennatem introduxit. Quo per litteras expulsi Guiscardus audito, relicto filio Boamundo cum militibus ut inchoata paterna persequeretur, Apuliam rediit, contractaque[a] uelociter Apulorum et Normannorum

4 manu Romam tendebat. Nec sustinuit nuntium aduenientis Henricus quin cum falso papa, sola fama territus, terga dampnaret.[b] Vacua ab obsessoribus Roma legitimum presulem accepit; sed non multo post eadem uiolentia qua prius amisit. Tunc quoque Alexius, audiens Rotbertum ad sua necessario reuocatum, summamque manum bello imponere sperans, supra Boamundum, qui partes relictas tuebatur, irruit; sed Normannus, gentilitii roboris tenax adolescens, arietantes Grecos et ceteras[c] quae conuenerant gentes usu militari, quanuis

5 multum numero inferior, fugae tradidit. Eodem quoque tempore Veneti, gens mari assueta, Guiscardum, propter quae uenerat sedatis, transfretare uolentem aggressi, superiorum[d] calamitatem sensere; pars mersi et cesi, pars fugati. Ille ceptam enauigans uiam multas ciuitates Alexii suae uoluntati applicuit. Sustulit imperator malefitio quem uirtute nequibat, uxori ipsius conubium augustale mentitus; cuius insidiis elaboratum uirus hauriens interiit, meliorem exitum si Deus uoluisset emeritus, inuincibilis hostili ferro et domestico obnoxius

6 ueneno. Sepultus est apud Venusam Apuliae, habens[e] epitaphium:

> Hic terror mundi Guiscardus. Hic expulit urbe
> quem Ligures regem, Roma, Lemannus[f] habent.
> Parthus, Arabs Macetumque falanx non texit Alexin,
> at fuga; sed Venetum nec fuga nec pelagus.[2]

---

[a] -que *om. CB*   [b] donaret *TBc' (mg.)*; daret *Cs (cf. e.g. 365. 2); we should probably read* nudaret *(cf. e.g. 233. 2 and 240. 1)*   [c] ceteros *A*   [d] *T (cf. 72. 2);* superiorem *ACB*   [e] hoc habens *Tt (not Tc), cf. 194. 2*   [f] Alemannus *Cs*

---

[1] From 188. 7.
[2] Walther, *Initia* 8129.

immediately, and was proceeding further against Alexius the emperor of Constantinople, when his ferocity was checked by a message from Pope Hildebrand. Henry emperor of Germany, son of that Henry of whom I have spoken previously,[1] indignant with the pope, who had published his excommunication in the matter of the investitures of churches, came to Rome with an army and besieged it, drove out Hildebrand, and installed Wibert of Ravenna. When he heard of this in a letter from the exiled pope Guiscard left his son Bohemond with the knights to continue what his father had begun, and himself returned to Apulia, where he swiftly gathered a force of Apulians and Normans and set off for Rome. Nor could Henry support the news of his coming: terrified by the mere report of his approach, he took his spurious pope and ran for it. Relieved of its besiegers, Rome took back its lawful pontiff, but lost him not long afterwards in a violent attack from the same source. Then Alexius too, hearing that Robert had been recalled by necessity to his own country, and hoping to finish the war, fell upon Bohemond, who was holding the position vacated by his father; but the Norman general, who was young and held fast to the toughness of his countrymen, withstood like the experienced fighter he was the charges of the Greeks and other assembled nationalities and, though much inferior in point of numbers, put them to flight. At the same time the Venetians, a people familiar with the sea, attacked Guiscard, who had settled the business for which he had come and was ready to take ship, but they suffered the same disaster as those who went before, some drowned or killed, some forced to flee. Guiscard, pursuing the course on which he had embarked, brought many cities belonging to Alexius under his sway. But the emperor removed by deceit the man he could not beat in fair fight, winning over Guiscard's own wife with lying promises that she should become his imperial consort, and she prepared and gave her husband secretly a poison which he drank, and died. He was a man who deserved a better end, had God so pleased; no enemy weapon could touch him; he succumbed to poison from those nearest to him. He was buried at Venosa in Apulia, with this epitaph:

> Here lies Guiscard, the terror of the world. He drove from the Eternal City him whom Ligurians, Romans, and Germans honour as their king. Not Parthians nor Arabs nor the famed Macedonian phalanx could save Alexius, only flight, and neither flight nor sea could save the Venetians.[2]

263. Verum quia Hildebrandi mentio se ingessit, de eo dicam quae*ᵃ* non friuolo auditu hausi, sed seria relatione eius*ᵇ* audiui qui se illa ex ore Hugonis abbatis Cluniacensis audisse iuraret.*ᶜ* Quae*ᵈ* ideo ammiror et predico, quia cogitationes aliorum prophetico mentis intuitu pronuntiabat. Alexander eum*ᵉ* papa, efficax ipsius studium conspicatus, cancellis apostolorum prefecerat. Circuibat ergo*ᶠ* pro sui contuitu offitii prouintias, ut perperam acta corrigeret.*ᵍ* Accurrebatur ab omnium*ʰ* ordinum hominibus, decisiones diuersorum negotiorum postulantibus. Cuncta ei submittebatur secularis potentia, cum pro
2 sanctitatis, tum pro ministerii ipsius reuerentia. Vnde die quadam, cum solito maior adequitantum*ⁱ* esset turma,*ʲ* abbas predictus in extremo agmine cum monachis suis sensim progrediebatur, uisoque eminus tanto uiri honore, quod tot mundanae potestates nutum illius prestolarentur, huiuscemodi*ᵏ* sententias*ˡ* uentilabat animo: homuntionem exilis staturae, despicabilis parentelae, quo Dei iuditio tot diuitum sepiri famulitio? tumere illum proculdubio et metiri altiora
3 merito pro tot obambulatorum obsequio. Vix haec, ut dixi, mente uersarat cum archidiaconus, reflexo equo et calcaribus incitato,*ᵐ* a longe clamans et abbatem obuncans*ⁿ* 'Tu, tu' inquit 'male cogitasti, falso infamans huiusce dumtaxat rei innocentem. Non enim michi hanc gloriam, si gloria dici potest quae cito transit, uel ego imputo uel ab aliis imputari uolo, sed beatis apostolis, quorum exhibetur priuilegio.' Suffusus ille pudore, nec quicquam infitiari ausus, hoc solum retulit: 'Queso, domine, quomodo nosti cogitatum meum, quem nulli communicaui?' 'Ab ore' ait 'tuo quasi per fistulas ad aures meas omnis illa*ᵒ* cogitatio deducta est.'

264. Item in eadem prouincia aecclesiam urbanam ingressi, ante aram continuatis et iunctis lateribus se prostrauerant. In multam horam protracta oratione, respexit archidiaconus abbatem turbulento rictu*ᵖ* infrendens. Ille, cum diutius oratum esset fores*ᑫ* egressus causamque
2 commotionis percunctatus, responsum accepit: 'Si me amare uis, caue

---

ᵃ quod T*t*   *ᵇ* illius T*t*   *ᶜ* iurasset T*t*   *ᵈ* quod T*t*   *ᵉ* om. T*t*A   *ᶠ* igitur T*t*   *ᵍ* corrigerent T*t*   *ʰ* omnibus A   *ⁱ* AapCe; ad equitandum T*t*A/C*s*B*c*; ad equitatum B*k*   *ʲ* turma esset T*t*   *ᵏ* huiusmodi T*t*   *ˡ* sententiam B   *ᵐ* T*t*; incito ACB   *ⁿ* aduncans T*t*   *ᵒ* om. T*t*   *ᵖ* ritu T*t*   *ᑫ* foras T*t**

263. Now, since I have had occasion to mention Hildebrand, I will give an account of him, which I have not absorbed open-mouthed from frivolous gossip but learnt from the serious narrative of someone who swore that he had heard the facts from the mouth of Hugh abbot of Cluny. What I find surprising in these facts, and worth repeating, is the way he declared the thoughts of other men with the inner vision of a prophet. For Pope Alexander, observing that he was competent and zealous, had appointed him chancellor of the Apostolic See, and therefore by virtue of his office he went round the provinces to correct whatever had been done wrong. Men of all ranks came to him in crowds, seeking decisions on a wide range of business; all secular jurisdictions submitted their problems to him, out of respect partly for his saintly character and partly for his actual office. And so one day, when the cavalcade of riders was larger than usual, the abbot of whom I spoke was at the end of the queue with his monks, making very slow progress; and when he saw from a distance the great honour paid to this man because so many secular authorities waited upon his nod, the thoughts that passed through his mind were something like this: This little man, short in stature and of contemptible origins—by what judgement of God is he so thickly beset with the fawning respect of all these rich men? He must be conceited and ambitious for more than he deserves, with so many visitors playing the toady. Scarcely had he formed, as I said, this train of thought, when the archdeacon, turning back his horse and urging it with his spurs, abused the abbot from a distance at the top of his voice. 'You!' he cried. 'You are quite wrong! Of this at least I am innocent, and your accusation is false. This show of glory, if glory you can call a thing that so swiftly passes, I do not claim, nor do I want others to claim it for me; it belongs to the holy Apostles to whose eminence it is shown.' The abbot was covered with shame. He could deny none of it; all he could reply was: 'Tell me, my lord, how do you know my thoughts, which I had not shared with anybody?' 'All that you thought', said the other, 'passed from your lips to my ears as if it were down pipes.'

264. Again, in the same province, they had gone into a city church and prostrated themselves side by side and touching each other before the altar. After they had prayed for a long time, the archdeacon looked at the abbot with a face of fury, grinding his teeth. When the abbot came out, after they had prayed for a while longer, and asked the reason for this indignation, he received the following reply: 'Pray be

ne ulterius hac me iniuria expungas.*ᵃ* Dominus*ᵇ* meus Iesus, spetiosus ille pre filiis hominum,[1] postulationibus meis uisibiliter astabat, intendens dictis et serenis fauens oculis; sed tuae orationis addictus uiolentia me deseruit, ad te conuersus. Puto quod tu ipse non diffiteberis esse genus iniuriae si amico eripias auctorem salutis suae. Preterea prenoueris mortalitatem hominum, et huic loco imminere excidium; cuius coniecturae signum habeo, quod angelum Domini super altare stantem uidi*ᶜ* euaginatum gladium stringere et huc illucque rotare. Futurae cladis notabilius habeo inditium, quod iam spissus et nebulosus aer prouintiam istam circumuolat, ut uides. Maturemus ergo pro-
3 fugium, nisi cum aliis uelimus subire exitium.' His dictis introeuntes diuersorium ad curam corporis assedere; continuoque dapibus appositis exortus in domo luctus auiditatem esurientium repressit, siquidem unus et alter, et mox plures e familia, dubium qua pernitie intercepti animas subito amisere. Tum eadem peste per uicinas edes grassante, ascensis mulis diffugiunt, festinationem uiae stimulis timoris accelerantes.

265. In Gallia uice papae*ᵈ* presederat concilio; ibi plures episcopi, olim per simoniam in aecclesias introducti, degradati potioribus locum dedere. Vnus erat quem suspitio istius apostasiae insimulabat, sed nullis testibus argui, nullis argumentis confutari poterat; quem cum putares constrictum maxime, more anguis lubrici elapsum mirareris;
2 ita dicendi arte callebat ut omnes eluderet. Tunc*ᵉ* archidiaconus: 'Cesset hominum eloquium, producatur in medium diuinum oraculum. Scimus profecto quod episcopalis gratia sancti Spiritus munus est, et quisquis episcopatum mercatur sancti Spiritus donum posse comparari pecunia opinatur. Coram nobis ergo, qui iuditio sancti Spiritus congregati sumus, dicat iste "Gloria Patri et Filio et Spiritui sancto"; quod si expresse et sine titubantia dixerit, constabit
3 apud me non illum uenaliter sed legitime presulatu functum.' Libens

---

ᵃ expugnes *TtBk* *ᵇ* Deus *B* *ᶜ* uidi *after the preceding* quod *Tt*
ᵈ papa *CeB* *ᵉ* tum *Tt* (cf. GP pp. 98, 109)*

[1] Ps. 44 (45): 3.

so kind as never again to treat me so abominably. My Lord Jesus, who is "fairer than the children of men",[1] stood by me as I offered my petitions, clear to see, listening to my words with a calm and favouring glance. But then, distracted by the violence of the way you pray, He left me in the lurch and turned wholly to you. You yourself will not, I think, deny that it is a serious injury to snatch from a friend the Author of his salvation. Besides which let me warn you in advance of the death of men and of the destruction that hangs over this place. Of this inference I have a token: I saw an angel of the Lord standing above the altar, and he drew his sword from its scabbard and swung it this way and that. And I have a more manifest signal of future disaster, in the thick and murky air which, as you see, now circulates in this province. Let us therefore make haste to escape, unless we wish to face destruction with the rest.' That said, they entered their inn, and addressed themselves to their bodily needs; and immediately, as they brought in dinner, there rose a sound of lamentation in the house which stifled all their appetite for food; for two or three of the household first of all, and soon more of them, were struck by some fatal disease whose nature is uncertain, and died suddenly. Then, as the same plague spread through the neighbouring houses, they mounted their mules and escaped, the hurry of their departure heightened by the spur of panic.

265. In Gaul he had presided in place of the pope at a council, where several bishops formerly promoted to their sees by simony were degraded and gave place to better men. There was one who was accused of this form of apostasy on suspicion, but no witnesses were forthcoming to expose him and no arguments to refute his case; when you might think he was really caught in the toils, he would astonish you by wriggling out like a slippery snake, and such was his skill in arguing that he was a match for them all. Then said the archdeacon: 'Let the language of men give way, and let the oracles of God take the central place. We all know well that the consecration of a bishop is a gift of the Holy Spirit, and whoever purchases a bishopric is of the opinion that a gift of the Holy Spirit can be bought for cash. Here are we, gathered together under the judgement of the Holy Spirit. Let this man say out loud before us all: "Glory be to the Father and to the Son and to the Holy Spirit", and if he utters those words clearly and without hesitation, I shall be certain that he holds a bishop's office not by purchase but in accordance with the law.' The man gladly

hanc conditionem ille accepit, nichil minus quam horum uerborum difficultatem ratus; et certe 'Gloria Patri et Filio' integre protulit, sed in 'Spiritu sancto' hesit. Suscitato cunctorum strepitu, nullo conatu uel tunc uel in uitae reliquo spatio Spiritum sanctum nominare potuit. Huius miraculi testis fuit abbas sepe nominatus, qui, deiectum episcopum per loca secum[a] ducens, illius rei experimentum sepe risit; de cuius uerborum certitudine dubitantem omnis Europa confutat, quae religionis Cluniacensis numerum per eum augmentatum non nescit.

266. Alexandro ergo[b] defuncto successit Hildebrandus, Gregorius septimus dictus. Hic quod alii mussitauerant palam extulit, excommunicans electos qui inuestituras[c] aecclesiarum de manu laici per anulum et baculum acciperent; unde Henricus imperator Alemannorum, fremens quod sine sua conscientia electus talia presumeret, illum, ut predixi,[1] post undecim annos Roma deturbauit, Wiberto inducto. Nec multo post letali papa[d] morbo ictus, quo se moriturum non ambigeret, rogatus est a cardinalibus ut papam constitueret, beati Petri exemplum referentibus, qui lactentis aecclesiae rudimentis uiuens Clementem prefecerat. Negauit ille id se exemplum secuturum quod ab antiquo conciliis esset uetitum, consilium uero[e] daturum: si uellent hominem in seculo potentem, eligerent Desiderium abbatem Cassinensem, qui salubriter et in tempore numero militari uiolentiam Wiberti infringeret; sin aecclesiasticum et eloquentem, acciperent episcopum Hostiensem Odonem. Ita obiit uir apud Deum felicis gratiae, et apud homines austeritatis fortassis nimiae. Denique fertur quod, inter eum et imperatorem primi tumultus initio, illum nudipedem et forcipes cum scopis portantem nec etiam foribus admiserit, abominatus hominem sacrilegum et sororii incesti reum. Abscessit Cesar exclusus, repulsam illam multorum necis causam protestans; statimque quaecumque posset incommoda Romanae sedi infligens, e diuerso fautores papae[f] in tirannidem excitauit. Siquidem rebellante quodam Radulfo, iussu

[a] sepe *Tt* morbo *Aa)* [b] om. *Tt* [c] inuestituram *Tt (cf. 288. 2)* [d] om. *TtAl (after* [e] om. *Tt* [f] eius papa *Tt*

[1] 262. 3.

accepted this proposal, thinking nothing less likely than any difficulty with these familiar words, and he produced 'Glory be to the Father and to the Son' at least without a hitch, but at 'and to the Holy Spirit' he stuck. There was universal uproar; but by no effort either then or in the remainder of his life could he name the Holy Spirit. Among eye-witnesses of this miracle was the abbot I have often named, who took the degraded bishop round with him, and was often moved to laughter by testing the truth of this story; and whoever doubts the veracity of his words has all Europe against him, which is well aware how Abbot Hugh has increased the number of religious vocations among the Cluniacs.

266. So on Alexander's death Hildebrand succeeded under the name of Gregory VII. He brought out into the open an issue which other men had been discussing in private, by excommunicating candidates for promotion who received the investiture of their churches from the hand of a layman by ring and staff. As a result the German emperor Henry, furious that a man elected without his being consulted should take so much upon himself, drove him out of Rome eleven years later, as I said before,[1] and put Wibert in his place. Not long afterwards, the pope was struck by a fatal illness, of which he had no doubt that he was going to die, and the cardinals asked him to appoint a pope, recalling the precedent of St Peter who, in the Church's infancy, had promoted Clement before his own death. The pope refused to follow an example which had been prohibited by councils from an early date, but said that he would give them some advice. If they wanted someone effective in the things of this world, they should choose Abbot Desiderius of Monte Cassino, who would promptly use armed force to put a salutary end to Wibert's violence; if they preferred a churchman and a good preacher, they should take Odo bishop of Ostia. Thus died a man who found grace in God's eyes, and in the eyes of men was perhaps unduly austere. It is said, for example, that at the start of the first dispute between him and the emperor, the emperor came barefoot and carrying scissors and a broom, and even so he would not admit him under his roof, such was his detestation of one who had committed sacrilege and was guilty of incest with his sister. Shut out, the emperor went his way, swearing that this rejection would cost many men their lives; and by immediately putting every possible obstacle in the path of the Roman See, he roused the pope's supporters to try to usurp the throne. The rebellion of a

ipsius Apostolici, qui ei coronam ex parte apostolorum miserat, bellorum fragoribus undique conflictatus est; sed ille, semper aduersis superior, et illum et ceteros improbe assurgentes tandem oppressit. Postremo non alienorum impetu sed domestico filii odio extrusus imperio, miserabilem uitae terminum habuit. Successit Hildebrando Desiderius, Victor appellatus; sed ad primam missam, incertum quo discrimine, cecidit exanimatus,[a] calice, si dignum est credere, ueneno infecto. Tunc in Odonem declinauit electio; is natione Gallus, primum Remensis archidiaconus, inde prior Cluniacensis, mox episcopus Hostiae, ultimo papa Romae, Vrbanus uocatus est.

267. Hactenus circumuagari licuerit, dum occasione gestorum Willelmi quaedam succurrebant quae pretermittenda non putabam; nunc familiarem eius uitam et mores interiores lector qui uolet audiet. In primis Dei[b] famulis humilis, subiectis facilis, in rebelles inexorabilis erat. Religionem Christianam, quantum secularis poterat, ita frequentabat ut cotidie missae assisteret, cotidie uespertinos et matutinos himnos audiret. Monasteria, unum in Anglia, alterum in Normannia
2 construxit. Primum Cadomis, quod sancto Stephano consecrauit, oportunis prediis et magnificentissimis donariis insignitum, ubi et[c] Lanfrancum abbatem, post etiam Cantuariae archiepiscopum, instituit, uirum antiquis scientia et religione comparandum, de quo serio dici potest: 'Tertius e celo cecidit Cato',[1] adeo caelestis sapor pectus eius et palatum infecerat, adeo Latinitas omnis in liberalium artium scientiam per doctrinam eius se[d] incitabat, adeo ipsius exemplo uel metu pro-
3 fessio monastica in religione sudabat. Non tunc episcoporum ambitus, non tunc abbatum uenalitas profitiebat; ille maioris gloriae, amplioris gratiae apud regem et archiepiscopum erat qui tenatioris sanctitudinis opinionem habebat. Alterum monasterium Hastingis edificauit[e] sancto Martino, quod cognominatur de Bello, quia in eo loco principalis aecclesia cernitur ubi inter confertos[f] cadauerum aceruos Haroldus inuentus fuisse memoratur.

[a] examinatus (sic) cecidit Tt [b] om. B [c] om. Cs, not unreasonably
[d] om. A [e] om. T; construxit B [f] Tc (cf. 241); consertos TtAl(consortes Aa)CB

[1] Juvenal ii. 40.

certain Rudolf under the orders of the Holy Father, who had even sent him a crown in the name of the Apostles, meant that he had to contend with the tumult of war on every side; but the emperor, always superior to adversity, at length suppressed both him and others who obstinately rose against him. In the end, it was not attacks by outsiders but the hatred of his own son that threw him out and brought his life to a pitiable close. Hildebrand was succeeded by Desiderius, under the name of Victor, but at his first mass for some unknown reason he fell dead, the chalice (though this is hardly credible) having been poisoned. The choice then fell upon Odo, a Gaul by race, who had first been archdeacon of Reims, then successively prior of Cluny and bishop of Ostia, and finally pope in Rome, under the name of Urban.

267. I hope this digression may be permitted me, for William's achievements put me in mind of certain topics, which ought not, I thought, to be passed over, and now the reader who so wishes shall hear of his private life and inner character. Above all else, he was humble-minded towards the servants of God, affable to the submissive, and inexorable in dealing with rebellion. He was a practising Christian as far as a layman could be, to the extent of attending mass every day and every day hearing vespers and matins. He built two monasteries, one in England and one in Normandy. The first, at Caen and dedicated to St Stephen, was endowed with appropriate estates and most lavish gifts, and there he installed as abbot Lanfranc, who was later archbishop of Canterbury, a man comparable with the Ancients for learning and religious fervour, of whom one can say in all seriousness: 'Here's a third Cato fallen from the sky.'[1] Such was the savour of Heaven that graced his heart and his tongue; such the way in which the whole Latin-speaking world was encouraged by his scholarship to pursue the liberal arts; such the zeal with which the votaries of monasticism toiled at the religious life, following his unique example or through fear of him. In those days bishops made no progress by ambition, and abbots none by bribes; the highest reputation and the warmest welcome in the eyes of king and archbishop were reserved for him who had a name for the most unshaken holiness of life. The other monastery he built at Hastings in honour of St Martin, and it is called Battle Abbey because the principal church is to be seen on the very spot where, according to tradition, among the piled heaps of corpses Harold was found.

4 Pene puer, et maturiora aetate sapiens, patruum suum Malgerium ab archiepiscopatu Rotomagensi remouit. Is erat litteris quidem non mediocriter cultus, sed, pro natalium conscientia professionis oblitus, uenationibus et auium certaminibus sepius iusto intendebat, et gazas aecclesiasticas conuiuiis profusioribus insumebat. Cuius rei fama crebrescente, tota uita pallii usu caruit, quod negaret sedes apostolica honoris huiusce priuilegium homini qui sacratum negligebat offitium. Vnde crebro conuentus, expostulante nepote patruelis offensas, cum nichilo reuerentius se ageret, cogente ultima necessitate degradatus
5 est. Ferunt quidam esse archanam depositionis causam: Mathildem, quam Willelmus acceperat, proximam sibi sanguine fuisse; id Christianae fidei zelo Malgerium non tulisse, ut consanguineo cubili fruerentur, sed in nepotem et comparem excommunicationis iaculum intentasse; ita cum irae adolescentis uxoriae querelae accederent, excogitatas occasiones quibus persecutor peccati sede pelleretur; sed postmodum prouectioribus annis pro expiatione sceleris illum sancto Stephano Cadomis monasterium edificasse, illam beatae Trinitati in eodem uico idem fecisse, utroque pro sexu suo personas inhabitantium eligente.

268. Malgerio successit Maurilius, Fiscamnensis monachus, multis uirtutibus sed maxime abstinentia laudatus. Is post bene et sancte actam uitam, cum ad extremum Deo uocante uenisset, uitali priuatus halitu ferme dimidia die iacuit defunctus. Veruntamen, cum iam pararetur in aecclesiam*a* ferri, anima resumpta circumstantes lacrimabili gaudio perfudit, stupentes hoc sermone corroborat: 'Attenti animo estote, ultima pastoris uestri uerba excipientes. Naturali morte resolutus fui, sed ut uobis intimarem quae uidi reductus sum, nec aliquanto
2 diutius subsistam, quia in Domino soporari delectat. Ductores spiritus mei uultibus et uestibus ad omnem elegantiam erant compositi; concordabat uerborum lenitas cum nitore uestium, ut nichil desiderarem preter talium uirorum obsequium. Itaque blandis assentationibus gauisus ibam, ut uere michi uidebatur, uersus orientem; promittebatur

a (a)ecclesia *TcA*

While still little more than a boy, and showing wisdom beyond his 4
years, he deposed his uncle Mauger from the archbishopric of Rouen.
Mauger was no mean scholar, but being conscious of his high birth he
used to forget his sacred calling, devoting himself more often than was
right to hunting and cockfighting and spending the treasures of his
church on over-lavish hospitality. Once this had become known, all
his life long he never received the pallium, the Apostolic See refusing
the honour of this privilege to a man who neglected his holy office.
He was frequently cited for this, and the nephew protested against his
uncle's misdeeds, but he showed no more reverence for his calling
than before; extreme measures were necessary, and he was removed
from office. Some say that there was a secret reason for his deposition: 5
Matilda, whom William had taken as his wife, was a near relation, and
in his zeal for the Christian faith Mauger had found it intolerable that
two blood-relations should share the marriage-bed, and had aimed the
weapon of excommunication against his nephew and that nephew's
consort. The young man was furious, his wife added her protests, and
so (it was said) they had been looking for opportunities to drive from
his see the man who had denounced their sin. Later, however, as William grew old, by way of atonement for the offence, he built the monastery at Caen in honour of St Stephen, and she built one for the Holy
Trinity in the same town, each founder choosing inmates of his or her
own sex.

268. Mauger was succeeded by Maurilius, a monk of Fécamp, with
a reputation for many virtues, abstinence in particular. When after a
good and holy life God summoned him and he had approached his
end, the breath of life left him, and for nearly half a day he lay dead.
When however preparations were already afoot to carry his body into
the church, his life returned, which reduced the bystanders to tears of
joy, and he comforted them in their amazement with the following
story: 'Listen attentively as you receive your shepherd's final words. I
died a natural death, but I have been brought back on purpose to tell
you what I saw, nor shall I be with you much longer, for it is my
delight to fall asleep in the Lord. Those who guided my spirit matched 2
the highest standard of elegance in countenance and in raiment; the
courtesy of their language was equal to the brilliance of their apparel,
so that I felt no lack of anything as long as I enjoyed the services of
men like them. These pleasing marks of respect filled me with joy, as
I made my way (so it really seemed to me) towards the East: I was

michi sedes paradisiaca *"*non multo post intranda. In momento preterita Europa,*"* ingressi Asiam uenimus Ierosolimam; ibi sanctis adoratis Iordanem pertendimus; citerioris ripae accolae, ductorum meorum contubernio mixti, laetum cetum fecere. Ego uisendi ulteriora studio
3 transitum maturabam. Tum comites Deum precepisse referunt ut ante demonum uisione terrificarer, quatinus ueniales culpae, quas confessione non dilueram, pauore horrendarum formarum purgarentur. Cum dicto astitit alteri parti tanta demonum uis, hastilia acuta uibrantium, ignes efflantium, ut ager ferreus, aer flammeus uideretur. Eorum horrore*"* ita sum affectus ut, si terra dehisceret, si caelum patesceret, tuto michi utrobique refugiendum non*"* estimarem. Ita meticulosus, dum quo euadam dubito, repente, ut*"* haec dicens uestrae saluti nisi negligitis consulerem, halitum recepi, confestim effusurus.' Dixit, et cum uerbo pene spiritum emisit. Corpus, in aecclesia sanctae Mariae tunc humi defossum, miraculo modo, ut aiunt, diuino altius tribus pedibus super terram eleuatum est.

269. Porro Willelmus, propositi quod in Normannia ceperat tenax, Stigandum perperam et falso archiepiscopum per cardinales Romanos et Ermenfredum episcopum Sedunensem deponi passus est. Successit ei in Wintonia Walkelinus, cuius bona opera famam uincentia uetustatem obliuionis a se repellent, quam diu ibi sedes episcopalis durabit; in Cantia Lanfrancus, de quo supra dixi,[1] qui talis Angliae Dei dono emicuit 'qualis discutiens fugientia Lucifer astra, cum roseo clarum prouehit ore diem',[2] ita ipsius industria monasticum*"* germen effloruit,
2 ita eo uiuente uigor pontificalis induruit. Eius consilio rex pronum se fecerat, ut nichil negandum duceret quod is faciendum diceret. Ipsius etiam*"* impulsu ambitum nebulonum fregerat qui consueto more mancipia sua Hiberniam uenditabant; cuius facti preconium cui*"* potius imputem, Lanfranco an Wlstano Wigorniae antistiti, pro uero

"–" om. *A*   *"* horrorum *A*   *"* om. *T*+   *"* ad *A*   *"* monachum *A* (monachicum *A*$^{p.c.}$)   *"* enim *T'**   *"* cuius *A*

[1] 267. 2.
[2] Cf. Seneca, *Apocolocyntosis* 4, lines 25, 27–8.

promised a home in Paradise, which not long hence I was to enter. In a moment we had passed out of Europe and entered Asia, where we arrived at Jerusalem. There we adored the saints and passed on to the Jordan, and the dwellers on the nearer bank, joining ranks with my escort, made a joyful company. For my part, in my longing to see the further country, I was hastening to cross; at which point my companions made known to me God's command that I must first be terrified by a vision of devils, that the fear of those horrible shapes might purge the venial sins which I had not atoned for by confession. As they spoke the words, there stood on the further bank such an army of demons, brandishing sharp spears and breathing fire, that the ground seemed to me made of iron and the air of flame. The horror of that sight so overwhelmed me that, had the earth gaped or the heavens opened, I would not have thought it safe for me to take refuge in either of them. In fear and trembling therefore, uncertain as I was of any means of escape, I suddenly received my breath again, that by this narrative, unless you neglect it, I might assist in bringing about your own salvation, though I shall shortly breathe my last.' Such were his words, and almost as he spoke he gave up the ghost. His body was at that time buried in the earth, in St Mary's church; but by a divinely-wrought miracle it has now, they say, been raised more than three feet above the ground.

269. Maintaining the strategy which he had adopted in Normandy, William then allowed Stigand, who was wrongfully and falsely archbishop, to be deposed by the Roman cardinals and Ermenfrid bishop of Sion. He had as successor at Winchester Walkelin, whose good works surpass their reputation and will keep at bay the oblivion of passing years as long as the see of Winchester endures; and at Canterbury Lanfranc, of whom I have already spoken,[1] who by God's grace dawned upon England 'as when the Daystar routs the fleeting stars and brings with blushing face the light of day':[2] so freely did his energy make monasticism flower, so much did episcopal discipline mature in his lifetime. To his wisdom the king had made himself subservient, and thought he should reject no course of action which Lanfranc recommended; it was at his instigation too that the king had frustrated the schemes of those rascals who had an established practice of selling their serfs into Ireland. Though whether I should give the credit for this achievement to Lanfranc or to Wulfstan bishop of Worcester, I cannot rightly decide; the king was reluctant, for he

non discerno, qui regem pro commodo uenalitatis quod sibi pensitabatur renitentem uix ad hoc coegerint*a* nisi quod Lanfrancus laudauerit Wlstanus preceperit, auctoritate episcopali pro conscientia sanctitatis abunde exuberans, homo quo nullus umquam iustior, nullus nostro seculo par illi apparuerit miraculorum potentia et prophetali gratia, quorum aliqua intendo dicere*b* posterius,[1] si tamen sanctissimis illius placuerit sensibus.

270. Veruntamen, quia alea fortunae incertis iactibus uoluitur, multa tunc tempore*c* aduersa prouenere. Feda inter abbatem Glastoniae et monachos eius discordia, ita ut post uerborum lites ad arma uentum sit. Coacti ergo intra aecclesiam monachi sancto altari miserias suas ingemebant,*d* sed irrumpentibus militibus duo ex eis interfecti, quattuordecim uulnerati, ceteri repulsi; nam et furor militum etiam crucifixum sagittis inhorrere fecerat. Huius noxae crimine infamatus abbas tota uita regis exilio deportatus est; eoque defuncto, pro redemptione peccati*e* auxiliaribus annumerata pecunia, honori restitutus est.

271. Miserabilis et infanda cedes Walkerii Dunelmensis episcopi, quem Northanimbri, populus semper rebellioni deditus, abiecto sacrorum ordinum respectu multis impetitum conuitiis trucidarunt. Fusus ibi non paucus numerus Lotharingorum, quod presul ipse nationis eius erat. *f*Causa cedis haec fuit. Erat episcopus preter pontificatum custos totius comitatus, prefeceratque rebus forensibus Gillebertum cognatum, interioribus Leobinum clericum, ambos in rebus commissis strenuos sed effrenes. Tolerabat episcopus eorum immodestiam, gratia strenuitatis inductus, et quia eos eleuarat cumulum benignitatis augebat. Indulget enim natura sibi, placidoque fauore suis arridet ipsa muneribus.[2] Is Leobinus Liulfum, beatissimi Cuthberti ministrum adeo dilectum ut ipse sanctus coram uigilanti assistens placita imperaret,—hunc, inquam, Liulfum per Gillebertum obtruncari fecit,

a coegerit T*t*   *b* om. T*t*   *c* temporis Savile, following William's practice   *d* applorabant T*t*A, GP p. 197 (well, for the dative is thus easier; cf. esp. HN 483)   *e* One expects ab to follow   *f-f* (p. 500) om. T*t*

[1] An apparent reference to the *Vita Wulfstani*.
[2] Unidentified. Cf. Letter 3. 2.

enjoyed a share of the profits from this traffic which they paid him, and they could hardly have brought him to agree, had not what Lanfranc advised been prescribed by Wulfstan, whose abundant authority as a bishop was much enhanced by his reputation for sanctity. He was a man of unsurpassed integrity, and without equal in our own day for miraculous powers and for the grace of prophecy, subjects on which I intend to say something later,[1] provided that this wins the approval of his saintly judgement.

270. But the roll of Fortune's dice is determined by random throws, and this was a period during which many disgraceful events occurred. There was a shocking dispute at Glastonbury between the abbot and his monks, such that after verbal conflicts they had recourse to arms. Obliged to take refuge in their church, the monks were lamenting their wretchedness to the altar, when knights burst in; two monks were killed, fourteen wounded, and the rest driven out, for the rage of the soldiery had left even the figure of the Crucified bristling with arrows. Discredited by the guilt for this outrage, the abbot spent the remainder of the king's lifetime in exile, and on his death, a sum of money having been paid by his supporters to obtain forgiveness for his sin, was restored to office.

271. A lamentable outrage was the murder of Bishop Walcher of Durham who, after a campaign of abuse, was killed in deliberate scorn for his sacred ministry by the people of Northumbria, who are always much given to rebellion. On that occasion a considerable number of Lotharingians were murdered, the bishop himself being of that nationality. The cause of this assassination was as follows. The bishop was not only diocesan but the warden of a whole county, and he had set his kinsman Gilbert over the external business and Leofwine, a cleric, over the internal. Both of them as administrators were energetic but undisciplined. The bishop, finding their energy valuable, tolerated their lack of restraint, and the fact that he had promoted them increased their large share in his goodwill; for human nature 'judges its own actions with indulgent eye, and with unthinking partiality approves the largess that itself has made.'[2] There was a man called 2 Liulf, an official so much beloved by his great master St Cuthbert that the saint himself appeared before him in a waking vision and dictated his legal decisions. This Leofwine had the Liulf of whom I speak put to death by Gilbert, being jealous of the more intimate

liuore ictus quod amplioris amicitiae locum apud pontificem pro conscientia*ᵃ* et aequitate iuditiorum haberet. Perculsus nuntio Walkerius furenti parentelae defuncti legalis placiti iuditium apposuit,*ᵇ* protestatus Leobinum suae suorumque necis auctorem. Vbi uentum ad placitum, nullis effera gens rationibus emolliri potuit quin in episcopum referret culpam, quod ambos homicidas in curia eius post necem Liulfi familiariter diuersatos uidissent. Surrectum ergo in clamores et iras, et Gillebertus de aecclesia, in qua cum episcopo sederat, ultro egrediens, ut suo periculo uitam domini mercaretur, impie occisus. Tum presul, pro ianuis pacem pretento ramo offerens, rabiem uulgi expleuit interemptus; fomes etiam mali Leobinus semiustulatus, quod nisi aecclesia cremata exire nolebat, exsiliens mille lanceis exceptus est.*ᶠ* Predictum id*ᶜ* ab Edgitha, relicta regis Eduardi; nam cum olim Walkerium uidisset Wintoniae ad consecrandum duci, cesarie lacteolum, uultu roseum, statura pregrandem, 'Pulchrum hic' ait 'martirem habemus,' coniectura uidelicet immodestae nationis ad presagiendum inducta. Successit ei Willelmus abbas Sancti Karilefi, qui monachos in Dunelmo posuit.

272. Preterea anno antequam moreretur proximo mortalitas hominum et iumentorum, uis tempestatum, frequens uiolentia fulgurum, quantam nemo uiderat, nemo audierat. Illo quoque anno quo obiit, promiscua febris plusquam dimidiam partem plebis depasta, adeo ut plures incommoditas morbi extingueret; deinde pro intemperie aeris fames subsecuta uulgo irrepsit, ut quod febribus erat reliquum ipsa corriperet.

273. Preter ceteras uirtutes, precipue in prima adolescentia castitatem suspexit, in tantum ut publice sereretur nichil illum in femina posse; ueruntamen ex procerum sententia matrimonio addictus ita se egit ut pluribus annis nullius probri suspitione notaretur. Tulit ex Mathilde liberos multos, quae, et marito morigera et prole fecunda, nobilis uiri animum in sui amoris incitabat aculeum: quamquam non desint qui ganniant eum celibatui antiquo renuntiasse cum regia potestas accreuisset, uolutatum*ᵈ* cum cuiusdam presbiteri filia, quam

---

ᵃ scientia *GP p. 272 p. 498*   *ᶜ* om. *T¹*
ᵇ *AaCB;* opposuit *Al;* obtulit *GP p. 272*
ᵈ uoluptatum *T⁺*
ᶠ See above,

place he occupied in the bishop's friendship on the ground of his upright and just judgements. Walcher, appalled by the news, countered the rage of the dead man's relations by going to court with them, affirming that Leofwine would be the death of himself and his friends. When the case came to court, there was no appeasing the fury of the people, who laid the burden of guilt on the bishop because they had seen the two murderers familiarly received at his court after Liulf's death. There arose a furious uproar, and Gilbert, who of his own accord left the church in which he had taken his seat with the bishop, in hopes of purchasing his master's life at the risk of his own, was foully murdered. Then, as the bishop stood before the doors of the church, proposing peace with a branch in his hand, the mob sated its frenzy by killing him. Leofwine too, the cause of this tragedy, half burnt to death because he would not leave the church until it was set on fire, leapt from the flames to be received on a thousand spears. This had been foretold by Eadgyth, King Edward's widow; for long before, when she had seen Walcher at Winchester going in procession to his consecration, fair-haired, fresh-complexioned, and very tall, she said: 'What a handsome martyr we have here!', inspired to prophesy no doubt by conjecture based on the native arrogance of the Northumbrians. He was succeeded by William, abbot of Saint-Calais, who installed monks in Durham. [3]

272. Besides this, in the year before the king's death there was a great mortality both of men and of beasts, severe storms, and constant lightning of a violence no man had ever seen or heard of. And in the year in which he died an epidemic fever preyed on more than half the ordinary population, so severely that many succumbed to the ill effects of the disease; and then, as a result of the corrupted air, a widespread famine followed, so that survivors of the fever fell victim to hunger.

273. Besides his other virtues, William had such respect for chastity, especially in early manhood, that public gossip told of his impotence. When, however, on the advice of his nobles he married, his conduct was such as to keep him free for many years of any suggestion of misbehaviour. He had many children by Matilda, and she, with her willingness to please her husband and her ability to bear him children, kindled a passionate attachment in the spirit of that great man; although there are scandal-mongers who maintain that he abandoned his early continence when royal power came to him, and wallowed in

per satellitem succiso poplite Mathildis sustulerit; quapropter illum
2 exheredatum, illam ad mortem freno equi cesam. Sed haec de tanto
rege credere dementiae ascribo, hoc constanter asseuerans, quod aliquantula simultas inter eos innata extremis annis fuerit pro Rotberto
filio, cui mater militarem manum ex fisci redditibus sufficere dicebatur. Verum propter hoc nichil coniugalis gratiae diminutum ipse
ostendit, dum quattuor annis ante se defunctam et magnificentissimis
inferiis extulit et lacrimis per multos dies ubertim prosecutus amissae
caritatem desiderauit; quin et ex eo tempore, si credimus, ab omni
uoluptate desciuit. Sepulta est regina Cadomis in monasterio sanctae
Trinitatis. Eiusdem[a] pietatis inditium in Edgithae reginae funere curando non minus fuit, quae, apud Westmonasterium studio eius
prope coniugem locata, habet tumbam argenti aurique expensis operosam.

274. Filios habuit Rotbertum, Ricardum, Willelmum, Henricum.
Posteriores duo post eum successione continua in Anglia regnauere.
Rotbertus, patre adhuc uiuente Normanniam sibi negari egre ferens,
in Italiam obstinatus abiit, ut, filia Bonefatii marchionis sumpta, patri
partibus illis adiutus aduersaretur; sed petitionis huiusce cassus,
Philippum Francorum regem contra patriam excitauit; quare et genitoris benedictione et hereditate frustratus, Anglia post mortem eius
2 caruit, comitatu Normanniae uix retento. Ea quoque post nouem
annos fratri Willelmo pro pecunia inuadata, Asiaticam expeditionem
cum ceteris Christianis aggressus est. Inde transactis quattuor annis
clarus militiae gestis regressus, Normanniae sine difficultate[b] immersit,
quod, germano Willelmo nuper defuncto, Henricus rex nouitate tener
Angliam in fide tenere satis habuit. Sed quia de hoc alias dicendum,[1]
nunc ceptam de filiis Willelmi Magni narrationem terminabo.

275. Ricardus magnanimo parenti spem laudis alebat, puer delicatus et,[c] ut id aetatulae pusio, altum quid spirans. Sed tantam[d] primeui

[a] eiusdemque B [b] Cs adds se, for good reason (cf. HN 506) [c] om. CB [d] tantum B

[1] See especially c. 389.

the embraces of a priest's daughter, whom Matilda sent packing after having her hamstrung by one of her vassals; the vassal (so the story goes) was deprived of his fief and Matilda was flogged to death with a horse's bridle. But to believe this of so great a king I regard as lunacy; what I do consistently assert is that some small disagreement arose between them in their last years on account of their son Robert, who is said to have been supplied with a troop of soldiers by his mother out of the revenues of the royal estates. But that this occasioned no lessening of their affection as man and wife he himself made clear; for when she died, four years before him, he gave her a most splendid funeral, and showed by many days of the deepest mourning how much he missed the love of her whom he had lost. Indeed from that time forward, if we believe what we are told, he abandoned pleasure of every kind. The queen was buried in the monastery of the Holy Trinity at Caen. There was evidence of the same deep feeling in the funeral which he arranged for Queen Eadgyth, who by his care was buried in Westminster Abbey near her husband, and has a tomb lavishly decorated with gold and silver.

274. His sons were Robert, Richard, William, and Henry. The last two followed him in immediate succession on the English throne. Robert, resenting that during his father's lifetime Normandy was denied him, obstinately went off to Italy, determined to marry a daughter of Marquis Boniface and secure help from those regions in opposing his father. When, however, his proposals were rejected, he roused Philip king of the French against his fatherland; and consequently, forfeiting both his father's blessing and his inheritance, failed to secure England after his father's death and was hard put to it to retain the duchy of Normandy. Even Normandy he mortgaged to his brother William nine years later, and set off on the expedition to Asia with the other Christians. There he spent four years, and returning with a distinguished military record entered Normandy without difficulty; for his brother William had recently died, and King Henry, who was vulnerable at the start of his reign, had his work cut out to retain England in its allegiance. But since I must speak of this elsewhere,[1] I will now complete the account on which I have embarked of the sons of the great William.

275. Richard encouraged in the mind of his great-hearted father the hope that he would make his mark: he was an elegant boy and, for a

floris indolem mors acerba cito depasta corrupit; tradunt ceruos in Noua Foresta terebrantem tabidi aeris nebula morbum incurrisse. Locus est quem Willelmus pater desertis uillis*a* per triginta et eo amplius miliaria in saltus et lustra ferarum[1] redegerat.

2 *b*Infando prorsus spectaculo, ut ubi ante uel humana conuersatio uel diuina ueneratio feruebat, nunc ibi cerui et capreoli et ceterae illud genus bestiae petulanter discursitent, nec illae quidem mortalium usibus communiter expositae. Vnde pro uero disseritur quod*b* *b*Ibi libenter aeuum exigere, ibi plurimis, omitto*c* diebus, certe mensibus uenationes exercere gaudebat. Ibi multa regio generi contigere*d* infortunia, quae habitatorum presens audire uolentibus suggerit memoria; nam postmodum*b* in eadem silua Willelmus, filius eius, et nepos Ricardus, filius Rotberti comitis Normanniae, mortem offenderint*e* seuero Dei iuditio, ille sagitta pectus, iste*f* collum traiectus, uel, ut quidam dicunt, arboris ramusculo*g* equo pertranseunte fauces appensus.

276. Filiae ipsius fuere quinque. Cecilia, Cadomensis abbatissa, uiuit; altera Constantia, comiti Britanniae Alano Fergant in coniugium data, austeritate iustitiae prouintiales in mortiferam sibi potionem exacuit; tertia Adala, Stephani Blesensis comitis uxor, laudatae in seculo potentiae uirago, nouiter apud Marcenniacum sanctimonialis habitum sumpsit. Duarum nomina exciderunt, unius quae Haroldo, ut diximus,[2] promissa infra maturos coniugio annos obiit; alterius quae,*h* Aldefonso Gallitiae regi per nuntios iurata, uirgineam mortem impetrauit a Deo. Repertus in defunctae genibus callus crebrarum eius orationum index.*i*

277. Patris memoriam quantis poterat occasionibus extollens, ossa, olim Niceae condita, sub extremo uitae tempore per legatum transferebat; sed ille prospere rediens, audita morte Willelmi, apud Apuliam resedit, sepultis ibi illustris uiri exuuiis. Matrem quantum uixit insigni

---

a *T+A add* subrutis (subreptis *Aap*) ecclesiis *(cf. JW s.a. 1100)*   *b–b* infando...quod *T+A;* ibi...postmodum *CB*   *c* *CsB add* quod   *d* contingere *B*   *e* offenderunt *C*   *f* ille *CBc*   *g* arboris ramusculo *before* collum *T+**   *h* om. *B*
i *T+A add* fuit *(and Ce* est*); cf. 211.1 n. d*

[1] Virgil, *Georg.* ii. 471.   [2] 228. 5.

child of that age, had high ambitions; but all that promise of a springtide flowering was quickly preyed upon and wasted by an early death. The story goes that while shooting stags in the New Forest he caught some sickness from breathing the foggy and corrupted air. This was a region which his father William, with villages abandoned, had reduced for thirty miles and more to 'woodland glades and lairs for the wild beasts'.[1]

T⁺A It is indeed a dreadful sight: where in old days human society or divine worship flourished, now red deer and roe and suchlike animals wander insolently, not even available to men at large for their benefit. So there is truth in the tradition that

CB There he would gladly pass his time, there he rejoiced to hunt for many—certainly months, for of days I say nothing. There many misfortunes have befallen the royal family, which the ready memory of the inhabitants prompts them to relate to those who wish to hear. For later

it was in that same forest that his son William and his grandson, Richard son of Robert duke of Normandy, met their deaths by God's strict judgement, one of them pierced by an arrow in the breast, the other [T⁺ *adds* by the branch of a tree] in the neck or, as some relate, hanged by the throat on the branch of a tree [T⁺ *omits* on . . . tree] when his horse ran underneath it.

276. William himself had five daughters. Cecilia, abbess of Caen, is still living. The second, Constance, married Alan Fergant, count of Brittany, and by the severity of her justice provoked her subjects to poison her. The third, Adela, wife of Stephen count of Blois, a powerful woman with a reputation for her worldly influence, has lately taken the veil as a nun at Marcigny. The names of two I have forgotten: one who, as I have said,[2] was promised to Harold, died before she was old enough to marry, the other, who had been betrothed through envoys to King Alfonso of Galicia, died as a virgin in answer to her prayers. After her death the callus found on her knees bore witness to her constancy in prayer.

277. William took every opportunity to honour the memory of his father, and at the very end of his life was engaged in bringing home his bones, which were originally buried at Nicaea, by means of a special envoy; the man was returning successful, but when he heard of William's death, he settled in Apulia and there buried the great man's

indulgentia dignatus est; quae ante patris obitum cuidam Herlewino de Comitis Villa, mediocrium opum uiro, nupserat. Ex eo Willelmus fratres habuit Rotbertum, quem comitem Moretonii fecit, crassi et hebetis ingenii hominem; Odonem, quem ad episcopatum Baiocensem prouexit comes, comitem Cantiae rex instituit. Callidioris pectoris ille totius Angliae uicedominus sub rege fuit post necem Willelmi filii Osberni. Itaque in aggerandis thesauris mirus tergiuersari, mirae astutiae,*a* pene papatum Romanum absens a ciuibus mercatus fuerat, peras peregrinorum epistolis et nummis infartiens. Cuius futuri itineris opinione cum certatim ex toto regno ad eum milites concurrerent, rex indigne ferens compedibus irretiuit, prefatus non se*b* Baiocarum episcopum sed comitem Cantiae prendere. Clientes eius minis impulsi tantam auri copiam prodidere ut nostri seculi estimationem superaret fului congeries metalli; denique et cullei plures e fluuiis extracti, quos per certa loca sullatis consciis infoderat, plenos auro molito. Post mortem fratris absolutus nepotique Willelmo aduersatus, partem Rotberti fouebat; sed tunc quoque male cedente fortuna, extorris Anglia Normannico nepoti et episcopatui insistebat. Deinde, cum eodem Ierosolimitanam uiam ingressus, Antiochiae in obsidione Christianorum finem habuit.

278. Exterarum nationum homines dignanter ad amicitiam admisit, indifferenter honoribus extulit; elemosinae curam habuit, transmarinis aecclesiis multas possessiones in Anglia largitus; nec ullum fere monasterium, presertim in Normannia, uel eius uel ducum munificentia pertransiit, ut Angliae*c* copia tenuitas illorum sustentaretur. Ita eius tempore ultro citroque cenobialis grex excreuit, monasteria surgebant religione uetera, edifitiis recentia. Sed hic animaduerto mussitationem dicentium melius fuisse ut antiqua in suo statu conseruarentur quam illis semimutilatis de rapina noua construerentur.

a abstinenti(a)e *A*   *b* *T*⁺ adds habere *(cf. 306. 3 capies . . . custodies)*   *c* Anglica *T*⁺*Al* (Anglia *Aa*)

remains. His mother he treated as long as she lived with distinguished generosity. Before his father's death she had married one Herluin of Conteville, a man of modest means. From him William acquired as brothers Robert, whom he made count of Mortain, dense and slow-witted, and Odo, whom as duke he promoted to the see of Bayeux, and as king installed in the earldom of Kent. He was a man of much livelier mind and, after the death of William Fitz Osbern, was deputy lord of all England under the king. In the accumulation of wealth he was a great double-dealer and showed great cunning, and had almost succeeded in buying the see of Rome from the citizens in his own absence, by stuffing the wallets of pilgrims with letters and coin. When rival throngs of knights from the whole kingdom hastened to join him on hearing of the journey he was planning, the king was furious and put him in chains, having explained that his fetters were not for the bishop of Bayeux but for the earl of Kent. His underlings, compelled by threats, divulged the existence of such a quantity of gold that the pile of tawny metal surpassed anything that our age could imagine; many sacks, for example, were hauled out of rivers, which he had sunk in particular places, and then made away with those who knew the secret; and these were full of beaten gold. Pardoned after his brother's death, he opposed his nephew William and supported Robert's cause; but then too things went wrong for him, and he was driven from England and took refuge with his Norman nephew and his Norman see. Later, when he set off with that same nephew on the journey to Jerusalem, he met his end at Antioch while the Christians were besieged there.

278. Men of foreign birth were generously admitted to William's friendship, and raised without prejudice to high positions. To almsgiving he devoted much attention, lavishly bestowing much English property on churches overseas, and there was scarcely a monastery, especially in Normandy, that was passed over by his munificence or that of his chief nobles, so that their poverty was relieved by English plenty. Thus the monastic population increased in his time on both sides of the Channel, and convents arose with a long history of devotion but new buildings. But at this point I should mention the grumbles of those who said it would have been better to preserve the old foundations in their former state than to rob them to build new ones while they fell into ruins.

279. Iustae fuit staturae, immensae corpulentiae, fatie fera, fronte capillis nuda, roboris ingentis in lacertis, ut magno sepe spectaculo fuerit quod nemo eius arcum tenderet, quem ipse admisso equo pedibus neruo extento sinuaret; magnae dignitatis sedens et stans, quamquam obesitas uentris nimis protensa corpus regium deformaret; commodae ualitudinis, ut qui numquam aliquo morbo periculoso preter in extremo decubuerit; exercitio nemorum adeo deditus ut, sicut predixi,[1] multa milia eiectis habitatoribus siluescere iuberet, in
2 quibus a ceteris negotiis auocatus animum remitteret. Conuiuia in precipuis festiuitatibus sumptuosa et magnifica inibat, Natale Domini apud Gloecestram, Pascha apud Wintoniam, Pentecosten apud Westmonasterium agens quotannis quibus in Anglia morari liceret. Omnes eo cuiuscumque professionis magnates regium edictum accersiebat, ut exterarum gentium legati spetiem multitudinis apparatumque delitiarum mirarentur. Nec ullo tempore comior aut indulgendi facilior erat, ut qui aduenerant largitatem eius cum diuitiis conquadrare ubique gentium iactitarent. Quem morem conuiuandi primus successor obstinate tenuit, secundus omisit.

280. *Sola est de qua merito culpetur pecuniae cupiditas, quam undecumque captatis occasionibus nichil umquam pensi habuit quin corraderet,[b] faceret diceret nonnulla, et pene omnia, tanta maiestate indigniora, ubi spes nummi affulsisset.[c a]

280. *Sola est de qua nonnichil culpetur pecuniae aggestio, quam undecumque captatis occasionibus, honestas modo et regia dignitate non inferiores posset dicere, congregabat. Sed excusabitur facile, quia nouum regnum sine magna pecunia non posset regere.[a]

2 Non est hic aliquid aliud [d] excusationis quod afferam, nisi quod quidam dixit: 'Necesse est ut multos timeat, quem multi timent'.[2] Nam ille pro timore inimicorum prouintias suas pecunia emungebat,[e] qua[f] impetus eorum uel tardaret uel etiam propelleret, persepe, ut fit in rebus humanis, uiribus cassatis[g] fidem hostilem premio pigneratus.

[a-a] sola...affulsisset T^+A; sola...regere CB [b] corroderet T^+ (cf. William's change at GP p. 310)   [c] effulsisset A [d] om. T^+A [e] emulgebat A
[f] quia B [g] quassatis T^+; the reading is not quite certain (cf. 388. 9 quassae uires, VD p. 274 cassis uiribus)

---

[1] 275. 1.
[2] Quoted from Laberius by Seneca, *De ira* ii. 11. 3 (Otto, *Sprichwörter*, p. 349).

279. He was of a proper height, immensely stout, with a ferocious expression and a high bald forehead; his arms extremely strong, so that it was often a remarkable sight to see no one able to draw his bow, which he himself, while spurring his horse to a gallop, could bend with taut bowstring. He had great dignity both seated and standing, although his prominent corpulence gave him an unshapely and unkingly figure. He enjoyed good health, for he was never laid up with any dangerous illness except at the end of his life; and he was so devoted to hunting in the forest that, as I have said already,[1] he ordered that many miles of country should be cleared of their inhabitants and turned over to woodland, in which he could be relieved of all other business and relax his mind. The dinners in which he took part on the major festivals were costly and splendid—Christmas at Gloucester, Easter at Winchester, Whitsun at Westminster in each of the years in which he was free to stay in England; all great men of whatever walk of life were summoned to them by royal edict, so that envoys from other nations might admire the large and brilliant company and the splendid luxury of the feast. Nor was he at any other season so courteous or so ready to oblige, so that foreign visitors might carry a lively report to every country of the generosity that matched his wealth. This custom of feasting was stoutly maintained by his first successor, and discontinued by the second.

T⁺A **280.** The only point on which he is rightly criticized is his passion for money, which no scruples restrained him from scraping together by seeking opportunities in all directions, doing and saying much—indeed everything—that was unworthy of so great a monarch, where dawned a glittering hope of gain.

CB **280.** The only point on which he is somewhat criticized is his accumulation of money, which he got together by seeking opportunities in all directions, if only he could call them honourable, and not unworthy of his royal dignity. But this will easily be excused by the thought that he could not rule a new kingdom without great expense.

Nor is there any other excuse I can suggest, except that, as someone said, 'He must fear many men, whom many fear'.[2] For it was fear of his enemies that drove him to squeeze the money from his provinces, with which either to slow up their attacks or even to drive them off entirely; very often, as happens in human affairs, when strength failed he secured the loyalty of his opponents by largesse. It still holds sway,

Regnat adhuc et in dies augetur huiusce dedecoris calamitas, ut et uillae et aecclesiae pensionibus supponantur, et ne hoc quidem perpetua exactorum fide, sed quicumque plus obtulerit statim pactis irritis prioribus palmam habeat.

281. Extremo uitae tempore in Normannia habitans, contractis inimicitiis cum rege Francorum aliquantisper se continuit; cuius abutens patientia Philippus fertur dixisse: 'Rex Angliae iacet Rotomagi, more absolutarum partu feminarum cubile fouens', iocatus in eius uentrem, quem potione alleuiarat. Quo prestrictus[a] conuitio, respondit: 'Cum ad missam post partum iero, centum milia candelas[b] ei libabo', talia 'per resurrectionem et splendorem Dei' pronuntians, quod soleret ex industria talia sacramenta facere quae ipso hiatu oris[c] terrificum quiddam auditorum mentibus insonarent.

282. Nec multo post, Augusto mense declinante, quando et segetes in agris et botri in uineis et poma in uiridariis copiam sui uolentibus fatiunt, exercitu coacto Frantiam infestus ingreditur. Omnia proterit, cuncta populatur; nichil erat quod furentis animum mitigaret, ut iniuriam insolenter acceptam multorum dispendio ulcisceretur. Postremo Medantum ciuitatem[d] iniectis ignibus cremauit, combusta illic aecclesia sanctae Mariae, reclusa una ustulata, quae speleum suum nec in tali necessitate deserendum putauit; fortunae omnes ciuium pessumdatae.

2 Quo successu exhilaratus, dum suos audatius incitat ut igni aditiant pabula, propius flammas succedens[e] foci calore et autumnalis estus inaequalitate morbum nactus est. Dicunt quidam quod preruptam fossam sonipes transiliens interranea sessoris diruperit,[f] quod in anteriori parte sellae uenter protuberabat. Hoc dolore affectus receptui suis cecinit, Rotomagumque reuersus crescente in dies incommodo lecto excipitur. Consulti medici inspectione urinae certam mortem predixere. Quo audito querimonia domum repleuit, quod eum preoccuparet mors emendationem uitae iam dudum meditantem. Resumpto animo, quae Christiani sunt exsecutus est in confessione et

3 uiatico. Normanniam inuitus et coactus Rotberto, Angliam Willelmo,

[a] perstrictus T^+CsBc *(but cf. GP p. 126)*   [b] candelarum T^+ *(William uses both constructions)*   [c] halitu oris *Al*, strictuosis *Aap*   [d] oppidum T^+ [e] succendens T^+Bc [f] disrupit *B*

it daily increases, this disgraceful and disastrous practice of subjecting both towns and churches to imposts; and even so, those who collect the money do not always keep faith, but if anyone offers more, away at once go all previous agreements and he wins the day.

281. At the very end of his life, when he was living in Normandy, he fell out with the king of the French, and for some time kept to his house; and King Philip, presuming on his forbearance, is reported to have said: 'The king of England lies in Rouen, keeping his bed like a woman who has just had her baby', joking at his corpulence, which he had reduced by a drug. Smitten by this offensive remark, William retorted: 'When I go to mass after my lying in, I will offer a hundred thousand candles on his behalf', and confirmed that with 'By the resurrection and glory of God!'; for it was his practice deliberately to use such oaths, so that the mere roar from his open mouth might somehow strike terror into the minds of his audience.

282. Not long after, towards the end of the month of August, when the harvest in the fields, the grapes in the vineyards, and the apples in the orchards offer their plenty to the first comer, he called his army together and entered France with hostile intent. He laid it all low, he ravaged everything; nothing could pacify his furious resolve to avenge, by injuring many, the insult he had received. Eventually he set fire with flaming missiles to the city of Mantes and burnt St Mary's church there; one recluse, who even in such an emergency thought she ought not to leave her cell, was burnt to death, and all the possessions of the citizens were destroyed. Encouraged by this success, he was urging his troops too rashly to add fuel to the fire, when he went too close to the flames, and the heat of the blaze with the exceptional warmth of the autumn brought on an illness. Some say that his horse, in jumping a steep ditch, ruptured its rider's internal organs because his stomach projected over the forward part of the saddle. Overcome by the pain, he sounded the retreat and retired to Rouen where, as the malady daily increased, he took to his bed. The doctors who were consulted inspected his urine and foretold certain death. On hearing the news, he filled the house with complaints that death should overtake him when he had long been planning to reform his life. Regaining his composure, he did all that a Christian should do in the way of confession and the last rites. Reluctantly and under pressure he entrusted Normandy to Robert; England he gave to William, and his maternal

possessiones maternas Henrico delegauit. Vinctos suos omnes educi et solui, thesauros efferri et aecclesiis dispergi precepit. Certum numerum pecuniae ad reparationem aecclesiae nuper crematae ipse indixit. Ordinatis ergo bene rebus, octauo idus Septembris decessit, anno regni uicesimo primo, comitatus quinquagesimo*a* secundo, uitae quinquagesimo nono, Dominicae incarnationis millesimo octogesimo septimo. Ille fuit annus quo Cnuto rex Danorum, ut supra diximus,[1] interemptus est; quo Saraceni Hispani in Christianos efferati, mox ab Aldefonso rege Gallitiae ad sua redire coacti, etiam urbibus quas olim tenuerant inuiti cessere.

283. Corpus regio sollemni curatum per Sequanam Cadomum delatum; ibi magna frequentia ordinatorum, laicorum pauca humi traditum. Varietatis humanae tunc fuit uidere miseriam, quod homo ille, totius olim Europae honor antecessorumque suorum omnium potentior, sedem aeternae requietionis sine calumnia impetrare non potuit: namque miles quidam, ad cuius patrimonium locus ille pertinuerat, clara contestans uoce rapinam[2] sepulturam inhibuit, dicens auito iure solum suum esse, nec illum in loco quem uiolenter inuaserat pausare debere. Quocirca uolente Henrico filio, qui solus ex liberis aderat, centum librae argenti litigatori persolutae audacem calumniam
2 compescuere. Nam tunc Rotbertus primogenitus in Frantia contra patriam bellabat; Willelmus antequam plane pater expiraret Angliam enauigauerat, utilius ducens suis in posterum commodis prospicere quam obsequiis paterni corporis interesse. Porro, in dispertienda pecunia nec segnis nec parcus, omnem illum thesaurum Wintoniae totis annis regni cumulatum*b* ab archanis sacrariis eruit in lucem, monasteriis aurum, aecclesiis agrestibus solidos quinque argenti, unicuique pago centum libras uiritim egenis diuidendas largitus. Patris etiam memoriam ingenti congerie argenti et auri cum gemmarum luce conspicue adornauit.

284. Fuit hoc tempore Beringerius Turonensis heresiarcha, qui panem et uinum in altari apposita post consecrationem sacerdotis

---

a primo... quinquagesimo *om. T*+   *b* accumulatum *TA*

[1] 261. 3.
[2] Cf. Lucan iii. 121–2.

possessions to Henry. He gave orders that all his captives should be brought out and set free, and his treasures produced and distributed to churches. A definite sum of money he himself earmarked for the repair of the church which he had lately burnt. Having thus set all his affairs in order, he passed away on 6 September in the twenty-first year of his reign, his fifty-second as duke, and the fifty-ninth of his life, in the year of our Lord 1087. That was the year in which, as I said above,[1] Cnut king of the Danes was killed, and in which the Spanish Saracens after a furious outburst against the Christians were soon forced to return to their own territory by King Alfonso of Galicia, and even reluctantly evacuated the cities which they had at one time held.

283. The king's body, honoured with the rites due to a monarch, was carried down the Seine to Caen, and there buried with a large attendance of clerics but few laymen. At that point the pitiful ups and downs of human life were well displayed: that great man, who at one time reflected honour on the whole of Europe and was the most powerful of all his line, could obtain no place for his eternal rest without due process of law; for there was a knight to whose ancestral property the land belonged, and he, 'maintaining with a loud voice that this was robbery',[2] forbade the interment, saying that the soil was his by inheritance from his forebears, and that the king ought not to rest in a place which he had seized by brute force. At the wish therefore of his son Henry, the only one of his children present, this bold claim was settled by paying a hundred pounds of silver to the claimant. For at that time Robert, the eldest son, was in France, making war on his fatherland; William, before his father had finally expired, had sailed away to England, thinking it more to the purpose to secure his own future interests than to attend the burial of his father's body. To this end, he was neither dilatory nor sparing in the distribution of funds; all the treasure which throughout the king's reign had been accumulated year by year in Winchester was brought out from its secret hiding-places into the light, and monasteries were given gold, country churches five silver shillings, and every county a hundred pounds to be divided individually among the poor. He also decorated his father's monument conspicuously with a mass of silver and gold and gleaming precious stones.

284. At this time lived a leading heretic, Berengar of Tours, who denied that the bread and wine laid upon the altar were, after their

uerum et substantiale corpus Domini, sicut sancta aecclesia predicat, esse denegabat; iamque scatebat omnis Gallia eius doctrina per egenos scolares, quos ipse cotidiana stipe sollicitabat, disseminata. Vnde soliditati catholicae timens, sanctissimae[a] memoriae Leo papa, Vercellis contra eum instituto concilio, tenebras nebulosi erroris euangelicorum testimoniorum fulgure depulit. Sed cum post obitum eius uirus hereseos, diu in sinibus quorundam nebulonum confotum, iterum erumperet, Hildebrandus cum archidiaconus esset Turonis, mox papa Romae, adunatis conciliis conuictum ad dogmatis sui anathema compulit; quae scripta suis locis[b] qui desiderat inueniet. Responderunt ei libris Lanfrancus archiepiscopus, sed precipue et fortiter Guimundus, prius[c] monachus de Sancto Leufredo Normanniae, postea episcopus Auersanus Apuliae, nostri temporis eloquentissimus. Porro, licet Beringerius primum calorem iuuentutis aliquarum heresium defensione infamauerit, aeuo austeriore ita resipuit ut sine retractatione a quibusdam sanctus habeatur, innumeris bonis maximeque humilitate et elemosinis approbatus; largarum possessionum dispertiendo[d] dominus, non abscondendo et adorando famulus; femineae uenustatis adeo parcus ut nullam conspectui suo pateretur admitti, ne formam uideretur delibasse oculo quam non pruriebat animo. Non aspernari pauperem, non adulari diuitem; secundum naturam uiuere; habens uictum et uestitum, iuxta apostolum,[1] his contentus esse. Vnde eum laudat Cinomannensis pontifex Hildebertus, in primis uersificator eximius, cuius uerba[2] propterea inserui, ut predicabilis episcopi affectum in magistrum ostendam; simul et doctrina eius erit exemplo posteris, qua quomodo uiui debeat instituit, etsi fortasse metas uerae laudis amore incitatus transilierit:

> Quem modo miratur, semper mirabitur orbis,
>   ille Berengarius non obiturus obit,
> quem sacrae fidei fastigia summa tenentem
>   Iani quinta dies abstulit, ausa nefas.
> Illa dies dampnosa dies et perfida mundo,
>   qua dolor et rerum summa ruina fuit;
> qua status aecclesiae, qua spes, qua gloria cleri,
>   qua cultor iuris iure ruente ruit.

[a] sanct(a)e *TCe (but cf. VD p. 304)*   [b] locis suis *T*   [c] primus *BkBc²*, primum *Bc¹*   [d] dispergendo *B*

[1] 1 Tim. 6: 8.

consecration by the priest, in truth and substance the Lord's body, as Holy Church asserts, and the whole of Gaul was already rife with his teaching, propagated as it was by poor scholars whom he personally recruited with a small daily allowance. Fearing therefore for catholic unity, Pope Leo of blessed memory called a council at Vercelli to refute him, and scattered the dark clouds of error with the lightning of Gospel testimony. When, however, after Leo's death the poison of heresy, long nurtured in the bosoms of sundry rascals, burst out again, Hildebrand, while archdeacon of Tours and later pope in Rome, called together councils which convicted Berengar and drove him to repudiate his teaching; this will be found on record in its proper place by anyone who needs it. He was answered in books by Archbishop Lanfranc and, with particular force, by Guitmund, first a monk of Saint-Leufroi in Normandy and later bishop of Aversa in Apulia, the most eloquent man of our time. In fact, though Berengar disgraced himself in the warmth of early manhood by defending some heresies, he repented as he grew more austere, to such effect that he is unhesitatingly held by some to be a saint, recommended by countless good qualities, humility and almsgiving in particular. By distributing his ample resources, not hiding them away and doing them obeisance, he proved himself their master, not their slave; where female beauty was concerned, he showed such abstinence that he allowed no woman to be brought within his sight, for fear he might be thought to have entertained his eye with beauty for which in his heart he had no desire. He did not despise the poor, nor cultivate the rich; he lived according to nature and, 'having food and raiment', in the Apostle's words,[1] 'he was therewith content'. For this he is praised by Hildebert bishop of Le Mans, poet of the first rank, whose words[2] I have inserted to show the feeling entertained for his master by that distinguished prelate; and at the same time his teaching will be an example to posterity, in which he showed how one ought to live, although perhaps affection moved him to overstep the boundaries of just praise.

He who is now the marvel of the world, and always will be, great Berengar, who cannot die, is dead. He held the topmost pinnacle of our holy faith, and the fifth day of January, with criminal temerity, has swept him away; that day when the world suffered loss and betrayal, a day of grief and utter ruin; on which the standing of the Church, the hope and glory of the clergy, and the pillar of the

---

[2] Hildebert, *Carm. min.* xviii.

Quicquid philosophi, quicquid cecinere poetae,
  ingenio cessit eloquioque suo.
Sanctior et maior sapientia, maius adorta,
  impleuit sacrum pectus et ora Deo.
Pectus eam uoluit, uox protulit, actio prompsit;
  singula factori sic studuere suo.
Vir sacer et sapiens, cui nomen crescit in horas;
  quo minor est quisquis maximus est hominum;
cui sensus peperit, partos seruauit honores;
  cui potior pauper^a diuite iusque lucro;
cui nec desidiam nec luxum res dedit ampla,
  nec tumidum fecit multus et altus honos;
qui nec ad argentum nec ad aurum lumina flexit,
  sed doluit quotiens cui daret haec aberat;
qui non cessauit inopum fulcire ruinas,
  donec inops dando pauper et ipse fuit;
cuius cura sequi naturam, legibus uti
  et mentem uitiis, ora negare dolis;
uirtutes opibus, uerum preponere falso;
  nil uacuum sensu dicere uel facere;
ledere nec quemquam, cunctis prodesse; fauorem
  et populare lucrum pellere mente, manu;
cui uestis textura rudis, cui non fuit umquam
  ante sitim potus nec cibus ante famem;
quem Pudor hospitium statuit sibi, quamque libido
  incestos superat, tam superauit eam;
quem Natura parens cum mundo contulit, inquit:
  'Degenerant alii, nascitur iste michi,'
quaeque uagabatur et pene reliquerat orbem,
  inclusit sacro pectore iustitiam.
Vir sacer a puero qui, quantum preminet orbi
  fama, tam famae preminet ipse suae.
Fama minor meritis cum totum peruolet orbem,
  cum semper crescat, non erit aequa tamen.
Vir pius atque grauis, uir sic in utroque modestus
  ut liuor neutro rodere possit^b eum.
Liuor enim^c deflet quem carpserat antea, nec tam
  carpsit et odit eum quam modo laudat, amat.
Quam prius ex uita, tam nunc ex morte gemiscit,
  et queritur celeres huius abisse dies.

canon law fell with the law itself. Whatever philosophers have written or poets have sung yielded to his mental acumen and his eloquence: his great and most sacred wisdom, with its high aims, filled his holy heart and mouth with God. His heart meditated it, his voice proclaimed it, and his actions showed it forth: thus every single part showed its zeal for its Creator. He was a holy and wise man, whose name grows hour by hour, and the greatest of men is less than he: it was his humanity that won him honour and preserved his honour won, and he preferred poor to rich and right to personal gain. His ample wealth caused in him neither sloth nor luxury, nor did many a high honour make him proud; he never turned his eyes to silver or gold, but grieved when there was no man at hand to whom he might give them; he did not cease to prop up the unfortunate until he himself was made poor by giving. His care was always to follow nature, to observe the laws, to keep his mind from wrongdoing and his mouth from guile, to prefer virtues to riches and truth to falsehood; to say or do nothing devoid of sense; to hurt no man and do good to all men; to drive popular favour and popular gain far from both mind and hand. The weave of his vesture was rough; never did he drink before he was thirsty, or before he was hungry, eat. Modesty made him a dwelling-place for herself, and as desire overcomes the lustful, even so he overcame desire. When mother nature made him a present to the world, 'The rest', she said, 'are degenerate, but this is my favourite son.' When justice was hard to find, and had almost left this present world, she gave her protection in her sacred bosom. A holy man from boyhood who, surpassing as his fame is throughout the world, himself surpasses his own fame—that fame so much less than his deserts which, though it run throughout the world and never cease to grow, will never for all that be equal to him. A pious and a serious man, and yet in both regards so modest that envy can carp at him in neither; for envy now mourns the man it had earlier faulted, and its faulting and its dislike were less than its praise and love now; it laments him in death now as once it did in life, and mourns that his days are so

^a pauper potior *T*   ^b posset *Bk, Hild.*   ^c eum *T*, Hild.*

Vir uere sapiens et parte beatus ab omni,
qui caelos anima, corpore ditat humum.
Post obitum uiuam secum, secum requiescam,
nec fiat melior sors mea sorte sua.

285. Videas in his uersibus quod laudis excesserit modum episcopus; sed sic se ostentat eloquentia, tali gestu procedit aureus lepos, eo modo 'purpureos flores fundit facundia diues'.[1] Beringerius plane, quanuis ipse sententiam correxerit, omnes quos ex totis terris deprauauerat conuertere nequiuit; adeo pessimum est alios exemplo uel uerbo a bono infirmare, quia fortassis peccatum te grauabit alienum, cum deletum fuerit tuum. Quod episcopum Carnotensem Fulbertum, quem Domini mater Maria olim egrotum lacte mamillarum suarum uisa fuerat sanare, predixisse aiunt. Nam cum in extremis positum multi uisitarent, et edium capacitas uix confluentibus sufficeret, ille inter oppositas cateruas oculo longe rimatus Beringerium nisu quo ualuit expellendum censuit, protestatus immanem demonem propter eum consistere, multosque ad eum sequendum blandiente manu et illice anhelitu corrumpere. Quin et ipse die Epiphaniorum moriens, gemituque producto recordatus quot miseros quondam adolescens primo erroris calore secta sua[a] infecerit, 'Hodie' inquit 'in die apparitionis suae apparebit michi Dominus meus Iesus Christus, propter penitentiam, ut spero, ad gloriam, uel propter alios, ut timeo, ad penam'.

286. Nos sane credimus, post benedictionem aecclesiasticam illa misteria esse uerum corpus et sanguinem Saluatoris, adducti et ueteri aecclesiae auctoritate et multis nouiter ostensis miraculis. Quale fuit illud[b] quod beatus Gregorius exhibuit Romae. Quale quod Paschasius[2] narrat contigisse Alemanniae, presbiterum Plegildum uisibiliter spetiem pueri in altari contrectasse, et post libata oscula in panis similitudinem conuersum aecclesiastico more sumpsisse; quod arroganti cauillatione ferunt Beringerium carpere solitum, et dicere: 'Spetiosa

---

[a] om. A   [b] om. T

[1] Unidentified.
[2] PL cxx. 1298–9, 1319–21.

soon over. A man of true wisdom and blessed on every side, whose soul is an enrichment of the heavens, as his body is of earth. O, after death may I live and rest with him!—for I could not wish for a better fate than this.

285. You may see in these lines that the bishop exceeded the limits of panegyric; but this is how eloquence makes a display of itself, such is the forward pace of golden charm, and in this fashion 'pours its bright blooms rich mastery of words'.[1] Clearly, though he himself corrected his views, it was impossible for Berengar to set right all those in every country whom he had led astray; such a very bad thing it is, by example or teaching to weaken other men's hold on the good, for it may be that other men's offences will burden your account, when your own have been struck out. This was foretold, they say, by Fulbert bishop of Chartres, who once, when he was ill, had a vision that he was cured by Mary, the mother of our Lord, with milk from her breasts. When he was at death's door and was receiving many visitors, so that the house would scarcely contain the crowd, Fulbert, peering deep into the throng surrounding him, said with all the force he could command that Berengar must be thrown out, asserting that a monstrous demon stood beside him, corrupting many people to follow him with winning gestures and alluring whispers. And Berengar himself, as he lay dying on the feast of the Epiphany, and recalled with a prolonged groan how many poor wretches he had long ago, as a young man in the first enthusiasm of his error, infected with his heresy, said: 'Today, on the day of His first appearance, my Lord Jesus Christ will appear to me, to bring me glory, as I hope, through my repentance, or punishment, as I fear, for what I have done to others.'

286. My own belief is that, once blessed by the Church, those mysteries are the very body and blood of the Saviour; and I am led to this both by the ancient authority of the Church and by the many miracles which have been displayed in later times. Among these was the miracle exhibited by St Gregory in Rome, or that which Paschasius[2] tells us took place in Germany, when a priest called Plecgils handled the form of a child on the altar for all to see: he kissed it, it resumed the appearance of bread, and he consumed it in the Church's traditional fashion. This they say Berengar used to criticize with impertinent

certe*a* pax nebulonis, ut cui oris prebuerat basium, dentium inferret
2 exitium'. Quale de pusione Iudaico, quod*b* in aecclesiam cum aequeuo*c* Christiano forte et ludibunde ingressus uidit puerum in ara membratim discerpi et uiritim populo diuidi. Id cum innocentia puerili parentibus pro uero assereret, in rogum detrusum ubi occluso hostio estuabat incendium, multis post horis sine iactura corporis exuuiarumque et etiam crinium a Christianis extractum; interrogatusque quomodo uoraces ignium globos euaserit, respondit: 'Illa pulchra femina quam uidi sedere in cathedra, cuius filius populo diuidebatur, semper michi in camino ad dexteram astitit, flammeas minas et fumea uolumina peplo suo*d* summouens'.

287. Tunc in prouintia Walarum quae Ros uocatur*e* inuentum est sepulchrum Walwen, qui fuit haud degener Arturis ex sorore nepos. Regnauit*f* in ea parte Britanniae quae adhuc Walweitha uocatur, miles uirtute nominatissimus, sed a fratre et nepote Hengesti, de quibus in primo libro dixi,[1] regno expulsus, prius multo eorum detrimento exilium compensans suum, communicans merito laudi auunculi, quod
2 ruentis patriae casum in plures annos distulerint. Sed Arturis sepulchrum nusquam uisitur, unde antiquitas neniarum adhuc eum uenturum fabulatur. Ceterum alterius bustum, ut premisi, tempore Willelmi regis repertum est super oram*g* maris, quattuordecim pedes longum, ubi a quibusdam asseritur ab hostibus uulneratus et naufragio eiectus, a quibusdam dicitur a ciuibus in publico epulo interfectus. Veritatis ergo notitia labat in dubio, licet neuter eorum defuerit famae suae patrocinio.

288. Illa fuit tempestas qua Henrici, de quo inter gesta Willelmi locutus sum,[2] miserabile et pene funestum per quinquaginta annos Alemannia ingemuit imperium. Erat is neque ineruditus neque ignauus, sed fato quodam ab omnibus ita impetitus ut rem religionis tractare sibi uideretur quisquis in illum arma produceret. Habebat filios duos,
2 Conradum et Henricum. Prior, nichil impium contra parentem ausus,

a certa *ABk*   *b* qui *T**   *c* coequeuo *B*   *d* om. *B*   *e* q. Ros uocatur *om. Tt*   *f* regnauitque *TtA*   *g* ora *Al*, eram *Aap*

---

[1] Ohta and Ebusa: 44. 1.
[2] e.g. 262. 3–4, 266. 3–4.

levity, on the ground that 'the rascal had a pretty idea of the sacrament, kissing it one moment and tearing it to pieces with his teeth the next'. Another is the story of the Jewish boy who happened to have gone 2 into a church when playing with a Christian boy of his own age, and saw a child on the altar being torn limb from limb and distributed individually to the people. When in his childish innocence he told this to his parents as the truth, they thrust him into an oven in which a fire was burning behind closed doors, from which many hours later he was rescued by Christians with no damage to his body or his clothes or even his hair; when asked how he escaped the flames of the devouring fire, he replied: 'That lovely lady whom I saw sitting on a throne, and whose son was divided among the people, stood all the time at my right hand in the furnace, driving off the threatening flames and the rolling smoke with her robe.'

287. It was then that, in the province of Wales called Rhos, they discovered the grave of Gawain, who was Arthur's nephew, being his sister's son, and not unworthy of his uncle. He ruled in the part of Britain still called Galloway, and was a knight with a heroic reputation; but he was driven from his kingdom by a brother and nephew of Hencgest, of whom I have spoken in the first book,[1] though he got some compensation for his exile from the great damage previously inflicted on them. And he deserved a share in his uncle's glory, because they postponed for many years the fall of their ruined country. Arthur's 2 grave, however, is nowhere to be found, whence come the traditional old wives' tales that he may yet return. In any case, the tomb of the other prince was found, as I have already said, in King William's time, on the sea-shore, fourteen feet long, in the place, as some assert, where he was wounded by the enemy and cast out to the winds and waves, or where, some say, he was killed by his fellow-citizens at a public feast. Thus our knowledge is shaky and the truth remains in doubt, though neither of them failed to defend his own fame.

288. That was the period when the pitiful and almost disastrous tenure of the imperial power by Henry, of whom I have spoken in the course of my account of William,[2] was for fifty years a grievous burden to the Germans. Himself neither uneducated nor idle, he became by some freak of fortune a general target, so much so that whoever took up arms against him thought himself to be serving the cause of religion. He had two sons, Conrad and Henry. The former of 2

subiugata Italia apud Aretium ciuitatem Tusciae dies expleuerat; alter patrem, aliquantulum ab externis feriatum, primo aeui tirocinio aggressus cedere imperio compulit, nec multo post defunctum imperialibus inferiis extulit. Viuit adhuc, eiusdem sententiae pertinaciter sequax pro qua patrem persequendum putauerat; nam et inuestituram aecclesiarum per baculum et anulum donat, et sine suo arbitratu papam electum non legitimum estimat, licet Calixtus, qui modo apostolicae sedi presidet, immodicam uiri auiditatem egregie inhibuerit. Verum de his plura me dicturum lector prestoletur,[1] cum series narrationis expetierit.

289. Porro Hildebrando papa, ut dixi,[2] mortuo et Vrbano a cardinalibus electo, imperator hesit in proposito ut Wibertum preferret et papam dictitaret, Romaeque altero expulso inferret. Sed aequiori, ut uidebatur, causae affuit militia Mathildis marcisae, quae oblita sexus nec dispar antiquis Amazonibus ferrata uirorum agmina in bellum agebat femina. Eius suffragio Vrbanus posteriori tempore thronum indeptus apostolicum securum per undecim annos actitauit otium. Post eum Paschalis consputa Henrici scientia a Romanis institutus est.

2 Grauabat superas adhuc uiuendo Wibertus auras, unicus scismatis sator, nec umquam quoad uixit peruicatiam deposuit, ut iustitiae manus daret, imperatoris iuditium pronuntians sequendum, non lanistarum uel pellificum Romanorum; quare ambo, ab Vrbano frequentibus*a* conciliis excommunicati, arguto sententiam suspendebant ludibrio. Inter haec erant multa quae in Cesare probares, quod esset ore facundus, acer ingenio, multa eruditus lectione, impiger elemosinis; prorsus in eo bona animi corporisque cerneres: ad arma prompte concurrere, ut qui sexagies et bis atie collocata*b* dimicarit; iuste lites componere; cum res non successisset, querelis in caelum conuersis inde opem expectare. Plures inimicorum eius uitam exitu miserando conclusere.

a sequentibus *CB (but cf. GP p. 13)*   *b* collata *TtAa*

[1] cc. 420–38.
[2] 266. 4.

these, with no spirit for any unfilial act against his father, had subdued Italy, but had ended his days at Arezzo, a city in Tuscany; the other, in the inexperience of youth, attacked his father, who was enjoying some respite from external pressures, and compelled him to retire from the imperial throne, though on his death not long after he buried him with imperial honours. This son is still alive, and remains obstinately of the same opinion which had made him think fit to persecute his own father: he grants investiture of churches by staff and ring, and regards any pope as illegitimate who has been elected without his approval; although Calixtus, who now presides over the Apostolic See, has brilliantly restrained the man's unlimited ambitions. But on this topic the reader must wait for me to say more,[1] when the order of my narrative calls for it.

289. So on the death of Hildebrand, of which I have spoken,[2] and the election of Urban by the cardinals, the emperor stood firm in his determination to promote Wibert and call him pope, and then to drive out his rival and establish him in Rome; but what was thought the better cause was supported by the troops of the Marchioness Matilda who, unmindful of her sex and a worthy rival of the Amazons of old, led into battle, woman as she was, the columns of men clad in mail. With her support Urban at a later date achieved the Apostolic throne, and held it in peace and quiet for eleven years. After him, treating with contempt the question of whether Henry should be informed or not, Paschal was installed by the Romans. Wibert lived on, still poisoning the air of heaven by his existence, a supreme begetter of schism who, as long as he lived, never abandoned his obstinacy and surrendered to justice, maintaining that the emperor's decision should be accepted, not that of butchers and cordwainers in Rome. Both, as a result, were excommunicated by Urban in frequent councils, but made light of his sentence with shrewd arguments. But at the same time, there were many other points which you would approve in an emperor: he was a powerful speaker with a keen intelligence nourished by wide reading, and active in charitable causes. In him good qualities of mind and body were immediately obvious: a ready warrior (he had fought it out in pitched battle sixty-two times), a just arbiter of disputes, a man who, when things had gone badly, turned his complaints towards Heaven and from Heaven expected help. The majority of his enemies came to a pitiable end.

290. Audiui uirum ueracissimum referentem quod quidam ex aduersariis eius, homo impotens et factiosus, dum resupinatis ceruicibus in conuiuio resideret, ita a muribus repente circumuallatus est ut nusquam esset effugium; tantus erat numerus bestiolarum ut in quamlibet ampla prouintia tot esse non putarentur. Itaque fustibus et subselliorum quae ad manum occurrissent fragminibus diu in eas*^a* seuitum, nec quicquam profectum; et quanuis a cunctis repellerentur, nulli tamen noxam uicariam referebant:*^b* illum solum dentibus, illum
2 terribili quodam occentu persequebantur. Quapropter a famulis ultra iactum sagittae in pelagus prouectus,*^c* nec sic uiolentiam euasit; continuo enim tanta uis murium ponto inundauit ut marmor paleis constratum iurares. Sed cum iam tabulata nauis corroderent, et naufragium indubitatum aqua per rimulas ingrediens minaretur, seruientes puppem ad litus retorquent. Tum uero animalia, iuxta carinam annauigantia, priora ad terram perueniunt; ita miser ille in aridam expositus, moxque totus dilaceratus, horrendam murium famem*^d* expleuit.

291. Id eo minus mirum iudico quod certum est in Asiaticis regionibus si leopardus aliquem mordicus attigerit, confestim murium copiam aduentare ut uulneratum commingant, immundum urinae diluuium comitari hominis exitium; sin uero sedulitate arcentium ministrorum intra nouem dies uitata fuerit pernities, aduocari medicorum industriam profecto ualituram. Conspicatus est relator meus quendam eiusmodi sautium, cum desperaret in terra salutem, in altum iactis anchoris processisse; nec mora, plures illo*^e* mures annasse corticibus malorum granatorum quorum medullas exederant inclusos (mirabile dictu), sed obstrepentibus nautis demersos. Nichil enim ille Parens rerum creatum destituit ingenio, nichil porro noxium sine remedio.

292. Sub isto imperatore regnante floruit Marinianus*^f* Scottus, qui primo Fuldensis monachus, post apud Mogontiacum inclusus, contemptu presentis uitae gratiam futurae demerebatur. Is, longo uitae otio chronographos scrutatus, dissonantiam ciclorum Dionisii Exigui

---

^a ea *A*   *^b* uic. ref. nox. *Tt*   *^c* proiectus *A*   *^d* famam *A*   *^e* plus mille *TtA* (William does not use* illo = illuc*)*   *^f* Marianus *Tt*

290. I have heard a man of the highest veracity telling how one of the emperor's adversaries, an uncontrollable and rebellious character, was leaning back one day as he sat at dinner, when he was suddenly so densely beset by a wall of mice that he had no means of escape; such was the multitude of these tiny creatures that in any region however wide one would not think there could be so many. A long and fierce attack was launched against them with sticks and such broken pieces of benches as were to hand, but it made no progress, and though all those present tried to drive them off, they turned against nobody else the fate intended for their victim, but attacked him alone with their teeth and with a terrible kind of squeaking. He was therefore conveyed by his servants further than a bowshot out to sea, and even so he did not escape their fury; immediately such a mass of mice filled the sea that one might swear the water was strewn with chaff. When, however, they were already gnawing the timbers of the craft, and water seeping through the crevices was unquestionably threatening shipwreck, the serving-men turned the ship back to shore. Then the creatures, swimming alongside the boat, reached the land first; and so, when that wretched man was set on dry land, he was soon entirely torn to pieces, and thus the horrible hunger of the mice was satisfied.

291. I am the less disposed to think that remarkable, because it is a known fact that in Asia, if anyone has been bitten by a leopard, an army of mice at once gathers to make water on the wounded man, and the victim's death is accompanied by a filthy flood of urine. If, however, his servants by their unsleeping defence have kept the plague at bay within the space of nine days, they send for the physicians, whose skill will assuredly prevail. The man who told me this had seen the victim of such an attack who, in despair of surviving on land, had put out to sea and cast anchor. Without delay, ever so many mice sailed after him, enclosed, believe it or not, in the rinds of pomegranates of which they had eaten the flesh, but the sailors went for them, shouting, and they were drowned. For the great Father of all has left no created thing without intelligence and no harmful thing without its remedy.

292. In the reign of this emperor flourished Marianus Scotus, who was at first a monk of Fulda and later a recluse at Mainz, and earned by his contempt for this present life the privilege of a life to come. The leisure of a long life he devoted to the detailed study of chronography, and he detected a discrepancy between the cycles of Dionysius

ab euangelica ueritate deprehendit. Itaque, ab initio seculi annos singulos recensens, uiginti duos annos*a* qui circulis predictis deerant superaddidit; sed paucos aut nullos sententiae suae sectatores habuit. Quare sepe mirari soleo cur nostri temporis doctos hoc respergat infortunium, ut in tanto numero discentium, in tam tristi pallore lucubrantium, uix aliquis plenam scientiae laudem referat: adeo inueteratus usus placet, adeo fere nullus nouis, licet probabiliter inuentis, serenitatem assensus pro merito indulget. Totis conatibus in sententiam ueterum reptatur, omne recens sordet; ita, quia solus fauor alit ingenia, cessante fauore obtorpuerunt omnia.

293. Sed quia Fuldense cenobium nominaui, dicam quod ibidem accidisse uir reuerendus*b* michi narrauit, Walkerius prior Maluerni, cuius uerbis qui non credit iniuriam religioni facit. 'Non' ait 'plusquam quindecim anni sunt quod in eodem loco exitialis lues grassata prius abbatem corripuit, mox multos monachorum extinxit. Superstites primo quisque sibi timere, orationes et elemosinas largiores facere; sed processu temporis, ut est omnium natura hominum, pedetemptim metu dempto omittere, cellerarius presertim, qui palam et ridicule clamitaret non posse penum tot expensis sufficere; sperasse se nuper*c* aliquod alleuiamentum pro tot elationibus funerum; nichil ultra spei esse, si quod uiui nequissent mortui consumerent. Itaque cum quadam nocte *d*pro re*d* necessaria soporem diu distulisset, tandem elaqueatis morarum retibus in dormitorium ire pergebat. Et ecce rem miram auditurus es: uidet in capitulo abbatem, et omnes qui obierant illo anno, eo quo excesserant ordine sedere. Timidus et effugere gestiens ui retractus est; increpitus et monastico more flagellis coercitus, audiuit uerba abbatis in hanc omnino sententiam: stultum esse de alterius morte emolumento inhiare, cum sors cuiusque sub eodem pendeat fato; impium esse, cum monachus omnem uitam in aecclesiae consumpserit obsequio, ut careat unius saltem anni post mortem stipendio; illum citissime obiturum, sed quicquid pro eo fieret ad aliorum

a om. A   *b* uenerandus T*t*   *c* semper (om. se) T   *d–d* propter T*A*

Exiguus and the Gospel truth. As a result, by reckoning years one at a time from the beginning of our era, he added twenty-two years which were wanting in the cycles of which I spoke; but he found few or none to follow his argument. This often makes me wonder why the learned of our own day should be infected with this misfortune, that in such a great number of students, pale and melancholy as they are with their researches, scarcely one wins a reputation for complete knowledge of his subject. Such is our devotion to the familiar and habitual; so true is it that almost no one accords to new discoveries, however plausible, the unimpassioned acceptance they deserve. With all our efforts we go plodding along after the opinions of the Ancients, and everything new is undervalued; and thus, since public credit is wit's only nursing-mother, where credit is slow in coming, sleep reigns supreme.

293. But, as I have mentioned the monastery of Fulda, let me tell of something which happened there, as I learnt from that reverend figure Walcher prior of Malvern; for anyone who does not believe what he says affronts the religious life. 'Not more than fifteen years ago', he said, 'in the place of which we speak a fatal pestilence broke out, which first seized the abbot and then carried off many of the monks. At first the survivors, fearing each for himself, offered up copious prayers and almsgiving; but as time went on, human nature being what it is, they gradually lost their fears, and did less and less. The cellarer in particular complained loudly and absurdly that their resources could not meet such great expense; he had lately hoped, he said, for some relief against the cost of all these funerals, but there was no hope in sight, if what the living had not been able to use was to be spent on the dead. So it happened one night that because of pressure of business he had stayed up very late, but at length he extricated himself from the toils that delayed him, and made his way towards the dorter. Now you are to hear something that will amaze you. He saw the abbot and all the monks who had died that year sitting in chapter in the order of their deaths. Terrified and longing to escape, he was haled back by force; he received a rebuke and a flogging, as is the monastic custom, and heard the abbot speaking to this effect. "It is foolish", he said, "to be greedy for gain from the death of a fellow man, for each man's lot depends on the same destiny, and it is impious, when a monk has spent his whole life in the service of the Church, to deprive him of even one year's allowance after his death. You yourself will die very shortly, but whatever is done for you will be diverted to the benefit of

quibus abstulerat refundendum commodum; iret modo, et alios corrigeret exemplo quos corruperat uerbo. Abiit ille, et nichil se*ᵃ* uanum uidisse tam recentibus plagis quam proximo sui obitu monstrauit.'

294. Interea, dum alia agimus, irrepsit materia et uoluntas accessit ut quid tempore Willelmi regis diffinitum sit de controuersia quae adhuc inter archiepiscopos Cantuariensem et Eboracensem uolutatur describam. De qua re ut plane norint posteri quid inde *ᵇ*rectius censeant, quid inde*ᵇ* antiqui patres senserint apponam.

295. 'Gregorius papa Augustino primo Anglorum archiepiscopo Doroberniae. 'Tua fraternitas non solum eos episcopos quos ordinauerit, neque hos tantummodo qui per Eboracae*ᵈ* episcopum fuerint*ᵉ* ordinati, sed etiam omnes Britanniae sacerdotes habeat, Deo*ᶠ* Domino nostro Iesu Christo auctore, subiectos.'

296. Bonefatius Iusto archiepiscopo Doroberniae.*ᵍ* 'Absit ab omni Christiano ut ex illa ciuitate Dorobernia aliquid minuatur aut in aliud mutetur nunc uel futuris temporibus, quae a predecessore nostro domno papa Gregorio statuta sunt, quoquomodo*ʰ* res humanae quassantur.*ⁱ* Sed magis ex auctoritate beati Petri apostolorum principis id ipsum precipientes firmamus, ut in Dorobernia ciuitate semper in posterum metropolitanus totius Britanniae locus habeatur, omnesque prouintiae regni Anglorum ut prefati loci metropolitanae aecclesiae subitiantur, immutilata et perpetua stabilitate decernimus. Hanc autem aecclesiam, utpote spetialiter consistentem sub potestate et tuitione sanctae Romanae aecclesiae, si quis conatus fuerit imminuere, eique de concessae potestatis*ʲ* iure quicquam abstulerit, auferat eum Deus de libro uitae, sciatque se sub anathematis uinculis esse nodatum.'

297. *ᵏ*Alexander Willelmo regi Anglorum. 'Causam Alricii, qui olim Cicestrensis aecclesiae dictus est episcopus,*ˡ* diligenter retractandam*ᵐ* et diffiniendam fratri nostro episcopo Lanfranco commisimus. Item*ⁿ* sibi negotium de discernenda lite quae inter archiepiscopum

ᵃ B adds in   *ᵇ⁻ᵇ* Tt; om. ACB, perhaps rightly   *ᶜ* The headings to 295–9 are omitted in B   *ᵈ* Eborac(a)e ACeBc¹, Bede HE i. 29; -censem TtAa (-cem BkBc², -ci Cs)   *ᵉ* fuerunt Tt   *ᶠ* om. Tt   *ᵍ* om. Tt. For the full text of the letter that follows see GP pp. 47–9 and ψ (fos. 235ᵛ–236ʳ)   *ʰ* AaCs, GP, ψ; quomodo TtAlCeB   *ⁱ* quassentur Aa, GP, ψ   *ʲ* pietatis Tt   *ᵏ* The complete letter is edited by Clover–Gibson, pp. 60–2; see also Counc. pp. 579–80   *ˡ* presul dictus est Tt (presul dictus Clover–Gibson)   *ᵐ* tractandam Tt   *ⁿ* ita A

those whom you have deprived of it. Go now and correct by your example others whom you have corrupted by your language." The man went his way, and demonstrated that this was no baseless vision both by his fresh scars and by his death, which befell soon after.'

294. All this time, while I have been engaged on other things, a fresh topic has intruded, and I have formed the desire to set down the decisions arrived at in the time of King William in the controversy which is still under discussion between the archbishops of Canterbury and York. To provide posterity with clear knowledge of how to form a right judgement on this subject, I will add the opinions of ancient Fathers on it.

295. Pope Gregory to Augustine first archbishop of the English in Canterbury. 'You, dear brother, are to have in subjection to you under the authority of our Lord God Jesus Christ not only those bishops whom you have ordained nor those alone who have been ordained by the bishop of York but also all the priests in Britain.'

296. Boniface to Justus archbishop of Canterbury. 'Far be it from every Christian to lower in any way the standing of the city of Canterbury or to make any change therein, either now or in the future, of those things which were established by our predecessor Pope Gregory, whatsoever upheavals may occur in human affairs. Rather, by authority of St Peter prince of the Apostles, we can establish and ordain the same principle, that in the city of Canterbury shall be the metropolitan see of all Britain for all time to come; and we decree absolutely, free of infringement or limitation of time, that all provinces of the kingdom of the English be subject to the metropolitan church of the aforesaid place. And whereas this church stands more particularly under the power and protection of the holy Roman church, whoever shall attempt to lower its standing and in any way to detract from the legal effect of the powers granted to it, may God remove him from the book of life, and let him know that he is fast bound in the bonds of excommunication.'

297. Alexander to William king of the English. 'The cause of Æthelric, who was sometime called bishop of Chichester, we have entrusted to our brother Bishop Lanfranc to be diligently re-examined and decided. We have also committed to him the business of

Eboracensem et episcopum Dorcacestrensem de pertinentia*a* diocesis eorum est firmiter iniungendo commendauimus, ut hanc causam diligentissima perquisitione pertractet et iusto fine determinet. In causis autem pertractandis et diffiniendis ita sibi nostrae et apostolicae auctoritatis uicem dedimus ut quicquid in eis iustitia dictante determinauerit, quasi in nostra presentia diffinitum,*b* deinceps firmum et indissolubile teneatur.'

298. *'*Generale concilium regni Anglorum de iure et primatu Dorobernensis siue Cantuariensis aecclesiae. 'Anno ab incarnatione Domini nostri Iesu Christi millesimo septuagesimo secundo, pontificatus autem domni Alexandri papae undecimo, regni uero Willelmi gloriosi regis Anglorum et ducis Normannorum sexto, ex precepto eiusdem Alexandri papae, annuente eodem rege, in presentia ipsius et episcoporum atque abbatum, uentilata est causa de primatu quem Lanfrancus Dorobernensis archiepiscopus super Eboracensem aecclesiam iure suae aecclesiae proclamabat, et de ordinationibus quorundam episcoporum, de quibus 2 ad quem spetialiter pertinerent certum minime constabat; et tandem aliquando diuersis diuersarum scripturarum auctoritatibus probatum atque ostensum est quod Eboracensis aecclesia Cantuariensi debeat subiacere, eiusque archiepiscopi ut primatis totius Britanniae dispositionibus, in his quae ad Christianam religionem pertinent, in omnibus obedire. Subiectionem uero Dunelmensis, hoc est Lindisfarnensis, episcopi atque omnium regionum a terminis Licifeldensis episcopii et Humbrae magni fluuii usque ad extremos Scottiae fines, et quicquid ex hac*d* parte predicti fluminis ad parrochiam Eboracensis aecclesiae iure competit, Cantuariensis metropolitanus Eboracensi archiepiscopo eiusque 3 successoribus obtinere concessit; ita ut si Cantuariensis archiepiscopus concilium cogere uoluerit, ubicumque uisum ei*e* fuerit, Eboracensis archiepiscopus sui presentiam*f* cum omnibus sibi subiectis ad nutum eius exhibeat, et eius canonicis dispositionibus obediens existat. Quod autem Eboracensis archiepiscopus professionem Cantuariensi archiepiscopo facere etiam cum sacramento debeat, Lanfrancus Dorobernensis archiepiscopus ex antiqua antecessorum consuetudine ostendit; sed ob amorem regis Thomae Eboracensi archiepiscopo sacramentum relaxauit, scriptamque tantum professionem recepit, non preiudicans

a pertinatia *CB* *b* definitum *AlC, Clover–Gibson* *c* *The judgement of the Council is edited from a number of MSS (including that of the shorter version in GP pp. 42–3) in Counc. pp. 601–4* *d* om. *B* *e* ei uisum *T', GP (and some other MSS used by Counc.)* *f* *B adds* et

determining the dispute between the archbishop of York and the bishop of Dorchester concerning what pertains to their dioceses, with strict instructions to consider this case after most diligent enquiry and pass just and final judgement. In the examination and decision of cases we have given him a share of our authority and that of the Apostle, to the intent that whatever his decision therein, as justice may dictate, shall be as though taken in our presence and be maintained thereafter firm and indissoluble.'

298. General council of the English kingdom touching the rights and primacy of the church of Dorobernia, otherwise Canterbury. 'In the year of our Lord Jesus Christ 1072, the eleventh year of Pope Alexander, and the sixth year of William glorious king of England and duke of Normandy, on the instructions of Pope Alexander aforesaid and with the approval of the aforesaid king, in the presence of the king himself and the bishops and abbots, a case was considered touching the primacy asserted by Lanfranc archbishop of Canterbury by right of his see over the see of York; also touching the ordinations of certain bishops concerning whom it was far from certain to whom they in particular belonged; and at length by the varying authority of various written documents it was proved and demonstrated that the church of York ought to be subject to the church of Canterbury, and to be obedient in all things to the dispositions of its archbishop as primate of all Britain in whatever pertains to the Christian religion. But the obedience of the bishop of Durham, that is of Lindisfarne, and of all regions from the boundaries of the bishopric of Lichfield and the great river Humber as far as the uttermost edge of Scotland, and whatever on this side of the aforesaid river rightly belongs to the province of the church of York—all this the metropolitan of Canterbury conceded as belonging to the archbishop of York and his successors. If, however, the archbishop of Canterbury wishes to call a council, wherever he may think fit, the archbishop of York must appear in person with all those subject to him on receipt of the summons, and must obey his canonical dispositions. That the archbishop of York is obliged to make his profession to the archbishop of Canterbury even with an oath was demonstrated by Lanfranc archbishop of Canterbury from the ancient custom of his predecessors; but out of love to the king he excused Thomas archbishop of York from taking the oath, and accepted only a written profession, without prejudice

successoribus suis qui sacramentum cum professione a successoribus
4 Thomae*a* exigere uoluerint. Si archiepiscopus Cantuariensis uitam
finierit, Eboracensis archiepiscopus Doroberniam ueniet, et eum qui
electus fuerit cum ceteris prefatae aecclesiae episcopis ut primatem proprium iure consecrabit. Quod si Eboracensis archiepiscopus obierit, is
qui ei successurus eligitur, accepto a rege archiepiscopatus dono, Cantuariam uel ubi Cantuariensi archiepiscopo placuerit accedet, et ab ipso
5 ordinationem canonico more suscipiet. Huic constitutioni consenserunt
prefatus rex, et archiepiscopi Lanfrancus Cantuariensis et Thomas Eboracensis, et Hubertus sanctae Romanae aecclesiae subdiaconus et prefati
Alexandri papae legatus, et ceteri qui interfuerunt episcopi et abbates.

'Ventilata est autem haec causa prius apud Wentanam ciuitatem in
Paschali sollemnitate in capella regia quae sita est in castello; postea in
uilla regia quae uocatur Windlesor, ubi et finem accepit in presentia
regis, episcoporum, abbatum, diuersorum ordinum, qui congregati
erant apud curiam in festiuitate Pentecostes.

6 '*b*+Signum Willelmi regis. *b*+Signum Mathildis reginae. Ego
Hubertus, sanctae Romanae aecclesiae lector et domni Alexandri
papae legatus, subscripsi. Ego Lanfrancus Dorobernensis archiepiscopus subscripsi. Ego Thomas Eboracensis archiepiscopus subscripsi.
Ego Willelmus Lundoniensis episcopus consensi. Ego Hermannus
Scireburnensis episcopus subscripsi. Ego Wlstanus Wigornensis episcopus subscripsi. Ego Walterus Herefordensis episcopus subscripsi.*c*
7 Ego Giso Wellensis episcopus consensi.*d* Ego Remigius Dorcacensis
episcopus subscripsi. Ego Walkelinus Wentanus episcopus subscripsi.*e*
Ego Herfastus Helmeanensis episcopus*f* subscripsi.*e* Ego Stigandus
Cicestrensis episcopus consensi. Ego Siwardus Rofensis episcopus consensi.*g* Ego Osbernus Exoniensis episcopus consensi.*g* Ego Odo Baiocensis episcopus et comes Cantiae consensi.*g* Ego Gosfridus
Constantiensis episcopus et unus de primatibus Anglorum consensi.
Ego Scotlandus abbas cenobii sancti Augustini consensi. Ego Elfwinus
8 abbas cenobii quod Ramesege dicitur consensi. Ego Elnothus Glastoniensis abbas consensi. Ego Turstanus abbas cenobii quod in insula
quae dicitur Heli situm est consensi. Ego Wlnothus abbas cenobii
quod Certesei dicitur consensi. Ego Elfwinus*h* abbas cenobii Euesandi
consensi. Ego Fridericus abbas Sancti Albani consensi. Ego Gosfridus

a om. *T¹* *b* The signs are preserved only in Cs *c* consensi *T¹A, Counc.* *d* concessi *Bk*, subscripsi *Bc* *e* consensi *T¹* *f* episcopus Helm. A *g* subscripsi *T¹* *h* Celwinus *T¹;* Elwius *Counc., correctly*

to his successors who may wish to receive an oath with the profession from Thomas's successors. If an archbishop of Canterbury reaches the end of his life, the archbishop of York will come to Canterbury, and together with all the other bishops of the church aforesaid he will duly consecrate as his own primate the man who has been elected. But if an archbishop of York dies, the man who is elected to succeed him, having received the grant of the archbishopric from the king, will go to Canterbury, or to such other place as the archbishop of Canterbury shall decide, and will accept ordination from him as the law directs. This constitution received the assent of the king aforesaid, of Archbishops Lanfranc of Canterbury and Thomas of York, and of Hubert subdeacon of the holy Roman church and legate of the aforesaid Pope Alexander, and of all the other bishops and abbots who were present.

'This case was first discussed in the city of Winchester at the Easter festival in the royal chapel which is within the castle; and afterwards in the royal town called Windsor, where it was finally decided in the presence of the king, bishops, abbots, and clergy of other ranks, who had assembled at court at the festival of Pentecost.

'+The mark of King William. +The mark of Queen Matilda. I Hubert, lector of the holy Roman church and legate of the lord Pope Alexander, have signed. I Lanfranc, archbishop of Canterbury, have signed. I Thomas, archbishop of York, have signed. I William, bishop of London, have assented. I Hereman, bishop of Sherborne, have signed. I Wulfstan, bishop of Worcester, have signed. I Walter, bishop of Hereford, have signed. I Giso, bishop of Wells, have assented. I Remigius, bishop of Dorchester, have signed. I Walkelin, bishop of Winchester, have signed. I Herfast, bishop of Elmham, have signed. I Stigand, bishop of Chichester, have assented. I Siward, bishop of Rochester, have assented. I Osbern, bishop of Exeter, have assented. I Odo, bishop of Bayeux and earl of Kent, have assented. I Geoffrey, bishop of Coutances and one of the chief men of England, have assented. I Scotland, abbot of the monastery of St Augustine, have assented. I Ælfwine, abbot of the monastery called Ramsey, have assented. I Æthelnoth, abbot of Glastonbury, have assented. I Thurstan, abbot of the monastery which is in the isle called Ely, have assented. I Wulfnoth, abbot of the monastery called Chertsey, have assented. I Ælfwine, abbot of the monastery of Evesham, have assented. I Frederick, abbot of St Albans, have assented. I Geoffrey, abbot of

abbas cenobii sancti Petri quod non longe a Lundonia situm est consensi. Ego Balduinus abbas cenobii sancti Edmundi consensi. Ego Turoldus abbas de Burgo consensi. Ego Adelelmus abbas Abbendoniae consensi. Ego Rualdus abbas Noui Monasterii Wintoniae consensi.'

299. Professio*a* Thomae Eboracensis archiepiscopi. 'Decet Christianum quemque Christianis legibus subiacere, nec his quae a sanctis patribus salubriter instituta sunt quibuslibet rationibus contraire. Hinc namque irae, dissensiones, inuidiae, contentiones,*b* ceteraque procedunt quae amatores suos in penas aeternas*c* demergunt. Et quanto quisque*d* altioris est ordinis, tanto impensius diuinis*e* debet obtemperare
2 preceptis. Propterea ego Thomas, ordinatus iam Eboracensis aecclesiae*f* metropolitanus antistes, auditis cognitisque rationibus, absolutam tibi, Lanfrance Dorobernensis archiepiscope, tuisque successoribus de canonica obedientia professionem fatio, et quicquid a te uel ab eis iuste et canonice michi iniunctum fuerit seruaturum me esse promitto. De hac autem re, dum a te adhuc ordinandus essem, dubius fui; ideoque tibi quidem sine conditione, successoribus uero tuis conditionaliter obtemperaturum me esse promisi.'

300. Habebat autem ex antiquo, sicut in libro primo dixisse me memini,[1] Cantuariensis archiepiscopus*g* hos episcopos: Lundoniensem, Wintoniensem, Rofensem, Scireburnensem, Wigorniensem, Herefordensem, Licitfeldensem, Selesiensem, Legecestrensem, Helmanensem, Sidnacestrensem, Dommucensem; additi sunt*h* tempore regis Eduardi senioris Cornubiensis, Cridiensis, Wellensis in Westsaxonia, et in Mer-
2 tiis Dorcestrensis, ut*i* secundo libro dixi.[2] Eboracensis autem archiepiscopus habebat omnes trans Humbram episcopos suae ditioni subiectos: Ripensem, Haugustaldensem, Lindisfarnensem, illum de Candida Casa quae nunc Witerne dicitur, et omnes episcopos Scottiae et Orcadum, sicut Cantuariensis habet episcopos Hiberniae et Walarum. Perierunt autem*j* iam dudum episcopatus Ripensis et Haugustaldensis ui hostilitatis, et Legecestrensis et Sidnacestrensis et*k* Dommucensis quo nescio modo. Porro autem tempore regis Eduardi simplicis Cornubiensis et
3 Cridiensis uniti sunt, et translatus est episcopatus in Exoniam. Sub rege Willelmo in isto eodem concilio pronuntiatum est secundum scita

a Prefatio A. *The Profession is edited from a number of MSS (including that of GP p. 42) in Counc. p. 605 (cf. Clover–Gibson, p. 44)* *b* om. T*t* *c* om. CB *d* quisquis B *e* T*t*, Counc.; om. ACB *f* om. B *g* episcopus T*t* *h* T*t* adds autem *i* T*t* adds in *j* om. B *k* om. T*t*

the monastery of St Peter which is not far from London, have assented. I Baldwin, abbot of the monastery of St Edmund, have assented. I Turold, abbot of Peterborough, have assented. I Æthelhelm, abbot of Abingdon, have assented. I Riwallon, abbot of New Minster at Winchester, have assented.'

299. The profession of Thomas archbishop of York. 'It is right for every Christian to be subject to Christian laws, and never for any reasons to go against the rules laid down by the holy Fathers for the good of all; for this is the source of wrath, dissensions, envy, contention, and other things which plunge those who love them into eternal punishment. And the higher a man's rank, the more earnestly he should obey the divine commandments. For this reason I Thomas, being now ordained as metropolitan prelate of the church of York, having heard and taken note of the arguments, make to you Lanfranc, archbishop of Canterbury, and to your successors my absolute profession of canonical obedience, and whatsoever is justly and lawfully enjoined upon me by you or by them I promise to observe. On this subject, while I was still awaiting ordination by you, I was in doubt, and therefore I have promised that I will obey you unconditionally, but your successors under conditions.'

300. The archbishop of Canterbury had of old, as I remember saying in the first book,[1] these bishops: London, Winchester, Rochester, Sherborne, Worcester, Hereford, Lichfield, Selsey, Leicester, Elmham, *Sidnacester,* Dunwich; there were added in the time of King Edward the Elder Cornwall, Crediton, and Wells in Wessex, and among the Mercians Dorchester, as I said in my second book.[2] The archbishop of York held subject to his power all the bishops across the Humber: Ripon, Hexham, Lindisfarne, him of *Candida Casa* now called Whithorn, and all the bishops of Scotland and the Orkneys, just as Canterbury has those of Ireland and Wales. The sees of Ripon and Hexham disappeared long ago through the violence of the enemy, Leicester, *Sidnacester* and Dunwich I know not how. Then, in the time of King Edward the Simple, Cornwall and Crediton were united, and the see was transferred to Exeter. Under King William in that same council it was decreed that, in accordance with canon law,

---

[1] cc. 99–103. [2] 129. 3.

canonum ut episcopi transeuntes de uillis constituerent sedes suas in urbibus diocesium suarum. Licitfeldensis ergo migrauit in Cestram, quae olim Ciuitas Legionum dicebatur; Selesiensis in Cicestram; Helmanensis in Tetford primo, nunc ab Herberto episcopo in Norwic; Scireburnensis in Salesberiam; Dorcestrensis in Lincoliam. Nam Lindisfarnensis pridem ueteri tempore transierat in Dunelmum, et nuper Wellensis in Bathoniam.

301. In hoc conuentu Lanfrancus, qui erat adhuc rudis Anglus, quesiuit a senioribus episcopis[a] qui esset ordo sedendi in concilio antiquo more statutus; illi uero, excusata difficultate responsi, in diem distulerunt posterum. Et tunc diligentissime aduocata memoria hunc se uidisse morem asseruere, ut Cantuariae archiepiscopus concilio presidens habeat a dextro latere archiepiscopum Eboraci, et iuxta eum episcopum Wintoniae, a sinistro autem Lundoniensem; quod si, ut contingit, pro aliqua necessitate Cantuariensis primas aduentum suum negauerit[b] uel obitu defuerit, Eboracensis archiepiscopus concilio presidens habeat[c] a dextra Lundoniensem episcopum, a sinistra Wintoniensem; ceteri secundum tempora ordinationum sedilia sua agnoscant.

302. Tunc quoque querela archiepiscopi Eboracensis de clamore in Wigorniensem et Dorcacestrensem episcopos decisa et sopita est. Namque dicebat eos suae ditioni subiacere debere; quod cum iam dudum muto silentio ruminasset, Romam cum Lanfranco profectus ut pallia sua ab apostolico reciperent, palam audiente senatu Romano extulit. Tunc[d] uero Lanfrancus, quanuis ad omnes iniurias inconcussae soliditatis esset, nonnichil tamen tam proterua et ante sibi inaudita postulatione turbatus, irae motum uultu prodidit, uerbis aliquandiu
2 intra fauces deuoratis. At Alexander papa, qui grauaretur Lanfrancum contristare (nam et uenienti dignanter assurrexerat, professus illud insigne reuerentiae non se detulisse honori archiepiscopii sed amori magisterii), tunc quoque iudicandi inuidiam a se reiecit,[e] litis arbitrium traiciens in Anglorum concilium. Quapropter, ut dixi, res multum diuque uentilata in hoc concilio hunc sortita est terminum, ut, quia

---

[a] Anglis *T'* (adding episcopis *after* sedendi)   [b] excusauerit *T'A* (cf. e.g. GP p. 159)   [c] habeatque *BkBc²*, habebatque *Bc'*   [d] tum *T'A*   [e] reicit *AlBk*, remouit *Bc²* (rom- *Bc'*)

bishops should quit villages and establish their sees in the cities of their dioceses: Lichfield therefore was moved to Chester (formerly called the City of Legions), Selsey to Chichester, Elmham first to Thetford and now by Bishop Herbert to Norwich, Sherborne to Salisbury, Dorchester to Lincoln. For long since, in ancient times, Lindisfarne had moved to Durham, and recently Wells to Bath.

301. In this assembly Lanfranc, who was still unfamiliar with England, asked the senior bishops what order of sitting in council was established by ancient custom, and they, giving the difficulty of the question as an excuse, put it off till next day. After very carefully recalling the tradition, they then declared that the usage they had witnessed was as follows: The archbishop of Canterbury as presiding over the council should have the archbishop of York on his right, and next to him the bishop of Winchester; on his left the bishop of London. If for any necessity, as sometimes happens, the primate of Canterbury has excused himself from attending, or if he has been prevented by death, the archbishop of York as presiding over the council should have the bishop of London on his right and Winchester on his left, and the others should identify their seats in accordance with their order of consecration.

302. At the same time the complaint of the archbishop of York touching his claim against the bishops of Worcester and Dorchester was decided and laid to rest; for he maintained that they ought to be subject to his jurisdiction, and this, after turning it over in his mind for a long time in complete silence, he had brought forward openly in the hearing of the Roman senate, when he and Lanfranc had gone to Rome so that each might receive his pallium from the pope. Whereupon Lanfranc, although firm and unmoved by all unfair attacks, was somewhat provoked by such an impertinent demand, the like of which he had never heard before, and showed signs of rising anger in his face, though for some time he choked back his words. Pope Alexander, however, who was reluctant to cause Lanfranc any distress—on his entrance he had graciously risen to his feet, declaring that he paid this sign of respect not to the credit of the archbishopric but to his love for his old teacher—on this occasion too declined the invidious task of passing judgement, and remitted the decision of the dispute to an English council. For this reason, as I have said, the question was long and deeply discussed in this council, and the following conclusion was reached: these

citra Humbram essent, hi episcopi Cantuariensi applicarentur, omnes uero Transhumbranos Eboracensis obtineret.

303. Hic sancta simplicitas beati Wlstani Wigorniensis episcopi, immo magnanima in Deo confidentia, laudanda et plausu excipienda est. Cum enim et de hac re et de parua scientia litterarum[a] pulsatus foras exisset ut strictiori[b] consilio responsum comeret suum, a tumultibus remoto animo 'Crede michi', inquit 'nondum cantauimus horam sextam. Cantemus ergo.' Tum[c] sotiis referentibus ut prius propter quod uenerant expedirent, quod satis superque sufficeret cantibus tempus, regem et proceres, si haec audierint, risui se haberi opinaturos, 'Prius, crede michi,' dixit 'fatiemus[d] Dei seruitium, et post agitabimus hominum litigium'. Hora igitur cantata,[e] nulla excogitata falsi tergiuersatione, nullo commentato ueri splendore, confestim aulam concilii 2 ingredi pergebat. Suis eum retinere temptantibus persuaderi non potuit; quin potius timentibus causae 'Pro certo' ait 'noueritis uisibiliter me hic uidere[f] beatos archiepiscopos Dunstanum Cantuariensem et Oswaldum Eboracensem, qui hodie suis me precibus[g] tuentes falsiloquorum acumen hebetabunt.' Ita data benedictione monacho,[1] minimae facundiae uiro sed Normannicae linguae sciolo, rem perorans obtinuit ut, qui suae diocesis ante indignus putabatur regimine, ab archiepiscopo Eboraci[h] supliciter rogaretur ut suas dignaretur lustrare, quo ipse pro timore hostium uel sermonis ignorantia cauebat accedere.

304. Verum ego non ulterius lectorum expectationem macerabo, qui haec forsitan non libenter intuentur, quia gesta Willelmi successorum prestolantur; quanuis, nisi me nimius amor mei fallit, nulli uarietatem relationum displicituram opinor, nisi si quis tam nubilus est ut Catonis supercilium emuletur. Sed alia in quarto et quinto libro qui uolet experietur; nam tertius debitum agnoscit modum.

[a] litt. sc. *T¹*   [b] astrictiori *CBk(-ore Bc), but cf. GP p. 284*   [c] *A adds* quo   [d] faciamus *B*   [e] *T¹* adds et   [f] uideri *A*   [g] precibus me *A*   [h] Eboracensi *T¹*

[1] Apparently the translator.

bishops, being on this side of the Humber, should be attached to Canterbury, and all those beyond should be assigned to York.

303. At this point the saintly simplicity—say rather, the greathearted confidence in God—shown by the blessed Wulfstan, bishop of Worcester, should be extolled, and received with acclamation. When he was being attacked both in this connection and for his own illiteracy, and had left the meeting in order to give more devoted attention to the framing of his reply, he distanced his mind from the hubbub, and 'I'll tell you what', he said: 'We haven't yet sung sext. Let's sing it now.' His companions replied that they should first finish what they had come for, and that there would be time enough and more for singing; the king and the nobles, if they heard of this, would think they were being made a laughing-stock. 'I'll tell you what', he said: 'We will perform our service to God first, and after that we'll deal with the disputes of men.' So they sang the office, and then, without thinking up any falsehood by way of subterfuge or contriving any dazzling presentation of the truth, he proceeded at once to enter the hall where the council was sitting. When his people tried to restrain him, he could not be persuaded—quite the reverse: while they feared for the success of his case, 'Let me tell you this', he said. 'Here, before my very eyes, I can see the saintly archbishops Dunstan of Canterbury and Oswald of York, who defend me this day with their prayers, and will blunt the arrows of those who speak lies.' So he gave his blessing to a monk[1] who was far from being a skilled speaker but had some knowledge of the Norman tongue, made his final summing-up, and won the case; so that the man who was previously considered unfit to rule his diocese was humbly begged by the archbishop of York to deign to conduct the visitation of his own dioceses, in places to which he was afraid to go, either from fear of the enemy or from ignorance of the language.

304. But I will not torment my readers any further with suspense, who maybe do not regard all this with any satisfaction, because they are waiting for the history of William's successors; although (unless excessive self-love deceives me) I take it that no one will object to some variety in my narrative, unless he is so clouded in mind that he imitates the critical disdain of a Cato. But he who so wishes will find other anecdotes in my fourth and fifth books; for my third book here accepts its proper end.

LIBER QVARTVS

Prologus libri quarti

Scio plerisque ineptum uideri quod gestis nostri temporis regum scribendis stilum applicuerim, dicentibus quod in eiusmodi scriptis sepe naufragatur ueritas et suffragatur falsitas; quippe presentium mala periculose, bona plausibiliter dicuntur. Eo fit, inquiunt, ut, quia modo*ᵃ* omnia magis ad peius quam ad melius sunt procliuia, scriptor obuia mala propter metum pretereat et bona, si non sunt, propter plausum confingat. Sunt alii qui nos ex segnitie*ᵇ* sua metientes impares tanto muneri existimant, et hoc studium praua sugillatione contaminant.

2 Quapropter iam pridem uel illorum ratiocinio uel istorum fastidio perculsus*ᶜ* in otium concesseram, silentio libenter adquiescens; sed dum aliquandiu solutus inertia uacassem, rursus solitus amor studiorum aurem uellit et manum iniecit, propterea quod nec nichil agere*ᵈ* possem, et istis forensibus et homine litterato indignis curis me tradere non nossem. Accessere amicorum meorum stimuli, quorum uel tacitae suggestioni deesse non debui, et illi quidem modeste iam prur-
3 ientem impulere ut ceptum persequerer. Illorum itaque quos penitus*ᵉ* reposito amore diligo hortatibus animatus assurgo, ut ex pectoris nostri promptuario uicturum apud se amicitiae pignus contineant. Quocirca illorum qui michi timent ut aut odiar aut mentiar beniuolentiae gratus, ita sub ope Christi satisfatiam ut nec falsarius nec odiosus inueniar; sic enim bene et secus acta perstringam ut, quasi inter Scillam et Caribdim illeso uolante nauigio, nichil desit sententiae, etsi aliquid deesse putetur
4 historiae. Porro illis qui alieni laboris onus sua estimatione premunt hoc respondeo quod olim sanctus Hieronymus canibus suis obiecit: 'Si placet, legant; si non placet, abitiant',[1] quia et ego haec*ᶠ* non tediosis ingero sed studiosis, si qui dignentur, consecro; quod et isti iuri

---

ᵃ T'A add pene   *ᵇ* segnitione A   *ᶜ* percussus T'Bc'   *ᵈ* addere T'   *ᵉ* om. T'   *ᶠ* om. T'

[1] Jerome, Praef. ad Ezram (PL xxviii. 1406).

BOOK FOUR

Prologue

MOST people, I know, will think it unwise to have turned my pen to the history of the kings of my own time; they will say that in works of this character truth is often disastrous and falsehood profitable, for in writing of contemporaries it is dangerous to criticize, while praise is sure of a welcome. Thus it is, they maintain, that with everything nowadays tending to the worse rather than the better, an author will pass over the evils that meet him on every hand, to be on the safe side, and as for good actions, if he cannot find any, he will invent them to secure a good reception. Others, judging my industry by their own lack of it, reckon me unequal to the greatness of my task, and try to poison my enterprise by their insinuations. Moved by the reasoning of one 2 party or the contempt of the other, I had long since retired to a life of leisure, content to remain silent; but after a period of idleness, my old love of study plucked me by the ear and laid its hand on my shoulder, for I was incapable of doing nothing, and knew not how to devote myself to those business cares which are so unworthy of a man of letters. Besides, there was the incitement of my friends, with whose slightest hints it was my duty to comply; and they for their part gently urged me, eager as I already was, to continue what I had begun. Quickened therefore by the encouragement of those whom I love with 3 the deepest affection, I set to work, that they may receive from my heart's treasure-house an enduring pledge of friendship. Grateful as I am therefore for the sympathy of those who fear on my behalf the alternatives of unpopularity or mendacity, I will give them satisfaction, with Christ's help, in such a way as to be found neither mendacious nor unpopular. I will so summarize doings, both good and bad, that as my ship speeds unhurt between Scylla and Charybdis, my information may perhaps be found wanting, but not my judgement. Those again 4 who depreciate the burden of another's toil, I would answer with the retort which St Jerome long ago cast at the dogs that barked at him: 'Let them read me if they like, and throw me away if they do not.'[1] Like him, I am not forcing my work upon those who are easily bored; I dedicate it to such lovers of learning as may deign to accept it; and even my critics will declare that this is reasonable, unless they are of

concinere pronuntiabunt, si non de his sunt de quibus dicitur: 'Stulti facile possunt conuinci, difficile compesci.'[1] Dicam igitur in hoc libro, qui huius operis est quartus, quicquid de Willelmo filio Willelmi Magni dici poterit, ut nec ueritas rerum titubet nec principalis de-
5 coloretur maiestas. Ibunt et in istas paginas quaedam quae sub eo uel in hac terra tristia uel alias gloriosa acciderunt, quantum dumtaxat nostra scientia attingere potuerit,[a] presertim de peregrinatione Christianorum in Ierusalem; quam hic apponere non erit iniurium, quia tam famosam his diebus expeditionem audire sit operae pretium et uirtutis incitamentum. Neque uero confido quod haec a me quam ab aliis qui scripserunt dicantur commodius, sed ut quod a multis scribitur a multis legatur. Verum ne tam diu prohemiari lecturo generet nausiam, iam nunc quod intendo incipiam.

305. Willelmus igitur filius Willelmi natus est Normanniae pluribus annis antequam pater Angliam adiret. Ingenti cura parentum altus, cum et illi naturaliter inesset ingentia parturiens animus, ad culmen supremae dignitatis euasit: incomparabilis proculdubio nostro tempore princeps, si non eum magnitudo patris obrueret, nec eius iuuentutem fata precipitassent, ne per aetatem maturiorem aboleret errores licentia
2 potestatis et impetu iuuenili contractos. Emensa pueritia in militari exercitio adolescentiam egit: equitare,[b] iaculari, certare cum primaeuis obsequio, cum aequaeuis offitio. Iacturam uirtutis putare si forte in militari tumultu alter eo prior arma corriperet, et nisi primus ex aduerso prouocaret uel prouocantem deiceret. Genitori in omnibus obsequelam gerens, eius se oculis in bello ostentans, eius lateri in pace obambulans. Spe sensim scaturiente iam successioni inhians, maxime post abdicationem fratris maioris, cum et tirocinium minoris nonnichil
3 suspiceret. Ita a patre ultima ualitudine decumbente in successorem adoptatus, antequam ille extremum efflasset ad occupandum regnum contendit, moxque uolentibus animis prouintialium exceptus et claues thesaurorum nactus est, quibus fretus totam Angliam animo subiecit suo. Accessit etiam fauori eius maximum rerum momentum, archiepiscopus Lanfrancus, eo[c] quod eum nutrierat et militem fecerat; quo

---

[a] potuit *T'A*   [b] equitari *CB*   [c] om. *T'A*

[1] Unidentified.

that sort of which it is said that 'Fools are easy to convince but difficult to control'.[1] I will tell therefore in this book, the fourth of my whole work, whatever there is to be told about William, son of William the Great, in such a way that the truth of history is not shaken, and no slur is cast upon the majesty of the Crown. These pages will also include certain events of his time, whether disasters in this country or great doings overseas, so far at least as my information can extend; in particular the Christians' pilgrimage to Jerusalem, which it will not be wrong to insert here, for to hear of such a famous enterprise in our own time is worthwhile in itself, and an inspiration to brave deeds. Not that I am confident of telling the story in more fitting language than others who have set it down; my purpose is to make the work of many writers accessible to many readers. But I must not sicken my future readers by the length of my preamble; so now to work.

305. King William's son, William, was born in Normandy several years before his father came to England. Brought up as he was by his parents with the greatest care, and naturally gifted with a spirit prolific of great ideas, he reached the highest point of supreme power—a prince unquestionably without peer in our own time, had he not been overshadowed by his father's greatness, and had fate not overtaken him at an early age, and thus prevented the faults developed by unlimited power and youthful spirits from being corrected by maturer years. His boyhood spent, he passed his youth in knightly exercises, riding and shooting, competing with his elders in courtesy, with his contemporaries in courtly duties; he thought it detrimental to his honour if anyone in a knightly affray set hand on sword before himself, and unless he was the first either to challenge the adversary or to unhorse the challenger. To his father he was always obedient, displaying himself in battle before his eyes, and walking by his side in peacetime. Thus his hopes gradually rose and he began to covet the succession, especially after his elder brother had 'abdicated'; although his younger brother, even in his adolescence, was giving him some cause for suspicion. Nominated on his father's deathbed as the successor, he made haste, before the king had breathed his last, to take possession of the kingdom; and being welcomed by the inhabitants, also secured the key of the royal treasure; by the power of which he subjected all England to his will. His popularity was increased by the support of Archbishop Lanfranc, the most powerful influence in affairs, for it was he who had reared him and made him knight; Lanfranc was the moving spirit in his

auctore et annitente die sanctorum Cosmae et Damiani coronatus, reliquo hiemis quiete et fauorabiliter uixit.

306. Qua exacta, mox in initio ueris primus illi conflictus, contra Odonem patruum, episcopum Baiocensem, fuit. Namque cum ille, ut dixi,[1] solutus a uinculis Rotbertum nepotem in comitatu Normanniae confirmasset, Angliam uenit recepitque a rege comitatum Cantiae. Sed cum omnia non suo arbitratu, ut olim, in regno disponi uideret (nam Willelmo Dunelmensi episcopo commendata erat amministratio rerum publicarum), liuore ictus a rege et ipse desciuit et multos eodem sus-
2 urro infecit: Rotberto regnum competere, qui sit et remissioris animi et iuueniles stultitias multis iam laboribus decoxerit; hunc delicate nutritum, animi ferotia quam uultus ipse demonstret pretumidum, omnia contra fas et ius ausurum; breui futurum ut honores iam dudum plurimis sudoribus partos amittant; nichil actum[a] morte patris, si quos ille uinxerit iste trucidet. Haec ipse, haec Rogerius de Monte Gomerico, haec Gaufridus Constantiensis episcopus cum nepote Rotberto comite Humbrensium et cum reliquis primo clam fremebant, post etiam
3 palam per ueredarios missis epistolis frequentabant. Quin etiam Willelmus Dunelmensis episcopus, quem rex a secretis habuerat, in eorum perfidiam concesserat; quod grauiter regem tulisse ferunt, quia cum amissae caritatis dispendio remotarum prouintiarum frustrabatur compendio. Itaque Odo predam omnem Rofecestram comportabat, regios fiscos in Cantia deuastans, maxime terras archiepiscopi, immortale in eum odium anhelans, quod eius consilio a fratre se in uincula coniectum asserebat. Sed nec fides uerborum uacillabat; nam cum olim Willelmus senior apud Lanfrancum quereretur se a fratre deseri, 'Tu' inquit 'prende eum et uinci'. 'Et quid' respondit ille 'quia clericus est?' Tum archiepiscopus lepida hilaritate, ut Persius ait,[2] crimina rasis librans in antithetis, 'Non' dixit 'episcopum Baiocarum capies, sed
4 comitem Cantiae custodies.' Gaufridus episcopus cum nepote, Bathoniam et Bercheleiam partemque pagi Wiltensis depopulans, manubias apud Bristou collocabat. Rogerius de Monte Gomerico, exercitum suum a Scrobbesberia cum Walensibus mittens, coloniam Wigorniensem predabatur, iamque Wigorniam infestus adueneratur cum regii

---

[a] auctum T[t]

[1] 277. 3.   [2] i. 85–6.

coronation on the feast of SS Cosmas and Damian; and for the rest of the winter he enjoyed peace and popularity.

306. Winter once over, he met his first opposition at the beginning of spring, from his uncle Odo bishop of Bayeux. When Odo, on being released from captivity as I have told,[1] had confirmed his nephew Robert as duke of Normandy, he came to England and received from the king the earldom of Kent. He saw, however, that he was no longer, as in former times, to have everything in the country all his own way, the conduct of public business having been entrusted to William bishop of Durham; and in a fit of jealousy he himself deserted the king and infected many others by the same insinuations. The throne belonged, he said, to Robert, who was of milder disposition, and by a long period of activity had corrected the follies of youth; William, with his delicate nurture, and the fierce arrogance so visible in the very expression of his face, would ride roughshod over law and justice. 'It will not be long before we lose the honour we have earned by long-continued effort; we shall have gained nothing by the father's death if those whom he made captive are slain by his son.' Such was the talk of Odo, of Roger of Montgomery, and Geoffrey bishop of Coutances, with his nephew Robert earl of the Northumbrians and the rest—secret, seditious talk at first, but soon they were corresponding by messengers, and developed it openly. Even William bishop of Durham, who was in the king's inner counsels, had joined in their revolt; which was, they say, a severe blow to the king, who lost personally a dear friend and politically the resources of the outlying counties. And so Odo set about collecting all his loot at Rochester, ravaging the royal domain in Kent, but especially the lands of the archbishop, against whom he had conceived a deathless hatred as allegedly responsible for his imprisonment by his brother William. Nor was Odo far wrong, for once when William was complaining to Lanfranc of his brother's treachery, the archbishop's reply was: 'Arrest him and lock him up!' 'What!', said the king, 'a clergyman?' The archbishop laughed, balancing, as Persius[2] says, 'charge against charge in neat antithesis'. 'No', he retorted, 'you will not be arresting the bishop of Bayeux, you will be taking into custody the earl of Kent.' Bishop Geoffrey, aided by his nephew, was ravaging Bath and Berkeley and part of Wiltshire, and storing his booty at Bristol. Roger of Montgomery, despatching his forces with the Welsh from Shrewsbury, was despoiling the territory of Worcester, and had already arrived before the city with hostile intent, when the king's troops who

milites qui pretendebant, freti benedictione Wlstani episcopi cui custodia castelli commissa erat, pauci multos effugarunt, pluribusque sautiis et cesis quosdam abduxerunt. Preterea Rogerius Bigot apud Norwic et Hugo de Grentemesnil apud Legecestram suis quisque partibus rapinas urgebant.

5   Ita totis defectionis uiribus in eum cui nec prudentia nec fortuna deerat frustra seuiebatur. Namque ille, uidens Normannos pene omnes in una rabie conspiratos, Anglos probos et fortes uiros, qui adhuc residui erant, inuitatoriis scriptis accersiit; quibus super iniuriis suis querimoniam fatiens bonasque leges et tributorum leuamen liberasque uenationes pollicens, fidelitati suae obligauit. Nec minori astutia Rogerium de Monte Gomerico, secum dissimulata perfidia equi-
6   tantem, circumuenit. Seorsum enim ducto magnam ingessit inuidiam, dicens libenter se*a* imperio cessurum si illi et aliis uideatur quos pater tutores reliquerat. Non se intelligere quid ita effrenes sint; si uelint pecunias, accipiant pro libito; si augmentum patrimoniorum, eodem modo prorsus quae uelint habeant. Tantum uideant ne iuditium genitoris periclitetur, quod si de se putauerint aspernandum, de se ipsis caueant exemplum; idem enim se regem qui illos duces fecerit. His uerbis comes et pollicitationibus incensus, qui primus factionis post
7   Odonem signifer fuit, primus defecit. Continuo ergo in desertores profectus, castella patrui sui Tunebrigge et Peuenesel effregit, ipso in posteriori intercepto; captum ad quod libuit iusiurandum impulit, ut Anglia decederet et Rofecestram traderet. Ad quod implendum eum cum fidelibus suis premisit, lento pede preeuntes subsecutus.*b* Erat tunc apud Rofecestram omnis pene iuuentutis ex Anglia et Normannia nobilitas, tres filii Rogerii comitis et Eustachius Bononiae iunior multique alii quos infra curam nostram existimo. Regii cum episcopo pauci et inermes (quis enim eo presente insidias timeret?) circa muros desiliunt, clamantes oppidanis ut portas aperiant; hoc episcopum
8   presentem uelle, hoc regem absentem iubere. At illi, de muro conspicati quod uultus episcopi cum uerbis oratorum non conueniret,*c* raptim apertis portis ruunt, equos inuolant, omnesque cum episcopo

---

a se libenter *T^t Bc*   *b* prosecutus *T^t*   *c* conuenirent *T^t Bk*

were defending it, inspired by the blessing of Bishop Wulfstan, who had been entrusted with the command of the castle, though greatly outnumbered put his men to flight, killed and wounded many, and took some prisoners. Besides which, Roger Bigod with his party was spreading destruction at Norwich, and Hugh of Grandmesnil with his at Leicester.

Such was the fruitless ferocity exerted by the rebels with all their might, against a king who lacked neither policy nor good fortune. He, when he saw the Normans almost to a man united in this mad conspiracy, sent a letter of invitation to all the English, good men and true, who yet remained; and complaining of his wrongs, bound them to his service, with the promise of good laws, lighter imposts, and freer hunting. With equal skill he got round Roger of Montgomery, who had kept his treachery a secret and was still riding in his train. Taking him on one side the king loaded him with complaints, saying that he would gladly resign the crown if he, and the others whom his father had appointed as his guardians, thought that right. 'I cannot understand', he said, 'why you are all so ungovernable. If you want money, take as much as you like, and the same with land; you are welcome. Only, mind you do not have my father's wisdom called in question; if you think he was wrong about me, take care that this does not reflect on yourselves. The same man who made me king chose you as magnates.' Such arguments and promises aroused the earl, and he who had been as standard-bearer of revolt second only to Odo, was the first to change sides. The king at once proceeded against the rebels, broke into his uncle's castles at Tonbridge and Pevensey, and in the latter seized the bishop himself. He made his captive take an oath at his dictation—to leave England and to surrender Rochester—and sent him on ahead with some reliable men of his own to carry this out, while he himself followed slowly. Rochester at that moment contained, one might say, the pick of the younger nobles from England and Normandy—the three sons of Earl Roger, the younger Eustace of Boulogne, and many others who need not, I think, be mentioned. The king's men who formed the bishop's escort were few and unarmed, for with the bishop in their keeping there was no fear of any unexpected turn; dismounting round the walls they called to the men in the town to open their gates, such being the wish of the bishop who was present and the order of the king, who was not. The townsmen, who could see from the walls that the bishop's face contradicted those who spoke on his behalf, opened their gates and sallied out at top speed, seized the horses, tied up the

uinctos abducunt. Rumor facti ad regem cito perlabitur. Seuerior ille malis, iramque intra conscientiam resorbens, Anglos suos appellat; iubet ut compatriotas aduocent ad obsidionem uenire, nisi si qui uelint sub nomine Nithing, quod nequam sonat, remanere. Angli, qui nichil miserius putarent quam huiusce uocabuli dedecore aduri, cateruatim ad regem confluunt, et inuincibilem exercitum fatiunt. Nec diutius potuere pati oppidani quin se traderent, experti quamlibet nobilem, quamlibet consertam manum nichil aduersus regem Angliae posse
9 proficere. Odo, secundo captus, perpetuo Angliam abiurauit. Dunelmensis episcopus ultro mare transiuit, quem rex uerecundia preteritae amicitiae indempnem[a] passus est effugere. Ceteri omnes in fidem recepti. Inter has obsidionis moras, homines regis mare custodientes quosdam, quos comes Normanniae in auxilium perfidorum miserat, partim cede partim naufragio oppressere; reliqui fugam intendentes et suspendere carbasa conati, moxque uento cessante destituti, ludibrio nostris, sibi exitio fuere, nam ne uiui caperentur e transtris se in mare precipitarunt.

307. Postero anno, ut dolor semper[b] retractatione acescit, magno scrutinio rex agere cepit quomodo iniurias suas ultum iret et uicariam fratri contumeliam referret. Itaque castrum sancti Walerici et portum uicinum et oppidum quod Albamarla uocatur sollertia sua adquisiuit, pecunia custodes corrumpens. Nec fuit animus comiti ut resisteret, sed domino suo regi Frantiae per nuntios[c] uiolentiam fratris exposuit, suppetias orans. Et ille quidem iners et cotidianam crapulam ructans ad bellum singultiens ingluuie ueniebat; sed occurrerunt magna pollicenti nummi regis Angliae, quibus infractus cingulum soluit et conuiuium
2 repetiit. Ita bello intestino diu laborauit Normannia, modo illis modo istis uincentibus; proceres utriusque furorem incitabant, homines leuissimi in neutra parte fidem habentes. Pauci quibus sanius consilium, consulentes suis commodis quod utrobique possessiones haberent, mediatores pacis fuere, ut comiti rex Cinomannis adquireret, comes regi castella quae habebat et Fiscamnum cenobium concederet.

[a] om. T¹   [b] om. T¹   [c] T¹ adds suos

bishop's escort and led them all off as prisoners. The news soon reached the king. The setback only made him more stern; he suppressed his anger, and appealed to his English followers, telling them to summon their fellow-countrymen to the siege, unless any wished to remain behind and be called *Nithing*, which means worthless. The English, who thought nothing more wretched than to be branded with this name, rallied to the king in crowds, and formed an invincible host. Nor could the townsmen hold out any longer without surrender, finding that no party however noble and well-disciplined could prevail against the king of England. Odo, taken prisoner for the second time, forswore England in perpetuity; the bishop of Durham voluntarily went overseas, being allowed to leave the realm unharmed out of respect for their former friendship, and the rest were admitted to take the oath of allegiance. While things were held up by the siege, the king's men who were guarding the sea wiped out, partly in action and partly by shipwreck, some of a force despatched by the duke of Normandy to aid the insurgents; the survivors tried to get away and attempted to hoist sail, but the wind soon dropped, leaving them becalmed, which ended in an entertaining spectacle for our men and disaster for them, for rather than be taken alive they plunged from their thwarts into the sea.

307. Next year, resentment as usual being embittered by retrospection, the king began exhaustive enquiries to discover how he could avenge his wrongs and inflict disgrace on his brother in turn. As a result, he employed his usual tactics to secure the castle and nearby harbour of Saint-Valery, and the town called Aumale, by bribing the men in charge. Nor had the duke any spirit to resist; he reported his brother's offensive action to his lord the king of France, and asked for help. Lazy as he was, and belching up his daily potations, the king was preparing with many a glutton's hiccup to take the field, when his lavish promises of help were forestalled by the coin of the English king. This melted him; he unbuckled his belt, and returned to the pleasures of the table. Thus Normandy suffered long from a civil war, in which first one side was successful and then the other, each party being roused to fury by the nobles, men of no worth at all and loyal to neither side. A few men of more sense, consulting their own interests as they had possessions both sides of the Channel, negotiated a peace, on terms that the king should acquire Maine for the duke, and the duke should relinquish to the king the castles which he held, and the monastery of

Iuratum est hoc pactum, et ab utrorumque hominibus sacramento firmatum.

308. Nec multo post rex mare transiit ut fidem promissorum expleret. Ergo uterque dux ingentes moliebantur conatus ut Cinomannis inuaderent; sed obstitit iam paratis iamque profecturis Henrici fratris minoris animositas, qui frenderet propter fratrum auaritiam, quod uterque possessiones paternas diuiderent, et se omnium pene expertem non erubescerent. Itaque Montem sancti Michahelis armatus insedit, et crebris excursibus obsidentem militiam germanorum contristauit. In ea obsidione precluum specimen morum in rege et comite apparuit, in altero mansuetudinis, in altero magnanimitatis; utriusque exempli notas pro legentium notitia affigam.

309. Egressus rex tabernaculo uidensque eminus hostes superbum inequitantes, solus in multos irruit, alacritate uirtutis impatiens simulque confidens nullum sibi ausurum obsistere; moxque occiso sub feminibus deturbatus equo, quem eo die quindecim marcis argenti emerat, etiam per pedem diu tractus est, sed fides loricae obstitit ne lederetur. Iamque miles qui deiecerat manum ad capulum aptabat ut feriret, cum ille periculo extremo territus exclamat: 'Tolle, nebulo! Rex Angliae sum.' Tremuit nota uoce iacentis uulgus militum, statimque reuerenter de terra leuato equum alterum adducunt.
2 Ille non expectato ascensorio sonipedem insiliens, omnesque circumstantes uiuido perstringens oculo, 'Quis' inquit 'me deiecit?' Mussitantibus cunctis, miles audacis facti conscius non defuit patrocinio suo, dicens: 'Ego, qui te non putarem esse regem sed militem.' Tum uero rex placidus uultuque serenus, 'Per uultum' ait 'de Luca,' (sic enim iurabat) 'meus amodo eris, et meo albo insertus laudabilis militiae premia reportabis'. Macte animi, amplissime rex, quod tibi preconium super hoc dicto[a] rependam?—a magni quondam Alexandri non degener[b] gloria, qui Persam militem se a tergo ferire conatum, sed pro perfidia ensis spe sua frustratum, incolumem pro admiratione fortitudinis conseruauit.

[a] dato B [b] degeneras T¹

Fécamp. So the treaty was sworn to, and ratified on oath by the men of both sides.

308. Not long after that, the king went overseas to fulfil his promises. Great were the feats of preparation set on foot by both commanders for the invasion of Maine; but when they were just ready and about to set out, they were brought to a halt by the enmity of their younger brother Henry, gnashing his teeth at the greed of two brothers capable of dividing up their paternal inheritance and shamelessly leaving him almost destitute. Consequently he occupied Mont-Saint-Michel with an armed force, and by frequent sallies did much mischief to his brothers' besieging troops. During the siege, both kings and duke gave a most characteristic display, the one of mildness and the other of generosity, and I will subjoin a brief account of each for the reader's information.

309. Coming out of his tent, the king saw the enemy arrogantly riding along at some distance, and charged the whole body, alone as he was, carried away by his intemperate courage, and confident that none would dare to stand against him. Soon his horse, which he had bought that day for fifteen marks of silver, was killed beneath him, and he was thrown and actually dragged for some distance by the foot; but his trusty corselet saved him from hurt. The knight who had unseated him was already grasping his sword-hilt to strike him dead, when shaken by the imminent danger he cried out: 'Lay off, you wretch! I am the king of England.' The whole troop heard the well-known voice, as he lay there, and trembled; at once they raised him respectfully from the ground and brought him another horse. Vaulting onto his charger without waiting for the mounting-block, he glared at them all with flashing eyes as they stood round. 'Who was it', he said, 'unhorsed me?' While they all hung back, the knight who had this deed of daring on his conscience showed that he was able to defend himself, saying: 'I, sire; I thought you were a knight and not the king.' At that the king was pacified, and his brow cleared. 'By the holy Face of Lucca!', he said (it was his favourite oath), 'henceforth you must be my man: you shall be entered on my list and win the rewards due to honourable service.' Bravo, most generous king! How can I praise you for words like these? You fall not short of the glory of great Alexander long ago, who, when a Persian knight tried to cut him down from behind and was foiled by the breaking of his sword, spared his life out of admiration for his courage.

310. Iam uero ut de mansuetudine comitis dicam, cum obsidio eo usque processisset ut aqua deesset obsessis,[a] misit Henricus nuntios comiti qui eum de siti sua conueniant: impium esse ut eum aqua arceant, quae esset communis mortalibus; aliter, si uelit, uirtutem experiatur, nec pugnet uiolentia elementorum sed uirtute militum. Tum ille, genuina[b] mentis mollitie flexus, suos qua pretendebant laxius
2 habere se iussit, ne frater siticulosus potu careret. Quod cum relatum regi esset, ut semper calori pronus erat, comiti dixit: 'Belle[c] scis actitare guerram, qui hostibus prebes aquae copiam; et quomodo eos domabimus, si eis et in pastu et in potu indulserimus?' At ille renidens illud come et merito famosum uerbum emisit: 'Pape, dimitterem fratrem nostrum mori siti? Et quem alium habebimus si eum amiserimus?' Ita rex, deridens mansueti hominis ingenium, resoluit prelium, infectaque re quam intenderat, quod eum Scottorum et Walensium tumultus uocabant, in regnum se cum ambobus fratribus recepit.

311. Statimque primo contra Walenses, post in Scottos expeditionem mouens, nichil magnificentia sua dignum exhibuit, militibus multis desideratis, iumentis interceptis. Nec tunc solum sed et multotiens parua illi in Walenses fortuna fuit; quod cuiuis mirum uideatur, cum ei alias semper alea bellorum felicissime arriserit. Sed ego intelligo pro soli inaequalitate et caeli inclementia sicut rebellionem eorum adiutam, ita eius uirtutem impeditam. Porro rex Henricus, excellentis ingenii uir, qui modo regnat, inuenit qua commenta illorum labefactaret arte, Flandritis in patria eorum[d] collocatis, qui eis pro
2 claustro sint et eos perpetuo coherceant. At uero tunc[e] satagente Rotberto comite, qui familiarem iam dudum apud Scottum locauerat gratiam, inter Malcolmum et Willelmum concordia inita. Veruntamen multis controuersiis utrobique habitis, et fluctuante propter utrorumque animositatem[f] iustitia, Malcolmus ultro Gloecestram uenit, aequis dumtaxat conditionibus multus[g] pro pace precator; nec quicquam obtinuit, nisi ut in regnum indempnis rediret, dedignante rege dolo capere quem uirtute subegisset. Idemque proxima hieme ab

[a] obsessis deesset T'A [b] gemina T' [c] bene B [d] illorum T'
[e] tum T' [f] animositate AapB [g] multis Al, multas Aap

310. Now for a word on the duke's mildness. The blockade had reached a point at which the besieged were short of water, and Henry sent envoys to the duke to discuss their need of water with him: it was monstrous, he maintained, to deprive him of something common to all mankind; he must please find some other means to test his resolution, and let the valour of his knights, not the violence of the elements, decide the fight. With his natural softheartedness the duke relented, and ordered his men to slacken their watch a little where they were on guard, so that his thirsty brother need not go without a drink. When 2 the king heard the news, he flared up as usual. 'A pretty way to wage war,' he said to the duke, 'giving your enemies access to water! How are we expected to beat them, if we let them have all the meat and drink they need?' The duke with a smile uttered that courteous reply which has deservedly become historic: 'Good heavens', he said, 'should I leave our brother to die of thirst? And where shall we look for another if we lose this one?' So the king, with a scornful laugh at the man's mild temper, broke off the contest, and leaving his intentions unfulfilled (for revolt among both Scots and Welsh demanded his return) retired to his own kingdom with both his brothers.

311. Without delay he set on foot an expedition, first against the Welsh and then the Scots, but the results were unworthy of his grand conception; many knights were lost and baggage animals cut off. Nor was this the only occasion; it happened many times that he had small success against the Welsh, which might surprise anyone who knew his constant good fortune in the hazards of war elsewhere. But, as I understand it, the roughness of the country and the inclement climate were as much a handicap to his prowess as they were a positive aid to the rebels. (It was King Henry who now reigns, a man of outstanding intelligence, who discovered the art of undermining their schemes, by planting Flemings in their home-country to act as a barrier against them and contain them permanently.) On this occasion, by the agency 2 of Duke Robert who had long before established friendly relations with the king of the Scots, an agreement was concluded between Malcolm and William; but as many causes of dispute arose on each side, and justice was always in jeopardy through their dislike of one another, Malcolm at his own suggestion came to Gloucester and pleaded eloquently for peace, at any rate if it were on fair conditions. He secured no concessions, except permission to return to his kingdom without harm, the king disdaining, as he said, to take by trickery a man whom

hominibus Rotberti comitis Humbronensium magis fraude quam uiribus occubuit. Cuius interitus accepto nuntio, uxor Margareta elemosinis et pudicitia insignis, fastidiens huius lucis moram, mortem precario*ᵃ* exegit a Deo. *ᵇ*Ambo cultu pietatis insignes, illa precipue. Namque toto uitae tempore uiginti quattuor pauperes habebat, ubicumque locorum erat, quos cibis et uestibus refitiebat. Ceterum in Quadragesima sacerdotum cantum preueniens noctibus in templo excubabat, triplicibus matutinis ipsa insistens de Trinitate, de Cruce, de sancta Maria; inde psalterium cum lacrimis uestem infundentibus, pectus succutientibus. Templo digrediens pascebat pauperes primo tres, mox nouem, inde uiginti quattuor, postremo trecentos, ipsa cum rege assistens et manibus aquam infundens.*ᵇ* Edgarum filium eius,*ᶜ* expulsum a patruo, Willelmus reformauit solio, egregia plane et quae tantum uirum decebat pietate, ut paternarum iniuriarum immemor filium suplicem restitueret regno.

312. Excellebat in eo magnanimitas, quam ipse processu temporis nimia seueritate obfuscauit; ita in eius furtim pectus uitia pro uirtutibus serpebant ut discernere nequiret. Diu dubitauit mundus quo tandem uergeret, quo se inclinaret indoles illius. Inter initia, uiuente Lanfranco archiepiscopo, ab omni crimine abhorrebat, ut unicum fore regum speculum speraretur; quo defuncto, aliquandiu uarium se prestitit aequali lance uitiorum atque uirtutum; iam uero postremis annis *ᵈ*omni gelante studio uirtutum,   *ᵈ*bonorum gelante studio, incomuitiorum in eo calor efferbuit,*ᵈ*   modorum seges succrescens incaluit,*ᵈ*
et erat ita liberalis quod prodigus, ita magnanimus quod superbus, ita seuerus quod seuus. Liceat enim michi, pace maiestatis regiae, uerum non occuluisse, quia iste parum Deum reuerebatur, nichil homines; quod indiscretum si quis dixerit, non peccabit, quia haec*ᵉ* a sapientibus tenenda sit moderatio, ut Deus timeatur omni tempore, homo pro tempore. Erat is foris et in conuentu hominum tumido uultu erectus, minaci oculo astantem defigens, et affectato rigore feroci uoce colloquentem reuerberans; quantum coniectari datur, metu inopiae et

---

ᵃ precaria B   *ᵇ⁻ᵇ* om. T¹   *ᶜ* eorum T¹   *ᵈ⁻ᵈ* omni (omnis Aa) ... efferbuit T¹A; bonorum ... incaluit CB   *ᵉ* om. CB

iv. 312. 3   THE HISTORY OF THE ENGLISH KINGS   555

he might have vanquished by force of arms; and the winter following he was done to death, more by fraud than force, by the men of Robert earl of the Northumbrians. Hearing the news of his decease, his queen 3 Margaret, famous for her generosity and holy life, lost her taste for the world; she prayed God for death, and won her wish. Both were famous for their devotion, especially the queen. All her life long, wherever she was, she kept twenty-four poor persons, whom she fed and clothed. In Lent, she would anticipate the chanting of her chaplains and keep nightly vigil in the church, herself attending triple matins, of the Trinity, of the Cross, and of the Blessed Virgin, and then reciting the Psalter, her dress wet with her tears, her bosom heaving. On leaving the chapel, she used to feed the poor: three at first, soon nine, then twenty-four, and finally three hundred; she was there to receive them with the king, and poured water on their hands. Her son Edgar, who had been driven out by his uncle, was put back on the throne by William, an outstanding instance of generosity; it was worthy of so great a man, to forget the wrongs done by the father and restore the son to the throne, at his petition.

312. He was a man of high principles, which he himself obscured as in process of time he became unduly harsh; in such a way did vices creep into his heart little by little in place of virtues that he could not tell the difference. Long was the world in doubt which way his character at length would turn and settle. At the beginning of his reign, while Archbishop Lanfranc was still living, he refrained from all wrongdoing, and it was hoped that he would turn out a paragon among princes. On Lanfranc's death, for some time he showed himself changeable, virtue and vice equally balanced; but now in his later years 2

T¹A all his love of virtue grew   CB his love of good grew cold, and
cold, while the heat of vicious- the undesirable features warmed into
ness boiled up within him.   life within him like springing corn.

His open-handedness became prodigality, his high-mindedness pride, his strictness cruelty. With all respect to the king's majesty, give me leave not to conceal the truth. He respected God too little, and man not at all; wherein if anyone sees an error of judgement, he will not be far wrong, for wise men should observe the moderate rule of fearing God all the time, and man as the time may dictate. Abroad and in the 3 gatherings of men his aspect was haughty and unbending; he would fix the man before him with a threatening gaze, and with assumed severity and harsh voice overbear those with whom he spoke; as far as can be

aliorum perfidiae plus iusto lucris et seueritati deditus. Intus et in triclinio cum priuatis omni lenitate accommodus, multa ioco transigebat; facetissimus quoque de aliquo suo perperam facto cauillator, ut inuidiam facti dilueret et ad sales transferret. Sed de liberalitate eius, qua se ipsum fallebat, post etiam de ceteris, sermo prolixior erit, ut ostendam quanta uitia in eo sub pretextu uirtutum pullularint.[a]

313. Sunt enim duo omnino[b] genera largorum: alteri prodigi, alteri liberales dicuntur. Prodigi sunt qui in ea pecunias suas effundunt quorum memoriam aut breuem aut nullam omnino sunt relicturi[c] in seculo, nec elemosinam habituri in Deo; liberales sunt qui captos a predonibus redimunt aut inopes subleuant aut aes alienum amicorum suscipiunt. Est ergo largiendum,[d] sed diligenter et moderate; plures enim patrimonia sua effudere inconsulte largiendo. Quid uero est stultius quam quod libenter fatias, curare ne diutius facere possis? Itaque quidam, cum non habeant quod dent, ad rapinas conuertuntur, maiusque odium assecuntur ab his quibus auferunt quam 2 benefitium ab his quibus contulerunt. Quod huic regi accidisse dolemus. Namque cum primis initiis regni metu turbarum milites congregasset, nichil illis denegandum putabat, maiora in futurum pollicitus. Itaque quia paternos thesauros[e] euacuarat et modicae ei tunc pensiones numerabantur, iam substantia defecerat; sed animus largiendi non deerat, quod usum donandi pene in naturam uerterat, homo qui nesciret cuiuscumque rei effringere pretium uel estimare commertium, sed cui pro libito[f] uenditor distraheret mercimonium et 3 miles pacisceretur stipendium. Vestium suarum pretium in immensum extolli uolebat, dedignans si quis alleuiasset.[g] Denique quodam mane, cum calciaretur nouas caligas, interrogauit cubicularium quanti constitissent. Cum ille respondisset tres solidos, indignabundus et fremens 'Fili' ait 'meretricis, ex quo habet rex caligas tam exilis pretii? Vade, et affer michi emptas marca argenti.' Iuit ille, et multo uiliores afferens, quanti preceperat emptas ementitus est. 'Atqui' inquit rex

---

[a] pullularunt *TpB* [b] omnino *om. T'Bc (the word is present in the source, Cic. Off. ii. 55, but there, as in Bk, before* duo) [c] relicturi sunt *Tp(and Bc),* sunt rel. sunt *Tt* [d] ergo largiendum est *T'* [e] *T'A** add impigre [f] libitu *T'*
[g] alleuasset *AapCeB*

guessed, it was fear of poverty or of other people's treachery that made him unduly avaricious and a martinet. At home and in the chamber with his private friends, he was all mildness and complaisance, and relied much on jest to carry a point, being in particular a merry critic of his own mistakes, so as to reduce the unpopularity they caused and dissolve it in laughter. Of his liberality, in which he deceived himself, and thereafter of his other qualities, I will speak at greater length, that I may show how in him great vices grew under the cloak of virtues.

313. There are in the main two kinds of generous men: the prodigal, as we call him, and the liberal. The prodigals are those who pour out their money on purposes of which they will leave a brief memorial in this world or none at all, nor will they win with God the credit of almsgiving; the liberal is he who ransoms a captive from the hands of pirates, or helps the poor, or takes upon himself the debts of his friends. We ought therefore to be generous, but carefully and in moderation, for many men by inconsiderate generosity have poured away their patrimony. And what can be more foolish than to go out of the way to make yourself incapable of any longer doing what you love to do? Thus it is that some men, when they have nothing to give away, betake themselves to violence, and the hatred they earn from the victims of their rapine is greater than the benefit they confer on the recipients of their bounty. So it was, regrettably, with William Rufus. When at the first beginning of his reign he had recruited knights for fear of popular disorders, he thought that nothing should be denied them, and promised still greater things for the future. Consequently, as he had [T¹A add smartly] exhausted his father's treasure, and his own cash income at the time was but modest, his resources had already failed; but his lavish intentions were unfailing, for he had turned the habit of giving almost into second nature, ignorant as he was how to beat down the price of anything or judge its proper value: the seller could dispose of his wares, the knight contract for his services, at a price of their own choosing. The cost of his clothes he liked to be immensely inflated, and spurned them if anyone reduced it. For instance, one morning when he was putting on some new shoes, he asked his valet what they had cost. 'Three shillings,' the man replied, at which the king flew into a rage. 'You son of a bitch!', he cried; 'since when has a king worn such trumpery shoes? Go and get me some that cost a mark of silver.' The servant went off and returned with a much cheaper pair, pretending they had been bought at the price specified.

'istae regiae conueniunt maiestati.' Ita cubicularius ex eo pretium uestimentorum eius pro uoluntate numerabat, multa perinde suis utilitatibus nundinatus.

314. Excitabat ergo totum Occidentem fama largitatis eius, Orientem usque pertendens.*a* Veniebant ad eum milites ex omni quae citra montes est prouintia, quos ipse profusissimis expensis munerabat. Itaque cum defecisset quod daret, inops et exhaustus ad lucra*b* conuertit animum. Accessit regiae*c* menti fomes cupiditatum, Rannulfus clericus, ex infimo genere hominum lingua et calliditate prouectus ad summum. Is,*d* si quando edictum regium processisset ut nominatum tributum Anglia penderet, duplum aditiebat, expilator diuitum, exterminator pauperum, confiscator alienarum hereditatum. Inuictus causidicus et cum uerbis tum rebus immodicus, iuxta in suplices ut in rebelles furens, 'subinde cachinnantibus quibusdam ac dicentibus*e* solum esse hominem qui sciret sic agitare ingenium,*f* nec aliorum curaret odium dummodo complacaret dominum. Hoc auctore sacri aecclesiarum honores mortuis pastoribus uenum locati; namque audita morte cuiuslibet episcopi uel abbatis, confestim clericus regis eo mittebatur, qui omnia inuenta*g* scripto exciperet, omnesque in posterum redditus*h* fisco regio inferret. Interea querebatur quis idoneus in loco defuncti substitueretur, non pro morum sed pro nummorum experimento, dabaturque tandem honor, ut ita dicam, nudus, magno tamen emptus. Haec eo indigniora uidebantur, quod tempore patris post decessum episcopi uel abbatis omnes redditus integre custodiebantur, substituendo pastori resignandi, eligebanturque personae religionis merito laudabiles. At uero pauculis annis intercedentibus omnia immutata. Nullus diues nisi nummularius, nullus clericus nisi causidicus, nullus presbiter nisi, ut uerbo parum*i* Latino utar, firmarius. Cuiuscumque conditionis homunculus, cuiuscumque criminis reus, statim ut de lucro regis appellasset, audiebatur; ab ipsis latronis faucibus resoluebatur laqueus si promisisset regale commodum. Soluta militari disciplina, curiales rusticorum substantias depascebantur, insumebant fortunas, a buccis miserorum cibos abstrahentes.*j* Tunc fluxus crinium, tunc luxus uestium, tunc usus calceorum cum arcuatis aculeis inuentus; mollitie

---

a protendens *C*   *b* rapinas *T'A*   *c* auid(a)e *T'A*   *d* iste *T'A*
e–e om. *T'*; subinde cachinnante rege ac dicente *A*   *f* *T'* adds ut   *g* inuento *T'*   *h* reditus *Tt*^{a.c.}*A*   *i* *CsB* add in   *j* abstr. cibos *T'*

'Why,' said the king, 'these are a good fit for the royal majesty.' So the servant henceforward paid what price he liked for the royal wardrobe, and made a good thing out of it.

314. Thus the fame of his generosity aroused all Europe, and even reached the East: knights came to him from every country this side the Alps, and he rewarded them at an enormous outlay. Consequently, when he had no more left to give, he turned with empty hands to some way of making money. The king's rapacious intentions were warmly seconded by Ranulf, a cleric whose ready tongue and wit had raised him from the lowest ranks of society to the top. Did a royal decree go forth that England should pay a specified sum by way of impost?— Ranulf doubled it; he skinned the rich, ground down the poor, and swept other men's inheritances into his net. Invincible in legal argument, and as much beyond control in speech as he was in affairs, he raged against the compliant no less than against the recalcitrant, while there were some who laughed, and said he was the only man who knew how to give his wits such good exercise, and cared nothing for other men's hatred provided he pleased his own master. It was his policy, when shepherds of the Church died, to put their sacred offices up for sale; for at the news of the death of any bishop or abbot, a royal clerk was at once sent down to make a written inventory of all he found and bring all subsequent income into the royal treasury. Meanwhile search was made for the most suitable successor to the deceased, the criterion being coin instead of character, and the honour when finally disposed of was, so to say, milked dry, yet bought at a great price. This seemed all the more outrageous because in his father's time, when a bishop or abbot died, all the revenues were preserved intact to be handed over to his successor, and persons praiseworthy for their religious life were chosen as shepherds of the Church. Now, after the passage of a very few years, all was changed. None became rich unless he was a money-changer, none a clerk unless he was a lawyer, none a priest unless he was—to use a somewhat foreign word—a rentier. No wretch however low in his station, no culprit however great his offence, but was sure of an audience the moment he made an appeal that would bring profit to the Crown; the noose itself was slackened from the bandit's neck if he had promised something to the king's advantage. The knightly code of honour disappeared; courtiers devoured the substance of the country people and engulfed their livelihood, taking the very food out of their mouths. Long flowing hair, luxurious garments, shoes with curved and

corporis certare cum feminis, gressum frangere, gestu soluto et latere
5 nudo incedere adolescentium specimen erat. Enerues, emolliti, quod
nati fuerant inuiti manebant, expugnatores alienae pudicitiae, prodigi
suae. Sequebantur curiam effeminatorum manus et ganearum greges:
ut non temere a quodam sapiente dictum

*a*est: 'Curia regis Angliae non *a*sit felicem fore Angliam si Henricus
est maiestatis diuersorium sed regnaret, talia coniectans quod is ab
exsoletorum prostibulum.' adolescentia obscenitates execraretur.

315. Ad dedecus tempo- 315. Adicerem his, si esset neces-
rum illorum pertinet*a* se,*a*
quod Anselmus archiepiscopus ista corrigere conatus, sed sotietate
suffraganeorum suorum destitutus, sponte discesserit, duritiae*b* temporis cedens, Anselmus quo nemo umquam iusti tenatior, nemo hoc
tempore tam anxie doctus, nemo tam penitus spiritualis fuerit, pater
patriae, mundi speculum. Hic cum iam iamque nauigaturus in portu
uentos expectaret, ut predo publicus*c* expilatus est, manticis omnibus
et bulgis in medium prolatis et exquisitis. De cuius iniuriis plura
dicerem si quicquam hoc solo sol uidisset indignius; simul et supersedendum est in historia quam reuerentissimi Edmeri[1] preoccupauit
facundia.

316. Vides quantus e liberalitate, quam putabat, fomes malorum*d*
eruperit. In quibus corrigendis quia ipse non tam exhibuit diligentiam
quam pretendit negligentiam, magnam et uix abolendam incurrit infamiam; immerito,*e* credo, quia numquam se tali supponeret probro qui
se tanto meminisset prelatum imperio. Haec igitur ideo inelaborato et
celeri sermone conuoluo, quia de tanto rege mala dicere erubesco, in
deiciendis et extenuandis malis*f* laborans.

a-a est (sit *Tp*) . . . temporum illorum *(ill. temp. T')* pertinet *T'A;* sit . . . necesse
CB   *b* nequiti(a)e *T'A*   *c* *T'A add* iussu regis   *d* fomes malorum *CB;*
gurges uitiorum *T'A*   *e* *William surely meant to write* non immerito *or* merito *(so translated)*   *f* criminibus *T'A*

[1] Eadmer, *The Life of St Anselm, Archbishop of Canterbury*, ed. R. W. Southern (NMT 1962, repr. OMT 1972 and 1980), p. 98.

pointed tips became the fashion. Softness of body rivalling the weaker sex, a mincing gait, effeminate gestures and a liberal display of the person as they went along, such was the ideal fashion of the younger men. Spineless, unmanned, they were reluctant to remain as Nature had intended they should be; they were a menace to the virtue of others and promiscuous with their own. Troupes of effeminates and gangs of wastrels went round with the court;

T¹A as a wise man said, with good reason: 'The court of the king of England is not the abode of majesty but a brothel for perverts.'

CB so that a wise man said, with good reason, that England would be fortunate if Henry were king—arguing from Henry's passionate hatred of indecency from youth onwards.

315. It shows how bad those times were,

315. I would add to this, did it need saying,

that Archbishop Anselm, having tried to put right this state of affairs but lacking the support of his fellow-bishops, gave in to the brazenness of the time, and departed of his own accord—Anselm, the most devoted champion of the right that ever was, than whom no one at this time was more meticulously learned, no one so genuinely spiritual, the father of his country, and a mirror for all the world. When he was at the very point of sailing, and in harbour waiting for a wind, he was [T¹A *add* on the king's orders] stripped like a common malefactor, every bag and purse brought out and ransacked. I would say more of the wrongs he suffered, had any single thing more outrageous ever been seen under the sun; besides which, it is right to omit an episode which has been anticipated by my religious and eloquent predecessor, Eadmer.[1]

316. You see what a hotbed of evils [T¹A whirlpool of vices] burgeoned from what he supposed to be generosity. He himself used no diligence to correct them, but rather made a display of negligence, so bringing on himself great and indelible discredit; which in my opinion he thoroughly deserved, for a man would never expose himself to such disgrace, who had once bethought him of the great kingdom he was called to rule. So I veil the topic in these few bald and hasty words, because I am ashamed to speak evil of so great a king, and I am devoting my efforts to refuting or palliating the evil spoken of him.

317. ᵃInsolentiae uel potius inscientiaeᵇ contra Deum hoc fuit signum. Iudei qui Lundoniae habitabant, quos pater e Rotomago illuc traduxerat, eum in quadam sollemnitate adierunt xenia offerentes. Quibus delinitus etiam ausus est animare ad conflictum contra Christianos, 'per uultumᵈ de Luca' pronuntians quod si uicissentᵃ in eorum sectam transiret. 317. ᵃInsolentiae in Deum Iudei suo tempore dedere inditium, semel apud Rotomagum ut quosdam ab errore suo refugos ad Iudaismum reuocarentᶜ muneribus inflectere conati; alia uice apud Lundoniam contra episcopos nostros in certamen animati, quia ille ludibundus, credo, dixisset quod, si uicissent Christianos apertis argumentationibus confutatos,ᵃ Magno igitur timore episcoporum et clericorum res acta est, pia sollicitudine fidei Christianae timentium. Et de hoc quidem certamine nichil Iudei preter confusionem retulerunt, quanuis multotiens iactarint se non ratione ᵉ sed factione superatos.

318. ᶠParis arrogantiae altera uice dedit inditium. Namᶠ 318. ᶠPosteriori tempore, id est anno regni eius ferme nono,ᶠ cum Rotbertus comes Normannorum Ierosolimam eundi, monitionibus Vrbani papae, ut posterius dicetur,¹ impetum cepisset, Normanniam fratri suo pro pecunia decem milium marcarum inuadatus est. Itaque importabilis pensionis edictum per totam Angliam cucurrit. Tunc episcopi et abbates frequentes curiamᵍ adeunt, super uiolentia querimoniam fatientes: non se posse ad tantum uectigal sufficere, nisi si

2 miseros agricolas omnino effugent. Quibus curialesʰ turbido, ut solebant,ⁱ uultu 'Non habetis' inquiuntʲ 'scrinia auro et argento composita, ossibus mortuorum plena?', nullo alio responso obsecrantes dignati.ᵏ Ita illi, intelligentes quo responsio tenderet, capsas sanctorum nudauerunt, crucifixos despoliauerunt, calices conflarunt, non in usum pauperum sed in fiscum regium; quicquid enim pene sancta seruauit auorum parcitas, illorum grassatorumˡ absumpsit auiditas.

319. Nichilo setius in homines grassabantur, primo pecuniam deinde terras auferentes.ᵐ Non pauperem tenuitas, non opulentum

---

ᵃ⁻ᵃ insolentiae ... uicissent T'A; insolentiae ... confutatos CB   ᵇ insciti(a)e T'   ᶜ reuocaret C   ᵈ A adds ait   ᵉ oratione CsB   ᶠ⁻ᶠ paris ... nam T'A; posteriori ... nono CB   ᵍ regem T'A   ʰ ille T'A   ⁱ solebat T'A   ʲ inquit T'A   ᵏ dignatus T'A   ˡ illorum grassatorum CB; unius hominis T'; hominis unius A   ᵐ grassabatur ... auferens T'A

---

¹ cc. 347, 350.

317. T¹A Let me give an example of his arrogance, or rather ignorance, towards God. Some London Jews, whom his father had transferred there from Rouen, came to him on some feast-day or other bearing gifts. Prompted by their flatteries, he dared encourage them—no less—to debate against the Christians, saying that 'By the holy Face of Lucca', if they prevailed,

317. CB The Jews in his time gave a display of arrogance towards God, on one occasion at Rouen trying by bribes to recall to the Jewish faith some who had abandoned their mistaken ways; another time, in London, they were encouraged to dispute with our bishops, because the king had said—in jest, I suppose—that if they refuted the Christians by clear proofs and beat them,

he would become a Jew himself. The contest was therefore held, to the great alarm of the bishops and clergy, who were filled with fear in their pious anxiety for the Christian faith. And from this dispute, at any rate, the Jews got nothing but confusion, although they have often boasted that they were beaten by party passion and not argument.

318. T¹A On another occasion he provided an example of similar arrogance; for

318. CB Later, about the ninth year of his reign,

Robert duke of Normandy, having caught the urge to go to Jerusalem, from the exhortations of Pope Urban II as will be told hereafter,[1] mortgaged Normandy to his brother for 10,000 marks in cash. An edict therefore ran throughout all England, levying an intolerable tax. Bishops and abbots flocked to the court, complaining of his brutality; they could not possibly meet such an impost, except by driving the wretched husbandmen from the land altogether. To this the courtiers [2] retorted, with their usual scowls: 'Have you no shrines adorned with gold and silver and filled with dead men's bones?' And that was all they vouchsafed the petitioners by way of answer. The churchmen therefore, discerning the purport of this reply, stripped their saints' reliquaries, despoiled their crucifixes, and melted down their chalices, not to help the poor but to fill the king's coffers; almost all that the holy parsimony of their ancestors had saved was consumed by the depredations of those robbers [T¹A one man].

319. Nor were they [T¹A was he] less ready to rob vassals, seizing first their money, then their lands. Poverty was no protection for the humble nor wealth for the opulent; hunting, which the king had at

copia tuebatur; uenationes, quas rex[a] primo indulserat, adeo prohibuit ut capitale esset suplitium prendidisse ceruum. [b]Quibus artibus ita amorem prouintialium a se effugauerat[b] [b]Quapropter multa seueritate, quam nulla condiebat dulcedo, factum est[b] ut sepe contra eius salutem a ducibus coniuraretur. Quorum unus, Rotbertus de Molbrei comes Humbronensium, orta inter eum et regem non modica controuersia uerborum, in prouintiam[c] iuris sui abiit, ingentia contra dominum suum molimina conaturus; sed subsequente
2 illo captus et aeternis uinculis irretitus est. Alter, Willelmus de Ou, proditionis apud regem accusatus delatoremque ad duellum prouocans, [d]dum se segniter expurgat,[d] cecatus et extesticulatus est. Plures illa delatio inuoluit, innocentes plane et probos uiros. Ex his fuit Willelmus de Alderia, spetiosae personae homo et compater regis. Is patibulo affigi iussus, Osmundo episcopo Salesberiae confessus et per omnes aecclesias oppidi flagellatus est. Itaque,[e] dispersis ad inopes uestibus, ad suspendium nudus ibat, delicatam carnem frequentibus super lapides
3 genuflexionibus cruentans. Episcopo et populo sequente ad locum suplitii ita satisfecit: 'Sic' inquit 'adiuuet Deus[f] animam meam et a malis liberet, ut de re qua accusor immunis sum; et quidem sententia de me prolata non reuocabitur, sed uolo [g]omnes homines[g] innocentiae meae esse conscios.' Tunc[h] dicta commendatione animae et aspersa aqua benedicta,[i] episcopus discessit,[j] ille appensus est, admirando fortitudinis spectaculo, ut nec moriturus gemitum nec moriens produceret suspirium.

320. Veruntamen sunt quaedam de rege preclarae magnanimitatis exempla, quae posteris non inuidebo. Venationi in quadam silua intentum nuntius detinuit ex transmarinis partibus, obsessam esse ciuitatem Cinomannis, quam nuper fratre profecto suae potestati adiecerat. Statim ergo ut expeditus erat retorsit equum, iter ad mare conuertens. Ammonentibus ducibus exercitum aduocandum, paratus componendos, 'Videbo' ait 'quis me sequetur. Putatis me non habiturum homines? Si cognoui iuuentutem meam, etiam naufragio ad
2 me uenisse uolet.' Hoc igitur modo pene solus ad mare peruenit. Erat

[a] om. T'A   [b-b] quibus ... effugauerat T'A; quapropter ... est CB
[c] prouintia A   [d-d] om. T'   [e] ita B   [f] Deus adiuuet T'   [g-g] uos omnes T'
   [h] tum T'A   [i] benedicta aqua ACsBk (cf. 323)
[j] T'Cs add et

first allowed, was so strictly forbidden that to take a stag was a capital offence.

T¹A This kind of behaviour had so alienated the affection of his subjects that there were

CB This great severity, unrelieved by charm of any kind, was the cause of

several conspiracies of magnates against his life. One of them, Robert of Mowbray earl of the Northumbrians, after high words had passed between him and the king, went off to the province that was under his jurisdiction, in order to set great operations on foot against his lord; but his lord went after him, and he was taken, and put in chains for evermore. A second, William of Eu, when accused of treachery in the king's presence, challenged his traducer to a duel, and being sluggish in justifying himself, was deprived of his eyes and testicles. Many people were involved in that accusation, perfectly innocent and worthy men. William of Aldery was one of them, a man of handsome person who had stood godfather with the king. Condemned to the gallows, he made his confession to Osmund bishop of Salisbury, and was scourged from church to church through the town. And so, having distributed his garments to the poor, he went naked to his hanging, drawing blood from his delicately-nurtured body by frequent kneeling upon the stony road. With the bishop and people following him to his place of punishment, he made this profession: 'So God assist my soul', he said, 'and deliver it from evil, I am innocent of that of which I am accused. The sentence passed upon me will not be revoked, but I wish all men to be aware of my innocence.' Then the bishop, having spoken the commendation of the departing soul and sprinkled him with holy water, withdrew, and he was hanged, giving an admirable display of courage, for he uttered no groan at the prospect of death, no sigh in the moment of it.

320. On the other hand, the king provided some examples of real greatness of spirit, which I will not conceal from posterity. Once, when he was intent on hunting in some forest, he was stayed by news from overseas of the siege of Le Mans, which he had lately added to his own power on his brother's departure. Lightly equipped as he was, he at once turned his horse's head and made instead for the coast. To the nobles who urged that he must summon an army and fit it out, his reply was: 'I shall see who will follow me. Do you suppose I shall be short of support? If I know my young men, they will willingly come to me, even at the risk of shipwreck.' In this fashion he arrived at the sea-

tunc nubilus aer et uentus contrarius; flatus uiolentia terga maris uerrebat. Illum statim transfretare uolentem nautae exorant ut pacem pelagi et uentorum clementiam operiatur. 'Atqui' inquit rex 'numquam audiui regem naufragio interisse. Quin potius soluite retinacula nauium; uidebitis elementa iam conspirata in meum obsequium.' Ponto transito obsessores eius audita*[a]* fama dissiliunt.

3 Auctor turbarum, Helias quidam, capitur; cui ante se adducto rex ludibundus 'Habeo te, magister!' dixit. At uero illius alta nobilitas, quae nesciret in tanto etiam*[b]* periculo humilia sapere, humilia loqui, 'Fortuitu' inquit 'me cepisti; sed si possem euadere,*[c]* noui quid facerem.' Tum Willelmus, pre furore fere extra se positus, et obuncans Heliam, 'Tu' inquit, 'nebulo, tu quid faceres? Discede, abi, fuge! Concedo tibi ut fatias quicquid poteris, et per uultum de Luca nichil, si me uiceris, pro hac uenia tecum paciscar.' Nec inferius factum uerbo fuit, sed continuo dimisit euadere, miratus potius quam insec-
4 tatus fugientem. Quis talia de illiterato homine crederet? Et fortassis erit aliquis qui, Lucanum[1] legens, falso opinetur Willelmum haec exempla de Iulio Cesare mutuatum esse. Sed non erat ei tantum studii uel otii ut litteras umquam audiret; immo calor mentis ingenitus et conscia uirtus eum talia exprimere cogebant.*[d]* Et profecto, si Christianitas nostra pateretur, sicut olim anima Euforbii transisse dicta est in Pitagoram Samium, ita posset dici quod anima Iulii Cesaris transierit in regem Willelmum.

321. Vnum edifitium*[e]* et ipsum permaximum, domum in Lundonia, incepit et perfecit, non parcens expensis dum modo liberalitatis suae magnificentiam exhiberet. Et mores quidem eius ex his quae diximus animaduertere poterit lector. Si quis uero desiderat scire corporis eius qualitatem, nouerit eum fuisse corpore quadrato, colore rufo, crine sufflauo, fronte fenestrata,*[f]*[2] oculo uario, quibusdam intermicantibus guttis distincto, precipuo robore, quamquam non magnae staturae, et uentre paulo proiectiore. Eloquentiae nullae, sed titubantia linguae notabilis,*[g]* maxime cum ira succresceret. Plura sub eo subita et tristia acciderunt, quae singulatim*[h]* per annos eius digeremus, ueritati maxime secundum cronicorum fidem inseruientes.

---

[a] audita eius $T'A*$ *[b]* etiam in tanto $T'Bc*$ *[c]* euadere possem $T'A$
[d] cogebat A *[e]* T' adds cepit   *[f]* fenestrato CsB *[g]* T' adds et (cf. e.g. 98.1 and 183.9)
[h] singillatim Bk, William's preferred form

[1] v. 493–4, 577–93; ii. 512–17.   [2] See ODML s.v. fenestrare 2b.

coast almost alone. The sky was overcast, the wind against him, the sea lashed into waves by the fury of the blast. He wished to cross at once; the sailors begged him to wait until the deep grew calmer and the winds relented. 'Why,' said the monarch, 'I never heard of a king being drowned. Cast off at once, and you will find the elements in league to obey me.' He crossed the Channel, and hearing the news of his arrival, the besieging forces melted away. The ringleader, a certain Helias, was taken, and brought before the king, who was very merry: 'I've got you, my fine fellow', he said. His captive had a lofty spirit, of the kind that knows not, even in a moment of such peril, the thoughts and language of humility. 'You have taken me by pure chance', he retorted, 'and if only I could get away, I know what I should do.' William was almost beside himself with rage, and stormed abusively at Helias. 'You!', he cried, 'You rascal! What could you do? Get out! Away with you! Clear off! I give you free leave to do your worst; and, by the Face of Lucca, if you beat me, I shall ask for no quarter in exchange for letting you go like this.' He was as good as his word, and at once let him go free, thinking the fugitive a cause for admiration rather than pursuit. Who would believe such behaviour in a man of no education? Some people, as they read their Lucan,[1] might perhaps wrongly suppose that William borrowed the inspiration for these actions from Julius Caesar; but he never had either the interest or the leisure to pay any attention to literature. Rather, it was his innate fire of mind, and conscious valour, that drove him to utterances such as these. Indeed, if our Christian faith admitted such a thing, it might be said that as the soul of Euphorbus is supposed to have passed into Pythagoras of Samos, so did the soul of Julius Caesar pass into King William.

321. He began and completed one building, and that on the grand scale, his palace in London, sparing no expense to secure an effect of open-handed splendour. Of his character, the reader can form an idea from what has been said. If anyone is curious to know his personal appearance, I would say that he was squarely built, ruddy in colouring, with rather yellow hair parted in the 'window' style,[2] eyes of no one colour but spangled with bright specks; of great strength, although of no great height, and inclined to be pot-bellied. He had no skill in speech, but was remarkable for his stammer, especially when his temper began to rise. Many sudden and tragic events befell in his time, which I will arrange one by one under their regnal years, with an eye to the truth, and following the Chronicle as my chief authority.

322. Secundo anno regni eius terrae motus ingens totam Angliam exterruit tertio idus Augusti, horrendo miraculo, ut edifitia omnia eminus resilirent et mox pristino modo resideret. Secuta est inopia omnium fructuum, tarda maturitas frugum, ut uix ad festum sancti Andreae messes reconderentur.

323. Quarto anno tumultus fulgurum, motus turbinum; denique idus[a] Octobris apud Wincelcumbam ictus de caelo emissus latus turris impulit tanta ui ut debilitata maceria in confinio tecti ingens foramen ad modum humanae grossitudinis aperiretur. Ibi ingressus trabem maximam perculit, ut fragmina [b]in tota[b] spargerentur aecclesia, quin et crucifixi caput cum dextra tibia et imaginem sanctae Mariae deiecit. Secutus est odor teterrimus, hominum importabilis naribus. Tandem monachi felici ausu irrumpentes benedictae aquae aspergine prestigias Inimici effugarunt.

324. Quid illud omnibus incognitum seculis? Discordia uentorum inter se dissidentium ab euroaustro ueniens sexto decimo kalendas Nouembris Lundoniae plusquam sexcentas domos effregit. Cumulabantur aecclesiae cum domibus, maceriae cum parietibus. Maius quoque scelus furor uentorum ausus tectum aecclesiae sanctae Mariae quae ad Arcus dicitur pariter sulleuauit, et duos ibi homines[c] obruit; ferebanturque tigna cum trabibus per inane, spectaculo a longe uisentibus, timori prope stantibus ne obruerentur. Quattuor tigna, sex et uiginti pedes longa, tanta ui in humum impacta[d] sunt ut uix quattuor pedes extarent; notabili uisu, quomodo duritiem[e] stratae publicae perruperint, eo ibi ordine posita quo in tecto manu artificis fuerant locata, quoad ob impedimenta transeuntium ad planitiem terrae sunt desecta, quod aliter erui nequirent.

325. Quinto anno eadem uiolentia fulminis apud Salesberiam tectum turris aecclesiae omnino disiecit, multumque maceriam labefactauit, quinta sane die postquam eam dedicauerat Osmundus, preclarae memoriae episcopus.

---

[a] One expects idibus (so JW s.a. *1091*) [b-b] per totam (. . . ecclesiam) Bc, om. Bk
[c] homines ibi CeB   [d] compacta T¹   [e] duriti(a)e A

322. In the second year of his reign, the whole of England was terrified by a great earthquake on 11 August, such that in fearful and wonderful fashion all buildings leapt into the air for some distance and then sank back as they had been before. This was followed by a shortage of all produce; the crops ripened so late that the harvest was barely got in by St Andrew's day.

323. In the fourth year there was violent lightning, and violent storms; for instance, on 15 October at Winchcombe a thunderbolt struck the side of the tower with such force that it broke down the masonry next to the roof, and a great hole opened, as large as a man. Through this it entered and struck a main beam, so that fragments were scattered all over the church, and it threw down the head of the Crucifix and its right leg, and also an image of the Blessed Virgin. Then followed a stench more frightful than men's sense of smell will tolerate. At length the monks with successful courage rushed in, and by sprinkling holy water put to flight the wiles of the Evil One.

324. What of this, the like of which has never been heard of? On 17 October, a great confusion of quarrelsome winds, coming from the south-east, demolished more than six hundred houses in London. Churches and houses, outer and partition walls were piled up together. The fury of the winds then proceeded to an even greater outrage: it at the same time lifted the roof of the church called St Mary-le-Bow, burying two men on the spot. Beams and rafters flying through the air filled those at a distance with amazement, and those standing nearby with terror that they would be overwhelmed. Four beams, each twenty-six feet long, were driven into the ground with such violence that scarcely four feet was left protruding, and it was curious to see how they penetrated the hard surface of the public street, standing there fixed in the precise order in which the builders had originally set them in the roof, until, being such an obstacle to passers-by, they were cut down to ground-level, because they could not be removed in any other way.

325. In his fifth year, the same violent lightning smashed the roof of the cathedral tower at Salisbury to pieces, and severely damaged the masonry, just four days after its dedication by Bishop Osmund of famous memory.

326. Sexto anno tantum fuit pluuiarum diluuium, tanta tempestas imbrium quantam nullus meminerat. Mox accedente hieme fluuii ita sunt congelati ut essent peruii equitantibus et plaustra ducentibus; nec mora, resoluto gelu impetu glatialium crustarum pontes effracti.

327. Septimo anno, propter tributa quae rex in Normannia positus edixerat, agricultura defecit; qua fatiscente fames e uestigio; ea quoque inualescente mortalitas hominum subsecuta, adeo crebra ut deesset morituris cura, mortuis sepultura. Tunc etiam Walenses in Normannos efferati Cestrensem pagum et partem Scrobbesberiensis*a* depopulati Anglesiam armis obtinuere.

328. Decimo anno kalendis Octobris apparuit cometes quindecim diebus, maiorem crinem emittens ad orientem, minorem uersus euroaustrum.*b* Apparuerunt et aliae stellae, quasi iacula inter se*c* emittentes. Ille fuit annus quo Anselmus, lux Angliae, ultro tenebras erroneorum effugiens, Romam iuit.

329. Vndecimo anno rex Noricorum Magnus cum Haroldo filio Haroldi regis quondam Angliae Orcadas insulas et Meuanias, et si quae aliae in oceano iacent, armis subegit. Iamque Angliam per Anglesiam obstinatus petebat; sed occurrerunt ei comites Hugo Cestrensis et Hugo Scrobbesberiensis, et antequam continentem ingrederetur*d* armis eum expulerunt. Cecidit ibi Hugo Scrobbesberiensis, eminus ferreo hastili perfossus.

330. Duodecimo anno fluctus marinus per Tamensem fluuium ascendit, et uillas multas cum hominibus mersit.

331. Tertio decimo anno, qui et extremus fuit uitae,*e* multa aduersa. Hoc quoque maxime horrendum, quod uisibiliter diabolus apparuit hominibus in saltibus et deuiis, transeuntes allocutus. Preterea in pago Berrucscire in uilla Hamstede continuis quindecim diebus fons sanguinem tam ubertim manauit ut uicinum uadum inficeret. Audiebat ille haec,*f* et ridebat,*g* nec sua somnia de se nec aliorum uisa curans.

---

a Scrobesberiensem *T¹*; Scrobbberienses *A*   *b* austrum *B*   *c* inter se iacula *A*   *d* ingrederentur *T¹*   *e* uit(a)e fuit *T¹ABc*   *f* h(a)ec ille *T¹A*   *g* garriebat *T¹A*

326. In the sixth year, there were greater floods and storms of rain than any in living memory. Then, on the approach of winter, the rivers were frozen until it was possible to ride horses and drive carts across them; and shortly afterwards, when the thaw came, bridges were broken down by the pressure of the ice-floes.

327. In the seventh year, the imposts decreed by the king when he was in Normandy caused a breakdown on the farms, and when farming collapsed, famine rapidly followed. As the famine grew more severe, plague came in its train, so universal that it was impossible to care for the dying or bury the dead. At that time too the Welsh broke out against the Normans, ravaged Cheshire and part of Shropshire, and seized Anglesey by force of arms.

328. In the tenth year, on 1 October, appeared a comet, which lasted a fortnight, shooting out a larger tail towards the east and a smaller one towards the south-east; and other stars also made their appearance, which seemed to be emitting shafts of light at one another. This was the year in which Anselm, England's brightest light, seeking to escape from the darkness of those in error, made his way to Rome.

329. In the eleventh year, Magnus king of the Norwegians, with Harold son of Harold the late English king, conquered the Orkney and Mevanian Isles and others lying in the Ocean, and was determined to make for England by way of Anglesey, had not Hugh earl of Chester and Hugh earl of Shrewsbury gone against him, and driven him off by force before he could set foot on the mainland. Hugh of Shrewsbury was killed there, pierced at long range by an iron spear.

330. In the twelfth year, a flood from the sea came up the Thames, and swamped many places and their inhabitants.

331. In the thirteenth year of William's reign, which was the year of his death, there were many sinister occurrences; among others, this was the most terrifying, that the Devil visibly appeared to men in woods and by-ways, and spoke to passers-by. Besides which, in the village of Hampstead in Berkshire for fifteen days on end a spring ran blood so abundantly that a nearby pool was stained with it. The king heard of these things and laughed, caring nothing either for his own dreams about himself or for what other people saw.

332. Multa de ipsius nece*^a* et preuisa et predicta homines serunt, quorum tria probabilium relatorum testimonio lecturis communicabo. Edmerus, nostrorum temporum historicus, sinceritate ueritatis laudandus, dicit[1] nobilem illum exulem Anselmum, cum quo pariter omnis religio exulabat, Marcenniacum uenisse, ut Hugonis abbatis Cluniacensis*^b* conscientiae querelas curarum suarum ingereret. Ibi cum de rege Willelmo sermo uolutaretur, abbatem predictum dixisse proxima nocte regem illum ante Deum ductum, et adiudicatum librato
2 iuditio tristem dampnationis subisse sententiam. Id quomodo nosset nec ipse tunc*^c* exposuit nec aliquis audientium requisiuit; ueruntamen pro contuitu religionis eius nulli presentium de fide dictorum inhesit ambiguum. Eius erat uitae Hugo, eius*^d* famae, ut omnes eius suspicerent eloquium, mirarentur consilium, quasi ex caelesti adito insonuisset oraculum. Nec multo post, occiso ut dicemus rege, uenit nuntius ut sedem suam dignaretur archiepiscopus.

333. Pridie quam 'excederet uita,' uidit per quietem se flebotomi ictu sanguinem emittere; radium*^f* cruoris in caelum usque protentum lucem obnubilare, diem interpolare. Ita inclamata sancta Maria, somno excussus, lumen inferri precepit, et cubicularios a se discedere uetuit. Tunc aliquot horis antelucanis nonnichil uigilatum. Paulo post, cum iam aurora diem inuehere meditaretur, monachus quidam transmarinus retulit Rotberto filio Haimonis, uiro magnatum principi, somnium
2 quod eadem nocte de rege uiderat mirum et horrendum: quod in quandam aecclesiam uenerit*^g* superbo gestu*^h* et insolenti, ut solebat, circumstantes despitiens; tunc,*ⁱ* crucifixum mordicus apprehendens, brachia illi corroserit,*^j* crura pene truncauerit; crucifixum diu tolerasse, sed tandem pede ita regem depulisse ut supinus caderet; ex ore iacentis tam effusam flammam exisse ut fumeorum uoluminum orbes etiam sidera lamberent. Hoc somnium Rotbertus non negligendum arbitratus, regi confestim, quod ei a secretis erat, intulit; at ille cachinnos ingeminans 'Monachus' inquit 'est, et causa nummorum
3 monachiliter somniat. Date ei centum solidos.' Multum tamen motus, diu cunctatus est an in siluam, sicut intenderat, iret,*^k* suadentibus

---

^a interitu *T¹A*   *^b* Clu(g)niacensis abbatis *T¹*   *^c* tunc ipse *A*   *^d* om. *A (gap in Al)*   *^{e–e}* periret *T¹A*   *^f* radiumque *T¹*   *^g* uenerat *CB*   *^h* om. *T¹*   *ⁱ* tum *T¹A*   *^j* corrosit *B*   *^k* adiret *T¹*

---

[1] Eadmer, *Life of St Anselm*, ed. Southern, pp. 123–4.

332. Of the visions and prophecies which foreshadowed the king's violent death, many stories are told, and three of these I will impart to my readers, on the evidence of narrators who can be trusted. Our contemporary Eadmer, a historian with a praiseworthy standard of truth, tells us[1] that Anselm, that noble exile, in whose person all religion in this country was in exile too, had gone to Marcigny to lay his troubles and his cares before Hugh abbot of Cluny. While there, when they were talking of King William, the abbot averred that on the previous night the king had been brought before his Maker, where solemn sentence had been passed on him, and he had received the desperate verdict of damnation. How he knew this, he did not then explain, nor did any of his hearers ask him; but such was his merit in religion that no one present had the slightest doubt that his words were true. Such was the life of Abbot Hugh and such his reputation that all men admired his words and marvelled at his wisdom, as though an oracle had spoken from inmost heaven. It was not long before the king was killed, as we shall hear, and a messenger arrived to urge the archbishop to resume his see.

333. The day before William's death, he dreamed that he was being bled, and a spurt of blood shooting up to the sky overcast the sun and brought darkness upon the day. He woke up suddenly, calling upon the Blessed Virgin, ordered lights to be brought in, and forbade his servants to leave him. Then, for several hours before the first light, they watched with him. Not long after, when dawn was already preparing to usher in the day, a certain foreign monk reported to Robert Fitz Hamon, a leading magnate, the dream he had had that night about the king, which was strange and horrible. The king had come into a church, looking scornfully round on the congregation with his usual haughty and insolent air; he had then seized the Crucifix in his teeth, gnawed away the arms of the Figure, and almost broken off its legs. The Figure endured this for some time, but at length gave the king such a kick with its foot that he fell over backwards; and as he lay there, such a gush of flame came out of his mouth that the rolling billows of smoke even reached the stars. This dream ought not, Robert thought, to be taken lightly, and being in the king's inner counsels, he went straight in and told him. The king roared with laughter. 'He's a monk', he said, 'and has these monkish dreams with an eye to the main chance. Give him a hundred shillings.' All the same, he was shaken, and spent a long time wondering whether to go hunting in the forest as he had intended, while his friends tried to

amicis ne suo dispendio ueritatem somniorum experiretur. Itaque ante cibum uenatu abstinuit, seriis negotiis cruditatem*ᵃ* indomitae mentis eructuans; ferunt ea die largiter epulatum crebrioribus quam consueuerat poculis frontem serenasse. Mox igitur post cibum in saltum contendit, paucis comitatus; quorum familiarissimus erat Walterius cognomento Tirel, qui de Frantia liberalitate regis adductus uenerat. Is, ceteris per moram uenationis quo quemque casus tulerat dispersis,
4 solus cum eo remanserat. Iamque*ᵇ* Phebo in oceanum procliui, rex ceruo ante se transeunti, extento neruo et emissa sagitta, non adeo seuum uulnus inflixit, diutile*ᶜ* adhuc fugitantem uiuacitate oculorum prosecutus, opposita contra uiolentiam solarium radiorum manu. Tunc*ᵈ* Walterius pulchrum facinus animo parturiens, ut rege alias interim intento ipse alterum ceruum, qui forte propter transibat, prosterneret, inscius et impotens regium pectus (Deus bone!) letali harundine traiecit. Sautius ille nullum uerbum emisit, sed ligno sagittae quantum extra corpus extabat effracto, moxque supra uulnus cadens,
5 mortem accelerauit. Accurrit Walterius; sed quia nec sensum nec uocem hausit, perniciter cornipedem insiliens benefitio calcarium probe euasit. Nec uero fuit qui persequeretur, illis coniuentibus, istis miserantibus, omnibus postremo alia molientibus; pars receptacula sua munire, pars furtiuas predas agere, pars regem nouum iamiamque circumspicere. Pauci rusticanorum cadauer, in reda caballaria compositum, Wintoniam in episcopatum deuexere, cruore undatim per
6 totam uiam stillante. Ibi infra ambitum turris, multorum procerum conuentu, paucorum planctu terrae traditum.

*ᵉ*Neque defuere opiniones quorundam dicentium ruinam turris, quae posterioribus annis accidit, peccatis illius contigisse, quod iniuria fuerit illum sacrato tumulari loco qui tota uita petulans et lubricus moriens etiam Christiano caruerit uiatico.*ᵉ*

*ᵉ*Secuta est posteriori anno ruina turris; de qua re quae opiniones fuerint parco dicere, ne uidear nugis credere, presertim cum pro instabilitate operis machina ruinam fecisse potuisset, etiamsi numquam ipse ibi sepultus fuisset.*ᵉ*

ᵃ crudelitatem *B*   *ᵇ* itaque *T¹Ce*   *ᶜ* diutine *Aac*; but cf. *GP* p. *419*
ᵈ tum *T¹A*   *ᵉ⁻ᵉ* neque ... uiatico *T¹A*; secuta ... fuisset *CB*

persuade him not to test the truth of dreams at the risk of his own life. So before dinner he did not go hunting, but relieved the vapours of his ungovernable mind by attention to serious business. That day, the story goes, he dined well, and cooled his fevered brow by drinking more heavily than was his custom. Shortly after dinner, therefore, he hastened into the forest with few companions; the most intimate of these was Walter surnamed Tirel, who had been attracted by the king's open-handedness to come over from France. All the others, as the hunt went on, had scattered where chance took them, and only Tirel had stayed with him. The sun was already sinking towards the west, when a stag passed within shot of the king; drawing his bow and letting his arrow fly, he wounded it, but not very severely. For some time, as it ran, he followed it with his keen eyes, putting his hand to his brow against the dazzling sun. At that moment Walter conceived a noble ambition, that he himself should lay low another stag that happened to pass within shot, while the king was temporarily otherwise engaged; and —God have mercy on us!—unknowingly and without power to prevent it he sent his fatal arrow through the king's breast. His victim uttered no word; but breaking off as much of the shaft as projected from his body, and then falling on the wound, he hastened his own death. Walter ran up, but finding him unconscious and speechless, he leapt hastily on his horse, and with good help from his spurs got clean away. Nor indeed was there any pursuit, one party conniving at his flight, others pitying him; but all had other things to think about, some fortifying their own places of refuge, some in secret carrying off what spoils they could, some looking about them every moment for a new king. A handful of the country folk, with a horse and cart, picked up the king's body and carried it to the cathedral at Winchester, with blood dripping freely the whole way. There it was laid in the ground, within the tower, many nobles being present, but few to mourn him.

T¹A Nor were there those lacking who said that the tower's fall, which occurred some years later, was due to his sins; that it had been wrong to inter, in such a sacred spot, him who had been his whole life wanton and lecherous, and even died without receiving the Last Rites.

CB Next year the tower fell; and this event gave rise to much comment, which I refrain from repeating, lest I be thought to lend an ear to idle talk. In particular, the fabric might easily have collapsed through unsound construction, even had he never been buried there.

7 Obiit anno Dominicae incarnationis millesimo centesimo, regni tertio decimo, quarto nonas Augusti,[a] maior quadragenario, ingentia presumens et ingentia, si pensa Parcarum euoluere uel uiolentiam fortunae abrumpere et eluctari potuisset, facturus. Tanta uis erat[b] animi ut quodlibet sibi regnum promittere auderet. Denique ante proximam diem mortis interrogatus ubi festum suum in Natali teneret, respondit Pictauis, quod comes Pictauensis Ierosolimam ire gestiens ei terram suam pro pecunia inuadaturus dicebatur. Ita paternis possessionibus non contentus, maiorisque gloriae spe raptatus,
8 indebitis incubabat honoribus. Vir sacrati ordinis hominibus pro dampno animae, cuius salutem reuocare laborent,[c] maxime miserandus; stipendiariis militibus pro copia donatiuorum mirandus;[d] prouintialibus, quod eorum substantias 'abradi sinebat,'[e] non desiderandus. Nullum suo tempore concilium fieri memini[f] in quo delictis eneruatis uigor aecclesiasticus confirmaretur.

[g]Sed quia in preceps pecuniae auiditate ferebatur, sacros honores sui iuris esse dictitabat,[g] [g]Aecclesiasticos honores diu antequam daret deliberabat, siue pro commodo siue pro trutinando merito,[g] utpote qui eo die quo excessit[h] tres episcopatus et duodecim abbatias
9 desolatas pastoribus in manu sua teneret. Quin et accepta occasione qua inter se dissiderent Vrbanus in Roma, Wibertus in Rauenna, tributum Romanae sedi negauit; pronior tamen in Wiberti gratiam, quod fomes et incentiuum inter eum et Anselmum fuerat discordiae quod[i] ille uir Deo dilectus Vrbanum apostolicum, alterum apostatam pronuntiaret.

334. Eius diebus religio Cistellensis cepit, quae nunc optima uia summi in caelum processus et creditur et dicitur. De qua hic loqui suscepto operi[j] non uidetur esse contrarium, quod ad Angliae gloriam pertineat, quae talem uirum produxerit qui huiusce religionis fuerit et auctor et mediator. Noster ille, et nostra puer in palestra primi aeui tirocinium cucurrit. Quapropter, si non inuidi sumus, eo illius bona

---

[a] *T¹ (cf. HN 491);* nonas Augusti quarto *ACB*   [b] erat uis *T¹A*   [c] nequeant *T¹A*   [d] miserandus *Tt^{a.c.} Tp*   [e-e] abradebat *T¹Al (Aap omits the context)*   [f] permisit *T¹A*   [g-g] sed ... dictitabat *T¹A;* aeccl. ... merito *CB*   [h] decessit *T¹*   [i] quo *CB*   [j] suscepti operis *CB*

He died in the year of our Lord 1100, and the thirteenth of his reign, 7
on 2 August, being over forty years of age. Immensely ambitious, he
would have been immensely successful, had he been able to complete
his allotted span, or to break through the violence of Fortune and fight
his way above it. His energy of mind was such that he was ready to
promise himself any kingdom. For instance, on the day before his
death, when he was asked where he would celebrate Christmas, he
replied 'Poitiers', because it was thought that the count of Poitou
desired to go to Jerusalem and would mortgage his territory to the king
for cash. Not content with his paternal inheritance, and carried away by
hopes of greater distinction, he was always intent on titles to which he
had no right. By those in holy orders he was a man greatly to be pitied 8
for the perdition of his soul, whose salvation they do their best to [T¹A
they cannot] re-establish; by the knights in his pay much to be admired
for his lavish generosity; and by his subjects not to be regretted, for he
allowed them to be denuded [T¹A he denuded them] of their substance. I do not remember that any council was held [T¹A He did not
allow any council to be held] in his time for the suppression of vices
and the strengthening of church discipline.

T¹A But because he was CB Ecclesiastical office he conferred
prompted above all by love of only after long deliberation, whether
money, he used to insist that from financial motives or for the
promotion to holy office was in weighing of the candidates' deserts,
his own power,

so that on the day he died, he had in hand three bishoprics and twelve
abbeys without shepherds. When Urban at Rome was in dispute with 9
Wibert at Ravenna, he seized the opportunity to withhold his tribute to
the Holy See; but he was more inclined to favour Wibert, for it had
been as tinder and fuel to the fire of hatred between himself and
Anselm that the man of God should have declared Urban to be pope
and his rival an apostate.

334. In his days began the Cistercian Order, which is now both
thought and said to be the high road of supreme progress toward
Heaven. To speak of it here does not, I think, conflict with the work I
have undertaken, for it is part of the glory of England to have produced
the great man who was the founder and promoter of this way of life. He
was our countryman, and it was in our schools as a boy that he ran the
first course of his early youth. Unless therefore we are of jealous
disposition, we welcome his achievements all the more gratefully

complectimur gratiosius quo agnoscimus propinquius; simul et laudes eius attollere michi est animus quia ingenua mens est si bonum in alio probes quod in te non esse suspires.

2 Is fuit Hardingus nomine, apud Anglos non ita reconditis natalibus procreatus, a puero Scireburniae monachus; sed cum adolescentem seculi urtica sollicitaret, pannos illos perosus, primo Scottiam, mox Frantiam contendit. Ibi aliquot annis litteris liberalibus exercitus, diuini amoris stimulos accepit. Namque cum pueriles ineptias robustior aetas excluderet, Romam cum consorte studiorum clerico profectus est; nec illos continuatio et difficultas itineris et facultatum penuria umquam cohibere potuit quin cotidie totum psalterium et euntes et redeuntes 3 cantitarent. Profecto iam predicabilis uiri spirabat animus quod non multo post per Dei gratiam est adorsus; nam Burgundiam regressus, in Molesmo, nouo et magno monasterio, crinem abiecit, et prima quidem elementa regulae olim uisa facile recognouit. Cum uero ei alia proponerentur obseruanda, quae nec in regula legerat nec usquam uiderat, rationem eorum efflagitare cepit, modeste sane et ut monachum decet, 'Ratione' inquiens 'supremus rerum[a] auctor omnia fecit, ratione omnia regit; ratione rotatur poli fabrica, ratione ipsa etiam quae dicuntur errantia torquentur sidera, ratione mouentur elementa; ratione et 4 aequilibritate debet nostra subsistere natura. Sed quia per desidiam sepe a ratione decidit, leges quondam multae latae; nouissime per beatum Benedictum regula diuinitus processit, quae fluxum naturae ad rationem reuocaret, in qua etsi habentur quaedam quorum rationem penetrare non suffitio, auctoritati tamen adquiescendum censeo. Ratio enim et auctoritas diuinorum scriptorum, quanuis dissonare uideantur, unum idemque sunt; namque cum Deus nichil sine ratione creauerit et recreauerit, qui fieri potest ut credam sanctos patres, sequaces scilicet Dei, quicquam preter rationem edicere, quasi soli auctoritati fidem 5 debeamus adhibere? Itaque illorum quae procuditis aut rationem aut auctoritatem afferte; quanuis non multum debeat credi, si quid humanae rationis possit allegari quod aequipollentibus argumentis ualeat eneruari. Quapropter ex regula, quae ratione et auctoritate nixa

[a] omnium *T¹* (cf. *GP* p. *418*)

because we recognize them as his kinsmen; and at the same time I have a mind to exalt his praise, because it shows generosity of spirit to praise in another man the virtue whose absence you lament in yourself.

This man's name was Harding; he was born in England of parents by no means obscure, and he had been from boyhood a monk of Sherborne, but as he grew up and felt an itch to live in the world, he came to hate his old sordid habit and made his way first to Scotland and then to France. Having spent some years there acquiring a liberal education, he felt the pricking of the love of God; for once maturity came to drive out the follies of boyhood, he and another clerk who was the companion of his studies set out for Rome. Nor could the unbroken hardships of the long journey, and shortage of funds, ever prevent them both going and coming from singing the whole Psalter every day. In fact, the heart of this outstanding man was already inspired by plans for the enterprise which by God's grace he set about soon afterwards. Returning to Burgundy, he took the tonsure in the big new monastery of Molesme. There he easily recognized the basic elements of the Rule he had seen long ago; but when other observances were set before him which he had neither read of in the Rule nor seen anywhere, he began to ask the reasons for them, though modestly of course and as befits a monk. 'It was by reason', he said, 'that the supreme Creator of the world made all things; by reason He governs all things; it is reason that makes the fabric of the world go round, reason that sends even what we call the wandering stars around their courses, reason that moves the elements, reason and balance by which our nature ought to subsist. But because through sloth that nature so often falls short of reason, many laws were laid down in the past. Most recently, in the work of St Benedict, under Providence a Rule went forth, intended to recall to reason the inconstancy of nature; and though the Rule has certain features the reason of which is too deep for me, I think none the less that its authority must be accepted. For reason and the authority of Holy Scripture, however much they may seem to differ, are one and the same: God having made nothing, and restored nothing, without reason, how can I believe that the holy Fathers, as followers of God, utter anything without reason, as though we were bound to give our allegiance to authority alone? Produce therefore either reason or authority for your new inventions—although one is not bound to give much credit to a proposition advanced by human reason alone, which can be weakened by contrary arguments of equal weight. Give me therefore parallels from the Rule, founded as it is on reason and

utpote omnium iustorum spiritu dictata est, date exempla; quod si non potestis, frustra profitemini illius prerogatiuam cuius contempnitis sequi doctrinam.'

335. Huiusmodi sententia ab uno, ut fit, serpens in alios merito mouit corda Deum timentium, ne forte in uacuum currerent aut cucurrissent. Frequentibus ergo capitulis disputatio agitata hunc finem habuit, ut ipse[a] abbas sententiam probaret, supersedendum superfluis, solam medullam regulae uestigandam.[b] Ita duo fratres electi, in quibus scientia litterarum cum religione quadraret, qui uicaria collatione auctoris regulae uoluntatem inquirerent, inquisitam aliis proponerent. Abbas sedulo agere ut totus conuentus assentiretur; sed quia difficile a mentibus[c] hominum auellitur quod ex antiquo insederit, quia inuiti expuunt quod prima saliua combiberint,[d] pene omnes suscipere recusarunt res nouas, quia[e] ⟨...⟩ antiquas. Soli decem et octo, in quibus Hardingus qui et Stephanus, sancta obstinatione peruicaces cum abbate suo cenobium derelinquunt, pronuntiantes non posse regulae puritatem custodiri in loco ubi et opum congeries et ciborum indigeries etiam reluctantem animum offocarent.[f] Igitur Cistellas uenere, locum prius saltuosum, nunc ita frequenti religione monachorum perspicuum ut diuinitatis ipsius conscius non immerito estimetur. Ibi suffragio archiepiscopi Viennensis, qui [g]nunc apostolicus est,[g] memorabile et omni seculo uenerabile opus ceptarunt.

336. Et plura certe uidentur aspera, sed haec precipue: nichil pellitium aut lineum uestiunt, nec illud quod subtiliter texitur laneum, quod nos staminium uocamus; numquam femoralia, nisi in itinere directi, habent, quae reuertentes lota restituunt. Duas tunicas cum cucullis habentes, hieme augmentum non assumunt,[h] sed aestate, si uolunt, leuamen accipiunt. Vestiti dormiunt et cincti, nec ullo tempore post matutinas ad lectos redeunt; sed ita horam matutinarum temperant ut ante laudes lucescat, ita regulae incubantes ut nec iota unum nec apicem pretereundum putent. Statim post laudes primam canunt, post primam in opera horis constitutis exeunt; quicquid fatiendum uel cantandum est, die sine aliena lucerna consummant. Nullus ex horis

[a] Tt(but not Tp)A add quoque   [b] inuestigandam T¹Cs   [c] sensibus T¹   [d] combiberunt B   [e] A corrector of Al adds diligebant; perhaps rather supply nesciebant esse   [f] offocarunt A   [g-g] tunc ... erat Bk; the allusion is to Calixtus II (d. 1124)   [h] adiciunt T¹

authority, for it is inspired by the spirit of all just men; and if you cannot do so, it is vain for you to claim as your leader a man whose teaching you scorn and do not follow.'

335. Such an argument made its way, as often happens, from one man to many others, and rightly moved the hearts of the devout with fears that they might be running, or might have run, in vain. And so, after frequent discussions in chapter, the upshot was that the abbot himself approved a proposal that they should abandon superfluities, and explore the very marrow of the Rule and nothing else. Two of the brethren were chosen whose piety was equal to their learning, with instructions to study the Rule on behalf of them all, to seek out the author's intentions, and to lay the result before their colleagues. The abbot did all he could to secure the consent of the whole community; but old-established ideas are hard to root out of the minds of men, reluctant as they are to reject what they have imbibed with their mother's milk, and almost all of them refused to accept ideas which seemed new because (?)they were old. Only eighteen, Harding (also called Stephen) among them, remained firm in pious obstinacy and left the convent with their abbot, declaring that it was not possible to maintain the purity of the Rule in a place where mounting wealth and overwhelming meals stifled even the spirit that fought against them. And so they came to Cîteaux, a place once buried in the forest, but now so famous for continuing monastic vocations that it might well be supposed to have some link with Heaven itself. There, with the support of the archbishop of Vienne, the present pope, they launched that memorable enterprise which all ages will revere.

336. Many things about it seem harsh, but these especially: they wear nothing made of fur or linen, nor the finely-woven woollen garment which we call an undershirt, and never use drawers except when sent on a journey, in which case they wash them on return and hand them in. They have each two tunics with cowls, and put on nothing extra in the winter, but are given some relief in summer if they wish. They sleep fully clothed and wearing their girdles, and do not return to their beds at any time after matins, but so arrange the time of matins that daybreak may precede lauds, keeping so closely to the Rule that they think it wrong to diverge by one letter, one iota. Immediately after lauds they sing prime, and after prime go out to work for the prescribed number of hours; all work or singing in choir is completed by daylight without artificial light. No one ever misses the day-hours or

diurnis, nullus ex completorio umquam deest, preter infirmos; cellararius et hospitarius*a* post auditum completorium seruiunt hospitibus, summo tamen*b* studio seruantes silentium. Abbas nichil sibi nisi quod aliis licere permittit, ubique presens, ubique gregis sui curam circumferens; solummodo edentibus non adest, quia mensa eius cum peregrinis et pauperibus est semper. Nichilominus, ubicumque sit, uerborum et obsoniorum abstemius, quia nec ipsi nec aliis umquam nisi duo fercula apponuntur, sagimen et carnes numquam nisi infirmis.

3 Ab idibus Septembris usque ad*c* Pascha nullius festiuitatis contuitu preter dies dominicos nisi semel in die ieiunium soluunt. Numquam claustrum nisi causa operandi egrediuntur, nec ibi nec usquam nisi abbati aut priori inuicem colloquentes. Horas canonicas indefesse continuant, nulla appenditia*d* extrinsecus aditientes preter uigiliam pro defunctis. *e*Cantus et himnos Ambrosianos, quantum ex Mediolano addiscere potuerunt, frequentant in diuinis offitiis.*e* Hospitum et infirmorum curam habentes, importabiles corporibus suis pro animarum remedio comminiscuntur cruces.

337. Haec abbas ille primo ingenti impetu et ipse fatiebat et alios*f* compellebat; sed temporis intercessu penituit homo delicate nutritus et egre ferens tam diutinam ciborum parsimoniam. Cuius uoluntatem monachi apud Molesmum residui cognoscentes, uerbis quibusdam incertum an et epistolis, per obedientiam papae astu quodam*g* ad monasterium retrahunt, uolentem cogentes. Quasi enim defatigatus improbitate suplicum, angustos parietes reliquit pauperum, augustiorem repetens thronum. Secuti eum ex Cistellis omnes qui cum eo 2 uenerant, preter octo. Illi, pauci numero sed multi merito, abbatem Albericum quendam ex suis, priorem Stephanum constituunt. Nec ille in uita moratus plus octennio, supremo feliciter conuentus est arbitrio. Tum, haud dubie nutu diuino, Stephanus absens etiam in abbatem eligitur, dux olim facti totius, spetiale et insigne nostrorum dierum*h* decus; cuius quanti sit meritum testantur abbatiae sedecim iam per eum factae, septem ceptae. Ita ipse, resona Dei tuba, circumpositos

a hospitalarius *T¹*   *b* om. *A*   *c* in *T¹Bc*   *d* appendentia *CsB*
e-e om. *T¹*   *f* *T¹A** add facere   *g* *T¹A** add eum   *h* dierum nostrorum *T¹*

compline except the sick. The cellarer and guest-master minister to the guests after hearing compline, though maintaining the strictest silence as they do so. The abbot allows himself no liberties that he does not allow to others; he is present everywhere, he bears about with him everywhere the care of his flock, and never parts from them except at mealtimes, for his table is shared always by pilgrims and poor people. None the less, wherever he may be, he is sparing of words and of victuals: neither he nor anyone else ever has more than two dishes set before him, and lard and meat are reserved for the sick. From mid-September until Easter they never break their fast more than once a day out of respect for any festival, but only on Sundays. They never leave the cloister except to go out to work, and neither in the cloister nor elsewhere do they talk to one another, only to the abbot and the prior. The canonical hours they maintain without flinching, adding nothing further from outside sources except the Vigils of the Dead. In the divine office they normally use the chants and hymns of the Ambrosian rite, so far as they have been able to learn them from Milan. Guests and the sick are properly looked after, but for their own bodies they invent torments hardly to be borne, for the salvation of their souls.

337. Such was the course which their abbot at first followed himself with such great enthusiasm and made the others follow; but, as time went on, he thought better of it, for he was a man of delicate nurture and found such prolonged abstinence hard to bear. When the monks who had remained at Molesme learnt of his change of mind (whether by word of mouth or by letter as well, is uncertain), they played what was really a trick: invoking his loyalty to the pope, they recalled him to the monastery. Though indeed the compulsion was not unwelcome: as if worn out by the importunity of their appeals, he left poverty's cramped quarters for the more exalted station which had once been his. In his departure from Cîteaux he was followed by all except eight of his original companions. A small number, those eight, but great in merit, and they appointed one of their own number, Alberic, as abbot and Stephen as prior. The abbot, however, survived no more than eight years, and then was summoned with good hope to his last account. Then, in accordance no doubt with the will of God, Stephen although absent was elected abbot—Stephen, the original leader of the whole enterprise, the special pride and glory of our times, to whose outstanding merit bear witness the sixteen abbeys which he has already founded, and seven begun. A sounding trumpet of the Lord, by his

cum uerbo tum exemplo in caelum dirigit, nichil infra preceptum fatiens, sermone comis, fatie iocundus, animo semper in Domino laetus. Hinc palam preclari uultus gaudium, hinc clam illud desuper ueniens irriguum, quia incolatum istum fastidiens patriam continuo amore desideret. Per haec fauorabilis cunctis habetur, quia Deus amorem uiri quem diligit in animos hominum dignanter refundit.[a] Quocirca beatum se computat terrae illius indigena, quisquis per illius manum pecunias suas transmittit[b] ad Deum. Plura quidem ille accipit;[c] sed paucis in suos[d] suorumque usus expensis, cetera in egenos et monasteriorum edificationem confestim dispertit; est enim Stephani marsupium omnium egentium publicum aerarium.

4 Abstinentiae illius est inditium, quod nichil ibi, sicut in ceteris cenobiis, uideas fulgurare auro, renidere[e] gemma, micare argento; nam, ut gentilis ait, 'in sancto quid facit aurum?'[1] Nos in sacratis uasis parum putamus actum nisi crassi crustam metalli obumbret honor lapidum uel topaziorum flamma uel ametistorum uiola uel smaragdorum lux herbida, nisi tunicae sacerdotales auro ludant: nisi multicoloribus parietes picturis renideant[f] et solem ad lacunar sollicitent. At uero illi, ea quae prima mortales falso estimant in secundis habentes, omne studium in ornandis moribus ponunt, magisque amant splendidas mentes quam auratas uestes, scientes quod benefactorum retributio optima est

5 munda frui conscientia. Quin etiam laudabilis abbatis clementia cum uel uult, uel uelle se simulat, aliquid de iugo[g] regulae inflectere, illi contra nituntur, non multum superesse uitae suae dicentes, nec tam diu se uicturos quam uixere; sperare se duraturos in proposito et successuris futuros exemplo, qui si flexi fuerint peccabunt. Et profecto fiet pro humana debilitate, cuius perpetua lex est ut nichil maximis laboribus partum diu possit consistere. Sed ut omnia quae de illis[h] dicta sunt, uel dici possunt, in summam conferam, sunt hodie monachi Cistellenses omnium monachorum exercitium, studiosorum speculum, desidiosorum oestrum.

[a] refudit *CBc* (effundit *Bk*)   [b] transmisit *Al*, transmiserit *Aa*   [c] accepit *Tt*[a.c.] *(not Tp)A*   [d] suis *A (but cf. GP p. 191)*   [e] renitere *T'*   [f] reniteant *T'*   [g] uigore *TtA*; rigore *Tp more naturally (cf. 341. 2 = GP p. 310)*   [h] illo *A*

own precept and example he shows to all the people round him the way to Heaven, nor does his practice fall short of his teaching: his speech courteous, his countenance cheerful, his spirit ever rejoicing in the Lord. Hence the outward joy of those distinguished features, and hence that secret outpouring that comes from on high: scorning our temporary sojourn here, he loves and longs continually for his heavenly home. If all men wish him well, it is because God in His mercy pours into the hearts of men love of the man whom He himself loves. So it is that any dweller in that country counts himself happy if he can convey his wealth to God by that man's hand. Great indeed is the wealth that comes his way; but he spends little on his own needs and those of his brethren, and the balance he distributes without delay for the poor and the building of monasteries, for Stephen's purse is the common treasury of all those who are in want.

It is an index of his self-denial that in those houses you nowhere see, as you do in other monasteries, the glitter of gold or flashing gems or gleaming silver; for, as the pagan poet says, 'To what purpose gold in holy places?'[1] The rest of us think our sacred vessels fall far short unless a solid sheet of precious metal is outshone by glorious gems, by flaming topaz, purple amethyst, or emerald that shines green as grass; unless our priestly vestments wanton with gold; unless our walls are bright with many-coloured paintings and invite the sun to play upon the ceiling. But the Cistercians put in second place what other mortals wrongly think most important; their efforts are all spent on the adornment of the character, and they prefer pure minds to gold-embroidered vestments, knowing that the best return for a life well spent is the enjoyment of a clear conscience. And more than that: when the abbot with well-meant kindliness wishes, or pretends to wish, to relax at some point the burden of the Rule, he meets with opposition from his monks. There is not much of their life left, they say, and they do not expect to live as long as they have lived already. Their hope is to abide by their resolution and set an example to their successors, whom any relaxation will dispose to sin. And so, to be sure, it will be—such is human weakness, whose unfailing principle it is that nothing won by great toil can long endure. But to sum up all that has been said or can be said about the Cistercians, they are today an example for all monks, a mirror for the zealous, and a gadfly for the easy-going.

[1] Persius ii. 69.

338. His temporibus in Anglia tres episcopatus ex antiquis sedibus transiere alias: Wellensis per Iohannem in Bathoniam, Cestrensis per Rotbertum in Couentreiam, Tetfordensis per Herbertum in Norwic, omnes *nummorum malefitio, omnes *maiori ambitu quam ut tantorum uenalitatis ambitu et sacrilegio.* uirorum debuisset interesse studio.* Denique, ut primum de postremo dicam, Herbertus cognomento Losinga, quod ei ars adulationis impegerat,[1] ex abbate Ramesiensi*b* emit episcopatum Tetfordensem, patre quoque suo Rotberto eiusdem cognominis in abbatiam Wintoniae intruso. Fuit ergo uir ille magnus in Anglia simoniae fomes, abbatiam episcopatumque nummis aucupatus, pecunia scilicet regiam sollicitudinem inuiscans et principum fauori non leues promissiones*c* assibilans. Vnde quidam egregie tunc temporis uersificus*d* ait:[2]

> Surgit in aecclesia monstrum genitore Losinga,
> Simonidum secta, canonum uirtute resecta.
> Petre, nimis tardas, nam Simon ad ardua temptat;
> si presens esses, non Simon ad alta uolaret.
> Proh dolor! aecclesiae nummis uenduntur et aere.

Et infra:

> Filius est presul, pater abba,*e* Simon uterque.
> Quid non speremus, si nummos possideamus?
> Omnia nummus habet; quod uult facit, addit et aufert.
> Res nimis iniusta, nummis fit presul et abba.

339. Veruntamen erroneum impetum iuuentutis aboleuit penitentia, Romam profectus seuerioribus annis; ubi loci, simonicum et*f* baculum et anulum deponens, indulgentia clementissimae sedis iterum recipere meruit, quod Romani sanctius et ordinatius censeant ut aecclesiarum omnium sumptus suis potius marsupiis seruiant quam quorumlibet regum usibus militent. Ita Herbertus, domum reuersus, sedem episcopalem, quae quondam fuerat*g* in Helman et tunc erat apud Tetford, ad insignem mercimoniis et populorum frequentia uicum transtulit, nomine Norwic. Ibi monachorum congregationem

---

a-a nummorum ... sacrilegio *T'A;* maiori *(-ore Bc)* ... studio *CB*   *b* Ramesiae *or sim. T'A, GP p. 151*   *c* prom. non leues *T'A, GP p. 151*   *d* uersificans *T'A*   *e* abbas *T'Cs (and the Leiden MS whose version of the whole poem is printed by H. Boehmer in MGH Lib. de lite iii. 615–17)*   *f* om. *GP p. 151, well*   *g* fuerit *B*

338. At that time three episcopal sees in England were transferred from their original cities to other places: Wells by John to Bath, Chester by Robert to Coventry, and Thetford by Herbert to Norwich—all T¹A acting out of lust for gold, all CB with more worldly ambition out of venal ambition and a dis- than ought to have found a place regard for ecclesiastical law. in the activity of such great men. For example, to speak first of the one last mentioned: Herbert, from his skill in adulation surnamed Losinga,¹ after being abbot of Ramsey purchased the bishopric of Thetford, having also thrust his father Robert, who enjoyed the same surname as himself, into the office of abbot of Winchester. Thus that man did much to foster simony in England, by his purchase of an abbacy and a bishopric in return for coin, using his money as bait with which to secure the king's interest and whispering generous promises to gain the favour of the great. As a contemporary poet admirably put it,²

In the Church a monster rises (Losinga was his father's name),
A disciple of Simon's school which canon law condemns.
Peter, you are too slow to act, while Simon scales the skies:
Were you here now, Simon would not wing his way heavenward.
O shame, that churches should now be sold for money, for mere cash!

And further on:

The son a bishop, the father an abbot: Simons both!
What might we too not hope for, if we had the money?
Money is now the master: it does what it would, it adds or takes away;
O the injustice of it! Bishop and abbot are made by money!

339. Yet he repented, and undid the errors of his impetuous youth; for, as his standards rose with age, he set off for Rome and there, having resigned the staff and ring which he had obtained by simony, was allowed by the great mercy of the Holy See to receive them back. In Rome they think it more in accordance with religion and good order that the funds of all the churches should be subservient to their own coffers, rather than be drafted into the service of some casual prince. So Herbert returned home, and transferred his episcopal see, which had once been at Elmham and was then at Thetford, to a busy and populous town called Norwich. There he installed a monastic community

---

¹ French *losenge*, adulation.   ² Walther, *Initia* 18920.

numero et religione percelebrem instituit, omnia eis necessaria ex nummis mercatus domesticis. Prouidens scilicet successorum querelae, nullas episcopii*ᵃ* terras monachis largitus est, ne illi Dei famulos fraudarent uictualibus, si quid donatum offendissent*ᵇ* quod suis competeret rebus. Preterea apud Tetford monachos Cluniacenses instituit, quod sint illius cenobii professores ubique pene gentium dispersi, locupletes in seculo et splendidissimae religionis in Deo. Ingenti ergo et numerosa uirtutum gratia preteritarum offensarum molem obumbrauit, disertitudinis et litterarum copia, nec minus secularium rerum peritia,
3 Romanae quoque celsitudini suspitiendus.*ᶜ* Fuitque Herbertus mutatus, ut Lucanus de Curione ait,*ᵈ*[1] momentum et mutatio rerum; sicut tempore istius regis simoniae causidicus, ita posterius propulsator inuictus, neque ab aliis fieri uoluit quod a se presumptum quondam*ᵉ* iuuenili feruore indoluit, pre se semper, ut aiunt, ferens Hieronimi dictum: 'Errauimus iuuenes, emendemus senes.'[2] Postremo quis in illius facti laudem digne pergat, quod tam nobile monasterium episcopus non multum pecuniosus fecerit, in quo nichil frustra desideres uel in edifitiorum sullimium spetie uel in ornamentorum pulchritudine uel in monachorum religione et ad omnes sedula*ᶠ* caritate? Haec et uiuum spe felici palpabant*ᵍ* et defunctum, si non uana fides penitentiae, super aethera*ʰ* tulerunt.

340. Iohannes erat Wellensis episcopus, natione Turonicus, usu non litteris medicus probatus. Is, defuncto abbate Bathoniensi, abbatiam a rege non grauate*ⁱ* obtinuit, eo quod et*ʲ* in curia omnia uenum agebantur, et auiditatem uidebatur palliare*ᵏ* ratio, ut urbs tam insignis nomen celebrius acciperet ex episcopio. Itaque primo in monachos*ˡ* seueritatem*ᵐ* exercere, quod essent et hebetes et sua estimatione barbari, omnes terras uictualium ministras subtrahens*ⁿ* pauculumque uictum
2 per laicos*ᵒ* exiliter inferens. Sed procedentibus annis, factis monachis nouis, mitius se agere, aliquantulum terrarum quo*ᵖ* se hospitesque suos quomodocumque*ᵍ* sustentarent indulgens priori.*ʳ* Et quanuis 'primo

---

ᵃ de episcopio T¹A, GP p. 151   *ᵇ* ostendissent T¹   *ᶜ* suscipiendus CsB   *ᵈ* dix(it) T¹A, GP p. 152   *ᵉ* quodam T¹   *ᶠ* sed. ad omnes T¹A, GP p. 152   *ᵍ* calcabant T¹   *ʰ* (a)ethera Tt*ᵖ⁻ᶜ*CeBk; (a)ethra T¹ACsBc, GP p. 152   *ⁱ* Tp(gratuito Tt)ABc, GP p. 194 (cf. p. 230); grauante CBk   *ʲ* om. T¹* (cf. GP p. 195 n. 1)   *ᵏ* pall. uid. T¹A   *ˡ* in mon. primo T¹   *ᵐ* tirannidem T¹A, GP p. 195 n. 1   *ⁿ* auferens (-ans Aap) T¹A, GP p. 195   *ᵒ* T¹A*, GP p. 195 add suos   *ᵖ* T¹A*, GP p. 195; qua CB   *ᵍ* quoquomodo B, GP p. 195   *ʳ* priori indulgens T¹A, GP p. 195   *ˢ⁻ˢ* (p. 590) CB; pene in omnibus insulsi esset animi et parum stabilis T¹A (cf. GP p. 195 n. 5)

distinguished by its size and fervour, providing all they needed from his personal resources; for to ensure against the complaints of his successors, he presented to the monks none of the lands belonging to the see, so that no later bishop might deprive God's servants of their daily bread if he found they had been given something that was really his own property. He also settled Cluniac monks at Thetford, for the religious of that convent are dispersed world-wide, rich in the things of this world and of glowing fervour in the service of God. So great and so many were his good deeds that he put into the shade the great mass of his past offences, and earned the respect even of the supreme power in Rome not less by his experience in worldly affairs than by his plentiful eloquence and learning. And so Herbert, thus changed, became, as Lucan[1] says of Curio, a hinge and pivot of affairs: he who in this king's time had been the rascally advocate of simony later became its pitiless opponent, and would not permit in others an offence which he had committed long ago in the rashness of youth and now regretted. He never forgot, they say, that remark of Jerome: 'We erred in youth; let us put it right in old age.'[2] Last but not least, who could adequately praise the achievement of a bishop who without great wealth founded such a noble monastery, which leaves nothing to be desired in the majestic beauty of its buildings, the splendour of its decoration, or the religious fervour and all-embracing charity of its monks? It was these actions that comforted him with good hope while still alive, and after death, if faith in repentance is not ill-founded, raised him to the skies.

340. The bishop of Wells was one John, a native of Tours and by practice rather than book-learning a skilled physician. On the death of the abbot of Bath he secured the abbey from the king, who raised no objection for two reasons: at court everything was bought and sold, and the king's greed could shelter behind reason if it made a city so distinguished even more famous as the seat of a bishop. So at first John treated the monks severely, on the ground that they were lazy and in his opinion barbarian, depriving them of all the land on which they grew their food and grudgingly supplying scanty victuals through lay servants. As the years passed by, however, and fresh monks were admitted, he relented, and allowed the prior a small quantity of land for the support, after a fashion, of himself and his guests. And although at first he had shown great austerity [T¹A at almost all points he had

---

[1] iv. 819.   [2] *Ep.* lxxxiv. 6.

cepisset austerius,[s] multa per eum ibi nobiliter cepta[a] et consummata in ornamentis et libris, maximeque monachorum congregatione, qui sunt scientia litterarum et sedulitate offitii[b] predicabiles. Ceterum numquam, nec etiam moriens, emolliri[c] potuit,[d] ut plena manu terrarum seruitium manumitteret, successoribus suis non imitandum prebens[e] exemplum.

341. Erat in Cestrensi diocesi cenobium Couentreia nomine,[f] quod comes magnificentissimus Lefricus, ut supra fatus sum,[1] cum uxore Godifa constituerat,[g] tanto auri et argenti spectaculo ut ipsi parietes aecclesiae angusti uiderentur thesaurorum receptaculis,[h] miraculo porro magno uisentium oculis. Hoc Rotbertus, eiusdem episcopus prouintiae,[i] inhians [j]non episcopaliter[j] inuolauit, ex ipsis aecclesiae gazis surripiens unde datoris manum suppleret,[k] unde papae occupationes falleret, unde auiditati Romanorum[l] irreperet,[m] pluresque ibi annos moratus nichil probitatis exhibuit: adeo tecta ruinam minitantia[n] numquam periculo exemit, adeo sacras opes dilapidans peculatus crimen incurrit, repetundarum reus futurus episcopus si esset accusator[o]
2 paratus. Monachos miserabili stipe cibans nec ad regularis ordinis amorem curauit accendere nec nisi ad popularem litteraturam passus est aspirare, ne uel ciborum affluentia delicatos uel regulae rigor et scientiae uigor[p] contra se faceret elatos. Agresti igitur uictu et triuiali littera[q] contenti, satis habebant si uel saltem quieti[r] uiuere possent. Quin etiam moriturus, paruifatiens scita canonum quibus edicitur pontifices in suis sedibus[s] sepeliri debere, non apud Cestram sed apud Couentreiam se tumulatum iri precepit, sua opinione relinquens successuris non indebitum calumpniandi sed quasi ius legitimum uendicandi.

342. Hic occasio temporum Willelmi translationem Augustini precellentissimi Anglorum apostoli cum sotiis suis exponi animaret, nisi

---

[s] *See above, p. 588*   [a] ibi nobiliter per eum incepta T'A, GP p. 195   [b] offiociorum iuxta T'A, GP p. 195   [c] T'A, GP p. 195; emendare C; emendari B   [d] uoluit C (potuit uel uoluit Bk)   [e] relinquens T'A   [f] nominatum T'A   [g] constituerant T'Al (see 169. 2n.)   [h] spectaculis B   [i] prou. ep. T'ABk   [j-j] more predonis T'A   [k] regis manum impleret T'A, GP p. 310 n. 1   [l] Rom. auid. T'A*, GP p. 310   [m] arriperet Al, surriperet Aa   [n] minancia Bk, GP p. 310   [o] acc. esset T'   [p] et sc. uigor om. T'   [q] literatura Aac, GP p. 310 (MSS CD)   [r] quiete T'A, GP p. 310 (cf. 235. 4)   [s] sedibus suis T'A, GP p. 310 n. 6

shown himself insensitive and unreliable], he began and carried through a notable programme at Bath in the field of decoration and books, and particularly in building up a monastic community notable for their learning and devotion. All the same, he could never, even on his deathbed, be so softened as with true generosity to give them free access to the income from their lands, thus leaving his successors a precedent that should not be followed.

341. There was in Chester diocese a convent by the name of Coventry, founded, as I have already said,[1] by the most noble Earl Leofric and his wife Godgifu, with such a display of gold and silver that the very walls of the church seemed too narrow to contain all its treasures, and it was a great wonder to all beholders. This excited the cupidity of Robert, bishop of the diocese, and in a most unepiscopal [T¹A thievish] fashion he pounced upon it, seizing enough of the actual treasures of the church to satisfy the hand which had given it to him [T¹A to fill the king's hands], to mislead the pope, busy as he was on other things, and to endear himself to the greed of the Romans; and in that see he spent several years without showing any symptoms of virtue. The roofs threatened to fall in, and he took no steps to rescue them; he despoiled his church of its wealth until he won a name for malversation; and, bishop as he was, he would have been forced by law to disgorge his takings, had there been anyone at hand to bring him to book. He allowed his monks a wretched pittance for their food, and neither tried to kindle within them love of the religious life nor suffered them to aim at anything above an elementary education, for fear that adequate victuals might soften them, or the rigour of the Rule and the vigour of increasing knowledge might encourage them to withstand him. Content therefore with country fare and a smattering of letters, they thought themselves lucky if they could only live unmolested. Even on his deathbed, despising the rules of canon law which lay down that a bishop ought to be buried in his cathedral church, he gave orders for his own interment at Coventry instead of Chester, in his own view leaving his successors in the position, not of claiming something which was not their due but of asserting their title to it as though it were a legal right.

342. At this point the opportunity offered by William's life and times would encourage me to recount the translation of St Augustine,

[1] 196. 2.

peritissimi Goscelini precurrisset ingenium,*a* Goscelini*b* qui monachus de Sancto Bertino cum Hermanno episcopo Salesberiae quondam Angliam uenerat, insignis litterarum et cantuum peritia. Is, multo episcopatus et abbatias perlustrans tempore, preclarae scientiae multis*c* locis monimenta dedit, in laudibus sanctorum Angliae nulli*d* post Bedam secundus, musicae porro*e* palmam post Osbernum*f* adeptus.
2 Denique innumeras sanctorum uitas recentium*g* stilo extulit, ueterum uel hostilitate amissas uel informiter editas comptius renouauit. Huius quoque translationis seriem ita expoliuit ut eam presentibus monstrasse digito futurorumque uideatur subiecisse oculo. Felix lingua quae tot sanctis seruierit, felix pectus quod tot uocales melodias emiserit, presertim cum in eius conuersatione certaret honestas doctrinae! Veruntamen quia de quibusdam episcopis parum laudanda huc usque contexui, aliquos alterius modi disparisque uitae, sed contemporaneos, introducam episcopos, ne ita uideatur nostrum obtorpuisse seculum quod non aliquem producat sanctum. Sed hanc sponsionem sequenti libro[1] post enarrata gesta Henrici regis cui placuerit experietur.

343. Nunc iter Ierosolimitanum scripto expediam, aliorum uisa*h* et sensa meis uerbis allegans. Proinde, sicut se occasio ingesserit, de situ et diuitiis Constantinopoleos, Antiochiae,*i* Ierusalem ex scriptis maiorum deflorata subtexam, ut qui ea*j* ignorat et haec forte inuenerit, in promptu habeat quae aliis cognoscenda ipse proponat. Sed ad haec enarranda feruentiore opus est spiritu, ut consummem efficaciter quod incipio tam hilariter. Appellata igitur in auxilium, ut mos est, Diuinitate, tale aucupabor exordium.

344. Anno ab incarnatione Domini millesimo nonagesimo quinto papa Vrbanus secundus, qui presidebat apostolico culmini, euasis Alpibus uenit in Gallias. Aduentus causa ferebatur perspicua quod uiolentia Wiberti Roma extrusus citramontanas ad sui reuerentiam sollicitaret aecclesias. Illud repositius propositum non ita uulgabatur, quod Boamundi consilio pene totam*k* Europam in Asiaticam

a ing. precurrisset *A*; om. *T¹* *b* Goscelinus *(Bc)Cs*; om. *T¹Bk* *c* pluribus *T¹A* *d* nulli *before* in laudibus *T¹A* *e* *T¹A add* primam *f* post Osbernum *om. T¹* *g* rec. uitas *T¹A** *h* uerba *T¹* *i* et Ant. et *T¹A* *j* illa *T¹A* *k* totam pene *T¹A*

[1] cc. 440–5.

the most excellent apostle of the English, and his companions, had I not been forestalled by the gifted and experienced pen of Goscelin— Goscelin, a monk of Saint-Bertin, who had at some time come to England with Hereman, bishop of Salisbury, and was distinguished as a scholar and as a skilled musician. He spent much time visiting cathedrals and abbeys, and in many places left evidence of his notable learning; for in the celebration of the English saints he was second to none since Bede, and in music he won the palm next after Osbern. He 2 composed, for example, lives of countless saints of modern times, and rewrote in more elegant fashion those of ancient saints either lost by enemy action or published with no grace of style. He also polished up the story of St Augustine's translation so vividly that he seemed to point a finger at every detail for his contemporaries and make future ages see it with their own eyes. Happy the tongue that rendered service to so many saints, the breath from which proceeded such sweet melodies!—not least because in his religious life learning was matched with integrity. But, since hitherto I have put together a story that does certain bishops little credit, I shall introduce a few prelates of a very different metal and another mode of life, although of our own time; for I would not have our generation thought to have grown so cold as to be unable to produce a single saint. But the fulfilment of this promise anyone who wishes will find in the following book, when I have told the story of King Henry.[1]

343. I will now recount the journey to Jerusalem, reporting in my own words what other men saw and felt. Next, as opportunity offers, I will subjoin selections from the work of ancient authors on the position and the riches of Constantinople, Antioch, and Jerusalem, so that anyone ignorant of those writings who may happen on my work may have something ready to his hand with which he can enlighten other people. But the telling of this story needs a touch of inspiration, if I am to finish effectively what I so light-heartedly undertake; and so I will call, as the custom is, upon God's help, and thus I will begin.

344. In the year of our Lord 1095, Pope Urban II, who then held the Apostolic See, crossed the Alps and arrived in Gaul. The ostensible and reported purpose of his journey was to seek recognition from the churches this side of the Alps, for he had been driven out of Rome by Wibert's violence. He had, however, a less immediate aim which was not so widely made known: to arouse almost all Europe, on the advice

expeditionem moueret, ut, in tanto tumultu omnium prouintiarum facile obaeratis auxiliaribus, et Vrbanus Romam et Boamundus Illir-
2 icum et Macedoniam peruaderent.[a] Nam eas terras, et quicquid preterea a Dirachio usque in Thessalonicam protenditur, Guiscardus pater super Alexium adquisierat. Iccirco illas Boamundus iuri suo competere clamitabat, inops hereditatis Apulae,[b] quam genitor Rogero comiti[c] filio delegauerat. Veruntamen quaecumque transeundi fuerit occasio, magno et illustri aduentus eius fuit emolumento Christianis.[d] Coactum ergo est[e] apud Clarum Montem concilium, quae clarissima est urbs[f] Aruernorum; numerus[g] episcoporum et abbatum trecentorum[h] decem; ubi aliquot diebus primo de catholica fide et inter se dissidentium[i] pace
3 tractatus prolixe habitus. Nam preter flagitia quibus singuli licenter[j] incubabant, ad hoc[k] calamitatis omnes Cisalpini deuenerant, ut nullis uel minimis causis extantibus[l] quisque alium caperet, nec nisi magno redemptum abire sineret. Preterea simonicus anguis ita lubricum caput erexerat, ita uenenato fotu[m] mortiferi germinis oua uaporauerat[n] ut totus orbis letali sibilo[o] infectus aecclesiasticos honores corrumperet. Tunc enim non dicam episcopi ad aecclesias, sed nec quislibet[p] ad quoscumque ordines nisi per pecunias aspirabat. Tunc legitimis uxoribus exclusis multi contrahebant diuortium, alienum expugnantes matrimonium. Quare, quia in his et in illis erat confusa criminum silua, ad penam quorundam potentiorum designata sunt nomina. Vnde, ne longum fatiam, totius[q] actionem concilii subnectam, quaedam meis sermonibus pro compendio breuians.

345. [r]In concilio apud Clarum Montem sub presentia domni Vrbani papae haec capitula finita sunt: Quod aecclesia catholica sit[s] in fide, casta,[t] libera ab omni seculari[u] seruitute. Vt episcopi uel abbates uel aliquis de clero aliquam aecclesiasticam dignitatem de manu principum uel quorumlibet laicorum non accipiant. Quod clerici in duabus aecclesiis uel ciuitatibus[v] prebendas non habeant. Quod aliquis simul

[a] peruaderet T^tA [b] Appul(a)e *(Apulie Aap, as Cs)* her. T^tA [c] minori T^tA^* [d] Chr. fuit emol. T^tA; fuit Chr. emol. *B*   [e] est ergo T^tA^* [f] urbs est T^tA [g] T^tA *add* fuit congregatorum   [h] *So the MSS that do not abbreviate the number*   [i-i] eorum qui inter se dissidebant T^tA [j] licenter singuli T^tA [k] haec *C*   [l] extantibus causis T^tA *(cf. GP p. 305)*   [m] fetu *CB*   [n] uaporauerant T^tA [o] sibilo l(a)etali T^tA [p] quilibet T^tA *(cf. VD p. 292)*   [q] totam T^t [r] *This chapter is one witness (and θκ , i.e. William's Liber Pontificalis, are two more) to an Anglo-Norman version of the canons of the Council of Clermont, ed. R. Somerville, Ann. Hist. Conc. Suppl. 1 (1972), 89–98*   [s] sit catholica T^tA [t] T^tA, θκ *add* pudicitia   [u] *om. CB*   [v] cui. uel(a)eccl. T^tA, θκ

of Bohemond, for an expedition into Asia, in order that in the great confusion that would ensue in every province, which would make it easy to hire auxiliary troops, Urban might overrun Rome, and Bohemond Illyricum and Macedonia. For those provinces, and whatever else stretches from Durazzo as far as Salonica, had been taken from Alexius by Bohemond's father Guiscard, and he therefore claimed that they rightly belonged to him, for he had been stripped of his inheritance in Apulia, which his father had handed over to his son Duke Roger. But whatever the motive for the pope's crossing of the Alps, his arrival did a great and glorious service to Christendom. So a council was summoned at Clermont, a famous city in the Auvergne. The number of bishops and abbots was three hundred and ten; and there some days were spent first in prolonged discussion of the catholic faith and the reconciliation of those who were in disagreement. For besides the criminal behaviour in which individuals used freely to indulge, all men this side of the Alps had reached such depths of calamity that for the very slightest reason or none at all anyone would take another man prisoner and not let him go free except on payment of a heavy ransom. Simony too had so raised its slimy head, and hatched such a poisonous brood of eggs fraught with death, that the whole world was noisome with its lethal hiss, and all promotion in the Church infected; for at that time, I will not say no bishop aspired to a see—no one aspired to any position in the Church, unless he backed his ambitions with coin of the realm. At that time many men, locking out their lawful wives, entered upon divorce by wrecking another man's marriage. As a result, since in both classes there was a tangled thicket of offences, some more powerful persons were mentioned by name with a view to punishment. And so, in order not to be tedious, I will subjoin the deliberations of the whole council, abbreviating some things in my own words to save space.

345. In the council held at Clermont in the presence of our lord Pope Urban the following resolutions were accepted: that the Church should be catholic in faith, chaste, and free from all worldly servitude. That bishops or abbots or any member of the clergy must accept no ecclesiastical dignity from the hands of princes or of any layman whatsoever. That clerks must not hold prebends in two churches or cities. That a man cannot be at the same time both a bishop and an

episcopus[a] et abbas esse non possit. Quod aecclesiasticae dignitates a
2 nullo emantur uel uendantur. Quod nullus cuiuslibet sacri ordinis
carnali commertio utatur. Quod eis qui ignorantes canonum prohibitionem canonias emerunt ignoscatur.[b] Quod eis qui scienter emptas a se uel a parentibus suis possederunt[c] auferantur. Quod nemo laicorum a capite ieiunii, nemo clericorum a Quinquagesima usque in Pascha carnes comedat. Quod omni tempore primum ieiunium quattuor temporum prima ebdomada Quadragesimae fiat. Quod ordines omni tempore uel in uespere sabbati uel perseuerante ieiunio in dominica celebrentur. Vt in sabbato Paschae non nisi post horam[d] nonam offitium celebretur. Vt ieiunium secundum in ebdomada Pentecostes celebretur.[e]
3 Quod ab Aduentu Domini usque ad octauas Epiphaniae, et a Septuagesima usque ad octauas Paschae, et a prima die Rogationum usque ad octauas Pentecostes,[f] et a quarta feria occidente sole omni tempore usque ad secundam feriam oriente sole treuia Dei custodiatur. Quod qui episcopum[g] ceperit, omnino exlex habeatur. Quod qui sacri ordinis uiros uel eorum famulos ceperit, anathema sit. Quod qui episcoporum uel clericorum morientium bona ceperit, anathema sit. Quod qui usque ad septimam[h] generationem
4 consanguinitati se copulauerit, anathema sit. Quod nemo in episcopum eligatur nisi presbiter aut diaconus aut subdiaconus, et cui natalium dignitas suffragatur, nisi maxima necessitate et licentia papae. Quod filii presbiterorum uel concubinarum ad presbiteratum non prouehantur,[i] nisi prius ad religiosam uitam transierint. Quod qui ad aecclesiam uel ad crucem confugerint,[j] data membrorum impunitate iustitiae tradantur uel innocentes liberentur.[k] Quod unaquaeque aecclesia decimas suas habeat, nec ad alteram transeant.[l] Quod laicus decimas[m] nec emat nec uendat.[n] Quod pro sepultura mortuorum pretium non recipiatur.[o]
5 In eo concilio excommunicauit domnus papa Philippum regem Francorum et omnes qui eum uel[p] regem uel dominum suum[q] uocauerint et ei obedierint [r]et ei locuti fuerint, nisi quod pertinet ad eum corrigendum;[r] similiter et illam maledictam coniugem eius et omnes qui eam reginam uel dominam nominauerint, quousque ad emendationem uenerint,[1] ita ut alter ab altero discedat. Similiter

[a] ep. simul *T'A, θκ*   [b] ignoscitur *T'Al*   [c] habuerunt (om. suis, as *θκ*) *T'A*   [d] om. *T'A* (cf. VW iii. 18)   [e] fiat *T'A*   [f] Pentecosten *T'Al, θ*   [g] episcopum qui *C*   [h] sextam (or VI) *CsB*   [i] promoueantur *CeBc, θκ*   [j] confugerit *T'A, θκ*   [k] tradatur (reddatur *θκ*) uel innocens liberetur *T'A, θκ*   [l] aliam transeat *CB*   [m] decimam *CB*   [n] nec emat nec uendat *CB*; nec (non *Aap*) uendat nec retineat *T'A, θκ*   [o] exigatur *T'A, θκ*   [p] om.

abbot. That ecclesiastical dignities may not be bought or sold by any man. That no man in any form of holy orders may indulge in sexual 2 activity. That those who have purchased canonries in ignorance of the canonical prohibition may be pardoned. That those who have knowingly held those purchased by themselves or by their relatives should be deprived of them. That no layman from Ash Wednesday and no cleric from Quinquagesima may eat meat until Easter. That for all time the first of the Ember Day fasts should take place in the first week of Lent. That for all time ordinations are to be celebrated either on the evening of Saturday or, the fast continuing, on a Sunday. That on the Saturday before Easter the office be not said except after the ninth hour. That the second fast be kept in the week of Pentecost. That from Advent to the octave of Epiphany and from Septuagesima 3 to the octave of Easter and from the first day of Rogationtide to the octave of Pentecost and from sunset on Wednesday for the whole of the time until sunrise on Monday the truce of God shall be kept. That he who has taken a bishop prisoner shall be treated as an outlaw in all respects. That he who has taken prisoner men in holy orders or their servants shall be anathema. That he who has seized the goods of bishops or clerics on their death shall be anathema. That he who has contracted marriage with his kindred unto the seventh generation shall be anathema. That no man shall be elected to a bishopric unless 4 he be priest or deacon or subdeacon and supported by legitimate birth, except in time of great need and under licence from the pope. That sons of priests or concubines shall not be promoted to the priesthood, unless they shall first have entered the religious life. That those who have taken sanctuary in a church or at a cross shall be granted immunity in life and limb before being handed over to justice, or if they are innocent shall be set free. That each individual church shall have its own tithes, nor shall they pass to any other church. That no layman shall buy or sell tithes. That a price shall not be accepted for the burial of the dead.

In that council our lord the pope excommunicated Philip king of the 5 French and all those who called him either their king or their lord and obeyed him and spoke with him, except as regards the correction of his errors. Likewise that accursed woman his wife and all those who called her either their queen or their lady, until they[1] be brought to mend their ways with the effect that each parts from the other. Likewise

T^tA (cf. qui eam reginam *below*) ^{q} om. A (cf. reginam uel dominam *below*)
$^{r-r}$ om. T^t

---

[1] i.e. the couple.

Wibertum Rauennatem, qui se papam appellat, et Henricum imperatorem Alemannorum, qui eum manutenet.*ᵃ*

346. Posteris diebus processit sermo*ᵇ* ad populum sane luculentus et efficax, qualem decet sacerdotis*ᶜ* esse, de Christianorum expeditione in Turchos; quem, sicut ab auditoribus accepi, placuit posteris transmittere, integro uerborum sensu custodito: illius enim facundiae uigorem seruare quis poterit? Nobiscum agitur*ᵈ* feliciter si, propinquam terentes orbitam, per aliquod diuerticulum redeamus*ᵉ* ad sententiam.

347. 'Multa' inquit, 'fratres carissimi, his diebus*ᶠ* uobis dicta recolitis: quaedam in concilio nostro iussa, quaedam inhibita. Inconditum et confusum scelerum chaos exigebat multorum*ᵍ* dierum interstitium; ueternus morbus uolebat cauterium. Dum enim indulgenti fune clementiae dimittimus lineam, multa modo apostolatus nostri offendit offitium quae precideret, nulla quibus parceret. Sed fuerit hactenus humanae fragilitatis quod peccastis, quod illecebrarum inuolucris sopiti caelestem exasperastis misericordiam, suspensam 2 paruipendendo iracundiam. *ʰ*Fuerit mundanae temulentiae quod, legitima non curantes matrimonia, alieni *ⁱ*cubilis non*ⁱ* pensastis iniuriam.*ʰ* Fuerit auiditatis nimiae quod fratres uestros, illo magno et eodem pretio emptos, ut quisque poterat illaqueantes contumeliose pecuniis emunxistis. Nunc uobis, inter ista peccatorum naufragia constitutis, portus placidae quietis aperitur, nisi negligitis.*ʲ* Parui laboris in Turchos compendio retribuetur uobis perpetuae salutis statio. Comparate nunc labores quos in scelerum exercitio habuistis, et 3 eos quos in itinere quod precipio habituri estis. Plures uel adulterii uel homicidii meditatio dat timores (nichil enim timidius nequitia, ut ait Salomon*ᵏ*[1]), multos labores (quid enim laboriosius iniustitia?); qui autem ambulat simpliciter, ambulat confidenter.[2] Horum laborum, horum timorum exitus erat*ˡ* peccatum; stipendium autem*ᵐ* peccati mors,[3] mors uero peccatorum pessima. Nunc a uobis "par labor atque metus pretio meliore petuntur".[4] Horum laborum erit causa caritas ut,

---

ᵃ *T'A add* et cetera *ᵇ* sermo processit *T'A* *ᶜ* pontificis *T'A* *ᵈ* agetur *T'A** *ᵉ* recurramus *T'A* *ᶠ* diebus hi(i)s *CsB* *ᵍ om. CB*
ʰ⁻ʰ om. A *ⁱ⁻ⁱ* laboris *T'* *ʲ* nisi neg. aperitur *T'A (cf. 268.3)*
ᵏ per Salomonem sapientia *T'A (cf. Boniface at c. 81 above)* *ˡ* erat exitus *T'A*
ᵐ stipendia enim *B, Vulg.*

---

[1] Wisd. 17: 10.
[2] Prov. 10: 9.
[3] Rom. 6: 23.
[4] Lucan i. 282.

Wibert of Ravenna who calls himself pope, and Henry emperor of Germany who supports him.

346. During the next days a sermon was delivered before the people which was truly brilliant and persuasive as a priest's words ought to be, on the subject of an expedition by Christians against the Turks; and this I have decided to hand down to posterity, as I received it from those who heard it, preserving intact the sense of what was said; the eloquence and force of the original who can reproduce? We shall be fortunate if, treading an adjacent path, we return by a circuitous route to its meaning.

347. 'You will remember, dearly beloved brethren,'—so he began—'all you have heard during these days, the ordinances and the prohibitions of our Council. Wild and confused was the abyss of wickedness; it demanded a long interval for consideration, and chronic disease cried out for cautery. While we pay out the line in mercy and slacken the rope of indulgence, my Apostolic office has now found much that needs the knife and nothing that should be spared. But let us call it human frailty hitherto if you have sinned, if you have been lulled in the embraces of temptation, have thought nothing of the wrath poised over your heads, and thus have tried the patience of the divine mercy. Let us call it the intoxication of life in the world if you have made light of lawful wedlock and thought nothing of violating another man's bed. Let us call it excess of appetite if you have taken every opportunity to ensnare your brethren, redeemed as they were for the same great price as you, and shamefully stripped them of their resources. But now, as you head for shipwreck among these dangerous reefs of sin, a haven of peace opens before you—unless you neglect it. Devote a little exertion to the Turks, and your effort will be rewarded by the anchorage of everlasting salvation. Do but compare the energy you have expended on criminal practices and what will be demanded by the journey I am recommending to you. Many are the terrors that spring from adulterous and murderous thoughts, for, as Solomon says, "Nothing is more timorous than wickedness";[1] many the toils (for what is more toilsome than injustice?). But "he that walketh uprightly, walketh surely."[2] Of these toils and these terrors the outcome was sin: "the wages of sin is death",[3] and the deaths of sinners are the worst of all. Now "no greater are the toil and fear you seek, but higher the reward".[4] The motive force of your toils will be

precepto Dominico¹ ammoniti, animas pro fratribus ponatis; caritatis stipendium erit Dei gratia; Dei gratiam sequetur uita aeterna.

4 'Ite ergo feliciter, ite confidenter ad inimicos Dei persequendos. Illi enim iam pridem (proh quantus Christianorum pudor!) Siriam, Armeniam, omnem postremo Asiam Minorem, cuius prouintiae sunt Bithinia Frigia Galatia Lidia Caria Pamphilia Isauria Litia Cilitia, occuparunt; nunc Illiricum et omnes inferiores terras insolentes inequitant, usque ad mare quod Brachium sancti Georgii uocatur. Quid quod Dominicum monimentum, unicum fidei pignus,ᵃ ditioni suae uendicant, et eius urbis introitum peregrinis nostris uenditant quae solis Christianis patere deberet, si aliquod solitae uirtutis uesti-
5 giumᵇ eis inesset? Hoc si solum esset, frontes nostras onerare sufficeret; iam uero quis ferat nisi multum iners, nisi Christianae gloriae inuidus, quod non ex aequo diuisimus orbem?² Illi Asiam, tertiam mundi partem, ut hereditarium nidum inhabitant, quae a maioribus nostris aequa duabus residuis partibus, et tractuum longitudine et prouintiarum magnitudine, non immerito estimata est. Ibi olim deuotionis nostraeᶜ rami pullularunt; ibi apostoli omnes, preter duos, mortes suas consecrarunt; ibi modo Christicolae, si qui supersunt, pauperculo agriculatu transigentes inediam nefandis illis uectigal pensitant, uel tacitis suspiriis nostraeᵈ libertatis desiderantes con-
6 scientiam, quia perdidereᵉ suam. Illi Affricam, alteram orbis partem, ducentis iam annis et eo amplius armis possessam tenent; quod ideo Christiani honoris periculum pronuntio, quia fuerit terra illa olim preclarorum ingeniorum altrix, quae diuinis scriptis omnem uetustatis situm a se repellent, quam diu fuerit qui Latinas litteras legat. Norunt litterati quod loquor. Tertium mundi clima restat Europa, cuius quantulam partem inhabitamus Christiani! Nam omnem illam barbariem quae in remotis insulis glatialem frequentatᶠ oceanum, quia
7 more beluino uictitat, Christianam quis dixerit? Hanc igitur nostri mundi portiunculam Turchi et Saraceni bello premunt, iamque, a trecentis annis Hispania et Balearibus insulis subiugatis, quod reliquum est spe deuorant, homines inertissimi et qui, comminus pugnandi fidutiam non habentes, fugax bellum diligunt. Numquam enim Turchus pede conserto martem audet, sed pulsus loco longe tendit

---

ᵃ mon. Dom. pig. fid. unicum T'A   ᵇ uest. uirt. T'A   ᶜ nostr(a)e deuotionis T'A   ᵈ uestr(a)e T'A   ᵉ amisere T'A   ᶠ frequentant C

¹ John 15: 13 conflated with 1 John 3: 16.   ² Lucan v. 495.

charity, that following the Lord's commands[1] you may lay down your lives for your brethren; the reward of charity will be God's favour, and God's favour will be followed by eternal life.

'Go forth then and prosper, go in good heart to attack the enemies of God. Long have they occupied, to the great shame of Christendom, Syria and Armenia and finally the whole of Asia Minor, of which the provinces are Bithynia, Phrygia, Galatia, Lydia, Caria, Pamphylia, Isauria, Lycia, Cilicia; and now in their insolence they raid Illyricum and all the nearer provinces as far as what is known as the Arm of St George. Nay more, they claim as theirs the Lord's sepulchre, that supreme monument of our faith, and take money from our pilgrims for entrance to a city that ought to be open exclusively to Christians, if they yet had in them some vestige of their wonted valour. If this were all, it would be shame enough for us; but he must be a real craven and hostile to the reputation of Christianity who can bear to see how "unfair is our division of the world".[2] They dwell in Asia as their ancestral home, the third part of the earth, which our forefathers not without reason regarded, for its wide open spaces and the greatness of its provinces, as the equal of the other two combined. There in old days the branches of our religion sprouted; there all the Apostles save two met their holy deaths; and there the Christians of today, those who remain, eke out a starveling livelihood by pitiful tillage of the soil while paying tribute to those rascals, longing even with suppressed sighs for knowledge of our liberty because they have lost their own. They hold Africa, the second part of the world, having won it two hundred and more years ago by force of arms; and this, I maintain, sets the honour of Christendom in peril, because that land of Africa was in old days the nurse of famous men of genius, whose inspired productions will preserve them from any taint of age and decay, as long as anyone remains who can read Latin. Every educated man knows what I mean. There remains Europe, the third division of the world; and how small a part of that do we Christians live in! For all those barbarous peoples who in far-distant islands frequent the ice-bound Ocean, living as they do like beasts—who could call them Christians? This small part, then, of our world is threatened by Turks and Saracens with war. For three hundred years ago they overran Spain and the Balearic Islands; now they fully expect to devour what remains, for all that they are the least valiant of men and, having no confidence in hand-to-hand combat, love fighting on the run. No Turk ever dares do battle at close quarters, and when driven from his

neruos et permittit uulnera uentis;[1] et quoniam*a* habet tela mortifero suco ebria, in homine quem percutit non uirtus sed uirus mortem facit. Quicquid igitur agit, fortunae, non fortitudini attribuerim, quod
8 pugnat*b* fuga et ueneno. Constat profecto quod omnis natio quae in Eoa*c* plaga nascitur, nimio solis ardore siccata, amplius quidem sapit, sed minus habet sanguinis; ideoque uicinam pugnam fugiunt, quia parum sanguinis se habere norunt. Contra, populus qui oritur*d* in Arctois*e* pruinis, et remotus est*f* a solis ardoribus, inconsultior quidem sed largo et luxurianti superbus sanguine promptissime pugnat. Vos estis gens quae*g* in temperatioribus mundi prouintiis oriunda, qui sitis et prodigi sanguinis ad*h* mortis uulnerumque contemptum et non careatis prudentia; namque et modestiam seruatis in castris, et in dimicatione utimini*i* consiliis.
9 'Itaque, scientia et fortitudine prediti,*j* aggredimini memorabile iter,*k* totis seculis predicandi si fratres uestros periculo exueritis.*l* Presentibus ex Dei nomine precipio, absentibus mando. Ituri et Christianitatem propugnaturi*m* specimen*n* crucis uestibus insigniant,*o* ut intestinae fidei foris amorem pretendant, habentes per Dei concessum et beati Petri priuilegium omnium absolutionem criminum, et hac interim laetitia laborem itineris alleuient, habituri post obitum felicis martirii
10 commertium. Ponentes ergo*p* ferias sceleribus, ut saltem in his regionibus liceat Christianis pacifice*q* uiuere, uadite, illam fortitudinem, prudentiam illam, quam in ciuili conflictu habere consuestis, iustiori effundentes prelio. Ite, predicabiles per orbem milites! Ite, et prosternite ignauas gentes! Eat famosa Francorum uirtus cum appenditiis sibi gentibus, solo sui nominis terrore totum orbem*r* motura.
11 'Sed quid uos diutius immoror, ut fortitudinem gentilium*s* uerbis extenuem? Immo proponite animis uestris deificam sententiam: "Angusta est uia quae ducit ad uitam."[2] Esto ergo ut sit semita itinerantium arcta, plena mortibus, suspecta periculis; sed haec eadem uos amissam ducet ad patriam; per multas nimirum tribulationes oportet nos*t* introire in regnum Dei.[3] Spectate ergo animo, si prensi fueritis,

a quia T'A   *b* pugnet T'A   *c* ea AapB   *d* oritur *after* pruinis T'A   *e* Arctos B   *f* om. T'Al   *g* om. A, *elegantly*   *h* et B *i* ut. in dim. T'A   *j* fort. pred. et sc. T'A   *k* iter mem. T'A   *l* exueritis periculo T'A   *m* propagaturi T'A* *(cf. GP p. 141* fidem... propagauit*)*   *n* speciem T'   *o* insignant Tt*a.c.*, -nat Tp   *p* igitur T*t*   *q* pac. Chr. T'A   *r* orientem T'A   *s* gentium CBc   *t* uos T'Al

[1] Lucan viii. 380-4.   [2] Matt. 7:14.   [3] Acts 14:21.

ground he "draws his bowstring from afar" and "trusts his missile to the wandering winds";[1] his bolts having drunk their fill of liquid poison, it is venom and not valour that brings death to the man they strike. If he achieves anything, therefore, I would ascribe it to fortune and not fortitude, seeing that his weapons of war are flight and poison. It is in fact well known that every nation born in an Eastern clime is dried up by the great heat of the sun; they may have more good sense, but they have less blood in their veins, and that is why they flee from battle at close quarters: they know that they have no blood to spare. A people, on the other hand, whose origin is in the northern frosts and who are far removed from the sun's heat, are less rational but fight most readily, in proud reliance on a generous and exuberant supply of blood. You are a race originating in the more temperate regions of the world, men whose readiness to shed your blood leads to a contempt for death and wounds, though you are not without forethought; for you observe moderation in camp, and in the heat of battle you find room for reason.

'And so, armed with experience and resolution, embark upon a memorable journey; you will be extolled by all future ages if you rescue your brethren from peril. To you who are here today I give orders in God's name, and to those who are not I issue His commission. Those who will take the road and act as champions of Christendom should fasten on their garments the image of the Cross, as an outward symbol of devotion to their inward faith, enjoying by God's grant and the privilege of St Peter absolution from all their offences, and with the joy of this they should lighten for the moment the labour of their journey, while expecting after death the compensation of a blessed martyrdom. Call a halt therefore to your crimes, that in these regions at least Christians may be free to live in peace, and go on your way, expending in a more righteous conflict the resolution and the foresight which you have become accustomed to display in civil strife. Go forth, you whose knightly reputation fills the world! Go forth, and lay these cowardly nations low! Let the celebrated valour of the Franks, with the nations under their sway, advance, and the mere terror of their name will shake the whole earth.

'But why should I delay any longer, in order to dispraise in words the courage of the gentiles? Much better set before your hearts that divine saying: "Narrow is the way that leadeth unto life."[2] It may well be that the path to be travelled is constricted, full of death in many forms, and overcast with perils; but this same road will lead you to the fatherland that you have lost, for indeed "We must through much tribulation enter into the kingdom of God".[3] Dwell therefore on the

cruces, spectate catenas, quaecumque postremo possunt tormenta*^a* infligi; operimini pro fidei uestrae robore horrenda suplitia, ut, si necesse fuerit, dampno corporum agatis animarum remedium. Mortemne timetis, uiri fortissimi, fortitudine et audatia*^b* prestantes? Nichil certe in uos poterit comminisci*^c* humana nequitia quo superna pensetur gloria; non enim sunt*^d* condignae passiones huius temporis ad futuram gloriam quae reuelabitur in nobis.[1] An nescitis quod uiuere hominibus est*^e* calamitas, mori felicitas? Haec uobis*^f* doctrina, si recordamini, cum lacte matrum*^g* affusa*^h* est sacerdotum uerbo; hanc maiores uestri martires pretenderunt exemplo. Mors enim a cenulento carcere liberat animas, ad proprium locum pro meritis euolaturas; mors accelerat bonis patriam, mors precidit reis malitiam. Per mortem ergo liberae animae uel oblectantur*ⁱ* gaudiis, spe meliora presumentes, uel fruuntur suplitiis, nichil peius timentes. Dum autem uinculis corporum irretiuntur, trahunt ab ipsis terrulenta contagia et, quod ueraciter quis dicat, mortuae sunt; nec enim luteum caelesti, diuinum mortali pulchre coheret. Plurimum quidem potest anima etiam nunc corpore uincta;*^j* instrumentum enim suum uiuificat, latenter id mouens et ultra mortalem naturam gestis producens. Veruntamen cum, sarcina*^k* qua in terram trahitur absoluta, proprium locum receperit, beatam et undique liberam participat fortitudinem, quomodocumque diuinae naturae inuisibilitati*^l* communicans. Gemino ergo functa offitio, corpori uitam ministrat cum adest, causam uero mutationis cum recedit. Videtis quam iocunde anima in dormienti*^m* corpore uigilet et, a sensibus seducta,*ⁿ* pro diuina cognatione multa futura prouideat. Cur ergo mortem timetis, qui somni requiem, quae instar mortis est, diligitis? Res est nimirum dementiae pro cupiditate breuis uitae inuidere sibi perpetuam.

Quin potius, fratres carissimi, si ita contigerit, ponite pro fratribus animas uestras; uacuate ab impiis Dei sacrarium, extrudite latrones, inducite pios. Nulla uos necessitudinis pietas contineat, quia prima hominis pietas*^o* in Deum. Nullum natalis soli caritas tricet, quia

---

^a torm. poss. *T'A*   *^b* aud. et fort. *T'A*   *^c* poterit comm. in uos *T'A*
^d sunt enim *T'*   *^e* om. *T'*; *after* uiuere *A*   *^f* uobiscum *T'A*   *^g* matris
T'   *^h* effusa *A*   *ⁱ* oblectentur *B*   *^j* iuncta *TpCeB, requiring* corpori *(so Cd)*   *^k* sarcinam *T'*   *^l* inuisibilitate *T'A*   *^m* dormiente *T'A**
ⁿ sed. a sens. *T'A*   *^o* pietas hominis *T'A*

[1] Rom. 8: 18.

crosses that await you if you are captured; dwell on the chains and in a word all the torments that can be inflicted on you; await for the strengthening of your faith those horrible punishments, so that, if it should prove necessary, you may procure by the loss of your bodies the salvation of your souls. Do you fear death, men of great courage as you are, and of outstanding fortitude and daring? Nothing that human wickedness can invent to use against you can outweigh the glories on high, for "the sufferings of this present time are not worthy to be compared with the glory which shall be revealed in us."[1] Do you not know that for men to live is a calamity and to die is happiness? This lesson, if you remember, was instilled into you with your mother's milk in the words of priests, and your martyred ancestors demonstrated it to you by their example. Death frees our souls from their filthy prisons, that they may fly up to the place where they belong in accordance with their deserts. Death brings the good more quickly to their fatherland; for the bad, it cuts short their career of wickedness. Thus our souls, set free by death, are either regaled with joys beyond all their hopes, or profit by punishment, than which they have nothing worse to fear. While they are bound fast in the meshes of the body, they draw the contagion of earth from those same bodies and (as a man might say with truth) are dead, for the earthy does not unite properly with the heavenly, nor the divine with the mortal. There is indeed much that the soul can do even now, bound as it is by the body, for it gives life to the body that is its tool, moving it in some hidden way and by its activity drawing that body beyond the limits of mortal nature. But once it has been liberated from the burden that drags it down to earth and has been allotted to its proper place, it wins a share in a fortitude that is blessed and in all directions free, because somehow or other it is in touch with the invisible mystery of the divine nature. Thus it performs a double office: it provides the body with life while it is in the body, and a reason for change when it departs. You see how cheerfully the soul keeps watch in the sleeping body and, now separate from the senses, can, because of its kinship with the divine, foresee many things that will come to pass. Why then fear death, when you love the repose of sleep, which is death's image? It is surely a crazy business, out of desire for this short life to deny oneself life everlasting.

'Rather, dearly beloved brethren, lay down your lives for your brethren if need be; clear the impious out of God's sanctuary, drive out the robbers and install the godfearing. Let no devotion to the ties of kinship restrain you, for man's first devotion must be towards God. Let no man be diverted by love of his native soil, because from different

diuersis respectibus Christiano totus est mundus[a] exilium et totus mundus patria; ita exilium patria, et patria[b] exilium. Nullum patrimoniorum amplitudo remoretur, quia ampliora sunt quae promittuntur, nec ea quae inani spe miseris adulentur uel ignauam mentem pigro[c] rerum meditamine[d] palpent,[1] sed crebris exemplis exhibita, frequenti usu comprobata. Et haec quidem sunt dultia,[e] sed caduca et quae centuplicatum contemptoribus suis[f] pretium important.

16 'Haec edico, haec mando, terminumque proximi ueris affigo. Aderit Deus euntibus, ut eis bonus[g] arrideat annus cum copia frugum, tum[h] serenitate temporum. Morituri caeli intrabunt triclinium, uicturi uidebunt sepulchrum Dominicum. Et quae maior felicitas quam ut homo, in terris agens, uideat loca illa in quibus caelorum Dominus conuersatus est[i] humanitus? Felices qui ad haec uocantur munia ut illa nanciscantur munera! Fortunati qui meditantur ista[j] prelia ut illa consequantur premia!'

348. Huiusce orationis tenorem scripsi, pauca propter ueritatem dictorum incastigato sermone depromens, plura manumittens. Hinc igitur populus auditorum accensus[k] iuditium animi clamore testatur, fauens sermocinationi, fauens peregrinationi; statimque in concilio proceres nonnulli, papae genibus affusi,[l] se suaque Dei militiae consecrarunt, e quibus fuit[m] Aimarus, insignis potentiae Podiensis episcopus, qui postea exercitum illum rexit prudentia, auxit[n] eloquentia. Igitur Nouembri mense,[o] in quo concilium actum fuit,[p] a singulis in
2 sua discessum. Continuoque fama boni, totum perlapsa orbem, dulci Christianorum animos infecit aura; qua circumquaque spirante, nulla fuit tam remota gens, tam abdita, quae non sui partem[q] mitteret. Nam non solum mediterraneas prouincias hic amor mouit, sed et omnes qui uel in penitissimis insulis uel in nationibus barbaris Christi nomen audierant. Tunc Walensis uenationem saltuum, tunc Scottus familiaritatem pulicum,[r] tunc Danus[s] continuationem potuum, tunc Noricus cruditatem reliquit piscium. Destituebantur agri cultoribus,

[a] mundus est (est om. Tt[a.c.]) T'Al* (Aap omits the context)   [b] patri Al (Aap omits the context)   [c] pigus Bk (and Cp; pignus Cs), pigrius Bc   [d] medicamine B   [e] dulcia sunt T'   [f] cont. suis centup. T'A   [g] bonis T'   [h] cum CsB   [i] est conu. Tt(not Tp)A   [j] ista (ita Tt) meditantur T'A*   [k] successus T'Bc'   [l] acclines T'ACe[v]   [m] om. CsB   [n] auxit ... rexit CsB   [o] mense Nou. T'A   [p] fuerat T'A   [q] partem sui T'A   [r] pel(l)icum T'   [s] Dac(c)us T'Al (datus Aap)

points of view a Christian must find the whole world exile and the whole world home, so that exile is home and home is exile. Let no man be held back by the greatness of his patrimony, for what is promised us is greater still: not things that flatter wretched victims with empty hope or "with idle musing on the event beguile"[1] a lazy mind, but things made known by frequent examples and established by common experience. The things I speak of are sweet but transitory, and such as for those who despise them bring a hundredfold reward.

'These are my orders, these my commissions, and the date I fix for them is the end of next spring. God will be with those who go, so that a good year smiles upon them, with plentiful harvest and fair weather. Those whose lot it is to die will enter the halls of Heaven, and those who live will see the Holy Sepulchre. And what greater happiness can there be than for a man during his life on earth to see the places in which the Lord of Heaven passed His earthly life? Happy are they who are called to perform these duties that they may win those rewards, and blessed they who plan to fight these battles that they may obtain those prizes!'

348. In giving the general tenor of this oration I have set down a few things without correcting the language, in order to preserve the truth of what was said, but have left more out. This then was the spark which kindled the multitudes who heard it, who voiced their opinion by acclamation, approving both the preacher and the pilgrimage. There and then in full council some of the nobles fell at the pope's feet and dedicated themselves and all that they had to God's service; among them was Adhemar, the very powerful bishop of Le Puy, who later guided the expedition by his wisdom and increased it by his eloquence. So in the month of November, in which the Council was held, they dispersed individually to their own homes; and immediately, as the good news spread over the whole world, it filled the hearts of Christians with a sweet wind that blew in every place, so that there was no nation so remote and well-hidden as not to send some part of itself. The central areas were not alone in feeling the force of this emotion: it affected all who in the remotest islands or among barbarian tribes had heard the call of Christ. The time had come for the Welshman to give up hunting in his forests, the Scotsman forsook his familiar fleas, the Dane broke off his long drawn-out potations, the Norwegian left his diet of raw fish. The fields were deserted with none to till them, houses

---

[1] Prudentius, *Psychomachia* 234.

3 edes habitatoribus; totis porro migrabatur urbibus.ᵃ Nullus necessitudinum amor, affectus patriae uilis, solus Deus pre oculis; quicquid in horreis, quicquid in tricliniis repositum responsurum erat uel auari uotis agricolae uel thesaurorum incubatorisᵇ deseritur; in solum Ierosolimitanum iter esuritur. Gaudium erat euntibus, meror remanentibus. Quid dico de remanentibus? Videres maritum cum matrona, cum omni postremo familia, euntem; rideres carpentis impositos totos in iter transferre penates.¹ Angustus erat limes transeuntibus, arctus
4 trames itinerantibus, sic ruebant agmina serie longa herentia. Opinionem hominum uincebat numerus, quanuis estimarentur sexagies centum milia itinerantium. Numquam proculdubio tot gentes in unam coiere sententiam, numquam tanta barbaries imperio uni, et pene nulli, ceruicositatem substrauit suam. Precipuum enimᶜ erat uidere miraculum, cum tam infinita multitudo sensim per terras Christianorum et non predabunda procederet, et non esset qui coherceret. Feruebat in omnibus alterutra dilectio, ut si penes aliquem quidᵈ repertum esset quod suum nonᵉ esse cognosceret, per multos dies passimᶠ agnoscendum proponeret, suspendebaturque interim inuentoris auiditas, dum forte illius qui perdiderat corrigeretur necessitas.

349. Iamque aduenerat desiderantibus mensis Martius, quando senecta brumali deposita mundus, uernali uestitus iuuenta, in plagam Orientis iturosᵍ inuitabat. ʰNec illi moras nexuere, tantus ardor animos inuaserat.ʰ Godefridus dux Lotharingorum per Pannoniam iter instituit, nulli umquam militi uirtute secundus, de antiqua Karoli Magni origine lineam trahens, et cui uere plurimus inerat Karolus tam sanguine quam mente. Sequebantur eum Frisones, Lotharingi,ⁱ Saxones, et quicquid gentium inter Renum et Garumnam fluuios iacet. Per Dalmatiam iter adorsi Raimundus comes de Sancto Egidio et Aimarus Podii episcopus, par insigne uirtutis, uiri armis in hostes, pietate in
2 Deum splendidi. Sub signis eorum militabant Gothi et Wascones et quicumque populus in Pireneum et Alpes diffunditur. Preuenerat eos compendio Boamundus, loco Apulus, gente Normannus; namque is, apud Brundisium nauibus conscensis Dirachioque appulsus, inde

---

ᵃ uiribus T¹   ᵇ incubatoriis T¹; one expects a noun parallel to uotis   ᶜ om. B   ᵈ om. CsB   ᵉ om. B   ᶠ om. CsB   ᵍ Turcos (!) B   ʰ⁻ʰ om. CsB   ⁱ Loth. Fris. T¹A

---

¹ Cf. Lucan ii. 729 (also Juvenal iii. 10).

with none to live in them; whole cities were emptied. The ties of kin- 3
dred lost their warmth, love of one's country was worth nothing; men
had God alone before their eyes. All that was stored in granary or hall
to answer the prayers, however greedy, of the farmer, or of the miser
brooding over his hoard, was left behind; they hungered solely for the
journey to Jerusalem. Those who went were full of joy, those who
stayed full of sorrow. Yet why do I speak of staying? You might have
seen husband and wife going, with all the family, and smiled at the
sight of them putting 'all their household gods'[1] in wagons to take the
road. The path was too narrow as they passed, the way constricted as
they journeyed; such was the press of traffic in its long unbroken
column. The numbers outstripped all conjecture, although it was 4
thought there were six million travellers. Never, beyond all doubt, had
so many nations united in one purpose; never had such a host of barbarians bowed its stubborn neck to one commander, indeed to almost
none. For the greatest marvel of it all was to see so numberless a multitude advancing slowly through lands held by Christians with no mind
for plunder, and yet with no man to restrain it. A burning love for their
neighbours was in every heart, so much so that, if anything was found
in anyone's possession which he knew not to be his, he would exhibit it
in public for many days to be identified, and the finder's desires were
held in suspense for the moment, until the loser had had a chance to
repair his loss.

349. The time came when the longed-for month of March arrived,
when the world, sloughing off the old age of winter and clothing itself
in youth and spring, summoned those who were to make the journey to
the East. Nor did they make excuses for delay; such was the ardour that
had filled their hearts. Godfrey duke of Lorraine, never second to any
in knightly valour, set off through Pannonia; he reckoned his lineage
from Charlemagne, and indeed there was much of Charlemagne in his
ability no less than in his veins. He was followed by Frisians, Lotharingians, Saxons, and all the nations that lie between the rivers Rhine
and Garonne. Dalmatia was the route taken by Count Raymond of
Saint-Gilles, and Adhemar bishop of Le Puy, a pair of outstanding
valour, famous for prowess against the enemy and piety towards God.
Under their banners served Goths and Gascons and all the peoples 2
who spread as far as the Pyrenees and the Alps. Ahead of them, using a
short cut, was Bohemond, whose home was in Apulia, his family
Norman; for he embarked at Brindisi and, having landed at Durazzo,

itinere pedestri*a* Constantinopolim per notos sibi tramites contendit. Ductu eius agebat prelium Italia et quaecumque contermina prouintia a Tirreno mari in Adriaticum*b* protenditur.

3 Hi omnes, pariter apud Constantinopolim conuenientes, nonnichil mutuae laetitiae habuere; ibique Hugonem Magnum, Philippi regis Francorum fratrem, inuenere, quod is, inconsulte et cum raro milite terras imperatoris ingressus et ab hominibus eius captus, in libera custodia habebatur.*c* At uero Alexius, eius ciuitatis imperator,*d* horum procerum aduentu territus, uolens sed quasi precibus coactus captionis gratiam fecit, homo tergiuersatione famosus et nichil umquam magnum*e* nisi dolo machinatus. Ipse Guiscardum, ut superius dixi,[1] ueneno uxoremque eius corruperat auro, fidem coniugalem falso per 4 nuntios pactus. Ipse denique Willelmum comitem Pictauensem in insidias Turchorum inductum, et sexaginta milibus armatorum priuatum,*f* pene solum effugere permisit, indignatus super eius responso, quo Greco negauerat hominium.*g* Ipsum postremo Boamundum, posteriori tempore contra se uenientem ut iniurias peregrinorum ulcisceretur, bis terque insidiis impetiuit; sed cum parum promoueret, Guidone fratre et*h* toto pene spoliauit exercitu,*i* notis 5 artibus toxica uel fluminibus uel uestibus infundens. Sed haec postmodum.[2] Tunc uero exercitum urbe arcens, proceribusque blande collocutus, tantum Graia facundia ualuit ut a singulis hominium*j* et sacramentum exigeret quod illi nichil doli machinarentur, quod urbes imperio suo appendices, si adquirere possent, redderent, sanguinis sui periculo alienum mercantes commodum. Soli Raimundo uisa est antiquior tuendae libertatis gratia, ut nec ipsi suum substerneret hominium nec profiteretur sacramentum.

6 Itaque, coactis omnibus uiribus, Niceam urbem Bithiniae aggrediuntur; ipsam enim primitus placuerat inuadi, quod et uiantibus obsisteret et mortem peregrinorum nuper ibi*k* occisorum ultum ire animati essent. Namque Walterus quidam, miles probatus sed preceps, quia uix in homine uno*l* sapientiam et audatiam conspicaberis, quod altera moretur altera precipitet, incircumspecte circum menia cursitans

---

a ped. it. T^tA *b* T^tA *add* mare *c* hab. cust. T^tA *d* eius ciu. imp. *om.* T^tA *e* *om.* T^t *f* priuatorum T^t *g* hominium (-num $Tp^{a.c.}$) neg. T^tA *h* *om.* B *i* exer. spol. T^tA *j* hominum T^tAaBk *k* ibi nuper T^tA *l* uno homine T^tAa (*and* $Al^{p.c.}$)

---

[1] 262. 5.
[2] 383. 2, 387. 6.

hastened from there to Constantinople overland by roads familiar to him. Under his leadership fought the Italians and all the adjacent region that stretches from the Tyrrhenian sea to the Adriatic.

They came together, all alike, at Constantinople, and this was a source of much common rejoicing. They found there Hugh the Great, brother of King Philip of the French, for he had entered the emperor's territories imprudently with a very small force and, having been seized by the emperor's men, was being held under house arrest. Alexius, however, the emperor of that city, who was terrified by the arrival of these great men, released him to oblige them, of his own accord, though he made a show of yielding to entreaty; for he was notoriously unreliable, and never did anything noteworthy except by some underhand trick. It was he who poisoned Guiscard, as I have already told,[1] and corrupted his wife with gold, having made her through intermediaries a false promise of marriage. It was he who led William count of Poitou into an ambush set by the Turks and, having stripped him of sixty thousand armed men, left him to escape almost alone, in resentment at the count's reply, when he refused to do homage to a Greek overlord. Finally, on a later occasion, when Bohemond himself moved against him to avenge wrongs suffered by the pilgrims, he attacked him treacherously two or three times; but, being unsuccessful, he robbed him of his brother Guy and almost all his army by his familiar tricks of putting poison into the streams or on their garments. But of this hereafter.[2] Now, however, he kept the army outside the city while ingratiating himself with its leaders, and made such good use of his Greek skill in words that he exacted homage from them individually, and an oath that they would do nothing surreptitiously but would restore to him any cities dependent on his empire which they might succeed in acquiring, thus purchasing another man's advantage at the risk of their own lives. Raymond alone thought it more important to preserve his freedom of action, and so neither offered the emperor homage nor took the oath.

And so, having got all their forces together, they moved against Nicaea, a city in Bithynia, having decided that it should be attacked first because it blocked their passage, and also because they had determined to avenge the deaths of some pilgrims who had lately been killed there. For a certain Walter, an experienced but headstrong knight—for you will rarely find wisdom and daring united in the same man, since one applies the brake and one the spur—had been killed with a large body of troops while riding round the walls without due precautions;

cum multa manu occubuerat. Eam manum Petrus heremita predicationibus suis de patria pellexerat.

350. Iam uero mense Septembri Rotbertus Normannorum comes, frater Willelmi regis, cuius titulum hic liber gestat, iter illud adoriri gestiens habuit sotios Rotbertum Flandrensem, Stephanum Blesensem sororis maritum, omnes amplae prosapiae comites et*[a]* quibus uirtus citra genus non erat. Parebant eis Angli et Normanni et Occidentales Franci et Flandritae, et omnium populorum cunei qui ab oceano Britannico usque ad Alpes mediterraneo tractu iacent. Ita uiam profecti reppererunt apud Lucas papam Vrbanum, qui Wiberto infensus, ut dixi,*[b]*[1] auxilio Mathildis Italiam et Vrbem circumsonabat armis,*[c]* iamque tantum promouerat ut Quirites, ad gratiam eius uersi, Wibertinos cum uerbis tum uerberibus lacesserent; nec erat alterutris uel in aecclesiis uel in triuiis parcendi animus, donec Wibertus uiribus impar Vrbano sedem uacuefecit, Alemanniam lapsus.*[d]*

351. De Roma, quae quondam domina orbis terrarum, nunc ad comparationem antiquitatis uidetur oppidum exiguum, et de Romanis olim*[e]* rerum dominis genteque togata,[2] qui nunc dicuntur*[f]* hominum*[g]* inertissimi, auro trutinantes iustitiam, pretio uenditantes canonum regulam—de Vrbe,*[h]* inquam, et urbicis quicquid conarer dicere preuenerunt uersus Hildeberti Cinomannensis *[i]*primo episcopi, post etiam Turonensis archiepiscopi;*[i]* quos hic cum inseruero, non ideo fatiam ut alieno labore partam gloriam in me transferam, sed erit ingenuae mentis inditium si, eius non inuidus gloriae,*[j]* apponam testimonium uenustae facundiae.[3]

> Par tibi, Roma, nichil, cum sis prope tota ruina;
>   quam magni fueris integra, fracta doces.
> Longa tuos fastus aetas destruxit: et arces
>   Cesaris et superum templa palude*[k]* iacent.
> Ille labor, labor ille ruit quem dirus Araxes
>   et stantem tremuit et cecidisse dolet;
> Quem gladii regum, quem prouida iura senatus,
>   quem superi rerum constituere caput;

---

[a] in C; om. B   *[b]* ut dixi infensus T'A*   *[c]* arm. circ. T'A   *[d]* elapsus C (cf. 232. 3); with lapsus in this sense William normally adds fuga   *[e]* om. CsB   *[f]* sunt C   *[g]* homines A   *[h]* Vrbano B   *[i-i]* episcopi T'A   *[j]* grati(a)e T'ABk   *[k]* plaude A*[a.c.]* Bk

this was a force which had been persuaded to leave its native land by the preaching of Peter the Hermit.

350. And now, in the month of September, Robert duke of Normandy, brother of the King William to whom this book is dedicated, who was longing to attempt this expedition, took as his associates Robert of Flanders and Stephen of Blois his sister's husband, all of them nobles of ancient lineage whose valour did not fall short of their ancestry. Under their orders were English and Normans, West Franks and Flemings, and bodies of men from all the peoples who lie inland from the British Ocean to the Alps. Setting out on their journey, at Lucca they found Pope Urban who in his hostility to Wibert, of which I have spoken,[1] was making warlike noises with Matilda's help around Italy and the city itself, and had already been so successful that the citizens of Rome had gone over to his side, and were assaulting Wibert's supporters with both words and blows. Nor had either side any mind to give quarter either in the churches or in the streets, until Wibert, whose strength was no match for his rival's, left the see to Urban and slipped away to Germany.

351. As for Rome, once mistress of the world and now, in comparison with Antiquity, more like a small town, and the Romans, in olden times 'lords of the world, those who the toga wore'[2] and now known as the most inactive of mankind, who put justice on the scales against gold and set a price on canon law—as for Rome, what I might try to say of the city and its citizens has been forestalled by those lines of Hildebert, first bishop of Le Mans and later archbishop of Tours; and if I insert them here, it will not be with the intention of transferring to my own account the honour earned by another man's toil, but it will be evidence of honesty on my part if I am not jealous of his achievement but append an example of his delightful style.[3]

> In ruins all, yet still beyond compare,
> How great thy prime, thou provest overthrown.
> Age hath undone thy pride: see, weltering there,
> Heaven's temples, Caesar's palace quite, quite down.
> Down is the masterpiece (Araxes dire
> Feared while it stood, yet grieved to see it fall),
> Which sworded kings and senate's wise empire
> And Heaven did stablish sovereign of us all.

---

[1] 289. 1.   [2] Virgil, *Aeneid* i. 282.   [3] Hildebert, *Carm. min.* xxxvi.

> quem magis optauit cum crimine solus habere
> Cesar quam sotius et pius esse socer;
> qui crescens studiis tribus hostes, crimen, amicos
> *ᵃ*ui domuit,*ᵃ* secuit legibus, emit ope;
3   in quem, dum fieret, uigilauit cura priorum,
> iuuit opus pietas hospitis, unda locum.
> Materiam,*ᵇ* fabros, expensas axis uterque
> misit; se muris obtulit ipse locus;
> Expendere duces thesauros, fata fauorem,
> artifices studium, totus et orbis opes.
> Vrbs cecidit de qua si quicquam dicere dignum
> moliar, hoc potero dicere: 'Roma fuit.'
> Non tamen annorum series, non flamma nec ensis
> ad plenum potuit hoc abolere decus.
> Cura hominum potuit tantam componere Romam
> quantam non potuit soluere cura deum.
4   Confer opes marmorque nouum superumque fauorem,
> artificum uigilent in noua facta manus:
> non tamen aut fieri par stanti machina muro
> aut restaurari sola ruina potest.
> Hic superum formas superi mirantur et ipsi
> et cupiunt fictis uultibus esse pares;
> non potuit natura deos hoc ore creare,
> quo miranda deum signa creauit homo.
> Vultus adest his numinibus,[1] potiusque coluntur
> artificum studio quam deitate sua.
> Vrbs felix si uel dominis urbs illa careret
> uel dominis esset turpe carere fide!

352. Paruane sunt haec*ᶜ* ad demonstrandam in tanta urbe uel olim bonorum*ᵈ* dignitatem uel modo malorum maiestatem? Sed, ne quid honori desit, aditiam et portarum numerum et multitudinem sacrorum cinerum; et, ne quis obscuritate uerborum se causetur a cognitione rerum*ᵉ* reici, erit sermo cotidianus et leuis.

2   Prima porta Cornelia, quae*ᶠ* modo dicitur porta sancti Petri, et Via Cornelia. Iuxta eam aecclesia beati Petri sita est, in qua corpus eius

---

ᵃ⁻ᵃ indomuit *CsB*   *ᵇ* materiem *T¹Al, most MSS of Hildebert*   *ᶜ B adds* enim   *ᵈ* honorum *CB*   *ᵉ* cog. rerum *C;* rer. cog. *T¹A;* cog. rerum uel *(uel om. Bk)* causarum *B*   *ᶠ* quo *Al,* quod *Aap*

Caesar to have her for his private ends
All loyalties, all kindred set at naught.
By threefold arts she grew: foes, crimes, and friends
By arms, laws, gold she vanquished, tamed, and bought.
Raised with unsleeping toil by men of old,   3
By generous strangers helped and neighbouring wave—
The whole round world sent craftsmen, marble, gold;
Nature herself the perfect setting gave.
Fortune her favour lavished, kings their treasure,
Artists their skill, all earth the best it had:
The City's fallen, whose greatness would you measure,
'Rome once stood here' is all that can be said.
Yet not the circling years, not sword nor fire
This glorious work could utterly lay low;
Man's toil could make of Rome a city higher
Than toiling gods could wholly overthrow.
Bring now Heaven's grace, bring gold, bring marble new,   4
And craftsmen eager for fresh feats of skill:
Your fabric yet the old shall not outdo;
E'en to restore it will defeat you still.
These sculptured gods the gods themselves amaze,
Content, could each but with his image vie;
Such godlike forms Nature in vain essays
As man creative here doth deify.
Art makes these gods and not divinity,
In godlike power and godlike beauty both.[1]
Thrice happy Rome, were she of tyrants free,
Or were her lords ashamed to break their troth.

352. Is this of no account as evidence either of the nobility of that great city in its ancient prosperity or of its present majesty in misfortune? But that it may lack none of its due honour, I will append the number of the gates and its long list of the remains of saints, and, that no one may complain that the obscurity of my language repels his attempt to learn the truth, I will use the casual words of everyday speech.

The first gate is the Cornelian, now called St Peter's gate, and the 2 Via Cornelia. Near it stands St Peter's church, in which his body lies,

---

[1] Literally 'These gods have a face' (as opposed to the Christian God).

iacet, auro et argento*a* et lapidibus parata; et*b* nullus hominum scit numerum sanctorum*c* martirum qui in eadem aecclesia pausant.*d* In eadem uia est altera aecclesia, in qua requiescunt sanctae uirgines Rufina et Secunda. In tertia aecclesia*e* sunt Marius et Martha, et*f* Audifax et Abacuc filii eorum.

3 Secunda porta Flamminia, quae modo appellatur sancti Valentini, et Via Flamminia; et cum ad pontem*g* Molbium peruenit, uocatur Via Rauennana, quia*h* ad Rauennam ducit. Ibi in primo miliario foris sanctus Valentinus in sua aecclesia*i* requiescit.

Tertia porta Porciniana, et uia eodem*j* modo appellata, sed cum peruenit ad Salariam nomen perdit; et ibi prope, in eo loco qui dicitur Cucumeris, requiescunt martires Festus Iohannes*k* Liberalis Diogenes Blastus Lucina, et in uno sepulchro ducenti sexaginta*l* et in altero triginta.

4 Quarta porta et uia Salaria, quae modo sancti Siluestri dicitur. Ibi iuxta uiam sanctus Hermes requiescit, et sancta Vasella et Protus et Iacinctus, Maxilianus*m* Herculanus Crispus, et in altero loco prope*n* requiescunt sancti martires Pamphilus*o* Quirinus septuaginta gradibus in imo terrae. Deinde basilica sanctae Felicitatis, ubi requiescit illa et Silanus filius eius, et non longe Bonefatius martir. Ibidem in altera aecclesia sunt Crisantus et Daria et Saturninus et Maurus et Iason*p* et
5 mater eorum Hilaria et alii innumerabiles. Et in altera basilica sanctus Alexander Vitalis Martialis, filii sanctae Felicitatis, et sanctae septem uirgines Saturnina Hilarina Dominanda Rogantina Serotina*q* Paulina Donata. Deinde basilica sancti Siluestri, ubi iacet marmoreo tumulo coopertus, et martires Celestinus Philippus et*r* Felix; et ibidem martires trecenti sexaginta quinque in uno sepulchro requiescunt, et prope Paulus et Crescentianus, Prisca*s* Semetrius Praxedis Potentiana pausant.

6 Quinta porta Numentana; ibi*t* sanctus Nicomedes*u* presbiter et martir, itemque uia eodem*v* modo dicitur. Iuxta uiam aecclesia sanctae Agnetis*w* et corpus; in altera*x* sancta Emerentiana et martires Alexander Felix*y* Papias. In septimo miliario eiusdem uiae sanctus papa Alexander cum Euentio et Theodolo pausat.*z*

7 Sexta porta et uia Tiburtina, quae modo dicitur porta*aa* sancti Laurentii. Iuxta hanc uiam iacet sanctus Laurentius in sua aecclesia et

---

a et argento *om. CB*   *b* etiam *CBc*   *c* *om. C*   *d* paus. eccl. *T'*
e basilica *T'A*   *f* etiam *C*   *g* pontum *A*   *h* qu(a)e *AC*   *i* (a)eccl.
sua *A*   *j* eadem *B*   *k* Ioh. Festus *T'A*   *l* quadraginta *A*   *m* *Properly* Maximilianus   *n* *om. T'*   *o* Pamphilius *A*; Pamphilinus *B*   *p* Iason et Maurus *T'A*   *q* Serantina *C*   *r* *om. T'A*   *s* B *adds* et   *t* ibidem

adorned with gold and silver and precious stones, and no man knows the number of the holy martyrs who rest in that same church. In the same street is another church, in which rest the holy virgins Rufina and Secunda; and in a third church are Marius and Martha with their sons Audifax and Abacuc.

The second gate is the Flaminian, now named St Valentine's gate, 3 and the Via Flaminia; and when it reaches the Milvian bridge, it is called the Via Ravennana, because it leads to Ravenna. There, at the first milestone outside the walls, rests St Valentine in his own church.

The third gate is the Pincian, and a road which bears the same name; but it loses that name when it reached the Via Salaria. Close thereby, in the place called the Cucumber, rest the martyrs Festus, John, Liberalis, Diogenes, Blastus, and Lucina, and in one tomb are two hundred and sixty, in another thirty.

The fourth gate and road is the Salarian, which is now called after 4 St Silvester. There by the road lies St Hermes, with St Basilla and Protus and Hyacinth, Maximilian, Herculanus, Crispus; and in another place nearby rest the holy martyrs Pamphilus and Quirinus seventy steps deep in the ground. Then the basilica of St Felicitas, where she rests and Silanus her son, and not far away is the martyr Boniface. There too in another church are Chrysanthus and Daria, and Saturninus, and Maurus and Jason and their mother Hilaria, and others past counting; and in another basilica St Alexander, Vitalis and Martialis 5 sons of St Felicitas, and seven holy virgins, Saturnina, Hilarina, Dominanda, Rogantina, Serotina, Paulina, and Donata. Then the basilica of St Silvester, where he lies, covered by a marble tomb, and the martyrs Celestine, Philip, and Felix; and there too rest three hundred and sixty-five martyrs in one sepulchre, and near them sleep Paul and Crescentian, Prisca, Semetrius, Praxedes, and Pudentiana.

The fifth gate is the Nomentan (there is St Nicomedes, priest and 6 martyr) with a road called by the same name. Near the road are both the church and the body of St Agnes, and in another church St Emerentiana and the martyrs Alexander, Felix, and Papias. At the seventh milestone on the same road rests the holy Pope Alexander with Eventius and Theodulus.

Sixth is the Tiburtine gate and way; the gate is now called the gate of 7 St Laurence. Near this road lies St Laurence in his own church, and

CBk " Nic(h)omedis *AaB* ^{v} eo *Bk*, eadem *Bc* ^{w} s. Agnetis et (a)eccl. *T'A* ^{x} *T'A* add (a)ecclesia ^{y} Felix *(T'* adds et*)* Alexander *T'A*
^{z} pausant *B (see 169. 2 n. a)* ^{aa} om. *B*

Habundius martir. Et ibi prope in altera aecclesia*ᵃ* pausant hi martires, Ciriaca Romanus Iustinus Crescentianus. Et ibi non longe basilica sancti Ipoliti, ubi ipse cum familia sua pausat, id est, decem et octo. Et ibi requiescunt beata Trifena*ᵇ* uxor Decii, et filia eius Cirilla*ᶜ* et Concordia nutrix eius.*ᵈ* Et in altera parte uiae illius est aecclesia Agapiti martiris.

8 Septima porta modo Maior dicitur, olim Sircurana dicebatur, et Via Lauicana quae ad beatam Helenam tendit. Ibi sunt*ᵉ* prope Petrus Marcellinus Tiburtius Genuinus*ᶠ* Gorgonius et quadraginta milites et alii innumerabiles; et non longe*ᵍ* sancti quattuor Coronati.

Octaua porta sancti*ʰ* Iohannis, quae apud antiquos Assenarica dicitur. Nona porta Metrosi dicitur, et coram istis ambabus*ⁱ* Via Latina iacet.*ʲ*

9 Decima porta et uia Latina dicitur. Iuxta eam quiescunt in una aecclesia martires Gordianus et Epimachus, Sulpitius Seruilianus*ᵏ* Quintus Quartus Sophia Triphenus.*ˡ* Et ibi prope in alio loco Tertullinus, et non longe aecclesia beatae Eugeniae, in qua iacet et Claudia mater eius et Stephanus papa cum clero suo, numero decem et nouem, et Nemesius diaconus.

10 Vndecima porta et uia dicitur Appia. Ibi requiescunt sanctus Sebastianus et Quirinus, et olim ibi requieuerunt apostolorum corpora.*ᵐ* Et paulo propius Romam sunt martires Ianuarius Vrbanus*ⁿ* Xenon Quirinus*ᵒ* Agapitus Felicissimus. Et in altera aecclesia Tiburtius Valerianus Maximus. Nec*ᵖ* longe aecclesia Ceciliae martiris, et ibi reconditi sunt Stephanus Sixtus*ᑫ* Zepherinus Eusebius Melchiades Marcellus Euticianus Dionisius Anteros Pontianus Lucius*ʳ* papae,*ˢ* Optatius Iulianus Calocerus*ᵗ* Parthenius*ᵘ* Tarsitius Policamus martires. Ibidem aecclesia sancti Cornelii et corpus. Et in altera*ᵛ* sancta*ʷ* Sotheris, et non longe pausant martires Ipolitus Adrianus Eusebius Maria Martha Paulina Valeria Marcellus; et prope Marcus papa in sua aecclesia.

11 Inter Viam Appiam et Ostiensem*ˣ* est Via Ardeatina, ubi sunt*ʸ* Marcus et Marcellianus. Et ibi iacet Damasus papa in sua aecclesia; et non longe sancta Petronilla, et*ᶻ* Nereus et Achilleus, et alii plures.

ᵃ om. *T¹A*   *ᵇ* Triphona *A*   *ᶜ* C. filia eius *T¹A*   *ᵈ* Ipoliti *T¹A**
ᵉ est *A*   *ᶠ* Geminus *T¹Bc*   *ᵍ* *T¹A* add sunt   *ʰ* om. *T¹Al (Aap omits the context)*   *ⁱ* om. *T¹*   *ʲ* iacet Latina *C*   *ᵏ* Valerianus *C;* Searserianus *or sim. B*   *ˡ* Triphonius *T¹A*   *ᵐ* corp. apost. *T¹A*   *ⁿ* om. *T¹*
ᵒ Quintinus *C*   *ᵖ* non *C*   *ᑫ* CsB add et   *ʳ* om. *T¹*   *ˢ* papa *B*   *ᵗ* Colocerus *C*   *ᵘ* Partemius *A*   *ᵛ* *A* adds (a)ecclesia   *ʷ* sancte Ce(and CpCdCr), om. Cs   *ˣ* Ost(i)ensam *AlC(Bk)*   *ʸ* *T¹** adds martires
ᶻ om. *T¹*

the martyr Abundius. And there nearby in another church rest these martyrs: Cyriaca, Romanus, Justin, and Crescentian. And there, not far away, is the basilica of St Hippolytus, where he himself rests with his family, that is, eighteen persons. And there lie the blessed Tryphonia, wife of Decius, and her daughter Cyrilla, and Concordia, her nurse [T¹A Concordia nurse of Hippolytus]. And in another part of that road is the church of the martyr Agapetus.

The seventh gate is now called the Greater gate, but was formerly the Sircuran, and there is the Via Labicana, which leads to St Helena. Near there are Peter and Marcellinus, Tiburtius, Genuinus, Gorgonius, and forty soldiers, and others past counting; and not far off are the Four Crowned Saints.

The eighth is called St John's gate, which in Antiquity was called the Asinaric.

The ninth is the Metrovian gate, and near both of these lies the Via Latina.

Tenth is the Latin gate, and the Via Latina. Near this lie in one church the martyrs Gordian and Epimachus, Sulpicius, Servilianus, Quintus, Quartus, Sophia, and Tryphenus; and near there in another place Tertullinus; and not far off is the church of St Eugenia, in which she lies and her mother Claudia, and Pope Stephen with his clergy to the number of nineteen, and the deacon Nemesius.

Eleventh is the Appian gate and the Via Appia. There rest St Sebastian and Quirinus, and there in old days rested the bodies of the Apostles. And a little nearer Rome are the martyrs Januarius, Urban, Zeno, Quirinus, Agapetus, and Felicissimus; and in another church Tiburtius, Valerian, and Maximus. Not far off is the church of the martyr Caecilia, and there are buried Popes Stephen, Sixtus, Zephyrinus, Eusebius, Miltiades, Marcellus, Eutychianus, Dionysius, Anterus, Pontianus, and Lucius, and the martyrs Optatius, Julian, Calocerus and Parthenius, Tarsicius and Policamus. There too is the church of St Cornelius and his body, and in another church St Soteris; and not far off rest the martyrs Hippolytus, Hadrian, Eusebius, Maria, Martha, Paulina, Valeria, and Marcellus; and nearby, Pope Marcus in his own church.

Between the Via Appia and the Ostian is the Via Ardeatina, where are [T¹*adds* the martyrs] Marcus and Marcellian; and there lies Pope Damasus in his own church, and not far off SS Petronilla, Nereus and Achilleus, and many others.

Duodecima porta et uia Ostiensis*a* dicitur; modo porta sancti Pauli uocatur, quia iuxta eam requiescit in aecclesia sua. Ibidemque Timotheus martir, et non longe in aecclesia sanctae Teclae sunt martires Felix et Adauctus et Nemesius. In Aqua Saluia est caput Anastasii martiris.

12 Tertia decima porta et uia Portuensis dicitur.*b* Ibi prope sunt in una aecclesia martires Felix Alexander, Abdon et Sennes, Simeon Anastasius Polion*c* Vincentius Milex Candida Innocentia.*d*

Quarta decima porta et uia Aurelia,*e* quae modo porta*f* sancti Pancratii dicitur, quia iuxta eam requiescit in aecclesia sua, et alii martires Paulinus Arthemius, sancta Sapientia cum tribus filiabus Fide Spe Caritate. Et in altera basilica*g* Processus et Martinianus, et in tertia Felices duo, et in quarta sanctus Calixtus et Calepodius, et in quinta sanctus Basilides.

13 Duodecimo intra urbem*h* miliario*i* in Monte Celio sunt martires Iohannes et Paulus in sua domo, quae est facta aecclesia post eorum martirium, et Crispinus et Crispinianus, et sancta Benedicta. In eodem monte est aecclesia sancti Stephani prothomartiris, et ibi reconditi sunt martires Primus et Felicianus. In Monte Auentino sanctus Bonefatius et in Monte Nola sancta Tatiana pausant.

353. Haec sunt Romana sanctuaria, haec sunt in terris diuina pignora; et tamen intra*j* hoc quasi caeleste promptuarium insano*k* furore gens ebria tum*l* cum illuc peregrini uenerunt fedo ambitu omnia turbabant, et supra ipsa sanctorum corpora ciuilem libabant sanguinem, dum non possent satiare pecuniarum libidinem. Vrbani ergo benedictione freti comites transita Tuscia et Campania per Apuliam Calabriam uenere, statimque mare transissent nisi consulti nautae
2 propter austrorum uiolentiam uetuissent. Quapropter Normannus et Blesensis comites, qua quisque poterat, hiemem fouere, apud amicos perhendinantes. Solus Flandrensis uentis uela*m* credidit, precipiti consilio feliciter usus; ideoque gregariorum uulgus pars propter inopiam domum reuertit, pars pro intemperie soli morbo defecit. Necnon et residui duces, ut uidere pacatum*n* classibus equor, uernali sole

a Ost(i)ensa *TpAlCB*   *b* Port. (et uia Ostiensis *Aap*) dic. et uia *T'A*   *c* Pilion *Bk*, Pelion *Bc*   *d* Annocentia *C*   *e* Aurea *C*   *f* porta *before* dicitur *T'A; om. C*   *g* *T'A* add* martires   *h* *T' (Tt^{t.l.})A add* Romam   *i* duodecimo . . . miliario *presents problems. Read either* Basilides, duodecimo miliario. Intra urbem *(so CCSL clxxv. 327–8) or* duodecimo extra urbem miliario. In Monte Celio   *j* inter *B*   *k* in suo *A*   *l* tunc *B*   *m* om. *B*   *n* placatum *T'Bc (*placitum *Bk)*

The twelfth gate is called the Ostian, and the road the Via Ostiensis; its name is now St Paul's gate, because near it rests the saint in his own church, and there too is the martyr Timothy, and not far off in the church of St Thecla are the martyrs Felix and Adauctus, and Nemesius. In Aqua Salvia is the head of the martyr Anastasius.

The thirteenth gate is called the gate of Porto, and the road the Via Portuensis. And nearby in one church are the martyrs Felix, Alexander, Abdon and Sennes, Simeon, Anastasius, Pollio, Vincent, Milex, Candida, and Innocentia.

The fourteenth gate is the Aurelian, with the Via Aurelia, which is now called the gate of St Pancras, because he lies near it in his church, and other martyrs, Paulinus, Arthemius, and St Sapientia with her three daughters Fides, Spes, and Caritas. And in another basilica are [T¹A *add* the martyrs] Processus and Martinianus, and in a third two called Felix, and in a fourth St Calixtus and Calepodius, and in a fifth St Basilides.

At the twelfth milestone within the city on the Caelian hill are the martyrs John and Paul in their house, which became a church after their martyrdom, and Crispin and Crispinian, and St Benedicta. On the same hill is a church of St Stephen the first martyr, and there are buried the martyrs Primus and Felicianus. On the Aventine hill rests St Boniface and on the Nola hill St Tatiana.

353. Such are Rome's holy places, such is its concrete testimony to God on earth; and yet, within this holy storehouse if I may so term it, a people intoxicated with raving madness were causing universal chaos by their foul ambition at the very moment when the pilgrims arrived in Rome, and over the very bodies of the saints were shedding the blood of fellow-citizens, as long as they could not satisfy their lust for gold. Relying therefore on Urban's blessing, the nobles passed through Tuscany and Campania and by way of Apulia reached Calabria, and would immediately have crossed the sea, had not the seamen they consulted forbidden this on account of the strong southerly gales. So the duke of Normandy and the count of Blois settled down for the winter where each best could, biding their time among their friends. Only the count of Flanders entrusted his sails to the winds, and his rash decision had a happy outcome. As a result, of the mass of common soldiers, some were driven home by shortage of supplies, and some from the intemperate climate fell victims to disease. And the rest of the leaders too, when they saw a smooth sea for their fleets as the spring sunshine

redeunte, maris fidem experti et Christi auxilio illesi, duobus portibus
3 excepti applicuere. Inde per Thessaliam, cuius metropolis est Thessalonica, Tratiam et hinc Constantinopolim uenere. Multi pauperum illa uia morbo et inedia extincti; multi in uado, quod pro rapiditate Diaboli dicitur, intercepti,*a* pluresque profecto perissent nisi equi emissarii, aduerso*b* amni*c* oppositi,*d* uiolenti gurgitis uortices fregissent; ita quibusdam uita procurata,[1] reliqui equis transducti. Omnis itaque multitudo quindecim dierum spatio preteritorum laborum indulsit solatio, positis castris in suburbano ciuitatis; de qua, quia 'se locus' obtulit, pauca dicenda.

354. Constantinopolis primum Bizantium dicta; formam antiqui uocabuli preferunt imperatorii nummi*f* bizantini uocati. Hanc diuinitus mutasse nomen sanctus Aldelmus auctor est in libro de Virginitate,[2] huiusmodi sententia. Constantino, in eadem urbe soporato, uisa est astitisse uetula rugis anilibus arata frontem;*g* mox imperiali clamide amicta*h* in iuuenculam refloruisse, uiridisque formae decore Constantini pellexisse oculum, ut non abstineret quin porrigeret ei oscu2 lum. Tum Helenam matrem, quae adesset, dixisse: 'Haec tua semper erit, nec umquam morietur, nisi in fine seculi.' Huius somnii solutionem Augustus extruso sopore ieiuniis et elemosinis extrahebat e caelo. Et ecce, post octo dies iterum soporatus, uisus est uidere Siluestrum papam, paulo ante defunctum, qui dulci luminum risu discipulum perstringens 'Consueta' inquit 'egisti prudentia, ut quod intellectum effugeret hominis, a Deo expectares soluendum nodum enigmatis. Haec igitur quam uidisti anicula est ciuitas ista, aeui situ decrepita, cuius iam uetustate quassa menia et uicinam ruinam minantia
3 reparatorem desiderant. Sed tu eam muris reformans et opibus uocabulo quoque insignies tuo, et regnabit in ea perpetuo imperatoria progenies. Non tamen tuo arbitratu fundamenta iacies, sed ascenso sonipede, cui quondam rudis Christicola insidens apostolorum Romae circuisti aecclesias, laxatis habenis quo uolet eundi promptum illi cedes arbitrium; habebisque*i* in manu hastam regiam, cuius cuspide in

a suffocati *T'A*   *b* aduerso (-si *Bk*) *CBk;* in (*om. Bc*) aduersum *T'ABc*
c amnem *T'A*   *d* appositi *B*   *c-c* locus se *Al (so too CeBc),* locus es *Aap; cf. GP p. 249*   *f* nummi (numini *Aap*) imp. *T'A*   *g* frontem arata *T'A*   *h* amictam *AB, equally well*   *i* habebis *A*

[1] i.e. forded the stream safely.
[2] *De uirginitate (prosa),* c. 25.

returned, took their chance of the treacherous sea and landed scatheless, by Christ's help, finding a welcome in two harbours. Thence by 3 way of Thessaly, of which the capital city is Salonica, they reached Thrace, and after that Constantinople. Many of those who had no money died on that journey from disease and hunger; many were drowned while trying to cross what from its violence is known as the Devil's Ford, and more would undoubtedly have perished, had not the advanced cavalry, positioned to breast the stream, broken the force of the whirling torrent, so that some of them saved their lives[1] and the rest were carried over on horseback. And so the whole multitude, for the space of a fortnight, enjoyed rest from their labours, having pitched their camp in the suburbs of the city of which, since the opportunity offers, something must be said.

354. Constantinople was first called Byzantium; the old form of the word survives in the imperial coins called bezants. The change of name was divinely inspired, as St Aldhelm tells us in his book *On Virginity*,[2] and this is the story. Once, when Constantine was sleeping in that same city, he dreamed that there stood by him an old woman, whose brow was furrowed with the wrinkles of age; then she became a maiden in the bloom of youth, clothed in the imperial mantle, whose fresh beauty so enchanted Constantine that he could not refrain from offering her a kiss. Whereupon his mother Helena, who was present 2 in the dream, declared: 'She will always be yours, nor shall she ever die until the ending of the world.' The emperor awoke, and by fast and almsgiving sought from Heaven the interpretation of this dream. Lo and behold, a week later he again fell asleep, and dreamed he saw Pope Silvester, who had died not long before. The pope smiled affectionately on his pupil. 'You have acted,' he said, 'with your usual prudence, in seeking from God the solution of a knotty riddle that escaped man's understanding. The old woman whom you saw is this timeworn city, whose walls, shattered by age and threatening immediate ruin, call for one to rebuild them. You are the man who 3 shall restore her in walls and in wealth; you shall call her by your own name, and here shall the imperial progeny reign for ever. Yet shall you not lay the foundations at your own sweet will. Mounting the charger on which once, as a new-made Christian, you rode round Rome to visit the churches of the Apostles, let fall the reins and leave it free to go wherever it will; hold in your hand your royal spear, and its point as it drags along the ground shall trace out the line of your

terram*a* tracta muri scribentur uestigia. Consules ergo in terra cuspidis*b* magisterium, quo ordine disponi debeant fundamenta menium'.

355. Paruit Augustus uisioni precluae, et ciuitatem aequam Romae constituit lege,*c* professus non debere imperatorem Romae principari, ubi a Christo coronati apostoli principabantur.*d* Fecit in ea duas aecclesias, quarum una Hirenis, altera dicitur Apostolorum, inuehens illuc numerosa sanctorum corpora, qui possint contra incursus hostium celeste*e* impetrare patrocinium. Statuas quoque triumphalium uirorum a Roma deductas et simulacra deorum ad uidentium ridiculum et tripodas Delphicos in circo dedit ad spectaculum simul et ad ciuitatis 2 ornamentum; gratumque admodum fuisse ferunt imperiali animo ut illic*f* urbem diuino iussu fundaret ubi et soli ubertas et caeli temperies mortalium saluti conueniret; quia enim in Britannia natus fuerat, ardores solis exosus erat. Est uero Tratia una Europae prouintia, ut poetae quoque canunt,[1] Hebri fluminis glatie et Bistonio aquilone perfrigida, uicina Mesiae cuius, ut ait Virgilius,[2] fecundas*g* 'mirantur Gargara messes'. At uero Contantinopolis, circumflua ponto, Europae atque Asiae carpit utrimque libratam temperiem, quod aquilonales*h* 3 hiatus mulceat e proximo ueniens Asiaticus eurus. Porrigitur ergo urbs ingentibus menibus, sed eam angustat conuenarum innumerus populus; quapropter rupium molibus et harenarum cumulis profundo iniectis longe itur in salum, et nouo commento tellus inuenta ueteres contrahit undas. Stupet itaque mare peregrinos uitreo in*i* gurgite campos, urbemque suam totis terrarum*j* commodis cingit et pascit. Est enim ciuitas undique, preter ad aquilonem, mari magno cincta, ambitu murorum iuxta situm pelagi angulosa, uiginti*k* milia*l* passuum muro 4 complexa. Danubius, qui et Hister, occultis canalibus sub terra influit urbi,*m* diebusque constitutis ablato pessulo inductus cenum platearum pelago importat. Certauere zelo imperiali Augusti singuli decorem addere, quisque*n* arbitrantes aliquid se institutae debere operae, iste sanctorum reliquiis, ille diuitiis, Constantinus omnibus.

---

a One expects terra (cf. Aldhelm p. 259. 13 Ehwald)   *b* cuspidis in terra T'A
c om. A   *d* cor. princ. apost. T'A; princ. cor. apost. B   *e* celestium C
f illuc ABc*1*   *g* om. CsB; before uicina Ce(and CpCr)   *h* aquilonales B; -nares T'; aquilonis Aa,Sidonius, carm. ii. 48, a source for this passage; there are other variants; we print William's normal form   *i* in uitreo T'A   *j* om. A   *k* duodecim T'ABk   *l* om. CBk   *m* urbi before sub T'A   *n* quique T'

---

[1] Cf. Horace, Ep. i. 16. 12–13.

wall. Thus, to learn the order in which the foundations of your walls must be laid out, you shall follow the instructions of your spear's mark in the soil.'

355. The august prince obeyed the wondrous vision, and founded by law a city the equal of Rome, stating that an emperor ought not to rule in Rome, where rule belonged to the Apostles crowned by Christ Himself. He built two churches in it, one called Eirene, the other the Holy Apostles, and installed the bodies of many saints, that they might secure the protection of Heaven against enemy attacks. He set up in the Circus statues of victorious generals brought from Rome, and images of the gods to excite the mockery of beholders, and Delphic tripods, as curiosities and as ornaments of his capital. They say that the emperor's heart was especially content to be founding a city at Heaven's bidding in a place where fertile soil and temperate climate conspired to make men healthy, for being born in Britain, he hated excessive heat. Now Thrace is a province of Europe kept really cool, as poets too tell,[1] by the icy river Hebrus and by blasts from the Bistonian north; neighbour to Moesia, whose fertile crops, as Virgil has it,[2] are the despair of Gargara. But Constantinople, washed around by the sea, enjoys a moderate climate, balanced between Europe on one side and Asia on the other, for the northern blasts are mollified by east winds from nearby Asia. The city is laid out with an immense circuit of walls, but the countless throng of those who gather there makes it seem small; so rocky breakwaters and piles of soil cast into the sea have taken it far out into the deep, and new-found land narrows the water's ancient bed. The sea, astonished to see immigrant fields usurp her glassy depths, girdles and feeds with all the good things of the earth the city that belongs to her; for the capital is washed by deep water on all sides except the north, being irregular in shape as the circuit of walls follows the water's edge, with a line of defences twenty miles long. The Danube, also called Hister, flows by hidden channels underground into the city; on appointed days it is admitted by the opening of a sluice, and carries the dirt of the streets into the sea. The emperors in turn have striven with imperial zeal to increase its beauty, each thinking it his duty to add something to the work begun, one relics of the saints, another riches, Constantine everything.

[2] *Georg.* i. 102–3 (*v.l.* Mysia).

356. Regnauerunt in ea post Constantinum Magnum imperatores quorum haec sunt nomina: Constantius filius eius, Iulianus apostata, Iouinianus,[a] Valens, Theodosius maior, Archadius,[b] Theodosius minor, Martianus, Leo primus, Zeno, Anastasius, Iustinus maior, Iustinianus (hic, litteris et bellis nobilis, fecit in Constantinopoli aecclesiam Diuinae Sapientiae, id est Domino[c] Christo, quam Agiam[d] Sophiam cognominauit; opus, ut ferunt,[e] omnibus per orbem edifitiis magnificentius, quodque certa rerum fatie inspectum uincat ampullata uerba refer-
2 entium), Iustinus minor, Tiberius, Mauritius primus Grecus, Focas, Heraclius, Heraclonas, Constans, Constantinus filius Heraclii[f] (iste Romam ueniens, et quod reliquum erat ornatus antiqui[g] corradens, tegulis etiam aereis fastigia aecclesiarum nudauit, triumpho scilicet apud Constantinopolim de hisce manubiis inhians; sed ei[h] infeliciter illa cessit auiditas, quia continuo apud Siracusas extinctus Saracenis Alexandriam deferentibus omnes illas reliquit exuuias), Constantinus, Iustinianus, Leo secundus,[i] Tiberius, iterum[j] Iustinianus, Philippicus,[k]
3 Anastasius, Theodosius, Leo tertius.[l] Hi omnes regnauerunt et[m] in Constantinopoli et in Roma, sequentes tantum in Constantinopoli: Constantinus, Leo, Constantinus,[n] Niceforus, Stauratius, Michael, Theophilus, Michael, Basilius, Leo, Alexander, Constantinus, Romani duo, Niceforus Focas, Iohannes, Basilius, Romanus, Michael, Constantinus, Theodora imperatrix, Michael, Sachius, Constantinus, Romanus Diogenes, Niceforus Butanius, Michael. Hic, per Alexium depulsus imperio, ad Guiscardum in Apuliam clandestinam fugam composuit, tradataque illi[o] potestate aliquid se opinatus est fecisse[p] quod[q] noceret Alexio. Vnde Guiscardo aggrediendi magna[r] increuit animus, ut inani spe mentiretur sibi adquiri posse[s] per industriam quod alter amiserat per ignauiam; sed quantum istis profecerit, precedens liber patefecit.[1]
4 Est in ea ciuitate lignum Domini ab Helena de Ierosolimis delatum. Requiescunt ibi apostoli Andreas, Iacobus frater Domini, Mathias; prophetae Heliseus, Samuel, Danihel et alii plures; Lucas euangelista; martires innumerabiles; confessores Iohannes Crisostomus, Basilius, Gregorius Nazanzenus, Spiridion;[t] uirgines Agatha, Lucia; omnesque

---

[a] Iouianus *Aac, correctly; Tt(not Tp) adds* Valentinianus, *but he was the corresponding western emperor*   [b] *om.* C   [c] T[t]A *add* Iesu   [d] Agio T[t]   [e] fertur A   [f] C. filius Her. *belongs after* Heraclius; *the parenthesis concerns Constans (II)*   [g] *om.* CsB   [h] enim T[t]ABk   [i] Leo sec. Iust. A   [j] item CB (iterum Iust. Tib. A)   [k] Philippus T[t]CBk (Anast. Philippicus A)   [l] Leo ter. Theod. A   [m] *om.* A   [n] Constantius T[t]Aa (constanter Al). *William makes several*

356. Of the emperors who have borne rule in the city since Constantine the Great, these are the names: Constantius his son, Julian the apostate, Jovinian, Valens, Theodosius I, Arcadius, Theodosius II, Marcian, Leo I, Zeno, Anastasius, Justin I, Justinian; famous alike for his writings and his battles, it was he who built in Constantinople a church in honour of the Divine Wisdom, that is, of the Lord Christ, which he called Hagia Sophia—the grandest building in the world, they say, and more remarkable when actually seen than in the inflated tales of travellers; Justin II, Tiberius, Maurice the first Greek, Phocas, Heraclius, Heraclonas, Constans, Constantine son of Heraclius; he went to Rome, and stealing what remained of its ancient adornment, even stripped the church roofs of their bronze tiles, in hopes of earning with these spoils a triumph in Constantinople; but his greed did him no good, for he was promptly killed at Syracuse, and left all his loot to the Saracens, who carried it off to Alexandria; Constantine, Justinian, Leo II, Tiberius, Justinian again, Philippicus, Anastasius, Theodosius, Leo III. All these ruled both in Constantinople and in Rome, those who follow in Constantinople only: Constantine, Leo, Constantine, Nicephorus, Stauracius, Michael, Theophilus, Michael, Basil, Leo, Alexander, Constantine, the two Romanuses, Nicephorus Phocas, John, Basil, Romanus, Michael, Constantine, the Empress Theodora, Michael, Isaac, Constantine, Romanus Diogenes, Nicephorus Botaniates, Michael. It was Michael who, when driven from the throne by Alexius, escaped secretly to Guiscard in Apulia, and handing over to him his power, thought he had done something that would hurt Alexius. Hence Guiscard's spirit for mighty enterprises grew so great that he deluded himself with the empty hope of gaining for himself by action what Michael had let slip by sloth; but how little this profited him has appeared in the preceding book.[1]

There is in that city our Lord's Cross, brought from Jerusalem by Helena. There too rest, of the Apostles Andrew, James the Lord's brother, and Matthias; of the prophets Elisha, Samuel, Daniel, and many more; Luke the evangelist; martyrs without number; the confessors John Chrysostom, Basil, Gregory of Nazianzus, and Spyridon; the virgins

omissions in what follows   " ei *T'A*   *p* effecisse *T'A*   *q* quo *TpA*
r magna aggrediendi *T'A*   *s* posse a(d)quiri *T'A*   *t* Spiridon *Bk, correctly*

---

[1] 262. 5–6.

postremo sancti quorum corpora illuc ex omnibus regionibus imperatores conuehere potuerunt.

357. Normannus itaque et Blesensis comites hominium suum Greco prostrauerunt;[a] nam iam Flandrita transierat et id facere fastidierat, quod se meminisset natum et educatum libere. Alii,[b] data fide acceptaque, Niceam pertendunt ebdomada Iunii[c] prima, quam iam ceteri a medio Maii obsederant.[d] Ita coniunctis uiribus multae utrimque mortes actae sunt, cum ab oppidanis facile in subiectos telorum omnia[e] genera rotarentur, nec alicuius licet inertissimi manus in confertos frustraretur. Quin et exanimatorum cadauera Turchi[f] uncis ferreis in murum trahebant, ludibrio nostrorum excarnificanda uel ablatis 2 uestibus deicienda.[g] Doluerunt id Franci, nec prius abstiterunt ferro exercere dolorem[1] quam Turchi, extremis malis fessi,[h] die solstitii aestiualis per clandestinos nuntios imperatori se dedidere. Ille, qui nichil preter commodum suum pensare nosset,[i] denuntiauit Francis ut abirent, malens urbem seruari Turchorum apertae perfidiae quam Francorum suspectae potentiae. Iussit tamen distribui argentum et aurum[j] optimatibus, nummos aereos inferioribus, ne se irremuneratos quererentur.

3 Ita Turchi, qui iam a quinquaginta annis Bithiniam, quae est pars Minoris Asiae, quam Romaniam dicunt, Eufrate transito possederant, in superiores fuga terras[k] concessere. Veruntamen ausi sunt obsidione soluta exercitum ultra progredientem incessere, auctore quodam Solimanno, cui dominium totius Romaniae obtigerat. Is, coactis sagittariorum milibus[l] estimatione trecentis sexaginta, nostros nichil minus quam bellum meditantes tanta ui aggressus est ut, ferreo imbre sagit- 4 tarum inundante[m] perterriti, omnes incunctanter dorsa nudarent. Et tum forte dux Godefridus et Hugo Magnus et Raimundus aliam uiam inuaserant, ut et inimicorum solum popularentur latius[n] et suis pabula compararent facilius. At uero Normannus, ancipiti discrimine permotus, aduentum Turchorum expeditis cursoribus Godefrido et ceteris per tutos tramites intimauit. Illi morae nescii signis in hostem conuersis

---

[a] prostituere T'A   [b] alteri T'Aa (altera Al)   [c] ieiunii AlB   [d] obs. a medio Maii T'A   [e] Savile; omnium T'ACB   [f] om. T'   [g] denudanda C   [h] fessi malis T'A   [i] nollet A   [j] aurum et argentum T'A   [k] terras fuga T'A*   [l] om. T'   [m] undante C   [n] largius T'

[1] Ovid, Met. xii. 534.

Agatha and Lucia; and lastly, all the saints whose bodies the emperors were able to bring together there from all parts of the world.

357. So the duke of Normandy and count of Blois did humble homage to the Greek emperor; the count of Flanders had already passed through Constantinople and refused to do so, remembering as he said, that he had not been born and bred a slave. The others, after exchanging pledges of loyalty, proceeded in the first week of June as far as Nicaea, which their colleagues had already been blockading since the middle of May. Their forces thus joined, there was considerable loss of life on either side, for the townsmen could easily roll missiles of all kinds onto the besiegers who lay below, and the most unskilful hand could not miss a target so densely packed. Besides which, the Turks hauled up the bodies of the dead onto the wall with iron hooks, to mock our men by tearing them to pieces, or stripping off their clothes before casting them down again. This infuriated the Franks, nor did they 'refrain from giving their fury full rein in battle',[1] until the Turks, exhausted by their privations, secretly sent messengers to the emperor on midsummer day, and surrendered. The emperor, incapable of considering anything but his own interests, gave the Franks notice to depart, preferring to reserve the city for the Turks with their undisguised treachery rather than for the suspect power of the Franks. He did, however, give orders for a distribution of gold and silver to the magnates, and of bronze coin to the other ranks, so that they might not complain that they were unrewarded.

So the Turks, who just fifty years before had crossed the Euphrates and made themselves masters of Bithynia, a part of Asia Minor (this they call Roum), retreated up country; but all the same, after the siege was lifted, they harassed the army as it advanced, inspired by a certain Suleiman, who had now become lord of all Roum. This man got together a force of archers estimated to be 360,000 strong, and fell upon our men, when their minds were set on anything rather than battle, with such violence that the continuous rain of iron arrows broke their spirit, and they at once turned tail, one and all. At that moment, as it happened, Duke Godfrey and Hugh the Great and Raymond had taken another line of advance, in order to ravage enemy territory on a wider front, and to make foraging easier for their own men. The Norman duke, much shaken by his critical position, sent express messengers by safe paths to report the Turkish onslaught to Godfrey and the rest. Without delay they turned against the enemy, and rescued

sotios eripuere periculo; namque hi[a] iam indiscrete[b] in tentoriis suis necabantur, nichil bello intenti sed solis lacrimis et precibus auras implentes. Nec rimabatur hostis uulneri aditum, sed in nothos fortunam emittens numquam pro densitate cuneorum inanem referebat manum. Sola erat mortis dilatio quod, quia iuxta quoddam harundinetum pugnabatur, equi Turchorum impediti liberis non exultabant cursibus. Sed tandem uisis antesignanis optimatum uenientium nostri ex harundineto prodeunt, et acclamato signo militari 'Deus uult!' dissipatos ordines hostium inuadunt, sotiis ut ex altera parte feriant innuentes. Ita Turchi, cum utrimque premerentur, nescio quid dirum stridentes ululatibus in caelum actis[c] diffugere, nec solito more pugna fugaci usi sed abiectis arcubus maius aliquid quam humanum timorem continua trium dierum fuga testati sunt. Nec erat qui eos fugaret, quia equi nostrorum, uix ieiuno cespite uitam sustentantes, alacrem persecutionem negabant, lasso statim ilium pulsu defectionem suam[d] ostendentes. Erat enim Asia, terra quondam frugum feracissima, ita moderno et antiquo tempore[e] Turchis seuientibus expilata ut uix raro exercitui alimoniam ministrare sufficeret, nedum tantae multitudini, quae totas segetes depastura, totos amnes epotatura uideretur; estimabantur enim cum a Nicea discessere septingenta milia, pars reliqua uel ferro interempta[f] uel ualitudine minuta, maior domos dilapsa.

358. Inde ergo per Antiochiam Pisidiae et Iconium urbes Eracleam uenere; ibi signum in caelo uiderunt modo ensis fulminei figuratum, mucrone uersus orientem protento. Iamque a kalendis Iulii,[g] cum Niceam deseruerant, Octobris mensis nonae uoluebantur[h] quando Antiochiam Siriae uenere. Cuius situm commemorarem, nisi auiditatem meam preoccuparet[i] Ambrosiana in Egesippo[l] facundia, simul et quod uereor ne michi uertatur uitio quod tam frequenter in digressionibus peregrinatur narratio. Veruntamen, quantum suscepti operis necessitas[j] postulat, dicam.

359. Ciuitas est maximo muro circumdata, montem etiam menibus complexa,[k] a Seleuco rege Asiae nomine Antiochi patris[l] cognominata;

---

[a] illi T'A   [b] indiscrete *after* suis T'A   [c] auctis T'   [d] defectum suum T'A* *(cf. GP p. 260; William elsewhere uses* defectio *of revolt)*   [e] om. CsB   [f] intercepta C   [g] Iunii B   [h] non euoluebatur C   [i] preoccupasset T'A   [j] necessitas T'A, *cf. 378. 2 and esp. GP p. 77;* narratio CB, *from above*   [k] circumplexa T'A   [l] patris Ant. T'A

their allies from peril; already they were being cut down indiscriminately in their tents, without a thought of fighting, and merely filling the air with lamentations and prayers. Nor need the enemy go searching for a deadly aim; he cast his luck upon the winds, and so densely were our men packed that he never missed. One thing alone delayed the massacre: they were fighting on the edge of a reed-bed, which impeded the Turkish horse from enjoying freedom to manoeuvre. At length our men sighted the vanguard of the approaching magnates, and advanced out of the reed-bed; shouting the war-cry 'God wills it!', they fell upon the enemy's disordered ranks, signalling to their friends to strike from the other side. The Turks, caught between two fires, with strange and terrible cries fled screeching to high heaven; nor did they retreat fighting, as their custom is, but threw away their bows, and showed by three successive days of flight that something more than human terror was upon them. Pursuit was out of the question: our horses, scarcely supporting life on the scanty grass, made a keen follow-up impossible, soon showing by the exhausted heaving of their flanks that they could do no more. For the land of Asia, once exceptionally fertile, had been in our own and earlier times so cruelly ravaged by the fury of the Turks that it could scarcely furnish supplies for a small force, let alone for so great a multitude, which might seem able to devour entire harvests and drink whole rivers dry. They were estimated on their departure from Nicaea to be 700,000 strong; of the balance, some were dead in battle or brought low by disease, but the majority had dropped off homeward bound.

358. So from there by way of Pisidian Antioch and Iconium they arrived at Heraclea, where they saw a portent in the sky in the shape of a flaming sword with its point stretching towards the east. From 1 July, when they had left Nicaea, it was already come to 7 October, when they reached Antioch in Syria. I would describe the situation of Antioch, were not my eagerness forestalled by the eloquence of Ambrose in his Hegesippus;[1] and were I not at the same time afraid that I may be blamed for allowing my narrative to wander so often into digressions. I will, however, say as much as the needs of my undertaking require.

359. The city is surrounded by a very high wall, and even includes a mountain within its defences. It was so called by Seleucus king of Asia

---

[1] i.e. Hegesippus' translation of Josephus, often attrib. to Ambrose. The reference is to iii. 5. 2.

post Romam et Constantinopolim et Alexandriam quarto per orbem loco cunctis*a* ciuitatibus prelata; menibus tuta, montibus ardua, magis ingenio quam ui, si umquam capiatur, obtinenda. Fluuius illi proximus, quem modo Fernum, quondam Orontem uocatum intelligo, duodecimo ab urbe miliario accipitur pelago,*b* fluentis rapacibus et ipso impetu frigidioribus salubris aurae temperie saluti*c* medetur ciuicae;*d* commeatum quoque nauium oppidanis inuehens, perseuerantiam obsidentium 2 quantolibet tempore deridet. Ibi primum Christiani olim nominis*e* uenerabile uocabulum excogitatum. Inde Paulus, huiusce*f* religionis incentiuum et fomes, ad predicandum processit. Ibi beatus Petrus primi antistitii*g* cathedram sedit; in cuius honore fundata illic aecclesia toto Turchorum tempore illibata permansit, nec minus altera, in honore sanctae Mariae consecrata, decore sui oculos spectantium*h* tenebat, mirum in modum, ut cuius persequebantur fidem reuererentur edem.

360. Hanc itaque ciuitatem Franci ab Octobri usque ad Iunium circumsedere,*i* tentoriis circum muros*j* amne transito*k* locatis. Perspectaque difficultate expugnandi, timiditati quorundam obuiandum arbitrati, omnes pariter proceres sacramento fecere obsidioni non ponendas ferias quoad uel ui uel ingenio prenderetur ciuitas; et, ut quod intendebant facilius implerent, castra cis fluuium constituerunt multa, quibus imposit militi excubias*l* pretenderent. Aoxianus quoque ciuitatis ammiratus, uidens Francos non ioco et ieiune agere sed ciuitatem serio impetere, Sansadolem filium ad Soldanum imperatorem*m* misit, qui Francorum audatiam exponens suppetias expeteret.*n* 2 Soldanus apud Persas qui apud Romanos Augustus, totius Orientis et omnium Saracenorum rector. Quod ideo, ut estimo, tam diu manet et propagatur imperium, quod gens illa, parum, ut dixi,[1] bellicosa et uiuacis sanguinis inops, semel acceptum nescit dediscere seruitium, ignorantque, ut Lucanus ait,[2] ideo 'datos ne quisquam seruiat enses'. At uero gens occidentalis,*o* audax et effera, diuturnam unius populi*p* dedignatur dominationem, sepe se seruitio exuens et de uno*q* in aliud

a loco cunctis per orbem *T'A**   *b* One expects a connective to follow   *c* sanitati *T'A*   *d* ciuium *C*   *e* Christianismi (*om.* olim nominis) *C; but cf. Acts 11: 26, and especially Fulcher i. 24. 13;* olim *remains strange*   *f* huius *B*   *g* antistitii *after* sedit *T'A*   *h* spec. oc. *T'*   *i* circumdedere *A*   *j* murum *B*   *k* transito amne *T'A*   *l* castra *CB, from above*   *m* *T'A* add Persidis; *cf. 364.1, Fulcher i. 15. 7*   *n* oraret *T'A*, more euphoniously*   *o* occ. gens *T'A*   *p* gentis *T'A*   *q* alio *T'A*

[1] 347. 8 (in Urban's speech, not suggesting its authenticity).

after his father Antiochus, and next to Rome, Constantinople, and Alexandria is exalted to fourth place among all the cities of the world; impregnably walled, amid precipitous mountains, if ever taken, it must be won by cunning and not by force. Near it is a river, now called, as I understand, the Fernus, but formerly the Orontes, which flows into the sea twelve miles from the city; with its fast-flowing waters, made even colder by their headlong course, it carries with it an admixture of fresh air to ensure the health of the inhabitants, and bringing transport by ship within reach of the citizens, it makes nonsense of the most obstinate siege, however long it lasts. It was there that the sacred name of Christian was first invented; from there that Paul, who propagated and enkindled the Christian religion, went forth to preach; there that St Peter occupied the first episcopal see. The church founded there in St Peter's honour remained untouched all through the Turkish occupation; and another, dedicated to St Mary, exercised by its beauty such a sway over the eyes of the beholder that, strange to relate, the Turks revered the shrine of her whose faith they persecuted.

360. This then was the city which the Franks besieged from October until June, crossing the river to pitch their tents round the walls; and when they had seen the difficulty of taking it, thinking precautions advisable against low morale in certain quarters, all the nobles alike took an oath that there should be no respite from the siege, until by force or cunning the city was taken. To make their purpose easier of fulfilment, they established many camps on the near side of the river, and installed knights to keep watch. Aoxianus the emir of the city, on his side, seeing that the Franks were not carefree or casual in their attack but meant business, sent his son Sansadoles to Soldan the emperor [T¹A *add* of Persia], to report the Frankish enterprise and ask for help. 'Soldan' in Persia is the equivalent of 'Augustus' among the Romans; he is ruler of the whole East and of all the Saracens. This empire, in my opinion, owes its great duration and still increasing extent to the unwarlike nature of the Persians, already referred to,[1] who being short of active blood cannot unlearn the servile habit they have once acquired, and do not understand how 'the sword's purpose' is, as Lucan has it,[2] 'that none need be a slave.' The western peoples, on the other hand, are bold and fierce, and reject the long-continued lordship of any one nation; often freeing themselves from servitude, they change from one to another. Thus the Roman rule

[2] iv. 579.

transferens. Denique Romanum imperium*a* prius ad Francos, post ad Teutones declinauit, orientale apud Persas semper durat.

361. Ad huius igitur*b* imperii principem Sansadoles missus uiam studio celerabat iuuenili; pater interim in custodia urbis imperatorio non deerat muneri.*c* Nec contenta uirtus inclusorum sua tutari nostros ultro lacessebat,*d* crebro illos et subito pabulantes et nundinantes aggressa;*e* nam de inuentis nauibus pontem facientes, nundinas ultra fluuium instituerant.*f* Ope igitur Christi pertinaces sumptis armis hostes audacter propellere, ut numquam eos*g* superiorem gloriam paterentur referre; cuius contumeliae ultionem in Siros et Armenios ciuitatis indigenas Turchi refundebant,*h* balistis et petrariis capita interemptorum in castra Francorum emittentes, ut illos eo modo ad dolorem incenderent.

362. Et iam, deuastatis omnibus circa urbem quae ad uictum poterant parari, temeraria fames, quae etiam tuta*i* expugnare solet, exercitum incessere ceperat, adeo ut, nondum*j* surgentibus in altam segetem culmis, quidam siliquas fabarum nondum adultarum pro summis delitiis amplecterentur. Alii carnes iumentorum, alii coria aquis mollita, quidam carduos parum coctos per abrasas fauces utero demittebant; quidam uel mures uel talium quid delitiarum poscentibus aliis uenundabant, et esurire sustinebat prolato ieiunus uenditor auro.*l*

2 Nec defuere qui cadauera cadaueribus infarcirent, humanis pasti carnibus; longe tamen et in montibus, ne nidore carnis adustae ceteri offenderentur. Plures spe reperiendae alimoniae ignotis uagabantur semitis, et a latrunculis uiarum gnaris trucidabantur.

*k*Tunc et Stephanus comes Blesensis clam effugit, mendatiis suis aduentantes retro agens, et magno proculdubio hominis improperio, quod sequenti statim die discessionis eius ciuitas deditioni consensit.*k*

*k*Sed non multo post ciuitas deditioni consensit.*k*

363. Boamundus enim, sollertis ingenii uir, ea parte qua pretendebat principem quendam Turchum, maximae turris custodem,

---

a om. T' *b* ergo B *c* muniri A *d* lacessebant T'A *e* aggressi T'A *f* constituerant C (but cf. GP p. 428) *g* eos after gloriam T'A *h* infundebant B *i* tuta etiam CB *j* om. C *k–k* tunc . . . consensit T'; sed . . . consensit CB; om. A

passed first to the Franks and later to the Teutons, while in the East the Persian Empire goes on for ever.

361. Such was the empire to whose head Sansadoles was sent. With the energy of youth he made good speed, while his father, in his careful watch over the city, acted as a general should. The besieged, not content to defend their own lines, bravely took the offensive against our troops, making frequent surprise attacks upon them as they foraged and marketed; for they had established a market for supplies across the river, making a bridge of the boats they found there. So our men took up arms with determination, by Christ's help, and bravely beat back the enemy, never allowing them the glory of any success. This disgrace the Turks avenged on the native Syrian and Armenian inhabitants, using their catapults and mortars to shoot the heads of those they killed into the Frankish camp in order to rouse their resentment.

362. By now they had consumed everything around the city that could be made fit for human food, and the headlong onset of famine, which often lays low what seems impregnable, began to assail the army. The corn being not yet grown up into the ear, some of them welcomed unripe beanpods as the greatest delicacy. Some ate the flesh of their baggage animals, others leather steeped in water to soften it; others stuffed half-cooked thistles down their bleeding throats. Dealers were found to meet the demand for mice and similar luxuries; 'the starving merchant' steeled himself to privation 'at the sight of gold.'[1] There [2] were actually some who made the dead support the dying, feeding on human flesh; but far away in the mountains, for fear their comrades might be revolted by the smell of burning meat. And many, in hopes of finding victuals, wandered along unknown byways, and were cut to pieces by robbers who knew the country.

T[1] Then it was that Stephen count of Blois fled secretly, using lies to turn back new arrivals; and without doubt it is a great reproach to the man, that on the day after his departure the city agreed to surrender.

CB It was not long, however, before the city agreed to surrender.

363. For the ingenious Bohemond, on the side of the city where he was encamped, making enormous promises by intermediaries, had

[1] Lucan iv. 97.

promissis ingentibus ad proditionem per internuntios sollicitauerat. Ille quoque, ut infamiam traditionis insigni excusatione palliaret, Boamundo filium in obsidatum dedit, Christi edicto, quod per somnium didicisset, id se facere professus. Suos igitur ad turrim Boamundus admouit, prius clandestino astu perpetuum a proceribus ciuitatis 2 donum nactus, si posset adquirere. Ita Franci, per funeas scalas nocte intempesta in murum euecti,*ᵃ* uexilloque Boamundi, quod uermiculatum erat, uentis in fastigio turris exposito, signum Christianum laetis fragoribus ingeminant: 'Deus uult! Deus uult!' Turchi experrecti et soporis penuria inertes fugam per angiportus inuadunt; districtis nostri gladiis*ᵇ* insecuti magnas de inimicis strages aceruant. In ea fuga occidit Aoxianus urbis ammiratus, a quodam rustico Siro*ᶜ* decollatus; caput eius Francis allatum ridiculo et gaudio fuit.

364. Nec diu opima uictoria laetati, postero die Turchorum obsidionem extra muros ingemuere. Venerant illi a Sansadole inuitati, duce Corbaguath satrapa orientali,*ᵈ* qui ab imperatore Persidis acceperat trecenta milia cum uiginti septem ammiratis. Horum sexaginta*ᵉ* milia*ᶠ* in arcem urbis per scopulos ascendere, aduocantibus eos Turchis qui adhuc ibidem remanserant. Itaque illi crebris excursibus Christianos*ᵍ* potissimum fatigabant, nec erat ulla spes nisi in Dei auxilio, cum bello infestatis cresceret*ʰ* inedia, inedia*ⁱ* semper magnorum*ʲ* comes prima 2 malorum.¹ Quapropter triduano prius*ᵏ* cum letaniis exacto*ˡ* ieiunio, legatus Petrus heremita mittitur ad Turchos.*ᵐ* Is familiari sibi eloquio ista prosecutus est, ut Turchi Christianorum terras, quas olim peruaserant indebite, nunc euacuent uolutarie: iustum esse ut, sicut Christiani non infestant*ⁿ* Persidam, ita Turchi non urgeant*ᵒ* Asiam; proinde*ᵖ* aut libenti discessu natiuum solum repetant, aut mane futuro bellum expectent; sortem per duos uel quattuor uel octo experiantur, ne periculum ad totum uergat exercitum.

365. Non erat Corbaguath eius facilitatis*ᵠ* ut legatum dignaretur responso, sed scacchis ludens et dentibus infrendens inanem dimisit,

ᵃ eiecti A   *ᵇ* gladiis nostri T'A   *ᶜ* suo T'Aap   *ᵈ* orientale B
ᵉ XL B   *ᶠ* om. C   *ᵍ* Christianos before crebris T'A   *ʰ* incresceret T'A   *ⁱ* om. T'AapBk   *ʲ* om. C   *ᵏ* prius trid. T'A   *ˡ* exaucto Tt(corr. from exauto)Tp   *ᵐ* ad. T. mittitur T'A   *ⁿ* urgent T'A   *ᵒ* Sarraceni non infestent T'A   *ᵖ* perinde C   *ᵠ* facultatis T'

¹ Lucan iv. 93.

been enticing a Turkish officer, the keeper of the principal tower, to betray his trust. The Turk, to cover the scandal of his treachery by an excuse that none could overlook, had given his son to Bohemond as a hostage, declaring that he did so by the express command of Christ given him in a dream. So Bohemond, having first with secret cunning obtained a perpetual grant of the city from the nobles on condition that he took it, moved his troops up to the tower. Scaling the walls by rope ladders at dead of night, and spreading Bohemond's crimson standard to the winds from the tower's top, with hoarse repeated shouts of glee the Franks gave the Christian war-cry: 'God wills it! God wills it!' The Turks awoke and, demoralized by their lack of sleep, took to their heels through the narrow streets, pursued by our men sword in hand, who cut their adversaries down in heaps. Among the victims of the rout was Aoxianus, the emir of the city, beheaded by some peasant from Syria; his head was brought to the Franks, and greeted with cheers and laughter.

364. They did not long enjoy this splendid victory, for next day they had the unpleasant shock of finding themselves blockaded by Turks outside the walls. These forces had arrived, at the invitation of Sansadoles, under command of Corbaguath, an eastern satrap, who had been given three hundred thousand men by the Persian emperor, with twenty-seven emirs. Sixty thousand of these made their way up over the rocks into the citadel, summoned by the Turks who had remained in occupation there. As a result, they wore down the Christians most effectively by frequent raids, nor had the Christians any hope but in God's help, for on top of their battle casualties was added increasing famine—'ever the first-lieutenant to disaster.'[1] So after holding a three-day fast with litanies, they sent Peter the Hermit to negotiate with the Turks. He argued, with his habitual eloquence, that the Turks, long wanton aggressors on Christian territory, should now willingly give it back; the Christians, he said, did not interfere with Persia, and it was fair that in return the Turks should leave Asia alone. They had two alternatives: to return voluntarily to their native land, or to expect battle next day; but they could try their luck with two, four, or eight champions on either side, so that their whole army need not be involved.

365. Corbaguath had not the courtesy to vouchsafe the envoy any answer. Sitting at the chess-board, grinding his teeth, he sent him away

hoc tantum*a* dicto, iam conclamatam esse Francorum superbiam. Ille quoque concite rediens exercitum de insolentia Turchi certiorem reddidit. Tunc omnes se alterutrum animantes etiam per preconem clamari fecere ut quisque nocte illa*b* equo suo pro posse prebendam*c* porrigeret, ne sequenti die multiformibus giris fatigatus deficeret. Iamque mane inclaruerat*d* cum per aties dispositi uexillis in hostem infestis prodeunt. Primam turmam duxere duo Rotberti,*e* Normannus et Flandrensis, et Hugo Magnus; secundam dux Godefridus; tertiam Podiensis episcopus. Boamundus in extremo agmine incedebat,*f* ceteris subsidio futurus. Raimundus in urbe remanserat, qui nostris receptui prouideret si necesse foret. Hoc Turchi eminus conspicati, primo quid esset hesere. Mox, cognito uexillo episcopi, quod eum maxime metuerent, quia illum*g* papam Christianorum et incentorem bellorum dictitarent,*h* antequam ferirentur, uidentes quod nostri tam animose et incunctanter procederent, terga dedere. Alteri quoque, insperato exsilientes tripudio, cedentes cecidere, quantum uel peditum ilia uel equitum calcaria sufficere potuerunt; persuadebantque sibi uidere se antiquos martires, qui olim milites fuissent quique mortis pretio parassent premia uitae, Georgium dico et Demetrium, uexillis leuatis a partibus montanis accurrere, iacula in hostes, in se auxilium uibrantes. Nec diffitendum est affuisse martires Christianis, sicut quondam*i* angelos Machabeis, simili dumtaxat causa pugnantibus. Reuersi uero in predam, tanta in castris illorum reppererunt quae cuiuslibet auidissimi*j* exercitus*k* satietatem*l* possent uel temperare uel extinguere. Hoc prelium actum est anno incarnationis Dominicae millesimo nonagesimo octauo, quarto kalendas Iulii; nam pridie nonas Iunii*m* capta fuerat urbs.*n* Mox, kalendis Augusti sequentibus, Podiensis episcopus,*o* Christianorum uexillifer, illius*p* boni auctor precipuus, communi mortalium conditioni feliciter manus dedit; et Hugo Magnus, concessu ut aiunt heroum, Frantiam rediit, causatus continuam uiscerum tortionem.

366. Sed cum, sex mensibus Antiochiae morati, preteritos labores tam diuturna quiete abstersissent, iter iam dudum inceptum resumere meditabantur. Primusque Raimundus, nullius umquam ignauiae

a tandem *T¹* *b* illa nocte *T¹A* *c* preb. pro posse *T¹A* *d* declaruerat *B* *e* Ro(t)b. duo *T¹A* *f* om. *CsB* *g* eum *T¹A* *h* dicerent *B* *i* quodam *Bk*, quosdam *Bc* *j* auarissimi *T¹A* *k* om. *B* *l* auiditatem *T¹* *m* Iulii *CB* (same variants in Fulcher i. 24. 4) *n* om. *T¹* *o* ep. Pod. *T¹A* *p* istius *T¹A*

empty, only remarking that it was all over with these Frankish popinjays. Peter for his part hastened back to inform the army of his insolent reception by the Turks. At that, all gave one another mutual encouragement, and they also had orders proclaimed by a herald that everyone that night should give his horse the best feed he could, that it might not sink from exhaustion next day in complicated movements. Day had just broken when they formed up in battle array, and advanced with flying colours against the enemy. The first squadron was commanded 2 by the two Roberts—of Normandy and Flanders—and by Hugh the Great; the second by Duke Godfrey; the third by the bishop of Le Puy. Bohemond brought up the rear, in reserve; Raymond had remained in the city, to secure the retreat of our men, should it prove necessary. When the Turks caught sight of this array in the distance, at first they were puzzled as to what was up. Soon they recognized the bishop's banner; and holding him as they did in special dread—for they called him the Christians' pope and the moving spirit in their wars—without waiting for a blow, when they saw our men advancing with such spirit and determination, they turned tail. The other side, exulting at this 3 unexpected triumph, cut them down as they fled, as long as the exertions of the footsoldiers or the spurs of the cavalry could keep it up. They were convinced they saw those ancient martyrs who had been knights in their own day, and who by their deaths had purchased the crown of life, St George and St Demetrius, with flying banners come charging from the hill-country, showering missiles on the enemy, and aid upon themselves; nor can we deny that martyrs have aided Christians, at any rate when fighting in a cause like this, just as angels once gave help to the Maccabees. When they turned back to the spoil, they 4 found enough in the enemy's camp to slake or extinguish the appetite of any soldiery, however greedy. This battle was fought on 28 June AD 1098, for it was on 4 June that the city had been taken. Shortly after, on 1 August following, the bishop of Le Puy, the Christians' standard-bearer and chief architect of that laudable enterprise, surrendered gladly to the common lot of mortality; and Hugh the Great, with the alleged agreement of the nobles, returned to France on the plea of unremitting internal pain.

366. When they had spent six months at Antioch, and by this lengthy rest had wiped out the effects of their previous exertion, they considered resuming the journey they had begun so long before; and Raymond, who was never guilty of slackness in any form, and always

conscius et cui semper cura primum in procinctu militari esse, et post eum Rotberti et Godefridus uiam moliti;^a solum Boamundum florentissimae ciuitatis aspectus et pecuniarum fames continuit ut interim differret. Sed latebat sub cupiditate ratio persuasibilis,^b qua diceret Antiochiam non sine principe Turchis exponendam continuo inuola-
2 turis. Resedit ergo in urbe, et Raimundi homines, qui uicum unum tenebant, improbus exactor menibus depulit. At uero ceteri per Tripolim et Beritum et Tirum et Sidonem et Acharonem et Caipham et Cesaream Palestinae transeuntes, ibi a dextra dimittentes maritima, peruenerunt Ramulam, a quibusdam ciuitatibus gratanter excepti, quarundam subiectione uirtutem suam insignientes. Non enim diutius moram protelari^c consilium erat, quod Aprilis mensis erat, et campestres fruges in maturas messes coaluerant.
3 Ramula est ciuitatula muro indiga, beati Georgii, si famae credimus, martirii conscia; cuius ibi ab antiquo fundatam aecclesiam Turchi nonnichil deformauerant, tunc metu Francorum subreptis omnibus suis in montana dilapsi. Sequenti mane, dubio adhuc diei et noctis confinio, Tancredus nepos Boamundi, prestans^d animi miles, sumptis armis, et quidam alii, Bethleem pertendunt, loca uicina explorare
4 cupientes. Siri qui essent in loco, progressi obuiam,^e letitiam suam desiderio lacrimante prodebant, saluti eorum pro paucitate nimirum^f metuentes; nam non multo plus quam centum milites uenerant. At illi, suplicibus uotis sacram edem uenerati, confestim Ierosolimam intentis animis inuadunt. Turchi quoque, pro fidutia uirium mentibus efferati, foras exsiliunt, in nostros^g aliquantisper arietantes; totus enim iam exercitus¹ aduentarat. Sed mox Francis annitentibus summoti hostes claustrorum muralium obiectu salutem suam tutabantur.

367. De situ et positione Ierusalem nichil me dicere copia scriptorum^h ammonet, nec necesse est ut in hoc campo nostraⁱ exultet^j oratio; adeo fere omnium notitiae patet quod Iosephus, quod Eucherius, quod Beda scripsere. Quis enim nesciat eam a Melchisedech Salem, a Iebuseis Iebus, a Salomone Ierosolimam uocatam? Quis non audierit quotiens sub aduerso marte cadens ciues ruinis sepelierit suis, uel Nabuchodonosor uel Tito uel Adriano agentibus? Adrianus ille fuit qui

^a iter adorti (-si Cs) C   ^b persuadibilis T^t   ^c protelare T^tA*   ^d prestantis T^t   ^e in loco essent obuiam prog. T^tA   ^f om. CsB   ^g nostris A   ^h scr. copia T^t   ⁱ mea B   ^j exulet Bc, extrahet Bk

---

[1] i.e. of Crusaders.

anxious to be first in every military exploit, led the way, followed by the two Roberts and by Godfrey. Only Bohemond was constrained, by the charms of that delightful city and by greed for money, to postpone his departure for the present. Beneath his self-interest lay a convincing reason: Antioch must not be left with no one in charge, a prey to the Turks, who would certainly attack it without delay. So he remained in 2 the city, and with outrageous violence drove out from its walls some men of Raymond's, who were in possession of a single street. The rest of them, passing by Tripoli, Beirut, Tyre, Sidon, Acre, Haifa, and the Palestinian Caesarea, there left the sea-coast on their right, and arrived at Ramlah; some of the towns made them welcome, and some they showed their prowess by reducing. To prolong their stay any further was not their design, for it was already April, and the corn in the fields had grown and ripened into harvest.

Ramlah is a small town without walls, the scene, if report is to be 3 believed, of the martyrdom of St George; he has a church there of ancient foundation, somewhat defaced by the Turks, who at that moment for fear of the Franks had scattered into the hills with all their belongings. Next morning, on the disputed frontier between night and day, Bohemond's nephew Tancred, a valiant knight, and some others took their arms and made their way as far as Bethlehem with the idea of exploring the neighbourhood. Such Syrians as were in the place came 4 out to greet them, with tears of longing displaying their joy, but full of anxiety for the safety of so small a party, for those who had come were not many more than a hundred knights. The Franks, after paying their respect to the sacred edifice with humble prayers, hastened eagerly onwards to Jerusalem. The Turks too, whose spirits rose with growing confidence in their numbers, sallied forth and for some time kept charging our men, for the whole army[1] had now arrived; but soon, when the Franks exerted themselves, the enemy were driven off, and took refuge within the shelter of their walls.

367. Of the site and setting of Jerusalem I am moved by the abundance of authorities to say nothing, nor is it necessary to give my pen free play in this field. Almost everyone has access to what Josephus, Eucherius, and Bede have written. Everyone knows that it was called Salem by Melchizedek, Jebus by the Jebusites, and Jerusalem by Solomon. Everyone has heard how often, as it fell before a foreign foe, it buried its citizens in its ruins, whether the aggressor were Nebuchadnezzar or Titus or Hadrian. It was Hadrian who called

Ierosolimam,[a] ex suo cognomine cognominatam Heliam,[b] orbiculato et maiori[c] murorum ambitu edificauit, ut locum sepulchri Dominici quod olim extra fuerat amplecteretur; nam et mons Sion intra urbem receptus[d] pro arce supereminet. Fons intra nullus, sed cisternis ad hoc preparatis colliguntur latices siti ciuium profuturi, quod ipsius urbis situs, supercilio ab aquilone montis Sion incipiens, ita sit molli cliuo dispositus ut pluuia ibi decidens nequaquam lutum fatiat, sed instar fluuiorum uel[e] cisternis excipiatur uel per portas defluens torrentem Cedron augeat. Ibi templum Domini et templum quod dicunt Salomonis, quibus incertum auctoribus edificata, Turchorum celebri frequentia colebantur,[f] templum presertim Domini, quod cotidianis uenerabantur excubiis Christianosque ingressu[g] arcebant, simulacro Mahumet ibidem collocato. Ibi decenti[h] opere compacta aecclesia sancti Sepulchri capax, a Constantino Magno edificata, nullam umquam ab inimicis fidei tulit iniuriam, metu, sicut[i] conitio, pro igne caelesti percussis,[j] qui quotannis in uigilia Paschae lampadibus serenus infulget. Quod miraculum quando ceperit, uel si ante tempora Saracenorum[k] fuerit, nullius historiae cognitione discernitur.

Legi ego in scripto Bernardi monachi[l] quod abhinc annis ducentis quinquaginta, id est, anno incarnationis octingentesimo[l] septuagesimo, idem Ierosolimam profectus ignem illum uiderit, hospitatusque fuerit[m] in xenodochio quod ibidem gloriosissimus Karolus Magnus construi iusserat, ubi et bibliothecam ingentis expensae compegerat. Tantamque et Egypti et per id locorum commemorat pacem Christianos sub Turchorum[n] dominio habuisse ut, si alicui uianti in mediis forte triuiis iumentum quo necessaria ueheret defungeretur,[o] ille relictis sarcinis ad proximam urbem expeditus[p] pro auxilio pergeret, omnia quae dimiserat illibata proculdubio reperturus. Nullus tamen ibi Christianus alienigena secure uiuere pro exploratorum suspitione poterat, nisi sigillo imperatoris Babilonii fretus; indigenae pacem Turchorum tribus annuis[q] talentis uel bizantinis[r] redimebant. Veruntamen quia Bernardus Theodosii tunc patriarchae nomen non tacet, ipsa me monet occasio ut omnium patriarcharum nomina proponam.

[a] Ierusalem T^1 [b] Heliam (Helia Aa) cognominatam T^1A [c] maiorum A [d] om. T^1 [e] T^1A add in [f] col. freq. T^1A [g] ingressi T^1 [h] tereti T^1A (cf. GP p. 300) [i] ut T^1A [j] perculsis $ACsB$ [k] paganorum T^1A [l] nongentesimo T^1, DCCCC B; so too Bernard's own manuscripts! [m] hosp. fuerit om. CsB [n] Sarracenorum T^1 [o] diffungeretur B [p] om. CsB [q] annis B [r] bizantiis B

the city Aelia, after one of his own names, and rebuilt it with a rounded and larger circuit of walls, so as to include the site of the Holy Sepulchre, which had previously been outside; Mount Sion too was brought within the city, which it dominates, forming the citadel. It contains no springs, but the rainwater is collected in cisterns provided for the purpose to supply the citizens with drinking-water; for the site of the city itself, beginning on the north with the escarpment of Mount Sion, tilts with a gentle slope in such a way that the rain which falls there never forms any mud, but runs off in streams, and if not collected in the cisterns, pours down through the gates to swell the Kidron torrent. In the city are the Lord's Temple and the one called Solomon's, the builders of both being unknown; both were thronged with Turkish worshippers, especially the Lord's Temple, for which they showed their reverence with daily devotions, forbidding any Christians to enter, and setting up in it an idol of Mahomet. There stands the church which contains the Holy Sepulchre, an elegant structure built by Constantine the Great, which has never suffered any injury from the enemies of the Faith; they are frightened, I suppose, on account of the fire from Heaven which glows untroubled from the lamps every year on Easter Eve. When this miracle took its rise, and whether it was before the days of the Saracens, there is no historical evidence to decide.

I have read in Bernard the Monk[1] that he saw the fire when he visited Jerusalem two hundred and fifty years ago, that is in the year 870, and that he stayed in the hospice built there to the order of Charlemagne of most glorious memory, where he had also put together a library at very great expense. According to Bernard, the Christians both in Egypt and in this part of the world enjoyed such peace under Turkish rule that if one of them were on a journey, and his beast of burden broke down, perhaps on the highroad, he could leave all his belongings and go for help empty-handed to the nearest town, in complete confidence that he would find all that he had left, untouched. But no foreign-born Christian could live there at his ease, because of their fear of spies, except in reliance on a permit under seal from the emperor of Babylon; the native Christian purchased immunity from the Turks for three talents or bezants a year. At this point, as Bernard mentions the name of Theodosius who was then patriarch, the opportunity prompts me to set forth the names of all the patriarchs of Jerusalem.

---

[1] *Itinera Hierosolymitana*, ed. T. Tobler and A. Molinier (Geneva, 1879), i. 309–20.

368. Iacobus frater Domini filius Alphei,[a] Simeon[b] filius Cleophae consobrinus Christi (Cleophas autem fuit frater Ioseph), Iustus, Zacheus, Tobias, Beniamin, Iohannes, Machabeus, Philippus, Seneca, Iustus, Leui, Effrem, Iustus,[c] Iudas (hi quindecim circumcisi fuerunt); Marcus, Cassianus, Publius, Maximus, Iulianus, Gaius (iste primus celebrauit Pascha et Quadragesimam more Romanorum), Simmachus, Gaius, Iulianus, Capito, Maximus, Antonius, Valens, Docilianus,[d] Narcisus, Dius, Germanio, Gordius, Alexander, Mazabanus, Irmeneus, Zabdas, Ermon, Macharius (huius temporibus inuenta est sancta crux ab[e] Helena), Ciriacus,[f] Maximus, Cirillus (iste construxit aecclesiam
2 sancti Sepulchri et montis Caluariae et Bethleem et uallis Iosaphat). Hi omnes uocati sunt episcopi. Post hos surrexere patriarchae: Cirillus protus patriarcha, Iohannes, Prailius, Iuuenalis, Iohannes, Zacharias (in cuius tempore uenit Cosdroe rex Persarum Ierusalem, et destruxit aecclesias Iudeae et Ierusalem, et occisa[g] sunt ab exercitu suo triginta sex milia[h] Christianorum), Modestus (iste constitutus est patriarcha ab Heraclio imperatore, postquam reuersus est uictor de Perside), Sophronius (cuius temporibus uenere Saraceni et eiecerunt Christianos omnes de Ierusalem, excepto patriarcha,[i] quem ob reuerentiam sanctitatis ibi
3 dimiserunt —illud fuit tempus quo Saraceni totam Egiptum et Affricam et[j] Iudeam et etiam[k] Hispaniam et Baleares insulas peruaserunt; partem Hispaniae abstulit eis Karolus Magnus, reliquam et omnes quas nominaui terras possident usque hodie, annis abhinc[l] quingentis), Theodorus, Ilia, Georgius, Thomas, Basilius,[m] Sergius, Salomontos,[n] Theodosius (hunc Theodosium fuisse abbatem Bernardus memorat, et raptum de monasterio suo, quod distabat ab Ierusalem quindecim milibus, et factum fuisse patriarcham Ierosolimae; tunc etiam[o] Michaelem dicit[p] fuisse patriarcham Babilonis super Egiptum, translato patri-
4 archatu Alexandriae in Babilonem), Ilia, Sergius, Leonthos, Athanasius,[q] Christodolus, Thomas, Ioseph, Orestes (in cuius tempore uenit Achim Soldanus de Babilonia, nepos Orestis patriarchae, et misit exercitum suum Ierusalem, et destruxit omnes aecclesias, scilicet quattuor milia, et auunculum suum patriarcham adduci fecit Babiloniam et ibidem occidi), Theophilus, Niceforus (hic edificauit casam[r] sancti Sepulchri quae nunc est, fauente Achim Soldano[s]), Sophronius (in cuius tempore Turchi

[a] Ioseph T'A   [b] Symon Tt(not Tp)Al, an alternative given by M. Le Quien (II), Oriens Christianus iii (Paris, 1740), 139 seq. (Roman numbers refer to his list)   [c] Iesse T'A; Ioseph Le Quien (XIV)   [d] Diocletianus T'; Dolichianus Le Quien (XXIX)   [e] a beata T'A (cf. 352. 8)   [f] C(h)irillus CsB. For Ciriacus see Le Quien, 155–6   [g] occisi C   [h] om. B   [i] extra patriarcham A   [j] om. T'

368. James the Lord's brother, the son of Alphaeus [T¹A Joseph]; Simeon the son of Cleophas, Christ's cousin (Cleophas was Joseph's brother); Justus [T¹A Jesse], Zacchaeus, Tobias, Benjamin, John, Maccabaeus, Philip, Seneca, Justus, Levi, Ephraim, Justus, Judas; these fifteen were circumcised. Mark, Cassian, Publius, Maximus, Julian, Gaius (he first celebrated Easter and Lent in the Roman manner), Symmachus, Gaius, Julian, Capito, Maximus, Antonius, Valens, Docilianus, Narcissus, Dius, Germanio, Gordius, Alexander, Mazabanus, Irmeneus, Zabdas, Hermon, Macarius (in his time the Holy Cross was discovered by Helena), Cyriacus, Maximus, Cyril (he built the churches of the Holy Sepulchre, of Mount Calvary, of Bethlehem, and of the Valley of Jehosephat). These were all called 2 bishops; after them arose the patriarchs: Cyril the first patriarch, John, Prailius, Juvenalis, John, Zacharias (in whose time Chosroes king of the Persians came to Jerusalem, and destroyed the churches of Judaea and Jerusalem, and thirty-six thousand Christians were killed by his army), Modestus (he was made patriarch by the emperor Heraclius on his victorious return from Persia), Sophronius (in whose time the Saracens came, and expelled all the Christians from Jerusalem, except the patriarch, whom they left there out of reverence for his sanctity—it was 3 at that time that the Saracens overran the whole of Egypt, Africa, and Judaea, and also Spain and the Balearic Islands; Charlemagne recovered part of Spain, but the rest of it, and all the other territories I have mentioned, they still possess, after [T¹A *add* about] five hundred years), Theodore, Ilia, George, Thomas, Basilius, Sergius, Salomontos, Theodosius (this Theodosius, according to Bernard, had been an abbot, and was removed from his monastery, which was fifteen miles from the city, and made patriarch of Jerusalem; at that time too, he says, Michael was patriarch of Babylon in Egypt, the patriarchate of Alexandria having been transferred to Babylon), Ilia, Sergius, 4 Leonthos, Athanasius, Christodoulos, Thomas, Joseph, Orestes (in whose time Hakim sultan of Babylonia, nephew of the patriarch Orestes, sent his army to Jerusalem, and destroyed all the churches to the number of four thousand; he ordered his uncle the patriarch to be taken to Babylonia, and there put to death), Theophilus, Nicephorus (he built the present 'hut' of the Holy Sepulchre, with the approval of Hakim the sultan), Sophronius (in whose time the Turks, coming to

ᵏ om. *C*   *ˡ* *T¹A add* circiter   *ᵐ* Basilidis *C*   *ⁿ* Salomontes *A*; Salomon *Le Quien (LXVII)*   *°* om. *C*   *ᵖ* dicunt *B*   *ᵍ* Anastasius *Tt(not Tp); v.* *Le Quien (LXXII)*   *ʳ* (a)cclesiam *C*   *ˢ* Soldano Achim *T¹A*

Ierosolimam uenientes pugnauerunt cum Saracenis et omnes interfecerunt et obtinuerunt ciuitatem; Christiani autem remanserunt ibi sub dominio Turchorum), Euthimius, Simeon (huius tempore uenerunt Franci et expugnauerunt Ierusalem, et liberauerunt eam de manibus Turchorum et regis Babiloniae).

369. Anno igitur Ierosolimitanae peregrinationis quarto, post captam Niceam tertio, post Antiochiam secundo, obsessa est a Francis Ierusalem, urbs bellorum maxima merces,[1] blandimentum laborum, supremae spei uiaticum. Erat tunc Iunii mensis dies[a] septimus, nec quicquam sibi obsessor uerebatur in cibatu uel in potu, quod messes in agris, uuae in uineis maturauerant;[b] sola iumentorum cura erat miserabilis, quae pro qualitate loci et temporis nullo sustentabantur irriguo; nam et fontis Siloe recessus, qui horis incertis dulcibus scatet
2 aquis, tunc calor solis ebiberat. Fons ille, si quando pluuialibus pascitur aquis,[c] torrentem Cedron auget, indeque undiuomo impetu in uallem Iosaphat decurrit; sed hoc admodum raro, quia nullus eius augmenti uel detrimenti serius[d] est terminus. Quocirca nostros, ad aquationem iumentorum crebro dispersos, hostes e cauernis egredientes inopine cedebant. Interea duces suo quisque muneri, Raimundus uero turri Dauiticae impiger assidebat.[e] Haec, ab occasu solis urbem muniens, ad medium fere tabulatu[f] quadratorum lapidum plumbo infuso compaginata, omnem metum obsidentium paucis intus defendentibus repellit.
3 Itaque uidentes urbem ad capiendum, propter prerupta montium et firmitatem menium et ferocitatem hostium, difficilem, machinas fieri precepere.[g] Et prius quidem, obsessionis die septimo, fortunam scalis erectis temptarunt, in resistentes uolaticas moliti sagittas; sed quia erant scalae paucae et[h] ascendentibus dampnosae, quod uulneribus exposti undique[i] nulla parte protegerentur, consilium mutarunt. Vnum fuit machinamentum quod nostri suem, ueteres uineam uocant, quod machina leuibus lignis colligata, tecto tabulis cratibusque contexto, lateribus crudis coriis munitis,[j] protegit in se subsidentes,[k] qui quasi
4 more suis ad murorum suffodienda penetrant fundamenta. Alterum fuit

[a] dies mensis *CsB* [b] maturarent *T¹* [c] aquis pascitur *T¹A* [d] certus *Bk;* serius *is very oddly used here* [e] as(s)istebat *T¹A* [f] *TpAlCs;* tabulatum *TιAaCeB* [g] precipere *A* [h] om. *C* [i] undique expositi *T¹A**
[j] communitis *CsB (cf. 424. 3)* [k] subsistentes *A*

---

[1] Lucan ii. 227–8, 655–6 (of Rome).

Jerusalem, fought with the Saracens and killed them all, and seized the city; the Christians, however, remained there under the dominion of the Turks), Euthymius, Simeon (it was in his time that the Franks arrived and captured Jerusalem, and delivered it from the hand of the Turks and of the king of Babylonia).

369. It was, then, in the fourth year of their pilgrimage to Jerusalem, the third year after the fall of Nicaea and the second after the fall of Antioch, that Jerusalem was besieged by the Franks—Jerusalem, 'the supreme reward of all their wars',[1] sweet solace of their toils, and sure resource of hope at the last. The date was 7 June. None of the besiegers had any fears in point of food or drink, for the harvest had ripened in the fields and the grapes in the vineyards; only their animals were in pitiful case, the country and season being such that there was no source of water to maintain them, and even the secret spring of Siloam, which flows with sweet water at irregular intervals, had been dried up by the heat of the sun. This spring, when it is fed by rain water, goes to swell the Kidron torrent, and then pours foaming down into the valley of Jehoshaphat; but this happens very rarely, because it has no proper period of increase or decrease. Consequently, as our men were constantly ranging about in search of water for their animals, the enemy could issue from the caves and cut them down unawares. Meanwhile, each of the leaders set about his task with energy, and Raymond in particular blockaded the Tower of David. This tower, which defends the city on the west, is built, to about half way up, of squared stones closely clamped with molten lead, and with a handful of defenders need have no fear of any siege.

So when they saw that, what with the precipitous cliffs and strong walls and stubborn enemy, the city would be difficult to take, they gave orders for the construction of engines. Before that, on the seventh day of the siege, they tried their luck by putting up scaling-ladders, having organized a barrage of arrows against the defence; but the ladders being too few in number, and very dangerous to the men on them, who were exposed to fire from all quarters and completely unprotected, they changed their plan. There was one engine in particular which we call a hog (it is the *vinea* of the Ancients): for it has a jointed framework of light scantling, with a roof of close-set planking and wicker hurdles, and sides protected with raw hide, and this gives protection to the men crouching in it, who, like a rooting hog, work their way forward to undermine the foundation of the walls. The other was a tower, of

pro lignorum penuria turris non magna, in modum edifitiorum facta (berfreid appellant), quod fastigium murorum aequaret. Hoc machinamentum dum fieret moram obsidioni dedit pro fabrorum inscitia*a* et lignorum inopia.*b* Et iam dies quartus decimus Iulii uoluebatur cum hi admotis*c* uineis murum suffodere, hi turrim promouere cepere; quod ut oportunius fieret, membratim disiunctam*d* ad muros tulere, ibique prope quantum a iactu sagittae cauere poterant compaginatam*e*
5 rotarum uolubilitate muro pene coniunxere. Interea funditores lapidibus, sagittarii*f* iaculis, arcubalistae telis quisque suum exercentes offitium instare, et propugnantes de muro summouere; milites quoque uirtute incomparabiles turrim ascendere, aequo iam pene marte telis et lapidibus in hostes agentes. Nec illi feriis uacabant, sed omnem uirtuti salutem committentes adipem et oleum ignitum in turrim et in milites fundibalis iaculabantur, multorum mortibus uoti sui se compotes gloriantes. Ita toto illo die certatum ut neutra pars se uictam putaret.

6 Sequenti die, qui erat quintus decimus Iulii, ad suprema uentum; namque Franci, pridiani certaminis euentu eruditiores, faces*g* oleagino suco uiuidas*h* in turrim muro proximam et eius custodes iecerunt. At flamma, uento agente in comas erecta, primo ligna, mox lapides corripiens custodes effugauit. Quin et tigna quae Turchi e muro pendula demiserant,*i* ut turrim, si propius admoueretur, reducto nisu brachiorum arietando effringerent, Franci funibus desectis ad se traxere, et de machina in murum iactis cratibusque constratis pontem qui turrim et menia continuaret fecere. Ita perfidis uersum in exitium
7 quod parauerant ad remedium. Tum uero et fumeis flammarum globis et nostrorum audatia hostes infracti fugam ineunt. Alteri, in murum et inde in urbem progredientes, quantum illa exigebat animorum laetitia*j* manibus egere. Et haec quidem uictoria in parte Godefridi et duorum Rotbertorum euenit. Ignorabat hoc Raimundus, donec fugitiuorum clamor et se de muro ultro precipitantium timor, qui dum mortem fugiunt mortem inuadunt, urbem captam prodidit. Quod intuitus, strictisque gladiis in fugitiuos*k* irruens, quantum animositati suae sufficere iudicauit iniurias Dei ultum ire festinabat.

a inscientia *T'Al (cf. 409. 1);* inconscientia *Aap*   *b* penuria *T'A*   *c* amotis *A*   *d* disiectam *A*   *e* compaginata *B*   *f* sagittarum *T'*   *g* fasces *B*   *h* uiridas *Tp,* linitas *Tt; one might expect* uuidas *or* umidas, *but cf. Fulcher i. 27. 6* ignem cum oleo et adipe uiuidum   *i* dimiserant *Tt(not Tp)ABk*   *j* anim. l(a)et. exig. *T'A*   *k* fugientes *T'A*

moderate size owing to shortage of timber, built-up after the fashion of a timber-framed house; they call it a belfry. It was designed to rise level with the top of the wall. This contrivance, while it was building, held up the siege for some time, the carpenters being unskilled and timber scarce. It was already 14 July when one party moved up their hogs to undermine the wall, while the others began to advance the tower. To do this more easily, they took it to pieces and brought it up to the wall in parts; there they assembled it, just out of bowshot, and rolling it forward on wheels moved it almost up to the wall. Meanwhile each 5 man kept to his allotted task, the slingers laying on with their stones, archers with arrows, crossbowmen with bolts, trying to drive the defenders from the wall; and the knights with incomparable valour climbed the tower and tackled the enemy, now almost on equal terms, with weapons and with stones. The enemy on their side were far from idle. Putting their whole hope of salvation in valour, they rained blazing fat and oil upon the tower and the knights with catapults, rejoicing in heavy casualties as a sign of their success. All that long day they fought, on such terms that neither side thought itself beaten.

Next day, which was 15 July, came the climax. The Franks, learning 6 their lesson from the outcome of the day before, hurled blazing missiles freshly fed with oozing oil against the nearest tower on the wall and its defenders. The fire, driven into a blaze by the force of the wind, caught first the timber and then the masonry, and drove back the defenders. Besides which, there were beams, which the Turks had lowered so that they hung from the wall, in order that by swinging them back with might and main they could smash the tower with a battering action, if it came too close; and these the Franks pulled across, cutting the ropes, and then laid them from their engine across to the wall, covered them with wicker hurdles, and so made a bridge to join tower and battlements. So what the heathen had made ready for their salvation was turned to their destruction. At this point, what with the rolling smoke and flames, and the bold 7 courage of our troops, the enemy's nerve broke, and he turned and ran. The other side, making their way onto the wall, and thence into the city, gave full expression by their prowess to the joy that was in their hearts. This victory was won in the sector of Godfrey and the two Roberts; Raymond knew nothing of it, till the shouts of the fugitives and the terror of men who jumped off the wall—fleeing one death only to rush upon another—showed that the city was taken. Seeing this, he fell with drawn sword on the runaways, and hastened to avenge the injuries done to God, until he judged that he had done justice to his own spiritedness.

8 Quingentos quoque*a* Ethiopas qui, in arcem Dauid refugi, claues portarum pollicita membrorum impunitate tradiderant, spectato presentis pacis commodo*b* incolumes Ascalonem dimisit. Nec ullum erat tunc*c* Turchis refugium, ita et*d* suplices et rebelles insatiabilis ira uictorum*e* consumebat. Decem milia in templo Salomonis interfecta, plura ex fastigiis templorum et arcis precipitata. Post haec cadauera cumulata igne immisso in aerium resoluta sunt elementum, ne sub 9 diuo in tabem fluentia inerti attraherent contagia mundo.[1] Ita cede infidelium expiata urbe, sepulchrum Domini, quod tam diu desiderauerant, *f*pro quo tot labores tulerant,*f* suplicibus cordibus et corporibus expetierunt.*g* Quot ibi precum thurificatione caelum incenderint,*h* quot lacrimis Deum in gratiam reuocauerint, nullus umquam profiteor*i* euolueret, nec si ueterum pompatica eloquentia procederet, non si Orpheus, qui uocalibus fidibus auritos ut dicitur scopulos flexit, resurgeret. Cogitetur igitur potius quam dicatur.

370. Illud insigne continentiae in omnibus optimatibus exemplum fuit, quod nec eo die nec consequentibus quisquam respectu predae auocauit animum, quin ceptum persequerentur triumphum. Solus Tancredus, intempestiua cupidine occupatus, quedam pretiosissima de templo Salomonis extulit; sed postmodum, sua conscientia et aliorum 2 conuentus colloquio, uel eadem uel appretiata loco restituit. Tum quicumque egenus uel*j* domum uel aliquas diuitias inuasit, numquam ulterius ullius locupletis tulit conuitium, sed semel possessa in ius adoptauit hereditarium. Nec mora, prelucidum illud Christianae nobilitatis specular, in quo uelut e*k* splendido lacunari omnium uirtutum repercutiebatur iubar, Godefridus in regem eligitur, omnibus non ignaua spe conferentibus, nullo modo posse decentius*l* prospici aecclesiae utilitatibus, dilato interim de patriarcha consilio, qui Romani papae deberet substitui iuditio.

371. At uero Babilonis imperator, non illius quae a Nembroth facta, a Semiramide aucta, *m*nunc asseritur deserta,*m* sed illius quam Cambises Ciri filius edificauit in Egipto,*n* in loco ubi quondam fuerat

---

a quingentosque *(om.* quoque*)* T'   *b* pacis comm. pres. C   *c* om. C   *d* ut Bk, om. Bc   *e* uictorum ira T'A   *f-f* om. T'   *g* petierunt B   *h* inciderint Al, inciderint Aap   *i* prof. unquam T'A   *j* om. T'A   *k* in T'A   *l* dec. posse T'A   *m-m* esse asseritur C   *n* fil. Ciri in Eg. edif. T'A

[1] Cf. Lucan vi. 88–9.

Five hundred Ethiopians, who had taken refuge in the Tower of David, and handed over the keys in return for a promise of bodily safety, he sent, with an eye to the advantage of immediate peace, unscathed to Ascalon. For the Turks there was now no escape; whether they cringed or fought back, the devouring anger of the victors was insatiable. Ten thousand were killed in Solomon's Temple; more were sent headlong from the parapets of the temples and the citadel. After this the bodies, piled in a heap, were set on fire, and thus dissolved into the elements of air, for fear that, if left to welter in dissolution under the open sky, they might 'draw down contagion on an idle world.'[1] Thus the city was purified by the massacre of the infidel, and with suppliant hearts and bodies bent low they made their way to the Holy Sepulchre, for which they had yearned so long and borne so many labours. The prayers with whose incense Heaven was then enkindled, the tears wherewith they called on God to renew His favour—these no man, I aver, could ever number, not even if the solemn eloquence of the Ancients were forthcoming, not even if Orpheus rose again, who, they say, could give ears to the rocks and sway them with the music of his lyre. Let this then be imagined rather than described.

370. A signal instance of self-restraint was seen in all the nobles, for neither on that day nor on those that followed did any of them with an eye for booty turn aside from the completion of the victory they had begun. Tancred alone, a prey to ill-timed avarice, took certain objects of great value out of Solomon's Temple; but afterwards, convicted by his own conscience and the reproach of others, he returned either the articles themselves or the equivalent in money. At that time any poor man who had seized a house or valuable property of any kind, never thereafter had to endure abuse from any rich man, but assumed as his hereditary right whatever he had once taken in possession. Without delay, that shining example of Christian chivalry, in whom was reflected as from a splendid ceiling the radiance of all the virtues, Godfrey was chosen king, all men agreeing in the lively hope that in no other way could the interests of the Church more fittingly be taken care of. A decision about the patriarch was deferred for the moment, as he needed to be replaced in accordance with the judgement of the Roman pontiff.

371. The emperor of Babylon, however—not the city said to have been founded by Nimrod and enlarged by Semiramis, thought now to be deserted, but the other Babylon in Egypt, built by Cyrus' son

Taphnis—imperator ergo Babilonis, diu conceptas in Francos iras parturiens, misit ducem militiae qui eos de regno, ut dictitabat, suo propelleret.[a] Ille precepta maturans munia, cum audisset captam Ierusalem, maiori cura stimulauit negotium, quamquam ante[b] nichil segnitiei admisisset; eratque barbaro animus ut Christianos in Ierusalem obsideret, et post uictoriam, quam iam mente somniabat falso presagus, sepulchrum Domini a fundo erutum dilapidaret.

2 Nostri, qui nichil minus diligerent quam obsidionales[c] erumnas denuo perpeti,[d] sumpta ex Dei parte audatia ex urbe uersus Ascalonem prodeunt, obuia hostibus inferentes pectora; portabantque secum partem Dominici ligni,[e] quam quidam Sirus ciuis Ierosolimitanus auita successione domi custoditam propalauerat. Felix plane et fidele furtum, ut toto tempore Turchis celaretur misterium! Ingentem ergo predam pecorum et pecudum secus[f] Ascalonem nacti, generale proposuerunt edictum ut omnia in patulis campis relinquerent, ne postero mane pugnaturis impedimento forent: satis superque se predam habituros si uincerent, dum modo expediti diuinas ulciscerentur iniurias. Itaque mane iam exercitu prodeunte[g] uideres, supero credo

3 instinctu, cornibus erectis pecora lateribus militum obambulantia, nec ulla posse abigi uiolentia. Quod eminus hostes intuiti, et solaribus radiis uisus hebetati, animis ante prelium conciderunt, quod crederent innumeram esse aduersariorum manum, quanuis ipsis non deesset militaris copia multo exercitio ad prelium preparata. Lentius itaque procedentes, Francos bipertito agmine et sinuatis alis includere conati sunt; sed duces, et maxime Rotbertus Normannus qui antesignanus erat, arte artem uel potius uirtute calliditatem eludentes, sagittariis et peditibus diductis[h] medias gentilium perruperunt aties. Eques

4 quoque Lotharingus, qui in extremo agmine cum domino suo erat, a lateribus inuolitans libertatem fugae et campos abstulit omnes.[1] Ita Turchi, ab anterioribus penetrati et ab exterioribus inclusi, ad uoluntatem[i] uictorum cesi sunt; reliqui noctis, quae imminebat, benefitio liberati. Multum aureae supellectilis in eorum castris inuentum, multum gemmarum, quarum raritas nostris regionibus incognita ibi

[a] proturbaret T'A   [b] antea T'A   [c] obsidiales T'Bc; obsidiones Al, -nis Aa   [d] experiri T'A   [e] lig. Dom. TpA   [f] iuxta T'A   [g] procedente exercitu T'A   [h] deductis CB   [i] satietatem T'A

---

[1] Lucan iv. 262–3.

Cambyses on the site of the former Taphnis—the emperor, I say, venting his long-conceived resentment on the Franks, sent the captain of his chivalry to sweep them, as he put it, out of his dominions. The general quickly took up the task assigned him, and when he heard of the fall of Jerusalem redoubled his efforts, although even before that he had tolerated no slackness. The paynim's plan was to besiege the Christians in Jerusalem, and after the victory of which he already dreamed with foolish optimism, to overthrow the Holy Sepulchre and pull it completely to pieces. Our men, who desired nothing less than another experience of the miseries of a siege, drew courage from the cause of God and took the offensive, advancing from the city towards Ascalon. With them they carried part of the Lord's Cross, which a Syrian citizen of Jerusalem had produced, whose family had preserved it as an heirloom. How fortunate, how faithful the guile that concealed the holy relic from the Turks all that time! Thus, having secured much booty in the way of cattle and sheep around Ascalon, they issued a general order that everything must be left in the open fields, for fear that next morning the beasts would get in their way as they prepared to fight; if they won the day there would be loot enough and to spare, provided they were unhampered in avenging the wrongs done to God. So when morning came, and the army advanced, you would have seen the cattle, as though by some heaven-sent instinct, walking alongside the knights with their horns held high, and refusing to be driven off by any use of force. When the enemy saw this from a distance, with their eyes dazzled by the rays of the sun, they lost heart before the battle began, thinking their adversaries were without number, although they themselves had no lack of chivalry made ready for the fray by constant practice. They advanced therefore rather slowly, and by dividing their forces in two and curving their wings round, attempted to encircle the Franks; but our leaders, and especially Robert of Normandy who was with the vanguard, met art with art, or rather cunning with valour, and deploying archers and foot-soldiery, broke through the centre of the heathen line. Besides which, the cavalry of Lorraine, who were in the rear of the column under their own lord, harassed their flanks, and leaving them no room to withdraw 'barred all extent of space.'[1] Penetrated by one enemy from in front and hemmed in by another on their flank, the Turks were cut down by the victors to their hearts' content; the remainder owed their escape to the approach of nightfall. Much gold plate was found in their camp, and many rare jewels, unknown in our part of the world, but there found native in their glittering beauty;

natiuo decore refulgurat; nec ulla uictoria laetior fuit Christianis, quod incruenti opima*ᵃ* retulere spolia.

372. Ierusalem itaque reuersi, cum statiua multorum dierum requie*ᵇ* uires reformassent, quidam suspirantes in natalis soli desiderium marinum adornarunt reditum. Soli Godefridus et Tancredus remanserunt, predicabiles profecto principes et quorum titulis nullas umquam affiget metas postera, si rectum*ᶜ* iudicet, aetas; uiri qui ab extremo Europae frigore in importabiles se Orientis calores immerserint, uitae suae prodigi dum modo Christianitati laboranti*ᵈ* concurrerent; qui preter metum barbaricorum incursuum semper pro incommoditate ignoti*ᵉ* poli suspecti, securitatem quietis et sanitatis in
2 patria contempserint, et pauculi numero tot inimicorum urbes fama et effectu uirtutum*ᶠ* presserint, memorabili fidutiae Dei exemplo, ut illic non dubitarent subsistere ubi uel pestifero afflarentur aere uel Saracenica occiderentur rabie. Cedant ergo poetarum preconia, nec priscos heroas uetus attollat fabula. Nichil umquam horum laudi comparabile ulla genuere secula; nam et si qua illorum fuit uirtus, in sepulchrales fauillas post mortem*ᵍ* euanuit, quod potius in mundialis pompae fumum quam in ullius boni solidum effusa fuerit. Istorum autem fortitudinis sentietur utilitas et ostendetur dignitas *ʰ*quam diu
3 orbis uolubilitas*ʰ* et sancta uigebit Christianitas. Quid uero de disciplina et abstinentia totius exercitus dicam? Nulla ibi uentris ingluuies, nulla fuit penis illuuies, quae non continuo uel ducum auctoritate*ⁱ* uel episcoporum sermone corrigeretur; nulli*ʲ* predandi per terras Christianorum cupido; nulla inter se controuersia quae non facile mediatorum iudicum cognitione recideretur. Quapropter, quia tam ordinati exercitus laus ad prelatorum redundat gloriam, singulorum procerum facta et exitus scripto insigniam, nec quicquam ueritati secundum relatorum meorum credulitatem subtraham. Nullus uero, cui amplior prouenit gestorum notitia, me pro incurioso*ᵏ* arguat, quia trans oceanum Britannicum abditos uix tenui murmure rerum Asianarum fama illustrat.

373. Initium*ˡ* laudum rex Godefridus occupat, qui Eustachii

ᵃ inopina *T'*   *ᵇ* quiete *T'A*   *ᶜ* si rectum postera *T'A*   *ᵈ* lab. Chr. *T'A*   *ᵉ* igniti *A*   *ᶠ* uirtutis *T'A*   *ᵍ* post mortem in sep. fau. *T'A*   *ʰ⁻ʰ* om. *A*   *ⁱ* austeritate *T'A*   *ʲ* nulla *T'**   *ᵏ* iniurioso *T'*   *ˡ* *T'A** add ergo

nor did the Christians ever win a happier victory, for they returned laden with loot but without loss of blood.

372. Once returned to Jerusalem, they recruited their strength by a long period of repose, and then some of them, filled with longing for their native land, made ready to return by sea. Only Godfrey and Tancred remained, leaders of high renown, to whose praises posterity, if it judge aright, will assign no limits; heroes who from the cold of uttermost Europe plunged into the intolerable heat of the East, careless of their own lives, if only they could bring help to Christendom in its hour of trial. Besides the fear of barbarian attacks, exposed to constant apprehension from the rigours of an unfamiliar climate, they made light of the certainty of peace and health in their own country; few as they were, they overwhelmed so many enemy cities by the fame and operation of their prowess, setting a noteworthy example of trust in God, in that they were ready to remain without hesitation in a place where either the air they breathed would be loaded with pestilence, or they would be killed by the fury of the Saracens. Let poets with their eulogies now give place, and fabled history no longer laud the heroes of Antiquity. Nothing to be compared with their glory has ever been begotten by any age. Such valour as the Ancients had vanished after their death into dust and ashes in the grave, for it was spent on the mirage of worldly splendour rather than on the solid aim of some good purpose; while of these brave heroes of ours, men will enjoy the benefit and tell the proud story, as long as the round world endures and the holy Church of Christ flourishes. Of the discipline and self-control of the whole army, what can I say? There was no gormandizing and no lechery that was not at once corrected by the captains' orders or the eloquence of the bishops; no man, while they were in Christian territory, lusted after loot; nor were there any quarrels among them that were not easily cut short by arbitration. And so, seeing that the wonderful discipline of the army redounds to the glory of its commanders, I will place on record the deeds and end of each of the leaders, abating nothing of the truth, according to the credibility of my authorities. Let no man who enjoys fuller knowledge of the facts upbraid me with lack of pains, for in our distant lair beyond the British Ocean, scarcely a rumour comes to enlighten our ignorance of events in Asia.

373. The place of honour is claimed by King Godfrey. The son of

comitis Bononiensis, de quo tempore regis Eduardi dixi,[1] filius materno excellentior genere ad Karoli Magni spectabat lineam. Siquidem mater, Ida nomine, Godefridi antiqui Lotharingorum ducis filia, habuit fratrem, a genitoris nomine Godefridum dictum, cognomento Bocardum. Illud fuit tempus quando Rotbertus Friso, de quo superius locutus sum,[2] mortuo Florentio Frisiae duce uxorem eius Gertrudem duxit, priuignum Theodericum in successionem ducatus prouehens. Non tulit hoc Bocardus, sed Frisonem expellens regionem
2 suis uoluntatibus addixit. Vltus se ille insidiis qui non posset preliis, per Flandritas suos sedentem ad *a*requisita naturae*a* extinxit, ferro per uerenda immisso. Ita priuignus benefitio uictrici successit ducatui. Vxor huius Godefridi fuit Mathildis marcisa, quam superior liber predicat,[3] quae mortuo marito ducatum impigre contra imperatorem retentauit, maxime intra Italiam; nam Lotharingiam et inferiores terras imperator obtinuit. Ida ergo, ut dicere ceperam, magnis spebus ad comitatum Lotharingorum petendum filium Godefridum erexit; namque seniori filio Eustachio hereditas paterna obtigerat, minor
3 Balduinus pueriles adhuc annos terebat. Godefridus, habilem ad arma aetatem nactus, imperatori Henrico, de quo proximus liber loquitur,[4] militiam suam consecrauit. Ingentibus ergo sudoribus eius in se transferens amicitiam, egregia liberalitate Cesaris totam pro stipendio accepit Lotharingiam. Vnde factum est ut, orta inter papam et Henricum simultate, cum eo ad oppugnandam Romam profectus, eam partem muri*b* quae uigiliis suis obseruabatur primus perrumperet, magnam fenestram irrupturis aperiens. Ita potissimum sudans et preferuidis uenis suspiriosus, cellarium subterraneum, quod forte se discursanti*c* obtulerat, ingressus est; ibi, cum nimio uini haustu
4 intemperantiam sitis placasset, febrim quartanam iniit. Dicunt alii uenenato Falerno infectum, quod soleant Romani et illius terrae homines totis infundere toxica tonnis.[5] Alii ei partem illam menium sorte*d* obtigisse ubi Tiberis influens mane seuas exhalat nebulas, quarum pernitie omnes milites eius preter decem interisse, ipsum amissis crinibus et unguibus dubie conualuisse. Veruntamen, quodlibet horum fuerit, constat eum numquam continuae sed lentae febris incommodo uacasse, donec, audita fama uiae Ierosolimitanae, illuc se

a-a necessaria *T'A;* nat. req. *Bk (cf. 180. 9),* secreta nature *Bc* *b* om. *CsB*
c discurrenti *T'A*   *d* forte *TpB*

[1] 199. 1. [2] First at 256. 3. [3] 289. 1.
[4] From c. 420. [5] Unidentified (medieval) quotation.

Eustace, count of Boulogne, of whom I have spoken in treating of King Edward,[1] he was of more distinguished lineage on his mother's side, and claimed descent from Charlemagne; for his mother, named Ida, was a daughter of Godfrey the elder, duke of Lorraine, and had a brother, called Godfrey after his father, and surnamed Bocard. That was the time when Robert the Frisian, of whom I have spoken above,[2] on the death of Floris count of Frisia married his widow Gertrude, promoting his stepson Theoderic to be heir to the county. This was too much for Bocard, and he drove out the Frisian and brought the province under his own sway; but the Frisian, seeking in stealth the revenge he could not secure in battle, had him killed by his Flemings as he sat fulfilling the demands of nature: they drove an iron spike through his privy parts. Thus the stepson by his stepfather's gift succeeded to the county. This Godfrey's wife was the marchioness Matilda told of in my last book;[3] on her husband's death she defended his dukedom actively against the emperor, especially in Italy; Lorraine and the Low Countries fell into the emperor's hand. So Ida, as I was about to say, encouraged her son Godfrey with high hopes to aim at the duchy of Lorraine, for the elder son, Eustace, had come into his father's inheritance, and Baldwin the younger was still a child. When Godfrey reached the fit age for bearing arms, he consecrated his knightly service to the emperor Henry, of whom my next book tells,[4] and having by great exertions earned the emperor's friendship, he was rewarded by the imperial generosity with the whole of Lorraine. Hence it was that on the outbreak of hostilities between Henry and the pope, he set off with Henry to lay siege to Rome, and was the first to break through the section of the wall under the surveillance of his own men, thus opening a wide gap for the troops who burst in after him. Streaming with sweat, gasping for breath, while the blood boiled in his veins, he found by chance, as he ranged about, an underground cellar, and went inside. There he satisfied his ungovernable thirst by excessive draughts of wine, and took a quartan fever. Some say he was poisoned by Falernian that had been tampered with, the Romans, like the Italians in general, being apt 'to pour in venom by the barrel full';[5] others, that by his allotted span of the wall the Tiber stream exhales dire morning mists, through whose poisonous influence all his knights died save ten, and he himself made a shaky recovery, losing his hair and nails. Whatever the facts, it is certain that he was never free from the affliction of a continual slow fever, until, hearing the news of the expedition to Jerusalem, he vowed that he would go thither, if God in His mercy

5 iturum uouit, si Deus propitius ei salutem*a* largiretur; quo uoto emisso ita ducis uires refloruisse ut nodosos integer artus et spatioso erectus pectore, quasi squalentibus annis exutus, recenti emicaret iuuenta.

Quare, diuinis benefitiis in se confluentibus responsurus, Ierosolimam iuit uel primus uel cum primis, magnas in bellum trahens cateruas, et quanuis durum et exercitatum militem haberet, nullus tamen eo uel prior in congressu uel promptior in effectu habebatur. Denique notum est quod Turchum, in Antiochena obsidione singularem pugnam*b* poscentem, medium a lateribus gladio Lotharingo dissecuerit, et iam palpitabat aruis medietas hominis cum alteram cornipes
6 uolucri cursu asportauit, adeo firme nebulo insederat; alterum aeque congressum librata in caput spatha a uertice ad inguina diffiderit, nec adhuc ictus horrendus steterit, sed sellam et spinam equi penitus disciderit. Audiui ueracem hominem referentem uidisse se quod subitiam: in ipsa obsidione militem ducis pabulari progressum, et a leone inuasum, obiectu clipei mortem aliquandiu distulisse;*c* indoluisse Godefridum uiso et uenabulo feram transfodisse; illam sautiam et dolore acrius seuientem in principem*d* irruisse, adeo ut ferro quod extabat e uulnere tibiam eius lederet,*e* et, nisi properasset gladio beluam euiscerare, illud uirtutis specimen potuisse dente ferino interire.

7 His successibus clarus, in regem Ierosolimae leuatur, propterea quod esset genere et uirtute*f* conspicuus, nec tamen superbus. Paruum admodum et finibus angustum fuit regnum, quod preter paucas in circuitu uillas nullas pene*g* urbes haberet; nam et infesta regis ualitudo, quam statim post bellum Babilonicum*h* incurrerat, ferias bellis dedit ut nichil adquireretur, et diuina sollertia barbaricas auiditates toto illo anno probe compescuit ut nichil amitteretur. Fama est regem otii desuetudine febrim antiquam nactum fuisse; sed ego conitio Deum placitam sibi animam et tot laboribus emeritam in melius regnum transferre mature uoluisse,*i* ne malitia mutaret animam*j* eius*k* aut*l* fictio
8 deciperet intellectum*m* illius.[1] Igitur, rota temporis referente annuum regni spatium, placida morte resolutus et sub Golgothana rupe tumulatus est; rex inuicti *"*sicut in ferrum sic in mortem*"* animi, qui

---

a sanitatem *T'A*   *b* pug. sing. *C*   *c* propul(s)asse *T'A*   *d* in principem om. *B*   *e* sauciaret *T'A*   *f* uirtute et genere *T'A*   *g* om. *CsB*   *h* Bab. bellum *T'A*   *i* uoluisse mature *C*   *j* i(ntellectum) *T'*, *Vulg.*   *k* il(lius) *T'*; ipsius *A*   *l* aut ne *Tt(not Tp)*, *Vulg.*   *m* a(nimam) *T'Bc'*, *Vulg.*   *n–n* in mortem sicut in ferrum *T'A*

---

[1] Wisd. 4: 11.

would grant him health. Having formulated this vow, he regained his strength to such a degree that, with limbs renewed, upright and broad-chested, as though he had put years of decrepitude from him, he shone with new-created youth.

And so, to make due response to this flow of heavenly blessings, he went first to Jerusalem or among the first, bringing great companies to battle in his train; and though his knights were tough and experienced, none was found either readier than he to join battle or more effective when it was joined. For example, it is well known how a Turk, who offered him single combat during the siege of Antioch, was cut in two by him from side to side with his sword of Lorraine; half the man already lay quivering on the bare ground, while the horse—so firm was the poor wretch's seat—galloped away with the other half. Or again how, when another man clashed with him, he swung his sword down on his head and cleft him in two from crest to fork; nor did the frightful blow stop there, but went on to split his saddle and his horse's back. What follows I have heard told by a trustworthy man who saw it happen. During the same siege, one of the duke's knights went out to forage, and was attacked by a lion. He held his shield in front of him, and for a time kept death at bay, until Godfrey saw it, and in a fit of passion transfixed the animal with a hunting spear. The wounded lion, maddened by the pain, charged the prince, and succeeded in damaging his leg with the weapon that projected from the wound; had he not speedily ripped its belly open with his sword, this paragon of valour might have fallen victim to the teeth of a wild beast.

Such was his brilliant record when he was exalted to be king of Jerusalem, for the reason that, though outstanding in birth and bravery, he was not proud. His kingdom was very small, its boundaries narrow, for, apart from a few villages round about, he had practically no towns: the king's health, which had failed him immediately after the war against the Babylonians, had meant a rest from fighting, so that nothing was gained, and Divine Wisdom repressed the ambition of the barbarians all that year, so that nothing was lost. The story goes that the king had an attack of his old fever as a result of this unwonted leisure; but my own conjecture is that it was God's will without delay to translate to a better kingdom that soul well-pleasing in His sight, the veteran of so many labours, 'lest wickedness should alter his soul, or deceit beguile his understanding.'[1] So, as the revolving year brought round the anniversary of his accession, he died a peaceful death, and was buried beneath the rock of Golgotha. His royal heart faced death, as it had

lacrimas astantium sepe benignus cohercuerit, interrogatusque de successore neminem nominatim sed*a* eum qui dignus foret*b* pronuntiauerit, nec umquam regium insigne ferre sustinuerit, professus unicam esse arrogantiam si coronaretur ipse*c* ad gloriam in ea urbe qua*d* Deus coronatus fuerat ad contumeliam. 'Obiit quinto decimo kalendas Augusti.*e*

374. Eo defuncto Tancredus et alii proceres Balduinum, fratrem eius, futurum regem pronuntiant, qui tum*f* in Mesopotamia morabatur; nam Eustachius senior, qui cum Godefrido Ierosolimam uenerat, iam dudum hereditarium solum repetierat. Balduini actus integra et breui*g* ueritate apponentur, fidei soliditate accommodata dictis Fulcherii Carnotensis; qui, capellanus ipsius,*h* aliquanta de ipso scripsit, stilo non quidem agresti*i* sed, ut dici solet,¹ sine nitore ac palestra, et qui alios ammonere potuit ut accuratius scriberent.
2 Balduinus igitur, iter sanctum cum ceteris adorsus, multos milites habuit indolis suae complices, quibus fretus nouos sibi exercitus ipse*j* moliri, splendidas occasiones aucupari quibus uirtus enitescere posset.

Denique, non contentus communi omnium laude, trium dierum ab Antiochia spatio a reliquis discedens Tarsum, Ciliciae urbem*k* nobilem, uoluntate ciuium suscepit;*l* Tarsum, Pauli quondam apostoli alumnam, in cuius honore ibi aecclesia episcopatus cernitur. Voluntarie Tarsenses se eius*m* clientelae subdidere, quod essent Christiani, et ipsius*n*
3 patrocinio se sperarent a Turchis protegi. Certatim itaque Cilices in eius ius*o* transiere, maxime post Turbexel flexum,*p* quod est oppidum natura munitum, cuius nutum inferiora spectarent castella; quo, ut dixi, dedito cetera eius iuditium secuta. Nec solum Cilitia sed et Armenia et Mesopotamia familiaritatem uiri*q* appetiuere; erant enim hae terrae pene Turchorum dominio liberae, sed inequitationibus infestatae. Quare dux Edessae urbis, qui et ciuium odio et hostium gladio premeretur, litteras necessitatis suae interpretes Balduino*r* misit: ueniret ergo quantotius, adoptionis premio laborem ueniendi con-
4 solaturus, namque ipse sexus utriusque*s* prole carebat. Ea est urbs in

a T*t*A *add* tantummodo   *b* esset T*t*A   *c* ipse cor. T*t*A   *d* in qua B   *c–e om.* CsB   *f* tunc T*t*A   *g* breui et integra T*t*A *h* eiusdem T*t*A   *i* agresti quidem T*t*   *j* ipse *before* sibi T*t*A   *k* urbem Cil. T*t*A   *l* recepit T*t*A   *m* eius se T*t*A   *n* eius T*t*A   *o* ius eius T*t*A   *p* deditum C; *but cf. 380. 1* ad deditionem . . . flecterent; *396.* 2 flexi se dedidere   *q* eius C   *r om.* A   *s* utriusque sexus T*t*A*

faced the naked sword, unconquerable: often he kindly rebuked those who stood weeping by his bed. When asked about his successor, he named no names, but advised them to choose the best man they could find; nor could he ever be brought to wear the royal crown, declaring that it would be supremely arrogant to wear himself a crown of majesty in that city where God Himself had worn a crown of shame. He died on 18 July.

374. On Godfrey's death, Tancred and the other chieftains proclaimed as king his brother Baldwin, who was then in Mesopotamia; for the elder brother Eustace, who had come with Godfrey to Jerusalem, had long since returned to the land of his fathers. Of Baldwin's doings I will append a brief and trustworthy narrative, placing entire confidence in the report of Fulcher of Chartres, who, having been his chaplain, wrote an account of him, in a style not indeed rustic but, as is commonly said,[1] without the polish of a practised writer, and such as might well warn others to take more trouble when they write. Baldwin then, when he set out on the crusade with the others, had many knights of his own temperament, on whom he could rely while he raised fresh armies for himself and sought out glorious opportunities for the display of valour.

For example, not satisfied with a success that was shared by all, he left the others at Antioch, and went off the distance of three days' journey to receive the voluntary surrender of Tarsus, a famous city in Cilicia, once the nurse of the Apostle Paul, to whom the cathedral there, still to be seen, is dedicated. The people of Tarsus willingly accepted him as their lord, because they were Christians and hoped under his suzerainty to be protected from the Turks. So the Cilicians hastened to transfer themselves to his control, especially after the surrender of Turbessel, a natural stronghold, which gave the lead to lesser fortresses, so that, as I have said, when it surrendered the remainder followed suit. Nor was it only Cilicia that sought his friendship, but Armenia and Mesopotamia as well; for these territories, while nearly free from Turkish domination, were harassed by Turkish raids. So the duke of Edessa, hard-pressed as he was by the hatred of his citizens and the sword of his enemies, sent Baldwin a letter to expound his plight, inviting him to come as soon as possible, and compensate the labour of coming by the privilege of becoming his adopted son, for he himself had no children of either sex. Edessa is a city in Syrian Mesopotamia,

---

[1] Cicero, *De legibus* i. 6.

Mesopotamia Siriae ubere glebae redditu^a et negotiatorum mercimoniis nominatissima, distans ab Eufrate uiginti miliariis, ab Antiochia centum; Edessam Greci,^b Siri Rothasiam dicunt. Ita Balduinus, exacto a legatis fidelitatis^c sacramento, cum octoginta solum militibus^d Eufratem transmeauit,^e spectaculo mirando seu dicere uelis fortitudinis seu temeritatis, ut inter circumfusas barbarorum nationes, quas alter haberet uel pro gente uel pro incredulitate suspectas, cum tantillo 5 exercitu non hesitaret procedere. Et ab Armeniis quidem et Siris grato excipiebatur gaudio et indulgenti fouebatur hospitio, cum crucibus et candelabris per tramites occurrentibus. Turchi autem, posterius agmen temptare aggressi,^f sollertia Balduini omnibus frustrati sunt insidiis, Samosatenis exemplum fugae fatientibus. Samosata est ciuitas ultra Eufraten, de qua Paulus fuit^g Samosatenus, cuius heresim confutatam in historia Eusebii[1] leget qui uolet; hanc etiam,^h si bene occurrit memoriae, dicit Iosephus[2] obsedisse Antoniumⁱ quando ad eum Herodes 6 uenit. Huius igitur urbis incolae Turchi, qui primi fuissent in Francos audatiae incentiuum, primi defectionis dedere auspitium. Itaque Balduinus, tuto Edessam perueniens, nichil ^jinferius quam sperabat inuenit;^j nam et inuitatoris profuso fauore^k susceptus et non post multum tempus, illo a perfidis ciuibus dilaniato, legitimum urbis ducatum adeptus, toto tempore quo Franci apud Antiochiam et Ierosolimam laborauerunt non immunis bellorum fuit, frequentibus assultibus hostes constristans suos.

7 At uero Nouembri mense ammonitus a Boamundo principe Antiochiae ut iter Ierosolimae iam tandem experirentur, profectionem composuit, propulsatisque solo candidi uexilli uisu, quod insigne in prelio habebat,^l Turchis, qui sperato eius discessu pacem leserant, a dextra relinquens Antiochiam uenit Laoditiam. Ibi liberalitate Raimundi comitis, qui ei ciuitati principabatur, tenui pretio suffitientiam stipis mercatus, Gibello transito recentibus uestigiis Boamundum insecutus est, qui eum fixis tentoriis operiebatur. Iunxit se cum eis communione uiae Daibertus Pisanus archiepiscopus, qui nauigio multis sibi sotiatis ciuibus Laoditiam applicuerat, et preterea 8 duo alii episcopi. Ita iunctis^m agminibus computabantur estimatione

^a reditu gleb(a)e T'A   ^b Greci Edessam T'A   ^c om. A   ^d milibus T'   ^e transfretauit CsB   ^f progressi B   ^g fuit Paulus T'ABc   ^h et C   ⁱ Ant. obs. T'A   ^{j-j} minus promissis desiderauit T'A   ^k fau. prof. T'A   ^l habebatur B   ^m mixtis T'A

of the greatest repute for the fertility of its soil and the wares of its merchants, twenty miles from the Euphrates and a hundred from Antioch; the Greeks call it Edessa, the Syrians Rothasia. Thereupon, having exacted an oath of fealty from the duke's representative, Baldwin crossed the Euphrates with no more than eighty knights; it was a remarkable display of courage—of foolhardiness, if you like—to advance unhesitatingly with that tiny force through surrounding nations of barbarians, whom anyone else would have held suspect for their nationality or their religion. By the Armenians and Syrians he was received with joy and gratitude, and entertained with lavish hospitality; they came to meet him along the way with crosses and flambeaux. The Turks, on the other hand, attempted to harass his rearguard, but were foiled in every stratagem by Baldwin's skill, the men of Samosata setting a precedent by taking to their heels. Samosata is a city across the Euphrates, the home of Paul of Samosata, of whose heresy and its refutation he who wills may read in the *History* of Eusebius;[1] Josephus[2] too, if I remember aright, says that Antony was besieging it when Herod came to visit him. It was, then, the Turkish inhabitants of this city, though they had been the first to urge bold resistance to the Franks, who provided the first example of abandoning the struggle. So Baldwin reached Edessa in safety, and found everything up to his expectations: his host received him with open arms, and not long after, when he was torn in pieces by disaffected citizens, Baldwin himself became lawful count. All the time that the Franks toiled at Antioch and Jerusalem, he was never free from fighting, making life hard for his enemies by constantly taking the offensive.

In the month of November, however, it was pointed out to him by Bohemond prince of Antioch that they ought now at last to attempt the journey to Jerusalem, and he made preparations to set out. The Turks, who in hopes of his departure had broken the peace, were put to flight at the mere appearance of the white banner which was his ensign in battle; and so, leaving Antioch on his right, he arrived at Laodicea. There by the liberality of Count Raymond, who was prince in that city, he bought a sufficiency of supplies at a low price, and passing the Jabala, followed the recent tracks of Bohemond, who had pitched camp and was waiting for him. Daimbert archbishop of Pisa, who had arrived at Laodicea by sea with many citizens of Pisa in his company, joined them to share their journey, and two other bishops as well. After this assembly of forces they were reckoned by careful estimate to be

---

[1] Eusebius, *Hist. eccl.* vii. 30 (tr. Rufinus). [2] *Antiq. Iud.* xiv. 25 (xiv. 439 Greek).

librata*a* uiginti quinque milia; quorum multi terras Saracenorum ingressi pro caritate mercimonii fame conclusi,*b* multi ex equitibus in pedites mutati equis inedia interceptis. Accedebat miseriis*c* imbrium affluentia, quod in illis terris quasi precipiti torrente pluuia hibernis dumtaxat mensibus inundet; itaque pauperes,*d* carentes mutatoriis, algido rigore moriebantur, quam pluribus diebus nulli tecto succedentes. Et huius quidem calamitatis nullum erat remedium, quod et
9 tentoria et ligna deficerent. At uero famem nonnichil leuabant harundines mellitas continue dentibus terentes, quas canamellas nomine*e* composito ex canna et melle uocant. Sic bis*f* omnino a Tripolitanis et Cesariensibus immenso*g* aere necessaria nacti, Ierosolimam uenere solstitii brumalis die. Occurrit illis ad portas rex Godefridus cum Eustachio fratre, quem ad hoc tempus detinuerat, nichil liberalitatis et gratiae*h* in eorum omittens obsequio. Illi,*i* peractis in Bethleem ex more Dominicae Natiuitatis sollemnibus, Daibertum patriarcham constituere. In quo facto Vrbani papae consensum obligatum non ambigo, quod esset is et reuerendus senio et potens eloquio et pollens marsupio.
10 Igitur post Circumcisionem Domini*j* sumptis*k* in Iericho palmis, quod insigne peregrinantium antiquitas instituit, sedes quisque suas raptim repetere*l* properarunt. Causa festinationis erat putor inconditorum cadauerum, quorum ita exhalabat cenum ut ipsum uiolaret caelum. Quocirca tabida pestis in auras effluens multos ex his qui nouiter uenerant leto dedit; ceteri per urbes maritimas, Tiberiadem dico et Cesaream Philippi, maturauerunt iter,*m* quod eos tenuitas uictus
11 et hostilis metus urgebant. Sed fami, ut dixi, consuluere pedum celeritate, et trecentorum militum, qui eos de Baldac castello infestabant, furori prospexerunt militaris artis calliditate; namque simulata paulisper fuga, ut ipsi de angustiis locorum euadentes Turchos inducerent, consulto cessere, sed mox retro uersi dispersos hostes pro libito fudere.*n* Putauerant illi nostros inhabiles pugnae,*o* quod essent clipei eorum et arcus pluuiali habundantia lentati, nesciebantque quod non in armorum uel in tegminum fiducia sed in excellenti ui animorum et crudo robore brachiorum uictoria uirorum consistat.*p*

a T'A add esse (but cf. 348. 4, 383. 1)   *b* inclusi A   *c* miseri(a)e T'A
d pauperiores T'A   *e* nomine after melle CsB, elegantly   *f* his Bc², hii Bc¹ (also Cs), om. Bk   *g* infinito T'A   *h* gratiarum et liberalitatis T'A   *i* illis Tt*a.c.*Tp   *j* om. B   *k* cesis T'A, Fulcher i. 34. 1 (where however adsumpsimus follows)   *l* rep. raptim T'A   *m* iter (ut Aap) maturauerunt T'A   *n* cecidere T'A   *o* pug. inh. T'A   *p* consistit CsB

twenty-five thousand, many of whom after entering Saracen territory were overwhelmed by famine through the high cost of supplies, and many were turned from knights into foot-soldiers when their horses died of starvation. Their misery was increased by the heavy rains, for in that part of the world rain falls, at any rate in the winter months, in torrents; and so the poor people, having no change of clothes, were frozen to death, lacking for many days on end the shelter of a roof. For this aspect of the disaster there was no remedy, as they had no tents and no wood. But for their hunger they found some relief by constantly chewing the reeds, sweet as honey, which they call 'cannamels', a word compounded of *canna* (reed) and *mel* (honey). Twice, and twice only, they secured what they needed, at an enormous price, from the inhabitants of Tripoli and Caesarea, and so arrived in Jerusalem on midwinter day. They were met at the gates by King Godfrey and his brother Eustace, whom he had kept with him down to that time, and Godfrey left nothing undone that could be of service in the way of generosity and favour. Having celebrated Christmas at Bethlehem with the traditional observances, they made Daimbert patriarch; in which action I have no doubt that they had secured the consent of Pope Urban, for Daimbert was venerable in years, and commanded both force of oratory and power of purse.

So, the Circumcision once past, they took up in Jericho the palms which since Antiquity have been the badge of pilgrims, and hurriedly set out on their return home. The reason for their haste was the stench of unburied bodies, whose rotting mass exhaled a breath that might poison the very sky. Thus did this foul corruption, rising into the air, bring death to many of the new arrivals; the rest made the best speed they could through the cities on the sea-coast, Tiberias and Caesarea Philippi, urged on as they were by the shortage of victuals and fear of the enemy. But famine they countered, as I have said, by speed of foot; and as for the fury of three hundred knights, who harassed them from the fortress of Baalbek, they found means to deal with them by skill in strategy. They feigned flight for a time, retiring deliberately as they came out of a narrow pass, in order to induce the Turks to follow them, then faced about, scattered their opponents, and routed them to their heart's content. The Turks had supposed our men incapable of action, because their shields and bows were relaxed by the constant rains; they did not realize that the victory of true men consists, not in confidence in weapons or armour, but in the high courage of their hearts and the raw strength of their right arms.

375. Et*a* tum quidem Balduinus Edessam, Boamundus uero*b* Antiochiam incolumes remearunt. Initio autem Iulii mensis licentia famae Balduini auribus detulit splendidum ducum nostrorum*c* margaritum obfuscatum, Boamundum scilicet captum et in catenas coniectum*d* a quodam Danisman gentili et in illis*e* terris potenti. Quapropter Edessenorum et Antiochenorum manu coacta insignem Christianorum contumeliam ulcisci sperabat. Porro Turchus, qui magis fraude et euentu quam uirtute et bellica militia*f* ducem cepisset, quod cum paucis ad Meletiniam urbem recipiendam uenerat, sciens Francos pro rei pudore uiribus extremis in se usuros,*g* in sua se recepit, compositis sane ordinibus, non quasi fugam intenderet sed quasi triumphum duceret. Tum Balduinus ultra Meletiniam duorum dierum uiam*h* progressus, cum uideret hostem belli necessitatem declinare, redeundum putauit; et ante tamen urbem in suos usus, non inuito prefecto Gabriele, transduxit.

376. Interea perlato ad se nuntio de fratris obitu et*i* prouintialium ac ducum*j* in eius electionem consensu, commendata Edessa Balduino cognato, arctissimae necessitudinis propinquitate coniuncto et preter haec neque imprudenti neque ignauo, ad Ierosolimitanum regnum mentem impulit. Congregatis ergo equitibus ducentis et peditibus septingentis, iter plenum mortis et periculorum*k* ingressus est;*l* unde audatiae tantae contuitu multi, quos falso fideles arbitrabatur, fuga clandestina*m* dilapsi. Ipse cum reliquis Antiochiam petiit, ingens momentum desolatis futurus,*n* consilio sagacis mentis informans ut Tancredum peterent in ducatum. Inde per Gibellum et Laoditiam uenit Tripolim; cuius urbis ammiratus,*o* natione quidem Turchus sed genio naturali*p* clementiae uisceribus profusus, extra muros illi uictui necessaria destinauit, adiecto quin etiam benignitatis mandato ut prudenter se ageret, quia Ducach rex Damascenorum tramitem angustum occupauerat per quem illum uenturum audierat.*q* Ille, quem puderet minis Saracenicis moueri, constanti animo quo proposuerat contendit;*r* sed, ad locum ueniens, fidem ammirati probauit. Est enim citra ciuitatem Beritum miliariis circiter quinque locus omnino angustus iuxta mare, quem et prerupta rupium et arcta callium*s* adeo cohercent ut centum uiri faucibus illis potiti quantumuis numerum itinerantium

a at *B*   *b* om. *T′A*   *c* nostrorum ducum *T′A*   *d* eiectum *B*
e hiis (om. in) *B*   *f* iustitia *T′A*   *g* nisuros *T′Al*   *h* uia *T′A*
i om. *CB*   *j* ducum et (et also Bk) prou. *T′A** (cf. 234. 2)   *k* periculosum *A*   *l* est ingressus *Aa*, ingressus (om. est) *Al* (also *Tt(not Tp)Bc)*   *m* om. *CsB*   *n* futurum *B* (?)   *o* admiratus urbis *T′*   *p* naturalis *T′Aa*
q aud. uent. *C*   *r* cucurrit *T′*   *s* collium *CsB*

375. For the moment, Baldwin returned safe to Edessa and Bohemond to Antioch. At the beginning of July, however, rumour with its usual freedom brought to Baldwin's ears the news that the bright pearl of all our generals was darkened—that Bohemond was taken, and thrown into chains, by one Danishmend, a heathen and a man of might in those parts. Consequently, he got together a force from Edessa and Antioch in hopes of avenging this signal insult to the Christians. The 2 Turk, who had captured the prince more by fraud and good luck than by valour and prowess in battle, because he had come with a small force to receive the surrender of Melitene, knew that the Franks, in view of the disgrace they had suffered, would use their utmost efforts against him, and retired to his own territory in good order, more like a triumphal procession than a retreat. Baldwin then proceeded two days' journey beyond Melitene, but when he saw the enemy refusing battle, he thought it best to return home, after bringing the city over to his side, not without support from Gabriel the prefect.

376. Meanwhile news had reached him of his brother's death and the agreement of the people of the province and the magnates to elect himself. He entrusted Edessa to a relative, Baldwin, who was connected with him by very close ties of kinship, and moreover neither rash nor idle, and turned his mind to the kingdom of Jerusalem. Collecting therefore two hundred knights and seven hundred men-at-arms, he set forth on a journey fraught with death and dangers; so that at the sight of such audacity, many whom he wrongly supposed faithful slipped secretly away. He himself with the remainder made his way to Antioch, where his good sense made all the difference to the city, forsaken as it was, for he suggested that they try to secure Tancred as their prince. Thence he proceeded by Jabala and Laodicea to Tripoli, where the 2 emir, a Turk by race but naturally generous and merciful, sent essential supplies to him outside the walls, adding moreover the kindly warning that he should act with great prudence, since Dukak king of Damascus had occupied the narrow pass through which he had heard that Baldwin would be advancing. Baldwin, as one who would be ashamed to be influenced by Saracen threats, advanced steadily on his chosen course; but when he reached the place, he found that the emir had spoken the truth. About five miles this side of Beirut, there is an extremely narrow 3 passage along the sea-coast, so much hemmed in with steep cliffs and constricted paths that a hundred men holding those narrows can keep any number of troops on the move from getting through; and travellers

aditu prohibere queant. Locus est ineuitabilis de Tripoli Ierosolimam euntibus. Huc ergo Balduinus perueniens speculatores misit qui situm loci et uires hostium renuntiarent. Regressi legati difficultatem fautium et aduersariorum qui insederant fidutiam uix pro timore intellecti anhelarunt. At Balduinus, qui parum ab optimo qui*a* umquam fuerit milite distaret, nichil perterritus atiem dispositam in eos constanter instituit. Tunc*b* Ducach mittit aliquos qui prelia prima lacessant elitiantque[1] incautos, retentans ampliores uires in locis oportunis. Itaque illi primo magno impetu uenire, mox subinde*c* subterfugere, ut nostros in angustias deducerent. Non latuit Balduinum huiuscemodi*d* calliditas; sed, antiquae militiae usu instructus, suis ut fugam simularent innuit, simul et, ut suspitionem metus urgeret, sarcinas et impedimenta quae iam deposuerant*e* resumi*f* et iumenta stimulis*g* agitari, quin et ordines laxari ut hostes incurrerent edixit. Tum uero hoc uiso Turchi exultare, et dirum frendentes, ut Eumenides exululare crederes, nostros insequi. Quidam ascensis nauibus littora preoccupare, quidam equis precurrere et peregrinos incaute iuxta mare ambulantes interimere. Nec Franci simulatam fugam omisere donec ad planitiem quam oculis destinauerant peruenirent, nullique tumultus excussere uiris mentes; quin immo necessitas qua intercepti erant aluit et ministrauit audatiam, et pauci terraque marique*h* innumeras sustinuere manus.[2] Namque, ut uisum est satis metum finxisse, consertis ordinibus et conuersis signis inimicos*i* iam iamque incursantes inclusere;*j* ita uersa rerum fatie, qui uicerant uicti et uicti fuere uictores. Turchi pernitiosa clade prostrati; reliqui ad naues precipiti studio fugientes, cum in altum plus iactu*k* sagittae processissent, ita nauigium remis et totis pectoribus innixi*l* propellebant quasi manibus aduersariorum ad terram retrahi possent. Et ut miraculum non sicut opinabile dubites sed sicut uisibile quodammodo palpes, solummodo quattuor Christiani milites fusi uictoriam ceteris sanguine peperere suo. Quapropter confirmo quod numquam Christicolae a paganis uincerentur, si ante bellum fortitudinem suam caelestibus fulcirent presidiis, et in bello armis suis

a quisquis *T'*   *b* tum *T'A*   *c* om. *CsB*   *d* huiusmodi *T'*
e posuerant *(om.* iam*) C*   *f* resumit *C*   *g* stim. ium. *T'A*   *h* et mari *A*   *i* inimicos *after* incursantes *T'A*   *j* includere *C*   *k* om. *A*
l om. *CsB*

[1] Cf. Lucan iv. 720-1.
[2] Cf. Lucan iv. 535-8.

from Tripoli to Jerusalem cannot avoid it. When Baldwin reached this point, he sent out scouts to report the lie of the land and the enemy strength. On return from their reconnaissance they recounted the difficulty of the passage, and the confidence of the enemy in occupation of it, in voices so breathless with fright that they could hardly make themselves understood. But Baldwin, being, as he was, not far short of the best soldier who ever lived, was quite unmoved and resolutely drew up his battle order. At this point Dukak despatched some of his troops 'to challenge first the fray and lure'[1] our men to advance imprudently, while he retained greater strength in key positions. So his men first advanced at high speed, and then quite soon withdrew, so as to draw our men on into the narrows. These clever tactics did not deceive Baldwin; drawing on his long years of fighting experience, he gave his men the signal to feign retreat, while at the same time, to reinforce the suggestion of panic, he ordered them to take up once more the baggage and gear which they had just parked, and to whip up the baggage animals, and even to open their formation so as to let in the enemy. At this sight the Turks were overjoyed, and with frightful yells, like screeching Furies, bore down on our men. Some of them jumped into boats and seized the foreshore, some rode ahead on their horses and cut down crusaders who were moving on foot improvidently near the sea. Nor did the Franks abandon their feigned withdrawal, till they reached an open space which they had marked down beforehand. 'No turmoil shook those hero-hearts'; on the contrary, the emergency in which they were caught supplied and fostered their courage, and 'few as they were, they bore up by land and sea against that countless host'.[2] For as soon as it appeared that they had pretended panic long enough, they closed their ranks and faced about, and the enemy who were continuously harassing them were hemmed in. The tables were turned: those who had been winning were defeated, and the losers won the day. The Turks were broken, and suffered heavy losses; the survivors fled headlong to the ships, and even when they had made more than a bowshot away from land, still kept on rowing with all the weight of their shoulders behind the oar, as though their adversaries might yet be able to pull them back to shore with their bare hands. This was a miracle; that you may not question it as a matter of opinion, but almost feel it as something visible, let me tell you that precisely four Christian knights were killed, and shed their blood to win victory for the rest. I reaffirm therefore that Christ's servants would never be defeated by the paynim, if before battle they would fortify their valour with the help of Heaven,

amicas superorum applicarent uirtutes; sed quia in pace omnibus se ingurgitant flagitiis, et in pugna sola nituntur audatia, ideo, nec immerito, multotiens fortitudo eorum deuiat a bona fortuna. Comes ergo*[a]* pulchro triumpho exultans, cum reuersus esset ad spolia cesorum detrahenda, non paucos Turchos offendit uiuos,[b] quos 8 dampni corporum immunes sed pecuniis inanes dimisit. Ipse cum suis, ne aliqua fraus lateret, retro secedens nocte illa sub oliuarum uirgultis requieuit; sed mox diluculo cum expeditis ad angustias accessit, fide oculata uisurus loci naturam, intuitusque omnia tuta esse (nam Turchi, qui pridie circa montem discursibus lasciuierant, nocte intempesta cede suorum uisa omnes diffugerant), significatione fumi facta, sicut conuenerat, sotiis discessum hostium intimauit. Illi, morarum uinculis absolutis, ducem continuo secuti. Tunc Beriti ammiratus uictum pre- 9 tereuntibus[c] misit, pro uirtute tam pauci exercitus stupefactus. Idem et Tirii et Sidonii et Acharonitae, qui et Ptholomaitae,[d] fecere, tacito metu Francorum fortitudinem[e] suspitientes. Nec minus homines Tancredi, qui in Caipha erant, liberales fuere, quanuis ipse absens esset. Castri illius nomen antiquum reperire nequeo, quia omnes mediterraneae ciuitates, quae in Iosepho leguntur quondam fuisse,[f] modo uel non sunt uel in uiculos mutatae nomina perdiderunt; maritimae integrae manent. Ita per Cesaream Palestinae et Azotum in Ioppen uentum, ubi prima illi gratulatio regni fuit, ciuibus ingenti gaudio portas aperientibus.

377. Igitur ab Ioppitis Ierosolimam deductus et ibi fauorabiliter exceptus, dierum sex spatio quieti satisfecit. Inde, ne Turchi dubitarent[g] indolem regni eius magno eorum malo adolescere, uersus Ascalonem expeditionem mouit. Cumque non longe ab urbe uires suas ostentaret, impetentes Ascalonitas facili opera depulit, oportunum[h] tempus ad id quod mente intendebat operiens. Denique repulsionem illorum gloriae suae tunc sufficere[i] arbitratus, in montana receptui[j] cecinit, ut hostes persequeretur, necnon et inimicorum dampno necessaria suis conquisiturus, qui pro penuria terrae fame singultiebant, quia illo anno messis egra uictum negauerat, spem prouintiae

---

[a] B adds a [b] Tur. non paucos uiu. off. *T'A* [c] preeuntibus *CsB* [d] qui et Pt. *om. T'A, cf. 382.1 (and Fulcher ii. 3. 9)* [e] fort. Fr. tac. metu *T'A* [f] quondam fuisse in Ios. leg. *T'A* [g] dub. Tur. *T'A* [h] oportunius *T'A* [i] sufficere tunc *TpA* (sufficere *om. Tt*) [j] rec. in montana *T'A*

and in battle would join to their own arms the favouring might of those above. As it is, in peace time they wallow in every vice, and in war depend simply on their own courage; no wonder if their valour often parts company with success.

So the count, overjoyed at this glorious victory, returned to strip spoil from the dead, and finding a number of Turks still alive, he spared their bodies but relieved them of money before letting them go. He himself and his men, for fear of surprise, withdrew, and rested that night under some olive trees. At first light he advanced to the narrows with a mobile force to see for himself how the land lay, and having established that all was safe—for the Turks, who had been gaily sallying forth round the mountain the day before, had all fled at dead of night after seeing the disaster to their army—he made a smoke signal as had been agreed, and informed his fellow-soldiers of the enemy's departure. They threw off all delay, and hastened to follow their leader. At that point the emir of Beirut sent them victuals as they passed by, being amazed at the valour of such a tiny force. His lead was followed by the people of Tyre, Sidon, and Acre (otherwise called Ptolemais), for they regarded the courage of the Franks with concealed apprehension. Tancred's men, who were in Haifa, were equally generous, though Tancred himself was absent. The ancient name of that fortress has eluded me, for all the inland cities of whose former existence we read in Josephus have now either disappeared, or have degenerated into villages and lost their identity; those on the sea-coast remain intact. Thus they passed through the Palestinian Caesarea and through Arsur, and reached Jaffa, where Baldwin for the first time was welcomed as king, the citizens opening their gates to him with unbounded joy.

377. So, being escorted by the people of Jaffa as far as Jerusalem, and made welcome there, he enjoyed six days' rest. Then, to leave the Turks in no doubt that they were to suffer severely as his kingdom grew, he set on foot an expedition towards Ascalon. As he was making a show of force not far from the city, the Ascalonites attacked him, but he easily beat them off, awaiting a suitable moment to put his plan into execution. At length, thinking this defeat of the enemy was sufficient glory for the moment, he gave the order to turn back into the hill-country, in order to pursue the enemy, and also to secure at their expense essential supplies for his own troops, who were retching with hunger because the land was so poor: a bad harvest that year had left them nothing to eat, and the hopes of the province were deceived by its

2 sterili prouentu decipiens. Itaque montana conscendit,[a] quo habitatores terrae Turchi relictis uillis concesserant, Siros secum in penitus abditos specus immergentes; sed inuenere Franci quo commenta fugitiuorum fallerent, fumo in ora cauernarum immisso, quo latrones fugati[b] pertinatiam amisere, uni et uni egredientes. Ita Turchi ad unum omnes[c] interfecti, Siri reseruati. Inde digressus exercitus Arabiamque petiturus busta preteriit patriarcharum Abrahae, Isaac et[d] Iacob, et trium matronarum Sarae, Rebeccae, Liae; locus est in Hebron, distans ab[e] 3 Ierosolimis tredecim milibus. Nam corpus Ioseph iacet in Neapoli, quae olim Sichem dicta est, marmore candido tectum omnibusque transeuntibus perspicuum; [f]ubi quoque fratrum uisuntur[f] mausolea, sed inferiori gloria.

Venit ergo exercitus in uallem ubi quondam[g] Deus Sodomam et Gomorram subuertit, caelestem flammam in scelestos iaculatus. Ibi lacus per octodecim milia diffunditur, nullius uiuentis capax; preterea tractatu adeo[h] horribilis[i] ut potantium ora torqueat et gustu amaro rictus distendat. Valli mons prominet, per loca scrobes salsas eructans, et quasi congelato uitro totus perlucidus, ubi colligitur quod quidam 4 nitrum, quidam salis gemmam uocant. Euadentes ergo lacum, uenerunt ad uillam sane locupletissimam et mellitis pomis quae dactilos dicunt[j] fecundam; quorum esu se infartientes uix lacunas uentrium implere,[k] uix ingluuiem fautium pre dulcedine temperare ualebant. Cetera timore[l] incolarum abrasa, preter aliquantos Ethiopas, ferruginea capillorum lanugine fuliginem pretendentes, quorum cedem nostri estimantes[m] infra uirtutem suam, non eos ira sed risu dignati sunt.

5 Huic uillae subiacet uallis, in qua hodieque silex cernitur quo percusso Moises mussitanti populo aquas infudit; latex adhuc tam uberi et precipiti riuo influit ut molendinorum uertigines impetu suo rotet. Tum in decliui montis extat aecclesia in honore legiferi Aaron edificata, ubi[n] mediante et cooperante fratre serebat[o] cum Deo alloquia.[p] Ibi a preuiis uiarum gnaris, qui ex Saracenis Christiani essent, addiscentes inde usque ad Babilonem nichil esse nisi ieiunum solum et omnium bonorum indigum, Ierosolimam reuersi sunt, primitias regni tot hostilium regionum subiectione Deo consecraturi.

[a] concendit *Al (and Bk)*, -tendit *Aa*   [b] fatigati *T'*, *probably rightly*   [c] omnes ad unum *T'A*   [d] om. T*t(not Tp)A, more elegantly; but cf. Fulcher ii. 4. 5*   [e] a *AlCeB (but cf. 386. 1, 403. 2)*   [f-f] uisunturque ibi fratrum eius (eius *also added by Bk*) *T'A*   [g] olim *T'Al* (enim *Aap*)   [h] adeo tractatu *A*   [i] terribilis *T'*   [j] uocant *T'A*   [k] impleuere *T'*   [l] pre timore *T'A*   [m] estimantes *after* suam *T'A*   [n] *T'A add* ipse   [o] ferebat *B*   [p] colloquia *T'A*(cf. GP p. 369)*

barren yield. So he advanced into the uplands, whither the Turkish 2
inhabitants had already fled, leaving their towns and concealing themselves and the Syrians with them in remote caverns. The Franks,
however, found a way to outwit this stratagem of the fugitives, by
driving smoke into the mouth of the caves; this dislodged the rascals,
who lost heart, and came out one by one. So the Turks to a man were
put to death, and the Syrians spared. The army then moved on, in the
direction of Arabia, and passed the monuments of the patriarchs
Abraham, Isaac, and Jacob, and the three matrons Sarah, Rebecca, and
Leah; the place is in Hebron, thirteen miles from Jerusalem. Joseph's 3
body lies in Nablus, formerly called Sichem, in a white marble tomb
which is a landmark for all who pass that way; the tombs of his brothers
are also shown, but they are less impressive.

Thus the army came into the valley where God once overthrew
Sodom and Gomorrah by casting fire from Heaven on the accursed
people. There is a lake there eighteen miles long, which supports no
living creature, and moreover is so repellent to the palate that it distorts
the faces of those who drink of it and distends their mouths with its
bitter taste. The valley is dominated by a hill which in places breaks out
in salt-pits, and glitters all over as though with crystals of glass; and
here they collect what some call nitre and others rocksalt. Making their 4
way past the lake, they came to a town which was clearly very rich, and
grows the honey-sweet fruit called dates. With these they stuffed
themselves, but could hardly fill their empty stomachs or restrain their
craving appetites because of the sweet taste. All else had been removed
by the frightened inhabitants, except for a certain number of Ethiopians, of sooty aspect and with rusty wool for hair; these our men
thought it unworthy of their mettle to put to death, regarding them as
objects for humour rather than hostility. Below this town lies a valley, 5
in which can still be seen the rock which Moses struck to give water to
the people when they murmured; the stream still flows so full and
gushing that its power is used to turn mill-wheels. Next, on the slope
of the hill, stands a church built in honour of Aaron the lawgiver,
where, with his brother as colleague and intermediary, he conversed
with God. There they learnt from guides who knew the routes, for they
were Saracens converted to Christianity, that there was nothing all the
way from there to Babylon but barren ground devoid of every useful
feature; and so they returned to Jerusalem, to offer God the first-fruits
of the kingdom in the subjection of so large an expanse of enemy
territory.

378. Paratis igitur regiis^a insignibus, magna gloria in Bethleem die Dominicae Natiuitatis a Daiberto patriarcha coronatus est Balduinus, fausta omnibus^b acclamantibus; nam ex tunc et deinceps nichil non uenerationis regiae et ipse labore suo^c est meritus et aliorum fauore adeptus, quanuis minimi et pene dico pudendi regni dominus. Quare decet Christi Domini^d clementiam suspicere et in potentiae illius contuitu spatiari, cuius suffragio timeri Christiani possent qui officere nequirent; uix enim^e in tota militia^f quadringenti milites erant et tot pedites qui Ierosolimam et Ramulam et Caipham et Ioppen^g custodirent. Nam qui ueniebant nauigio, intuto tamen inter tot hostium portus animo, sanctis adoratis statim repatriandum censebant, pedestri uia penitus interclusa. Cumulabat quin immo difficultatem quod Martio mense Tancredus discesserat Antiochiae principaturus, et nec ipse regi nec rex ipsi auxilium pro uiae longitudine ferre^h ualebat;ⁱ adde quod, si necessitas exposceret, sine irreparabilis discriminis metu gentem suam de uno in aliud castrum non transduceret. Euidens ergo miraculum pronuntio, quod Dei solius tutum suffragio tanta barbarorum horrebat natio.

379. Illo anno, qui fuit Dominicae incarnationis millesimus centesimus primus, ignis sacratus, qui solebat uigiliam Paschae illustrare, tardauit plus solito. Sabbato enim lectis alternatim lectionibus Grece et Latine repetitoque ter 'Kirieleison' et^j clara Sirorum melodia perstrepente, cum necdum appareret ignis et iam occiduus sol uesperam urgeret, noctem inueheret, ab omnibus cum merore in domos discessum. Placuerat enim perpenso^k consilio ut illa nocte omni homine uacaret sancti Sepulchri aecclesia, ne aliquis cui ulcerosa squalebat conscientia Deum magis irritaret ingerendi^l impudentia. Iamque diluculo sensim in lucem serpente processio Latinorum ad templum Salomonis edicitur, ut ibi oraturi Dei misericordiam inuitarent; idem circa sepulchrum Domini fatiebant Siri, ui doloris barbas et capillos^m uellicantes. Nec diu potuere pati diuina uiscera, confestim igne in unam lampadem Sepulchri immisso. Quem cum animaduertisset Sirus per fenestrellasⁿ scintillantem, plausu manuum laetitiam prodens cursum patriarchae

---

^a regis *A; om. T¹*   ^b *om.* fausta *T¹A*   ^c suo labore *T¹A**   ^d *om. T¹A*   ^e *om. A*   ^f milia *A(hence* inter tot *Aa)Ce*   ^g Ioppe *AlCB*   ^h conferre *T¹A*   ⁱ ualebant *B*   ^j *om. T¹*   ^k propenso *C*   ^l One misses a reflexive   ^m capillos (-lo *Aap*) et barbas *T¹A*   ⁿ fenestras *Ce (and CdCr;* per fen. sc. *om. CsB);* fenestrulas *Fulcher cod. L, p. 833 Hagenmayer*

378. So the royal insignia were made ready, and Baldwin was crowned with great splendour in Bethlehem on Christmas Day by the patriarch Daimbert amid scenes of great enthusiasm; for from that day forward he deserved by his own exertions, and received from the loyalty of others, every whit of the reverence due to a king, although only the lord of a minute, and one might almost say humiliating, realm. For this we ought to admire the mercy of Christ our Lord and to walk in contemplation of His power, seeing that it was His support that enabled the Christians to command respect, although they could do no hurt; in their whole force there were scarcely four hundred knights and as many foot-soldiers, to garrison Jerusalem and Ramlah and Haifa and Jaffa. For those who came by sea, though with an unquiet mind on account of the enemy harbours all around, were in favour of an immediate return home, once they had adored the holy places, the overland route being completely cut off. The difficulties were increased by Tancred's departure in March to take up his rule as prince in Antioch, the distance between them being now so great that neither could be of any assistance to the other; besides which, it would be impossible, if need arose, for either of them to move his men from one stronghold to another without fear of irreparable disaster. I declare it therefore a manifest miracle that a man with no protection but the help of God was able to strike fear into such a horde of barbarians.

379. In that year, AD 1101, the sacred fire which usually illuminated Easter Eve was slower in coming than usual. On the Saturday, the lessons were read alternately in Greek and Latin, the *Kyrie eleison* was three times repeated, the sound of Syrian chanting filled the place, and still the fire did not come; the setting sun brought evening on apace and was now making way for night, and all dispersed to their lodgings in despair. It had been judiciously decided that on that night no one should be admitted into the church of the Holy Sepulchre, for fear that someone with a bad and festering conscience might anger God still more by shamelessly intruding. Already first light was gradually broadening into dawn, when it was announced that the Latins would go in procession to Solomon's Temple, to pray there and ask God for His mercy; the Syrians were doing the same around the Holy Sepulchre, tearing their beards and hair in the violence of their grief. The bowels of Divine compassion could not long endure this, and fire suddenly descended upon one of the lamps in the Sepulchre. A Syrian saw it sparkling through the window, and clapping his hands for joy,

3 accelerauit. Ille, clauibus quas gestabat aditum ediculae sepulchralis aperiens, caeleste munus cereo accenso extulit, omnibus ad hoc concurrentibus communicans. Mox per omnem aecclesiam ceterae diuinitus accensae sunt lampades, mirum in modum illa quae proxime illuminanda esset fumo premisso uicinam accensionem docente. Sic nimirum Christi uetus[a] artificium nouit quos amat terrere ut mulceat, et in materiam transeat laudis comminatio potestatis. Quia enim dona Dei[b] usitata assiduitate ipsa uilescunt[c] hominibus, plerumque assensum indulgentiae suae raritate commendat, ut ametur gratius quod desideratum fuerat ardentius.

380. Tunc stolus nauium Ianuensium et Pisanorum Laoditiam applicuerat, et inde Ioppen prospero cursu[d] nauigauerat, nautaeque tractis ad terram ratibus[e] Ierosolimae cum rege Pascha exegerant. Quorum ipse uirtutem pretio uadatus, tertiam partem pecuniae pepigit de omnibus urbibus quas adquirere pariter[f] possent, et uicum unum ciuitatis quem eligerent. Ita precipites aurique cupidine cecos[1] magis quam pro Dei amore impulit ut sanguinem suum nundinantes statim
2 Azotum obsiderent, et ad deditionem post tres dies flecterent. Nec uero difficulter[g] oppidani se dedidere, iram regis si ui caperentur reueriti, quia preterito anno Godefridum idem aggressum acriter repulerant, malefitio fortunae adiuti. Siquidem cum ille suos ascensu scalarum in murum erigeret,[h] iam uictores, iam fastigia menium tenentes repentinus ligneae turris casus, quae forinsecus muro adiecta erat, uiros uictoria priuauit et plures extinxit; plures capti, et seuitia Saracenorum dilaniati. Inde Cesaream Palestinae Balduinus totis uiribus et offirmato robore obsidens, cum uideret ciuium pertinatiam et expugnandi diffi-
3 cultatem, machinas compaginari precepit.[i] Factae ergo petrariae, facta turris ingens, uiginti cubitis muri altitudinem uincens. At uero nostri, morae impatientes et tam diutinae impotes expectationis,[j] scalis erectis murum superare aggressi obstinatione uirium ad superiora euasere, conscientia uirtutis frementes quod, iam quindecim diebus Saracenicis

---

[a] uetus Christi T'A*   [b] Dei dona T'A   [c] uiluerunt T'   [d] flatu T'A (cf. 238. 9)   [e] nauibus T'   [f] om. AB   [g] dif(f)icile T'A   [h] promouisset T'Al (promouissent Aap)   [i] fecit T'   [j] exp. impotes T'A

---

[1] Lucan vii. 747.

hastened the approach of the patriarch. The patriarch opened the inner 3
chapel of the Sepulchre with the keys which he always carried, and
lighting a wax candle, brought out the gift of Heaven and distributed it
to all who came running up to receive it. Soon the other lamps all
through the church were kindled by heavenly agency, the next lamp to
be lit always giving notice in a wonderful way that its moment of kindling was at hand, by a warning wisp of smoke. So well does Christ, with
practised skill, know how to put fear into those whom He loves, that He
may calm their fears, and that a threatening glimpse of His power to
hurt may be turned into matter for His praise. God's ordinary gifts men
hold cheap for their mere familiarity; He often gives the expression of
His loving-kindness value by its rarity, that what had been the object of
more passionate longing may earn more loving gratitude.

380. At that point the flotillas of Genoa and Pisa had put in at
Laodicea, and had sailed on thence with favourable winds to Jaffa,
where the sailors hauled their ships ashore and spent Easter at Jerusalem with the king. The king struck a bargain for their military service, promising them a third part of the money from all the cities they
might be able to acquire together, and a street of their own choosing in
the city; and thus he drove them headlong, and 'in lust of lucre blind'[1]
rather than from the love of God, to set a price on their own lives, so
that they immediately laid siege to Arsur, and forced it after three days
to surrender. Nor were the townsmen at all reluctant to give in, for 2
they feared the king's wrath if they had to be taken by force: the previous year, when Godfrey had attempted the same thing, they had
roundly repulsed him, aided by a malevolent stroke of fortune. He was
getting his men onto the walls with scaling ladders; they were just
winning the day, and already held the parapet, when the sudden collapse of a wooden tower, which had been built against the wall from
outside, robbed them of their victory and killed many of them; yet
more were captured, and butchered by the cruel Saracens. Next,
Baldwin laid siege with all his resources, and with stubborn resolution,
to Palestinian Caesarea; but finding the citizens obstinate, and the place
hard to take by storm, he gave orders to make siege-engines. Catapults 3
were therefore constructed, and an enormous tower, twenty cubits
higher than the wall. Our men, however, chafing at the delay, and
unable to endure such a long period of waiting, tried to scale the wall
by putting up ladders, and by sheer strength and determination got to
the top; knowing their own valour, they raged at the thought that they

bellis intenti, tanti temporis spatium perdidissent. Quanuis igitur extrema ui a Cesariensibus certaretur, multos molares in ascendentes uoluentibus, illi dissimulato periculo cuneos obstantes perrumpere,*a* 4 brachiis exertis*b* et strictis gladiis rem agentes. Turchi, ulterius non ferentes fugamque adorsi, uel ipsi se precipitauerunt uel hostili manu occubuerunt; plures seruituti, pauci redemptioni seruati, inter quos ammiratus urbis et episcopus, quem archadium uocant. Eratque spectaculum quod uidenti cachinnum excuteret, cum Turchus, in collo Christiani pugno*c* percussus, bizantinos euomeret; nam miseri extremae inopiae metu, mares intra gingiuas, feminae intra non dicenda, nummos absconderant. Vides quod aperte loqui erubescit oratio; sed intelligit profecto lector quod uolo, immo quod nolo, dicere.

381. Nec adhuc quieuit imperator Babilonis quin ducem et exercitum ad expugnandos Francos missitaret. Illi, nauigio Ascalonem appulsi, mox iuxta Ramulam cursitarunt, curis regis abutentes, qui tunc Cesariensi bello tenebatur. Agrorum igitur*d* depopulatione ad congrediendum crebrius illum irritarunt. At ille*e* non impari callidate, ut calor indomitus deferuesceret, uetito instantes passus languescere bello,[1] hac effecit*f* cunctatione ut plerique morarum pertesi*g* dilaberentur; reliquos, qui essent undecim milia equitum, uiginti unum milia*h* 2 peditum, cum suis ducentis quinquaginta equitibus, peditibus paulo minus septingentis inuasit. Paucaque militibus locutus (quibus si perstarent uictoriam, si morerentur gloriam promitteret; si fugerent, longe Frantiam esse*i* commoneret), primus in hostes irruit, productoque aliquantum certamine, cum aties suas labare cerneret, desperatis rebus occurrit. Itaque*j* nota sui spetie Turchos proturbans,*k* conto ducem prostrauit, quo interempto tota diffugere agmina. Nostri, qui principio pugnae*l* ita circumsepti fuerant ut nullus*m* alterum uideret, tunc Dominicae crucis uexillo preuio adeo uirtutem*n* exercuerunt*o* ut quinque milia trucidarent; ex Francis octoginta equites, pedites paulo plus*p* desiderati.

3 Porro sequens successus*q* solatio fuit, quod quingentos equites

a perrupere *ACs(not Ca)B*   *b* ex. br. *T'A*   *c* pug. Chr. *T'A*   *d* ergo *T'A*   *e* illi *A*   *f* fecit *T'*; efficit *B*. The *word follows* cunctatione *in T'A*   *g* mor. pert. *om*. *CB*   *h* *om*. *T'Bk*   *i* esse Fr. *T'A*   *j* ita *A*   *k* prorobans *Bk*, probans *Bc*   *l* *om*. *Tt*   *m* neuter *TtA (cf. GP p. 86)*   *n* *om*. *Tt; before* adeo *A*   *o* exterruerunt *Tt*   *p* plus ped. paulo *Tt*   *q* succ. seq. *Tt*

[1] Lucan iv. 281.

had now devoted a fortnight to fighting the Saracens, and had nothing to show for all that period of time. And so, although the men of Caesarea fought with the greatest violence, rolling down numerous millstones on them as they made their way up, they made light of the danger, and broke through the serried ranks before them, doing the work with drawn sword and strong right arm. The Turks could stand no more; they broke, and either threw themselves down, or met their death at the enemy's hand. Many were spared to become slaves, a few to be ransomed, among whom was the emir of the city and the bishop, whom they call *al kadi*. It was enough to make the beholder burst out laughing, to see a Turk struck on the neck by a Christian fist and spewing out his bezants; for the poor wretches in fear of utter penury had hidden their coin, the men in their cheeks, the women in their unmentionables. You see my pen is ashamed to write it openly; but the reader no doubt understands what I wish, or rather do not wish, to say.

381. Nor did the emperor of Babylon remain quiet all this time, but was for sending a general with an army to drive out the Franks. The force landed from the sea at Ascalon, and then proceeded to range up and down near Ramlah, taking advantage of the king's preoccupation, for he was then engaged in the fighting at Caesarea. By ravaging the countryside, they tried frequently to provoke him to an engagement. But his tactics were as good as theirs: in order that their indomitable spirit might evaporate, he 'suffered their eagerness to wane, denying battle'.[1] By this inactivity he ensured that most of them, weary of waiting, melted away; the remainder, being 11,000 horse and 21,000 foot, he attacked with his own troops, who numbered 250 horse and rather less than 700 foot. After a short address to his men, designed to promise them victory if they stood their ground and glory if they died, and to warn them that, if they turned tail, France was very far away, he led the charge against the enemy; the struggle was somewhat prolonged, and whenever he saw his own ranks waver, he rushed up to deal with the crisis. The mere sight of his well-known form broke the Turks' morale; he laid low their commander with a lance; and when he fell, the whole force fled. Our own men, who when the battle began had been so hemmed in that none of them could see his neighbour, behaved at this point with such courage, led by the banner with the Lord's Cross, that they cut down five thousand; the Franks lost eighty horsemen, and rather more foot.

A success which immediately followed was some consolation for this

Arabas interemerunt. Illi ante Ioppen biduo cucurrerant, sed parum explicantes Ascalonem redibant, uisoque eminus exercitu nostro, suos esse sperantes, tamquam triumphantibus congratulaturi obuiam ibant; sed tandem aliquando in se iaculis*a* emissis intelligentes Francos esse, perinde palluerunt sicut 'nudis pressit qui*b* calcibus anguem', ut poetae uerbo[1] utar; itaque ipso hebetes stupore*c* terga cedentibus exhibuere. Ita rex Ioppen perueniens errorem epistolae quae, Tancredo a*d* Ioppitis missa, falso regem cum exercitu extinctum nuntiauerat ueratiori scripto correxit; iamque Tancredus iter ad Ierosolimam parauerat, cum nuntius ueniens ostenso sigillo regio*e* mestitiam depulit, laetitiam reformauit.

382. Longum est si uelim explicare omnia eius certamina: quomodo Tiberiadem Sidonem Acharonem, id est Ptholomaidem,*f* quomodo postremo cunctas maritimas urbes*g* subegerit; quomodo pene omnem diem Turchorum mortibus*h* insignierit, aut assultu clandestino aut bello publico. Ingentes operas eiusmodi desiderat oratio*i* hominis qui ampullato eloquio*j* et curioso habundet otio. Nobis utrumque deest, et, quod maxime obest, rerum expedita scientia; omnia uero*k* indulgenti famae credere, et facilitatem auditorum fallere, ueracis historici non 2 debet esse. Quocirca illa*l* solummodo quae scripto comperi apponam, quibus ad unguem comprobetur gloriosa uiri deuotio et gratia uictura in seculo; illudque constanter asseruerim, parua*m* manu magna illum prelia persepe lusisse, nec umquam campum fugisse, preter apud Ramulam et apud Acharonem. Enimuero ambas fugas predicabiles exceperunt uictoriae, quod magis inconsiderata uirtute quam timore prouenerint, sicut paucis insertis lector agnoscet.[2]

383. Eo Septembri cuius septimo idus predictum*n* prelium fuit, Willelmus comes Pictauensis Ierosolimam perrexit, multa secum ducens agmina, ut estimarentur sexaginta milia militum et multo plura peditum. Iuit cum eo Stephanus comes Burgundiae et Hugo Lizianensis, frater Raimundi comitis, et Hugo Magnus et Stephanus

---

a iaculis in se *TtA* *b* qui pressit *TtA, against Juvenal's order* *c* stupore hebetes *TtA* *d* ab *Tt (also a minor variant at 377. 2* ab Ierosolimis*)* *e* sig. regio (regio *om. Tt*) ostenso*TtA* *f* id est Pt. *om. TtA (cf. 376. 9)* *g* urbes maritimas *TtA* *h* mortibus Turcorum *Tt* *i* relatio *TtA; the whole expression seems oddly inverted* *j* colloquio *Tt* *k* autem *TtA* *l* illas *B* *m* pauca *TtA* *n* om. *CB*

---

[1] Juvenal i. 43. [2] c. 384 (Ramlah), 385. 1–2 (not specified there as before Acre).

loss—the annihilation of five hundred Arab horsemen. These men had manoeuvred in front of Jaffa for two days, but doing no good there, were returning to Ascalon, and seeing our force in the distance, hoped it was their own, and went to meet it as though to congratulate the winning side. When the receipt of a flight of missiles warned them that it was the Franks, they turned pale 'like one that barefoot on a viper treads', as the poet puts it,[1] and dumbfounded with astonishment fled, exposing themselves to slaughter from behind. So the king came to Jaffa, and there corrected by a more exact report the error of a letter sent to Tancred by the local inhabitants, which had falsely reported that the king and his army had been wiped out. Tancred had already made preparations to go to Jerusalem, when the arrival of a messenger, who displayed the king's seal, dispelled his sorrow, and made him happy once again.

382. It would take too long to recount all the struggles in which Baldwin was engaged; how he subdued Tiberias, Sidon, Acre (otherwise Ptolemais), and eventually all the cities of the sea-coast; how almost every day was distinguished by Turkish casualties, either in secret raid or open battle. Colossal exploits of this kind require as their narrator someone rich in rhetoric and with leisure for taking pains. I stand in need of both, and also (which is a greater hindrance still) of accurate knowledge of the facts; but to trust in all respects to partial reports, and trade upon the credulity of one's hearers, ought to be outside the province of the honest historian. I will serve up therefore only what I have learnt from written sources; and this will suffice accurately to establish his glorious devotion to God and undying merit in this world. There is one point I would emphasize: how often he staked all on a major battle with scanty forces, and how he never retreated from the field, except at Ramlah and at Acre. And those retreats were both followed by brilliant victories, because they were brought about by reckless courage rather than fear, as the reader will learn after a brief interlude.[2]

383. The battle was fought on 7 September, and that same month William count of Poitou set out for Jerusalem, bringing large forces with him, so that the estimated total was sixty thousand knights and many more thousand footmen. With him came Stephen count of Burgundy and Hugh of Lusignan, Count Raymond's brother, and Hugh the Great and Stephen of Blois, all anxious to mend the

Blesensis, antiquae discessionis improperium noua et excogitata uirtute sarcire cupientes. Ita per Constantinopolim profectus, cum insolenti responso,[a] ut superius dixi,[1] Alexium offendisset, illo non curante uel potius procurante, Solimanni incurrit insidias;[b] qui sciens exercitum fame ac siti laborare, quod aliquantis diebus errabundi per palustria et inuia loca iuerant, cum trecentis milibus sagittariorum occurrit. Nulla umquam luctuosior Francis pugna uisa, quia nec timidum fuga nec audacem uirtus poterat[c] eripere discrimini, quod in arcto loco pugnaretur et in consertos sagittarum nubes[d] non frustraretur. Interfecta igitur[e] plusquam centum milia, preda omnis abducta; ita Solimannus, ex manubiis Francorum claras manibus suorum[f] nactus inferias, dispendium Niceae ultus est. Sed quia multis tramitibus itum erat, nec omnes cesi nec omnia direpta; nam preter Pictauensem, qui pene ad pudenda nudatus erat, ceteri comites prompte sua defensitauerant. Omnes ergo recollectis ex fuga militibus, preter Hugonem Magnum, quem mortuum Tarsensis ciuitatis urna excepit, Antiochiam conuolarunt. In quibus Tancredus,[g] egregiae pietatis miles, ingentem munificentiae suae[h] gratiam ostendit, cunctos quatenus poterat pecuniis sustentans, Willelmum precipue, quem fortunae uicissitudo eo afflictauerat inuidiosius quo ante prouexerat serenius; qui preter gazas, quarum dampno non adeo affitiebatur, quod caducae sunt et reparabiles, ex tot eximiis militibus[i] solus pene remanserat superstes. Ita recreatis animis iter moliti, undecumque belli occasiones querebant. Sensit sitim furentium prima Tortuosa ciuitas, qua peruasa et direpta non modicum preteritas[j] erumnas releuarunt. Inde ad angustias, de quibus superius dixi,[2] uenerunt, ubi eos rex iam pridem operiebatur, contra Turchos, si prohibere uellent, opem laturus. Eius uirtute defensi, et benigno apud Ioppen hospitio suscepti, Ierosolimam proximo Pascha contenderunt; ubi sacrosanctum ignem laetis hauserunt oculis, deuotis adorarunt animis. Post haec reuersi Ioppen,[k] ascensis nauibus patriam quisque suam redire meditabatur; quorum Pictauensis continua uenti prosperitate prouectus[l] patriam tenuit, ceteri retro uiolenter[m] acti.

[a] resp. ins. *TtACs(not Ca)*   [b] ins. Sol. incurrit *TtA*   [c] pot. uirtus *Tt*
[d] nub. sag. *TtA*   [e] igitur interfecta *TtA*   [f] suis *Tt*   [g] Tancredus *after miles CsB*   [h] su(a)e mun. *TtA*   [i] *Tt inserts* preter Hugonem Magnum *(cf. above)*   [j] pretentas *A*   [k] Iop. reuersi *TtAa*   [l] om. *Tt*   [m] uiolenter retro (reus *Aap*) *TtA*

[1] 349. 4.   [2] 376. 3.

disgrace of their former departure by some fresh act of deliberate valour. He set out therefore by way of Constantinople, where, as I have already told,[1] he gave great offence to Alexius by an insolent reply. Thereafter—without Alexius caring, or perhaps because he took care over it—he fell into a trap laid by Suleiman, who, knowing that after some days of wandering through trackless marshes the army was suffering from hunger and thirst, confronted him with three hundred thousand bowmen. Never did the Franks face a battle of more disastrous aspect: flight was no refuge for the coward, nor valour for the brave, for they had to fight in a restricted space, and so closely packed together that the cloud of arrows could not miss its mark. More than a hundred thousand were killed, and all the booty carried off; and thus Suleiman avenged the loss of Nicaea, and with the Frankish spoils gave a brilliant send-off to the spirits of his own dead. They had however been journeying by many paths, and consequently all were not killed, nor was all the booty dissipated; apart from the count of Poitou, who was stripped almost to a state of nature, the other nobles had actively defended their own possessions. They therefore reassembled the knights who had fled, and hastened to converge on Antioch, all save Hugh the Great, who died and was buried at Tarsus. In these circumstances they benefited from a great display of munificence on the part of Tancred, a soldier of most generous heart, who relieved them all with money to the extent of his power, and especially William. William had been dealt by the treachery of Fortune a blow all the more cruel, in that he had previously flourished in her smiles; besides his treasure, the loss of which did not affect him unduly, for treasure is quick to go, and can be won back again, of all those distinguished knights he was almost the only survivor. Having thus refreshed their spirits, they set off again, seeking every excuse for battle. The first city to feel their raging appetite was Tortosa, which they overran and plundered, thereby doing much to recoup their previous losses. Next they came to the defile of which I have spoken above[2] where the king had long been waiting for them, to second them against the Turks if they tried to stand in their way. Being protected by his valour, and kindly received at Jaffa, they hastened to Jerusalem, as Easter was at hand, where they joyfully beheld, and reverently adored, the sacred fire. After that, they returned to Jaffa, boarded their ships, and prepared to return each of them to his own country. The count of Poitou, sailing all the way with a favourable wind, reached home; the others were violently driven back.

384. Iam uero mense Maio inchoante,^a Turchi et Arabes Ramulam obsederunt, superioris anni dampnum noui exercitus supplemento eodem refitientes numero. Episcopus urbis, prudenter oportunitate spectata, cauit sibi loco, Ioppen latenter profectus. Iamque rex exierat, credens falso asserentibus non esse hostes plusquam quingentos; itaque nec atiem dirigere nec pedites conuocare curauit; tantum milites regem sequi cornicines monuerunt, multum amicis suadentibus ut Turch-
2 orum fraudes caueret. Stephani duo, Blesensis et Burgundus, regem equis insecuti, ne desides et inglorii sed triumphalis pompae conscii terras repeterent suas; sed aliam quam opinabantur gloriam, aliam uictoriam parabant fata^b uiris. Namque rex, uisa hostium multitudine,^c dum se frustratum opinione cognosceret, ira mentem sautius et magnanimitatis conscientia fremens, quid faceret hesitabat; si cederet, preteritae gloriae ignominiam, si pugnaret, suorum mortes animo uolutabat.^d Veruntamen uicit calor ingenitus, et terga iam dabat metus[1] cum, commilitonum hortatibus animatus, ut fugam in castellum per
3 medios hostes intenderet adquieuit. Ceteri, cum clamore secuti, densissimas perruperunt aties, animas suas Deo consecrantes et mortes impigre ulti; comites quoque, feriendo defatigati adeo ut manus gladiis obrigescerent, neci succubuerunt. Rex, in arcem lapsus, ex ducentis quos duxerat aliquantos sotios habuit; quibus orantibus ut uitam dignaretur fugiendo^e producere (sua pericula mundo parui ponderis esse, illius uitam ad multorum profectum ualere, utpote qui omni seculo sit uirtutis spectaculum), quanuis in fractis rebus ingenti animi
4 constantia, dignum se credidit uita. Itaque quinque militibus comitatus, in montana rependo insidiantes elusit. Militum fuit unus Rotbertus Anglus, ut superius dixi;[2] ceteros notitiae nostrae fama tam longinqua occuluit. Ille cum tribus^f comprehensus est; unus euasit cum rege.^g Turchi extremam uim furoris in illos qui euaserant in arcem^h effuderunt, in quibus fuit Hugo Lizianensis et Gaufredus Vindocinensis; tres tantum superstites Ierosolimitanis nuntii miseriarum fuere.
5 Rex interdiu latens, noctu per auiaⁱ cornipedem cursu exhaustum^j

^a mediante *TtA (cf. Fulcher ii. 15. 1)*   ^b fata parabant *TtA*   ^c mult. host. *TtA*   ^d proponebat *Tt*   ^e fug. dign. *TtA*   ^f *TtA* add* aliis ^g quintus cum rege euasit *TtA*   ^h qui in arcem refugerant (-ent *Aap*) *TtA* ⁱ noctu per auia *om. CB*   ^j exh. cursu *TtA*

---

[1] Perhaps not a quotation.
[2] 251. 2.

384. It was now the beginning [TtA middle] of May, and the Turks and Arabs laid siege to Ramlah, making good their losses of the year before by reinforcements of the same extent. The bishop of Ramlah wisely waited for a suitable moment and found safety in flight, making secretly for Jaffa. The king had already sallied forth, relying on misleading reports that the enemy were not more than five hundred strong; as a result he had taken no trouble to organize his line or get his infantry together, but the knights were simply summoned by trumpet to follow the king, although his friends urgently warned him to look out for a Turkish trap. The two Stephens, of Blois and Burgundy, followed the king on horseback, in hopes of returning home as partners in his triumph neither idle nor undistinguished; but fate had in store for them distinction and victory of a kind they did not look for. For when the king saw the enemy's numbers and realized his mistake, he was very angry, and being passionately conscious of his own heroic record, was in two minds what to do: retreat would be a betrayal of his glorious past, and to engage, he thought, would mean death for his men. None the less, inborn valour won the day and fear was like to flee away,[1] when, encouraged by the support of his knights, he agreed to attempt an escape into the fortress through the thick of the enemy. The others followed him with loud shouts, and burst through the enemy's concentrated ranks, commending their souls to God and selling their lives dearly. The counts too laid about them, until they were exhausted, and their hands stiffened with cramp about the sword-hilt; then they succumbed. The king escaped into the citadel with a few companions out of the two hundred he had set out with; they besought him not to be too proud to prolong his life by flight, saying that their own peril was of little importance to the world, whereas his life was essential to the good estate of many men, seeing that he was the model of valour to every age; and although of indomitable courage in disaster, he accepted the necessity for self-preservation. Accompanied therefore by five knights, he stole out into the hill-country, and eluded those who were on the watch for him. One of the knights was Robert, an Englishman, as I have already said;[2] the distance the news has to cover has denied us knowledge of the others. Robert and three more were taken prisoner, and one escaped with the king. On those who had escaped into the citadel the Turks expended the full violence of their fury (they included Hugh of Lusignan and Geoffrey of Vendôme), and only three survived to bear the news of the disaster to Jerusalem.

The king, lying hid by day and urging his exhausted horse by night

stimulans, Azotum peruenit, pulchro et ad miraculum Dei prono salutis euentu, quod paulo ante Turchi[a] discesserant, qui iam biduo circa urbem predas egerant. Inde Ioppen nauigio ueniens, Ierosolimitanis[b] epistolam de uitae suae certitudine legauit. Portitor cartae fuit homuntio Sirus, qui etsi inueniretur habitus uilitate et sermonis noti commertio insidiantes falleret. Hic, notis sibi per deuia compendiis perfidorum pericula declinans, tertio die Ierosolimam peruenit.

6 Tum equites qui urbem tutabantur, iunctis sibi auxiliarium peditum turmis, ad Ioppen profecturi iter mari proximum direxerunt,[c] mediterraneis deuitatis;[d] extremi tamen agminis Turchis urgentibus interfecti, quod uel equis uel pedibus destituebantur. Ita congregatis ex Ierosolimis nonaginta equitibus, ex Tiberiade octoginta, quos Hugo dux strenuissimus adduxerat in subsidium,[e] [f]armigeri quoque[f] pro penuria in locum militum allecti. Postera ergo die[g] moram pugnae absoluit, Turchis iam adeo ferocibus ut paratis machinis murum 7 Ioppes aggredi meditarentur.[h] Preuentum hoc Balduini diligentia, et Dominica cruce preuia, qua superius bellum caruerat, totis uiribus[i] in hostes alacriter itum, acriter certatum. At illi, more solito nostros circumgirantes, actum de Christianis putarunt, hilari ululatu uociferantes. Sed affuit et[j] de celo[k] tandem respexit Dominus Iesus, Francisque animositatem ingerens inimicos campo priuatos coniecit in fugam. Hoc et in[l] anteriori prelio factum est, ut non semel eiecti tentoriis[m] postea multitudine superarint;[n] tum autem, cum pedites eminus sagittis et equites lanceis comminus ferirent, omni spe pedibus commissa fugere perseuerauere.

385. Altera illi pugna posterioribus annis fuit, in qua milites nostri, Turchorum copia pressi et in fugam acti,[o] etiam salutare uexillum amisere, sed, cum longiuscule fugissent, reuersi sunt; pudor famae trepidos animauit ut ignominiam propulsarent. Ingens ibi pugna uirorum fuit, collato pede et aduerso pectore rem agentium. Nostri

[a] Tur. paulo ante *TtA*   [b] Ierosolimitis *Tt* (cf. *386. 2*)   [c] dilexerunt *TtA*   [d] uitatis *TtA*   [e] *Tt adds* contractos   [f-f] armigerique *Tt*   [g] om. *Tt*   [h] deliberarent *TtA*   [i] totis regni uiribus *Al*, totis regiminibus *Aa*   [j] qui *B*   [k] *TtA add* uel   [l] om. *TtACs*   [m] tent. eiecti *TtA*   [n] superarunt *TtB*   [o] aucti *Tt*

through a pathless country, made his way to Arsur; by a wonderful piece of good fortune, which might well be a divine miracle, the Turks, who had been plundering round the town for two days, had left shortly before. Thence he went to Jaffa by sea, and despatched a letter to Jerusalem to confirm that he was still alive. The bearer of his missive was a miserable Syrian, whose ragged clothes and knowledge of the language would have enabled him to deceive the pickets even if he had been caught. Avoiding the peril of the paynim by using byways he knew through the outlying country, on the third day he reached Jerusalem. Thereupon the cavalry who were protecting the city, taking with them some companies of auxiliary foot, set out for Jaffa, avoiding the inland route and keeping as close to the sea as they could; even so, the rearguard of their force, as it was unprotected by either horse or foot, was cut down by the Turks. Thus were assembled ninety knights from Jerusalem and eighty from Tiberias, whom Count Hugh with his usual energy had brought up to assist them; and esquires were promoted to act as knights as a further remedy for the shortage of men. So on the following day the king put an end to delay in engaging, the Turks being by now so confident that they had got their engines ready and were proposing to attack the walls of Jaffa. Their plans were foiled by the activity of Baldwin. The Lord's Cross going before them, which had been absent in the previous battle, with all their strength they moved against the enemy courageously. The contest was fierce. The Turks in their usual fashion rode round our men, and with howls of triumph gave utterance to their conviction that the Christians were doomed. But the Lord Jesus was at hand; at long last He looked down from Heaven, and breathing valour into the Franks, He banished their adversaries from the field and put them to flight. It had happened in the previous battle too that, although more than once driven from their encampment, the Turks had afterwards won the day by sheer numbers; but this time, harassed by the arrows of the infantry at long range, and at close quarters by the lances of the knights, they put all hope of safety in flight, and ran without drawing breath.

385. In later years he fought a second battle, in which our knights, hard pressed by the Turkish numbers, were forced to retire, and even to abandon the standard of their salvation; but after a flight of some duration they rallied, for, shaken though they were, concern for their reputation inspired them to fight back against disgrace. It was a heroic struggle: hand to hand, breastplate against breastplate was the order of

crucem reportarunt, fusis aduersariis campum uendicantes. Ceciderunt ibi plures quos ego quoque noram, inter quos Godefridus, abnepos eius nothus, iam inde a pueritia umbram uirtutis uultu colorans, ueritatem animo spirans.

2 Ambae ergo fugae fuere in principio quasi fomentum ignominiae, sed in fine uerax alimentum gloriae; illa nominatior, sed ista fructuosior. Denique ad supplementum rerum quas amiserat, simul et ad legitimum conubium, non multo[a] post comitissa Siciliae Ierosolimam uenit, tantas gazas cubiculo regis inferens ut mirum cuiuis[b] uideatur unde mulier tam infinitos pretiosae supellectilis cumulos coaceruarit. Et tunc quidem illam thoro recepit,[c] sed non multo post dimisit; aiunt incommodo tactam, quo eius genitalia cancer, morbus incurabilis, exederit.[d] Illud constat, regem prolis inopem fuisse; nec mirum[e] si homo, cuius otium erat egrescere, uxorios amplexus horruerit, omnem aetatem in bellis deterens.

3 Quibus laboribus effecit ut ammirabilis et pene diuina uirtus eius fuerit presentibus stimulo, futura[f] posteris miraculo. Obiit in expeditione Arabica mense Aprili, et publico funere Ierosolimis iuxta fratrem tumulatus, cum septimo decimo anno regni[g] quartus accresceret mensis. Vir multis laboribus emeritus, et cuius gloriae nullus pretendit nubila liuor,[1] nisi quod fuerit pecuniae iusto tenatior; sed huius culpae facilis ut uera erit excusatio, si consideretur quod necessaria in remanentes effusio munerum inhibuerit quo minus mercaretur fauorem abeuntium.

386. Successit ei Balduinus cognatus dux Edessae, quem moriens regem denuntiauerat, antiquis iam stipendiis laudatum. Ille [h]multis annis[h] regnum impigre tutatus, etiam auxit Antiocheno principatu, quem occiso Rogerio filio Ricardi obtinuit. Vtrasque ergo regiones egregio moderamine rexit,[i] minori quidem presumptionis roncho sed maiori et consultiori prouidentia; quanuis sint qui opinionem eius lacerent, tenacitatis eum nimiae arguentes. Quare, cum preterito anno non longe ab Ierosolima equitantem Turchi cepissent, paucis aut nullis gemitibus[j] sui eum desiderarunt, latuitque pene anno et incolas et

---

[a] multum B   [b] cuius A   [c] recepto B   [d] excederit Bk, exesit Bc   [e] TtA add erat   [f] futuro A   [g] regni anno (annis Aa) TtA   [h-h] ad hoc tempus TtA   [i] regit TtA   [j] TtA add ut ferunt

[1] Statius, Theb. xii. 818.

the day; but our men won back the Cross, routed their adversaries, and remained masters of the field. There fell on that spot many men whom even I knew, among them Godfrey, the king's bastard nephew(?), who from his early boyhood had embodied the ideal of courage in his countenance, and in his spirit breathed the air of truth.

Both these retreats, to start with, were the stuff of which disgrace is made, but in the end they proved the true material of reputation; the first was more widely celebrated, the second more fruitful in results. For instance, not long afterwards, by way of making good his losses and at the same time giving him the benefits of lawful wedlock, the countess of Sicily came to Jerusalem, bringing such treasure with her to the king's marriage chamber that anyone might wonder how a woman could accumulate such infinite store of precious things. At the time, he accepted her as his consort, but not long afterwards dismissed her, because (it is said) she was afflicted with some disorder, which caused an incurable cancer to attack her privy parts. It is certain at least that the king had no children; nor is it surprising that a wife's embraces should prove repellent to a man for whom leisure was a form of illness and whose whole time was spent in battle.

By these endeavours he made his astonishing and almost superhuman courage an inspiration to his contemporaries, just as it will be the admiration of posterity. He died in April, on an expedition to Arabia, and was buried after a state funeral in Jerusalem beside his brother, having reigned seventeen years and something over three months. He was the veteran of many toils, whose glory is 'by envy's mist undimmed',[1] save that he was, they say, unduly sparing of his money. This fault, however, will be readily, and properly, excused, if we consider that the need to shower gifts on those who stayed by him prevented him from purchasing the goodwill of those who departed.

386. He was succeeded by his kinsman Baldwin count of Edessa, a veteran of former campaigns, whom he had named as king upon his deathbed. For many years he vigorously defended his kingdom, and even increased it by adding the principality of Antioch, which he secured on the death of Roger son of Richard. His rule in both places was distinguished by its moderation; he showed little conceit of himself, and great wisdom and foresight, although some attack his reputation with the charge of avarice. As a result, when last year he was captured by the Turks while out riding not far from Jerusalem, his subjects [TtA *add* so it is said] wasted few or no sighs of regret; and

rumigerulos quo terrarum abductus,[a] si superis[b] auris uesceretur[c] necne. Refutarunt porro Ierosolimitae uel regem facere uel ordinem et ducatum militum interrumpere quoad rei certitudo sciretur, propter eius absentiam in nullo infractiores. Postmodum uero, cognito loco quo uinculatus fuerat, milites audacissimi spetiem negotiatorum mentientes, armis sub uestibus occultatis, oppidum ingressi regem eripuere discrimini, protestati non conferre se id[d] eius auaritiae, sed Gozelini de Turbexel gratiae, qui nichil umquam pensi fecerat quin omnia quae posset militibus erogaret. Vixit diu[e] frugi homo, et nulli preter hanc culpam infamiae obnoxius. Principatus Antiochenus ad Boamundi spectat filium, de quo nunc dicam.[f]

387. Boamundus Rotberti Guiscardi ex Normanna[g] filius fuit; alter Rogerus ex Apula genitus, qui cognomen Marsupii a patre meruit, quod paterno et curioso intuitu deprehendisset eum iam a tenero libenter nummos numerare. Nam Boamundus aetatis maiusculae nichil erat quod retineret, sed etiam puerilia[h] xenia dispertiret. Itaque Rogerus Apuliam, quae sibi materno genere[i] competere uidebatur, accepit; Boamundus cum genitore ad bellum Durachinum profectus est. Cumque oppidani fidutia menium iactitarent ideo urbem Durachium nominatam, quod contra omnes obsidiones imperterrita duraret, 'Et ego' inquit[j] 'uocor Durandus; et eo usque in obsidione durabo quo[k] ciuitati nomen auferam, ut non Durachium sed Mollitium amodo dicatur.' Cuius responsi constantia effecit ut confestim pauefacti portas aperirent. Ita tutus a tergo, ceteras urbes usque ad[l] Thessalonicam leuiore labore subegit. Iamque illuc peruenerat, iam Alexium cum per se tum per filium uinci posse docuerat, cum uxoria fraude deceptus ingens dispositum[m] morte destituit. Tum uero Boamundus, Apuliam reuersus, aliquot castella fraterna indulgentia tenuit, multa ipse uirtute et prudentia conquisiuit;[n] nam ad fratrem spetietenus ducatus peruenerat, alterum bello meliores[o] secuti. Nec uero parui momenti fuit

[a] *One expects* abductus sit, si conferre TtA *(B gives* uel *for* id*)* dicam, *leaving a gap* B [i] iure Tt *(cf. 75) the story must concern him* niensem coloniam*)* TtA [b] superius A [e] uiuit adhuc TtA [g] Normanna Tt[b.c.]Ce; Normannia TtACsB [j] TtA add Guischardus *(variously spelt), probably rightly:* [k] quod Tt [m] depositum Tt[a.c.]Ce [o] meliore sunt C; meliorem B [c] uesc. auris TtA [f] Tt omits (Bo)amundi... [h] *in* uirilia [l] *om.* TtA *(cf. GP p. 285* usque Wigor- [n] prud. et uirt. adquisiuit [d] se id

for nearly a year the local inhabitants and the gossip-mongers did not know where he had been taken, and whether or no he were still in the land of the living. The people of Jerusalem, in fact, refused either to elect a king or to effect any changes in the organization or leadership of their knights, until they knew for certain what had happened, and did not allow his absence to dismay them in the least. Later, however, when they discovered the place where he had been put in chains, the boldest of his knights, disguising themselves as merchants, with weapons hidden under their clothes, entered the town and rescued the king from his predicament, assuring him that they did so not out of any affection for his close-fistedness, but because of what they owed to Joscelin of Turbessel, who without the slightest hesitation had distributed among the knights all that it was in his power to give. Baldwin lived long in good repute, untouched by any criticism except for this one failing. The principality of Antioch belongs to the son of Bohemond, of whom I must now speak.

387. Bohemond was the son of Robert Guiscard by a Norman woman; his other son, Roger, was the child of an Apulian, and was nicknamed Moneybags by his father, whose parental insight had detected in him from his earliest years a love of counting money. As for Bohemond, who was somewhat older, nothing stuck to his fingers, and even as a child he gave away his presents. Roger, then, was given Apulia, which seemed appropriately his by his mother's nationality, and Bohemond set off with his father to make war on Durazzo. When the townspeople, confident in their fortifications, boasted that their town was called Durazzo because of its duration undismayed by any siege, '*My* name', retorted Guiscard, 'is Durand, and I propose to show endurance in this siege until I make your city change its name, and be called for the future not Durazzo but Mollezzo.' By this obstinate rejoinder they were frightened into opening their gates forthwith. Having thus protected his rear, he had less trouble in subduing the other cities as far as Salonica; and he had already got that far, and had shown that Alexius could be defeated both by himself and by his son, when he fell a victim to the plots of his wife, and by his death left those great hopes unfulfilled. Bohemond thereupon returned to Apulia, where he held a certain number of castles by his brother's generosity and added many more by his own skill and courage; for while the duchy had ostensibly passed to the one brother, it was the other who was followed by the soldiers of repute. It was also of considerable

quod, paterni propositi sequax, Wibertum repellens Vrbano ualidissime astitit, et cunctantem*a* impulit ut Gallias ad concilium*b* Clari Montis accederet, quo eum Raimundi Prouintialis comitis et episcopi Caturcensis epistolae inuitabant. Concilioque celebrato, libens occasionem accepit et in Gretiam copias traiecit; subindeque promouens exercitum, modeste Raimundum et Godefridum uenturos operiebatur. Quibus uenientibus sotiatus, magnum incitamentum ceteris erat, disciplinae militaris scientia et uirtute nulli secundus.

4 Sed quia quae cum ceteris fecit communi laudi sors attribuit, et quomodo captus fuerit anterior sermo notitiae*c* dedit,[1] nunc qualiter se seruitio exuerit dicendum. Danisman enim, cum uideret nichil utilitatibus suis applicari quod tantum uirum teneret, inflexus animo*d* de pacis conditionibus actitare cepit; nam nec illum occidere, ne in se odia Christianorum effusa*e* concitaret, nec sine spebus in perpetuum ualiturae pacis dimittere uolebat. Pollicitus ergo Boamundus continuam gentili concordiam, reuertit*f* Antiochiam, argenteos compedes quibus
5 illigatus*g* fuerat secum deferens. A suis ergo exceptus plausibiliter,*h* Laoditiam et ceteras urbes*i* quas Tancredus adquisierat suscepit, ne*j* uideretur oscitare otio dum auunculus suspiraret in ergastulo. Nec multo post Gallias uenit, offerens catenas sancti Leonardi honori, quae sibi fuerant oneri. Fertur enim in primis ille sanctus absoluendorum uinculorum potens, ut, uidentibus nec mutire audentibus aduersariis, pondera sua captiuus liber asportet. Ita ducta uxore filia regis Francorum, et altera Tancredo missa, repetiit Apuliam, sequentibus se Francorum proceribus, qui spe maioris commodi patriam deserebant; simul et spectaturi comminus quid uiua uirtutis speties*k* efficeret,
6 quam*l* tam insignis fama ubique loqueretur.*m* Itaque ille,*n* dispositis apud Apuliam rebus suis, denuo in Alexium efferatus est, pretendens belli causam peregrinorum iniuriam, qua ille perinfamis erat. Sed parum et prope nichil gessit prospere, sollertis imperatoris deceptus astutia, qui omnes duces eius aut pecuniis oberatos ab eo alienauit*o* aut ueneno, ut dixi,[2] sustulit. Quapropter animo deiectus Apuliam rediit; ibique post paucos dies, dum ad*p* Antiochiam iter meditatur,*q*

a cunctantemque (*om.* et) T*t*A   *b* ad concilium *om.* B   *c* not. sermo ant. T*t*A   *d* animi mollitie T*t*A   *e* effusa in se Chr. odia T*t*A   *f* reuertitur T*t*Cs   *g* alligatus C   *h* plaus. exceptus T*t*A   *i* *om.* T*t*   *j* *The final clause is to be taken with* adquisierat, *not* suscepit, *despite the order*   *k* spes B   *l* quamquam T*t*   *m* loquebatur T*t*A*   *n* *om.* T*t*   *o* abalienauit T*t*A   *p* apud T*t*   *q* meditaretur A

[1] 375. 1.   [2] Apparently referring to 262. 5, 349. 3 (Robert Guiscard).

importance that, in continuation of his father's policy, he rejected Wibert and gave his most effective support to Urban, urging him for all his reluctance to go into Gaul and attend the Council of Clermont, to which he had been invited by a letter from Raymond count of Provence and the bishop of Cahors. The Council once over, he readily seized the opportunity and crossed with his forces into Greece, thence, advancing by short stages, he modestly awaited the arrival of Raymond and Godfrey. On their appearance he joined them, and was a great encouragement to all the rest, being second to none in prowess and in knowledge of the art of war.

But since the exploits which he shared with other people came to be attributed to the common credit of them all, and since I have already explained how he was taken captive,[1] I must now tell how he escaped from his captivity. Danishmend, seeing that it brought him no benefit to have so great a man in his power, relented, and opened discussions on the terms of peace; he was reluctant to put Bohemond to death, for fear of rousing against himself an outburst of resentment from the Christians, and unwilling to let him go without some hope of lasting peace. Bohemond therefore promised the heathen an enduring treaty, and returned to Antioch, bringing with him the silver fetters with which he had been bound; and being received by his own people with enthusiasm, he took over Laodicea and the other cities which Tancred had acquired in order not to seem idle while his uncle was languishing in prison. Not long afterwards he came to Gaul, and there offered as a guerdon to St Leonard the gyves that had been such a burden to himself. For St Leonard is foremost, it is said, in power to loose a man from bondage, so that the captive is set free and bears away his chains, while his enemies look on and dare not say a word. So, having taken to wife a daughter of the king of the French, and sent another to Tancred, he returned to Apulia, followed by the Frankish nobles who were leaving their own country in hope of bettering themselves, and also of seeing in action at close quarters that living image of valour, whose glorious fame made him talked of everywhere. Having disposed of his affairs in Apulia, he let fly once more against Alexius, the pretext being the ill-treatment of pilgrims, for which he was notorious. But he had little or no success, being deceived by the craft and cunning of the emperor, who either weaned his generals away from him by binding them to himself with presents, or despatched them, as I have said,[2] with poison. He therefore returned in dejection to Apulia, and after a few days there, while proposing to return to Antioch, he died, being in

defungitur, aetate citra senium, prudentia infra nullum, relicto tenerioris aeui filio. Vir in aduersis constans, in prosperis*a* circumspectus; nam et pro suspitione noxiae potionis paratum commentus erat remedium, cultellum qui, ante ora comedentis infixus, sudore (mirum dictu) prodebat manubrii, si quid tecto illatum esset uenefitii.

Post eum Tancredus Antiochiae principatui*b* prefuit, haud pudendus auunculo nepos; qui cum et ipse 'communem mortalium' uiam obitu prepropero triuisset, successit Rogerius filius Ricardi. Is, gloriae antecessorum in bellis non impar, ignominiam tamen auaritiae incurrit; quapropter cum eum milites cauerent, stipendiario milite pene nullo et indigena raro Turchis congressus occubuit, mortem suam non ignaue ultus. Nam cum *d*ab eis*d* captus et diloricatus iuberetur ensem reddere, negauit se ulli nisi duci daturum, quod omnes infra dignitatis suae deditionem aspiceret. Credidit infelix ammiratus simulatis uocibus, et iam galea caput nudatus porrexit manum, ut reciperet Rogerii gladium. Tum*e* uero ille infrendens et totis fortitudinis reliquiis in ictum se cogens, Turcho caput decussit, moxque perfossus excogitato genere uirtutis dedecus seruitutis effugit. Eius mortem Balduinus secundus rex Ierosolimorum ultus insigniter,*f* principatum ciuitatis*g* *h*et filiam suam Boamundo filio Boamundi seruauit*h* fideliter.

388. Raimundus fuit filius Willelmi antiquissimi Tolosae comitis, qui uir acer et efficax patriam, antecessorum suorum*i* socordia obscuram, titulis suis reddidit illustrem. Vxor eius Almodis, multis uicissim desponsata, multam ex omnibus sobolem tulit, insano muliercula pruritu et irreuerenti, ut cum ei longo usu uir displicuisset, alias migraret nouos impletura penates.[1] Denique primum Arelatensi comiti nupta, mox illius pertesa huic Willelmo se coniunxit; cui cum duos peperisset filios, Barcinonensem ad conubium illexit comitem. Porro Willelmus, mortis confinis foribus,*j* Tolosanum comitatum dedit filio aequiuoco sed moribus absono, quod esset crassioris ingenii,*k* et*l*

---

a (ad)uersis . . . prosperis *om. Tt, leaving a gap (cf. 386. 2 n.)* *b* princ. Ant. *TtA* *c–c* mortalium publicam *Tt;* publicam mortalium *A* *d–d* a Turc(h)is *TtA* *e* tunc *Tt* *f* insegniter *TtAlC* *g* seruitutis *Tt* *h–h* Boamundi filio reseruat *TtA* *i* om. *TtA* *j* for. conf. *TtA* *k* animi *TtA* *l* om. *B*

[1] Cf. Lucan ii. 331–2.

years still short of old age but in wisdom second to none, and leaving a son of tender years. He was a man inflexible in adversity, and in prosperity circumspect; suspicious as he was of poisoning, he had even provided an immediate remedy in the shape of a knife which, if driven into the table in front of him as he sat at meat, extraordinarily enough indicated by the sweating of its handle if any poison had been brought under his roof.

After him Tancred ruled over the principality of Antioch, a nephew not unworthy of his uncle; and when he too by an untimely death had taken the common road of mortal men, he was succeeded by Roger son of Richard. Although in battle not unworthy of his glorious ancestors, Roger incurred the disgrace of avarice; and being therefore regarded with suspicion by his knights, so that he had almost no paid cavalry, and very few from his own land, he met his end in an engagement with the Turks. But he bravely made them pay for his death. When taken by the Turks, stripped of his defensive armour, and ordered to surrender his sword, he refused to give it up to anyone except the general, on the ground that the others were all unfit to receive the surrender of a man of his rank. The poor emir believed this fairy-story, and having already taken off his helmet, held out his hand to receive Roger's sword. At that instant Roger, grinding his teeth, and gathering all the strength he had left into a single blow, struck off the Turk's head, and being instantly cut down, escaped the shame of slavery by this deliberate valour. His death was gloriously avenged by Baldwin II king of Jerusalem, who faithfully kept the principality and his daughter's hand for Bohemond's son of the same name.

388. Raymond was the son of William, the most distinguished count of Toulouse, an energetic and successful man, who by his own exploits brought fame to his native country, which had languished in obscurity under the inaction of his forebears. His wife Almodis had in turn had many husbands, and had borne many children by them all; she was a woman of crazy and unprincipled appetite, such that when through long familiarity she had grown tired of one husband, she would go elsewhere to 'stock another's home'.[1] Thus she had first been married to the count of Arles, but soon growing tired of him, had allied herself with the William of whom we speak; and when she had borne him two sons, she enticed the count of Barcelona into marriage with her. William, when at death's door, gave the county of Toulouse to his son, who bore the same name but in character was very different, being

nichil Tolosani contra eum nouarent, familiae illius dominatui assueti. Raimundus uero, uiuatioris spiritus, Caturcensem accepit, et *non mediocriter* auxit, Arelatensi et Narbonensi et Prouintiali et Lemouicensi adiunctis.*b* Tolosam quoque a germano emit, pluribus annis ante magni motus uiam profecto Ierosolimam. Sed haec multi temporis intercessu et aetate impensa labori. Itaque pugnis semper assiduus legitimam uxorem non desiderauit, multinubo concubinatu uoluptatem 3 exercens. Denique ex una pelicum filium natum Bertrannum cognitione et hereditate dignatus est, quod in aliquantis patrissaret; cui uxorem coniunxit Mathildis marcisae neptem, ex Longobardia natam, ut illius affinitate illas prouintiae partes*c* tutaretur. Ipse quoque extremis fere*d* annis uxorem asciuit filiam regis Tarraconensis, splendidam dotem pactus, aeternam scilicet conterminarum prouintiarum pacem. Nec multo post, niuem capitis respitiens, Ierosolimitanum iter uouit, ut lassi et effeti corporis uires iam uel sero Deo deseruirent, auctore precipue Caturcensi episcopo, cuius precipua opera ipse impugnatus semper*e* fuerat; etiam in quodam duello altero lumine priuatus;*f* cuius insigne calamitatis pre se ferens non solum non occultabat, sed etiam 4 gloriabatur ultro*g* specimen nobilis militiae ostentans. Tunc autem mutua federati amicitia, ut senectutem suam diuinis consumerent cultibus, Vrbano iam in predicationem prono stimulos addidere, ut transitis Alpibus potissimum apud Clarum Montem concilium cogeret, quod esset ea ciuitas et illorum patriae propinqua et ex tota Gallia uenientibus oportuna. Veruntamen in ipso ad concilium itinere pontifex obitu defecit. Successit curae illius presul*h* Podii, de quo supra diximus;[1] cuius hortatibus animatus et umbone protectus, Raimundus primus omnium laicorum crucem accepit, aditiens uoto ut numquam in patriam rediret, sed potius duraturo in Turchos labore aruinam preteritarum iniquitatum extenuaret.

5 Iam uero in itinere plura*i* dedit inditia fortitudinis, ad laborem primus, ad quietem ultimus; plura etiam patientiae, quod parte*j* Antiochiae quam occupauerat*k* Boamundo et turri Dauid Godefrido

a-a immane quantum T*t*A*l*; in immensum (mensum *Aap*) *Aa*   *b* adiectis T*t*A   *c* partes prou. T'A   *d* fere extremis T'A   *e* om. T'A; after ipse Ce   *f* priuaretur Bk, om. Bc   *g* ultro before etiam T'A (but cf. 449. 1)
h pontifex T'A   *i* plura in itinere T'A   *j* arce C   *k* preoc(c)upauerat B

---

[1] First at 348. 1.

something of a blockhead; for the people of Toulouse would not rebel against him, accustomed as they were to be ruled by a member of the family. But Raymond, who was a more lively spirit, was given the county of Cahors and considerably enlarged it, adding those of Arles, Narbonne, Provence, and Limoges. He also bought Toulouse from his own brother, who was departing for Jerusalem, several years before the great movement thither. But this demanded a long interval of time, and a life spent on the task. Being thus continually engaged in warfare, he felt no need of a lawful wife, and satisfied his desires with a succession of mistresses. By one of his concubines he had a son Bertram, whom he thought worthy of recognition as his son and heir, because in many ways he took after his father; and gave him to wife a niece of the marchioness Matilda of Lombard birth, in order by this alliance to safeguard that flank of his dominions. He too, almost at the end of his life, married a daughter of the king of Tarragona, stipulating for a splendid dowry—no less than a treaty of perpetual peace between their adjacent provinces. Not long after that, in consideration of his grey hairs, he vowed to make the journey to Jerusalem, that his bodily strength, weary and worn out as it was, might even at that late hour be devoted to the service of God. In this the prime mover was the bishop of Cahors, of whose special ill will he himself had always been the target; and he had even lost one of his eyes in a duel, but bore the marks of this calamity proudly, not only not concealing them, but actually glorying in the display of this evidence of notable service. But now, being united in mutual friendship with a view to spending their old age in God's service, they spurred on Urban, who was already inclined to preach the crusade, urging him to cross the Alps and hold a council, preferably at Clermont, on the ground that that city was not far from their own country and convenient for persons attending from the whole of Gaul. The bishop, however, died while actually on his way to the Council, and his mission was taken up by the bishop of Le Puy, of whom we have already spoken.[1] Fired by his exhortations and secure in his protection, Raymond was the first layman of all to take the Cross, adding to his vow the resolution never to return to his own country, but to work off the gross flesh of his past iniquities by continuing toil against the Turk.

While on his journey he set many an example of courage, for he was the first in action and the last to seek repose; many of tolerance too, for he willingly handed over to Bohemond a part of Antioch which he had seized himself, and made way for Godfrey in the Tower of David. At

libenter cesserit. Sed tandem, nimiis exactionibus quorundam fracta patientia, in deditione urbis Ascalonensis decidit. Siquidem in primo Francorum aduentu oppidani, exploratis omnium ducum nostrorum*a* moribus, ipsum in patronum elegere, quod multi, eo ante*b* a Monte Pessulano*c* nauigio uenientes negotiatum,*d* fidem eius et uirtutem in
6 caelum tulerant. Itaque traditis clauibus sacramento ducem adegere ut nulli Christianorum potestatem urbis refunderet, si ipse uel*e* nollet tenere uel nequiret. Tunc a proceribus mussitatum est, expostulantibus urbem regis dominio, quod parum ei ualeret*f* regnum si non haberet Ascalonem, quae hostibus esset*g* receptaculo, nostris obstaculo. Et rex quidem leniter,*h* ut omnia, et uultu tranquillis conueniente moribus rem allegabat, ceteri peruicatius. Haec ille uerba paruipendebat, non infirmis rationibus dicta eorum cassans: omnes sotios suos iam sibi receptui consuluisse, partim patriam deuectos, partim adquisitam inhabitantes prouintiam; se solum, abiurata natali*i* terra, nec illuc posse
7 redire nec hic*j* receptum habere. Cessisse se in aliis; hoc modo paterentur, ut Ascalonem in fidelitatem*k* sancti Sepulchri teneret; ceterum ne redderet sacramento fecisse. Quo audito cuncti strepere, perfidum et cupidum uocare, ut uix manibus temperarent. Contumeliae huius rubore comes*l* suffusus, ab aequi bonique uiri desciuit offitio, inimicis Dei claues ciuitatis*m* contradens et metum peierandi multorum in posterum sanguine compensans. Neque enim ad hunc diem ciuitas illa capi uel ui uel ingenio potuit; quin et plures ex hominibus illius, affluenti urbis*n* opulentia delectati, fidei transfugio ciuium caritatem meruere.
8 Ita uir*o* ille, Ierosolima*p* egressus, Laoditiam uenit, qua subiugata aliquantum*q* ibi morarum nexuit; cumque Constantinopolim iuisset, obtinuit Laoditiam Tancredus, ui an amore ambiguum. Ille interea Bizantio commoratus prudentia qua uigebat effecit ut Alexii gratiam haberet; unde contigit ut, imperatoris benignitate per tuta deductus, sotietati erumnarum non implicaretur quas Willelmum Pictauensem et ceteros*r* superius incurrisse diximus;[1] cum quibus Tortuosam ciuitatem
9 cepit, sed illis ultra euntibus solus possedit. Et, ut latius uires suas

a nostrorum ducum *A* *b* antea *T'A* *c* Pislerio *T'A* *d* negotiatorum *C* *e* uel ipse *CB* *f* ualeret ei *T'A* *g* esset hostibus *T'A* *h* leuiter *CB* *i* naturali *TpC* *j* hac *B* *k* in fidelitatem *(or* infid-*) AaBc, cf.* 392. 2; in fidelitate *(or* infid-*) T'AlCBk* *l* ille rubore *(om.* comes*) T'A* *m om. ABc* *n* urbis affluenti *T'A* *o om. T'A* *p* Ierosolimam *B* *q* aliquantulum *T'* *r* et ceteros *after* diximus *T'A*

[1] 349. 4, 383. 2.

length however his patience, which had been much tried by the greed of others, was exhausted when it came to surrendering the city of Ascalon. When the Franks first arrived, the townsfolk after enquiry into the character of all our generals chose Raymond to be their patron, having heard his sense of honour and his courage raised to the skies by many people who had earlier made the voyage from Montpellier to Ascalon on business. Handing their keys to him, therefore, they bound him by an oath that if he were unwilling or unable to hold the town himself, he would not hand over possession to any of the Christians. The magnates protested at this, claiming the city for the lordship of the king, on the ground that his kingdom would be worth almost nothing without Ascalon, which would serve as a refuge for his enemies and an obstacle to our own side. The king for his part argued the case mildly, as usual, his peaceful nature being reflected in his face; but the others were more forceful. Raymond made light of their representations, refuting what they said with arguments of some force: all his companions, he said, had already made good their own retreat, some by returning home, some by acquiring a province to dwell in; he alone had foresworn his native soil, and could neither return thither nor find a refuge here. He had already given way in other matters; they ought now to allow him to hold Ascalon as a vassal of the Holy Sepulchre; in any case, he had sworn an oath not to hand it over. At these words there was universal uproar; they called him treacherous and greedy, and could scarcely keep their hands off him. Filled with resentment at these insults, the count did what no fair and right-minded man should have done, and handed over the keys of the city to the enemies of God, purchasing freedom from the fear of breaking his oath at the price of many men's blood in after time; for to this day that city has never been taken either by force or cunning, and many of his men, delighted by the wealth of that rich city, actually earned the affection of the citizens by abandoning their faith.

So Raymond left Jerusalem and went to Laodicea, which he conquered, and rested there for some time; but on his departure for Constantinople Tancred obtained Laodicea, whether amicably or by force is disputed. Meanwhile, during his stay in Byzantium, he obtained with characteristic skill the support of Alexius, so that, being conducted with the emperor's kind assistance by safe routes, he was not involved in a share of the misfortunes which befell William of Poitou and the others, as we have said above.[1] In their company he took the city of Tortosa, but when they went on, he held it by himself. In order to distribute his

spargeret, oppidum contra Tripolim, quod Castellum Peregrinorum uocant, firmauit, et ibi Herbertum episcopum ex abbate constituit;[a] et, ut quassae suorum uires aliquanta quiete coalescerent, cum Tripolitanis in septennium fedus iecit. Veruntamen ante prestitutum terminum pax rupta est, deprehenso intra castellum quodam oppidano cum pugione toxicato, quem sub femore occuluerat. Tum[b] profecto Tripolitanae uictoriae supremam manum imposuisset, nisi prope diem mors adueniens presenti uitae spiritum subduxisset ingentia parturientem. Cuius morte audita, Willelmus de Monte Pessulano[c] et ceteri duces prouintiae Willelmum peregrinum, quem in ipsa obsidione ex Hispana[d] susceperat, uix[e] quadrimum, patriam deuehendum curarunt, sollicita omnium spe in successionem educandum. Nec inuitus Bertrannus factum, quanuis se inconsulto, audiuit, ut paternas adoreas instauraret. Itaque innumero succinctus milite, precipueque Ianuensibus et Pisanis, qui de coniugis cognatione erant, annitentibus,[f] Tripolim terra marique aggressus est, diuturnaque obsidione fractam in potestatem redegit. Successit ei filius[g] Pontius ex Longobarda,[h] adolescens maiorum emulus gloriae,[i] sortitusque[j] est iugalem Tancredi quondam Antiocheni principis uxorem. Id enim ille moriens preceperat, protestatus[k] in ephebo et Christianorum commodum et Turchorum omnifariam dispendium. Pontius ergo Tripoli principatur, sancti Sepulchri se profitens seruum, auitum scilicet et paternum secutus exemplum.

389. Rotbertus filius Willelmi Anglorum regis primi natus in Normannia[l] spectatae iam uirtutis habebatur adolescens quando pater Angliam uenit, fortitudinis probatae, quamquam exilis corporis et pinguis aqualiculi. Inter bellicas patris alas excreuit, primaeuo tirocinio parenti morem in omnibus[m] gerens. Veruntamen iuuenilem[n] indutus calorem, Normanniam se a patre adhuc uiuente, fatuorum sodalium instinctu, impetrare[o] posse sperauit. Quod cum ille negasset, terrisonae uocis roncho iuuenem abigens, iratus abscessit Rotbertus,[p] multisque assultibus patriam infestauit, primo quidem genitore cachinnos excutiente[q] et subinde dicente: 'Per resurrectionem Dei! Probus erit Robelinus Curta Ocrea.' Hoc enim erat eius cognomen, quod esset[r]

[a] ex abbate episc. instituit T'A   [b] tunc T'   [c] Pislerio T'A (cf. 388. 5)
[d] Hispania TpCsB   [e] om. C   [f] annitentibus before qui T'A   [g] filius after Long. T'A* (cf. 387. 1)   [h] Longobardia B   [i] glor. mai. em. T'A   [j] consortius Bk, et sortitus Bc   [k] T'A* add adolescere (cf. 94. 2, 377. 1)   [l] Normanniam T'   [m] in omnibus morem T'A   [n] iuuent(a)e uiridem T'A   [o] CBc add se   [p] om. T'A   [q] excut. gen. cac. T'A   [r] sit T'A

forces more widely, he fortified a town opposite Tripoli which they call Castel Pelerin, and there installed Abbot Herbert as bishop; then, in order that his weary troops might regain strength by a period of repose, he made a seven-year treaty with the people of Tripoli. The peace was broken, however, before its appointed term, when one of the townsfolk was caught within the citadel carrying a poisoned dagger which he had hidden inside his thigh. He would then certainly have put the finishing touches to his victory at Tripoli, had not Death promptly visited him, and robbed him of the breath of life in this world, full of great schemes though he was. On hearing the news of his death, William of Montpellier and the other chiefs of the province took William the Pilgrim, the son born to him of a Spanish mother actually during the siege, who was then barely four years old, and had him conveyed into his own country to be brought up with all men's watchful care and hope as the successor. Nor was Bertram sorry when he heard the news, although it had been done without consulting him, to have the opportunity to renew his father's triumphs. Aided therefore by a large force of knights, mainly from Genoa and Pisa, who were of the same kin as his wife, he attacked Tripoli by land and sea, broke its resistance by a long siege, and got it into his power. He was succeeded by Pons, his son by the Lombard woman, a young man keen to vie in glory with his ancestors, who took as his consort the wife of Tancred, former prince of Antioch. Such had been Tancred's dying wish, for he affirmed that in the youth was stored up great profit for the Christians and loss of every kind for the Turks. Pons therefore is now prince of Tripoli, and following the example of his father and grandfather, he declares himself the servant of the Holy Sepulchre.

389. Robert, son of William I king of England, had been born in Normandy, and was already a young man of established prowess when his father came to England; his courage was proven, although he was small in stature, and pot-bellied. He grew up among his father's warlike squadrons, and in his prentice days did exactly as his father told him. When filled, however, with the hot blood of youth, he was encouraged by foolish companions to hope that he could secure Normandy from his father during his lifetime. When his father refused, driving the young man away with jeers in that terrific voice of his, Robert went off in a passion, and harried his own country with frequent attacks. At first his father merely laughed. 'By God's resurrection!', he used to say, 'He'll be a hero, will our Robin Curt-hose!' This was his nickname

exiguus, ceterum nichil habens quod succenseres,ᵃ quia nec illepidae formae nec infaceti eloquii nec uirtutis imbecillaeᵇ nec eneruis eratᶜ consilii.ᵈ Posterius uero rex adeo effera succensus est ira ut eum et benedictione ultima et hereditate fraudaret Anglica. Comitatu tamen Normanniae egre licet et improbe retento, post nouem annos Ierosolimitanae uiae laboribus periculumᵉ suae fortitudinis fecit, et in multis quidem mirabilis apparuit, ut numquam a Christiano uel pagano potuerit ex equiteᶠ pedes effici; tum uero maxime in bello Antiocheno, cuius ipse uictoriam pulchra experientia nobilitauit. Nam cum Turchi, ut diximus,¹ subito terrefacti fugae se dedissent,ᵍ nostrique palantes uehementius impeterent, Corbaguath dux, genuinae uirtutis memor, retento equoʰ suos inclamauit,ⁱ famulos ignauos et annosarum uictoriarum oblitos uocans, ut uictores quondam Orientis paterentur se ab aduena et pene inermi populo finibus excludi. Quo clamore multi resumentes animum Francos conuersi urgere et propiores cedere cepere, Corbaguath suos animante et hostes feriente, ut imperatoris et militis probe offitiumʲ exsequeretur. Tum uero Normannus comes et Philippus clericus, filius Rogerii comitis de Monte Gomerico, et Warinus de Tanea,ᵏ castello Cinomannico, mutua se uiuacitateˡ inuicem hortati, qui ante simulataᵐ fuga cedebant, conuertunt cornipedes, et quisque suum comparem incessens deiciunt. Ibi Corbaguath, quanuis comitem cognosceret, solo tamen corpore mensus, simul et fugere inglorium arbitratus, audatiam congressus morte propinqua luit, uitali statim spiritu priuatus; cuius nece uisa Turchi, qui iam gloriabundi ululabant, spe recenti exinaniti fugam iterarunt. In eo tumultu Warinus cecidit, Rotbertus cum Philippo palmam retulit; Philippus hac militia precluus, sed Ierosolimis, ut fertur, bono fine functus, preter exercitium equestre litteris clarus. Ita Rotbertus, Ierosolimam ueniens,ⁿ indelebili macula nobilitatem suam respersit, quod regnum, consensu omnium sibi utpote regis filio delatum, recusarit, non reuerentiae, ut fertur,ᵒ contuitu sed laborum inextricabilium metu. Veruntamen patriam regresso, in qua licenter se delicatis uoluptatibus inseruiturum putauerat, affuit pro hac culpa, credo,ᵖ Deus misericorditer ubique seuiens et omnes eius dulcedines amarissimis offensionibus offuscans, sicut consequenti scripto palam fiet.

ᵃ succenseas T¹A   ᵇ inbecillis Cs (cf. 228. 10 imbecillis animi, GP p. 143 imbecilles)   ᶜ om. T¹; est A   ᵈ consilio T¹   ᵉ periculum before fecit C   ᶠ ex equite om. T¹   ᵍ com(m)isissent T¹A   ʰ equos A   ⁱ inclamat CB   ʲ officium prob(a)e T¹A*   ᵏ Taneo A   ˡ uiu. se T¹A   ᵐ sim. ante T¹A   ⁿ perueniens T¹A   ᵒ ferunt Tt(not Tp)A   ᵖ ut credo T¹A

¹ 365. 2.

because of his small size; in other respects there was nothing to criticize, for he was neither unattractive in feature nor unready in speech, not feeble in courage nor weak in counsel. Later, the king grew so fierce with anger that he deprived him of his deathbed blessing and of the English succession. He managed, however, to retain rather doubtfully 3 and improperly the duchy of Normandy; but after nine years put his valour to the test by making the laborious voyage to Jerusalem, and achieved by many feats a great reputation, such that neither Christian nor pagan could unhorse him, but particularly in the fighting at Antioch, where he adorned the victory with a brilliant exploit. When the Turks, as we have said,[1] had taken to their heels in sudden panic, and our men were eagerly pursuing them while they were disordered, their general Corbaguath did not forget his proper courage, but reined in his horse and shouted to his men: cowards and slaves he called them, to forget their time-honoured victories, and allow the former conquerors of the East to be driven from their country by a pack of half-armed foreigners. Hearing his shouts, many of them took heart; they faced 4 about and went for the Franks, killing those nearest them, Corbaguath all the time encouraging his men and striking at the enemy, so that he roundly did his duty as a general and a warrior too. At that point the duke of Normandy and Philip the Clerk, son of Roger of Montgomery, and Warin of Taney, a castle in Maine, shouted mutual encouragement at one another—for they were retiring in pretended flight—turned their horses, made each for his adversary, and overthrew him. Corbaguath recognized the duke, but took his measure by his size alone, and in any case thought it inglorious to run away; he paid for this rash encounter by immediate death, for he was killed at once. The Turks were already voicing yells of triumph, but when they saw him fall, deprived of their new-found hope they fled a second time. In the rough 5 and tumble Warin was killed, and Robert together with Philip was the victor. Philip won distinction in this fight, but made a good end, it is said, at Jerusalem; besides his knightly skill, he was distinguished by his education. So Robert came to Jerusalem, where he brought a lasting stain upon his noble reputation by refusing the kingdom when it was offered to him by common consent as a king's son, not from any consideration of modesty, it is supposed, but through fear of its insoluble difficulties. However, when he returned home, expecting to be free to devote himself to pleasure and delight, God visited him for this fault, as I suppose, who shows His anger everywhere in mercy, and darkened all his pleasures with most bitter pains, as will appear in the sequel.

6 Vxorem filiam Willelmi de Conuersana, quam rediens in Apulia duxerat, cuius elegantissimae spetiei prodigium uix ullius disertitudinis explicabit conatus, post paucos annos morbo amisit, deceptam, ut dicunt, obstetricis*a* consilio, quae pro affluentis lactis copia puerperae mammas stricta preceperat illigari fascia. Sed accessit, tantorum malorum grande solatium, filius ex coniuge sublatus, qui, Willelmus dictus uaticinio nominis auiti, spem egregiae probitatis*b* aleret in posterum. Pecuniam infinitam, quam ei socer*c* dotis nomine annumerauerat, ut eius commertio Normanniam exueret uadimonio,
7 *d*ita dilapidauit*d* ut pauculis diebus nec nummus superesset. Precipitauit quoque infamiam eius*e* inconsultus aduentus in Angliam, ut fratri Henrico*f* regnum eriperet; sed desertorum qui eum inuitauerant destitutus auxilio, germani paci facile adquieuit utriusque partis ducum arbitrio,*g* trium milium marcarum annuum donum ab Anglia uerbotenus habiturus. Nam promiserat ista rex, non daturus; sed, fratris facilitatem non nesciens, blandam credulitatem luserat, dum interim calor bellicus deferuesceret. Porro ille, quasi cum Fortuna certaret utrum plus illa daret an ipse dispergeret, sola uoluntate reginae tacite postulantis comperta, tantam massam argenti benignus in perpetuum ignouit, acclines feminei fastus preces pro magno exosculatus; erat enim eius*h* in baptismo filiola.
8 Offensarum igitur erat immemor, culparum quatenus non deberet remissor, omnibus pro uoto respondens adeuntibus,*i* ne tristes dimitteret, et*j* quod*k* dare non posset compromittens.*l* Qua morum dulcedine, qui laudari et subiectorum amorem mercari debuerat, adeo in contemptum sui Normannos exacuit ut nullius eum momenti estimarent. Tunc enim potentum quisque sibi aduersari, tunc*m* manubiae predarum per totam regionem agi, tunc uulgus expoliari. Quas incommoditates comiti prouintiales deferentes nullum referebant auxilium, dum ille primo commotus, mox uel munusculis uel
9 temporis intercessu ira languescente leniebatur. Iccirco, extremis malis

a pelicis *T'Al* (-ces *Aap*)   *b* pietatis *CBk*, indolis *Bc*   *c* socer ei *T'A*
d-d mimorum (nummorum *Tp*) et nebulonum sinibus ita ingessit *T'A*   *e* eius inf. *T'Al*
(eius *om. Aap*)   *f* hoc *A*   *g* auxilio *CB, from above*   *h* om. *T'*
i adeuntes *B*   *j* etiam *TpAB*   *k* qu(a)e *T'A*   *l* repromittens *C (cf. GP*
p. 48)   *m* om. *C*

He had married in Apulia on his way home a daughter of William of 6
Conversano, to whose miraculous beauty the efforts of the most eloquent
pen could scarce do justice; but after a few years she fell sick and died,
having been misled (so the story goes) by the advice of a midwife [T¹A
mistress], who had told her when she was in childbed to restrain the
superabundant flow of milk by very tight lacing of her breasts. One
consolation there was to lighten this great misfortune, the son born to
him by his wife, who was called William for the good omen of his
grandfather's name, and encouraged hopes of great worth in the future.
His father-in-law had paid him vast sums in cash by way of dowry, that
by use of these he might free Normandy from mortgage; and these he
dissipated [T¹A he flung into the laps of actors and wastrels] to such a
tune that in a very few days there was not a penny left. His reputation 7
also suffered severely from an imprudent expedition into England,
intended to wrest the kingdom from his brother Henry; those who had
invited him deserted and left him in the lurch, and he was glad to make
peace with his brother with the support of the leaders on both sides, in
return for the nominal payment of an annual gift of three thousand
marks from England. The king had promised him this with no intention
of paying it; he knew his brother's easy-going ways, and had made game
of his complaisance and credulity to give the passions of war time to cool
down. In fact the duke, as though he had a competition with Fortune
whether she could give him more than he could throw away, simply
because he understood that the queen so wished it from her silent
pleading, blandly forgave in perpetuity the payment of this enormous
sum of coin, welcoming the humble supplications of that proud woman
as though they were some great thing; for she was his god-daughter.

He was, then, a man with no memory for wrongs done to him, and 8
forgave offences beyond what was right; to all who came to him he gave
the answer they desired, rather than send them away disappointed, and
anything that he could not give, he promised. By this gentleness of
character, a man who ought to have been praised for it, and to have
won the affection of his subjects, goaded the Normans into such contempt that they thought him of no account at all. At that time the
powerful men were all at odds with one another, there was plunder and
rapine throughout the province, and the common people were stripped
of all they had. When the people of the province brought these disorders to the notice of the duke, they came away empty-handed; he was
stirred to begin with, but a little money, or lapse of time, soon cooled
his resentment, and he was pacified. Consequently they were moved by 9

ammoniti, opem regis Henrici censuere implorandam, ut laboranti*a* patriae succurreret.*b* Ille Cesarianae sententiae assistens: 'Si uiolandum est ius, gratia ciuium uiolandum est; aliis rebus pietatem colas',[1] non semel in Normanniam uires traiecit, ut laboranti iustitiae manum daret; tantumque postremo ualuit ut totam terram preter Rotomagum et Falesium et Cadomum subiugaret. Iamque ad hoc Rotbertus uenerat, ut in uicis illis pene se altero uagaretur, precarium uictum a burgensibus nundinans.*c* Quare offensi Cadomenses non diu in fide mansere, sed, rege per nuntios ammonito, portis seratis et repagulis obiectis urbem clausere. Quo Rotbertus cognito effugere gestiens, uix permissus est, armigero tamen cum cubiculi*d* pannis retento. Inde raptim Rotomagum ueniens, dominum suum regem Francorum et cognatum comitem Flandrensem de suffragio conuenit; sed nullo impetrato ad bellum publicum uenit, ultimam fortunam experturus. Qua illum infelici pede prosequente captus, ad

*e*hunc diem in libera tenetur custodia, laudabili fratris pietate quod nichil preter solitudinem patiatur mali, si solitudo dici potest ubi et custodum diligentia et iocorum preterea et obsoniorum non deest frequentia. Tenetur ergo omnium sotiorum uiae superstes, et utrum aliquando sit exiturus uero uacillante in dubio.*e*

*e*diem mortis in libera tentus est custodia, laudabili fratris pietate quod nichil preter solitudinem passus sit mali, si solitudo dici potest ubi et custodum diligentia et iocorum preterea et obsoniorum non deerat frequentia. Tenebatur ergo sotiorum omnium uiae superstes, nec umquam usque obitum relaxatus.*e*

Patria lingua facundus, ut sit iocundior nullus; in aliis consiliosus, ut nichil excellentius; militiae peritus, ut si quis umquam; pro mollitie tamen animi numquam regendae reipublicae idoneus iudicatus. Veruntamen quia*f* superius dixi quaecumque noram de Hugone Magno et Blesensi et Flandrensi*g*[2] comitibus, non incongrue, ut opinor, quartum librum hac meta concludam.

---

a labanti *T'A** (*cf. 8. 2;* laboranti *appears below*)   *b* subueniret *T'*   *c* nundinaturus *Bk,* -natus *Bc*   *d* cubili *B*   *e-e* hunc ... dubio *T'A;* diem ... relaxatus *CB*   *f T'A add* iam   *g* Flandrita *T'A* (*cf. 357. 1*)

[1] Suet. *Iul.* xxx. 5 (citing Cicero, *De officiis* iii. 82).
[2] See Index s. nn. Robert II, count of Flanders and Stephen, count of Blois.

their desperate straits to implore the help of King Henry, and beg him to succour his native land in its necessity. Henry, subscribing to Caesar's opinion: 'If you must break the law, break it in the interest of your fellow citizens; in every other case, you should mind your duty',[1] took his forces across to Normandy more than once to rescue justice in its extremity, and so strong was he in the end that he subdued the whole country except Rouen, Falaise, and Caen. Robert was by now reduced to the point of wandering from one of those towns to another, with hardly a single companion, haggling with the burgesses for a precarious livelihood. This was too much for the people of Caen, and they did not long remain in their allegiance, but sending messengers to inform the king, they bolted and barred their gates and closed the town. When Robert discovered this and wanted to get away, he obtained permission with difficulty, and the squire was forced to remain behind with his sorry bed-linen. He hurried thence to Rouen, and appealed to his lord the king of the French and his kinsman the count of Flanders for support; but not receiving any, he was reduced to overt war, to try a last throw with Fortune. But she pursued him with hostile intent. He was captured,

T¹A and remains in open confinement until the present time, having to thank his brother's praiseworthy sense of duty that he has nothing worse to suffer than solitude, if solitude it can be called when he enjoys the continual attention of his guards, and plenty of amusement and good eating. He is held, then, surviving all the companions of his journey, and it is uncertain whether he will ever be allowed free again.	CB and kept in open confinement until the day of his death, having to thank his brother's praiseworthy sense of duty that he had nothing worse to suffer than solitude, if solitude it can be called when he was enjoying the continual attention of his guards, and plenty of amusement and good eating. So he was held in captivity until he survived all the companions of his journey, and was never released until the day of his death.

He was a good speaker in his native tongue, and no one was better company; in the case of other men a wise counsellor, surpassed by none; an experienced soldier if any man ever was; yet for his softheartedness never thought fit to rule a commonwealth. In any case, as I have already set down all I know of Hugh the Great and the counts of Blois and Flanders,[2] this will, I think, be a suitable place to conclude my fourth book.

LIBER QVINTVS

Prologus libri quinti

Ordine rerum uocante[a] tempus Henrici regis ingressi sumus, cuius gesta stili offitio posteris tradere maioris quam a nobis debeat exquiri[b] est operae; nam et si sola quae nostras aures attigerunt scripto mandarentur, cuiuslibet eloquentissimi neruos fatigare et grandia possent armaria grauare. Quis ergo conetur omnia illa consiliorum pondera, illa gestorum regalium[c] molimina enucleatim retexere? Altioris sunt ista negotii et otiosioris animi. Vix haec auderet uel Cicero in prosa, cuius adorat sales tota Latinitas,[d] uel si quis uersuum fauore Mantuanum lacessit poetam. Adde quod, dum ambiguis relatoribus fidem[e] detraho, homo procul ab aulicis misteriis secretus, maiora gesta ignorans, paucis manum appono. Quare uerendum est ne, dum litterae distant[f] ab animi uoto, minor [g]uideatur cuius gesta multa preterero.[g] Veruntamen huius culpae, si culpa dicenda est, bona erit apud illum deprecatio qui meminerit me nec omnia eius gesta potuisse nosse,[h] [i]nec omnia quae noueram[i] scriptum iri debuisse; alterum exegerit personae meae exilitas, alterum coactura sit lecturorum satietas. Pauca igitur rerum eius liber hic quintus suo uendicabit gremio; cetera proculdubio et seret fama et uictura in posteros feret memoria. Nec uero a proposito priorum quattuor degenerabit, sed quaedam quae hic et alias eius acciderunt tempore procudet, quae forsitan uel non scripta uel multis sunt incognita. Occupabunt itaque ista[j] magnam partem uoluminis, prefata uenia tam longarum digressionum et in hoc et in aliis.

390. Henricus, iunior filius[k] Willelmi Magni, natus est in Anglia anno tertio[l] postquam pater eam adierat, infans iam tum[m] omnium uotis conspirantibus educatus egregie, quod solus omnium[n] filiorum Willelmi natus esset regie, et ei[o] regnum uideretur[p] competere. Itaque tirocinium rudimentorum in scolis egit[q] litteralibus, et librorum[r]

---

[a] ducente T^l [b] om. AB   [c] reg. gest. T^l [d] Lat. tota T^l
[e] fidem amb. rel. T^l [f] distent T^l [g-g] putetur quem ueraciter laudare intendo T^l [h] nosse potuisse T^l [i-i] nec ea que noueram omnia T^l [j] ita B   [k] filius iunior T^l [l] tercio anno T^l [m] non $BkBc^2$, om. Bc^l
[n] om. T^l [o] T^l adds quandoque   [p] uidebatur T^l [q] transegit T^l
[r] T^lC; littera Al(lit(t)erarum $Aa)BkBc^2$ (litteralia Bc^l)

BOOK FIVE

Prologue

Following the order of events, I have arrived at the time of King Henry; but to record his actions in writing for the benefit of posterity is a larger task than can fairly be demanded of me. Even were I to set down those deeds alone which have come to my knowledge, they might exhaust the strength of the readiest writer, and overload many a capacious book-cupboard. Who then can try to recount in detail all his weighty counsels and his great kingly enterprises? They need further research and greater leisure than I can command. Scarcely would Cicero hazard them in prose, whose brilliance makes him the idol of the Latin world, nor any rival of the bard of Mantua (if such there be) in verse. Besides which, resolved as I am not to trust dubious authorities, yet being a man remote from the mysteries of the court, I am ill-informed about his greater achievements, and can lay my hands on little; with the resultant risk that what I write will fall far short of what I should like, and I shall make him seem a lesser man by omitting many of his exploits. Yet this deficiency, if it is one, will readily obtain forgiveness from one who bears in mind that I could not possibly know the whole story, and indeed was under a duty not to set down all I knew; my personal insignificance made the first inevitable, the second will be demanded by my reader's patience. This fifth book therefore will embrace only a selection of his acts; the rest no doubt will be spread abroad by fame, and tradition long-enduring will transmit them to posterity. It will, however, maintain the principle of the previous four, and set forth some events which happened in his time both here and elsewhere, and are perhaps either unrecorded, or unknown to many. These then will claim a large part of the book, and let me for such long digressions, both in this and in the earlier books, bespeak the reader's pardon.

390. Henry, the youngest son of William the Great, was born in England two years after his father's arrival. The centre of all men's hopes while still an infant, he received a princely education, for he alone of all William's sons was born a prince, and the throne seemed destined to be his. So he served his apprenticeship to learning in the

mella adeo auidis medullis indidit ut nulli postea bellorum tumultus, nulli curarum motus eas excutere illustri animo*a* possent. Quanuis ipse nec multum palam legeret nec nisi summisse cantitaret, fuerunt tamen,*b* ut uere confirmo, litterae, quanuis tumultuarie libatae, magna supellex ad regnandum scientiae, iuxta illam Platonis sententiam, qua dicit[1] beatam esse rempublicam si uel philosophi regnarent uel reges
2 philosopharentur. Philosophia ergo non adeo exiliter informatus, sensim discebat ut successu temporis prouintiales mitius contineret, milites nonnisi diligentissime explorata necessitate committere sineret. Itaque pueritiam ad spem regni litteris muniebat, subinde, patre quoque*c* audiente, iactitare prouerbium solitus 'rex illiteratus asinus coronatus'.[2] Ferunt quin etiam genitorem, non pretereunter notata morum eius compositione quibus uiuacem prudentiam aleret, ab uno fratrum lesum et lacrimantem his animasse: 'Ne fleas, fili, quoniam et tu rex eris.'

391. Vicesimo ergo primo regni paterni anno, *d*etatis suae nono decimo,*d* in Pentecoste apud Westmonasterium sumpsit arma a patre, cum quo tunc Normanniam nauigans, *e*non multo post presens funeri eius*e* astitit, ceteris fratribus quo quemque*f* spes tulerat dilapsis, ut superior sermo non occuluit.[3] Quapropter paterna benedictione et materna hereditate, simul et multiplicibus thesauris nixus, supercilium germanorum parum fatiebat, utrique uel assistens uel aduersans pro merito; inclinatior porro Rotberto pro mansuetudine, eius lenitatem suo rigore satagebat acuere. *g*Contra ille, noxia facilitate delatoribus credulus, fratrem immeritum iniuriis uexabat, quas uel breuiter taxare non erit incongruum.

392. Eo tempore quo, frementibus aduersus Willelmum secundum Angliae proceribus, Rotbertus in Normannia uentum prosperum expectabat ad nauigandum, Henricus in Britanniam eius iussu abscesserat. Tum ille occasione aucupata omnem illam pecuniarum uim testamento patris adolescentulo legatam, quae erat trium milium

a ill. an. exc. *T'*   *b* *T'* * *adds* ei   *c* quoque patre *T'*   *d–d* *om.* *T'*
e–e post annum presens eius funeri *T'*   *f* quecumque *CBk*   *g–g* (*p. 712*) *om.* *T'*

---

[1] Plato, *Republic* 473c–d, known to William from Lactantius, *Div. inst.* iii. 21. 6, or Jerome, *Comm. in Ionam* 3: 6–9 (*PL* xxv. 1143A). Cf. also 126. 3, 449. 1.
[2] Walther, *Proverbia* 26852.

grammar school, and with such eagerness did he absorb the honeyed sweets of books that in later life war's alarms and the thronging cares of peace were alike unable to dislodge them from his noble heart. Though he himself read little openly and never chanted except in an undertone, yet I can affirm for a truth that literature, despite his haphazard acquaintance with it, was to him a great storehouse of political wisdom, which bears out Plato's opinion[1] that a state would be happy if philosophers were kings, or kings philosophers. So, as he acquired more than a tincture of philosophy, he gradually learnt how to ride his subjects with a lighter rein as time went on, and to withhold his knights from every engagement that was not most clearly seen to be inevitable. In this way while still a youth he equipped himself by education to realize his royal hopes, and used even in his father's hearing to make play with the proverb 'a king unlettered is a donkey crowned'.[2] They say too that his father, who had a more than passing knowledge of his character, in which he sought to develop energy and prudence, found him one day in tears after one of his brothers had hurt him, and encouraged him by saying: 'Do not cry, my son; you too shall be a king.'

391. In the twenty-first year of his father's reign, when he was nineteen, he was knighted on Whitsunday at Westminster by his father. He then crossed with him into Normandy, and there, not long after, was present at his funeral, the other brothers being scattered each in pursuit of his own ambitions, as has been already told.[3] Thus enjoying his father's blessing and his mother's inheritance, and being well supplied with money, he made light of his brothers' disdain, supporting or opposing either as they happened to deserve. Robert's good nature made him the favourite, but Henry tried to put an edge on this mildness by his own severity. His brother in return showed a dangerous readiness to believe malicious gossip, and wronged the innocent Henry in ways of which a brief account will not be out of place.

392. At the time when the nobles of England were in revolt against William II, and Robert was in Normandy awaiting a favourable wind before he crossed, Henry at his bidding had retired to Brittany. Robert seized the opportunity, and spent on the payment of his troops the whole sum of money, amounting to three thousand marks,

[3] c. 283.

marcarum, in stipendiarios suos absumpsit. Id Henricus reuersus, licet forsitan egre tulisset, taciturna preteriit industria; enimuero, nuntiata pacis compositione in Anglia, deposita militia ferias armis dedere.
2 Comes in sua, iunior in ea quae frater suus uel[a] dederat uel promiserat discessit. Namque et in acceptum promissa referebat, custodiens turrem Rotomagi in eius fidelitatem; sed delatione pessimorum cessit in aduersum fidelitas, et nulla sua culpa in ipso eodem loco Henricus libere custoditus est, ne seruatorum diligentiam effugio luderet. Post medium annum laxatus, fratri Willelmo inuitanti seruiturum se obtulit; at ille, nichilo modestius ephebum remunerans, plus anno inanibus sponsionibus egentem distulit. Quapropter, Rotberto emendationem facti per nuntios promittente, Normanniam uenit, amborum fratrum
3 expertus insidias. Nam et rex pro repulsa iratus ut retineretur frustra mandarat, et comes accusatorum lenociniis mutatus uoluntatem uerterat, ut blanditiis attractum non ita facile dimitteret. Verum ille, Dei prouidentia et sagaci sui diligentia cuncta euadens pericula, occupatione Abrincarum et quorundam castellorum coegit fratrem libenter paci manum dedere.

Nec multo post, Willelmo ueniente in Normanniam ut se de fratre Rotberto[b] ulcisceretur, comiti obsequelam suam exhibuit, Rotomagi positus. Denique regios eo interdiu uenientes, qui dolo ciuium totam iam pridem occupauerant urbem, probe[c] expulit, ammonito per nuntios comite ut ille a fronte propelleret quos ipse a tergo
4 urgeret.[g] Vnde factum est ut Conanum quendam, proditionis apud comitem insimulatum, quem ille uinculis irretire uolebat, arbitratus nichil calamitosius posse inferri[d] misero quam ut exosum spiritum in ergastulo traheret—hunc ergo Conanum Henricus suae curae seruatum iri postulauit. Quo concesso, in superiora Rotomagensis turris duxit, iussoque ut late circumposita diligenter ex arcis edito[e] specularetur, sua per hironiam omnia futura pronuntians, inopinum ex propugnaculo deturbans[f] in subiectum[g] Sequanam precipitauit,
5 comitibus qui secum aderant pariter impellentibus, protestatus nullam

[a] om. ABc   [b] om. A   [c] proprie Al, om. Aa   [g] See above, p. 710
[d] inferre A   [e] edito arcis T[t]   [f] turbans T[t]   [g] subiectam Aac

left to young Henry in his father's will. Henry on his return, resent this as he might, deliberately overlooked it and said nothing; indeed, hearing that peace was concluded in England, they laid aside their arms and brought their warfare to an end. The duke retired to his own territory, and the younger prince to the lands given or promised to him by his brother; the promised lands he reckoned as already his, and garrisoned the castle of Rouen as Robert's loyal vassal. But by malice and misrepresentation this loyalty turned to Henry's hurt, and though he had done no wrong, he was placed under open arrest in that same castle, so that he could not elude the vigilance of his keepers and escape. After half a year he was released, and accepted an invitation to enter the service of his brother William; but William showed no greater sense of decency in rewarding the young man, and fobbed him off in his necessity for more than a year with empty promises. So when Robert sent and offered him redress, he returned to Normandy, having found that neither of his brothers was to be trusted. The king had taken his defection badly, and had in vain commanded that he should be detained; and the duke, converted by the winning words of Henry's opponents, had changed his policy, and after tempting him with kind offers, was not so ready to let him go. But Henry, through God's providence and his own prudence and energy, avoided every danger, and by occupying Avranches and several castles, forced his brother gladly to come to terms.

Not long after, William crossed into Normandy to take reprisals on his brother Robert, and Henry, who was then at Rouen, lent his support to the duke. For instance, the royal troops, aided by treachery among the citizens, had occupied the whole city some time before; but when they advanced in daylight on the castle, he roundly drove them out, sending a message to advise the duke to make a frontal attack while he pressed hard upon their rear. As a result, when a certain Conan was charged with treason before the duke, and Robert was minded to load him with chains, thinking that no direr penalty could be inflicted on the wretch than a long and hateful life in prison, Henry demanded that the fellow should be reserved for his own attentions. This being granted, he took him up to the summit of the keep at Rouen, and told him carefully to survey the wide prospect visible from the tower's top, with the assurance (it was a bitter jest) that all would soon be his; then caught him off his guard, and, with a helping hand from the companions who were with him, threw him from the battlements down headlong into the Seine below. A traitor, he assured

uitae moram deberi traditori: quoquo modo alieni hominis posse tolerari iniurias; illius uero qui tibi iuratus fecerit hominium*a* nullo modo posse differri suplitium, si fuerit probatus perfidiae. *b*Parum hic labor apud Rotbertum ualuit, uirum animi mobilis, qui, statim ad ingratitudinem flexus, bene meritum urbe cedere coegit. Illud fuit tempus quo, ut supra lectum est,[1] apud Montem sancti Michahelis ambobus fratribus Henricus pro sui salute simul et gloria restitit.*b* Ita, cum utrique germano*c* fuerit fidelis et efficax, illi, nullis adolescentem possessionibus dignati, ad maiorem prudentiam eui processu*d* penuria uictualium*e* informabant.

393. Occiso uero rege Willelmo, ut supra dictum est,[2] post iusta funeri regio persoluta in regem electus est, aliquantis tamen ante controuersiis inter proceres agitatis atque sopitis, annitente maxime *f*comite Warwicensi Henrico, uiro*f* integro et sancto, cuius familiari iam dudum usus fuerat contubernio. Itaque edicto statim per Angliam misso iniustitias a fratre et Rannulfo institutas prohibuit, pensionum et uinculorum gratiam fecit; effeminatos curia propellens, lucernarum usum noctibus in curia restituit, qui fuerat tempore fratris intermissus; antiquarum moderationem legum reuocauit in solidum, sacramento 2 suo et omnium procerum ne luderentur corroborans. Laetus ergo dies uisus est*g* reuirescere populis, cum post tot anxietatum nubila serenarum promissionum infulgebant lumina. Et ne quid perfecto gaudio accumulato*h* abesset, Rannulfo nequitiarum fece*i* tenebris ergastularibus incluso, propter Anselmum pernicibus nuntiis directum. Quapropter certatim*j* plausu plebeio concrepante, in regem coronatus est*k* Lundoniae nonis Augustis,*l* quarto post obitum fratris die. Haec eo studiosius celerabantur,*m* ne mentes procerum electionis quassarentur penitudine, quod ferebatur rumor Rotbertum Normanniae comi- 3 tem ex Apulia aduentantem iam iamque affore. Nec multo post, suadentibus amicis ac*n* maxime pontificibus ut remota uoluptate pelicum legitimum amplecteretur conubium, die sancti Martini accepit Mathildem filiam Malcolmi regis Scottorum, cuius amori iam pridem animum impulerat, paruipendens dotales diuitias, dum modo diu cupitis potiretur amplexibus. Erat enim illa, licet genere sullimis

a hominum *CeB*   *b–b* om. *T¹*   *c* fratri *T¹*   *d* successu *T¹*
e inactualium *A*   *f–f* Henrico com. Waruicensi uiro fide *T¹*   *g* est uisus *A*
h profecto *(so also Aap, rightly?)* acc. gaud. *T¹*   *i* face *Barlow*   *j* statim *A*   *k* om. *B*   *l* Augusti *T¹Bk*   *m* celebrabantur *CeB*   *n* et *T¹*

[1] c. 308.   [2] 333. 4.

them, deserves no respite; wrongs done by another man's man can somehow or another be tolerated, but if a man who has done homage on his oath is proved a traitor, his punishment can in no wise be deferred. This effort did Henry little good with his brother Robert, a man of inconstant temper; and Robert, turning at once ungrateful, drove his benefactor out of the city. It was at this time that, as has been told above,[1] Henry had to resist both his brothers, in defence of his own safety as well as reputation, at Mont-Saint-Michel. So it was: he was faithful and helpful to each in turn, but neither of them thought fit to give the young man any lands of his own, and they let him learn greater knowledge of the world with the passage of time in the hard school of poverty.

393. On the killing of King William, related above,[2] when the last rites had been paid to the royal corpse, Henry was chosen king, some preliminary disputes among the nobles having first been settled, chiefly by the efforts of Henry earl of Warwick, a man of the highest character whose intimate friendship he had long enjoyed. In a proclamation immediately despatched throughout England, he prohibited the unjust practices of his brother and Ranulf, remitted imposts, freed prisoners, and purged his court of effeminates, restoring the use of lamps at night which had been given up in his brother's time; the just rule of our ancient laws he re-established to the full, confirming them by his own oath and the oath of all his nobles, that none should make game of them. A day of happiness seemed to 2 dawn once more upon the nation; all the clouds of anxiety were past, and the morn shone bright with promise of fair weather. That their cup of happiness might be full, he plunged the arch-villain Ranulf in the darkness of the prison-house, and sent in haste for Anselm. And so the crowds vied with each other in their hurrahs when he was crowned king, in London on 5 August, three days after his brother's death. These measures were taken with all speed, for fear that the nobles might repent of his election, shaken by the rumour that Robert duke of Normandy was on his way from Apulia and would at any moment be upon them. Not long after, urged by 3 his friends and especially the bishops to abandon the embrace of his mistresses and to enter lawful wedlock, he married at Martinmas Matilda, daughter of Malcolm king of the Scots. To love of her his mind had long since been turned, and a rich dowry was in his eyes of no account, if he could but secure the affections of one whom he

utpote regis Eduardi ex fratre Edmundo abneptis, modicae tamen*a* domina supellectilis, utroque tunc parente pupilla. De qua posterius uberior erit*b* narrandi materia.[1]

394. Rotbertus interea, Normanniam ueniens, comitatum suum obsistente nullo recepit. Quo audito, omnes pene huius terrae*c* optimates fidei regi iuratae transfugae fuere, quidam nullis extantibus causis, quidam leuibus occasiunculis emendicatis, quod nollet eis terras quas uellent ultro*d* pro libito eorum*e* impertiri. Soli Rotbertus filius Haimonis et*f* Ricardus de Retuers et Rogerius Bigot et Rotbertus comes de Mellento cum fratre Henrico iustas partes fouebant. Ceterum*g* omnes uel clam pro Rotberto, ut rex fieret, mittere, uel palam contumeliis dominum inurere, Godricum eum et comparem Godgiuam 2 appellantes. Audiebat haec ille, et formidabiles cachinnos iram differens eitiebat, stultitias fatuorum insania obiectas artifitioso silentio dissoluens, blandus odii dissimulator, sed pro tempore immodicus retributor. Accessit temporum turbini uersutia Rannulfi; namque ille, sollicitato per nuntios dapifero suo, funem afferri sibi impetrauit. Funem minister aquae baiulus, proh dolus,*h* amphora immersum detulit;*i* quo ille muro turris demissus, si lesit brachia, si excoriauit manus, parum curat populus. Inde Normanniam euadens, comiti iam anhelanti et in feruorem prelii prono addidit calcaria ut incunctanter ueniret.

395. Secundo ergo Henrici anno, mense Augusto, allitans apud Portesmuthe copias suas in omnem regionem exposuit, effudit, obiecit. Nec uero rex segnitiei deditus fuit, sed innumeram e regione manum contraxit,*j* dignitatem suam si necesse foret asserturus. Nam, licet principibus defitientibus, partes eius solidae manebant, quas Anselmi archiepiscopi cum episcopis*k* suis, simul et omnium Anglorum tutabatur fauor. Quapropter ipse prouintialium fidei gratus et saluti prouidus, plerumque cuneos circuiens docebat quomodo, militum ferotiam eludentes, clipeos obiectarent et ictus remitterent; quo effecit ut ultroneis uotis pugnam deposcerent, in nullo Normannos 2 metuentes. Sed satagentibus sanioris consilii hominibus, qui dicerent

a om. T' *b* erit uberior T' *c* terr(a)e huius (om. pene) T' *d* om. A *e* eorum libito T' *f* om. C *g* ceteri Bk, preferably *h* proh dolus (dolor CsB) om. T' *i* attulit T' *j* traxit C *k* coepiscopis T'A

[1] c. 418.

had long desired; she was in fact, although of exalted rank as a great-great-niece of King Edward through his brother Edmund, mistress of only a modest fortune, being an orphan without either parent. Of her there will be more to be said hereafter.[1]

394. Robert meanwhile reached Normandy, and resumed his domain without opposition; on hearing which, nearly all the English nobles threw over the homage they had pledged to the king, some of them for no obvious reason, and others on some slight and trumped-up excuse, for instance because he was unwilling to satisfy their appetites with grants of land. Only Robert Fitz Hamon, Richard de Redvers, and Roger Bigod, and also Robert count of Meulan with his brother Henry, supported the true cause. All either sent secretly for Robert offering to make him king, or openly insulted their own lord, calling him Godric and his consort Godgifu. Henry listened to their gibes, with sudden bursts of ferocious laughter, biding his time; in politic silence he let the crazy attacks of fools expend themselves, hiding his resentment under a mask of courtesy, but ready to strike back hard when the time should come. The cunning of Ranulf added to the stormy scene; he sent repeated appeals to his steward asking for a rope, and the servant who brought him water (O the cunning of it!) conveyed a rope coiled up in the water-jar. With this he let himself down from the tower wall, and if he bruised his arms and grazed his hands, all's one for that. Thence he made his way to Normandy, where he found the duke already panting with eagerness for the fray, and spurred him on to come forthwith.

395. So in the second year of Henry's reign, in the month of August, Robert landed in Portsmouth, and rapidly deployed his forces in the surrounding country. Nor was the king a prey to inaction; he got together a large force in opposition, to defend his authority should need arise; for his party held solidly together though its leaders had deserted, and the support of Archbishop Anselm with his fellow bishops and of all the English was a tower of strength. So Henry himself, grateful for his subjects' loyalty and careful for their safety, went constantly through their ranks, teaching them how to counter fierce cavalry attacks by holding their shields before them and returning blow for blow. As a result, they lost all their fear of the Normans, and actually demanded to be allowed to fight. But wiser heads were active, saying that the law of natural affection must be broken if brother with

pietatis ius uiolandum si fraterna necessitudo prelio concurreret, paci animos accommodauere, reputantes quod, si alter occumberet, alter infirmior remaneret, cum nullus fratrum preter ipsos superesset. Sed et trium milium marcarum[a] promissio lenem comitis fallebat credulitatem,[b] ut procinctu soluto de tanta pecunia menti blandiretur suae: quam[c] ille posteriori statim anno uoluntati reginae libens, quod illa peteret, condonauit.

396. Posteriori anno rebellauit Rotbertus de Belesmo, maior filiorum Rogerii de Monte Gomerico, offirmans contra regem castella Brigas et Arundellum. Comportatum eo frumentum ex omni regione Scrobbesberiae, et quicquid necessarium bellum efflagitat diuturnum; nec minus castellum Scrobbesberiense rebellioni consensit, Walensibus pro motu fortunae ad malum pronis. Rex itaque animo ingens omniaque aduersa uirtute premens, militia coacta[d] Brigas obsedit, unde iam in[e] Arundellum transierat Rotbertus, alimentorum copia et militum ferotia satis habundeque munitum locum presumens; sed paucos post dies oppidani, et formidine conscientiae et fortitudine militiae regiae[f] flexi, se dedidere. Quo audito, ab incepto tumore Arundellum destitit, regali[g] se addicens[h] clientelae, egregia sane conditione, ut dominus suus integra membrorum salute Normanniam permitteretur abire. Porro Scrobbesberienses per Radulfum tum[i] abbatem Sagii, postea Cantuariae archiepiscopum, regi misere castelli claues, deditionis presentis indices, futurae deuotionis[j] obsides. Ita dissensionis incendium, quod putabatur fore magnum, paucissimis[k] diebus in cineres consenuit et desertorum semper nouis[l] rebus inhiantium auiditatem cohercuit. Rotbertus cum fratribus Ernulfo, qui paternum cognomen[m] sortitus fuerat, et Rogerio Pictauensi (quod ex ea regione uxorem acceperat sic dicto) Angliam perpetuo abiurauit, sed uigorem sacramenti temperauit adiectio, nisi regi placito quandoque satisfecisset obsequio.

397. Tunc fax bellorum immissa Normanniae, perfidorum admixtione quasi rogalibus alimentis animata, conualuit, circumquaque posita corripiens. Est enim Normannia oportuna et patiens malorum

[a] marc(h)arum milium *A*   [b] credulitatem (crudel- *Tt; so too Aap*) fallebat *T'*   [c] quas *T'*   [d] *T' adds* primo   [e] om. *T'*   [f] reg. mil. *A*   [g] regi(a)e *T'*   [h] adiciens *T'*   [i] tunc *T'A (cf. esp. 445. 2)*   [j] deu. fut. *T'*   [k] paucis *A*   [l] nouis semper *T'*   [m] cog. pat. *T'*

brother were to meet in battle; so they resigned themselves to the prospect of peace, and reflected that if one were killed, the other would be left weaker, since no brother still lived except themselves. Besides this, the easy and credulous duke was taken in with the promise of three thousand marks, with the idea that he could disband his expedition, and indulge his fancy with this large sum of money; but the following year at the queen's request he relinquished it of his own accord to give her pleasure.

396. The following year Robert of Bellême, eldest son of Roger of Montgomery, rebelled, and fortified against the king the castles of Bridgnorth and Arundel, collecting in Bridgnorth corn from the whole of Shropshire and everything required for a war of some duration. The castle of Shrewsbury also joined in the rebellion, the Welsh being always ready to do ill, as changing fortune leads. The king's spirit ran high, and bearing down everything in his way by his personal courage, he got together a force of knights and laid siege to Bridgnorth. Robert had already left for Arundel, supposing the place fully secured by its ample supplies and brave defenders; but after a few days' siege, the townsmen were moved to surrender by their own bad consciences and the strength of the royal force. On hearing the news, Arundel abandoned its ambitious intentions and joined the king's allegiance, though on unusual terms, for its lord was allowed without physical harm to leave for Normandy. Then the defenders of Shrewsbury, by the hand of Ralph at that time abbot of Séez and afterwards archbishop of Canterbury, sent the king the keys of the castle as an indication of surrender at the moment and an earnest of loyalty for the future. Thus the fires of rebellion, instead of the expected conflagration, died down in a very few days into ashes, checking the ambition of those traitors who are always ready for revolution. Robert with his brothers, Arnulf who had inherited his father's name, and Roger of Poitou, so called as having married a wife from that part of the world, foreswore England for life; but the rigour of his oath was moderated by the proviso 'unless he should at some future date satisfy the king by acceptable submission'.

397. At that time a torch was set to the fire of conflict in Normandy, and encouraged by these disloyal elements, which were as fuel to the flames, it was soon well alight and spreading all around. Normandy has no great expanse of territory, but she is a convenient

nutricula, quanuis non multo tractu regionum diffusa; itaque diu seditiones intestinas probe tolerat, et pace reddita in fecundiorem statum mature resurgit, turbatores suos illius prouintiae diffisos*a* cum libuerit in Frantiam*b* liberis anfractibus emittens. Contra Anglia nec diu infestos patitur, sed semel intra sinum suum receptos uel dedit uel extinguit, nec populatibus attrita rediuiuum cito caput*c* attollit. Quocirca Normanniam Belesmitanus ueniens et tunc et deinceps habuit malignitatis suae complices et, ne parum uideretur, illices. In his erat Willelmus comes Moretolii, filius Rotberti regis patrui. Is semper a puero Henrici gloriae inuidus, tum maxime in aduentu Normanni[1] prauum animum extulit; non enim contentus duobus comitatibus,*d* Moretolii in Normannia, Cornugalliae in Anglia, comitatum Cantiae, quem Odo patruus habuerat, a rege exigebat, infestus et improbus adeo ut infami arrogantia se deuotaret non induturum clamidem nisi a patruo, ut dictitabat,*e* sibi refusam consequeretur hereditatem. Sed tunc quidem suspensi calliditate responsi frustratus est rex prudentissimus hominem; discussis uero turbinibus serenoque pacis reddito, non solum quae petebat non annuit uerum etiam indebite retenta repetere cepit, modeste*f* tamen et iuditiali placito, ut nichil quod faceret uideretur resultare iuri et calcitrare ab aequo. Tunc*g* uero Willelmus, sententia iuditii expunctus, indignabundus et fremens Normanniam abiit. Ibi, preter assultus quos regiis castellis irritus fecerat, in Ricardum quoque comitem Cestrensem, Hugonis filium, debachatus nonnulla partibus eius*h* appenditia inuasit, carpsit, abrasit. Erat ille tunc pro aetate paruulus, et regis fidei tutelaeque accommodatus.

398. Hi ergo duo, factionum capita, rebellionum incentiua, cum aliis quos nominare pudet, patriam populationibus late contristabant, consumebanturque frequentes sed cassae apud comitem*i* querelae prouintialium de uiolentia clamantium. Mouebatur his ille, sed rebus suis timens, ne exacerbati eius interpolarent otium, dissimulabat. At uero rex Henricus pro fratris infamia, quam cumulabat patriae miseria, dolorem transeunter ferre nequibat, crudele et a boni principis *j*offitio longe*j* esse permensus, quod impii homines pauperum fortunis

a diffusos *T'Bk* *b* frementiam (*om.* liberis) *B* *c* caput cito *T'*
d com. duobus *T'* *e* dictabat *ABc'* *f* modesto *T'* *g* tum *T'*
h illius *B* *i* apud com. sed cass(a)e *T'* *j–j* cura longe abhorrens *T'*

[1] i.e. Robert of Bellême.

and long-suffering fosterer of the wicked. She has a high tolerance of prolonged internal discord, and when peace is restored soon regains her old fertility, giving the authors of the disorder who dare not trust themselves within her bounds free passage into France whenever it suits. England, on the other hand, cannot put up with an enemy for long; once he has gained admittance, she either surrenders him, or wipes him out, and if she has been much ravaged, she does not quickly lift her head again. So Robert of Bellême, on arriving in Normandy, found both then and afterwards plenty of people to share—more than that, to encourage—his evil designs. Among them was William count of Mortain, son of Robert the king's uncle. From boyhood he had envied Henry his success, and the Norman's[1] arrival was a great moment to give free reign to his ill-will. Not content with two earldoms, Mortain in Normandy and Cornwall in England, he was claiming from the king the earldom of Kent, which his uncle Odo had held. Such was his bitterness and obstinacy that with hideous arrogance he vowed that he would not wear a cloak, until he was allowed to inherit what he asserted passed to him from his uncle. For the moment, however, by a skilful and temporizing reply, the king with his usual wisdom put the man off. When the storm had blown over and all was clear and peaceful once again, he not only refused his request but proceeded to demand the return of what he held wrongfully; this however the king did reasonably and by due process of law, so that none of his actions seemed inequitable or unjust. At that point William, having lost the verdict of the court, flounced off to Normandy in a passion, and there, over and above the fruitless attacks he had made on the king's castles, vented his rage on Richard earl of Chester, Hugh's son, by the invasion, seizure, or pillage of sundry lands which formed part of his possessions, Richard being at that time a minor and the king's ward.

398. So these two ringleaders and firebrands of revolt, with others whom I am ashamed to mention, were reducing their native land to misery by their extensive depredations. Frequent and fruitless were the appeals made to the duke by the provincials complaining of their wrongs; he sympathized, but selfishly fearing that if he provoked the rebels, they would interrupt his own slumbers, he did nothing. As for King Henry, the pain of his brother's dishonour, intensified by the country's wretchedness, was more than he could lightly bear; he clearly saw how outrageous it was, how far from the standard to be expected

2 ingluuiem suam urgebant. Itaque fratrem ad se accitum in Angliam semel blande uerbis, post uero in Normanniam ueniens[a] non semel dure bellis ammonuit, ut comitem non monachum ageret; nam et incentori Willelmo omnia quae habebat[b] in Anglia abstulit, castella ad solum complanauit. Sed cum ad pacem nichil promoueret, diu deliberatione consilii regia sullimitas curis pectus exercuit, utrum fraternae necessitudinis oblitus patriam discrimini eriperet, an indiscreta pietate 3 fluctuare permitteret; et profecto commune commodum et pietas priuatae necessitudinis intuitu terga dedisset, nisi, ut aiunt, Paschalis[c] apostolicus dubitantem ad opus epistolis impelleret, asseuerans facundia qua uigebat non fore ciuile bellum[d] sed preclare patriae predicandum emolumentum. Itaque Normanniam ueniens breui totam cepit,[e] uel potius recepit, omnibus[f] ad eius dominium confluentibus, ut 4 fessae prouintiae uigore quo pollebat consuleret. Non[g] tamen sine sanguine tantam uictoriam consummans, multos ex carissimis amisit, inter quos Rogerium de Gloecestra, probatum militem, in obsessione Falesii arcubalistae iactu in capite percussum; [h]preterea Rotbertum filium Haimonis, qui conto ictus timpora hebetatusque ingenio, non pauco tempore quasi captus mente superuixit. Merito multatum ferunt, quod eius liberandi causa rex Henricus Baiocas ciuitatem cum principali aecclesia ignibus absumpserit. Sed utrique, ut speramus, purgabile fuit; nam et detrimenta aecclesiae rex mirifice resarciuit, et Rotbertus monasterium Theokesberiae suo fauore non facile memoratu quantum exaltauit, ubi et edifitiorum decor et monachorum caritas aduentantium rapit oculos et allicit animos.[h]

5   Horum[i] dispendium ut Fortuna sarciret, summam manum incruente[j] bello imposuit, uenientemque contra se cum non contempnenda manu fratrem[k] et Willelmum comitem Moretolii et Rotbertum[l] Belesmi ditioni eius facili opera contradidit. Hoc bellum actum est apud Tenerchebrei, castellum comitis Moretoliensis, sabbato in sancti Michahelis uigilia. Idem dies ante quadraginta circiter annos fuerat[m] cum Willelmus primus Hastingas appulit, prouido forsitan Dei[n] iuditio ut eo die subderetur Angliae Normannia quo ad eam subiugandam

[a] transiens *T'*   [b] agebat *Tt(corr. to* ab-*)Tp*   [c] *T' adds* episcopus
[d] prelium *T'*   [e] subiugauit *T'*   [f] *T' adds* certatim   [g] *For the version of* CsCa *here see Appendix, pp. 830–32*   [h-h] *om.* *T'*   [i] quod *T'*   [j] ingruente C*(not* Ca*)*B   [k] fratrem *after* se *T'*   [l] Willelmo comite Moritolii et Roberto *T'*   [m] fuerat *after* dies *T'*   [n] Dei forsitan *T'*

of a prince, that criminals should sate their ravenous appetites with the patrimony of the poor. And so he summoned his brother to England, and remonstrated with him once gently by word of mouth, urging him to play the duke and not the monk; after that he went to Normandy and did the same more than once, far from gently, by armed force. William, the ringleader, he deprived of all his possessions in England, and razed his castles to the ground. But finding he made no progress towards peace, the king—his royal heart weary with care—wondered long and anxiously whether to forget the love he owed his brother and save the country from its peril, or with ill-timed affection to leave things to take their course. And really the public interest, the cause of duty, would have retired defeated by his observance of the ties of blood, had not Pope Paschal, as the story goes, sent him a letter urging him in his uncertainty to act, with all his vigorous eloquence maintaining that it would be no civil war, but a historic deliverance to be unreservedly praised by his country. So he entered Normandy, and soon gained—or rather regained—the whole of it; for all men crowded to acknowledge him as lord, hoping that with his characteristic vigour he would take steps to restore the exhausted province. But this great victory was not achieved without bloodshed, and he lost many of his dearest friends, among them the veteran soldier Roger of Gloucester, who was struck on the head by a bolt from a crossbow at the siege of Falaise; besides him Robert Fitz Hamon, who was wounded on the temple with a pike and lost his reason, surviving some considerable time in a state of dotage. They say he deserved his punishment, because in order to set him free King Henry burnt the town of Bayeux with its principal church; but both, we hope, were permitted to earn absolution: the king magnificently restored the damaged church, and Robert by his patronage raised to remarkable eminence the abbey of Tewkesbury, whose splendid buildings and devoted monks dazzle the eyes and charm the heart of their visitors.

To make good these losses, Fortune put the finishing touch to the war without bloodshed, and when his brother advanced against him with a far from negligible force, accompanied by William count of Mortain and Robert of Bellême, she delivered them without effort into his hand. This battle was fought at Tinchebray, a castle of the count of Mortain, on a Saturday, the eve of Michaelmas. It was on the same day, about forty years before, that William the First landed at Hastings; perhaps it was a judgement of Providence that Normandy should submit to England on the very day on which the Norman host

6 olim uenerat Normannorum copia. Captus est ibi comes Moretolii, qui eo uenerat studiosam sui operam[a] oppidanis pollicitus, simul et iniurias suas ultum iri sperans; sed, ut dixi, prensus[b] squaloris carcerei tota uita accolatum accepit, uiuacitate mentis et alacritate iuuentutis nonnichil laudandus, sed pro perfidia finem asperum emeritus. Et tunc quidem Belesmensis in ipso belli exordio mortem cauit effugio; sed dum[c] postmodum clandestinis factionibus regem irritasset, et ipse captus ceterorum inuolutus est periculo, ad mortem perpetuo inclusus 7 ergastulo. Vir [d]pro incompositis moribus intolerabilis[e] et[d] in aliorum delicta inexorabilis; preterea seuitia notabilis cum in aliis[f] tum in hoc, quod puerulum ex baptismo filiolum, quem in obsidatum acceperat, pro modico delicto patris excecarit, lumina miselli unguibus nefandis abrumpens; simulationis et argutiarum plenus, frontis sereno et sermonum affabilitate credulos decipiens, gnaros autem malitiae exterritans, ut nullum esset maius futurae calamitatis inditium quam pretensae affabilitatis eloquium.

399. Ita rex clarus, successibus ouans, regnum regressus[g] est, composita[h] pace in Normannia qualem nulla aetas meminit, qualem nec ipse pater magno illo rerum et uerborum fastu[i] umquam efficere potuit. In ceteris quoque genitoris emulus, rapinas curialium,[j] furta, stupra edicto compescuit, deprehensis oculos cum testibus[k] euelli precipiens. Contra trapezetas, quos uulgo monetarios uocant, precipuam sui diligentiam exhibuit, nullum falsarium, quin pugnum perderet, impune abire permittens qui fuisset intellectus falsitatis suae commertio fatuos irrisisse.

400. Scottorum reges lenitate sua palpauit, morem fratris emulatus; siquidem ille Dunecanum, filium Malcolmi nothum, et militem fecit et regem Scottorum mortuo patre constituit.[l] Sed eo patrui Duuenaldi fraude interempto, Edgarum in regnum promouit, prefato Duuenaldo astutia Dauid iunioris et[m] uiribus Willelmi extincto. Edgaro fatali sorte occumbente, Alexandrum successorem Henricus affinitate[n] detinuit, data ei in coniugium filia notha, de qua ille uiua nec sobolem,

---

[a] operam sui *T'* [b] pressus *B* [c] dum *before* regem *T'* [d-d] omni corporis obscenitate infamis, nec minus *T'* [e] om. *CB* [f] pluribus *T'* [g] ingressus *T'A* [h] magnifico composita apparatu *Tt*, comp. mag. app. *Tp* [i] roncho *T'A* [j] *T' adds* in agrestes [k] cum testibus *om. T'*; cum testiculis *Al*[p.c.]*Aap* [l] mortuo patre reg. Sc. statuit *T'* [m] om. *T'* [n] aff. Henricus *T'*

had once arrived to conquer her. Among the prisoners was the count of Mortain, who had come to fulfil a promise that he would actively support the inmates, but was hoping at the same time to avenge the wrongs he had endured; but, as I say, he was taken captive, and condemned for the rest of his life to the rigours of a prison cell. A man of lively mind and youthful energy, he had many good points, but deserved a harsh ending because of his treachery. Robert of Bellême for the moment escaped death by flight at the very onset of the battle; but later, having provoked the king by his intrigues, he too was captured, and being involved in the others' peril, was imprisoned for life. He was a man of intolerable looseness of conduct, and pitiless towards others' failings; notorious for his cruelty, of which this is an outstanding example. Having taken one of his godsons as a hostage, in return for some small misconduct of the father he blinded the son, gouging out the poor child's eyeballs with his own ghastly nails. Full as he was of pretence and blarney, he would deceive the simple-hearted with his unclouded brow and friendly tongue, while those who knew his black heart shook with fear; for there was no surer sign of impending trouble than a show of fair words from him.

399. And so our famous king returned in triumph to his kingdom, having established such a peace in Normandy as no age has ever seen, and even his father, with his proud record in deed and word, could never make. In other respects too he followed his father's example, and put a stop by proclamation to the ravages, the rape and rapine of his courtiers, ordaining that convicted offenders should lose their eyes and testicles. With the mintmasters, commonly called moneyers, he was particularly strict; no forger was allowed to escape without the loss of a hand, who was found to have deluded simple folk by putting his false coin into circulation.

400. Towards the kings of the Scots he was conciliatory, following the precedent set by his brother. For William knighted Duncan, Malcolm's bastard son, and made him king of the Scots on his father's death. When Duncan was treacherously killed by his uncle Donald, he advanced Edgar to the throne, Donald having been done to death by the intrigue of the younger David with William's powerful aid. Edgar in his turn having died, Henry bound his successor Alexander by ties of relationship, giving him his own illegitimate daughter in marriage; during her lifetime, however, he had no children by her, as far as I

quod sciam, tulit nec ante se mortuam multum suspirauit; defuerat enim feminae, ut fertur, quod desideraretur uel in morum modestia uel in corporis elegantia. *Alexandro maioribus suis apposito, Dauid minor[b] filiorum Malcolmi, quem rex comitem fecerat et conubio insignis feminae donauerat, solium Scottorum ascendit, iuuenis ceteris curialior et[c] qui, nostrorum conuictu et familiaritate limatus a puero, omnem rubiginem Scotticae barbariei deterserat. Denique regno potitus mox omnes compatriotas triennalium tributorum pensione leuauit qui uellent habitare cultius, amiciri elegantius, pasci accuratius. Neque uero umquam in acta historiarum relatum est tantae sanctitatis tres fuisse pariter reges et fratres, maternae pietatis nectar redolentes; namque preter uictus parcitatem, elemosinarum copiam, orationum assiduitatem ita domesticum regibus uitium euicerunt ut numquam feratur in eorum thalamos nisi legitimas uxores isse, nec eorum quemquam pelicatu aliquo pudicitiam contristasse. Solus fuit Edmundus Margaretae[d] filius a bono degener, qui, Duuenaldi patrui nequitiae particeps, fraternae non inscius necis fuerit, pactus scilicet regni dimidium; sed captus et perpetuis compedibus detentus ingenue penituit, et ad mortem ueniens cum ipsis uinculis se tumulari mandauit, professus se plexum merito pro fratricidii delicto.[a]

401. Walenses rex Henricus,[e] semper in rebellionem surgentes, crebris expeditionibus in deditionem premebat, consilioque salubri nixus, ut eorum tumorem extenuaret, Flandrenses omnes Angliae accolas eo traduxit. Plures enim, qui tempore patris pro materna[f] cognatione confluxerant, occultabat Anglia, adeo ut ipsi regno pro multitudine onerosi uiderentur; quapropter[g] cum substantiis et necessitudinibus apud Ros, prouintiam Walliarum, uelut in sentinam congessit, ut et regnum defecaret et hostium brutam temeritatem retunderet.[h] Nec eo setius illuc expeditionem[i] pro temporum oportunitate dirigebat; in quarum una, incertum cuius audatia, eminus insidianti[j] harundine impetitus probe et pulchre euasit, fideliter hamatae thoracis adiutus benefitio et simul perfidiam frustrante Dei consilio.

[a-a] *om. T*[1]   [b] *iunior A*   [c] *etiam A*   [d] *Margare B*   [e] *rex H. om. T*[1]   [f] *T*[1] *adds* scilicet   [g] *T*[1]*A* add* omnes   [h] *minueret T*[1]   [i] *William surely meant to write* expeditiones *(so translated)*   [j] *insidiante T*[1]

know, and when the lady predeceased him, he did not waste many sighs on her, for she was wanting, it is said, in correctness of manners and charm of person. When Alexander was gathered to his fathers, Malcolm's youngest son David, whom the king had made an earl and honoured with the hand of a lady of noble birth, ascended the throne of the Scots. A young man of more courtly disposition than the rest, he had from boyhood been polished by familiar intercourse with the English, and rubbed off all the barbarian gaucherie of Scottish manners; for example, soon after his accession he gave a three-year exemption from the payment of dues to any of his countrymen who was prepared to raise his standard of comfort in housing, of elegance in dress, and of civility in diet. History can show no parallel to these three brothers, each a king and each so holy, breathing the fragrance of their mother's pious life; for besides their abstinence, their copious almsgiving and their constancy in prayer, they successfully overcame the vice most prevalent in kings, and it is recorded that no woman entered their bedchamber except their lawful wives, nor did any of them bring a stain upon his innocence by keeping any mistress. Edmund was the only son of Margaret who sank from this high standard: his uncle Donald's partner in crime, he cannot be held innocent of his brother's death, for he bargained that he should receive half the kingdom. Being taken, however, and imprisoned for life, he frankly repented, and on his deathbed gave instructions that his fetters should be buried with him, admitting that he was rightly punished for the crime of his brother's murder.

401. The Welsh were in constant revolt, and King Henry maintained pressure on them by frequent expeditions until they surrendered; also, in reliance on an admirable plan for reducing their ebullience, he removed into Wales all the Flemings who were living in England. Many Flemings who had trooped over in his father's time, relying on their kinship with his mother, were lying low in England, in such numbers as actually to seem a burden on the realm itself; and so he collected them all together, as though into some great midden, in the Welsh province of Rhos, with all their belongings and relatives, thereby simultaneously purging his kingdom and putting a brake on his headstrong and barbarous enemies. None the less, he sent expeditions in that direction at any suitable opportunity, on one of which he was himself attacked from a distance, no one knows thanks to whose daring, by a stealthy arrow, but well and truly escaped, thanks to the trusty protection of his coat of mail and the aid of Providence, which

Sed nec tunc auctor teli eminuit, nec umquam postea inuestigari ualuit, quanuis ille statim non hesitasset dicere sagittam non a quolibet Walense sed a prouintiali emissam, 'per mortem Domini nostri' talia pronuntians, quem morem iurandi uel irae nimietas uel rei serietas ab
3 ore principis extorquebat.*a* Nam et ea hora in proprio solo, non in hostica regione progrediebatur sensim et caute exercitus, ut nichil minus quam insidias quis opinari posset. Nec tamen intestini discriminis metu pedem ab incepto retulit, donec Walenses, datis obsidibus nobilium suorum filiis cum aliquanta pecunia et multo peculio, regiae magnanimitatis motum sedarent.

402. Britones transmarinos, quos adolescens uicinos castellis*b* Danfronto et*c* sancti Michahelis habuerat, pecuniis ad obsequium transducebat. Est enim illud genus hominum egens in patria, aliasque externo aere laboriosae uitae mercatur stipendia; si dederis, nec ciuilia sine respectu iuris et cognationis detrectans prelia, sed pro quantitate munerum ad quascumque uoles partes obnoxium. Huius consuetudinis ille non inscius, si quando opus habuisset stipendiariis militibus, multa perdebat in Britones, fidem perfidae nationis nummis suis mutuatus.

403. Rotbertum comitem Flandriae primis regni sui temporibus offendit hac causa. Balduinus senior, huius Rotberti auus, Willelmum in Angliam uenientem arguto, quo pollebat, consilio et militum additamento uiuaciter iuuerat. His ille illustres crebro retributiones refuderat, omnibus, ut ferunt, annis trecentas argenti marcas pro fide et affinitate socero annumerans. Ea munificentia, in filio Balduino non imminuta, hesit in*d* Rotberti Frisonis malitia, quam superior non preteriit sermo.[1] Porro iste Rotbertus, Frisonis filius, omissum munus a Willelmo secundo non difficulter impetrauerat, quod et is cognationem pretenderet et ille inuictum animum in spargenda pecunia haberet.
2 Verum Henricus maiori pondere rem uentilans, ut nec indebite adunaret pecunias nec nisi debite dilapidaret habitas, Rotberto ab

a excutiebat *T^t* (the last word of this version) Monti   *d* om. A   *b* A* adds suis   *c* A* adds

---

[1] 257. 1.

brought that treachery to nought. The man responsible for that shot did not become known at the time, and could never afterwards be traced, although Henry had declared at once without hesitation that the arrow was sent, not by some chance Welshman, but by one of his own subjects, affirming this 'By our Lord's death'—a form of oath wrung from him by extreme anger or some matter of great moment; for at the time the army was on his own land, not in enemy territory, advancing slowly and cautiously, so that an ambush was the last thing to be expected. Yet fear of danger from within did not make him withdraw from what he had begun, until the Welsh handed over the sons of their nobles as hostages, and allayed the king's generous resentment with a certain amount of money and a great deal of property.

402. The Bretons, whom as a young man he had had as his neighbours in the castles of Domfront and Mont-Saint-Michel, he used to bring into his service for money. As a race they are penniless at home, and happy to earn the rewards of a laborious life elsewhere at the expense of strangers. Pay them, and they will throw justice and kinship to the winds, and not refuse to fight even in a civil war; and the more you give, the readier they will be to follow wherever you lead. Henry knew this habit of theirs, and if ever he needed mercenary troops, spent a great deal on Bretons, taking a short lease of that faithless people's faith in return for coin.

403. At the very beginning of his reign he quarrelled with Count Robert of Flanders, for the following reason. The elder Baldwin, this Robert's grandfather, had given energetic help to William on his expedition into England, with the wise counsel in which he abounded and with reinforcements of knights. William had made frequent and generous acknowledgement of these services, paying three hundred marks of silver every year (so it is said) to his father-in-law in recognition of his loyalty and kinship. This generosity, which persisted undiminished towards his son Baldwin, came to a stop with the treachery of Robert the Frisian which has been mentioned above.[1] Now this Robert, son of Robert the Frisian, had without difficulty secured from William II the interrupted pension, one side putting forward ties of kinship and the other having an inexhaustible passion for squandering money. Henry's attitude, however, was more serious: he did not accumulate money that was not properly his, and when he had money, did not

Ierosolima reuerso, et quasi pro imperio trecentas argenti marcas exigenti, in hanc respondit sententiam: non solitos reges Angliae Flandritis uectigal pendere, nec se uelle libertatem maiorum macula suae timiditatis fuscare.[a] Quapropter, si suo committat arbitrio, libenter se quod oportunitas siuerit ut cognato et amico dare; si uero in exactione permanendum putauerit, omnino negare. Hac ille ratione deiectus animum multo tempore in regem tumuit; sed parum aut nichil simultatibus adiutus, mansuetudini mentem accommodauit, expertus regem posse flecti precario, non fastu tirannico.

Iam uero Balduino filio eius uarietas temporum causas irarum in regem dedit. Siquidem Willelmum filium Rotberti Normanni uolens hereditati intrudere, alienis se sponte negotiis immiscuit, crebroque castella regis in Normannia inopinatis fatigabat assultibus, magnum incommodum si fata siuissent terrae minatus; sed apud Archas maiori manu militum[b] quam timebat exceptus mortem maturauit, crebris ictibus galea quassata cerebrum uiolatus. Causam ferunt morbi augmentati quod ea die allium cum auca presumpserit, nec nocte uenere abstinuerit. Hic intuebuntur posteri eximium regalis pietatis exemplum, quod medicum peritissimum decumbenti miserit, illacrimatus (si credimus) morbo perire quem pro ammiratione fortitudinis saluari maluisset. Successor eius Karolus nulla molestia uires regis inquietauit, primo federe suspenso, mox etiam consummato,[c] amicitiam eius amplexus.

404. Philippus rex Francorum regi nostro nec utilis nec infestus fuit, propterea quod esset uentri magis quam negotiis deditus, nec preterea in[d] castellis eius collimitaneus; pauca enim quae tunc habebat in Normannia magis Britanniae quam Frantiae uicina[e] erant. Adde quod, ut superius dixi,[1] Philippus accedente senio libidine grauis, comitissaeque Andegauensis spetie lusus, illicitis ardoribus defeneratus famulabatur. Quocirca ab Apostolico excommunicatus, cum in uilla qua mansitabat nichil diuini seruitii fieret, sed discedente eo tinnitus signorum undique concreparent, insulsam[f] fatuitatem cachinnis

[a] AaCe[b.c.]; fucare AlCB   [b] manum mi Al, manum Aap   [c] confirmato A   [d] om. A, rightly?   [e] om. A   [f] insulam ABk

[1] 235. 5.

pour it out except for proper purposes. When Robert returned from Jerusalem, and asked for his three hundred marks of silver almost in a tone of command, he was informed that the kings of England do not normally pay tax to Flemings, and the present king was not prepared to blot the record of his forebears' independence by any cowardice of his own. If it were left to his discretion, he would gladly give what circumstances might indicate, as to a friend and kinsman; but if he felt it necessary to persist in his demands, the answer was an uncompromising no. Thus disappointed, the count was for a long time resentful against the king; but when quarrelling did little or no good, he made up his mind to be milder, finding that the king could be moved by appeals but not by imperious insolence.

At the time we have now reached, however, the changing course of events had given his son Baldwin reasons for discontent with the king. Wishing to install William, son of Robert the Norman, in his inheritance by force, he meddled deliberately in other people's business, and wearied the king's castles in Normandy with frequent and unexpected attacks, threatening the land with disaster, had fate allowed it. However, he was received at Arques by a larger force of knights than he was anticipating, and died an early death, suffering severe brain-damage from a rain of blows which pounded his helmet. They say his condition was aggravated by a meal, earlier that day, of goose and garlic, and by sexual indulgence that night. At this point, posterity will contemplate an outstanding instance of kingly generosity: the king sent his most skilled physician to the sick-bed, and shed tears (if we can believe it) at the death from sickness of a man whose recovery he would have welcomed as an admirer of valour. Charles his successor gave the royal power no trouble by any hostile act, and welcomed his friendship first with a provisional treaty, but soon with a permanent one.

404. Philip, king of the French, was neither helpful nor hurtful to our king, being devoted more to his belly than to business, nor did his castles march with Henry's, for the few that he possessed at that time in Normandy were nearer Brittany than France. Besides which, Philip, as I have said above,[1] with advancing years was absorbed in lechery, and being deluded by the fair countess of Anjou, became the bondslave and plaything of adulterous passion. For this he was excommunicated by the Holy See; in any place where he was staying, divine service was suspended, and on his departure the ringing of bells burst

2 exprimebat, 'Audis,' inquiens, 'bella, quomodo nos effugant?' Adeo erat omnibus episcopis prouintiae suae derisui ut nullus eos desponsaret preter Willelmum archiepiscopum Rotomagensem; cuius facti temeritatem luit multis annis interdictus et uix tandem aliquando per Anselmum archiepiscopum apostolicae communioni redditus. Philippo interea nulla mora insanae temulentiae satietatem fecit, nisi quod in extremo uitae tactus morbo monachicum apud Floriacum accepit habitum. Pulchrius et fortunatius illa, quod aetate et sanitate integra, nec spetie rugata, apud Fontem Euraldi sanctimonialium appetiit uelum, nec multo post presenti uitae ualefecit, Deo forsitan prouidente non posse delicatae mulieris corpus religionis laboribus inseruire.

405. At uero Ludouicus filius Philippi uarium se prestitit, in^a neutra parte bene constans. Primo enim tempore plurimus in fratrem irarum auctor Henrico^b ad capiendam Normanniam fuit, corruptus uidelicet Anglorum spoliis et multo regis obrizo: non quod ille obtulerit, sed quod alter inuitauerit, ultro adhortans^c ne clarissimae olim patriae neruos dissimulatione sua succidi sineret. Postea uero simultas inter eos exorta est pro Thetbaldo comite Blesensi, filio Stephani qui apud Ramulam occubuit, quod Thetbaldus susceptus esset Stephano
2 ex Adala filia Willelmi Magni. Diu igitur ex parte regis nostri labores uiarum consumpserunt nuntii, ut dignaretur Ludouicus satisfactionem Thetbaldi. Ille uero, parum fatiens preces, Thetbaldum ab Apostolico deuotari fecit quasi arrogantem et Deo rebellem, qui preter austeritatem morum, quae^d omnibus uidebatur intolerabilis, ferebatur dominum suum priuare auitis possessionibus. Itaque diu productis inimicitiis, cum uterque grossum tumeret, nec alter alteri pro persona cederet, Ludouicus Normanniam uenit, inflatiori anhelitu late omnia exhauriens. Nuntiabantur haec regi,^{e} qui apud Rotomagum se continebat, adeo ut uulgus militum aures eius infestaret: pateretur repelli Ludouicum, hominem aqualiculi pondere olim lectum fouentem, sed
3 nunc pro dissimulatione^f minis auras onerantem. Ille, paterni memor exempli, fatuitatem Franci patientia extundere quam uiribus repellere malebat. Quin etiam milites benigne appellando hac ratione mulcebat:

^{a} ut in B ^{b} om. A ^{c} ultro adhortans om. A ^{d} qua ABk* (cf. 165. 12) ^{e} regi h(a)ec A ^{f} A* adds sua (cf. 405. 1)

out everywhere. Whereat he gave vent to his folly in half-witted laughter: 'Do you hear, my fair one,' he said, 'how they scare us away?' The bishops of his province all held him in such contempt that none would marry them except William archbishop of Rouen, and he paid the penalty of his imprudence by many years of excommunication, until at length he was reconciled to the Holy See through the good offices of Archbishop Anselm. No lapse of time, meanwhile, sated Philip's appetite for mad self-indulgence, except that at the end of his life, when he fell ill, he took the monastic habit at Fleury. The lady's lot was happier and more honourable, for in the prime of life and health, without a wrinkle on her lovely face, she sought the veil of a nun at Fontevrault, and not long after bade farewell to this present world, God maybe foreseeing that her delicate body could not support the austerities of the religious life.

405. Philip's son Louis proved unreliable, and supported neither side for long. At first he was active in encouraging Henry to be hostile to his brother, and to seize Normandy, beguiled by the prospect of spoils from the English and the king's abundant gold. Not that Henry made any offer; the advances came from Louis, who urged him not to let his country, once so famous, be crippled by his own inactivity. Later, they quarrelled over Theobald count of Blois, the son of Stephen who fell at Ramlah, because Theobald was Stephen's son by Adela, daughter of William the Great. Long did the messengers on our king's behalf toil to and fro to persuade Louis to accept satisfaction from Theobald; but Louis was deaf to the king's prayers, and had Theobald denounced by the Holy See as an arrogant renegade, who besides being universally intolerable for his rigid behaviour, was trying to oust his lord, as was alleged, from his ancestral possessions. The quarrel was long drawn out, for passion ran high on both sides, and each was too conscious of his own position to give way. At length, Louis invaded Normandy, and started spreading destruction with overbearing violence. This was reported to the king, who was then at Rouen, showing such restraint that his knights in a body beset him with protests, demanding leave to drive out that tunbelly Louis, who had been wont to keep his fat self in bed, and was now loading the air with threats because their own king let him be. Henry, with his father's example in mind, thought this empty-headed Frenchman better given time to exhaust himself than driven off by force. He also appealed to his knights as their well-wisher, and pacified them on

non debere illos mirari si sanguinis eorum prodigus esse caueret quos sibi fideles non modicis experimentis approbasset; impium esse ut ad regnum sibi parandum eorum glorietur*a* mortibus qui uitam suam pro eius salute ultroneis deuoueant certaminibus; illos regni sui nutritos,*b* pietatis alumnos. Quapropter boni principis se uelle sequi exemplum, ut modestia sua eorum remoretur impetum quos ita paratos
4 pro se uideat ad moriendum. Postremo, cum uideret prudentiam suam sinistra interpretatione turbari et ignauiam uocari, in tantum ut Ludouicus prope Rotomagum quattuor miliariis ignes faceret, predas ageret, maiori fortitudine uim animi concussit, et procinctu parato uicit egregie, preteritas dissimulationes feroci puniens uictoria. Veruntamen aliquanto post pax parta est, quia et omnium rerum est*c* uicissitudo, et nummi quaslibet iniurias leuant, ad persuadendum quod intendunt potentes. Quare Willelmus, filius regis nostri, hominium*d* regi Francorum de Normannia fecit, iure legitimo de eo prouintiam cogniturus. Illud fuit tempus quo idem puer filiam Fulconis comitis Andegauensis despondit et accepit, patris prudentia satagente ut hinc pecunia, hinc affinitate mediante nichil contra filium turbaretur.

406. His diebus Calixtus papa, de quo posterius dicam plura,[1] presentiam suam prope Normanniam exhibuit; cuius colloquio potitus, rex Angliae Romanos prudentiam Normannorum mirari et predicare coegit. Namque ille, ut fertur, infesto uenerat animo, ut eum asperius conueniret quare fratrem et sancti Sepulchri peregrinum in captione teneret; sed responso principis, quod erat simile ueri, et probabilibus argumentis perstrictus, parum contra retulit. Possunt enim communes loci ad quamlibet partem inflecti pro facundia oratoris, presertim cum
2 non contempnatur eloquentia quam pretiosa condiunt xenia. Et ut nichil cumulatae pompae deesset, adolescentulos clarissimi generis, filios comitis de Mellento, ut contra cardinales de dialectica disputarent subornauit, quorum tortilibus sophismatibus cum*e* uiuacitate rationum obsisti nequiret,*f* non puduit cardinales confiteri maiori occiduas

---

a grauetur *A* *b* nutricios *Cs* *c* est *C (after* uicissitudo *Aac, Terence, Eun.* 376); om. *AB* *d* hominum *B* *e* *A adds* pro *f* nequirent *B*

---

[1] Starting at 432. 1.

these lines: 'Do not be surprised', he said, 'if I shrink from reckless shedding of your blood: I have proved your loyalty to me in no mean time of trial, and it would be outrageous for a man intent on securing a kingdom for himself, to exult in the deaths of those who risk their lives to secure his safety in battles of their own choosing. You are born and bred in my own kingdom, the foster-children of my affection; I propose to behave as a good king should, who by his moderation will always restrain the eagerness of men whom he sees to be so ready to die for his own sake.' Finally, when he saw that a sinister interpretation was being put on his policy of prudence, and that it was passing for cowardice, to such an extent that Louis lit his fires and drove off his booty within four miles of Rouen, he steeled his heart, and, mobilizing his forces, roundly defeated him in a pitched battle, reversing his previous negligence by a bold stroke of victory. None the less, it was not long before peace was brought about; all things are subject to change, and coin can alleviate any wrong with its persuasive power of getting its own way. So William, our king's son, did homage to the king of the French for Normandy, acknowledging that he would hold the province from him by legal right. It was at this time that the same son was betrothed to a daughter of Fulk count of Anjou, and had her to wife, his wise father thus providing that with money as the go-between on one side and family ties on the other, his son should remain undisturbed.

406. About this time Pope Calixtus, of whom more hereafter,[1] made his appearance in the region of Normandy; whereupon the king of England, having arranged an interview with him, compelled the Romans to admire and praise the wisdom of the Normans. For the pope—so it is reported—had come with hostile intent, to lodge an emphatic protest at his holding in captivity his own brother, who was also a pilgrim of the Holy Sepulchre; but he was so overborne by the king's defence, which was plausible, and by his cogent arguments, that he could say little in reply. General considerations can be adapted to either side of an argument according to the skill of the advocate, and, in particular, eloquence is sure of a hearing when spiced with rich gifts. To complete the splendid effect, he put up some young men of the highest rank, sons of the count of Meulan, to meet the cardinals in a debate on dialectic; and when it proved impossible by force of reasoning to withstand their volleys of argument, the cardinals were not ashamed to confess that these western territories had a far more

plagas florere litterarum peritia quam ipsi audissent uel putassent in patria. Itaque haec collocutio hunc finem emeruit, ut pronuntiaret Apostolicus nichil Anglorum regis causa iustius, prudentia eminentius, facundia uberius.

407. Horum puerorum pater erat comes de Mellento Rotbertus, ut dixi, filius Rogerii de Bellomonte, qui Pratellum cenobium Normanniae construxit, homo antiquae simplicitatis et fidei qui, crebro a Willelmo primo inuitatus ut Angliam ueniret largis ad uoluntatem possessionibus munerandus, supersedit, pronuntians patrum suorum hereditatem se uelle fouere, non transmarinas et indebitas possessiones 2 uel appetere uel inuadere. Hic duos filios habuit, Rotbertum istum et Henricum. Henricus comes Warwicensis, dulcis et quieti animi uir, congruo suis moribus studio uitam egit et clausit. Alter astutior et pronioris ad uersutiam cordis preter paternam hereditatem in Normannia et ingentia predia in Anglia castellum, quod matris suae frater Hugo filius Gualeranni tenuerat, Mellentum nomine, a rege Frantiae nundinatus est pecunia. Qui cum superiorum regum tempore, spe sensim pullulante, in gloriam procederet, huius aetate summo prouectu effloruit, habebaturque eius consilium quasi quis diuinum consuluisset 3 sacrarium. Idque*a* non immerito assecutus estimabatur, quod esset aeui maturus ad consulendum, suasor concordiae, dissuasor discordiae, et prorsus ad quod intenderet pro uiribus eloquentiae citissimus persuasor,*b* ingentis in Anglia momenti, ut inueteratum uestiendi uel comedendi exemplo suo inuerteret morem. Denique consuetudo semel prandendi in omnium optimatum curiis per eum frequentatur, quam ipse causa bonae ualitudinis acceptam nuntiis a Constantino-4 politano imperatore Alexio suo, ut dixi, ceteris refudit exemplo. Quod tamen magis parcitate dapsilitatis fecisse et docuisse quam timore cruditatis et indigeriei immerito culpatur, quia nemo eo, ut fertur, in dapibus aliis sumptuosior uel sibi moderatior fuit. In placitis propugnator iustitiae, in guerris prouisor uictoriae; dominum regem ad seueritatem legum custodiendam exacuens, ipse non*c* eas sequens sed proponens; expers in reges perfidiae, in ceteros eius persecutor.

408. Habebat preterea rex Henricus episcopum Salesberiensem Rogerium a secretis, cuius maxime nitebatur consilio; nam et ante

---

a idque *Aa;* iamque *AlCB*   *b* perorator *B*   *c* The sense seems to demand the addition of solum *(so translated)*

flourishing literary culture than they had ever heard of or imagined in their own country. So the outcome of this meeting was a declaration by the pope that for the justice of his case, his eminent wisdom, and copious eloquence, the English king had no superior.

407. The young men's father, as I have said, was Robert count of Meulan, the son of Roger of Beaumont, who founded the Norman monastery at Préaux, a simple-hearted, honourable man of the old school, who refused many invitations from William I to come to England and receive as much land as he wanted in return, saying that he would rather look to the inheritance of his fathers than go soliciting or snatching possessions overseas to which he had no claim. He had two sons, the 2 Robert of whom I speak, and Henry. Henry earl of Warwick, a man of kindly and peaceable disposition, lived and died engaged in pursuits congenial to his character. His brother, who was cleverer and more disposed by nature to intrigue, besides his inheritance in Normandy and large estates in England, had purchased from the king of France for cash the castle of Meulan, which had been held by his mother's brother, Hugh son of Waleran. In previous reigns, as his ambitions gradually blossomed, he was making his way to the front; but in this reign he flourished exceedingly, and his opinion was regarded as the utterance of an oracle. This reputation was not thought undeserved, for he had good 3 judgement, used his influence on the side of unity and peace, and could employ his powerful eloquence to secure his ends speedily. So great was his influence in England that his example could reverse traditional habits in dress or diet. For instance, the habit of dining once a day owes to him its universal adoption in the courts of the nobility. He himself had taken it over, for his health's sake, from Alexius emperor of Constantinople, by messengers, and passed it on to others, as I have said, by his example. He is blamed for having adopted and encouraged this practice 4 more from reasons of economy than from fear of digestive disorders, but unfairly; for no one had a greater reputation for extravagant hospitality to others, combined with personal moderation. A champion of justice in the courts, in war he was an architect of victory; inspiring his lord the king to maintain the severity of the laws, and himself not merely obeying the existing laws but proposing new ones; without a disloyal thought towards his masters, and a scourge of disloyalty towards others.

408. Besides him, King Henry had in his inner counsels Roger bishop of Salisbury, and leant heavily on his advice; for he had put

regnum omnibus suis prefecerat, rex primum cancellarium, mox episcopum constituerat, prudentiam uiri expertus. Sollerter administrati episcopatus offitium spem infudit quod maiori dignus haberetur munere; itaque totius regni moderamen illius delegauit iustitiae, siue ipse adesset Angliae siue moraretur Normanniae. Refugit episcopus tantis se curis inuoluere, nisi tres archiepiscopi Cantuarienses, Anselmus, Radulfus, Willelmus, et postremo papa iniunxissent ei munus obedientiae. Sategit ita fieri Henricus, non nescius quod fideliter sua tractaret commoda Rogerius; nec defuit ille spei regiae, sed tanta integritate, tanta se agebat industria ut nulla contra eum conflaretur inuidia. Denique rex plerumque triennio, nonnumquam quadriennio et eo amplius, in Normannia moratus, cum in regnum reuerteretur, deputabat iustitiarii modestiae quod nichil aut parum inueniebat molestiae. Inter haec aecclesiastica offitia non negligere, sed cotidie mane omnia honeste persoluere, ut expeditius et tutius ceteris posset accedere. Pontifex magnanimus et nullis umquam parcens sumptibus, dum quae fatienda proponeret, edifitia presertim, consummaret; quod cum alias, tum maxime in Salesberia et Malmesberia*ᵃ* est uidere. Fecit enim ibi edifitia spatio diffusa, numero pecuniarum sumptuosa, spetie formosissima, ita iuste composito ordine lapidum ut iunctura perstringat intuitum et totam maceriam unum mentiatur esse saxum. Aecclesiam Salesberiensem et nouam fecit et ornamentis excoluit, ut nulli in Anglia cedat sed multas precedat, ipseque non falso possit dicere Deo: 'Domine, dilexi decorem domus tuae.'[1]

409. Hibernensium regem Murcardum et successores eius, quorum nomina fama non extulit, ita deuotos habuit noster Henricus ut nichil nisi quod eum palparet scriberent, nichil nisi quod iuberet*ᵇ* agerent; quanuis feratur Murcardus nescio qua de causa paucis diebus inflatius in Anglos egisse, sed mox pro interdicto nauigio et mercimonio nauigantium tumorem pectoris sedasse. Quanti enim ualeret Hibernia si non annauigarent merces ex Anglia? Ita pro penuria, immo pro inscientia cultorum ieiunum*ᶜ* omnium bonorum solum agrestem et squalidam multitudinem Hibernensium extra urbes producit; Angli uero et Franci cultiori genere uitae urbes nundinarum commertio inhabitant.

ᵃ et Malm. *om. A*   *ᵇ* iuberet *Al*ᵖ·ᶜ*C;* iuberent *A;* iuberetur *B*   *ᶜ* leocini (-inium *after corr.*) *Al,* ei unum *Aap*

[1] Ps. 25 (26): 8.

him in charge of his household before his accession, and as king, having had experience of his sound judgement, he had appointed him first chancellor and then bishop. His prudent conduct of the bishopric inspired the hope that he might be found worthy of higher office, and so the king entrusted to his judgement the administration of justice throughout the realm, whether he were himself in England or detained in Normandy. The bishop was for refusing to involve himself in so great a charge, had not three archbishops of Canterbury, Anselm, Ralph, and William, and finally the pope, enjoined on him the duty of obedience. Henry pressed for this to happen, knowing that Roger would manage his affairs loyally; nor did he disappoint the king, but conducted himself with such integrity and energy that no ill-feeling was aroused against him. For example, the king remained in Normandy often for three years at a time, sometimes for four or even more, and on returning to his kingdom set it down to the moderation of his justiciar that he found little or no discontent. With all this, he would not neglect his religious duties, but performed all duly every morning, that he might more speedily and safely proceed to other things. As a bishop he was liberal, and never spared expense provided he could accomplish what he had in mind to do, especially his buildings. This can be seen above all at Salisbury and Malmesbury; for there he erected buildings large in scale, expensive, and very beautiful to look at, the courses of stone being laid so exactly that the joints defy inspection and give the whole wall the appearance of a single rock-face. Salisbury cathedral he rebuilt and richly furnished, so that it is passed by no church in England and surpasses many, and he himself can say to God with perfect truth: 'Lord, I have loved the beauty of Thy house.'[1]

409. Muirchertach king of the Irish, and his successors, whose names are not reported, were so devoted to our King Henry that they wrote nothing except what would please him and did nothing except what he told them to do, although it is said that Muirchertach for some unknown reason once for a short time took a high line with the English; but finding communications by sea cut off, and all sea-borne trade, he soon piped down. What would Ireland be worth without the goods that come in by sea from England? The soil lacks all advantages, and so poor, or rather unskilful, are its cultivators that it can produce only a ragged mob of rustic Irishmen outside the towns; the English and French, with their more civilized way of life, live in the towns,

2 Paulus Orcadum comes, quanuis Noricorum regi hereditario iure subiectus, ita regis amicitias suspitiebat ut crebra ei munuscula missitaret. Nam et ille prona uoluptate exterarum terrarum miracula inhiabat, leones, leopardos, linces, camelos, quorum fetus Anglia est inops, grandi, ut dixi,[1] iocunditate a regibus alienis expostulans; habebatque conseptum quod Wdestoche dicitur, in quo delitias talium rerum con-
3 fouebat, posueratque ibi animal quod strix uocatur, missum sibi a Willelmo de Monte Pislerio. De quo animali Plinius Secundus in octauo Naturalis[a] Historiae libro et Isidorus de Ethimologiis memorant,[2] esse animal in Affrica quod Affri eritii genus dicant,[b] coopertum hispidis setis, quas in canes insectantes naturaliter emittant.[c] Sunt uero setae, ut uidi, palmo et plus longae, in utraque summitate acutae, similes pennis aucarum ubi desinunt plumae, sed paulo plus grossae, nigro et albo quasi intertinctae.

410. Illud preter cetera Henricum insigniebat, quod, quanuis pro tumultibus Normannicis sepe et diu regno suo deesset, ita timore suo rebelles frenabat ut nichil pacis in Anglia desiderares; quocirca etiam exterae gentes illuc, uelut ad unicum tutae[d] quietis portum, libenter appellebant. Denique Siwardus rex Noricorum, primo aeui processu fortissimis conferendus, incepto itinere Ierosolimitano rogataque regis pace in Anglia tota resedit hieme; plurimoque per aecclesias auro expenso, mox, ut fauonius ad serenitatem pelagi uernales portas aperuit, naues repetiit, prouectusque in altum Baleares insulas, quae Maiorica et Minorica dicuntur, armis territas faciliores ad subigendum
2 prefato Willelmo de Monte Pislerio reliquit. Inde pertendit[e] Ierosolimam, nauibus omnibus incolumibus preter unam, quae, dum retinacula a portu soluere tardat, absorta est immani uoragine quam inter Sequanica et Aquitanica littora esse Paulus historicus Longobardorum asseuerat,[3] tanto undarum impetu ut ad triginta miliaria garrulitas discernatur aquarum. Ierusalem ueniens Tirum et Sidonem, urbes quas mare allambit, ad Christianitatis gratiam obsedit, effregit, subegit. Mutato itinere Contantinopolim ingressus, nauem aureis rostratam
3 draconibus fastigio Sanctae Sophiae pro tropheo affixit. Hominibus

[a] naturali *A* [b] dicunt *A* [c] emittat *Aap, more correctly* [d] tuti *B* [e] protendit *A*

[1] Does not seem to refer to anything earlier, though later cf. 412. 1 (*iocundus*).
[2] Pliny, *Nat. hist.* viii. 125; Isidore, *Etymol.* xii. 2. 35.
[3] Paul the Deacon, *Hist. Lang.* i. 6 (*PL* xcv. 445).

and carry on trade and commerce. Paul earl of the Orkneys, although 2
by hereditary right a subject of the king of the Norwegians, valued his
friendship with our king highly enough to send him frequent presents;
for Henry took a passionate delight in the marvels of other countries,
with much affability, as I have said,[1] asking foreign kings to send him
animals not found in England—lions, leopards, lynxes, camels—and
he had a park called Woodstock in which he kept his pets of this
description. He had put there an animal called a porcupine, sent him 3
by William of Montpellier, which is mentioned by Pliny in the eighth
book of his *Natural History* and by Isidore in his *Etymologies*;[2] they
report the existence of an animal in Africa, called by the Africans a
kind of hedgehog, covered with bristling spines, which it has the
power to shoot out at dogs pursuing it. The spines, as I have seen for
myself, are a palm or more in length, and sharp at both ends, something like goose quills at the point where the feather-part leaves off,
but rather thicker, and as it were striped black and white.

410. The most remarkable thing about Henry was his power of
keeping rebellion in check by the fear of his name, in such a way that
in spite of long and frequent absences from his kingdom caused by disorder in Normandy, the peaceful condition of England never left anything to be desired, so that even foreign peoples readily came over
here as to the one haven of peace and safety. For instance, Sigurd
king of the Norwegians, who in his early days could be counted
among the bravest, when starting on his journey to Jerusalem, obtained
our king's leave and settled in England for a whole winter. He spent
gold liberally on sundry churches; and then, when the western breeze
opened the gates of spring and calmed the deep, he took ship again,
and bearing out to sea, terrified the Balearic Islands, whose names are
Majorca and Minorca, and left them an easier prey to the William of
Montpellier of whom we were speaking. Thence he made for Jerusalem 2
with all his ships intact except one which, being slow to cast off from
harbour, was swallowed up in the great whirlpool which lies, according
to Paul the historian of the Lombards,[3] between the shores of the
Seine region and Aquitaine, its waves being so violent that the roar of
waters can be heard for thirty miles. Coming to Jerusalem, he laid
siege to the sea-washed cities of Tyre and Sidon for the advantage of
Christendom, stormed, and subdued them. By a change of route he
came to Constantinople, and there fixed a ship with golden serpents
for its figurehead on the pinnacle of St Sophia as a trophy. In that 3

suis in eadem urbe cateruatim morientibus remedium excogitauit, ut reliqui parcius et aqua mixtum uinum biberent, ingenti[a] ingenii acrimonia ut, porcino iecore mero iniecto moxque pro asperitate liquoris resoluto, idem in hominibus fieri primo presagiret, post etiam quodam defuncto exinterato uisu addisceret. Quare contuitu prudentiae et fortitudinis, quae grande quid pollicebantur, imperatore illum retinere temptante, spem eius, qua iam aurum Noricum deuorabat, pulchre cassauit, impetrata ad proximam urbem licentia cistas thesaurorum plumbo impletas et obsignatas apud eum deponens, quasi citissimi reditus uades. Ita ille illusus est; alter pedes domum contendit.

411. Sed enim ut ad Henricum regrediatur oratio, erat ille in rebus suis prouidendo efficax, defendendo pertinax; bellorum quatinus posset cum honestate repressor, cum uero decreuisset non pati, impatiendus iniuriarum exactor, obuia pericula uirtutis umbone decutiens; odii et amicitiae in quamlibet[b] tenax, in altero nimio irarum estui, in altero regiae magnanimitati satisfatiens, hostes uidelicet ad miseriam deprimens, amicos et clientes ad inuidiam efferens; nam et hanc curam uel primam uel maximam boni principis philosophia proponit, 2 ut parcat subiectis et debellet superbos.[1] Iustitiae rigore inflexibilis, prouintiales quiete, proceres dignanter continebat, fures et falsarios latentes maxima diligentia perscrutans, inuentos puniens, paruarum quoque rerum non negligens: cum nummos fractos, licet boni argenti, a uenditoribus non recipi audisset, omnes uel frangi uel incidi precepit. Mercatorum falsam ulnam castigauit, brachii sui mensura adhibita omnibusque per Angliam proposita. Curialibus suis,[c] ubicumque uillarum esset, quantum a rusticis gratis accipere, quantum et quoto pretio emere debuissent, edixit, transgressores uel graui pecuniarum 3 multa uel uitae dispendio affitiens. Principio regni, ut terrore exempli reos inureret, ad membrorum detruncationem, post ad pecuniae

---

[a] om. CB (but cf. GP p. 126)   [b] quemlibet CB; one expects quamlibet without in   [c] Al ends here

[1] Virgil, Aen. vi. 853.

same city his men began to die like flies, and he himself thought out a remedy, making the survivors drink wine more sparingly, and not unless mixed with water. Such was his penetrating intelligence: he put a pig's liver into the unmixed wine, and finding it soon dissolve away in the harsh liquor, he first foretold that the same thing would happen in the human body, and then obtained visual confirmation by post-mortem examination of one who had died. In view of his sagacity and courage, which promised great things, the emperor endeavoured to detain him, but when he was already in imagination battening on their Norwegian gold, Sigurd fairly made nonsense of his hopes: obtaining leave to go as far as some neighbouring city, he deposited his treasure-chests with the emperor, filled up with lead and sealed, as though guaranteeing a speedy return. So the emperor was double-crossed, and Sigurd made his way home on foot.

411. But to return to King Henry. In the management of his affairs, he was capable in administration and obstinate in defence, striving to avoid open hostilities as long as he honourably could; but once he had decided that a situation could no longer be supported, he became insupportable himself in the quest for revenge, armed with resolution like a shield to beat down the dangers in his path. His hatreds and his friendships were maintained to any extreme, the one serving as outlets for his great fits of rage, the other for his kingly generosity, as he plunged his enemies in misery, and exalted friends and supporters until all were jealous of them: does not philosophy prescribe that the first or greatest care of a good prince should be 'to spare the humble and beat down the proud'?[1] The standard of his justice was inflexible; 2 he kept his subjects in order without disturbance and his nobles without loss of dignity; he showed the greatest diligence in seeking out thieves and forgers in their dens, and punishing them when found. Even details did not escape his notice; having heard that broken coins, although made of good silver, were not being accepted in payment, he gave orders that all coins alike should be broken or cut. He punished the false ell in use among merchants, introducing his own forearm as a standard for universal use throughout England. Wherever he might be on his estates, he notified the persons of his court by proclamation as to how much they might receive from the country people as a gift, how much it was their duty to buy, and at what price; and the disobedient were visited with heavy fines or loss of life. At the beginning 3 of his reign, in order to set a fearful example and make a lasting impression on evildoers, he was more inclined to exact loss of a limb,

solutionem procliuior. Pro morum*a* prudentia, ut fere fert natura mortalium, optimatibus uenerabilis, prouintialibus amabilis habebatur. Quod si qui maiorum, iurati sacramenti immemores, a fidei tramite exorbitarent, continuo et consiliorum efficatia et laborum perseuerantia erroneos reuocabat ad lineam, per asperitatem uulnerum detrectantes reducens ad sanitatem animorum. Nec facile quam diuturnos sudores in talibus effuderit enumerem, dum nichil patitur inultum quod a delinquentibus commissum dignitati suae non esset consenta-
4 neum. Pugnarum erat maxima causa Normannia, ut ante dixi,[1] in qua ipse pariter multis annis degens Angliae quoque prospitiebat, nullo audente caput erigere dum ille audatiam, ille suspiceret prudentiam. Nec uero propter rebellionem aliquorum procerum umquam suorum appetitus est insidiis, nisi semel. Auctor earum fuit quidam cubicularius, plebeii*b* generis patre sed pro regiorum thesaurorum custodia famosi nominis homine natus; is deprehensus et facile confessus, penas perfidiae acriter luit. Preter hoc tota*c* uita securus, animos omnium timori, sermones amori obstrictos habebat.

412. Statura minimos supergrediens, a maximis uincebatur, crine nigro et iuxta frontem profugo, oculis dulce serenis, thoroso pectore, carnoso corpore. Facetiarum pro tempore plenus, nec pro mole negotiorum, cum se communioni dedisset, minus iocundus. Minus pugnacis famae, Scipionis Affricani dictum representabat: 'Imperatorem me mea mater, non bellatorem peperit.'[2] Quapropter sapientia nulli umquam*d* modernorum regum secundus, et pene dicam omnium antecessorum in Anglia facile primus, libentius bellabat consilio quam gladio; uincebat, si poterat, sanguine nullo, si aliter non poterat,
2 pauco. Omnium tota uita omnino obscenitatum cupidinearum expers, quoniam, ut a consciis accepimus, non effreni uoluptate sed gignendae prolis amore mulierum gremio infunderetur, nec dignaretur aduenae delectationi prebere assensum, nisi ubi regium semen procedere posset in effectum, effundens naturam ut dominus, non obtemperans libidini ut famulus. Cibis indifferenter utens magisque

---

a [A] adds ergo   *b* plebei B   *c* om. [A]Bk   *d* om. [A]

[1] cc. 397–8.
[2] Frontinus, *Strat.* iv. 7. 4.

and later to require monetary payments; and by this characteristic prudence, as is the way of human nature, he won the respect of his nobles and the affection of his countrymen. If any of the more important lords, forgetting their oath of allegiance, swerved from the narrow path of loyalty, he used at once to recall the strays by prudent counsel and unremitting efforts, bringing the rebellious back to toeing the line by the severity of the wounds he inflicted on them. Nor could I easily recount the long-continued labours he expended on such people, leaving no action unpunished which could not be committed by the disaffected without some impairment of his royal dignity. The chief source of his wars, as I have said before,[1] was Normandy, in which he himself spent many years, without however neglecting England; no one dared to raise his head, for some respected his energy, others his wisdom. Never was he exposed, on account of rebellion among his nobles, to treachery from his own servants, save once only: the traitor was one of his chamberlains, son of a man of lowly origin who had achieved a great name as keeper of the royal treasure, and having been detected and easily brought to confess, he paid a bitter price for his disloyalty. With this one exception, he had no trouble all his life, maintaining fear of himself in all men's hearts and love upon their lips.

412. In person he was more than short and less than tall, with black hair retreating from his forehead, a glance serene and kindly, muscular chest and thickset limbs. In season, he was full of fun, and once he had decided to be sociable, a mass of business did not damp his spirits. As a fighter he was of less repute than some, and embodied that saying of Scipio Africanus: 'My mother bore me for command, not combat'.[2] As a result, being in political wisdom second to none among the kings of our day, and I would almost say, easily first among all his predecessors in England, he preferred to do battle in the council-chamber rather than the field, and won his victories without bloodshed if he could, and with very little if he could not. All his life he was completely free from fleshly lusts, indulging in the embraces of the female sex (as I have heard from those who know) from love of begetting children and not to gratify his passions; for he thought it beneath his dignity to comply with extraneous gratification, unless the royal seed could fulfil its natural purpose; employing his bodily functions as their master, not obeying his lust as its slave. At table he was not particular, eating

explens esuriem quam multis obsoniis urgens ingluuiem; potui numquam preter sitim indulgens; continentiae minimum excessum cum in suis tum in omnibus execrans. Somni grauis, et quem*ᵃ* frequens roncatio interrumperet. Facultatis in dicendo magis fortuitae quam elaboratae, nec precipitis, sed maturae.

413. Pietatis in Deum predicandae, monasteria in Anglia et Normannia construxit; quibus quia nondum supremam manum imposuit, ego quoque interim iuditium meum differrem, nisi me Radingensium fratrum caritas tacere non sineret. Hoc ille cenobium inter duo flumina Kenetam et Tamensem constituit, loco ubi pene omnium itinerantium ad populosiores urbes Angliae posset esse diuersorium, posuitque ibi monachos Cluniacenses, qui sunt hodie preclarum sanctitatis exemplum, hospitalitatis indefessae et*ᵇ* dulcis inditium: uideas ibi quod non alibi, ut plus hospites totis horis uenientes quam inhabitantes insu2 mant. Preproperum me et adulatorem fortasse quis dixerit, quod nunc primum nascentem religionem tanto efferam preconio, nesciens quid uentura pariat dies;[1] sed ipsi, ut spero, cum Dei gratia enitentur ut in bono durent. Ego non erubesco si sanctis uiris blandiar, et bonum quod in me non habeo in aliis ammirer. Inuestituras aecclesiarum Deo et sancto Petro remisit, post multas controuersias inter eum et Anselmum archiepiscopum habitas uix tandem ad consentiendum, pro ingenti Dei gratia, ingloriosa de fratre uictoria[2] inflexus. Sed harum causarum tenorem multo uerborum circuitu egit domnus*ᶜ* Edmerus;[3] nos pro pleniori notitia Paschalis sepe dicti[4] apostolici scripta ad hanc rem pertinentia subnectemus.*ᵈ*

414. 'Paschalis episcopus Henrico regi salutem.

'In litteris quas nuper ad nos per familiarem tuum, nostrae dilectionis filium, clericum Willelmum transmisisti, et personae tuae sospitatem cognouimus et successus prosperos quos tibi superatis regni aduersariis benignitas diuina concessit; audiuimus preterea optatam uirilem sobolem ex ingenua te et religiosa coniuge suscepisse. Quod

ᵃ quam [A]   *ᵇ* om. CB   *ᶜ* dom(i)nus CB; om. [A] (Edmerus om. a, E. egit Aa)   *ᵈ* The following letters are also found in θ and in Eadmer, Hist. nov. pp. 155–7, 149–51, 178–9 (checked in ψ, fos. 247–9)

[1] Prov. 27: 1.
[2] Referring to Henry's victory at Tinchebray, seen as due to the grace of God, and therefore reason for reconciliation with Anselm. See 414. 1.

to stay his appetite rather than plying his stomach with a succession of delicacies, and never drinking except to quench his thirst; the least intemperance, whether in his own servants or in general, met with severe rebuke. His sleep was heavy, and broken by frequent snores. He was a ready speaker, but owed more to chance than art, not hasty, but deliberate.

413. Being a man of praiseworthy devotion towards God, he built monasteries in England and in Normandy, of which, as he has not yet set the finishing touches to them, I too would withhold my judgement for the moment, did not brotherly love for the monks of Reading forbid me to keep silence. This house was founded by him between the two rivers of Kennet and Thames, in a place well suited to provide a lodging for almost all travellers to the more populous cities of England. In it he established monks of Cluny, who are at this time a distinguished exemplar of holy life and a model of inexhaustible and delightful hospitality. One can see there, as nowhere else, how the guests, who arrive at all hours, get more provision than the inmates. I may be thought hasty, or over-anxious to please, if I pay such a tribute to a religious life which is so lately born into the world, not knowing 'what the coming day may bring forth';[1] but my hope is that the monks themselves, with God's grace, will win through to be steadfast in well-doing. For my part, I feel no shame in praising men of holy life, and admiring in others the good qualities I lack in myself. As for the investitures of churches, he returned them into the hand of God and St Peter, after long controversy with Archbishop Anselm, being with difficulty, through God's great goodness, brought to consent by that inglorious victory over his brother.[2] But the course of this legal wrangle has been told at length by Dom Eadmer,[3] and I, just to make the story clear, will subjoin the documents on the subject issued by Pope Paschal, to whom I have often referred.[4]

414. 'Paschal, bishop, to King Henry, greeting.
'From the letter which you lately sent us by the hand of your servant, our beloved son, William your clerk, we learnt of your good health, and of the successes vouchsafed you by the Divine goodness in defeating the enemies of your kingdom. We have heard moreover that you have been blessed by your noble and devout consort with the

---

[3] In his *Historia novella*, pp. 118–86.   [4] In fact only in 289. 1 and 398. 3.

profecto cum nos laetificauerit, oportunum rati sumus nunc tibi precepta et uoluntatem Dei ualidius inculcare, cum amplioribus benefitiis benignitati eius te perspicis debitorem. Nos quoque diuinis benefitiis benignitatem nostram penes te sotiare optamus; sed graue nobis est quia id a nobis uideris expetere quod prestare*ᵃ* non possumus. Si enim consentiamus aut patiamur inuestituras a tua excellentia fieri, et nostrum proculdubio et tuum erit immane periculum. Qua in re contemplari te uolumus quid aut non fatiendo perdas aut fatiendo conquiras. Nos enim in prohibitione hac nichil amplius obedientiae, nichil liberalitatis per aecclesias nanciscimur, nec tibi debitae potestatis aut iuris subtrahere quicquam nitimur, nisi ut erga te Dei ira minuatur,*ᵇ* et sic tibi prospera cuncta contingant. Ait enim Dominus: "Honorificantes me honorificabo; qui autem contempnunt me erunt ignobiles."[1] Dices itaque: "Mei hoc iuris est." Non utique; non est imperatorium,*ᶜ* non regium, sed diuinum; solius illius est qui dixit: "Ego sum hostium."[2] Vnde pro ipso te rogo cuius hoc munus est, ut reddas hoc ipsi, ipsi dimittas cuius amori etiam quae tua sunt debes. Nos autem cur tuae obniteremur uoluntati, cur obsisteremus gratiae, nisi Dei in huius negotii consensu sciremus nos uoluntati obuiare, gratiam amittere? Cur tibi quicquam negaremus quod cuiquam esset mortalium concedendum, cum benefitia de te ampliora sumpserimus?

'Perspice, fili carissime, utrum decus an dedecus tibi sit quod sapientissimus ac religiosissimus Gallicanorum episcoporum Anselmus propter hoc tuo lateri adherere, tuo uereter in regno consistere. Qui tanta de te bona hactenus audierant, quid de te sentient, quid loquentur, cum hoc fuerit in regionibus diuulgatum? Ipsi qui coram te tuos excessus extollunt, cum presentia tua caruerint, hoc profecto ualidius infamabunt. Redi ergo, carissime fili, ad cor tuum; propter misericordiam Dei et propter amorem Vnigeniti deprecamur. Reuoca pastorem tuum, reuoca patrem tuum; et si quid,*ᵈ* quod non opinamur, grauius aduersus te gesserit, si inuestituras aduersatus*ᵉ* fueris, nos iuxta uoluntatem tuam, quantum cum Deo possumus, moderabimur. Tu tantum

---

ᵃ *[A], θ, Ead. p. 155 add* omnino *ᵇ* imminuatur *(om.* ira*) [A]* *ᶜ* imperatorum *[A]* *ᵈ* *CeBk, θ, Ead. p. 156;* quis *[A]CsBc* *ᵉ* auersatus *θ, Ead. p. 156, correctly*

---

[1] 1 Kgs. (1 Sam.) 2: 30.
[2] John 10: 7.

male issue you so much desired. This news gave us great joy; and we think it opportune to impress upon you with greater force the commandment and will of God at this moment, when in His increasing favours you can see so clearly the debt you owe to His benevolence. So we for our part wish to associate in your person our own benevo- 2 lence with the favour of Heaven; but it lies heavy upon us that you seem to demand of us something that we can by no means grant, for if we concur in or endure the exercise of investitures by your Excellency, it will assuredly bring grievous peril upon both you and us. In this matter we would have you contemplate what you lose by the non-exercise or gain by the exercise of them; for by this prohibition we ourselves acquire no further right to obedience or scope for generosity from the churches; we are not trying to take from you anything of the powers or legal rights that are your due, but only to mitigate the wrath of God towards you, that so all things may have for you a happy issue. As the Lord saith: "Them that honour me I will honour, 3 and they that despise me shall be lightly esteemed."[1] You will say therefore: "This is mine of right." Not so, indeed, for it belongs not to emperors or kings, but to God; it is His alone, who has said: "I am the door."[2] Wherefore I beg you on behalf of Him whose gift this is, that you give it back to Him; restore it to Him, to whose love you owe even what is truly yours. For our part, why should we resist your will and strive against your favour, unless we knew that by consent in this matter we should contravene the will of God and forfeit His favour? Why should we deny you anything that might be in our power to grant to any mortal, seeing we have received from you such ample kindness?

'Consider well, beloved son, whether it be to your glory or your 4 shame that Anselm, wisest and holiest of the Gallican bishops, for this cause fears to remain at your side, and to abide within your kingdom. Those who had hitherto heard such good things of you, what will they think of you, what will they say, when this is spread abroad among the nations? The very men who laud your overweening acts before your face, will, when you are absent, all the more forcibly reject this one. Return therefore, my beloved son, by God's mercy and by the love of His only Son we beseech you, return to your senses; recall your shepherd and your spiritual father; and if he has committed any serious fault against you, which we do not suppose, then, if you give up investitures, we will order all things according to your will, so far as under God we can. You have only to relieve your person and realm 5

talis repulsae[1] infamiam a persona tua et regno remoueas. Haec si feceris, et, si grauia quaelibet a nobis petieris quae cum Deo preberi facultas sit, profecto consequeris, et pro te Dominum ipso adiuuante exorare curabimus et de peccatis tam tibi quam coniugi tuae sanctorum apostolorum meritis indulgentiam et absolutionem fatiemus. Filium etiam[a] tuum, quem ex spectabili[b] et gloriosa coniuge suscepisti, quem, ut audiuimus, egregii patris Willelmi nomine nominasti, tanta tecum imminentia confouebimus ut qui te uel illum leserit Romanam aecclesiam uideatur lesisse.

'Data Lateranis nono kalendas Decembris.'

415. 'Paschalis Anselmo.

'Suauissimas dilectionis tuae accepimus litteras, caritatis calamo scriptas. In his reuerentiam deuotionis tuae complectimur, et perpendentes fidei tuae robur et piae sollicitudinis instantiam exultamus, quia, gratia Dei tibi prestante auxilium, te nec promissa sustollunt nec minae concutiunt. Dolemus autem quia, cum fratres nostros episcopos, legatos regis Anglorum, benigne susceperimus, quae nec diximus eis
2 nec cogitauimus redeuntes ad propria retulerunt. Audiuimus enim eos dixisse quia, si rex in aliis bene ageret, nos inuestituras aecclesiarum nec prohibere nec factas excommunicare, et quod ideo nolebamus cartae committere, ne sub occasione ea ceteri principes in nos inclamarent. Vnde Iesum, qui corda et renes scrutatur, in animam nostram testem inuocamus si, ex quo huius sanctae sedis curam suscepimus gerere, hoc immane scelus uel descendit in mentem.'
3 Et infra:
'Si ergo uirgam pastoralitatis signum, si anulum signaculum[c] fidei tradit laica manus, quid in aecclesia pontifices agunt? Episcopos autem qui ueritatem in mendatium commutarunt, ipsa ueritate, quae Deus est, in medium introducta a beati Petri gratia et a nostra sotietate secernimus, donec Romanae aecclesiae satisfatiant. Quicumque uero intra[d] predictas indutias inuestituras consecrationum acceperunt,[e] a consortio nostro et aecclesiae alienos habemus.'

[a] autem *[A]*   [b] ex spectabili *Cs, Ead. p. 156;* ex(s)pectabili *[A]CeB, θ*   [c] *om.* *[A]*   [d] inter *[A]Bk*   [e] acceperint *[A]*

of the shame of this rejection.[1] Do this; and then, if you ask us for things of moment, such as it may be possible under God to grant, they shall be yours; and we shall be careful, with his help, to endeavour to win the Lord over on your behalf, and by the merits of the holy Apostles we will grant both you and your consort indulgence and absolution from your sins. As for your son, born to you of your noble and illustrious consort, to whom we hear that you have given the name of your great father William, we will cherish him like yourself with such care that whoso wrong yourself or him, it shall be as if he wronged the Roman Church.

'Given at the Lateran, 23 November.'

415. 'Paschal to Anselm.
'We have received your most sweet letter, beloved son, written with a pen steeped in affection. We welcome your reverent devotion, and when we consider the strength of your faith and your zeal and pious care, we rejoice that, God's grace being your helper, you are neither carried away by promises nor shaken by threats. We regret, however, that after our kindly reception of our brother bishops, the emissaries of the king of England, they have reported on returning to their own country things that we have neither said nor thought. For they say (as we have heard) that if the king did well in other ways, we would neither forbid the investitures of churches nor declare them invalid when performed, and that we were unwilling to commit this to writing, only for fear that it would give other princes an opportunity to make demands upon us. For which cause we call Jesus, the searcher-out of heart and reins, to bear witness against our soul if, since the first day that we assumed the charge of this Holy See, this monstrous crime even entered into our mind.'

And further on: 'If then the staff, the emblem of the shepherd's office, if the ring, sign-manual of the Faith, can be bestowed by the hand of laymen, what part in the Church can prelates play? As for those bishops who have turned truth into falsehood, we call before their eyes the very Truth which is God Himself, and cut them off from the favour of St Peter and from converse with ourselves, until they make satisfaction to the Roman Church. Whoever within the aforesaid truce has received investiture and consecration, we consider alienated from communion with the Church and with ourselves.'

[1] i.e. of Anselm.

416. 'Paschalis Anselmo.

'Quod Anglici regis cor ad apostolicae sedis obedientiam omnipotentis Dei dignatio inclinauit, eidem miserationum Domino gratias agimus, in cuius manu corda regum uersantur. Hoc nimirum tuae caritatis gratia tuarumque orationum instantia factum credimus, ut in hac parte populum illum cui tua sollicitudo presidet miseratio superna respiceret.[a] Quod autem et regi et his qui obnoxii uidentur adeo condescendimus, eo affectu et compassione factum noueris ut eos qui iacebant erigere ualeamus; te autem, in Christo uenerabilis et carissime frater, ab illa prohibitione siue, ut tu credis, excommunicatione absoluimus, quam ab antecessore nostro sanctae memoriae Vrbano papa aduersus inuestituras ac hominia factam intelligis. Tu uero eos qui aut inuestituras accepere aut inuestitos benedixere aut hominia fecere cum ea satisfactione quam tibi per communes legatos Willelmum et Balduinum, uiros fideles ac ueridicos, significamus Domino cooperante suscipito, et eos uice nostrae auctoritatis absoluito;[b] quos uel ipse benedicas uel a quibus uolueris benedici precipias, nisi in his aliud forte reperias propter quod a sacratis[c] honoribus sint repellendi. Si qui uero deinceps preter inuestituras aecclesiarum prelationes assumpserint, etiamsi regi hominia fecerint, nequaquam ob hoc a benedictionis munere arceantur, donec[d] omnipotentis Dei gratia ad hoc omittendum cor regium tuae predicationis imbribus molliatur. Preterea super episcopis qui falsum, ut nosti, a nobis rumorem retulerunt, cor nostrum commotum est uehementius, quia non solum nos leserunt sed multorum simplicium animas deceperunt et regem aduersus caritatem sedis apostolicae impulerunt. Vnde et inultum eorum flagitium Domino cooperante non patimur; sed quia filii nostri regis instantia pro eis nos pulsat attentius, etiam ipsis communionis tuae participium non negabis. Sane regem et coniugem, et proceres illos qui pro hoc negotio cum rege ex precepto nostro laborauerunt, quorum nomina ex supradicti Willelmi suggestione cognosces, iuxta sponsionem nostram a peccatis et penitentiis absolues. Rotomagensis episcopi causam tuae deliberationi committimus, et quod ei indulseris indulgemus.'

---

[a] despiceret *AtAap*   [b] absoluto *[A]*   [c] sacris *[A], θ, Ead. p. 178*
[d] *[A], θ, Ead. p. 179 add* per *(then* gratiam α, θ*)*

416. 'Paschal to Anselm.

'Forasmuch as it hath pleased almighty God to turn the heart of the king of England into obedience to the Apostolic See, we give thanks to Him, the Lord of all mercies, in whose hand are set the hearts of kings. This we surely believe to be the outcome of the favour won by your love, and of your earnestness in prayer, that in this regard Heaven should look down in mercy on the people over whom you preside with loving care. But if we condescend thus far both to the king and to those who appear to be guilty, be sure that this is done with such compassionate affection as may enable us to set upright those who were fallen. For your part, reverend and most beloved brother in Christ, we absolve you from the prohibition and (as you suppose it to be) invalidation, which you understand to have been decreed by our predecessor of blessed memory, Pope Urban, against investitures and homage. But you are, God being your helper, to receive those who have either accepted investitures or blessed those who have been invested, or have done homage, exacting such satisfaction as we notify to you by our common emissaries William and Baldwin, faithful and true men, and grant them absolution as the minister of our authority; consecrate them yourself, or order their consecration by whoever you wish, unless perchance you find in them some other reason why they should be rejected from the dignity of consecration. But if any henceforward accept preferment not involving investitures of churches, although they may have done homage to the king, they are not for that reason to be refused the benefit of consecration, until through the grace of almighty God the king's heart be softened by the gentle rain of your admonitions into a readiness to forego the homage. Moreover, as concerning the bishops who brought back from our presence (as you know) a lying rumour, our heart is sorely vexed, for they have not only done us an injury, they have deceived the hearts of many simple folk and urged the king to oppose the kindly affection of the Apostolic See. For which cause we cannot, with God's help, allow their offence to remain unpunished; yet, forasmuch as the king, our son, importunes us on their behalf, even they shall not be forbidden the right of converse with you. As for the king and his consort, and those nobles who along with the king suffered under our sentence, whose names you will learn from the aforesaid William, all these you will absolve according to our promise from their sins and penances. The case of the bishop of Rouen we commit to your discretion, and whatsoever relief you may grant him, that we grant.'

417. Haec Paschalis summus papa pro aecclesiarum Dei libertate sollicitus agebat. Fuerunt autem episcopi quos mendatii arguit Girardus archiepiscopus Eboracensis et Herbertus Norwicensis; quorum errata reprehenderunt ueratiores legati, Willelmus postea Exoniensis episcopus et Balduinus Beccensis monachus. Eratque tunc Anselmus archiepiscopus iterum tempore istius regis Lugduni exul apud Hugonem eiusdem ciuitatis archiepiscopum, quando epistola prima quam apposui emissa est, quia nec ipse ullo desiderio ueniendi tenebatur nec rex animositatem suam pro copia susurronum sedari patiebatur.
2 Diu ergo et reuocare illum et monitionibus apostolicis obsecundare distulit, non elationis ambitu sed procerum, et maxime comitis de Mellento, instinctu, qui, in hoc negotio magis antiqua consuetudine quam recti tenore rationem reuerberans, allegabat multum regiae maiestati diminui si omittens morem antecessorum non inuestiret electum per baculum et anulum. Veruntamen rex, diligentius inspecto*ᵃ* quid uiuida epistolarum ratio, quid diuinorum munerum in se ubertim confluens ammoneret largitio, inuestituram anuli et baculi indulsit in per-
3 petuum, retento tantum electionis et regalium priuilegio. Coacto ergo apud Lundoniam magno episcoporum et procerum abbatumque concilio, multa aecclesiasticarum et secularium rerum ordinata negotia, decisa litigia. Nec multo post, uno die quinque sunt ordinati episcopi in Cantia ab Anselmo archiepiscopo: Willelmus ad Wintoniam, Rogerius ad Salesberiam, Willelmus ad Exoniam, Reinalmus*ᵇ* ad Herefordum, Vrbanus ad Clamorgan. Itaque controuersia frequentibus dissensionibus agitata, plurimoque Anselmi ad Romam itu et reditu uentilata, laudabilem finem accepit.

418. Vxor regis*ᶜ* ex antiqua et illustri regum stirpe descendit Mathildis, filia regis Scottorum, ut predixi.¹ A teneris annis inter sanctimoniales apud Wiltoniam et Rumesium educata, litteris quoque femineum pectus exercuit; unde, ut ignobiles nuptias respueret plusquam semel a patre oblatas, peplum sacratae professionis index gestauit. Quapropter, cum rex suscipere uellet eam thalamo, res in disceptationem uenit, nec nisi legitimis productis testibus, qui eam iurarent sine professione causa procorum uelum gessisse, archiepiscopus adduci potuit
2 ad consentiendum. Haec igitur duobus partubus,*ᵈ* altero alterius

ᵃ inspe a, re inspecta *Aac (Aap omits the context)*   *ᵇ* Rainaldus *(or* Rein-*)* CB   *ᶜ* regi *[A]*C   *ᵈ* partibus *[A]*

¹ 393. 3.

417. Thus did Paschal the supreme pontiff act, in his anxiety to secure the freedom of the churches of God. The bishops whom he accused of falsehood were Gerard archbishop of York and Herbert bishop of Norwich, whose errors were refuted by more truthful emissaries, William afterwards bishop of Exeter, and Baldwin monk of Bec. Archbishop Anselm was now in this king's reign an exile for the second time, living at Lyon with Hugh, archbishop of that city, when the first letter which I have quoted was issued. For the archbishop himself had no desire whatsoever to return, nor did the king suffer his hostility to be assuaged, for there were mischief-makers in plenty. He was therefore very slow to recall Anselm and obey the pope's admonitions, not from pride and vainglory, but at the urging of his nobles and especially the count of Meulan, who, beating back reason on this point more by appeal to ancient custom than to any moral principle, urged that the king's majesty would suffer severely if he forewent the custom of his predecessors and did not invest the elected person by staff and ring. The king, however, after carefully considering the lessons of the pope's letter with its vigorous argument, and of the flood of heavenly blessings that poured in upon him, gave up in perpetuity the investiture by ring and staff, reserving only the privilege of election and regalian rights. A great council of bishops, nobles and abbots was therefore summoned in London, and much business both ecclesiastical and secular was settled, and many suits decided. Not long after, five bishops were consecrated in one day at Canterbury by Archbishop Anselm: William to Winchester, Roger to Salisbury, William to Exeter, Reinhelm to Hereford, Urban to Glamorgan. Thus did the controversy, the source of frequent disagreements, and the cause of so many journeys by Anselm to and from Rome, find a satisfactory conclusion.

418. The king's wife Matilda, a daughter of the king of the Scots as I have already said,[1] was descended from an ancient and illustrious line of kings. She had been brought up from her earliest years among nuns at Wilton and Romsey, and had even exercised her intelligence, though a woman, in literature. Hence, so as to find a reason to reject the unworthy offers of marriage which her father laid before her more than once, she wore the veil that marks a professed religious; and consequently, when the king wished to marry her, there was much dispute, nor could the archbishop have been brought to give his consent if lawful witnesses had not been produced to swear that she had worn the veil because of her suitors and had never been professed. The bearing

sexus, contenta in posterum et parere et parturire destitit, aequanimiterque ferebat rege alias intento ipsa curiae ualedicere, Westmonasterio
multis annis morata. Nec tamen quicquam ei regalis magnificentiae
deerat, sed indefessa frequentia undae salutantium et totis apportantium temporibus accipiebantur et uomebantur superbis edibus; hoc
regis iubebat liberalitas, hoc ipsius grata et dulcis attrahebat benignitas.

3 Sanctitudinis egregiae, non usquequaque despicabilis formae, maternae
pietatis emula, nichil sinistrum quantum ad se moribus admittens,
preter regium cubile pudoris integra, nulla etiam suspitione lesa. Cilitio
sub regio cultu conuoluta, nudipes diebus Quadragesimae terebat aecclesiarum limina, nec horrebat pedes lauare morbidorum, ulcera sanie
distillantia contrectare, postremo longa manibus oscula protelare,
mensam apponere. Erat ei in audiendo seruitio Dei uoluptas unica,
ideoque in clericos bene melodos inconsiderate prouida[a] blande quos-
4 cumque alloqui, multa largiri, plura polliceri. Inde, liberalitate ipsius
per orbem sata, turmatim huc aduentabant scolastici cum cantibus
tum[b] uersibus famosi, felicemque se putabat qui carminis nouitate
aures mulceret dominae. Nec in[c] his solum expensas conferebat, sed
etiam omni generi hominum, presertim aduenarum, qui muneribus
acceptis famam eius longe per terras uenditarent. Est enim cupiditas
gloriae ita innata mentibus hominum ut uix aliquis bonae conscientiae
pretiosis contentus fructibus, si quid bene fecerit, non dulce habeat
5 efferri in uulgus. Vnde aiunt, et constat, dominae esse surreptum ut
extraneos quos posset premiis deliniret, ceteros promissis aliquando
efficacibus, aliquando et sepius inanibus suspenderet. Eo effectum est
ut prodige donantium non effugeret uitium, multimodas colonis suis
deferens calumnias, inferens iniurias, auferens substantias, quo bonae
largitricis nacta famam suorum paruipensaret contumeliam. Sed haec
qui recte iudicare uolet, consiliis ministrorum imputabit, qui, more
arpiarum, quicquid poterant corripere unguibus, uel infodiebant marsupiis uel insumebant conuiuiis; quorum feculentis susurris aures
oppleta neuum honestissimae menti contraxit, de reliquo factis omnibus approbanda et sancta.

[a] prodiga *[A]*, *perhaps rightly* [b] cum *[A]* [c] *Better deleted*

of two children, one of either sex, left her content, and for the future she ceased either to have offspring or desire them, satisfied, when the king was busy elsewhere, to bid the court goodbye herself, and spend many years at Westminster. Yet she forewent none of the state due to a queen; the throng of visitors was inexhaustible; the tide of well-wishers and contributors(?) continually ebbed and flowed through her proud portals. Such was the effect of our king's generosity, such the attraction of her own sweet kindliness. She was a woman of exceptional holiness, and by no means negligible beauty, in piety her mother's rival, and in her own character exempt from all evil influence; outside the royal marriage-bed of unblemished chastity, and untouched even by the breath of suspicion. Under her royal robes she wore a shift of hair-cloth, and trod the church floors barefooted during Lent; nor did she shrink from washing the feet of the diseased and handling their foul discharging sores, after which she would kiss their hands at length, and set food before them. She took especial pleasure in hearing divine service, and for that reason took more thought than was wholly wise for the clerks with sweet voices; she had a winning word for each, and would give them rich gifts, and promise richer. The news of her liberality consequently spread through the world, and hither flocked in troops any scholars who had a name for singing or for turning verses; happy he thought himself, the man who could please his lady's ear with a new song. Nor were they the only recipients of her bounty; it went to all sorts of men, especially to foreigners, who might accept her presents, and then advertise her fame in other countries. So deeply is the love of glory set by nature in the minds of men that scarce anyone is content with the precious fruits of a good conscience, and does not count it sweet, if he does something well, to have it spread abroad. Hence it was, they say—and indeed it is true—that our lady was beguiled into sweetening with presents all the foreigners she could, and kept the others dangling with promises that were sometimes honoured, and sometimes—indeed, more often—empty. Thus it came about that she did not escape the vice of prodigality, laid all kinds of claim against her tenantry, used them despitefully and took their livelihood, winning the name of a generous giver but ignoring the wrongs of her own people. But a right judgement of her conduct will attribute it to the cunning of her servants, who like harpies seized with their talons all they could, and either buried it in their own moneybags, or wasted it in riotous living; their poisoned whispers filled her ears, and made an unsightly blemish grow on her most honourable mind, who in all her other actions was admirable and godly.

6   Inter haec erepta est patriae, magno prouintialium dampno, suo nullo; nam et funus, nobiliter curatum apud Westmonasterium, quietem accepit et spiritus se caelum incolere non friuolis signis ostendit. Obiit regno post septemdecim annos et sex menses libenter relicto, fatum parentum experta, qui pene omnes uirente potissimum aeuo excessere mundo. Successit thoro eius, sed non ita cito, Adala filia ducis de Louanio, quod est castellum, caput Lotharingiae.

419. Filium habuit rex Henricus ex Mathilde nomine Willelmum, dulci spe et ingenti cura in successionem educatum et prouectum; nam et ei, uix dum^a duodecim annorum esset, omnes liberi homines Angliae et Normanniae cuiuscumque ordinis et dignitatis, cuiuscumque domini fideles, manibus et^b sacramento se dedere coacti sunt. Filiam quoque Fulconis comitis Andegauensis uix nubilem ipse etiam impubis despondit et accepit, dato sibi a socero comitatu Cinomannico pro munere sponsalitio; quin et Ierosolimam Fulco ire contendens comitatum commendauit regi suum si uiueret, futurum profecto
2   generi si non rediret. Plures ergo prouintiae spectabant nutum pueri, putabaturque regis Eduardi uaticinium[1] in eo complendum; ferebaturque spes Angliae, modo arboris succisa, in illo iuuenculo iterum floribus pubescere, fructus protrudere, et ideo finem malorum sperari posse. Deo aliter uisum; huiuscemodi enim opinionem tulerunt aurae, quod eum proxima dies urgebat fato satisfacere. Enimuero socero tunc annitente simulque Thetbaldo filio Stephani et Adalae amitae,[2] Ludouicus rex Frantiae Normanniam concessit puero, ut facto sibi
3   hominio possideret eam iure legitimo. Ordinabat haec et effitiebat prudentissimi patris prudentia, ut hominium, quod ipse pro culmine imperii fastidiret facere, filius delicatus et qui putabatur uiam seculi ingressurus non recusaret. His agitandis et placita^c concordia componendis quattuor annorum tempus rex impendit, in Normannia toto hoc tempore moratus. Veruntamen tam splendidae et excogitatae pacis serenum, tam omnium spes in speculam erectas confudit humanae sortis uarietas.

Namque indicto in Angliam reditu, rex sub ipso crepusculo septimo kalendas Decembris apud Barbeflet naues soluit, eumque qui

---

^{a} uix cum *Aa*, uix α *(but cf. 217. 1 = GP p. 174)* ^{b} om. *[A]* ^{c} placida *[A]Cs(after corr.?)*

[1] 226. 2.
[2] i.e. William's.

Amid all this, she was taken from among her people to their great loss, 6
but not to hers; for her body was honourably buried at Westminster and
is now at peace, while her spirit showed by tokens more than ordinary
that it inhabits Heaven. At her death she gladly gave up the throne after a
reign of seventeen years and six months, sharing the lot of her relations,
who almost all departed this life in the flower of their age. She was succeeded as the king's consort, but not immediately, by Adela, daughter of
the duke of Louvain, which is a castle, the capital of Lorraine.

419. King Henry had a son by Matilda named William, who with
affection and hope and every care was educated and brought up to be
his successor. When he was scarcely twelve years old, all the free men
of England and Normandy, whatever their order and dignity and whoever their lord, were compelled to bind themselves to him by the
giving of homage on oath. He was betrothed to a daughter of Fulk
count of Anjou, when she was scarcely of marriageable age, and he yet
a boy, and had her to wife, receiving as a betrothal-present from his
father-in-law the county of Maine; further, when Fulk was setting out
for Jerusalem, he entrusted his county to the king, if he lived, for if he
did not return, it would go to his son-in-law. Thus many provinces 2
looked to the boy's lightest wish, and in him it was supposed King
Edward's prophecy[1] was to be fulfilled: the hope of England, it was
thought, once cut down like a tree, was in the person of that young
prince again to blossom and bear fruit, so that one might hope the evil
times were coming to an end. But God had other plans; these expectations went down the wind, for the day was already at hand when he
must fulfil his fate. Thanks to the efforts of his father-in-law, assisted
by Theobald the son of Stephen and his[2] aunt Adela, Louis king of
France granted the young man Normandy, on terms that he would do
him homage for it and hold it by lawful right. This was the outcome 3
of his wise father's policy, that the homage which he himself as a sover-
eign prince was too proud to pay, should not be refused by his son,
who was an elegant youth, and likely it was thought to make a name in
the world. In the discussion of this and its expression in a formal agreement, the king spent four years, remaining in Normandy the whole
time. And now peace dawned, the bright fruit of so much labour, the
hopes of all men were lifted as to a tower's top, when all was thrown
into confusion by the mutability of human things.

Having appointed his return to England, the king left Barfleur just at
twilight on 25 November, and the wind that filled his sails wafted him

impleuerat carbasa uentus feliciter regno et amplae fortunae inuexit.
4 At uero adolescentulus, iam septemdecim annorum et paulo plus, cui nichil delitiarum preter nomen regis pro paterna indulgentia deesset, aliam sibi nauem parari precepit, omnibus pene adolescentulis*a* procerum filiis quasi pro colludio aetatis puerilis eo accurrentibus. Quin et remiges, immodice mero ingurgitati, uoluptate nautica quam potus ministrabat mature illos qui precesserant post tergum relinquendos clamitabant; erat enim nauis optima, tabulatis nouis et clauis recenter compacta. Itaque ceca iam nocte iuuentus sapientiae indiga simulque
5 potu obruta nauem a littore impellunt. Volat illa pennata pernitior harundine et crispantia maris terga radens imprudentia ebriorum impegit in scopulum, non longe a littore supra pelagus extantem. Consurgunt ergo miseri et magno clamore ferratos contos expediunt, diu certantes ut nauem a rupe propellerent; sed obsistebat Fortuna, omnes eorum conatus in irritum deducens. Itaque et remi in saxum obnixi crepuere concussaque prora pependit.[1] Iamque alios undis exponebat, alios ingressa per rimas aqua enecabat, cum*b* eiecta scafa filius regis excipitur; saluarique potuisset ad litus regressus, nisi soror eius notha, comitissa Perticae, in maiori naue cum morte luctans femineo ululatu[2]
6 fratris opem implorasset, ne tam impie se relinqueret. Ille misericordia infractus lembum carinae applicari iussit, ut sororem exciperet, mortem misellus pro clementiae teneritudine indeptus; continuo enim multitudine insilientium*c* scafa uicta subsedit, omnesque pariter fundo inuoluit. Euasit unus, et ille agrestis, qui tota nocte malo supernatans mane totius tragediae actum expressit.

Nulla umquam fuit nauis Angliae tantae miseriae, nulla toti*d* orbi
7 tam patulae famae. Periit ibi cum Willelmo alter[3] filius regis Ricardus, quem ante regnum ex prouintiali femina susceperat, iuuenis magnanimus et patri pro obsequio acceptus; Ricardus comes Cestrae et frater eius Otuelus, nutritius et magister filii regis; filia regis, comitissa Perticae, et neptis eius soror Thetbaldi, comitissa Cestrae; preterea quisquis erat in curia lectissimus miles uel capellanus, et optimatum filii ad militiam prouehendi. Accurrerant enim undique, ut dixi, non leue gloriae

a adolescentibus *[A]*   *b* *B adds* iam   *c* in silentium *[A]*   *d* toto *B; om.* *[A]*

---

[1] Cf. Virgil, *Aen.* v. 205–6. William echoes other details of the shipwreck in Virgil.
[2] Virgil, *Aen.* iv. 667.
[3] This is the strict meaning of the Latin; but there were other illegitimate sons.

safely back to his kingdom and his ample wealth. The young man, 4
however, who was now seventeen or a little more, and through his
father's indulgence enjoyed all the sweets of kingship except the name
of king, gave orders that another ship should be got ready for himself,
and almost all the young men who were sons of nobles flocked to join
him, as though for a youthful frolic. The rowers too, who were deep
sunk in liquor, and filled with glee, as sailors are, by what they had
drunk, were clamorously insistent that they would soon leave behind
them those who had started first. They had a splendid ship, provided
with new planking and nails. It was already night and pitch dark,
when those young hotheads, drunk as well as foolish, put out from
the shore. The ship sped swifter than a feathered arrow, and skimming 5
the sea's curling top, she struck, through the carelessness of her
besotted crew, a rock projecting from the surface not far from the
shore. Hapless souls, they jump to their feet and in a babel of shouting
unship iron-shod poles for a long struggle to push their vessel off the
rock; but Fortune was against them, and brought to nought all their
endeavours. So 'the oars smashed against the crags, fast hung the bat-
tered prow'.[1] Already some were being washed overboard, and others
drowned by the water that came in through the cracks, when they got
off a boat with the king's son in it, and he might have made his way
back to shore and been saved, had not his half-sister, the countess of
Perche, wrestling with death in the main ship, implored her brother
'with shrieks as women will'[2] to help, and not to leave her so heart-
lessly. Overcome with pity, he ordered them to bring the boat alongside 6
the hull to take his sister off, and this soft-hearted kindness cost the
poor prince his life; for a mob jumped at once into the boat, and she
was swamped, and took them all together to the bottom. One man
escaped, a country fellow, who floated all night on a spar, and in the
morning told the whole tragic story.

No ship that ever sailed brought England such disaster, none was so
well known the wide world over. There perished then with William 7
the king's other[3] son Richard, born to him before his accession by a
woman of the country, a high-spirited youth, whose devotion had
earned his father's love; Richard earl of Chester and his brother Otuel,
the guardian and tutor of the king's son; the king's daughter the
countess of Perche, and his niece, Theobald's sister, the countess of
Chester; besides all the choicest knights and chaplains of the court,
and the nobles' sons who were candidates for knighthood, for they
had hastened from all sides to join him, as I have said, expecting no

suae numeraturi commodum si filio regis uel deferrent ludicrum uel
8 conferrent obsequium; accumulauitque calamitatem*a* difficultas inueniendorum cadauerum, quia dispersis per littora quesitoribus nullum facile repertum est, sed ierunt tam delicata corpora 'equoreis crudelia pabula monstris'.[1] Iuuenculi ergo morte cognita res mirum in modum mutatae. Parens enim celibatui renuntiauit, cui post mortem Mathildis studuerat, futuros heredes ex noua coniuge iamiamque operiens. Socer, ex Ierosolimis domum reuersus, partibus Willelmi filii Rotberti Normanni comitis improbus astitit, tradens ei alteram filiam nuptum et Cinomannicum comitatum; irarum stimulos in regem acuebat dos filiae, post mortem filii in Anglia retenta.

420. Filiam Mathildem ex Mathilde susceptam dedit rex Henricus Henrico imperatori Alemanniae, filio Henrici de quo tertius liber memoriam fecit.[2] Fuit hic Henricus quintus eius nominis apud Teutonicos imperator, qui licet pro contumeliis apostolicae sedis patri grauiter succensuisset, ipse tamen eiusdem sententiae sequax et propugnator suo tempore fuit infestus. Namque cum Vrbano papae Paschalis successisset, uir nullo uirtutis genere carens, rursus questio de inuestituris aecclesiarum, rursus bella, rursus lites agitari, neutris partibus loco
2 cedentibus. Imperator omnes episcopos et abbates regni sui quod citra montes est fautores habebat, quia Karolus Magnus pro contundenda gentium illarum ferotia omnes pene terras aecclesiis contulerat, consiliosissime perpendens nolle sacri ordinis homines tam facile quam laicos fidelitatem domini reicere; preterea, si laici rebellarent, illos posse et*b* excommunicationis auctoritate et potentiae seueritate compescere. Papa ultramontanas aecclesias suae rationi subiecerat, parumque suspitiebant*c* urbes Italae*d* Henrici dominium, seruitio se putantes exutas post Conradi fratris eius interitum, qui a patre relictus Longo-
3 bardiae in regem apud Aretium obierat diem. At uero Henricus, antiquis Cesaribus in nullo uirtute deiectior, post pacatum regnum Teutonicum presumebat animo Italicum, rebellionem urbium subiugaturus questionemque de inuestitura suo libito recisurus. Sed iter illud

a With this word the old hand of Cs ceases   *b* om. [A]   *c* suscipiebant B
d Itali(a)e AaB, rightly?

[1] Statius, Theb. ix. 300.
[2] cc. 288–9.

small gain in reputation if they could show the king's son some sport or do him some service. The disaster was deepened by the difficulty of recovering the dead, for though search-parties were sent up and down the shore, none was found easily, but those pampered bodies went to make 'a cruel feast for monsters of the deep'.[1] When the young man's death was known, the face of things was wonderfully changed. His father abandoned the celibate life on which he had been intent since Matilda's death, looking impatiently for fresh heirs from a new wife. The father-in-law, on his return from Jerusalem, showed a complete lack of principle by joining the party of William son of Robert the Norman duke, to whom he gave the hand of his other daughter and the county of Maine; his first daughter's dowry put an edge on his resentment against the king, for after his son's death the king kept it in England.

420. His daughter Matilda, Queen Matilda's child, was given in marriage by King Henry to Henry emperor of Germany, son of that Henry of whom I told in my third book.[2] This Henry was the fifth emperor of that name among the Teutons. Though he had taken strongly against his father because of his outrages against the Apostolic See, yet for his part he followed the same policy, and fought for it in his own day vigorously. When Pope Urban had been succeeded by Paschal, a man endowed with every virtue, the controversy over investitures of churches broke out once more; once more all was battling and strife, and neither party would give way. The emperor was supported by all the bishops and abbots of his realm on this side the Alps; for Charlemagne, in order to break the fierce spirit of those nations, had given almost all the land to churches, very wisely considering that clerks in holy orders would not throw off their fealty to their lord so easily as laymen; besides which, he thought, if the laity rebelled, the authority to excommunicate would be there to control them as well as the severity of civil power. The pope had subjected the churches beyond the Alps to his own way of thinking, and the cities of Italy had little respect for Henry's rule, thinking themselves set free from servitude after the death of his brother Conrad, who had been bequeathed by his father to Lombardy as its king, but had died at Arezzo. Henry, however, whose spirit in no way fell short of the Caesars of Antiquity, once his Teuton dominions were at peace, was already in imagination recovering his realm in Italy: he would subdue those rebellious cities, he would cut the knot of the investiture

ad Romam magnis exercitationibus pectorum, magnis angoribus corporum consummatum Dauid Scottus Bancornensis episcopus exposuit, magis in regis gratiam quam historicum deceret acclinis. Denique et inauditam uiolentiam, quod Apostolicum cepit, quanuis libere custodierit, laudi ducit ab exemplo quod Iacob, angelum uiolenter tenens, benedictionem ab eo extorserit.[1] Preter haec laborat asserere dictum apostoli 'nemo militans Deo implicat se negotiis secularibus'[2] non aduersari cupiditatibus pontificum per laicos inuestitorum, quia non sit seculare negotium si clericus laico fecerit hominium; quae quantum sint friuola, cuiuslibet diiudicabit prudentia. Ego interim, ne bonum uirum uerbo uidear premere, statuo indulgendum, quia non historiam sed panagericum scripsit. Nunc uero priuilegium et conuentionem, uiolenta trium septimanarum captione a papa extorta, ueraciter inseram, et qualiter non multo post religiosiori consilio*a* eneruata sunt subitiam.

421. *b*'Dominus papa Paschalis non inquietabit dominum regem nec eius imperium uel regnum de inuestitura episcopatuum et abbatiarum neque de iniuria sibi illata et suis in persona et bonis neque aliquod malum reddet sibi uel alicui personae pro hac causa et penitus in personam regis Henrici numquam anathema ponet nec remanebit in domino papa quin coronet eum sicut in ordine continetur et regnum et imperium offitii sui auxilio eum tenere adiuuabit pro posse suo. Et haec adimplebit dominus papa sine fraude et malo ingenio.

'Haec sunt nomina illorum episcoporum et cardinalium qui precepto domini papae Paschalis priuilegium et amicitiam domino Henrico imperatori sacramento confirmauerunt: Petrus Portuensis episcopus, Centius Sabinensis episcopus, Robertus cardinalis Sancti Eusebii, Bonefatius cardinalis Sancti Marci, Anastasius cardinalis Sancti Clementis, Gregorius cardinalis Apostolorum Petri et Pauli, item Gregorius cardinalis Sancti Crisogoni, Iohannes cardinalis Sanctae Potentianae,*c* Risus cardinalis Sancti Laurentii, Reinerus cardinalis Sanctorum Marcellini et Petri, Vitalis cardinalis Sanctae Balbinae, Teuzo*d* cardinalis Sancti Marci,*e* Thetbaldus cardinalis Iohannis et Pauli, Iohannes decanus in Scola Greca, Leo decanus Sancti Vitalis, Albo decanus Sergii et Bachi.'

---

a concilio [A] *b* This document and those in 422 and 424 are also found in θ and JW s.a. 1111; edition in MGH Constit. i. 142–5 *c* Properly Pudentianae *d* Euzo B (Duuzo JW; Diuizo MGH); cf. 431. 3 *e* Properly Martini

---

[1] Gen. 32: 24–9. [2] 2 Tim. 2: 4.

controversy at his good pleasure. But his expedition to Rome, accompanied at such a cost in anguish of heart and bodily discomfort, has been told by David the Scot, bishop of Bangor, though with more prejudice in favour of the king than is proper for an historian. For instance, even the unexampled violence of seizing the Holy Father, although he was kept in open captivity, is represented as creditable, on the analogy of Jacob, who held the angel by force till he had wrung a blessing from him.[1] Besides which, he strives to maintain that the Apostle's words 'No man that warreth in God's service entangleth himself with the affairs of this life'[2] are not fatal to the ambition of prelates who have received lay investiture, on the ground that it is not an affair of this life if a clerk does homage to a layman; and how flimsy this is, any man of sense will see for himself. But, as at present advised, rather than seem to condemn a good man out of hand, I think one should be lenient with him, on the ground that he was writing panegyric and not history. And now I will truthfully set down the privilege and form of agreement extracted from the pope by three weeks' forcible confinement, to which I will add how, not long after, a more spiritual policy took away their effect.

421. 'Our lord Pope Paschal will not molest our lord the king, his realm and empire, in the matter of investiture of bishoprics and abbacies, nor in the matter of injuries suffered by him and his in their person and possessions; nor will he return evil of any kind to him or any other person in this regard; and he will certainly never lay an anathema on the person of King Henry; nor will our lord the pope retain the right of refusal to crown him as the ordinal provides; and he will, aided by his office, as best he may, assist the king to maintain his realm and empire. And this our lord the pope will fulfil without fraud or malice.

'These are the names of the bishops and cardinals who by command of our lord Pope Paschal, have by oath confirmed this privilege and act of friendship offered to our lord and emperor Henry: Peter bishop of Porto, Cencio bishop of Sabina, Robert cardinal of St Eusebius, Boniface cardinal of St Mark, Anastasius cardinal of St Clement, Gregory cardinal of the Apostles Peter and Paul, Gregory cardinal of St Chrysogonus, John cardinal of St Pudentiana, Riso cardinal of St Laurence, Reiner cardinal of SS Marcellinus and Peter, Vitalis cardinal of St Balbina, Teuzo cardinal of St Martin, Theobald cardinal of SS John and Paul, John deacon of the Schola Graeca, Leo deacon of St Vitalis, Albo deacon of SS Sergius and Bacchus.'

422. Ipse etiam rex hoc sacramentum fecit:

'Ego Henricus rex liberos dimittam quarta uel quinta feria proxima et dominum papam et episcopos et cardinales et omnes captiuos et obsides qui pro eo uel cum eo capti sunt, et secure perduci fatiam intra portas Transtiberinae ciuitatis, *a*nec ulterius capiam aut capi permittam eos qui in fidelitate domini papae Paschalis permanent, et populi Romani et Transtiberinae*a* ciuitatis*b* pacem et securitatem seruabo tam per me quam per meos in personis qui pacem michi seruauerint. Dominum papam fideliter adiuuabo ut papatum suum quiete et secure teneat. Patrimonia et possessiones Romanae aecclesiae quae abstuli restituam, et cuncta quae habere debet more antecessorum suorum*c* recuperare et tenere adiuuabo bona fide sine fraude et malo ingenio, et domino papae Paschali obediam saluo honore regni et imperii, sicut catholici imperatores catholicis pontificibus Romanis.

2 'Et isti sunt iuratores ex parte ipsius regis: Fridericus Coloniensis archiepiscopus, Godebardus*d* Tridentinus episcopus, Bruno Spirensis episcopus, Berengarius comes, Albertus cancellarius, Herimannus comes, Fridericus comes palatinus, Bonefatius marchio, Albertus comes de Blandriaco, Fridericus comes, Godefridus comes, Warnerius marchio.'

423. Hac conuentione expleta et predictorum episcoporum et cardinalium sacramento confirmata,*e* osculo utrimque dato, domnus papa quarto idus Aprilis dominica Quasi modo geniti missam celebrauit, in qua post communionem suam et ministrorum altaris imperatori corpus et sanguinem Domini dedit in haec uerba: 'Hoc Dominicum corpus, quod sacrosancta tenet aecclesia, natum ex Maria uirgine, eleuatum in cruce pro redemptione humani generis, damus tibi, fili carissime, in remissionem peccatorum tuorum et in conseruationem confirmandae pacis et uerae amicitiae inter me et te, et regnum et*f*
2 sacerdotium.' Altero uero die Apostolicus et rex ad columnas quae sunt in foro conuenerunt, dispositis presidiis loricatorum ubicumque uidebatur opus esse, ne impediretur regis consecratio. Et in Argentea Porta receptus est rex ab episcopis et cardinalibus et toto clero Romano, et cepta oratione quae in ordine continetur ab Hostiensi episcopo, quoniam Albanus deerat a quo debuisset dici si adesset, ad

a–a om. [A]   *b* ciuitatis θ; -tati [C]B; om. [A]. JW and MGH both give ciuitatis, but with different constructions. The correct reading is not certain   *c* meorum JW, MGH (suorum uel meorum Bk)   *d* Gedebardus [A], θ; Gebehardus JW, MGH (correctly)   *e* confirmata Cd; confirmato [C]B; om. [A]   *f* om. AgAap

422. The king for his part swore the following oath:
'I, King Henry, will send away scot-free on Thursday or Friday next my lord the pope and the bishops and cardinals, and all the captives and hostages taken on his behalf or in his company, and will cause them to be conveyed safely within the gates of Trastevere; nor will I hereafter take, or suffer to be taken, those who abide in fealty to our lord Pope Paschal; and for the people of Rome and Trastevere I will maintain peace and security as concerns myself and my men, for such persons as keep the peace towards me. My lord the pope I will faithfully assist to maintain his papal see in peace and security. The patrimony and possessions of the Roman church which I have taken away I will restore, and I will aid the pope to recover and to maintain all that he ought to have by the custom of his predecessors, in good faith, without deceit or malice. And I will render obedience to my lord Pope Paschal, saving the honour of my realm and empire, even as catholic emperors render it to catholic Roman pontiffs.

'And these are they who swore on the king's side: Frederick archbishop of Cologne, Gebhard bishop of Trento, Bruno bishop of Speyer, Count Berengar, Chancellor Adalbert, Count Hermann, Frederick count palatine, Marquis Boniface, Albert count of Biandrate, Count Frederick, Count Godfrey, Marquis Werner.'

423. This agreement having been completed, and confirmed by the oaths of the bishops and cardinals aforesaid, they exchanged the kiss of peace, and our lord the pope on 10 April, which was Low Sunday, celebrated Mass; wherein, after he and the ministers of the altar had communicated, he gave the emperor the body and blood of the Lord with these words: 'This body of the Lord, which the most holy Church has in its keeping, born of the Virgin Mary and lifted up on the Cross for the redemption of the human race, we here give thee, dearly beloved son, for the remission of thy sins and the preservation of the peace and true friendship to be confirmed between me and thee, and between kingship and priesthood.' Next day, the pope and the king met at the columns in the Forum, pickets of men in armour being posted wherever seemed necessary, that nothing might hamper the king's consecration. So the king was received at the Silver Gate by the bishops and cardinals and the whole clergy of Rome, and the prayer contained in the ordinal being begun by the bishop of Ostia, in the absence of the bishop of Albano by whom it should have been said had he been present, he was taken to the middle of the Rota, and

mediam rotam ductus est; et ibi recepit secundam orationem a Portuensi episcopo, sicut precipit Romanus ordo. Deinde duxerunt eum cum letaniis usque ad confessionem apostolorum, et ibi unxit eum Hostiensis episcopus inter scapulas et in brachio dextro. Post haec a domino Apostolico ad altare eorundem apostolorum deductus et ibidem, imposita sibi corona, ab ipso Apostolico in imperatorem est consecratus. Post impositam coronam missa de resurrectione Domini est celebrata, in qua ante communionem domnus Apostolicus priuilegium imperatori propria manu dedit, in quo sibi et regno suo quod hic scriptum est concessit et in eodem loco sub anathemate confirmauit.

424. 'Paschalis episcopus seruus seruorum Dei carissimo in Christo filio et per Dei omnipotentis gratiam Romanorum imperatori augusto Henrico salutem*a* et apostolicam benedictionem.

'Regnum uestrum sanctae Romanae aecclesiae coherere diuina dispositio constituit; predecessores siquidem uestri probitatis et prudentiae amplioris gratia Romanae urbis coronam et imperium consecuti sunt. Ad cuius uidelicet coronae et imperii dignitatem tuam quoque personam, fili carissime Henrice, per nostri sacerdotii ministerium maiestas diuina prouexit. Illam igitur dignitatis prerogatiuam, quam predecessores nostri uestris predecessoribus catholicis imperatoribus concesserunt et priuilegiorum paginis confirmauerunt, nos quoque tuae dilectioni concedimus et presentis priuilegii pagina confirmamus, ut regni tui episcopis uel abbatibus libere preter uiolentiam uel simoniam electis inuestituram uirgae et anuli conferas; post inuestitionem uero canonice consecrationem accipiant ab episcopo ad quem pertinuerit. Si quis autem a clero uel populo preter assensum tuum electus fuerit, nisi a te inuestiatur, a nemine consecretur, exceptis nimirum illis qui uel in archiepiscoporum uel in Romani pontificis solent dispositione consistere. Sane archiepiscopi uel episcopi libertatem habeant a te inuestitos episcopos uel abbates canonice consecrandi; predecessores enim uestri aecclesias regni sui tantis regalium suorum benefitiis ampliarunt ut regnum ipsum maxime episcoporum uel abbatum presidiis oporteat communiri, et populares dissensiones, quae in electis omnibus sepe contingunt, regali oporteat maiestate compesci. Quam ob rem prudentiae tuae et potestati cura debet sollicitius imminere, ut Romanae aecclesiae magnitudo et ceterarum salus tuis,

a salutes *[C]Bk*

there was the recipient of a second prayer from the bishop of Porto, as the Roman ordinal prescribes. They then took him with litanies to the shrine of the Apostles, and there the bishop of Ostia anointed him between the shoulders and on the right arm. Next he was taken by the Holy Father to the altar of the same Apostles, and there the pope himself set the crown upon his head, and he was consecrated emperor. After the crowning a Mass of the Lord's Resurrection was celebrated, in which before making his communion our lord the pope gave a privilege to the emperor with his own hand, in which he granted to him and his realm the concession hereafter written, and confirmed it in the same place with an anathema.

424. 'Paschal, bishop, servant of the servants of God, to his beloved son in Christ, and by the grace of almighty God august emperor of the Romans, Henry, greeting and our Apostolic blessing.

'That your realm should be closely bound to the holy Roman church is ordained by divine Providence, for your predecessors, thanks to their surpassing uprightness and wisdom, have received the crown and empire of the city of Rome. To the dignity of this same crown and empire you too, our beloved son Henry, have now been promoted by the Divine Majesty through the ministry of ourself as priest. Now therefore that same most excellent dignity which our predecessors granted to the catholic emperors your predecessors, and confirmed by written privileges, we do now grant to you, beloved, and confirm it by this present deed of privilege, that you should confer upon the bishops and abbots of your realm, who have been freely elected without violence or simony, investiture of staff and ring; but after investment let them receive lawful consecration from the bishop to whom it shall pertain so to do. But if any be elected by clergy or people without your consent, unless he be invested by you, let none consecrate him, excepting such as normally lie within the disposition of archbishops or of the Roman pontiff. Let archbishops and bishops enjoy freedom lawfully to consecrate bishops and abbots who have been invested by you; for your predecessors so generously endowed the churches of their realm with their royal possessions that the realm itself ought to enjoy the support of bishops and abbots in particular, and the popular dissensions so often provoked by elections ought to be subdued by the king's majesty. For this cause it should be a principal care of your wisdom and power to maintain the greatness of the Roman church and the whole estate of other churches, with God's aid, by your

4 Domino prestante, benefitiis et seruitiis conseruetur. Si qua igitur aecclesiastica uel secularis persona, hanc nostrae concessionis paginam sciens, contra eam temerario ausu uenire temptauerit, anathematis uinculo, nisi resipuerit, innodetur, honorisque ac dignitatis suae periculum patiatur; obseruantes autem haec misericordia diuina custodiat, et personam potestatemque tuam ad honorem suum et gloriam feliciter imperare concedat.'

425. Peracto itaque toto ipsius consecrationis offitio, Apostolicus et imperator complexis inuicem dextris iuerunt cum celebri pompa ad cameram quae est ante confessionem sancti Gregorii, ut ibi deponerent Apostolicus sua sacerdotalia, imperator autem sua regalia. Imperatori autem exeunti de camera et suis regalibus exuto occurrerunt Romani patritii cum aureo circulo, quem imposuerunt imperatori in capite, et per eum dederunt sibi summum patritiatum Romanae urbis communi consensu omnium et uolenti animo.

426. Omnem hanc ambitionem priuilegiorum et consecrationis uerbo de scriptis prefati Dauid transtuli, quae ille, ut dixi,[1] pronius quam deberet ad gratiam regis inflectit. Sequenti uero anno congregatum est concilium Romae, non tam precipiente quam coniuente papa, et priuilegium illud irritum factum est. Auctores fuere huiusce mutationis archiepiscopus Viennensis, qui postea sedem apostolicam rexit, et episcopus Engolismensis, Girardus nomine, qui coepiscopos ad haec exinanienda[a] irritabant. Eius ergo concilii actio[b] haec est:

427. 'Anno ab incarnatione Domini millesimo centesimo duodecimo, indictione quinta, anno pontificatus domini papae Paschalis secundi tertio decimo, mense Martio, quinto decimo kalendas Aprilis, celebratum est concilium Romae Lateranis in basilica Constantiniana. In qua cum dominus papa Paschalis resedisset, cum archiepiscopis et episcopis et cardinalibus et uaria multitudine clericorum et laicorum, ultima die concilii facta coram omnibus professione catholicae fidei, ne
2 quis de fide ipsius dubitaret, dixit: "Amplector omnem diuinam scripturam Veteris ac Noui Testamenti, legem a Moise scriptam et a sanctis prophetis; amplector quattuor euangelia, septem canonicas epistolas,[c]

[a] exinaniendo B   [b] a'uo Bk, antioc Bc. The proceedings are also given in θ, in JW s.a. 1112, and in η; edition in MGH Constit. i. 571–3   [c] [C] adds et

munificence and services. If therefore any person ecclesiastical or secular, knowing this our grant in writing, shall essay in his rash audacity to contravene it, let him, unless he repents, be bound by the chain of anathema, and be brought in peril of his honour and dignity; but as for those who observe its provisions, may the Divine Mercy watch over them, and grant that your imperial person may reign in felicity to His glory and honour.'

425. After the whole rite of consecration had been completed, the pope and emperor, hand in hand, and followed by a great company, went to the chamber which is before the shrine of St Gregory, that there the pope might put off his priestly vestments and the emperor his vestments as king. But as the emperor came forth from the chamber, having laid aside his regalia, the Roman patricians met him with a gold circlet, which they set upon his head, and therewith confirmed upon him the supreme patriciate of the city of Rome, by the common consent and general will of all the citizens.

426. All this parade of privileges and consecration rites I have copied word for word from David's book, in which, as I have said,[1] he shows undue prejudice in favour of the king. In the following year, however, a council met in Rome, not so much at the pope's command as with his connivance, and this privilege was quashed. The leaders in this reversal were the archbishop of Vienne, afterwards pope, and the bishop of Angoulême, Gerard by name, who aroused their fellow bishops to annul the whole transaction. The proceedings of this council run as follows:

427. 'In the year of our Lord 1112, being the fifth indiction and the thirteenth year of the pontificate of our lord Pope Paschal II, on 18 March, was held a council at Rome, in the Lateran, in the basilica of Constantine. Wherein, when our lord Pope Paschal had taken his seat, with the archbishops, bishops, and cardinals, and a diverse multitude of persons both clerical and lay, on the last day of the council he made in the sight of all his profession of the catholic faith, that none might doubt of his orthodoxy, and said. "I embrace the whole Divine Scripture of the Old and New Testaments, the law written by Moses and by the holy prophets; I embrace the four gospels, the

---

[1] 420. 3.

epistolas gloriosi doctoris beati Pauli apostoli, sanctos canones apostolorum, quattuor concilia uniuersalia sicut quattuor euangelia, Nicenum Ephesinum Constantinopolitanum Calcedonense; preterea Antiochenum concilium, et decreta sanctorum patrum Romanorum pontificum et precipue decreta domini mei papae Gregorii septimi et beatae memoriae papae Vrbani. Quae ipsi laudauerunt laudo, quae tenuerunt teneo, quae confirmauerunt confirmo, quae dampnauerunt dampno, quae repulerunt repello, quae interdixerunt interdico, quae prohibuerunt prohibeo; in omnibus et per omnia in his semper perseuerabo." Quibus expletis, surrexit pro omnibus Girardus Engolismensis episcopus, legatus in Aquitania, et communi assensu domini papae[a] Paschalis totiusque concilii legit hanc scripturam:

428. '"Priuilegium illud, quod non est priuilegium sed uere debet dici prauilegium, pro liberatione captiuorum et aecclesiae a domino Paschali papa per uiolentiam regis Henrici[b] extortum, nos omnes, in hoc sancto concilio cum domino papa congregati, canonica censura et aecclesiastica auctoritate iuditio sancti Spiritus dampnamus et irritum esse iudicamus atque omnino quassamus[c] et, ne quid auctoritatis et efficatiae habeat, penitus excommunicamus. Et hoc ideo dampnatum est, quia in eo prauilegio continetur quod electus canonice a clero et populo a nemine consecretur nisi prius a rege inuestiatur, quod est contra Spiritum sanctum et canonicam institutionem." Perlecta uero hac carta, acclamatum[d] ab omnibus et uniuerso concilio "Amen, Amen! Fiat, Fiat!"

429. 'Archiepiscopi qui cum suis suffraganeis interfuerunt hi sunt: Iohannes patriarcha Veneticus, Semies[e] Capuanus, Landulfus Beneuentanus, Amalfitanus, Regitanus, Hidrontinus, Brundisinus, Capsanus, Girontinus, et Greci Rosanus et archiepiscopus Sanctae Seuerinae. Episcopi uero: Centius Sabinensis, Petrus Portuensis, Leo Hostiensis, Cono Prenestinus, Girardus Engolismensis, Galo Leonensis legatus pro Bituricensi et Viennensi archiepiscopis,[f] Rogerius Vulturnensis, Gaufridus Senensis, Rollandus Populonensis, Gregorius Terracinensis, Willelmus Troianus,[g] Willelmus Siracusanus legatus pro omnibus Siculis, et alii fere centum episcopi. Siwinus[h] et

---

[a] om. [C], θ   [b] Henrici regis [A], MGH   [c] i.e. cassamus (so MGH)
[d] [A], θ, JW, η, MGH add est   [e] CB, θ, JW, η (and MGH[v]); Sennes [A], MGH (rightly)   [f] Viennensi archiepiscopis (-pus Aap) Aa, θ, JW, η, MGH; Viennensis (or sim.) archiepiscopus At (def. Ag) [C]B; archiepiscopus Biennensis MGH[v]   [g] Willelmus Troianus om. [C]B   [h] Siguinus JW, η; Bruno Signinus (i.e. of Segni) MGH, rightly

seven canonical epistles and the epistles of the glorious doctor and apostle St Paul, the holy canons of the Apostles, the general councils—four in number, even as there are four gospels—of Nicaea, Ephesus, Constantinople, and Chalcedon; and in addition the council of Antioch, the decrees of our holy fathers the Roman pontiffs, and especially the decrees of my lord Pope Gregory VII and Pope Urban of blessed memory. What they approved, I approve; what they held, I hold; what they confirmed, I confirm; what they condemned, I condemn; what they rejected, I reject; what they forbade, I forbid; what they prohibited, I prohibit; and these principles in and through all things I will ever maintain." When this was concluded, Gerard bishop of Angoulême, legate in Aquitaine, arose on behalf of all, and by common consent of our lord Pope Paschal and the whole council, read the document which follows:

428. '"Whereas the violence of King Henry wrested from our lord Pope Paschal, to obtain the liberation of prisoners and of the captive Church, a privilege which is no privilege but ought rather to be called a depravilege: Now therefore all we who are gathered together in this holy council with our lord the pope by lawful sentence and with the authority of the Church do by the judgement of the Holy Spirit condemn the same and judge it to be worthless and declare it altogether null and void and utterly anathematize it that it may be of no authority or effect. For this cause we do condemn it, because in that depravilege it is contained that a person canonically elected by clergy and people is by no means to be consecrated unless first he be invested by the king, a thing which is contrary to the Holy Spirit and to established law." When this document had been read, all present and the whole council cried: "Amen, amen! So be it! So be it!"

429. 'The archbishops who with their suffragans were present were these: John patriarch of Venice, Sennes of Capua, Landulf of Benevento, those of Amalfi, Reggio, Otranto, Brindisi, Conza, Acerenza; of the Greeks, the archbishop of Rossano and the archbishop of Santa Severina. The bishops were Cencio of Sabina, Peter of Porto, Leo of Ostia, Kuno of Palestrina, Gerard of Angoulême, Galo of Saint-Pol-de-Léon, legate for the archbishop of Bourges and the archbishop of Vienne, Roger of Volterra, Geoffrey of Siena, Roland of Massa Marittima, Gregory of Terracina, William of Troia, William of Syracuse, legate for all the Sicilians, and about one hundred other bishops. Siwin,

Iohannes Tusculanus episcopus,[a] cum essent Romae illa die, concilio non interfuerunt; qui postea, lecta dampnatione prauilegii, consenserunt et laudauerunt.'

430. Ferebantur ista per orbem, nec dissimulabat omnis Gallia imperatorem execrari, aecclesiastici zeli in eum uigore intentato. His commotus Romam septimo decimo anno Paschalis papae contendit, acrius in illum ulturus; sed is felici transitu mundanas effugerat erumnas, ridebatque in requie positus ex alto contumacis Cesaris minas. Cuius morte accepta, alacrius imperator celerabat uiam, ut Iohanne Gaitano superioris papae cancellario, qui iam electus et Gelasius dictus fuerat, eiecto Mauritium Bracarensem episcopum, cognomento Burdinum, intruderet. Sed haec epistola Gelasii certius proponet.

431. [b]'Gelasius seruus seruorum Dei archiepiscopis, episcopis, abbatibus, clericis, principibus et ceteris per Galliam fidelibus salutem. 'Quia uos Romanae aecclesiae membra estis, quae in ea nuper acta sunt dilectioni uestrae significare curamus. Siquidem post electionem nostram dominus imperator, furtiue et inopinata uelocitate Romam ueniens, nos egredi compulit. Pacem postea[c] minis et terroribus postulauit, dicens quae posset se facturum, nisi nos ei iuramento pacis certi-
2 tudinem faceremus. Ad quae nos ista respondimus: "De controuersia quae inter aecclesiam et regnum est, uel conuentioni uel iustitiae libenter adquiescimus loco et tempore competenti, uidelicet Mediolani uel Cremonae in proxima beati Lucae festiuitate, fratrum nostrorum iuditio, qui a Deo sunt iudices constituti in aecclesia, et sine quibus haec causa tractari non potest. Et quoniam dominus imperator a nobis securitatem querit, nos uerbo et scripto eam promittimus, nisi ipse interim impediat. Alias enim securitatem[d] facere nec honestas
3 aecclesiae nec consuetudo est." Ille statim die post electionem nostram quadragesimo quarto Bracarensem episcopum, anno preterito a domno predecessore nostro Paschali papa in concilio Beneuenti excommunicatum, in matris aecclesiae inuasionem ingessit; qui etiam,

---

[a] episcopi *Aa, θ, JW, MGH pp. 247–8* [c] *[A] adds* et
[b] *This letter is also found in* θκ, *and in Eadmer, Hist. nov.*
[d] securitates *[A], θκ, Ead. p. 247*

and John bishop of Tusculum, although in Rome that day, were not present at the council; but afterwards, having read the condemnation of the depravilege, they concurred and approved it.'

430. This being spread throughout the world, the whole of Gaul was not slow to load the emperor with imprecations, and the zeal of churchmen everywhere was concentrated against him. Aroused by this, he hastened to Rome in the seventeenth year of Pope Paschal to take violent steps against him; but the pope by a blessed passing had escaped the troubles of the world, and being at peace on high laughed to scorn the stubborn Caesar's threats. Hearing the news of his death, the emperor hastened still more eagerly, his purpose being to eject John of Gaeta, the late pope's chancellor, who had already been elected and had taken the name of Gelasius, and to foist in Maurice bishop of Braga, surnamed Bourdin. But this will be more authoritatively set forth in a letter of Pope Gelasius:

431. 'Gelasius, servant of the servants of God, to the archbishops, bishops, abbots, clergy, princes, and all the faithful throughout Gaul, greeting.

'Seeing that you are members of the Roman Church, we would have you know, beloved, what has lately passed within her. After our election, our lord the emperor, coming to Rome by stealth and with unlooked-for speed, compelled us to give place. Thereafter he demanded peace with threats and menaces, saying that he would do his worst, unless we gave him assurance of peace on oath. Thereto we replied as follows: "As concerning the controversy now on foot between Church and empire, we gladly submit to any agreement or judicial decision that may be made at the appropriate place and time, to wit, in Milan or Cremona at the feast of St Luke next ensuing, according to the judgement of our brethren, who are appointed by God to be judges in the Church, and without whom this case cannot be dealt with. And forasmuch as our lord the emperor is asking security from us, we promise him the same by word of mouth and in writing, unless he himself in the meanwhile is an impediment; for to grant him immunity on any other footing is neither honourable for the Church nor customary." Without delay, on the forty-fourth day after our election, he took the bishop of Braga, who the year before had been excommunicated by our predecessor Pope Paschal in the council of Benevento, and foisted him by force upon his mother the Church;

cum per nostras olim manus pallium accepisset, eidem domino nostro et catholicis successoribus, quorum primus ego sum, fidelitatem iurauit. In hoc autem tanto facinore nullum de Romanis dominus imperator, Deo gratias, sotium habuit; sed Wibertini soli, Romanus de Sancto Marcello, Centius qui dicebatur Sancti Crisogoni, Teuzo*a* qui multo per Datiam debachatus est tempore, tam infamem gloriam celebrarunt. Vestrae igitur experientiae litterarum presentium perceptione mandamus ut, super his per Dei gratiam communi deliberatione tractantes, ad matris aecclesiae ultionem communibus prestante Deo auxiliis, sicut oportere cognoscitis, accingamini.

'Data Gaitae, septimo decimo kalendas Februarii.'

432. Expulsus autem Gelasius, Salerni nauibus conscensis, inde uenit Genuam; indeque*b* itinere pedestri Cluniacum contendens ibidem obiit. Tunc, id est, anno Dominicae incarnationis millesimo centesimo nono decimo, cardinales qui cum Gelasio uenerant, simulque omnis aecclesia Cisalpina, Guidonem archiepiscopum Viennensem in papam grandi paratu leuantes Calixtum uocarunt, religionis et efficatiae ipsius contuitu,*c* sperantes se per illius potentiam, quod esset in auxiliando facultatis maximae, imperatoris uiribus obniti posse. Nec ille credulos spei effectu exinaniens, mox concilio Remis celebrato inuestitos uel inuestiendos a laicis ab aecclesiis remouit, pariter et imperatorem, nisi resipisceret, inuoluens. Ita tempore aliquanto in inferioribus plagis moratus, ut partes suas augeret, Romam compositis in Gallia rebus uenit, libenterque a ciuibus (nam iam imperator discesserat) receptus est. Tum Burdinus, in medio relictus, Sutrium effugit, multis peregrinorum calamitatibus papatum suum fouere meditatus; sed quomodo inde sit eiectus, sequenti epistola cognosces.

433. 'Calixtus episcopus seruus seruorum Dei dilectis fratribus et filiis archiepiscopis, episcopis, abbatibus, prioribus et ceteris tam clericis quam laicis beati Petri fidelibus per Gallias constitutis salutem et apostolicam benedictionem.

'Quia dereliquit populus legem Domini et in iuditiis eius non ambulat, uisitat Dominus in uirga iniquitates*d* eorum et in uerberibus peccata eorum; paternae tamen conseruans uiscera pietatis, de sua confidentes misericordia non relinquit. Diu siquidem, peccatis

---

a Teuzo *[C]*, θκ *(cf. 421. 2)*; Teutzo *[A]*; Teuto *B (as it seems)*; et Euzo *Ead, p. 247*
b itideque *a*, itidemque *Aa*   *c* intuitu *[A]*   *d* peccata *[A]Bc¹*

a man who, when he received the pall aforetime at our own hand, swore fealty to our lord Pope Paschal and to his lawful successors, of whom I am the first. In this monstrous outrage, the emperor had no assistance from the Romans—praise be to God! Only Wibert's supporters, Romanus of St Marcellus, Cencio so-called of St Chrysogonus, and Teuzo who for long ranged in frenzy over Dacia, lent countenance to this disgraceful elevation. We therefore charge you, as men well versed 4 in affairs, on receipt of this present letter to take counsel in common on this subject by the grace of God, and gird yourselves to avenge your mother the Church with mutual assistance under God, as you know to be your duty.

'Given at Gaeta, 16 January.'

432. On his expulsion, Gelasius took ship at Salerno and sailed to Genoa; thence he made his way overland to Cluny, and there died. Whereupon, that is to say, in the year 1119, the cardinals who had accompanied him, together with the whole Church on this side the Alps, elected Guy archbishop of Vienne with full solemnities as pope under the name Calixtus, having regard to his holiness of life and his abilities, and hoping that by his influence—for he was a most effective ally—they would be able to make head against the imperial power. Nor did he disappoint those who believed in him, but soon afterwards 2 held a council at Reims, at which he dismissed from their churches any who had received or might hereafter receive lay investiture, including the emperor in his censure, unless he should repent. For some time he remained in the west to strengthen his party; then, having arranged affairs in Gaul, he came to Rome, where he was welcomed by the citizens, for the emperor had already left. Bourdin, thus left in the lurch, escaped to Sutri, planning to build up his tenure of the papacy by levying heavy toll on pilgrims, but was ejected, as you will learn from the following letter:

433. 'Calixtus, bishop, servant of the servants of God, to his beloved brothers and sons, the archbishops, bishops, abbots, priors, and other faithful servants of St Peter both clerical and lay who are in Gaul, greeting and the Apostolic blessing.

'Since the people have deserted the law of the Lord and walk not in His judgements, the Lord is visiting their iniquities with His rod and their sins with stripes; but He retains the bowels of His fatherly affection, and deserts not them that trust in His mercy. Long indeed, as 2

exigentibus, per illud Teutonicorum regis idolum, Burdinum uidelicet, fideles aecclesiae conturbati sunt, et alii quidem capti, alii usque ad mortem carceris maceratione afflicti sunt. Nuper autem, festis Paschalibus celebratis, cum peregrinorum et pauperum clamores ferre penitus non possemus, cum aecclesiae fidelibus ab urbe digressi sumus, et tam diu Sutrium obsedimus donec diuina potentia et supradictum aecclesiae inimicum Burdinum, qui diabolo nidum ibidem fecerat, et locum
3 ipsum omnino in nostram tradidit potestatem. Rogamus itaque caritatem uestram ut pro tantis benefitiis una nobiscum Regi regum gratias referatis, et in catholicae aecclesiae obedientia et seruitio constantissime maneatis, retributionem debitam in presenti et futuro ab omnipotente Domino per eius gratiam recepturi. Rogamus etiam ut has litteras alter alteri presentari omni remota negligentia fatiatis.

'Data Sutrii, quinto kalendas Maii.'

434. Vrbana omnino et excogitata facetia, ut eum quem oderat regis Teutonici uocaret idolum, quod ille Mauritii peritiam cum[a] in litteris tum in ciuilibus negotiis magni pensaret! Erat is, ut dixi,[1] Bracarensis archiepiscopus, quae est ciuitas Hispaniae; quem multum quislibet reuereri et pene adorare pro uiua magnae industriae spetie debuisset, nisi tam famoso facinore enitescere maluisset. Nec enim sacratissimam sedem nummis nundinari dubitasset, si tam desperatus inueniretur uenditor quam paratus erat emptor. Tum[b] autem captus et monachus factus in Caueam (monasterium ita uocant) directus est.

435. Processit ulterius in augendo bono laudabilis papae magnificentia, ut illam effrenem et ingenitam Romanorum cupiditatem cohiberet. Nullae ipsius tempore uiantibus circa Romam insidiae, nullae urbem ingressis iniuriae. Oblationes apud Sanctum Petrum, quas pro petulantia proque libidine potentes diripiebant, anteriores apostolicos qui uel mutire auderent indignis affitientes contumeliis, Calixtus reuocauit ad medium, scilicet ad apostolicae sedis rectoris publicum
2 usum. Nec quicquam in eius pectore pecuniarum uel habendarum ambitus uel habitarum amor operari bono abhorrens potuit, adeo ut Anglos peregrinos magis ad Sanctum Dauid quam Romam pergere ammoneret pro uiae longitudine: ad illum locum bis euntibus idem

---

[a] tum *MSS*   [b] tunc *[A]*

[1] c. 430.

their sins required, have the faithful of the Church been troubled by Bourdin, that idol of the Teuton king, and some of them have been taken captive, others afflicted with the torment of prison even unto death. Of late, however, after celebrating the festival of Easter, since we could no longer endure the crying of the pilgrims and the poor, we went forth from the city with the faithful sons of the Church and laid siege to Sutri, until the Almighty utterly subjected to our power both the place itself and the aforesaid enemy of the Church Bourdin, who had made his devil's nest therein. We beg you therefore, beloved, to give thanks with us for these great benefits to the King of Kings, and to abide unflinchingly in your duty and service to the catholic Church, knowing that you will receive a due reward now and in the future from almighty God by His grace. We ask also that you cause this letter to be made known one to another without delay.

'Given at Sutri, 27 April.'

434. It was an apt and ingenious pleasantry to call the object of his hatred 'the idol of the Teuton king', for the emperor had a high opinion of Maurice as an expert both in academic studies and in politics. As I have said,[1] he was archbishop of Braga, a town in Spain, and a man whom anyone might have admired and almost venerated as a living example of great energy, had he not chosen rather to achieve notoriety by such infamous conduct. For he would not have hesitated to purchase the most holy See for cash, had his readiness to buy been matched by recklessness in a seller. But now he was taken prisoner, became a monk, and was sent to a monastery called La Cava.

435. The pope's admirable statesmanship went further in welldoing, by restraining the unbridled and congenital avarice of the Romans. In his time, no ambush awaited travellers in the neighbourhood of Rome, and no outrage after they had entered the city. The offerings at St Peter's used to be forcibly divided by powerful nobles motivated by insolence or greed, who replied with shameful insults to any previous popes who dared so much as open their mouths to protest; Calixtus restored them to the general good, that is, to the public purposes of the ruler of the Apostolic See. In his heart, riches—the desire of getting them or the love of them when got—could have no effect at variance with what was right, so much so that he encouraged English pilgrims to go to St David's rather than Rome, because of the length of the journey; those who went twice to St David's should

benedictionis refundendum commodum quod haberent qui semel Romam irent. Quid quod illam inueteratam inuestiturae*ᵃ* controuersiam inter regnum et sacerdotium, quae iam plus quam quinquaginta annis turbas fecerat, adeo ut aliquo heresis fautore morbo uel morte succiso ilico quasi hidrae capita plura pullularent, ipse sua industria abrasit, decidit, deleuit,*ᵇ* Teutonicae animositatis colla uigore securis apostolicae decutiens. Quod et eius et Apostolici professiones mundo his dictis ostendent.

436. '"Ego Calixtus episcopus seruus seruorum Dei tibi dilecto filio Henrico, Dei gratia Romanorum imperatori augusto,*ᵈ* concedo electiones episcoporum et abbatum Teutonici regni qui ad regnum pertinent in presentia tua fieri, absque simonia et absque ulla uiolentia, ut, si qua inter partes discordia emerserit, metropolitani uel prouintialium consilio uel iuditio saniori parti assensum et auxilium
2 prebeas. Electus autem regalia a te recipiat, et quae ex his iure tibi debet fatiat; ex aliis uero partibus imperii consecratus infra sex menses regalia a te per sceptrum recipiat, et quae ex his iure tibi debet fatiat, exceptis omnibus quae ad Romanam aecclesiam pertinere noscuntur. De quibus uero michi querimoniam feceris et auxilium postulaueris, secundum offitii mei debitum auxilium tibi prestabo. Do tibi ueram pacem, et omnibus qui in tua parte sunt uel fuerunt tempore huius discordiae. Vale.'

437. 'In nomine sanctae et indiuiduae Trinitatis. Ego Henricus, Dei gratia Romanorum imperator augustus, pro amore Dei et sanctae Romanae aecclesiae et domni Calixti papae, et pro remedio animae meae, dimitto Deo et sanctis Dei apostolis Petro et Paulo sanctaeque catholicae aecclesiae omnem inuestituram per anulum et baculum, et concedo in omnibus aecclesiis quae in regno uel imperio meo sunt canonicam fieri electionem et liberam consecrationem. Possessiones et regalia beati Petri, quae a principio huius discordiae usque ad hodiernam*ᵉ* diem siue tempore patris mei siue etiam meo ablata sunt, quae habeo, eidem sanctae Romanae aecclesiae restituo; quae non habeo, ut
2 restituantur fideliter iuuabo. Possessiones etiam omnium aliarum aecclesiarum et principum et omnium aliorum tam laicorum quam

---

ᵃ om. [A]   *ᵇ* euellit Ag*ᵃ·ᶜ*Aa   *ᶜ* cc. 436–7 are edited in MGH Constit. i. 159–61   *ᵈ* om. [C]B   *ᵉ* hodiernum At Aa

have the same privileges in the way of benediction as those who went once to Rome. As for the long-standing investiture controversy between empire and priesthood, which had now troubled the world for more than fifty years to such an extent that, when one leader of the heresy was cut off by disease or death, more heads promptly sprouted on the hydra, this by his own efforts he wiped out, cut short, and made away with, severing the sprouting necks of Teuton fury with the axe of Apostolic power. This will be made clear to the world by the proclamations of pope and emperor, which ran as follows:

436. 'I Calixtus, bishop, servant of the servants of God, to you, my beloved son Henry, by God's grace august emperor of the Romans, do grant that the elections of bishops and abbots in the Teuton kingdom who pertain to the royal power be effected in your presence, without simony or any use of force, on condition that if any dispute arise between the parties, after counsel or judgement given by the metropolitan or bishops of the province, you give consent and aid to the better party. Let the elect receive from you his temporalities, and render to you that which he rightly owes in respect of them; but from other parts of the empire let the candidate after consecration within six months receive from you his temporalities by sceptre, and render to you that which he rightly owes in respect of them, all things excepted which pertain to the church of Rome. In the matters whereupon you complain to me and ask my help, I will give you due assistance, as by my office I am bound to do. True peace I give unto you, and to all who are or were on your side during the time of this dispute. Farewell.'

437. 'In the name of the holy and undivided Trinity. I, Henry, by God's grace august emperor of the Romans, for the love of God and of the holy Roman Church and of my lord Pope Calixtus and for the salvation of my soul, relinquish unto God and His holy Apostles Peter and Paul and the holy catholic Church all investiture by ring and staff; and I grant that in all churches within my realm and empire there shall be canonical election and free right to consecrate. As concerns the possessions and temporalities of St Peter which from the beginning of this dispute until the present day, in my father's time and mine, have been taken away: those which I hold, I restore to the holy Roman church; and as for those which I do not hold, I will give faithful aid towards their restoration. As for the possessions of all other churches and princes and all other men, be they clerics or laymen,

clericorum, quae in werra*a* ista amissae sunt, consilio principum uel iustitia, quas habeo, reddam; quas non habeo, fideliter ut reddantur*b* iuuabo. Et do ueram pacem domno papae Calixto et sanctae Romanae aecclesiae et omnibus qui in parte ipsius sunt uel fuerunt; et*c* in quibus sancta Romana aecclesia auxilium postulauerit, fideliter iuuabo; et de quibus michi querimoniam fecerit, debitam sibi fatiam iustitiam.

3 'Haec omnia acta sunt consensu et consilio principum quorum nomina subscripta sunt: Albertus archiepiscopus Mogontiae, Fredericus Coloniensis archiepiscopus, Ratisbonensis episcopus, Babenbergensis episcopus, Bruno Spirensis,*d* Augustensis, Traiectensis, Constantiensis, abbas Foldensis, Heremannus dux, Fredericus dux, Bonefatius marchio, Thetbaldus marchio, Ernulfus comes palatinus, Otbertus comes palatinus, Berengarius comes.'

438. Sedato itaque tam ueterno morbo, qui aecclesiae statum conturbauerat, magnum gaudium quisquis Christiane sapuit accepit, quod is imperator, qui proxima fortitudinis gloria acriter Karoli Magni inuaderet uestigia, etiam a deuotione ipsius in Deum non degeneraret, qui, preter Teutonici regni nobiliter sopitas rebelliones, etiam Italicum ita subegit ut nullus adeo. Ter enim in decennio Italiam ingressus urbium tumorem compescuit, primo aduentu Nouariam, Placentiam, Aretium, secundo et tertio Cremonam et Mantuam incendio exterminans. Sed et Rauennae motum paucorum obsidione dierum leniuit; namque Pisani et Papienses cum Mediolanensibus amicitiam eius quam uim experiri malebant. Huic, ut ante fatus sum,[1] filia regis Angliae nupta exhibebat patrem fortitudine, matrem religione; contendebat in ea pietas industriae, nec quod magis probares discerneres facile.

439. Erat tunc Willelmus comes Pictauorum fatuus et lubricus; qui postquam de Ierosolima, ut superiori libro lectum est,[2] rediit, ita omne uitiorum uolutabrum premebat quasi*e* crederet omnia fortuitu agi, non prouidentia regi. Nugas porro suas salsa quadam uenustate condiens ad facetias reuocabat, audientium rictus cachinno distendens. Denique apud castellum quoddam Nior habitacula quaedam quasi

---

a guerra B   *b* ut reddantur *om. [A]*   *c om. [C]B*   *d Bc¹, MGH add* episcopus   *e [A]adds* non

[1] 420. 1.   [2] 383. 4.

which have been lost in this strife, by the counsel of princes or by process of law, those which I hold I will restore; and as for those which I do not hold, I will give faithful aid towards their restoration. True peace I give unto my lord Pope Calixtus and to the holy Roman Church and to all those who are or were on her side, and wheresover the holy Roman church shall ask aid of me, I will faithfully give aid; in what point soever she lays claim against me, I will render her justice as is due.

'All this is enacted with the consent and counsel of the princes whose 3 names are hereafter written: Adalbert archbishop of Mainz, Frederick archbishop of Cologne, the bishop of Regensburg, the bishop of Bamberg, Bruno bishop of Speyer, the bishops of Augsburg, Utrecht, Konstanz; the abbot of Fulda; Duke Hermann, Duke Frederick, Marquis Boniface, Marquis Theobald, Arnulf count palatine, Otbert count palatine, Count Berengar.'

438. The healing of such an ancient sore, which had much disturbed the good estate of the Church, brought great joy to all wise and Christian hearts, with the thought that this emperor, who in repute of valour stood next to Charlemagne and was his zealous rival, equally maintained Charles's standard of devotion towards God. Not counting the spirited suppression of revolts in his Teuton realm, he subdued his Italian dominions as no emperor had done hitherto. Three times in ten years he descended on Italy and tamed the pride of her cities: Novara, Piacenza, and Arezzo were destroyed by fire on his first expedition, on his second and third Cremona and Mantua; rebellion at Ravenna was pacified by a few days' siege; the people of Pisa and Pavia, with those of Milan, preferred to risk his friendship rather than his enmity. His consort, as I have already said,[1] was the daughter of the king of England, who displayed her father's courage and her mother's piety; holiness in her found its equal in energy, and it would be hard to say which was more admirable.

439. At that time lived William count of Poitou, a lecher and a fool. On his return from Jerusalem, related in the previous book,[2] he set himself to wallow in every vice, like one who thought this world the plaything of chance, not the domain of Providence. Gilding his foolish sports with a spurious veneer of wit, he took nothing seriously, making his audience roar with laughter. For instance at Niort, one of his castles, he built a suite of rooms like monastic cells, with the fantastic notion

monasteriola construens, abbatiam pelicum ibi se positurum delirabat, nuncupatim illam et illam, quaecumque famosioris prostibuli esset, abbatissam uel priorem ceterasue*ᵃ* offitiales instituturum cantitans.
2 Legitima quoque uxore depulsa, uicecomitis cuiusdam coniugem surripuit, quam adeo ardebat ut clipeo suo simulacrum mulierculae insereret, perinde dictitans se illam uelle ferre in prelio, sicut illa portabat eum in triclinio. Vnde increpitus et excommunicatus a Girardo Engolismorum episcopo, iussusque illicitam uenerem abicere, 'Antea'*ᵇ* inquit 'crispabis pectine refugum a fronte capillum quam ego uicecomitissae indicam repudium', cauillatus in uirum cuius pertenuis cesaries pectinem non desideraret.
3 Nec minus, cum Petrus preclarae sanctitatis Pictauorum episcopus eum liberius argueret et detrectantem palam excommunicare inciperet, ille precipiti furore percitus crinem antistitis inuolat, strictumque mucronem uibrans 'Iam' inquit 'morieris, nisi me absolueris.' Tum uero presul timore simulato indutias petens loquendi, quod reliquum fuerat excommunicationis fidenter perorauit, ita comitem a Christianitate suspendens ut nec cum aliquo conuiuari nec etiam loqui auderet, nisi mature resipisceret. Ita offitio suo, ut sibi uidebatur, peracto, martiriique tropheum sitiens, collum protendit, 'Feri' inquiens, 'feri!'
4 At Willelmus*ᶜ* refractior consuetum leporem intulit, ut diceret: 'Tantum certe te odio ut nec meo te digner odio, nec caelum umquam intrabis meae manus ministerio.' Veruntamen post modicum uipereo meretriculae*ᵈ* infectus sibilo, incesti dissuasorem detrusit exilio; ubi beato fine conclusus, frequentibus et magnis miraculis innuit mundo quam gloriose uiuat in caelo. Quibus auditis, comes dicacitate insolenti non abstinuit, professus palam penitere se quod non ei iam dudum mortem accelerasset, ut ipsi anima sancta grates haberet potissimum cuius furore caeleste mercatus esset commodum.
5 Vitam Petri et mortem uersus isti commendant. De uiuo dictum est:[1]

    Corpus: opes: studium: mores   cibus asper: egenus:
    lectio: probra   domat: carpit: alit: fugiunt.

ᵃ ceteras uero *[A]*   *ᵇ* ante o *a*, ante d *Aap;* ante *Aac (as one expects)*   *ᶜ* nichilo has probably fallen out; cf. e.g. GP p. 155   *ᵈ* muliercul(a)e *[A]*

[1] Walther, *Initia* 3362.

that he would found there a cloister of courtesans, and repeatedly sang of his intention to promote this girl or that by name to be abbess or prioress or to some other monastic office, according to the notoriety of the brothel they came from. Putting away his lawful spouse, he carried 2 off the wife of a certain viscount, whom he loved with such passion as to set his strumpet's picture on his shield, often saying that he would serve under her ensign in battle as she did under him in the bedchamber. When Gerard bishop of Angoulême rebuked and excommunicated him, ordering him to abandon his illicit passions, 'You first use a comb,' he replied, 'to curl those runaway locks of yours, and then I will pack off my viscountess,' the point of the insult being that the bishop's scanty hairs needed no comb.

In the same way when Peter, bishop of Poitiers, a man of outstand- 3 ing holiness, reproved him with great freedom, and on his rejecting the rebuke began openly to excommunicate him, the count flew into a sudden rage, grabbed the bishop by the hair, and waving his drawn sword shouted: 'You die this instant unless you absolve me!' The bishop pretended to be frightened, and begged a respite in which he could speak; then boldly finished the sentence of excommunication, cutting off the count from all converse with Christendom, that he might not dare to share a meal or even speak with anyone until he should come to his senses. Having thus, as he thought, performed his duty, and longing for the crown of martyrdom, he stretched out his neck, crying 'Strike, strike!' William, however, was somewhat shaken, 4 but back came his usual wit: 'I hate you so much,' he said, 'that I regard you as beneath the notice of my hatred. If you are bound for Heaven, expect no help from me.' Soon afterwards, however, poisoned by the whispers of that hissing viper his mistress, he drove into exile the man who had rebuked his vice; and there Peter came to a blessed end, and by many and great miracles demonstrates on earth the glory he enjoys in Heaven. On hearing the news, the count could not repress an insolent witticism, openly expressing regret that he had not sent Peter to his death long ago; for surely the holy soul would be particularly grateful to the man whose rage had secured for him the comforts of Paradise.

Peter's life and death are commended in the lines which follow. Of 5 him when in life, it was written:[1]

> Hard tack his body tames, poor raid his purse,
>   Books feed his mind, sins 'fore his virtues quail;

Virtutes: culpas: fructum   colit: amputat: auget;
   ius: litem: pacem   protegit: odit: amat.
Fert misero: tribuit peccanti: seruat amico
   auxilium: ueniam: continuamque fidem.
Mente Maria uacat, sed in actu[a] Martha laborat;
   est intenta gregi Martha, Maria Deo.
Sic apud hunc regnat Deus intra, proximus extra,
   hic desiderio, proximus obsequio.
Diligit ille Rachel, nec Liam ferre recusat,
   uxoremque nouus duxit utramque Iacob;
huius amat uultum, iuuat huius carpere fructum,
   cum sit pulchra Rachel fertiliorque Lia.

6 De mortuo dictum est:[1]

Exutus rebus, ui tentus,[b] pulsus ab urbe,
   presul pauperiem, uincla fugamque tulit;
nunc   diues: liber: stabilis   sua premia: Christum:
   astra   capit: sequitur: possidet   iste Petrus.
Vitam religio, mentem discretio, famam
   lux operum, studium lectio, uerba modus,[c]
iuditium ius, iustitiam rigor, ora uenustas
   ornabant, pietas uiscera, uirga manum.
Promouit: priuauit eum: profugumque recepit
   papa: comes: Christus   ordine: sede: polo.

440. Huius Petri fuerunt contemporanei et in religione sotii Rotbertus de Arbreisel et Bernardus abbas Tirunensis. Quorum primus omnium huius temporis sermocinatorum famosissimus et profusissimus, tantum non spumea sed mellea uiguit eloquentia ut, hominibus certatim opes congerentibus, illud egregium sanctimonialium monasterium apud Fontem Ebraldi construeret, in quo, tota seculi uoluptate castrata, feminarum Deo deuotarum quanta nusquam multitudo in Dei feruet obsequio; nam preter ceterarum illecebrarum abdicationem, quantulum illud est quod in nullo loco loquuntur nisi in capitulo, proposita a magistro perhennis taciturnitatis regula, quia semel laxato silentio
2 feminae pronae sint ad mussitandum friuola. Alter, famosus paupertatis amator, in saltuosum et desertum locum, relicto amplissimarum

---

[a] actum [C]B   [b] ui tentus Ce; intentus [A]CrB   [c] modus Ce; modum [A]CrB

Virtue's, fault's, goodness' patron, pruner, nurse;
  Law's, concord's, strife's protector, lover, flail.
To sad, to sinners, and to friends he gives
  Assistance, pardon, faith that does not vary;
Still Mary, busy Martha—both he lives,
  Martha on man intent and on Heav'n Mary.
Thus God within him reigns; without, his neighbour,
  For God he longs for, and his neighbour serves;
Rachel he loves, for Leah content to labour;
  Both wives our second Jacob well deserves.
One's harvest rich he loves, the other's bloom:
  Though Rachel's fair, Leah's is the fruitful womb.

Of him when dead:[1]

  Spoiled, hunted, ousted from his see,
    In poverty, exile, and chains,
  Our Peter now, strong, rich, and free
    Prize wins, Christ follows, Heaven gains.
  Religion, wisdom, deeds renowned
    In life and mind and fame appear;
  His words discreet, his learning sound,
    His judgement just, his doom severe.
  With comely mien, and staff in hand,
    True piety his heart did grace;
  Whom pope promoted and count banned,
    Christ welcomed in his heavenly place.

440. Contemporaries of this Peter and his fellows in the religious life were Robert of Arbrissel and Bernard abbot of Tiron. The first of these was the most famous and eloquent of all the preachers of our time; his eloquence was honey and not froth, and such its power that men hastened to load him with their offerings, and he was able to build that famous monastery of nuns at Fontevrault, where a throng of devoted women such as can be seen nowhere else, having cut away all the pleasures of the world, are fervent in God's service. Not to speak of the other pleasures they have abandoned, think what a thing it is that they speak nowhere save in Chapter; their master set before them a rule of unbroken silence, for if such a rule is once relaxed, women are prone to chatter and gossip. The other was a famous devotee of poverty; leaving a monastery that had great possessions, he

[1] Cf. Walther, *Initia* 6192a.

diuitiarum cenobio, cum paucis concessit, ibique, quia lucerna sub modio latere non potuit, undatim multis confluentibus monasterium fecit, magis insigne religione monachorum et numero quam fulgore pecuniarum et cumulo.

441. Et, ne Anglia expers boni putetur, quis possit preterire Serlonem abbatem Gloecestrensem, qui locum illum ex humili et pene nullo ad gloriosum prouectum extulit? Nota est omnibus Anglis Gloecestrensis discreta religio, quam infirmus possit suspicere nec possit fortis contempnere. Hoc illis signifer Serlo intulit, ut ne quid nimis; quanuis ut erat bonis humilis, ita superbis minax ac terribilis. Ad quod firmandum uersus de eo Godefridi prioris adducam in medium:[1]

2   Aecclesiae murus cecidit Serlone cadente,
    uirtutis gladius, bucina iustitiae.
    Vera loquens et non uanis sermonibus utens,
    et quos corripuit principibus placuit.
    Iuditium preceps, contrarius ordinis error
    et leuitas morum non placuere sibi.
    Tertius a Iano mensis, lux tertia mensis,
    cum nece suppressum uita leuauit eum.

442. Quis Lanzonem taceat, qui ea aetate nullo inferius sanctitate floruit, monachus Cluniacensis et prior Sancti Pancratii in Anglia? qui probitate sua ita locum illum reuerentiae monachilis gratia nobilitauit ut unicum bonitatis pro uero asseratur esse domicilium. De cuius uita quia quicquid dixero infra illius merita esse denuntio, solum illius obitum, uerbis quibus scriptum inueni, apponam, ut liquido pateat quam gloriose uixerit qui tam gratiose obiit.

443. 'Pius Dominus, qui flagellat omnem filium quem recipit,[2] qui iustos suae sotios passionis simul et consolationis fore promittit, tam acerbo languore domnum Lanzonem triduo passionem suam preuenire permisit ut, si aliquis ex terrena conuersatione mundissimae menti eius puluis adhesit, illa eum tribulatione excussum esse non sit

---
[1] Walther, *Initia* 5194.
[2] Heb. 12: 6.

retired with a few companions into a deserted place in the woods, and there, when many came flocking to him, for his light could not be hid under a bushel, he erected a monastery more famous for the piety and number of its monks than for the quantity and brilliance of its riches.

441. Again—for let no one think England without her share of credit—who could pass over Serlo abbot of Gloucester, who raised that house from being lowly and almost nothing to be great and glorious? Everyone in England knows the well-balanced life they lead at Gloucester, which earns the admiration of the weak without incurring the contempt of the strong. It was Serlo, their standard-bearer, who established its principle of nothing in excess; although, humble as he was in good men's company, he was no less an object of fear and apprehension to the proud. To confirm this, let me quote some lines by Prior Godfrey:[1]

> The Church's wall is fall'n! Serlo lies here.
>   Trumpet of justice he, and virtue's sword.
> The princes he rebuked did hold him dear;
>   The truth he spoke, and wasted ne'er a word.
> No headstrong judgement his, no flighty way;
>   Error, the foe of discipline, he hated.
> The year's third month it was, the month's third day,
>   When, by death o'ercome, to life he was translated.

442. Who would not tell of Lanzo, who flourished at this time, and was no one's inferior in holiness? A monk of Cluny he was, and prior of St Pancras in England; and by his noble character raised that house to such an admirable pitch of monastic excellence that it is truly said to be, as a dwelling-place of goodness, in a class by itself. Whatever I might say of his life would be, I give fair warning, unworthy of his deserts, and I will therefore set down only his death, just as I have found it on record; a death so blessed will make it clear enough how glorious his life must have been.

443. 'Our merciful Lord, who "chastiseth every son whom He receiveth"[2] and promises that the just shall be partakers both of His passion and of His reward, permitted Dom Lanzo to prepare for his passing with three days of such bitter agony that if any speck or stain from his earthly life still clung to that most pure spirit, we may be

ambiguum. Cum enim dicat tantus apostolus, qui super Dominicum recubuit pectus, "Si dixerimus quia peccatum non habemus, ipsi nos seducimus, et ueritas in nobis non est",[1] cumque peccatum omne aut leuius hic aut in futuro grauius iudicet Christus, noluit ei aliquid offensionis post mortem occurrere quem se toto corde sciebat amare; ideoque, si quid in eo examinandum iudicabat, uoluit[a] in uiuente[b]
2 decoquere. Huic nempe assertioni fiducia[c] morientis attestata est. Nam cum quinta feria ante Passionem Domini incolumis, dicto ex cotidiana Quadragesimae consuetudine psalterio, se hora tertia missam celebraturus usque ad casulam induisset, et usque ad incipiendam missam quaequae dicenda erant predixisset, subito languore tam molesto corripitur ut ipse, quae induerat uestimenta exuens, etiam non plicata reliquerit, egressusque oratorio sine intermissione per biduum, hoc est, usque ad sabbatum conteritur, non sedendo, non ambulando, non iacendo, non stando neque dormiendo ullam omnino
3 requiem habens. Numquam tamen noctibus locutus, rogantibus fratribus[d] ut silentium solueret non adquieuit, rogans ne monachatus sui pudicitiam libarent, quod numquam, postquam monachicum habitum accepisset, a completorio exiens usque ad sequentis diei primam locutus fuisset. Sabbato autem sequente, dum ita quassatus se putaret iamiamque defungi, surgentes ad matutinam sinaxim fratres ad se inungendum uenire precepit; quos cum inunctus ex more osculari uoluisset, nimio eorum compulsus amore, non iacendo nec sedendo sed, quanuis ad mortem anxiatus, inter brachia sustentatus stando
4 osculatus est. Die illucescente in capitulum ductus, cum sedisset, fratres ante se omnes uenire rogauit, quibus paternam benedictionem et absolutionem impertiens idem sibi ab eis uoluit impertiri. Postea docuit quid, si obiret, eis esset agendum, sicque regressus est unde uenerat, reliquum diei cum sequenti dominica aliquanto quietius transigens; cum ecce post haec, id est, post dominicam imminentis mortis inditia deprehenduntur, et ipse manibus ablutis, pexo capite missam auditurus oratorium ingreditur, sumptoque corpore et san-
5 guine Domini ad lectum regressus est. Post modicum obmutuit; fratres ante illum uenientes singillatim benedicebat, simili modo totum

[a] uel ut *a*, ut luit *Aa* [b] in iuuentute *CrB* [c] confidentia *[A]* [d] om. *[C]B*

[1] 1 John 1: 8.

sure that those days of suffering drove it clean away. The great Apostle who lay on our Lord's breast has said that "If we say that we have no sin, we deceive ourselves, and the truth is not in us";[1] Christ judges every sin, either more lightly in this world or more severely in the next, and He did not wish any unpleasantness after death to befall a man whom He knew to love Him with all his heart. Consequently, if He judged that anything in him needed scrutiny, He wished to purge it away in his lifetime. These words of mine are confirmed by Lanzo's confidence on his deathbed. On the Friday in Passion week, being in good health, he said the Psalter, as was his daily custom in Lent, and at the third hour had vested himself as far as the chasuble with a view to saying Mass and had pronounced the opening sentences up to the beginning of the Canon, when he was struck by a sudden illness so severe that, having taken off the vestments he had just put on, he left them there without even folding them. Leaving the chapel, he was kept in continuous pain for two days—until the Saturday, that is—being unable to obtain any rest, whether sitting down or walking, lying, standing, or sleeping. Yet at night-time he said nothing, and would not consent when the brethren asked him to break silence, begging them not to tamper with his stainless record as a monk; for ever since taking the habit, he said, he had never spoken between Compline of one day and Prime of the next. On the Saturday following, he felt that after such a buffeting he might die at any moment, and told the brethren, when they rose for their morning Office, to come and give him extreme unction. Having received it, he wished to give them the customary kiss, and, moved by his exceeding love for them, did so not lying down nor sitting but standing up, although in agony even unto death, supported by their arms on either side. At daybreak he was taken into the chapter-house, and having sat down, asked all the brethren to come before him; then blessed them as their father and gave them absolution, and wished to receive the same from them in return. After that, he told them what they must do if he died, and so went back whence he had come, spending the rest of that day and the Sunday which followed somewhat more peacefully. Suddenly, when Sunday was past, the signs of approaching death became manifest. Having washed his hands and combed his hair, he went to the chapel to hear Mass, and having received the Lord's body and blood, went back to his bed. Shortly afterwards, he lost the use of his voice. He gave the brethren his blessing, as they came before him one at a time, and in the same way blessed the convent as a whole. And then, lifting

conuentum; at uero oculis in caelum erectis utraque manu domnum
abbatem cum omnibus sibi commissis benedicere nitebatur. Rogatus
autem a fratribus ut apud Deum, ad quem ibat, eorum memor esset,
caput inclinando benignissime adquieuit. Haec et his similia cum fecisset, innuit sibi porrigi crucem, quam capite, immo toto corpore incli-
nato adorans, manibus amplexans, laeto ore salutare uidebatur et
iocundo affectu[a] deosculabatur; cum ilico astantes migrando percellit,
raptusque in manibus eorum uiuus adhuc in presbiterium ante altare
6 sancti Pancratii defertur. Vbi aliquandiu superuiuens, roseo fatiei
rubore suauis, eadem diei hora qua purgandus infirmatus est, cariturus
perhenniter omni malo purus migrauit ad Christum.

'Et uide quam mirabiliter[b] in eo cuncta concurrerunt: passio serui
cum passione Domini, hora incipientis infirmitatis cum hora incipientis aeternae salutis, quinque dies quos sustinuit egritudinis quinis corporis[c] sensibus, quibus nemo uitat peccatum, emundandis. Porro
quod quinto die necdum transacto decessit, ut remur,[d] innuit eum in
7 ultimo sensu, qui tactus dicitur, non perfecisse peccatum. Tertia uero
diei hora, qua et infirmatus est et moriendo in uitam ingressus est[e]
eternam, quid aliud insinuat quam eandem Spiritus sancti gratiam,
qua omnem eius uitam gubernatam cognoscimus, et infirmato et
obeunti euidenter affuisse? Vt etiam esse supparem illis patribus nostris, Odoni scilicet atque Odiloni, et merito et premio non ambigamus,
8 insigne quiddam illis concessum huic quoque collatum est. Cum enim
illis contulerit Dominus ut octaua die sollemnitatum quas pre ceteris
diligebant transirent (nam et beatus Odo festiuitatem beati Martini et
sanctus Odilo Natiuitatem Domini precipue amabant, in quorum
octaua die uterque decessit), domno Lanzoni, qui pre ceteris huius
aeui hominibus regulam sancti Benedicti obseruabat, et beatam Dei
genitricem eiusque sollemnia singulari uenerabatur affectu, contulit ut
solita sibi consuetudine et in transitu sancti Benedicti et in festiuitate
sanctae Mariae quae Annuntiatio Dominica dicitur maiorem missam
in conuentu celebraret, et octauo [f]a predicto sancti Benedicti transitu
die preuentus infirmitate, octauo[f] nichilominus die ab Annuntiatione
Dominica migraret ad Christum.'

9   Igitur qui uitam domni Lanzonis ignorat, quam placens Deo fuerit
ex fine colligat; nec usitato morientium more predicta illi contigisse

[a] om. CeB (et . . . deosc. om. Cr)   [b] mutabiliter [C]B   [c] corporibus [A]   [d] reor [A]   [e] om. [C]B   [f-f] om. [C]B

his eyes to Heaven, he tried with both hands to bless the abbot and all committed to his charge. When asked by the brethren to bear them in mind in the presence of God, whereunto he was bound, he signified his assent most lovingly with a nod of the head. After this and more of the same kind, he asked by signs for a crucifix; bending his head, or rather his whole body, in reverence before it, he grasped it in his hands, seemed to welcome it with smiling face, and kissed it with love and joy. At that moment those who stood round were shaken to see that his passing had come, and they took him quickly in their arms before he died, and carried him into the sanctuary before the altar of St Pancras. There he lived for a while longer with a lovely flush on his face, and then, at the same hour of the day at which that illness had begun which was to purify him, he passed in his purity to Christ, where no evil shall touch him any more.

'And now observe how wondrously in him all things answered, one to another: the passion of the servant to the passion of his Lord; the onset of his sickness to the onset of his eternal salvation; the five days of suffering which he endured to the purifying of the five bodily senses, wherein no man can escape sin. Indeed, the fact that he died when the fifth day was not yet far spent shows, I take it, that he was not far gone in sin with the last sense, the sense of touch. That it was the third hour at which he fell ill, and the third at which by death he entered into eternal life, surely indicates that the same grace of the Holy Spirit, by which we know that all his life was governed, was clearly present with him on his sickbed and at the hour of death. Nor need we hesitate to think him the equal both in merit and reward of our great fathers, Odo and Odilo, for a wondrous gift vouchsafed to them was given also to him. The Lord permitted them to pass over on the octave of the feasts which they loved above all others, for Martinmas was Odo's special love and Christmas Odilo's, and each died on the octave. So too Dom Lanzo, who kept the Rule of St Benedict above all other men of our time, and revered with special affection God's blessed Mother and her festivals, was permitted, in accordance with his usual custom, to celebrate High Mass in the convent both on the obit of St Benedict and on that feast of the blessed Virgin which is called the Annunciation of the Lord; and then it was on the octave of St Benedict that the sickness took over, and equally on the octave of the Annunciation that he passed over unto Christ.'

Let him therefore who knows not the life of Dom Lanzo infer from his ending how pleasing it was to God, and believe with us that it was

nobiscum credat, quem Spiritus sancti carismatibus nemine huius temporis inferius ditatum sciat.

444. Nec memoria Godefridi prioris Wintoniensis ire debet in perditum, qui temporibus his litteratura et religione insignis fuit. Litteraturam protestantur libri plures, et epistolae familiari illo et dulci stilo editae, maximeque epigrammata quae satirico modo absoluit, preterea uersus de primatum Angliae laudibus. Quid? omne diuinum offitium, quod agresti quadam uetustate obsoletum per industriam suam natiua excultum uenustate fecit enitescere? Religionis et hospitalitatis normam pulchre inchoatam deliniauit in monachos, qui hodieque ita in utrisque prioris terunt uestigium ut aut nichil aut parum eis desit
2 ad laudis cumulum. Denique est in ea domo hospitum*ᵃ* terra marique uenientium quantum libuerit diuersorium, sumptu indefitienti, caritate indefatigata. Inter haec inerat sancto uiro morum humilitas, ut nichil ex illo unico philosophiae promptuario redoleret nisi humile, procederet nisi dulce. Quantula uero potest uideri haec eius laudatio! Quotus enim quisque est qui uel minimum litteris imbutus non alios infra dignitatem suam opinetur, tumido gestu et pompatico incessu pre se ferens conscientiam litterarum! Veruntamen, ne quid perfectionis sanctae deesset animae, multis ille annis*ᵇ* grabatum fouit, camino diuturnae tabis medullas et peccata excoctus.

445. Sed quid de talibus plura? Erant prorsus tunc in Anglia multi scientia illustres, religione celebres, quorum uirtus eo probabilior quo seculo senescente constantior et uiridior. Laudabiliter igitur uiuendo fidem preteritis fatiebant historiis, ne uetera possint falsitatis argui, cum nouorum exemplo probentur potuisse fieri. Quin etiam si qui essent*ᶜ* aecclesiarum prelati qui uiderentur ab antiquorum sanctitate degeneres, in mundialibus scilicet efficaces, in spiritualibus desides, tales, inquam, si qui essent, sumptuosis locorum cultibus conabantur
2 errata obumbrare. Erigebat quisque templa recentia, sanctorumque suorum argento et auro amiciebat corpora, nichil pretermittendo

---

ᵃ hospitium *[A]*, *GP p. 173*   *ᵇ* annis ille *[A]*   *ᶜ* om. *[A]*

by no ordinary deathbed chance that these privileges fell to his lot, knowing that he was endowed as richly as any man in our time with the gifts of the Holy Spirit.

444. Nor ought the memory of Godfrey prior of Winchester to pass into oblivion, who in these days was remarkable for piety and literary gifts. As evidence of his gifts we have his many books, and his letters written in an intimate and delightful style; above all, the epigrams written by him in satiric mood, and his poem in praise of the primates of England. Still more, the whole Divine Office, which had become a kind of rustic survival, was by his energy developed in its natural beauty, and given a new brilliance. He made a fine beginning in raising the standard of religious life and of hospitality, leaving a pattern for his monks, who to this day follow their prior's lead in both departments, to such good purpose that in little or nothing do they fall short of the highest praise. For example, there exists in that house a resting-place for visitors who come by sea and land, to their heart's content, in expense unfailing, in affection inexhaustible. Amidst all this, there was in that holy man such humility of character that, though a priceless storehouse of philosophy, he savoured only of what was humble and uttered only what was delightful. But how great this encomium may appear! How few there are that have even a tincture of letters, and do not think other men beneath them, revealing pride in their own education by a haughty air and self-important gait! However, that the perfecting of that holy soul might be completed, he kept his bed for many years, while the fire of long-continued sickness dried up his bones, and burned away his sins.

445. But of such men I need say no more. There were at that time in England many persons distinguished for their learning and famous for their religious life, whose virtue deserves the higher praise, in that it grows fresher and stronger as the world waxes old. By their admirable lives they made the stories of the past time seem credible; we cannot accuse old tales of being untrue, when recent facts prove that they might easily have happened. And further: it may be there were prelates who seemed to fall short of the holiness of early times, able administrators in the affairs of this world, in spiritual things less active; it may be so. But such men did their best to put their shortcomings in the shade by the wealth they lavished on holy places. Each one would build a new cathedral, and clothe in silver and gold the bodies of the

caritate sumptuum quod ad gratiam possit allicere oculos intuentium. Quorum est Rannulfus superius nominatus,[1] qui apud Dunelmum factus episcopus in edifitiis monachorum nouis et beati Cuthberti ueneratione nonnullam gloriam nomini suo commentus est; cuius extulit famam sacrati corporis translatio, quod e mausoleo leuatum cunctis uolentibus fecit conspicuum. Tractauit illud ausu felici Radulfus tunc abbas Sagii, postea Cantuariae archiepiscopus, et propalam illibatum protulit, quod quibusdam uenisset in dubium, utrum olim uulgatum[a]
3 adhuc de integritate compaginis duraret miraculum. Eodemque fere tempore in Heliensi cenobio sub abbate Ricardo uirginales exuuiae beatae Etheldridae integrae uisae uidentibus stupori et plausui fuere. Monasterium illud, nuper a rege Henrico in episcopatum mutatum, primum Herueum accepit episcopum, qui pro penuria uictualium Bancornensem, ubi intronizatus fuerat, deseruerat locum; et ne Lincoliensis pontifex mutilatam suam quereretur diocesim, ex rebus Heliensis cenobii dampnum rex sarciuit, querelam composuit.

4   Sane quid[b] eius tempore de primatu duorum metropolitanorum, Cantuariensis et Eboracensis, sit uel iustitiae surreptum uel uiolentia presumptum, dicam cum ad ordinem uenero.[2] Iam enim terminata serie regum, de successione totius Angliae pontificum michi uideo esse dicendum; in quo utinam afflueret uber dicendi copia, ne ulterius sub obliuione iaceant tam preclara patriae lumina. Et quidem erunt multi fortassis in diuersis regionibus Angliae qui quaedam aliter ac
5 ego dixi se dicant audisse uel legisse. Veruntamen, si recto aguntur iuditio, non ideo me censorio expungent stilo; ego enim, ueram legem secutus historiae, nichil umquam posui nisi quod a fidelibus relatoribus uel scriptoribus addidici. Porro, quoquo modo haec se habeant, priuatim ipse michi sub ope Christi gratulor, quod continuam Anglorum historiam ordinauerim post Bedam uel solus uel primus. Si quis ergo, sicut iam susurrari audio, post me scribendi de talibus munus attemptauerit, michi debeat collectionis gratiam, sibi habeat electionis materiam.

[a] diuulgatum *[A]*   [b] quod *[A]*

[1] First at 314. 1.
[2] In *GP* pp. 39 seq.

saints of his devotion, leaving nothing undone by way of generous expense that might attract and win over the eye of the beholder. Among these is that Ranulf of whom I have told above.[1] Made bishop of Durham, he contrived to win no small glory for his name by his new buildings for the monks, and by his veneration for St Cuthbert; and what increased his fame was the translation of the holy body, which he raised from its tomb and exposed to the view of all who wished to see it. With well-judged boldness Ralph, then abbot of Séez and afterwards archbishop of Canterbury, handled the body, and published abroad that it was still unimpaired; otherwise certain people might have come to doubt whether the famous wonder of old time, the incorruptibility of the body, was still true. About the same time, in the monastery of Ely, under Abbot Richard, the relics of the virgin St Æthelthryth were found to be incorrupt, and filled all beholders with wonder and enthusiasm. Ely, lately turned by King Henry from a monastery into the seat of a bishopric, received Hervey as its first bishop, who had left Bangor, where he had held the see, for lack of livelihood; and that the bishop of Lincoln might not complain of the mutilation of his diocese, the king made good the loss out of the possessions of the monastery of Ely, and put an end to any dispute.

In his time too the rights of primacy between the two metropolitans of Canterbury and York were the object of judicial chicanery or forcible aggression; but of this I will speak in due course.[2] For now I have finished the line of kings, and perceive that I ought to tell of the succession of bishops in all England; and would that for such a subject I enjoyed a copious abundance of eloquence, that those glorious luminaries of their country might no longer be left lying in oblivion. There will be many, perhaps, in diverse parts of England, ready to say that they have heard or read about some things a different account from that which I have given. But if they judge aright, they will not therefore with critical pen dismiss me as worthless: I have followed the true law of the historian, and have set down nothing but what I have learnt from trustworthy report or written source. Moreover, be that as it may, I have this private satisfaction, by God's help, that I have set in order the unbroken course of English history, and am since Bede the only man so to do, or at any rate the first. If anyone therefore, as I already hear suggested, has a mind to follow me in writing on this subject, let him give me the credit for the collection of the facts, and make his own selection from the material.

446. Haec habui, domine uenerabilis Comes, de gestis Anglorum quae dicerem, ab aduentu eorum in Angliam usque in annum uicesimum octauum[a] felicissimi regni patris uestri; cetera proprium occupabunt libellum, si benignum istis non negaueritis uultum. Hoc autem opus postquam absolui, circumspectis plurimis, uobis potissimum delegandum credidi. Cum enim alios considero, in uno nobilitatem, in altero militiam, in isto litteraturam, in illo iustitiam, in paucis munificentiam inuenio; itaque in aliis aliqua, in singulis singula, in
2 uobis ammiror uniuersa. Si quis enim umquam fuit nobilis, uos in ea re precellitis, cuius genus a precellentissimis regibus et comitibus lineam trahit, animus a moribus imitationem conducit. Habetis ergo a Normannis bellandi peritiam, a Flandrensibus liniamentorum gratiam, a Francis generositatis eminentiam. De militiae porro uestrae industria quis hesitet, cum eam excellentissimus pater in uobis suspitiat? Cum enim aliqui motus in Normannia nuntiantur, uos premittit, ut uirtute uestra profligentur suspecta, sagacitate redintegretur concordia; cum redit in regnum, uos reducit, ut sitis ei foris tutelae, domi laetitiae, ornamento ubique.

447. Litteras ita fouetis ut, cum sitis tantarum occupationum mole districti, horas tamen aliquas uobis surripiatis, quibus aut ipsi legere aut legentes possitis audire. Digno itaque moderamine fortunae uestrae celsitudinem componitis, dum nec militiam propter litteras postponitis nec litteras propter militiam, ut quidam, conspuitis; in quo etiam scientiae uestrae patescit miraculum, quia, dum libros diligitis, datis inditium quam auidis medullis fontem eorum combiberitis. Multae siquidem res, etiam cum[b] non habentur, desiderantur; philosophiam nullus amabit qui eam extrema satietate non hauserit.

448. Iustitiae uestrae fama regiones[c] etiam nostras attigit; a uobis siquidem prauum iuditium numquam extorsit uel personae sullimitas uel fortunae tenuitas. Nichil reperit in uestro pectore quod suis conducat artibus, qui iustitiam labefactare conatur seu oblatione muneris seu delinimento fauoris.[d]

[a] om. [A]   [b] cum etiam [A]   [c] religiones [C]Bk   [d] Ce ends with this word

446. Here then, right honourable Lord, is what I have found to say about the history of the English, from their coming into England down to the twenty-eighth year of your most glorious father's reign; what follows shall fill a small volume of its own, if you do not refuse a kind welcome to what lies before you. When I had finished my work, I considered many names, and chose you above all others as its recipient. When I look at other men, I find in one high birth, in another knightly valour, in this man literary gifts, in that man justice, in a few generosity; in short, other men have their excellences, each to his own; it is in you that I admire all these at once. If ever a man was nobly born, you are pre-eminently so, whose family traces its descent from famous kings and dukes, whose spirit derives from their high character the urge to imitate them. From the Normans you inherit your skill in battle; from the Flemings your good looks; from the French your eminent nobility of character. As for your energy in knightly deeds, who can question it, seeing that your most famous father regards it as something to admire in you? For when news is brought of any disturbance in Normandy, he sends you on before him, that your valour may crush what is disloyal, and your wisdom restore peace; when he returns to his kingdom, he brings you back with him, that you may be his defence abroad, his happiness at home, his glory everywhere.

447. To literature you are so devoted that, burdened as you are by such a load of business, you yet snatch a few hours to yourself in which to read or listen to others reading. In your exalted station you steer a praiseworthy middle course, neither neglecting knightly exercises for the sake of letters, nor rejecting letters, as some do, for the sake of knighthood. In this point too your knowledge appears remarkable, that in your love of books you show how deeply you have drunk of the fountain-head; many things are an object of desire even when they are entirely absent, but no one can love learning who has not satisfied his uttermost thirst with draughts of it.

448. Your reputation for justice has reached even to the region where we dwell, for no man by the grandeur of his position or the modesty of his means ever deflected your judgement into falsehood. Your bosom harbours nothing that might encourage the man who tries to weaken the force of justice by the proffer of gifts or the blandishments of influence.

449. Munificentiae uestrae*a* pecuniaeque contemptum pretendit Theokesberiae cenobium; de quo, ut audio, non solum xenia non corraditis sed etiam ultro missa remittitis.*b* Quantum hoc sit, isto presertim tempore, quantae in seculo gloriae, quantae apud Deum gratiae, ipsi certe intelligitis. Beata est igitur, secundum sententiam Platonis,[1] respublica cuius rector est philosophus, cuius princeps non delectatur muneribus. Plura de talibus dicerem, nisi et suspitio meae adulationis et laudanda modestia uestri pudoris dicturientem cohiberet.

2 Sane quae dixi non pretermittere fuit consilium, ut per offitium linguae meae probitas uestra posteros non lateat, et ipsa de uirtute in uirtutem proficere contendat. Et quidem iam dudum, quibusdam persuadentibus, ferebat animus ut, quae pretereunda non putarem, per succiduos semper annos huic operi apponerem; sed consultius uidetur alium de talibus librum procudere quam iam absoluto frequenter noua insuere. Nec uero quisquam superfluam me operam dicat insumere, si clarissimi omnium sua aetate regum gesta propono. Multa enim sullimitati

3 eius mea humilitas debet, et adhuc plura debebit, ut (si nichil aliud esset) quod se talem filium habere gaudet.*c* Nam et olim felici sorte susceptum non perfunctorie, ut hodie claret, litteris erudiri precepit; post etiam amplissimarum possessionum fecit dominum; nunc postremo patrium in uos reclinat affectum. Sit ergo hic liber, ut est, uestrae gloriae absolute consecratus; in altero erit idem uitae qui scripturae terminus. Quod superest, munus meum dignanter suscipite, ut gaudeam grato cognitoris arbitrio, qui non erraui eligendi iuditio.

a *An accusative noun has dropped out*   *b* mittitis *CrB*   *c* gauderet *B*

---

[1] Cf. above, p. 710 n. 1.

449. Your generosity and your contempt of coin are advertised by the community of Tewkesbury; for, as I hear, so far from raking in presents from them, you even send back what they proffer of their own accord. How great a thing this is, especially in our own day; what good report it wins in the world and what favour with God, I am sure you already know. Blessed therefore, as Plato holds,[1] is the state whose ruler is a philosopher, and whose prince takes no delight in gifts. I would say more on this head, did not the fear of being thought to flatter, and your own admirable modesty, restrain my eager pen. What I have said, I have deliberately included, that by the dutiful service of my words your prowess may not be hid from posterity, but you may be encouraged to progress from one excellence to another. And indeed it had long been in my mind, at the persuasion of certain friends, that whatever seemed worthy of preservation should be added to this work year by year; but to make another book of those additions seems a better plan than to be frequently tacking new pieces onto a fabric already finished. And let no one say that I pursue a needless task, if I set forth the history of the most famous of all kings in his day; for lowly as I am, I owe much to his royal highness and shall owe still more; for example, if there were nothing else, that he is the happy father of such a noble son. For you were born in a lucky hour, and the schooling in literature that he ordained for you was, as we now see, far from superficial; afterwards he made you master of great possessions, and now finally he rests on you his fatherly affection. Let this book, then, be—as indeed it is—dedicated wholly to your glory; the writing of the other will end only with life itself. For the rest, deign to accept this offering of mine, that, as I have not chosen wrongly, so I may rejoice in the favourable verdict of my judge.

APPENDIX I
ADDITIONS OF B AND C

At 12 n. r (after effecerint) *B adds*

Sed et hoc, et quicquid boni potest diebus Egberti ascribi, attenuat facinus quo Elbertum[a] et Egelbrihtum filios patrui aut interemit[b] aut interimi aequanimiter[c] passus fuit.

At 19. 2 n. j (after uestigia) *C adds a long passage, conventionally numbered cc. 19 (in part)–29 (in part). There is much overlap with AG.*

3 Sed quia Kenwalkii tempora attigimus et Glastoniensis cenobii[d] se obtulit locus, eiusdem aecclesiae exortum[e] et processum, quantum e strue monimentorum corradere potero, repetens ab origine pandam.[1] Tradunt bonae credulitatis annales[2] quod Lucius rex Britannorum ad Eleutherium, tertio decimo loco post beatum Petrum papam, miserit oratum ut Britanniae tenebras luce Christianae predicationis illustraret. Mactus animi rex, magnae prorsus laudis factum adorsus, ut fidem, quam tunc temporis pene omnes reges et populi persequerentur exhibitam, ipse ultro appeteret uix auditam. Venerunt ergo Eleutherio mittente predicatores Britanniam, quorum in aeuum durabit efficatia,
4 quanuis longae situs aetatis consumpserit nomina. Horum fuit opera uetusta in Glastonia sanctae Mariae aecclesia, sicut fidelis per succidua secula non tacuit antiquitas. Sunt et illae non exiguae fidei litterae in nonnullis locis repertae ad hanc sententiam: 'Aecclesiam Glastoniae non fecerunt aliorum hominum manus, sed ipsi discipuli Christi eam edificauerunt.' Nec abhorret a uero, quia si Philippus apostolus Gallis predicauit, sicut Freculfus libro secundo, capitulo quarto dicit,[3] potest credi quod et trans oceanum sermonis semina iecit. Sed ne uidear per opinionum[f] nenias lectorum expectationem fraudare, illis quae discrepant in medio relictis ad solidae ueritatis gesta enarranda succingar.

[a] *Properly* Egelredum [b] interimit *Bk(and BpBph)* [c] om. *Bc*
[d] monasterii *Cs* [e] rudimentum *Cs (cf. AG p. 40), omitting* aecclesiae [f] opinionem *Cs*

[1] Cf. Virgil, *Georg.* iv. 286, *Aen.* i. 372.

APPENDIX I

12

But both this, and any other good thing that can be marked up to Ecgberht's reign, is diminished by a crime: he either killed or looked complacently on the killing of, his uncle's sons, Æthelred and Æthelberht.

19

Now, as we have reached the reign of Cenwealh, and the proper place to mention the monastery of Glastonbury, let me 'e'en from its birth tell o'er'[1] the rise and progress of that house, so far as I can gather it from the formless mass of the documents. We are told by trustworthy annals[2] that Lucius king of the British sent to Eleutherius, thirteenth successor of St Peter, to beg that he would lighten the darkness of Britain with the rays of Christian preaching. O brave king, and worthy of all praise his undertaking! That faith which in those days nearly all kings and people persecuted when it was presented to them, he went out of his way to ask for when he had scarce heard of it. So preachers sent by Eleutherius came to Britain, where their work shall endure for ever, although many years' oblivion has devoured their names. The ancient church of St Mary at Glastonbury was their handiwork, as the faithful tradition of succeeding centuries recounts. There is too that trustworthy record found in several sources, which declares that no other hands made the church of Glastonbury, but it was Christ's disciples themselves that built it. Nor is this unlikely; for if the Apostle Philip preached to the Gauls, as Freculf says in Book 2, Chapter 4,[3] we can well believe that he also sowed the seed of his preaching across the sea. But I would not be thought to deceive my readers' expectations with romantic fancies; and therefore, leaving these points of difference undecided, I will set to and tell a story of solid truth.

3

4

---

[2] *ASC* s.a. 167.
[3] Freculf of Lisieux, *Chronicon* (*PL* cvi. 1148B).

20. Aecclesia de qua loquimur, quae pro antiquitate sui celebriter ab Anglis Ealdecirce, id est Vetusta Aecclesia nuncupatur, primo uirgea, nescio quid diuinae sanctitatis iam inde a principio redoluit, spirauitque in omnem patriam quanuis ex deformi grandis reuerentia cultu.[1] Hinc confluentium illuc populorum totis callibus undae, hinc opulentorum deposita pompa conuentus, hinc religiosorum et litteratorum frequens perhendinatio. Nam, sicut a maioribus accepimus, Gildas neque insulsus neque infacetus historicus, cui Britanni debent si quid notitiae inter ceteras gentes habent, multum annorum ibi exegit loci sanctitudine captus. Est ergo aecclesia illa omnium quas quidem nouerim in Anglia uetustissima, et inde cognomen sortita. In ea multorum sanctorum, quorum aliquos in processu notabimus, corporales seruantur exuuiae, nec a beatorum cineribus uacat ullus fani ambitus: adeo pauimentum lapide polito crustatum, adeo altaris latera ipsumque altare supra[a] et infra reliquiis confertissimis aggeruntur.[b] Vbi etiam notare licet in pauimento uel per triangulum uel per quadratum lapides altrinsecus ex industria positos et plumbo sigillatos, sub quibus quiddam archani sacri contineri si credo, iniuriam religioni non fatio. Antiquitas et sanctorum[c] congeries exciuit reuerentiam loco, ut uix ibi quis noctu presumat excubias agere, uix interdiu excrescens flegma proicere, illusoriae feditatis conscius toto cohorreat corpore. Nullus intra contiguum cimiterium uel auem uenatoriam aduexit uel quadrupedes[d] induxit, qui sui uel rei possessae indempnis abierit. Ferro uel aqua examinandi si orationem ibi deposuerunt, omnes quos presens memoria complectitur, uno excepto, de salute sua tripudiarunt. Si quis e uicino aliquod edifitium locandum putasset, quod obumbratione sua lucem inuideret aecclesiae, patuit ruinae; satisque constat homines illius prouintiae nullum sanctius uel crebrius iuramentum habere quam per Veterem Aecclesiam, nichil magis uitantes metu celeris uindictae quam peierare. Labantem ueritatem dictorum quae proposuimus in libro quem de antiquitate eiusdem aecclesiae scripsimus pro successu annorum testimoniis fulciemus.[2]

21. Interim palam factum est merito dici caeleste in terris sanctuarium tot sanctorum reconditorium. Quantum uero is locus fuerit etiam

---

[a] super *Cs (and Cr)*   [b] aggerantur *some witnesses at AG p. 66, rightly?*   [c] antiquitas et sanctorum *AG p. 66;* antiquitas sanctorum et *Ce (and CdCr);* antiqua sanctorum *Cs*   [d] quadrupes *Cs (and Cr)*

---

[1] Unidentified.

20. The church of which I speak, commonly called by the English *Ealdecirce*, that is Old Church, on account of its antiquity, was at first made of wattle, and from its very beginning it possessed a mysterious aura of sanctity, and although 'rough was the fabric that inspired such awe',[1] the whole country felt the breath. Hence the floods of common folk streaming in by every road; the gatherings of rich men, their grandeur laid aside; the frequent visits of the saintly and the learned. Gildas, for instance, a historian not without style and insight, whom the British have to thank for such knowledge of them as exists among other peoples, spent (so our forefathers tell us) many years at Glastonbury, attracted by the holiness of the place. This church then is the oldest of all that I know in England, and thence derives its name. In it are preserved the bodily remains of many saints, some of whom we shall touch on in due course, and there is no part of the sacred building without the ashes of holy men, so thickly piled with relics are the floor, tiled with polished stone, the sides of the altar, and the altar itself, above and below. One may also notice in the pavement on both sides stones carefully placed in triangular and square patterns, and sealed with lead; and I am not irreligious if I believe that some secret holy thing lies beneath them. The age of the place and its multitude of saints inspires such reverence for the shrine that men would scarcely dare keep vigil there by night, or void their overflowing rheum by day; one conscious of pollution by the visions of sleep would tremble in every limb. No one ever carried hawk or drove animal into the neighbouring graveyard, and yet went his way unscathed in person or possession. Persons obliged to undergo ordeal by fire or water who made their supplications here have been, with one sole exception in living memory, triumphantly vindicated. If anyone had thought to raise nearby a building that might overshadow the church's light, he laid it open to ruin. It is notorious that the men of that region have no more solemn or familiar oath than to swear by the Old Church, and shun nothing more, from fear of immediate penalty, than to be forsworn. Any weakness in the truth of what I say I shall remedy with evidence, in chronological order, in my book on the antiquity of Glastonbury.[2]

21. Meanwhile, I have made it clear that the resting-place of so many saints richly deserves to be esteemed a little heaven on earth.

---

[2] *AG* pp. 2, 6–7, 18. What follows is also indebted to *AG*.

primatibus patriae uenerabilis, ut ibi potissimum sub protectione Dei genitricis opperirentur diem resurrectionis, plura sunt documento, quibus pro cautela fastidii abstineo. Illud quod pene clam omnibus est libenter predicarem, si ueritatem exculpere possem, quid illae piramides sibi uelint quae, aliquantis pedibus ab aecclesia illa positae, cimi-
2 terium monachorum pretexunt. Procerior sane et propinquior aecclesiae habet quinque tabulatus, et altitudinem uiginti octo pedum; haec, pre nimia sui uetustate etsi ruinam minetur, habet tamen antiquitatis nonnulla spectacula, quae plane possunt legi, licet non plene possint intelligi. In superiori enim tabulatu est imago pontificali scemate facta; in secundo imago regiam pretendens pompam et litterae[a] Her Sexi et Bliswerh; in tertio nichilominus nomina Wencrest Bantomp Winethegn; in quarto Bate Wulfred et Eanfled; in quinto, qui et inferior est, imago et haec scriptura: Logwor[b] Weaslieas et Bregden
3 Swelwes Hiwingendes Bearn. Altera uero piramis habet uiginti sex pedes et quattuor tabulatus, in quibus haec leguntur: Centwine Hedde episcopus et Bregored et Beorward. Quid haec significent non temere diffinio, sed ex suspitione colligo eorum interius in cauatis lapidibus contineri ossa quorum exterius leguntur nomina. Certe Logwor is pro uero asseritur esse de cuius nomine quondam Logweresberh[c] dicebatur, qui nunc Mons Acutus uocatur; Bregden a quo Brentacnol et Brentemeirs; Bregored et Beorward[d][1] abbates eiusdem loci tempore Britonum, de quibus et ceteris qui occurrere poterunt exhinc liberiori campo exultabit oratio. Iam enim abbatum seriem, et quid cuique et a quo rege monasterio delegatum sit, sermo explicare contendet.

22. Ac primum de beato Patritio, a quo monimentorum nostrorum series elucescere[e] cepit, pauca libabimus. Saxonibus enim Britannorum infestantibus pacem, et Pelagianis eorum expugnantibus fidem, sanctus Germanus Autisiodorensis contra utrosque suppetias tulit. Illos enim alleluiatico cantu fudit, istos euangelicis et apostolicis tonitribus fulminauit. Inde in patriam molitus reditum, Patritium ad familiare contubernium asciuit, eundemque post aliquot annos Hibernensibus, iubente Celestino papa, predicatorem misit. Vnde scriptum est in Cronicis:[2]

[a] *The mysterious names are usually given as they appear in Ce; but that MS (like Cd) represents wynn and thorn by an ordinary p, and the evidence of Cs and AG has been used in this respect*   [b] *AG p. 84 (so too below); Logor CeCs (like Ce below)*   [c] *AG p. 84; Logp- Ce (Cs uncertain)*   [d] *Beorwald AG p. 84*   [e] *illucessere Cs*

[1] i.e. Berhtwald.

How sacred was that place, even among the princes of the land, so that there above all other they preferred, under the protection of the Mother of God, to await the Resurrection, there is much to show, which, for fear of being tedious, I omit. One thing generally unknown I would gladly tell, could I discover the truth, and that is, the meaning of those pyramids which stand on the edge of the monastic graveyard a few feet from the church. The taller, which is nearer the church, has five tiers, and is twenty-eight feet high. It threatens to collapse from old age, but still displays some ancient features, which can be deciphered though they can no longer be fully understood. In the uppermost tier is a figure habited like a bishop, in the second one like a king in state, and the inscription 'Here are *Sexi* and *Bliswerh*'. In the third too are names, *Wencrest*, *Bantomp*, *Winethegn*. In the fourth *Bate*, *Wulfred* and *Eanfled*. In the fifth, which is the lowest, is a figure, and this inscription: '*Logwor Weaslieas* and *Bregden Swelwes Hiwingendes Bearn*'. The other pyramid is twenty-six feet high, and has four tiers, on which are inscribed *Centwine*, *Hedde* bishop, and *Bregored*, and *Beorward*. The meaning of these I am not so rash as to determine, but I suppose the stones are hollow, and contain within them the bones of those whose names are to be read on the outside. Certainly, it is maintained with perfect truth that Logwor is the man who once gave his name to *Logworesburh*, the present Montacute; that Bregden is the origin of Brent Knoll and Brent Marsh; and that Bregored and Beorward[1] were abbots of Glastonbury in the days of the Britons. To them, and to such others as we may meet with, I shall henceforward gladly devote more space; for it will now be my endeavour to set out the succession of the abbots, the gifts conferred on each for the use of the monastery, and the king from whom they came.

22. First I will say a few words about St Patrick, with whom light first dawns on our recorded history. At a time when the Saxons were molesting the peace of the British, and the Pelagians assailing their orthodoxy, St Germanus of Auxerre came to our aid on both fronts: the enemy he routed with the Alleluia triumph-song, the heretic he blasted with the Apostolic thunders of the Gospel. Returning thence to his own country, he called Patrick to be a member of his household, and some years later with the authority of Pope Celestine despatched him to evangelize the Irish. Hence the entries in the Chronicles:[2]

---

[2] Cf. *ASC* s.a. 430, but this was presumably not William's source.

'Anno Dominicae incarnationis quadringentesimo uicesimo quinto sanctus Patritius ordinatur a Celestino papa in Hiberniam.' Item: 'Quadringentesimo tricesimo tertio anno Hibernia insula conuertitur ad fidem Christi predicante sancto Patritio cum multis mirabilibus.'

2 Ille igitur munus iniunctum gnauiter exsecutus, et extremis diebus in patriam reuertens, super altare suum Cornubiam appulit, quod hodieque apud incolas magnae uenerationi est propter sanctitudinem et utilitatem propter infirmorum salutem. Ita Glastoniam ueniens ibique monachus et abbas factus, post aliquot annos naturae cessit. Cuius assertionis omnem[a] absoluit scrupulum uisio cuiusdam fratris, qui post obitum beati uiri, iam nutante memoria utrum ibi monachus et abbas fuerit, cum de hoc frequens uerteretur questio, tali confirmatus 3 est oraculo. Resolutus enim in soporem, uisus est audire quendam legentem post multa eius miracula haec uerba: 'Hic igitur metropolitani pallii sanctitate decoratus est; postmodum uero hic monachus et abbas factus.' Adiecit etiam ut non integre credenti litteris aureis quod dixerat scriptum ostenderet. Excessit ergo Patritius anno aetatis centesimo undecimo, incarnationis Domini quadringentesimo septuagesimo secundo, qui fuit annus ex quo Hiberniam missus est quadragesimus septimus. Requiescit in dextro latere altaris Vetustae Aecclesiae in piramide saxea, quam argento uestiuit posterorum diligentia. Hinc Hibernensibus mos inolitus ad exosculandas patroni reliquias locum frequentare.

23. Vnde et sanctum Indrahtum et beatam Brigidam, Hiberniae non obscuros incolas, huc olim commeasse celeberrimus sermo est. Brigida, relictis quibusdam suis insignibus, monili uidelicet pera et textrilibus armis, quae adhuc pro sanctitatis memoria ostentantur et morbis diuersis medentur, utrum domum reuersa an ibi acceperit pausam incertum. Alterum iuxta Glastoniam martirizatum cum sotiis septem, postmodum in Veterem translatum Aecclesiam,[b] liquebit per narrationis consequentiam.[1]

24. Successit Patritio in abbatis regimine Benignus, sed quot annis incertum. Quis autem fuerit, et quomodo patria lingua dictus, non infacete uersus exprimunt qui in epitaphio apud Ferramere scripti fuerunt:

[a] omne Cs   [b] Cs adds sicut

'AD 425 St Patrick is ordained by Pope Celestine for service in Ireland', and 'AD 433 Ireland converted to Christianity by the preaching of St Patrick, with many miracles'. After executing his mission with vigour, at the end of his life he came back home, and landed in Cornwall, voyaging on his altar, which is still held in great veneration by the Cornish for its holiness, and its value in the treatment of the sick. So he came to Glastonbury, and having become a monk and abbot there, after some years paid the debt of nature. Any hesitation about this statement is dispelled by the vision of one of the monks, who after the saint's death, when the tradition was already uncertain whether he had been monk and abbot there, and the question was much discussed, had his faith established by the following oracle. In his sleep, he seemed to hear someone reading, at the end of an account of St Patrick's many miracles, the following words: 'So he was honoured with the sacred pallium of an archbishop; but afterwards became a monk and abbot here.' The reader added that, if he did not fully believe, he would show what he had said, written in letters of gold. So Patrick died in the one hundred and eleventh year of his age and the year of our Lord 472, which was the forty-seventh year after his sending into Ireland. He rests on the right side of the altar of the Old Church, in a stone pyramid, which the devotion of later times has overlaid with silver. Hence it is an ancient custom amongst the Irish to visit Glastonbury to kiss the relics of their patron saint.

23. According to a well-established tradition, this later attracted hither two eminent natives of Ireland, St Indract and St Brigid. Brigid left behind her some personal relics, a necklace, a purse, and some weaving implements, which are still displayed as a memorial of her sanctity, and heal various diseases; but whether she returned home or entered into rest at Glastonbury, is uncertain. Indract, as we shall see in the course of our narrative,[1] was martyred near Glastonbury with seven companions, and later translated into the Old Church.

24. Patrick was succeeded in the office of abbot by Benignus, but for how many years is uncertain. Who he was, and what his name in his native tongue, is neatly given in his epitaph at Meare:

---

[1] 35C. 3.

Hoc patris in lapide Beonnae sunt ossa locata,
qui pater extiterat monachorum hic tempore prisco;
hunc fore Patritii quondam fortasse ministrum
fantur Hibernigenae, et Beonnam de nomine dicunt.

Is quantae apud Deum gratiae fuerit et sit, et ueteris quondam uitae et nouae in maiorem aecclesiam translationis preconantur magnalia.

25. Iam uero quanti hunc locum penderit magnus ille Dauid Meneuensium archiepiscopus celebrius est quam ut nostro indigeat illustrari relatu. Ille antiquitatem et sanctitudinem aecclesiae diuino comprobauit oraculo. Dedicationi enim eius intendens cum episcopis septem, quorum primas erat, ad locum uenit; paratis autem omnibus quae offitii usus[a] exposceret, nocte precessura, ut putabat, festiuitatem somno indulsit. Omnes ergo sensus in quietem solutus, uidit Domi-
2 num Iesum assistere, causam aduentus blande sciscitantem. Quam cum ille incunctanter aperuisset, reuocauit eum a sententia Dominus hoc dicto, dedicatam a se dudum aecclesiam in honorem matris suae; iteratione humana sacramentum temerari non oportere. Simulque cum dicto, digito uolam terebrare[b] uisus subiecit, hoc haberet[c] signum repeti non debere quod ipse anticipasset facere; sed quia intentionis illius non tam fuisset audatia quam deuotio, penam non prolongandam. Denique mane futuro, cum in missa 'Cum ipso et per ipsum et in ipso' dicturus esset, plenum ei salutis uigorem refundendum.
3 His terroribus antistes somno excussus, sicut tunc ulcerosa[d] sanie impalluit, sic postea ueritati prophetiae applausit. Sed ne nichil uideretur egisse, aliam aecclesiam citato fecit et dedicauit opere. De hoc sane egregio et incomparabili uiro, utrum ibi obierit an in sede propria uitam finierit,[e] incertum habeo. Nam eum cum beato Patritio esse affirmant,[f] et Walenses orationum frequentatione et multiplici sermone id proculdubio astruunt et corroborant, illud in medium proferentes, Bernardum episcopum semel et secundo eum quesisse, et multis reclamantibus non inuenisse. Haec de beato Dauid dixisse suffitiat.

26. Multum temporis in medio, et uenit in Britanniam sanctus Augustinus, a beato Gregorio directus, anno incarnationis Domini

---

[a] usus officii *Cs*   [b] temerare *Cs*   [c] habet *Cs*   [d] exulcerosa *Cs*
[e] finierunt *Cs*   [f] *A subject seems to be lacking (*quidam *AG p. 64,* uiri religiosi recordatione digni *CdCr)*

> Within this tomb his bones Beonna lays,
> Was father here of monks in ancient days.
> Patrick of old to serve he had the honour
> (So Erin's sons aver, and name Beonna).

The favour that he found, and still finds, in the sight of God, is clearly shown by the miracles worked during his life in olden days, and since his recent translation into the larger church.

25. The esteem for Glastonbury felt by the great St David, archbishop of Menevia, is too well known to need any advertisement from me. The antiquity and holiness of the church was established through him by a heavenly vision. With seven other bishops, whose metropolitan he was, he came to take part in the dedication; and when all things needful for the ceremony were made ready, on the night preceding (as was thought) the festival, he fell asleep. When he was sound asleep, he saw standing beside him the Lord Jesus, who gently asked the reason of his coming. He explained without hesitation; whereupon the Lord turned him from his purpose, saying that He had long since dedicated the church in honour of His Mother, and it was wrong for such a sacrament to be repeated, and so profaned, by the hand of man. At the same moment, in the dream, the Lord pierced with His finger the palm of his hand, and said: 'Behold a sign that what I have done already must not be repeated. Nevertheless, inasmuch as you were motivated by piety and not presumption, your penalty shall not last long. In the morning, at Mass, when you come to the "With Him and through Him and in Him", you shall be fully restored to health and strength.' The bishop awoke in terror. He grew pale then at the running sore on his hand, and later no less surely welcomed the truth of the prophecy. And, that his journey might not seem fruitless, he quickly built and dedicated another church. Concerning this famous and incomparable man, I find no certainty whether he died at Glastonbury, or ended his life in his own see. They say he lies with St Patrick, and the Welsh, by their habit of praying to him, and often in conversation, definitely confirm this, telling how Bishop Bernard more than once looked for his body, and in face of many protests could not find it. So much for St David.

26. Long after, in the year of our Lord 596, came St Augustine's mission to Britain, sent by St Gregory; and it was one of his fellow-

quingentesimo nonagesimo sexto; cuius predicationis commilitonem Paulinum, ex archiepiscopo Eboracensi Rofensem episcopum, asserit maiorum traditio aecclesiae contextum, dudum ut diximus[1] uirgeae, ligneo induisse tabulatu. Egit nimirum predicabilis uiri sollertia ut nichil decederet sanctitati et plurimum accederet ornatui; et certe solet aecclesiarum cultus augustior quamlibet brutas mentes ad orandum accendere, quamlibet ceruicositatem ad suplicandum inflectere.

27. Anno incarnationis sexcentesimo primo, id est, aduentus beati Augustini quinto, rex Domnoniae terram quae appellatur Ineswitrin ad Aecclesiam Vetustam concessit, quae ibi sita est, ob[a] petitionem Worgrez abbatis, in quinque cassatis: 'Ego Maworn episcopus hanc cartam conscripsi. Ego Worgrez eiusdem loci abbas subscripsi.'

28. Quis iste rex fuerit, scedulae uetustas negat scire. Veruntamen quod Britannus fuerit hinc non ambigitur, quod Glastoniam sua lingua Ineswitrin appellauit; sic enim eam Britannice uocari apud eos[b] constat. Illud quoque animaduertere par est, quantae antiquitatis sit aecclesia quae tunc etiam dicebatur uetusta. Fuerunt sane eiusdem abbates, Britannicam barbariem nominibus pretendentes, preter Worgrez, Lademund et Bregored. Prelationis eorum tempora sunt in obscuro, sed nomina illorum et dignitates in maiori aecclesia, prodente secus altare pictura, sunt in propatulo. Felices ergo eius loci habitatores, quos ipsa sanctuarii reuerentia ad morum compositionem inuitat. Nullum de his crediderim deperire caelo quos egressos corpore tot patronorum excipit laus uel excusatio.

29. Anno Dominicae incarnationis sexcentesimo septuagesimo Kenwalh, regni sui uicesimo nono, dedit Berhtwaldo Glastoniensi abbati Ferramere duas hidas, archiepiscopo Theodoro interueniente. Hic idem Berhtwaldus, renitente rege et diocesis episcopo Glastoniae renuntians, ad regimen monasterii Raculf secessit. Quocirca Berhtwaldus, et fama religionis nominatissimus et generis nobilitate precluus, quippe fratris Ethelredi regis Mertiorum filius, et loci oportunitate Cantuariae proximus, Theodoro archiepiscopo decedente, illius successit cathedrae. Haec de Glastoniensis antiquitate aecclesiae me dixisse suffitiat.

2 Nunc ad Kenwalkium ex ordine reuertar, qui . . .

[a] ad Cs   [b] *One expects* omnes

campaigners, Paulinus archbishop of York and later bishop of Rochester, who according to the tradition of our fathers clothed the church, which had long been made of wattle as we have said,[1] in a covering of wooden planking. His admirable skill contrived, while taking nothing from its sanctity, greatly to increase its beauty; and true it is that churches, when they are made more beautiful and solemn, can kindle even the dullest mind to prayer and bend to supplication the most obstinate.

27. In the year of our Lord 601—the fifth, that is, after the arrival of St Augustine—the king of Dumnonia gave the Old Church land called *Ineswitrin*, in which it stands, comprising five hides, in answer to the prayer of Abbot Worgrez. 'I, Bishop Maworn, drew up this deed. I, Worgrez, abbot of the same place, set my hand thereto.'

28. Who this king was, the ancient charter cannot tell us. That he was British is quite clear from his calling Glastonbury in his native tongue *Ineswitrin*, for that is known to have been its British name. Another point is worth notice; how ancient a foundation must be, that even then was called Old Church. Among its abbots, with their barbarous British names, were, besides Worgrez, Lademund and Bregored. The dates of their reigns are obscure, but their names and dignities are on public record in the larger church, painted up near the altar. Happy the dwellers in that place, whom reverence for their ancient sanctuary of itself encourages to holiness of life; nor, I believe, can any perish from the way to Heaven, of those who at their departing find so many patron saints to recommend or to defend them.

29. In the year of our Lord 670 Cenwealh, then in the twenty-ninth year of his reign, gave to Berhtwald abbot of Glastonbury, by the mediation of Archbishop Theodore, two hides at Meare. This Berhtwald, against the wishes of the king and his diocesan, resigned from Glastonbury, and retired to rule the monastery at Reculver. So Berhtwald, as he was celebrated for holiness of life, of distinguished lineage (being brother's son to Æthelred king of the Mercians), and most conveniently situated for Canterbury, succeeded on the death of Theodore to the archiepiscopal throne. I need say no more about the antiquity of the church of Glastonbury.

Now let me return in due order to Cenwealh, who (was so generous) 2 ... [*continued in main text*]

---

[1] 20. 1.

At 35. 3 n. g (after precipue) *C proceeds with a passage conventionally numbered 35 (in part)–36 (in this edition 35C and 36C).*

3 Glastingense, in quo*ᵃ* beati martiris Indrahti et sotiorum eius corpora, de loco martirii translata, iussit inferri: ipsius quidem in lapidea piramide ad sinistrum altaris, cum quo posterorum diligentia beatam Hildam locauit, ceterorum in pauimento, prout uel casus tulit uel industria locauit. Hic etiam Beatorum Apostolorum Aecclesiam huic Vetustae, de qua loquimur, appendicem a fundamentis edificauit, et magnis possessionibus ditauit, et priuilegium in haec uerba concessit:

36C. *ᵇ*'In nomine Domini nostri Iesu Christi. Ego Ina regali a Domino fretus dignitate, cum consilio Sexburgae reginae et licentia Beortwaldi Dorobernensis aecclesiae pontificis et omnium suffraganeorum suorum, necnon etiam*ᶜ* hortatu Baldredi et Adelardi subregulorum, Aecclesiae Vetustae quae est in loco qui dicitur Glasteie, quam magnus Sacerdos et summus Pontifex suo et angelorum obsequio sibi ac perpetuae uirgini Mariae beato Dauid multis et inauditis miraculis olim se sanctificasse innotuit, ex his quae paterna hereditate possideo et in dominium peculiare teneo locis continuis et congruentibus, concedo ad supplementum uitae regularis et ad usum monachorum: Brente decem hidas, Soweie decem hidas, Piltune uiginti hidas,
2 Dulting uiginti hidas, Bleddanhid*ᵈ* unam hidam, cum his omnibus quae antecessores mei eidem aecclesiae contulerunt: Kenewalchius, qui Theodoro archiepiscopo interueniente Ferramere, Bregereie, Coneneie,*ᵈ* Martineseie, Ederedeseie; Kentwinus, qui Glastingeie matrem sanctorum uocare solitus fuerat, et eam ab omni seculari et aecclesiastico obsequio immunem statuit et hanc priuilegii dignitatem concessit, ut habeant fratres eiusdem loci potestatem eligendi et constituendi sibi rectorem iuxta regulam sancti Benedicti; Hedde episcopus qui, Cedwalla annuente et propria manu licet paganus confirmante, Lantocai; Baldred, qui Pennard sex hidas; Adelard, qui Poelt sexaginta
3 hidas, me annuente et confirmante, dederunt. Quorum ego deuotioni et benignae petitioni assentio, et contra malignantium hominum et oblatrantium canum insidias regalium munimine inuigilo litterarum, quatinus aecclesia Domini nostri Iesu Christi et perpetuae uirginis Mariae, sicut in regno Britanniae est prima et fons et origo totius

ᵃ One expects quod   *ᵇ* A longer version of this document (Sawyer 250) is found in AG pp. 98–102 (and a number of related later MSS, including δρστ)   *ᶜ* om. Ce
ᵈ Beokerie Godenie AG p. 98

35C

Glastonbury, to which he ordered to be translated the bodies of the blessed martyr Indract and his companions after removal from their place of martyrdom. Indract himself he placed in a stone pyramid on the left of the altar, where the care of later generations has also laid St Hild; the others beneath the pavement, as chance or purpose decided. Ine also built from its foundations the church of the Holy Apostles, as an appendage of the Old Church of which I am speaking, and enriched it with great possessions, granting a charter in the following terms:

36C. 'In the name of our Lord Jesus Christ. I, Ine, endowed of the Lord with the dignity of a king, on the advice of Seaxburh my queen, and with the leave of Berhtwald archbishop of Canterbury and all his suffragans, and at the request of Baldred and Æthelheard my subkings, unto the Old Church which is in the place called Glastonbury, which long ago our great High Priest and Supreme Pontiff consecrated by His own ministry and the ministry of angels to Himself and to Mary ever virgin, as he made manifest to St David by many unheard-of miracles, from among those lands, contiguous and convenient, which I possess by inheritance from my father and hold for my especial domain, do grant for the further increase of the religious life and for the use of the monks: in Brent ten hides, in Zoy ten hides, in Pilton twenty hides, in Doulting twenty hides, in Bleadney one hide, together with all those gifts which my predecessors have given to the church aforesaid, to wit: Cenwealh, who by the mediation of Archbishop Theodore gave Meare, Beckery, Godney, Marchey, and Nyland; Centwine, who had been wont to call Glastonbury the mother of saints, and appointed that it should be free from all services both ecclesiastical and lay, granting it also this honourable privilege, that the brethren of that place should enjoy the power of choosing and appointing their own ruler in accordance with the Rule of St Benedict; Bishop Hædde, who gave Leigh [in Street], Cædwalla approving and confirming it with his own hand, albeit a pagan; Baldred, who gave six hides at Pennard; Æthelheard, who gave sixty hides at Polden Hill, with approval and confirmation from myself. To the devotion and the generous request of all these persons I accede, and against the wiles of men of ill-will and barking dogs I set the unsleeping bulwark of my royal charter, that as the church of our Lord Jesus Christ and of Mary ever virgin is first in the kingdom of Britain and the source and

religionis, ita et ipsa supereminentem priuilegii obtineat dignitatem, nec ulli omnino hominum ancillare obsequium fatiat in terris,*a* quae
4 super choros angelorum dominatur in caelis. Igitur summo pontifice Gregorio annuente et ut matrem Domini sui in sinum et protectionem Romanae aecclesiae, meque licet indignum cum ipsa, suscipiente, consentientibus etiam omnibus Britanniae regibus archiepiscopis episcopis ducibus atque abbatibus, statuo ego atque confirmo quatinus omnes terrae et loca et possessiones beatae Mariae Glasteie sint quieta et ab omnibus regiis exactionibus et operibus quae indici solent, uidelicet expeditione et pontis arcisue constructione, et ab omnium archiepiscoporum et episcoporum promulgationibus et perturbationibus,*b* sicut in antiquis eiusdem aecclesiae cartis confirmatum esse inuenitur, et a predecessoribus meis Kenewalchio, Kentwino, Cedwalla, Baldredo astipu-
5 latum esse dinoscitur, inconcussa et illibata permaneant. Et quaecumque emerserint causae in homicidiis, sacrilegis, uenefitiis, furtis, rapinis, in dispositione aecclesiarum et descriptione, in ordinatione clericorum, in conuenticulis sinodalibus et in omnibus iuditiariis examinationibus absque ullius hominis preiuditio abbatis et conuentus dispositione finiantur. Sed et omnibus regni mei regibus archiepiscopis episcopis ducibus et principibus super honorem suum et amorem meum precipio, et omnibus tam meis quam eorum ministris super salutem corporis sui precipio, ne ullus eorum insulam Domini nostri Iesu Christi et perpetuae uirginis Mariae Glasteie, nec eiusdem aecclesiae possessiones, causa placitandi perscrutandi rapiendi uel aliquid fatiendi quod ibidem Deo famulantibus possit esse in scandalum
6 audeat intrare. Illud sane omnipotentis Dei et perpetuae uirginis Mariae et beatorum apostolorum Petri et Pauli et omnium sanctorum interdictione prohibeo, ne in ipsa Glastingensi aecclesia, nec in aecclesiis sibi subditis, uidelicet Soweie, Brente, Merlinch, Sapwic, Stret, Budecalech, Piltune nec in earum capellis, sed nec in insulis aliqua interueniente occasione episcopus sibi episcopalem cathedram statuere nec ⟨missas⟩*c* sollemnes celebrare nec altaria consecrare nec aecclesias dedicare nec ordines facere nec aliquid omnino disponere presumat, nisi
7 ab abbate uel a fratribus eiusdem loci inuitatus fuerit. Quod si ad hoc uocatus uenerit, nichil de rebus aecclesiae sed nec de ipsis oblationibus ipse sibi aliquid usurpet, sciens duobus in locis ex ipsius aecclesiae

a in terris faciat *Ce*   *b* proturbationibus *Ce*   *c* *AG p. 100; om. CeCs*

fountain-head of all religion, so it may enjoy a privilege and dignity above all others, and that she may never do humble service to any man on earth, who rules over the angel-choirs in Heaven. Therefore, 4 with the approval of Gregory the supreme pontiff, who receives in the protective embrace of the Roman Church both [Glastonbury], as the Mother of his Lord, and me (unworthy as I am) with her; and with the consent of all the kings of Britain, the archbishops, bishops, thegns, and abbots; I determine and confirm that all the lands, the territories and possessions of St Mary of Glastonbury should remain quit and be for ever inviolate and free of all such royal exactions and services as may be decreed from time to time, to wit military service and the building of bridges and fortresses, and from the decrees and interference of all archbishops and bishops, even as is found to be confirmed in the ancient charters of that same church and is known to have been provided by my predecessors Cenwealh, Centwine, Cædwalla, and Baldred. Whatsoever cases shall arise of homicide, sacrilege, 5 poisoning, theft, rapine, in the ordering of churches and appointing of their boundaries, in the ordination of clerks, in synodal assemblies and in judicial investigations of every kind, let them without the prejudgement of any man be determined as the abbot and convent may dispose. To all the kings of my kingdom, the archbishops, bishops, thegns, and princes, I ordain as they value their honour and my love for them, and to all servants mine as well as theirs I ordain as they value their bodily safety, that none of them presume to enter the island of our Lord Jesus Christ and of Mary ever virgin, to wit, Glastonbury, nor the possessions of the said church, for the purpose of impleading or making search or forcible removal or any other act that might be to the scandal of the servants of God in that place. This too I prohibit by 6 the authority of almighty God and of Mary ever virgin and of the blessed Apostles Peter and Paul and of All saints, that in the mother-church of Glastonbury or in its daughter-churches of Zoy, Brent, Moorlinch, Shapwick, Street, Butleigh, and Pilton, or in their chapels, or in the islands, for any reason whatsoever any bishop should presume to establish his episcopal see or celebrate solemn masses or consecrate altars or dedicate churches or conduct ordinations or make any dispositions whatsoever, unless he be invited by the abbot or brethren of the aforesaid place. Should he come for this purpose at their invitation, 7 let him not usurp for his own use any of the goods of the church or of the offerings made thereat, knowing that in two places two lodgings have been set apart for him out of the possessions of the church, one

possessionibus duas sibi delegatas mansiones, unam in Piltuna, alteram in uilla quae Poelt dicitur, ut habeat ubi uel adueniens hospitetur uel inde ueniens sese recipiat. Neque enim eum ibi, nisi importunitate temporis aut molestia corporis detentus fuerit, aut ab abbate uel fratribus rogatus fuerit, nec amplius quam cum tribus aut cum quattuor clericis
8 pernoctare licet. Hoc etiam preuideat idem episcopus, ut singulis annis cum clericis suis qui Fontaneto sunt ipsam matrem suam, Glastoniensem aecclesiam uidelicet, feria secunda post ascensionem Domini, cum letania recognoscat. Quod si superbia inflatus eam distulerit, et quae superius dicta et confirmata sunt preuaricauerit, mansiones sibi superius delegatas amittat. Abbas uel monachi a quocumque uoluerint, qui Pascha canonicum celebret, aecclesiastica sacramenta in Glastingensi aecclesia et in
9 aecclesiis sibi subditis et in earum capellis percipiant. Quisquis autem huius munificentiae meae et liberalitatis testamentum quouis deinceps tempore, aliqua occasione, cuiuslibet etiam dignitatis uel professionis uel gradus, peruertere uel in irritum deducere temptauerit, sciat se cum Iuda proditore aeterna confusione edacibus ineffabilium tormentorum periturum flammis.

'Scripta est huius donationis pagina anno Dominicae incarnationis septingentesimo uicesimo quinto, indictione quarta, sub presentia Inae regis et Beortwaldi Dorobernensis pontificis.'

At 38 n. h (after reliquit) *C adds a passage conventionally numbered 38 (in part)–39.*

Hic Glastingensi aecclesiae multa benefitia intulit, et priuilegium in haec uerba concessit:

39. *a*"In nomine Domini nostri Iesu Christi. Ego Cuthredus rex Westsaxonum*b* uniuersa priorum regum suppetitia, Centwines Baldredes Cedwallan Ines Ethelardes, Ethelbaldes regis Mertiorum, in uillis et in uicis atque agris ac prediis massisque maioribus, ut est pristina urbs Glestingi corroborata, sicque propriae manus subscriptione crucisque signo confirmatum hoc donatiuum stabili iure gratum et ratum regum predictorum decerno durare, quamdiu 'uertigo poli terras atque aequora circa ethera sidereum*c* iusso*d* moderamine
2 uoluet'.[1] Si quis autem huius meae donationis*e* testamentum tirannica

---

a *A version of this document (Sawyer 257) is found in AG p. 104 (and some later MSS, including ξσ)*   *b* Westseaxana *Ce, perhaps rightly*   *c* Cd*p.c.*, ξ; siderum *CeCs,* σ, *AG p. 104*   *d* iusto *Cs (and Cd), cf. Juvencus, Evang. ii. 575*   *e* donationis mee *Cs*

in Pilton and one in the vill called Polden Hill, that he may have a place of entertainment on his arrival or a resting-place on his departure. For it is not lawful for him, unless he be detained by stress of weather or bodily infirmity, or be invited by the abbot or the brethren, to pass the night there or to do so in the company of more than three clerks or four at the most. And let the said bishop look well to this, that every year with those of his clerks who are at Wells he acknowledge his mother the church of Glastonbury with a solemn litany on the Monday after Ascension Day. But if, being puffed up by pride, he fail to do so, or contravene what has been above ordained and confirmed, let him lose the lodgings above appointed for him. Let the abbot and monks be free to receive the sacraments of the Church from anyone of their choice who observes the canonical Easter, whether in the church of Glastonbury or in its dependent churches or in their chapels. Whosoever at any future time and for any occasion whatsoever, of whatever dignity, profession or rank, attempts to pervert or bring to nought this record of my generous liberality, let him know that he will perish in everlasting confusion with the archtraitor Judas in the devouring flames of inexpressible torment.

'This charter of donation was drawn up in the year of our Lord's Incarnation 725, the fourth indiction, in the presence of King Ine and of Berhtwald archbishop of Canterbury.'

38

Cuthred bestowed many benefits on Glastonbury, and gave them a charter in the following words:

39. 'In the name of our Lord Jesus Christ. I, Cuthred king of the West Saxons, confirm all the gifts of previous kings, of Centwine, Baldred, Cædwalla, Ine, Æthelheard, and of Æthelbald king of the Mercians, in towns and in villages, in farms and fields and greater estates, with which the ancient city of Glastonbury was endowed, and this benefaction of the kings aforesaid, confirmed as it is with the subscription of my own hand and the sign of the Cross, shall endure for ever approved and ratified, as I hereby decree, "while the revolving sky with ordered sway round earth and sea the starry ether wheels".[1] But if any man, full of tyranny and insolence, attempts for any reason to

---

[1] Juvencus, *Evang.* praef. 13–14.

fretus insolentia qualibet occasione interrumpere atque in irritum deducere nisus fuerit, sit a consortio piorum ultimi uentilabro examinis sequestratus, rapatiumque collegio combinatus uiolentiae suae presumptionem luat in aeuum. Qui uero beniuola potius preditus intentione haec probare roborare ac defendere studuerit, uoti compos ipse Altithroni gloriam auscultet indefecta perhennitate cum faustis agminibus angelorum atque omnium sanctorum.

'Exemplar huius largitionis promulgatum est in predicto cenobio sub presentia Cuthredi regis, quod propriae manus munificentia altario sacro commendauit in lignea basilica qua fratres abbatis Hemgisli sarcofagum sortiuntur in die,[1] anno ab incarnatione septingentesimo quadragesimo quinto.'

At 50. 5 n. l (after perdidit) *C gives an expanded version of one sentence.*

nam et beati Aidani episcopi et Celfrithi abbatis et sanctissimae uiraginis Hildae et aliorum plurimorum ossa, sicut in libro quem de antiquitate Glastoniensis aecclesiae nuper edidi locutus sum,[2] tunc Glastoniam translata, et aliorum sanctorum alias nonnulla.

At 66 n. a (after fecit) *B adds*

Iacet[a] in Frantia apud Sanctum Paulum de Cormarico, quod cenobium Karolus Magnus eius consilio construxit; unde hodieque[b] quattuor monachorum uictus et potus pro eiusdem Alcwini anima cotidianae infertur elemosinae in eadem aecclesia.

At 138 n. e, B replaces primaria . . . edificata *with a longer passage, here numbered 138B. 1-5.*

1 quae nunc destructa est, quam amplam pro more uetustatis uidimus, primaria in cenobio fuerit, aecclesia beatae Mariae, quam ante istam quae nunc est monachi frequentabant, postea regis Edgari diebus sub
2 Elfrico abbate edificata. Cuius autem opinionis fuerit apud Gallos, cum in belli sudoribus tum in Christiano cultu, non parum epistola quam subitio facit inditium.

[c]'Summae et indiuiduae Trinitatis honore omniumque sanctorum precellentissima intercessione glorioso et munifico regi Adelstano Samsonis summi pontificis ego Rohbodus prepositus istius seculi gloriam et aeterni beatitudinem.

[a] latet *Bk (and Bph)*   [b] hodie *Bk (but not Bph)*   [c] *Radbod's letter was also copied by William into the margin of MS A of GP pp. 399-400. It is here edited from BkBp and Bc¹Bc² = Bc (but the private readings of the individual manuscripts are normally ignored).*

break the witness of this my gift and bring it all to naught, let him be separated by the winnowing-fan of the Last Judgement from the company of the saints, and being joined with the society of the rapacious pay to all eternity the price of his violence and presumption. But whoso with good intent is zealous to approve, support, and confirm it, may his prayers be answered, and may he behold(?) the glory of the Most High for ever and ever together with the blessed hosts of angels and of all the saints.

'The text of this deed of gift was published in the monastery aforesaid in the presence of King Cuthred, and he with his own generous hand laid it upon the high altar in the wooden church where the brethren do honour to the burial-place of Abbot Hæmgils,[1] in the year of the Incarnation 745.'

50.5

For, as I have described in my recent book on the antiquity of the church of Glastonbury,[2] the bones of the holy Bishop Aidan, of Abbot Ceolfrith, of the most holy virgin St Hild, and of many others were at that time translated to Glastonbury, and some bodies of other saints elsewhere.

66

He lies in France at St Paul's Cormery, a house built by Charlemagne on his advice. That is why even today in that church food and drink for four monks are distributed as daily alms for the soul of Alcuin.

138B

[St Peter's church,] which is now destroyed but which I know from my own eyes was large by the standard of ancient times, came first in the monastery; St Mary's, which the monks used prior to the church which now stands, was built later, in King Edgar's days, under Abbot Ælfric. Of the reputation Æthelstan enjoyed among the Gauls, both in the toils of war and in Christian piety, the letter which I subjoin gives some indication:

'To Æthelstan, by the honour of the most high and undivided Trinity and with the most distinguished intercession of all saints king glorious and munificent, I Radbod, prior of St Samson the bishop, wish glory in this world and in the next, eternal blessedness.

---

[1] The Latin is obscure and doubtless corrupt; one expects the sense 'on the day on which the brethren venerate Hæmgils' tomb at the anniversary of his death'.

[2] *AG* p. 68.

'Benignitatis ac sullimitatis uestrae, piissime et in omnibus huius temporis regibus terrenis famosa laude precellentissime rex Adelstane, nouerit optime pietas, manente adhuc stabilitate nostrae regionis, quod pater uester Eduardus per litteras se commendauit consortio fraternitatis sancti Samsonis summi confessoris ac Louenani[a] archiepiscopi senioris ac consobrini mei ac clericorum eius. Vnde usque hodie indefessas Regi Christo pro eius animae salute et pro salute uestra fundimus preces, et die noctuque, uidentes super nos magnam[b] misericordiam uestram apparere, in psalmis et missis et orationibus nostris, quasi prouolutus ego et duodecim canonici mei genibus uestris fuissemus, promittimus Deum clementem orare pro uobis. Et modo reliquias, quas uobis omni terrena substantia scimus esse cariores, transmitto uobis, id est, ossa sancti Senatoris, sancti Paterni atque sancti Scubilionis eiusdem sancti[c] Paterni magistri, qui similiter uno die eademque hora cum supradicto Paterno migrauit ad Christum. Isti certissime duo sancti cum sancto Paterno leua dextraque iacuerunt in sepulchro, atque illorum sollemnitates nono kalendas Octobris, sicut et Paterni, celebrantur. Igitur, rex gloriose, sanctae exaltator aecclesiae, gentilitatis humiliator prauae, regni tui speculum, totius bonitatis exemplum, dissipator hostium, pater clericorum, adiutor egentium, amator omnium sanctorum, inuocator angelorum, deprecamur atque humiliter inuocamus, qui in exulatu et captiuitate nostris meritis et peccatis in Frantia commoramur,[d] ut non nostri obliuiscatur uestrae felicissimae largitatis[e] magna misericordia.' Haec epistola.

Ceterum rex reliquias beati Paterni Malmesberiae, reliquorum Mideltune commendauit, quo loci monasterium a fundamentis procuderat. Tunc enim, ut superius dixi,[1] piratis Normannorum omnem oram marini littoris, simul et urbes quae super Ligerim sitae sunt, infestantibus, corpora sanctorum, de Britannia Minori et e parte Galliae quae nunc Normannia uocatur translata et ad tutiora loca delata, facile cuilibet pro penuria baiulorum uenum patebant, presertim Adelstano, regi opinatissimo et talium rerum appetentissimo.

At 139. 5 n. m (instead of accepta ... fratris) *B gives*
(ut fertur) apud Lamport spontaneum carcerem subiuit. Vnde cum proximam aecclesiam Miclaniensem humili statu compactam uideret,

[a] *Bc¹, GP;* Leuenani *BkBc²;* Leuonani *Bp*   [b] magnam super nos *Bc*   [c] *om. Bc*
[d] *BpBc¹, GP;* commorantur *BkBc²*   [e] felicitatis largissime *Bc*

'May it please your most generous and exalted Majesty, O most religious and among all the earthly kings of our own day most excellent and illustrious King Æthelstan, I would have you know well, most godly prince, that while the stability of this our country still endured, your father Edward introduced himself by letter to the community of the brethren of St Samson the great confessor and to Archbishop Levenanus, my senior and cousin, and his clerks. As a result down to this day we offer our untiring suffrages to Christ the King for the salvation of his soul and for your salvation, and by day and night, as we behold your great kindness to us, in our psalms and masses and prayers, as though I and my twelve canons had been prostrate at your knee, we promise to beseech God's mercy for you. And now I send you relics which we know are dearer to you than all property on earth, to wit, bones of St Senator, St Paternus, and St Scubilio, master of the aforesaid St Paternus, who likewise passed to live with Christ the same day and hour as St Paternus. These two saints beyond question lay with St Paternus on his left and right in the sepulchre, and their festivals are celebrated on 23 September, as is that of St Paternus. And so, glorious king, pillar of Holy Church, humbler of heathen wickedness, mirror of your realm, exemplar of all goodness, scatterer of your enemies, father of clerks, helper of the needy, lover of all saints, suppliant of the angels, we who for our deserts and our transgressions live in exile and captivity in France, pray and humbly beseech you that in your felicity, in your generosity, in your great pity you should not forget us.' Such was the letter.

For the rest, the king entrusted the relics of St Paternus to Malmesbury, and those of the other saints to Milton, a place where he had established a monastery from its foundations. For at that time, as I have said above,[1] while the piratical Northmen were infesting the whole sea-coast as well as the cities which lie on the Loire, the bodies of saints translated from Brittany and that part of Gaul now called Normandy and carried to safer places were, because of the poverty of their bearers, easily available for sale to anyone, and especially to Æthelstan, a well-known king with a great appetite for such things.

139.5
[submitting to a seven-year penance,] (so the story goes) underwent voluntary restraint at Lamport. Hence, when he saw that the neighbouring church of Muchelney was a very modest building, he is said

---

[1] 121. 7.

uouisse plusquam semel dicitur ut, si umquam exiret, eam in sullime culmen eueheret. Sed haec quomodocumque se habeant, illud reuera constat, quod, sicut in cartis eiusdem aecclesiae legi, rex Ethelstanus aecclesiam Miclaniensem sancto Petro excelsiorem fecit, multis redditibus habitatores consolatus. Nec illud uacat a gloria, quod in delatorem fratris, si tamen credimus,

BkBc[2] (Bc[1] omits 150–53) omit 151, and give 150 in the following form:

150B. [a]"Gloriosae recordationis Edgarus Anglorum rex, filius Edmundi regis, cuius studium diuinis cultibus potissimum inuigilabat, ad monasterium sanctae Dei genitricis Mariae in Glestingabiri frequenter adueniens et eundem locum clariori pre ceteris dignitate extollere summo elaborans studio, plura admodumque magnifica priuilegia contulit communi episcoporum abbatum primorumque prouintiae consilio. Quorum primum est ut nullus nisi eiusdem loci monachus ibidem fungatur abbatis nomine uel offitio, nec alius nisi quem secundum 2 tenorem regulae concorditer elegerit parilis conuentus assensio. Quod si alterius loci abbatem uel monachum eidem loco prefici necessitas ingruerit, non alium assumi censuit nisi quem congregatio ipsius monasterii secundum timorem Dei sibi preesse elegerit; tamen ne hoc fiat, obseruato omnimodis si ibidem quispiam uel extremus congregationis illi offitio aptus reperiri potuerit. Monachis itaque electionem sui abbatis perpetuo manere censuit; sibi uero suisque heredibus tribuendi fratri electo pastoralem baculum potestatem retinuit. Sanxit etiam ut quotiens abbas loci uel monachi aliquos suorum sacris ordinibus insigniri decernerent, a quocumque presulum canonice ordinatorum[b] aut in illius sede aut in eodem sanctae Mariae Glestingensi monasterio tam monachos quam clericos,[c] quos idoneos iudicarent, ad titulum 3 sanctae Mariae ordinari facerent. Concessit etiam ut, sicut ipse in propria, ita totius insulae causas in omnibus tam aecclesiasticis quam secularibus negotiis absque ullius contradictione abbas aut conuentus corrigeret. Nec ulli[d] omnino insulam natiuitatis suae[1] consciam, siue episcopus siue dux[e] aut princeps aut cuiuscumque ordinis alius, licitum foret intrare causa quippiam fatiendi quod contrarium inibi

---

[a] *A briefer version of the information given in 1–4 appears in AG p. 122. For 6–7 see AG p. 128. 8 overlaps with 150. 7 (main text) (cf. AG p. 128). The version is edited here from Bk Bp Bc[2], but individual readings of Bk and Bp are normally ignored.*   [b] Stubbs; ordinatum *BkBpBc[2]; perhaps* ordinato?   [c] cleros *BkBc[2]*   [d] illi *Bc[2]*   [e] dux siue episcopus *Bc[2]*

to have vowed more than once that, if he were ever released, he would raise it to great distinction. Whatever be the truth of this, one thing is certain, that, as I have read in the muniments of the church, King Æthelstan raised the church of Muchelney to greater heights in honour of St Peter, helping those who dwelt there with many rents. It is also to his credit that, if we may believe it, he [took passionate vengeance on] the man who had informed against his brother.

150B. Edgar of glorious memory, king of England, son of King Edmund, whose attention was especially directed towards the worship of God, frequently came to the monastery of Mary, holy Mother of God, at Glastonbury, and made every effort to exalt that place beyond all others in fame and importance; hence he made a gift of many splendid privileges with the common consent of the bishops, abbots, and leading men of the province. The first is that no one except a monk of the house should enjoy the name and office of abbot there, and then only after undisputed election, according to the provisions of the Rule, by the unqualified assent of the house. If it proves necessary for the abbot or monk of some other place to be put in charge, Edgar decreed that no one should be chosen save one elected by the congregation of the monastery to rule them, as fear of God dictates to them; but to prevent such an outcome, they are to take every trouble to discover whether someone, even the least of the congregation, can be found suitable for the office. He thought it proper, therefore, that the monks should for ever retain the right to elect their abbot, though he reserved to himself and his heirs the power to present the pastoral staff to the brother chosen. He also laid down that whenever the abbot and monks of the place decided that some of their own people should be marked out with holy orders, they should have them ordained in the name of St Mary, monk or clerk, as they thought suitable, by any canonically ordained bishop, either in his see or in the monastery of St Mary at Glastonbury. He also agreed that, just as he did in his own property, so too the abbot and convent should decide causes affecting the whole island, in all secular or church business, without anyone saying them nay. Nor would it be permitted to anyone to enter the island of his[1] birth, whether he be bishop or thegn or prince or another of whatever rank, in order to do anything that might be prejudicial to the servants of God there, just

---

[1] i.e. the king's.

Deo seruientibus esse possit, sicut et predecessores[a] sui sanxerunt et priuilegiis confirmauerunt, uidelicet Cenwines Ines Ethelardus Cuthredus Elfredus Edwardus Ethelstanus Edmundus, omnino prohibuit.

4   Vbi ergo generali assensu, ut dictum est, pontificum abbatum optimatumque suorum haec priuilegia ipsi[b] loco conferre disposuit, lituum proprium ebore decentissime formatum auroque decoratum super altare sanctae Dei genitricis posuit, ipsiusque donatione eidem sanctae Dei[c] genitrici ac suis monachis ea perpetualiter possidenda attribuit. Eundem quoque lituum mox in sui presentia fecit secari per medium, ne eum cuiquam dare uel uendere posset quilibet abbatum sequentium, precipiens partem illius seruari in loca[d] ad iam dictae donationis perhenne testimonium. Recogitans uero quam multa temeritas humanae leuitatis quibusque solet surrepere, uerensque ne forte quis in posterum uel haec priuilegia loco illi auferre uel monachos inde moliretur eicere, inclito domno Iohanni papae, qui Octauiano in regiminis honore successerat, direxit idem cirographum regiae liberalitatis, orans ut et ipse haec[e] roboraret scripto apostolicae auctoritatis.[f]

5   Qui benigne directam[g] suscipiens legationem, concordi assensu Romani concilii sancita ab eis firmauit scribendo apostolicae auctoritatis preceptionem, terribiliter intorquens in uiolatores, si qui forte emerserint, perpetui anathematis ultionem. Igitur domni predicti apostolici eidem loco directum testamentum uenustae recordationis rex Edgarus super aram beatissimae Dei genitricis Mariae itidem ad perpetuale posuit monumentum, iubens diligenter asseruari in posterum ad notitiam quorumque sequentium. Ea etiam utraque, ne uideremur talia commentari, his gratum habuimus subindere aduersus eos qui non ut pastores per hostium intrare sed ut fures et latrones in idem ouile sanctae Mariae[h] aliunde querunt irrumpere.[1]

6   'Nouerit cunctorum notitia fidelium quod ego Iohannes, pii Conditoris clementia sanctae Romanae sedis existens indignus papa, gloriosi Anglorum regis Edgari, necnon et sanctae Dorobernensis aecclesiae archipresulis Dunstani, summisso pulsatus rogatu pro monasterio sanctae Mariae, uidelicet Glastingebiri, quod ipsi acti amore superni Regis in multis et magnis possessionibus ditauerant, monachorum inibi multiplicantes normam, preceptoque regali firmauerant; quod[i] et ipse facere non differam. Quorum assentiens benignae petitioni, in sinu Romanae aecclesiae et beatorum apostolorum protectione

---

[a] predecessoris Bc^2 [b] ipso Bc^2 [c] om. $BkBp$ [d] One expects loco   [e] ipse hec Bk; ipse hoc Bp; haec ipse Bc^2 [f] auct. apost. Bc^2 [g] directum Bc^2 [h] om. Bc^2, leaving a gap   [i] $Bc^{2a.c.}$; quo $BkBpBc^{2p.c.}$

as his predecessors laid down and confirmed by privilege, namely Centwine, Ine, Æthelheard, Cuthred, Alfred, Edward, Æthelstan, and Edmund.

When, therefore, as has been said, he had decided to confer these privileges on the place in accordance with the general agreement of his bishops, abbots, and nobles, he placed his own beautifully wrought ivory and gold staff on the altar of the holy Mother of God, and by that gift handed the privileges over for possession for all time to the holy Mother of God and her monks. Presently, he had the staff cut in half in his presence, so that none among later abbots could give it away or sell it, giving instructions that half of it should be kept *in situ* as a perpetual reminder of the said gift. But recalling the wanton fickleness to which men can succumb, and fearing that someone might one day try to remove these privileges or drive the monks out, he sent this charter, witness of his kingly munificence, to the glorious lord Pope John, successor to Octavian, praying that he strengthen them in writing with the papal authority. The pope received the embassy kindly and confirmed what had been ordained with the unanimous agreement of the Roman council, putting in writing the papal instruction and turning the dreadful vengeance of everlasting anathema against any future violator. The confirmation sent to Glastonbury by the pope King Edgar of fragrant memory placed on the altar of Mary the blessed Mother of God as a lasting memorial, ordering that it be carefully preserved from then on for the information of posterity. In case we should appear to be making all this up, we have found it agreeable to insert both these documents to thwart those who seek not to enter the fold of St Mary like shepherds through the door, but like thieves and robbers, to break into it by some other way.[1]

'Let all the faithful be aware that I John, by the mercy of our pious Maker the unworthy pope of the Holy See of Rome, have been moved by the humble request made by Edgar, glorious king of the English, and Dunstan archbishop of Canterbury, on behalf of the monastery of St Mary at Glastonbury, a house which they themselves had, through love of the King on high, enriched with many great possessions, increasing the monastic [population and instituting a stricter] observance there, and had shored up by the royal command; I too will do the same, without delay. Assenting to their well-meant request, I receive that place into the bosom of the Roman Church and the

---

[1] Cf. John 10: 1.

eundem locum suscipio, et priuilegiis astruo et corroboro, quo finetenus in eo quo nunc pollet permaneat monachali ordine, ipsique
7 monachi de suis sibi adhibeant pastorem. Ordinatio uero tam monachorum quam clericorum in arbitrio abbatis et conuentus sit. Decernimus etiam ut nulli omnino hominum eandem insulam placitandi causa[a] uel aliquid aliud ibi[b] perscrutandi aut corrigendi intrare liceat. Si quis autem id molitus fuerit contraire, aut possessiones eiusdem aecclesiae auferre retinere minuere uel temerariis uexationibus fatigare, ex auctoritate Dei, Patris et Filii et Spiritus sancti, sanctaeque Dei genitricis Mariae ac sanctorum apostolorum Petri et Pauli omniumque sanctorum, perpetuae sit addictus maledictioni, nisi resipuerit. Omnibus uero eidem loco iusta seruantibus sit pax Domini nostri Iesu Christi Amen, nostraque stipulatio inconuulsa permaneat.

'Actum tempore Elfwardi eiusdem monasterii abbatis.'

8 Haec igitur predictus rex Edgarus duodecimo anno regni sui sacro scripto Lundoniae confirmauit, eodemque anno, qui fuit nongentesimus sexagesimus quintus Dominicae incarnationis, papa Iohannes[c] Romae in generali sinodo auctorizauit, cunctosque potioris dignitatis, qui prefuerunt eidem concilio generali, ea corroborare imperauit. Perpendant ergo contemptores tantae interminationis quantae subiaceant sententiae excommunicationis; et quidem beato Petro apostolo principi apostolorum Christus[d] ligandi soluendique presulatum clauesque regni caelorum simul tradidit.[e] Cuique autem fideli[f] constat perspicuum atque euidens quod huius apostoli uicarius potestatisque potissi-
9 mum sit[g] heres Romanae aecclesiae presidens. Huic sanctae memoriae Iohannes laudabiliter prefuit suo tempore, ut hodieque uiget gloriosa recordatione, promotus ad id Dei totiusque populi electione. Si ergo decretum beati Petri apostoli ratum, consequenter et Iohannis apostolici ratum. Sed nemo uel demens ratum esse Petri apostoli decretum denegat; nemo igitur sanae mentis dissimile fore Iohannis apostolici decretum repugnat. Aut isti itaque,[h] concedentes beato Petro suisque successoribus collatam a Christo potestatem, transgredi cessabunt tanti interdictus auctoritatem, aut floccipendentes cum diabolo suisque complicibus prescriptae maledictionis sibi adquirent perpetuitatem.
10 Constat ergo neminem extraneorum idem cenobium sibi preripuisse quem non constiterit, nec sine dedecore, amisisse, nullaque monachorum machinatione, sed Dei iuditio ob sanctae auctoritatis ultionem

[a] causa placitandi *BkBp*   [b] om. *BkBp*   [c] papa Ioh. *Bc²* (and 150. 7); prefatus papa Ioh. *Bp*, prefatus papa *Bk*   [d] Christi *Bc²*   [e] simul trad. reg. cel. *BkBp*   [f] om. *Bc²*   [g] sto *Bc²*   [h] itaque isti *BkBp*

protection of the blessed Apostles, and I affirm and confirm by privilege that until the end it remain in the monastic order under which it now flourishes, and that the monks choose their shepherd from among their own number. But the ordination both of monks and clerks is to be at the discretion of the abbot and convent. We also decree that no man whatever may enter the island to hold court or to investigate or correct anything else there. If anyone plots to disobey, or to remove, retain, diminish, or rashly assault the possessions of the church, let him be subject to perpetual curse unless he regains his senses, on the authority of God, the Father, Son, and Holy Spirit, and Mary, the holy Mother of God, and the holy Apostles Peter and Paul, and all the saints. But on all who do right by the place let the peace of our Lord Jesus Christ rest, Amen, and let these conditions remain unshaken.

'Done in the time of Ælfweard, abbot of the monastery.'

These things, therefore, the said King Edgar confirmed by his holy writ at London in the twelfth year of his reign. And in the same year, AD 965, Pope John gave them his authority in a general synod at Rome, and ordered all the distinguished men who controlled the council to confirm them. Let, therefore, those who disregard such a curse realize under what hard sentence of excommunication they lie; and indeed Christ handed to St Peter, prince of the Apostles, the power of binding and loosing, together with the keys of Heaven. It is clear and patent to any one of the faithful that he who presides over the Roman Church is the vicar of the Apostle and the especial heir to his power. John of holy memory in his time presided in a praiseworthy manner over that Church, just as even today he flourishes in glorious recollection; for he was advanced to that position by the choice of God and the whole people. If then the decree of the Apostle Peter is fixed, so consequently is that of Pope John. But no one can be so mad as to deny that the decree of Peter is fixed; so no sane man can argue otherwise for John's. These people then must allow to the blessed Peter and his successors the power given them by Christ and cease to flout the authority of such an interdict. Otherwise, if they disregard it, they will, like the Devil and his lackeys, fall perpetually under the curse. It is therefore beyond question that no outsider who has snatched the monastery for himself has failed to lose it disgracefully, and that this has befallen each of them not by any machination of the monks but by the judgement of God in

id cuique eorum accidisse. Nemo itaque haec legens despitiat, nemo uel subirascendo se palam notabilem fatiat. Nam si irascitur, pro alio forte prolatum de se dictum fatebitur.

At 398. 4 n. g (instead of Non tamen . . . Praeterea*) Cs (whose orthography we follow), and from* uirum ac C*a, give*

Neque tamen uictoriam hanc sine sanguine consummauit; nam ex carissimis suis multos amisit, et inter eos egregium uirum ac strenuissimum militem Rogerium de Gloecestra. Is, in obsidione Fallesii telo arcubaliste grauiter uulneratus in capite, donauit aecclesie sancti Petri de Gloecestra manerium quod appellatur Culna sancti Andree, et in hoc assensum et concessionem regis, qui statim ad se uidendum uenerat, impetrauit, ita quod manum ipsius, cum eam huius rei gratia deoscularetur, frontis sanguine cruentauit. Cuius donationis confirmationem et testimonium regis aduersus Gilebertum de Mineriis ad maiorem rei euidentiam operi huic inserere dignum duximus.

'Henricus rex Anglorum Samsoni episcopo Wigornensi et Walterio uicecomiti de Gloecestra, et omnibus baronibus suis Francis et Anglis de Gloecestresira salutem.

'Notum sit uobis quod dedi et concessi manerium de Culna aecclesie[a] sancti Petri de Gloecestra ad communem uictum monachorum, sicut Rogerius de Gloecestra eis dedit et concessit, et sicut melius tenuit, pro anima mea et uxoris mee et pro animabus antecessorum meorum. Teste Girmundo abbate Winchelcumbe et Rogero de Gloecestra et Hugone paruo.'

'Henricus rex Anglorum archiepiscopis, episcopis, abbatibus, comitibus, baronibus, uicecomitibus et omnibus fidelibus suis Francis et Anglis totius Anglie salutem.

'Sciatis quia monachi de Gloecestra et Gilebertus de Mineriis in curiam meam uenerunt coram me ad terminum inter eos positum, de placito manerii de Culna quod Gilebertus uersus eos et abbatem suum clamabat, et Adam de Port et Willelmus filius Odonis coram me testificati fuerunt quod ipsi affuerunt ubi Rogerius de Gloecestra manerium illud aecclesie sancti Petri et monachis ibidem Deo seruientibus in elemosinam dederat, et ubi ego requisitione ipsius Rogerii donationem illam eis concessi, et inde isdem Gilebertus iudicium recusauit.

'Testibus Willelmo archiepiscopo Cantuarie et Rogerio episcopo Salesberie et Willelmo episcopo Wintonie et Bernardo episcopo de

---

[a] aecclesia C*a*

enforcement of His holy authority. Let therefore no one who reads these words underrate their force; let no one draw attention to himself by even a mild show of anger. For if he is angry, he will be acknowledging that words perhaps written for another apply to him too.

398.4

But this great victory was not achieved without bloodshed; for he lost many of his dearest friends, among them that distinguished man and valiant knight Roger of Gloucester. Severely wounded in the head by a bolt from a crossbow at the siege of Falaise, he gave to the church of St Peter's Gloucester the manor called Coln St Andrew, and for this he sought the assent and concession of the king, who had come at once to see him, on which occasion he besmirched with blood from his forehead the king's hand when he kissed it by way of thanks. As further evidence of this action we have thought good to insert here the confirmation of the donation and the testimony of the king against Gilbert of Minières.

'Henry, king of the English, to Samson bishop of Worcester and Walter sheriff of Gloucester, and all his barons of Gloucestershire both French and English, greeting.

'Be it known to you that I have given and conceded the manor of Coln to the church of St Peter's Gloucester for the common sustenance of the monks, as Roger of Gloucester gave and conceded it to them, to hold as securely as he did, for the souls of myself and my wife and those of my predecessors. Witnesses: Girmund abbot of Winchcombe and Roger of Gloucester and Hugh Small.'

'Henry, king of the English, to his archbishops, bishops, abbots, earls, barons, sheriffs, and all his faithful followers, both French and English, throughout all England, greeting.

'Know that the monks of Gloucester and Gilbert of Minières came before me in my court, on a date set between them, to settle the dispute between them concerning the manor of Coln, which Gilbert claimed as his against them and their abbot; and Adam de Port and William son of Odo testified before me that they were present when Roger of Gloucester gave that manor as alms to the church of St Peter and the monks serving God there, and when I confirmed that donation to them at Roger's request, and that Gilbert refused judgment for it.

'Witnesses: William archbishop of Canterbury, and Roger bishop of Salisbury, and William bishop of Winchester, and Bernard bishop of

Sancto Dauid, et Willelmo episcopo Exonie et Vrbano episcopo de Glamorgan et Gaufrido cancellario et Roberto de Sigillo et Milone de Gloecestra et Henrico de Port et Walterio de Amfreuilla et Willelmo de Folia et Rogerio et Willelmo filiis[a] Adam de Port.

'Apud Wintoniam anno ab incarnatione Domini millesimo centesimo uicesimo septimo.'

Porro

[a] filius *Ca*

St David's, and William bishop of Exeter, and Urban bishop of Glamorgan, and Geoffrey the chancellor, and Robert de Sigillo, and Miles of Gloucester, and Henry de Port, and Walter of Amfreville, and William of La Folie, and Roger and William sons of Adam de Port.

'Given at Winchester in the year of our Lord 1127.'

Further,

APPENDIX II
ADDITIONS OF THE Aa GROUP

In this Appendix we have not imposed the uniform orthography used elsewhere in this volume.

(a) *Aa readings of interest (found in AapAac)*

49. 2	ut ipse ⟨de se⟩ dictitabat
94. 2	hortatu ⟨prefati⟩ Ethelardi (cf. Index s.n. Æthelheard archbp. of Canterbury)
98. 2	⟨post eum⟩ regnauerunt
107. 3	post annos ⟨regni⟩
112. 1	apposui, ⟨unde et 'glomerem' masculino genere, sicut[a] in exemplari corrupte habebatur, posui.⟩
125. 5	Aldredus . . . instaurauit] tunc quidem quomodocumque remansit, tempore uero Normannorum per Serlonem abbatem caput extulit.
126. 2	idem germanus ⟨ut prefatus sum⟩ (cf. 112. 2)
131. 3	in matrimonium ⟨ut prelocutus sum⟩ (cf. 126. 1)
134. 1	sororis copula ⟨ut iam bis asserui⟩ (cf. 126. 1, 131. 3)
135. 1	sororem eius ⟨ut ante dictum est⟩ (cf. 126. 2)
166. 1	Iohannes ⟨huius nominis⟩ quintus
167. 1	De hoc . . . dictus est] Decedente hoc Iohanne successit Gregorius, ei[b] item Iohannes sextus decimus; illi Siluester, qui et Gerbertus, de quo
167. 6	Iohannes . . . decem] Siluester, qui Gerbertus, annis quattuor, mensem unum, dies decem:

[a] om. *Aap*   [b] et *Aac*

---

112. 1
That is why I have put even *glomer* in the masculine form, this being the corrupt reading of my source.

125. 5
For the time being it continued somehow or other, but in the time of the Normans it raised its head thanks to Abbot Serlo.

167. 1
On the death of this John Gregory succeeded, then John XVI, then Silvester, also known as Gerbert, concerning whom

167. 6
Silvester, also known as Gerbert, four years, one month, ten days.

180. 11	Porro ⟨post eum*a*⟩ Robertus
199. 9	Senex ille et ⟨fama clarus et⟩ lingua potens
201. 1	Gregorius ⟨illius uocabuli⟩ sextus
212	famoso ⟨sicut in primo libro dixit*b*⟩ monasterio (cf. 42. 3)
220. 2	transmarinis ⟨monachis⟩ (cf. *Vita Ædwardi Regis*, ed. F. Barlow (OMT, 2nd edn., 1992), p. 62)
223	ut ⟨cecus⟩ lotus est
228. 6	rex ⟨E(a)dwardus⟩
257. 1	uxoremque ⟨ut ante dixi⟩ (cf. 235. 5)
276	⟨Prima⟩ Cecilia
282. 3	comitatus quinquagesimo secundo] nondum expleto comitatus quinquagesimo primo
306. 2	⟨barones⟩ amittant
311. 2	hieme ⟨ut supra tetigi⟩ (cf. 250)
333. 2	ut fumeorum . . . lamberent] ut fumi magnitudo etiam sidera obnubilaret
336. 1	habentes ⟨in illis dumtaxat regionibus⟩
343	diuitiis ⟨Rome⟩
355. 2	natus] conuersatus et imperator creatus
374. 5	⟨primo⟩ exemplum
385. 1	abnepos eius] abnepos regis
395. 2	anno ⟨ut supra tetigi⟩ (cf. 389. 7)
419. 1	comitis ⟨ut ante dixi⟩ (cf. 405. 4)

(*b*) *Aac readings of interest (confirmed in essentials by Aa²Aa³)*

15. 1	porrexit. ⟨Ipse est qui monasterium sancti Martini apud Doferam fecit.⟩
15. 4	quadringentesimo quadragesimo sexto
29. 2	in gestis ⟨pontificum⟩ Anglorum
120. 2	interemptus ⟨anno Dominice incarnationis octingentesimo septuagesimo, duodecimo kalendas Decembris⟩
121. 1	octo] nouem
122. 3	alterum . . . confouerat] Intimum uero Grimbaldum sanctissimum monachum et cantorem et hostelarium ecclesie sancti Bertini, qui, se euocante et archiepiscopo Remensi Fulcone mittente Angliam uenerat, cognitus quod se puerum olim, ut ferunt, Romam euntem

a cum *AapAac* *b* So *AapAac*

---

122. 3
His close friend Grimbald, that most holy monk, chanter and hosteller of the church of Saint-Bertin, who had come to England at his invitation and sent by Fulk archbishop of Reims, and whom he knew because, as the story goes, Grimbald had received him kindly long ago, when he was a boy, on his way

836   APPENDIX II

benigno hospicio confortauerat, in famosa ciuitate Wenta sibi gratissima, facto interim monasteriolo,*ª* collocauit, ubi frequentius uisitando et commorando eius melliflua exhortatione pasceretur, donec illum eminentiori dignitati, quod mire optabat, inthronizaret.

124. 1 Elfredus . . . instruendas] Commendatio et obitus*ᵇ* Ælfredi regis. Famosus, bellicosus, uictoriosus; uiduarum, pupillorum, orphanorum pauperumque prouisor studiosus; poetarum Saxonicorum peritissimus; sue genti carissimus, affabilis omnibus, liberalissimus; prudentia fortitudine temperantia iusticia preditus; in infirmitate qua assidue laborabat patientissimus; in exequendis iudiciis indagator discretissimus, in seruitio Dei uigilantissimus et deuotissimus; Angul Saxonum rex Ælfredus piissimi regis Athulfi filius, uiginti et nouem annis sexque mensibus regni sui peractis, morte obiit, indictione quarta, quinto kalendas Nouembris, feria quarta, et Wintonie in Nouo Monasterio sepultus immortalitatis stolam et resurrectionis gloriam cum iustis expectat. Ad cuius predicti Monasterii Noui officinas instruendas Edwardus filius eius

124. 2 filium successorem ⟨Edwardum⟩
126. 1 Lodouici ⟨Balbi⟩*ᶜ* filii Karoli Calui
139. 2 nutricem ⟨suam⟩
147. 1 Eadmundi ⟨fratris Ethelstani⟩
157. 3 Warewelle ⟨que uocatur Harewode⟩
165. 13 sedes apostolica duos Christianos duces*ᵈ* inter se decertare misit (*Aap omits the context*)

   ª monasterio *Aa²*   *ᵇ* ob *Aa²*; obitu *Aac*   *ᶜ* Not in *Aa²*   *ᵈ* duc. Chr. *Aa²*

---

to Rome, he established in the famous city of Winchester, his favourite, meanwhile constructing a small monastery there. Here he proposed to visit him and reside frequently, and to feed on his honeyed exhortations, till he could fulfil his heart's desire by installing him in a higher office.

124. 1
Commendation and death of King Alfred: Renowned, warlike, victorious; assiduous carer for widows, wards, orphans, and the poor; most skilled of Saxon poets; dear to his people, approachable to all, most generous; gifted with prudence, bravery, temperance, and justice; most long-suffering during the disease that constantly plagued him; a discreet investigator when giving judgement, alert and devout in the service of God: Alfred, king of the Anglo-Saxons, son of the most pious King Æthelwulf, after 29 years and six months of his reign died in the fourth indiction, on 28 October, a Wednesday, and was buried at Winchester in New Minster, where with the just he awaits the robe of immortality and the glory of the resurrection. To construct the buildings of the aforesaid New Minster, his son Edward [purchased]

205. 1   ciuis ⟨Lucianus⟩ [a]
         uxorem ⟨Eugeniam⟩ [b]
213. 3   eundem] Eadmundum (!)
214. 3   *om.* nouiter
230. 3   nepos] pronepos
242. 2   prelium ⟨utrimque⟩ consertum

297   *After* teneatur *is added*:

'Explicit de Willelmo Magno, Norm' comite et rege Anglorum. Incipiunt leges eiusdem.

Willelmus rex Anglorum omnibus ad quos scriptum hoc perueniet per totam Angliam salutem et amicitiam.

Mando et precipio per totam Anglie nationem custodiri:

Si Anglicus homo compellat [d] aliquem Francigenam per bellum de furto uel homicidio [e] uel aliqua re pro qua bellum fieri debeat uel iudicium inter duos homines, habeat plenam licentiam hoc faciendi. Et si Anglicus bellum nolit, Francigena compellatus allegiet [f] se iureiurando contra eum per testes suos secundum legem Normannie.

Item: Si Francigena compellet Anglicum per bellum de eisdem rebus, Anglicus plena licentia defendat se per bellum, uel per iudicium si magis ei placeat. Et si untrum sit, id est inualidus, et nolit bellum uel non possit, querat sibi legalem defensorem. Si Francigena uictus fuerit, persoluat regi

---

[a] *Above the line in* Aa²Aa³   [b] *Above the line in* Aa²Aa³   [c] *This first extract from the Quadripartitus (Liebermann, Gesetze p. 483) is also found in two MSS in the British Library, Cotton Tit. A. xxvii, fo. 148ᵛ (Tit.) and Royal 11 B. ii, fo. 166ʳ⁻ᵛ (R)*   [d] com- pellet *Tit.,* R *(rightly)*   [e] homidio *Aac*   [f] allegiat *Aa³*

297

End [of the sections] concerning William the Great, duke of Normandy and king of the English. Here begin his laws.

William king of the English to all to whom this document shall come through all England, greeting and friendship.

I order and command [the following] to be observed throughout the realm of England:

If an Englishman challenges a Frenchman to [trial by] combat concerning theft or homicide or anything for which combat or ordeal should take place between two men, let him have full licence to do this; and if the Englishman refuses combat, let the Frenchman who is challenged clear himself by oath against him by means of his witnesses, according to the law of Normandy.

Also: if a Frenchman challenge an Englishman to combat concerning the same things, let the Englishman with full licence defend himself in combat, or by ordeal, if he so prefers. And if he is *untrum*, i.e. infirm, and refuses combat or is incapable of it, let him seek a legal defender for himself. If the

sexaginta solidos. Et si Anglicus nolit se defendere per bellum uel per testimonium, allegiet se per Dei iudicium.

De omnibus uthlagii rebus rex instituit ut Anglicus purget se ad iudicium. Et si Anglicus appellet Francigenam de uthlagaria, et hoc super eum inueritare*ᵃ* uelit, defendat se Francigena per bellum. Et si Anglicus non audeat eum probare per bellum, defendat se Francigena plano iuramento, non in uerborum obseruantiis.

1. *ᵇ*Regem Anglie singulari maiestate regni sui dominum esse manifeste ueritatis intuitus et singulorum denique cognouit effectus. Quod cum inclita benignitate regis et iure debita subditorum fidelitate proueniat, situs quoque patrie confidenter adiuuat, nature beneficiis et maris uicinitate conclusus, ut sine gratuita dominorum licentia nullus exitus, nulli relinquatur*ᶜ* ingressus. Vnde tanta genti securitas, tanta bonorum omnium copia successit ut, si uere rationis honestate regeretur, etatis auree pristina tempora conformaret. Sed hoc tantis eam promotionibus elicit, quod, cum omni forinseca perturbatione sit libera, tantis gaudiorum uoluptatibus euehatur, sicut miseranda mortalium conditio est, malo scilicet acclinis et lapsui prona, intestinis animi seditionibus et ceco nouorum molimine semper infrendit.

ᵃ in ueritate *AacAa²Aa³*   *ᵇ* *The second extract (Liebermann, Gesetze pp. 542–3) is also found in Tit. A. XXVII, fos. 151ʳ–153ʳ (Tit.)*   *ᶜ* relinquantur *Tit.; but one expects rather* nullus ... nullus *or* nulli ... nulli

---

Frenchman is defeated, let him pay 60 shillings to the king. And if the Englishman refuses to defend himself either in combat or by testimony, let him clear himself by ordeal of God.

Concerning all matters of outlawry the king provides that an Englishman should purge himself by ordeal. And if an Englishman accuses a Frenchman of outlawry and wishes to make this good against him, let the Frenchman defend himself by combat. And if the Englishman does not dare to put him to the test by combat, let the Frenchman defend himself by straightforward oath, not by clever word-play.

1. That the king of England is with unique majesty lord of his realm is known to the gaze of clear truth and by the results of individual actions(?). Although this is a result of the king's outstanding goodness and the justly owed loyalty of his subjects, it is firmly backed up by the geographical situation of the country, shut in as it is by the favours of nature and the proximity of the sea, so that no one can go in or out without the willing permission of the lords. Hence so great a freedom from worry, so great an abundance of all good things has come upon England that, if it were ruled by the virtue of true reason, it would return to the Golden Age of yore. But what deprives it of such a prospect(?) is that, though it is free from all outside interference and is transported by all its joys and pleasures, yet—such is the wretched lot of mortals, prone as they are to sin and backsliding—it ever gnashes its teeth in deep divisions of mind and blind striving after novelty.

2. Hinc a primeuo mundi nascentis exordio, quos rerum Deus artifex equa libertate ditauerat, inobedientie motus inflammantis eiecit, et qui celi Dominum ferre non poterant hominum seruiunt prauitate distincti, continuis malorum prosecutionibus in deteriora queque proiecti. Et licet immeritos diuina tamen miseratio tanta prosequitur et tali dominos informatione componit ne uel*ᵃ* aliquos seruitus adnichilet aut impunita securitas elata precipitet. Reges etiam qui perfunctoria ceteros pompa preueniunt, ne potentatibus insolescant, carnis infirmitatibus et humanis admodum*ᵇ* necessitatibus expositos utili penitus sollicitatione*ᶜ* frequentat.

3. Regem quippe non faciunt uulgi de fascibus fabulosa commenta uel furentes*ᵈ* insanie uel infinita iugera uel amica putredinis ingeniosa crapula uel de lamentis pauperum conuulsa pecunia. Regem non faciunt uestes Tyrie, non auro nitide trabes, non color frontis uel uota*ᵉ* regia. Sed rex est qui posuit metus et diri mala pectoris, quem non ambitio impotens et nunquam stabilis fauor uulgi precipitis mouet. Rex est qui se diri pectoris fetoribus euacuat et prodesse singulis sollerter inuigilat, quales nuper ad fastigium huius culminis non ambitio popularis sed spectata inter bonos moderatio prouexit.

ᵃ uilis *Tit.*, *no doubt rightly*   *ᵇ* om. *Tit.*   *ᶜ* sollicitudine *Aa³*   *ᵈ* furentes *Tit.*; furentis *AacAa²Aa³*. *The text is not certain*   *ᵉ* nota *Liebermann*

---

2. So it was that, at the very beginning of the newly born world, those who had been endowed by God, creator of the world, with equal liberty were expelled by the impulse of the disobedience that inflamed them; and those who could not bear [to obey] the Lord of Heaven are become slaves, marked with human depravity, and cast into ever greater evil by continual escort of ills. And though they do not merit it, yet God's pity is in such constant attendance, and endows lords with such qualities, that not all men are destroyed by slavery or cast headlong by unpunished licence. Kings too, who exceed all others in careless pomp, it exposes, lest they grow insolent in their power, to infirmities of the flesh and human necessities, and visits with a salutary series of troubles.

3. For a king is not made by mythical fabrications of the vulgar concerning the trappings of royalty, or fits of madness, or endless acres, or that friend of corruption, a hangover induced by elaborate menus, or money torn from the lamenting poor. A king is not made by purple garments, or roof-beams gleaming with gold, or the colour(?) of the forehead or the prayers offered up for royalty. But he is a king who has laid aside fears and the evils inhabiting a sinful breast, who is not moved by uncontrolled ambition and the shifting favours of the headlong mob. He is a king who purges himself of the stench of his wicked heart and carefully strives to be of use to such men as have recently been carried to the heights not by wooing the people but by a reputation among the good for moderation.

4. Necessaria siquidem est prelatis mansuetudo*a* et disciplina subiectis. Postquam enim ad singula queque sagax hominum penetrauit intentio et nichil ad pecuniam uisum est incommodum, creuit opulentia, creuit inuidia, ex inuidia odium, ex odio bellum, nulli fides, nulli profuit elemosina. Si qua tamen natiue bonitatis remanserant monimenta, sanxere leges et uiuendi iura, constituerunt urbes et fida receptacula quo tuta fieret inter improbos innocentia, et quos ipsa probitatis hortamenta non excitant saltem conquiescant ad pene formidinem. Lex alia naturalis, que apud omnes eadem est, alia consuetudinis, in qua habet unaqueque patria suum aliquid proprium.

445. 2   abbas Sagii] episcopus Roffe

a mans. prel. $Aa^2 Aa^3$

---

4. The ruler needs to show kindness and the subject obedience. For ever since the sagacious attention of man penetrated into every nook and cranny and nothing seemed inconvenient if money resulted, opulence has grown, envy has grown, and from envy hatred, and from hatred war; and neither loyalty nor alms-giving has done anyone any good. But where any relics of natural goodness remained, people laid down laws and ordinances for living, and founded cities and trustworthy hiding-places, so that innocence might find safety in the midst of the wicked, and those who are not spurred on by exhortations to rectitude are at least silenced by fear of punishment. One law is by nature, the same for all; another is by custom, in which each and every country has its own particularity.

INDEX

Almost all proper names mentioned in *GR* are listed, with the main exception of: (*a*) the gates, roads and persons found in 352, unless they are also mentioned elsewhere; (*b*) the Eastern emperors listed in 356 and the patriarchs of Jerusalem listed in 368, except for those about whom William gives further information. Where persons appearing in the Index are alluded to, but not named, in the text, the reference is added; but allusions to persons not appearing in the Index are excluded. Thus 'the three sons of Earl Roger' alluded to at 306.7 are indexed under Roger of Poitou, Robert of Bellême and Hugh earl of Shrewsbury. But the unnamed daughter of King Baldwin II at 387.8 (= Alice) is not indexed. Identifications can normally be found in the Commentary.

Passages are referred to by chapter and sub-section. Where no sub-section is given, either the chapter has no sub-sections or the reference extends throughout the chapter.

'ep.' refers to the Letters printed before Book i, 'pr.' to the prologues of the five books. Bracketed letters (e.g. B) signal passages found only in individual versions, some printed in the apparatus, some in the appendices. It should be noted that 19.3–29.1 appear in Appendix I; 35.3–36 in the main text have parallel 35C.3–36C in Appendix I; 38 (in part)–39 appear in Appendix I; 138 is printed in the main text, 138D.1 5 in Appendix I; 150–1 in their C version appear in the main text (150C and 151C), the parallel 150B in Appendix I.

So far as possible, personal names are spelt as in *Handbook of British Chronology*, ed. 3, ed. E. B. Fryde, D. E. Greenway, S. Porter, and I. Roy (London, 1986).

Aaron 377.5
Abingdon (Berks.) 135.3; abbots of, *see* Æthelhelm, Æthelwold, Siward
Abraham 377.2
Acca, bp. of Hexham (709–31) 208.3
Acerenza (Basilicata) 429
Acha, d. of K. Ælle, w. of K. Æthelfrith 47.5; 49.1 (Tt)
Acre (*also called* Ptolemais) 366.2; 376.9; 382
Adalbert, archbp. of Mainz (1111–37), chancellor of Henry V 422.2; 437.3
Adalbold II, bp. of Utrecht (1010–26) 168.1
Adam, first man 115
Adela, d. of K. William I (d. 1137) 276; 405.1; 419.2
Adela, d. of Godfrey VII count of Louvain, 2nd w. of K. Henry I (m. 1121) 418.6
Adhemar, bp. of Le Puy (1087–98) 348.1; 349.1; 365.2,4; 388.4
Adriatic Sea 262.3; 349.2
Adulf, count of Boulogne (918–35) 123.5; 135.3
Aedan, Irish k. of Dal Riata (574–608) 47.2
Ælfflæd, d. of K. Alfred 121.13
Ælfflæd, w. of K. Edward the Elder 126.1–2
Ælfflæd, d. of K. Oswiu (654–713/4) 50.4

Ælfgar, s. of Leofric (d. 1062?) 199.7; 200.3; 252.1
Ælfgifu (*properly* Æthelgifu?), d. of K. Alfred 121.13; 122.3
Ælfgifu, w. of K. Edmund I (d. 944) 154.3–155
Ælfgifu, d. of K. Edward the Elder 126.2; 135.2; *see also* Ealdgyth
Ælfheah, prior of Glastonbury, abt. of Bath (*c*. 963–84), bp. of Winchester (984–1006), archbp. of Canterbury (1006–12) 165.5–6; 176; 181.3,5; 184; 207.4
Ælfhelm, earl, f. of Ælfgifu 'of Northampton' 188.1
Ælfhere, ealdorman of Mercia (d. 983) 161.2; 162.4; 165.9
Ælfric, ealdorman 165.3,9 (*see* Commentary)
Ælfric, recipient of papal letter 150C.7–151C (*see* Commentary)
Ælfric, abt. of Malmesbury (*c*. 965–*c*. 977), bp. of Crediton (977/9–986/7) 138 (and 138B.1); 153.2
Ælfric Puttoc, archbp. of York (1023–51) 183.1; 188.4
Ælfthryth, w. of Ealdorman Æthelwold and of K. Edgar I (m. 964) 157; 159.2; 161.1; 162; 164

Ælfwald (*called* Elcwold *by William*), k. of E. Angles (*c*. 713–49) 97.4
Ælfwald I, k. of Northumbria (778/9–788) 72.1
Ælfweard, abt. of Glastonbury (*c*. 975 x 1009; *see Commentary on 150C.7*) 150B.7
Ælfweard, *see also* Æthelweard, k. of W. Saxons
Ælfwine, grandson of K. Alfred (d. 937) 135.6; 136
Ælfwine (*elsewhere* Æthelwig), abt. of Evesham (1058–77) 298.8
Ælfwine, s. of K. Oswiu (d. 679) 51.2; 77
Ælfwine, abt. of Ramsey (1043–1079/80) 298.7
Ælfwold, f. of Leofstan (10c.) 166.2–3
Ælle, k. of Deira (560–588/90) 45–6; 47.4–5; 49.1
Æscwine, k. of W. Saxons (674–6) 33
Æthelbald, k. of Mercia (716–57): reign 79; letter of Boniface to 80–1; holds council and issues charter to monasteries 83–4; mentioned in a charter 39.1; also mentioned 40; 86
Æthelbald, k. of W. Saxons (855–60) 113.1,4; 117–18
Æthelberht, k. of E. Angles (d. 794) 86; 97.5; 210
Æthelberht, s. of Eormenred 12(B); 209; 215
Æthelberht I, k. of Kent (560–616) 9.1; 10; 17.1; 98.1
Æthelberht II, k. of Kent (725–62) 15.2
Æthelberht, k. of W. Saxons (860–5) 113.4; 117–8
Æthelberht, *see also* Æthelred I k. of Northumbria, Eadberht Præn
Æthelburh, d. of Anna, abbess of Faremoutiers-en-Brie 214.1–2
Æthelburh, w. of K. Edwin (m. 625) 48.2
Æthelburh, w. of K. Ine 36.2–37
Æthelflæd, d. of K. Alfred, w. of Æthelred II k. of Mercia (d. 918) 121.10, 13; 125.4; 133.2
Æthelflæd Candida, w. of K. Edgar I 159.2
Æthelflæd, w. of Wigmund 212
Æthelfrith, k. of Bernicia (592/3–616) 47; 49.1; 97.2
Æthelgar, abt. of New Minster, Winchester (964–?988), bp. of Chichester, i.e. Selsey (980–8), archbp. of Canterbury (988–90) 184.2
Æthelheard, archbp. of Canterbury (792/3–805): favoured by K. Cenwulf 87.3; letter and visit to pope 88.9; 89.1, 3; judgement of pope concerning 89.4–6; letters from Alcuin 70.4; 82.2; 87.4; and Malmesbury 94.2 (*see Commentary*)
Æthelheard, *subregulus* of K. Ine 36C.1–2; 39.1 (*see Commentary*)
Æthelheard, k. of W. Saxons (726–?740) (*see Commentary*) 38; 150B.3
Æthelhelm, abt. of Abingdon (1071–83) 298.8
Æthelhelm, ealdorman, f. of Ælfflæd w. of K. Edward the Elder 126.1
Æthelhelm, *see* Athelm
Æthelhere, k. of E. Angles (654–5) 97.4
Æthelhild, d. of K. Edward the Elder 126.2
Æthelmær (Eilmer), flying monk of Malmesbury (11c.) 225.6
Æthelmær, ealdorman of Devon in the time of K. Swein Forkbeard 177.3
Æthelnoth, archbp. of Canterbury (1020–38) 183.1; 184–185.1; 186.1
Æthelnoth, contentious magnate under K. Edgar I 153.2
Æthelnoth, abt. of Glastonbury (1053–1077/8) 298.8
Æthelnoth, son of Wigstan (ambassador of K. Æthelred the Unready) 166.2–3
Æthelred, k. of E. Angles (mid-8c.) 97.5
Æthelred, s. of Eormenred 12 (B) (Elbertus); 209; 215
Æthelred I, k. of Mercia (675–704): reign 77; and Bardney 49.9; 77; also mentioned 29.1; 49.8; 51.2; 74.3; 76.2; 78–9
Æthelred II, k. of Mercia (?879–911) 121.10–11,13; 125.1, 133.2
Æthelred I (*also known as* Æthelberht), k. of Northumbria (774–9, 790–6) 70.3; 72–73.1; 93.2
Æthelred, k. of W. Saxons (865–71) 118–20; 125.2
Æthelred 'Mucill', father-in-law of K. Alfred 121.13
Æthelred the Unready, k. of England (978–1016): promoted by stepmother 161.1; 162.1; reign 164–6; 176–180.3; treaty with Richard I duke of Normandy 165.13–166; exile and return 178.1; 179.2; death 180.3; also mentioned 159.2; 173; 180.11; 181.3; 183.9; 188.1,3,5; 196.1,6
Æthelric, k. of Bernicia (568–72) 46–47.1
Æthelric II, bp. of Chichester, i.e. Selsey (1058–70) 297

Æthelsige I, bp. of Sherborne (978/9–991/3) 166.2–3
Æthelstan, bp. of Ramsbury (*c.* 909 × 927) 129.3 (*see Commentary*)
Æthelstan, k. of England (924–39): relatives 126; reign 131–40; old volume (poem) concerning 132; 133.2–5; 135.6–9; character 132; 134.4–5; 138; liking for relics 138B.5 (cf. 135.6); unites kingship of England 121.6; 134.1; defeat of Anlaf 131.4–7; 135.6–9; betrothal of sisters 112.2; 126; 131.3; 134.1; 135.2–6; 140; praised by Europe 135.1; relations with monasteries 131.2; 135.6; 138B.2–5; 139.5 (B); 140; 150B.3; issues charter 137; stories concerning 138–9; death 140; also mentioned 141.1; 146.1; 147.1(Aa); 185.2
Æthelstan, *subregulus* of S.E. counties (839–851/5) 108.1
Æthelswith (*rightly* Ealhswith), w. of K. Alfred 121.13
Æthelswith, d. of K. Alfred 121.13; 123.5; 135.3 (*where wrongly called* d. of K. Edward the Elder)
Æthelswith, w. of K. Burgred (m. 853) 96.2–3; 113.4
Æthelthryth, St, w. of K. Ecgfrith (d. 679/80) 51.1; 207.4; 214.1–2; 445.3
Æthelwald, s. of Æthelred k. of W. Saxons (d. *c.* 903) 125.2–3
Æthelwald, k. of E. Angles (655–?664) 97.4
Æthelwald Moll, k. of Northumbria (758/9–765) 72.1–2
Æthelwalh, k. of S. Saxons (?/674–680/5) 34.2; 76.1
Æthelweard, s. of K. Alfred (d. 922) 121.13; 130; 135.6
Æthelweard, abt. of Glastonbury (*c.* 1024–53) 160.2
Æthelweard, historian (d. 998+) i pr. 2,7
Æthelweard (*also known as* Ælfweard), k. of W. Saxons (924) 126.1; 131.1; 133.2; 139.2
Æthelwine, grandson of K. Alfred (d. 937) 135.6; 136
Æthelwold, St, abt. of Abingdon (*c.* 954–63), bp. of Winchester (963–84) 149.4–6; 161.2; 218.2
Æthelwold, ealdorman of E. Anglia (d. *c.* 962) 157.1–2
Æthelwulf, k. of W. Saxons (*also known as* Athulf: 108.1; 124.1 (Aa)) (839–58): genealogy 115–16; early career 106.4; reign 107.3–109; 113; grant of church liberties

109; 114; 122.2; also mentioned 96.2; 112.2; 117–8; 121.1; 124.1(Aa); 126.1
Africa, Africans: conquered by Vandals 5.2; ruled by Saracens 91.2–92; 347.6; 368.3; animal of 409.3
Agatha, virgin 356.4
Agatha, w. of Edward s. of K. Edmund II 180.10
Agilbert, bp. of Dorchester (*c.* 650–*c.* 660) 29.2; 50.3
Agrippa, son-in-law of Augustus 175.1
Agrippina, *see* Colonia
Aidan, bp. of Lindisfarne (635–51) 49.4; 50.5 (C)
Alan III, count of Brittany (1008–40) 236.3 (*but see Commentary*)
Alan IV Fergant, count of Brittany (1084–1112) 276
Alans 68.1
Alban, St 87.1 (alluding to abbey at St Albans (Herts.), q. v.)
Albano (Lazio) 423.2
Alberic, abt. of Cîteaux (1099–1109) 337.2
Albert, count of Biandrate (*fl.* 1112) 422.2
Albion 153.1
Albo (*rightly* Aldo?), cardinal deacon of SS Sergius and Bacchus (*fl.* 1111) 421.2
Alcuin (*sometimes called* Albinus *by William*) 65.2; 66 (also B); 69; 73.1; 79; letters cited 65.3; 70; 72.2–3; 82.2; 87.4; 91; 94.2
Aldfrith, k. of Northumbria (686–705) 36.1; 52; 76.2
Aldhelm, bp. of Sherborne (*c.* 705–9): praises of 31; 35.4–5 (cf. 66); kinsman of K. David ep. i.5, of kings of Wessex ep. ii.4; 35.5; 131.7 (B); and K. Ine 35.4; and monastery of Malmesbury ep. i.5; ep. ii.1; 29.3–31; 153.2; books on virginity 31.1; 36.1; 354.1; visits Rome 35.4; 77; tomb at Malmesbury 136; elevation 147.3
Aldwulf, k. of E. Angles (663/4–713) 97.4
Aldwulf, bp. of Lichfield (799/801–814/6) 87.1
Alemanni(a) 68.1,8; 110.2,5. Later occurrences are translated 'German(y)', q. v.: emperors of Alemanni 126.2; 188.7; 251.3; 262.3; 266.1; 345.5; 420.1 (of Alemannia; cf. 288.1)
Alençon (Orne) 231.3–4
Alexander the Great 309.2
Alexander II, pope (1061–73), formerly Anselm bp. of Lucca (1057–61): William (the future Conqueror) appeals to 238.7

Alexander II, pope (1061–73) (*cont.*) (cf. 241); and dispute of York and Canterbury 297; 298.1,5–6; 302; also mentioned 263.1; 266.1
Alexander I, k. of Scots (1107–24) 228.2; 250; 400.1–3
Alexandria 356.2; 359.1; 368.3; patriarch of, *see* Michael I
Alexius I Comnenus, emperor (1081–1118): and Edgar the Ætheling 251.3; attitude toward English 225.4; relations with Crusaders 225.4; 349.3–5; 357.1–2; 383.1; with Guiscard and Bohemond 262.3–6, 344.2; 349.3–4; 356.3; 387.2, 6, with Emperor Michael 356.3, with Raymond of Saint-Gilles 388.8, with K. Sigurd 410.3; dietary principles 407.3
Alfonso VI, k. of (*inter alia*) Galicia (1072–1109) 167.2; 276; 282.3; *see also* Tarragona
Alfred, s. of K. Æthelred the Unready (d. 1037) 165.13; 177.6–178.1; 180.10–11; 181.3; 188.1, 3, 5; 197.6
Alfred, rebel against K. Æthelstan 131.1; 136–7; 139.2–3
Alfred, k. of W. Saxons (871–99): seizes Mercia 96.3; anointed by pope 109; 121.1; at battle of Ashdown 119; reign 121–3; and learning 122.3–6; 123.1–3; 149.1; children 121.13; 123.5; death and burial 124 (with 124.1(Aa)); mentioned in charters 143.2; 150B.3; 185.2; also mentioned 97.5–6; 125.1,3; 126.1; 133.2; 134.1; 139.1–2; 141.2
Alhandreus, Arab astronomer 167.2
Alhheard, bp. of Elmham (781/5–805/14) 87.2
Alhred, k. of Northumbria (765–74) 72.1–2
Almodis, w. of 'William' count of Toulouse (*see Commentary*) 388.1
Alphaeus, f. of James 'the Lord's brother' 368.1
Alps, Alpine: crossed 68.6; 170.1; 344.1–2; 388.4; 'this side the Alps' 262.1; 314.1; 344.1, 3; 420.2; 432.1; 'duke near' 112.2; 126.2 (cf. 110.1); also mentioned 349.2; 350.1
Alric, joint k. of Kent (725–?) 15.2
Alwih, br. of K. Penda 79
Amalfi (Campania) 429
Amazons 289.1
Ambrose (339–97), St, bp. of Milan 61.1; 336.3 (Ambrosian rite), 358 (his Hegesippus)

Ambrosius Aurelianus, last Roman survivor in Britain 8.2
Anastasius, cardinal priest of St Clement (1102–25) 421.2
Andover (Hants.) 159.1
Andrew, St 165.1; 356.4; *see also* Coln St Andrew
Angles (*see Commentary on 6 and 121.3*): arrive in Britain 1.1; 4.2; 5.1,3; Angles and angels 45.2; also mentioned 15.4; 97.1,5–6; 116.2
Angles, East (and East Anglia); and West Angles 125.1; kingdom of 97 (*see also* i pr.5; 98.1; 213.1); its extent 102; allusions elsewhere to relations with E. Saxons 98.2; Mercia 74.2; 86; 96.1; 107.1, Northumbria 47.4; 48.1, Wessex 19.1; 35.2; 107.1; 121.11; 125.1; and the Danes 120.2; 121.6,11; 125.1; 165.10; 176; 177.2; 180.7; 181.1; 213.2; bishops of 87.2; 102; ealdormen of, *see* Æthelwold, Ulfcytel; king of 19.1; *see also* Ælfwald, Æthelberht, Æthelhere, Æthelred, Æthelwald, Aldwulf, Anna, Beonna, Earpwald, Ecgric, Edmund, Eohric, Guthrum, Rædwald, Sigeberht
Anglesey, Mevanian Isles 48.3; 260.2; 327; 329
Anglia, Old (N. Germany) 116.2
Anglo-Saxons 124.1(Aa)
Angoulême (Charente), bishop of, *see* Gerard de Blavia
Anjou, Angevin: counts of 235; *see also* Fulk III, IV and V, Geoffrey II Martel, Geoffrey III the Bearded, Geoffrey IV Martel; countess of (= Bertrada of Montfort) 257.1; 404
Anlaf s. of Guthfrith II, k. at York (939–41) 141 (*see Commentary*)
Anlaf (Olaf), s. of K. Sihtric, k. at York (941–52, d. 981) 131.4–7; 134.2; 135.6–7, 9; 141 (where conflated with Anlaf, s. of K. Guthfrith II)
Anlaf (Olaf Tryggvasson), k. of Norway (995–1000) 165.4
Anna, k. of E. Angles (d. 654) 19.1; 74.2; 97.4; 214.1
Ansbert, son-in-law of Chlotar II 68.4
Anschis, s. of Arnulf bp. of Metz 68.4
Anscytel, s. of Riulf 145.1–2
Ansegisel, f. of Pippin II 68.3–4
Anselm, archbp. of Canterbury (1093–1109): exiles 315; 328; 332.1; 417.1; favours

INDEX

Urban 333.9; under K. Henry I 393.2; 395.1; 408.1; 413.2; 414.4; 417.3; and K. Philip I 404.2; letters from Pope Paschal II 415–16; death i pr. 3
Anselm of Lucca, *see* Pope Alexander II
Antioch (mod. Antakya, Turkey): fighting in and riches of 358–9 (cf. 343); fighting in and around in 1098 277.3; 360–65; 369.1; 373.5–6; 374.6; 388.5; 389.3; taken over by count of Edessa 386.1; emir of, *see* Aoxianus; princes of, *see* Bohemond I and II, Roger of Salerno; regent of, *see* Tancred; bishop of, *see* Paul of Samosata; Council of 427.2; also mentioned 366.1; 374.2,4,7; 375.1; 376.1; 383.3; 387.4,6–7
Antioch, Pisidian (nr. mod. Yalvaç, Turkey) 358
Antiochus, f. of Seleucus I 359.1
Antony = Marcus Antonius (d. 30 BC) 374.5
Aoxianus (Yagi Siyan), emir of Antioch (1087–98) 360.1; 361; 363.2
Apollinaris, St 160.2
Apulia, Apulian(s): in connection with family of Robert Guiscard 262.2–3,6; 344.2; 349.2; 356.3; 387.1–2,5–6; burial place of Duke Robert I 277.1; also mentioned 284.2; 353.1; 389.6; 393.2; dukes of, *see* Robert Guiscard, Roger Borsa
Aquitaine: in Carolingian period 110.2–3; monk from and his tales 170–172.1; also mentioned 410.2; 427.3; 'prince' of, *see* Louis; duke of, *see* William IX; kings of, *see* Pippin I and II; *praefectus* of, *see* Ranulf
Arabia, Arabian, Arab(s): 'nation hostile to Christ' 225.4; in Crusade 377.2; 381.3; 384.1; 385.3; in epitaph of Guiscard 262.6
Araxes, River (mod. Aras, Armenia) 351.2
Ardennes 254.1
Arezzo (Toscana) 288.2; 420.2; 438
Argences (Calvados) 178.3
Arians 167.1
Arles (B.-du-Rhône), count and county of 388.1–2
Armenia, Armenian(s) 347.4; 361; 374.3,5
Arnold, f. of Arnulf bp. of Metz 68.4
Arnulf III, count of Flanders (1070–1) 256.3–257.1
Arnulf, count palatine (*see Commentary*) 437.3
Arnulf, k. of Germany (888–99, emperor from 896) 112.1; 121.10

Arnulf I the Great, count of Flanders (918–65) 123.5; 145.4
Arnulf, bp. of Metz (615–26, d. 643/7) 68.4
Arnulf, br. of Robert of Bellême (d. after 1102) 396.3
Arques (Seine-Mar.) 232; 403.4; count of, *see* William
Arsur (N. of Jaffa) 376.9 (*see Commentary*); 380.1–2; 384.5
Arthur, K. 8.2; 287
Arundel (Sussex) 396.1–2
Ascalon (S. of Jaffa), Ascalonites 369.8; 371.2; 377.1; 381.1,3; 388.5–7
Ashdown (ridge in Berks.), battle of 119
Asia: Major 91.2–92; 225.4; Minor 225.4; 347.4; 357.3 (its provinces 347.4); expedition to (first Crusade) 257.2; 274.2; 344.1; king of 359.1; 'our ignorance of events in' 372.3; despoiled by Turks 357.6; mice in 291; also mentioned 92; 268.2; 347.5; 355.2; 364.?
Assandun (Ashdon or Ashingdon, Essex) 180.7; 181.4
Asser, bp. of Sherborne (*c*. 895–909) 122.4; 123.3
Asylum, instituted by Romulus at Rome 172.2
Athelney (Somerset) 121.2–5; 122.3; abbot of, *see* John the Old Saxon
Athelm (*or* Æthelhelm), bp. of Wells (*c*. 909–923/5), archbp. of Canterbury (923/5–926) 129.3; 184.2
Athulf, *see* Æthelwulf
Augsburg (Bavaria) 437.3
Augustine, St, archbp. of Canterbury (597–604/9): mission to England from Pope Gregory 26; 88.6–7; 89.6; 129.1; 295; converts K. Æthelberht 9.2; 10.3; translation 342; festival 144.1; also mentioned 10.1; 18.3; 27
Augustine, St (354–430), relics of 184.1
Augustine's, St *see* Canterbury
Augustus, first Roman emperor (d. 14) 175.1; *see also* Octavian; used of Charlemagne 65.3; 68.7, of Emperor Henry III 194.3; *see also* 360.2 (Soldan *as* Persian *equivalent*)
Aumale (Seine-Mar.) 307.1
Austrasia 110.2; Austrasian Franks 110.5; *see also* Pippin II
Auvergne 344.2
Auxerre (Yonne) 110.3; 121.7; *see also* Germanus

Avars 91.1; 110.2
Aventine, hill in Rome 352.13
Aversa (Campania; wrongly said to be in Apulia), bishop of, *see* Guitmund
Avranches (Manche) 392.3
Azariah 202.10

Baalbek (in mod. Lebanon) 374.11
Babylon, Semiramis' city 371.1
Babylon in Egypt (mod. Cairo), Babylonia(ns): foundation 371.1; emperor of 367.4; 371.1; 381.1; sultan of 368.4; king of 368.4; patriarch of 368.3; 'war against Babylonians' 373.7; scene of martyrdom of Robert s. of Godwine 251.3, of Orestes 368.4; also mentioned 377.5
Badon, Mount (unidentified) 8.2
Bældæg (*otherwise* Baldr), ancestor of K. Æthelwulf 44.3; 116.1
Baldred, *subregulus* of K. Ine 36C.1–2,4; 39.1
Baldred, k. of Kent (exp. 825/7) 15.3; 107.1
Baldwin, monk of Bec, legate of Anselm 416.2; 417.1
Baldwin, abt. of Bury St Edmunds (1065–1097/8) 298.8
Baldwin I, count of Edessa (1098–1100), k. of Jerusalem (1100–18): his father 199.1; as a child 373.2; activities in the Crusade: becomes count of Edessa 374.3–6, actions there 375, first trip to Jerusalem 374.7–9, second, ending in coronation 376–378.1 (cf. 374.1), siege of Arsur and Caesarea 380, at Ramlah 251.2 (cf. 384.1–3), other feats as king 381–2; 383.4–385.2; marriage 385.2; death 385.3–386.1
Baldwin II of Le Bourg, count of Edessa (1100–18), k. of Jerusalem (1118–31) 376.1; 386; 387.8
Baldwin II, count of Flanders (879–918) 123.5; 135.3
Baldwin V, count of Flanders, father-in-law of K. William I (1035–67) 188.2; 234.2; 256.3; 403.1
Baldwin VI, count of Flanders (1067–70) 256.3; 403.1
Baldwin VII, count of Flanders (1111–19) 257.2; 403.3
Baldwin II, count of Hainault (1071–98) 256.3; 257.1
Balearic Islands 92; 347.7; 368.3; 410.1
Balzo the Short, murderer of Duke William I 145.3–4
Bamberg (Bavaria) 437.3

Bamburgh (Northumberland) 49.7
Bangor (Gwynedd, *but see Commentary*) 47.3; bishops of, *see* David the Scot, Hervey
Bantomp, name on pyramid at Glastonbury 21.2
Barcelona 170.1: count of (= Raymond-Berengar I, d. 1076) 388.1
Bardney (Lincs.) 49.8–9; 77; 125.5
Barfleur (Manche) 419.3
Barking (Essex) 36.1; abbess of, *see* Hildelith
Basil, St 356.2
Bate, name on pyramid at Glastonbury 21.2
Bath (Somerset): in days before K. Ceawlin 17.1; K. Edgar I crowned at 160.1; under K. Swein Forkbeard 177.3; under K. William II 306.4; monastery 340; abbot of, *see* Ælfheah (*see also* 340.1); seat of bishop 100; 300.3; 338.1; 340.1; bishop of, *see* John of Villula
Battle Abbey (Sussex) 267.3
Bavaria 91.1; 110.3,5; *see also* Norica
Bayeux (Calvados) 398.4; bishop of, *see* Odo; viscount of, *see* Ranulf I
Bearn, name on pyramid at Glastonbury 21.2
Bec (-Hellouin), le (Eure), monastery 417.1; monk of, *see* Baldwin
Beckery (Somerset) 36C.2; 150.4 (= Little Ireland)
Bede (d. 735): and Northumbria 47.1; 54.1; Alcuin on 70.1; alleged visit to Rome 57; 58.2; death 54.1; 60–1; epitaph 62; panegyric of 54.1 (cf. 51.2; 54.6); 57; 59 (cf. 66); his *Hist. Eccl.* (referred to as the *Gesta Anglorum* at 29.2, 51.1, 65.1, 123.1, and 208.1; as the *Aecclesiastica Anglorum Historia* at 54.6; cf. 53.2 'Anglorum Historia'): W. comments on his own use of i pr. 4; 47.1; 54.6, style of i pr.1; 59.1, cited *in extenso* 55–6, testimony of also noted 5.3; 9.1; 10.3; 33; 49.3, 7; 51.2; 53.2; 78; 98.2; 100; 208.3; 213.1; 214.1,3; 367.1, discrepancies with *ASC* 9.1; 33 (*cf. also* 29.3), translated by Alfred 123.1; his *Vita Abbatum* 51.2; 54.3; history and literature since i pr.1–3; 62–3; 69; 342.1; 445.5
Bedfordshire 101
Bedwig 116.2
Beirut 366.2; 376.3,8
Belgian Gaul 233.1
Benedict, St (*c.* 480–*c.* 550) 36C.2; 334.4; 443.8

INDEX

Benedict I, pope (574–8) 45.2
Benedict X, pope (1058–9) 199.10
Benedict Biscop, founder of St Peter's, Monkwearmouth (d. 689) 54.2–4; 55.1
Benevento (Campania) 431.3; archbishop of, *see* Landulf II
Benignus (*also* Beonna), abt. of Glastonbury 24
Benson (Oxon.) 42.1
Beonna, k. of E. Angles (749) 97.5
Beonna, *see* Benignus
Beorn, cousin of Swein s. of Earl Godwine 200.2 (*see* Commentary)
Beornheah, bp. of Selsey (c. 909–930/1) 129.3
Beornred, k. of Mercia (757) 79
Beornwulf, k. of Mercia (823–5) 96.1; 106.4–107.1
Beorward, *see* Berhtwald
Beow (*also* Beaw), ancestor of Woden 116.1
Berengar, count of Sulzbach (*fl.* 1111–22) 422.2; 437.3
Berengar of Tours (d. *c.* 1088) 284–286.1
Berhtfrith, murderer of St Wigstan 212
Berhtwald, abt. of Glastonbury and of Reculver, archbp. of Canterbury (692/3–731) 21.3 (*where called* Beorward); 29.1 (*see* Commentary); 36C.1,9; 184.2
Berhtwulf, k. of Mercia (840–?852) 96.2
Berkeley (Glos.) 204.1; 306.4
Berkshire 100; 331
Bernard the Monk, pilgrim (travelled *c.* 870) 367.3–4; 368.3
Bernard, bp. of St David's (1115–48) 25.3; 398.4(Cs)
Bernard, founder of Tiron (1107–9) 440
Bernicia, Bernicians 49.1; 50.1; 80.5; kings of, *see* Æthelfrith, Æthelric, Eanfrith, Ida, Oswald, Oswiu; *see also* Northumbria
Bertram of Toulouse, count of Tripoli (1109–12) 388.3,10–11
Bethlehem 366.3; 368.1; 374.9; 378.1
Beverstone (Glos.) 199.4
Biandrate (Piemonte), count of, *see* Albert
Bigod, *see* Roger
Birinus, bp. of Dorchester (634–*c.* 650) 18.3
Distonian (i.e. Thracian) 355.2
Bithynia (now N.W. Turkey) 178.6; 347.4; 349.6; 357.3
Bladon, River (now Evenlode, Oxon.) 30
Bleadney (Somerset) 36C.1
Bleddyn ap Cynfyn, Welsh king (d. 1075) 228.8

Bliswerh, name on pyramid at Glastonbury 21.2
Blithhild, w. of Ansbert 68.4
Blois (Loir-et-Cher), counts of, *see* Stephen, Theobald I and II
Boethius (consul 510) 122.4; 123.1; 167.5–6
Bohemond I, prince of Antioch (d. 1111): early career 262.3–4; 344.2; 387.1–2; advises Crusade 344.1 (cf. 387.3); and Alexius 262.4; 344.2; 349.4; 387.2,6; comes to Constantinople 349.2; at Antioch 363; 365.2; 366.1–2; 375.1; 388.5; journey to Jerusalem 374.7; capture of 375; career summarized 387.1–7; also mentioned 366.3; 386.2; 387.8
Bohemond II, prince of Antioch (1126–30) 386.2; 387.6, 8
Boniface V, pope (619–25) 296
Boniface, archbp. of Mainz (747–55): letters of 79–83; also mentioned 85
Boniface, cardinal priest of St Mark (?/ 1111–1119 x ?1122) 421.2
Boniface, marquis (*fl.* 1111) 422.2; 437.3 (*see* Commentary)
Boniface I, marquis of Montferrat (1060–*c.* 1100) 274.1
Bordeaux (Gironde) 231.1
Bosham (Sussex) 228.3
Botaniates, i.e. Nicephorus III (emperor 1078–81) 225.4; 356.3
Boulogne (-sur-mer) (Pas-de-Calais), counts of, *see* Adulf, Eustace II and III
Bourdin (Bordinho), *see* Maurice
Bourges (Cher) 429
Braga (in mod. Portugal) 434; bishop of, *see* Maurice Bourdin
Bregden, name on pyramid at Glastonbury 21.2–3
Bregored, abt. of Glastonbury (7c.) 21.3; 28
Brent (Somerset) 36C.1,6; 151C.1
Brentford (Middlesex) 180.5–6
Brent Knoll (Somerset) 21.3
Brent Marsh (Somerset) 21.3
Bridgnorth (Shropshire) 396.1–2
Brie (= Faremoutiers-en-Brie) (Seine-et-Marne), nunnery 214.2; abbess of, *see* Æthelburh
Brigid, St 23
Brihtric, k. of W. Saxons (786–802) 43; 90; 106.1,3; 113.2
Brihtwold, 'bp. of Wiltshire', i.e. Ramsbury (1005–45) 221
Brill (Bucks.) 224.1

Brindisi (Puglia) 349.2; 429
Brionne (Eure) 230.3,5; counts of, *see* Gilbert, Guy of Burgundy
Bristol 306.4
Britain (*for William's use of* Britannia *see* Commentary *on 121.3*); world of 12; 'another world' 54.1; voyage round 7.3; British sea, ocean 5.1; 127.1; 179.3; 199.8; 350.1; 372.3; northern 44.1; western 134.6; as opposed to Scotland 54.1; Galloway in 287.1; and Romans 1.1; 2; Constantine born in 355.2; nations of 48.3; rich in culture 53.2; stone buildings in 54.3; and Anglo-Saxon invasions i pr. 1,5; 1.1; 5.1, 3; 16.1; 116.2; and Danes 43.2; and Christianity 19.3; 26; subject to archbishops of Canterbury 295–6; 298.2 (cf. 88.9); importance of Glastonbury in 151C.1; ruled by kings of Wessex 228.7, by K. Edwin 48.2, by K. Ecgberht 106.1; 107.2; luminaries of 74.2; used of William's own day 16.1 (?); 213.6; kingdom of 36C.3; 106.1; king of, *see* Vortigern
British = Britons q.v. (the translation preserves William's variation between *Britanni* and *Britones*): in time of Romans 1.2; and Saxons 22.1; and kings of Wessex 17.1; 18.1; 19.2; 33; 135.7; and Chester 47.3; and Northumbria 49.2–3; what they owe to Gildas 20.1; British king of Dumnonia 27–8; in Cornwall 106.3; North British = Welsh 106.3; 134.6; in 'ancient poem' 135.7; language 28; king of, *see* Lucius
Britons: ancient 239.2; and Romans 3; and Picts and Scots 3.2; Gildas wisest of 70.4; *History* of 4.1; and Angles, English 8.1–3; and kings of Wessex 16.2; 17.1–2; 40; 108.1; 125.1; 133.1; and Mercia 108.1; 'in the days of the Britons' 21.3; in William's day 1.2; 8.2; 'whom we call the Welsh' 125.1; Northern Britons = Northwalians 134.5; Western Britons = Cornwallians 134.6; king of, *see* Cadwallon
Brittany, Bretons: contrasted with 'Britons of our own island' 1.2; 'Bretons on the Continent' 2.2; under Carolingians 110.2; and Danes 121.10 (cf. 138B.5); relics from 138B.5; 140; and K. William I 228.5; 236; 258.1; and K. Henry I 392.1; 402; 404.1; Ralph of Gael from 255.1; relics from 140; portent in 207.1; counts of, *see* Alan III and IV, Conan I

Brond, ancestor of K. Æthelwulf 116.1
Brunefeld (unidentified), battle of (*ASC* Brunanburh) 131.4–7; 135.6–9
Bruno, bp. of Speyer (1107–23) 195 (*see* Commentary); 422.2; 437.3
Bryne, priest under K. Cenwulf 88.9
Buckinghamshire 101
Burgred, k. of Mercia (?852–873/4) 96.2–3; 108.1
Burgundy 80.4; 97.3; 110.2; 334.3; king of, *see* Rudolf III; counts of, *see* Stephen, William I; *see also* Guy
Bury St Edmunds (Suffolk), abbot of, *see* Baldwin; *see also* St Edmund
Butleigh (Somerset) 36C.6; 150C.4; 151C.1
Byrhthelm, bp. of Wells (956–9 and 959–73) 150C.2
Byzantium 354.1; 388.8; *see also* Constantinople

Cadwallon, prince of Gwynedd (d. 634) 48.4–49.2
Cædwalla, k. of W. Saxons (685–9) 14; 34.1–3; 36C.2,4; 39.1; 74.2
Caelian, hill in Rome 352.13
Caen (Calvados) 267.2,5; 273.2; 283.1; 389.9–10; abbess of, *see* Cecilia
Caesar, used of ancient emperors 420.3; of German emperors normally translated 'emperor' and the like, but see 194.2–3; 430; *see also* Julius
Caesarea (Palestinian), S. of Haifa: on route of Crusaders 366.2; 376.9; overcharges 374.9; taken by K. Baldwin 380.2–4; 381.1
Caesarea Philippi (also known as Paneas, mod. Banyas), E. of Tyre 374.10
Cahors (Lot) 388.2; bishop of (Gerald of Cardaillac, 1093–*c*. 1112) 387.3; 388.3
Cairo, *see* Babylon
Calabria 262.2; 353.1
Calixtus II, pope (1119–24): as archbp. of Vienne (1090–1119) 335.2; 426; 429; 432.1; elected pope 432.1; and K. Henry I 406; 408.1; and the Romans 435; and investitures 288.2; 432.2; 435.2–437.1; letters of 433; 436; also mentioned 405.2; 437.2
Calne (Wilts.) 161.2–3
Calvary, Mt 368.1
Cambridgeshire 102
Cambyses, k. of Persia (530–522 BC) 371.1
Campania 353.1

INDEX

Candida Casa, see Whithorn
Canterbury (called *Cantuaria, Dorobernia,* and even *Cantia*): as a city 29.1; 88.7; 129.3; 165.5; 296; 298.4; 417.3; riot at 199.2–3; archbishopric 87.1–2, 4; 95.1; 99; 150C.5; 165.5; 184.1; dispute with York 88.6–8; 294–9; 301; 445.4; subordinate bishops 87.2; 300.1–2; 302.2; cathedral 165.6; 184.1 (cf. 181.5); archbishops of, *see* Ælfheah, Æthelgar, Æthelheard, Æthelnoth, Anselm, Athelm, Augustine, Berhtwald, Cuthbert, Dunstan, Eadsige, Jænberht, Justus, Lanfranc, Laurence, Lyfing, Oda, Plegmund, Ralph of Escures, Robert of Jumièges, Sigeric, Stigand, Theodore, William of Corbeil; *see also* Osbern; St Augustine's 10.2; 54.4; 76.2; 215, abbots of, *see* Hadrian, Scotland
Capua (Campania), prince of, *see* Richard; archbishop of, *see* Sennes
Caria (now S.W. Turkey) 347.4
Carloman, s. of Charles Martel (d. 754) 68.5
Carloman, s. of Pippin III, k. 768 (d. 771) 68.6
Carloman, s. of Louis the German (830–80) 110.5
Carloman, s. of Louis II the Stammerer (879–84) 110.7–8
Carmentis, mother of Evander 206.2
Castel Pelerin (nr. Tripoli) 388.9
Catigis, s. of Vortigern 8.1
Cato (the Elder, 234–149 BC) 59.2; (Younger, d. 46 BC) 304. *Cf. also* 267.2
Ceawlin, k. of W. Saxons (560–91, d. 592) 16.3–17; 34.1; 116.1
Cecilia, d. of K. William I, abbess of Caen (1113–27) 276
Cedd, bp. of London (*c.* 653–64) 98.2
Celestine I, pope (422–32) 22.1
Celtic Gaul 233.1
Cencio (Cinthius), Wibertine cardinal bp. of St Chrysogonus 431.3
Cencio (*rightly* Crescentius), cardinal bp. of Sabina (?/1102–1121/?) 421.2; 429
Cenred, f. of K. Ine 36C.1; 116.1
Cenred, k. of Mercia (704–9) 76.2; 78; 98.3
Cenred, k. of Northumbria (716–8) 53.1
Centwine, name on pyramid at Glastonbury 21.3
Centwine, k. of W. Saxons (676–85): as king 33; mentioned in charters 36C.2,4; 39.1; 143.2; 150B.3; 185.2
Cenwealh, br. of K. Penda 94.2

Cenwealh, k. of W. Saxons (642–72) 19.1–3; 29.1–2; 32; 36C.2,4; 74.2; 76.1
Cenwulf, bp. of Dorchester (*c.* 909–909/25) 129.3
Cenwulf, k. of Mercia (796–821): accession, reign and death 94.2–95; correspondence with pope 88–9; also mentioned 96.1; 211.1
Ceol, *see* Ceolric
Ceolberht, *minister* of K. Cenwulf 88.9
Ceolfrith, abt. of Monkwearmouth (688–716) 50.5 (C); 54.5; 55; 58
Ceolred, k. of Mercia (709–16) 77; 79; 80.5
Ceolric (*also* Ceol), k. of W. Saxons (591–?597) 17.3–18.1
Ceolwald, f. of Cenred f. of K. Ine 116.1
Ceolwulf I, k. of Mercia (821–3) 96.1; 212
Ceolwulf II, k. of Mercia (873/4–?) 96.3
Ceolwulf, k. of Northumbria (729–37, d. ?764) 53–54.1; 64–65.1
Ceolwulf, k. of W. Saxons (597–?611) 17.3
Cerdic, k. of W. Saxons (519–34) 16; 43.1; 116.1; 228.7
Chalcedon (on Asiatic side of Bosphorus) 427.2
Charlemagne, Charles Augustus (768–814, emperor from 800): lineage and reign 67–68.7; and Alcuin 65.2–66; 69; 70.2; 72.3; 90–1; and Archbishop Æthelheard 82.2; and Eadburh 113.3; and K. Offa 90; 91.2–94.1; and the Church 68.7; 202.6–7; 420.2; 438; founds Cormery 66(B), hospice at Jerusalem 367.3; defeats Saracens 135.4; 167.2; 368.3; and Spain, *see that entry*; lance of 135.4; language spoken by 68.2; *Life* of 68.2; descendants of 68.8; 110.1; 128.2; 135.2; 349.1; 373.1; also mentioned 106.3
Charles the Bald, k. (840–77, emperor from 876): career and death 110.1–3,6; children 109; 113.1; 126.1; grandsons 127.3; and John the Scot 122.5; brings relics from Constantinople 127.2
Charles the Fat, k. (876–87, emperor from 880, d. 888) 110.5,8; his vision 111–112.1
Charles the Good, count of Flanders (1119–27) 257; 403.4
Charles Martel (Tudites, the Hammer), mayor of the palace (d. 714) 68.4; 80.5; 82.2; 204.7
Charles, k. of Provence (845–63) 110.4
Charles the Simple, k. of E. Franks (898–923, d. 929) 112.1; 126.1–2; 127.1,3–4; 128.1; 236.3

850 INDEX

Chartres (Eure-et-Loir) 127.2; 186; bishop of, *see* Fulbert; *see also* Fulcher
Charybdis iv pr. 3
Cheilaion, Mt (at Ephesus) 225.2
Chelles (Seine-et-Marne), monastery 11.2
Chertsey (Surrey), abbot of, *see* Wulfnoth (Wulfwold)
Cheshire 101; 327
Chester (Cheshire; formerly called the City of Legions (*Legaceaster*) 47.3, 300.3; and so named 101; 133.1; 148.2; 214.3) 76.2; 341.2; see 338.1; 341.1; bishop of, *see* Robert of Limesey; earls of, *see* Hugh of Avranches, Richard (also 212); countess of 419.7 (*see Commentary*)
Chichester (Sussex) 100; 300.3; bishops of, *see* Æthelgar, Æthelric II, Stigand
Chlodulf, bp. of Metz (*c.* 659) 68.4
Chlotar II (583–629), Merovingian king 68.4
Chosroes II, k. of Persia (591–628) 368.2
Christina, d. of Edgar the Ætheling 228.1
Chur (in mod. Switzerland), *Churwelsch* 110.5 (*see Commentary*)
Cicero 132; v pr. 1
Cilicia (now in S. E. Turkey), Cilicians 347.4; 374.2–3
Cirencester (Glos.) 17.1; 18.1
Cistercians 334–7
Cîteaux (Côte-d'Or) 335.2; 337.1; abbots of, *see* Alberic, Stephen Harding
City of Legions, *see* Chester
Clement, St, bp. of Rome (d. *c.* 100) 266.2; *see also* Wibert
Cleophas, br. of Joseph 368.1
Clermont (-Ferrand, Puy-de-Dôme) 344.2; 387.3; 388.4; Council of 344.3–345
Cluny, abbey (Sâone-et-Loire): Gelasius dies at 432.1; abbots of, *see* Hugh, Odilo, Odo; prior of, *see* Urban; monk of, *see* Lanzo; Cluniac monks 265.3; 413, at Reading 413.1, Thetford 339.2, Wenlock 216
Cnut, k. of England (1016–35), of Denmark (1019–35), of Norway (1028–35): Danes choose as king 179.2 (cf. 181.5; 183.3); campaigns in England 179.2–3; 180.1–10; as king of England 181; 183.9; his titles 183.1; 185.1; attitude to English 254.2; and Glastonbury 184.2–185; in Rome and Scotland 182; in Sweden and Norway 181.6; and Chartres 186; letter of 183.1–8; death 187.2; successors 259.1 (cf. 188.1); also mentioned 188.3, 7; 196.4; 200.1; 221; 258.3

Cnut IV, k. of Denmark (1080–86) 249.2; 257.1; 258.3; 261–262.1; 282.3
Coln St Andrew (= Coln Rogers, Glos.) 398.4 (Cs)
Cologne (Köln) 175.1,3; archbishops of, *see* Frederick, Heribert, Pilgrim (*also* 175)
Colonia, formerly Agrippina, mod. Cologne 175.1
Compiègne (Oise) 110.7; 112.1
Conan, killed by K. Henry I 392.4
Conan I, count of Brittany (d. 992) 178.5
Conrad, s. of Henry IV, king of Lombardy (d. 1101) 288; 420.2
Conrad I, k. of Germany (911–18) 68.8; 112.1; 135.1
Conrad II, k. of Germany (1024–39, emperor from 1027) 183.2–4; 193.1
Constance, d. of K. William I (d. 1090) 276
Constans II, emperor (641–68) 356.2 (*see Commentary*)
Constantine, abt. of Saint-Mesmin-de-Micy nr. Orléans (989–95) 168.1
Constantine I (the Great), emperor (306–37); acclaimed emperor 1.2; basilica of in Rome 427.1; and Constantinople 354; 355.1–2,4; builds church of Holy Sepulchre 367.3; sword of 135.4; also mentioned 356.1
Constantine III, emperor (407–11) 2.1
Constantine II, k. of Scots (900–43) 131.3–4,7; 134.2; 135.7
Constantinople: foundation and description of 354–5 (cf. 343); one of three most important cities 359.1; emperors of generally 68.5,7; 92; list of emperors 356.1–3; for emperors discussed further or elsewhere, *see* Alexius I, Botaniates, Constans II, Constantine I and III, Diogenes, Heraclius, John II, Justinian I, 'Maniches', Michael VII; unnamed emperor 260.1; Crusaders at 349.2–3, 5; 353.3; 357.1; 383.1; 388.8; K. Sigurd at 410.2–3; relics from 127.2, at 356.4; Council of 427.2; churches of St Irene and the Holy Apostles in 355.1; church of St Sophia in 356.1; 410.2; bishops of, *see* Gregory of Nazianzus, John Chrysostom; *see also* Byzantium
Constantius I, Western emperor (305–6) 1
Conteville (Eure), viscount of, *see* Herluin
Conza (E. of Salerno, Campania) 429
Corbaguath (Kerbogha, atabeg of Mosul, d. 1102) 364.1; 365.1; 389.3–4
Cormery (Indre-et-Loire), monastery 66 (B)

Cornwall, Cornish 22.2; 100 ('Cornubia, now Cornwall'); 106.3; 129.3 *(see Commentary)*; 134.6; 300.1–2; bishop of, *see* Lyfing; earl of, *see* William count of Mortain
Corsica 92
Cosham (Hants) 180.1
Cotentin, viscount of, *see* Nigel II
Coutances (Manche), bishop of, *see* Geoffrey
Coventry (Warwickshire) 101; 184.1; 196.2; 338.1; 341; bishop of, *see* Robert of Limesey
Crediton (Devon) 100; 300.1–2; bishops of, *see* Ælfric, Eadwulf, Lyfing
Cremona (Lombardia) 431.2; 438
Creoding, ancestor of K. Æthelwulf 116.1 (A)
Crescentius, *see* Cencio
Crete 92
Crowland (Lincs.) 253.2
Cumberland, Cumbrians 141.2; 196.2; kings of, *see* Malcolm, Owain
Cumbra, ealdorman (d. 757) 41
Curio, C. Scribonius (d. 49 BC) 339.3
Cutha, s. of K. Ceawlin 17.2–3
Cutha, br. of K. Ceawlin 17.2; 34.1
Cutha, ancestor of K. Æthelwulf 116.1
Cuthbald, br. of K. Cynegils 35.1
Cuthbert, archbp. of Canterbury (740–60) 82–3
Cuthbert, abt. of Malmesbury (late 8c.) 94.2
Cuthbert, St, bp. of Lindisfarne (685–7); and K. Oswiu 51; and K. Alfred 121.2–3; church of (at Durham) 70.3; buried and venerated at Durham 49.8; 61.4; 64; 271.2; 445.2; incorrupt 207.4
Cuthburh, sister of K. Ine, w. of K. Aldfrith 36.1
Cuthgils, br. of K. Cynegils 33
Cuthred, k. of Kent (798–807) 15.3; 95.2
Cuthred, k. of W. Saxons (740–56) 29.2; 38–40; 143.2; 150B.3; 185.2
Cuthwine, ancestor of K. Æthelwulf 116.1
Cwenburh, sister of K. Ine 36.1
Cwenthryth, sister of St Kenelm 95.3; 211
Cwichelm, k. of W. Saxons (626–36) 18
Cyneburh, d. of K. Penda 74.3; 76.2
Cynegils, k. of W. Saxons (611–?642) 18.1,3; 33; 35.1
Cyneheard, br. of Sigeberht k. of W. Saxons 42
Cyneswith, w. of K. Penda 74.3
Cyneswith, d. of K. Penda 74.3; 98.3

Cynewulf, k. of W. Saxons (757–86) 42–43.1; 86
Cynric, k. of W. Saxons (534–?560) 16; 116.1
Cyprus 92
Cyril I, bp. of Jerusalem (350/1, with exiles; *see Commentary*) 368.1
Cyrus, k. of Persia (559–29 BC) 371.1

Dacia 431.3
Dacre (Cumbria) 134.2
Daedalus, mythical craftsman 170.2; 225.6
Dagobert, k., ancestor of Pippin (621–37) 68.4
Daimbert, (arch)bp. of Pisa (1088–99), Latin patriarch of Jerusalem (1099–1102, d. 1105) 374.7,9; 378.1
Dalmatia 349.1
Damascus 376.2; *see also* Dukak
Danes, *see* Denmark
Daniel, prophet 356.4
Danishmend (i.e. Malik Ghazi, Danishmend emir, d. 1106) 375.1; 387.4
Danube, River 355.4
David, k. of Israel 169.4; tower of (in Jerusalem) 369.2,8; 388.5
David, 'archbp. of Menevia' (d. 589 or 601) 25; 36C.1
David I, k. of Scots (1124–53) ep. i; 228.2; 400.1
David the Scot, bp. of Bangor (1120–?1139) 420.3–4; 426
Dee, River (at Chester) 148.2
Degsa, stone of (*Degsastan*) 47.2
Deira, Deirans 45.2; 49.1; 50.1; 80.5; kings of, *see* Ælle, Edwin, Guthfrith II, Osric, Oswine; *see also* Northumbria
Delphic tripods 355.2
Demetrius, St 365.3
Deneberht, bp. of Worcester (?800–22) 87.2
Denmark, Danes: language 253.1; potations 348.2 (cf. 148.3); axe 188.6; slave trade with 200.1; raids on Continent 121.7, 10; Danish invasions of England, early or general 43.2; 50.5; 54.2, 5; 73.1 (cf. 70.2–3); 96.2–3; 107.2–108.2; 118–120; 134.4; 154.5; 213.2, under K. Alfred 97.5; 121.1–2,5,10–12; 122.1, under K. Edward the Elder 97.6; 125.2–3, under K. Æthelstan 121.6; 131.3–7; 135.6–9, under K. Æthelred the Unready 164.3; 165.2–12; 176–177.4; 179.1–4; 180.1–3; massacre of 165.12; under K. Edmund II 180.4–9; destroy churches and libraries

Denmark, Danes (*cont.*)
123.2; 125.5 (cf. 181.4); and London 188.1, 4; merge with Northumbrians 125.1 (cf. 200.2, 248.2); under K. William I 249.2; 261.1; 262.1; jarls 97.6; 118; 119.2; 177.1; also mentioned 181.6; 183.3,7; 188.1; 200.2; 248.2; 254.2; kings 118–119.1; 259; *see also* Cnut, Cnut IV, Eohric, Eric I, Guthrum, Harold III, Harthacnut, Niels, Olaf the Hungry, Osecg, Sihtric, Swein I and II
Derbyshire 101
Desiderius, Lombard king (757–74) 68.6
Desiderius, *see* Victor III
Devil's Ford (*see Commentary*) 353.3
Devon(shire) 100; 157.1; 165.5; *see also* Æthelmær, Dumnonia, Ordgar
Dijon (Côte-d'Or), abbot of, *see* William of Volpiano
Diogenes, i.e. Romanus IV (emperor 1067–71) 225.4; 356.3
Dionysius the Areopagite, work falsely attributed to 122.5
Dionysius Exiguus (d. *c.* 540) 292.1
Dionysius, St, and his church at Wilton 218.3–4; *see also* Saint-Denis
Dives, River (Orne and Calvados) 234.1
Divizo, *see* Teuzo
Dol (-de-Bretagne, Ille-et-Vilaine) 258.1; *see* Levenanus, Radbod, Samson
Domfront (Orne) 231.3–232.1; 402
Donald Bane, k. of Scots (1093–7) 311.3; 400.1,3
Dorchester (Oxon.): see of 101; 300.1,3; and archbishop of York 297; 302.1; bishops of, *see* Agilbert, Birinus, Cenwulf, Remigius
Dorobernia 298.1; *see also* Canterbury, Dover
Dorset 100
Doulting (Somerset) 36C.1
Dover (Kent) (*twice called* Dorobernia) 15.1 (Aa); 139.4; 199.1; 228.5
Dukak (Shams al-Muluk), ruler of Damascus 1095–1104 376.2,4
Dumnonia 27; 100 (*where wrongly said to be old name for Devonshire*)
Duncan II, k. of Scots (1094) 400.1, 3
Dunfermline (Fife) 250
Dunstan, abt. of Glastonbury (940–57/?), bp. of Worcester (?957–9), archbp. of Canterbury (959–88); at Glastonbury 143.1; 144.2; and K. Eadred 146.2; and K. Eadwig 147.2,4; and K. Edgar I 148.1; 150.2,5; 150B.6; 158; 159.2; and K. Edward 161; and K. Æthelred the Unready 164–165.2; panegyric of 149.1–4, 6; also mentioned 149.5; 184.2; 218.3–4; 303.2
Dunwich (Suffolk) 87.3; 300.1–2; bishops of, *see* Felix, Tidferth
Durazzo (mod. Dürres, Albania) 262.3; 344.2; 349.2; 387.1–2
Durham, monks at 271.3; 445.2; burials at 49.8; 61.4; see of 104; 298.2; 300.3; bishop of (*see Commentary*) 177.7, *see also* Geoffrey Rufus, Ranulf Flambard, Walcher, William of Saint-Calais; dean of, *see* Leofwine
Dyfnwal, k. (*see Commentary*) 148.2

Eadbald, k. of Kent (616–40) 10–11.1; 48.2
Eadberht, k. of Kent (725–?748) 15.2
Eadberht Præn, k. of Kent (796–8) 15.3 (Æthelberht); 95.2
Eadberht, *see* Ecgberht k. of Northumbria
Eadburh, d. of K. Edward the Elder 126.3; 217; 219
Eadburh, d. of K. Offa 90; 113.2–3
Eadflæd, d. of K. Edward the Elder 126.2
Eadgifu, w. of K. Edward the Elder (d. 966/7) 126.3; 217.1
Eadgifu, d. of K. Edward the Elder 126.1–2; a second d. of same name 126.3 (*see Commentary on 126*); 135.2
Eadgyth, d. of K. Edgar I 159.2; 218–19
Eadgyth, d. of K. Edward the Elder 112.2; 126.2; 135.2
Eadgyth, d. of Godwine, w. of K. Edward the Confessor 196.6; 197.2–3; 199.7; 220.1; 271.3; 273.2
Eadhild, d. of K. Edward the Elder 126.2; 128.2; 135.2
Eadmer, historian and hagiographer (d. *c.* 1124) i pr.3; 315; 332.1; 413.2
Eadnoth the Staller (d. 1067) 254.2
Eadred, k. of England (946–55) 126.3; 146
Eadric, k. of Kent (685–6/7) 13–14.1; 34.2 ('k. of S. Saxons')
Eadric Streona, ealdorman of Mercia (d. 1017) 165.9; 177.1; 179.4; 180.1,4, 6–7,9–10; 181.1–2
Eadsige, archbp. of Canterbury (1038–50) 197.2
Eadwig, s. of K. Æthelred the Unready (d. 1017) 180.10

INDEX 853

Eadwig, s. of K. Edmund II (*see* Commentary) 180.10
Eadwig, k. of England (955–9) 147–148.1
Eadwulf, bp. of Crediton (*c.* 909–34) 129.3
Eadwulf, bp. of Lindsey (796–836/9) 87.2
Eafa, ancestor of K. Æthelwulf 116.1
Ealdgyth (*properly* Ælfgifu), d. of K. Edward the Elder 112.2
Ealdred, archbp. of York (1062–9) 125.5; 247.2–3; 251.1
Ealdwulf, rebel against K. Æthelstan 131.3
Ealhmund, f. of Ecgberht k. of W. Saxons 116.1
Ealhstan, bp. of Sherborne (816/25–867) 106.4; 108.2–109; 113.1; 114.3
Ealhswith, *see* Æthelswith
Eanbald I, archbp. of York (779/80–796) 65.2
Eanfled, name on pyramid at Glastonbury 21.2
Eanfrith, k. of Bernicia (633/4–634) 49.1
Eanwulf, ealdorman of Somerset (mid-9c.) 113.1
Earconberht, k. of Kent (640–64) 11; 76.2; 209.1; 214.2–215
Earcongota, d. of K. Earconberht 11.2; 214.3
Earpwald, k. of E. Angles (616/27, d. 627/8) 97.2
Ebroin, Neustrian mayor (d. 679) 68.4
Ebusa, relative of Hencgest (*see* Commentary) 44.1; 287.1
Ecgberht I, k. of Kent (664–73): and arrival of Theodore 12; 50.4; killing of Æthelberht and Æthelred 12 (B); 13; 209.1; 215; also mentioned 15.1
Ecgberht (*rightly* Eadberht), k. of Northumbria (737–58) 65.1–2; 69; 70.3; 72.1
Ecgberht, k. of West Saxons (802–39): lineage 116.1; exile 43; 106.1–2; reign 43.2; 106.3–107; other references to dealings with Kent 15.3; 98.3; 215, Northumbria 73.2, Mercia 96, E. Saxons 98.3; 'sole ruler of almost the whole island' i pr. 5 (cf. 106.1, 107.2); as end of period covered by Book i pr. 5; 15.4; 43.2; 73.2; 105; also mentioned 108.1; 228.7
Ecgberht, archbp. of York (?732–66) 65; 72.1
Ecgfrith, k. of Mercia (796) 94; 210
Ecgfrith, k. of Northumbria (670–85) 51–2; 77; 214.1
Ecgric, k. of E. Angles in the time of K. Penda 74.2; 97.3–4

Ecgwine, St, bp. of Worcester (693/?–717) 98.3
Ecgwynn, w. of K. Edward the Elder 126.1
Edessa (or Rothasia [374.4]; mod. Urfa, S. E. Turkey) 374.3–4,6; 375.1; 376.1; 386.1; counts of, *see* Baldwin I and II, Joscelin I
Edgar, k. of Scots (1097–1107) 228.2; 311.3; 400.1,3
Edgar I, k. of England (959–75): reign 148–9; 160.3; and Glastonbury 149.7; 150B; 150C; and Malmesbury 152–3; vision of 154–5; character and general behaviour 155–6; cruelty and lechery 157–9; death and incorruption 160 (cf. 180.9); son called 'Edgaring' 68.2; mentioned in charter 185.2; also mentioned i pr. 3; 138; 138B.1; 161.1–2; 164.1; 180.9; 196.6; 209.2; 218.1
Edgar II the Ætheling ('reigned' 1066): elected king 'by some' 228.1; candidate for throne 238.1; 247.2; 249.1; at York 248.2; and Scots 249.1; 251.1; in Normandy and the East 251; still alive 228.1; 251.3
Edmund, s. of K. Edgar I (d. 971) 159.2
Edmund, St, k. of E. Angles (855–69): king 97.5; 213.1–2; martyrdom 97.5–6; 120.2; 213.2–3; monastery built in honour of 181.4 (cf. 213.4, 6; 298.8); vision of seen by K. Swein 179.1; incorruption of 207.4; 213.4–5; *see* Bury St Edmunds
Edmund, s. of K. Malcolm III 400.3
Edmund I, k. of England (939–46): reign 141; and Glastonbury 142–3; death and burial 144 (cf. 150C.2); son called 'Edmunding' 68.2; mentioned in charters 150B.1,3; 185.2; also mentioned 126.3; 146.1; 147.1; 148.1
Edmund II Ironside, k. of England (1016): lineage and early life 179.5; career and death 180.1–9; as 'brother' of K. Cnut 181.2; 184.2; 185.1; fate of killers of 181.1–2; also mentioned 180.10; 228.1; 393.3
Edward, s. of K. Edmund II (d. 1057) 180.10; 228.1–2
Edward, s. of K. Malcolm III (d. 1093) 228.2; 250
Edward the Elder, k. of W. Saxons (899/900–924): fathering of Æthelstan 139.2; successes against Danes 97.6; reign 125; wives and children 112.1; 126; 128.2; 131.1; 135.3; 139.2; 140; 146.1; 217; and New Minster, Winchester 124.1 (Aa); and

Edward the Elder (*cont.*)
  bishoprics 128.2–129.2; 300.1; death 130; 133.1–2; mentioned in charters 143.2; 150B.3; 185.2; also mentioned 121.13; 124.2 (wth Aa); 127.1; 133.4; 138B.2
Edward I the Martyr, k. of England (975–8) 159.2; 161–164.1; 165.7, 9
Edward II the Confessor, St, k. of England (1042–66): mother 165.13; early years 177.6–178.1; 179.2; 180.10–11; 181. 3; 188.1, 3; 221–2; 226.1; reign 196–200; character 220; marriage 197.2–3; called the Simple 259.1; 300.2; alleged grant of England to William the Conqueror 240.2; attitude to overseas kingdoms 259.1; visions, prophecies and miracles 221–7 (cf. 419.2); last days and death 228.1, 6 (cf. 200.3, 238.1, 252.1); oath by 183.9; also mentioned 228.7–8; 271.3; 373.1; 393.3
Edwin, k. of Deira (616–33): exile with K. Rædwald 47.4; 48.1; 97.2; reign 48; and W. Saxons 18.2; becomes Christian 45.3; 48.3–4; a luminary 74.2; also mentioned 47.5; 49.1,3; 50.3; 97.4
Edwin, s. of K. Edward the Elder (d. 933) 126.2; 139.3–140
Edwin, br. of Morcar earl of Northumbria (d. 1071) 228.9; 247.2; 252
Egypt, Egyptians 189.2; 367.4; 368.3; 371.1
Eilaf, Swedish king, worsted by K. Cnut (1025) 181.6
Eilmer, *see* Æthelmær
Eisc (*otherwise* Oisc, Æsc), k. of Kent (488–?512) 8.4
Elcwold, *see* Ælfwald
Elesa, f. of K. Cerdic 116.1
Eleutherius, pope (*c.* 174–89) 19.3
Elisha, prophet 356.4
Elmham (Norfolk) 102; 300.1,3; 339.1; bishops of, *see* Alhheard, Herfast, Stigand
Ely (Cambs.), diocese of 102; 445.3; monastery of St Peter and St Æthelthryth 149.4; 188.5; 214.3; 298.8; 445.3; bishop of, *see* Hervey; abbots of, *see* Richard, Thurstan
Emma, w. of K. Eadbald 11.1
Emma, w. of K. Æthelred the Unready and K. Cnut (d. 1052): parentage and marriage to K. Æthelred 165.12–13; sent to Normandy 177.6–178.1; sent to Flanders 188.2; marriage to K. Cnut 180.11; 181.3; 196.4; treatment by K. Edward the Confessor 196.3–4; children 180.10; 188.1,7; 228.2; prodigality 181.5; also mentioned 179.5

England, English, *passim* (*for William's use of Anglia see Commentary on 121.3*): English words, language and style of writing i pr. 4; 20.1; 31.2; 49.4; 60.2; 68.3; 114.2; 122.4; 123.1–3; 153.2; 179.5; 183.8; 211.2; Anglo-Saxons 124.1 (Aa); Schola Anglorum in Rome 96.2; 109; 137.1; characteristics of the English: credulity 124.2, dislike of superiors 198, moustaches 239.2, drunkenness 245.4–5; 255.1 (cf. 241), do not like being called *Nithing* 306.8, more cultivated than the Irish 409.1; contrasted with Normans 198; 228.12; iii pr. 1; 236.2; 241; 245.5; 397.1; *Anglo-Saxon Chronicle* alluded to i pr. 2; 8.4–9.1; 15.2(?); 22.1; 29.3; 33; ii pr. 2; 115; 148.2; 188.5; *Gesta Anglorum, see* Bede; kings of, *see* Æthelred the Unready, Æthelstan, Cnut, Eadred, Eadwig, Edgar I and II, Edmund I and II, Edward I and II, Harold I and II, Harthacnut, Henry I, Swein Forkbeard, William I and II; *see also* Angles
Eni, f. of K. Anna 97.4
Ennius, Roman poet (239–169 BC) 206.2
Eohric, Danish k. of E. Angles (d. 905) 97.6
Eoppa, ancestor of K. Æthelwulf 116.1
Eormenburh, w. of K. Merewald 76.2; 215
Eormenhild, d. of K. Earconberht 76.2; 214.3
Eormenred, br. of K. Earconberht 12 (B); 76.2; 209.1; 215
Eormenric, k. of Kent (?512–*c.* 560) 8.4; 9.1
Ephesus 225.2–4; 427.2
Epicureans 237.3
Eric I, k. of Denmark (1095–1103) 261.3
Eric Bloodaxe, k. at York (947–54) 146.1
Eric of Hlathir, earl of Northumbria under K. Cnut (1016–*c.* 1023) 180.3; 181.1,3
Ermenfrid, bp. of Sion (1055–84), papal legate 269.1
Ermengard, w. of Louis the Pious (d. 818) 110.1
Ermengard, w. of Lothar I 110.4
Esla, ancestor of K. Æthelwulf 116.1
Essex, East Saxons: Essex (Latin only in 103) 97.5; 103; 107.1; kingdom of i pr. 5; 97.1; 98; its extent 103; kings of 213.1, *see also* Offa, Sæberht, Sæweard, Seaxred, Sebbi, Selred, Sigeberht I and II, Sigeheard, Sigehere, Sledd, Swæfred, Swithhelm, Swithred
Ethel-, *see* Æthel-
Ethiopian(s) 121.6; 369.8; 377.4

INDEX 855

Eu (Seine-Mar.), counts of, *see* Gilbert, Robert, William
Eucherius, bp. of Lyon (*c.* 428–50) 367.1 (*but the work alluded to is not his*)
Eudo (*see Commentary*) 236.3
Eugenia, w. of Lucianus 205.1 (Aa)
Euphorbus, Trojan 320.4
Euphrates, River 357.3; 374.4–5
Europe: 'third division of the world' 347.6; as opposed to Africa and/or Asia 92; 268.2; 355.2, to Britain 135.7; Constantinople on border of 355.2; Thrace a province of 355.2; 'uttermost' 372.1; praises K. Æthelstan 135.1; mounts Crusade 257.2 (cf. 344.1); European Christians 92 (cf. 314.1); approves of Hugh abbot of Cluny 265.3; brought honour by K. William I 283.1
Eusebius, church historian (d. *c.* 340) 374.5
Eustace II, count of Boulogne (*c.* 1047–*c.* 1092, but see *Commentary on 306.7*) 199.1–3; 373.1
Eustace III, count of Boulogne (*c.* 1092–*c.* 1125, but see *Commentary on 306.7*) 228.2; 306.7; 373.2; 374.1,9
Evander, f. of Pallas 206
Evesham (Worcs.) 212; abbot of, *see* Ælfwine
Évreux (Eure) 233.2
Exeter (Devon): Cornish driven from 134.6; burned by Danes 165.6; subdued by K. William I 248.1; seat of bishopric 100; 300.2; bishops of, *see* Osbern, William Warelwast
Exmes (Orne) 234.1
Eystein I, k. of Norway (1103–22) 260.2
Ezekiel 202.8

Falaise (Calvados) 389.9; 398.4 (also Cs)
Falernian wine, from Campania 373.4
Faramund, first k. of the Franks 68.2
Farndon (Cheshire) 133.1
Faustinianus 171.3
Fécamp (Seine-Mar.) 165.13; 178.1–4; 230.1; 268.1; 307.2; *see also* William de Ros, William of Volpiano
Felix, bp. of Dunwich (630/1–647/8) 97.3
Fernus, later name of R. Orontes 359.1
Fildas, *minister* of K. Cenwulf 88.9
Finan, bp. of Lindisfarne (651–61) 98.2
Finn, ancestor of Woden 116.1
Firmicus Maternus, Julius, author of astrological treatise (wr. 334–7) 167.2
Flanders, Flemish, Flemings: as place of exile 147.2; 188.2; 199.7; 200.3 (cf. 228.9); William Fitz Osbern in 256.2–5; Flemings settled in Wales 311.1; 401.1; in Crusades 350.1; bad effect on English 148.3; good looks of Earl Robert derived from 446.2; also mentioned 373.2; 403.2; counts of 123.5, *see also* Arnulf I and III, Baldwin II, V, VI and VII, Charles the Good, Robert I and II
Fleury, monastery (Saint-Benoît-sur-Loire, Loiret) 149.5; 167.1; 404.2
Florence, bishop of, *see* Nicholas II
Floris I, count of Holland (1049–61) 373.1
Fontenay (-en-Puisaye, Yonne), battle of 110.3
Fontevrault (mod. Fontevraud, Maine-et-Loire), nunnery 404.2; 440.1
Formosus, pope (891–6) 128.2–129.1
France (*W.* uses Frantia *geographically from the eighth century on, passim*); western half of 110.2; as opposed to Normandy 145.4; 232.3; 233.3–234.1; 282.1; 283.2; 397.1; 404.1; 'the region now properly called France' 68.8; *W. normally speaks of kings* 'of the French'; *but* 'in France' 128.2, 257.1, 'of France' 168.2, 407.2, 419.2; lineage of kings 67–8; 112; kings of, *see* Henry I, Hugh Capet, Louis VI, Philip I, Robert I; *see also* Gaul
Franks (*used in the translation conventionally to c. 950, and later of French crusaders; note* 92 '*Franks and European Christians of every kind*'), Frankish, French *passim*: Franks across the Rhine properly so called 68.1; Austrasian 110.5; West 110.6; 350.1; early 9; name and origin 68.1; language 68.3; history of sketched 68; apostle of 111.9; effect of education among 97.2; seemly dress of Frankish clerks 82.2; polish and warlike character of 106.2; lifestyle of French and Normans 245.5, of French and English in Ireland 409.1; Earl Robert gets noble character from 446.2; severance of kingdom of French and empire of Romans 112; inherit Roman rule 360.2; rulers of, unnamed, 9.1; 11.1, *see also* Carloman, Charles k. of Provence, Charles the Bald, Charles the Fat, Charles Martel, Charles the Simple, Charlemagne, Chlotar II, Dagobert, Faramund, Lothar I and II, Louis the Pious, Louis II, III and IV, Louis the Stammerer, Merovech, Pippin I, II and III, Theuderic III

Frealaf, ancestor of Woden 116.1
Freawine, ancestor of K. Æthelwulf 116.1
Freculf of Lisieux, historian (d. c. 853) 19.4
Fredegar (*elsewhere* Frithogar etc.), ancestor of K. Æthelwulf 116.1
Frederick, abt. of St Albans (c. 1072) 298.8
Frederick, archbp. of Cologne (1100–31) 422.2; 437.3
Frederick, count (*fl.* 1111; *see Commentary*) 422.2
Frederick I von Somerschenburg, count palatine of Saxony (*fl.* 1111) 422.2
Frederick, duke of Swabia (*fl.* 1122) 437.3
Frideswide, St, church of at Oxford 179.4
Fridewald, f. of Woden (*elsewhere* Frithowald) 116.1
Frig, w. of Woden 5.3
Frisia, Frisian(s) 91.1; 256.3; 349.1; 373.1; *see also* Robert I the Frisian
Frithestan, bp. of Winchester (909–932/3) 129.3
Fulbert, bp. of Chartres (1006–28) 186; 285
Fulcher of Chartres, historian of first Crusade (1059–c. 1127) 374.1
Fulda, monastery (Saxony) 192.1; 292.1; 293; 437.3
Fulk III Nerra, count of Anjou (987–1040) 235.1–3
Fulk IV Rechin, count of Anjou (1067–1109) 235.5–6; 257.1
Fulk V, count of Anjou (1106–29), k. of Jerusalem (1131–43) 235.6; 405.4; 419.1–2, 8
Fulk, archbp. of Reims (883–900) 122.3 (Aa)

Gabriel, lord of Melitene (d. 1103) 375.2
Gaeta (Lazio) 431.4; *see also* Gelasius
Gaius, bp. of Jerusalem (c. 160) 368.1
Galatia (now central Turkey) 347.4
Galicia (Spain) 167.2; king of, *see* Alfonso VI
Gall, St 192.1
Galloway 287.1
Galo, bp. of Saint-Pol-de-Léon (1108–29) 429
Galwalas, Gauls 68.1
Gargara, peak in the Troad 355.2
Garonne, River 233.1; 349.1
Gascony, Gascons 110.2; 349.2
Gaul (*William employs* Gallia (*normally sing., occasionally plur.*) *for all periods, including his own, though less frequently than* Frantia (*for his usage see s.v.* France). *Only selected refs. are given.*): part inhabited by Normans 5.2 (cf. 127.1); horn of 134.6; Celtic and Belgian 233.1; in the Roman period 1.2; 2.1; Bretons settled in 1.2; seized by Franks 68.1
Gauls, Gaulish (*for* Galwalas *see* 68.1): allies of Caesar 254.1; pride in learning 59.1; preached to by St Philip 19.4; brilliant style 31.2; Gallican bishops 414.4
Gauts (people of S. Sweden) 259.2; *see also* Goths
Gawain, nephew of K. Arthur 287
Geat, ancestor of Woden 116.1
Gebhard I, bp. of Trento (1106–20) 422.2
Gelasius II, pope (1118–19), formerly John of Gaeta, cardinal deacon of S. Maria in Schola Graeca 421.2; 430–432.1
Genoa (Liguria) 380.1; 388.10; 432.1
Geoffrey III the Bearded, count of Anjou (1060–7) 235.4
Geoffrey, bp. of Coutances (1049–93) 298.7; 306.2,4
Geoffrey II Martel, count of Anjou (1040–60) 230.6–231; 233.3; 235.1, 4; dealings with his father Fulk 235.2; burns Le Mans 236.1; death 234.2
Geoffrey IV Martel, count of Anjou (1103–6) 235.6
Geoffrey Rufus, chancellor of K. Henry I (?1123–33), bp. of Durham (1133–41) 398.4 (Cs)
Geoffrey, abt. of St Peter's, Westminster (c. 1072) 298.8
Geoffrey, bp. of Siena (1085–1127) 429
Geoffrey, count of Vendôme (d. 1102) 384.4
George, St 365.3; 366.3; Arm of (Sea of Marmora and Bosphorus) 347.4
Gerard de Blavia, bp. of Angoulême (1101–36) 426; 427.3; 429; 439.2
Gerard, archbp. of York (1100–8) 417.1 (cf. 415.1–2, 416.3–4)
Gerberoi (Oise) 258.2
Gerbert = Pope Silvester II (999–1003), prev. archbp. of Reims (991–8) and Ravenna (998–9) 167–9 (cf. 170.3); 172
Germans: in time of Caesar 254.1; invited to Britain 5.1; in Robert Guiscard's epitaph (*Lemannus*) 262.6; obstinacy of 192.2
Germanus, St, of Auxerre 22.1; 121.7–9
Germany: etymology of name 5.1; source of Angles, Saxons and Jutes 4.2; 5.1 (cf. 5.3); 7.3 (cf. 16.1); source of Franks and English 68.3; Lotharingia part of 110.1; Scandza part of 116.2; Franks seize 68.1;

also mentioned 80.1; 286.1; 350.2; kings and emperors of, *see* Arnulf, Conrad I and II, Henry I, III, IV and V, Otto I, II and III, *see also* Louis the German; *see also* Alemannia, Teutons
Gertrude of Saxony, w. of Floris I count of Holland, then of Robert I the Frisian (m. 1063) 256.3; 373.1
Gewis, ancestor of K. Æthelwulf 116.1
Gewisse, i.e. W. Saxons 129.1–2
Giferth (*elsewhere* Siferth), k. (*fl.* 973) 148.2
Gilbert, count (of Brionne or Eu) (d. 1040/1) 230.1–2
Gilbert, relative of Walcher bp. of Durham (d. 1080) 271
Gilbert of Minières (*fl.* 1127) 398.4 (Cs)
Gildas, historian (*fl. c.* 540) 20.1; 70.4
Gillingham (Dorset) 180.4. (Kent) 188.5 (*see* Commentary); 197.1
Girmund, abt. of Winchcombe (1095–1122) 398.4 (Cs)
Gisela, d. of Charles the Simple 112.1; 236.3
Giso, bp. of Wells (1060/1–1088) 298.6
Glamorgan, bishop of, *see* Urban
Glastonbury (Somerset): history of summarized 19.3–29.1; 'ancient city' 39.1; Old (wattle, then wooden) Church (St Mary's) 19.4–21; 22.3–23; 25.1–2; 26–8; 35C.3; 36C.1–8; 39.2; 143.1–2, 4; 184.2; 185.4 (also called 'the larger church' 24, 28); church of the Holy Apostles ('an appendage of the Old Church') 35C.3; 'another church' built by St David 25.3; the pyramids 21; William's book *De Antiquitate* ... 20.3; 35.3 (B); 50.5 (C); benefactions to 27; 29.1; 35C.3; 38; 142; 149.7; 184.2; charters concerning 36C; 39; 143; 150C.1–6 (cf. 150B.1–3); 185; papal letter concerning 150B.5–7; 150C.7–151C; relics 20.2; 23; 35C.3; 50.5 (with addition in C); 54.5; kings buried at 144.3; 160.1–2; 180.9; 184.2; visited by Brihtwold 221; riot at 270; monks of 22.2; 149.4; 184.2; prior of, *see* Ælfheah; abbots of, *see* Ælfweard, Æthelnoth, Æthelweard, Benignus, Berhtwald, Bregored, Dunstan, Hæmgils, Lademund, Patrick, Worgrez
Gloucester: early fate of 17.1; St Oswald's bones at 49.9; 125.5; K. Æthelstan dies at 140; St Peter's 125.5 (*where see* Commentary); 398.4 (Cs); 441.1; abbot of, *see* Serlo; under K. Cnut 180.8; council at 199.4–5;

visited by K. William I 279.2, by K. Malcolm III 311.2; earl of, *see* Robert; sheriff of, *see* Walter; *see also* Miles, Roger
Gloucestershire 101; 398.4 (Cs)
Goar, St 85
Godfrey 'abnepos nothus' of K. Baldwin I (d. 1113) 385.1
Godfrey II, duke of Lower Lorraine (grandfather of Godfrey of Bouillon) (*c.* 1047–69) 373.1
Godfrey III Bocard (= Hunchback), duke of Lower Lorraine (1069–76) 373.1–2
Godfrey IV of Bouillon, duke of Lower Lorraine, 'advocatus S. Sepulchri' (1087–1100): lineage and career summarized 373 (cf. 349.1); his father 199.1; early stages of Crusade 349.1 (cf. 373.5, 387.3); 357.4–5; at Antioch 365.2; 373.5–6; on route to and at Jerusalem 366.1; 369.7; 388.5; at Arsur 380.2; as king 370.2; 373.7; 374.9; at Ascalon 371.4; 388.6; praised 372.1; death 373.8; 376.1; also mentioned 374.1; 385.3
Godfrey, count of Calw (*fl.* 1111) 422.2
Godfrey, prior of St Swithun's, Winchester (1082–1107) 441; 444
Godgifu, sister of K. Edward the Confessor 199.1, 7
Godgifu, w. of Ealdorman Leofric 196.2; 341.1
Godgifu, nickname of Queen Matilda 394.1
Godney (Somerset) 36C.2; 150C.4
Godric, nickname of K. Henry I 394.1
Godwine, earl of Wessex (d. 1053): character 197.1 (cf. 5); in Sweden 181.6; and K. Harthacnut 188.5–6; and K. Edward the Confessor 196.2–3, 5–6; 197.1–2; 198; 199.2–9; exiled to Flanders 199.7 (cf. 196.3); and K. Harold I 188.1; and 'grant' of England to Duke William I 240.2; sons listed 200, referred to collectively 196.3, 6; 197.5; 199.9; 228.1 (cf. 241); death 197.6 (cf. 199.7)
Godwine (of Winchester), f. of Robert 251.2
Godwine, ancestor of Woden 116.1 (A)
Godwulf, ancestor of Woden 116.1
Golgotha, rock of (Jerusalem) 373.8
Gomorrah 377.3
Goscelin, hagiographer (*fl.* 1100) 342
Gothia 110.2
Goths 5.2; 116.2 (*see* Commentary); 167.1–2; 349.2; king of (Visigoths), *see* Reccared; *see also* Gauts

Gratian = Pope Gregory VI, q. v.
Greece (in Latin only 387.3), Greek(s): as opposed to Latins 12; 122.5, to Syrians 374.4; language 68.1; 122.5; 179.3; 189.1; 379.1; style and eloquence 31.2; 349.5; in Europe 262.4; 429; Eastern emperors listed 356.1–3 (first Greek 356.2); cf. 349.4; also mentioned 225.3
Gregory I, St, pope (590–604): sends Augustine to England 26; 88.7; 129.1; Angles and angels 45.1–2; lays down rules for English bishops 88.6; 89.6; 129.1; 295–6; miracle in Rome 286.1; his *Pastoral Care* 123.1–2; his *Dialogues* 122.4; 204.7; quoted 295; *Life* of 45.3; shrine of 425; also mentioned 167.1
Gregory II, pope (715–31) 36C.4
Gregory III, pope (731–41) 82.2
Gregory IV, pope (827–44) 114.4
Gregory V, pope (996–9) 167.1 (Aa)
Gregory VI, (formerly Gratian, 201.1) pope (1045–6) 201–3
Gregory VII, pope (1073–85), normally called Hildebrand: as archdeacon of Tours 284.2 (called archdeacon 263.3, 264.1); as chancellor 263.1; at a council in France 265; made pope 266.1; driven from Rome 262.3–4; 266.1 (cf. 373.3); wonderful powers 263–5; illness and death 266.2–3; 289.1; also mentioned 266.4; 427.2
Gregory, cardinal priest of SS. XII Apostoli (*rightly* Peter and Paul) (?–1112) 421.2
Gregory, cardinal priest of St Chrysogonus (?/1111–1113) 421.2
Gregory of Nazianzus, bp. of Sasima and Constantinople (329–89) 356.4
Gregory, bp. of Terracina (1106–26) 429
Grimbald, called abt. of New Minster, Winchester (d. 903) 122.3 (with Aa) (*see Commentary*); 123.3
Gruffydd ap Llywelyn ap Seisyll (d. 1063) 196.3 (*but see Commentary*); 228.8
Gruffydd ap Rhydderch (d. 1055) 196.3 (*but see Commentary*)
Guiscard, *see* Robert
Guitmund, bp. of Aversa (1088–?1095) 284.2
Gunnhild, d. of K. Cnut (d. 1038) 188.3, 7–8
Gunnhild, sister of K. Swein Forkbeard (d. 1002) 177.1
Guorongus, ruler of Kent (5c.) 7.2
Gurmund, *see* Guthrum

Guthfrith II, k. of Deira (927, d. 934) 134.2–3
Guthrum (*or* Gurmund) Danish k. of E. Angles (d. 889/90) 97.5–6; 121.5–6; 134.1; 141.2
Guy, archbp. of Vienne, *see* Calixtus
Guy, br. of count of Poitou (William V [VII duke of Aquitaine], 1039–58) 232.3 (*see Commentary*)
Guy I, count of Ponthieu (1053–1100) 228.4–5; 233.3
Guy, (half-) br. of Bohemond I 349.4
Guy of Burgundy, count of Brionne and Vernon, br. of William I count of Burgundy (pretender to Normandy 1047) 230.3–5
Gwala (*also* Hwala), ancestor of Woden 116.2
Gyrth, s. of Godwine 200.1; 239.3

Hadrian I, pope (772–95) 68.6; 87.2–3; 88.2,7–8; 93.2; 202.6
Hadrian, abt. of St Augustine's, Canterbury (d. 709/10) 12; 54.4
Hadrian (P. Aelius Hadrianus), Roman emperor (117–38) 367.1
Hædde, bp. of Winchester (676–?705) 36C.2; *see also* Hedde
Hæmgils, abt. of Glastonbury (c. 680–c. 705) 39.2
Hæsten, Viking leader (late 10c.) 121.7; 127.1; 145.4
Hagarenes, descendants of Hagar, i.e. Saracens 91.2; 225.4
Haifa 366.2; 376.9; 378.1
Haimo Dentatus (Longtooth) (d. 1047) 230.4–5
Hainault (region on mod. French/Belgian border) 257.1; count of, *see* Baldwin II
Hakim, Fatimid caliph of Egypt (996–1021) 368.4
Hakon, companion of K. Cnut IV 261.1
Hampshire 41; 100; 121.2
Hampstead (? Finchampstead) (Berks.) 331
Harding, s. of Eadnoth the Staller 254.2
Harding, *see* Stephen
Harewood, *see* Wherwell
Harold III, k. of Denmark (1074–80) 261.2
Harold Fairhair (Harfagri), k. of Norway (c. 880–930, d. 945) 135.1
Harold Fairhair (*properly* Harold III Hardrada, k. of Norway 1045–66) 228.9,11; 238.2; 252.2; 260

INDEX 859

Harold I Harefoot, k. of England (1035/6–40) 188.1–2, 4–5; 259.1
Harold II Godwinesson, k. of England (1066): summary of life 200.1; reduces Welsh 196.3; 199.1; 228.8; at his father's death 197.6; exile to Ireland 199.6–7; earldom (of Wessex) lost and restored 199.7; and Northumbrians 200.2–3; 252.1–2; and K. Magnus II 260.2; visit to Normandy 228.3–5; 236.2, to Brittany 228.5; 236.2; betrothal 228.5; 238.2–4; 276; seizes crown 228.7; right to it 238.1–4; 240.2; at Stamford Bridge 228.9–11; 239.1; 252.2; 260.1; at Hastings 228.11; 239.1–2; 240–1; 242.3–243; death 242.3; 267.3; burial 247.1; see also Harold his son; also mentioned 200.2; 225.1–3; 228.1; 238.7; 247.2; 252.3
Harold, s. of K. Harold II Godwinesson 260.2; 329
Harthacnut, k. of England (1040–2) and Denmark (from 1035) 188.1,3,5–7; 196.5; 259.1
Hastings (Sussex): Duke William lands at 238.10; 398.5; battle at described 239–44, reflected on 228.11–12; 245.1, alluded to 200.1; 245.5; 252.2; monastery of St Martin 267.3
Hathra (also Hrathra), ancestor of Woden 116.2
Hebron, nr. Jerusalem 377.2
Hebrus, river of Thrace (mod. Maritsa, Bulgaria) 355.2
Hedde, bp. named on pyramid at Glastonbury 21.3; see also Hædde
Hedeby (Schleswig-Holstein) 116.2 (see Commentary); see also Slaswic
Hegesippus, see Ambrose
Helena, mother of Constantine the Great 1.2; 352.8; 354.2; 356.4; 368.1
Helgrim, Norwegian ambassador to K. Æthelstan 135.1
Helias, count of Maine (1092–1109) 320.3
Hellendune (nr. Wroughton, Wilts.) 106.4
Hencgest, k. of Kent (c. 455–c. 488): lineage and arrival in Britain 5.3; and Britons 7–8; also mentioned 16.2; 44.1–2; 74.1; 287.1
Henry I, k. of England (1100–35): author's policy on iii pr. 3; v pr.; character iii pr.3; 411–12; hatred of indecency 314.5; upbringing 390; in Normandy 389.9; 391; 397–9; 408.1–2; 403.3–404.1; 405; 408.1–2; 411.4; 419.3; 446.2; kills Conan 392.4–5; at his father's burial 283.1; 391; inheritance 282.3; and Robert Curthose 310; 389.7,9–10; 391–2; 393.2; 394–5; 398.1–2,5; 405.1; 413.2; crowned 393.2; charters of 398.4 (Cs); difficulty of early reign 274.2; 395–6; Laws 399; 407.4; 411.2–3; and Welsh 311.1; 401; and Scots 400.1; and Irish 409.1; and Robert of Bellême 396–8; and the Church 398.3; 406; 413–7; 445.3; and the Continent 402–5; 410.1; his marriage 228.2; 393.3; 418.1; his children 419–420.1; his councillors 407–8; his zoo 409.2–3; also mentioned ep. ii.1 ('our king'); 68.8 (B); 235.6; 257.2; 274.1; 279.2; 305.2; 308; 342.2
Henry I, k. of France (1031–60): crowned 187; and Duke William 230.1–2, 4–6; 232.2–234; death 188.2; 225.5; 234.2; also mentioned 128.2; 258.1
Henry I the Fowler, k. of Germany (919–36) 112.2; 126.2; 135.1
Henry III, emperor (1039–56): conquests 189; humour 190–1; other stories about 192–194.1; marriage 188.7–8; death 225.5; 'epitaph' 194.2–3; also mentioned 195; 202.8–9; 262.3
Henry IV, emperor (1056–1106): his qualities 289.2; his folly 225.5; 288.1; and Wibert 262.3–4; 266.1; 289; 345.5; and Gregory VII 266.3; and Edgar the Ætheling 251.3; retirement and death 288.2 (cf. 266.4); also mentioned 290.1; 292.1; 420.1; 437.1
Henry V, emperor (1106–25): lineage 68.8; and the Church: generally 288, in time of Paschal 420–9, later 431–8; and Italy 373–3; 420.3; 430; 438; his wife 420.1; 438
Henry of Beaumont, earl of Warwick (1089–1119) 393.1; 394.1; 407.2
Heraclea (mod. Eregli, E. of Konya, Turkey) 358
Heraclius, emperor (610–41) 356.2; 368.2
Herbert (rightly Albert), abbot of Saint-Erard, bp. of Tripoli (1103/5–1115) 388.9
Herbert Losinga, abt. of Ramsey (1087–1090/1), bp. of Norwich (1090/1–1119) 300.3; 338–9; 417.1 (cf. 415.1–2, 416.3–4)
Herbert I 'Wake Dog', count of Maine (d. c. 1035) 235.1
Herbert II, count of Maine (1051–62) 236.1
Hereford(shire): visited by K. Æthelstan 134.5, by Earl Godwine 199.4; abandoned by Earl Ralph 199.1; William Fitz Osbern's laws for 256.2; cathedral 210; bishopric

Hereford(shire) (*cont.*)
101; 300.1; bishops of, *see* Reinhelm, Walter, Wulfheard; earls of, *see* Miles, Ralph, Roger, William Fitz Osbern; sheriff of, *see* Port

Hereman, bp. of Ramsbury-Sherborne (then Salisbury) (1045–78) 298.6; 342.1

Heremod, ancestor of Woden 116.2

Herfast, bp. of Elmham (1070–84) 298.7

Heribert, archbp. of Cologne (999–1021) 174.2

Herluin, viscount of Conteville, husband of Herleve mother of K. William I 277.1

Hermann, count of Winzenburg, marquis of Meissen (*fl.* 1111) 422.2

Hermann (*rightly* Henry), duke of Bavaria (*fl.* 1122) 437.3

Hermenigild, s. of Liuvigild k. of Visigoths (d. 585) 167.1

Herod the Great (d. 4 BC) 169.5; 374.5

Hertfordshire 101; 103

Hervey, bp. of Bangor (1092–1109), bp. of Ely (1109–31) 445.3

Hexham (Northumberland) 72.1; 104; 300.2; bishops of, *see* Acca, John of Beverley

Hezekiah 88.4

Hild, abbess of Whitby (d. 680) 35C.3; 50.4–5 (and C); 54.5

Hildebert, poet, bp. of Le Mans (1096–1125), archbp. of Tours (1125–33) 284.4; 285.1; 351.1; poems cited 284.5–9; 351.2–4

Hildebrand, *see* Gregory VII

Hildelith, abbess of Barking (*c*. 675–716/?) 36.1

Hinguar, killer of St Edmund 97.5; 213.2

Hispalis, *see* Seville

Hister, another name for the (Lower) Danube 355.4

Hiwingendes, name on pyramid at Glastonbury 21.2

Hlothhere, k. of Kent (673–85) 13

Holland, counts of, *see* Floris I, Theoderic V

Honorius, Flavius, Roman emperor (393–423) 2.2; 167.1

Honorius I, pope (625–38) 65.1

Horsa, br. of Hencgest 5.3; 8.1

Hubba, killer of St Edmund 213.2

Hubert, subdeacon and papal legate (?/1072–1080/?) 298.5–6

Hugh of Avranches, earl of Chester (1071–1101) 214.3; 260.2; 329; 397.3

Hugh Bardulf, lord of Nogent and Pithiviers (1026–58) 232.1

Hugh Capet, k. of France (987–96) 68.8; 128 (*see Commentary*); 168.1

Hugh, abt. of Cluny (1049–1109) 263–4; 265.3; 332

Hugh Falconberg of Saint-Omer, prince of Galilee (d. 1105) 384.6

Hugh of Gournay (*fl. c*. 1054) 233.2

Hugh of Grandmesnil (d. 1098?) 306.4

Hugh the Great, count of Paris (*c*. 895–956) 126.2; 135.2 (*see Commentary, as also on* 128)

Hugh the Great (Hugh of France), count of Vermandois, br. of K. Philip I (d. 1101): hired by K. William I 262.1; on Crusade 349.3; 357.4–5; 365.2; returns home 365.4; goes back East 383.1; dies 383.3; also mentioned 389.11

Hugh VI, count of Lusignan (d. 1102) 383.1; 384.4

Hugh, archbp. of Lyon (*c*. 1083/92–1106) 417.1

Hugh IV, count of Maine (1032/5–1051) 236.1–2

Hugh II of Montfort (?/1054–1089) 233.2

Hugh of Montgomery, earl of Shrewsbury (1094–8) 260.2; 306.7; 329

Hugh, s. of Robert count of Montdidier, heir of K. Louis IV (*see Commentary*) 128

Hugh Small 398.4 (Cs)

Hugh, count of Tours, father-in-law of Lothar I 110.4

Hugh, son of Waleran, count of Meulan (1069–80) 407.2

Hugh, *see* Rudolf

Humber, River 228.9; seen as boundary 97.1; 104; 141.1; 180.1; 228.9; 298.2; 300.2; 302.2

Huns 91.1; 110.2; 180.10; 228.1; Hunnish sword 93.2

Huntingdonshire 101

Hwicce, bps. of, *see* Ecgwine, Wærferth

Hyrcanus, high priest of Jerusalem (at time of siege in 135/4 BC) 169.4

Hywel ab Idwal (*see Commentary*) 148.2

Iago ab Idwal (the Bald), k. of Gwynedd (950–79) 148.2

Iconium (mod. Konya, Turkey) 358

Ida, k. of Bernicia (547–59) 7.3; 44.2–3; 46; 49.1; 53.2

Ida, mother of Godfrey IV (d. 1113) 373.1–2

INDEX

Idwal (Foel ab Anarawd, d. 942), Welsh k. 131.3; (Ieuaf, s. of former, d. 988) 155
Illyricum 344.1; 347.4
India 122.2
Indract, St 23; 35C.3
Ine, k. of W. Saxons (688–726): reign 35; Laws 35.3; visit to Rome 37; and Aldhelm 35.4–5; and Glastonbury 35.3; 35C.3–36C; 39.1; 143.2; 150B.3; 151C.1; 185.2; sisters and wife 36–7; descendants 106.1; 116.1; also mentioned 14.2; 38; 43.1; 77; 79
Ineswitrin (i.e. glassy island), old name for Glastonbury 27–8
Ingild, br. of K. Ine 35.5; 106.1; 116.1
Ireland, Irish: evangelized 22; 'Erin's sons' in epitaph 24; and Glastonbury 22.2–24; attacked by K. Oswiu 51.1; K. Magnus III killed in 260.1; refuge for exiles 52.1; 134.2 (cf. 141.1); 199.7; 254.2; slave-trade with 269.2; innocence 51.1; learning 52.1; general character 409.1; bishops of 300.2; king of, *see* Muirchertach; *see also* Brigid, David the Scot, Indract, John the Scot, Little Ireland, Marianus Scotus, Meildulf, Patrick
Isaac, patriarch 377.2
Isaiah, Book of 189.2
Isauria (S. Central Turkey) 347.4
Isembard, pagan under Louis IV (*see Commentary*) 128.1
Isembard (= Ingelram), count of Ponthieu (1052–3) 232.2
Isidore, St, bp. of Seville (599–636) 167.2; 409.3
Italy, Italian: 'still' occupied by Lombards 5.2; under Lombards 68.5; attacked by Huns 91.1; in Carolingian period 110.1,4,6; under Gregory VI 201.1; Robert Curthose in 274.1; subdued by Conrad 288.2 (cf. 420.2); in Crusade 349.2; and Countess Matilda 350.2; 373.2; and Henry V 420.2–3; 438; magic mountain in 170.1; morals of 80.4; duke of 145.2 (*see Commentary*); emperor of 168.3
Iudethil, Welsh k. (*fl.* 975) 148.2

Jabala, (mod. Jeble, S. of Laodicea) 374.7 (*where apparently thought to be a river*); 376.2
Jacob, patriarch 377.2; 420.3; 439.5
Jænberht, archbp. of Canterbury (765–92) 87.1,3; 88.7

Jaffa (part of mod. Tel-Aviv): K. Baldwin I at 376.9; 381.3; 384.5–6; kindness to Crusaders 377.1; 383.4; garrison of 378.1; as port 380.1; 384.5; also mentioned 384.1
James, br. of Our Lord, bp. of Jerusalem 356.4; 368.1
Jebusites 367.1
Jehoshaphat, valley of (in Jerusalem) 368.1; 369.2
Jericho 374.10
Jerome, St (d. 420) 189.2; iv pr. 4; 339.3
Jerusalem: various names of 367.1 (cf. 172.1); church so called in Rome 172; position and riches 367 (cf. 343); Church of Holy Sepulchre 367.3; 368.1, 4; 379.1; Holy Fire 367.3; 379; 383.4; Cross brought from 356.4 (cf. 371.2); in story about Gerbert 172; ravaged by Saracens 225.4; lost by Saracens 92; Crusaders hasten to 366.4; siege and fall 369–371.1 (cf. 374.6); later in Crusades e.g. 372.1; 374.9; 376.3; 377.1–2,5; 378.1; 380.1; 381.3; 383.1,4; 384.4–6; 385.1–3; 386; 388.8; 389.5 (cf. 403.2, 439.1); bishops and patriarchs of listed 368 (only those given further detail appear in the Index: Cyril I, Gaius, Jacob, Macarius I, Modestus, Nicephorus I, Orestes, Simeon, Simeon II, Sophronius I and II, Theodosius, Zacharias, *see also* Daimbert); high priest of, *see* Hyrcanus; kingdom of 373.7; kings of, *see* Baldwin I and II, Fulk V, Godfrey of Bouillon; *see also* David, Solomon; visits to by individuals: Bernard the Monk 367.3, K. Edgar II 251.2, K. Eric I 261.3, Fulk III count of Anjou 235.3, Fulk V count of Anjou 419.1, 8, Maurilius (in a vision) 268.2, Robert le Frisian 257.2, Robert I duke of Normandy 178.5; 180.11; 187.2; 229–230.1, K. Sigurd I 260.2; 410.1–2, Swein s. of Earl Godwine 200.2, William IV count of Toulouse 388.2; 'journey to Jerusalem' (or sim.) used of Crusade 277.3; iv pr. 5; 318.1; 333.7; 343; 348.3; 369.1; 373.4 (cf. 5); 374.1; 388.3; 389.3; 410.1
Jew(s), Jewish 135.4; 170.6; 286.2; 317
John, St, 60.2; 352.8; 443.1
John II, emperor (1118–43) 225.4
John VIII, pope (872–82) 110.6
John XI, pope (931–935/6) 137
John XII, *see* Octavian

John XIII, pope (965–72) 150B.4–5, 8–9; 150C.7; letters of 150B.6–7; 151C
John XV, pope (985–96), letter of 166. Confused with Gerbert 167.1,6 (corrected in Aa)
John XVI, pope (997–8) 167.1 (Aa)
John XIX, pope (1024–32) 183.2–4
John, cardinal priest of St Pudentiana (*fl.* 1111) 421.2
John, cardinal deacon of Schola Graeca, *see* Gelasius
John of Beverley, bp. of Hexham (687–706) 55.2
John I Chrysostom, patriarch of Constantinople (398–404, d. 407) 356.4
John of Gaeta, *see* Gelasius
John Gradenigo, patriarch of Venice (transferred see to Venice from Grado 1112) 429
John II de Marsico, bp. of Tusculum (1093–1112) 429
John the Old Saxon, abt. of Athelney under K. Alfred 122.3
John, s. of Robert the German priest 174.2
John the Scot (9c.) 122.5–6; 123.3
John of Villula, bp. of Wells (later Bath) (1088–1122) 338.1; 340
Jordan, River 268.2
Jordanes, historian of Goths (*c.* 550) 116.2
Joscelin I of Courtenay, count of Edessa, lord of Turbessel (1123–31) 386.2
Joseph, husband of Mary 368.1
Joseph, patriarch 377.3
Josephus (Flavius) (b. 37–8), Jewish historian 169.4–5; 367.1; 374.5; 376.9
Judaea 368.2–3
Judas 36C.9; 151C.2
Judith, w. of K. Æthelwulf (m. 856) and of K. Æthelbald his son 109; 113.1; 117; 126.1
Judith, w. of Louis the Pious (d. 843) 110.1
Judith, w. of Richard II duke of Normandy 178.5
Judith, niece of K. William I 253.2
Julius Caesar (100–44 BC) 1.1; 239.2; 254.1; 320.4; 351.2; 389.9
Jumièges (Seine-Mar.) 145.4; 197.4; 199.9
Justinian I, emperor (527–65) 356.1
Justus, archbp. of Canterbury (624–627/31) 296
Jutes 5.1,3

Kenelm, St, s. of K. Cenwulf (d. ?821) 95.3; 211–12
Kennet, River (Berks.) 413.1
Kenneth II, k. of Scots (971–95) 148.2; 156.1
Kent: as dowry of Vortigern's daughter 7.2; and Cadwallon 14.1; kingdom of i pr. 5; 9–15; 97.1; its extent 99; references elsewhere to relations with: Mercia 77; 87.1; 88.7; 95.1–2, Northumbria 44.1–2; 48.2, Wessex 17.1; 34.2; 35.2; 98.3; 106.4–107.1; 117; and Danes 108.1; 117; 165.5; 180.1; and Earl Godwine 199.3; ravaged by Odo 306.3; sees of 99; also mentioned 215; kings of (*called* reges Cantuariorum ,-itarum), *see* Æthelberht I and II, Alric, Baldred, Cuthred, Eadbald, Eadberht, Eadberht Præn, Eadric, Earconberht, Ecgberht I, Eisc, Eormenric, Guorongus, Hencgest, Hlothhere, Ohta, Wihtred; earldom of 397.2, *see* Odo
Kenten, br. of K. Ine 35.5
Kerbogha, *see* Corbaguath
Kidron, torrent in Jerusalem 367.2; 369.2
Kingston (-upon-Thames, Surrey) 131.1; 133.2
Konstanz (Baden) 437.3
Kuno, cardinal bishop of Palestrina (*c.* 1108–22) 429

La Cava, monastery near Salerno 434
Lademund, abt. of Glastonbury (6c.) 28
Lambeth (London) 188.3
Lamport (Northants.) 139.5 (B)
Landulf II, archbp. of Benevento (1108–19) 429
Lanfranc, archbp. of Canterbury (1070–89): panegyric on 267.2–3; 269.1; as abbot of Caen 267.2; and conspiracy of Waltheof 255.2; and slave-trade 269.2; and Berengar 284.2; influence with K. William I 269.2; and dispute over Æthelric 297; and dispute between York and Canterbury 298.1,3,5–6; 299.2; on precedence of bishops 301; in Rome 302; and K. William II 305.3; 306.3; 312.1
Langres (Haute-Marne) 54.5
Lanzo, monk of Cluny, prior of St Pancras (Lewes, Sussex) (1077–1107) 442–3
Laodicea (mod. Lattakieh, Syria) 374.7; 376.2; 380.1; 387.5; 388.8
Lateran, the seat of the popes in Rome 414.5; 427.1
Latin, allusions to speaking, writing, knowledge of etc. i pr. 1–2; 59.1; 60.2; 122.5; 123.3; 211.2; 267.2; 314.3; 347.6; 379.1; v pr. 1; alphabet 206.2

Latins 12; 122.5; 379.2
Laurence, archbp. of Canterbury (604/9–619) 10.1–2; 88.7
Laurence, St (d. 258) 193.2; gate and burial place of in Rome 352.7
Le Mans (Sarthe) 236.1; 320.1; *see also* Hildebert, Maine
Leah, d. of Laban, w. of Jacob 377.2; 439.5
Leander, bp. of Seville (579–99) 167.1–2
Leicester(shire) 87.3; 101; 300.1–2; 306.4; bishop of, *see* Wernberht; earl of, *see* Robert of Beaumont
Leigh in Street (Somerset) 36C.2
Leo III, pope (795–816) 68.7; letter to 87.3; 88; his reply 89
Leo IV, pope (847–55) 109; 121.1
Leo IX, pope (1048/9–54) 171.3; 194.3–195; 284.1–2
Leo, cardinal bp. of Ostia (1101–15) 423.2–3; 429
Leo, bp. of Trier (*rightly* Trevi) in 991 165.13; 166.1
Leo, cardinal deacon of St Vitalis (*rightly* SS. Vitus and Modestus) (*fl.* 1111) 421.2
Leofric, earl of Mercia (1023 × 1032–57) 196.2; 199.4 ('of Northumbrians'),7; 252.1; 341.1
Leofstan, desecrator of tomb of St Edmund 213.5
Leofstan, s. of Ælfwold (*fl.* 991) 166.2–3
Leofwine, dean of Durham (d. 1080) 271
Leofwine, s. of Earl Godwine 200.1
Leominster (Heref.) 196.2
Leonard, St 387.5
Le Puy (-en-Velay, Haute-Loire), bishop of, *see* Adhemar
Leuthere, bp. of W. Saxons (670–?/676) 29.2–30
Levenanus (*name uncertain*), archbp. (of Dol?) 138B.2
Lichfield (Staffs.) 79; 87.1–2; 101; 298.2; 300.1, 3; bishop of, *see* Aldwulf
Ligurians 262.6
Lillebonne (Seine-Mar.) 238.8
Limoges 388.2
Lincoln 49.8; 101; 223; 300.3; 445.3; bishop of, *see* Remigius
Lincolnshire 101
Lindisfarne (Northumberland); St Oswald's head buried at 49.8; K. Ceolwulf takes habit there 64; see of 104; and bishopric of Durham 298.2; 300.3; and archbishopric of York 300.2; bishops of, *see* Aidan, Cuthbert, Finan
Lindsey (district of Lincs.) 179.2; bishop of, *see* Eadwulf
Liofa, murderer of K. Edmund I 144.1
Little Ireland, estate at Glastonbury = Beckery, q.v.
Liudhard, Frankish bp. (*c.* 590) 9.2
Liulf (d. 1080) 271.2
Liuticii (branch of Slavs) 189
Logwor, name on pyramid at Glastonbury 21.2–3
Logworesburh (Montacute) 21.3
Loire, River 121.7; 138B.5
Lombardy, Lombard(s): 'still hold Italy' 5.2; tyrannize in Italy 68.5; 'marches against Slavs and Lombards' 110.5; Paul historian of 410.2; also mentioned 93.1; 388.3, 11; kings of, *see* Conrad, Desiderius
London, Londoners: and East Saxons 98.1; 103; and Mercians 98.3; 121.10; K. Edgar I signs a charter at 150B.8; 150.C7; and Danes 108.1; 165.3–4; 177.2–4; 180.1–5; 188.1; Danish cemetery 188.4; K. Edward the Confessor wears crown in 228.6; K. Harold II elected by 'Danes and citizens of London' 188.1; and K. William I 247.1–2; and K. William II 317; 321; and K. Henry I 393.2; 417.3; Jews in 317; tempest in 324; bishopric of 76.1; 87.2; 88.6; 103; 300.1; 301; churches 324 (*see also* St Paul); also mentioned 188.3; 199.6, 9; 252.2; 298.8; bishops of, *see* Cedd, Mellitus, Robert of Jumièges, Robert de Sigillo, Theodred, William, Wini
Lorraine 371.4; 373.2–3, 5; 418.6; dukes of, *see* Godfrey II, III and IV
Lothar I, k. (814–55, emperor from 817) 110.1,3–4; 111.7–10
Lothar II, k. (835–68) 110.4
Lotharingia, Lotharingians 68.1; 110.1; 271.1; 349.1
Louis the Blind (d. 928) (*see Commentary on 111*) 111.10–112.1
Louis the Child, k. of E. Franks (900–11) 112.1 (*see Commentary*)
Louis the German, k. of E. Franks (817–76) 110.1–3,5,8; 111.6–9
Louis the Pious, emperor (814–40) 68.7; 110.1–3,5
Louis, 'prince of Aquitaine' (*see Commentary on 126*) 126.3; 135.2

Louis II, s. of Lothar I (840–75, emperor from 850) 110.4; 111.7–8,10
Louis the Stammerer, s. of Charles the Bald (877–9) 110.7; 112.1; 126.1 (with Aa); 127.3
Louis III (d. 882) 110.5; 127.3 (*see Commentary on* 128)
Louis IV d'Outremer (936–54) 128 (*see Commentary*); 145.3
Louis VI the Fat, k. of France (1108–37) 68.8; 128.2; 257.1; 389.10; 405; 419.2
Louvain (in mod. Belgium) 418.6
Lucan, Roman poet (39–65) 320.4; 339.3; 360.2
Lucca (Toscana) 350.2; Face of (in oath of William Rufus) 309.2; 317 (T^{1}A); 320.3; bishop of, *see* Alexander II
Lucia, virgin 356.4
Lucianus, young Roman 205.1 (Aa)
Lucius, 'k. of the British' (*fl.* 167) 19.3
Ludeca, k. of Mercia (825–7) 96.1; 107.1
Ludgershall (Bucks.) 224.1
Luke, St 115; 356.4
Lull, archbp. of Mainz (754–86) 85
Lusitania (mod. Portugal) 167.2
Lycia (now S. Turkey) 225.4; 347.4
Lydia (now W. Turkey) 347.4
Lyfing, abt. of Tavistock (*c.* 1009–27), bp. of Crediton, Cornwall and Worcester (1027–46) 182; 188.6
Lyfing, archbp. of Canterbury (1013–20) 176; 184.1
Lyon (Rhône) 417.1; archbishop of, *see* Hugh; *see also* Eucherius

Macarius I, patriarch of Jerusalem (314–33) 368.1
Macbeth, k. of Scots (1040–57) 196.2
Maccabees 365.3
Macedonia, Macedonian 262.6; 344.1
Macrobius (*c.* 400) 168.1
Maeotis, Lake (Sea of Azov) 68.1
Magnus, St 174
Magnus I the Good, k. of Norway (1035–46) and the following two kings appear in an inextricably confused account at 259–60
Magnus II Haroldsson, k. of Norway (1066–9) 228.11
Magnus III Olafsson [Barelegs], k. of Norway (1095–1103) 329
Mahomet 189.1; 367.2
Maine 236.1–2; 258.1; 307.2–308; 389.4; 419.1,8; counts of, *see* Helias, Herbert I and II, Hugh IV
Mainz (Hesse) 192.1; 292.1; archbishops of, *see* Adalbert, Boniface, Lull
Majorca 410.1
Malcolm, king of Cumbrians (973–97) 148.2
Malcolm I, k. of Scots (943–54) 141.2
Malcolm II, k. of Scots (1005–34) 182
Malcolm III, k. of Scots (1058–93): installed by Siward 196.2; uses York as base 248.2; subdued by K. William I 249–50; and Edgar the Ætheling 251.1; and K. William II 311.2; marriage 228.1; 249.1; children 228.2; 393.3; 400; death 250.1; 311.2–3; 400.1
Malmesbury (Wilts.): foundation and early history of monastery 29.3–31; various depredations 87.3; 94.2; 108.3; 135.6; favoured by K. Ecgfrith 94.2, K. Æthelstan 135.6; 136–8; 138B.5; 140, K. Edgar I 152; 153.2; under K. Eadwig 147.3; translation of St Aldhelm 147.3; flight of Æthelmær (Eilmer) 225.6; letters from convent of ep. i–ii; St Peter's and St Mary's 138 (cf. 138B.1); also mentioned 122.6; 170.1; 179.5; 408.3; abbots of, *see* Ælfric, Cuthbert (*also* Æthelheard archbishop of Canterbury); *see also* Meildulf, William of Malmesbury
Malvern (Great, Worcs.), prior of, *see* Walcher
Maniches (*see Commentary on 225.3*) 225.3–4
Mantes (-la-Jolie, Yvelines) 282.1–2; *see also* Walter
Mantua (Lombardia) 438; *see also* Virgil
Marchey (Somerset) 36C.2; 150C.4
Marcigny (Saône-et-Loire) 276; 332.1
Margaret, w. of K. Malcolm III (m. *c.* 1069, d. 1093) 228.1–2; 249.1; 311.3; 400.3; 418.3
Marianus Scotus, Irish monk (d. 1082–3) 292.1
Marinus I, pope (882–4) 122.2
Mars, Field of (at Rome) 169.1
Martha, St 149.1; 439.5
Martin, duke, son of Chlodulf 68.4
Martin of Tours, St (d. 397): translated 121.7–9; monastery of: at Dover 15.1 (Aa), at Hastings 267.3, at Tours 69
Mary, St, mother of Christ: vision of seen: by Jewish boy 286.2, by Fulbert 285.1; image

INDEX   865

at battle of Badon 8.2, Winchcombe 323; her shift protects Chartres 127.2; revered by Lanzo 443.8; and Martha 149.1; 439.5; also mentioned (esp. in oaths, et sim.) 36C.6; 114.4; 150B.2, 7; 153.2; 179.1; 185.2–3; 196.1; 224.2; 311.3; 333.1; 423.1; 443.8; churches of, at Antioch 359.2, Chartres 186, Glastonbury (q.v.), Jumièges 199.9, London 324, Malmesbury 138.1 (and 138B.1); cf. ep. ii.1, Mantes 282.1, Rome 96.2, Rouen 268.3, Stow 196.2

Mary, d. of K. Malcolm III (d. 1115) 228.2

Mascusius, *archipirata* under K. Edgar I (*see* Commentary) 148.2

Matilda, countess of Tuscany (1046–1115) 274.1; 289.1; 350.2; 373.2; 388.3

Matilda, d. of K. Henry I, w. of Henry V (d. 1167) ep. i.3,7; ep. ii.1,3,7; 420.1; 438

Matilda, d. of K. Malcolm III, w. of K. Henry I (d. 1118): lineage 418.1; marriage 228.2; 393.3; 418.1; children 414.1, 5; 420.1; 438; and Robert Curthose 389.7; 395.2; favours Malmesbury and writing of *GR*: ep. i.3,5–7; ep. ii; i pr. 4 (Tt); character 418; also mentioned 398.4 (Cs); 416.4; 419.8

Matilda, w. of K. William I (m. *c.* 1050–1, d. 1083): parentage and relations 234.2; 256.3; 258.1; 401.1; character 234.2; dispute over marriage 267.5; treatment by K. William 273; also mentioned 298.6; 305.1; 391

Mattathias 202.10

Matthias, apostle 356.4

Mauger, archbp. of Rouen (*c.* 1037–*c.* 1054) 267.4–268.1

Maurice, St, leader of Theban legion 135.5

Maurice Bourdin (Bordinho), bp. of Braga (1111–14) 430; 431.3; 432.2; 433.2; 434

Maurilius, archbp. of Rouen (*c.* 1054–67) 268

Maworn, bp. (*fl.* 601) 27

Maximus, Magnus, Roman emperor (383–8) 2

Meare (Somerset) 24; 29.1; 36C.2; 150C.4

Medway, River (Kent) 180.6

Meildulfesburh, i.e. Malmesbury 30

Meildulf (Maeldubh), founder of Malmesbury 29.3

Melchizedek 367.1

Melitene (mod. Malatya, Turkey) 375.2

Mellitus, bp. of London (604–17) 98.1–2

Menevia (St David's), *see* David

Merchelm, s. of K. Penda 74.3

Mercia (*used only three times by W.*: 122.4; 180.5,9), Mercians: extent of 101; London capital of 121.10; southern 75; kingdom of i pr. 5; 73.2–96; 125.1; references elsewhere to relations with E. Anglia 97.3–5; 107.1 (*see also* Angles, East), E. Saxons, 98.1,3, Kent 15.2–3 (*see also* Kent), Northumbria 48.4; 49.6, 8; 50.3; 51.2 (*see also* Northumbria), Wessex 18.1; 19.1; 33; 34.2; 40; 42.1; 43.1; 106.1–2,4; 107.1; 108.1; 120.1; 122.4; 125.1 (*see also* Wessex); and Danes 120; in time of K. Cnut 180.1, 3, 5, 9; 181.1; patrician of 70.4; bishop(s) of 87.2; 88.7; 101; 129.3; 300.1; *see also* Hwicce; monasteries in 161.2; kings of, descent from Woden 44.3; kings of, *see* Æthelbald, Æthelred I and II, Beornred, Beornwulf, Berhtwulf, Burgred, Cenred, Cenwulf, Ceolred, Ceolwulf I and II, Ecgfrith, Ludeca, Offa, Penda, Wiglaf, Wulfhere; *see also* Ælfhere, Eadric Streona, Leofric, Osberht

Merefin, s. of Merewald br. of Wulfhere k. of Mercia (late 7c.) 76.2

Merewald, s. of K. Penda 74.3; 76.2; 215

Merovech, head of the Merovingian dynasty (5c.) 68.2

Merovings 68.2–3

Mesopotamia (Syrian), used of Edessa region 374.1, 3–4

Metz (Moselle), bishops of, *see* Arnulf, Chlodulf

Meulan (Yvelines) 407.2; counts of, *see* Hugh son of Waleran, Robert of Beaumont, Waleran I

Mevanian Isles, *see* Anglesey

Michael, archangel 114.4

Michael I, patriarch of Alexandria (860–70) 368.3

Michael VII Ducas Parapinakes, emperor (1071–8) 225.4; 356.3 (out of sequence)

Milan 336.3; 431.2; 438; bishop of, *see* Ambrose

Mildburh, St, nun of Wenlock 76.2; 215–6

Mildred, St, sister of Merefin 76.2; 215

Mildred (*properly* Mildgyth), sister of Merefin 76.2

Miles of Gloucester, earl of Hereford (1141–3) 398.4 (Cs)

Milton (Abbas, Dorset) 138B.5

Milvian Bridge, Rome 352.3

Minorca 410.1

Modestus, patriarch of Jerusalem (632–633/4) 368.2
Moesia (in mod. Bulgaria) 355.2
Molesme (Yonne) 334.3 (cf. 335); 337.1
Moll, *see* Æthelwald
Monkwearmouth (Durham), monastery of 54.4; 55.1; 70.1; *see also* Benedict Biscop, Ceolfrith
Mont Cenis 110.6
Montacute (Somerset) 21.3
Montdidier (Somme), count of, *see* Robert
Monte Gargano (Puglia) 183.2
Montecassino (Lazio) 68.5; abbot of, *see* Victor III
Montferrat (Var), marquis of, *see* Boniface I
Montlhéry (Essonne) 110.8
Montpellier (Hérault) 388.5; count of, *see* William V
Mont-Saint-Michel (Manche) 308 (cf. 309–10); 392.5; 402
Moorlinch (Somerset) 36C.6; 150C.4; 151C.1
Morcar, earl of Northumberland (1065–71) 200.3; 228.9; 247.2; 248.2; 252
Morcar, thane of the Seven Boroughs (d. 1015) 179.4
Mortain (Manche), counts of 398.5; *see* Robert, William
Mortemer (Seine-Inférieure) 233.2
Moses 377.5; 427.2
Mouliherne (Maine-et-Loire) 230.6
Moulins (-la-Marche, Orne) 232.3
Muchelney, abbey (Somerset) 139.5 (B)
Muirchertach, Irish k. (1086–1119) 409.1
Mul, br. of K. Cædwalla (7c.) 14; 34.2; 35.2

Nablus (Neapolis, formerly Sichem, N. E. of Jaffa) 377.3
Nantes (Loire-Atl.) 236.3 (miracle there described in 237)
Narbonne (Aude), county of 388.2
Nebuchadnezzar 367.1
Nemetum, *civitas* = Speyer q.v. 110.2
Neustria 110.2; *see also* Ebroin
New Forest (Hants.) 275
Nicaea (mod. Iznik, Turkey): Council of 427.2; Duke Robert I dies there 178.6; 277.1; attacked and taken by Crusaders 349.6; 357.1–2; 369.1; Suleiman avenges loss of 383.2; also mentioned 357.6–358
Nicephorus I, patriarch of Jerusalem (1020–48) 368.4
Nicephorus III, *see* Botaniates

Nicholas II, formerly bp. of Florence (1046–58/9), pope (1058/9–61) 199.11; 225.5
Niels, k. of Denmark (1104–34) 261.3
Nigel II, viscount of the Cotentin (d. 1092) 230.4–5
Nimrod 371.1
Nineveh 226.2
Niort (Deux-Sèvres) 439.1
Nithing, villain (OE) 306.8
Noah 116.2
Nola, hill at Rome (the Quirinal?) 352.13
Norfolk 102; earl of, *see* Ralph of Gael
Norica ('otherwise Bavaria') 110.2,5,8; *see also* Bavaria
Normandy (*selected refs. only*): name 5.2; 127.1; 138B.5; given to Rollo 112.1; 127.1; relics from 138B.5; K. Æthelred the Unready and his family in 178.1; 180.10; 181.3; 188.1–2; 196.5; 221–2; 226.1; portent interpreted as bearing on relation of with England 207.1–2; visit of Harold Godwinesson 228.3–5; 236.2; under William as duke and king, *see* William, II duke of Normandy; under K. William II, *see that entry*; and Robert Curthose, *see* Robert II Curthose; and K. Henry I, *see that entry*; homage for to France 405.4; 419.2–3; law of 297 (Aa); characterized 397.1; dukes of, *see* Richard I, II and III, Robert I and II, William II, William Longsword
Normans (*selected refs. only*): coming of to England i. pr. 6; 15.4; ii pr. 3; 216; 245.3; 246.2; ravages of in the north 54.2; 'in the time of' 125.5 (Aa); in Apulia 262.2–3; in Sicily 92; treatment under K. Edward the Confessor 197.4–5; 199.9; military usages of 236.2; 241; 395.1 (cf. 446.2); character and attitudes 228.12; iii pr. 1; 245.5–246; 253.2; 254.3–255.1; contrasted with English, *see* England; and Angevins 231.4; contempt for in Exeter 248.1; language 303.2
Northamptonshire 101
Northmen 110.7; 127.1, 3–4; 138B.5
Northumbria, Northumbrians: name 7.3; description of 54.2; extent of 104; provinces of 45.2; 49.1; Bede's concern with 47.1; royal line 7.3; 44.3; kingdom of i pr. 5; 44–73; references elsewhere to relations with E. Saxons 98.2, Kent 9.1 (cf. 44.2) (*see also* Kent), Mercia 74.2–3; 77 (*see also*

Mercia), Wessex 18.2; 36.1; 107.2; 120.1; 121.11; 125.1 (*see also* Wessex), *see also* Angles, East; under K. Æthelstan 131.3; 134.1; 141.1, K. Edmund I 141, K. Eadred 146.1, K. Edmund II 179.5; and Danes 120; 121.6,11; 125.1; 165.3; 177.2; 180.3; 181.1; 213.2; under: K. Edward the Confessor 200.2–3; 252.1, K. William II 319.1; pride and stubbornness of 44.2; 48.1; 271.1, 3; as slavers 45.1; monks at Selsey 208.1; sees of 104; also mentioned 43.2; 247.2; kings of, *see* Ælfwald I, Æthelred I, Æthelwald Moll, Aldfrith, Alhred, Cenred, Ceolwulf, Eadberht, Ecgfrith, Osberht, Osred I and II, Osric, Oswiu, Oswulf; earls of Northumbria (Northumberland after the Conquest), *see* Eric, Morcar, Robert of Mowbray, Siward, Tostig, Uhtred, Waltheof; other rulers in, *see* Edwin, Eric Bloodaxe, Leofric, Rægnald, Sigeferth, Sihtric

Northwalians, 'that is, the Northern Britons' 134.5

Norway, Norwegian(s): history of 258.3–260; subdued by Earl Godwine 181.6; attack on England in 1066 228.9–11; 238.2; 239.1; 252.2; driven off under K. William II 329; and the Orkneys 260.3; 329; 409.2; Norwegian gold 410.3; eaters of raw fish 348.2; jarls 131.7; also mentioned 127.1; 131.7; kings of 127.1. *See* Anlaf, Cnut, Eystein I, Harold Fairhair, Magnus I, II and III, Olaf II and III, Sigurd I, Swein Cnutsson

Norwich (Norfolk): busy and populous 339.1; Ralph of Gael takes ship at 255.3; see 102; 300.3; 338.1; 339.1; monastery 339.2–3; also mentioned 306.4; bishop of, *see* Herbert Losinga

Nottinghamshire 101

Novara (Piemonte) 438

Nyland (*Ætheresig*) (Somerset) 36C.2; 150C.4

Octavian = the Emperor Augustus (q.v.) 170.1

Octavian = Pope John XII (955–64) 150B.4

Oda, archbp. of Canterbury (941–58) 147.2; 149.5

Odda, earl in w. country (d. 1056) 199.8

Odilo, abt. of Cluny (994–1048) 443.7–8

Odo, bp. of Bayeux, earl of Kent (d. 1097) 277; 298.7; 306.1–3, 6–9; 397.2

Odo, abt. of Cluny (927–42) 443.7–8

Odo, br. of K. Henry I of France 233.1–2

Odo, s. of K. Robert the Pious 187.1

Odo, *see* Urban, William son of Odo

Offa, k. of E. Saxons (abd. 709) 98.3

Offa, k. of Mercia (757–96): reign of 86–94.1; defeats K. Cynewulf 42.1; and E. Angles 96.1; and Kent 88.7; 95.2; and K. Ecgberht 106.1; kills K. Æthelberht 86; 97.5; 210, K. Beornred 79; and Church 87.1,3; 94.2; splits province of Canterbury 88.7–8; and Charlemagne 90; 91.2; 92–94.1; letters from Alcuin 70.2; 72.3; and Schola Anglorum 109; marriage of daughter 43.1; 90; 106.2; 113.2 (cf. 210)

Ohta, br. of Hencgest (5c.) 44.1; 287.1

Ohta, k. of Kent (from 512) 8.4

Olaf II Haraldsson, St, k. of Norway (1012–30) 181.6; 259.1; 260.1

Olaf the Hungry, k. of Denmark (1086–95) 261.2–3

Olaf III Kyrre, k. of Norway (1067–93) 260.1

Olaf, *see* Anlaf

Ordgar, ealdorman of Devon (10c.) 157; 159.2

Ordmær, father-in-law of K. Edgar I 159.2

Orestes, patriarch of Jerusalem (986–1006) 368.4

Orkneys, Orkney Islands: Angles make for 7.3; obey K. Edwin 48.3; conquered by K. Magnus III 260.2 (*see Commentary*); 329; subject to Norway 409.2; bishop of 300.2; earl of, *see* Paul

Orléans (Loiret) 168.1; 204.7

Orne, River (Orne, Sarthe) 230.4

Orontes, River (mod. Asi) 359.1

Orosius, historian (early 5c.) 123.1

Orpheus 369.9

Osberht, ealdorman of Mercia (*c*. 800) 70.4; 94.2

Osberht, k. of Northumbria (d. 867) 120.2

Osbern of Canterbury, writer and musician (d. after 1087) 149.3; 342.1

Osbern Fitz Osbern, bp. of Exeter (1072–1103) 298.7

Osbjorn, br. of K. Swein II 261.1

Osecg (*elsewhere* Bagsecg), Danish k. killed in Battle of Ashdown 119.2

Osfrith, Norwegian ambassador to K. Æthelstan 135.1

Osmund, bp. of Salisbury (1078–99) 319.2; 325
Osred I, k. of Northumbria (705/6–716) 53.1; 80.5
Osred II, k. of Northumbria (788–90) 72.2
Osric, ealdorman under K. Cynewulf 42.3
Osric, k. of Deira (633–4) 49.1; 50.1
Osric, k. of Northumbria (718–29) 53.1
Osthryth, d. of K. Oswiu (d. 697) 49.8; 77
Ostia (Lazio), road and gate leading to 352.11; bishops of, *see* Leo, Urban
Oswald, St, k. of Bernicia (634–42) 47.5; 49; 50.1,3; 74.2–3; 97.4; 125.5; 208
Oswald, member of royal family of W. Saxons (d. 730) 38
Oswald, St, bp. of Worcester (961–92, also archbp. of York from 971) 149.5–6; 150C.2; 209.2; 303.2
Oswen, holy woman 213.5
Oswine, k. of Deira (644–51) 50.1–2
Oswiu, k. of Bernicia and then Northumbria (642–70): flight and return 47.5; 49.1; reign 50.1–4; and Mercia 50.3; 74.3–75; kills K. Æthelhere 97.4; and relics of K. Oswald 49.7–8; also mentioned 51.1; 52.2; 98.2
Oswulf, k. of Northumbria (?757–?758) 72.1
Otbert, of Saxony, dances for a year 174
Otbert (*rightly* Otto) of Wittelsbach, count palatine of Bavaria (*fl.* 1122) 437.3
Otranto (Apulia) 429
Otto I the Great, emperor (962–73) 68.8; 112.2; 126.2; 135.1
Otto II, emperor (967–83) 168.1
Otto III, emperor (996–1003) 168.1,3
Otuel, br. of Richard earl of Chester (d. 1120) 419.7
Owain, k. of Strathclyde (= Cumbrians) (d. *c.* 937) 134.2
Oxford, Oxfordshire 10.1; 177.2; 179.4; 188.2

Palestrina (Lazio), bishop of, *see* Kuno
Pallas, s. of Evander 206
Pallig, Danish jarl (d. 1002) 177.1
Palumbus, priest 205.3,6
Pamphylia (now S. Turkey) 347.4
Panborough (Somerset) 150C.4
Pancras, St, his church in Rome 352.12; his monastery at Lewes (Sussex) 442 (cf. 443), prior of, *see* Lanzo
Pannonia (north of Dalmatia) 349.1
Paris 121.7; 145.4; count of, *see* Hugh the Great
Parthians 262.6
Paschal II, pope (1099–1118): installed 289.1; and Anselm 415–417.2; and K. Henry I 398.3; 413.2–414; and Henry V 420; documents in quarrel with Henry V 421–2; 424; 427–9; excommunicates Maurice Bourdin 431.3; death 430; also mentioned 261.3; 341.1; 439.6
Paschasius = Radbert abt. of Corbie (*c.* 845) 286.1
Paternus, St 138B.3–5
Patrick, St 22; 24; 25.3
Paul, St (d. *c.* 65), associated with St Peter (esp. in Rome) 36C.6; 55.1; 58.2; 89.1; 113.4; 150B.7; 151C.2; 153.2; 183.1; 208.1–2; 437.1; alone 359.2; 374.2; 427.2; churches or monasteries at: Cormery 66 (B), Jarrow 54.2 (cf. 55.1), London 180.3; 181.5; 213.4; 228.1; gate of at Rome 352.11
Paul the Deacon, historian of Lombards (d. ?797) 410.2
Paul, earl of the Orkneys (*c.* 1123–36) 409.2
Paul of Samosata (bp. of Antioch *c.* 260–8) 374.5
Paulinus, archbp. of York (625/6–633), bp. of Rochester (633–44) 26; 48.3; 65.1; 70.3
Pavia (Lombardia) 96.3; 145.2; 184.1; 438
Peada, s. of K. Penda (d. 656) 74.3–76.1
Pelagians 22.1
Penda, k. of Mercia (?626–55): reign 74 (cf. 96.3); and E. Angles 74.2; 97.3–4; and Northumbria 48.4; 49.6, 10; 50.3; 51.2; 74.2–3; and Wessex 18.1; 19.1–2; 74.2; children 51.2; 74.3–75; 76.2; 98.3; descendants 79; 86; 94.2
Pennard (Somerset) 36C.2
Penne, hill (?Penselwood, Somerset) 19.2
Penselwood (Somerset) 180.4
Perche (Orne), countess of = Matilda, illegitimate d. of K. Henry I (d. 1120) 419.5,7
Pershore (Worcs.) 217.2; 219
Persia, Persian(s) 309.2; 360; 364; 368.2; kings of, *see* Cambyses, Chosroes II, Cyrus
Persius, Latin poet (d. 62) 306.3
Peter, St, apostle, often associated with St Paul, q.v.: alone (often in connection with papacy) 19.3; 89.1, 5; 109; 111.7,9; 114.4; 129.1; 137; 150B.8–9; 151C.2; 166.2; 183.2,8; 201.2, 4; 221; 266.2; 296–7; 338.2; 347.9; 359.2; 413.2; 415.3; 433.1; 437.1;

churches or monasteries of, at: Antioch 359.2, Canterbury 88.7, Gloucester 125.5, 398.4 (Cs), Malmesbury 138.1, Monkwearmouth 54.2 (cf. 55.1), Muchelney 139.5(B), Rome 68.7; 201.5–6 (cf. 203); 211.1; 352.2; 435.1,Westminster 298.8, Winchester 114.4, York 70.3; gate of at Rome 352.2
Peter Damiani, Italian cardinal and poet (1007–72) 171.3
Peter the Hermit (d. 1115) 349.6; 364.2–365.1
Peter II, bp. of Poitiers (1087–1115) 439.3; 440.1
Peter, cardinal bp. of Porto (?/1102–1130/?) 421.2; 423.2; 429
Peterborough (Northants.) 149.4; abbot of, 177.7, see also Turold
Pevensey (Sussex) 306.7
Philip, St, apostle 19.4
Philip the Clerk, s. of Roger of Montgomery 389.4–5
Philip I, k. of France (1060–1108): lineage 128.2; minority 188.2; 234.2; and Robert I of Flanders 257.1; and K. William I 258.1–2; 281; and Robert Curthose 258.2; 274.1; 307.1; and K. Henry I 404.1; first wife 257.1; and Bertrada of Montfort 235.5; 257.1; 345.5; 404; daughters 387.5; excommunication 345.5; 404; takes habit 404.2; also mentioned 256.3; 262.1; 349.3; 405.1
Phinehas 202.10
Phrygia (now W. Central Turkey) 347.4
Piacenza (Emilia-Romagna) 438
Picts 3.1; 7.3; 48.3; 51.2; 52.2
Pilgrim, archbp. of Cologne (1021–36) 174.2
Pilton (Somerset) 36C.1,6–7; 151C.1
Pippin I, k. of Aquitaine (797–838) 110.1–2
Pippin II, mayor in Austrasia (d. 714) 68.3–5
Pippin II, k. of Aquitaine (c. 838–64) 110.2–3
Pippin III, k. (751–68) 68.2 (B), 5–6
Pisa (Toscana), Pisans 92; 380.1; 388.10; 438; archbishop of, see Daimbert
Pisidia (now S. Turkey), see Antioch
Plato 237.3; 390.1; 449.1
Plegils, priest in Germany (c. 830) 286.1
Plegmund, archbp. of Canterbury (890–923) 123.3; 129.2
Pliny (the Elder, d. 79) 409.3
Poitiers (Vienne) 333.7; bishop of, see Peter II

Poitou, count of, see William VII; see also Roger
Polden Hill (Somerset) 36C.2,7
Pons, count of Tripoli (1112–37) 388.11; see also William count of Toulouse
Ponthieu (Somme) 128.1; 228.3; counts of, see Guy I, Isembard
Popes: see Alexander II, Benedict I and X, Boniface V, Calixtus II, Celestine I, Clement (bishop), Eleutherius, Formosus, Gelasius II, Gregory I–VII, Hadrian I, Honorius I, John VIII, XI–XIII, XV–XVI, XIX, Leo III–IV, IX, Marinus I, Nicholas II, Paschal II, Sergius I, Silvester I (bishop), II (see Gerbert), Stephen II and IX, Urban II, Victor II and III, Zacharias; see also Wibert
Populonia (Massa Marittima), bishop of, see Roland
Port, Adam de, sheriff of Herefordshire (c. 1111–23, d. c. 1138), his sons Roger and William, (another relation) Henry 398.4 (Cs)
Porto (Portus Romanus, Lazio), bishop of, see Peter
Portsmouth (Hants) 395.1
Préaux (Eure), monastery 407.1
Proteus 86
Provence 80.4; 110.4; 388.2; see also Charles, Raymond
Ptolemais, see Acre
Ptolemy, mathematician (1c.) 167.2
Pucklechurch (Glos.) 144.1
Pybba, f. of K. Penda 74.1
Pyrenees 349.2
Pythagoras of Samos, philosopher (6c. BC) 167.1; 320.4

Rachel, w. of Jacob 439.5
Radbod, prior of St Samson's Dol (fl. c. 927) 138B.2
Rædwald, k. of E. Angles (d. c. 620) 47.4–48.1; 97.1–2,4
Rægenhere, s. of K. Rædwald (d. 616) 47.5
Rægnald (Rognvald), regulus in Northumbria under K. Edmund I 141.2
Ralph of Escures, abt. of Séez, archbp. of Canterbury (1114–22) i pr. 3 (B); 396.2; 408.1; 445.2
Ralph, earl of Hereford (1049/55–1057) 199.1, 8
Ralph Mowin, murderer of Duke Robert I (1035) 178.6

Ralph of Gacé, cousin and murderer of Gilbert count of Brionne (c. 1041) 230.2
Ralph of Gael, earl of Norfolk (1070–5, d. c. 1096) 253.2; 255 (also earl of Suffolk: 255.1)
Ramlah (S. E. of Jaffa): described 366.3; K. Baldwin I besieged in 251.2; 384.1–3 (cf. 382.2); 405.1; Crusaders at 366.2; 378.1; also mentioned 381.1
Ramsbury (Wilts.) 100; bishops of, see Æthelstan, Brihtwold, Hereman
Ramsey (Hunts.) 97.3; 149.5; 209.2; 338.1; abbots of, see Ælfwine, Herbert Losinga
Ranulf, *praefectus* of Aquitaine (*fl.* 864) 110.2
Ranulf I, viscount of Bayeux, conspirator against Duke William II 230.4–5
Ranulf Flambard, bp. of Durham (1099–1128) 314.1–2; 393.1–2; 394.2; 445.2
Ravenna (Emilia-Romagna) 333.9; 438; Via Ravennana in Rome 352.3; see also Gerbert, Wibert
Raymond IV of Saint-Gilles, count of Toulouse, marquis of Provence (387.3) (c. 1088–1105): lineage and career 388; first layman to take Cross 388.4; early stages of Crusade 349.1 (cf. 387.3); 349.5; 357.4–5; at Antioch 365.2; 366.2; 388.5; at Jerusalem 369.2,7; 388.5 (cf. 11); at Ascalon 388.5–7; prince of Laodicea 374.7 (cf. 388.8); at Tripoli 388.9–10; death 388.10; also mentioned 366.1; 383.1
Reading (Berks.) 413
Rebecca, w. of Isaac 377.2
Reccared, k. of Visigoths (became Catholic 587) 167.1
Reculver (Kent), abbot of, see Berhtwald
Regensburg (Bavaria) 437.3
Reggio (di Calabria) 429
Reims (Marne) 432.2; archbishops of, see Fulk, Gerbert; archdeacon of, see Urban
Reiner, cardinal priest of SS Marcellinus and Peter (*fl.* 1111) 421.2
Reinhelm, bp. of Hereford (1107–15) 417.3
Remigius, bp. of Dorchester (then Lincoln) (?1067–92) 297; 298.7; 302.1
Remigius, St 111.7,9
Rennes (Ille-et-Vilaine) 237.7
Repton (Derbyshire) 42.3; 212
Rhine, River 68.1–3; 233.1; 349.1
Rhiwallon ap Cynfyn, Welsh k. (d. 1070) 228.8

Rhodes 92
Rhos, region of Wales 287.1; 401.1
Rhys, br. of Gruffydd ap Rhydderch (d. 1053) 196.3
Ricberht, killer of K. Earpwald (627/8) 97.2
Richard, earl of Chester (1101–20) 397.3; 419.7
Richard, abt. of Ely (at least 1100–2) 445.3
Richard, illegitimate s. of K. Henry I (d. 1120) 419.7
Richard I, duke of Normandy (942–96) 145.4; 165.13–166; 178.1
Richard II, duke of Normandy (996–1026); connection with K. Æthelred 177.6–178.1; 180.11; 228.2; and K. Cnut 181.3; character, life at Fécamp, and death 178.1–4; also mentioned 178.5; 188.2; 229; 230.3
Richard III, duke of Normandy (1026–7) 178.5; 188.2
Richard of the Principate (d. 1112) 386.1; 387.7
Richard de Redvers (d. 1107) 394.1
Richard, s. of Robert Curthose (d. 1101) 275.2
Richard, 'br.' of Robert Guiscard, prince of Capua (*see Commentary*) 262.2
Richard, s. of K. William I (d. 1069/74) 274.1; 275.1
Richildis, w. of Baldwin VI count of Flanders 256.3–5
Ricula, sister of K. Æthelberht I 98.1
Ripon (Yorks.) 104; 300.2
Riso, cardinal priest of St Laurence in Damaso (1105–12) 421.2
Riulf, rebel against Duke William I 145.1,3
Riwallon, abt. of New Minster, Winchester (1072–88) 298.8
Robert of Arbrissel, founder of Fontevrault (1100; d. 1117) 440.1
Robert of Beaumont, count of Meulan and earl of Leicester (d. 1118) 394.1; 407; 417.2 (his sons 406.2)
Robert of Bellême, earl of Shrewsbury (1098–1102, d. after 1130/1) 306.7; 396; 397.2; 398.1, 5–7
Robert II Curthose, duke of Normandy (d. 1134): nickname 389.2; character and career 389; his 'abdication' 305.2; and K. Philip I 258.2; 274.1 (cf. 283.2); 307.1; and Edgar the Ætheling 251.1–2; and his mother 273.2; in Italy 274.1; and Normandy 251.1–2; 274; 277.3; 282.3; 307–8;

INDEX

310; 389.3 (cf. 1); 392.1–4; 394; mortgages Normandy 274.2; 318.1; 389.6; Crusade: goes on 274.2; 277.3; 318.1 (cf. 320.1); 350; 389.3, early stages 350; 353; 357.1,4, at Antioch 365.2; 389.3, to and at Jerusalem 366.1; 369.7, battle with Egyptians 371.3; later in Normandy 274.2; 389.8–10; and K. Henry I, *see that entry*; and Odo 277.3; 306.1–2; raids on England 306.9; 389.7; 392.1; 393.2; 395; and Scotland 311.2; marriage 389.6; imprisonment and death 389.10–11; 406.1; sons, *see* Richard, William Clito

Robert, count of Eu, supporter of K. William I (*c*. 1047/8–1091/3) 233.2

Robert, cardinal priest of St Eusebius (?/1100–1112, ?1123–?) 421.2

Robert Fitz Hamon (d. 1107) 230.4; 333.1–2; 394.1; 398.4

Robert II, count of Flanders (1087–1111): on Crusade 257.2, early stages 350; 353.1–2; 357.1, at Antioch 365.2, to and at Jerusalem 366.1; 369.7; quarrel with K. Henry I 403.1–3; death 257.2; also mentioned 389.11

Robert I the Frisian, count of Flanders (1071–87, d. 1093): and Frisia 256.3; 373.1–2; takes Flanders 256.4–5; and K. William I 257.1; 403.1; and K. Cnut IV 257.1; 258.3; 261.2; pilgrimage 257.2

Robert, German priest 174

Robert, earl of Gloucester (1122–47), s. of K. Henry I ep. iii; 446–9

Robert, s. of Godwine of Winchester 251.2–3; 384.4

Robert Guiscard (called Durand 387.1), duke of Apulia (d. 1085) 262; 344.2; 349.3; 356.3; 387.1–3

Robert of Jumièges, bp. of London (1044–51), archbp. of Canterbury (1051–2) 197.4–5; 199.9

Robert of Limesey, bp. of Chester (later Coventry) (1086–1117) 338.1; 341

Robert Losinga, f. of Herbert, abt. of New Minster, Winchester (?1088–98) 338

Robert, count of Montdidier 128.1

Robert, count of Mortain, uterine br. of K. William I (?/1063–1090) 277.1; 397.2

Robert of Mowbray, earl of Northumberland (1086–95) 250; 306.2, 4; 311.2; 319.1

Robert I, duke of Normandy (1027–35): may have plotted to kill Duke Richard III 178.5; boasts he would invade England

180.11 (cf. 238.9); as father of Duke William II 187.2; 228.2; 229–230.1; 277.1; pilgrimage 178.5; 180.11; 187.2; 229–230.1; death at Nicaea 178.6; 277.1 (cf. 230.1); also mentioned 230.4

Robert I the Pious, k. of France (d. 1031) 128.2; 168.1–2; 187.1

Robert I, archbp. of Rouen (989–1037) 178.4

Robert de Sigillo, keeper of the seal (*c*. 1121–31), bishop of London (1141–50) 398.4 (Cs)

Rochester (Kent): the Medway at 180.6; Paulinus dies at 65.1; dispute between K. Æthelred and bishop 165.1; and Odo 306.3, 7–8; see 87.2; 99; 300.1; bishop unnamed (*see Commentary*) 165.1; bishops of, *see* Paulinus, Siward

Roger of Beaumont, father of Robert of Beaumont (d. 1090+) 407.1

Roger Bigod (d. 1107) 306.4; 394.1

Roger (Borsa 387.1), s. of Robert Guiscard, duke of Apulia (d. 1111) 262.3; 344.2; 387.1–2

Roger of Gloucester, killed at siege of Falaise (1105) 398.4 (and Cs)

Roger I of Hauteville, count of Sicily, br. of Robert Guiscard (d. 1101) 262.2

Roger, earl of Hereford (1071–5, d. after 1089) 255.2–3

Roger, bp. (perhaps of Lisieux, 990–1022) 166.3

Roger I of Montgomery, earl of Shrewsbury (*c*. 1035) 231.3

Roger II of Montgomery, earl of Shrewsbury (1074–94) 306.2, 4–7; 389.4; 396.1

Roger of Poitou, br. of Robert of Bellême 306.7; 396.3

Roger of Salerno, s. of Richard of the Principate, prince of Antioch (1112–19) 386.1; 387.7–8

Roger, bp. of Salisbury (1107–39) 398.4 (Cs); 408; 417.3

Roger, bp. of Volterra (1099–1131) 429

Roland, bp. of Populonia (= Massa Marittima) (1112–38) 429

Roland, Song of 242.2

Rollo (Rolf), count of Rouen (d. *c*. 930) 112.1; 127; 145.1; 236.3

Romanus, (Wibertine) cardinal priest of St Marcellus 431.3; *see also* Diogenes

Rome (*selected refs. only*): one of the three greatest cities 359.1; people of 68.7; 110.6; 195; 205.6; 422.1; gates and sanctuaries

Rome (*cont.*)
of 352; cf. 343 (Aa); Asylum in 172.2; church called Jerusalem in 172; various Roman *tituli* mentioned in 421.2 and 431.3 are not indexed; Schola Anglorum, *see* England; visits to, assorted (mainly Englishmen): general 245.2; individual 34.3–35.1; 37; 54.5; 57–8; 68.7; 77; 78 (cf. 98.3); 82.2; 87.4; 88.9–89.1; 96.2; 98.3; 109 (cf. 113.4; 126.1); 109 (cf. 121.1; 122.2–3 with 122.3 Aa); 110.6; 129.2; 137.1; 182–3; 184.1; 199.9; 302.1; 328 (cf. 417.3); 334.2; 339.1; 356.2; slaves taken to 45.1; synod at 150B.8; 150C.7; stories set in 169; 205; 'high road to' 171.1; dangers of journey to 183.3–4; 201.1–2 (cf. 202.5); 435.1; grief for Henry III 194.3; in time of Pope Gregory VI 200–3; body of Pallas found in 206; miracles at 211.1–2; 286.1; and Urban II 333.9; 344.1; 350.2; Hildebert on 351; and Constantinople 355.1; 359.1 (cf. also 354.3); and Henry IV 262.3–4; 266.1; 289; and Henry V 373.3; 420.3–438; 'pope of Rome' and the like e.g. 151C.1, *see also* Popes; Roman: world 225.5, kingdom 110.4, empire 110.8; 111.9, 11; 112.2; 360.2, patrician of the Romans 68.5; 93.1; 111.1 (Roman patricians 425), church 36C.4; 68.5–6; 80.1; 137.1; 150B.6,8; 150C.5; 166.1; 296; 298.5–6; 414.5; 415.3; 422.1; 424.1,3; 431.1; 436.2; 437.2, cardinals 199.11; 269.1, senate 201.4; 302.1, council 150B.5; ordinal 423.2 (cf. 421.1), clergy 423.2, polish i pr. 4; 149.3, eloquence 132; Roman(s): in ancient Gaul 254.1, in Britain 1–3; 8.2; 54.2, in Spain 167.1, in Germany 175.1, ruled by Lothar I 110.1, greed of 339.1; 341.1; 351.1; 353.1; 435.1, prose style of 31.2, wine 373.4, admire Normans 406; Roman (Holy, Apostolic) see e.g. 57; 288.2; 415.2
Romsey (Hants) 159.2; 228.1; 418.1
Romulus 172.2
Rossano (Calabria) 429
Rothasia, *see* Edessa
Rouen (Seine-Mar.): and Rollo 127.3–4; treaty signed at 166.3; old ships to be seen at 180.11; K. William I at 281; 282.2; Jews in 317; and K. Henry I 389.9–10; 392.2–5; 405.2,4; 'bishop' of (see *Commentary*) 416.4; count of, *see* Rollo; archbishops of, *see* Mauger, Maurilius, Robert I, William
Roum, Turkish name for Asia Minor 357.3
Rudolf III, k. of Burgundy (993–1032) 183.3–4
Rudolf, s. of Hugh, witness on behalf of Duke Richard I 166.3
Rudolf, duke of Swabia (1057–80) 266.4

Sabina (Magliano, Lazio), bishop of, *see* Cencio
Sæberht, k. of E. Saxons (d. 616/7) 98.1
Sæweard, k. of E. Saxons (*c*. 617) 98.1–2
St Albans (Herts.) 87.1; abbot of, *see* Frederick
Saint-Bertin, monastery of (at Saint-Omer, Pas-de-Calais) 122.3 (Aa); 342.1
Saint-Calais (Sarthe), abbot of, *see* William
St David's (Dyfed) 122.4; 435.2; *see also* Bernard, David, Menevia
Saint-Denis (nr. Paris) 68.5; 204.7
St Edmunds, *see* Bury
St Germans (Cornwall) 100
Saint-Leufroi (La Croix-, Eure), monastery 284.2
Saint-Médard, monastery at Soissons (Aisne) 110.2
Saint-Melaine, abbey of (at Rennes) 237.7–8
Saint-Mesmin, abbot of, *see* Constantine
Saint-Pol-de-Léon (Finistère), bishop of, *see* Galo
Saint-Valery (-sur-Somme, Somme) 238.8; 307.1
Saintes (Charente-Mar.) 235.1
Salerno (Campania) 432.1; *see also* Roger
Salisbury (Wilts.) 319.2; cathedral 325; 408.3; Wulfnoth in chains at 200.1; see 100; 300.3; bishops of, *see* Hereman, Osmund, Roger
Salonica (mod. Thessaloniki, N. Greece) 344.2; 353.3; 387.2
Samosata (mod. Samsat, Turkey) 374.5; *see also* Paul
Samson, bp. of Worcester (1096–1112) 398.4 (Cs)
Samson, St, bp. of Dol (6c.) 138B.2
Samuel, prophet 59.3; 356.4
Sandwich (Kent) 177.1; 179.3; 180.1
Sansadoles (Shams ad-Daula), s. of Aoxianus 360.1; 361; 364.1
Santa Severina (Calabria) 429
Saracen(s): summary of their conquests 92; 347.6–7; 368.3; in Africa and Asia 91.2

(cf. 178.5; 200.2); 356.2; 368.3; in Gaul 68.4; 80.4; 204.7; in Judaea 367.3; 368.2–4; in Sicily 356.2; in Spain 80.4; 91.2; 135.4–5; 167.1–2; 204.7; 282.3; 347.7; 368.3; and Charlemagne, *see that entry*; and Charles Martel 204.7; and Mahomet 189.1; some converted to Christianity 377.5; a Saracen known to Gerbert 167.3–5; and the abacus 167.3; ruled by 'Soldan' 360.2; in connection with the Crusades 260.2; 372.2; 374.8; 376.2; 380.2–3; *see also* Hagarenes
Sarah, w. of Abraham 377.2
Sardanapalus, Assyrian king 36.3
Sardinia 92
Saxony, Saxons: Old 80.3; 91.1; 122.3; on Continent 110.2,5; 116.2; 173–174.1; 192.1; 349.1; in Britain 1.1; 4.2; 5.1, 3; 22.1; 88.7; 97.1; province of 89.1; see of Saxony 30; used of West Saxons 113.3; bad effect of 148.3; Saxon poets 124.1 (Aa); Saxon sword 133.2; *see also* Anglo-Saxons, Essex, Sussex, Wessex
Scandza (*see Commentary*) 116.2
Sceaf, ancestor of Woden 116; *see also* Streph
Sceld (*also* Sceldw(e)a), ancestor of Woden 116.1
Scipio Africanus (Numantinus, 185/4–129 BC) 412.1 (*see also* 61.2)
Scotland, Scot(s), Scottish: position 54.1; 104; 125.1; 298.2; in time of Romans 3; and Angles 6; 7.3; and Christianity 49.1–2; 50.3; and K. Edwin 48.3; and Charlemagne 72.3; and K. Edward the Elder 125.1; and K. Eadred 146.1; and K. Cnut 182; and K. William I 249.1–2; 250; and K. William II 310.2–311; and K. Henry I 400.1–2; place of refuge 47.5; 134.2; 249.1; bishops 298.2; 300.2; troubled by fleas 348.2; language 49.4; manners 400.2; also mentioned 228.9; 334.2; kings of 400.1, *see* Aedan, Alexander I, Constantine II, David I, Donald, Duncan II, Edgar, Kenneth II, Macbeth, Malcolm I, II and III. For Irishmen called 'Scots' *see* David the Scot, John the Scot, Marianus Scotus, Meildulf
Scotland, abt. of St Augustine's, Canterbury (1070–87) 298.7
Scubilio, St 138B.3–5
Scylla iv pr. 3
Seaxburh, w. of K. Cenwealh (reigned alone 672–?674) 32; 36C.1

Seaxburh, w. of K. Earconberht 214.1–3
Seaxred, k. of E. Saxons (*c.* 617) 98.1
Sebbi, k. of E. Saxons (*c.* 664–*c.* 694) 98.2
Séez (Savoie), abbot of, *see* Ralph of Escures
Segni (Lazio) 429 (*see Commentary*)
Seine, River: noble river 121.7; as boundary 233.1; 'shores of the Seine region' 410.2; also mentioned 145.4; 283.1; 392.4
Seleucus I (*c.* 358–281 BC) 359.1
Selred, k. of E. Saxons (?738–46) 98.3
Selsey (Sussex) 87.2; 100; 208; 300.1, 3; bishops of, *see* Æthelgar, Æthelric II, Beornheah, Stigand
Semiramis, Assyrian queen 371.1
Senator, St 138B.3–5
Seneca (the Elder, d. *c.* 40) 59.2
Senlis (Oise) 110.2
Sennes, archbp. of Capua (1098–1118) 429
Sergius I, pope (687–701) 34.3; 35.4; letter of 58
Serlo, abt. of St Peter's, Gloucester (1072–1104) 125.5 (Aa); 441
Severus, L. Septimius, Roman emperor (193–211) 1.1
Seville (formerly Hispalis, S. Spain) 167.2; bishops of, *see* Isidore, Leander
Sexi, name on pyramid at Glastonbury 21.2
Shaftesbury (Dorset) 122.3; 162.4–163; 187.2; 219
Shapwick (Somerset) 36C.6; 150C.4; 151C.1
Sherborne (Dorset) 100; 117; 300.1,3; 334.2; bishops of, *see* Æthelsige I, Aldhelm, Asser, Ealhstan, Hereman, Wærstan, *see also* Sigehelm; monk of, *see* Stephen Harding
Sherston (Wilts.) 180.4
Shrewsbury (Shropshire) 306.4; 396.1–2; earls of, *see* Hugh of Montgomery, Robert of Bellême, Roger of Montgomery
Shropshire 101; 327; 396.1
Sichem, *see* Nablus
Sicily, Sicilians 92; 429; count of, *see* Roger I; countess of (= Adelaide of Salona, queen of Jerusalem) 385.2
Sidnacester (*see Commentary*) 87.2–3; 300.1–2
Sidon (S. of Beirut) 36.3 (adj. trsl. 'Phoenician'); 260.2; 366.2; 376.9; 382.1; 410.2
Sidonius Apollinaris (5c.) 121.7
Siena, bishop of, *see* Geoffrey
Sigebald, f. of K. Sigeberht II 98.1
Sigeberht, k. of E. Angles (630/1–?) 74.2; 97.2–3

Sigeberht, k. of W. Saxons (756–?757) 41–42.1
Sigeberht I the Little, k. of E. Saxons (from *c*. 617) 98.1–2
Sigeberht II the Good, k. of E. Saxons (from *c*. 653) 98
Sigeferth, thane of the Seven Boroughs (d. 1015) 179.4–5
Sigeheard, k. of E. Saxons (*c*. 694–before 709) 98.2
Sigehelm (*fl*. 883) 122.2 (*see Commentary*)
Sigehere, k. of E. Saxons (*c*. 664–?) 98.2–3
Sigeric, archbp. of Canterbury (990–4) 165.2; 184.2
Sigurd I, k. of Norway (1103–30) 260.2; 410
Sihtric (Sigtrygg), Danish k. in Northumberland (d. 926) 126.1; 131.3–4; 134.1–2
Siloam, spring in Jerusalem 369.1
Silvester I, bp. of Rome (314–35) 354.2–3
Silvester II, pope, *see* Gerbert (see Aa at 167.1,6)
Simeon, cousin of Christ, bp. of Jerusalem 368.1
Simeon II, patriarch of Jerusalem (before 1092–9) 368.4
Simon Magus 171.3 (cf. also 338.2)
Sion (Sitten, Switzerland), bishop of, *see* Ermenfrid
Sion, Mt 367.1–2
Siward, abt. of Abingdon (1030–44) 197.2
Siward, earl of Northumbria (*c*. 1041–55) 196.2; 199.4; 200.2; 240.2; 253.1
Siward, bp. of Rochester (1058–75) 298.7
Siwin 429 (*see Commentary*)
Slaswic (*see Commentary*) 116.2
Slavs 91.1; 110.5; *see also* Liuticii, Wends
Sledd, k. of E. Saxons (late 6c.) 98.1
Sodom 377.3
Solomon 81; 169.4–5; 347.3; 367.1; temple of, in Jerusalem 367.2; 369.8; 370.1; 379.2
Somerset 100; 113.1; 121.2; *see also* Eanwulf
Sophronius I, patriarch of Jerusalem (633/4–638) 368.2
Sophronius II, patriarch of Jerusalem (?/1059–1064/?) 368.4
Southampton (Hants) 117; 164.3; 177.4
Spain, Spanish: history 167.1–2; Goths in 5.2; 167.1–2; Saracens in, *see* Saracens; and Charles Martel 204.7; and Charlemagne 91.2; 135.4–5; 167.2; 368.3; also mentioned 388.10; 434
Speyer (Bavaria) 194.1; bishop of, *see* Bruno; *see also* Nemetum

Spyridon, St (d. *c*. 348) 356.4
Staffordshire 101
Stamford Bridge (Yorks.) 228.10
Stephen, St, churches of: in Caen 267.2, 5; in Rome 352.13
Stephen II (III), pope (752–7) 68.5
Stephen IX (X), pope (1057–8) 225.5
Stephen, count of Blois (1088–1102): wife 276; early stages of Crusade 350; 353; 357.1; flight from Antioch 362.2 (T^1)(cf. 383.1); return to East 383.1; death at Ramlah 384.2–3; 405.1; also mentioned 389.11; 419.2
Stephen, count of Burgundy and Maçon (d. 1102) 383.1; 384.2–3
Stephen Harding, monk of Sherborne, abt. of Cîteaux (1109–33) 334; 335.2; 337.2–5
Stermon (*also* Itermon), ancestor of Woden 116.2
Stigand, bp. of Elmham ('of South Saxons' 199.10) (1043, 1044–7), bp. of Winchester (1047–70) and archbp. of Canterbury (1052–70): chequered career 199.10–11; mocks at K. Edward the Confessor's vision 227; advice on K. Edward's heir 240.2; and K. William I 247.2–3; 251.1; 269.1
Stigand, bp. of Selsey, then Chichester (1070–87) 298.7
Stow, St Mary's (Stow St Mary, nr. Gainsborough, Lincs.) 196.2
Street (Somerset) 36C.6; 150C.4; 151C.1
Streneshalh (Whitby) 50.4
Streph, s. of Noah (*also* Seth, Sceaf, q.v.) 116.2
Suffolk 102; 255.1
Suleiman (= Kilij Arslan, sultan of Roum, 1092–1107) 357.3; 383.1–2
Surrey 100; 107.1
Sussex, South Saxons: Sussex (Latin only in 100) 100; 107.1; and W. Saxons 34.2; bishops 129.3; 199.10 (*see Commentary*); kings of, *see* Æthelwalh, Eadric
Sutri (Lazio) 432.2; 433.2–3
Swabia 110.8; duke of, *see* Rudolf
Swæfred, k. of E. Saxons (*c*. 694–before 709) 98.2
Sweden, Swedes 180.10; 181.5–6; 183.1; 189.1; 259.2
Swein Cnutsson ('Hardhand'), k. of Norway (1030–35) 260.1
Swein I Forkbeard, k. of Denmark

(987–1014), k. of England (1013–14) 176–177.3; 179.1–2; 180.7
Swein II Estrithsson, k. of Denmark (1046–74) 249.2; 259; 261.1
Swein, son of Earl Godwine 199.4,6–7; 200.1–2
Swelwes, name on pyramid at Glastonbury 21.2
Swithhelm, k. of E. Saxons (653/64–653/64) 98.2
Swithhun, bp. of Winchester (852/3–862/5) 108.2; 109; 114.3
Swithred, k. of E. Saxons (*c*. 746–?) (*W. calls him* Swithhæd) 98.3
Syracuse 356.2; bishop of, *see* William
Syria, Syrian(s): and Saracens 225.4 (cf. 347.4); in connection with: Antioch 358; 361; 363.2, Bethlehem 366.4, Edessa 374.4, Jerusalem 371.2; 379.1–2; also mentioned 374.5; 377.2; 384.5

Tamar, River (Cornwall and Devon) 134.6
Tancred, prince of Galilee, regent of Antioch (1106–12): praised 372.1; generosity 383.3; at Bethlehem 366.3; at Jerusalem 370.1; and Antioch 376.1; 378.2; 387.5,7; 388.11; at Laodicea 387.5; 388.8; wife 387.5; 388.11; also mentioned 374.1; 376.9; 381.3
Taney, unidentified castle in Maine, *see* Warin
Taphnis, alleged predecessor of Egyptian Babylon 371.1
Tarragona (Catalonia), k. of (= Alfonso VI, q.v.) 388.3
Tarsus (in S. E. Turkey) 374.2; 383.3
Tavistock (Devon) 180.10; abbot of, *see* Lyfing
Terracina (Lazio), bishop of, *see* Gregory
Tetti (*elsewhere* Tætwa), ancestor of Woden 116.1
Teutons: empire and emperors 68.1; 360.2; 420.1; kingdom and kings 68.8; 112.1; 135.1; 420.3; 433.2; 434; 436.1; 438; obstinacy 192.2; fury 435.2; *see also* Germany
Teuzo, cardinal priest of St Mark (*rightly* Divizo, cardinal priest of St Martin) (*c*. 1103–21) 421.2
Teuzo, Wibertine legate (*see Commentary*) 431.3
Tewkesbury, abbey (Glos.) 398.4; 449.1
Thames, River: fords, bridges 177.3; 180.5; people thrown into 181.2; 188.4; flood comes up 330; also mentioned 107.1; 200.1; 413.1
Thanet, Isle of (Kent) 6; 13; 117; 215
Theban Legion 135.5
Theobald, cardinal priest of SS John and Paul (*fl*. 1111) 421.2
Theobald (Dietpold), marquis of the Bavarian Nordgau (*fl*. 1122) 437.3
Theobald I, count of Blois (1037–89) 231.2
Theobald II, count of Blois (1109–52) 405.1–2; 419.2,7
Theodbald, br. of K. Æthelfrith 47.2
Theoderic V, stepson of Robert the Frisian, count of Holland (1076–91) 373.1–2
Theodore, archbp. of Canterbury (668/9–90): arrival and learning of 12; 50.3–4; and Canterbury 29; 54.4; and Glastonbury 29; 36C.2; also mentioned 77
Theodosius, patriarch of Jerusalem (?/ 867–*c*. 878) 367.4; 368.3
Theodosius I, Roman emperor (379–95) 2.2; 356.1
Theodred, bp. of London (909/26–951/3) 213.4
Theseus, Greek hero 170.2
Thessaly (in mod. N. Greece) 353.3
Thetford (Norfolk) 102; 300.3; 338.1; 339.1–2
Theuderic III, Merovingian king (633–91) 68.3
Thomas, St 122.2
Thomas of Bayeux, archbp. of York (1070–1100) 297; 298.3,5–6; 299; 302.1; 303.2
Thorney (Cambs.) 149.4
Thrace 353.3; 355.2
Thunor, servant of K. Ecgberht I 209.1
Thuringia 110.2,5
Thurkil (the Tall), earl under K. Cnut (1017–23/?) 176; 181.1,3
Thurstan, abt. of Ely (?1066–1072/3) 298.8
Thurstan (Turstenc), s. of Turgis, witness on behalf of Duke Richard I 166.3
Tiber, River 373.4
Tiberias (on Sea of Galilee) 374.10; 382.1; 384.6
Tidferth, bp. of Dunwich (798–816/24) 87.2
Tinchebray (Orne), battle of 398.5
Tiron (Eure-et-Loir), abbey of 440
Titus, Roman emperor (79–81) 367.1
Toledo 167.2
Tonbridge (Kent) 306.7

Tortosa (mod. Tartus, N. of Tripoli) 383.3; 388.8
Tostig, earl of Northumbria (1055–65) 200.1–3; 228.9,11; 252.1–2
Toulouse (Haute-Garonne) 388.2; *see also* Bertram, Raymond IV, William (*rightly* Pons), William IV
Tours (Indre-et-Loire): and Alcuin 65.3; dispute with Auxerre 121.8–10; and Danes 121.7; and Geoffrey Martel 231.2; also mentioned 340.1; *see also* Berengar, Gregory VII, Hildebert, Hugh, Martin
Trajan, Roman emperor (98–117) 175.1
Trastevere (Rome) 422.1
Trento (Trentino), bishop of, *see* Gebhard I
Trier (*rightly* Trevi), 'bishop of', *see* Leo
Tripoli (N. of Beirut) 366.2; 374.9; 376.2–3; 388.9–11; bishop of, *see* Herbert; counts of, *see* Bertram, Pons
Troia (Apulia), bishop of, *see* William
Tudites, *see* Charles Martel
Turbessel, stronghold (mod. Tell Bashir, N. E. Syria) 374.3; *see also* Joscelin I
Turfrith, friend of K. Guthfrith II 134.2–3
Turgis, *see* Thurstan
Turk(s), Turkish: conquests of 347.6–7; 357.3; 364.2 (cf. 374.3); peace under their rule 367.4; at Antioch 359.2; in Jerusalem 235.3; 368.4; at Ramlah 251.2; 384.1; Crusade directed against 257.2; 346; 347.2; *passim* during the Crusade sections; tactics of 347.7; 357.5; treachery of 363.1; 375.2; religion of 189.1; 367.2; deface a church 366.3; 'the Turkish cause' 260.2; 'Turk but generous and merciful' 376.2; also mentioned 225.4; 349.4
Turnus, killer of Pallas 206.1
Turold, abt. of Peterborough (1070–98) 298.8
Tuscany 288.2; 353.1; countess of, *see* Matilda
Tusculum (nr. mod. Frascati, Lazio), bishop of, *see* John II de Marsico
Tynemouth (Northumberland) 250
Tyre (S. of Sidon), Tyrian 49.4; 297 (Aa); 366.2; 376.9; 410.2
Tyrrhenian Sea 121.7; 127.1; 349.2

Uhtred, earl of Northumbria (d. 1016) 177.2; 180.2–3
Ulf, Swedish king, worsted by K. Cnut (1025) 181.6
Ulfcytel, ealdorman of E. Anglia (d. 1016) 165.10; 180.7
Urban, bp. of Glamorgan (i.e. Llandaff) (1107–34) 398.4 (Cs); 417.3
Urban II, pope (1088–99), formerly Odo archdeacon of Reims, prior of Cluny, and (1078–88) cardinal bp. of Ostia: as bishop of Ostia 266.2,4; election 266.4; 289.1; and Wibert 289.2; 333.9; 344.1; 350.2; 387.3; excommunicates Henry IV 289.2, King Philip I 345.5; 404.1; favours Crusade 318.1; 344.1–2; 353.1; 388.4; at Clermont 345.1, 5; 387.3; speech there 346–348.1; on investitures 416.1; also mentioned 337.1; 374.9; 420.1; 427.2
Utrecht (Holland), bishop of 437.3; *see also* Adalbold II
Uzziah, k. of Judah 202.10

Valenciennes (Nord) 257.1
Valentinian I, Roman emperor (364–75) 68.1; 356.1 (*see apparatus criticus*)
Val-ès-Dunes (Calvados) 230.4
Vandals 5.2
Vendôme (Loire-et-Cher), count of, *see* Geoffrey
Venice, Venetians 262.5–6; patriarch of, *see* John Gradenigo
Venosa (Apulia) 262.6
Venus 205.2,6
Vercelli (Piemonte) 284.1
Vernon (Eure) 230.3; *see also* Guy of Burgundy
Vexin, count of the, *see* Walter of Mantes
Victor II, pope (1055–7) 225.5; 265.1
Victor III, pope (1087), formerly Desiderius abt. of Montecassino (1057–87) 266.2,4
Vienne (Isère), archbishop of, *see* Calixtus
Vimeu (part of Ponthieu) 110.7
Vincent, St 160.2
Virgil (70–19 BC) 124.2; 135.3; 206.1; 355.2; v pr. 1 ('the bard of Mantua')
Vitalis, cardinal priest of St Balbina (?/ 1111–16) 421.2
Volterra (Toscana), bishop of, *see* Roger
Vortigern, 'k. of Britain' 4; 6–8.3
Vortimer, s. of Vortigern 8.1

Wada, abbot, messenger of K. Cenwulf 88.9
Wægdæg 45.1 (Tt)
Wældæg, s. of Woden 44.3
Wærburh, St 76.2; 214.3
Wærferth, bp. of Worcester (872–915) 122.4

INDEX 877

Wærstan, bp. of Sherborne (*c*. 909–?918) 129.3
Walaric, St 238.9
Walcher, bp. of Durham (1071–80) 271
Walcher, prior of Great Malvern (d. 1125) 293
Waleran I, count of Meulan (d. *c*. 1068) 407.2
Wales, Welsh(man): under K. Edward the Elder 125.1; reduced by Earl Harold 196.3; 228.8; around Hereford 199.1,4–5; and K. William I 258.1; and K. William II 306.4; 310.2; 311.1; 327; and K. Henry I 311.1; 396.1; 401; pays tribute of wolves 155; given to hunting 348.2; reverence for St David 25.3; under Canterbury 300.2; Welsh kings, *see* Bleddyn, Cadwallon, Dyfnwal, Giferth, Gruffydd, Hywel, Iago, Idwal, Iudethil, Rhiwallon; *see also* British, Britons, Northwalians, Rhos, Rhys
Walkelin, bp. of Winchester (1070–98) 269.1; 298.7
Walter ('a certain', at Moulins) 232.3
Walter of Amfreville (*fl.* 1127) 398.4 (Cs)
Walter, sheriff of Gloucester (*c*. 1097–1127/?) 398.4 (Cs)
Walter, bp. of Hereford (1061–79) 298.6
Walter of Mantes, count of the Vexin (d. 1063) 199.1 (*see Commentary*); 236.2
Walter Sans-Avoir (d. 1096) 349.6
Walter Tirel, slayer of K. William II 333.3–5
Waltham Abbey (Essex) 247.1
Walthchis, s. of Arnulf bp. of Metz 68.4
Waltheof, earl of Northumberland (1072–5) 248.2; 253; 255.2
Wandregesil (Wandrille), St 68.4
Wareham (Dorset) 43.2; 162.2
Warin of Taney, crusader (d. 1102) 389.4–5
Warwick, earl of, *see* Henry of Beaumont
Warwickshire 101
Wear, River (Durham), 54.2; *see also* Monkwearmouth
Weaslieas, name on pyramid at Glastonbury 21.2
Wells (Somerset): and Glastonbury 36C.8 (cf. 150C.4–5); see 100; 300.1,3; 338.1; bishops of, 150C.4–5, *see* Athelm, Byrhthelm, Giso, John of Villula
Wencrest, name on pyramid at Glastonbury 21.2
Wends (i.e. W. Slavs) 80.3; 189; 202.9; 259.2
Wenlock, Much (Shropshire) 76.2; 196.2; 216; nun of, *see* Mildburh

Wernberht, bp. of Leicester (801/3–814/16) 87.2
Werner, marquis (*fl.* 1111) 422.2
Wessex (Westsexa *only 16.2, occasionally* Westsaxonia), West Saxons: kingdom of i pr. 5; 15.4–19.2; 29.2–43; 97.1; ii pr. 3 (and Book ii *passim*); 105; 125.1; 228.7; references after 43 to relations with: E. Angles 97.6 (*and see* Angles, East), E. Saxons 98.1,3, Kent, *see that entry*, Mercia 74.2; 76.1; 77; 79; 86; 90; 96.1 (*and see* Mercia), Northumbria 73.2 (*and see* Northumbria); and K. Cnut 180.1,3,5,9; 181.1; allow no queens 113.2–3 (*where also called* Saxons); see(s) of 29.2; 100; 129 (cf. 300.1); bishop of, *see* Leuthere; earls of, *see* Godwine, K. Harold II; kings of ep. ii.4; 44.3; 97.6, *see* Æscwine, Æthelbald, Æthelberht, Æthelheard, Æthelred, Æthelweard, Æthelwulf, Alfred, Brihtric, Cædwalla, Ceawlin, Centwine, Cenwealh, Ceolric, Ceolwulf, Cerdic, Cuthred, Cwichelm, Cynegils, Cynewulf, Cynric, Ecgberht, Edward the Elder, Ine, Sigeberht; *see also* Gewisse
Westminster (London): burials at 188.2; 228.6; 273.2; 418.6; church consecrated 228.6; feasts at 225.1; 279.2; Henry knighted at 391; Q. Matilda at 418.2; abbot of, *see* Geoffrey
Wherwell (Hants) 157.3 ('called Harewood' Aa); 162.4; 199.7
Whitby (Yorks., formerly *Strenesalh*) 50.4; abbess of, *see* Hild
Whithorn (Wigtownshire), also called *Candida Casa* 104; 300.2
Wibert of Ravenna, installed as Pope Clement III by Henry IV (1084; d. 1100): intruded 262.3–4; 266.1–2; 289.1; 344.1; disfavoured by Robert Guiscard and Bohemond 387.3; excommunicated at Council of Clermont 345.5 (cf. 289.2); favoured by K. William II 333.9; escapes to Germany 350.2; supporters named 431.3
Wig, ancestor of K. Æthelwulf 116.1
Wight, Isle of 16.2–3; 34.2; 76.1; 177.4
Wiglaf, k. of Mercia (827–40) 96.2; 107.1; 212
Wigmund, s. of K. Wiglaf 212
Wigstan, f. of Æthelnoth 166.2–3
Wigstan, St 212
Wihtburh, d. of K. Anna (d. 743) 207.4
Wihtgar, nephew of K. Cerdic 16.3

Wihtlæg, son of Woden 44.3
Wihtred, k. of Kent (690–725) 15.1 (with Aa)
Wilfrid I, archbp. of York (669–78) 50.3; 51; 52.2; 100; 208.1
William, II duke of Normandy (1035–87), I k. of England (1066–87) (*selected references only*): author's policy on iii pr. 1–2; as child and youth 178.6; 187.2; 188.2; 229–230.3; 267.4; warfare as duke in Normandy 230.5–6; 231–232.1; 233–4; 236; 238.1; given succession of England 228.2; and Harold 228.4–5; 236.2; 238.2–4; 239–40; 247.1; lead up to landing in England 238.5–10; 256.1; 398.5; 403.1; victory at Hastings, *see* Hastings; crowned 247.3; warfare as king in Britain 248–50; 252.3; 258.1, on continent 251.1; 257.1; 258.1–2; 281–282.1 (cf. 399); and church 254.3; 267; 269.1; 278; 280.2; 297–8; 300.3; 314.3; and English nobility 253–254.2; 255; and Lanfranc 269; 306.3; and New Forest 275 (cf. 279.1); and Scotland, *see that entry*; and Danes 262.1 (cf. 258.3); census 258.2; laws of 297 (Aa); wife 234.2; 267.5; 273; daughters 276; sons 274–5; and Robert Curthose 389.1–2; and William 305.1–2; 306.6; and Henry 390.2–391; half-brothers 277.1; character 228.2; 267.1; 273.1; 277.1; 279–80; appearance and habits 279; 'in time of' 197.3; 199.11; 287.2; 294; illness and death 282 (cf. 305.3; 389.2); burial 283; 391; also mentioned e.g. 308.2–3, 6; 401.1; 407.1
William II, k. of England (1087–1100): author's policy on iii pr. 3; iv pr. 4; 316; early years and accession 282.3; 283.2; 305; and Normandy 258.2; 307–10; 318.1; 327; 392.3; revolts in England 306 (cf. 392.1–3); 319; and Wales 311; and Scots 250; 311; 400.1; and Jews 317; and Flemish pension 403.1; character iii pr.3; 309; 312–13; 320; prodigal, greedy and extortionate 312.2–316; 318–319.1; 333.2, 8; 340.1; 341.1; appearance 321; 'in time of' 260.2 (cf. 334.1); portents before death 332–333.2; death and burial 275.2; 333.3–6; 393.1–3; obituary 333.7–9; also mentioned 274; 277.3; 279.2; 342.1; 350.1
William of Aldery, executed by K. William II 319.2–3
William, VII count of Poitou, IX duke of Aquitaine (1071–1126) 333.7; 349.4; 383; 388.8; 439.1–4, 6
William, count of Arques (1037/48–1051, d. ?) 232.1,3
William I, count of Burgundy (1057–87) 230.5
William Clito, s. of Robert Curthose (d. 1128) 389.6; 403.3; 419.8
William of Conversano (*see Commentary*) 389.6
William of Corbeil, archbp. of Canterbury (1123–36) 398.4 (Cs); 408.1
William Crispin, supporter of Duke William II (d. 1074) 233.2
William, count of Eu (mutilated under K. William II) 319.2
William Fitz Osbern, earl of Hereford (1067–71) 231.3; 255.1; 256; 277.2
William Giffard, bp. of Winchester (1107–29) 398.4 (Cs); 417.3
William, s. of K. Henry I (d. 1120) 405.4; 414.1, 5; 418.2; 419
William of La Folie (*fl.* 1127) 398.4 (Cs)
William, bp. of London (1051–75) 298.6
William Longsword, s. of Rollo (933–42) 145; 165.13; 229
William of Malmesbury, letter to earl Robert ep. iii; *see also e.g.* i pr.1; 29.3; ii pr.; 149.3; 228.12; iii pr.; iv pr.; v pr.; 445.4–5
William V, count of Montpellier (1077–1121) 388.10; 409.3–410.1
William, count of Mortain (1090–1106), earl of Cornwall (1090–1104) 397.2–3; 398.1–2,5–6
William, s. of Odo (*fl.* 1127) 398.4 (Cs)
William (*rightly* William-Jordan) the Pilgrim, relative of Raymond IV of Saint-Gilles (confused by W. with Alfonse-Jordan, Raymond's son; *see Commentary*) 388.10
William de Ros, abt. of Fécamp (1079–1107) 178.4
William, archbp. of Rouen (1079–1110) 404.2
William, abt. of Saint-Calais, bp. of Durham (1080–96) 271.3; 306.1,3,9
William, bp. of Syracuse (1105–15) 429
William (*rightly* Pons), count of Toulouse (d. *c.* 1060) 388.1–2 (*see Commentary*)
William IV, count of Toulouse (*c.* 1060–93) 388.1–2 (*see Commentary*)
William, bp. of Troia (1106–33) 429
William of Volpiano, abt. of Saint-Bénigne,

INDEX

Dijon and reformer of Fécamp (from 1001; d. 1031) 165.13
William Warelwast, clerk, later bp. of Exeter (1107–37) 398.4 (Cs); 414.1; 416.2,4; 417.1,3
Wilton (Wilts.) 126.2; 218.1 (cf. 3–4); 219; 418.1
Wiltshire 100; 121.2; 306.4; bishop of, *see* Brihtwold
Wimborne (Dorset) 36.1; 120.2
Winchcombe (Glos.) 95.2–3; 211.2; 323; abbot of, *see* Girmund
Winchester (Hants): burials at 42.3; 107.3; 113.4; 124 (and 124.1 Aa); 126.3; 130 (cf. 133.1); 131.1; 146.2; 147.4; 187.2; 188.3; 197.6; 333.5; attacks by Danes and 'pirates' 117; 177.2; and Grimbald 122.3 (Aa); charters dated at 114.4; 398.4 (Cs); synod at 161.2–3; case of York and Canterbury discussed at 298.5; benefactions 181.5; 196.4; K. William I at 279.2; 298.5; bishopric 87.2; 100; 269.1; 300.1; 301; cathedral 19.2; 124.2; 146.2; 333.5–6; 'small monastery' 122.3 (Aa); K. Alfred's monastery, later moved 124; clerks expelled 149.6; also mentioned 137.1; 159.1; 164.3; 197.2; 217.2; 271.3; 283.2; bishops of, *see* Ælfheah, Æthelwold, Frithestan, Hædde, Stigand, Swithhun, Walkelin, William Giffard; St Swithun's 444, prior of, *see* Godfrey; New Minster 122.3; 124.1 (Aa); 147.4, abbots of, *see* Æthelgar, Grimbald, Riwallon, Robert Losinga; *see also* Godwine, Wulfsin
Windsor (Berks.) 224.2; 298.5
Winethegn, name on pyramid at Glastonbury 21.2
Wini, bp. of London (666–?before 672) 76.1
Wirtgeornesburh 19.2
Wissant (Pas-de-Calais) 139.4; 199.1
Woden: worshipped by English 5.3; ancestor of royalty of: E. Angles 97.1, E. Saxons 98.1, Kent 5.3; 44.3, Mercia 44.3; 74.1, Northumbria 44.3; 45.1, West Saxons 16.1; 44.3; 116.1
Wodnesdic 17.2 (*see Commentary on 17*)
Woodstock (Oxon.) 409.2
Worcester(shire): part of Mercia 101; under K. Harthacnut 188.4; expulsion of clerks 149.6; despoiled by Roger of Montgomery 306.4; see of 101; 300.1; and archbishop of York 302.1; *see also* Hwicce; bishops of, *see* Deneberht, Dunstan, Ecgwine, Lyfing, Oswald, Samson, Wærferth, Wulfstan II
Worgrez, abt. of Glastonbury (6c.?) 27–8
Wulfheard, bp. of Hereford (799/801–822/4) 87.2
Wulfhere, k. of Mercia (658–75): and W. Saxons 19.2; becomes king 75; reign 76–7; marriage 76.2; 214.3; brothers and sisters 29.1; 74.3; 76.2; 215; also mentioned 78
Wulfmær of Ludgershall 224.1
Wulfnoth, exiled by K. Æthelred the Unready 165.8
Wulfnoth (*rightly* Wulfwold), abt. of Chertsey (?1058–84) 298.8
Wulfnoth, s. of Earl Godwine 200.1; 240.2
Wulfred, name on pyramid at Glastonbury 21.2
Wulfstan, precentor of Winchester (d. *c.* 1000) 149.5
Wulfstan II, bp. of Worcester (1062–95) 269.2; 298.6; 302.1; 303; 306.4
Wulfstan I, archbp. of York (931–56) 146.1
Wulfthryth, w. of K. Edgar I 159.2
Wulfwine Spillecorn, s. of Wulfmær, cured by K. Edward the Confessor 224
Wye, River 134.6

York: as capital 70.4; and Alcuin 65.3; 70.1,3; library 65.2; and Danes 120.2; 134.2,4; Norwegian envoys received in 135.1; Norwegians besiege 228.9; under K. William I 248.2; 249.2; 252.2; 253.1; early bishops 65.1–2; archbishopric 88.6; 101; 104; 249.2; 300.2; 301–2; 445.4; dispute with Canterbury, *see* Canterbury; also mentioned 50.4; archbishops of, *see* Ælfric Puttoc, Ealdred, Eanbald I, Ecgberht, Gerard, Oswald, Paulinus, Thomas of Bayeux, Wilfrid I, Wulfstan I
Yvelines (Essonne), forest of 110.8

Zacharias, patriarch of Jerusalem (609–*c.* 631) 368.2
Zacharias, pope (741–52) 68.5
Zoy (Middlezoy, Somerset) 36C.1,6; 150. C4; 151C.1

Printed in the USA/Agawam, MA
March 14, 2023

806993.004